COUNTRIES
AND THEIR
CULTURES

EDITORIAL BOARD

Countries and Their Cultures was prepared under the auspices and with the support of the Human Relations Area Files, Inc. (HRAF) at Yale University. The foremost international research organization in the field of cultural anthropology, HRAF is a not-for-profit consortium of 19 Sponsoring Member institutions and more than 400 active and inactive Associate Member institutions in nearly 40 countries. The mission of HRAF is to provide information that facilitates the cross-cultural study of human behavior, society, and culture. The HRAF Collection of Ethnography, which has been building since 1949, contains nearly one million pages of information, indexed according to more than 700 subject categories, on the cultures of the world. An increasing portion of the Collection of Ethnography, which now covers more than 365 cultures, is accessible via the World Wide Web to member institutions. The HRAF Collection of Archaeology, the first installment of which appeared in 1999, is also accessible on the Web to those member institutions opting to receive it.

COUNTRIES
AND THEIR
CULTURES

VOLUME 4

SAINT KITTS AND NEVIS
TO
ZIMBABWE
•
INDEX

Melvin Ember and Carol R. Ember, Editors

Macmillan Reference USA
an imprint of the Gale Group
New York • Detroit • San Francisco • London • Boston • Woodbridge, CT

Countries and Their Cultures

Copyright © 2001 Macmillan Reference USA, an imprint of Gale Group

All rights reserved. No part of this book may be reproduced or transmitted in any form or by any means, electronic or mechanical, including photocopying, recording, or by any information storage and retrieval system, without permission in writing from the Publisher.

Macmillan Reference USA
1633 Broadway
New York, NY 10019

Macmillan Reference USA
27500 Drake Rd.
Farmington Hills, MI 48331-3535

Library of Congress Cataloging-in-Publication Data
Countries and their cultures / Melvin Ember and Carol R. Ember, editors.
     p.cm.
   Includes bibliographical references and index.
   ISBN 0-02-864950-8 (set : hc.)
1. Ethnology-Encyclopedias. I. Ember, Melvin. II. Ember, Carol R.
GN307 .C68 2001
306'.03-dc21

2001030188

Volume 1: 0-02-864947-8
Volume 2: 0-02-864948-6
Volume 3: 0-02-864949-4
Volume 4: 0-02-864946-X

Printed in the United States of America

Printing number
  2 3 4 5 6 7 8 9 10

Front cover photos (clockwise from top): Aymara man with llamas © Gian Berto Vanni/Corbis; Japanese kindergarten students © Don Stevenson/Mira; Hooded men at Oaxaca Festival © Liba Taylor/Corbis; Kava Ceremony, Fiji © Charles & Josette Lenars/Corbis; Wedding service in a Russian Orthodox church © Dean Conger/Corbis; Egyptian ranger battalion demonstration © Corbis; Boy eating lobster at Friendship Regatta festivities © Dean Conger/Corbis; Akha villagers perform a Chi Ji Tsi ritual © Michael Freeman/Corbis. Background: Desert Rose block print by Arlinka Blair © Jonathan Blair/Corbis.

SAINT KITTS AND NEVIS

CULTURE NAME

The inhabitants of the two islands are referred to as Kittitians (or Kitticians) and Nevisians, respectively.

ORIENTATION

Identification. Both islands were discovered by Christopher Columbus on his second voyage to the New World in 1493. Originally, Columbus named the larger island for his patron saint, Saint Christopher, but in the early seventeenth century, British settlers shortened the name to Saint Kitts. Columbus named the smaller neighboring island *Nuestra Señora de las Nieves* ("Our Lady of the Clouds") because the volcanic mountain in its center usually was encircled by snowlike clouds. When the British arrived, they altered the spelling to Nevis.

Location and Geography. Two miles apart, Saint Kitts and Nevis are in the northern part of the Leeward Islands, approximately two hundred fifty miles (402 kilometers) southeast of Puerto Rico. Saint Kitts, the larger island, is twenty-three miles (thirty-seven kilometers) in its greatest length, with an area of sixty-eight square miles (176.8 square kilometers). Nevis is thirty-six square miles (93.6 square kilometers) in area. Formed by similar mountain-building forces, both islands have dormant volcanoes in their central regions. The capitals Basseterre (Saint Kitts) and Charlestown (Nevis) are ports that are involved in tourism.

Demography. The population has been estimated (1999) to be forty-four thousand, with thirty-five thousand on Saint Kitts and nine thousand on Nevis. However, many more Kittitians and Nevisians live abroad than inhabit the islands. Ninety-five percent of the populace consists of Afro-Caribbeans who are largely descendants of slaves imported to work on sugar plantations, with the remainder made up of descendants of British settlers and early and later migrants.

Linguistic Affiliation. All the inhabitants speak English, and all the Afro-Caribbean residents have access to a local dialect based partly on English and partly on several West African languages. English is the language of business, religion, and tourism and is the medium of instruction in schools. The local dialect, referred to as Kittitian on Saint Kitts and Nevisian on Nevis, is used in the family, at social gatherings, and among men socializing together. It also is employed by Nevisians to communicate with one another without being understood by tourists.

Symbolism. The eclectic nature of contemporary society on Saint Kitts/Nevis and the varied origins of the Afro-Caribbean populace militate against deeply held and widely shared cultural symbols. Both islands have traditional dances, music, garb, and tales, but neither one is committed to a constellation of symbols that could anchor a cultural identity. Instead, the richness and variety of the cultural background is celebrated in a series of festivals. The roots of those festivals go back to the seventeenth century, when they were often associated with Christmas and May Day celebrations. A strong association with Christmas remains, partly because of tradition and partly from the holiday visits of many Kittitians and Nevisians living elsewhere.

HISTORY AND ETHNIC RELATIONS

Emergence of the Nation. The development of political independence was the final link in a process of increasing autonomy for the Afro-Caribbean population of Saint Kitts/Nevis that began in the early nineteenth century. In the eighteenth century, partly because whites feared the slave population, which outnumbered them nearly ten to one, slaves were treated harshly. Although forced to work long hours on sugar plantations, they managed to maintain limited gardens of their own. Some slaves escaped to the mountainous interior, where they set up small holdings and tried to succeed at farming and remain unnoticed. Over the years, former

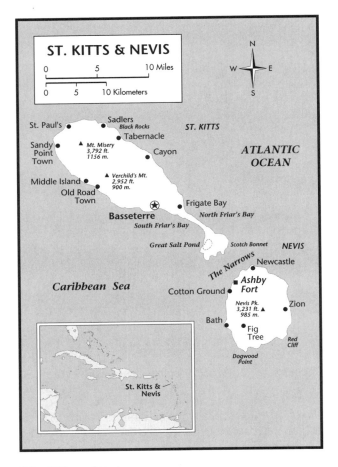

Saint Kitts and Nevis

In the 1950s, the elimination of sugar and cotton production and an assortment of agricultural problems led to increasing waves of emigration, largely to Great Britain, Commonwealth members, and other English-speaking countries. Emigration resulted in significant changes that were accelerated by political changes in the mid-1960s, when Great Britain established the associated state of Saint Kitts/Nevis, which became fully independent in 1983. Nevisians were unhappy with their connection to the numerically dominant Kittitians and agreed to independence only if they could retain the right to secede and have internal self-rule.

The lengthy economic decline left the islands in an unpromising position. Initial efforts to establish more productive agricultural and other pursuits involving manual labor were stymied by the strong preference of Kittitians and Nevisians for white-collar work. The development of tourism in the 1970s and the increasing ability of emigrants to send funds home have led to better economic circumstances on both islands, which maintain excellent public school systems, resulting in a literacy rate in excess of 90 percent, and good public health programs.

National Identity. The coat of arms appears to owe as much to colonial influence as its does to indigenous traditions.

The contemporary national identity is complex and strongly affected by emigration and the opportunities afforded by education. Emigration in the 1970s reduced the population. That trend seems likely to continue, as current population projections for the years 2000 and 2010 indicate a maintenance of the 1995 figure of thirty-nine thousand. Current estimates suggest that far more inhabitants live abroad than at home, by a factor of four or five to one. Kittitians and Nevisians abroad are employed in a wide range of positions that reflect their education. Nonetheless, they retain strong ties to their homes, visit frequently on holidays, especially on Christmas, and regularly send home money and goods. Family ties are strongly maintained through frequent visits. Many younger islanders look forward to completing their educations abroad and then taking up residence in a foreign country. The result is a complex identity rooted partly in place and tradition and partly in the wider world and educational accomplishment. Emigration makes the achievement of white-collar work ever more possible.

slaves established villages in parts of the interior not suitable for plantations. When emancipation began in 1834, there were well-established Afro-Caribbean villages capable of maintaining elements of their traditional culture and developing a complex web of social relations.

Most inhabitants of the islands engaged in basic agriculture and lived very simply. Religion, particularly the Anglican faith, played a major role in education and the formation of concepts of respectability, with an admixture of African traditions centering on mortuary practices and holiday celebrations. By the early twentieth century, the British colonial government provided free basic public education and some amenities. Still, the situation of most islanders remained one of poverty with comparatively little social stratification based on wealth. Members of society who could sustain an elite status generally were connected either to religion or to education, and they maintained some visible material goods, such as a house and furnishings.

URBANISM, ARCHITECTURE, AND THE USE OF SPACE

Basseterre, the largest city on the islands, has eighteen thousand people, while Charlestown has an approximate population of 1,500. Both cities are seats of government and tourism and the major mercantile centers and ports of the islands. Both feature a combination of contemporary architecture mixed with colonial structures. Scattered throughout the islands, there are many fine buildings, often the homes of former plantation owners, some of which have been transformed into inns for tourists.

People usually live in towns and villages ranging from twenty to a few hundred residents in size. The villages often contain a general store and sometimes a post office and are characterized by groupings of houses that reflect kinship connections. Most of these village houses are fairly modest wood frame affairs, and the tropical clime obviates the need for complex insulation and weatherproofing. The largest problem faced by homeowners is the hurricanes that appear late in every summer.

House design usually includes a porch on which the occupants can observe passers by. Socializing occurs easily and frequently at home and in public settings. There is an expectation of and pressure for sociability, and adults try to be accessible. Men generally meet on street corners or frequent small bars, rum shops, and pubs where they can socialize. Women generally confine their interactions to social visits, shopping, and church, though chance encounters are always welcome. Sociability is a distinguishing characteristic of the islands and often is commented on by visitors.

There are good paved road systems totaling seventy-eight miles around each island, though some of the interior roads are either dirt or in poor repair. There are 4,500 automobiles on the islands, and far more people own cars than possess scooters or mopeds. The reason for this pattern seems to be status and the appearance of respectability.

FOOD AND ECONOMY

Food in Daily Life. There are a variety of mixed dishes, including many that betray their off-islands origins, such as spaghetti, but there are also local culinary traditions. In addition to staples such as rice and beans, the islands are known for "goat water," a stew usually made from the neck bones and meat of goats. Accompanying most meals are a range of vegetables, especially squashes and peas, and hot sauces. While fresh fish are available, mutton or goat is the staple meat and is served in a variety of ways ranging from curried to creole style. Fried chicken is also popular, especially for entertaining guests. Beverages range from softdrinks to fruit juices to beer and rum. Of all these purchased drinks, beer is significantly the cheapest, as there is a brewery on Saint Kitts.

Basic Economy. Most coastal families maintain small gardens and a few chickens to round out the menu, but most people living along the more populous coast purchase their needs from general stores, and most of the goods are imported and expensive. Sugar production still accounts for a significant part of the income on Saint Kitts. Both islands produce a range of agricultural products for export, and Nevis has a small stock of cattle, most of which are exported.

The monetary unit is the Eastern Caribbean dollar, which is pegged to the U.S. dollar. The need to import many necessities, including foodstuffs, makes the cost of living high.

Both islands have enterprises that assemble electronics goods for export. In addition, there is significant production of beverages, beer, plastics, and ethanol. The biggest element in the current economy is clearly tourism, which accounts for approximate 53 percent of the national revenue. While locals own and run the great majority of the mercantile enterprises and many popular tourist locales, the largest resorts are owned by off-island concerns, principally American.

SOCIAL STRATIFICATION

With the exception of moneyed expatriates from America and Great Britain, the inhabitants do not have a significant class structure based on wealth. The major sociocultural concern of most islanders is to appear "respectable," meaning that one manages an acceptable appearance in possessions and in one's person and behaves in socially appropriate ways, as defined largely by cultural patterns originating in British colonial society. While poverty is inimical to respectability, wealth is not essential for it. Material possessions are important, but as demonstrations of respectability rather than of wealth. Education matters greatly; young people are serious about their studies, and good students are praised by adults and respected by their peers.

POLITICAL LIFE

Government. The islands are a constitutional monarchy with a single elected representative

Masquerade dancers on Saint Kitts.

body, the National Assembly. The government is headed by the prime minister, and for administrative purposes, the country is divided into fourteen parishes.

The most singular aspect of the government is that it is bifurcated. While the head of government is in Basseterre, as a condition of union, Nevis demanded internal self-rule. Thus, that island has its own assembly and its own elected premier. The increasing disenchantment of most Nevisians with their treatment by the central government has led to a movement for independence. Although Saint Kitts/Nevis is already the smallest country in the Western Hemisphere, in August 1998, Nevisians voted on secession. The 62 percent of the population that supported secession fell only 4 percent short of the two-thirds required.

Social Problems and Control. The United States and other countries in the Caribbean are concerned that the islands could come under increasing pressure from drug cartels. While there is very little crime against persons or property, in the last ten years there have been increasing problems, especially on Saint Kitts, with drug smugglers who wish to use the islands for transshipment to the United States. Both Saint Kitts and Nevis maintain small police forces that seldom carry arms. Saint Kitts also maintains a coastal watch program in an effort to impede drug smuggling. If the islands become independent of one another, many observers fear that their size would make them vulnerable to outside pressures for illegal activities.

GENDER ROLES AND STATUSES

Generally, gender roles owe far more to the pattern of the colonial British then to that of West Africa, with one exception. While the male status has more rights and privileges than the female, especially in the public arena, women have significant rights and, as they approach middle age, may even have authority. Some of the better known and more successful entrepreneurs and political figures are women.

During most of the period before independence, the "respectable" pattern was for men to be the breadwinners and women to tend children at home and confine their social activities to the church and the marketplace. However, many families were matricentric, with the woman and extended kin providing much of the material and affective needs of children. With increased education, women have found new ways to realize their potential and gain public respect.

A man harvesting sugar cane. Most citizens are descendants of the slave labor population.

MARRIAGE, FAMILY, AND KINSHIP

Marriage. Marriage is undertaken as both a social responsibility and a sign of adulthood. The reasons given for marriage emphasize love, though parents pressure children, especially females, who are old enough to marry but are not involved in socializing. Sexual experimentation is reluctantly accepted, and that has resulted in 20 percent of the children on Saint Kitts/Nevis being born out of wedlock.

A newly married couple may reside with either set of parents at first but will prefer to live in their own domicile, though usually close to other relatives. With the high percentage of educated citizens living abroad, there are an increasing number of mixed marriages. However, the kinship ties between off-islanders and residents continue to be strong.

SOCIALIZATION

Child Rearing and Education. Mothers are differentially involved in child care. Child rearing tends to be mild, with both males and females kept close until boys begin to explore at about school age. Both genders learn appropriate skills and are taught to respect their parents and elders.

Education is valued, and nearly all young people complete primary school. Most then attend secondary school system modeled on that of Great Britain, and a number of the better students obtain scholarships to study in the United States, Great Britain, or other Commonwealth countries.

ETIQUETTE

Etiquette reflects the concept of respectability in which reciprocity and decorum define both interpersonal relations and social acceptability. It is based largely on colonial British models and relaxed only for close friends and family members.

RELIGION

Some 95 percent of islanders are Protestants, principally Anglican and Methodist, though there are a number of smaller Protestant sects. Religion remains a very important institution in the society and culture. It is a major vehicle for maintaining community solidarity and providing guidelines to and reinforcing the importance of respectable behavior.

While virtually all islanders identity themselves as Christians, many older and some younger islanders believe in *obeah*, a form of witchcraft in which an individual can be supernaturally harmed by another person for reasons ranging from a perceived wrong to simple envy.

MEDICINE AND HEALTH CARE

Saint Kitts and Nevis have good health care with a sufficiency of doctors who are usually British or Canadian trained. There is a hospital on Saint Kitts and an infirmary on Nevis. Pharmaceutical services are widely available.

SECULAR CELEBRATIONS

Held in early August, Culturama is a celebration of traditional Nevisian culture in which music, arts, crafts, and dramatic presentations play dominant roles. It has proven to be a venue though which Nevisians can both expose the young to, and reaffirm pride in their cultural heritage.

THE ARTS AND HUMANITIES

Graphic and Performance Arts. There is a theater group on Saint Kitts and a society of craftspeople. On Nevis, there is a small dramatic society and theater in Charlestown, The Hamilton Arts Center,

Two women cut hair outside a house on Saint Kitts Island.

next to the Alexander Hamilton Museum. There are several reading societies and artists on the island, but little of an organized nature.

BIBLIOGRAPHY

Browne, Whitman T. *From Commoner to King: Robert L. Bradshaw, Crusader for Dignity and Justice in the Caribbean*, 1992.

Hubbard, Vincent K. *Swords, Ships, and Sugar: A History of Nevis to 1900*, 1993.

Merrill, Gordon Clark. *The Historical Geography of Saint Kitts and Nevis*, 1958.

Mills, Frank L., S. B. Jones-Hendrickson, and Bertram Eugene. *Christmas Sports in Saint Kitts–Nevis: Our Neglected Cultural Tradition*, 1984.

Moll, Verna Penn. *St Kitts-Nevis*, 1995.

Motley, Constance Baker. *Equal Justice under Law: An Autobiography*, 1998.

Olwig, Karen Fog. *Global Culture, Island Identity: Continuity and Change in the Afro-Caribbean Community of Nevis*, 1993.

Richardson, Bonham C. *Caribbean Migrants: Environment and Human Survival on Saint Kitts and Nevis*, 1983.

—DOUGLAS RAYBECK

SAINT LUCIA

CULTURE NAME

Saint Lucian

ALTERNATIVE NAMES

Hewanorra, Iounaloa (Island Carib)

ORIENTATION

Identification. The origins of the name Saint Lucia are lost in history. The commonly held notion that Columbus sighted the island on Saint Lucy's Day, 13 December 1498, is dubious, for there is no good evidence of his "discovery." A more plausible explanation attributes the naming to one of various French visitors during the sixteenth century. It appears that the original designation was "Sainte Alousie," the name used in Father DuTetre's 1664 volume on the Antilles.

Saint Lucians identify by this name, distinguishing themselves from residents and nationals of neighboring islands. Although many thousands have emigrated to various parts of the Americas and Europe, especially during the twentieth century, this identification remains strong, even among those born in the diaspora. The question of a shared culture is contentious, for Saint Lucians are divided along many lines, yet there is a sense of belonging to a place, a locality, of which they have a sense of possession. One compelling item of common culture might be *Kwéyòl* or *Patwa*, the French-derived creole language spoken by most Saint Lucians. However, many born and raised abroad do not speak the language, and Saint Lucians also recognize that their *Kwéyòl* is virtually identical to that spoken on Dominica and the French islands of Martinique and Guadeloupe.

Location and Geography. Saint Lucia has an area of 238 square miles (616 square kilometers). It is 27 miles (43 kilometer) long on its north-south axis and 14 miles (22 kilometer) at its widest east-west dimension. Saint Lucia lies between Saint Vincent to the south and Martinique to the north. It is a mountainous island born of ancient volcanic activity, some of which remains in the form of a sulphur springs area near the southwest coastal town of Soufriere. Rainfall is plentiful but variable, with heaviest precipitation in the mountainous interior and drier regions at the north and south extremities. There is also an annual wet-dry cycle, but it is not pronounced.

The island is ringed by a number of settlements, many of which had their origins as fishing villages and residential areas associated with plantations. The capital, Castries, is in the northwest. Castries is situated on a natural harbor that accounts for its preeminence from earliest colonial times. In recent decades there has been a substantial growth of some interior settlements associated with banana cultivation.

Demography. The 1991 census puts Saint Lucia's population at 133,308; the 1995 population estimate was 145,213. This represents a 17.5 percent increase since 1980, and a 33.6 percent increase since 1970. Population growth is slowed only by a substantial outward migration. Nearly 40 percent of the population lives in the greater Castries area, a percentage that did not change much in the 20 years between 1970 and 1991. However, the Castries population has shifted from the central city and its densely populated residential areas to more dispersed suburban neighborhoods as new housing has been built. The area of most rapid growth is the Gros-Islet region in the north of the island, the center of tourism development and upper middle-class and expatriate housing construction.

Most of the population, approximately 90 percent, is of African or African-mixed descent, reflecting Saint Lucia's history of slavery. A small minority, less than 10 percent, has East Indian ancestry—descendants of indentured workers brought to the island after 1858. This minority has dispersed in the

guages. English is the language of instruction in the schools and the language used in business, governmental institutions, and most formal settings. Some older Saint Lucians, especially in rural areas, have only rudimentary skills in English.

The use of the two languages represents socioeconomic differences. *Kwéyòl*, although spoken by nearly all Saint Lucians, was denigrated and its monolingual speakers disadvantaged until the emergence of a recent cultural movement which has sought to celebrate and restore dignity to *Kwéyòl*. English remains the language of official Saint Lucia, but there is a concerted effort to establish *Kwéyòl* as a second national language.

Symbolism. The language issue reflects the cultural struggle of a mini-state, only recently emerging from its colonial past, to define and identify itself. Until the 1970s most of what passed for national symbols in Saint Lucia were of European derivation. The large square in central Castries was named Columbus Square, and the cricket ground, Victoria Park. An annual event was held on Morne Fortune above Castries to recognize the recapture of the island from the French by English forces in 1796 (and incidentally, the reimposition of slavery).

With the establishment of constitutional independence in 1979, a movement to give recognition to local figures and cultural expression, and to redefine Saint Lucian identity, took on great significance. When the island attained internal self-government in 1967, some symbols of national status appeared—a flag, an anthem, and a crest. The central square has been renamed Derek Walcott Square for Saint Lucia's Nobel Laureate in literature, and the park is now called Mindoo Phillip Park after a legendary Saint Lucian cricketer. But the task of creation or recreation of national symbols and national identity is still in process, and is frequently controversial.

HISTORY AND ETHNIC RELATIONS

Emergence of the Nation. Saint Lucia had a long colonial history under both French and British rule. During a turbulent period of the eighteenth century, the island changed hands fourteen times and was finally ceded to the British in 1814. British colonialism came to an end in 1979 after a succession of constitutional changes involving increasing degrees of self-rule and autonomy, especially after 1951. The African population was brought to the island as slaves, mostly during the last half of the 1700s. Saint Lucia's formal institutions are evi-

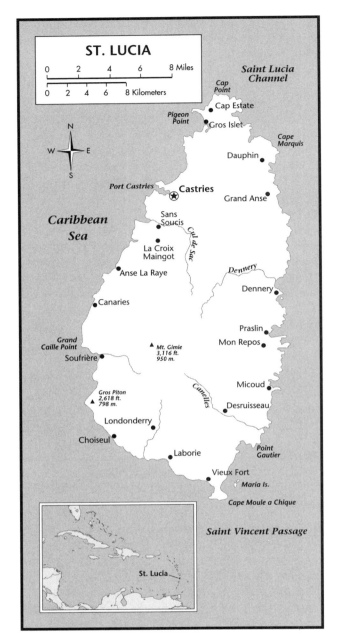

Saint Lucia

last forty years, but is still concentrated in a few rural villages. There remain a few old families of European origin, but there are no settlements of poor whites like those found in some neighboring islands. A more recently arrived Middle-Eastern population is mostly settled in the city.

Linguistic Affiliation. Most Saint Lucians are functionally bilingual, especially those under 40 years of age. The language most commonly spoken in village and rural areas is *Kwéyòl*, a creole language that is a mixture of French and African lan-

dence of the European colonial heritage, but the vital folk culture is a product of the African population.

National Identity. The search for a national identity is ongoing. Independence for Saint Lucia, as for most of her neighbors only recently emerged from a profoundly colonial experience, has involved an examination of cultural traditions that were suppressed in the past. Because culture is conflated with class and color, this is sometimes a difficult exercise.

Ethnic Relations. Ethnic relations in Saint Lucia are a product of the economic history of the island. The virtual demise of the Amerindian population and the establishment of an export-driven plantation economy dependent on African slave labor determined the fundamental social formation. Colonial domination by a European minority over an enslaved African majority established the social dynamic. The basic black-white opposition is complicated by the addition of other populations: East Indians from the sub-continent arrived in the 1850s as indentured labor for the plantations, and more recently a small number of "Syrians," mostly Christian Lebanese, have settled in urban areas as merchants. Unlike some larger Caribbean societies where there have been serious political divisions along ethnic lines, Saint Lucian race relations mostly reflect a continuing black-white tension.

URBANISM, ARCHITECTURE, AND THE USE OF SPACE

In recent times urban-rural divisions have been reduced. The island is small enough that, with improvements in roads and the proliferation of motor vehicles, especially public transport mini-buses, the capital Castries and the southern urban center of Vieux-Fort are within easy reach from nearly all localities. The consequence is that many now live outside these centers but commute daily to jobs. The days of rural isolation have ended.

Architecture reflects changes in materials and styles over time. The graceful tropical house styles characteristically made of wood, with steep-pitched roofs with dormers, jalousied windows, and filigreed trim, typical of upper-class dwellings four decades ago, are now things of the past. Cinder block construction has become ubiquitous, resulting in houses that are heavy in appearance, hot in the tropical climate, and occasionally given to collapse in a hurricane. Some public buildings are in the old colonial style, resembling British municipal construction throughout the Empire, but a disastrous fire in Castries in 1947 reduced three-fourths

of the town to rubble and most new construction was box-like and utilitarian. Newer public construction has followed the same pattern.

Private homes with sufficient space used to have a sitting room, used only on rare occasions. Family heirlooms such as china and tapestries were kept in sideboards there, to be displayed on special occasions. Many of these spaces have been given over to the television set in the last two decades, as Saint Lucians have moved leisure time indoors from the stoop and veranda where neighborhood gatherings once took place after dark. New private homes incorporate kitchens with electric appliances and full bathrooms, replacing backyard cook sheds and outdoor latrines. It should be noted that many Saint Lucians still live in quarters much sparer than these, an indication of a continuing serious housing problem; in 1991 the modal dwelling size was two rooms.

FOOD AND ECONOMY

Food in Daily Life. Food habits reflect the plantation past: the typical diet contains a lot of starches, animal protein content that varies by location, and until recently, little in the way of green vegetables. Starches include various kinds of yams, dasheen, eddos, bananas and plantains, sweet potatoes, and breadfruit. Most of these are boiled, served with some kind of stewed fish or meat, and accompanied by a sauce. Pepper (*capsicum*) sauce is always present at the table, as most dishes are not prepared spicy hot. Animal protein sources reflect the historical scarcity of this element: pork hocks, pig tail, chicken back, and saltfish (cod) have been staples. Imported processed foods have been available for decades, but more recently account for larger parts of many meals.

Food Customs at Ceremonial Occasions. Ceremonial observances are occasions for celebration and lavish food and drink consumption. Celebrations usually mark rites of passage in the lives of Saint Lucians—christenings, first communions, confirmations, weddings, and funerals—while calendrical events are not especially marked. A first communion celebration, for example, usually includes a significant outlay in food and drink for guests, who come from around the island. Hosts try to serve prestigious drinks—whiskey, brandy, gin, rum—and a sumptuous meal centered on meat—chicken for the poorest and as much as a side of beef for the more affluent. Everyone in attendance must leave satisfied, and one never can be sure how many might stop in.

Basic Economy. Throughout Saint Lucia's colonial and post-colonial history, agricultural production has been export-oriented. More than some of its neighbors, Saint Lucia has undergone a series of booms and busts. Agricultural production under colonial rule focused on sugar cane, only giving way to bananas as a principal cash crop in the 1950s. Cane was grown under a number of systems—plantation, sharecropping (*metayage*), and smallholder—reflecting changing market conditions and capital investment over time. The shift to bananas opened up the market for large numbers of rural small producers, and ushered in an era of prosperity that lasted from 1960 to the early 1990s.

The focus on commercial export-driven production has meant that agriculture for local consumption has suffered. Research and development of locally consumed foodstuffs has received scant attention, credit facilities for food production have been non-existent, and storage and preservation of local foods has never been on the agenda of economic planners. One recent consequence of this bias has been that imported foods, mass-produced in countries like the United States, have often been cheaper for consumers than locally-produced alternatives.

Land Tenure and Property. Saint Lucia still supports the institution known as "family land" (*té fami*). This is a tenure and transfer practice that exists outside the legal system, although it is partially supported by the old French legal system (the Napoleonic Code) which is still extant. Briefly, the principles of the system are these: land is held not individually, but communally by family members; transfer, when one dies intestate, is in undivided parcel to all descendants; sale is proscribed, that is, land is retained by the family; rights in land are inherited without legal division. Family land exists alongside individual tenure and land transfers are often accomplished through wills.

Commercial Activities. Much commercial activity is concerned with importing goods from industrial economies. Trading in locally produced goods is largely in foodstuffs. The Castries marketplace is a daily market established and regulated by government where vegetables, fruits, meat and fish are sold. The market also has an area where locally produced crafts and utility items are sold to tourists and local customers.

Major Industries. Industrial growth during the last thirty years has been largely in the area of export processing plants producing garments, electronics assembly, paper products, and leather goods. These employ local labor but are often foreign-owned. Local industries are small-scale and involve food processing and craft production.

In recent years the growth of tourism, mostly associated with the development of facilities in the Castries-Gros-Islet corridor, has overtaken banana production as the most important earner of foreign exchange. Employment generation attributed to tourism has been significant, with more than twelve thousand full-time jobs in the industry. The Saint Lucia Tourist Board has promoted tourist-oriented events, including a jazz festival featuring international and local talent.

Trade. Trade, which in colonial times was dominated by exchange with Great Britain, has shifted to the United States, from which a variety of finished goods are imported, and Japan, which supplies motor vehicles and electronics. By far the most important export is bananas, an economic mainstay for the past forty years. The market for Saint Lucian bananas is in the European Union, primarily Great Britain, and depends on preferential treatment. This trade is currently threatened by regulations imposed by the World Trade Organization.

Division of Labor. The division of labor is very much like that of any modernizing economy, with workers hired based on skills and education.

SOCIAL STRATIFICATION

Classes and Castes. Although in recent years a middle class has developed, the disparities between rich and poor are extreme. Rural prosperity based on banana cultivation is now seriously threatened. The growth of suburban areas around Castries is indicative of the economic primacy of the capital; village areas continue to be marked by poverty and substandard living conditions.

Symbols of Social Stratification. Race remains an important social marker, but it is probably of less consequence than in former times. Likewise, language (English vs. *Kwéyòl*), while still significant, is less important, particularly with the increase in spoken English and decreasing numbers of monolingual *Kwéyòl* speakers.

POLITICAL LIFE

Government. Saint Lucia has a parliamentary system, constructed on a British model. Universal adult suffrage has been in place since 1951, and by 2000,

Boats in a cove in Sonfiere. Many original settlements began as fishing villages.

the island had conducted thirteen elections under this system. The House of Assembly has seventeen elected members, with the majority party forming the government. The term of office is usually five years, but elections are occasionally called before this term elapses. A ministerial system is in place whereby a professional civil service is answerable to a Minister of Government, usually an elected member of the House.

Leadership and Political Officials. Control of the government has shifted between two parties during the last half of the twentieth century. The Saint Lucia Labour Party (SLP), formed out of the trade union movement in 1947, controlled the first elected government after 1951. The United Workers Party (UWP) succeeded them in 1964 after its inauguration earlier that year. In the intervening years the UWP has led the government for all but seven years. In 2000, an SLP government was in place.

Social Problems and Control. The legal system is mostly founded on British common law, with some continuing Napoleanic Code influence from the earlier French period. A professionally trained police force serves the island. Criminal activity has been on the rise in recent years; the presence of guns in the hands of a criminal element is increasingly troubling, and violent crimes that are gun- and drug-associated have multiplied. Saint Lucia, like many of its neighbors, has become a locale for drug transshipment, leading to the rise in crime.

Military Activity. The island currently has no standing army, but a unit of the Police Force is assigned to the Regional Security System Unit.

SOCIAL WELFARE AND CHANGE PROGRAMS

At the national level, social welfare is divided between two government ministries: Health; and Education, Human Resource Development, Youth and Sports. In the latter, the Department of Human Resource Development carries out skills and training programs, often in conjunction with nongovernmental organizations (NGOs). The Ministry of Health is more concerned with the care and welfare of the sick and the elderly, particularly the indigent population. A number of church-affiliated and private organizations also address social welfare concerns.

A market vendor examines onions in Castries. The market is regulated by the government.

NONGOVERNMENTAL ORGANIZATIONS AND OTHER ASSOCIATIONS

Numerous civic organizations like Rotary and Lions clubs are present, along with many church-affiliated organizations. Older organizations like friendly societies, once found in all communities, have become less important in recent times. Development activities and training in this sphere are overseen by the National Research and Development Foundation, an NGO that receives government support and operates training programs for entrepreneurship. Another important NGO is the Folk Research Centre (FRC), which is involved in social and cultural research, programming, and education.

GENDER ROLES AND STATUSES

Division of Labor by Gender. Although there is a patriarchal bias in the society, occupational differentiation has declined in recent times. Both men and women perform most agricultural labor, and the professional ranks are open to both. Some traditional occupations continue to be gender specific— fishing is a male activity, paid domestic labor is done by women. Assembly factories hire a mostly female workforce. The significantly greater success

by girls than boys in school may affect gender parity in positions that demand education and training.

The Relative Status of Women and Men. Much has been made of the so-called "matrifocal" character of West Indian domestic life. This is reflected in Saint Lucia, where men are frequently not dominant figures in households, or are absent. As more women are gainfully employed outside the home, and with the relative success of female schoolchildren, traditional male dominance in the society may be severely challenged.

MARRIAGE, FAMILY, AND KINSHIP

Marriage. Marriage takes place between consenting adults, but is frequently not entered into until middle age. Other living or domestic arrangements often precede a legal marriage, especially within the lower class. These may include "friending," a visiting relationship that often results in childbirth and which may involve the performance of domestic services by the woman in return for a measure of financial contribution on the part of the man. Another arrangement is a cohabitational relationship without benefit of legal marriage. This may be an enduring union eventually given the legal legitimacy of marriage; expectations of the partners and the enactment of the relationship parallel those of a legal union. The cohabitational union is usually not an option for the middle class, for whom the respectability conferred by a legal union is an important consideration.

Relationships outside of marriage are commonplace for men, who may have "friending" alliances despite being in a cohabitational union. When children are born of such unions, the man is expected to financially contribute to the care of the child, but among the poor these contributions are likely to be meager. The opportunity for women to engage in similar activity outside a cohabitational union is limited.

Domestic Unit. Household composition evidences considerable variation. Although domestic units include everything from nuclear family groupings to three-generational households with no resident males, there are a large number of female-headed domestic units. The incidence of these is often class-determined, much more commonplace among poor women than in the middle class. Males resident in such units may be transient.

Kin Groups. The most important kin grouping is the family, which is defined both matrilineally and patrilineally. Family and residential groups often include extended family and others included though non-formal mechanisms. Other extensions include godparenthood, especially for the Roman Catholic majority.

SOCIALIZATION

Child Rearing and Education. Children are often fostered in the homes of relatives, especially grandparents. In part this is a function of the mobility of Saint Lucians, who have long migrated to work opportunities leaving dependent children behind. From an early age village and rural children have considerable freedom to explore their environment without much adult supervision. With young girls this freedom is curtailed as they approach puberty, in the effort to avoid early pregnancies. Childless women are considered unfortunate, but they often acquire maternal status through customary fosterage or adoption.

Children enter infant school at age five. At about eight years old, they move on to primary school. These two institutions are found in most communities and most are coeducational. For the majority of Saint Lucian children, formal schooling

An elderly man weaves a fish trap from dried palm fronds. Fishing is still considered only a man's profession.

ends when they reach the age of fifteen. Although the opportunities for secondary schooling have expanded greatly during the past forty years, there are not enough places for all who desire admittance and entrance exams determine who will continue.

Higher Education. There are no universities in Saint Lucia, but students can prepare for admittance to the University of the West Indies, which has three campuses, by attending classes at the Sir Arthur Lewis Community College.

RELIGION

Religious Beliefs. Reflecting early French colonial control, the majority of Saint Lucians are Roman Catholics, although in recent years Protestant sects have converted many. Every village and many rural settlements have Catholic churches. Much of the clergy is now Saint Lucian, a change from colonial times when nearly all churches had French priests. All the Catholic holidays and sacraments are celebrated.

Death and the Afterlife. Along with conventional religious funeral and burial practices, Saint Lucians stage and participate in wakes, the most important of which occurs in the evening of the death. A wake is presumably attended by at least one representative from each household in the village. Preparations include laying out the deceased in their best clothing inside the house for viewing by guests. Attendees are served white rum and strong coffee at intervals throughout the event, which may continue well into the night. Inside the house a group of singers renders hymns by Ira Davis Sankey, the late-nineteenth-century American gospel singer and hymn composer; and the atmosphere is solemn. Outside, the tone is festive and boisterous. Games are played, jokes are told, and vignettes, sometimes of a ribald nature, are performed. The wake, in somewhat subdued terms, may be repeated a week after the death, and a Mass is often said for the deceased on the occasion of the first anniversary of the death.

MEDICINE AND HEALTH CARE

Saint Lucia has a primary health care system that includes health centers throughout the island, each with a resident nurse and visited weekly by a doctor. Hospitals are situated at Vieux-Fort and Castries, with a smaller unit in Dennery. Private medical practitioners are mostly located in Castries, and those who can afford it seek them out. Apart from biomedical facilities and personnel, there are many who practice traditional alternative therapies. These range from the use of locally grown plants and herbs, combined in a variety of tinctures, poultices, and remedies, to practitioners of Obeah, locally known as *tchenbwa* or *zeb*. These practitioners treat not only medical ailments but also spells, mental afflictions, and troubles of a supernatural origin. Saint Lucians are eclectic in their choice of treatment for various maladies, a phenomenon that reflects their creolized heritage.

SECULAR CELEBRATIONS

Two significant secular events draw many participants. The first of these is Carnival, traditionally a pre-Lenten festival, similar to those found elsewhere in the Caribbean, Brazil, and Louisiana. Although it had some religious overtones, Carnival has become a purely secular event. Recently the Saint Lucian Carnival has been shifted to July, possibly to attract tourists and to avoid the congestion of many events occurring in the spring. Carnival includes costuming, parades, Calypso contests, queen contests, and general celebratory behavior. A second event, of more recent vintage, is *Jounen Kwéyòl* (Creole Day), a week-long festival cele-

brating traditional music, dance, storytelling, costuming, crafts, and *Kwéyòl* language. Another pair of celebrations are the flower festivals, *La Rose* and *La Marguerite*, observed annually by local societies in many villages on the feast days of the patron saints, Saint Rose de Lima (30 August) and Saint Marguerite D'youville (17 October).

THE ARTS AND HUMANITIES

Support for the Arts. Governmental interest in the arts has grown since independence, and the state sometimes collaborates with an NGO, the Folk Research Centre. Sponsorship of the arts by local business has also grown, reflecting a concern for local enterprise beyond its economic utility.

Literature. Saint Lucia boasts a Nobel prize-winning poet and playwright, Derek Walcott. The island has also produced a number of other writers of somewhat less renown. Interest in literature and its production continues to be significant.

Graphic Arts. Graphic arts have received less attention than literature or performance, but the Saint Omer family, under the guidance of its artistic patriarch, Dunstan, has produced remarkable art in the form of public murals, some found in the churches of the island. Another artist of international reputation is Joseph Eudovic, a wood sculptor who maintains a studio and shop near Castries.

Performance Arts. Performance art receives much attention and participation in Saint Lucia. Perhaps the early work of Derek Walcott and his brother, Roddy, also a playwright, set the stage for an interest in drama. It has continued, also inspired by the creolization movement, and a number of performances are staged throughout the year in different venues.

Production of popular music has also flourished during the last thirty to forty years of the twentieth century. Many Saint Lucian groups have participated in the explosion of popular forms that came from the Lesser Antilles beginning about 1970. Recordings of local groups are found in record stores and can be heard on local radio stations. The growth of the creolization movement has given new vitality to traditional musical and performance forms, culminating in the annual celebration of *Jounen Kwéyòl*. These forms, often denigrated in the past, are now seen as components of a national cultural expression, to be nurtured and respected.

The State of the Physical and Social Sciences

Social science research has been carried out for many years in Saint Lucia, mostly by foreign researchers but sometimes with local counterparts. In the 1970s the Folk Research Centre was founded to monitor this research, and to recover research that was locally unavailable. Currently the FRC engages in programming and oversight, and works with visiting scholars. Physical research has been mostly of a biomedical nature or dealing with agriculture. The most significant research has been the Rockefeller-financed bilharzia (schistosomiasis) study, which operated during the 1960s and 1970s, and the work of the WINBAN (Windward Island Banana Association) laboratory on banana propagation.

Bibliography

Acosta, Yvonne and Jean Casimir. "Social Origins of the Counter-Plantation System in Saint Lucia." P. I. Gomes, ed., *Rural Development in the Caribbean*, 1985.

Alleyne, Mervin. "Language and Culture in Saint Lucia." *Caribbean Studies* 1 (1): 1–10, 1961.

Barrow, Christine. *Family Land and Development in Saint Lucia, Monograph Series #1*, 1992.

Beck, Jane C. *To Windward of the Land: The Occult World of Alexander Charles*, 1979.

Breen, Henry H. *Saint Lucia: Historical Statistical and Descriptive*, 1970.

Crichlow, Michaeline. "An Alternative Approach to Family Land Tenure in the Anglophone Caribbean: The Case of Saint Lucia." *New West Indian Guide/Nieuwe West-Indische Gids* 68: 77–99, 1994.

Dressler, William. *Hypertension and Culture Change: Acculturation and Disease in the West Indies*, 1982.

Guilbault, Jocelyn. "Fitness and Flexibility: Funeral Wakes in Saint Lucia, West Indies." *Ethnomusicology* 31: 273–299, 1987.

Jordan, Peter. *Schistosomiasis—The Saint Lucia Project*, 1985.

Midgett, Douglas. "Performance Roles and Musical Change in a Caribbean Society." *Ethnomusicology* 21: 55–73, 1977.

———. "The Saint Lucia Labour Party Electoral Victory of 1997 and the Decline of the Conservative Movements." *Journal of Eastern Caribbean Studies* 23 (4): 1–24, 1998.

Momsen, Janet H. (compiler). *Saint Lucia*, (World Bibliographic Series, Vol. 185), 1996.

Mondesir, Jones E. *Dictionary of Saint Lucian Creole*, 1992.

Potter, Robert B. "Housing and the State in the Eastern Caribbean." R. B. Potter and D. Conway, eds., *Self-Help Housing, the Poor, and the State in the Caribbean*, 1997.

Romalis, Rochelle. "Economic Change and Peasant Political Consciousness in the Commonwealth Caribbean." *Journal of Commonwealth and Comparative Politics* 8: 225–241, 1975.

Walcott, Derek. "What the Twilight Says: An Overture." *Dream on Monkey Mountain and Other Plays*, 1970.

———. *The Antilles: Fragments of Epic Memory (The Nobel Lecture)*, 1992.

Welch, Barbara. "Banana Dependency: Albatross or Liferaft for the Windwards?" *Social and Economic Studies* 43: 123–149, 1994.

—Douglas Midgett

SAINT VINCENT AND THE GRENADINES

CULTURE NAME
Vincentians

ALTERNATIVE NAMES

The locals sometimes call the main island "Hairoun," its Carib name. The term "Saint Vincent" is often used for the whole group, including the Grenadines.

ORIENTATION

Identification. The name "Saint Vincent" was bestowed by Columbus on his discovery of the island on 22 January 1498, in honor of Saint Vincent of Saragossa, a Spanish saint. The name "Grenadines" derives from the Spanish for "pomegranate" (in reference to the distribution of the smaller islands; pomegranate fruits do not grow on the islands).

Location and Geography. The area of Saint Vincent and the Grenadines is 150 square miles (389 square kilometers), with the 133 square miles comprising the mainland and 17 square miles in the Grenadines.

Demography. Saint Vincent and the Grenadines has a population of approximately 120,000 (2000 estimate), with about 110,000 residing on Saint Vincent and the remainder distributed among the Grenadines. On Saint Vincent, most of the population lives in the southern two thirds of the island because the volcano occupies the northern third of the island. The capital, Kingstown, and its suburbs have a population of around 25,000.

Linguistic Affiliation. The official language of Saint Vincent and the Grenadines is English. Most, however, normally speak a creole known locally as "dialect." This would be unintelligible to the casual visitor, but it is based on an English vocabulary and can be learned in a short time.

Symbolism. The national flag is a tricolor of green, gold, and blue, with a stylized *V* in the center—representing the rich foliage of the island, the sun, and the sea. All public buildings display the flag, as do many private homes. Vincentians dwell on the natural beauty of the islands: the volcano and the "black sand" of the beaches; the Vincentian parrot, an endangered endemic species; the rainforest of the interior; the beautiful views.

HISTORY AND ETHNIC RELATIONS

Emergence of the Nation. Saint Vincent was one of the last Caribbean islands to be colonized by Europeans. The aboriginal Caribs existed there in sufficient force to hold off European incursions until the eighteenth century. In the early seventeenth century, the Black Caribs—a population composed of the descendants of Caribs and African maroons from other islands—emerged on Saint Vincent.

In 1763, the Treaty of Paris granted Saint Vincent to the British who quickly set up plantations with large numbers of slaves. The Carib lands in the northern part of the island had been excluded from expropriation by the British, but the promise of profitable sugar cultivation led to encroachment by planters and eventually to two Carib wars. After the Second Carib War (1793–1795), the Black Caribs were removed to Central America. The "Red" Caribs, whose descendants still live in Saint Vincent, were allowed to stay.

By the beginning of the nineteenth century, the British colony had settled into a sugar plantation economy maintained by the importation of slaves. Slavery ended on 1 August 1834.

The importation of Africans by Europeans established the basic Afro-European foundation of Vincentian society. The labor shortage created by emancipation occasioned the immigration of East Indians, Portuguese, and Barbadian whites. Many of the freed slaves were turned into agricultural wage earners, but most became peasants. A combi-

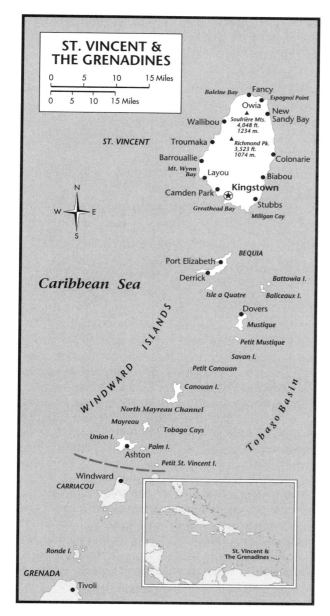

Saint Vincent and the Grenadines

National Identity. The poor people in Saint Vincent, whether of African, European, Native American, or Asian descent, derive a strong sense of identity from the history of the resistance activities of the Caribs in the eighteenth century, while the wealthier Vincentians identify with English or North American models of behavior. More than that, the environmental features of Saint Vincent unify the country. The national anthem emphasizes the natural beauty of the islands.

Ethnic Relations. The population of the nation at the 1991 census was 106,499, with over 82,000 describing themselves as African/Negro/Black (77.1 percent), 17,501 as mixed (16.4 percent), 3,341 as Amerindian/Carib (3.1 percent), 1,477 as East Indian (1.4 percent), 511 as Portuguese (0.5 percent), 982 as white (0.9 percent), and 140 describing themselves as "other."

Each of the ethnic minorities has been successfully integrated into the nation state and a Vincentian identity. All ethnicities intermarry with the black majority, although the Barbados-descended local whites of Dorsetshire Hill are said to be more reclusive.

URBANISM, ARCHITECTURE, AND THE USE OF SPACE

Saint Vincent and the Grenadines is primarily rural. Most of the population lives in small villages of 100 to 500 people. The only large town in the country is the capital, Kingstown.

Saint Vincent has a reliable electric supply to the entire island, along with telephone service and safe drinking water. Many people cannot afford utilities in their homes, and the government has supplied most villages with public showers and water taps. Most buildings are made of cinder block or wood frames, painted white or the pastel colors common to the Caribbean.

FOOD AND ECONOMY

Food in Daily Life. The daily dish of most Vincentians is *pilau*, a preparation of rice and pigeon peas to which is added any meat or fish available. Locally grown vegetables, "ground provision," include yams and sweet potatoes, dasheens, eddoes, tannies, and cassava. Among the island's abundant fruits are bananas, mangos, breadfruit, guavas, plumrose, coconuts, passion fruits, and pineapples.

The main meal is usually eaten in the early evening when the heat of the day has dissipated. A

nation of peasant and plantation agriculture remains the character of Saint Vincent in modern times.

In the latter half of the twentieth century, Vincentians gradually came to have more control over their own political life. Universal suffrage granted by the British Crown in 1951 gave common people a measure of power that was formerly possessed by the planters. Independence was granted in 1979. Due to the reliance on an export economy of bananas, Saint Vincent remains dependent on the trade policies of the United States, Great Britain, and the European Union.

light lunch or snacks of fruit make up the midday meal. Breakfast is normally a hearty affair, typically consisting of fried salt fish with onions and peppers, bread, and a pot of cocoa or coffee.

Fish of all kinds are caught by the local fishermen. Cetaceans also are hunted and eaten, the most common being porpoises, killer whales, and pilot whales. Fishsellers travel to the villages in pickup trucks when a catch is in, blowing conch shells to announce that fish are for sale. On holidays, it is common for everyone to fish for crawfish in the mountain streams or to catch land crabs to add to the evening meal.

Food Customs at Ceremonial Occasions. Whenever guests are invited for a meal, they must be fed until they are satisfied. Rum is drunk before or after a special meal, or even during a break in the day. Strong rum (70 percent alcohol) is the Vincentian drink and is offered to all male guests. Women may have beer, but usually they do not drink strong alcohol. Sea moss—a mixture of milk, seaweed, and spices—is considered an aphrodisiac and appears at Christmas and other special occasions. For birthdays and other celebrations cakes are usually eaten.

Basic Economy. Bananas and tourism are the main forces in the Vincentian economy: bananas on the mainland, tourism in the Grenadines. Plantations continued to exist after the end of slavery and remained powerful, but small farming employed more people in contemporary times. Few households can subsist entirely from their farming, and most have some members engaged in wage labor. Remittances from abroad have become an essential part of the Vincentian economy.

Land Tenure and Property. The current pattern of land distribution and use began during slavery, and a few families own most of the land. Agricultural land may be owned outright, rented or sharecropped. Land may also be held jointly by a number of siblings and their heirs—a uniquely Caribbean form of land tenure known as "family land." All who have a share in the land have a right to its produce.

Commercial Activities. The economy is a mixture of subsistence and plantation agriculture. In the capital, Kingstown, a market square is occupied on most days by women selling "ground provision," produce from their gardens. Women also sell their produce in neighboring countries. A separate market in the capital is set up for fishermen. Funded by Japan, it is called "Little Tokyo." Whales, caught on the western side of Saint Vincent, are butchered and sold out of the town of Barroullie. All fish products are produced for local consumption.

On Saint Vincent, there is a cigarette factory, a plastics factory, a various food processing facilities directed to the local market. Occasionally, European and American investments provide jobs, including a tennis racket factory, clothing manufacture, and a marina.

On Canouan, a traditional boat-building industry continues to employ a few people.

On the other islands, subsistence agriculture and tourism are the primary factors in the economy.

Major Industries. Apart from agriculture, and tourism in the Grenadines, there is no major industry. Saint Vincent is a major world producer of arrowroot.

Trade. The main trade partners are the United States, other CARICOM (Caribbean common market) countries, the United Kingdom, and the European Economic Community. Saint Vincent has very little manufacturing, so most of the trade is in bananas, arrowroot, and other agricultural produce. In spite of the peasant economy, all of the food staples used daily by Vincentians—flour, rice, sugar, salt cod—are imported.

Division of Labor. Unemployment ranged from 20 to 50 percent throughout the twentieth century, with the highest rates coming in the 1990s. These figures are misleading, as nearly everyone is engaged in some subsistence activity. Most Vincentians engage in multiple economic activities.

SOCIAL STRATIFICATION

Classes and Castes. Vincentian society consists of a small elite composed of foreign-educated black Vincentians and the white planter families, a small middle class of government employees and business professionals, and a large class of poor people. The Caribs, whose villages flank the volcano, are the poorest people on the island. A community of foreign expatriates who have taken Vincentian citizenship live in the southeast section of the main island. Foreign whites control Mustique, Petit Saint Vincent, and Palm Island.

Symbols of Social Stratification. A sharp difference is visible between the very small local elite and the activities of the poor who make up the majority of the Vincentian population. The middle class differentiate themselves from the poorer people by their use of standard English speech, private automobiles, and expensive dress, as well as lodge memberships and such activities as beauty contests.

POLITICAL LIFE

Government. Saint Vincent and the Grenadines is a constitutional monarchy with Elizabeth II as head of state in 2000. Her representative on the island then was Governor-General David Jack.

Leadership and Political Officials. Power is divided between the Unity Labor Party (social democrat) and the New Democracy Party (conservative), with the conservatives holding the balance for most of the years since independence. Sir James Mitchell has been prime minister since 1984. Ralph Gonsalves, a scholar and lawyer, was the minority leader in 2000.

Social Problems and Control. Unemployment, underemployment, and the drug trade are the main problems Saint Vincent has had to face in modern times. The Grenadines, with their many uninhabited islets, are a transhipment point for illicit drugs from South America to the United States.

Military Activity. The country has no formal military. The duties of a military have been taken over by the Saint Vincent and the Grenadines Royal Police Force. The U.S. military has a training and advisory role.

SOCIAL WELFARE AND CHANGE PROGRAMS

The U.S. Peace Corps and Canadian Crossroads organizations maintain a presence in Saint Vincent. Scandinavian, Taiwanese, and Japanese aid agencies all have active projects in the islands. The World Health Organization had some success in an AIDS awareness campaign, with the result that Saint Vincent and the Grenadines has one of the highest rates of condom use in the world near the end of the 1990s.

NONGOVERNMENTAL ORGANIZATIONS AND OTHER ASSOCIATIONS

Churches organize many activities, but secular clubs are plentiful. These include drama groups, lodges, nature organizations, the girl and boy scouts, and domino playing, soccer, and cricket clubs.

GENDER ROLES AND STATUSES

Division of Labor by Gender. Men and women work together on many activities, but typically men do the farming, women do the gardening, and men work at sea. Traditionally, only women sell produce in the market square; only men sell fish. Women are paid less than men at service jobs.

The Relative Status of Women and Men. Although women have more economic power than in many peasant economies and are often heads of households, men have a higher status. Relationships between men and women are placed overtly in a context of monetary/sexual favor exchange.

MARRIAGE, FAMILY, AND KINSHIP

Marriage. Three forms of conjugal relationship are recognized: "visiting" (the couple reside separately), "keeping" (cohabitation), and legal marriage. Among the majority of the population, the tendency is to marry later in life, usually after a couple has had several children together. It is common for women and men to have a number of children by different partners.

Domestic Unit. Households in Saint Vincent and the Grenadines may be composed of extended families, nuclear families, or individuals. The matrifocal, multigeneration family is typical. Overall, the composition of the household is flexible. In times of need, children are "lent" or "shifted" to the households of kin to lighten the subsistence needs of a household.

Inheritance. Inheritance is bilateral according to British law. Family land is always inherited jointly and cannot be broken up.

Kin Groups. People recognize kin of any degree and will go out of their way to be especially courteous and generous to them, but there are no kin groupings larger than the extended family.

SOCIALIZATION

Infant Care. For most Vincentians, the umbilicus or "navel string" is planted under a fruit-bearing tree shortly after birth, so that the child will have a healthy and productive life. The child is not given a name until about four weeks after birth. Meanwhile, the infant is coddled and cuddled and played with by all in the household. Care is taken not to become too attached to the infant unless it should sicken and die from too much love—a condition known as *love maljo*.

Men loading plastic-wrapped banana bunches onto a lighter for transfer to a freighter anchored in deeper water. Bananas are one of the major exports of Saint Vincent.

Child Rearing and Education. Children are raised by everyone in the household and in the extended family. Children early develop a sense of security about their place in society. At the age of five or six, the child may begin to attend school. Education is free but not compulsory up to about eight years of age. After that, tuition must be paid. Many families cannot afford to send their children to school at any age, and their children work on the farms as soon as they are able. Literacy is in excess of 80 percent, and given their occupational opportunities, Vincentians are over educated on the whole. People often must have several O-levels (equivalent to one or two years of American college) to be hired as a clerk in a store.

Higher Education. Saint Vincent has a small teacher's college, a nursing school, and a medical college on the main island. The medical college is geared to foreign students, only admitting one or two Vincentians on scholarship per class. A University of West Indies Extension office offers some classes but no degrees.

ETIQUETTE

Generosity is the main feature of Vincentian conduct. Vincentians give of themselves and their resources to an extraordinary degree. Two customs that may strike the visitor as unusual are that it is a serious breach of etiquette to call someone's name in public and that the use of cameras by foreigners is likely to elicit an angry or violent response.

RELIGION

Almost everyone in Saint Vincent is a Christian, and most Christian denominations are represented. A native religion, a combination of African rituals and Christian liturgy, has formed on Saint Vincent. Its followers are known as the Converted, or Spiritual Baptists. Believed by the rest of the population to have a particular facility with spirits, they are utilized by most Vincentians to conduct rituals at wakes and at other times of spiritual unrest. The local "pointer," the Converted ritual specialist, may also be consulted for illness or psychological unease. Rastafarians also have a presence in Saint Vincent.

Religious Beliefs. Saint Vincent is a Christian country, although a few Bahai can be found. Main denominations are Anglican, Catholic, Methodist, and Pentecostal. About 10 percent of the population belongs to the local "Converted" religion (also known as "Spiritual Baptist"), a combination of African and Christian rituals. Several hundred Vincentians are Rastafarians.

Among a large portion of the Vincentian population, dreams are interpreted as real spiritual events and many ordinary Vincentians fear dreams, as they may predict misfortune. "Jumbies" (evil spirits), "Rounces" (spirit-animals that produce night terrors), "Ghosts" (the spirits of lie people seeking their graves), "Diablesses" (demon temptresses), "Haggs" (vampire-like creatures), and other supernatural beings inhabit Saint Vincent and many small ritual actions are required to protect one from them. These include keeping a bottle of hot pepper sauce by one's bed, placing a jar of urine in one's yard, and spinning around before entering one's home. Some young people scoff at these practices.

Religious Practitioners. The ordinary Christian denominations have ministers, priests, and bishops as they are found in other Christian countries. The Rastafarians have elders, who do not conduct any special rituals but instead are respected interpreters of scripture (the Bible). The Converted have a host of religious practitioners, the most important of which is the office of "pointer." The local pointer is the person to whom most Vincentians will turn in times of spiritual trouble. Although the Converted are persecuted socially and their religion was actually illegal until 1965, they are still revered and feared for their powers. The Converted say, "They curse us in the day, but they seek us out at night."

Rituals and Holy Places. There are no pilgrimage locations on Saint Vincent. Church buildings themselves are the only permanently holy places. Rituals by the Converted temporarily sanctify specific locations—a house, the market square, a crossroads, a beach—for services they hold there.

Traditionally the Converted conduct a wake for a family (regardless of the denomination) on any one of the third-, ninth-, fortieth-night, or six-month or one-year anniversary of the death—but the "nine nights" and the "forty days" are the most important. The Converted receive a ritual payment of hot cross buns and cocoa tea.

The celebrations of Carnival (originally before Lent) and Nine Mornings (before Christmas) began as religious rituals, but now are primarily secular in nature.

Death and the Afterlife. The dead in Saint Vincent are remarkably mobile. On All Saint's Eve (31 October) and on All Soul's Eve (1 November), souls of the deceased are believed to leave the grave and to wander about Saint Vincent visiting their favorite places. Lighted candles are placed on the graves of departed family members to guide the souls back to their resting places.

The dead also roam on the third, ninth, and fortieth days after death, and on the six-month and one-year anniversary of the death. The Converted traditionally are called to conduct rituals in the home of the deceased on any of these days.

MEDICINE AND HEALTH CARE

Health care is accessible to people in all parts of the island. Basic health care is free or low cost to all, but any special services and all surgery are expensive. Many of the poor forgo operations that would be considered necessary in other countries.

SECULAR CELEBRATIONS

The two most important events in the Vincentian calendar are Christmas and Carnival. There are, besides, twelve national holidays throughout the year: New Year's Day, Saint Vincent and the Grenadines Day (22 January, celebrating the discovery of the islands by Columbus), Good Friday, Easter Monday, Labor Day (1 May, also known locally as "Fisherman's Day"), Whit Monday, CARICOM Day (celebrating the Caribbean common market), Carnival Tuesday, August Monday (1 August, Emancipation Day), Independence Day (27 October), Christmas Day, and Boxing Day (26 December).

Christmas includes three segments: Nine Mornings, Christmas Day, and "the two days following Christmas." Following a custom begun during slavery, on the Nine Mornings Vincentians hold parties each day in the pre-dawn hours, then go to work, and party again the next day for each of the nine days. In Kingstown, large sections of the town are taken over by the party goers. Christmas Day is spent with one's family. Boxing Day and the day after are spent visiting neighbors. The Christmas season coincides with a cooling "Christmas breeze" and is looked forward to for the temporary relief from the tropical heat as much as for the celebrations.

Carnival celebrations, with their attendant calypso and costume contests, are sponsored by the government.

THE ARTS AND HUMANITIES

Support for the Arts. The visual arts are not highly elaborated on Saint Vincent. Several musical groups do support themselves, although mainly by tours and record sales off the island. The government sponsors the Carnival celebration which formerly was held according to the religious calendar, but was moved to July to encourage tourism.

Literature. There is almost no written literature produced by Vincentians themselves. Myths, folktales, and other stories are rarely passed down in any formal way. However, Vincentians place great value on the ability to create good stories, jokes, and riddles and to present them in a convincing and entertaining way. Impromptu speaking contests and joke contests may be arranged in any gathering. Moonlit nights in the rural villages are especially noted as a time for these performances.

Graphic Arts. There is little in the way of graphic arts in Saint Vincent and the Grenadines. Occasionally an individual self-taught artist will gain attention.

Performance Arts. Calypso, Soka, Reggae, and Gospel are the main forms of music heard in Saint Vincent. Competitive caroling groups also perform at Christmas time.

Dramatic presentations are held by school and church groups throughout the islands as fund-raising events. The most important of these are "concerts," variety shows featuring short plays, jokes, and singing for which a small entrance fee is charged.

THE STATE OF THE PHYSICAL AND SOCIAL SCIENCES

Local development of the sciences is negligible; however, the islands themselves are the focus of much scientific activity. Scientists from around the world are attracted by Saint Vincent's volcano and its endemic wildlife. Dozens of sociologists and anthropologists have conducted major research on aspects of Vincentian society.

BIBLIOGRAPHY

Abrahams, Roger D. *The Man-of-Words in the West Indies: Performance and the Emergence of Creole Culture,* 1983.

Austin, Roy L. "Family Environment, Educational Aspiration and Performance in Saint Vincent." *The Review of Black Political Economy* 17 (3): 101–122, 1989.

Betley, Brian James. "Stratification and Strategies: A Study of Adaptation and Mobility in a Vincentian Town." Ph.D. dssertation, University of California, Los Angeles, 1976.

Brittain, Ann W. "Anticipated Child Loss to Migration and Sustained High Fertility in an East Caribbean Population. *Social Biology* 38 (;ef): 94–112, 1991.

Gearing, Margaret Jean. "Family Planning in Saint Vincent, West Indies: A Population History Perspective." *Social Science and Medicine* 35 (10): 1273–1282, 1992.

Gullick, Charles (C. J. M. R.). *Myths of a Minority: The Changing Traditions of the Vincentian Caribs,* 1985.

Jackson, Jane. "Social Organization in Saint Vincent." B.Litt. thesis, Oxford University, 1972.

Landman, Bette Emeline. "Household and Community in Canouan, British West Indies." Ph.D. dissertation, Ohio State University, 1972.

Price, Neil. *Behind the Planter's Back: Lower Class Responses to Marginality in Bequia Island, Saint Vincent,* 1988.

Shacochis, Bob. *Swimming in the Volcano,* 1993.

Thomas-Hope, Elizabeth M. *Explanation in Caribbean Migration: Perception and the Image: Jamaica, Barbados, Saint Vincent,* 1992.

Zane, Wallace W. *Journeys to the Spiritual Lands: The Natural History of a West Indian Religion,* 1999.

—WALLACE W. ZANE

SAMOA

CULTURE NAME
Samoan

ORIENTATION

Identification. Oral tradition holds that the Samoan archipelago was created by the god Tagaloa at the beginning of history. Until 1997, the western islands were known as Western Samoa or Samoa I Sisifo to distinguish them from the nearby group known as American Samoa or Amerika Samoa. The distinction was necessitated by the partitioning of the archipelago in 1899. All Samoans adhere to a set of core social values and practices known as *fa'a Samoa* and speak the Samoan language. The official name today is Samoa.

Location and Geography. Samoa includes nine inhabited islands on top of a submarine mountain range. The largest islands are Savai'i at 703 square miles (1820 square kilometers) and Upolu at 430 square miles (1114 square kilometers), on which the capital, Apia, is located. The capital and port developed around Apia Bay from an aggregation of thirteen villages.

Demography. The population is estimated at 172,000 for the year 2000, 94 percent of which is is ethnically Samoan. A small number of people of mixed descent are descendants of Samoans and European, Chinese, Melanesians, and other Polynesians who settled in the country in the late nineteenth and early twentieth centuries.

Linguistic Affiliation. Samoan belongs to a group of Austronesian languages spoken throughout Polynesia. It has a chiefly or polite variant used in elite communication and a colloquial form used in daily communication. Samoan is the language of instruction in elementary schools and is used alongside English in secondary and tertiary education, government, commerce, religion, and the broadcast media. The language is a cherished symbol of cultural identity.

Symbolism. A representation of the Southern Cross appears on both the national flag and the emblem of state. The close link between Samoan society and Christianity is symbolized in the national motto "Samoa is founded on God" (*Fa'avae ile Atua Samoa*) and in a highlighted cross on the national emblem. The sea and the coconut palm, both major food sources, also are shown on the emblem. An orator's staff and sinnet fly whisk and a multilegged wooden bowl in which the beverage kava is prepared for chiefs are symbolic of the authority of tradition. A political movement, *O le Mau a Pule*, promoted independence in the first half of the twentieth century, calling for Samoa for Samoans (*Samoa mo Samoa*) and engaging in confrontations with colonial powers over the right to self-government. For some, the struggles of the Mau, in particular the martyrdom of a national chief in a confrontation with New Zealand soldiers, are symbols of the nation's determination to reclaim sovereignty. Samoans celebrate the peaceful attainment of constitutional independence in 1962 on 1 June.

The national anthem and a religious anthem, *Lota Nu'u ua ou Fanau ai* ("My Village in Which I Was Born") are sung to celebrate national identity. Samoans refer to their country in these anthems as a gift from God and refer to themselves in formal speech as the children of Samoa, brothers and sisters, and the Samoan family.

HISTORY AND ETHNIC RELATIONS

Emergence of the Nation. In the mid-nineteenth century, Germany, Britain, and the United States established consular presences and attempted to impose their authority. Mutual suspicion, disunity, and a lack of military resources meant that the powers were largely unsuccessful until they agreed

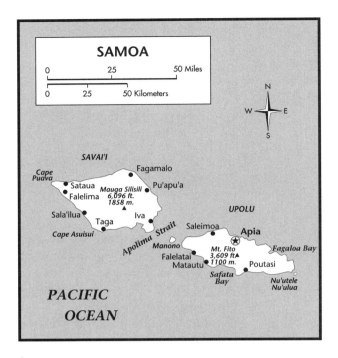

Samoa

After World War II, the United Nations made Samoa a trusteeship and gave New Zealand responsibility for preparing it for independence. A better trained and more sympathetic administration and a determined and well-educated group of Samoans led the country through a series of national consultations and constitutional conventions. That process produced a unique constitution that embodied elements of Samoan and British political traditions and led to a peaceful transition to independence on 1 January 1962.

National Identity. The national and political cultures that characterize the nation are unambiguously Samoan. This is in large part a consequence of a constitutional provision that limited both suffrage and political representation to those who held chiefly titles and are widely regarded as protectors of culture and tradition. These arrangements continued until 1991, when the constitution was amended to permit universal suffrage. While representation is still limited to chiefs, the younger titleholders now being elected generally have broader experience and more formal education than their predecessors.

Ethnic Relations. Samoan society has been remarkably free of ethnic tension, largely as a result of the dominance of a single ethnic group and a history of intermarriage that has blurred ethnic boundaries. Samoans have established significant migrant communities in a number of countries, including New Zealand, Australia, and the United States, and smaller communities in other neighbors.

URBANISM, ARCHITECTURE, AND THE USE OF SPACE

The spatial arrangement of villages beyond the capital has changed little. Most villages lie on flat land beside the sea and are connected by a coastal road. Clusters of sleeping houses, their associated cooking houses, and structures for ablutions are arranged around a central common (*malae*). Churches, pastors' homes, meeting houses and guest houses, and women's committee meeting houses also occupy prominent positions around the malae. Schools stand on land provided by villages and frequently on the malae.

The availability of migrant remittances has transformed the design and materials used in private homes and public buildings. Houses typically have large single rectangular spaces around which some furniture is spread and family portraits, certificates, and religious pictures are hung. Homes

to "rationalize" their Pacific interests at the turn of the century.

The western part of the archipelago came under German control, and the eastern part under American naval administration. The German administration was determined to impose its authority and tried to undermine the Samoan polity and replace its titular heads with the kaiser. These attempts provoked varying degrees of anger between 1900 and 1914, when a small New Zealand expeditionary force, acting on British orders, ended the German administration.

After World War I, New Zealand administered Western Samoa under a League of Nations mandate. It too was determined to establish authority and pursued a course similar to that of the Germans. It proved an inept administration, and its mishandling of the *S.S. Talune's* arrival, which resulted in the death of 25 percent of the population from influenza and its violent reaction to the Mau procession in 1929, left Samoans suspicious and disillusioned. These and other clumsy attempts to promote village and agricultural development strengthened Samoans' determination to reclaim their autonomy. Their calls found the ear of a sympathetic Labor government in New Zealand in the mid-1930s, but World War II intervened before progress was made.

increasingly have indoor cooking and bathing facilities. The new architecture has reshaped social relations. Indigenous building materials are being replaced by sawn lumber framing and cladding, iron roofing, and concrete foundations. The coral lime cement once used in larger public buildings has been replaced by concrete and steel.

FOOD AND ECONOMY

Food in Daily Life. Samoans eat a mixture of local and imported foods. Local staples include fish, lobster, crab, chicken, and pork; lettuce and cabbage; root vegetables such as *talo*, *ta'amu*, and yams; tree crops such as breadfruit and coconut; and local beverages such as coffee and cocoa. Imported foods include rice, canned meat and fish, butter, jam, honey, flour, sugar, bread, tea, and carbonated beverages.

Many families drink beverages such as tea throughout the day but have a single main meal together in the evening. A range of restaurants, including a McDonald's, in the capital are frequented largely by tourists and the local elite.

Food Customs at Ceremonial Occasions. Sharing of food is a central element of ceremonies and features in Sunday meals known as *toana'i*, the feasts that accompany weddings and funerals and the conferring of chiefly titles, and annual feasts such as White Sunday. Special meals are marked by a larger than usual amount of food, a greater range of delicacies, and formality. Food also features in ceremonial presentations and exchanges between families and villages. The presentation of cooked whole pigs is a central feature of such events, and twenty-liter drums of salted beef are increasingly popular. Kava (*'ava*), a beverage made from the powdered root of *Piper methysticum*, made and shared in a ceremonially defined order at meetings of chiefs (*matai*) and less formally among men after work.

Basic Economy. The agricultural and industrial sectors employ 70 percent of the workforce and account for 65 percent of the gross domestic product (GDP). The service sector employs 30 percent of those employed and accounts for 35 percent of the GDP. Much of this sector is associated with the tourist industry, which is limited by intense competition from other islands in the region and its dependence on economic conditions in source countries.

The economy ran large trade deficits in the 1990s. Products are exported to New Zealand, American Samoa, Australia, Germany and the United States, and imports, intermediate goods,

Samoan artist Fatu Feu'u attends the South Pacific Arts Festival.

foods, and capital goods come from New Zealand, Australia, Fiji, and the United States. The economy is highly dependent on remittances from expatriates in New Zealand, Australia, the United States, and American Samoa and aid from New Zealand, Australia, and Germany. These remittances are declining because overseas-born children of migrants have attenuated their connections with the nation, whose geopolitical significance has declined since the Cold War ended.

Land Tenure and Property. Much agricultural production comes from the 87 percent of the land held under customary tenure and associated with villages. The control of this land is vested in elected chiefs (*matai*), who administer it for the families (*aiga*) they head. The remaining 13 percent is land held by the crown and a small area of freehold residential land around the capital.

Trade. Samoa produces some primary commodities for export: hardwood timber, copra and coconut products, root vegetables, coffee, cocoa, and fish. Agricultural produce constitutes 90 percent of exports. The most promising export crop, taro, was effectively eliminated by leaf blight in 1993. A small industrial sector designed to provide import substitution and exports processes primary commodities such as coconut cream and oil, animal feed, soap, biscuits, cigarettes, and beer. A multinational corporation has established a wiring harness assembly plant whose production is reexported; and a clothing assembly plant is planned.

SOCIAL STRATIFICATION

Classes and Castes. Samoan society is meritocratic. Those with recognized ability have traditionally been elected to leadership of families. Aside from four nationally significant chiefly titles, the influence of most titles is confined to the families and villages with which they are associated. Title holders gained status and influence not only from accumulating resources but also from their ability to mobilize and redistribute them. These principles work against significant permanent disparities in wealth. The power of chiefs has been reduced, and the wealth returned by expatriates has flowed into all sectors of society, undermining traditional rank-wealth correlations. The public influence of women is becoming increasingly apparent. A commercial elite that has derived its power from the accumulation and investment of private wealth has become increasingly influential in politics.

POLITICAL LIFE

Government. The legislative branch of the government consists of a unicameral Legislative Assembly (*O Le Fono a Faipule*) elected to five-year terms by universal suffrage. A twelve-member cabinet nominated by the prime minister is appointed by the head of state, Malietoa Tanumafili II, who has held that position since 1962. Forty-seven members are elected by Samoans in eleven electorates based on traditional political divisions. Two members at large represent general electors. Only holders of matai titles can be elected to the Fono.

Legislation is administered by a permanent public service that consists of people chosen on the basis of merit. The quality of public service has been questioned periodically since independence. Concern with the quality of governance has led the current government to engage in training programs aimed at institutional strengthening.

The judicial branch includes a Supreme Court, a court of appeals, and a lands and titles court. These agencies deal with matters that cannot be dealt with by village polities. Village polities (*fono a matai*) are empowered by the Village Fono Act of 1990 to make and administer bylaws for the regulation of

Upolu police officer in traditional dress.

village activities and to punish those who break them.

Social Problems and Control. The role of village politics in the maintenance of order is important because the state has no army and a relatively small police force. This limits the ability of the state to enforce laws and shapes its relations with villages, which retain significant autonomy.

Samoans accept and trust these institutions but have found that they are ineffective in areas such as the pursuit of commercial debts. Recent cases have pointed to tension between collective rights recognized, emphasized, and enforced by village polities, and the individual rights conferred by the constitution in areas such as freedom of religion and speech.

SOCIAL WELFARE AND CHANGE PROGRAMS

The government is responsible for health, education, and welfare in cooperation with villages and churches. Health care and education are provided for a nominal cost. Families provide for their members' welfare. The state grants a small old-age pension, and the Catholic Church runs a senior citizens' home.

People under the portico of the immigration office as traffic passes by in Apia. Ethnic tensions are virtually non-existent in Samoa.

Nongovernmental Organizations and Other Associations

The most influential nongovernmental organizations (NGOs) are the churches, in which 99 percent of Samoans participate actively and which actively comment on the government's legislative program and activity. A small number of NGOs work for the rights of women and the disabled, environmental conservation, and transparency in government. Professional associations exert some influence on the drafting of legislation. These organizations have a limited impact on the life of most residents.

Gender Roles and Statuses

The organization of traditional production was clearly gendered, and the parts of this mode of production that remain intact are still gendered. The constitution provides for equality of opportunity, and there are no entrenched legal, social, or religious obstacles to equality for women. There is some evidence of growing upward social mobility by women.

Marriage, Family, and Kinship

Samoan society is composed of extended families (*aiga potopoto*), each of which is associated with land and a chiefly title. All Samoans inherit membership and land use rights in the *aiga* of their parents' parents. They may choose to live with one or more of *aiga* and develop strong ties with those in which they live. Choices are determined by matters such as the availability of resources and status of various groups and personal preference. Aiga potopoto include resident members who work the land, "serve" the chief, and exercise full rights of membership and nonresident members who live outside the group but have some rights in its activities. Resident members live in clusters of households within the village, share some facilities and equipment, and work on family-land controlled by the matai.

Inheritance. Rights to reside on and use land are granted to members of a kin group who request them, subject to availability. Rights lapse at death, and matai may then reassign them. There is a growing tendency to approve the transmission of rights to parcels of land from parents to children, protecting investments in development and constituting a form of de facto freehold tenure. Since neither lands nor titles can be formally transmitted without the consent of the kin group, the only property that can be assigned is personal property.

Many residents die intestate and with little personal property. With increasing personal wealth, provision for the formal disposition of wealth may assume greater importance. This is not a foreign concept, since matai have traditionally made their wishes known before death in a form of will known as a *mavaega*. The Public Trust Office and legal practitioners handle the administration of estates.

SOCIALIZATION

Child Rearing and Education. Younger people are expected to respect their elders and comply with their demands. Justification for this principle is found in Samoan tradition and Christian scripture. The only exception exists in early childhood, when infants are protected and indulged by parents, grandparents, and older siblings. After around age five, children are expected to take an active, if limited, part in the family economy. From then until marriage young people are expected to comply unquestioningly with their parents' and elders' wishes.

Great importance is attached to the family's role in socialization. A "good" child is alert and intelligent and shows deference, politeness, and obedience to elders and respect for Samoan custom (*aganu'u fa'a samoa*) and Christian principles and practices. The belief that the potential for learning these qualities is partly genetic and partly social and is defined initially within the family is grounded in both Samoan and Christian thought.

Formal education is provided in secular and religious institutions. There are elementary, intermediate, and secondary secular schools run by the government or churches and church-linked classes that provide religious instruction. There is great respect and desire for higher education, and a significant part of the education budget is committed to supporting the National University of Samoa, the nursing school, the teachers training college, the trades training institute, and overseas training.

RELIGION

Religious Beliefs. Samoa is overwhelmingly Christian. The major denominations— Congregationalist, Methodist, Roman Catholic, and Latter-Day Saints—have been joined recently by smaller ones such as the SDA and charismatic Pentecostal groups such as Assembly of God. Clergy and leaders are prepared at theological training institutions at home and abroad. Small Baha'i and Muslim groups have formed in recent years.

MEDICINE AND HEALTH CARE

Parallel systems of introduced and indigenous knowledge and practice coexist. Certain conditions are believed to be "Samoan illnesses" (*ma'i samoa*) that are explained and treated by indigenous practitioners and others to be "European illnesses" (*ma'i papalagi*), which are best understood and treated by those trained in the Western biomedical tradition.

BIBLIOGRAPHY

Ahlburg, D. A. *Remittances and Their Impact. A Study of Tonga and Western Samoa*, 1991.

Boyd, M. "The Record in Western Samoa to 1945." In A. Ross, ed., *New Zealand's Record in the Pacific in the Twentieth Century*, 1969.

Davidson, J. W. *Samoa mo Samoa*, 1967.

Fairbairn Pacific Consultants Ltd. *The Western Samoan Economy: Paving the Way for Sustainable Growth and Stability*, 1994.

Field, M. *Mau: Samoa's Struggle against New Zealand Oppression*, 1984.

Gilson, R. P. *Samoa 1830–1900: The Politics of a Multicultural Community*, 1970.

Macpherson, C., and L. Macpherson. *Samoan Medical Beliefs and Practices*, 1991.

Meleisea, M. *Lagaga: A Short History of Western Samoa*, 1987.

———. *Change and Adaptations in Western Samoa*, 1992.

Moyle, Richard M., ed. *The Samoan Journals of John Williams 1830 and 1832*, 1984.

O'Meara, T. "Samoa: Customary Individualism." In R. G. Crocombe, ed., *Land Tenure in the Pacific*, 3rd ed. 1987.

———. *Samoan Planters: Tradition and Economic Development in Polynesia*, 1990.

Pitt, D. C. *Tradition and Economic Progress in Samoa*, 1970.

Shankman, P. *Migration and Underdevelopment: The Case of Western Samoa*, 1976.

University of the South Pacific. *Pacific Constitutions Vol. I: Polynesia*, 1983.

World Bank. *Pacific Island Economies: Toward Higher Growth in the 1990s*, 1991.

———. *Pacific Island Economies: Building a Resilient Economic Base for the Twenty-First Century*, 1996.

—CLUNY MACPHERSON

SAN MARINO

CULTURE NAME
Sammarinese

ALTERNATIVE NAME
La Serenissima Repubblica di San Marino (The Most Serene Republic of San Marino)

ORIENTATION

Identification. San Marino takes its name from its founder, Marinus, who according to legend founded the republic in 301 C.E. San Marino is comprised of native Sammarinese and Italian citizens. Although Italian-speaking and heavily influenced by the surrounding Italian culture, the Sammarinese have maintained their individuality through the centuries, have a strong sense of identity, and are proud of their unique culture.

Location and Geography. San Marino, one of the smallest republics in the world, is located in the Emilia-Romagna region of Italy, south of the city of Rimini on the northern part of the Adriatic coast. Approximately 24 square miles (61 square kilometers) in size, San Marino is completely landlocked. Situated in the central part of the Apennine mountains, San Marino is dominated by the three-peaked Mount Titano, which is 2,437 feet (743 meters) high. There are several streams and small rivers, including the Ausa, Marano, and the San Marino. The terrain is rugged but the climate is Mediterranean with mild to cool winters and warm, sunny summers. The capital is located in the main town, also called San Marino. Other important towns include Serravalle, Borgo Maggiore, and Domagnano.

Demography. A 1997 survey put the population of San Marino at 24,714 of which 14 percent are were fourteen years old and younger, 68 percent were between fifteen and sixty-four years old, and 18 percent were sixty-five years old and over. The population is divided ethnically between Sam-

marinese and Italians. San Marino is one of the most densely populated countries in the world with an average of more than 860 people per square mile (332 per square kilometers). The republic is approximately 5.5 miles (9 kilometers) across and 8 miles (13 kilometers) long. It is estimated that sixteen thousand Sammarinese live in other countries.

Linguistic Affiliation. The official number of languages spoken in San Marino is two: a Sammarinese dialect and standard Italian. Approximately 83 percent of the population speak Sammarinese, which is considered a variation of the Emiliano-Romagnolo dialect found in the surrounding Italian region. Standard Italian is the language of everyday use, although typical Sammarinese phrases and expressions are used regularly.

Symbolism. The Sammarinese flag consists of two equal bands of white (above) and light blue (below) with the national coat of arms placed in the center. The coat of arms features a shield with three towers on three peaks flanked by a wreath, with a crown above and a scroll below bearing the word Libertas (Liberty). The towers represent the three fortified towers on Mount Titano which have been strategic in the defense of the republic throughout its history. The national holiday is 3 September, the Anniversary of the Foundation of the Republic.

HISTORY AND ETHNIC RELATIONS

Emergence of the Nation. San Marino was founded in 301 C.E. by a Christian stonemason, Marinus, who fled the island of Arbe off the Dalmation coast to escape the anti-Christian persecution of the Roman Emperor Diocletian. Taking refuge on Mount Titano, Marinus founded a small community of Christians. The area had been inhabited since prehistoric times, although records date back only to the Middle Ages. In memory of Marinus, the area was named the Land of San Marino,

San Marino

then the Community of San Marino, and finally the Republic of San Marino. The state of San Marino maintained its independence despite frequent invasions by the rulers of Rimini, and in 1291 Pope Nicholas IV recognized San Marino's independence.

The territory of San Marino consisted only of Mount Titano until 1463 when the republic formed an alliance against Sigismondo Pandolfo Malatesta, Lord of Rimini, who was later defeated. As a reward, Pope Pius II gave San Marino the towns of Fiorentino, Montegiardino, and Serravalle. In the same year the town of Faetano voluntarily joined the young state. The nation has remained the same size ever since.

San Marino has been occupied by invaders only twice, both for short periods of time. In 1503 Cesare Borgia, known as Duca Valentino, occupied the country until his the death of his father Rodrigo Borgia, Pope Alexander VI, the same year. The political unrest following the Pope's death forced Cesare Borgia to withdraw his forces from San Marino. In 1739 Cardinal Alberoni, in an attempt to gain more

political power, used military force to occupy San Marino but civil disobedience and clandestine communications with the current Pope, Clement XII, helped to ensure recognition of San Marino's rights and restoration of its independence. Since 1862 San Marino has had an official treaty of friendship, revised several times, with Italy.

National Identity. The Sammarinese are proud of their history and have a strong sense of unity due to San Marino's small size and unique place in the world.

Ethnic Relations. There is a large resident Italian population in the republic, and contact with the surrounding Italian regions have helped ensure close cultural and ethnic ties between the Sammarinese and the Italians. Although there is a free flow of people in and out of San Marino, it is extremely difficult to acquire citizenship. A person can become a citizen only by being born in the republic, and only if both parents are citizens; or by marrying a Sammarinese. Citizenship through naturalization is rare. As a consequence, San Marino has a population that is still almost exclusively native Sammarinese.

URBANISM, ARCHITECTURE, AND THE USE OF SPACE

San Marino is a mountainous nation consisting of small hill towns. Stone, brick, and tile are some of the principal building materials and like many Italian towns, the center of town is piazza which also serves a social function as a gathering place. The capital, the City of San Marino, is a fortified town as are many of the other towns of San Marino. Much of the original medieval fortifications remain, including three fortified towers located on the peaks of Mount Titano. These towers, called La Guaita, La Cesta, and Il Montale, are still linked by ramparts and walls constructed from the local sandstone. The oldest part of the capital dates from the early twelfth century. In the older sections of San Marino there are still many buildings dating from the Renaissance period in the early 1400s.

FOOD AND ECONOMY

Food in Daily Life. Food and meals are an important part of life in San Marino. The cuisine is Mediterranean, emphasizing fresh and locally grown produce, pasta, and meat. Although it is similar to that of the Italian Romagna region which borders San Marino, the cuisine of San Marino features its own typical dishes. Traditional recipes include *faggioli con le cotiche*, a dark bean soup flavored with bacon and traditionally prepared at Christmas; *pasta e cece*, a soup of chickpeas and noodles flavored with garlic and rosemary; and *nidi di rondine* (literally, "swallow's nest"), a dish of pasta with smoked ham, cheese, beef, and a tomato sauce, which is then covered with a white sauce and baked in the oven. Roast rabbit with fennel is also a popular Sammarinese dish. Other popular local dishes include *bustrengo*, a cake made with raisins; *cacciatello*, a mixture of milk and eggs; and *zuppa di ciliege*, cherries stewed in red wine and sugar and served on local bread. San Marino also produces high quality wines, the most famous of which are the *Sangiovese*, a strong red wine; and the *Biancale*, a dry white wine. There are many small family-owned restaurants, often providing outdoor seating in the summer, which play an important role in the lives of the Sammarinese, as meals are a daily part of family life and socializing.

Basic Economy. Tourism is one of the most important parts of San Marino's economy and many businesses cater to the tourist trade. The sale of collectible postage stamps and coins also constitutes a major part of the republic's revenue. Until the latter part of the twentieth century, farming, mining, and stone working formed the core of San Marino's economy. White sandstone was once abundant but most of the quarries are now closed. Sandstone is now extracted in limited quantities for decorative and artistic purposes rather than for construction. In addition to wine, the production and export of alcoholic spirits and liqueurs is a significant industry, along with other agricultural products such as wheat, grapes, corn, olives, cattle, pigs, horses, beef, cheese, and hides. Although San Marino still has a strong agricultural sector, it is dependent on imports from Italy in order to meet all of its needs.

San Marino's standard of living is high with an average per capita yearly income of about $32,000 (U.S.). San Marino's GDP is around $500 million (U.S.) annually with the rate of inflation at 2.2 percent. Unofficial estimates put the GDP growth rate at 8 percent.

Land Tenure and Property. Approximately 65 percent of San Marino is covered by farmland and pine forests with the rest consisting of parks, public spaces and buildings. Both private and public ownership of property exists in the republic.

Commercial Activities. The tourist sector generates more than 50 percent of the gross domestic product (GDP) of San Marino, with an average of 3.2 million tourists visiting the republic San Marino every year. Small businesses such as souvenir shops and restaurants depend heavily on tourism. Other important commercial activities include the sale of historic coins and postage stamps. In 1894 San Marino issued the first commemorative stamps which have been an important source of income for the republic ever since.

Major Industries. Important industries include banking and the manufacturing of clothing, electronics, paint, synthetic rubber, telecommunications equipment, and ceramics. Important export products include building stone, lime, wood, chestnuts, wheat, wine, baked goods, hides, and ceramics. San Marino's main trading partner is Italy, accounting for 85 percent of exports. Agricultural products and consumer goods are imported from Italy, eastern Europe, South America, China and Taiwan.

Trade. Italy is San Marino's major trading partner. Trade statistics are included with those for Italy.

Division of Labor. According to a 1998 study, the workforce of San Marino was divided as follows: 4,254 (25 percent) worked in the broad public sector; 5,637 (34 percent) worked in industry; 3,140 (16.5 percent) worked in the commercial sector; 1,492 (9.1 percent) worked in construction; 505 (2.7 percent) worked in banking and insurance; 355 (2.1 percent) worked in transportation and communications; 248 (1.6 percent) were involved in agriculture; 1,779 (9.3 percent) worked in a variety of businesses and services. The unemployment rate is around 2 percent. Recent figures place the unemployment rate at about 2.2 percent for women and at 1.8 percent for men.

SOCIAL STRATIFICATION

Classes and Castes. San Marino's small population and high standard of living have helped ensure a relatively balanced distribution of wealth. The government maintains a policy of full employment for all its citizens and works with the private sector to ensure that all Sammarinese who wish to work are employed. San Marino's small size, power-sharing government, high standard of living, and educated population have made it a country with very little social stratification.

Uniformed guards in San Marino. The country is neutral and has no military nor any alliances with other countries.

POLITICAL LIFE

Government. Created in the early Middle Ages, the original governing body was the Arengo, made up of the heads of each family. Today the Arengo is the electoral body, while the main governing body is the Great and General Council. In 1243, the first two captains regent were nominated by the council and this system has continued to this day. The council is composed of sixty members who are elected every five years under a proportional representation system. The duties of the Council consist of approving the budget and nominating the captains regent and heads of the executive.

Every six months, the council elects two captains regent to be heads of state for a six-month term. The regents are chosen from opposing parties in order to provide a balance of power. The investiture of the captains regent takes place on 1 April and 1 October every year. Once a regent's term is completed, citizens have three days to file any complaints about the regent's activities. If warranted, judicial proceedings against the ex-head of state may be initiated.

Executive power is held by the State Congress, which is composed of three secretaries and seven ministries. The Council of Twelve is elected by the Great and General Council for the duration of the legislature and serves as a jurisdictional body as well as a court of appeals. Two government officials represent the state in financial and patrimonial matters.

The judicial system of San Marino is entrusted to foreign executives for both historical and social reasons. The only Sammarinese judges are the justices of the peace, who handle only civil cases where sums do not exceed 25 million lire (around $16,000 [U.S.]).

Leadership and Political Officials. San Marino is a democratic republic with several political parties. The three main parties are the Democratic Christian Party of San Marino, the Socialist Party of San Marino, and the Progressive Democratic Party of San Marino; there are several other smaller parties. Because of San Marino's small size and population, it is difficult for any one party to gain a pure majority, and most of the time the government is ruled by a coalition. The current parties in power are the Democratic Christian Party and the Socialist Party.

Social Problems and Control. San Marino faces economic and administrative problems related to its status as a close financial and trading partner with Italy while at the same time remaining separated from the European Union. Another important issue facing the government is improving relations among the parliament, the cabinet, and the captains regent.

Military Activity. San Marino is officially neutral and does not have an army or any alliances with other nations. The last battle in which San Marino actively participated was in 1463. The republic has been invaded and occupied several times since then but has always maintained its position of neutrality. There is a symbolic military force of eighty men who participate in San Marino's ceremonial events and occasionally assist the police. In a time of crisis, however, the government can call all adult males to arms as happened during World War II when San Marino was directly involved in the war as the target of heavy bombing and as a haven for thousands of refugees.

SOCIAL WELFARE AND CHANGE PROGRAMS

The Institute for Health and Social Security, a public organization that is independently managed, provides health care, social services, and social security. San Marino provides cradle-to-grave health care for all its citizens as well as retirement pensions.

GENDER ROLES AND STATUSES

The Relative Status of Women and Men. In San Marino today, women have most of the social and political rights that men have. Women received the right to vote in 1960 and the right to hold office in 1973. The first female captains regent were elected shortly thereafter. Nevertheless, slightly more men than women receive some form of higher education, and the unemployment rate is higher for women as well. These differences are in part due to the changing role of women in San Marino and the transition the republic has undergone in the late twentieth century, as its economy has moved away from agriculture and deemphasized industrialization.

MARRIAGE, FAMILY, AND KINSHIP

Domestic Unit. In a small and unified country like San Marino, family plays an important role. Extended family and kin are an important part of the social structure of the republic. With the transition from an agricultural to a more industrialized economy following World War II, the nuclear family has replaced the extended family as the basic domestic unit. There are approximately eight marriages per one thousand and the divorce rate is relatively low. If they are no longer able to care for themselves, older family members usually live with their younger relatives. Children often continue to live at home with their parents well into adulthood, until higher education is completed or they start their own families.

SOCIALIZATION

Infant Care. Public day care and nursery schools are available for children under the age of five.

Child Rearing and Education. The school system in San Marino is very similar to that in Italy and is obligatory until the age of sixteen. Children attend state-run primary and secondary schools, choosing a particular type of school when they reach the high school level.

Higher Education. There are no universities or colleges in San Marino and those students who decide to pursue higher education usually attend university in Italy where San Marino's high school diplomas are recognized.

Formula One cars in the Imola Grand Prix.

ETIQUETTE

Standards of etiquette are similar to those in Italy. Due to the important tourist industry, the Sammarinese are accustomed to welcoming people from all over the world.

RELIGION

Religious Beliefs. The predominant religion, Roman Catholicism, is still regarded as the principal religion. Historically, the Sammarinese have been against the Vatican's political control over their republic but have embraced the pope's spiritual authority on religious matters. The importance of Catholicism in San Marino has led to the involvement of the church in many state occasions; many of San Marino's official ceremonies are held in the Basilica, the republic's main church, or in other churches. There are a total of nine Catholic parishes all of which comprise the diocese of San Marino.

Religious Practitioners. There is no official state religion but practitioners of Roman Catholicism predominate. There are no figures available for the number of non-Catholic practitioners.

Rituals and Holy Places. The Basilica dates from the fourteenth century and contains the remains of Saint Marino.

MEDICINE AND HEALTH CARE

San Marino is able to provide low-cost health care for its citizens through clinics and a small hospital. Although the level of care is high, for certain types of health care the Sammarinese must turn to hospitals outside of the republic. The average life expectancy is placed at seventy-seven for men and eighty-five for women. The Sammarinese birthrate is around 11 births per 1,000 people, while the infant mortality is rate 3 out of every 1,000 births.

SECULAR CELEBRATIONS

There are five official national festivals in San Marino all of which celebrate important events in the republic's history: 5 February, the anniversary of the republic's liberation from the occupying forces of Cardinal Alberoni in 1740; 25 March marks the day in 1906 when the Arengo implemented the democratic form of government that exists today; 1 April and 1 October, the two days when the captains regent take office; and 3 September, the feast day of the patron saint and founder of the republic, Saint Marino.

THE ARTS AND HUMANITIES

Support for the Arts. The Sammarinese proudly support and maintain several small museums as well as take an active interest in cultural activities including film, music, and literature.

Graphic Arts. San Marino's long history and extended periods of peace have endowed it with a substantial artistic legacy including paintings by several important Italian artists from the Renaissance and Baroque periods. There are also numerous sculptures placed throughout public spaces. Traditional crafts, such as stone carving and ceramics, have been able to survive in part from the tourist industry.

THE STATE OF THE PHYSICAL AND SOCIAL SCIENCES

San Marino's small population and its lack of a university means that it is not able to support academic research at the postsecondary level. Many Sammarinese, however, go on to pursue successful careers in academia and research outside the republic.

BIBLIOGRAPHY

Cardinali, Marino. *San Marino e la sua Storia*, (San Marino and its history), 1982.

Carrick, Noel. *San Marino*, 1988.

Edwards, Adrian. *San Marino*, 1996.

Grimes, Barbara. *Ethnologue*, 13th ed., 1996.

Ricci, Corrado. *La Repubblica di San Marino* (The Republic of San Marino), 1906.

Rogatnick, Joseph H. "Little States in a World of Powers: A Study of Conduct of Foreign Affairs by Andorra, Lichtenstein, Monaco, and San Marino," Ph.D. dissertation, University of Pennsylvania, 1976.

Web Sites

Il Portale della Repubblica di San Marino (The Gateway to the Republic of San Marino). Electronic document. Available from http://www.omniway.sm

San Marino. Electronic document. Available from http://www.photius.com/wfb/wfb1999/san_marino

U.S. Department of State. *Background Notes: San Marino*. Electronic document. Available from http://www.stategov/www/background_notes/sanmarino_9811_bgn.html

—M. CAMERON ARNOLD

SÃO TOMÉ E PRÍNCIPE

CULTURE NAME

São Toméan Creole

ORIENTATION

Identification. São Tomé e Príncipe is the second smallest country in the Organization of African Unity. Culturally, it is a Luso-African creole nation peopled by descendants of Africans brought to work on plantations. Inhabiting two lush equatorial islands, the people of São Tomé e Príncipe are poor.

Location and Geography. The Republic of São Tomé e Príncipe is composed of two inhabited islands with a total area of 385 square miles (996 square kilometers). São Tomé accounts for 330 square miles (857 square kilometers) and contains close to 95 percent of the population. São Tomé is in the equatorial zone. Its strategic location in the center of the Gulf of Guinea has been an important factor in the island's history and culture. The island has served as a trading post and its strategic location was noticed by both sides during the Cold War. The topography is extremely rugged, with the exception of a small coastal plain on the northern coast where the capital and major population center, the city of São Tomé, is located. Steep hills, mountains, and ravines with narrow areas of flat terrain characterize the interior. Pico São Tomé in the west-central part of the island is the highest point. Steep hills known as *morros* that dominate the landscape and are heavily forested.

Agriculture is labor-intensive, and the percentage of people dependent on agriculture continues to decline. The beauty of the island's tropical ecology has potential for the development of tourism. Poor communications and lack of infrastructure have kept the islands relatively isolated and undeveloped, but there has been steady growth in the number of visitors.

Demography. The population of 140,000 (1999 estimate) is overwhelmingly of West African stock. It is a young population, with the majority under the age of thirty. Historically, the country has always been an agrarian society with settlements in small holdings and concentrations of laborers in widely dispersed plantations. Since independence in 1975, there has been a trend toward urbanization, with 44 percent of the population now considered urban and 60 percent of the population living near the capital, which has approximately 60,000 persons. Small towns are focal points for the religious, commercial, and administrative life of people living outside the plantations.

Linguistic Affiliation. The language is a Luso-African creole derived from the languages spoken by Africans brought by the Portuguese, with a great many words from Portuguese. This language was formed in the fifteenth and sixteenth centuries when a significant number of white Portuguese resided in the country. Portuguese was widely spoken until the mid-seventeenth century, by which time most of the whites had left.

Portuguese is the official language and the language of education. São Tomeans refer to their creole language as *Forro*, *lunga santome* or *dialecto*. A mutually intelligible dialect of *Forro* called *ling'le* is spoken on Príncipe. In the south of São Tomé a refugee community of Angolan slaves speaks a dialect called *lunga ngola*. Since independence, children learn Portuguese at an early age. Television broadcasts in Portuguese since the mid-1980s have eroded the use of the local languages.

Symbolism. The Cross, the Trinity, and the saints are important Christian symbols. Historical symbols derived from the early days of colonization include various symbols of the Portuguese king. Local cults typically use African symbols of red cloth, iron, and wooden dolls. Other healing cults invest particular plots of land with symbolic and ritual significance as the dwelling places of spirits. During

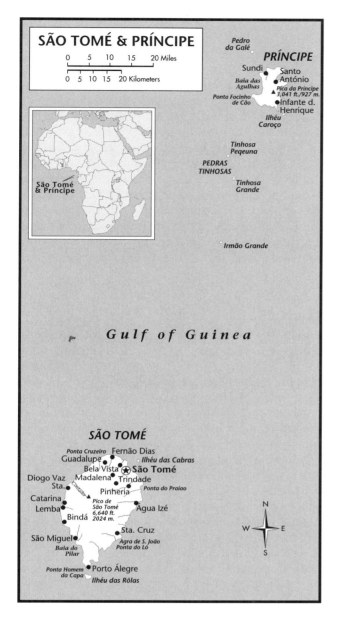

SÃO TOMÉ & PRÍNCIPE

0   5   10   15   20 Miles

0   5   10   15   20 Kilometers

Pedro
da Galé

PRÍNCIPE

Sundi
Baía das
Agulhas
Ponta Focinho
de Cão

Santo
António
Pica da Príncipe
3,041 ft./927 m.
Infante d.
Henrique

Ilhéu
Caroço

Tinhosa
Pequena

**PEDRAS
TINHOSAS**

Tinhosa
Grande

Irmão Grande

Gulf of Guinea

SÃO TOMÉ

Ponta Cruzeiro   Fernão Dias
Guadalupe
Ilhéu das Cabras
Bela Vista   ★ São Tomé
Diogo Vaz   Madalena   Trindade
Sta.
Pinhéria
Catarina   Ponta do Praiao
Lemba   Pico de
São Tomé
6,640 ft.
2024 m.   Água Izé
Bindá
São Miguel   Sta. Cruz
Baía do
Pilar   Agra de S. João
Ponta do Ló
Ponta Homem   Porto Álegre
da Capa   Ilhéu das Rôlas

N
W   E
S

São Tomé and Príncipe

the first twenty years of single-party Marxist-Leninist rule, internationalist Marxist symbols predominated. After multiparty democracy was introduced in 1990, the parties developed unique symbols, and several newspapers use cartoons and symbolic drawings. A wooden doll with a sliver of iron embedded in its chest and red cloth wound around its neck placed at the base of a tree constitutes a potent symbol.

HISTORY AND ETHNIC RELATIONS

Emergence of the Nation. São Tomé e Príncipe was uninhabited when it was sighted by Portuguese explorers, in 1471. A succession of estate and plantation systems brought Africans from the mainland, and their descendants shaped creole culture. The emergence of the nation is linked to the roles and attitudes developed in response to the plantations and to the processes by which Africans became assimilated as free persons. The term *Forro* is synonymous with the national identity.

The first Portuguese settlers landed in 1486 on the southwest coast. The settlement was abandoned as climate and disease took its toll, and there were no indigenous inhabitants from whom the settlers could buy food. The colonizers were unable to produce sugar or wheat, as the royal charter had urged. The king, Joao II, then gave the captaincy of the island to Alvaro de Caminha who began a settlement on the Bahia de Ana Chaves, the site of the present capital. Among the settlers were two thousand Jewish children taken from their parents and converted to Christianity. In addition to the Jewish children, there were exiled convicts and prostitutes known as *degredados.* The free whites were government officials, soldiers, and traders sent to exploit the West African slave, spice, and sugar trade.

The royal charter directed the Jewish settlers and *degredados* to marry slave women and populate the island with their offspring. A second royal decree of 1515 granted free status to all African slave women given to the settlers and their offspring, and a decree in 1517 extended free status to the male African slaves of the early Jewish and convict settlers. Royal orders and actions by the king's magistrates prevented whites from trading in slaves born on the island. This created a large free black and mixed-race population that formed the nucleus of São Toméan culture. The African and European settlers transformed the island into a prosperous center of the slave and spice trades and an early sugar producer.

The granting of political rights to mulattos and free blacks gave considerable power to the more prosperous free Africans, who served in the municipal council.

National Identity. By the early nineteenth century, free and degredado whites had merged into a single white category. Mulattos had the rights and privileges of whites and were grouped together in the censuses. The largest group was the *Forros,* or free blacks. The more prosperous and politically prominent free blacks referred to themselves as *filhos da terra,* the descendants of the earliest settlers, to distinguish themselves from blacks who were freed in the nineteenth century. Basically all those who lived away from the plantations and could claim a small plot of land, membership in a religious brotherhood, or political patronage were considered Forros.

Most of the rural population is tied to the *roças*, (plantations). These people are the descendants of Angolan and Mozambican contract laborers and Cape Verdians. The word *tonga* is a pejorative term by which some Forros refer to these people. Descendants of Cape Verdians remain a small and distinct community, many of whom still seek to migrate.

The process of assimilation to the national culture is accelerating as the plantations decline in economic importance, and the social distinctions based on race that characterized the colonial period no longer exist.

Ethnic Relations. Mulattos were always few in numbers and never held a high status. Under the Portuguese, they were given special privileges that ceased at independence, and they do not constitute a bloc in economic or cultural terms. They tend to assimilate to the Forro category over time. Whites are often expatriate workers on one of the many technical missions associated with development assistance. Other whites are engaged in business and are not permanent residents. The island has remained essentially African, with the closest ties and influences coming from the African mainland.

URBANISM, ARCHITECTURE, AND THE USE OF SPACE

Urban spaces were designed and built by the Portuguese colonial administration and include imposing cement administrative buildings, commercial houses, and the lodgings of the former colonial administrators and civil servants built in a Salazarist style known as luso-tropical. They were designed to evoke the grandeur and permanence of the Portuguese overseas empire. In the capital city and in the small towns, buildings are arranged in a centralized pattern with a Catholic church, the administrative building, postal and telecommunications offices, and a commercial house that formerly belonged to Portuguese overseas companies. Near these buildings are solid cement houses built for Europeans and now occupied by well-connected Forros. In São Tomé City, the streets follow a grid pattern. In small towns, concrete buildings are strung along the few roads that traverse the islands. Fort São Sebastião, built by the Portuguese in the sixteenth century to guard the entrance to the Bay of Ana Chaves and the port of São Tomé, houses the national museum.

Indigenous architecture consists of wooden houses raised on stilts that are surrounded by small patches of garden (*kintéh*). Most people in urban or rural spaces live in these small houses. There is no coordinated plan other than the continual subdivision of house plots as families grow and access to land in urban areas decreases. A variety of shanties and shelters can be attached to these houses as households engage in petty commerce and services. Footpaths that follow the contours of the smallholdings to reach the main roads connect these large and sprawling settlements. Public buildings are rare except for Christian meetinghouses. People on plantations are housed in large cement barracks and houses known as *sanzalas* above which loom the spacious houses of the plantation administrators.

FOOD AND ECONOMY

Food in Daily Life. The cuisine is based on tropical root crops, plantains, and bananas, with fish as the most common source of protein. The vegetables that are eaten consist of gathered indigenous greens that are cooked in red palm oil. Production of these foodstuffs is inadequate as a result of the islands' history as a plantation economy. Traditional palm oil stews are the national dish. Corn is eaten as a snack food. The traditional food culture includes fruit bats and monkey meat. Asian fruits are well established, but New World fruits such as papayas and guavas are the most widespread and abundant. Citrus trees can be found in most houseyards. Since colonial times, the country's reliance on food from abroad has begun to change the food culture. Imported rice and bread made of imported wheat flour are staple foods of urban dwellers.

Generally people eat a hot meal cooked before sunset. Breakfast consists of reheated food from the night before or tea and bread. People generally eat around the hearth, which in most dwellings is a separate structure made of wood or fronds.

Food Customs at Ceremonial Occasions. At weddings, baptisms, and funerals, people prepare a lavish table set in the Portuguese manner with a large array of dishes that are admired by the guests. Bottled beverages grace the table setting. These occasions are marked by roasted goat, chicken, or beef among the affluent. Wealthy families also prepare the traditional luso-African-Brazilian *feijoada*, a rich bean stew, for Sunday lunch or for guests. Palm wine is the primary local beverage. The intermittent production of the local brewery is avidly consumed, and bottled soft drinks are a luxury. A local cane alcohol, *cacharamba*, is of dubious quality.

Basic Economy. Agriculture and small service industries are the major sectors of the economy. Fisheries are potentially important. Fishing remains an important activity in coastal communities.

As a poor island microstate, São Tomé has limited options as a result of small markets, poor infrastructure, high transportation costs, and a lack of trained personnel and entrepreneurs. The traditional pattern of seeking state patronage remains entrenched, and avoiding labor on the plantations is still a paramount concern of most people. Overseas development aid is the main source of income for the state. In this economic climate, corruption and inefficiency abound, public indebtedness is growing, and there are periodic riots over shortages.

Land Tenure and Property. At independence in 1975, twenty large Portuguese *roças* owned 93 percent of the land. Over eleven thousand native smallholders were crowded into the remaining land with tiny holdings called *glebas*. Squatters moved into abandoned areas on the *roças* to grow native crops for subsistence and sale. In 1992, land redistribution was begun to give squatters and small farmers secure ownership of their land and make more land available to households that wanted to farm.

Commercial Activities. Smallholders grow root crops, vegetables, plantains, and bananas for local consumption.

Major Industries. Industry is virtually nonexistent except for a few processing plants for food, beverages, and soap. Logging has contributed to the economy but has had a negative effect on the environment. The natural beauty and relatively healthy and safe environment have potential for tourism and ecotourism. Some investment in hotels and other tourist facilities has taken place.

Trade. Traditionally, the plantation economy exported cocoa and coffee and imported rice, beans, and salt fish to feed the plantation workers. Today, cocoa is the major export, accounting for over 90 percent of foreign exchange earnings. Cocoa and export crops such as coffee, coconuts, and palm kernels are still grown on the plantations. Small amounts of high-quality cocoa are exported. Major export partners are the Netherlands, Germany, and Portugal. Imports include machinery and electrical equipment, food, and petroleum products. Import partners include Portugal, France, and Angola.

SOCIAL STRATIFICATION

Classes and Castes. Descent from a Forro family that owns land in one of the small native holdings assures kin ties and the influence needed to secure state patronage. The old African creole families that figured prominently in the history of the islands in seventeenth to nineteenth centuries still control politics and resources. Achieved status through education is important but depends on patronage; it is rare for non-Forros to advance through education alone. Thrift and hard work may advance the economic status of small farmers, traders, and fishers, but their low status gives these people little access to credit. Decades of economic stagnation and the fact that most resources are funneled through the state restrict people's opportunities to achieve social and economic mobility. Workers on the plantations are the most marginal citizens in social and economic terms.

Symbols of Social Stratification. On an island with no locally produced consumer goods, travel and access to the outside world are symbols of high status. Educating one's children and shopping in Lisbon or Gabon are symbols of power and status. Participation in traditional religious and dance societies is a symbol of status that is being eclipsed by the adoption of the Western consumer culture.

POLITICAL LIFE

Government. After fifteen years of rule by a Marxist party, the Movimento Libertador de São Tomé e Príncipe (MLSTP), the country became a multiparty democracy in 1990. There is an elected National Assembly headed by a prime minister, a judiciary, and a president who is the head of state. Three main parties vie for power and the ability to dispense government resources and patronage. While political expression was restricted under the former state, there is now a fervent and active political debate carried out in photocopied newspapers and broadsheets, radio and political rallies, and word of mouth.

Leadership and Political Officials. There are three political parties: the MLSTP-Partido Social Democrata, the Acção Democrática Independente, and the Partido da Convergencia Democratica-Grupo de Reflexão. The political officials who seek power within and between these parties have been the same persons since 1975. Democratization has not raised the standard of living, increased the opportunities for marginalized people, or reduced corruption.

Social Problems and Control. Petty theft and larceny are caused by poverty and frequent shortages of consumer goods, but violence is rare.

Military Activity. The armed forces consist of a small army and a police force with six hundred members. For defense, the country previously relied on Cuban and Angolan troops; it is assumed that foreign troops are no longer present. While police forces are an important institution for social control, more commonly social control is achieved through ritual and the use of spirits.

GENDER ROLES AND STATUSES

Division of Labor by Gender. São Tomé e Príncipe is a male-dominated society, although women play important roles in all major formal and informal institutions. Women have held important posts in government. For several years after independence, the president of the National Assembly and the minister of foreign affairs were women.

The Relative Status of Women and Men. Women can manage their own business enterprises independently of their husbands and brothers. The market traders who sell produce and fish are all women, some of whom accumulate and manage large amounts of cash.

In a household, women manage their money independently of their husbands. Marriage to a woman with land or other property does not give the husband access or control over those resources. A third of households are headed by women.

MARRIAGE, FAMILY, AND KINSHIP

Marriage. Three types of conjugal union are common: the Christian monogamous marriage, the coresidential customary union, and the visiting relationship. Christian marriage is largely confined to the educated elite and has the highest social prestige. Among members of evangelical Christian churches and the elite, formal marriage is an accepted institution, but men often maintain conjugal relations with other women and support multiple households. Most couples live in coresidential customary unions. Typically, women and men have several partners over the course of their adult lives and have children by different partners. In plantation households, marriages are less stable, with women maintaining visiting relations with a series of men. The visiting relationship is the most common form of conjugal union for poor Forro or *tonga* females. Polygyny is not accepted but has been known to occur in rural areas. In all forms of conjugal unions, the father and husband are expected to contribute to the expenses of the wife and child.

DOMESTIC UNIT

Inheritance. Women can inherit land, and small freehold plots held by a family often were registered in the name of the senior women in the family.

Kin Groups. People reckon descent bilaterally and tend to keep the property inherited from their paternal or maternal lines distinct. Following the Portuguese custom, children take their surname from the father. Descent normally can be traced back at least three to four generations. Annual family gatherings and funerals reinforce these ties.

Infant Care. On average, a woman has five to seven children. Great status is attached to having children regardless of their paternity. Typically, children remain with the mother until adolescence, after which time they may begin to spend more time with the father's family. There is also coparenting in which godparents play an important role. Children often move to be raised by a parent or relative when there is an economic crisis.

SOCIALIZATION

There is universal compulsory primary education, and children have access to schools throughout the island. For people residing on roças or in rural Forro settlements, secondary education implies sending a child to live with relatives or as a dependent in an urban family.

Higher Education. There are no institutions of higher education on the islands. Many high school graduates want to receive a university education abroad, but few people can afford this.

ETIQUETTE

Manners and etiquette are considered important, and greeting a person and inquiring about his or her health and family is essential in social encounters. Recognizing and paying deference to the status of a person is important. Older men and women tend to be treated with great respect, particularly if they have many children and grandchildren. Entry into a person's home or garden is a privilege, and acquaintances often converse in the road or across a garden hedge rather than enter a house or yard.

RELIGION

Religious Beliefs. Over 80 percent of the people claim to be Roman Catholic, less than 3 percent are Evangelical Christians, and 1 percent are Seventh Day Adventists. There are twelve catholic parishes and a cathedral in the capital. The roots of Catholicism go back to the fifteenth century.

There is a deep and widely held set of spiritist beliefs derived from the religions of African coastal societies. These beliefs centered on the spirits of ancestors and spirits that reside in sacred places. Places containing the remains of hastily buried persons are considered dangerous, and people leave offerings to those spirits to permit them to farm nearby. Spiritist rituals often center on healing and appeasing spirits that have been forgotten or wish to return to the world of the living.

Religious Practitioners. People also belong to local religious brotherhoods. There are few native priests with most being sent from Europe. Religious festivals organized around the patron saints of towns and parishes are a feature of the annual religious calendar, and people may travel from other parts of the island to attend. Religious brotherhoods and sisterhoods play an important role in organizing these ceremonies and festivals. The most important Catholic rituals are baptism and the wake, followed by a funeral mass. Other sacraments are rarely observed.

Forros have a communal religious ritual called *djambí* in which an entire neighborhood or village gathers to drum, dance, and witness spirit possession. Individuals can seek out a ritual specialist to obtain protection from rivals, restore their health, or gain the attention of a potential lover. On the *roças*, ritual specialists perform healing, divination, and ritual protection.

Death and the Afterlife. Forros believe that the spirits of the dead are never disconnected from the world of the living. There remains a bond that requires the living to remember and propitiate the dead. Misfortune often is attributed to spirits of the dead that have been forgotten or not propitiated. While a spirit can reach a person who has emigrated illness and misfortune, the spirit remains bound to the island and to the place where he or she died.

MEDICINE AND HEALTH CARE

There is a hospital in the capital city, smaller clinics on the large roças and in the towns, and health dispensaries that reach most of the population. Health facilities are inadequately staffed, and there is a chronic shortage of pharmaceuticals. Over 80 percent of the population has access to safe drinking water.

Traditional herbal healers and masseurs use a combination of herbal treatments and rituals. These practitioners diagnose disease by the visible symptoms, feeling the body or examining the urine.

SECULAR CELEBRATIONS

Independence Day on 12 July commemorates independence from Portugal in 1975. It is an official holiday and the largest celebration on the islands. The Labor Day holiday is celebrated on 1 May.

THE ARTS AND HUMANITIES

Support for the Arts. There is a national theater company that performs plays in Forro. It has a wide following, but limited financial support from the government restricts the number of dramas that are performed.

Literature. Poetry is the most highly developed form of literary expression. Francisco Tenreiro and Alda Graça do Espiritu Santo are among the most noted published poets. Historical events are often the subject of local poetry. Tomas Ribas is among the better known writers of folktales and short stories.

Graphic Arts. Pascoal Viegas Vilhete (Canarim) Almada Negreiros, and Vianna da Mota painted folk scenes with artistic and historical value. Artists today who combine traditional folk art themes with an abstract expressionist style exhibit at the Francisco Tenreiro Cultural Center or the National Museum.

Performance Arts. Dance and drama are widely practiced and appreciated. Folklore pageants such as the Danço Congo and the Tchiloli are interpretations of sixteenth century Portuguese historical plays. They are performed by masked performers in colorful attire and are accompanied by drums, flutes, and dancers. Other dance forms include the *pwita* and the *bulaweh*, both of which are organized and performed by dance societies. Older, more sedate dance forms such as the *ussua* and *socopé* are performed rarely.

THE STATE OF THE PHYSICAL AND SOCIAL SCIENCES

The physical and social sciences are not supported, as there is no institution of higher education. The little research that is done is primarily in the areas of environmental science and social science studies related to economic development and social welfare projects. Expatriate scientists and São Toméans trained abroad and funded through development assistance carry out these projects. There is a national library.

BIBLIOGRAPHY

Ambrosio, Antonio. "Para a historia do Folclore Sao Tomense." *Historia*, 81: 60–88, 1985.

Clarence-Smith, W. G. *The Third Portuguese Empire 1825–1975: A Study in Economic Imperialism*, 1985.

Eyzaguirre, Pablo B. "The Ecology of Swidden Agriculture and Agrarian History in São Tomé." *Cahiers d'Etudes Africaines*, 26 (101–102): 113–129, 1986.

———. "The Independence of São Tomé e Príncipe and Agrarian Reform." *Journal or Modern African Studies*, 27 (4): 671–678, 1989.

———. "São Tomé e Príncipe." In John Middleton, ed. *The Encyclopedia of Africa South of the Sahara*, 1997.

Ferraz, Luiz Ivens. *The Creole of São Tomé*, 1979.

Garfield, Robert. *A History of São Tomé Island 1470–1655: The Key to Guinea*, 1992.

Hodges, Tony, and Malyn Newitt. *São Tomé and Príncipe: From Plantation Colony to Microstate*, 1988.

Neves, Carlos Agostinho das. *S. Tome e Príncipe Na Segunda Metade do Sec. XVIII*, 1989.

Seibert, Gerhard. *Comrades, Clients and Cousins, Colonialism, Socialism and Democratization in São Tomé e Príncipe*, 1999.

Tenreiro, Frasncisco. *A Ilha de São Tomé*, 1961.

—PABLO B. EYZAGUIRRE

SAUDI ARABIA

CULTURE NAME
Saudi Arabian

ALTERNATIVE NAMES
Arabia, Saudi, North Arabia, Desert Arabia; informally, the Kingdom

ORIENTATION

Identification. The Kingdom of Saudi Arabia (in Arabic, *al-Mamlaka al-Arabiya as-Saudiya*) occupies most of the Arabian Peninsula, the original homeland of the Arab people and of Islam. The cultural identities Saudi Arabian citizens express are principally those of Muslim and Arab, linking them to millions of people beyond the nation's borders. They also identify with the contemporary state and its national culture; the country's name links the ruling dynasty, Al Saud, with the state's cultural and geographic setting.

Identities connected to the traditional ways of life of the Bedouin and of oasis-dwelling farmers, fishers, craftspeople and artisans, and merchants, caravaneers, and long-distance traders remain in force even as economic changes have transformed or ended those ways of life. Regional and kin-based tribal and clan identities are shared among Saudi Arabian citizens.

Location and Geography. Saudi Arabia occupies 868,730 square miles (2,250,000 square kilometers). It is bounded on the east by the Arabian (Persian) Gulf; on the west by the Red Sea; to the south and southeast by Yemen, Oman, the United Arab Emirates, and Qatar; and to the north and northeast by Jordan, Iraq, and Kuwait.

Saudi Arabia has a hot desert climate with high humidity on the coastal fringes. Rainfall is scarce except in the area of Asir, where it is sufficient for agriculture on terraced farms and upper slopes and alluvial planes.

Rainfall is adequate for the nomadic herding of sheep, goats, and camels and for the sustenance of nondomesticated desert fauna, but crop production is dependent on irrigation from underground aquifers. Saudi Arabia has no rivers or permanent bodies of water other than artificial lakes and pools. Wadis, the dry beds of ancient rivers, sometimes flow with runoff from downpours and seep with underground water.

Saudi Arabia has four main regions. Najd, the geographic center and political and cultural core, is a vast plateau that combines rocky and sandy areas with isolated mountains and wadi systems. Agricultural oases are the sites of villages, towns, and cities. This area's rangelands have long sustained nomadic pastoral production and are the homelands of the main Bedouin communities. Najd is bordered to the west by the regions of Hijaz and Asir along the Red Sea. A narrow coastal plane known as Tihama is predominant in the south, while a mountain chain with a steep western escarpment runs through these areas.

Hijaz has strong and ancient urban traditions and is the location of Mecca (Makkah) and Medina (al-Madinah). Other important Hijazi cities are Jiddah, a seaport, a commercial center, and formerly diplomatic capital; Taif, summer capital; and Yanbu, a newly developing industrial and longtime port city. Hijaz has agricultural oases, and a history of tribally organized nomadic pastoralism.

Asir has several cities and some nomadic presence, yet it is rural, with farmers living in settled communities largely organized in accordance with tribal and clan identities. The seaports of Hijaz and Asir also have populations traditionally oriented toward the sea, for trade or fishing, a characteristic they share with the Eastern Province.

The largest oasis, al-Ahsa (al-Hasa), is watered by artesian wells and springs in the interior of the Eastern Province and provides dates and other crops. The Eastern Province is also the main source

Saudi Arabia

of oil wealth. Oil and gas wells, refineries and other processing and distribution plants, and the headquarters of the national oil industry are located there. Trade and urban centers have long existed in this area, but the tricity complex of Dammam, al-Khubar, and Dhahran has been predominant since the 1960s, while Jubail is becoming a large industrial city.

Each geographic region has diverse local customs and histories. However, all the regions share traditional ways of life in a harsh desert environment and from a long history that includes the creation of the contemporary state and its culture in the last three centuries. They also share a common history of development since the 1950s, including a vast oil-revenue-induced boom between the mid-1970s and the mid-1980s, military events that led to the presence of foreign troops on Saudi Arabian soil in the 1990s, and the process of "globalization" at the end of the twentieth century.

Demography. The population in 1992 was about 16,900,000 and was increasing at a rate of 3.3 percent annually. A population of twenty million was projected for the year 2000, almost triple the roughly seven million enumerated in the early 1970s. The 1992 population consisted of 12,300,000 Saudi Arabian citizens and 4,600,000 resident foreigners, of whom about half were other Arabs. Just over three-quarters of the population was urban, with the remainder classified as rural, including the few remaining nomads. More than half the citizens were less than 20 years old.

Linguistic Affiliation. Arabic is the language of all Saudi Arabian citizens and about half the immigrants. Classical Arabic (*fusha*) in its Koranic, high literary, and modern standard forms is used for prayers and religious rituals, poetry, lectures, speeches, broadcasts, written communications, and other formal purposes. Conversationally, people use colloquial Arabic (*amiya*). There are many subdialects and internal variants. English is the main second language.

Symbolism. The national flag is green, the color of Islam, and bears a white inscription that translates as, "There is No God but God, and Muhammad is the Messenger of God." A white saber, the sword of Islam, was added in 1906 and symbolizes the military successes of Islam and of Abd al-Aziz Al Saud, the founder of the contemporary state. The national logo depicts two crossed swords and a date palm tree. The national day is 23 September, marking the unification in 1932 of the regions of Najd and its dependencies, Hijaz, and Asir to form the Kingdom of Saudi Arabia.

The national day is celebrated with speeches, receptions, and school-related activities but usually lacks pomp and ceremony. The king, leading princes, and government ministers often are seen on television performing their culturally prescribed roles.

The state and people engage in the creation of a national cultural heritage through the preservation or reconstruction of elements from the past that are seen as embodying the traditional culture. Examples are the preservation of old houses and mosques, the use of traditional motifs in new buildings, the holding of camel races, and the setting up in museums and hotels of tents with rugs and paraphernalia typical of traditional Bedouin tented households.

The national culture also embraces the new and the modern: a national airline (Saudia), oil industry and petrochemical installations, wheat growing in the irrigated desert, skyscrapers, shopping malls with artificial waterfalls and ice-skating rinks, and supermodern highways, ports, and airports. The contemporary consumer culture includes automobiles, pickup trucks, videocassette recorders, multichannel televisions, and telephones as well as computers and mobile phones.

Other dimensions of the national culture and its symbolism include performances such as the *ardah*, where men dance waving swords in the air; the recitation of epic poems about historical events related to tribal affairs; and national sports competitions. The distinctive clothing worn by both men and women conforms with Muslim dress codes that prescribe modesty for both sexes but especially women.

Saudi Arabia's most powerful cultural symbols are those linked to Islam. The ritual celebrations that have the strongest hold on people's imaginations are the holy month of Ramadan, the holy pilgrimage (*haj*) to Mecca, and the Muslim feasts of *Id al-Fitr* and *Id al-Adha*, which occur after the end of Ramadan and in conjunction with the pilgrimage, respectively. Other important rituals are the more private social celebrations of weddings, visits (especially among women) for joyous and sad occasions, extended family and clan reunions and other kin-based socializing, and the expression of condolences and participation in funerals.

HISTORY AND ETHNIC RELATIONS

Emergence of the Nation. Saudi Arabia's cultural roots lie deep in antiquity. Although remote from centers of ancient civilizations, Arabia's people had a multiplicity of contacts with Egypt, Syria, and Iraq and with the Roman and Byzantine empires. Ancient Arabia was home to states, cities, and other manifestations of complex cultures and societies. Of particular significance to ancient Arabia was the domestication of the dromedary (one-humped camel) in the southern part of the peninsula between 3000 and 2500 B.C.E. By 1000 B.C.E., camels were important in the lucrative caravan trade, especially for the transport of incense, between southern Arabia and markets in the north. The invention of the north Arabian camel saddle between about 500 and 100 B.C.E. allowed tribally organized camel raisers to enhance their power and influence.

Armed camel raisers did not subsist on their own in desert Arabia but depended on foods produced by farmers in the region's oases and on a wide range of products, including weapons, manufactured by local craftspeople. The Bedouin obtained some of their necessities through tribute in return for their protection of farmers and craftspeople.

Market exchange also existed, and the output of nomadic and sedentary producers was marketed locally and, in the case of camels and horses, through long-distance trade.

Markets and their specialized personnel of merchants and traders are as indigenous to the culture of Arabia as are Bedouin camel raisers and oasis-dwelling farmers. Knowledge of the state as an institution has also long been present, although the exercise of effective state power was often lacking in the past.

The foundation and legitimacy of the state are linked to Islam, which is itself historically linked to Arabia. Muslims believe that God (Allah) sent His final revelation "in clear Arabic," in the form of the holy Koran, through His Messenger, Muhammad. This occurred first in and around Mecca and then in Medina beginning in 622 C.E., which marks the first year of the Islamic era (1 A.H.). By the time of Muhammad's death in 632, almost all the tribal and local communities in Arabia had declared their loyalty to him as a political leader and most had accepted Islam. The process of conversion was completed under the leadership of Islam's first caliph, Abu Bakr. The religion was then carried by Arabian converts throughout the Middle East and north Africa.

Islam brought not only a new religion but a new way of life that included innovations in legal and political concepts and practices and a new identity that was universalistic and cosmopolitan. The new Muslim identity, politics, and laws transcended the social and cultural borders of existing communities that had been organized as localities or kin-based tribes.

National Identity. Contemporary Saudi Arabia arose from a process of state development that began in the late seventeenth century, when leaders of the Bani Khalid tribe created a state in the al-Ahsa area of today's Eastern Province. Other attempts at state building involved the Al Rashid and Al Idrisi dynasties in Najd and Asir, respectively. However, the most effective movement was initiated in the late 1730s by Sheikh Muhammad Al Abd al-Wahab (died 1792). After studying in the Hijaz and Iraq, he returned to Najd and preached and wrote against practices that deviated from Islam. He stressed the unity of God and urged his followers, who became known as *muwahidun* ("unitarians"), to end polytheistic practices and adhere strictly to the Koran and the *Hadith* (the sayings and doings of the Prophet).

In 1744, the sheikh swore an oath with Muhammad Al Saud, the emir of ad-Diriyah, that they would collaborate to establish a state orga-

Urban houses in Al-Balad Medina, Jeddah. Gender-segregated space still exists in many households.

nized and run according to Islamic principles. Their goal was religious reform, a phenomenon that involved a new leadership structure that placed Al Saud in the position of *umara* (princes, rulers) and Al Abd al-Wahab (also known as Al Sheikh) in the position of *ulama* (learned in religion). The reform movement also involved military struggle, preaching, the establishment of Koranic schools, the setting up of new communities, and the creation of a bureaucratic state that ruled in Najd from 1765 and in Hijaz from 1803 until 1818, when it was defeated by an Ottoman army from Egypt. This state was reestablished in the mid-nineteenth century, overthrown by Al Rashid, and re-created through reconquest and religious reform under the leadership of Abd al-Aziz Al Saud beginning in 1902 and culminating with the declaration of the present kingdom in 1932.

Never a colony of a foreign power or a province of the Ottoman Empire, the Saudi Arabian state resulted from an indigenous local process of sociopolitical change and religious reform. Some think of that state as having a strong tribal dimension, in part because the Al Saud are of tribal origins. However, merchants provided loans and financial assistance, preachers and teachers built a consciousness among Muslims and imparted religious knowledge, and jurists and bureaucrats labored to carry out the work of a state without regard to tribal identity.

The legitimacy of the state is derived from Islam, along with the will of the citizens, who swear an oath of allegiance (*bayah*) to the ruler. The constitution is the Koran, and *Sharia* (Islamic law) is the law of the land. The ruler has the title "Custodian of the Two Holy Mosques," which implies an Islamic role, yet he also carries the title of *malik* ("king"), which may be seen as symbolic of the state's technical, administrative, and policing functions.

Ethnic Relations. As Muslims, Saudi Arabians participate in a community (*ummah*) in which issues of race, ethnicity, and national origin should be of no significance and never form the basis for social action, political behavior, and economic organization. The identity of Muslim transcends the borders of states and ideally takes precedence over all other identities.

Socially, however, the concept of origin (*asl*) is strong among many Saudi Arabians. Some people, mainly in Hijaz, are recognized descendants of Muhammad and are known as *Ashraf*. Many others throughout the kingdom assert patrilineal descent from eponymous ancestors from ancient Arab tribes. Still others stress Arabian origins but without tribal connections. However, Saudi citizenship embraces people with historical origins outside the Arabian Peninsula. Considerations of origin are important markers and influence social interaction, including marriage, but do not translate directly into economic or power differentials in the national society. Moreover, the social significance of such considerations is waning, especially among younger people.

The more prominent cultural division within Saudi Arabian society is between citizens and immigrants. That division sometimes is muted by the common bonds of Islam and/or Arabism, yet many immigrants are neither Muslim nor Arab. In these cases, religious, linguistic, and other cultural barriers accentuate the social cleavage between the local person and the foreigner. Moreover, class divisions separate citizens from the many immigrants who are low-skilled workers. The immigrants come temporarily and mostly as individuals without families. They are thus in the society but not of it, and little effort is made to assimilate them.

URBANISM, ARCHITECTURE, AND THE USE OF SPACE

In 1950, roughly 40 percent of the population was nomadic and resided in tents in highly dispersed patterns on vast rangelands, where they migrated with herds of camels, sheep, and goats to seasonal pastures and for access to water. Another 40 percent lived in villages in the rural areas of oases or the Asir highlands and worked mainly in agriculture. The remaining 20 percent were urbanites in the old cities of Mecca, Medina, Jiddah, Taif, Abha, Buraydah, Unayzah, Ha'il, Hufuf, and Riyadh. In 1992, three-quarters of the population was classified as urban.

Major changes accompanied the growth of the oil industry in the 1950s. New cities developed rapidly, while older ones increased in size. Nomadic Bedouin settled in villages and in and around cities, and villagers left their communities for rapidly growing urban areas. This geographic mobility was accompanied by occupational mobility as Bedouin and villagers worked as wage laborers or small-scale traders and taxi drivers and then became government and private sector employees, professionals, and businesspeople. People from old cities also moved to newly developing cities and experienced occupational change.

The new cities and the transformed areas of old ones depend on the use of automobiles. They sprawl over large areas, have neighborhoods separated by open spaces, and are linked by wide thoroughfares, freeways, and ring roads. The new urban fabric contrasts sharply with urban scenes that lingered into the 1970s. The old cities were walled and had compact residential areas with mazes of narrow paths, parts of which were covered by the upper stories of houses. Most houses had inward-looking courtyards, and some used wind catches to circulate air. The old cities also had date palm gardens with wells and other greenery between and among neighborhoods. Mosques were within easy walking distance from residences, and there was always a main central mosque, a major market area, and a principal seat of government that was usually part of a fort.

Similarities in the social use of domestic space transcended the categories of nomad, villager, and urbanite and continue today. The tents of nomads and the permanent houses of others were divided into sections for men and women, which also served as the family living quarters. Among the nomads, men sat on kilims and carpets around a hearth outside the front of the tent to visit, drink coffee and tea, and eat. Boys past puberty and male visitors slept there. Women made similar use of the space set aside for their visiting in the tents.

The same pattern of gender-segregated space continues to exist in the homes of sedentary people. Modern housing often has separate entrances and separate reception areas or living rooms for each gender. In many houses, people sit on carpets or cushions alongside the walls of the room, and most of those houses have areas with chairs and sofas around the walls. The central space of the room is left open.

People in both cities and smaller communities now live mainly in individual dwellings with exterior surrounding walls. Although apartment buildings exist, they usually are inhabited by immigrants. The tents and old houses usually housed extended families of three or more generations. Although nuclear family households are increasingly the norm, relatives continue to cluster together, and it is not uncommon for brothers to locate their dwellings on adjacent lots or inside a common compound. Many immigrants live in camps specifically created for them or in abandoned housing in the older parts of towns; some guest workers live on farms.

FOOD AND ECONOMY

Food in Daily Life.
The traditional staple foods were dates; goat, camel, and cow's milk; ghee, cheese, and other milk products; bread and other foods from wheat, millet, and barley; squash, eggplant, okra, pumpkin, beans, leeks, onions, and a few other vegetables; mint, coriander, parsley, and cumin; and occasionally mutton, goat, or camel meat and, on the coasts, fish. Elderly people remember meals of the past as simple but adequate, without a morsel wasted. They regularly ate at home and started the day with a breakfast of coffee and a few dates soon after the dawn prayer. A meal of dates, milk and/or milk products, and bread was served at midmorning. The last and main meal often was taken before the sunset prayer and consisted of a hot grain-based dish, vegetables among sedentary people in oases, milk among the nomadic Bedouin, rarely some meat, and dates.

Meals today are eaten later, and the foods are more copious and elaborate. Cheese, yogurt, jam, eggs, beans, and bread may be consumed around eight a.m. A lunch of mutton or chicken on a plate of rice with side dishes of vegetables and salads followed by fresh fruit is shared by family members around 2:30 P.M. The evening meal is usually a lighter version of lunch and is eaten well after eight o'clock. Less common today are dates, grain-based dishes, and milk. Rice has become ubiquitous, and chicken very common. Light roasted Arabic coffee without sugar but spiced with cardamom remains the national beverage; tea is also popular.

Foods that are taboo are those forbidden by Islam, notably pork and wine and other alcoholic beverages. Restaurants were uncommon and considered somewhat improper in the past, but a wide spectrum now serves Middle Eastern, north African, Italian, Indian and Pakistani, Korean, Japanese, Chinese, and other cuisines in addition to American and Middle Eastern fast food.

Food Customs at Ceremonial Occasions.
The arrival of a guest at one's home is an event that leads to a special meal in honor of the visitor. Traditional etiquette required that sheep, goat, or camel be sacrificially slaughtered, and this is still often done. However, chicken may be substituted, and in many urban households meat dishes have replaced eating the whole animal. Major ritual occasions associated with Islamic feasts, weddings, reunions of family and kin, and other social events still require the sacrificial slaughter of sheep or, less commonly, goats or young camels.

For these events, meat is boiled in huge pots, and part of the soup is passed among the guests, with the rest poured over large trays of rice on top of which the cooked meat is placed. Traditionally, male guests and older men gather around the tray and eat first, using the right hand; they are followed by younger men and finally boys. Women and girls eat separately, often food prepared specially for them but sometimes eating what the men and boys have not consumed. Multiple rounds of coffee and tea are served before and after the meal, and incense is burned.

Basic Economy.
Saudi Arabia produced all its staple foods until the 1940s. Coffee, tea, sugar, cardamom, rice, cloth, and some manufactured

A Saudi man using the Internet in his office in Riyadh. There are substantial variations in the amount of income and accumulated wealth among Saudi Arabians.

items were the main imports. Exports consisted of dates, camels, horses, and sheep, with western India, Iraq, greater Syria, and Egypt being the main centers of long-distance trade. Saudi Arabia also received a modest income related to the holy pilgrimage and other travel to shrines. Generally, the country was self-reliant, but for a smaller population and at a lower consumption level. The majority of the population worked in food production; however, most people depended on local exchange for food and other items. Today, a vastly richer country is dependent on international trade for much of its food and almost everything else.

In the 1970s and 1980s, Saudi Arabia invested heavily in new commercial agriculture. Spectacular increases have been achieved in the production of wheat, sorghum, barley, poultry and eggs, and new vegetable and fruit crops. However, much of this expansion depends on the use of fossil water (not replenishible), guest workers, imported machinery, and state subsidies. Saudi Arabia has regained self-sufficiency in wheat, and range-based livestock raising is increasingly commercial in orientation. Many Saudi Arabians still work in agriculture and ranching, but as owners and managers rather than workers; some are absentee owners, and many have other occupations and other sources of income.

Land Tenure and Property. Land developed for agricultural, residential, commercial, and industrial uses that has been demarcated is usually owned as private property (*mulk*) and can be bought and sold freely. Some property, however, may be held as a trust (*waqf*) for the support of a religious institution or an owner's descendants. Nondemarcated, undeveloped land in the desert belongs to the state, but traditional rights of access to rangeland and the ownership of water wells dug by nomads or their ancestors are informally attributed to lineages and clans in Bedouin communities. Much land in older settlements is encumbered by informal but powerful ancestral claims of ownership and tenure.

Commercial Activities. Saudi Arabia has banks, foreign exchange houses, and gold and jewelry shops; import houses and agencies of international companies; engineering and contracting firms; supermarkets, grocery stores, butcheries, and bakeries; hotels and restaurants; coffeehouses (for men only); and retail firms selling clothing, home wares, electronics, automobiles, and other consumer items. There are tailors, small repair shops, and other service shops.

Major Industries. The Saudi Arabian oil industry began in 1933, when Americans obtained concessions to explore for oil. Commercial quantities of "black gold" were discovered in 1938, but development of the industry was interrupted by World War II. The Arabian American Oil Company (ARAMCO) was formed in 1944, and the industry's expansion followed rapidly. Saudi Arabia has more than 261 billion barrels of proven oil reserves— more than a fourth of the world total—and perhaps a trillion barrels of potentially recoverable oil. It is the world's leading oil producer and exporter, has the world's greatest capacity for oil production, and has the world's fifth largest proven reserves of natural gas. Saudi Arabia also has large and expanding refinery projects and an ambitious program to develop petrochemical production. In the late 1990s, oil revenues accounted for 85 percent of export earnings and 40 percent of gross domestic product (GDP).

Gradual nationalization of the oil industry started in the 1970s. Control and ownership shifted to the state-owned Saudi Arabian Oil Company (Saudi Aramco) for crude production, refining, and marketing. Petrochemical production falls under the Saudi Arabian Basic Industries Corporation (SABIC), while much of the downstream parts of the industry are controlled by state companies. The state holds title to all the country's mineral resources, and the oil industry as a whole is governed by the Supreme Petroleum Council headed by the king.

Trade. The bulk of exports are crude oil, refined products, and natural gas liquids. The main customers are Japan and other Asian countries, western Europe, and the United States. Aside from military items, the principal imports include machinery, appliances, electrical equipment, foodstuffs, chemical products, jewelry and metals, and transport items. The major source of imports is the European Union, followed by the United States, and Japan, with only 3 to 4 percent from other Middle Eastern countries.

Division of Labor. Unskilled manual work and that of servants and nannies is performed almost exclusively by immigrants. Medium- to high-skilled private sector salaried employment has also been dominated by guest workers. Saudi Arabian citizens prevail in government employment and ownership and management positions in business enterprises. A process of "Saudization" of the modern workforce has been a national goal since the 1980s. With rapidly rising levels of higher education and the local development of specialized expertise, young Saudi Arabians increasingly have taken

A group of Saudi men gather in front of a store in Jeddah. Men have substantially more rights than women, who must remain out of public view.

on positions requiring advanced professional knowledge. Economic and demographic forces have contributed to the replacement of immigrants by local citizens in middle-level private sector jobs.

SOCIAL STRATIFICATION

Classes and Castes. A major social division is that between guest workers and local citizens. The working class is largely composed of temporary immigrants, who also occupy middle-class positions and a few positions in the upper class.

Major variations in income and accumulated wealth exist, with the major categories including the super-rich, the very rich, and the rich alongside a large middle-income group and some with limited incomes. Only small pockets of poverty persist. A strong ideology of egalitarianism is traditional among Saudi Arabians, whose social and verbal patterns of interaction stress equality and siblinghood rather than status differentiation. However, degrees of luxury vary greatly. Differences in lifestyle are increasing as wealthy elites interact less commonly with middle-class people. Common attitudes, beliefs, and practices are shared across economic divides, which also are bridged by ties of kinship and religion.

POLITICAL LIFE

Government. Saudi Arabia is a monarchy whose king serves as both head of state and head of government. The Koran is the constitution. Legislation and other regulations are promulgated by royal decree or ministerial decree sanctioned by the king. The monarch appoints cabinet ministers, governors of provinces, senior military officers, and ambassadors. He is also commander in chief of the armed forces and the final court of appeal with the power of pardon. Since the rule of King Abd al-Aziz Al Saud (died 1953), the kings have all come from among King Abd al-Aziz's sons, a provision that has been extended to include his grandsons.

The government also consists of the Royal Divan, which includes the king's private office; advisers for domestic, religious, and international issues; the chief of protocol; and the heads of the office of Bedouin affairs, along with the department of religious research, missionary activities, and guidance and the committees for the propagation of virtue and prevention of vice. The king holds court in the divan, where citizens can make requests or express complaints.

The Council of Ministers is the main executive organ and is composed of the king, the crown prince, several royal ministers of state without portfolio, other ministers of state, the heads of twenty ministries and the national guard, several main provincial governors, and the heads of the monetary agency and the petroleum and mineral organization. The kingdom has a large civil service that began to expand rapidly in the early 1970s and employed an estimated 400,000 persons in the early 1990s. Saudi Arabia has fourteen provinces, each governed by an emir, usually from the royal family, who reports to the minister of the interior.

Leadership and Political Officials. There are no political parties, but the royal family is a large grouping with significant political influence. It consists of about twenty thousand people and has several main branches and clans. Some princes are especially influential in politics, while others are active in business. The ulama also play important leadership roles and consist of members of the Al Sheikh family and several thousand religious scholars, *qadis* (judges), lawyers, seminary teachers, and imams (prayer leaders) of mosques. Business and merchant families often exert political influence, but there are no labor unions or syndicates for pro-

fessional groups. Opposition groups exist outside the country. Political upheavals, some of them violent, have taken place, yet the political system has remained relatively stable over decades of rapid economic, social, and demographic change.

Social Problems and Control. Adherence to Islamic values and maintenance of social stability in the context of rapid economic change have been consistent goals of Saudi Arabia's development plans. Religion and society combine to foster significant social control. A powerful deterrent to deviant behavior is that such behavior brings shame to one's family and kin and is considered sinful. Crimes related to alcohol and drugs and to sexual misconduct sometimes are linked to rapid modernization. Theft is rare, and other economic crimes are relatively uncommon, with the exception of smuggling. Assault and murder are limited mainly to segments of tribal communities and usually involve issues of honor and revenge.

The justice system is based on the *Sharia*, which defines many crimes and specifies punishments. Crimes not specifically identified in the Sharia are defined on the basis of analogy and often are punished by prison sentences. Sharia-prescribed punishments usually have a physical component. An individual arrested on a criminal charge is detained in a police station until a judgment is rendered by a court of first instance presided over by one or more qadis. A court of cassation, or appeals court, also exists, and the king functions as a final court of appeal. A person found not guilty is released. If a physical punishment is prescribed, it is carried out in a public place, usually outside a main mosque on Friday, where the criminal's name and ancestral names are called out loudly for all to hear and where the shame is said to be more painful than the physical blow. Prison sentences, typical for cases involving drugs, are less public. Foreigners convicted of crimes are punished and then deported.

Islam is strict about issues of law and order and rigorous in the use of witnesses. For a man to be convicted of theft, four Muslims must swear a religious oath that they saw the theft take place. Alternatively, an individual may confess. Physical punishment usually is applied only to serious repeat offenders. The state employs the police, supports the qadis and the court system, provides the prisons, and assures that maximum media attention is given to punishments.

Military Activity. Saudi Arabia maintains an army, navy, air force, coast guard, national guard, and frontier guard with a combined total of about two hundred thousand men. These all-volunteer forces have state-of-the-art equipment and a reputation for professionalism.

NONGOVERNMENTAL ORGANIZATIONS AND OTHER ASSOCIATIONS

The giving of alms or a tithe (*zakat*) is one of the five pillars of Islam. This religious obligation sometimes is paid as a tax to Islamic states. Considerable private donations are made to philanthropic societies that address the changing needs of the poor and the handicapped. Other private voluntary organizations deal with community needs, establish sports and cultural clubs, and contribute to development programs that complement state activities. These associations normally are registered with the ministry of social affairs and often receive financial support from the state in addition to contributions from citizens.

GENDER ROLES AND STATUSES

Division of Labor by Gender. Strict gender segregation is sanctioned by the state and society. Males and females who are not not barred from marriage by incest rules should not interact in individual or group settings. Women may work outside the home in settings where they do not have contact with unrelated men. Women are employed in girls' schools and the women's sections of universities, social work and development programs for women, banks that cater to female clients, medicine and nursing for women, television and radio programming, and computer and library work. Sections of markets are set aside for women sellers. However, only about 7 percent of Saudi Arabia's formal workforce is female.

The Relative Status of Women and Men. Men have more rights than do women. Women are not allowed to drive; cannot travel abroad without the permission or presence of a male guardian (*mahram*); are dependent on fathers, brothers, or husbands to conduct almost all their private and public business; and have to wear a veil and remain out of public view. However, women can own property in their own names and invest their own money in business deals. Women's status is high in the family, especially in the roles of mothers and sisters. Significant numbers of women have had high levels of success in academia, literary production, business, and other fields, yet their achievements go publicly unremarked and they are barred from most aspects of public life.

An Arabian coffee pot.

MARRIAGE, FAMILY, AND KINSHIP

Marriage. Traditionally, marriage was between paternal first cousins or other patrilineally related kin. It was customary for potential spouses not to meet before the wedding night, and marriages had to be arranged by fathers, mothers, and other relatives. These practices are changing slowly and unevenly, but the tendency is toward fewer close-cousin marriages and for the couple to communicate with each other before the wedding. Parents still arrange marriages but are more likely to manage indirectly and from the background. Men are allowed to have four wives at a time as long as they can treat them equally, but polygyny is uncommon in most of the population. Marriage is considered a necessary part of life, and almost all adults marry. Marriage is usually a costly affair. Divorce is relatively easy for men and difficult for women. Divorce rates are high, and remarriage is common, especially for men.

Domestic Unit. In traditional residence pattern, a bride joined her husband in his father's household. Authority was held by the husband's father, and the new wife was under the control of her mother-in-law. Neolocal residence is now the norm, or at least the ideal, for newly married couples. In these smaller conjugal families, the roles of husbands and wives feature greater equality and more sharing of responsibilities. Authority formally rests with the husband, who also has the religiously sanctioned duty of providing for the needs of his wife and children.

Inheritance. The stipulations of Islam are widely followed in the inheritance of property. Sons inherit twice the share of daughters from their fathers. Provisions exist for a widow to inherit a small portion, but sons are enjoined to support their mothers, especially widowed or divorced mothers. Custom, but not the Sharia, allows immobile property to be inherited intact by male descendants; in such cases, daughters are usually given a ''share'' of a potential inheritance in money or other items when they marry.

Kin Groups. Kinship is patrilineal, and women continue to remain members of their kin groups after marriage. Among Bedouin and many rural settlers, kin groups identified by ancestral names in larger aggregations include lineages, clans, and tribes and have major social significance. Genealogy is of great interest; although corporate kin groups have largely ceased to exist, many people continue to identify with and take pride in their lineage, clan, and tribal names and descent.

SOCIALIZATION

Child Rearing and Education. Mothers used to give birth at home, perhaps with the assistance of a midwife. Infants were cared for by their mothers, who carried them everywhere and nursed them. Other women in extended households, including longtime domestic servants, participated actively in rearing children, teaching them Arabian culture and mores. Fathers and uncles and grandfathers did not take part in child care but played with the children, kissed them, and taught them genealogies and morality. They taught them generosity and hospitality by example.

Intense family and kin-based socialization at home is now mainly a memory. Birth takes place at a hospital, and infant boys are circumcised there before going home (girls are not circumcised). A foreign maid or nanny who may speak little or no Arabic often does much of the work of child rearing. This is an issue that troubles many Saudi Arabians. Breast-feeding sometimes is rejected for not being modern. While much visiting goes on among relatives, conjugal family households today do not provide the rich family learning setting of the past.

Boys and girls go to kindergarten and the rest of the educational system. In 1970, the literacy rate was 15 percent for men and 2 percent for women. In 1990, the rate was 73 percent for men and 48 percent for women, and it is even higher now. The increased role of the school in society represents a break with the past, yet there is also continuity. Religious subjects and the Arabic language are strongly represented in curricula but are not always taught in traditional ways. Universities have produced tens of thousands of graduates in a single generation. Half or more of those graduates are women.

ETIQUETTE

Social interaction is marked by strong gender segregation and respect for age differentials. An egalitarian ethos and a high valorization of polite behavior also prevail. Men and women seldom interact across the gender divide outside the domestic space of families, and many of the society's most powerful do's and don'ts aim to regulate such interaction beyond the confines of a home. Thus male-female interaction in a commercial shop should be formal and strictly limited to the process of buying and selling. Generally, men and women should refrain from making specific references to individuals of the other gender, although it is appropriate and common for one to inquire about the well-being of another individual's ''family'' or ''house''— concepts which are understood as circumlocutions for significant others of the opposite gender. Deference should be shown to those who are older, and relations between generations are often characterized by strict formality and the maintenance of decorum in social gatherings.

Most social interaction takes place in groups that are gender- and age-specific. Social visiting within such contexts is very common and occurs on both an everyday basis and for special events. The latter especially include visits to convey condolences for a death or, conversely, to express congratulations for a happy occurrence such as a wedding, a graduation or promotion, or a safe return from a trip. A guest, upon arrival, should greet individually the host and all others present by shaking hands or, if well-known to each other and of similar age, by kissing on the cheeks three or more times. The individual being greeted should stand. The guest must be offered refreshments of coffee and tea. An invitation to lunch or dinner should also be offered by the host. An animated and relatively long exchange of greetings is expected between host and guest and between the guest and others present, as

A Bedouin tribesman at a market in Abha.

patterns, but in attenuated forms, apply between local citizens and immigrants.

RELIGION

Religious Beliefs. All Saudi Arabian citizens are Muslims. Except for a small minority of Shia, Saudi Arabians are Sunni and mainly follow the Handbali school of Islamic law (*madhab*). Half or more of the immigrants are also Muslims. Non-Muslim faiths are not allowed to practice in Saudi Arabia.

Religious Practitioners. Islam does not have ordained clergy or priests. The person most learned in Islam is the one who leads the prayers. The learned (*ulama*) include judges, preachers, teachers, prayer leaders, and others who have studied Islam.

Rituals and Holy Places. The major everyday rituals are related to the five daily prayers that constitute one of the five pillars of Islam. Those who pray face Mecca, ideally in a mosque or as a group. The *haj* (pilgrimage) is another of the five pillars and should be performed at least once in one's life. Visits also take place to the mosque and tomb of Muhammad in Medina. The other three pillars of Islam are witnessing that there is no God but God and Muhammad is His Messenger, fasting during the day throughout the month of Ramadan, and the giving of alms.

Death and the Afterlife. The dead are washed, wrapped in seamless shrouds, and buried in graves facing Mecca without coffins or markers. Burial takes place before sunset on the day of death. The dead go to heaven or hell.

MEDICINE AND HEALTH CARE

A rich body of traditional medicine previously existed in Saudi Arabia. Physical ailments were treated with the use of herbs and other plants and also by cauterization or burning a specific part of the body with a hot iron. Severe mental health problems were often addressed through special readings of the Koran. Modern Western medicine is now wide-spread and is used by all segments of the society. Public and private hospitals and clinics are established throughout the country, and several specialist hospitals with state-of-the-art medical technologies and practice exist in the major cities. Still, travel abroad to other Arab countries and to Europe and the United States for medical treatment remains common and is supported by the state.

each individual inquires about the other's health and wishes him/her God's protection. The offering of refreshments and the exchange of greetings is extended to office and shop settings (at least among people of the same gender); failure to observe them is very rude. Meanwhile, gender segregation is maintained in public places such as airports or banks, where separate lines for men and women are usual.

People tend to remain in close physical contact during social interaction. Walking arm-in-arm or holding hands and gently slapping or touching a person's outstretched palm while talking is common, especially among people of the same gender who know each other well. Gazing, and especially staring, at strangers is rude. In public, people should avoid direct eye-contact with passers-by. When greeting a stranger or an acquaintance, it is appropriate for the person who arrives first to say, in Arabic, "Peace be upon you," to which the proper reply is, "And upon you peace." When saying goodbye, it is proper to say, in Arabic, "In the custody of God," the reply being "In the custody of the Generous One." Generally, the same patterns of etiquette hold throughout Saudi Arabia. Greater formality, however, prevails among Bedouin and rural people, while more relaxed, informal interaction occurs among younger urbanites. The same

THE ARTS AND HUMANITIES

Literature. The main art form in Saudi Arabia is in the realm of literature. Classical Arabic poetry is highly valued, while a wide range of colloquial poetic forms is popular and are widely used in different social settings. Recitations of poetry are common at weddings and to mark other important public events. The novel has also become popular among both men and women authors. Local publishing houses exist, while authors also have access to publishers in other Arab countries. The state censor of publications, however, plays a powerful role in deciding what can be published.

Graphic Arts. Painting and sculpture are practiced, but a rich variety of folk art in weaving, decorative arts, furniture making, and similar work is of a high quality. The making of jewelry in both traditional and modern styles is also common.

THE STATE OF THE PHYSICAL AND SOCIAL SCIENCES

The physical and social sciences are all taught in Saudi Arabian universities, which exist in all the main cities. Medical sciences are especially popular among both women and men students. One university is specifically devoted to study and research relevant to petroleum. Agriculture and agricultural engineering is a specialty at several other universities, while courses and programs in social studies bring anthropology, sociology, and social work to a wide spectrum of students. Psychology is also taught, as are economics and business. Research centers tied to universities, government entities, and to Islamic entities have a significant presence. Meanwhile, Saudi Arabia has a long history of state sponsorship of large numbers of university students and scholars abroad, especially in the United States.

BIBLIOGRAPHY

Al-Farsy, Fouad. *Saudi Arabia: A Case Study in Development*, 1982.

Almana, Mohammed. *Arabia Unified: A Portrait of Ibn Saud*, 1980.

Al-Naqeeb, Khaldoon. *Society and State in the Gulf and Arab Peninsula*, 1990

Al Rasheed, Madawi. *Politics in an Arabian Oasis: The Rashidi Tribal Dynasty*, 1991.

Altorki, Soraya. *Women in Saudi Arabia: Ideology and Behavior among the Elite*, 1986.

———, and Donald P. Cole. *Arabian Oasis City: The Transformation of 'Unayzah*, 1989.

Al-Yassini, Ayman. *Religion and State in the Kingdom of Saudi Arabia*, 1985.

Birks, J. S., and C. A. Sinclair. *Saudi Arabia into the '90s*, 1988.

Carter, J. R. L. *Merchant Families of Saudi Arabia*, 1984.

Cole, Donald P. *Nomads of the Nomads: The Al Murrah Bedouin of the Empty Quarter*, 1975.

Dahlan, Ahmed Hassan, ed. *Politics, Administration, and Development in Saudi Arabia*, 1990.

Field, Michael. *The Merchants: The Big Business Families of Saudi Arabia and the Gulf States*, 1985.

Habib, John s. *Ibn Sa'uds Warriors of Islam: The Ikhwan of Najd and their Role in the Creation of the Saudi Kingdom, 1910–1930*, 1978.

Helms, Christine Moss. *The Cohesion of Saudi Arabia: Evolution of Political Identity*, 1981.

Hopwood, Derek, ed. *The Arabian Peninsula: Society and Politics*, 1972.

Ingham, Bruce. *Bedouin of Northern Arabia: Traditions of the Al-Dhafir*, 1986.

Lacey, Robert. *The Kingdom: Arabia and the House of Saud*, 1982.

Looney, Robert E. *Economic Development in Saudi Arabia: Consequences of the Oil Price Decline*, 1990.

Metz, Helen Chapin, ed. *Saudi Arabia: A Country Study*, 1992.

Niblock, Timothy, ed. *State, Society, and Economy in Saudi Arabia*, 1982.

Sirageldin, Ismail A., Naiem A. Sherbiny, and M. Ismail Serageldin. *Saudis in Transition: The Challenges of a Changing Labor Market*, 1985.

Sowayan, Saad Abdullah. *Nabati Poetry: The Oral Poetry of Arabia*, 1985.

Winder, R. Bayly. *Saudi Arabia in the Nineteenth Century*, 1961.

—DONALD POWELL COLE

SCOTLAND

CULTURE NAME

Scottish or Scots; Scotch is considered antiquated and belittling.

ALTERNATIVE NAMES

Historically, Scotland was referred to as Caledonia and by the Gaelic name Alba.

ORIENTATION

Identification. An imaginary line running roughly from Aberdeen to Glasgow separates the Highlands in the north and west from the Lowlands in the south and east. This line still distinguishes a more Gaelic and rurally oriented Highland cultural sphere from a more hybrid and urban Lowland culture. Gaelic traditions and language are strongest on the northwest coast, especially in the Hebridean Islands. The Northern Islands, Orkney and Shetland, with strong historical ties to Norway, are culturally distinct from the Highlands. To the south, the heavily urbanized Central Belt encompasses Dundee, Edinburgh, Saint Andrews, Stirling, Paisley, and Glasgow. The premier cities of Edinburgh in the east and Glasgow in the west embody important cultural contrasts and antagonisms within this urban frame. The more mountainous Borders region to the south and east of this belt is more rural. There is population flow between Scotland and England and between Scotland, Ireland, and Northern Ireland. There is a small Asian Muslim community.

Location and Geography. Scotland occupies approximately the northern third of the United Kingdom's (UK) mainland, encompassing 7.5 million hectares. The area of Scotland is 29,795 square miles (77,168 square kilometers). The climate is cool, wet, and often windy. Much land in the Highlands and Borders is rugged and difficult to cultivate, but the Lowlands and parts of the Borders include prime agricultural land. Scotland is surrounded by the North Sea, offering fish, oil and natural gas, and potentially tidal and wave power.

Demography. In 1997, the population was 5,122,500, with over 3 million persons in the Central Belt. This distribution shows the effects of rural depopulation, especially during the "Highland Clearances" (c. 1790–1830), when landlords forced tenants off their land to modernize the economy, especially through sheep raising. Some tenants were resettled in coastal villages and encouraged to supplement farming with fishing, linen weaving, and kelp manufacture, while many others migrated to the Central Belt or emigrated abroad. Industrialization led to massive urbanization in the nineteenth century during which the population increased from around 1.5 million to 4.5 million, with the growth concentrated in and around Glasgow. Immigrants from the Highlands and Ireland played a major role in this growth. Today there are around sixty-five thousand native Gaelic speakers. There are approximately twenty thousand Pakistanis, ten thousand Indians, ten thousand Chinese, six thousand blacks (Africa, Caribbean, other), four thousand five hundred "other" Asians, one thousand one hundred Bangladeshis, and eight thousand five hundred from other ethnic groups. There are many people of Italian and Polish extraction. People raised in Scotland will often identify as Scottish, regardless of non-Scottish ancestry.

Linguistic Affiliation. The Gaelic spoken in Scotland derives from Q-Celtic. Only a portion of the Highland-Island population speaks it as a first language in a bilingual milieu, although those areas have bilingual education and road signs and Gaelic newspapers. Major governmental policy statements and the slogans and publications of political parties are translated into Gaelic.

Scots is a cognate of modern English with a strong Danish influence. Borrowings from Gaelic, Norse, and Norman French have created a diverse patchwork of regional dialects. However, extensive

Scotland

interactions with English and the urban mixture of regional dialects have yielded a Scots to Scottish-English continuum. Scots can be used situationally to emphasize cultural and political identification.

Symbolism. Dominant national symbols evidence a growing demand for political devolution and/or independence. The imagery stemming from the Wars of Independence (1296–1371) produced na-

tional heroes such as William Wallace and Robert the Bruce. The images of the Scottish thistle, the lion rampant, and the Saint Andrew's cross (Saltire) on the national flags come from that period. Symbols that evoke the past of the Highlands include the system of clan tartans and bagpipes. Those images were incorporated into Scotland's modern martial traditions through the Highland regiments in the British Army. A third strain emphasizes Lowland

Protestant political history since the Reformation, revolving around the national Presbyterian Church (the "Kirk"). Images of the national covenants from the seventeenth century protesting against interference in Scottish religious affairs are often invoked. The fortunes of the national soccer teams and the dramatic landscape are heavily invested with national meaning.

HISTORY AND ETHNIC RELATIONS

Emergence of the Nation. In the eleventh century, the Scottish kingdom was a politico-ethnic patchwork of Scots, Picts, Angles, and Britons. Under Anglo-Norman feudal institutions, many cities were founded, often populated by Flemish, Norman, English, and Scandinavian immigrants recruited for craft and artisanal skills. These changes mark the growing cultural divergence between the Lowlands and the Highlands.

Between the late thirteenth and fifteenth centuries, the political system became unstable and fragmented when the royal line died without a clear heir and rulership was contested, leading to the "Wars of Independence," during which the kings of England and rival Scottish noble houses competed for overlordship. The church went into a long decline, and urban growth set the stage for the Scottish Reformation (1560–67) and the establishment the Calvinist Kirk. Sustained in part by a new class alliance of lesser nobility (lairds), burghers, lawyers, and the ministers of the new Kirk, the authority of the Kirk spread rapidly throughout the Lowlands.

The links between Scotland and England were reinforced by dynastic strategy when King James VI of Scotland acquired the English throne as James I. The next century saw internecine religious war and a shift in power from the monarch and court to the parliaments. In 1707, the Scottish aristocracy agreed to a Union of the Scottish and English parliaments, securing Scotland's part in the coming British Empire. A crucial aspect of this treaty was the preservation of the autonomy of Scotland's Kirk, legal and educational systems, and organs of local government.

In its pre-Reformation conflicts with England, Scotland often sought an alliance with France. After 1707, aristocratic clan chiefs called Jacobites, with French assistance, attempted to reinstate the deposed Stuart royal line. The result of the defeat at the Battle of Culloden (1746) was the harsh oppression of Gaelic culture, including the outlawing of kilts, bagpipes, and the bearing of arms. The Highlands were treated by British and Scottish Lowland authorities as a culturally backward internal colony.

National Identity. Major processes shaping the national identity since 1707 have been Calvinist Protestantism, participation in the British Empire, a mixture of pride and shame involving the cultural and demographic decimation of the Highlands, the sense of a national working class, a weakening sense of attachment to the British Empire and Commonwealth, and an increasing orientation toward a larger European framework.

Ethnic Relations. Cultural tensions still exist between Catholics and Protestants and Highlanders and Lowlanders. However, the Labor Party has been a major force in integrating the Protestant and Catholic communities. There are ethnic tensions between the Scots and English in some areas over access to jobs and housing, and non-white Scots often encounter racism.

URBANISM, ARCHITECTURE, AND THE USE OF SPACE

Coastal fishing villages are oriented around a bay or inlet, and farm towns usually have a central "high street." Larger market towns are more free form and often contain the ruins of a castle or abbey. Such towns generally have an old central core of small stone residences and shops.

After World War II, many "New Towns" were established as a response to urban decay in the Central Belt and a way to attract new "lighter" industries. Generally inland, they often have a central business district and recreational spaces surrounded by low-lying, semi-detached suburban housing estates.

Suburban sprawl surrounds the two major northern cities of Inverness and Aberdeen. Glasgow is oriented around the Firth of Clyde, the focus of the declining shipbuilding industry. Its architecture reflects the investments of shipping and tobacco magnates. In the 1980s and 1990s the decaying town center was redeveloped. The architecture of Edinburgh retains the central core of the medieval city. The Georgian New Town, planned and built on a rectilinear design from the late eighteenth century, became a residential alternative for the new upper and middle classes.

Interspersed within and outlying these major cities are turn-of-the-century tenements, new suburbs, and newer but decaying housing estates where unemployment often runs around 50 per-

A weaver sits at his loom to weave Harris Tweed, Harris Island, Outer Hebrides. The textiles industry was predominant until 1900.

FOOD AND ECONOMY

Food in Daily Life. The diet features prepared foods and an expanded choice of fruits and vegetables. Meals such as mince and tatties (ground beef and boiled or mashed potatoes) and homemade curries are common, along with take-out options. Scots are heavy consumers of sugar, chocolate, salt, and butter, but recently they have begun eating less meat and more fish, whole-meal bread, and vegetables.

Food Customs at Ceremonial Occasions. Whiskey often serves as a symbolic marker of special occasions. Christmas dinners tend to feature turkey, and haggis provides the centerpiece of the Burns Supper. There is also a strong baking tradition exemplified in tea room fare of fudges and scones.

Basic Economy. By 1900 the textile industry was eclipsed by heavy industries such as coal, iron, steel, engineering, and shipbuilding. Despite state support, the heavier industries have been in decline, increasingly being replaced by electronics and chemicals. Whiskey-making is a stable industry. Manufacturing's share of employment and gross domestic product (GDP) has declined, primarily replaced by the growth of services and the banking and financial sector. Tourism has stimulated the growth of the service sector. Agriculture makes only a modest contribution to employment and GDP. North Sea oil discovered in the early 1970s boosted the economy, but the development of cheaper sources elsewhere has halved production rates. There are chronically high unemployment rates. Manufacturing's share of employment and gross domestic product (GDP) has declined, primarily replaced by the growth of services in public administration and the banking and financial sector.

Land Tenure and Property. Formally, land ownership is still organized in a system of publicly registered feudal conveyances. Until the Succession Act (1964), male primogeniture governed land inheritance. In the 1970s, a process of phasing out feudal tenure and creating legal provision for direct title holding was begun, but there is pressure for the acceleration of land reform. Land ownership can be highly secretive and often is concentrated in a few absentee landlords. Recent moves by some local Highland and Island communities to "buy out" their owners and establish collective ownership have elicited widespread popular support. Historically, land issues have been particularly contentious in the Highlands.

SOCIAL STRATIFICATION

Classes and Castes. Scotland has a high proportion of the UK's hereditary nobility. By the turn of the century, the landed gentry and the industrial bourgeoisie were developing complex patterns of intermarriage and corporate ownership. The current class structure reflects deindustrialization. The transformation of the classic industrial working class into a more varied series of manual and non-manual occupational segments has made the distinction between working class and middle class difficult. Severe poverty is concentrated in public housing estates in the major urban areas.

The Catholic community is largely Labour-voting and urban working class. The rural and urban working and middle classes are associated more with Presbyterian Protestantism, and the aristocracy has a historical association with the Episcopal Church.

Symbols of Social Stratification. Speech is a key marker of class. Several rural and urban working-class varieties of Scots coexist with rural and urban middle class varieties. Linguistic convergence with received pronunciation English is viewed as a sign of education and middle to upper class status.

There is a strong tendency for Scots to identify as working class despite occupations and levels of education that indicate a middle class status. Scotland has a social democratically inclined middle class with a strong sense of its roots in the industrial working class and the formation of the welfare state; there is a widespread belief that egalitarianism is inherent in the national culture.

POLITICAL LIFE

Government. Scotland is a nation within the multinational UK state, administratively distinct, with its own legislature. Since 1885, it has been administered through the Scottish Office, led by the secretary of state for Scotland, who is appointed by the UK Parliament. Beneath the Scottish Office are thirty-two local authorities that administer basic services, and a separate system of laws and courts. The Scotland Act of 1998 established the first mod-

An aerial view of Edinborough. The city's architecture is still indicative of medieval times.

ern parliament, which receives a yearly block grant from the UK treasury and has the power to vary the UK personal income tax rate. It legislates on health, education and training, local government, social work and housing, economic development and transport, law and home affairs, environment, agriculture, forestry and fishing, sport and the arts, and public registers and records. The UK Parliament retains power over defense, foreign affairs, central economic planning (including business taxation), social security, and immigration. The one hundred twenty-nine ministers to the Scottish Parliament (MSPs) are elected for fixed four-year terms through a system combining proportional representation and popular election. The first parliament included representatives from six parties and was 37 percent female.

Leadership and Political Officials. The thirty-two local authorities are coordinated through the Convention of Scottish Local Authorities (COSLA), which has been increasingly Labour-dominated and includes large urban authorities with a "party machine" style of local politics. The Conservative Party is stronger in rural agricultural regions. The Scottish National Party (SNP) has rural and urban support but has had more success in rural areas. Because of its size and dominance, the Labour Party is more bureacratized than are the SNP, the Conservatives, and the Liberal Democrats. The SNP, limited to Scotland, has been more informal and less professionalized.

Despite internal dissent, Labour has supported Scottish devolution since the 1980s. The SNP is a left-of-center social democratic party to the left of Labour. It supports full national independence for Scotland as a member of the European Union. The Conservatives lost control of all UK parliamentary seats in Scotland in 1997. Many Scottish Conservatives support moderate devolution and rejected the party's traditional resistance to constitutional change. The Liberal Democrats have maintained a commitment to federalism in Britain for over a hundred years. They tend to be liberal on both social and economic issues, though they favor more state intervention than do the Conservatives. Although small, the Scottish Socialist Party and the Greens managed to get one representative each elected to the parliament.

Social Problems and Control. The legal system combines civilian and common law traditions. Law is based on judge-made precedents, authoritative legal texts, and legislation. Judgments are made by a judge or a simple majority of a fifteen-member jury, depending on the magnitude of the crime. There are three possible verdicts: guilty, not guilty, and "not proven," meaning the jury suspects guilt, but the evidence is not sufficient to warrant a guilty verdict. The courts are divided into civil and criminal systems, with overlapping judges. The highest civil court of appeal is the UK House of Lords, and for criminal cases it is the High Court of Criminal Appeal, which is Scottish. There are specialized tribunals presided over by laypersons and specialists to adjudicate minor juvenile offenses and industrial disputes. The former, called Children's Hearings, are primarily welfare-based rather than punitive. There is system of legal aid combined with various bodies that offer legal advice.

Drugs, especially heroin, and drug-related crime are a problem in larger cities. Police report an increasing frequency of fraud, auto theft, and violent crimes involving guns. Drunk driving has been reduced, and the use of a designated driver has become a common practice. There has been an effort to raise awareness of domestic violence against women.

Military Activity. Militarism has been an important stimulus for industry. Scotland was called "a landlocked aircraft carrier" because of its role as part of NATO's forward defense strategy during the Cold War. The nuclear presence has been reduced by popular anti-nuclear, anti-war pressures and a new NATO strategy oriented toward smaller-scale, non-nuclear capabilities. In the early 1990s around twenty-two thousand servicepersons were based in Scotland. However, restructuring of the military and related industries is leading to reductions in military jobs.

SOCIAL WELFARE AND CHANGE PROGRAMS

Beyond the government, Scottish life is managed through a network of Scottish- and UK-based Non-Departmental Public Bodies (NDPBs, sometimes called "quangos") whose members are appointed and are responsible for various aspects of public spending and administration. Those concerned solely with Scotland are now accountable to the Executive of the new Parliament, while most cross-border public bodies are accountable to both the Scottish and UK parliaments. Most have executive or advisory functions, often linked to the National Health Service. Those responsible for local spending are concerned with education, local enterprise, and housing.

NONGOVERNMENTAL ORGANIZATIONS AND OTHER ASSOCIATIONS

In the civil society, important players include the major churches (Church of Scotland, Catholic, and Episcopal), which often coordinate their efforts through ACTS (Action Together by Churches in Scotland), the Scottish Trades Union Congress (STUC), the Confederation of British Industry (Scottish branch), the Scottish Federation of Small Businesses, the Educational Institute of Scotland, the Scottish Council of Voluntary Organizations, other professional associations, interest groups, and around forty thousand smaller bodies concerned with the general public benefit. The political parties and COSLA mediate between civil society and the government. In conjunction with the political parties and campaigning groups, this network (with the general exception of business-oriented bodies) was crucial in achieving constitutional change in the late 1990s.

GENDER ROLES AND STATUSES

Division of Labor by Gender. Women are beginning to outstrip men as a percentage of total employees. Scottish machismo, bolstered by laborism, Calvinism, militarism, and soccer is adjusting to a

A view of Braemar Castle. The Scottish aristocracy agreed in 1707 to join England's and Scotland's parliaments.

world where the association of women with domesticity and reproduction and men with public life and paid employment are weakening. However, life chances are far from equal. Men far outnumber women in elected political offices, the legal profession, and managerial and administrative positions in business. Women earn 72 percent of what men earn on average, and are concentrated in certain economic sectors (shops, hotels, financial and business services, education, health, and social work) and the voluntary sector. Subject choices by sex in education suggest that gendered work expectations endure, with construction, engineering, manufacture and production, and transport being overwhelmingly male and personal care, office and secretarial, and social work overwhelmingly female.

The Relative Status of Women and Men. Men and women are notionally equal, but there is still room for reform. The feminist movement has opposed sex discrimination, fought to ensure greater participation by women in the new parliament, and had some success heightening awareness about violence against women. Still, many young men and women consider it acceptable to hit a woman or force her to have sex in certain circumstances. Women, especially as single parents and pensioners, are more vulnerable to poverty than men are, and the vast majority of single parents with dependent children are women.

MARRIAGE, FAMILY, AND KINSHIP

Marriage. Over a third of marriages are civil rather than religious. Scots law requires that marriages be monogamous and be between consenting adults (over age 16) and provides for the recognition of marriage "by habit and repute."

Traditional weddings take place on Friday or Saturday, with the groom in formal attire (often kilted) and the bride usually in white, forbidden to see the groom until the ceremony. Weddings normally are conducted near the bride's home. The bride enters last and is "given away" by her father or a senior male relative. Divorce can be obtained on the bases of adultery, intolerable behavior, desertion, and de facto separation.

Domestic Unit. An increasing number of households (around 30 percent) contain a single adult, while those with one male and one female with children (around 20 percent) have been decreasing. Around a quarter include one male, one female, and no children, and just over 10 percent include three or more adults with no children. At least a third of households are headed by women, a fifth of those widowed or divorced, whereas two thirds of households are headed by men, over half of which are married.

Inheritance. Until the 1960s, the incomes, savings, and properties of both spouses were considered totally separate, with marriage conferring no claims. Parliamentary acts in 1964 and 1985 established equal claims at divorce on most property acquired during marriage, and household goods and savings from housekeeping allowances are equally shared. A peculiarity of Scots law is that minors can enter into binding contracts.

Kin Groups. The clan system today has significance primarily for historians and tourists. Ties of kinship are activated by conditions of class and economic opportunity, with poverty, family businesses, and extreme wealth tending to heighten the importance of kin group obligations. Scotland is a small country with a high degree of overlap in social and kinship networks. Thus, urban networks involving politics and public life can be very dense, creating a sense of familiarity across a wide social field.

SOCIALIZATION

Child Rearing and Education. Child rearing is primarily women's work, sometimes aided by play groups. Mass literacy and education developed early, creating a popular conception of Scots as deeply commited to education, self improvement, and access to education. However, this tradition also produced the stern authoritarian "dominie" (parish teacher) teaching a narrow curriculum backed by corporal punishment. In recent decades, more child-centered teaching methods and diverse curricula built around national standards have developed. Scottish education is distinctive in its integration of denominational schools (almost all Catholic) into the broader system of public funding and management.

Higher Education. There are four ancient universities, four established in the twentieth century, fifty-four technical and vocational colleges of further education, and 16,233 adult community education groups. The university course lasts four years, not three as in most English universities. Scottish students used to make the transition from secondary to higher education at age 17; now most take an extra year to prepare for university.

ETIQUETTE

Rules of etiquette are situational, affected by status, class, and familiarity. An initial reserve toward strangers is likely to be heightened if one party is of higher status. However, friendliness and verbal politeness are expected in everyday life. Light, humorous banter, often about soccer, facilitates such interactions. The notion that Scots are more friendly and open than the English is common. Similarly, many believe that people are more friendly in Glasgow than in Edinburgh. Two somewhat ritualized markers of politeness are the offering of tea, coffee, and sweets to house visitors and taking turns buying rounds of drinks at a pub.

RELIGION

Religious Beliefs. The Church of Scotland has around 770,217 members, and around 774,550 people are members of the Catholic Church. The Episcopalians have around thirty-five thousand communicants, with a similar number distributed among smaller Protestant denominations, including many strict Sabbatarians in the Highlands, Islands, and fishing ports of the northeast coast. There are around fifteen thousand to twenty thousand Muslims; a handful of Hindus, Sikhs, and Buddhist; and four Jewish congregations.

Although mainstream church attendance is in decline, Scotland bears the impress of its Protestant history. Today's adherents range from scriptural fundamentalists to liberals who view the Bible interpretively. In addition to the Protestant distaste for symbolic elaboration and emphasis on the individual's personal relationship to God, a strong sense of guilt and righteousness pervades Presbyterian discourses. Traditional supernatural beliefs (ghosts, fairies, etc.) endure as literary themes and in revived forms in Celticist New Age beliefs. Belief in the gift of second sight persists among some Highlanders.

Religious Practitioners. Leading members of the Presbyterian, Catholic, and Episcopal churches regularly make public pronouncements in the media regarding social issues and government policies. In recent years, this has involved the critical rejection of some aspects of neoliberalism and support for devolution.

Rituals and Holy Places. Easter and Christmas are the major ceremonial occasions. Medieval sites of pilgrimage are visited primarily by tourists and antiquarians. The Scottish landscape, with ancient religious structures from stone circles to ruined abbeys, often is said to have a sacred quality. The Isle

A stone footbridge in the highlands of Scotland. The highlands have rugged terrain that is difficult to cultivate.

of Iona, the base for Saint Columba's early missions to Scotland in the fifth century, is home to the Iona Community, an ecumenical religious retreat founded in the 1930s.

Death and the Afterlife. Funerary practices normally involve a simple ceremony of blessings and remembrance by family members and friends in a chapel or funeral parlor, leading to interment or cremation. Until recently, women did not go to the gravesite, and in some parts of the western Highlands and Islands the postburial mean can still become an extended alcoholic ritual. Catholic ceremonies may be preceded by a traditional wake.

MEDICINE AND HEALTH CARE

The National Health Service (NHS) was anticipated by the Highlands and Islands Medical Scheme, which subsidizes medical practices in the poor and sparsely populated Highlands. The NHS made general health care more available and, continues to enjoy strong popular support. Despite its strong medical tradition, Scotland has a long history of high morbidity and mortality as a result of the climate, the diet, and poverty-related diseases such as tuberculosis. High consumption of tobacco, alcohol, and fatty foods, along with a lack of exercise

and an increasing incidence of cancer is creating a new profile of ill health.

SECULAR CELEBRATIONS

Christmas was hardly observed in the Lowlands after the Reformation but is broadly observed as a relatively secularized holiday. New Year's Eve, called Hogmanay, has long been the main midwinter celebration. Fairlike events and public gatherings for the changing of the year are promoted by major cities. Customarily, some entertained guests at home, while others went ''first-footing.'' First-footers carry a bottle of whiskey and perhaps some food and, if traditional, a lump of coal or something black.

Celtic seasonal rituals fused to medieval saints' days survive in modern secularized celebrations. Traditionally, Halloween (31 October) involved children ''guising,'' or dressing up in costumes and entertaining for treats, engaging in mischief, and young girls performing divination to find out about their future spouses. The May Day celebration of Beltane, involving bonfires on hilltops, has seen a revival. Many towns have fairs and gala weeks, especially during the summer. Annual Highland Gatherings serve a similar civic function, as do the Common Ridings in the Borders towns, in which a

A small house in Gorstan. The poor quality of housing is a concern in both urban and rural areas.

horseback procession ''beats out'' the boundaries of the medieval burgh.

Saint Andrew's Day (30 November), named after the national patron saint, is not marked ritually, but events of national significance are often timed to fall on that day. Perhaps the most symbol-laden holiday is Burns Day (25 January), named after the ''national'' poet, Robert Burns. Set around a ritual ''peasant'' meal of haggis (a mixture of oats, offal, and seasonings boiled inside the lining of a sheep's stomach), neeps (turnips), and tatties (potatoes), accompanied by whiskey, the event involves an elabo-

rate series of speeches and set readings from Burns's opus. This ceremony plays upon Burns's bawdy celebration of the common people and penchant for deflating the self-righteous and highborn. Traditionally very male-dominated and chauvanistic affairs, gender participation is now more equal, and even feminist readings of Burns's radicalism can be found.

THE ARTS AND HUMANITIES

Support for the Arts. The Scottish Arts Council is advised by specialist committees about funding for theaters, art galleries, musical and literary organizations, art centers, and major festivals. Almost half the budget goes to support the four national companies: Scottish Opera, Scottish Ballet, Royal National Orchestra, and Scottish Chamber Orchestra. Local authorities and economic development agencies have become major contributors. In the popular arts, self-financing and ticket charges are important.

Literature. Passion for the spoken word has arisen from linguistic diversity and the tradition of public oration and dispute on scriptural subjects. The ability to tell a good story or joke is prized. There are rich poetry and prose traditions in Gaelic, Scots, and Scots-inflected English. Gaelic literature derives from bardic verses celebrating heroes and political leaders. The development of Gaelic communities in the major cities, particularly Glasgow, around 1870–1914 stimulated new linguistic and literary awareness.

Scottish literature oscillates between romantic flourishes and mordant commentary, often suggesting a preoccupation with dialectical tensions: reason-passion, reality-fantasy, natural-supernatural, solemnity-satire. There was a notable revival after the World War I, spearheaded by the poet Hugh MacDiarmid. Many twentieth century prose writers wrote about Scottish locales and themes. Recent works such as Alasdair Gray's *Lanark* and Irvine Welsh's *Trainspotting* combine gritty reality and wild imagination with Scots language and caustic visions of a deindustrializing world.

Graphic Arts. Scottish painting has struggled to establish a distinctive identity. Scottishness has been a question of subject matter more than style. Since 1900, French impressionism and post-1960s conceptual approaches have been influential. The absence of a major Scottish-based art market has tended to keep the fine arts semiprofessional.

Stylized animals and objects in bas relief on Pictish symbol stones mixed with the curvilinear designs of Celtic Christianity in the first millennium C.E. French and Flemish influences appear in medieval church sculpture. In the nineteenth century, neoclassical styles dominated. Only with the rise of modernism has the long connection between architecture and ornamental sculpture been broken, allowing freer, more experimental modes to develop.

At a more popular and functional level, jewelry and textiles sustain artistic traditions that often allude to Pictish and Celtic design themes. Major art colleges provide support, particularly in the area of textiles.

Performance Arts. The national ballet, opera, and orchestras and the Edinburgh festival ensure that a high art tradition is maintained. Traditional music and dance have had a revival, sustained by dedicated groups and associations, major nationwide competitive events, and a tradition of informal music-making in pubs, along with the new popularity of the Ceilidh, a public event of traditional set dances to fiddle tunes. There is an active folk scene, and a strong popular music scene. Since the 1970s there has been a flourishing of new theaters and companies performing new works in Scots and translations of plays into that language.

THE STATE OF THE PHYSICAL AND SOCIAL SCIENCES

Scotland was in the forefront of the development of the physical and social sciences, including groundbreaking work in the eighteenth century in mathematics by Colin MacLaurin, geology by James Hutton, and in chemistry by Joseph Black, sociological data gathering in the Statistical Account (1790s), and the moral philosophy and political economy of David Hume, Adam Smith, John Millar, and Adam Ferguson.

During the heyday of industrialization, Scotland became preeminent in the field of engineering, and the social sciences were eclipsed by the physical sciences, exemplified by the physicists Lord Kelvin (William Thomson) and James Clark Maxwell. The sciences atrophied during the post-World War I industrial decline. Since the 1960s, there has been a push to strengthen the role of physical sciences in higher education. Technology transfer between industry and university has been a core goal, supported by the establishment of university-associated research institutes. Offshore engineering, aquaculture, veterinary medicine, and computers are key research areas along with medicine. Scotland has been a leader in cloning research, and the school of linguistics at Edinburgh has stimulated work on the interface of speech and computers.

Whereas corporate funding has provided major support for the physical sciences, the social sciences have had to compete for funds from the Economic and Social Research Council and smaller sources. Political change has stimulated revivals in history and legal studies and reestablished Scotland as a topic for political and sociological study.

BIBLIOGRAPHY

Berry, Christopher J. *Social Theory of the Scottish Enlightenment* 1997.

Brown, Alice, David McCrone, and Lindsay Paterson. *Politics and Society in Scotland*, 2nd ed., 1998.

———, and Paula Surridge. *The Scottish Electorate: The 1997 General Election and Beyond*, 1999.

Cohen, Anthony P. *Whalsay. Symbol, Segment and Boundary in a Shetland Island Community*, 1987.

Daiches, David, ed. *The New Companion to Scottish Culture*, 1993.

Harvie, Christopher. *No Gods and Precious Few Heroes: Scotland since 1914*, 3rd ed., 1998.

Hassan, Gerry, ed. *A Guide to the Scottish Parliament: The Shape of Things to Come*, 1999.

Hunter, James. *The Making of the Crofting Community*, 1976.

Kay, Billy. *Scots: The Mither Tongue*, 1986.

Kellas, James. *The Scottish Political System*, 4th ed., 1989.

Linklater, Magnus, and Robin Denniston, eds. *The Anatomy of Scotland: How Scotland Works*, 1992.

Maan, Bashir. *The New Scots: The Story of Asians in Scotland*, 1992.

MacKay, Fiona, Chrisma Bould, and Georgie Young, eds. *Gender Audit 1998–99: Putting Scottish Women in the Picture*, 1999.

McCrone, David. *Understanding Scotland: The Sociology of a Stateless Nation*, 1992.

Nadel, Jane. "Stigma and Separation: Pariah Status and Community Persistence in a Scottish Fishing Village." *Ethnology* 23 (2): 101–115, 1984.

Nairn, Tom. *The Break-Up of Britain*, 1977.

Neville, Gwen Kennedy. "Community Form and Ceremonial Life in Three Regions of Scotland." *American Ethnologist* 6 (1): 93–109, 1979.

Parman, Susan. *Scottish Crofters: A Historical Ethnography of a Celtic Village*, 1990.

Paterson, Lindsay. *The Autonomy of Modern Scotland*, 1994.

———, ed. *A Diverse Assembly: The Debate on a Scottish Parliament*, 1998.

Smout, T. C. *A History of the Scottish People, 1560–1830*, 1972.

———. *A Century of the Scottish People, 1830–1950*, 1987.

Withers, Charles W. J. *Gaelic Scotland: The Transformation of a Culture Region*, 1988.

Woman's Claim of Right Group. *A Woman's Claim of Right in Scotland: Women, Representation, and Politics*, 1991.

—JONATHAN HEARN

SEE ALSO: UNITED KINGDOM

SENEGAL

CULTURE NAME

Senegalese

ORIENTATION

Identification. The area that today is Senegal once was part of the West African Empire of Mali, Ghana, and Tekrur. The country takes its name from the river that runs along its northern and eastern borders, forming the frontier with Mauritania and Mali. A poetic etymology from the Wolof people states that the name derives from the local term *Sunugal*, meaning ''our dugout canoe'' (everyone is in the same boat). The Republic of Senegal became independent in 1960 after three centuries of French colonial rule. Dakar, the capital since independence in 1960, lies on the Cap Vert peninsula, the most westerly point in Africa. Before independence, Dakar was the capital of French West Africa (AOF, or *l'Afrique Occidentale Française*), which included nine French-speaking West African states.

Although predominantly Muslim, Senegal is a tolerant secular state, whose peoples have lived together peacefully for several generations and have intermingled to some extent. Islam is a potential unifying factor. Wolof is the national language. The spread of education and increased economic opportunity have modified a traditional social structure based on kinship, but the majority of the people adhere to the traditional values of *Kersa* (respect for others) and *Tegin* (good manners). *Terranga* (hospitality) is a common word used by almost all of the country's twelve ethnic groups.

This sense of a national identity is not shared by the Diola populations in the forest areas of the Casamance, who since December 1982 have been engaged in an armed insurgency to separate from the Islamized northerners. The first president, Léopold Sédar Senghor, a Roman Catholic who presided over the nation for over twenty years, was a fervent advocate of African unity.

Location and Geography. Senegal, situated on the western tip of Africa, covers an area of 76,000 square miles (196,781 square kilometers). It is bordered on the north by Mauritania, on the east by Mali, on the south by Guinea and Guinea-Bissau, and on the west by the Atlantic Ocean. The long, narrow Republic of the Gambia is approximately two hundred miles long, surrounded by Senegal's southern region. Agriculture is based largely on the cultivation of peanuts, millet, and sorghum. Like most Sahelian countries, Senegal has an important livestock sector that periodically is decimated by drought. Niokolo Koba National Park is situated in the southeast and is one of the most important reserves for large mammals in West Africa.

Demography. The population of approximately ten million includes indigenous peoples, and a non-African population that is mostly French and Lebanese. There are heavy population concentrations in the urban centers (Dakar, Thiès, Kaolack, Saint-Louis, Ziguinchor) because of rapid growth of the population and deteriorating environmental conditions that have made it difficult for people to live off the land.

Linguistic Affiliation. The population is divided into twelve ethnic groups, each with its own customs and dialect. The largest single ethnic group is the Wolof, who makes up over one-third of the population. Although French is the official language, it is spoken only by an educated minority, and Wolof has become a lingua franca towns and markets, schools, and interethnic marriages.

Symbolism. Animals, songs, flags, and colors have served as national symbols since before independence. The national flag has bands of green, yellow, and red. A green five-pointed star appears in the center of the yellow band. The color green symbolizes the forest and hope. Yellow stands for the savanna, and red for the blood spilled in the fight for liberty. In preparation for Independence Day, there

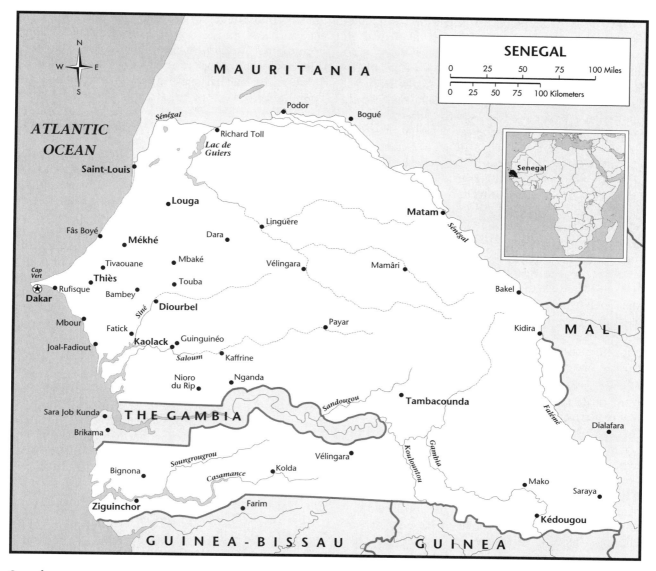

Senegal

is a week of celebrating the flag and the national anthem. The words of the national anthem were written by Senghor. The coat of arms shows a gold lion in profile on a green base, framed by the rays of a gold five-pointed star in the upper left corner. The state seal has the coat of arms on one side and a baobab tree on the other, with the national motto: "One people, one aim, one faith." The baobab tree is the traditional meeting place (the *pencha*) where discussions and political rallies take place.

HISTORY AND ETHNIC RELATIONS

Emergence of the Nation. Paleolithic and Neolithic wall paintings, tools, and pottery have been found in the Senegal River valley. After the tenth century, the people of Senegal were in constant contact with North Africa. Arab and Berber caravans came regularly to trade and arrived periodically as invaders looking for territories to conquer and convert to Islam. In the fourteenth century, the Wolof empire, which extended from the Senegal River to the Gambia River, included six states: Baol, Walo, Cayor, Sine, Djolof, and Saloum. In 1444, the Portuguese turned the island of Gorée into a graveyard for sailors and established a profitable trade in slaves and gold along the coast of Senegal. Gradually, other European merchants followed, including the French, who established their first settlements in 1638 in the Senegal River, on the island of Saint-Louis, which became the base of all French activity and expansion in West Africa.

In 1840, the French government declared Senegal a permanent French possession, abolished all forms of slavery, and granted full citizenship to those born in Senegal. This enabled the people of Senegal to elect and send a deputy to the National Assembly in Paris. In 1854, General Louis Faidherbe, a colonial administrator, was given the assignment of pacifying the continuously battling kingdoms along the Senegal River. He created the *Tirailleurs Senegalais* (corps of Senegalese riflemen), an army of local volunteers under French commanders who achieved international fame during World War II. By 1902, the French government, which had embarked on a "Grand Design" to conquer as much territory as possible, had completed the conquest of most of the parts of West Africa not occupied by the British, the Portuguese, and the Germans, and Dakar was designated the capital of all French West African territories. The development of state schools provided education for Africans, and scholarships gave them the opportunity to receive higher learning in France, creating an educated African elite.

After World War II, France's relations with some of its territories were marked by major colonial wars, a crisis that resulted in the acceleration of the decolonization process in West Africa. In 1959, Senegal and the French Sudan decided to merge and form the independent Mali Federation, but it was not a success. Both countries then declared individual independence. On April 1960, Senegal was proclaimed an independent nation. The country's governing political party is the Senegalese Progressive Union (Union Progressiste Sénégalaise, or UPS), which was founded in 1949 and led by Léopold Sédar Senghor.

National Identity. Senegal is a land of traditions, and its people, although heterogenous, share a strong sense of national identity deeply rooted in *Thiossane*, a word used by the Wolof as well as the Serer (Fulani), that means "history, tradition, and culture." Since the World Festival of Negro Arts was organized at Dakar in 1966, institutions have been created or reoriented toward African traditions, including the Fundamental Institute of Black Africa; the Houses of Youth and Culture; the craft village of Soumbedioune in Dakar, which has become a center for Senegalese sculpture and goldsmithing; the Dynamique Museum; the Daniel Sorano Theater; and the tapestry factory of Thiès. Although French is the official language and the main language of instruction in the schools, even the most educated people are far from being "black Frenchmen" culturally. The Dakar Wolof dialect has become the national language, especially in the urban areas and among the youth. The nation's precolonial traditions and long colonial history have helped forge a strong sense of national identity among the majority of the people, particularly the populations north of the Gambia River, who share similar hierarchical social structures and Islamic traditions and adherence to Muslim brotherhoods.

Ethnic Relations. The largest single ethnic group is the Wolof (43 percent of the population), followed by the Pular (also called Peulh or Fulani, nearly 25 percent, and the Serer (more than 15 percent). Smaller groups include the Diola, Mandink, and Soninke. Despite this cultural heterogeneity, interethnic strife does not exist and generally no group seeks autonomy on ethnic grounds or political independence except in the Casamance region. Since the early 1980s, the Casamance has seen the development of a separatist movement, and since 1990, there has been conflict between local guerrillas and the army. Casamance is substantially less Islamic and less Wolof than the rest of the country.

The presence of Europeans, mostly French (usually called *Toubabs* by the Senegalese) and Lebanese (each accounting for 1 percent of the population) has not caused serious friction or hostility. The country was tolerant of non–Senegalese Africans who came to live and work until the 1989 outbreak of violence Mauritania over grazing disputes curtailed their immigration.

The Wolof have preserved their ethnic identity as a result of their openness to other groups and people. For centuries they have lived side by side with the Serer, Tukulor, Fulani, Mandink, and Diolas and have traded and intermarried with these neighbors. Although they have fought neighbors in the past, today the relationship is one of tolerance and mutual jokes, which are known among the Wolof and the Fulani as *Kal*. The Wolof accept any person who easily identifies with others' customs.

URBANISM, ARCHITECTURE, AND THE USE OF SPACE

Lebou fishing people who settled in Dakar in the eighteenth century were looking for a safe haven. They founded their new site in 1795 and called it Ndakarou. Dakar occupies the southern end of the Cap Vert peninsula. On a plateau about hundred feet above the sea, the administrative structures left from the colonial era include the Presidential Palace, City Hall, the Chamber of Commerce with its yellow bricks, and the Court House, which was built in 1906. The tall modern buildings, handsome resi-

Women harvest rice from a field in the Casamance River region. The main Senegalese dish is chep-bu-jen *and consists of rice with vegetables and a spicy sauce.*

dences, and tree-lined avenues of the business and administrative district are thoroughly French in appearance. Adjoining the business section is the old and crowded quarter called the Medina, a jumble of old buildings, shacks, and narrow streets. On the western side, beyond the Medina, are the impressive buildings of the University of Dakar and the fashionable suburb of Fann. Dakar has many mosques, the most impressive of which is the Great Mosque, and numerous churches and cathedrals. On Goree Island, with its "House of Slaves," fortified bunkers and huge naval guns built during World War II are overgrown with vegetation.

In rural areas, dwellings differ in type and in the materials used for construction but are adapted to the climate and the village way of life. Important activities and social occasions are shared on the *pen-cha*, where people gather to chat and discuss village matters.

FOOD AND ECONOMY

Food in Daily Life. The basic food is rice cooked with a spicy sauce and vegetables. The national dish is *chep-bu-jen*, the Wolof word for rice with fish. Cooked in a tomato sauce with boiled fish and a few vegetables (carrots, cabbage, and green peppers),

chep-bu-jen is originally from the city of Saint-Louis. *Yassa*, a dish from Casamance is chicken or fish marinated in lemon juice, pepper, and onions and then baked. It is accompanied by plain white rice. Other sauces include *mafé*, *domada* and *soupe kandja*, (which is made from okra with fish and palm oil).

Food Customs at Ceremonial Occasions. On ceremonial occasions, festive meals that include roasted or grilled meat with beans or French fries are eaten. Couscous (steamed millet) with vegetables, mutton, and gravy is a ceremonial dish. At the end of each meal, strong and sweet tea is drunk. Except in areas where it is prohibited, alcohol is available.

Basic Economy. The country's market economy is based largely on agriculture. The limited economic growth it has achieved since independence is interrupted periodically by drought conditions that can send the economy into severe recession. The most important food crops are millet and sorghum; large quantities of rice are imported. Cotton, rice, sugar, and market-garden produce are grown. The national currency is called the CFA franc.

Land Tenure and Property. Primarily small family farms are worked chiefly by family labor. More than two-thirds of the country's farms are less than ten acres in size; only 5 percent are more than twenty-five acres. After independence, the National Land Tenure Law of 1964 gave the state rights over all rural land and in theory abolished rents paid to absentee landlords. Under this arrangement, the state would become the steward of the land and allocate land rights to those who worked it. Before independence, traditional local systems of land tenure were based on African customary law, which allowed the local nobility or the head or chief of a village to receive crop shares and land rents from former slaves and people without land. Under the new law, which was part of a package of socialist reforms, owners with permanent buildings on their land were given six months to establish deeds for their plots. All land was divided into four categories: urban areas, reserves (including national forests and parks), farmland, and "pioneer zones." The law permitted the government to declare some of the less intensively occupied pioneer zones and cede them to groups and organizations that were willing to develop them. The country's most prominent Muslim leaders own large estates in the pioneer zones. The government's decision in 1991 to transfer large tracts of protected forestland to the head of the *Mouride* brotherhood to be used by his followers for planting peanuts dealt a serious blow to the credibility of the land tenure policy. In a few weeks, thousands of Mouride followers *talibés* had cleared the land, a process accompanied by the eviction of six thousand pastoralists and one hundred thousand animals from the forest area. The press and the international donor community sharply criticized the government's decision, which followed a pattern dating back to colonial days, when the French ceded large tracts of land to the Mourides to encourage peanut production.

Other reforms included the establishment of farmers' cooperatives and rural councils to replace traditional kin and patron-client networks. The cooperatives became the basic sources from which farmers could obtain seeds, tools, credit, and marketing facilities for their crops.

Commercial Activities. Agricultural and manufactured products are sold, including foodstuffs and household goods. The informal sector provides inexpensive goods and services for the urban poor who cannot afford to buy the goods produced by the formal industrial sector. There is an enormous market for cheap used clothing, which often is smuggled into the country and permits families to clothe their children at a relatively low cost.

Major Industries. Industrial output is determined largely by agricultural performance. Most major manufacturing is located in and around Dakar. Food processing is the largest activity, accounting for 43 percent of industrial production. Groundnut extraction is the major agricultural industry. Other industrial production includes fishing, phosphate mining, chemicals and oil, metal and mechanical industries, and the construction material and paper industries. In terms of light industry, the craft sector is very active. It includes handmade textiles; gold, silver, and iron smithing; pottery making; woodworking; basketry; leatherworking; and other traditional crafts.

Trade. Peanuts, phosphates, cotton, and fish and fishing products are exported. Fishing products, mostly canned tuna, provide direct and indirect employment for more than 150,000 people. As part of its diversification policy, Senegal became one of the first African countries to develop tourism as a major national economic activity. However, tourism suffered a major blow from the Casamance insurgency and the conflict with Mauritania. Cash crops include rice, cowpeas, maize, sugar, and livestock. Cement, refined sugar, fertilizers, and tobacco products are exported to neighboring countries. Food, capital goods, and petroleum are imported from France, Cote d'Ivoire, Nigeria, Algeria, China, and Japan.

Division of Labor. In the past, division of labor was practiced in farming. Before the rainy season, young men did the hard work of clearing the bush and preparing the land for sowing. Once it rained and the seeds began to sprout, women and children weeded. The constitution bans child labor, but instead of attending school, many children work in the family's fields.

SOCIAL STRATIFICATION

Classes and Castes. The society historically was organized into a hierarchy of castes, a rigid structure in which descendants of royal lines and nobles ruled over artisan castes and slaves. After independence, a new set of status criteria emerged. New means for achieving wealth, power, and status were introduced through the market economy and the development of the educational system. The modern elite includes successful businessmen, managers and professionals in the private sector as well as influential politicians, and highly educated individuals. The deterioration of living conditions has affected the life of the masses. Lepers, polio victims, and beggars are a common sight in the cities.

View of Dakar's Independence Square. Many rural lands are still owned by city dwellers.

Symbols of Social Stratification. During the colonial era, nearly all the profits generated by the largest firms went to foreigners and the local nobility. The nationalization programs led by the government after independence favored a small number of citizens who entered into a new competition for status and power. The clans included successful businessmen, highly educated or politically well-connected individuals who were able to afford European-style living standards, including cars, modern appliances, luxurious villas or apartments, good schools, higher education for their children, and travel abroad. Investments in real estate, commerce, and agriculture were signs of achievement. In the rural hinterlands of the Cap Vert region, city dwellers own as much as 70 percent of the land. *Jardiniers du Dimanche*, or ("Sunday farmers") have invested in truck farms, orchards, and cattle-fattening operations, using loans from state-run banks. Corruption has contributed to the growing gap between the elite and the masses who are struggling to survive.

POLITICAL LIFE

Government. Senegal is a moderately decentralized republic dominated by a strong presidency. The president is elected by popular vote for a seven-year term and appoints a prime minister. The 1963 constitution provides for a civilian government composed of a dominant executive branch, a National Assembly, and an independent judiciary. A second legislative chamber, the Senate, was established in 1999.

Leadership and Political Officials. Called the "Poet President," Senghor was elected in 1960. As a student during the Depression years in Paris, he wrote poetry that helped launch the concept of *Négritude*. Inspired by the romantic vision of Africa of Harlem Renaissance authors and European ethnographers, Senghor exalted African culture. During his reign, the arts were well funded; he organized the Festival of Negro Arts in Dakar in 1966. His contribution to the founding of the Organization of African Unity (OAU) and Senegal and Gambia River Basin development associations won him respect as an elder statesman. Although a practicing Roman Catholic, Senghor developed strong ties with the Muslim brotherhoods, who supported him. Some Senegalese respected and revered him as the "Father of the Nation" even though they did not share his political views.

Senghor's political legacy was mixed. He provided the nation with a level of peace, political stability, tolerance, and freedom of expression that was rare in Africa. Unlike most African leaders, he knew when and how to give up power. However, by establishing a de facto one-party system, he contributed to the decline of his party's dynamism and thwarted the development of an opposition that could openly challenge national policies that had failed to stem economic decline.

President Abdou Diouf, who held office from 1981 to 2000, was a handpicked successor who peacefully stepped down after two decades in power. In a presidential election held in the year 2000, the forty-year dominance of the Socialist Party and Diouf's nineteen-year reign ended. In a second round of elections, he was defeated by Abdoulaye Wade, the leader of the main opposition party, the Senegalese Democratic Party.

Social Problems and Control. In the 1980s, Senegal, which had been largely free of ethnic, racial, and religious strife, began to experience those problems. Anti-Moor rioting and the mass exodus of Moors in 1989, the insurrection of separatist rebels, the fundamentalist Islamists who have emerged to challenge the brotherhoods' religious authority and the legitimacy of the secular state, and students' unrest and frustration at the lack of employment opportunities after graduation are signs of a more turbulent and less tolerant society. Theft occurs frequently, and most of the time people beat the criminal before the police arrive; on many occasions, vigilante groups and mobs have tried to lynch suspected thieves. Civilians have no access to guns, which are used mostly by the military and the police. In urban areas, alcoholism and drug use (mostly cannabis) have become a major issue.

Military Activity. The army has demonstrated a firm commitment to civilian rule and loyalty to the regime in power. Diouf continued Senghor's policy of building up the army and using it as an instrument of foreign policy. The army was used to put down the insurgency in the Casamance and ensure peace and order on the borders with Mauritania and Guinea-Bissau in the late 1980s and early 1990s. The military forces number about fifteen thousand and are among the best trained in Africa.

SOCIAL WELFARE AND CHANGE PROGRAMS

Poor economic management has led to the intervention of the International Monetary Fund and the World Bank in State programs and policies. Two decades of structural adjustment programs have reduced government spending in all public sector activities, including social services. Urban and rural dwellers have adopted creative survival strategies, that have helped them cope with difficult times.

NONGOVERNMENTAL ORGANIZATIONS AND OTHER ASSOCIATIONS

In difficult economic times, individuals and communities increasingly rely on social ties to create solidarity networks. These ties include family, friends, ethnic groups, neighborhood associations, religious brotherhoods, and hometown networks. Nongovernmental organizations such as UNICEF, the Red Cross Society of Senegal, Medecins sans Frontières, CARE, the Ford Foundation, and the Peace Corps help these networks in their initiatives. Village-based parent student associations have played an important role in financing school construction and providing school supplies and materials in rural areas. Village health committees have been organized to build maternity and village health centers and manage the distribution of medicines. In the countryside, farmers have launched their own irrigated agricultural projects. Nongovernmental organizations have helped finance these small-scale development activities.

GENDER ROLES AND STATUSES

Division of Labor by Gender. Women generally do most of the household chores of cooking, cleaning, and child rearing. With the growing exodus of young men from the villages, rural women have become increasingly involved in managing village forestry resources and operating millet and rice mills. The government has established a rural development agency designed to organize village women and involve them more actively in the development process. Women play a prominent role in village health committees and prenatal and postnatal programs. In urban areas, despite women's second-class status within Islam, change has proceeded rapidly in big cities, where women have entered the labor market as secretaries, typists, salesclerks, maids, and unskilled workers in textile mills and tuna-canning factories.

The Relative Status of Women and Men. The position of women in most ethnic groups is one of dependence: husbands, fathers, brothers, and uncles all have rights over women and much of what they produce. Despite constitutional protections, women face extensive societal discrimination, especially in rural areas, where Islamic and traditional customs, including polygyny and Islamic rules of inheritance, are strong and women generally are confined

A house in Sokone, Senegal, has protected privacy with a painted metal fence.

to traditional roles. About half of all women live in polygynous unions. It is estimated that only 20 percent of women are engaged in paid employment. Due to the fact that men are legally considered heads of the household, women pay higher taxes than men and employers pay child allowances to men and not to women. In urban areas, several women's groups have formed to address violence against women, usually wife beating, which is a common problem. The police usually do not intervene in domestic disputes, and most people are reluctant to go outside the family for help.

MARRIAGE, FAMILY, AND KINSHIP

Marriage. In rural areas, parents often arrange marriages for their children. A young man may want a young woman, but his father decides whether she is suitable. A go-between often is appointed to investigate the woman's family background. If the father finds the family satisfactory, he sends the go-between to deliver kola nuts to the woman's parents. The parents accept the kola nuts if they approve of the young man. In matrilineal ethnic groups such as the Wolof, the mother's brother is sent on behalf of the groom to ask for the bride's hand. Along with kola nuts, money is given. Gifts such as a television set, a sewing machine,

jewelry, and fashionable clothes are required from the groom. In Muslim families, most marriages are conducted at the mosque by the iman, or religious leader. Then a civil marriage takes place at city hall or the family court.

The bride moves to the groom's house with great ceremony in which relatives and friends participate. In rural areas, young women sing ribald songs to provoke and entertain. Usually many days of festivities follow.

Domestic Unit. The core of a domestic group or compound is a nuclear polygynous or family. After marriage, a man brings his wife to his father's compound, but such residence is not necessarily permanent. In any domestic group, other people often live with the family, sometimes permanently and sometimes temporarily. Often these are kin such as the male head's unmarried or divorced sister, a sister's child, or a wife's child by a divorced spouse.

Inheritance. The debts of the deceased are paid before the estate is distributed among the heirs. If all the deceased's children are minors, his brother acts as trustee for the estate. He may marry the deceased's widow, but this is not common. If there is an adult son of the deceased, he acts as the trustee. When a married man with children dies, each son receives a full share in the estate, each daughter gets

A Senegalese family having a meal together, Ile de Goree. Traditional housekeeping and child-rearing roles are expected from Senegalese women, particularly in rural areas.

half a share, and the wives each receive an eighth of a share. A learned man often is called in to see that the distribution follows Islamic law, because few people make wills.

Kin Groups. The traditional social structure based on kinship and rigid stratification remains important but is being modified by the spread of education, the market economy, and the movement of people to urban and industrial centers. The presence of kin at life-cycle ceremonials is necessary for the achievement and maintenance of status.

SOCIALIZATION

Infant Care. People value children greatly. A child is seen as neighborhood property, and so child care responsibilities are shared. Using a *Mbotu*, a brightly colored rectangular shawl, mothers carry babies closely tied to their backs during their daily occupations. Neighbors and family members take turns helping busy mothers. Abandonment of infants is rare, and the strength of family bonds limits the need for institutional care of orphans.

Child Rearing and Education. By the time a child is five or six years of age, he or she is taught good

values and etiquette. A child should greet elders, help parents with household chores, avoid foul language, and listen to the wisdom of elders. In their early years, boys and girls play together. As they grow older, gender roles become more sharply defined, with the girls remaining more with their mothers to learn household chores. In almost all ethnic groups, boys are circumcised as part of the process of reaching maturity, but the practice of female genital mutilation has been made a criminal offense. Muslim children attend Koranic school until they are six or seven at which time they start a formal education. Corporal punishment in schools has become unacceptable to parents, particularly in urban areas. Formal education is free. The school system has primary, secondary, and advanced levels. Education is available to both sexes. There are many private schools, run primarily by Catholic religious orders.

Higher Education. Universities include the University of Dakar and the University of Saint-Louis. There are also several vocational institutes. As a result of student unrest and deteriorating conditions at the universities, the elite often sends its children to study abroad.

ments when they meet even if they do not know one another. Comments frequently focus on eating habits, cleanliness, and intelligence. A person's social rating often is linked to how well he or she respects community values such as *Jom* (dignity or self-respect) and *Ham-sa-bop* (self-knowledge).

RELIGION

Religious Beliefs. Ninety percent of the people identify themselves as Muslims and are affiliated with one of the three principal brotherhoods: the *Mourides*, the *Tijaniyya*, or the *Qadiriyya*. Each brotherhood is distinguished by slight differences in rituals and codes of conduct. Each year, wealthy and middle-class people make the pilgrimage to Mecca. Despite the small size of the Catholic community (approximately 5 percent of the population), Senegal has produced one of black Africa's few cardinals.

Aspects of traditional religion are fused with Islam or Christianity. Many urbanized people still regard their ancestors as important spiritual leaders of everyday life, although Allah or God is worshiped formally.

Religious Practitioners. Many Senegalese believe that living people and spirits may control supernatural forces, and malevolent men often are feared more deeply than are evil spirits. The Wolof seek help from a *Jabaran-kat* ("healer"), who asks them to sacrifice a chicken to ward off the evil powers of a *doma* ("witch").

Death and the Afterlife. Death is considered a path by which one joins one's ancestors. When a person dies, loud mourning echoes from the house of the bereaved. Others sing and dance to celebrate the dead person and to send his or her spirit to heaven. The cult of the ancestors is practiced among many of the ethnic groups. Among the rural Wolof, household water jars are seldom cleaned because the spirit of an ancestor could come to drink at that moment and find no water.

A woman making fish pastilles on the street, Goree Island. Fish products are a major export.

MEDICINE AND HEALTH CARE

As a tropical country and a poor nation, Senegal is challenged by numerous health problems, including parasitic, intestinal, venereal, and respiratory diseases. Poor sanitation is the main environmental factor that affects the level of health. Malaria is endemic and is a cause of premature death. Intestinal parasites are common because of polluted water. Gonorrhea is present in urban centers. AIDS is a

ETIQUETTE

The day starts with greetings. Young men often shake hands, and young women curtsy and often bend down slightly on one knee to greet their elders. Foul language is not tolerated in public, and people usually resort to communication or "dialogue" to diffuse hostility and aggressiveness. People employ Kal, an institutionalized joking relationship that permits individuals within extended families, caste groups, and ethnic groups to exchange blunt com-

major concern for the population and the health services. Other diseases include hepatitis, trachoma, and tuberculosis. The quality of medical care has deteriorated because of the decline in the number of hospital beds and medical personnel, the lack of medicines in public health facilities, and the appalling conditions of public hospitals.

SECULAR CELEBRATIONS

The major state holidays are New Year's Day (1 January), Independence Day (4 April), International Workers' Day (1 May). During the holidays, people cook ceremonial food and dress up in bright traditional outfits. Religious holidays include Christmas (25 December), and Good Friday, Easter Monday, Eid-al-Fitr, Eid-al-Adha, the Islamic New Year, and Muhammad's birthday.

ARTS AND HUMANITIES

Support for the Arts. Artists are self-supporting and are forced to seek markets outside the country.

Literature. There is a strong tradition of oral literature that reflects the country's history, philosophy, morality, and culture. Since the 1930s, writers have produced novels, short stories, tales, and essays dealing almost exclusively with African themes. The country also has produced successful filmmakers.

Graphic Arts. Glass painting, a new popular art, depicts religious and historical scenes and personalities. Goldsmiths, weavers, and tailors produce jewelry, carpers, and clothing.

Performance Arts. The performance of traditional dances is a popular form of recreation, and children learn to dance at a very young age. Popular sports include soccer and a form of wrestling called *Lamb* (the Wolof word for "fight").

THE STATE OF THE PHYSICAL AND SOCIAL SCIENCES

Despite the solid reputation of the University of Dakar, which was built in the mid-1900s, the development of the physical and social sciences remains limited primarily because of a lack of funding. However, attempts has been made to develop methods of utilizing solar energy.

BIBLIOGRAPHY

American University. *Area Handbook for Senegal*, 1963.

Clark, Andrew F., and Lucie Colvin Phillips. *Historical Dictionary of Senegal*, 2nd ed. 1994.

Dilley, R. M., and J. S. Eades. *Senegal*, 1994.

Gellar, Sheldon. *Senegal: An African Nation between Islam and the West*, 1995.

Hudgens, Jim, and Richard Trillo. *West Africa*, 1995.

Sallah, Tijan M. *Wolof*, 1996.

U. S. Department of State, *Senegal*, 1999.

—MADJIGUENE DIAJAYETTE

SERBIA AND MONTENEGRO

CULTURE NAME

Serbian; Montenegrin; also Yugoslav or Yugoslavian

ALTERNATIVE NAMES

The local name for the region is Srbija-Crna Gora

ORIENTATION

Identification. The name Yugoslavia previously designated six republics (Serbia, Montenegro, Macedonia, Bosnia-Herzogovia, Croatia, and Slovenia), but now includes just Serbia and Montenegro. The word means "land of the southern Slavs." Montenegro, which means "black mountain," takes its name from its rugged terrain. Within Serbia there are several national cultures. In addition to the dominant Serb tradition, there is a large Hungarian population in the northern province of Vojvodina, where Hungarian is the common language and the culture is highly influenced by Hungary (which borders the province to the north). In southern Serbia, the province of Kosovo is primarily Albanian, and has an Islamic culture that bears many remnants of the earlier Turkish conquest.

Location and Geography. Serbia is a landlocked territory in the Balkan Peninsula of Eastern Europe, bordering Montenegro, Bosnia-Herzegovina, Croatia, Hungary, Romania, Bulgaria, Macedonia, and Albania. Montenegro is to the west of Serbia, also bordering Bosnia and Herzogovina, Albania, and the Adriatic Sea. Serbia covers 34,136 square miles (88,412 square kilometers); Montenegro has an area of 5,299 square miles (13,724 square kilometers). Together they are slightly smaller than the state of Kentucky. The terrain varies widely. In the north there are fertile plains that produce most of Serbia's crops, as well as marshlands along the Sava and Danube Rivers. At the northern border, the Danube River runs along the Iron Gate Gorge. Cen-

tral Serbia is hilly and forested and is the most densely populated region of the country. In the east, there are the Carpathian and Rhodope Mountains, as well as the Balkan range, which forms the border with Romania. The Dinaric Alps rise in the western central region. Kosovo, in the south, is considered the cradle of Serbian civilization. Its geographical formation is two basins surrounded by mountains, including the highest peak in Yugoslavia, Daravica, with an elevation of 8,714 feet (2,656 meters). Kosovo's rocky soil does not produce much, with the exception of corn and rye, but there are grazing fields for livestock, as well as mineral resources of lead, zinc, and silver. Montenegro, the smallest of the former Yugoslav republics, is largely forested. Its terrain is rough and mountainous, better suited for animal husbandry than for farming. Its coastal plain along the Adriatic is narrow, dropping off to sheer cliffs in the north.

Belgrade is the capital of Serbia and is the largest city in the country, with a population of 1.5 million. It takes its name, which translates as "white fortress," from the large stone walls that enclose the old part of the city. It is in the north of the country, on a cliff overlooking the meeting of the Danube and Sava Rivers.

Demography. Since the civil wars began in the early 1990s, the population has become more heavily Serbian. Many Croats have fled, particularly from Belgrade and Vojvodina, and many ethnic Serbs have fled from other former Yugoslav republics, Bosnia and Croatia in particular. The 2000 estimate for Serbia's population was 9,981,929, and for Montenegro 680,158. However, these numbers are uncertain due to forced dislocation and ethnic cleansing. Serbs constitute 62.6 percent of people in the area; 16.5 percent are Albanian; 5 percent Montenegrin; 3.4 percent Yugoslav; and 3.3 percent Hungarian. The remaining 9.2 percent are composed of other minorities, including Croats, Gypsies, and Magyars.

Serbia

Linguistic Affiliation. Serbian, the official language, is spoken by 95 percent of the population. It is virtually identical to Croatian, except that Serbian is written in the Cyrillic, or Russian, alphabet, and Croatian uses Roman letters. Five percent of the people speak Albanian, most of these concentrated in the southern province of Kosovo. German, English, and French are commonly learned in school as second languages.

Symbolism. The national symbol of Serbia is a double-headed white eagle, a creature considered the king of animals. The new flag of Serbia and Montenegro is three vertical bars, blue, white, and red (from top to bottom). The flag of the former Yugoslavia was the same but with a red star outlined in yellow in the center.

HISTORY AND ETHNIC RELATIONS

Emergence of the Nation. There is archaeological evidence that civilization in present-day Serbia dates to between 7000 and 6000 B.C.E. The first known inhabitants were the Illyrians, followed by the Celts in the fourth century, and the Romans a century after that. Slavic tribes, whose descendants today form most of the population of the region, arrived in the sixth century. The Byzantine Empire ruled the Balkans for centuries, until the 1150s, when Stefan Nemanja, a leader of a Serb clan, united many smaller clans to defeat the foreign power. Nemanja became king, and in 1220 passed the crown to his son Stefan II. The Nemanja Dynasty continued to rule for the next two hundred years, a period considered a golden age in Serbian history. During this period the Serb Empire expanded to include Serbia, Montenegro, and Albania, reaching as far as Greece in the south.

The Ottoman Turkish Empire to the south also was growing, however, and in 1389 arrived in Kosovo and demanded that Serbian forces surrender to them. The Turks ruled for nearly five hundred years. During their reign, many of the people were enslaved, and the cultural and economic development of the region was stifled.

Throughout the nineteenth century, however, the Serbs began to reassert their desire for self-rule, and in 1878, with the aid of Russian forces, Serbia defeated the Ottomans. In that same year, the Congress of Berlin declared Serbia independent, but it also partitioned the country so that Bosnia-Herzogovina, a region with a large Serb population, became part of Austria. Overall, the Congress's redistribution of land decreased the domain of the Turks and the Russians and increased that of Austria–Hungary and Great Britain. This shift in the balance of powers exacerbated tensions among the various nations involved.

National borders in the Balkans shifted again with the First Balkan War of 1912, when Serbia, along with the other Greece and Bulgaria, took Macedonia back from Turkish rule. In 1913, in the Second Balkan War, Serbia took possession of Kosovo from Albania. They also attempted to take Macedonia from Bulgaria, which had claimed it the year before.

Tensions with Austria continued to build, and in 1914 Gavrilo Princip, a Serb nationalist, assassinated the Austrian archduke Francis Ferdinand. Austria declared war on Serbia, and within several months occupied the entire region. The assassination of the archduke is often named as the immediate act initiating World War I, which would in many ways reconfigure the European continent. When the war ended in 1918, a kingdom uniting Serbia, Montenegro, Bosnia-Herzogovina, Croatia, Slovenia, and Macedonia was formed. In 1929 this kingdom was named Yugoslavia. Despite strong disagreements among the different regions (particularly Serbia and Croatia) as to how to govern, Serbia prevailed, and Yugoslavia was declared a constitutional monarchy under the rule of the Serb king Aleksandar Karadjordjevic.

In 1941 Yugoslavia joined the Tripartite Alliance of Germany, Italy, and Spain, hoping that this would allow them to expand their borders into Greece. Later that same year, however, they decided to pull out of the alliance, and closed their borders to prevent Hitler from invading. The Germans ignored this move, and proceeded to bomb Belgrade. Hitler divided the Balkans among Germany, Italy, Bulgaria, and Hungary. In Croatia, the people greeted German troops as a way to escape the rule of the Serbs, and Croatia, aligned with the Axis powers, became a Fascist puppet state. The Croatian government waged a campaign to rid the territory of Serbs, Jews, and Gypsies, ultimately killing 750,000 people.

The end of World War II saw the rise to power of Josip Tito, who ruled Yugoslavia under a Communist dictatorship from 1945 until 1980. All businesses and institutions were owned and managed by the government. Tito declared himself president for life. He did away with the monarchy, and while he greatly consolidated the power of the central government in Yugoslavia, he also gave republic status to Bosnia-Herzegovina, Montenegro, and Macedonia. Tito managed to keep his nation unaligned with either the Soviet Union or Western countries. He refused to submit to the control of the Soviet Union, which held sway in many of the other Eastern European nations, and for this reason, in 1948 Joseph Stalin expelled Yugoslavia from the Communist Information Bureau.

When Tito died in 1980, the country established a collective presidency: each republic had a representative, and the body worked together to make decisions; the presidency of the country rotated among these different leaders. Slobodan Milosevic became president in 1989, advocating a vision of ''Greater Serbia'' free of ethnic minorities. Slovenia and Croatia disagreed with Milosevic's policies, and both regions declared independence in June 1991. Milosevic sent troops in, and thousands of people died before the 1992 cease-fire. The European Community granted recognition to the republics, and two other regions of the former Yugoslavia—Macedonia, and Bosnia and Herzogovina—called for independence.

Milosevic refused to recognize the sovereignty of any of these states, and on 27 April 1992 declared Serbia and Montenegro the Federal Republic of Yugoslavia. They officially withdrew troops from Bosnia, but many of these forces were Bosnian Serbs, who stayed on of their own accord and continued to perpetrate horrible violence against the Muslims in the area. In May 1992 the U.N. Security Council responded by passing economic sanctions against Yugoslavia.

In 1996 a peace treaty was negotiated between Yugoslavia and Croatia, and Bosnia was divided between Serbs and Croat Muslims.

In that same year, Milosevic was defeated in a presidential election but refused to accept the result. Protests and demonstrations ensued, which the government put down using violence. Elections were held again the following year, and Milosevic won.

In March 1998 the largely Albanian province of Kosovo began fighting for independence. Milosevic's government proceeded to destroy villages and kill thousands of Albanians in the region. An arms embargo by the European nations and the United States had no effect, and in early 1999 NATO intervened on the behalf Kosovo and bombed Yugoslavia. In June 1999 a peace treaty was worked out between Yugoslavia and NATO, but the underlying causes of the conflict were not resolved, and violence continues in the region, which remains under the temporary control of NATO and the U.N. Security Council.

A presidential election in September 2000 resulted in a victory for opposition candidate Vojislav Kostunica, but Milosevic refused to admit that he had lost. Protests ensued; Milosevic's troops attempted to put them down, but eventually troops joined the crowds in agitating for the president's ouster. Milosevic was forced to admit defeat. The European Union responded by lifting certain sanctions against Yugoslavia, including bans on commercial flights and oil shipments. Kostunica supports a free-market economy and increased autonomy for Montenegro, and acknowledges the possibility of self-determination for Kosovo. While his stance is much more moderate than Milosevic's,

Kostunica has refused to advocate the prosecution of his predecessor as a war criminal.

National Identity. The people of Yugoslavia identify primarily with their region. Serbs are more likely than other groups to subscribe to an identity as Yugoslav; many minorities see this identity as attempting to subsume significant regional, ethnic, and religious differences. Montenegrins also have a tradition of Pan-Slavism, which led them to remain with Serbia even as other republics were demanding independence. However, Montenegro has had differences with Serbia, particularly over policy in Bosnia, Croatia, and, most recently, Kosovo. Religion also plays an important role in national identity, in particular for Muslims, the largest religious minority (and the majority in certain areas, such as Kosovo and parts of Bosnia).

Ethnic Relations. The Balkan Peninsula is a hodgepodge of cultures and ethnicities. While most of the people are of Slavic origin, their histories diverged under the varying influences of different governments, religions, and cultures. For example, Slovenia and Croatia are primarily Roman Catholic, whereas most of Serbia is Eastern Orthodox; in Kosovo and Bosnia there is a large Islamic population. The north has a strong influence from Hungary, and the south displays more remnants of Turkish culture. The union of these different cultures under a repressive regime makes for a volatile situation; for this reason the entire region has been referred to as the ''Balkan tinderbox.'' The virulent animosity among different groups has, in recent years, led to civil war. The Serb government has brutally suppressed virtually all minorities to consolidate Serb power. Under Milosevic, a policy of ethnic cleansing has attempted to rid the country of Croat Muslims in Bosnia and ethnic Albanians in Kosovo when these groups have agitated for self-rule; the results have been ongoing violence and the oppression of ethnic minorities.

Yugoslavia also has one of the world's largest Gypsy populations, who are also treated with intolerance. In the 1980s there was a movement among Yugoslav Gypsies for separate nationhood, but it never materialized and eventually lost steam.

URBANISM, ARCHITECTURE, AND THE USE OF SPACE

Belgrade is home to the old royal palace of Yugoslavia, as well as current government buildings. Many of these are in an area called New Belgrade, on the outskirts of the city. Belgrade also boasts centuries-

Radio B92 is the only station that preserves its own network of correspondence.

old churches, mosques, and several national museums. Due in part to its advantageous location at the junction of two rivers, the city has a history of possession by various foreign powers: It has been captured sixty times (by the Romans, Huns, Turks, and Germans, among others) and destroyed thirty-eight times. Many of the city's older structures were damaged by the Nazis during World War II. Some were later restored, but the recent civil war has again devastated the city.

The largest city in Montenegro is Titograd (known as Podgorica before Tito renamed it in 1946). It is an industrial center. Much of the architecture in Titograd reflects the Turkish influence of the Ottoman Empire.

Pristina, with a population of about 108,000, is the capital of the province of Kosovo. It served as capital of the Serbian Empire before the invasion of the Ottoman Turks in the fourteenth century. The city's architecture, exhibiting both Serbian and Turkish influence, testifies to its long history.

Novi Sad, a city with a population of 179,600, in the northern province of Vojvodina, boasts a fortress from the Roman era, as well as a university and the Serbian National Theater. It also is a manufacturing center.

Subotica, with a population of about 100,000, is Serbia's northernmost city and serves as an important center for commerce, agriculture, and intellectual activity.

In the cities, most people live in apartment buildings, although there are also older houses. In the countryside most houses are modest buildings of wood, brick, or stone. They are generally surrounded by courtyards enclosed by walls or fences for privacy. Even in rural areas, houses tend to be relatively close together. Some villages in Kosovo are laid out in a unique square pattern. The houses have watchtowers, and are surrounded by mud walls for protection from enemies.

Serbia is famous for its religious architecture: Huge, beautiful churches and monasteries are not just in the big cities, but also are scattered throughout the nation. Some date back centuries; others, such as the Church of Saint George in the town of Topola, were built in the twentieth century. They are awe-inspiring structures adorned with elaborate mosaics, frescoes, and marble carvings.

FOOD AND ECONOMY

Food in Daily Life. Staples of the Serbian diet are bread, meat, fruits, vegetables, and dairy products. Breakfast generally consists of eggs, meat, and bread, with a dairy spread called *kajmak.* Lunch is the main meal of the day and usually is eaten at about three in the afternoon. A light supper is eaten at about 8:00 P.M.

Peppers are a common ingredient in many dishes. The national dish, called *cevapcici,* is small meat patties, highly spiced and prepared on a grill. Other Serbian specialties include *proja,* a type of cornbread; *gibanica,* a thin, crispy dough often served with cheese and eggs; *sarma,* cabbage leaves filled with meat; and *djuvéc,* a vegetable stew. *Pita* (a type of strudel) and *palacinke* (crepes) are popular desserts. Coffee is prepared in the Turkish style, boiled to a thick, potent liquid and served in small cups. A fruit concoction called *sok* is another favorite drink. For alcohol there is beer and a fruit brandy called *rakija.*

Food Customs at Ceremonial Occasions. The Christmas feast is an elaborate occasion. On Christmas Eve, people eat Lenten foods (no meat or dairy products) and drink hot toddies (warm brandy with honey). The following day, the meal generally consists of roast pork and a round bread called *cesnica.* On Krsna Slava, a family's patron saint's day, another round bread, called *kolac,* is served, as well as *zito,* a boiled, sweetened wheat dish. For Easter, boiled eggs are a traditional food. The shells are dyed and decorated in elaborate patterns.

Basic Economy. The collapse of the Yugoslav Republic in 1991 wreaked havoc on the economy of the region. Trade links were interrupted, and ongoing warfare has destroyed many physical assets. Economic sanctions further stunted the growth of the economy during these years. There is currently an unemployment rate of 30 percent.

Industry accounts for 50 percent of the GDP and employs a large number of people in the fabrication of machines, electronics, and consumer goods. Three-quarters of the workforce is in the business sector (either agriculture or industry). Agriculture accounts for 20 percent of the GDP. Before World War II, more than 75 percent of the population were farmers. Today, due mainly to advances in agricultural technology, this figure has shrunk to fewer than 30 percent; this includes a million people who support themselves through subsistence farming. Crops include wheat, corn, oil seeds, sugar beets, and fruit. Livestock also are raised for dairy products and meat. A quarter of the labor force is in education, government, or services. The tourist industry, which grew steadily throughout the 1980s, has been virtually extinguished by the civil war of the 1990s.

Petrol, imported goods, food, or loot from occupied territories is bought and sold on the black market at the borders of Serbia.

Land Tenure and Property. Under the Communist system, virtually everything was owned by the government. However, even under Tito, many farmers opposed collective farms, and while the government did run several such large-scale operations, small, privately owned farms were permitted as well. Since Tito's demise, the country has been moving toward a capitalist economy. More privatization has been allowed, and people have begun to open stores and businesses. However, this economic development has been hindered by sanctions and by the chaos of civil war.

Commercial Activities. Serbia produces agricultural products and manufactured goods (textiles, machinery, cars, household appliances, etc.) for sale. However, the civil war has slowed or halted production in many areas, and along with economic sanctions, has created a situation of shortages and rationing. Many goods are bought and sold on the black market; they are brought into the country illegally and sold for high prices. Many people, especially in rural areas, also rely on their own gardens and animals to supplement their diets.

Major Industries. Industries include machine-building (aircraft, trucks, tanks, other weapons, and agricultural equipment), metallurgy, mining, production of consumer goods, and electronics. Serbia has one of the largest hydroelectric dams in Europe, and supplies electricity not just to the former Yugoslav republics but to neighboring countries as well.

Trade. Trade has been restricted by sanctions imposed by many Western countries. Major partners include the former Yugoslav republics of Macedonia and Bosnia and Herzogovina, as well as Italy, Germany, and Russia.

Division of Labor. It is traditional for children to continue in the trade or occupation of their parents. However, with more educational opportunities, this is not necessarily the case now. There are approximately two million people in the socialized sector, of which 75 percent are in business (agriculture or industry) and 25 percent are in education, government, and other services. There is also a significant unemployment rate (26 percent in 1996).

SOCIAL STRATIFICATION

Classes and Castes. Before World War II the base of society was the peasant class, with a small upper class composed of government workers, professionals, merchants, and artisans, and an even tinier middle class. Under communism, education, Party membership, and rapid industrialization offered possibilities for upward mobility. Since the fall of Tito's government and the rise of the free-market economy, people have been able to attempt to better their status through entrepreneurship. However, economic sanctions have had the effect of decreasing the overall standard of living; shortages and inflation make even necessary items unaffordable or unavailable. This situation has created more extreme differences between the rich and the poor, as those who have access to goods can hoard them and sell them for exorbitant rates.

Symbols of Social Stratification. Most young people and city-dwellers wear Western-style clothing. In the villages, women wear the traditional outfit of a plain blouse, long black skirt, and head scarf. For festive occasions, unmarried women wear small red felt caps adorned with gold braid, and married women don large white hats with starched wings. Albanian men in Kosovo wear small white caps, which reflect their Muslim heritage.

POLITICAL LIFE

Government. The Federal Republic of Yugoslavia elects a president for a four-year term (although during his eleven-year tenure, Slobodan Milosevic refused to recognize the outcome of these elections if they were not to his advantage). The president appoints a prime minister. The legislative branch of the government, called the Federal Assembly, consists of two houses. The Chamber of Citizens, with 138 seats (108 from Serbia and 30 from Montenegro), is elected by popular vote. The Chamber of Republics, with 20 representatives from each republic, is chosen by republic assemblies. However, since 1998, Serbia has superseded Montenegro's right to have representatives in the Chamber of Republics.

Both Serbia and Montenegro also have their own governments, which are similar in structure to the federal one. Each has its own president, legislature, and court system. The voting age is sixteen if one is employed, or eighteen otherwise.

Leadership and Political Officials. Serbia has a history of powerful, demagogic leaders who have maintained control by manipulating the media and other forceful methods. This has created a certain distance between the highest government officials and the people, which can manifest itself in the populace as either fear, admiration, or a combination of the two.

Today, there are eleven political parties represented in the Yugoslav Federal Assembly, four from Montenegro and seven from Serbia. Until the September 2000 elections, Milosevic's Socialist Party of Serbia, and Milosevic himself, exercised ultimate power. Kostunica managed to unite eighteen opposition groups as the Democratic Opposition of Serbia, but this coalition is fraught with dissension.

Social Problems and Control. There are local court systems in each republic, as well as a Federal Court, which is the highest court of appeals and which also resolves property disputes among the republics. There is a high rate of corruption in government and in business. Refugees, economic strain, and social unrest have also been major social problems. Political dissidents have been dealt swift and harsh punishments.

Military Activity. The military consists of an army made up of ground forces with border troops, naval forces, and air defense forces. It is under the command of the Yugoslav president, in conjunction with the Supreme Defense Council, which includes the presidents of both Serbia and Montenegro. All men are required to serve one year in the armed forces. The police (both federal and republican) have the responsibility of maintaining order in the coun-

Church Island, Bay of Kotor. Montenegro borders the Adriatic Sea.

try, and in many cases are better armed than the military.

SOCIAL WELFARE AND CHANGE PROGRAMS

The Communist regime instituted an extensive social welfare system, much of which is still intact. This system provides retirement and disability pensions as well as unemployment and family allowances. There is also a socialized health care system, and the government runs shelters and homes for orphans and the mentally and physically disabled. However, civil war and economic sanctions have left the government in many instances unable to pay its Social Security checks, and many older and disabled people have suffered as a result.

NONGOVERNMENTAL ORGANIZATIONS AND OTHER ASSOCIATIONS

Western nongovernmental organizations, including Red Cross and USAID, have provided assistance in dealing with the sizable problems of food, housing, and medical needs. However, Yugoslavia is not recognized by the international community as a whole, and has been denied admission to the United Nations and other international organizations.

GENDER ROLES AND STATUSES

Division of Labor by Gender. Traditionally, women perform only domestic work. Under communism, however, they began to take other types of jobs in large numbers. The number of women wage earners increased from 400,000 in 1948 to 2.4 million in 1985. The percentage of women who work outside the home varies greatly from region to region. Most women take positions in cultural and social welfare, public service and administration, and trade and catering. Almost all of the nation's elementary school teachers are women. However, even when women work outside the home, they are still expected to cook, clean, and take care of other domestic tasks.

The Relative Status of Women and Men. Serbian culture is traditionally male-dominated. Men are considered the head of the household. While women have gained significant economic power since World War II, many vestiges of the patriarchal system are still evident in women's lower social status.

MARRIAGE, FAMILY, AND KINSHIP

Marriage. Wedding celebrations often last for days. Before a couple enters their new house for the first time, the bride stands in the doorway and lifts a baby boy three times. This is to ensure that the marriage will be blessed with children. Marriages are generally not arranged. Under Tito, women gained equal rights in marriage and divorce became easier and more common.

Domestic Unit. It is customary for several generations to live together under the same roof. Ethnic Albanians tend to have large families, of eight to ten children, and extended families often live together in a compound of houses enclosed by a stone wall. Even in Serbian families, which tend to be smaller, cousins, aunts, uncles, and other family members often live, if not in the same house, then in close proximity to one another. The Serbian language does not distinguish between cousins and siblings, which is an indication of the particular closeness of extended families.

Inheritance. Inheritance customs follow a system of male primogeniture: The firstborn son inherits the family's property.

Kin Groups. Until modern times, rural Montenegrins lived in clans. Feuding among the different clans was legendary and could go on for generations. In rural areas the land was traditionally worked under the administration of *zadrugas*, groups of a hundred or more people made up of extended families, which were overseen by male elders. The zadrugas were religious groups, each with its own patron saint, and served the social function of providing for orphans, the elderly, and the sick or disabled. In the 1970s the organizations began to evolve from the traditional patriarchal system to a more cooperative one. They also declined in prevalence as the population became more urban than rural.

SOCIALIZATION

Infant Care. Infant care is largely the role of the mother. Godparents also play a significant part, and there is a fairly elaborate ceremony soon after birth that involves the godparent cutting the child's umbilical cord. Under the Communist regime, the government set up day nurseries to care for babies, allowing women to return to their jobs soon after childbirth.

Child Rearing and Education. The godfather (*kum*) or godmother (*kuma*) plays an important role in a child's upbringing. They are not related by blood, but are considered part of the spiritual family. He or she is responsible for the child if anything happens to the parents. The kum or kuma is in charge of naming the baby, and has a role of honor in the baptism and later in the child's wedding. Both boys and girls are expected to help with household chores.

Education is free and compulsory between ages seven and fourteen. Primary school lasts for eight years, after which students choose the vocation or field they will study in secondary school. This lasts three or four years, depending on the area of study. Seventy-one percent of children attend primary school. This number drops to 64 percent at the secondary level. Albanians, and Albanian girls in particular, are much less likely to receive an education. In 1990, all Albanian schools in Kosovo were closed down because the Serbian government did not approve of their curriculum, which emphasized Albanian culture. Some underground schools have been started, but many children continue to go without schooling.

Higher Education. The largest university, in Belgrade, was founded in 1863. There are other universities, in the cities of Novi Sad, Nis, and Podgorica. Kosovo's only university, in Pristina, was closed in 1990, when all ethnic Albanian faculty were fired and the Albanian students were either expelled or resigned in protest. Albanian faculty and students are now attempting to run an underground university. In 1998 the government took control of all the universities in the country, curtailing all academic freedom.

ETIQUETTE

Kissing is a common form of greeting, for both men and women. Three kisses, alternating cheeks, are customary. Serbs are a hospitable people and love to visit and chat. When entering a home as a guest for the first time, one generally brings a small present of flowers, food, or wine. It also is customary to remove one's shoes and put on a pair of slippers before going into the house. Hosts are expected to serve their guests; *slatko*, a sweet strawberry preserve, often is provided.

RELIGION

Religious Beliefs. Sixty-five percent of the population belongs to the Eastern Orthodox Church. Nineteen percent are Muslim (most of these people live in Kosovo, and the majority are Sunni, although there are some Shi'ite as well); 4 percent are Roman Catholic; 1 percent are Protestant; and the remaining 11 percent practice other religions. Be-

Belgrade city center. The city boasts both centuries' old and modern-day architecture.

fore World War II there was a sizable Jewish population. It shrunk from 64,405 in 1931 to 6,835 in 1948. Many of those who were not killed in the Holocaust emigrated to Israel. Today the Jewish population is about 5,000, organized into 29 communes under the Federation of Jewish Communities in Yugoslavia. The Eastern Orthodox Church split off from the Roman Catholic Church in 1054, in what became known as the Great Schism. Many of the fundamental beliefs of the two churches remain the same, the fundamental difference being that the Eastern Orthodox religion does not recognize the authority of the pope. Instead they have a group of patriarchs who have equal status. The Serbian Orthodox Church was founded in 1219, and its rise was tied to the rise of the Serbian state at that time. A central figure in the church is Saint Sava, the brother of Stefan Nemanja, Serbia's first king. Since its founding, the church has promoted Serbian nationalism, and has struggled against the dominance of the central authority of the Greek Orthodox Church in Constantinople.

Religious Practitioners. The patriarchs hold the highest position in the Eastern Orthodox Church and are responsible for most official decisions. Priests are the primary religious figures in the community and are responsible for conducting services and counseling their parishioners. Unlike in Roman Catholicism, they are permitted to marry. There also are monks, who are celibate. Only monks, not priests, can obtain the position of bishop.

Rituals and Holy Places. Religious ceremonies are held in churches—elaborate, beautifully designed buildings, many of which date back hundreds of years. Each family has a patron saint, who is honored once a year in a large celebration called Krsna Slava. A candle is lit in the saint's honor, and special foods are consumed, including the round bread *kolac.* A priest comes to the house to bless it with holy water and incense. The family and priest stand in a circle around the *kolac* and sing a special song.

Christmas (observed on 6 and 7 January in the Eastern Orthodox Church) is a major holiday. Christmas Eve, called Badnje Vece, is feted with a large bonfire in the churchyard and the singing of hymns. On Christmas morning a selected young person knocks on the door and ''brings Christmas into the house,'' poking a stick into the fireplace. The number of sparks that are released predicts how much luck the family will have in the year to come. Easter also is a big holiday. In addition to church services, it is celebrated by dying eggs and performing traditional *kolo* dances.

Death and the Afterlife. Funerals are large, elaborate occasions. In the cemetery, a spread of salads and roasted meats is presented in honor of the deceased; this is repeated a year after the death, at which point the gravestone is placed in the ground. Gravestones often bear photographs as well as inscriptions. Eastern Orthodox Christians believe in heaven, hell, and purgatory, a concept of an afterlife in which one is rewarded or punished according to one's actions in this life.

MEDICINE AND HEALTH CARE

Comprehensive health care is provided for pregnant women, infants, children up to age fifteen, students up to age twenty-six, and people over age sixty-five. All people are ensured treatment for infectious diseases and mental illness. However, at least one-fifth of the population does not receive health care. The post-World War II Communist government did a good job of eliminating many of the country's health problems, including typhus, typhoid, dysentery, and tuberculosis. Infectious diseases are problems in the less developed regions, such as Kosovo. The leading causes of death are circulatory diseases and cancer, due in part to the increase in environmental pollution and cigarette smoking since the 1970s. Traffic accidents and suicide also are significant health issues.

SECULAR CELEBRATIONS

The principal secular celebrations are New Year's Day, 1 January; International Labor Day, 1 May; Day of Uprising in Serbia, 7 July; and Republic Day, 29 November.

THE ARTS AND HUMANITIES

Support for the Arts. The communist government had a policy of fairly strict censorship but state-approved artists did receive funding. Today there are virtually no funds (public or private) for the support of the arts. The National Theater in Belgrade hosts ballet performances. There are also traveling folklore groups that perform around the country.

Literature. Serbian literature traces its roots to the thirteenth-century epic poetry of Kosovo. The nineteenth-century Serbian poets Jovan Jovanovic Zmaj and Djura Jaksic gained prominence beyond the nation's borders. Contemporary Serbian writers include Milorad Pavic, Vladimir Arsenijevic, and Ivo Andric, who won the 1961 Nobel Prize for literature for his novel *Bridge Over the River Drina.* The Montenegrin Milovan Djilas was a prominent critic of the Communist system, and composed works in a number of genres, including fiction, nonfiction, memoir, and history.

Graphic Arts. Serbia is known for its textiles made of wool, flax, and hemp. These materials are also woven into carpets of complex geometric patterns. The decoration of Easter eggs is another traditional art form. They are colored with natural dyes and adorned with intricate patterns and designs.

Many churches and monasteries are decorated with frescoes and mosaics. Contemporary painting often incorporates religious and historic concepts as well as modern aesthetic principles. Serbia has produced several nationally recognized painters, including Milic Stankovic and Olja Ivanicki. Ivan Generalic is well known for his primitive-style depictions (some of them fairly political) of Yugoslav life.

A typical house in Montenegro. Most houses in rural areas are still relatively close together.

Artists have not been deterred by the economic or political situation, and have begun displaying installations in bombed-out buildings in Belgrade, shows they call ''Phobjects.'' Contemporary art also can be seen on the street in popular surrealistic political posters that are hung in towns and cities.

Performance Arts. One type of traditional Serbian music is performed on a *guslari*, a single-stringed instrument played with a bow, which the musician accompanies by singing ballads that relay both news and historical events. Another kind of folk music is called *tamburitza*. It is played by groups of musicians on stringed instruments similar to mandolins and banjos. The *gadje*, a bagpipe like instrument, also is common. Albanian music in Kosovo has a more Arabic sound, echoing the influence of the Turks, and Gypsies dance to a type of music called *blehmuzika*, using a brass band.

Serbian folk dances are called *kolos*, and are performed by professional troupes, or by guests at weddings and other special occasions. They involve a group of people holding hands and moving in a circle. A specific kolo music accompanies the dance.

During the Turkish rule, when people were forbidden to hold large celebrations, they often transmitted news through the lyrics and movements of the kolo tradition. Traditional accompaniment to the dance is a violin, and occasionally an accordion or a flute. Costumes also are important parts of dance; even today, traditional regional dress is worn for the performances.

Western rock music is extremely popular with younger audiences, and Yugoslavia has produced some homegrown stars. Many of them use the form to convey political messages.

There also is a long tradition of filmmaking in the entire former Yugoslavia. The first film recordings date to 1905, and the first full-length film was made in 1910. After World War II the industry grew considerably, thanks to government funding for productions. In 1939, the director Mihail Popovic gained acclaim for his historical film *Battle of Kosovo*. In the 1980s, director Emir Kusturica, from Sarajevo, won first place at the Cannes Film Festival for *When Father Was Away on Business*. His films depicted the terror that the Communist government inspired in the people. The 1990s saw decreased production in the film industry, but some of the movies that were produced took on the difficult subject of the civil war, including *Pretty Village, Pretty Flame*, directed by Srdjan Dragojevic. Goran Paskaljevic, another Serbian director, produced the widely acclaimed film *Powder Keg* in 1998.

THE STATE OF THE PHYSICAL AND SOCIAL SCIENCES

Serbia has produced several well-known scientists, including Mileva Maric Einstein (the first wife of Albert Einstein), Mihajlo Pupin, and Nikola Tesla. The civil wars that began in the early 1990s took a severe toll on the economy, and today there is little money available for the study of either the physical or social sciences.

BIBLIOGRAPHY

Allcock, John B. et al., eds. *Conflict in the Former Yugoslavia: An Encyclopedia*, 1998.

Anzulovic, Branimir. *Heavenly Serbia: From Myth to Genocide*, 1999.

Campbell, Greg. *Road to Kosovo: A Balkan Diary*, 1999.

"Country Report: Yugoslavia (Serbia-Montenegro)." In *The Economist Intelligence Unit*, 1998.

Erlanger, Steven. "Yugoslavs Bicker over Army and Secret Police." *New York Times*, 8 November 2000.

"Former Yugoslavia." *U.N. Chronicle*, 1 March 1999.

Gall, Carlotta. "Bosnians Vote with a Hope: To Break Ethnic Parties' Rule." *New York Times*, 12 November 2000.

Gojkovic, Drinka. *The Road to War in Serbia: Trauma and Catharsis*, 2000.

Greenberg, Susan. "The Great Yugoslav Failure." *New Statesman*, 9 August 1999.

Hawkesworth, Celia. *Voices in the Shadows: Women and Verbal Art in Serbia and Bosnia*, 2000.

Lampe, John R. *Yugoslavia as History: Twice There Was a Country*, 2000.

McGeary, Johanna. "The End of Milosevic." *Time*, 16 October 2000.

Milivojevic, JoAnn. *Serbia*, 1999.

"More Trouble in the Balkans." *The Economist*, 15 July 1999.

Muravchik, Joshua. "The Road to Kosovo." *Commentary*, June 1999.

Nelan, Bruce, et al. "Into the Fire." *Time*, 5 April 1999.

Ramet, Sabrina P. *Gender Politics in the Western Balkans*, 1999.

Ranesar, Romesh. "Man of the Hour." *Time*, 16 October 2000.

Sopova, Jasmina. "Talking to Serbian Filmmaker Goran Paskaljevic." *UNESCO Courier*, February 2000.

"Still Pretty Nasty." *The Economist*, 23 September 2000.

U.S. Department of State. *Erasing History: Ethnic Cleansing in Kosovo*, 1999.

Wachtel, Andrew. *Making a Nation, Breaking a Nation: Literature and Cultural Politics in Yugoslavia*, 1998.

Web Sites

U.S. Department of State, Central Intelligence Agency. "Serbia and Montenegro." In *CIA World Factbook 2000*, http://www.odci.gov/cia/publications/factbook/geos/sr

—ELEANOR STANFORD

SEYCHELLES

CULTURE NAME

Seychellois

ORIENTATION

Identification. The name "Seychelles" derives from the 1756 French expedition that led to the annexation of the islands. The commander of the expedition named the islands *Séchelles* after the controller of finance, Vicomte Moreau des Séchelles.

Location and Geography. Located in the Indian Ocean south of the equator, with a land area of 118 square miles (455 square kilometers), the Seychelles is technically the smallest continent. The central islands have a continental shelf and are granitic, while the outlying ones are flat coral islands. The granitic islands are mountainous. The capital, Victoria, is on the main island, Mahé, at a spot where the island of Saint Anne creates natural harbor. The country has a large number of native species, especially birds and plants.

Demography. The population was 79,164 in 1999 and is growing slowly as a result of out-migration.

Linguistic Affiliation. The official languages are Seychelles Creole, French, and English. Seychelles Creole has a strong resemblance to the Creoles of Mauritius and Reunion and those of the Caribbean. There has been disagreement about the use of French versus English and the extent to which Creole should be used. Most people speak Creole at home. The English-French divide occurs in debates about how new words should be integrated into Creole.

Symbolism. The flag consists of wedges or rays emanating from the lower left corner. The colors are yellow, red, white, and green, with a blue wedge at the upper left. The flag symbolizes the ocean, the link to Africa, and the multicolored nature of the population. The government that gained power through a coup in 1977 had Marxist leanings and used rhetoric appropriate to that ideology. The country has used a national rhetoric of development and the pioneering spirit, especially in regard to the development of the outer islands.

HISTORY AND ETHNIC RELATIONS

Emergence of the Nation. The country was not inhabited when Europeans discovered and settled the islands. While the French originally settled in 1770, the British took control during the Napoleonic Wars, but without throwing out the French upper class. The settlers brought slaves, and the society featured white domination and black slavery. After the British prohibited slavery in 1835, the influx of African workers did not end because British warships captured Arab slavers and forced the liberated slaves to work on plantations as "apprentices" without pay. The *Gran'bla* ("big whites") of French origin dominated the economy and political life, with a British colonial administration that at times was supportive but was often hostile to them. The administration did not permit the importation of Indian indentured laborers. Therefore, the Indian component of the population is small and, like a similar minority of Chinese, is confined to a merchant class.

The country became independent from Britain in 1976, with the exception of the islands retained as the British Indian Ocean Territory. This included Diego Garcia, which was developed as U.S. military base.

National Identity. Independence brought public debate about issues of national identity and allegiance. The winner of the first election for the presidency, James Mancham, favored integration or close ties with Britain; his main opponent, France Albert René, saw this as a danger to the national identity, which he considered African. He also had

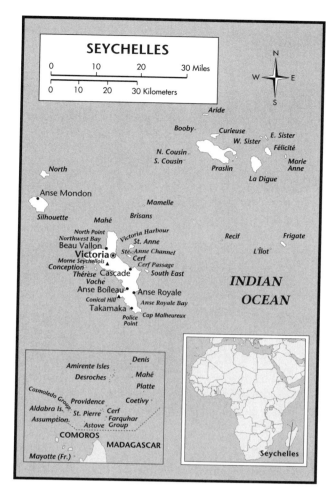

Seychelles

URBANISM, ARCHITECTURE, AND THE USE OF SPACE

Traditional architecture had two distinct forms: plantations and town houses. The plantation was focused on a *lakou* (courtyard with an owner's or manager's house), the *kalorife* (drying oven for copra), and storage houses. Separate from the courtyard were the workers' houses with thatched roofs, and on some plantations also with walls made from coconut leaves. The workers' houses often were divided into two parts: a sleeping room and a living room. The living room often was filled with furniture and seldom was used, as most social life took place outdoors. The kitchen was usually in a separate house. The typical town house had a general Victorian form, but both the roof and the walls might be made of corrugated iron sheets. With the decline of the plantation sector and agriculture in general the traditional lay out of the courtyards are disappearing. New houses are often constructed in an architecture common to many former British colonies, such that there is often a flat roof with a slight slope and windows with many horizontally arranged panes that can be tilted in order to allow easy circulation of air.

FOOD AND ECONOMY

Food in Daily Life. The staple is curry and rice, which may be eaten two or three times a day. The curry may be based on fish or meat. Coconut milk often is used in the curry. Upper-class Creoles eat meals that consist of both fish and meat. Alcoholism has been prevalent, partly because the plantations used drinks as payments and incentives. Among the working classes drinking tended to be solitary. A typical drink is palm wine, fermented sap tapped from coconut palm fronds.

Food Customs at Ceremonial Occasions. There are no specific foods for ceremonial occasions, but meat is preferred.

Basic Economy. In a land-based plantation economy, copra and in some periods cinnamon and vanilla were the main exports. In 1960, about a third of the economically active population worked on plantations, and about 20 percent in the public sector. After the opening of the international airport in 1971, tourism became important. Segmentation of the economy into the tourism and plantation sectors developed. Wages were much higher in the tourism sector. There was little scope for expansion of the plantation economy or for increases in wages, since the wage-paying potential was fixed by inter-

strong socialist leanings. The *Gran'bla* wanted to reestablish ties with France. René toppled the first elected government in a coup in 1977 and established a one-party state that lasted until 1992. However, his party, the Seychelles People's Progressive Front (SPPF), remained in power after the election of 1992, and René won the presidential election of 1993 and has been president since.

Ethnic Relations. The Indian and Chinese merchants form two distinct ethnic communities, as do the *gran'bla*. Those that were evicted from Diego Garcia when the U.S. military base was established are called Illois. They are also found in Mauritius and regard themselves as distinct from Seychellois although they historically and culturally belong to the mobile plantation worker class in Seychelles. Ethnic relations are mainly relations of class in Seychelles.

national prices of plantation crops. The plantation sector declined, and agriculture now accounts for about 4 percent of the gross domestic product (GDP) and less than 10 percent of the workforce. Although Seychelles copra is of very high quality, it is likely that the plantation sector will disappear completely. Tourism now employs 30 percent of the labor force and accounts for 13 percent of GDP and 60 percent of foreign exchange earnings. Although the country is now classified as an upper-middle-income economy by the World Bank, it has retained an unequal income distribution, and in 1992, about 7 percent of the population was considered poor. The Seychelles Rupee (SRS) is the national currency. There is approximately 5 SRS to the USD.

Land Tenure and Property. While historically the *gran'bla* owned nearly the all land, the postindependence period saw the sale of land being to outsiders. In 1960, fifty-six landowners held two-thirds of the agricultural land. In 1976, 56 percent was held by foreigners.

Major Industries. Tourism is focused on the upper part of the market. Tuna fishing and canning are becoming increasingly important, as is aquaculture. A small manufacturing sector is linked to the establishment of an international trade zone. The country also offers registration facilities for foreign companies.

Trade. Apart from the export oriented manufacturing, tuna and plantation crops, trade is limited to locally produced fish and vegetables and imported manufactured goods. Souvenirs are produced and sold to tourists.

SOCIAL STRATIFICATION

Classes and Castes. Social stratification is symbolized largely by skin color and ethnic origin. There is hierarchy of color terms, from *ble* ("blue") to *bla-rose* ("white-pink") that coincides with the historical continuum of status from plantation worker to landowner. Seychellois use the color terms to identify the people they are talking about. The degree to which color and class determine the social order is a contested issue.

Symbols of Social Stratification. There are no particular symbols of social stratification apart from skin color and complexion.

Fish hang from the handlebars of a fisherman's bicycle. Seychelles is located in the Indian Ocean.

POLITICAL LIFE

Government. Since 1992, the Republic of Seychelles has been a multiparty state. The present constitution was adopted in 1993 and stipulates that the head of government is also the chief of state and appoints the council of ministers. A direct election of the president is held every five years, as are elections for the unicameral thirty-five-seat National Assembly. The president appoints the members of the supreme court and appeals court. Civil law and commercial law derive from the French, while the penal code is influenced by the British model.

Leadership and Political Officials. The SPPF is the dominant party. Other parties include the Democratic Party, United Opposition Party, Seychelles Party, Seychelles Liberal Party, and Seychelles Democratic Movement.

Social Problems and Control. The main social problems recognized by the government and nongovernmental organizations (NGOs) are domestic violence, sexual abuse of children and alcoholism.

Military Activity. The country has never fought in a war. There is little emphasis on fighting prowess or martial arts. Seychellois participated in World War II in the British Army. The coup in 1977 and a subsequent attempted countercoup led to the establishment of military forces; there is also a coast guard.

NONGOVERNMENTAL ORGANIZATIONS AND OTHER ASSOCIATIONS

Several Seychelles-based nongovernmental organizations exist. Among these are several organizations that address social problems such as CAREDA (Committee on Awareness, Resilience and Education against Drugs and Alcohol) and the Association for the Promotion of Solid Humane Families. The important National Council for Children is a semigovernmental organization. There are two human rights NGOs that both were established in 1998: the Center for Rights and Development, and the Friends for a Democratic Society. There are also a number of NGOs focusing on natural preservation or the study of nature.

GENDER ROLES AND STATUSES

Division of Labor by Gender. There are no strict norms for the division of labor by gender, but several statistical tendencies. In particular, women rarely fish. In the plantation economy, both men and women worked as wage laborers. The tourism industry also employs women, although the labor force participation of women relative to men has been reduced by the decline of the plantation economy. Female employment is about 40 percent of that of males in administration and 14 percent in clerical and professional jobs.

The Relative Status of Women and Men. Women generally have a high status in the working class, but not in other social strata. Women control economic resources within the family and often pursue economic careers. Traditionally, violence between spouses has been a problem, usually with women as the victims.

MARRIAGE, FAMILY, AND KINSHIP

Marriage. Consensual unions are common but less so among the gran'bla and the Indian and Chinese communities. Polygamy is not practiced, but unions are unstable and divorce or breakup is common. Fifty to 60 percent of births are to women who are not married and often are not acknowledged by the child's father. The partners generally arrange the marriage. There is a strong contractual aspect to marriage, with a clear division of responsibilities between men and women. Among working-

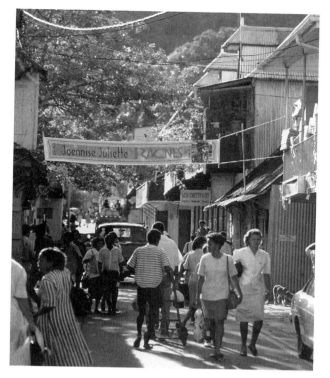

Market Street, the crowded shopping street in Victoria. Tourism employs 30 percent of the workforce.

class people, the man gives his spouse his wages, which are used for daily expenditures for food, clothes, and the children. Women use their own income for durables, which they keep if the union dissolves. To a large extent, marriages occur within the same social and color strata.

Domestic Unit. The form of the domestic unit varies with class. The ideal gran'bla family is nuclear. Among plantation workers, serial monogamy is prevalent, with the woman as the stable center of a domestic unit that consists of herself, her husband (married or in a consensual union), her children regardless of their father, and fostered children. Plantation workers developed a highly regulated system of fosterage in which firstborn children were given to the maternal grandmother or an aunt. A young women who gave away a child early would receive children later from her daughters or younger sisters. This fostering occurred in all classes. The nature of the system differed with the relative social class of the child giver and the child recipient: with large asymmetry in favor of the recipient, this became a system of domestic child work. With the sharp reduction in fertility rates in recent years, the system has been impossible to maintain. Each member of a household is assigned his or her own tasks.

Women process copra, or coconuts, in the Seychelles. The plantation sector of the economy is expected to decline.

Inheritance. Inheritance is bilateral, with men and women having equal rights.

Kin Groups. Descent is generally bilateral and no descent groups are formed. However, descent has a strong matrilateral bias, especially in the working class. That and the practice of fostering children create networks of women that resemble kin groups. Gran'bla families were formed in the same manner as European families, with an emphasis on patrilineal succession to a name and attempts to keep property within the family.

SOCIALIZATION

Infant Care. Infants sleep with their parents, especially the mother. Toddlers have freedom to roam but often are watched by older siblings. They are given small tasks from an early age in accordance with the precise assignment of tasks within the household.

Child Rearing and Education. Early initiation to an active sexual life has been considered a problem by health authorities. The number of children born to women below age twenty is high. Enrollment in primary education is universal but drops off at the secondary stage. Girls enroll as often as boys. The post-1997 revolutionary regime established a National Youth Service (NYS) along socialist lines. The NYS was replaced in 1999 with the fifth grade of secondary school.

Higher Education. Those who want higher education attend schools and universities overseas. No higher education is available domestically except for polytechnic training, including teacher training, nursing, tourism, and arts.

ETIQUETTE

Seychellois are usually described as laid-back and easygoing. Dress codes are relaxed, and formal clothing is seldom worn. Interpersonal distance is somewhat greater than it is in Europe. Complimentary statements to or about other persons, especially children, are avoided because they may bring misfortune. Greetings are simple.

RELIGION

Religious Beliefs. Most of the people are Roman Catholic (90 percent) or Anglican (8 percent). What the priests teach is somewhat different from the beliefs and practices of the layperson. Seychellois traditionally had a strong belief in spirits (*nam*) and sorcery (*gri-gri*). Some sorcerers were very influential.

Religious Practitioners. Religious practitioners are priests of the various churches as well as the healers/sorcerers.

Rituals and Holy Places. There are no religious rituals specific to the Seychellois, and the Christian religious feasts are celebrated.

Death and the Afterlife. In general, people follow Christian conceptions of death and the afterlife. Linked to ideas about sorcery was the belief that the spirit of a person prematurely killed by sorcery could be made to serve the sorcerer for the duration of that person's natural life span.

MEDICINE AND HEALTH CARE

Major tropical diseases such as malaria have never established in the islands. The primary health care system is well established. Advanced care is not available, but there is a hospital in the capital. The nature of current beliefs and practices involving traditional medicine is not documented. Sorcerers traditionally were involved in healing through the use of medicinal plants.

SECULAR CELEBRATIONS

The national day is celebrated on 18 June to commemorate the adoption of the constitution in 1993. On 5 June Liberation Day is celebrated in remembrance of the 1977 coup, and on 29 June Independence Day is observed. Labor Day is on 1 May. New Year is celebrated on 1 and 2 January. Christian holidays that are also public holidays include All Saints Day (1 November), Immaculate Conception (8 December), and Christmas Day (25 December).

THE ARTS AND HUMANITIES

Literature. Seychelles Creole is a written language and the only daily newspaper, the *Nation* publishes partly in Creole. Apart from folk tales which have been published in Creole there is no literature.

Graphic Arts. There are few arts and crafts in Seychelles that derive from a Seychellois tradition. There is a small crafts industry in conjunction with tourism.

THE STATE OF THE PHYSICAL AND SOCIAL SCIENCES

There is not much research either in physical or social sciences based in Seychelles. A journal that covers the sciences in general appears sporadically. Seychelles has nevertheless been the focus of research, in particular marine biology, ornithology, botany, and geology because of the uniqueness of the islands.

BIBLIOGRAPHY

Benedict, Burton. *People of the Seychelles*, 1966.

———. "The Equality of the Sexes in Seychelles." In M. Freedman, ed. *Social Organization*, 1967.

Benedict, Marion, and Burton Benedict. *Men, Women and Money in Seychelles*, 1982.

Berge, Gunnvor. *Hierarchy, Equality and Social Change: Exchange Processes on a Seychelles Plantation*, 1987.

Pedersen, Jon. *The Social Construction of Fertility: Population Processes on a Plantation in the Seychelles*, 1985.

———. "Plantation Women and Children: Wage Labor, Adoption and Fertility in the Seychelles." *Ethnology* 26 (1): 51–61, 1987.

Scarr, Deryck. *Seychelles since 1770: History of a Slave and Post-Slavery Society*, 1999.

—JON PEDERSEN

SIERRA LEONE

CULTURE NAME

Sierra Leonean

ALTERNATIVE NAMES

The Republic of Sierra Leone

ORIENTATION

Identification. The name "Sierra Leone" dates back to 1462, when Portuguese explorer Pedro da Cintra, sailing down the West African coast, saw the tall mountains rising up on what is now the Freetown Peninsula and called them the "Lion Mountains," or "*Serra Lyoa*." Successive visits by English sailors and later British colonization modified the name to "Sierra Leone." Despite distinctive regional variations in language and local traditions, Sierra Leoneans today are united by many factors, such as their shared lingua franca Krio, widespread membership in men's and women's social associations and societies, and even sporting events, especially when the national football (soccer) team plays. At the same time, a worsening domestic economy, declining infrastructure, and deteriorating health conditions have prevented the country's progress, and have to some extent hindered the development of a strong sense of collective pride or shared national identification, especially in the rural areas outside the capital city.

Location and Geography. Sierra Leone is located on the west coast of Africa, north of the equator. With a land area of 27,699 square miles (71,740 square kilometers), it is slightly smaller than the state of South Carolina. Sierra Leone is bounded by Guinea to the north and northeast, Liberia to the south and southeast, and the Atlantic Ocean to the west.

There are a wide variety of ecological and agricultural zones to which people have adapted. Starting in the west, Sierra Leone has some 250 miles (400

kilometers) of coastline, giving it both bountiful marine resources and attractive tourist potential. This is followed by low-lying mangrove swamps, rain-forested plains and farmland, and finally a mountainous plateau in the east, where Mount Bintumani rises to 6,390 feet (1,948 meters). The climate is tropical, with two seasons determining the agricultural cycle: the rainy season from May to November, followed by the dry season from December to May, which includes *harmattan*, when cool, dry winds blow in off the Sahara Desert. The capital Freetown sits on a coastal peninsula, situated next to the world's third largest natural harbor. This prime location historically made Sierra Leone the center of trade and colonial administration in the region.

Demography. The population of Sierra Leone is 4.7 million people, the majority being children and youth. The population had been increasing at just over 2 percent per year, though this has declined somewhat since civil conflict began in 1991. Thirty-six percent of the people live in urban areas. The average woman bears six children during her lifetime. There are also numerous Sierra Leoneans living and working abroad, especially in England and the United States. They generate active discussion concerning events in their country, and provide an important source of resources for their families at home.

Linguistic Affiliation. Different reports list between fifteen and twenty different ethnic groups. This is a discrepancy not so much as to whether a certain group of people "exists" or not, but whether local dialects once spoken continue to be mutually distinct in the face of population expansion, intermarriage, and migration. For example, the two largest ethnic groups, the Temne and Mende, each comprise about 30 percent of the total population, and have come to "absorb" many of their less populous neighbors. For instance, Loko people will admit to being heavily culturally influenced by the Temne people surrounding them, the Krim and the Gola by

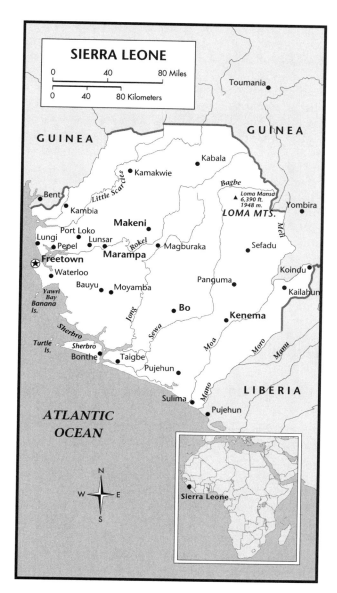

Sierra Leone

ten associate the tall cotton tree, white sandy beaches, or the large natural harbor with home; people from the east often think of coffee and cocoa plantations. Yet the palm tree and the rice grain are the national symbols par excellence, immortalized in currency, song, and folklore, and valued for their central and staple contributions to everyday life. Different species of palms contribute to cooking oil, thatch roofs, fermented wine, soap, fruits, and nuts. Perhaps the only thing more important than the palm tree is rice, the staple food, usually eaten every day. It is often hard for outsiders to grasp the centrality of rice to daily existence in Sierra Leone. Mende people, for example, have over 20 different words to describe rice in its variant forms, such as separate words for "sweet rice," "pounded rice," and "the rice that sticks to the bottom of a pot upon cooking."

HISTORY AND ETHNIC RELATIONS

Archaeological evidence suggests that people have occupied Sierra Leone for at least twenty-five hundred years, and early migrations, expeditions, and wars gave the country its diverse cultural and ethnic mosaic. Traders and missionaries, especially from the north, were instrumental in spreading knowledge of tools, education, and Islam. The emergence of a modern national identity, however, did not begin until the seventeenth and eighteenth centuries, when Bunce Island, off the coast of Freetown, became one of the centers of the West African slave trade. Over two thousand slaves per year were channeled through this port, thus increasing the incidence of warfare and violence among the local population. The slaves were especially valued off the coast of South Carolina on rice plantations, where it was discovered they had considerable agricultural expertise.

There are between fifteen and twenty ethnic groups in Sierra Leone, depending on one's linguistic tendency to "lump" or "split" groups of people speaking different dialects. Relations have been generally cordial among them, and Sierra Leone has largely avoided the racial tension characteristic of other parts of the world. In the recent conflict, for instance, one family may have children fighting for opposing sides, a fact which makes the violence difficult, as well as deeply and personally felt. When ethnic problems do arise, they often do so around the time of national elections, when politicians become accused of catering to the desires of one particular constituency (usually their own ethnic group) in order to gain votes.

the Mende, and so on. In addition, there are a number of people of Lebanese descent, whose ancestors fled Turkish persecution in Lebanon in the late nineteenth century. While each ethnic group speaks its own language, the majority of people speak either Mende, Temne, or Krio. The official language spoken in schools and government administration is English, a product of British colonial influence. It is not unusual for a child growing up to learn four different languages—that of their parent's ethnic group, a neighboring group, Krio, and English.

Symbolism. To some extent symbolic imagery is regionally based—people from the western area of-

Emergence of the Nation. When the slave trade began to be outlawed near the close of the eighteenth century, Sierra Leone became a resettlement site for freed slaves from England and the Americas, thus the name of the capital, "Freetown." English philanthropists, concerned about the welfare of unemployed blacks on the streets of London, pushed a "benevolent" movement to round them all up and take them back to Africa to settle, where they could begin life anew. Other migrants had been ex-slaves from America who had fought for the British during the Revolutionary War. The English loss had forced them to move to Canada, where they were not entirely welcome. Still others were ex-slaves who had revolted and were living freely in the mountains of Jamaica, until the British conquered the area and deported them to Nova Scotia, from where they emigrated en masse to Sierra Leone. Finally, from the time when the English officially outlawed the slave trade in 1807 up until the 1860s, the British navy policed the West African coast for trading ships, would intercept them, and release their human cargoes in Freetown, in what became a rapidly expanding settlement.

In 1808 Sierra Leone became a British crown colony, ruled under a colonial governor. The British administration favored a policy of "indirect rule" whereby they relied on slightly reorganized indigenous institutions to implement colonial policies and maintain order. Rulers who had been "kings" and "queens" became instead "paramount chiefs," some of them appointed by the administration, and then forced into a subordinate relationship. This allowed the crown to organize labor forces for timber cutting or mining, to grow cash crops for export, or to send work expeditions to plantations as far away as the Congo. Sierra Leoneans did not passively accept such manipulations. The 1898 "Hut Tax rebellion" occurred as a response to British attempts to impose an annual tax on all houses in the country. The Temne and Mende people especially refused to pay, attacking and looting trading stations, and killing policemen, missionaries, and all those suspected of assisting the colonial government.

Pressures to end colonialism had as much to do with Britain's weakened position following World War II as it did with the pan-African demands for autonomy. Sierra Leone became an independent, sovereign state on 27 April 1961 with Milton Margai as its prime minister. Ten years later, on 19 April 1971, the country became a republic, with an elected president as the head of state.

National Identity. National identity has been influenced by several factors. Besides the common experiences shared under colonialism or since independence, one of the most important has been the development of the regional lingua franca Krio, a language that unites all the different ethnic groups, especially in their trade and interaction with each other. Another has been the near universal membership, across ethnic lines, in men's and women's social organizations, especially *Poro* among the men, and *Bundu*, or *Sande*, among the women.

Ethnic Relations. There are between fifteen and twenty ethnic groups in Sierra Leone, depending on one's linguistic tendency to "lump" or "split" groups of people speaking different dialects. Relations have generally been good between them, and Sierra Leone has largely avoided the racial tension characteristic of other parts of the world. When problems do arise, they often originate at the time of national elections, with politicians being accused of catering to the desires of one particular constituency (usually their own ethnic group) in order to gain votes.

URBANISM, ARCHITECTURE, AND THE USE OF SPACE

Around the capital, Freetown, the architecture of the houses is somewhat unique. Often wood and clapboard in structure, they are noticeably influenced by Krio and colonial English styles. Also in Freetown, large buildings have become a source of national pride, especially the government State House and the national football stadium, which is a central gathering place for many large events.

Outside of Freetown, the "traditional" house in Sierra Leone is a clay and earth structure, built with a thatch roof. Construction can either be "wattle and daub" (wattle is the frame of a group of poles secured by the intertwining of twigs and vines; this frame is then "daubed" or plastered with soft earth to cover it), or clay and earth blocks, which are dried and hardened in the sun. These construction techniques have the advantage of allowing the house to stay relatively cool inside during the season of hot and dry months. Modern materials are now often incorporated into building techniques, especially zinc sheets for roofs and cement to cover floors and walls. While making the interior of the house considerably less cool during the heat, these materials do allow for more permanent structures needing less maintenance.

Houses are either round or rectangular, and typically offer a veranda, a central parlor, and two or three interior rooms. These may function as bedrooms or food storage areas, or both. More well-to-

A group of women belonging to a cooperative make garas, a traditional tie-dyed cloth.

do people may cluster a group of houses together into a "compound," sometimes walled off, to separate it from the rest of the village. Kitchens are often located outside the main house, and may be open structures supporting only a roof, as adequate ventilation is needed to maintain the cooking fire. During the sunny days, however, the kitchen is often wherever a woman moves her "three stones," the large rocks that support a pot, underneath which is built a stick fire. This same area during cool harmattan evenings then becomes a place where children gather to hear stories told from their elders. During the rainy season, however, it is not unusual to see a woman move her pots inside the parlor of the main house to get away from the damp.

Older towns and villages are "traditional" in that there are no gridlike "streets" per se, and the houses appear in irregular and sometimes densely packed clumps. More recently constructed areas that have sprung up since the expansion of trade and commerce tend to be organized along railroad lines or streets, and are thus more linear in their order. Depending on the size, almost any village will include shops or market areas, a centralized public court space, a church and/or mosque, a school, wells, and latrines. Near the outside of the village is typically a cemetery, and at either edge of town a carefully defined "Poro" or "Bundu" bush, one area

strictly off-limits for women, the other area off-limits for men.

FOOD AND ECONOMY

Food in Daily Life. For almost all Sierra Leoneans, rice is the staple food, consumed at virtually every meal. A Sierra Leonean will often say, without any exaggeration, "If I haven't eaten rice today, then I haven't eaten!" Other things are of course eaten—a wide variety of fruits, seafood, potatoes, cassava, etc.—but these are often considered to be just "snacks" and not "real food." Real food is rice, prepared numerous ways, and topped with a variety of sauces made from some combination of potato leaves, cassava leaves, hot peppers, peanuts, beans, okra, fish, beef, chicken, eggplant, onions, and tomatoes. Bones, particularly chicken bones, are a delicacy, because their brittle nature makes the sweet marrow inside easily accessible.

Along the street one can find snacks such as fresh mangoes, oranges, pineapple, or papaya, fried plantains, potato or cassava chunks with pepper sauce, small bags of popcorn or peanuts, bread, roasted corn, or skewers of grilled meat or shrimp. Local bars in some towns and villages will also sell poyo the sweet, lightly fermented palm wine tapped from the high tops of palm trees. Poyo bars can be areas of lively informal debate and conversation among men.

Sometimes villages, and sometimes families within villages, will have specific taboos or proscriptions against eating certain foods. These are usually attributed to a law handed down from someone's ancestor, perhaps the founder of the village. The taboo can be a restriction against certain kind of meat or a certain oil, or even against food prepared a certain way. Violation is usually seen as a risky proposition, and can incur the ill feelings of would-be guardians either living or dead.

Food Customs at Ceremonial Occasions. Almost all ceremonial occasions such as weddings, funerals, initiations, and memorial services demand the preparation of large platters of rice, distributed to guests until they are full. Depending on the occasion, a portion may also be offered to the ancestors, to honor their memory. Another common practice in this sense is to pour liquor in the ancestors' honor in the corners of a house. Other food traditions vary with region or religion: Mende Muslims, for instance, will mark a burial ceremony with *lehweh*, a ball of rice flour mixed with water and sugar, served with a kola nut on top.

Kola nuts are highly valued in and of themselves, and are often associated with greetings, diplomacy, provisions of respect, religious rites, and initiation ceremonies. High in caffeine concentration, they are also used as a stimulant, a clothing dye, and even in the preparation of medicines.

Basic Economy. Subsistence agriculture comprises the mainstay of the rural Sierra Leonean economy. Cash crops such as coffee, cocoa, peanuts, and tobacco are also important, as are small-scale marketing and commodity trade. Sierra Leone is rich in diamonds, bauxite, and gold, but the national economy receives little of the benefits that could come from the official export of these items, due to mismanagement, widespread smuggling, and corruption.

Land Tenure and Property. All the territory of an administrative chiefdom is technically held by the paramount chief. Underneath this authority, older families who can prove descent from a village founder then control the land close to their home. An elder male of the lineage usually administers land to those who request a plot to farm. This is most often to members of his extended family, but may include strangers who provide a gift of respect, and usually some portion of the ensuing harvest.

Commercial Activities. Sierra Leone's economy is largely informal, with small-scale marketing and trading of basic commodities, especially cloth, cigarettes, shoes, pots and pans, and mats. Women particularly dominate the market trade in foodstuffs.

Major Industries. Food processing (especially of flour, oil, rice, and fish) is one of the major industrial activities in Sierra Leone. Mining was for years the dominant industry, especially of rutile, bauxite, and diamonds. Also, because of Sierra Leone's beautiful beaches and "exotic" wildlife (hippos, chimpanzees, and monkeys), the tourist industry once thrived. Since the beginning of the 1991 conflict, however, official mining and tourism have stopped.

Trade. Besides the cash crops listed above, illegally smuggled diamonds have become a dominant item of trade. High in value only to foreign countries, they have played a major part in subsidizing the rebellion that has spread across Sierra Leone. International marketers who bought them came to recognize their own role in inadvertently funding the conflict, and publicly renounced any dealing in Sierra Leonean diamonds. Yet small and easily concealed, Sierra Leonean diamonds are now simply carried across national borders where they are sold to the same international marketers as "Liberian" or "Guinean" in origin.

Division of Labor. Like most big cities, Sierra Leone's urban areas offer a variety of occupational specialties, especially in small-scale trading, government, and industry. Downturns in the national economy, however, have made full-time salaried jobs extremely hard to procure, especially if one's family is not well connected. Village-level occupations are dominated by farming, but include traders, hunters, midwives, marketers, religious specialists, educators, policemen, and blacksmiths. Young men aged eighteen to twenty-nine are often attracted to mining jobs and the idea of "striking it rich," but the poor and exploitative conditions of the work often make their ventures short or seasonal, lasting between a few months and several years.

SOCIAL STRATIFICATION

Classes and Castes. Sierra Leonean society is in some ways a stratified one. The traditional elite families are those who can trace descent (usually through the father's line) to a warrior or hunter who first settled in the area. These families then control and administer land, a valuable asset in a

A thatched hut stands in a village on the south coast of Sierra Leone. Such traditional buildings stay cooler than those with zinc roofs and cement walls and floors but require more maintenance.

subsistence society, which puts them in an advantageous relationship to non-landholders. People who want to acquire the right to farm must show respect to an elder from this family (usually, but not always, a male), who may then grant them use of the land.

Colonial administrators in some ways exacerbated these differences between people, by favoring those elite families who supported their agenda with urban employment opportunities, political appointments, and education.

Symbols of Social Stratification. Some Sierra Leoneans will claim that one of the most persistent and negative impacts of colonialism was to pass along a taste for Western values and European goods, and the belief that anything African is relatively inferior. Thus one indicator of a high social status is the accumulation and display of Western accoutrements: Western clothing, English speech, satellite television, and Mercedes-Benz cars (or increasingly, sport-utility vehicles).

POLITICAL LIFE

Government. Under the terms of the constitution, executive power is vested in the president, who is directly elected by the people. The president appoints a cabinet of ministers, responsible for various government departments. There is also multiparty legislative power vested in an eighty-member Parliament, whose members are elected to five-year terms. Paramount chiefs serve in "District Councils," which in turn elect representatives to the legislature. Finally, there is a system of courts with a chief justice as head.

Leadership and Political Officials. Sierra Leone's political customs are often referred to as "patrimonial," in that elected officials become "patrons" to their voter base, the "clients." Clients expect patrons to share some of the benefits or entitlements of their office, and in return give them electoral support. This system became somewhat strained in the last thirty years of the twentieth century, as widespread political corruption drained many resources that would otherwise have been distributed. Yet in general, Sierra Leoneans respect almost any high-ranking official, regardless of political affiliation. Deference may be shown upon meeting with a slight bow, formal speech, and supporting the right arm with the left when shaking hands.

Social Problems and Control. In March 1991, an attack on a small southern village by a group of armed Sierra Leoneans, Liberians, and Burkinabes calling themselves the Revolutionary United Front (RUF) began what has become a nine-year civil conflict. Tens of thousands of people have lost their lives, and almost all of the population has at one time been displaced, either within or across national boundaries. Though initially supported by the National Patriotic Front of Liberia, the RUF later claimed its own populist political reform agenda to end corruption, reduce reliance on foreign aid, and usher in peace between all ethnic groups. Dramatic violence waged against innocent civilians, however, and the failure of government actions—including genuine political reforms and concessions granted to the RUF—to produce a consistent peace, has fueled popular skepticism about the legitimacy of RUF claims. Unlike conflicts in Europe or other parts of Africa, the Sierra Leone war has largely avoided ethnic divisiveness. Most analysts attribute the current violence to a mixture of war-inspired, socially marginalized youth fighting continued exclusion, and increased criminal control over the highly profitable, illicit diamond trade.

A problematic legacy of the war will certainly be the large number of guns and light weapons that have entered Sierra Leone since the breakup of the Soviet Union. Kalashnikov rifles, usually channeled into Sierra Leone by foreign arms merchants, can be bought for several dollars. Their widespread prevalence coupled with the intense poverty of the country is a virtual guarantee that extortion, highway banditry, and attacks on civilians will remain a dire social problem for years to come.

Military Activity. Sierra Leone's military is currently attempting reorganization. There are an estimated forty-five thousand total combatants that previously made up the different factions of the war—ex-Sierra Leone army soldiers, civilian militias, and RUF rebels. Few of these have followed up on agreements made to disarm and return to civilian life. Nigeria maintains some troop presence in the country, and a force of over ten thousand United Nations peacekeepers is currently in place, although their mandate has proven somewhat limited.

SOCIAL WELFARE AND CHANGE PROGRAMS

Steady economic decline coupled with rising international debt has severely limited Sierra Leone's ability to provide basic social welfare programs to its citizens. Smuggling, corruption, worldwide recession, and a large informal economy have all posed real problems to official attempts to remedy

Buyers and sellers at the Freetown open air market. Sierra Leone's economy is largely informal, and women dominate the food market.

the situation. Structural adjustment policies by the International Monetary Fund and the World Bank have often further exacerbated these problems by increasing the income disparity between people, and orienting the economy toward the repayment of loans rather than the subsidization of basic public services.

NONGOVERNMENTAL ORGANIZATIONS AND OTHER ASSOCIATIONS

The state's declining ability to meet basic health, education, and welfare needs has meant a corresponding increase in the number and activities of nongovernmental organizations (NGOs) in the country. There are a wide variety of local and international NGOs who compete for funding from international donors in order to implement projects in economic and infrastructural development, health and sanitation, agriculture, and education. Most of their programs are "vertical," so called because they are designed and funded by external agencies according to Western priorities. Since 1991, international relief agencies have become an even bigger presence, bringing aid to Sierra Leonean refugees and internally displaced people who have fled the violence surrounding their homes.

GENDER ROLES AND STATUSES

Division of Labor by Gender. Women are the backbone of Sierra Leonean labor. Men do the physically intense work of clearing fields and plowing swamps, but planting, harvesting, weeding, gathering wood, cooking, cleaning, marketing, and child care are duties often shouldered by women. Young children, especially girls, are encouraged to help their parents with minor household chores and farm work, and early in life take pride in their ability to contribute to the welfare of the household.

The Relative Status of Women and Men. The relative status of women is a bit paradoxical. On the surface, they seem to have low status—women technically live under the authority of the men they marry, have fewer legal rights, less formal education, and lower literacy rates. Yet in reality, women's relationship to men is more complementary than subordinate, due mostly to the considerable power and solidarity gained through the collective formed by the near universal membership in the women's Bundu or Sande societies.

Though some have pointed out that the women's societies stratify as much as they unify, others have noted how they provide substantial resources and skills that allow women to independently manage problems and control their lives. A society can, for example, autonomously determine laws that regulate proper social conduct and relations between genders, with codes as binding for men as they are for women. A girl's initiation gives her womanly status, allowing her to marry and bear children, activities which help her gain further prestige. A less tangible but important benefit is that society membership often enshrouds women with a certain mystique that confounds men, who become unable to explain the "womanly knowledge" and secrets over which the society presides.

MARRIAGE, FAMILY, AND KINSHIP

Marriage. For all Sierra Leoneans, marriage is a mark of adult maturity and brings considerable prestige to both bride and groom. Specific customs vary by ethnic group and socioeconomic status, but usually begin when a man is able to assemble enough brideprice (often a mixture of money and fine cloth) to give to the prospective bride and her family. He may be able to amass this himself, but often has to ask his father and his father's brothers for support. Almost all marriages used to be arranged between families, sometimes while the girl was still quite young. Increasingly, "love marriages" are more common, especially among those who have been to school.

Domestic Unit. The basic household structure is an extended family, organized for the majority of people around the farm and its rice production. Many households are polygynous, where a husband may have more than one wife; the first or "senior" wife usually has some authority over "junior" wives, such as in training and organizing them into a functional unit. Monogamy is also common, especially among urban and Christian families. Sierra Leoneans love children, and larger households tend to have more prestige. Having many children is in fact an investment of sorts, which, though initially expensive to maintain, eventually allows a family to accumulate wealth by creating a large and diverse labor pool, by gaining brideprice for its daughters, and by strategically marrying off children to create new alliances with other families.

Inheritance. Inheritance laws most often favor the male heirs. Upon the death of a male household head, rights of inheritance usually pass first to his eldest living brother. This is most often land and personal property, but may even include the deceased's wives, if they are willing, and any young children. If there are no living brothers, inheritance passes to the eldest adult son. There are exceptions to this, most notably among the coastal Sherbro women, who may be heads of households, village chiefs, or even lineage heads; it is not unusual in these circumstances for women to become trustees of land or property.

Kin Groups. Kinship networks are extremely important in everyday matters, in that one is obligated to assist one's family members throughout life. The majority of people are patrilineal, and so sons (and sometimes daughters) usually obtain rights to land through their father's side. Kin groups also play an important part in hearing legal cases and settling disputes before they are referred to a neutral third party. Thus, upon marriage, a man and a woman may each prefer to settle near their own kin, as this confers them distinct political and economic advantages. Though rights and responsibilities exist on both sides of one's family, maternal uncles are often particularly important figures, offering both obligations and entitlements to an individual.

A colonial period house in Freetown, Sierra Leone.

SOCIALIZATION

Infant Care. Mothers carry infants close to them at all times, strapped to their backs by a brightly colored cloth or *lappa*. Babies are breast-fed on demand, often for well over a year, although solid foods, usually rice pap, may be introduced at a young age. Both the extended family and the community share responsibility in rearing infants and children. It is not even unusual for a mother to "give" her child to a trusted friend or relative, though she of course would still play an active part in the child's life.

Child Rearing and Education. Providing they can afford school fees, most parents will try to send their children to at least several years of formal schooling. This is often Western-style education, although Arabic schools are an option in many areas. Outside the formal system, the men's and women's societies have historically provided important instruction for proper behavior—boys may learn the arts of proper male social conduct, including conflict mediation and forest survival; girls similarly learn crucial social, household, and childbearing skills to prepare them for womanhood. Traditionally this instruction could last more than a year; increasingly, however, pressures from school and urban environments have shortened this time to a month or less.

Higher Education. Many schools outside Freetown (both primary and secondary) have been closed since the beginning of the 1991 conflict. There has thus arisen some social concern over what the effects may be of a generation raised without access to formal education. This is one advantage recognized by refugees who have crossed over into Guinea and Liberia—relief agencies usually provide free schooling for refugee children and youth.

ETIQUETTE

Sierra Leoneans as a rule are extremely polite and manner-conscious. Much attention is given, especially in urban areas, to one's neatness of dress and style of presentation. Courteous and eloquent greetings are a way of life. Elders are especially respected. The "good" host is always a giving host, one who will call any passerby to join in a meal by a whole-hearted, "Come, let's eat." It is polite as a guest to leave some food on the plate, thanking the host profusely for his or her generosity.

Churchgoers outside a church in Freetown. About 10 percent of the population is Christian, but Christians sometimes continue to observe indigenous religious customs.

RELIGION

Religious Beliefs. Reports often list Sierra Leoneans as 60 percent Muslim, 10 percent Christian, and 30 percent "indigenous believers." These kinds of numbers often mask the degree to which religious beliefs in Sierra Leone may be flexible and accommodating. One can go to a Christian church on Sunday, for example, and still make a sacrifice to one's ancestors for good fortune. Likewise, Muslim rituals may appear to dominate in some areas, yet these can become mixed with indigenous ideas or customs.

Religious Practitioners. Besides Muslim and Christian holy leaders, there are a number of indigenous religious practitioners who are able to mediate with the spirit world. These include diviners, healers, men's and women's society elders, and witchcraft specialists.

Rituals and Holy Places. Churches, mosques, and society clearings in the forest or town occupy central positions in Sierra Leonean religious life and serve as focal points for organizing religious activities, especially toward God or ancestral spirits. Water is often considered especially important and many religious rituals take place near the edges of lakes, rivers, or streams.

Death and the Afterlife. Specific burial customs may vary by region or religion, yet practically all of them encompass a firm conviction in the existence of God and the spirit world, and especially in the abilities of one's deceased ancestors to intervene in the activities of everyday life. Sacrifices, ritual remembrances, and prayer are made in order enlist ancestors' support and good favor.

MEDICINE AND HEALTH CARE

The United Nations estimates that Sierra Leone has the highest death rate in the world, and the second highest infant morality rate (195 out of every 1,000 infants die within a year of birth). Life expectancy at birth in 1995 was only 34.1 years, down significantly from previously improving figures.

Even factoring in war-related violence, malaria is still the number one health threat. Schistosomiasis, bloody diarrhea, tetanus, measles, and polio are also endemic in some areas. Access to clean drinking water and adequate sanitation, especially in the rural countryside, is limited.

Medical facilities are extremely strained and are continuing to decline, especially since the 1991 conflict began. Yet even before this, the centrally organized national health service reached only an estimated 35 percent of the population, with less than 1 percent of annual government expenditures being allocated to health care. There are also an array of widely used indigenous practitioners, including midwives, broken-bone specialists, herbalists, society leaders, and Muslim-based ritual specialists.

SECULAR CELEBRATIONS

Outside of the major Muslim and Christian holidays, Sierra Leoneans also celebrate New Year's Day (1 January), National Independence Day (27 April), Labor Day (1 May), and National Day (9 August).

THE ARTS AND HUMANITIES

Support for the Arts. Government funding for the arts has been extremely limited and most artists are self-supported.

Literature. There are rich and lively traditions of storytelling across Sierra Leone. The most famous storytellers (sometimes endearingly called "liars") can manage to earn a living from their trade, though mostly these traditions are informal affairs, and start when children gather around an elder under the full moon once the evening chores are done. There are also critically acclaimed Sierra Leonean novels, such as *The Last Harmattan of Alusine Dunbar*, by Syl Cheney-Coker (Heinmann Books).

Graphic Arts. Among the graphic arts practiced in Sierra Leone are woodcarving, tie-dyeing, batik-printing, textile and fabric design, and basket making.

Performance Arts. A few famous Sierra Leonean musicians have gained widespread appeal both at home and abroad, such as "S. E. Rogers," "Calendar," "Dr. Oloh," and "Salliah." There is even a national dance troupe that travels around the world. To a large extent, however, participation in the arts is widely diffused and informal; dancing, painting, singing, storytelling, tie-dying, weaving, and drumming are widely practiced skills, the learning for which is often begun in childhood.

THE STATE OF THE PHYSICAL AND SOCIAL SCIENCES

Fourah Bay College (now the University of Sierra Leone) was the first university in West Africa, and was historically one of the centers for African scholars of law, medicine, and education. Its operation is currently severely strained, however, from inadequate funds, decaying infrastructure, and poorly paid professors. Several teachers' colleges around the country have similarly become either strained or closed, especially since the 1991 conflict.

BIBLIOGRAPHY

Abdullah, Ibrahim, and Patrick Muana. "The Revolutionary United Front of Sierra Leone: A Revolt of the Lumpenproletariat." In Christopher Claham, ed., *African Guerrillas*, 1998.

Abraham, Arthur. *Mende Government and Politics Under Colonial Rule: A Historical Study of Political Change in Sierra Leone, 1890–1937*, 1978.

Bangura, Yusuf. "Underdevelopment and the Politics of Sierra Leone's Trade Relations." *Africa Development* 9 (2): 71–91, 1984.

Blyden, Nemata. *West Indians in West Africa, 1808–1880: The African Diaspora in Reverse*, 2000.

Center for Health Information. *Sierra Leone: Health Statistics Report*, 1996.

Ferme, Mariane. "'Hammocks Belong to Men, Stools to Women': Constructing and Contesting Gender Domains in a Mende Village." Ph.D. dissertation, University of Chicago, 1992.

Fyfe, Christopher. *A Short History of Sierra Leone*, 1969 (1962).

Fyle, C. Magbaily. "Precolonial Commerce in Northeastern Sierra Leone." African Studies Center Working Paper No. 10, 1979.

Gittins, Anthony. *Mende Religion: Aspects of Belief and Thought in Sierra Leone*, 1987.

Gueye, M., and A. Bohannen. "African Initiatives and Resistance in West Africa, 1880–1914." In Adu Boahen, ed., *UNESCO General History Africa*, Vol. 7: *Africa Under Colonial Domination, 1880–1935*, 1985.

Jambai, Amara, and C. MacCormack. "Maternal Health, War, and Religious Tradition: Authoritative Knowledge in Pujehun District, Sierra Leone." In R. Davis-Floyd and C. Sargent, eds., *Childbirth across Cultures: The Social Production of Authoritative Knowledge*, 1996.

Joko Smart, H. M. "Recent Trends in Law Reform in Sierra Leone." *Journal of African Law* 31 (1/2): 136–150, 1987.

Kallon, Kelfala. *The Economics of Sierra Leonean Entrepreneurship*, 1990.

Kandeh, Borbor Sama. "Causes of Infant and Early Childhood Deaths in Sierra Leone." *Social Science and Medicine* 23 (3): 297–303, 1986.

Kandeh, Jimmy. "Politicization of Ethnic Identities in Sierra Leone." *African Studies Review* 35 (2): 81–99, 1992.

Kargbo, Thomas. "Traditional Midwifery in Sierra Leone." In Una Maclean, Christopher Fyfe, eds., *African Medicine in the Modern World*, 1987.

———. *Rainforest Relations: Gender and Resource Use among the Mende of Gola, Sierra Leone*, 1994.

Luke, David F., and Stephen Riley. "The Politics of Economic Decline in Sierra Leone." *Journal of Modern African Studies* 27 (1): 133–141, 1989.

MacCormack, Carol. "Mende and Sherbro Women in High Office." *Canadian Journal of African Studies* 6 (2): 151–164, 1972.

Margai, Sir Milton. "Welfare Work in a Secret Society." *African Affairs* 47: 227–230, 1948.

Reno, William. *Corruption and State Politics in Sierra Leone*, 1992.

———. *Fighting for the Rain Forest: War, Youth, and Resources in Sierra Leone*, 1996.

Richards, Paul, Ibrahim Abdullah, Joseph Amara, Patrick Muana, Teddy Stanley, and James Vincent. "Reintegration of War-Affected Youth and Ex-Combatants: A Study of the Social and Economic Opportunity Structure in Sierra Leone." Report prepared for the Sierra Leone Ministry of National Reconstruction, 1996.

United Nations. *World Development Report*, 1998.

United Nations Secretariat. *World Population Prospects: The 1998 Revision*, Vol. 1: Comprehensive Tables, 1998.

White, Frances. *Sierra Leone's Settler Women Traders: Women on the Afro-European Frontier*, 1987.

Zack-Williams, A. B. ''Sierra Leone: Crisis and Despair.'' *Review of African Political Economy* 49: 22–33, 1990.

—M. Douglas Henry

SINGAPORE

CULTURE NAME

Singaporean

ORIENTATION

Identification. The place name "Singapore" is derived from *Singa-pura* ("City of the Lion"), a commonly used term since the fourteenth century. The main cultural traditions are Malay, Indian, Chinese, and to some extent Western (British). The different communities do not regard themselves as sharing a culture; instead, they consider themselves parts of a whole. This is illustrated by reference to a popular local dish, *Rojak*, a salad in which the various ingredients are covered by the same peanut sauce, forming a distinct whole with each ingredient clearly discernible. The peanut sauce is Singaporeanness; the other ingredients are the different cultural traditions.

Location and Geography. Singapore lies at the tip of the Malay peninsula. It borders Malaysia, Indonesia, and Brunei. Its area is 248 square miles (642 square kilometers), including the main island and some sixty islets. The main island is flat with a hilly region in the middle. The highest point is Bukit Timah, feet (206 meters) above sea level. The climate is tropical with high humidity and abundant rainfall, especially during the northeast monsoon in December to March. The period of the southwest monsoon (June to September) is usually the driest.

The main island is fully urbanized with a dense commercial city center to the south. Around the city center are new townships that house about 86 percent of the population. The townships are self-contained and have high-rise apartment blocks, shops, medical and social service buildings, religious buildings, and schools; they are well connected by the Mass Rapid Transport System (MRT), which circles the island.

Demography. Singapore has a population of about three million, 2.7 million of whom are citizens and permanent residents. The other three hundred thousand are mainly foreign workers. The Chinese constitute about 78 percent, the Malays 14 percent, the Indians 7 percent, and others 1 percent of the population. The ethnic composition of the population has been relatively stable.

Linguistic Affiliation. Singapore is a multilingual state. The national language is Malay, and the four official languages are Malay, English, Indian (Tamil), and Chinese (Mandarin). English is the administrative language and the medium of instruction in schools. Pupils also choose one of the "mother tongues": Malay, Tamil, and Chinese. There are various subdialects of the different languages.

Symbolism. Economic prosperity and political stability are associated with the national culture, as is the Singaporean concept *kiasu*. Kiasu means "afraid to lose" and refers to the wish to come in first in lines, competitions, negotiations, and so forth. Some say kiasu keeps standards high, but others claim it leads to a graceless society.

The flag is divided into equal red and white horizontal sections symbolizing unity and purity. A white crescent moon and five stars in a circle symbolize a growing nation and the ideals of democracy, peace, progress, justice, and equality. The national anthem and national motto are in Malay. Other symbols draw on the distinct ethnic traditions. Chinese, Malays, and Indians draw on symbolic materials and ritual practices from their own traditions and for their own purposes.

HISTORY AND ETHNIC RELATIONS

Emergence of the Nation. Singapore emerged as a nation after 1965. For nearly one hundred fifty years it had been a British colony that was intimately linked to the whole Malay peninsula. Singa-

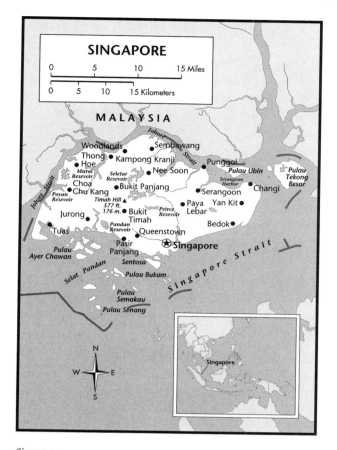

Singapore

pore came into being as a British trade port in 1819 and continued as one of the three British "Strait Settlements." In that period, Malays from nearby areas, large numbers of immigrants from China, and later Indian convict laborers moved into the island. The British did little to integrate the population, largely leaving each community to itself. Singapore gained independence in 1959 and joined the Union of Malaya in 1963 but was expelled in 1965. The next five years were marked by the "policy of survival." From 1945 until the early 1970s, the island had severe housing shortages and a poor infrastructure, high criminality and unemployment, racial riots, and communist uprisings. The "survival policy" was based on the attraction of foreign investment through low taxes, the development of an efficient infrastructure, a disciplined workforce, and strict political control. In thirty years Singapore changed from a rough trading port to a rich, orderly, industrialized society. The remembrance of social and economic difficulties influenced the development of a national culture with a focus on wealth and stability and the idea of multiculturalism.

National Identity. There is no single dominant national identity. Instead, there are complex identities that draw on a variety of sources and are relevant in different situations, although ethnic identity takes precedence in most situations.

Ethnic Relations. Cultural links to India, China, Malaysia, and Indonesia give Singaporeans orientations and loyalties that stretch far beyond the national borders. These differences are superseded by an identification with Singapore as a homeland with wealth and stability. Distance and distinction mark ethnic relations within the country.

URBANISM, ARCHITECTURE, AND THE USE OF SPACE

Singapore is a green city, but it has a very groomed greenness. There are two small national parks. Only at the fringes of the island and on the islets is there rural life, and it is disappearing fast. Highways crisscrossing the island, the huge port on the southern tip, vast industrial areas to the west, and the airport to the east create an air of swift efficiency.

The most striking features of the landscape are the high-rise buildings. This is a distinctly modern architecture with roots in the functionalism of the 1960s. In the 1980s and 1990s, there was more diversity in building styles. The typical domicile is a small apartment off the ground. Ethnicity is not an issue in the public use of space; communal differences are clearly discernible in the layout of the interiors of homes and certain town areas.

FOOD AND ECONOMY

Food in Daily Life. Rice, fish, chicken, and vegetables are the staples. When these ingredients are mixed with a rich variety of spices, chilis, coconuts, lime, and tamarind, the variations are endless. Food is often eaten outside the home in food centers where food is cheap, tasty, and freshly made. There are many cafés, coffeehouses and teahouses, and formal restaurants. Forks and spoons are used, but Chinese food is eaten with chopsticks, and Indian and Malay food may be eaten with the hand. The three main meals are breakfast, lunch, and dinner. Most meals are eaten hot. Malays do not eat pork, Indians do not eat beef, and many Buddhist Chinese are part-time vegetarians. Many people do not drink alcohol.

Food Customs at Ceremonial Occasions. Special dishes are eaten during the major ceremonial occasions of all three ethnic groups, but none are connected to national celebrations.

Basic Economy. Singapore has a fully developed industrial international economy. The country depends heavily on imports, as there are few natural resources on the island. There has been a consistent surplus in the overall balance of payments. There is a large degree of state control of the economy.

Land Tenure and Property. There is a large degree of private ownership of houses and apartments. Land tenure is firmly regulated by the government and there are government plans for the use of every inch of the island's territory. Foreigners usually are allowed only to lease land, but they may buy apartments.

Commercial Activities, Major Industries, and Trade. Manufacturing is the most important economic sector, followed by financial and business services, commerce, transportation, and communications. Production is mainly for export. The main exports are electronics, refined petroleum products, natural rubber, and palm oil. The main trading partners are Malaysia, the European Union (EU), the United States, Hong Kong, and Japan.

Division of Labor. About two-thirds of the resident population is employed. Only 0.2 percent of the members of the workforce are employed in the primary sector, and about 37 percent of employed persons work in commerce and finance and the business sector. Twenty-three percent work in manufacturing, 21 percent in other services, and 18 percent in transportation and communications and construction. The unemployment rate has long been below 3 percent but increased during the recent economic downturn. Chinese are overrepresented in professional, technical, administrative, and managerial jobs, whereas Malays are the most underrepresented in highly skilled jobs, with Indians in the middle. The substantial numbers of foreign workers are overrepresented in production and related work.

Shutters open out onto clotheslines in downtown colonial-style housing in Singapore.

SOCIAL STRATIFICATION

Classes and Castes. There are wide income and wealth differences, but the country is more differentiated by ethnicity than by class. All the ethnic groups have experienced upward occupational mobility. There is an intense focus on education. Good marks are a sure path to good positions with good wages. In this respect, Singapore is a meritocracy.

Symbols of Social Stratification. Singaporeans jokingly refer to their desire for the "five C's": car, condominium, credit card, club membership, and career. These are important symbols of wealth and status regardless of ethnicity. There is no national costume, but the orchid is used as a national symbol, and textiles with orchid patterns may be employed as a national symbol on formal occasions.

Boats and buildings in Inner Harbor. High-rises are a striking feature of Singapore's landscape.

POLITICAL LIFE

Government. Singapore is a republic with a parliamentary system. The head of state is the president, who is elected for a fixed term of six years. The parliament is elected in a general compulsory election every five years. There are also six nominated members of the parliament. The cabinet is the executive organ of the state, and execution of government policies is carried out by ministries and statutory boards.

Leadership and Political Officials. The People's Action Party (PAP) has maintained a large majority in the parliament since 1965, with only a few seats held by politicians from opposition parties. The road to a political position through the cadre system of the PAP lies in educational and professional merit as well as loyalty. The other parties are led by politicians with strong personalities.

Social Problems and Control. The crime rate is low. The judiciary system is based on the British legal system. The death penalty is imposed for drug smuggling, and caning is still used as a punishment. In addition, there are fines or other penalties for a wide range of transgressions, such as throwing litter on the floor, urinating in the elevator, and engaging in politics outside registered political parties.

Military Activity. Both military and civil defense are well developed, and the armed forces are equipped. Two and a half years of compulsory military service are required for males.

SOCIAL WELFARE AND CHANGE PROGRAMS

Social welfare is financed through the Central Provident Fund (CPF), a public savings scheme. Employees under age 55 and their employers contribute a fixed amount of a worker's salary into an individual account administered by the CPF. This account provides financial security for old age and can be drawn on for housing and medical and educational costs. Charity is an important aspect of the financing of social welfare. Care of the old, sick, and disabled is in the hands of families and relatives. Three different agencies provide some social services for members of the three ethnic groups. Independent social work units also carry out some social work.

NONGOVERNMENTAL ORGANIZATIONS AND OTHER ASSOCIATIONS

Many of the nearly five thousand registered societies are directly or indirectly linked to the government. Among the rest, very few can be defined as

Workers riding bicycles to Sembahong Shipyard, one of the two repair facilities in Singapore. Cars are a symbol of wealth and status.

nongovernmental organizations (NGOs) in a strict sense, but they form the basis of the civil society. A pattern of division according to ethnic distinction exists, but there are many nonethnic associations and societies.

GENDER ROLES AND STATUSES

Nearly 80 percent of men and about 50 percent of women are employed. Women have joined the workforce in large numbers but are underrepresented in leadership positions in all areas and institutions.

MARRIAGE, FAMILY, AND KINSHIP

Marriage. Polygamy is allowed among Muslim Malays, but otherwise monogamy is the rule. Interethnic marriages are not common. Divorce is becoming more common. The average age at first marriage has increased, and it is customary for young people to live with their parents until they marry.

Domestic Unit. The basic household unit is the nuclear family, which constituted 85 percent of res-

ident households in 1990. Close links with relatives on both the husband's and the wife's sides are usually maintained. The proportion of households without a family nucleus shrank from 26 percent in 1957 to 8 percent in 1980, reflecting the changes from an immigrant to a settled population. Males dominate as heads of households.

Inheritance. Traditionally, sons inherited family assets, while daughters were expected to marry out of the family. This pattern is less common today.

Kin Groups. Kin groups play a significant role in all ethnic groups, and people often move within wide networks of relatives. Privately, kin groups are important, but politically and economically, they play a marginal role.

SOCIALIZATION

Infant Care. Children are brought along in most situations except business and very formal events. Small children are showered with affection. Generally, children are expected to be quiet and obedient and may be physically punished for misbehaving. There is very little free space where children can play and few areas designed specially for children.

Child Rearing and Education. Children are thought to hold the key not only to their own future but also to the future of their families, and education is regarded as extremely important. There is a range of private and public nurseries, kindergartens, and play schools. Children start school at age six.

Higher Education. There is a great emphasis on higher education. Children spend six years in primary school and four years in secondary school and then go on to a vocational school or university, depending on their grades (a sure way to higher education in Singapore) or money (a university education abroad). Competition for entrance to the best schools is fierce.

ETIQUETTE

Older people ideally are treated with respect, but wealth and status may supersede age distinctions. A social superior or an authority is treated with much formality. There are great differences between formal and informal events, situations, and places. In social interaction, a certain physical distance is kept, especially between men and women. Food rules of the ethnic groups are always respected.

RELIGION

Religious Beliefs. There is freedom of religion with some exceptions. Singapore has been described as one of the most religious countries in the world. The major religions are Islam (Malay), Hinduism (Indians), Buddhism, Taoism, and folk religion (Chinese), along with a substantial number of Christians of various denominations.

Religious Practitioners. Religious experts vary from formally installed priests and teachers representing the institutionalized religions to self-ordained shamans, healers, and sorcerers.

Rituals and Holy Places. The many Chinese and Indian temples, Malay mosques, and Christian churches are the main public arenas for religious activities. Much religious activity is also carried out in the home. There are different "street festivals" according to the ritual calendars of the different ethnic groups

Death and the Afterlife. A funeral is a major ritual for all ethnic group. The idea of an afterlife is generally shared.

MEDICINE AND HEALTH CARE

A well-developed modern medical system consists of private and public clinics and hospitals. Traditional medical beliefs and practices are also common.

SECULAR CELEBRATIONS

The national holiday is on 31 August and is celebrated with military parades and culture shows at the national stadium. The ethnic public holidays are divided nearly equally among Chinese, Malay, Indian, and Christian holidays. The most important ethnic holidays are the Chinese New Year and the Malay Muslim Rahmadan, both celebrated in January–February, and the Indian Deepavali or Festival of the Light, celebrated around September–October.

THE ARTS AND HUMANITIES

Literature, Graphic Arts, and Performance Arts. A common complaint is that Singapore has no culture, and the fine arts have a limited public. The government subsidizes some art institutions and events, but generally there is little public funding. The different ethnic groups have their own artistic traditions and focus on arts. The contemporary generation is more focused on contemporary art forms.

THE STATE OF THE PHYSICAL AND SOCIAL SCIENCES

Singapore has well-developed scientific institutions. Priority is given to technology and applied science. There are two universities: the National University of Singapore, a full-scale university with all disciplines, and the Nanyang Technical University.

BIBLIOGRAPHY

Bloodworth, Dennis. *The Tiger and the Trojan Horse*, 1986.

Brazil, David. *Street Smart Singapore*, 1991.

Census of Population, Monograph No. 5. Singapore, 1990.

Cheng, Lim Keak. *Geographical Analysis of the Singapore Population*, 1995.

Chua, Beng Huat. *Political Legitimacy and Housing. Stakeholding in Singapore*, 1997.

Clammer, John. *The Sociology of Singapore Religion: Studies in Christianity and Chinese Culture*, 1991.

Craig, JoAnn. *Culture Shock: Singapore and Malaysia*, 1979.

Drysdale, John. *Singapore: Struggle for Success*, 1984.

Hill, Michael, and Kwee Fee Lian. *The Politics of Nation Building and Citizenship in Singapore*, 1995.

Ho, Kong Chong, and Chua Beng Huat. *Cultural, Social and Leisure Activities in Singapore*, 1995.

Huff, W. G. *The Economic Growth of Singapore: Trade and Development in the Twentieth Century*, 1994.

Kuo, Eddie C. Y., and Tong Chee Kiong. *Religion in Singapore*, 1995.

Lai, Ah Eng. *Meanings of Multiethnicity: A Case-Study of Ethnicity and Ethnic Relations in Singapore*, 2nd ed., 1995.

Lee, Edwin. "Community, Family and Household." In Chew C. T. Ernest and Edwin Lee, eds., *A History of Singapore*, 2nd ed., 1996.

Lim, Catherine. *Little Ironies: Stories of Singapore*, 1978.

Pugalenthi Sr. *Elections in Singapore*, 1996.

Tamney, Joseph B. *The Struggle over Singapore's Soul: Western Modernization and Asian Culture*, 1995.

Toh, Mun Heng, and Tay Boon Nga. *Households and Housing in Singapore*, 1995.

Turnbull, C. M. *A History of Singapore, 1819–1988*, 1989.

Yeoh, B. S. A., and L. Kong, eds. *Portraits of Places. History, Community and Identity in Singapore*, 1995.

—BENEDICTE BRØGGER

SLOVAKIA

CULTURE NAME

Slovak

ORIENTATION

Identification. "Slovak" is derived from the Slovakian term for Slav: *Slovan*. There are three main regional culture areas: western, central, and eastern. *Slovensko* is the shortened local name for Slovakia, or the Slovak Republic. Slovaks share a common culture despite regional and even local differences in dialect, local customs, and religion. Hungarians (Magyars) in Slovakia are generally bilingual and have been acculturated but wish to maintain their national culture, especially their language.

Location and Geography. Slovakia (the Slovak Republic) is a landlocked country with ports on the Danube River at Bratislava and Komarno; it is bordered by the Czech Republic, Poland, Ukraine, Hungary, and Austria. Slovakia has a total area of 18,928 square miles (49,035 square kilometers). Its range of elevation runs from a low of 308 feet (94 meters) at the Bodrok River to a high of 8,711 feet (2,655 meters) at Gerlachovsky peak in the High Tatras. Slovakia's topography is extremely varied for such a small total area. Physiographic provinces range from the High Tatras in the north to the rich agricultural lands of the plains and the Danube Basin to the south. Other components of the Carpathian Mountains are the Little Carpathians and White Carpathians of western Slovakia and the Low Tatras and Slovak Ore Mountains in the north-central area. Bratislava, the capital, is a city of 441,453 population on the Danube in southwestern Slovakia. It appears on older maps as Pressburg and was once the Hungarian capital.

Demography. The July 1999 population estimate was 5,396,193, approximately 85.7 percent of which is ethnically Slovak. Hungarians are the largest cultural minority at 10.7 percent (nearly six

hundred thousand) and are concentrated in the southern lowlands near the Hungarian border. Rom or Roma (Gypsies) account for 1.5 percent and probably are underreported in census figures, although there has been a substantial migration to Austria, the Czech Republic, and other nations since 1989. Rom occasionally self-identify as Hungarian in census records. Other groups include Czechs, 1.4 percent; Ruthenians (Rusyns), 0.3 percent; Ukrainians, 0.3 percent; Germans, 0.1 percent; and Poles, 0.1 percent. Rusyns are eastern Slavs who live in Slovakia, Ukraine, and Poland. The population growth rate is estimated to be 0.08 percent (1998), with an age structure of 0-14 years, 21 percent; 15-64 years, 68 percent; and 65 and over, 11 percent.

Linguistic Affiliation. Slovak, the national language, uses the Roman alphabet. Along with Czech and Polish, it is classified as a western Slavic tongue in the Indo-European language family. Slovak is very closely related to Czech. Political circumstances beginning nearly a thousand years ago separated populations, but Slovak and Czech are still mutually intelligible. There are three main dialects of Slovak, corresponding to the western, central, and eastern regions. It is said that the pronunciation of particular sounds in the western region is hard, while the dialect of central Slovakia is said to be softer sounding and was adopted historically as the norm. In all but parts of eastern Slovakia, the stress is on the first syllable of a word; longer words (three or more syllables) have secondary accents. There are Slovak words that appear to be formed entirely or mostly of consonants, such as the term for death: *smrt'*.

Slovak was designated the official language by the Slovak State Language Law of 1 January 1996. This measure curtailed the use of minority languages in the public sphere and mostly affected the Hungarian minority. The language law has now been revised and is less restrictive. Many Slovaks

Slovakia

and most non-Slovaks know a second language. Besides Magyar (spoken by Hungarians) and Rusyn (spoken by Rusyns in eastern Slovakia), German, English, Russian, French, and Czech are used.

Symbolism. Slovakia's national flag consists of three equal horizontal bands of color, from top to bottom white, blue, and red. Superimposed over the bands on the left (hoist) side is a shield displaying the national emblem: a double apostolic cross in white sits atop the middle peak of three blue mountaintops, all on a red background. The emblem predates the national flag by centuries (elements of the emblem were used in the Great Moravian Empire) and appears in many contexts both in Slovakia and abroad among people of Slovak descent. The national flag became official on 1 January 1993, Independence Day. The national anthem, *Nad Tatrou Sa Blýska*, translates as ''Lightning over the Tatras.'' The lyrics refer to stormy times and the belief that Slovaks survive them, while their oppressors and opponents lose. In the former Czechoslovakia, the Slovak anthem was played after the Czech anthem. Folk culture has had a broad impact on the symbols and metaphors of national culture.

For example, the *fujara*, or shepherd's flute, a bassoonlike tube of wood over a meter long, and the *valaška*, or shepherd's ax, are markers of Slovak culture, along with folk costumes and designs.

HISTORY AND ETHNIC RELATIONS

Emergence of the Nation. Slovaks trace their origins to the Slavic peoples who migrated from the European-Asian frontier to the area between the Danube and the Carpathians in the fifth and sixth centuries C.E. As increasingly sophisticated agricultural peoples, those Slavs established permanent communities in the Morava, Ipel', Torysa, Vah, and Nitra river valleys. This region of early western Slavic occupation, especially east of the Morava River, correlates almost exactly with the historical and contemporary geographic distribution of Slovaks. The settlement of Nitra became an early focus of political importance and the home of western Slavic rulers, such as King Svätopluk (870–894 C.E.). The first Christian church in east-central Europe was established at Nitra, and in the ninth century, the Great Moravian Empire reached its greatest development, occupying all the land currently within Slovakia. The empire's estimated one million inhabitants included all the western Slavs (peoples who became the Czechs, Moravians, Slovaks, and Poles).

After the invasion of nomadic Hungarian peoples in the tenth century, the peoples who became the Slovaks were isolated from other western Slavic groups as a result of the conquest of the Great Moravian Empire after the Battle of Bratislava in 907. Hungarian rule over Slovaks lasted a thousand years until the end of World War I and the breakup of the Austro–Hungarian Empire. Halfway into that millennium, the Turks invaded this region.

The emergence of Slovak national consciousness is fairly recent, dating to about the 1700s, and has been punctuated by nationalistic movements, especially as the originally multiethnic Hungarian state attempted to transform itself into an ethnic Magyar state through programs of assimilation. Written Slovak appeared before the eighteenth century in literary texts, and near the end of that century a national movement began to delineate Slovak ethnic identity, especially in the work of Anton Bernolák, who codified written Slovak based on the western Slovak dialect. In the nineteenth century, this process continued with Ján Kollár and Pavol Šafárik, who developed a written form of Slovak that combined the western and central dialects. L'udovit Štùr finally codified written Slovak by 1844, basing it on the central dialect. Štùr also encouraged the development of Slovak romanticism, with its focus on patriotism and nationalism and identification with popular and folk traditions. The formation of the Austro–Hungarian state in 1867 led to increased efforts to assimilate the Slovaks under Magyarization. *Matica Slovenská*, the Slovak cultural organization known in English as the Slovak Institute of Sciences and Arts, founded in 1863, was suppressed by 1875. Slovak secondary schools were closed. Compulsory language training in Hungarian was forced on Slovak children, and Hungarian became the official language. As the state grew more alien to Slovaks, they responded with increased tenacity in retaining their language and customs and emphasizing their ethnic identity through literature, music, and folk traditions. At the end of World War I, Slovak identity was fully formed, and in 1919 Slovakia joined with Czechia to form union of two western Slavic nations: Czecho-Slovakia. Slovakia became an independent nation on 1 January 1993.

National Identity. Slovak national culture and identity crystallized between about 1700 and World War I, in part as a reaction to centuries of attempted assimilation by other peoples, primarily Hungarians. Slovaks who emigrated to the United States in the last quarter of the nineteenth and the first quarter of the twentieth centuries promoted elements of national identity abroad.

Ethnic Relations. Slovaks have experienced adversarial relationships with four major ethnic groups as a consequence of wars, conquests, and political configurations: Hungarians, Czechs, Germans, and Russians. Nomadic Hungarian peoples conquered the ancestors of the Slovaks in 907 C.E. and retained control over them until the end of World War I. While closely related to Czechs culturally, Slovaks generally felt marginalized in the various permutations of the unified or federated Czecho–Slovakia and Czechoslovakia from 1919 to the end of 1992. This nonviolent ethnic conflict, sometimes called the "Slovak Question," ended in the recent "Velvet Divorce."

During the regime of Jozef Tito and the formation of a pro–Nazi state between 1939 and the end of World War II, Czech domination was replaced by German control. After 1948, Russian influence appeared with the re-creation of the Czechoslovak state and the establishment of the Warsaw Pact. Russian military personnel and Soviet armaments and aircraft were stationed in Slovakia after the 1968 Soviet–led invasion of Czechoslovakia by Warsaw Pact troops, during which the Prague Spring movement, led by Prime Minister Alexander Dubček (a Slovak), was crushed.

Currently, the most significant ethnic conflicts are with Hungarians and Rom. The large Hungarian minority concentrated in the lowlands of southern Slovakia has been more vocal and politically unified since 1989. In 1996, when the Slovak State Language Law took effect, Hungarian communities were further galvanized against the nationalistic government of Prime Minister Vladimir Mečiar. This led Hungarian political parties to join with the Slovak opposition to gain the majority in the fall 1998 parliamentary elections. Meanwhile, the Slovak and Hungarian governments have been at odds over the partially completed Gabčikovo-Nagmoros dam project on the Danube, a dispute that went to the World Court. Hungarians have long protested the project, mostly on the grounds that it poses a flood threat to Budapest and other Hungarian communities.

Rom have been physically attacked and even killed by ethnic Slovak skinheads in the past few years. While skinhead groups are relatively rare, racist attitudes toward the Rom persist among many Slovaks.

URBANISM, ARCHITECTURE, AND THE USE OF SPACE

The Slovak settlement pattern includes hamlets or colonies, villages, towns, and cities. They are distinguished by population size (with hamlets differing in both size and composition). Cities typically have populations over ten thousand, towns have between four thousand and about ten thousand people, villages have a few hundred to three thousand people, and hamlets or colonies have a few households with perhaps several dozen related people. Hamlets are rapidly depopulating in some areas, and many have ceased to exist; empty houses in others are being purchased by city dwellers for use as vacation homes.

Historically, ethnic Slovak dwellings consisted of one room where all activities took place: sleeping, food preparation and eating, and social and economic tasks. Over time, an additional room was added primarily for sleeping and entertaining. Furniture for sitting (long, narrow benches in older-style kitchens) and sleeping is placed along the walls, while tables for entertaining or providing work surfaces are moved near the benches in kitchens or remain in the center of the second room–bedroom. Family photographs and hand-painted ceramics adorn the walls of most rooms. Two-room houses of the older type can still be found in hamlets and villages. Occasionally rooms were added to accommodate newly married sons. Since the 1950s, most dwellings have indoor plumbing, although outdoor privies can still be found even in homes with running water and flush toilets. Structures for housing livestock frequently are attached to dwellings but are separated by walls and have their own entrances. Other outbuildings may include a rabbit hutch, a barn, and a separate structure where a hog is kept and fattened. Traditional Slovak homes had a fence with a gate leading into the yard as the only entrance visible from the street. The house usually was situated lengthwise on the property, with the door opening onto the little courtyard, not the street (there was little frontage.) The street side usually featured a flower garden, and a vegetable garden was located in back of the courtyard. In towns and cities, dwellings became more diverse over time. Some cities now exhibit suburban sprawl with high-rise apartment building away from the old town centers. Some towns and cities have incorporated nearby villages, and so within the same urban center one can see modern hotels and restaurants in one sector and decades-old peasant cottages in another. Vegetable gardens continue to be popular even in towns as a source of fresh produce.

Non-Slovak influence in the architecture of towns and cities is widespread. In eastern Slovakia, there are Gothic buildings in Spiš and Levoča, while Renaissance structures can be seen in Šariš. Baroque and rococo buildings can be found in Bratislava. There are castles and strongholds from before the Crusades. Elements of Slovak folk architecture include the wooden churches and wooden and log dwellings of northern and eastern Slovakia, along with the plastered-over mud-brick homes of western and central Slovakia. There are central places and parks in towns and cities with benches, and virtually all communities except for hamlets have soccer fields. Most monuments commemorate wars, battles, and military, political, and cultural heroes. The most noteworthy Slovak monument is Bradlo, the massive hilltop tribute to General Milan Rastislav Štefánik (1880–1919) near Košariská in western Slovakia. Stefanik, a hero of World War I, is a national icon, and his monument is the site of pilgrimages. The second most popular type of monument commemorates the Slovak National Uprising of 1944 against Germany in World War II.

FOOD AND ECONOMY

Food in Daily Life. Slovak food exhibits much regional variation, but generally is based on soups, stewed and boiled vegetables, stewed fruits, smoked meats (especially sausages), roasted meats, gruels, and dairy dishes. Sheep cheese with small dumplings, *bryndzové halušky*, is among the most typical Slovak dishes. Traditionally in peasant households, five meals would be taken: early in the morning upon rising (*raňajky*), a snack at about ten A.M. (*desiata*), the main meal of the day at noon (*obed*), another snack around four P.M. (*olovrant*), and supper in the evening after chores (*večera*). Tea with sugar is the most popular hot beverage. Bread is served with every meal, and hot soup is a fixture as the first course at the main noon meal, with meat dishes commonly served at that time as well. The evening meal is usually light and may include bread, cheese, and vegetables. Beer, wine, juices, and carbonated water or flavored sodas are served with most meals. The main distilled beverage is plum brandy (*slivovica*), and *borovička*(gin) is quite popular.

Food Customs at Ceremonial Occasions. Special foods are prepared for a number of religious holi-

Religious sculptures stand on the side altar of the Church of Saint Egidius in Bardejov, Slovakia. Approximately three-quarters of the population is Christian.

days. On Christmas Eve, the meal is meatless and usually begins with a blessed wafer that is drizzled with honey. An alcoholic beverage based on honey called *medové* also is prepared for this occasion. A vegetable-based based soup is served first, followed by small baked pieces of dough that are moistened in milk and coated with a sweetened poppyseed mixture. On Christmas and other occasions for feasting, a roasted goose may be served, along with sausage (*klobása*). Fresh sausages (*jaternica*, for example) made from barley, pork meat, blood, and

rice also appear on special occasions. There is toasting with alcoholic beverages and a dessert of small cakes made with fruit or cheese fillings or log-shaped strudels with nut or poppyseed fillings. Salads tend to be made from sliced cucumbers prepared with a clear sweet and sour dressing or sour cream.

Basic Economy. Slovakia is an industrialized nation with a growing service sector. The economy was privatized amid accusations of racketeering in the 1990s. Many former collective farms have been transformed into agricultural cooperatives, with varying degrees of success. Earlier in the 1990s, some cooperatives were cash-poor and had to pay their workers with produce or livestock. The agricultural sector accounts for about 5 percent of the gross domestic product (GDP), industry contributes nearly 40 percent, and services account for around 55 percent. The labor force exceeds 2,300,000 and is divided (approximate percentages in 1994) as follows: services, 45.6 percent; industry, 29.3 percent; agriculture, 8.9 percent; transportation and communications, 8.2 percent; and construction, 8 percent. The unemployment rate, which was negligible before 1989 because of the structure of the command economy, has increased throughout the 1990s and is now nearly 20 percent (19.07 percent in June 2000). Unemployment is particularly high in areas that formerly produced armaments. Inflation was about 6 percent in 1997, and prices have been increasing for many goods and services.

Land Tenure and Property. Land, homes, and privatized businesses and factories can be owned by individuals, bought and sold, and passed on to heirs. Much agricultural land is owned and operated by members of cooperatives. Many Slovaks in rural areas retain ownership and exclusive use over plots of land that are used to generate food for family consumption or provide pasturage for livestock.

Commercial Activities. Agricultural production includes grains (rye, wheat, corn, barley), silage (clover), potatoes, sugar beets, hops, fruit, hogs, cattle, poultry, and wood products. There is growing travel and tourist industry, with hotels, restaurants, spas, car rental firms, and ski resorts. Privately owned retail stores now include some foreign investment.

Major Industries. Slovakia produces metal and metal products, fossil fuels (oil, gas, coke), chemicals, synthetic fibers, machinery, paper, ceramics, transportation vehicles, rubber products, optical and electrical apparatus, food and beverages, electricity, and nuclear fuel.

Trade. Slovakia's exports to major trading partners are as follows: Germany, 20.9 percent; Austria, 6 percent; other European Union countries, 14.4 percent; the Czech Republic, 30.6 percent; and countries of the former Soviet Union, 7.1 percent (1996). Exports totaled nearly $9 billion in 1996 and included machinery and transport equipment, chemicals, raw materials, and manufactured goods. Slovakia imports more than it exports. In 1996, it took in about $11 billion of imports in machinery and transport equipment, fuels, intermediate manufactured goods, and miscellaneous manufactured goods. Slovakia imports primarily from Germany, 14.7 percent; Italy, 6 percent; the Czech Republic, 24.8 percent; and countries of the former Soviet Union, 17.7 percent (1996 figures).

SOCIAL STRATIFICATION

Classes and Castes. Slovakia is characterized by socioeconomic classes, with the divisions falling along educational and occupational lines. However, income is not always an accurate indicator of class because some professions requiring advanced study have depressed pay scales.

Symbols of Social Stratification. Higher socioeconomic standing is marked by automobile ownership, stylish clothing, the size of a home or apartment, a home's furnishings and location, and even speech. People in lower socioeconomic groups take public transportation and are more likely to use regional dialects. A relatively small percentage of the population experienced great gains in wealth in the 1990s. An undocumented percentage of Slovaks receive financial help from relatives working in the West.

POLITICAL LIFE

Government. Slovakia is a parliamentary democracy with legislative, judicial, and executive branches. The legislative branch consists of a single-chamber parliament that meets in Bratislava, has one hundred fifty elected members, and is called the National Council of the Slovak Republic (*NR SR*). Members of parliament are elected for four-year terms through universal suffrage; the voting age is 18. The judicial system is represented by the Supreme Court (with judges elected by the parliament) and the Constitutional Court. Executive power is held by the prime minister and other ministers. After the general elections of 1998, Slovakia planned for the direct popular election of its president (the post was vacant after March 1998, when Michal Kovač, Slovakia's first president, left office).

Leadership and Political Officials. After the Velvet Revolution of 1989 in Czechoslovakia that ended communist rule, politicians who promoted national interests became popular in many areas of Slovakia. A charismatic leader named Vladimir Mečiar headed the Movement for a Democratic Slovakia and became prime minister. However, Slo-

Bratislava Castle, a former palace, on a hilltop overlooking Slovakia's capital city, which is situated on the shores of the Danube River.

vaks have become disenchanted with politicians as concerns over economic problems have grown. Many Slovaks blamed politicians for the Velvet Divorce that divided Czechoslovakia into two nations at the end of 1992. The 25–26 September 1998 Slovak elections produced a new governing coalition composed of former opposition parties, and Meciar was replaced by Mikulaš Dzurinda, chair of the Slovak Democratic Coalition (SDK). The agenda of the Dzurinda government includes the direct election of a president, membership in NATO, and admission to the European Union. In 1999, Rudolf Schuster (the chair of SOP, the Party of Civic Understanding) became the first directly elected Slovak president.

Current major political parties and movements include the Movement for a Democratic Slovakia (HZDS), Slovak Democratic Coalition (SDK), Slovak Workers' Association (ZRS), Christian Democratic Party (KDH), Democratic Union (DS), Slovak National Party (SNS), and Party of the Hungarian Coalition (SMK). In June 1998, there were upwards of twenty political parties and/or movements. On the local level, candidates for local office (mayor, vice mayor) are typically lifelong residents of their communities and are elected by popular vote.

Social Problems and Control. Slovak civil law is based on the former Austro-Hungarian codes of law, and its system has been modified to comply with the Organization on Security and Cooperation in Europe (OSCE). Property crimes became more common after 1989, and while most are committed by Slovaks, a steady influx of foreigners from Russia and other former Soviet bloc countries has contributed to the problem. Car theft, theft of merchandise, and burglary are much more common than they were before 1989. Pickpockets are active in urban areas and on buses and trains, assaults are more common, and there have been car bombings and political assassinations. Organized gangs of criminals have become powerful in some areas, and skinheads have committed assaults and other atrocities against Rom. Slovak law enforcement is understaffed. Informal social control is more likely to take place in villages where there is no resident police force and law enforcement must be called in from another town.

Military Activity. Before 1989, Slovakia was a major manufacturer of military equipment and a major arms-trading partner with the Soviet Union. That industry has been curtailed. The Czechs and Slovaks divided up military equipment when they split, with Slovakia receiving the smaller share.

There is a military draft for males when they reach age 18; in 1998, it was estimated that total military manpower stood at 1,125,200. Military expenditures in 1998 totaled $436 million (U.S.), which represented 2.1 percent of GDP. The military branches are the army, the air and air defense forces, and the reserve force (home guards).

NONGOVERNMENTAL ORGANIZATIONS AND OTHER ASSOCIATIONS

Nongovernmental organizations (NGOs) have proliferated since 1989 and number in the thousands. Slovak organizations and associations include trade unions, environmental and/or conservation groups, associations of artists and performers, folklore ensembles, political lobbying groups, and religious organizations. Examples are the Party of Entrepreneurs and Businessmen of Slovakia, the Christian Social Union, the Metal Workers Union (KOVO and METALURG), and the Confederation of Trade Unions (KOZ). There are also Slovak chapters of international organizations, including environmental groups such as the Greens.

GENDER ROLES AND STATUSES

Division of Labor by Gender. Until the second half of the twentieth century, political, medical (excluding nursing), religious, construction, architectural, engineering, managerial, and administrative roles were almost always restricted to men. Women could enter teaching, clerical positions, nursing, sales, and factory jobs. Change came about slowly, and today women are seen in most professions; there are female physicians, politicians, professors, managers, pastors, and administrators. However, in the household, women still are expected to perform child care and basic maintenance.

The Relative Status of Women and Men. Slovak men retain a privileged position in the home and the outside world. While women have been entering occupations traditionally held by men and more women are acquiring education beyond the secondary level and opting to remain unmarried longer, they still experience difficulties in certain areas, especially business and politics above the local level. Wealth remains largely in the hands of men.

MARRIAGE, FAMILY, AND KINSHIP

Marriage. Slovaks practice monogamy, and individuals have free choice in the selection of marriage partners, though marrying within one's religion is

Men cutting grass in Ladomirova. Much agricultural land is owned and operated by cooperatives.

expected in many areas. In rural sectors, it was once expected that everyone would marry except individuals who were disabled. In modern Slovakia, people have other options, including remaining single and living with a partner. The majority of Slovaks marry and enjoy some economic benefit, especially if they have children. Parents still receive, in many instances, a cash bonus when a child is born and mothers are given ample maternity leave. Divorce has become common since the 1980s, along with remarriage. Gay and lesbian partnerships remain mostly closeted, and same-sex marriages are not legal.

Domestic Unit. The basic household unit has increasingly become the nuclear family. Traditional households, especially in rural areas, consisted of extended families that were three generations deep. Grandparents, particularly grandmothers, cared for the offspring of married sons or daughters. Slovaks were at one time more likely to live with the groom's family. Men retain authority in the household, though women informally negotiate decision making and exert considerable influence. Today both spouses are likely to work outside the home.

Inheritance. The children of a couple inherit property equally. In the past, a dowry system operated among the peasantry, and daughters who wanted to accumulate a dowry might sell their future share of property to their brothers for cash. As a result of land reallocations in the past, partible inheritance practices among landowners resulted in plots of dwindling size in only a few generations. The resulting ribbonlike strips of land could seldom support a family. Today, the grown children of deceased parents feud over shares in houses and property. If one of them already occupies the house, he or she may have to sell it to satisfy the claims of siblings.

Kin Groups. Rural-urban migration has resulted in a dispersing of kin, as has emigration to the West. Young people no longer expect to remain in the hamlets, villages, or towns of their birth but seek to move to cities. Today there are no kin groups larger than the extended family. Slovaks have bilateral kinship and trace descent through both parents.

SOCIALIZATION

Infant Care. Slovaks place infants in cribs to sleep in the parents' bedroom. Babies play in little pens or in safely confined areas on a blanket on the floor. They are wheeled around outside in strollers but are picked up and carried in the home. Very active or crying babies are entertained and/or pacified with a variety of toys and teething objects.

Child Rearing and Education. Children are supposed to behave like miniature adults. They are expected to be quiet, attentive, and respectful and to keep their clothing clean. Parents and other caregivers attempt to set parameters of behavior and then assess sanctions when rules are broken. Corporal punishment is still common, although less violent methods are increasingly employed. Families try to instill a serious work ethic in children and may assign them substantive chores as early as age seven. In rural areas, once it was common for elementary school-age children to take geese and other small livestock to pasture. There is compulsory formal education for children through the tenth grade.

Higher Education. Slovaks value postsecondary education, and many parents encourage their children to prepare for it by attending academic high schools. However, there appear to be many more students eligible to attend universities than there are places for them.

ETIQUETTE

Slovaks maintain a typically Western distance (about three feet) when conversing. Greetings are expected, and consist of "good morning," "good day," and "good evening." "Good night" is reserved for the last leave taking of the evening. Both men and women shake right hands with acquaintances and newly introduced strangers, and men and women may kiss close friends and relatives on both cheeks during greeting and leave taking. For business and other professional activities, men are expected to wear suits and ties, while women still adhere to a code that involves dresses or two-piece suits with skirts or skirts and blouses.

Lunches tend to be lengthy with several courses served because the noon meal is the main meal of the day. During a visit to a home, food and drink are immediately placed on the table. Refreshments are supposed to be accepted graciously, and emptied plates and glasses are refilled promptly. It is customary to bring flowers, food (cakes), or a beverage when visiting people's homes. Business lunches and home visits are likely to include the offer of alcoholic beverages. Women usually can refuse politely and request a soft drink or hot tea. Men are expected to drink but may decline if they are driving.

RELIGION

Religious Beliefs. The monks Cyril and Methodius brought Christianity to the Great Moravian Empire in the ninth century, but there is evidence of an earlier traditional religion among western Slavs that involved a pantheon of supernatural beings. Today, 70 to 75 percent of Slovaks are Christian, and the majority (60.3 percent) are Roman Catholics. This figure includes Rom, most of whom are Catholic. Other major religions include Evangelical Lutheran, nearly 7 percent; Orthodox Christian, 4.1 percent; and Judaism (greatly reduced by the Holocaust), around 1 percent). Atheists may constitute nearly 10 percent of the population, and other faiths (especially Christian) account for the rest.

Religious Practitioners. Full-time religious practitioners include priests, pastors, and rabbis. In many communities, religious leaders participate in secular events and celebrations alongside political officials. Political leaders no longer control their activities, as they did before 1989.

Rituals and Holy Places. Slovaks affiliated with the major religions worship in established churches or synagogues. Christians conduct burial rites in cemeteries, and some groups visit special sacred areas. The Roman Catholic Church of Saint Jacob in Levoča ranks as one of the most significant shrines. In eastern and parts of central Slovakia, Roman

A Slovakian woman embroiders a piece of fabric. Slovakia has an extensive arts and crafts heritage.

Catholics place offerings of flowers and sometimes scarves at free-standing crosses in the countryside.

Death and the Afterlife. Slovak Christians believe that the soul survives death, and they bury their dead below ground in cemetery plots rather than cremating. In many villages, embalming was introduced as late as the 1980s, and wakes commonly were held at home before the widespread construction of *houses of sorrow* at or in cemeteries. In some communities, children from the same village are buried together in one or more rows of individual plots rather than with their families. Mourning lasts for nearly a year, and traditionally adult daughters and widows wear only black or subdued colors. Christian cemeteries tend to be located near churches, and it is common to see weeds and unmown grass there. Jewish cemeteries fell into neglect after the Holocaust. Many Christians in rural areas believed that ghosts of the deceased could come back and cause mischief; some people still attribute various types of misfortune to the activities of ghosts.

MEDICINE AND HEALTH CARE

Slovaks used to attribute illness and misfortune to supernatural causes and sought curers to diagnose their problems and provide remedies. They made extensive use of medicinal plants and mud poultices. Linden (*lipa*) blossoms were collected and dried to make infusions for various maladies. Serious cuts could be treated with the sap of red milkweed, and a beverage brewed from the plant called mouse's tail reportedly lowered blood pressure. Numerous medicinal spas, such as Piešťany in western Slovakia, have attracted patients for centuries. Slovakia's spas enjoy international renown and tend to be associated with specific types of ailments.

In the 1970s, curers for diagnosing and treating the evil eye could be found in rural areas, but modern medicine is Western in character. Villages typically have clinics staffed by resident nurses and midwife-paramedics. Regular visits by nonresident dentists, pediatricians, general practitioners, and obstetrician-gynecologists before 1989 provided free health care for all citizens, with nominal charges for prescriptions. After 1989, socialized medicine ended and medical care moved toward privatization. In general, the cost of medical care and equipment is the responsibility of individuals.

SECULAR CELEBRATIONS

Slovaks celebrate a number of public holidays, several of which are associated with the Christian calendar and beliefs. January 1 is both New Year's Day

Mountains and trees surround a small white church and graveyard. Slovakia has extremely varied topography for its size; its elevation ranges from 308 feet (94 meters) to 8,722 feet (2,655 meters).

and Independence Day. January 6 is Epiphany, a Christian festival celebrated especially in Catholic communities, where boys dress up as the Magi and go in a procession from house to house. Other Christian spring holidays on the public calendar include Good Friday, Easter Sunday, and Easter Monday, when young men used to visit homes of single young women and switch them with whips made of willow branches tied with ribbon and douse them with cologne. May Day (1 May), a survival from a much older annual round of Slavic and Slovak festivals signifying the major spring celebration, was transformed during the decades of communism into a celebration of workers, with political speeches and shows of military force. The liberation of the Slovak Republic is commemorated on 8 May. Another Christian and national holiday (observed mostly by Catholics), 5 July, honors Saints Cyril and Methodius, who brought Christianity to the Slavs. The anniversary of the Slovak national uprising in World War II is celebrated on 29 August. Constitution Day of the new Slovak Republic is celebrated on 1 September, and 15 September marks another Christian holiday: Our Lady of the Seven Sorrows. All Souls' (Saints') Day on 1 November is observed by many Christians; visits are made to relatives' cemetery plots, where candles are lit. Christmas, the final holiday of the calendar year is celebrated on 25 December, and 31 December marks the celebration of Sylvester (New Year's Eve).

Annual local secular celebrations usually include an end-of-the-school-year festival and parade, and in agricultural areas there are events marking the end of the grain harvest. This festival is called *dožinky* and usually occurs in August. In the early fall, *oberačky* celebrates the harvesting of apples and other late orchard crops. These local secular events include feasting and dancing.

THE ARTS AND HUMANITIES

Support for the Arts. Folk arts and crafts have enjoyed government support through the Center for Folk Art Production (ULUV). The center has promoted these arts abroad through numerous exhibitions. However, in many areas, state subsidies for the arts dried up after 1989, and artists have had to find other means of support.

Literature. Slovak folklore has a long oral tradition of storytelling. Stories generally fall into two categories: folktales that have broad geographic distribution in Slovakia and stories that stem from personal accounts that may be told for only one or two generations in an individual family.

The formal written literary language arose in the eighteenth century and was codified in the nineteenth century. Poetry became established in the nineteenth and twentieth centuries as a vehicle of the national spirit. While male poets were prominent in the public sphere, the recent publication of *Incipient Feminists: Women Writers in the Slovak National Revival* by Norma Rudinsky has revealed poems written by women.

While books were affordable before 1989 because of government support, the communist regime controlled and monitored what was published. After 1989, state financial sponsorship of publishing entered a period of transition, resulting in price increases for most books.

Graphic Arts. Slovakia has an extensive heritage of arts and crafts. Modra in southwestern Slovakia has been a center for the production of fine ceramics that began in the 1600s and now exhibits a distinctive folk-art form incorporating historical designs and firing techniques. Painting, sculpture, wood carving, glass (crystal) making, and other graphic arts enjoyed a decade of expansion and access to new markets after 1989. There are stores operated by regional artists' associations where works are sold, and new outlets to Western markets have been established. Modern art has roots both in Slovak folk themes and in European art in general. Most graphic artists belong to special associations or organizations; there are galleries and shows in cities and towns and in many museums. Art exhibits appear occasionally in villages.

A particular type of graphic art involving wire and metalworking was produced by Slovak tinkers from the Upper Vah River Valley or Spis. Their production of utilitarian household items such as candleholders is considered an art form.

Performance Arts. Performance arts fall into three main categories: folk, formal and/or classical, and modern and contemporary. Folk performances are usually local events, many in rural areas, and most often are held in the summer. They frequently are associated with particular festival dates or special commemorative events, such as the first mention of a village in historical records. Folk music, folk dances, minidramas and musicals, and mock weddings with the participants dressed in traditional costumes remain popular. Some folk performances are national or even international in scope, such as the festival in Východná in July. Traditional music ranges from groups playing string instruments and clarinets to groups playing brass instruments. Slovak music is said to have been influenced by both liturgical and chamber music, but a national musical tradition arose in the first half of the nineteenth century that was based primarily on folk themes.

Formal and/or classical and modern and/or contemporary performances are numerous. There are orchestras and chamber groups in many cities, with the most significant groups having their primary homes in Bratislava. A chamber opera was founded in 1986 to provide an outlet for newer performers in a kind of alternative theater.

There are theaters throughout Slovakia where skits, plays, operas, and puppet shows are performed before enthusiastic audiences. Motion pictures have become important in Slovak performance art since the 1960s. While many restrictions were placed on films made before 1989 and those films were expected to promote a political agenda, some works achieved international renown, such as *The Shop on Main Street*. In the 1990s, because of a lack of state financing, the main film studio closed, but Slovak filmmakers have continued their work.

THE STATE OF THE PHYSICAL AND SOCIAL SCIENCES

The physical and social sciences are extremely active in Slovakia. Numerous scientific journals are published, and some now appear in electronic form online. Many institutions of higher learning offer courses of study leading to advanced degrees in natural, behavioral, and social sciences as well as engineering, environmental science, and agricultural engineering. Comenius University and Slovak Technical University, both in Bratislava, are leading institutions in the physical and social sciences. While higher education was free before 1989, there has been a transition to a tuition-based program. In recent years, students in the social sciences numbered about 15.5 percent of the total university population, while natural science accounted for 3 percent and engineering, architecture, mathematics, and other sciences together accounted for 37 percent. There are twenty-one state institutions of higher learning: eighteen civilian schools, two military academies, and one policy institute.

BIBLIOGRAPHY

Baylis, Thomas A. ''Elite Change after Communism: Eastern Germany, the Czech Republic, and Slovakia.'' *East European Politics and Societies* 12 (2): 265–299, 1998.

Bugaski, J. *Ethnic Politics in Eastern Europe: A Guide to Nationality Policies*, 1995.

El Mallakh, Dorothea H. *The Slovak Autonomy Movement, 1935–1939: A Study in Unrelenting Nationalism,* 1979.

Erdmann, Yvonne. "The Development of Social Benefits and Social Policy in Poland, Hungary and the Slovak Republic since the System Transformation." *East European Quarterly* 32 (3): 301–314, 1998.

Fish, M. Steven. "The Determinants of Economic Reform in the Post-Communist World." *East European Politics and Societies* 12 (1): 31–78, 1998.

Jelinek, Yeshayahu, *The Parish Republic: Hlinka's Slovak People's Party, 1939–1945,* 1976.

Johnson, Owen V., *Slovakia 1918–1938: Education and the Making of a Nation,* 1985.

Kirschbaum, Stanislav J., and Anne C. Roman, eds. *Reflections on Slovak History,* 1987.

Leff, Carol Skalnik. *National Conflict in Czechoslovakia: The Making and Remaking of a State, 1918–1987,* 1988.

Mikus, Joseph A. *Slovakia and the Slovaks,* 1977.

Oddo, Gilbert. *Slovakia and Its People,* 1960.

Portal, Roger. *The Slavs: A Cultural and Historical Survey of the Slavonic Peoples,* 1969.

Pynsent, Robert B. "Tinkering with the Ferkos: A Kind of Slovakness." *Slavonic and East European Review* 76 (2): 279–295, 1998.

Rudinsky, Norma L. *Incipient Feminists: Women Writers in the Slovak National Revival,* 1991.

Seton-Watson, R. W. *A History of the Czechs and Slovaks,* 1943.

Stolarik, Marian Mark. *Immigration and Urbanization: The Slovak Experience, 1870–1918,* 1989.

Teleki, Ilona. "Loss and Lack of Recognition: Identifying Fears in the Slovak-Hungarian Relationship." *Slovo* 10 (1–2): 199–218, 1998.

—JANET POLLAK

SLOVENIA

CULTURE NAME
Slovenian

ALTERNATIVE NAMES
Slovenia is officially known as the Republic of Slovenia and called Slovenija by its residents.

ORIENTATION

Identification. Slovenia takes its name from the Slovenes, the group of South Slavs who originally settled the area. Eighty-seven percent of the population considers itself Slovene, while Hungarians and Italians constitute significant groups and have the status of indigenous minorities under the Slovenian Constitution, guaranteeing them seats in the National Assembly. There are other minority groups, most of whom immigrated, for economic reasons, from other regions of the former Yugoslavia after World War II.

Location and Geography. Slovenia is situated in southeastern Europe on the Balkan Peninsula and is bordered by Austria to the north, Hungary to the northeast, Croatia to the south and southeast, and Italy and the Adriatic Sea to the west. A mountainous country, Slovenia sits in the foothills of the eastern Alps just south of the Julian Alps, the Kamnik-Savinja Alps, the Karawanken chain, and the Pohorje Massif on the Austrian border. The Adriatic coast of Slovenia is about 39 miles (50 kilometers) in length, running from the border with Italy to the border with Croatia. Slovenia's Kras plateau, between central Slovenia and the Italian frontier, is an interesting area of unusual geological formations, underground rivers, caves, and gorges. Three main rivers located in the northeast, the Mura, the Drava, and the Sava, provide valuable sources of water. On the Pannonian plain to the east and northeast, near the borders with Hungary and Croatia, the landscape is primarily flat. Nevertheless, the major-ity of the country is hilly to mountainous with about ninety percent of its land at least 650 feet (200 meters) above sea level. Slightly smaller than the state of New Jersey, Slovenia is approximately 7,906 square miles (20,273 square kilometers) in area. In addition to the capital, Ljubljana, other important cities include Maribor, Kranj, Novo Mesto, and Celje. Areas along the coast enjoy a warm Mediterranean climate while those in the mountains to the north have cold winters and rainy summers. The plateaus to the east, where Ljubljana is located, have a mild, more moderate climate with warm to hot summers and cold winters.

Demography. In 2000, Slovenia had an overall population of about 1,970,056 with an overall population density of 252 people per square mile (97 per square kilometer). The majority of the population was ethnically Slovene, a Slavic group. The rest of the population was made up of Croats (2.7 percent), Serbs (2.4 percent), Bosnians (1.3 percent), Hungarians (0.43 percent), Montenegrins (0.22 percent), Macedonians (0.22 percent), Albanians (0.18 percent) and Italians (0.16 percent). Almost half of all Slovenes live in urban areas, mostly in Ljubljana and Maribor, the two largest cities, with the rest of the population distributed throughout rural areas.

Linguistic Affiliation. The official language of the republic, Slovene, is a Slavic language. About 7 percent of the population speaks Serbo-Croatian. Most Slovenes speak at least two languages. Unlike other Slavic cultures, the Slovenes have been greatly influenced by German and Austrian cultures, a result of centuries of rule by the Austrian Habsburgs. Italian influence is evident in the regions that border Italy. These non-Slavic influences are reflected in the Slovene language, which is written in the Latin alphabet, while most Slavic languages use the Cyrillic alphabet. The variety of dialects is also a result of the shared borders with four different nations. During the Protestant Reformation and the Catholic Counter-Reformation, Slovenia's language, which

Slovenia

had been considered a peasant language compared to the more prestigious German, was used by political and religious factions as an instrument of propaganda. Although initially a political tool, Slovene eventually gained a new level of prestige and provided a linguistic identity that helped shape Slovenia's national identity.

Symbolism. Two important national symbols are the linden tree and the chamois, a European antelope, both of which are abundant throughout the country. Slovenia's flag consists of three horizontal bands of white on the top, blue, and then red on the bottom with a shield in the upper left. On the shield are three white mountain peaks with three gold six-pointed stars above them. The stars were taken from the coat of arms of the Counts of Celje, the Slovenian dynastic house of the late fourteenth–early fifteenth centuries.

HISTORY AND ETHNIC RELATIONS

Emergence of the Nation. Starting in the sixth century C.E., the area that is now Slovenia was perpetually invaded by the Avars, a Mongol tribe, who were in turn, driven out by the Slavs. In 623 C.E., chieftain Franko Samo created the first independent Slovene state, which covered an area from Lake Balaton, now located in Hungary, to the Mediterranean. This independent state persisted until the latter part of the eighth century when it was absorbed into the Frankish empire. In the tenth century, Slovenia fell under the control of the Holy Roman Empire and was reorganized as the duchy of Carantania by the Holy Roman Emperor Otto I (912–973). With the exception of four years of rule by Napoléon (1809–1813), when, along with Croatia, it was a part of the Illyrian Provinces, Slovenia was a part of the Austrian Hapsburg Empire, from 1335 to 1918.

In 1918, at the end of World War I, Slovenia joined with other Slavic groups to form the Kingdom of Serbs, Croats, and Slovenes. Renamed the Kingdom of Yugoslavia in 1929 by a Serbian monarch, Slovenia and its neighboring Yugoslav states fell under Nazi Germany's control in World War II. Communist partisans, under the leadership of Josip

Broz Tito, fiercely resisted the German, Italian, and Hungarian occupation, leading to the establishment of a socialist Yugoslavia toward the end of the war. During the postwar Communist period, Slovenia was the most prosperous region of Yugoslavia.

After Tito's death in 1980, serious disagreements and unrest among Yugoslavia's regions began to grow, and the central government in Belgrade sought to further strengthen its control. The local Slovene government resisted and in September 1989, the General Assembly of the Yugoslav Republic of Slovenia adopted an amendment to its constitution asserting the right of Slovenia to secede from Yugoslavia. On 25 June 1991, the Republic of Slovenia declared its independence. A bloodless ten-day war with Yugoslavia followed, ending in the withdrawal of Belgrade's forces and official recognition of Slovenia's status as an independent republic.

As a newly independent state, Slovenia has sought economic stabilization and governmental reorganization, emphasizing its central European heritage and its role as a bridge between eastern and western Europe. With its increased regional profile, including its status as a nonpermanent member of the United Nations Security Council and as a charter member of the World Trade Organization, Slovenia plays an important role in world politics considering its small size.

National Identity. Under the Austro-Hungarian Empire, Slovenia was a part of the Austrian crown lands of Carinthia, Carniola, and Styria, except for a minority of Slovenes living under the republic of Venice. During the Napoleonic Wars, when Slovenia was part of the Illyrian Provinces, a period of relative liberal rule helped fuel the growth of Slovene and Slav nationalism, which ultimately triumphed at the end of World War I. Despite forced transfers during World War II, most Slovenes have managed to remain in Slovenia, and in 1947 Istria, the Slovenian-speaking area of Italy on the Adriatic coast, also joined the republic. More than 87 percent of the population identifies itself as Slovene although minorities are an integral part of the society.

Ethnic Relations. Although Slovenia was a part of Yugoslavia from 1918 to 1991, the country has always identified strongly with central Europe, maintaining a balance between its Slavic culture and language and Western influences. The ethnic conflicts and civil unrest that have plagued other regions of the former Yugoslavia in the 1990s and early twenty-first century, have been avoided in Slovenia. Conscious of its unique position as a bridge between east and west, Slovenia is developing its identity as a newly independent republic while maintaining a balanced relationship with the different cultures of its neighbors.

URBANISM, ARCHITECTURE, AND THE USE OF SPACE

Slovenia's towns have many well-preserved buildings representing various styles of architecture dating from the 1100s on. Fine examples of Romanesque architecture can be found throughout Slovenia, including the church at Sticna Abbey and Podsreda Castle. Architecture from the late Gothic period also survives. Many buildings in older sections of Slovenia's towns are in the Italian Baroque style, particularly in Ljubljana. After a serious earthquake in 1895, extensive sections of Ljubljana were rebuilt in the Art Nouveau style. Throughout Slovenia the focus of town life revolves around the older city centers, squares, churches, and marketplaces.

FOOD AND ECONOMY

Food in Daily Life. Slovenia has a rich culinary tradition that is a product of both its climate and its location at the crossroads of central Europe. Slovene culinary heritage is reflective of Mediterranean, Alpine, and Eastern European cultures. Meals are an important part of Slovene family life, and enjoying a snack or a glass of wine at a café with friends is a typical social activity. Although every region in Slovenia has its own specialties, most of Slovenia's oldest traditional dishes are made using flour, buckwheat, or barley, as well as potatoes and cabbage. The town of Idrija, west of Ljubljana, is known for its *idrija zlikrofi*, spiced potato balls wrapped in thinly rolled dough, and *zeljsevka*, rolled yeast dough with herb filling. The town of Murska Sobota, Slovenia's northernmost city, is famous for its *prekmurska gibanica*, a pastry filled with cottage cheese, poppy seeds, walnuts, and apple. Slovenia also produces a variety of wines, an activity dating back to the days when the country was a part of the Roman Empire.

Food Customs at Ceremonial Occasions. There are some particular dishes prepared for special occasions including *potica*, a dessert with a variety of fillings, and braided loaves of traditional bread for Christmas. In country towns the slaughtering of a pig, all parts of which are used to make a variety of pork products, is still a major event.

Basic Economy. After its independence from Yugoslavia in 1991, Slovenia went through a period of transition as it adjusted to economic changes as a new, small republic moving away from socialism. Although the first few years were difficult, Slovenia has now emerged as one of the strongest economies among the former socialist countries of Eastern Europe. The economic outlook, however, remained unclear in the early twenty-first century as the rate of inflation hovered around 10 percent with unemployment at 14.5 percent. Slovenia's loss of its markets in the former Yugoslavia, which once accounted for 30 percent of its exports, has caused the country to modernize its factories and production methods as it seeks to attract foreign investment. Slovenia's growth rate in 2000 was estimated at 3.8 percent with per capita income around $9,000 (U.S.).

Land Tenure and Property. Primogeniture, inheritance by the oldest son, historically determined land distribution in Slovenia. Land and property were kept intact and passed down through families, a tradition that helped limit land fragmentation, which was common in other parts of the Balkans. Despite its years under Yugoslavia's socialist government, Slovenia's strong tradition of family-owned property helped it maintain its distribution of property. Agricultural land, accounting for almost 43 percent of the territory, and forests, covering more than half, make Slovenia the "greenest" country in Europe next to Finland. Nevertheless, 52 percent of Slovenes live in urban areas in small houses and apartment buildings. Formerly state-owned farms and land have been reprivatized.

Commercial Activities. Among the numerous commercial activities in Slovenia, many cater to tourism. Slovenia's proximity to the Alps and the Mediterranean, along with its climate, makes it a popular tourist destination. The business derived from tourist hotels, ski resorts, golf courses, and horseback-riding centers provides employment for a growing number of Slovenes.

Major Industries. Major industries include the production of electrical equipment, processed food, paper and paper products, chemicals, textiles, metal and wood products, and electricity. Other important industries include the manufacturing of shoes, skis, and furniture. Coal mines and steel mills continue to operate and new factories, such as the French Renault car assembly plant, reflect recent foreign investment in Slovenia.

Trade. Germany is Slovenia's most important trading partner both for exports and imports. Other important trading partners include Croatia, Italy, France, and Austria. Exports include chemical products, food and live animals, furniture, machinery, and transportation equipment. Slovenia imports manufactured products and consumer goods.

Division of Labor. In 1994 the process of privatizing state-owned businesses was begun and many Slovenes have taken advantage of these changes to become owners of or shareholders in companies. A large section of the population works in the tourism industry, but only one out of ten people work in agriculture. Many Slovenes, however, pursue small-scale agricultural activities, such as beekeeping and grape growing, as side businesses.

SOCIAL STRATIFICATION

Classes and Castes. According to the 1998 census, 87 percent of people are Slovenes. There are approximately 8,500 ethnic Hungarians, 3,000 Italians, and 2,300 Gypsies living in Slovenia. The Hungarian and Italian populations are recognized by the government as indigenous minorities and are protected under the constitution. The Gypsies, however, are viewed with suspicion and are frequently targets of ethnic discrimination. Despite government attempts, past and present, to provide employment and increase school attendance among Gypsies, most of them continue to hold on to their nomadic way of life, shunning mainstream education and jobs. Since the start of civil unrest in other regions of the former Yugoslavia, Slovenia has become a refuge for those escaping from both violence and poor economic conditions. There are also several thousand migrants from Croatia who enter Slovenia every day to work. The peasants, who once accounted for a large part of the population, decreased dramatically in numbers during the post-World War II era as Slovenia, along with the rest of Yugoslavia, underwent a rapid transformation from an agricultural to an industrial society. By the early 1980s, over half of agricultural workers were women. Postwar industrialization created a new class of workers, including government employees who achieved desirable positions through education and political connections. A small intellectual caste has been present in Slovenia since the nineteenth century. A large section of Slovenia's population is now a part of the well-educated, urban-dwelling middle class. Extreme class differences between rich and poor are not present.

Symbols of Social Stratification. Symbols of social stratification include the types of consumer goods found in many Western countries. As Slove-

A Slovenian peasant removes corn from the dried cobs while his wife holds his new hat. Clothing is one sign of Slovenia's new affluence; the country has one of the strongest economies among the formerly socialist East European nations.

nia's economy and standard of living have grown, the demand for and ability to purchase consumer goods have increased. Cars, electronic appliances, and clothing are the most immediate signs of social stratification and the new affluence.

POLITICAL LIFE

Government. The process of government reform has been ongoing since the country's emergence as an independent nation in 1991. While some aspects of the former socialist rule have been maintained, the Slovene government has adopted several democratic measures, including a parliamentary form of government. A 1991 constitution guarantees basic civil rights, including universal suffrage for all Slovenes over the age of eighteen, freedom of religion, and freedom of the press. The National Assembly, or Drzavni Zbor, has exclusive control over the passage of new laws and consists of ninety deputies elected for four years by proportional representation. There is also a forty-member Council of State, the Drzavni Svet, which functions as an advisory body and whose members are elected for five-year terms by region and special interest group. The president is the head of state and supreme commander of the armed forces and cannot

be elected for more than two five-year terms. Executive power is held by the prime minister and a fifteen-member cabinet.

Leadership and Political Officials. The seven political parties in Slovenia support ideologies ranging from the far right to the center-left. In the 1996 parliamentary elections a centrist alliance of three parties gained the majority. President Milan Kucan was elected for a second term in 1997, and Janez Drnovsek has served as prime minister since the first elections were held in 1992.

Social Problems and Control. Important social problems and issues include the country's transition to a free market economy, an aging population (the average age for men is thirty-five, for women, thirty-eight), creating jobs for an educated population, and coping with the increasing number of migrant workers and refugees.

The crime rate is low but there has been a rise in organized and economic crime since Slovenia's independence and change to privatization. Money laundering is a particularly increasing problem. Slovenia's location between Italy, Austria, and Hungary puts it in the middle of international money-laundering schemes. The Slovene government is actively fighting the resulting problems.

Foundry workers pouring molten metal into molds. While women comprise 45 percent of the workforce, they are largely confined to the welfare, public services, and hospitality fields.

Military Activity. Slovenia requires seven months of military service for all males at age eighteen. As of 1998, the country had an army of 9,550 active duty soldiers as well as a reserve force. A member of the United Nations, Slovenia has signed defense accords with Austria and Hungary.

GENDER ROLES AND STATUS

Division of Labor by Gender. In Slovenia women comprise 45 percent of the overall workforce and more than 60 percent of the workforce in the agricultural sector. In addition, primary school teachers are almost exclusively women. Industrialization and education have dramatically changed women's roles in the workplace, but aspects of Slovenia's traditionally patriarchal society still persist. Women work primarily in three fields: cultural and social welfare, public services and administration, and the hospitality industry.

The Relative Status Women and Men. Although women were granted complete civil and political rights after World War II, feminist groups state that industrialization has not eradicated the traditional patriarchy but has only created a situation where women are exploited. Women are often treated as sex objects and are still expected to take care of all domestic matters even if they work full-time outside the home.

MARRIAGE, FAMILY AND KINSHIP

Marriage. Despite years of socialism, Slovenian society is still oriented around the extended family. Rights and duties are more rigorously defined by family relationships than in the West. Although the average age for a first marriage has increased, marriage is considered important for maintaining and strengthening family bonds. Religious and cultural influences help keep the divorce rate low.

Domestic Unit. In urban areas, the domestic unit is typically married adults and their children, if they have any, and sometimes older relatives. In rural areas, extended families—often larger than those found in cities—live together or share property. Relatives who are unable to care for themselves usually reside with family members.

Kin Groups. Before the twentieth century, family-based organizations called *zadruga* held property and farmed land in common. Both formal and customary law determined the obligations and rights of zadruga members.

SOCIALIZATION

Child Rearing and Education. Education is mandatory and free until age fifteen. After this, students can choose a school that is more specialized if they wish to continue education. Most of the population has some basic education; another 42 percent have secondary schooling (past age fifteen at a high school; and approximately 9 percent receive higher, university education. There is a national, standardized curriculum. Competition for university places is strong. For Slovenes over ten years old, the literacy rate is placed at 99 percent.

Higher Education. Around 36 percent of the people receive postsecondary or higher levels of education. There are thirty institutions of higher learning but only two universities, the University of Ljubljana, founded in 1595, and the University of Maribor. Admittance to the universities is competitive but there are numerous schools that offer professional degrees. It is also possible to obtain a two-year "first stage" degree, equivalent to an associate degree, at the universities.

A bridge leading to a Baroque-style church in Ljubljana. Slovenia's towns have many well-preserved buildings representing various styles of architecture dating from the 1100s on.

RELIGION

Religious Beliefs. The majority of Slovenes, approximately 71 percent, identify themselves as Roman Catholic; Roman Catholicism has undoubtedly influenced Slovene culture more than any other religious belief. Protestantism gained a strong position during the Reformation in the 1500s but later saw its numbers of practitioners diminish.

Eastern Orthodox Christians comprise 2.5 percent of the population, Protestants, 1 percent, and Muslims, 1 percent. Most of the Protestants belong to the Lutheran church in Murska Sobota. There was once a small Jewish population in Slovenia but Jews were banished from the area in the fifteenth century. Although the ruins of a synagogue can still be seen in Maribor, there is no longer an active Jewish temple anywhere in Slovenia today. The rabbi of Zagreb, Croatia, occasionally holds services for the tiny Jewish community that lives in Ljubljana.

Rituals and Holy Places. There are several churches that are considered pilgrimage sites and places of spiritual renewal. In Brezje, a basilica dedicated to Saint Vid was first established in the 1100s. At the center of this church is a chapel dedicated to the Virgin Mary, with paintings by Leopold Layer.

The Gothic church of Ptujska Gora, located on top of a mountain, was erected at the end of the fourteenth century and is famous for its beautiful altar. Another pilgrimage church is located at Sveta Gora in the foothills of the Alps. The feast days of the Virgin Mary are the central pilgrimage days for all three churches. There are two monasteries, Sticna Monastery and Pleterje Carthusian Monastery, which are open to visitors who often come not only for spiritual reflection but also to purchase the herbal remedies for which the monks are famous.

MEDICINE AND HEALTH CARE

Health care is provided by the government for all of Slovenia's citizens. Life expectancy has increased and is almost at western European levels: seventy years for men and seventy-eight years for women. The birthrate is low, under 10 per 1,000 people, and infant mortality is 5.5 per 1,000 births.

SECULAR CELEBRATIONS

Important secular celebrations include 8 February, Preseren Day, a Slovene cultural day; 1 May, worker's holiday; 25 June, Slovenia Day, and 26 December, Independence Day.

THE ARTS AND HUMANITIES

Support for the Arts. There is generally a strong interest in supporting the arts in Slovenia and enthusiastic patronage of cultural events. Under the Yugoslav socialist government, arts and culture received state support. As an independent nation, Slovenia is seeking to maintain the same level of support for the arts, although privatization is changing the way institutions and artists are funded.

Literature. Literature has always been enthusiastically supported in Slovenia, and with the country's high literacy rate, this interest continues to grow. The earliest written texts in Slovene, which were religious, date from around 970 C.E. The first published book in Slovene appeared in 1550, and in 1584 a Slovene grammar text and Bible were published. Until the late eighteenth century, however, almost all books published in Slovenia were in Latin or German. Slovenian literature flourished in the early 1800s during the Romantic period and began to develop an identity. During this period France Prešeren, considered Slovenia's greatest poet, published his works. In the second half of the nineteenth century, Fran Levstik published his interpretation of oral Slovene folktales, and in 1866 Josip Juri published the first long novel completely in Slovene, entitled *The Tenth Brother.* Slovenian literature immediately before and after World War II was heavily influenced by socialist realism and the struggles of the war period. Various other literary styles, such as symbolism and existentialism, have influenced Slovene writers since the 1960s.

Graphic Arts. Slovenia has an unusual variety of art ranging from Gothic frescoes to contemporary sculpture. The late nineteenth century saw the rise of a Slovene Expressionist school led by the painter Boñidar Jakac. In the early twentieth century a new trend in art emerged as a group of artists joined to form the Club of Independents, some of whom continued working under Tito's socialist government. Slovenia has a small but vibrant art community today that is dominated by the multimedia group Neue Slowenische Kunst and a five-member artists' cooperative called IRWIN. There is also a rich tradition of folk art which is best exemplified by the painted beehives illustrated with folk motifs that are found throughout Slovenia.

Performance Arts. Folk music and dance are an important part of Slovenia's culture. The Institute of Music and National Manuscripts in Ljubljana maintains an archive of the wide variety of traditional songs and fables set to music. Folk dances are still a part of traditional celebrations, and the first ballet school, which was established in Slovenia in 1918 as a part of the Ljubljana Opera, continues to perform. Other dance companies, including contemporary and avant-garde, have also been formed.

THE STATE OF THE PHYSICAL AND SOCIAL SCIENCES

Slovenia has a strong tradition in the sciences, with several important figures, including Janez Vajkard Valvasor, a seventeenth-century mathematician and Fritz Pregl, who won the Nobel Prize for chemistry in 1923. The Slovenian Academy of Arts and Sciences has a research center with fourteen institutes conducting research on all aspects of science, history, and culture.

BIBLIOGRAPHY

Arnez, John. *Slovenia in European Affairs: Reflections on Slovenian Political History,* 1958.

Curtis, Glenn E. *Yugoslavia: A Country Study,* 1992.

Dickey, Karlene. *Slovenia: A Study of the Educational System of the Republic of Slovenia,* 1995.

Dizdarevic, Jasmina, and Lucka Letic. *Slovenia,* 2000.

Fallon, Steve. *Slovenia: Lonely Planet Guide,* 1995.

Fink-Hafner, Danica, and John Robbins. *Making a New Nation: The Formation of Slovenia,* 1997.

Minnich, Robert Gary. *The Homemade World of Zagaj: An Interpretation of the "Practical Life" among Traditional Peasant Farmers in West Haloze, Slovenia,* 1979.

Svetlik, Ivan. *Social Policy in Slovenia: Between Tradition and Innovation,* 1992.

Tollefson, James W. *The Language Situation and Language Policy in Slovenia,* 1981.

Web Sites

U.S. Department of State Bureau of European Affairs. Background Notes: Slovenia. Electronic document. Available from: http://www.state.gov/www .background_notes/slovenia;_9902_bgn.html

—M. CAMERON ARNOLD

SOLOMON ISLANDS

CULTURE NAME
Solomon Islander

ALTERNATIVE NAME
Melanesia; Melanesians; *Wantoks* (''one people,'' people from the Melanesian region sharing certain characteristics, especially the use of pidgin English).

ORIENTATION
Identification. When Spanish explorer Álvaro de Mendaña de Neira visited the Solomon Islands in 1568, he found some gold at the mouth of what is now the Mataniko River. By a turn of an amused fate, he erroneously thought that this could be one of the locations in which King Solomon (the Israelite monarch) obtained gold for his temple in Jerusalem. Mendaña then named the islands after King Solomon—Solomon Islands.

The islands are most widely known to the outside world for the World War II battles that were fought there, especially on Guadalcanal. Peace prevailed for most of the rest of the century in a country that was sometimes called the ''Happy Islands,'' until ethnic conflict erupted in late 1998.

Location and Geography. The Solomon Islands lie northeast of Australia in the South Pacific Ocean. They are part of a long chain of archipelagos called Melanesia, which stretches from Papua New Guinea in the north to New Caledonia and Fiji in the south. Second largest in the Melanesian chain, the Solomon Islands archipelago covers approximately 310,000 square miles (803,000 square kilometers) of ocean and consists of 10,639 square miles (27,556 square kilometers) of land. There are a total of 992 islands in the Solomon Islands, including the six main islands of New Georgia, Choiseul, Santa Isabel, Guadalcanal, Malaita, and San Cristóbal.

The climate of the Solomon Islands is equatorial, tempered by the surrounding ocean. Rainfall is often heavy especially in the interior near the mountains and on the windward sides of the large islands. Coastal areas of the main islands sheltered from the prevailing wind get less rain and, therefore, are drier. Honiara, the capital, is situated on Guadalcanal, in a rain shadow cast by a high mountain range.

Demography. The population of the Solomon Islands is estimated to be approximately 450,000. It is comprised predominantly of Melanesians with the rest of the population consisting of Polynesians, Micronesians, and small pockets of Chinese and Europeans. The annual growth rate is around 3.5 percent.

Most of the population (85 percent) live in villages. Only those with paid employment are found in the urban centers and provincial headquarters of Honiara (the capital), Auki, Gizo, Buala, Kira Kira, and Lata.

Linguistic Affiliation. The Melanesian region of the Pacific is known for its polylinguism. Among Melanesians and Polynesians in the Solomon Islands, approximately 63 to 70 distinct languages are spoken and perhaps an equal number of dialects. Each of the languages and several of the dialects are associated with distinct cultural groups.

Solomon Islanders also speak a variant of English called pidgin English (a form of Creole). And in formal places, such as in church services and in schools, English is spoken although it is usually interspersed with pidgin English and the native languages.

Symbolism. The multiplicity of ethnic groups made it quite difficult for the nation to agree on one symbol for itself. The leaders at independence, therefore, chose an amalgam of symbols to closely represent the different islands and their cultures. This is shown in the national coat of arms, which displays a crocodile and a shark upholding the government (represented by a crown) and a frigate bird

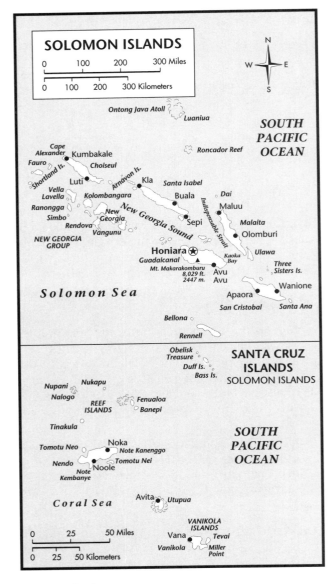

Solomon Islands

fishing and other marine skills, especially in the lagoons.

Subsequent migrants, finding that the big islands were occupied, settled on the outlying islands, most of which are coral outliers. Sikaiana, Reef Islands and the Temotu Islands. These migrants were mostly Polynesians, and they mastered fishing and navigation.

The first contact with Europeans was in 1568 with Spanish explorer Álvaro de Mendaña de Neira. Mendaña left and returned a second time in 1595 with the intent to settle. He died of malaria, and the settlement was short-lived.

Until 1767, when English explorer Philip Carteret landed in the islands, contact with outsiders was limited. It was in the 1800s, when traders and whalers arrived, that contact with Europeans became constant and enduring. Entrepreneurs, church missionaries, and the British colonial government officers soon arrived thereafter.

Before Britain proclaimed protectorate status over the islands in 1893, there was no single centralized politico-cultural system. What existed were numerous autonomous clan-based communities often headed by a male leader with his assistants. Unlike Polynesian societies, there had not been a known overall monarch ruling the islands.

Within the islands, there was intercommunity trading and even warring networks. These networks were further cemented by intermarriages and mutual help alliances.

With the arrival of churches and government, communication was made easier between the islanders, and further networks then developed. The British also put an end to intertribal warfare and conflicts. As a result, the predominant cultures of Melanesia and Polynesia were deeply intertwined with the cultures of the different churches, and both urban and rural lifestyles. Added to this was the introduction of western popular culture.

Emergence of the Nation. The emergence of nationhood came late to most Pacific nations so that the Solomon Islands was given political autonomy from Britain only in 1978, in a peaceful transfer of power. Calls for political independence, however, preceded the 1970s. Starting in the 1990s, Solomon Islanders made several attempts at independence through indigenous movements. Government was an anathema to the leaders of these movements because they did not see why they had to pay taxes when they received little in return from the government.

supporting both. Also displayed are an eagle, a turtle, a war shield, and some fighting spears. The coat of arms also includes the phrase "to lead is to serve," which characterizes the general belief of the founding fathers who called on every member of the new nation to cherish duty and responsibility.

HISTORY AND ETHNIC RELATIONS

The first discoverers of the Solomon Islands were the island peoples themselves. They settled the main islands and developed land-based communities, first with agriculture and then through animal husbandry, particularly pigs. They also developed

National Identity. In the Solomon Islands, national culture developed from the convergence of a number of factors. One of the most important is the high level of tolerance and comity developed between different churches in the last century. Unlike the government, church missions have done a lot for the people. They have provided schools, clinics, church buildings, and overall good will. The churches have enabled different cultures to assimilate such teachings as the social gospel of sharing and caring.

Another factor that congeals national culture is the sharing of a lingua franca, the "Solomon Islands pidgin English." Although pidgin English is not a compulsory subject in schools, it is the social glue that cements relationships particularly in a country with multiple languages.

Concomitant with the above is the concept of *wantokism*. Wantokism is a rallying philosophy that brings together, in common cause, people who are related, those who speak similar languages, those from the same area or island, and even the country as a whole. Its social malleability means that it can be applied in more than one situation especially when one is new to a place or unfamiliar to a group of people. It is a concept in which mutual hospitality is shared among and between different individuals and groups. The concept also traverses national boundaries. It is shared particularly among the three main Melanesian nations, the Solomon Islands, Vanuatu, and Papua New Guinea.

The development of a national culture was also influenced by the battles Solomon Islanders experienced during World War II. Although the "war was not our war," the fact that many Solomon Islanders had common experiences, including putting their lives at risk to save their country from the enemy (the Japanese), helped unite them into one people.

Ethnic Relations. The ethnic groups of the Solomon Islands reflect the natural division of the islands. A Guadalcanal person would readily identify with others from Guadalcanal. This would equally apply to a Malaita person who would easily relate to another Malaita person. But within the islands, ethnic associations follow the different languages. Having more than seventy languages in the Solomon Islands means, then, that there are more than seventy ethnic groups as well. It was only in the late twentieth century that ethnic relations became politicized, resulting in violence.

URBANISM, ARCHITECTURE, AND THE USE OF SPACE

With a relatively small population and large land area, space is affordable in the Solomon Islands. In urban areas, however, the choice of space is limited because of the restricted availability of houses and the nature of freehold land tenure. In such circumstances, Solomon Islanders have to fit into these new environments and quickly adapt to what is generally known as the *taon kalsa* ("town culture"). This includes developing relationships with one's neighbors from other islands and sharing transportation.

Houses in towns usually take the form of the Western bungalow with three bedrooms on average. These are built mostly of cement and timber, with corrugated iron roofing. A kitchen and other convenient amenities are included therein. Often, however, the practice of having in-house toilets infracts the tradition, as still practiced in rural areas, of having separate toilets for men and women as a sign of deep respect for one's siblings.

In rural areas, large villages are often situated on tribal land. Villages comprise individual families placing their homes next to other relatives. There is usually a village quad (square) where children can play and meetings can be held. Sometimes, village squares are used for games consisting of intervillage competitions. In other areas, family homes are made on artificial islands built over shallow shoals in a lagoon by gathering rocks and piling them together to make a "home over the sea." This lifestyle has several advantages: living over the sea is generally cooler, most of these artificial islands are mosquito-free, and families have greater privacy so they can bring up their children as they wish without the undesirable influences from other children.

In rural areas, most Solomon Island dwellings are made of sago-palm thatching often with a separate kitchen. Most dwellings are rectangular in shape, raised on stilts with windows for ventilation to take advantage of the frequent land and sea breezes. A separate kitchen is convenient where open-stove cooking is done especially with the family oven, which is used for large Sunday cooking or for public festivals, such as weddings and funerals.

For those who live in mountain areas, which often experience cold nights, houses are generally built low. Often the living area includes a fireplace for heat. In places such as the Kwaio Mountains, on Malaita, where traditional worship is still practiced, men's houses are built separate from family houses. Also, the separately built *bisi* (menstruating and birthing hut) is where women go during monthly menses and during childbirth.

An important piece of national architecture is the parliament house, which was built as a gift from the United States to Solomon Islands. The building features rich frescoes in the ceiling telling stories of various life-phases in the islands. On the pinnacle of the roof overlooking the whole town are carvings of ancestral gods, which are totemic guides to the different peoples. The building epitomizes the unity of the country besides being a symbolic haven for democratic deliberation and decision making.

FOOD AND ECONOMY

Food in Daily Life. Traditionally, yams, panas, and taros are the main staples in the Solomon Islands. These are usually eaten with fish and sea-shells, for those on the coast, or greens, snails, eels, and opossums, for those inland and in the mountains. The traditional diet does not distinguish between breakfast, lunch, and dinner. What is eaten is usually what is available at that time. Solomon Islanders do not use many spices in their cooking except for coconut milk. During harvesting seasons, breadfruits and ngali nuts are gathered, and eaten or traded.

Today, the traditional diet has changed markedly, especially in urban areas. Rice is becoming the main staple, and is often eaten with tea. For lunch and dinner, rice is eaten with canned meat or fish. The locally-produced Solomon Taiyo (canned tuna) has become a favorite protein source.

For urban families with limited income, breakfast consists of tea with leftovers from previous meals. More affluent families drink tea or coffee and eat buttered bread, rolls, or biscuits. Lunch and dinner are usually the big meals of the day. Eating does not necessary follow time, but as they say, "it follows the tummy." Most families eat together so they can talk. Traditionally, the habit of eating at tables was not the norm. Today, it is becoming one.

Food Customs at Ceremonial Occasions. There is a saying that "everyone who goes to a feast expects to eat." Usually a lot of preparation is required for ceremonial occasions. This might involve preparing a pig for the oven, making manioc, taro, yam or swamp-taro pudding, and roasting fish; when it can be afforded, a cow is prepared.

Traditionally, there are no special drinks (particularly alcoholic ones) that go with the food. Water is the main drink. But if the hosts prefer, green coconuts are prepared, to be drunk after the main courses.

Often, in kastom feasts, guests are provided with betel nuts to chew. Similar to desserts, betel nuts are eaten as the final food that tops off a good meal.

Basic Economy. Most of the people are rural villagers who depend on subsistence agriculture for sustenance. Therefore, agriculture and fishing are the mainstays of village life. Any surplus food or fish is bartered or sold at the markets.

Land Tenure and Property. In the Solomon Islands, 85 percent of land is managed under customary tenure, meaning that local clans and members of clan groups have control over it. Traditionally, people do not own the land; the land owns them. People merely have stewardship over the land which is held in "good faith" for them and for subsequent generations.

Commercial Activities. Beginning in the early 1990s, small-scale industries were encouraged, resulting in goods that are sold mostly in the local area at retail and wholesale stores. Examples of these locally-produced products are beer, furniture, and noodles. Otherwise, agricultural products have been the main commodities for sale. In the service sector, hotels and small motels were established in the late twentieth century to encourage small-scale tourism.

Major Industries. Except for Marubeni Fishing Company, which produces canned tuna, and Gold Ridge mine, which produces gold, most of the industries are comprised small or medium-sized businesses. The main industries are geared toward local markets, including the food processing sector, which produces such items as rice, biscuits, beer, and *twisties*, a brand of confectionery. Other manufacturers produce twisted tobacco, corrugated roofing sheets, nails, fibro canoes and tanks, timber, and buttons.

The tourism industry has only been recently encouraged. The Solomon Islands has stellar scenery, including lagoons, lakes, fauna and flora. The government has encouraged controlled tourism to attract Australians, Japanese, Americans, and scuba divers.

Trade. The export of palm oil and kernels, copra (dried coconut), cocoa, fish, and timber constitute the bulk of the country's trade. The main destinations for these products are Japan, the United Kingdom, Thailand, South Korea, Germany, Australia,

A family relaxes on benches in front of their house in Falamai Village. Stilts and windows provide needed ventilation in the equatorial climate.

the Netherlands, Sweden, and Singapore. Other exported products that are traded in relatively smaller quantities include beer, buttons, precious stones, shell money, and wooden carvings.

Division of Labor. Most Solomon Islanders are self-employed. According to the most recent census data available (1986), 71.4 percent of the economically active population (133, 498) was engaged in non-monetary work in villages, including subsistence farming. The labor force engaged exclusively in wage-earning activities was only 14 percent. A further 14.5 percent was engaged in both wage-earning and subsistence production.

In the formal monetary sector, there were approximately 34,000 employed persons in 1996. Looking at the distribution of this number in terms of economic sectors, 58 percent of the employed were in the service sector including the public service, financial services, and trade; 26 percent in the primary sector, which includes agriculture, fisheries, and forestry; and 16 percent in the secondary sector including manufacturing and construction. It is also useful to look at the relative roles of the public and private sectors in providing employment. In the year under consideration the public sector accounted for 32 percent of the total wage employment while the private sector accounted for the remaining two-thirds.

SOCIAL STRATIFICATION

Classes and Castes. The Solomon Islands does not have caste or class divisions as found among some Asian cultures. Instead, the country has different tribal groups found on the different islands. Individuals and groups gravitate towards their own kith and kin. Broader still, they move along island lines or interisland groupings according to various affiliations, including marriages, church memberships, and general friendship.

The emergence of a semblance of class was brought about during the colonial days between those who moved to urban centers and those who remained in villages. Today, those who are employed in the formal sector form a sort of elite class, in contrast to those who are not formally employed either in the public or the private sector. The late twentieth century saw the emergence of another class, a small group of businesspeople.

Symbols of Social Stratification. Social stratification is more obvious in urban areas where people are known by where they live. The well-to-do often live in suburbs such as Ngosi, Tandai, and Lingakiki. Those who live in Kukum Labor line or at the mouth of Mataniko River are usually less affluent. In a similar manner, people are known by the cars they drive, the houses they live in, and the restaurants and bars they frequent.

POLITICAL LIFE

Government. On the eve of political independence in 1978, Solomon Islands' government leaders decided to retain the parliamentary system of government that had been employed during the colonial era. The nation has a governor-general who represents the British monarch, a prime minister as the head of the executive, a speaker of the house who heads parliament, and a chief justice as the highest legal officer. There is no limit to the term a person can serve as prime minister. The speaker is voted for a five-year term, while the chief justice remains in office until retirement unless he or she has proven unable to carry out his or her constitutional duties. The fifty-member parliament is elected every four years.

Leadership and Political Officials. Leadership in traditional culture follows the "big man system." People become leaders when they gain influence by the manipulation of their abilities around followers and resources. Today, most leaders are elected through either consensus or popular ballot.

National leadership in the Solomon Islands has long been dominated by Solomon Mamaloni, who died in January 2000, and Peter Kenilorea. Mamaloni's style of leadership was the "all rounder" who rubs shoulders with almost everybody whom he comes across. He was ready to help those who seek his assistance. It was his professed belief that Solomon Islanders should do things for themselves, as much as possible. Kenilorea, on the other hand, takes a different stance—a gentleman's approach with the usual formality and selectivity. Kenilorea is a real statesman and his contributions to the country have been well-recognized by the jobs he has been given after his occasional spells from politics.

By and large, most Solomon Islanders respect the members of parliament because many leaders have established close rapport with their people. Solomon Islands has experience with coalition governments, resulting from a weak party system, shifting party alliances, and frequent "number contests," often devoid of political merit. Inevitably, this leads to a lot of personal politics and the cult of individuals.

Social Problems and Control. For a long time the Solomon Islands has been free from large-scale social problems. Most problems were concentrated in urban areas, particularly Honiara. Otherwise the rural areas were quite free of conflicts other than the occasional land dispute cases and community arguments that emerged among villagers.

Unlike other countries where sectarian conflicts have flared among members of different religious groups, religious comity in the country is enviable. In the early twenty-first century, the most serious conflict was centered on Guadalcanal, where Guadalcanal residents faced off against resident Malaita people. The conflict arose when the police without due cause or care shot a Guadalcanal man. Thereafter, the conflict raged on. The Guadalcanal people formed an ethnic freedom fighters group called Isatabu Freedom Fighters and chased 20,000 people from Malaita who lived on Guadalcanal. Guadalcanal militants asserted that Malaitans have contributed to many of their problems. Later, a Malaita force was formed, called the Malaita Eagle Force. More than 50 people were killed in the early years of the conflict.

Other social problems prevalent mostly in urban areas include burglary, theft, break-ins, and general social discord between neighbors. During soccer matches, fights often break out between rival supporters. These fracas take serious dimensions when games are held between different island groups, especially during the annual competition between the best provincial teams, competing for the Solomon Cup.

Military Activity. The nation has no standing army or navy. It was only when the Bougainville Crisis spilled over from Papua New Guinea into the Solomon Islands in the early 1990s that the Police Field Force (PFF), a paramilitary unit, was established. Since the Guadalcanal conflict began in late 1998, the PFF has been instrumental in keeping order, arresting offenders and troublemakers and maintaining imposed government decrees in Honiara and around Guadalcanal.

SOCIAL WELFARE AND CHANGE PROGRAMS

The government of Bartholomew Ulufalu, which gained power in the 1997 election, was accommodating to major structural adjustment programs (SAPs) pushed by the International Monetary Fund (IMF) and the World Bank. For a long time, various governments were skeptical about SAPs. The fear was that devaluing the dollar, wage cuts, and other economic stringencies were meant to help only the urban economy. Rural areas, it was believed, would be adversely affected.

Ulufalu, however, as a trained economist, was inclined to adopt the program of the IMF and World Bank, and did so. Although the economy began recovering and revenue collection improved markedly, rural villagers saw their purchasing power diminished. The cost of essential services began to soar. School fees, for example, increased by more than 100 percent. Many rural parents could no longer afford to send their children to school. Thus, the structural adjustment program that was meant to improve social conditions merely exacerbated them.

NONGOVERNMETAL ORGANIZATIONS AND OTHER ASSOCIATIONS

Except for the churches, Nongovermental organizations (NGOs) arrived in the Solomon Islands in a big way only in the 1980s. There are the usual ones, which include the Red Cross, Rotary Club, Save the Children, and Catholic Relief. The best known NGO and the one that can be regarded as indigenous is the Solomon Islands Development Trust (SIDT). Well organized, well funded, and innovative in its aims and approach, SIDT has contributed to development in quite a revolutionary way with its emphasis on total change for the person (*metanoia*). It has mobile teams spreading their network in all corners of the country. In addition to a women's group, SIDT also offers opportunities for training and learning for those who would like to look at development and life in more innovative and empowering ways.

GENDER ROLES AND STATUSES

Division of Labor by Gender. In traditional societies, kastom dictates the roles of women and men. This was true in all the villages. Household duties were the preserve of the women, as were such gardening tasks as organizing garden boundaries, planting, and weeding. Men took care of felling trees to clear areas for gardens, building canoes, hunting, and fishing.

As Solomon Islanders encounter the Western lifestyle, there is a blurring of these traditional roles. Many Solomon Islanders, however, do not challenge traditional roles, rather they attempt to reconcile these roles with their new ones as doctors, lawyers, teachers, or even ministers and pastors in the churches.

MARRIAGE, FAMILY AND KINSHIP

Marriage. Traditionally, parents and adult relatives often arranged marriages. One of the reasons for this was to ensure not individual but social/communal compatibility. Love was developed not outside of marriage but within marriage. Marriage outside of the clan was often the norm but sometimes arrangements were made for marriage within the clan for exceptional reasons. Great care was taken that close relatives, ranging from first to third cousins, were not involved. The existence of a bride price (better termed ''bride gift'') differed from one group to the other and from one island group to another. The bride price was not a payment but compensation to the parents and the family for the ''loss'' of a family member.

Today marriage has changed markedly. Although traditional arranged marriage is still practiced, many marriages are a mixture of individuals making their choice with the blessings of the family. Today marriage can take the form of a court marriage, kastom marriage, church marriage, private marriage, or mere cohabiting. Cohabiting is not widely practiced because it is still socially stigmatized.

Domestic Unit. The family, by definition and through socialization, is ''extended'' in the Solomon Islands. Even in urban areas, family comes before money and food. As the saying goes, ''one cannot cry for money and food but certainly one weeps when one's relative or family member passes away.''

Who makes a family decision depends on the criticalness of the issue. Men often make critical decisions because they have to negotiate and account for the decisions if need be. Women often make decisions pertaining to the household, those that involve women's affairs, and those that involve her own relatives. Although men take on the critical decisions, women often play a role in these decisions in the background, out of the gaze of others.

Inheritance. In the Solomon Islands inheritance differs from one group and one island to another, with both patrilineal and matrilineal inheritance being practiced. For example, on Malaita it is patrilineal while on Guadalcanal it is matrilineal. Custom courts in these islands are cognizant of this. Even the national court system considers these differences in its decision making.

Inheritance includes not only material things but also knowledge, wisdom, and magical powers, which are often regarded as heirlooms of the tribe.

Residents of Honiara stroll on the street. As many as seventy distinct languages are spoken in the islands; one legacy of British colonizers is the use of English in formal places.

Fathers often pass on canoes, adzes, spears, and the necessary skills to use onto their sons. Where these are scarce, the first born is often given custody of the items, although the other sons may seek permission for their use from time to time. Mothers often pass on to their daughters body decorations, gardening and fishing skills, and magical incantations.

In towns, inheritance mostly involves money and Western goods and properties, such as houses and cars. In such cases, Western laws apply, especially the British laws of property.

Kin Groups. Belonging to a kinship group is still important in the Solomon Islands. The stigma that comes with not belonging to a kinship group is a heavy one—tantamount to be regarded a bastard.

As mentioned above, there are matrilineal kinship groups on islands such as Guadalcanal, Isabel, Shortlands, and Bougainville, and patrilineal groups on islands such as Malaita. Although one belongs to one's father's group or one's mother's group, secondary membership in the other side is never discounted. Today, there is a mixing of both sides and the strength of such relationship is regarded in terms of ''how often and easy people do things together.'' Being visible during a kinship event is important in order to make oneself known to other members, especially the young ones.

SOCIALIZATION

Infant Care. It is the parents' primary and foremost responsibility to care for their children. In the Solomon Islands, members of the extended family often help. Solomon Islanders believe that a child, especially an infant, should not have unrelated people close to her or him all the time; a close relative should look after the child. It is believed that infants should be soothed, calmed, or fed every time they cry for attention. It is only when children start to speak and think for themselves that they are slowly left alone.

Child Rearing and Education. Again, it is the parents and relatives who are responsible for the formative education and training of children. Children are taught to watch carefully, ask few questions, and then follow through by participating when asked. A good child is said to behave very much like her mother, if she is a girl, or father, if he is a boy. Good children carry family values with them in life. When one makes a mistake, the parents are often blamed. If the children do well, the parents receive the credit first.

A boy is said to be mature when he can build a house and canoe and make a garden. A girl is regarded as grown up when she can cultivate food gardens, hew wood, carry water, and look after her family and family members even when her mother is absent.

Higher Education. Higher education is highly prized in the Solomon Islands. Although fees are high, parents go to great lengths to pay for at least one of their children to get a decent education. Some wealthy families send their children to such places as New Zealand and Australia for their high school education. Only in 1992 did the first Solomon Islander receive a Ph.D.

ETIQUETTE

In the Solomon Islands, respect for elders and women, particularly in rural areas, is a must. On Malaita, infraction of such rules, especially those pertaining to the dignity of married women, often incurs the immediate payment of compensation. When one is talking to a woman who is not a relative, one is expected to look away as a sign of respect. Strangers are expected to be respected particularly as they are regarded as new and know little of community kastoms. Often when they make mistakes, strangers are gently reminded of community protocols.

Girls are not to show signs of friendliness to strangers, or even boyfriends, when they are with their brothers or relatives. Boys are mutually required to do the same as sign of respect to their sisters and relatives. When guests come to one's house, it is hospitable to allow them to eat first and eat the best. To do otherwise is a sign of moral weakness and lack of respect and dignity for oneself and one's family.

RELIGION

Religious Beliefs. Traditionally, Solomon Islanders believe that ancestors, although invisible, are still around. Therefore, one can invoke their help if need be or ask that their wrath or curse befall one's enemies. Animism was practiced before Christianity reached the islands. For believers in animism, most living things have spirits and it bodes well to maintain a cordial relationship with one's ancestors and the whole ecosystem. For those who live near the coast, totem gods include sharks,

octopi, and stingrays. Inland people worship crocodiles, snakes, the eagle, and the owl as deity totems.

Today Christianity pervades most of the country. There is a lot of syncretism between Christian worship and traditional beliefs. People usually pray to the Christian God but use ancestors or those who have recently died as mediators. The belief is that those who have passed on are closer to God and can "see" better.

Today, 90 percent of Solomon Islanders are professed Christians. The five main Christian churches are the Catholic, Anglican, South Sea Evangelical, Seventh Day Adventist, and Christian Fellowship (a derivative of Methodism). Beside Christians, there are traditional practitioners, Mormons, Muslims, and Baha'is.

Religious Practitioners. Teaching and preaching are accented in churches. Healing is one of the sacraments but not the major one. Some people in the Solomon Islands still practice traditional healing. In the Western Solomons, there are healers who can fix broken bones, massage swollen bodies, and cure aching heads. Others have the power to pull cursed objects from a victim's body by sucking them out or by sending another spirit to bring them back. Still others practice black magic.

Rituals and Holy Places. In the Solomon Islands, shrines are always taboo places. These are the places where ancestral remains are kept and ancestral spirits live. Small children are not allowed as the spirits would cause them harm. Nowadays, very few of these places have sacrifices offered as many people have become Christianized.

Today, only Christian rituals are regularly practiced and performed. For example, during the Easter season the stations of the cross is performed and special prayers offered. There are prayer walks in the night as faithful prayer warriors stage spiritual warfare against Satan and his host of angels.

Death and the Afterlife. Death is as important as birth in the Solomon Islands. When people are born, there is celebration. When they die, there is festivity to mark the passing away of a life.

It is believed that when people die, they merely "take the next boat" to the other world. But spirits do not go away immediately after death. They linger for a while as they find it difficult parting from their loved ones. Then after some time, the deceased spirits move on.

When there is a death, the corpse is kept above ground as long as possible. This is to allow all the

Workers tying thatch onto a new house in Honiara, Guadalcanal.

loved ones and family members to pay their last respects. After the deceased is buried, people resume their normal lives. The widow or widower and close relatives then cleanse themselves and continue life again.

MEDICINE AND HEALTH CARE

In traditional Solomon Island society, every disease has a spiritual cause or explanation to it. Before Western-introduced diseases, there were traditional cures for most diseases. With the introduction of Western diseases and medicine, the whole equation changed drastically.

Today, the Solomon Islands is accosted in varying degrees with diseases and medical challenges like most third world countries. Lifestyle diseases—including cardiovascular disease, stroke, cancer, and diabetes—have been blamed on dietary changes, namely the increasing dependence on imported foods such as white flour, white rice, sugar, and canned meat, as well as an increase in smoking and alcohol consumption. Among vector-borne diseases, malaria is prevalent in the country.

Despite the above, great strides have been made in the country. In the 1990s the average life expectancy was 63 years for men and 65 years for women.

SECULAR CELEBRATIONS

The Solomon Islands has a number of secular celebrations. The first is Independence Day (7 July), which is a colorful day when most island people converge on the capital (Honiara) to celebrate. Queen's birthday (12 June), is usually co-celebrated with Independence Day, and commemorates the birth of Queen Elizabeth II of England. Honors and medals are given to those who have done heroic and great things for the country and people. Christmas Day (25 December) is always a time when families disperse from the capital and meet with their loved ones at their homes to celebrate Christ's birthday. The Christmas holiday is not only a religious holiday, but also the longest holiday of the year for most people. New Year (1 January) is the most celebrated day of each year. There is a tradition of playing a lot of games, especially water games, and competitions between villages.

THE ARTS AND HUMANITIES

Support for the Arts. Artists in the Solomon Islands are mostly self-supporting. With the encouragement of tourism in the late twentieth century, many more people have taken up the arts, with the specific intention of making money from their artistic skills.

Literature. Literature, both written and oral, has had a sporadic history in the Solomon Islands. It has been seriously studied only since the 1970s. There is a writers' association that has an open membership for all who are interested. This has encouraged both oral and written literatures.

Graphic Arts. The graphic arts are also a relatively new area promoted mostly through touristic advertisements and salesmanship. Graphic arts courses are now offered during summer semesters at the University of the South Pacific Center in Honiara. With more businesses being set up in the capital, many graphic artists have had tremendous income earnings. Sign writing, for example, has been a big moneymaker.

Performance Arts. Music has been a popular pastime in the Solomon Islands. In most of the islands, music is made to keep people together and enhance their companionship. Many Solomon Islanders are natural song composers. The Sulufou Islanders and the Fuaga Brothers are two of the more popular bands.

Drama is valued for its ability to pass on certain messages and influence decisions. Many schools have drama groups that perform historical stories, such as World War II battle tales.

THE STATE OF THE PHYSICAL AND SOCIAL SCIENCES

The Solomon Islands College of Higher Education (SICHE) is an institution founded in 1984 that grew out of the old Teachers' Training College. Since its inception, its achievements have been remarkable. SICHE's schools include industrial arts, agriculture, nursing and health studies, and education. SICHE also has a Solomon Islands studies program, which has not yet been fully developed.

BIBLIOGRAPHY

Akin, David. Negotiating culture in East Kwaio, Malaita, Solomon Islands, Ph.D. diss., University of Hawaii, Honolulu, 1993.

Australian Agency for International Development. *The Solomon Islands Economy: Achieving Sustainable Economic Development*, 1995.

Gegeo, David. "History, Empowerment, and Social Responsibility: Views of a Pacific Islands Indigenous Scholar." Keynote address delivered at the 12th meeting of the *Pacific History Association*, Honiara, Solomon Islands, June 1998.

———. Kastom and Binis: towards integrating cultural knowledge into rural development in Solomon Islands." Ph.D. diss., University of Hawaii at Manoa, 1994.

———, "Indigenous Knowledge in Community and Literacy Development: Strategies for Empowerment from Within." Unpublished paper, 1997.

Hogbin, Ian H. "Coconuts and Coral Islands," *National Geographic Magazine* 65 (3), 1934.

Kabutaulaka, Tarcisus. "Solomon Islands: A Review." *Contemporary Pacific: A Journal of Island Affairs* 11 (2): 443–449, 1999.

LaFranchi, Christopher. *Islands Adrift? Comparing Industrial and Small-Scale Economic Options for Maravovo Lagoon Region of the Solomon Islands*, 1999.

Lockwood, Victoria S., Thomas G. Harding, and Ben J. Wallace. *Contemporary Pacific Societies: Studies in Development and Change*, 1993.

O'Callaghan, Mary-Lousie. *Solomon Islands: A New Economic Strategy*, 1994.

O'Connor, Gulbun Coker. The Moro movement of Guadalcanal, Ph.D. diss., University of Pennsylvania, 1973.

Talu, Alaimu, and Max Quanchi, eds., *Messy Entanglements*, 1995.

Tryon, Darrell T., and B. D. Hackman. *Solomon Island Languages: An Internal Classification*, 1983.

United Nations Development Program. *Pacific Human Development Report, 1999: Creating Opportunities*, 1999.

—JOHN MOFFAT FUGUI

SOMALIA

CULTURE NAME
Somali

ALTERNATIVE NAMES
Somali Democratic Republic, Soomaaliya (in Somali)

ORIENTATION

Identification. Somalia was known to the ancient Egyptians as the Land of Punt. They valued its trees which produced the aromatic gum resins frankincense and myrrh. Punt is also mentioned in the Bible, and ancient Romans called it Cape Aromatica. Somalia is named for the legendary father of the Somali people, Samaal (or Samale).

The Somali people share a common language, Somali, and most are Muslims of the Sunni sect. Somalis also live in northern Kenya; in the Ogaden region of eastern Ethiopia; and in Djibouti, to the northwest of Somalia. In spite of national boundaries, all Somalis consider themselves one people. This unity makes them one of Africa's largest ethnic groups.

Location and Geography. Somalia is on the outer edge of the Somali Peninsula, also called the Horn of Africa, on the East African coast. It is bordered on the north by the Gulf of Aden, on the east by the Indian Ocean, on the southwest by Kenya, and on the west and northwest by Ethiopia and Djibouti.

At approximately 246,200 square miles (637,658 square kilometers), Somalia is about the size of Texas. Its coastline extends about 1,800 miles (2,896 kilometers). Somalia is hot for much of the year, with two wet and two dry seasons. Vegetation is generally sparse, except in the area between the Jubba and the Shabeelle Rivers in south-central Somalia.

A semiarid plain called the Guban runs parallel to the northern coast of Somalia. The Karkaar Mountains extend from Somalia's northwestern border to the eastern tip of the Horn of Africa, with the highest point, Shimber Berris, at 7,900 feet (2,408 meters). South of the mountain ranges, a central plateau known as the Haud extends to the Shabeelle River and westward into the Ogaden region of eastern Ethiopia. During the rainy seasons, from April to June and from October to November, this area provides plenty of water and grazing lands for livestock.

Somalia's two rivers, the Jubba and the Shabeelle, flow from the Ethiopian highlands into southeastern Somalia. The Shabeelle (Leopard) River does not enter the Indian Ocean but instead turns parallel to the coast and runs southward for 170 miles (274 kilometers) before drying up in marshes and sand flats. The Jubba flows year-round into the Indian Ocean.

The port city of Mogadishu, in southeastern Somalia on the Indian Ocean, is the largest city and the traditional capital of Somalia. Mogadishu was largely destroyed in the fighting between clans during the civil war of the 1990s. In 2000 a Somali assembly voted to make Mogadishu the new president's base but to move other government functions to the city of Baidoa, northwest of Mogadishu, until the capital could be rebuilt.

Demography. No census was taken in Somalia until 1975, and those figures were not reported. The large number of nomads makes it difficult to get an accurate population count. Population estimates have been made based on the 1986–1987 census, which recorded a population of 7.1 million. In spite of the death toll due to famine and civil war in the 1990s, 2000 population estimates range from 9 million to 14.5 million. About three-quarters of the people live in rural areas and one-quarter in the cities. Ethnic Somalis make up about 95 percent of the population. The remainder are Indians, Pakistanis, other Asians, Arabs, Europeans, and groups of mixed ancestry.

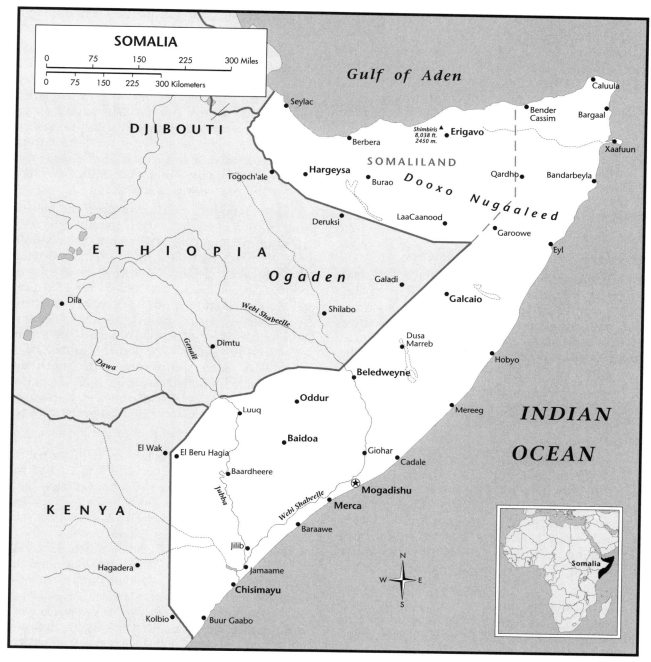

Somalia

Linguistic Affiliation. All Somalis speak Somali, the official language. In the Afro-Asiatic family of languages, Somali is an Eastern Cushitic language. Somali did not become a written language until January 1973. Common Somali is the most widely spoken dialect, but Coastal Somali and Central Somali also are spoken. Somalis frequently use wordplay and humor in everyday communication.

Arabic, the language of the Qur'an, is spoken and read for religious purposes. A small percentage of Somalis also speak Italian, and a growing number speak English. Educated young adults from well-to-do urban families may speak five or more languages.

Symbolism. The most widely recognized symbol is the camel, because it provides transportation, milk, meat, income, and status to a majority of Somalis.

Other symbols of Somalia are the five-pointed white star on the Somali flag and the crescent, which represents the new moon and is a universal symbol of the Islamic faith. Each point of the star represents a land that is home to Somali people: the portion within the national boundaries, once divided into two territories, Italian and British; the Ogaden region of Ethiopia; the Northern Frontier District of Kenya; and Djibouti. Somalis hope that one day all these territories can become a unified Somali nation.

The leopard is considered the national symbol of Somalia. Two African leopards adorn the national emblem, a five-pointed white star on a light blue shield with a gold border.

HISTORY AND ETHNIC RELATIONS

Emergence of the Nation. The origin of the Somali people is uncertain. Current theory suggests that the Somali originated in the southern Ethiopian highlands and migrated into northern Kenya during the first millennium B.C.E. They then gradually migrated northward to populate the Horn of Africa by C.E. 100.

The Somalis are tall and wiry in stature, with aquiline features, elongated heads, and light brown to black skin. Somali women are known for their beauty.

Arabs introduced the Islamic faith to Africa beginning in the seventh century. By the tenth century, Arab trading posts thrived in southern Somalia, along the Indian Ocean. These included Mogadishu, established as the first Arab settlement in East Africa. The city was at the height of its influence and wealth during the thirteenth century, when it controlled the gold trade on the East African coast.

Most Somalis converted to Islam by about 1100. They joined with the Arabs in fighting the Islamic holy wars against Ethiopian Christians in the fifteenth and sixteenth centuries. By the eighteenth century the Somalis had defeated the Oromo people, who had threatened both Muslims and Christians in Ethiopia and Somalia. The Somalis became the dominant people in the land.

Europeans became interested in Somalia during the nineteenth century, beginning with its exploration by British adventurer Sir Richard Burton in 1854. Interest grew when the Suez Canal opened in 1869, and in 1887 Britain declared the northern Somalia coast a protectorate, known as British Somaliland. The French claimed the far western coast (now Djibouti) at about the same time, naming it French Somaliland. Italy took control of southern Somalia, including Mogadishu, in 1889, naming it Italian Somaliland.

In 1899 Somali Islamic teacher Muhammad Abdullah Hasan (1856–1920), known to the British as "the Mad Mullah," gathered an army. They hoped to gain the Ogaden region of Ethiopia for Somalis and to drive out the non-Islamic Europeans. Hasan and his army, called Dervishes, fought the Ethiopians and later the British from 1900 to 1920. The British bombed the Dervish capital in 1920 and Hasan escaped, but he died later that year, ending the resistance movement.

At the beginning of World War II the Italians drove the British from northern Somalia. The British recaptured Somalia and drove out the Italians in 1941. In 1949 the United Nations (U.N.) General Assembly awarded Italy administrative control over southern Somalia as a trust territory for a ten-year period that would then lead to Somalia's independence. British Somaliland was awarded its independence on 26 June 1960 and united with Italian Somaliland to establish the Somali Republic on 1 July 1960. After independence, parliamentary leader Aadan Abdullah Usmaan was appointed president by the legislature. He appointed Abdirashiid Ali Shermaarke the first prime minister of Somalia.

National Identity. Although united as one nation in 1960, northern and southern Somalia had for years functioned as two separate countries, with separate school systems, taxes, currencies, police, and political and legal administrations. As early as December 1961, northern Somali military leaders pushed for separation of the north and the south. At the same time, most Somalis wanted to unite the regions outside of Somalia that were populated with many Somalis—the Ogaden, the NFD in Kenya, and Djibouti. In the 1960s, a guerrilla warfare campaign by Somali *shiftas* (bandits) in Kenya and skirmishes over the Ogaden region resulted in a mutual defense agreement against the Somalis by Kenya and Ethiopia.

Former prime minister Shermaarke was elected president in 1967, and his prime minister, Muhammad Ibrahim Egal, focused on internal development and restoration of peace with Ethiopia and Kenya.

Shermaarke was assassinated by a bodyguard on 15 October 1969. Somali military took control of Mogadishu in a *coup d'état* on 21 October 1969.

The new government, called the Supreme Revolutionary Council (SRC), chose army commander Major General Muhammad Siad Barre as president and renamed Somalia the Somali Democratic Republic. Based on principles of Marxism as well as on the Qur'an and on Siad Barre's ideas about self-reliance for the Somali people, this new political ideology for Somalia was known as "scientific socialism."

Somalia was engaged in the Ogaden War with Ethiopia in 1977–1978. Defeated, Somalia suffered an economic decline, and there was growing national opposition to Siad Barre's leadership, nearly a one-man government by 1982. Siad Barre was severely injured in a car accident on 23 May 1986, and a power struggle for control of the government began between political leaders and clan leaders. Siad Barre recovered and was nominated for another seven-year term, but various clans whose members had been terrorized by Siad Barre's Red Berets (a military terrorist unit from his own clan, the Mareehaan) rose up against him.

In 1990, members of the Hawiye clan of south-central Somalia formed the United Somali Congress (USC), and in December they stormed Mogadishu and defeated the Red Berets. Siad Barre escaped to Nigeria. The USC's leader, Muhammad Ali Mahdi, was appointed president, but Hawiye subclan leader General Muhammad Farah Aidid, of the Habir Gedir subclan, also claimed power. The two disagreed on forming a central government for Somalia, and civil war began.

Somali civilians suffered the most in the unstable years that followed. It was estimated that some three hundred thousand Somalis died between 1991 and mid-1993. Although international relief organizations sent food and supplies, much was stolen by bandits and warring clan members before it could reach those who needed it most.

U.N. secretary-general Boutros Boutros-Ghali arranged a truce between Mahdi and Aidid in December 1992, but clan members continued to fight. The United States led Operation Restore Hope in 1992, and U.N. countries sent food and supplies, along with soldiers to ensure that they reached the people. In mid-1993 the U.N. Security Council resolved to turn the operation into a "nation-building" effort that would include disarming militias and restoring political and civil institutions. The operation deteriorated as Somalis and U.N. troops committed acts of violence against one another. U.S. troops were pulled out of Somalia in early 1994, and the last U.N. troops left in March 1995.

Aidid died in the fighting in Mogadishu in August 1996, but his son, Hussein Muhammad Aidid, took his place and continued his father's mission to put their subclan in control of Somalia.

After U.N. aid slowed and troops were withdrawn, the situation gradually improved in Somalia. Farmers returned home and produced a good harvest in 1995. Although clan fighting continued in 1997 and 1998 and no central government was established, local governments continued to function.

In August 2000, after twelve failed attempts to organize a central government, some two thousand Somalis representing the clans and subclans met in Djibouti to discuss forming a government for Somalia.

During the clan wars of the early 1990s, northern Somalia declared itself the independent Somaliland Republic, appointed former Somali prime minister Muhammad Ibrahim Egal as its president, wrote a constitution, developed an assembly, and governmental institutions, and began to function successfully apart from the warring to the south. Although it has not been recognized as a separate nation, the Somaliland Republic continues to declare itself independent. Members of the Murjateen clan in northeastern Somalia also formed their own government during the 1990s, calling their territory Puntland, although they agreed to rejoin Somalia if a central government was formed.

Ethnic Relations. Some 95 percent of the people of Somalia are ethnic Somalis, and relations with the small percentage of Arabs, Indians, Pakistanis, Asians, Europeans, and mixed groups living in Somalia are generally peaceful. With a history of colonization by the British, French, and Italians, the Somalis are said to be wary of foreigners, even fearful of possible renewed colonization. Somali civilians, however, welcomed U.N. troops arriving during Operation Restore Hope in the early 1990s, and most Somalis welcome the international relief workers who have become a part of daily life in post-civil war Somalia.

Urbanism, Architecture, and the Use of Space

Nomadic herders spend nearly all of their time outdoors. A large shade tree might provide a meeting place or a classroom.

The traditional shelter of the herders is the *aqal*, a dome-shaped, collapsible hut made from poles covered by hides, woven fiber mats, or sometimes cloth or tin. Easy to break down and reassemble, the aqal is carried on a camel's back and set up by the women of the family once a new camp is made. A bed made from wooden stakes covered with hides is

Somalian famine victims wait in line for food in Baidoa. Although said to be wary of foreigners, Somalis have welcomed the international relief workers present since the 1990s.

the only furniture in the aqal. Nomads have few possessions, and each item has practical uses. Cooking utensils, storage boxes, stools, woven mats, and water bags are among the family's only household goods.

A nomad camp may be surrounded by a fence made from thorn bushes to keep out predators. Animals are also kept in corrals made from thorn bushes. A prayer area may be set apart within the camp by a circle of stones.

Farmers make permanent homes that are similar to the aqal. Round huts called *mundals* are made from poles and brush or vines plastered with mud, animal dung, and ashes and covered with a broad, cone-shaped thatched roof. Rectangular huts, often with flat tin roofs, are called *arish*. Other homes are built from logs, stone, brick, or cement. Farmers have a few pieces of wooden furniture and decorative pottery, gourds, or woven goods.

City dwellers often live in Arab-style white-washed houses made of stone or brick covered with plaster or cement. These are one-or two-story houses, with a flat roof. Bars cover the lower windows, which rarely have screens or glass. Wealthy Somalis, Europeans, and others may have traditional Western-style homes with tile roofs and walled courtyards. Many Somalis, even in the cities, do not have electricity and running water in their homes.

Somalia's largest cities are the ports of Mogadishu, Merca, Baraawe, and Kismayu on the Indian Ocean, and Berbera on the Gulf of Aden. Other significant cities are Hargeisa and Burao in the north and Baidoa in the south. Mogadishu's oldest sector, Hammawein, contains the mosque of Fakr al-Din as well as many old Arab-style buildings. Italian occupants also built their own neighborhoods in Mogadishu. Much of this architecture was heavily damaged in the civil war, along with modern Somali government buildings such as Parliament House and Somali National University. The former palace of the sultan of Zanzibar still stands, although in poor condition, as a museum in Mogadishu. A few statues and monuments were erected in Mogadishu but several were destroyed, among them an equestrian statue of Muhammad Abdullah Hasan, erected after Somalia's independence in 1960. A monument to independence also was built in Mogadishu. The city's oldest mosque, the mosque of Sheik Abdul Aziz, built in 1238, survived the civil war, along with a Roman arch built in the early twentieth century.

FOOD AND ECONOMY

Food in Daily Life. Milk from camels, goats, and cows is a major food for Somali herdsmen and nomadic families. Young men tending camel herds during the rainy season may drink up to ten quarts of milk a day. Aging camels may be slaughtered for their meat, especially when guests are expected for a celebration, and the fatty camel's hump is considered a delicacy. Meat, including liver, from sheep and goats also is popular, but meat is served only a few times a month, usually on special occasions. Durra (a grain sorghum), honey, dates, rice, and tea are other food staples for nomads. Farmers in southern Somalia grow corn, beans, sorghum, millet, squash, and a few other vegetables and fruits. Boiled millet and rice are staples, but rice must be imported. The most popular bread is *muufo*, a flat bread made from ground corn flour. Somalis season their food with butter and ghee, the clear liquid skimmed from melted butter. They also sweeten their food with sugar, sorghum, or honey. A holdover from Italian occupation in the south is a love for pasta and marinara sauce. Although fish is plentiful in the waters off the Somali coast, Somalis generally do not like fish. In accordance with the Muslim faith, they do not eat pork or drink alcohol. Milk, tea, coffee, and water are favorite drinks. Carbonated drinks are available in cities.

Among nomads and farmers, cooking is usually done over a wood or charcoal fire outdoors or in a communal cooking hut, because homes are large enough only for sleeping. Grain is ground by hand, using primitive tools.

Restaurants are popular in cities, but women seldom dined out with men until the late 1990s. Arab cuisine is popular fare in many restaurants, Italian at others. Especially in Mogadishu, international restaurants serve Chinese, European, and sometimes American foods.

At home it is customary for women to serve the men first, and then eat with their children after the men have finished. Rural Somalis eat by scooping food from a bowl with the first three fingers of their right hand or with a spoon (as in many other Muslim and African cultures, the left hand is considered unclean because it is used for washing the body). A rolled banana leaf also may be used for scooping. Urban Somalis may use silverware when they dine, but many still enjoy eating with their fingers.

Food Customs at Ceremonial Occasions. Weddings, births, circumcisions, and Islamic and secular holidays call for celebrations involving food. Families slaughter animals, make bread, and prepare food for guests and for the poor, who are often invited to join the celebration.

Basic Economy. Somalia is one of the world's poorest countries, and many gains made during the years after independence were lost in the destruction brought about by civil war in the 1990s. However, in 2000, individuals had begun to help rebuild cities through independent businesses. Among the factors hindering economic development is lack of adequate transportation. The country has no railroads, only one airline, and few paved roads. Financial assistance from the United States helped improve Somalia's major seaports and Mogadishu International Airport during the 1980s. Telecommunication systems were largely destroyed during the civil war. However, in 1999, independent businessmen in some towns established satellite telephone systems and electricity, and Somali livestock traders and other entrepreneurs conducted much of their business by telephone. Banking networks also were being established.

The basic monetary unit is the Somali shilling, with one hundred cents equal to one shilling. A large amount of the income received by Somalis comes from Somalis who have migrated to other countries to find work and send money and goods home to relatives.

Land Tenure and Property. In precolonial times, land claims were made by families and through bargaining among clan members. During European colonization, Italians established plantations in the riverine area and settled many poor Italian families on the land to raise crops. Since independence much of this land has been farmed by Somalis.

Somali nomads consider pastureland available to all, but if a family digs a water well, it is considered their possession. Under Siad Barre's socialist regime there was an effort to lease privately owned land to government cooperatives, but Somalis resented working land they did not own. Some land was sold in urban areas, but grazing land continued to be shared.

Commercial Activities. In the colonial era Italians developed banana, sugarcane, and citrus fruit plantations in southern Somalia. These again thrived in the late twentieth century with Italian assistance after a decade of decline due to high government taxation of exports in the 1980s. Livestock and animal products make up a large portion of the goods produced in Somalia.

The country's few natural resources, such as gypsum-anhydrite, quartz, uranium, iron ore, and possibly gold, have not been widely exploited.

Major Industries. Although Somalia is not an industrialized nation, there are some industries, such as fish and meat canneries, milk-processing plants, sugar refineries, leather-tanning factories, and pharmaceutical and electronics factories. Many of these were built with the help of foreign nations such as the former Soviet Union. Some mining and petroleum exploration has been done, with the help of Middle Eastern countries.

Trade. Transportation equipment, machinery, cement and other building materials, iron, and steel are major imports of Somalia. Most of the imports come from Italy, Ethiopia and Kenya, China, Saudi Arabia, India and Pakistan, the United States, and Great Britain. Livestock is the country's main export, especially camels, which are sold to Saudi Arabia and other Arab nations. Animal hides also are exported. Bananas are the chief crop export. Coffee, cotton, peanuts, mangoes, citrus fruits, and sugarcane are other important crops. Fishing and the export of frankincense and myrrh add to the economy.

Division of Labor. More than half of all Somalis are self-employed, as herders, farmers, or independent business owners. In the cities, some workers once held government jobs, and in 2000 a growing percentage of workers had factory, plantation, or fishing-industry jobs. Among rural Somalis of the Saab clan-family, lower castes still provide certain types of goods and services.

SOCIAL STRATIFICATION

Classes and Castes. The Samaal believe that their clan-family is superior to the Saab. The Saab clan-family developed a caste system that awards status to different groups based on their heritage or occupation. Lower-class groups among the Digil and Rahanwayn were identified by occupation. The largest group was the *midgaan* (a derogatory name), who served as barbers, circumcisers, and hunters. The Tumaal were blacksmiths and metalworkers. The Yibir served as fortune-tellers and makers of protective amulets and charms. In the late twentieth century, many from these groups found work in towns and cities and raised their status, and the old arrangements whereby they served certain clans had largely disappeared by the 1990s.

A small percentage of the peoples of the riverine and southern coastal area are descendants of a pre-Somali people who lived in the Horn of Africa. Added to this group are descendants of Africans once enslaved by the Somalis. These cultural groups are called *habash*. While not poorly treated, habash are considered inferior by the Somalis. Most habash are Muslims and speak Somali, although some, such as the coastal groups Bajuni and Amarani, speak Swahili.

Symbols of Social Stratification. Among the nomads, wealthier men were traditionally those who owned more camels and other livestock. Warriors and priests were considered to have the most prestigious vocations. In some Rahanwayn and Digil settlements, members are divided between Darkskins and Lightskins, with those of darker skins having slightly more prestige in ceremonies, although the two are considered equal in other ways.

By 2000, education, income, and the ability to speak foreign languages had become standards by which status was attained among urban Somalis.

POLITICAL LIFE

Government. During most of the 1990s there was no central government in Somalia. However, some of the fifty districts and eight regional councils formed at the Addis Accords of March 1993 survived into 2000.

In August 2000, Somalis met in a representative council in Djibouti and took the first steps toward reestablishing a government for Somalia. A 245-member assembly made up of men and women representing all clans chose a new president and wrote a transitional constitution. The assembly was to function as a transitional government for three years. It appointed a new Somali president, Abdikassim Salad Hassan, a leader of the Habir Gedir subclan in the Mogadishu region. Allied with the Islamic courts and Somali businessowners, Salad proposed unity, peace, and prosperity for all of Somalia. After three years under the transitional government, national elections were to be held.

Leadership and Political Officials. Somalis are traditionally an independent and democratic people but are fiercely loyal to their clan and its associated political party. Ceremonial clan leaders are called sultans, or *bokor* in Somali, a term referring to binding the people together. Actual rule and enforcement of clan laws usually fall to the elders and a council made up of the clan's adult males.

Somalia's first modern political party, the Somali Youth Club (SYC), was formed in Mogadishu in 1943, at the urging of British colonial officials. A

Women greeting each other in Mogadishu. Somali women generally do not socialize with men in public places.

multiclan organization that favored Somali unity, it was renamed the Somali Youth League (SYL) in 1947. Throughout Somalia's modern history it remained the strongest political party.

During Siad Barre's dictatorship, political parties were prohibited in Somalia, but several organized outside the country and sought to overthrow the regime. Among them was the Somali National Movement (SNM), a militant party organized by Isaaq clan members living in London. In alliance with the rebel United Somali Congress (USC) and the Somali Patriotic Movement (SPM), it was able to overthrow Siad Barre in 1991.

After ousting the dictator, however, disagreements and fighting broke out among the three parties as well as the clans, subclans, and various guerrilla groups, plummeting the nation into civil war that lasted throughout the 1990s.

Social Problems and Control. Under the central government formed at independence, Somalia developed a Western-style judicial system, with a penal code, a code of criminal court procedures, and a four-tiered court system. Islamic law (*Shari'a*) and Somali customary law (*heer*) were retained in many civil and interclan matters. The Somali Police Force evolved from forces organized during colonial administration by the Italians and the British. The most common crimes committed are shootings, robbery and theft, looting, and kidnapping for ransom.

Somali clans have a traditional means of compensating for lives lost in interclan disputes, thereby discouraging violence and encouraging peaceful settlement. The clan responsible for the death pays the victim's clan a fine, called *dia*, traditionally a set number of camels or other livestock. A certain percentage of the dia—called *jiffo*—is paid by the immediate relatives of the one responsible for the death to the immediate family of the deceased. Dia is also paid, in a lesser amount, for other crimes, such as rape, adultery, and theft. Dia-paying groups are formed by agreement among closely related clan members. Enforcement of dia customs falls to the elders and the clan council. If a matter cannot be settled peacefully, fighting breaks out between clans, followed by another peace council.

Military Activity. The Somali National Army (SNA) was formed at independence from military groups created under British and Italian colonial rule. Somalia was allied with the Soviet Union during the 1960s, receiving both military training and weapons from the Soviets, as well as from Egypt and other Muslim states. Before the Ogaden War of 1977–1978, Somalia's military was one of the largest and best-armored and mechanized in sub-Saharan Africa. After it lost the war and the Soviets withdrew support, however, the Somali military declined.

During the early 1980s it received training and weapons from the United States, France, Italy, and Saudi Arabia. However, when the Western world learned of human-rights violations under Siad Barre, it withdrew military support. After Siad Barre's fall, the Somali military ceased to exist.

SOCIAL WELFARE AND CHANGE PROGRAMS

Probably the largest efforts at social welfare and change in Somalia came during the 1960s and 1970s, the years after independence, and the early years of Siad Barre's socialist regime. Barre attempted to do away with the clan system and create a heterogeneous society. Some nomads were settled as farmers, ranchers, or fishermen. Under Barre the status of women improved, a written alphabet was created for Somalia, and there were increased efforts in the areas of literacy and education.

NONGOVERNMENTAL ORGANIZATIONS AND OTHER ASSOCIATIONS

Associations active in providing relief to the starving and the ill in Somalia during the late 1980s and 1990s were the International Red Cross, Doctors Without Borders, the Red Crescent, the United Nations (U.N.) World Food Program, Save the Children Service, Cooperative for Assistance and Relief Everywhere, Inc. (CARE), Irish Concern, and many others. Somalis provided a large portion of this care as well.

In 2000 and 2001, a dozen U.N. agencies, among them the World Health Organization (WHO), the U.N. Children's Fund (UNICEF), and the U.N. Development Program (UNDP), provided all types of aid to Somalia. They continue to be assisted by NGOs both from around the world and within Somalia.

In 1994 a group of Somali women educated in Western countries returned to their homeland to help Somali women who were striving to rebuild the economy by starting their own businesses. The group, called the Somali Women's Trust, also helped establish girls' schools and women's health centers, and helped reestablish refugees in Somalia. Another Somali women's group, Candlelight, provides similar services.

GENDER ROLES AND STATUSES

Division of Labor by Gender. In traditional Samaal clans, men and older boys do the important work of tending camels and cattle, the most valuable animals. Girls and young boys tend sheep and goats. Somali men are considered warriors (*waranle*), except for those few who choose the religious life. Adult men are also expected to serve on their clan-family council. Urban men may work as businessmen, blacksmiths, craftsmen, fishermen, or factory workers.

Women in nomadic clans are responsible for caring for children, cooking, and moving the family aqal. Women and girls in farming clans are responsible for planting and harvesting crops, caring for children, and cooking. Urban women may hold jobs in shops or offices or may run their own business.

The Relative Status of Women and Men. Somali women are expected to submit to men and to fulfill their duties as daughters, wives, and mothers. Although they do not wear the Muslim veil, they generally do not socialize with men in public places. Somali women living in the cities, especially those

A Somali nomad woman ties roof supports together to reconstruct a portable hut after moving to a new location. The aqal is easy to breakdown and reassemble.

educated in other countries, dress and behave more like Western women.

Given the right to vote in newly independent Somalia, women began to take an active interest in politics and served on government committees and the People's Assembly. They served in military units and played sports. Opportunities for secondary and higher education had increased for women before the collapse of the government in 1991.

With many Somali men killed during the civil war or lost to diseases such as tuberculosis, women have learned to fend for themselves. They have shown remarkable adaptability and a talent for business. The United Nations and other international organizations launched campaigns in the late 1990s to help Somali women and girls get better health care, an education, and job skills training. Somali natives who have been educated abroad are returning to help with these endeavors. Several programs have been started to promote nomadic women's enterprises, such as the collecting of henna leaves for grinding into natural cosmetics. Women in urban areas sell wares in the streets or marketplaces or run their own shops.

In spite of condemnation by the United Nations and by modern Muslim leaders, nearly all Somali girls are forced to undergo the dangerous and dis-

figuring circumcision rite known to the United Nations as "female genital mutilation" (FGM). Somalia also has one of Africa's highest maternal mortality rates; approximately sixteen mothers die for every one thousand live births. Widespread efforts to correct unsafe practices in reproductive health are expected to improve these conditions in the twenty-first century.

MARRIAGE, FAMILY, AND KINSHIP

Marriage. Somali marriages have traditionally been considered a bond between not just a man and a woman but also between clans and families. Until very recently, most Somali marriages were arranged, usually between an older man with some wealth and the father of a young woman he wished to wed. These customs still hold true in many rural areas in the twenty-first century. The man pays a bride price—usually in livestock or money—to the woman's family. Samaal traditionally marry outside their family lineage, or, if within the lineage, separated from the man by six or more generations. Saab follow the Arab tradition of marrying within the father's family lineage, with first cousins often marrying. A Somali bride often lives with her husband's family after marriage, with her own parents providing the home and household goods. She keeps her family name, however.

Weddings are joyous occasions, but the couple often signs an agreement giving the bride a certain amount of property should the couple divorce, which is common in Somalia. The husband holds the property in trust for her. Tradition calls for the wife to relinquish her right to the property if she initiates the divorce.

Islamic law permits a man to have up to four wives if he can provide them and their children with equal support. If a man repeats three times to his wife, "I divorce you," the couple is considered divorced. The wife is given a three-month grace period, however, in case she should be pregnant.

Today many urban Somalis choose a mate based on love and common interests rather than accepting an arranged marriage.

Domestic Unit. The Somali domestic unit consists of a man, his wife or wives, and their children. Elderly or unmarried relatives may live with the family. In homes with more than one wife, each wife usually lives with her children in her own house, and the husband and father divides his time among them. In the case of a divorce, children usually remain with their mother. The male is considered the head of the household, except where it is headed by a divorced or widowed woman.

Inheritance. Inheritance passes from father to son in Somali families. A wife remains a part of her father's lineage, while her children belong to her husband's lineage.

Under Islamic law, daughters are entitled to inherit half of what sons get, but in Somali society daughters usually did not receive valuable animals or land. Under Siad Barre's regime, social reforms included equal inheritance rights for women, although this was opposed by some Islamic leaders.

Kin Groups. Somali society is based on a clan-family structure. The two major clan groups are the Samaal (or Samale) and the Saab (or Sab), named for two brothers who are said to have been members of the prophet Muhammad's tribe, the Quraysh of Arabia. Many Somalis believe that their ancestor from Old Testament times was Noah's son Ham.

The Samaal, which make up about three-quarters of the Somali population, are divided into four main clan-families: the Dir, Daarood, Isaaq, and Hawiye. The Saab are divided into the Digil and Rahanwayn clan-families. Major clans can have thousands of members, each claiming descent from a common ancestor. These clans are subdivided into subclans and into primary lineage groups. Somali men trace their membership in a particular clan-family through their patrilineage, going back a dozen or more generations. Clan groups with the longest ancestry have the most prestige. Clans and subclans are associated with the territory they occupy for most of the year.

SOCIALIZATION

Child Rearing and Education. Somali children are raised with much love but are also disciplined and taught to work from age five or six, with little time for play. In spite of numerous hardships, Somali children are known for their sense of joy and abundant laughter. Children are taught independence and self-reliance and to carefully observe the world around them.

Both boys and girls are circumcised during a ceremony and celebration. Boys and girls are kept separated, according to Islamic law, and traditionally do not date, although a group of teenage males do a courtship dance for girls of marriageable age.

Because of the high incidence of divorce, many children grow up with only one parent, usually the mother, although boys may stay with their father and his wives. Multiple wives make for family groups with many children.

Education for Somali children in all but the wealthiest urban families was practically nonexistent, except for training in reading the Qur'an, before the early 1970s. Boys in rural areas attended outdoor schools where they learned Arabic using wooden slates. Before independence some attended Roman Catholic schools, where they learned Arabic or Italian. Under Siad Barre, a Latin-based alphabet was created for the Somali language, which previously had no written form. The leader undertook a massive literacy campaign in Somalia and achieved some success, although many nomadic children still did not attend school, and many others, especially girls, dropped out after four years of primary school.

Students learned reading, writing, and arithmetic as well as Arabic, animal husbandry, and agriculture. A lack of trained teachers, materials, and schools, however, made secondary-school classes inadequate, and only about 10 percent of students went on to secondary school.

When civil war broke out, most secular education stopped, as schools were bombed and the government, which had hired teachers, collapsed. However, some dedicated teachers struggled on during

A woman and child in Og Village, Ainabo. Somali children are raised with much love, combined with discipline.

the 1990s, often without pay. Students continued to come, eager to learn even when there were no chairs or desks and no roof on the school. In the absence of a government, parents contributed what they could toward supplies so their children could continue to get an education.

Higher Education. Somali National University in Mogadishu, founded in 1970, was the nation's principal university before the civil war. Courses were offered in education, sciences, law, medicine, engineering, geology, economics, agriculture, and veterinary science. The National Adult Education Center was established in the late 1970s to combat a relapse in literacy among the adult nomadic population.

In 1981 the Nomad Education Program was created by the Barre government, which established boarding schools in ten regions and selected students from various clan-families to attend school for sixty days. Students ranged in age from fourteen to fifty, but most were in their twenties. After completing the course, they went home and taught what they had learned to other members of the clan-family. The most relevant courses for the nomad students were those related to geography and the environment. Other valuable classes were those in personal hygiene, nutrition, first aid, and mid-

wifery for female students. The Nomad Education Program, like so many others, died during the civil war.

Somali National University was largely destroyed in the fighting in Mogadishu. University professors and Somali intellectuals began working in 1993 to establish a private university in Mogadishu. The new Mogadishu University was finally opened in September 1997. It offers programs in Shari'a and Law, Education, Arts, Business and Economics, and Computer Science. Somaliland also opened a private university, Amoud University, in 1997. It is largely supported by international funding and by Somalis living in the United Arab Emirates.

ETIQUETTE

In the Somali language *soo maal*, a common greeting of welcome, refers to the act of milking, offering a guest the opportunity to milk an animal and get himself something to drink. Somalis offer a milky tea and burn incense to welcome visitors.

Somalis greet one another by saying, *"Maalin wanaagsan"* (Good day) or *"Nabad myah?"* (How are you?). Men of the same clan-family then share a long handshake. Women greet one another informally and may hug and kiss one another on the cheek. Members of unrelated clan-families do not shake hands or exchange intimacies. Somalis also use certain Arab hand gestures to communicate.

RELIGION

Religious Beliefs. Religion is a major influence on the lives of Somalis. They are Sunni Muslims of the Shafi'ite rite, with great interest in Sufi spiritualism, characterized by chanting, whirling, chewing *qat*, (a narcotic leaf), and falling into a trance as a way of communing with Allah. They also include the veneration of Somali saints in religious worship.

Added to the daily practice of Islam is a belief in mortal spirits called *jinn*, said to be descended from a fallen heavenly spirit. According to folk beliefs, jinn can cause misfortune and illness or can help humans.

Somalis believe the poor, weak, or injured have special spiritual powers given by Allah, so Somalis are always kind to the less fortunate in hopes that they will not use this power for evil against them.

Religious Practitioners. Unlike other Muslims, Somalis believe that both their religious and secular leaders have the power to bless and to curse people. This power, believed to be given by Allah, is called *baraka*. Baraka is believed to linger at the tombs of Somali saints and to help cure illness and resolve other troubles upon a visit to the tomb. Islamic teachers and mosque officials make up a large portion of religious practitioners (Islam has no priests).

Somali followers of Sufiism, given the name Dervishes, dedicate themselves to a life of religion by preaching Islam and giving up all possessions. The Sufi are also known for the farming communities and religious centers they established in southern Somalia, called *jamaat*.

Among nomads, a respected male leader or religious devotee might be appointed *wadad*. His duties are to lead prayers and to perform ritual sacrifices on religious holidays and special occasions. He also learns folk astronomy, which is used for healing, divination, and to determine times for migration.

Other religious practitioners include the Yibir clan of the Saab. Yibir practitioners are called on to exorcise spirits and restore health, good fortune, or prosperity to individuals through prayers and ceremonies, including animal sacrifice.

Rituals and Holy Places. Mosques can be found in all Somali cities and towns. Nomads worship wherever they are, with men and women praying and studying the Qur'an separately. In accordance

A pedestrian passes a billboard in Mogadishu. Somali did not become a written language until 1973.

with Islam, Somalis are to pray five times each day, facing Mecca. They should recite the creed of Islam and observe *zakat*, or giving to the poor, if able. They should make a pilgrimage to Mecca at least once and should observe the fast of Ramadan.

Tombs of the Somali holy men or sheiks, venerated as saints, have become national shrines. Pilgrims visit on the saint's annual feast day, usually in the month of his birth, when his power is believed to be the strongest.

Religious holidays include the Islamic holidays of Ramadan (the month of fasting); Id al-Fitr (the Little Feast); the First of Muharram (when an angel is said to shake the tree of life and death); Maulid an-Nabi (the birth of the prophet Muhammad); and Id al-Adha (commemorating the story of Abraham and his son Ishmael). Islamic holidays fall at different times of year according to the Islamic calendar. Holidays are celebrated with feasting and storytelling, visiting graves, giving to the poor, parades, plays, and ceremonies.

Death and the Afterlife. Somalis hold the Muslim view that each person will be judged by Allah in the afterlife. They also believe that a tree representing all Muslims grows at the boundary between Earth and Heaven (some believe the boundary is on the

Moon). Each person is represented by a leaf on the tree. When an angel shakes the tree on the first day of the new year, in the Islamic month of Muharram, it is said that those whose leaves fall off will die within the coming year. Muslims also believe that a person who dies while fasting during Ramadan is especially blessed by Allah.

When a Somali dies, feasting and celebration are held, as they are at a birth. A Somali wife must mourn her husband's death in seclusion at home for four months and ten days, according to Islamic practice.

MEDICINE AND HEALTH CARE

Before the civil war of the 1990s, Somalia's Ministry of Health regulated all medical practices and personnel, but with the breakdown of the government and the destruction of most hospitals and clinics, Somalia's health care system has declined. There are few doctors and hospitals, and many unqualified persons practice a form of medicine at private facilities, especially in Mogadishu and other cities. The absence of regulation carries over to prescription drugs, which are often improperly dispensed by pharmacies. The World Health Organization (WHO) and the United Nations Children's Fund (UNICEF), along with international and Somali nongovernmental organizations (NGOs), provide much of the health care and health information services in Somalia. Most health care is free, but some hospitals charge patients a fee to help recover costs.

Tuberculosis and malaria are the two major causes of illness and death in the nation. Somalia had one of the world's highest tuberculosis rates in 2000, but it also had one of the highest cure rates, thanks to U.N. and other international organizations and their Somali health workers. In 2000 these organizations launched an aggressive program to fight malaria. They have also conducted ongoing polio, measles, and tetanus vaccination campaigns.

Cholera and other gastrointestinal diseases had become endemic in Mogadishu and other areas by 2000, largely because of the piles of rubbish and poor sanitation conditions resulting from civil war. Malnutrition and starvation, schistosomiasis, tetanus, leprosy, venereal disease, and skin and eye infections claim life and limb unnecessarily. Somalia is estimated to have a low prevalence of HIV and AIDS, compared with other African countries. In late 1999 studies showed from 8 to 9 percent of the subjects were HIV positive. Health workers are be-

ing trained in prevention and management of sexually transmitted diseases.

Somali folk medicine is often practiced by nomads and farmers who have no immediate access to medical care. Somalis believe that some kinds of illnesses are caused by possession of the body by spirits, which can be exorcised through ritual.

SECULAR CELEBRATIONS

Somalis celebrate Independence Day on 26 June, the date in 1960 when British Somaliland gained its independence. They celebrate the Foundation of the Republic on 1 July. At the beginning of August they hold a secular New Year celebration called Dab-Shid (Fire-Lighting) when they light a stick and jump over the fire.

THE ARTS AND HUMANITIES

Literature. Somalia has long been known as a nation of poets. A people with few possessions and no written language until the 1970s, Somalis developed an oral tradition of poetry and storytelling, that has been passed down through generations. Many of these poems and stories were written down in the late twentieth century. A popular new genre of song on the radio in the late twentieth century was *heello*, taken from Somali poetry. Some themes of Somali poetry are history, philosophy, and clan politics, as well as praise or ridicule of humans or animals. Probably the best-known Somali poet is spiritual and military leader Muhammad Abdullah Hasan, leader of the Muslim Dervishes.

Islamic poetry is also a Somali tradition; many poets were great religious leaders and are now considered saints. Somali Islamic poetry is written in Arabic, often in the form of prayer. Although Somali poets have been writing since at least the twelfth century, the most well-known Somali Islamic poets of recent times are Seylici (d. 1882), "Sheik Suufi" (d. 1905), and Sheik Uweys Maxamed (1869–1905).

Somali Islamic prose written in Arabic is called *manqabah*. Writers record the deeds and virtues of Somali sheiks, or religious leaders, some with miraculous powers. Somalis also read Arabic religious classics.

Modern Somali novelist Nuruddin Farah (b. 1945) has become internationally famous for his novels about African women's issues and the struggle for human rights in postcolonial Africa. His novels include *From a Crooked Rib* (1970), *Maps*

(1986), and *Gifts* (1992). He was awarded the Neustadt International Prize for Literature in 1998.

Performance Arts. Somali plays were performed in the late twentieth century at the National Theater in Mogadishu and at small theaters in other cities. Somalis began to write plays under the influence of British and Italian colonists. Somali plays are now written in Somali, Arabic, English, and Italian. A well-known modern Somali playwright is Hassan Mumin (*Leopard Among the Women*, 1974; *Contes de Djibouti*, 1980).

THE STATE OF THE PHYSICAL AND SOCIAL SCIENCES

Astronomy has been a popular career for Somalis; astronomer Muusa H. Galaal wrote *The Terminology and Practice of Somali Weather Lore, Astronomy, and Astrology* (1968). Science and engineering students who might have studied in Somalia if not for civil war have emigrated to other countries to study, where they have successful careers in medicine and the physical and social sciences. Some have returned to Somalia to help their people. In the late twentieth century, telecommunications and computer science became popular areas of study and enterprise for Somalis as they sought to rebuild their war-torn country and keep pace with new technology. In 2000 Somalia had one of Africa's most well developed telecommunications systems, as well as Internet service for its expanding computer networks.

BIBLIOGRAPHY

Abdi Sheik-Abdi. *Divine Madness: Mohammed Abdulle Hassan (1856–1920)*, 1993.

Andrzejewski, B. W. "Islamic Literature of Somalia." Hans Wolff Memorial Lecture at Indiana University, 1983.

Brook, Diane L., and Brook, George A. "Social Studies for Somali Nomads." *The Social Studies* 84 (1): 5, 1993.

D'Haem, Jeanne. *The Last Camel: True Stories of Somalia*, 1997.

Ditmars, Hadani. "Women Rebuild Shattered Economy." *African Business* December 1994, p. 31.

"A Failed State That Is Succeeding in Parts." *The Economist* 28 August 1999, p. 33.

Fisher, Ian. "Somalis Get Leader; Now They Need a Nation." *New York Times* 31 August 2000, p. A1.

———. "With Warlords at Home, Somalis Talk Peace." *New York Times* 6 August 2000, p. N3.

Fox, Mary Virginia. "Somalia." In Mary Reidy, ed., *Enchantment of the World*, 1996.

Hassig, Susan M. "Somalia." In *Cultures of the World*, 1997.

Howe, Jonathan T. "The United States and United Nations in Somalia: The Limits of Involvement." *Washington Quarterly* 18 (3) 1995.

"Infibulation Still Practiced by Somalis in North-Eastern Kenya." *WIN News* 25 (1): 1999.

Larson, Charles R. "Full Disclosure." *World and I* 13 (12): 1998.

Lewis, Ioan M. *Blood and Bone: The Call of Kinship in Somalia Society*, 1995.

———. *The Modern History of Somalia: Nation and State in the Horn of Africa*, 1988.

Metz, Helen Chapin, ed. *Somalia: A Country Study*, 1993.

Press, Robert. *The New Africa: Dispatches from a Changing Continent*, 1999.

Web Sites

Bower, Hilary. "World Health Organization Somalia Health Update." www.unsomalia.org

United Nations Development Programme Somalia. "Somalia: A Health System in Crisis." www.unsomalia.org/sectors/health_nutrition/stories/20001221.htm

—ANN H. SHURGIN

SOUTH AFRICA

CULTURE NAME

South African

ORIENTATION

Identification. South Africa is the only nation-state named after its geographic location; there was a general agreement not to change the name after the establishment of a constitutional nonracial democracy in 1994. The country came into being through the 1910 Act of Union that united two British colonies and two independent republics into the Union of South Africa. After the establishment of the first colonial outpost of the Dutch East India Company at Cape Town in 1652, South Africa became a society officially divided into colonizer and native, white and nonwhite, citizen and subject, employed and indentured, free and slave. The result was a fragmented national identity symbolized and implemented by the white minority government's policy of racial separation. Economic status has paralleled political and social segregation and inequality, with the black African, mixed-race ("Coloured"), and Indian and Pakistani ("Asian") population groups experiencing dispossession and a lack of legal rights. Since the first nonracial elections in 1994, the ruling African National Congress (ANC) has attempted to overcome this legacy and create unified national loyalties on the basis of equal legal status and an equitable allocation of resources.

Location and Geography. South Africa has an area of 472,281 square miles (1,223,208 square kilometers). It lies at the southern end of the African continent, bordered on the north by Namibia, Botswana, Zimbabwe, Mozambique, and Swaziland; on the east and south by the Indian Ocean; and on the west by the Atlantic Ocean. The independent country of Lesotho lies in the middle of east central South Africa.

Among the prominent features of the topography is a plateau that covers almost two thirds of the center of the country. The plateau complex rises toward the southeast, where it climaxes in the Drakensberg range, part of an escarpment that separates the plateau from the coastal areas. The Drakensburg includes Champagne Castle, the highest peak in the country. The larger portion of the plateau is known as the highveld, which ends in the north in the gold-bearing Witwatersrand, a long, rocky ridge that includes the financial capital and largest city, Johannesburg. The region north of the Witwatersrand, called the bushveld, slopes downward from east to west toward the Limpopo River, which forms the international border. The western section of the plateau, the middleveld, also descends towards the west and varies in elevation between the highveld and bushveld. Between the Drakensburg and the eastern and southern coastline, the land descends to the sea. Toward the eastern coast there is an interior belt of green, hilly country that contains the Cape and Natal midlands. Nearer the coast there is a low-lying plain called the eastern lowveld. Southwest of the plateau the country becomes progressively more arid, giving way to the stony desert of the Great Karroo, bordered on the east by the lower, better watered plateau of the Little Karroo. Separating the dry southern interior from the sandy littoral of the southern coast and West Cape is another range, the Langeberg. On the southwest coast is Table Mountain, with Cape Town, the "Mother City," set in its base, and the coastal plain of the Cape Peninsula tailing off to the south. The southern most point in Africa, Cape Agulhas, lies sixty miles to the east. South Africa also includes part of the Kalahari Desert in the northwest and a section of the Namib Desert in the west. The chief rivers, crossing the country from west to east, are the Limpopo, Vaal, and Orange, which are not navigable but are useful for irrigation. A major new water source was created by the damming of the Orange and the Malibamatso below their sources in the Lesotho Drakensburg. This se-

South Africa

ries of dams, the Lesotho Highlands Water Project, is the largest public works project in Africa.

Demography. The population numbers approximately forty million, comprised of eight officially recognized Bantu-speaking groups; white Afrikaners descended from Dutch, French, and German settlers who speak Afrikaans, a variety of Dutch; English-speaking descendants of British colonists; a mixed-race population that speaks Afrikaans or English; and an immigrant Indian population that speaks primarily Tamil and Urdu. A small remnant of Khoi and San aboriginal populations lives in the extreme northwest. Rural areas are inhabited primarily by Bantu speakers (black African) and Coloured (Khoisan, European, Southeast Asian, and Bantu African) speakers of Afrikaans. The largest language group, the Zulu, numbers about nine million but does not represent a dominant ethnic grouping. Black Africans make up about seventy-seven percent of the population, whites about eleven percent, Coloureds about eight percent, Indians over two percent, and other minorities less than two percent. Most South Africans live in urban areas, with twenty percent of the population residing in the central province of Gauteng, which contains Johannesburg, the surrounding industrial towns, and Pretoria, the administrative capital. Other major urban centers include Durban, a busy port on the central east coast; Cape Town, a ship refitting, wine, and tourist center; and Port Elizabeth, an industrial and manufacturing city on the eastern Cape coast. During the 1990s, urban centers received immigration from other sub-Saharan African countries, and these immigrants are active in small-scale urban commercial ventures.

Linguistic Affiliation. South Africa has eleven official languages, a measure that was included in the 1994 constitution to equalize the status of Bantu languages with Afrikaans, which under the white minority government had been the official language along with English. Afrikaans is still the most widely used language in everyday conversation, while English dominates in commerce, education, law, government, formal communication, and the media. English is becoming a lingua franca of the country, but strong attachments to ethnic, regional, and community linguistic traditions remain, supported by radio and television programming in all the nation's languages. Linguistic subnationalism among ethnic groups such as the Afrikaners remains an important feature of political life.

Symbolism. The nation's racially, ethnically, and politically divided history has produced national and subnational symbols that still function as symbols of the country, and others symbols that are accepted only by certain groups. The monuments to white settler conquest and political dominance, such as the Afrikaner *Voortrekker* ("pioneer") Monument in Pretoria and the Rhodes Monument honoring the British colonial empire builder and Cape prime minister Cecil Rhodes, remain sectarian symbols. Government buildings that once represented the white minority but now house national democratic institutions, such the union buildings in Pretoria and the parliament buildings in Cape Town, have become national symbols. The nation's wildlife, much of it housed in Kruger National Park, has replaced white "founding fathers" on the currency since 1994. Cape Town's Table Mountain remains the premier geographic symbol. Symbols of precolonial and colonial African nationalism such as the Zulu king Shaka have been promoted to national prominence. Names and symbols of the previous rulers have been retained, such as Kruger National Park and Pretoria, both named for prominent Afrikaner founding fathers, and the springbok, an antelope that is the emblem of the national rugby team.

HISTORY AND ETHNIC RELATIONS

Emergence of the Nation. South Africa has early human fossils at Sterkfontein and other sites. The first modern inhabitants were the San ("bushman") hunter-gatherers and the Khoi ("Hottentot") peoples, who herded livestock. The San may have been present for thousands of years and left evidence of their presence in thousands of ancient cave paintings ("rock art"). Bantu-speaking clans that were the ancestors of the Nguni (today's amaZulu, amaXhosa, amaSwazi, and vaTsonga peoples) and Tswana-Sotho language groups (today's Batswana and Southern and Northern Basotho) migrated down from east Africa as early as the fifteenth century. These clans encountered European settlers in the late eighteenth and early nineteenth centuries, when the colonists were beginning their migrations up from the Cape. The Cape's European merchants, soldiers, and farmers wiped out, drove off, or enslaved the indigenous Khoi herders and imported slave labor from Madagascar, Indonesia, and India. When the British abolished slavery in 1834, the pattern of white legal dominance was entrenched. In the interior, after nearly annihilating the San and Khoi, Bantu-speaking peoples and European colonists opposed one another in a series of ethnic and racial wars that continued until the democratic transformation of 1994. Conflict among Bantu-speaking chiefdoms was as common and severe as that between Bantus and whites. In resisting colonial expansion, black African rulers founded sizable and powerful kingdoms and nations by incorporating neighboring chieftaincies. The result was the emergence of the Zulu, Xhosa, Pedi, Venda, Swazi, Sotho, Tswana, and Tsonga nations, along with the white Afrikaners.

Modern South Africa emerged from these conflicts. The original Cape Colony was established though conquest of the Khoi by the Dutch in the seventeenth century and of the Xhosa by the British in the eighteenth and nineteenth centuries. Natal, the second colony, emerged from the destruction of the Zulu kingdom by Afrikaners and the British between 1838 and 1879. The two former republics of the Orange Free State and Transvaal (South African Republic) were established by Afrikaner settlers who defeated and dispossessed the Basotho and Batswana. Lesotho would have been forcibly incorporated into the Orange Free State without the extension of British protection in 1869. The ultimate unification of the country resulted from the South African War (1899–1902) between the British and the two Afrikaner republics, which reduced the country to ruin at the beginning of the twentieth century. Even after union, the Afrikaners never forgot their defeat and cruel treatment by the British. This resentment led to the consolidation of Afrikaner nationalism and political dominance by mid century. In 1948, the Afrikaner National Party, running on a platform of racial segregation and suppression of the black majority known as *apartheid* ("separateness"), came to power in a whites-only election. Behind the struggles between the British and the Afrikaners for political dominance there loomed the "Native question": how to keep the aspirations of blacks from undermining the dominance of the white minority. Struggles by the black population to achieve democratic political equality began in the early 1950s and succeeded in the early 1990s.

National Identity. Afrikaners historically considered themselves the only true South Africans and, while granting full citizenship to all residents of European descent, denied that status to people of color until the democratic transition of 1994. British South Africans retain a sense of cultural and social connection to Great Britain without weakening their identity as South Africans. A similar concept of primary local and secondary ancestral identity is prevalent among people of Indian descent. The Bantu-speaking black peoples have long regarded themselves as South African despite the attempts of the white authorities to classify them as less than full citizens or as citizens of ethnic homelands ("Bantustans") between 1959 and 1991. Strong cultural loyalties to African languages and local political structures such as the kingdom and the chieftaincy remain an important component of identity. National identity comes first for all black people, but belonging to an ethnic, linguistic, and regional grouping and even to an ancestral clan has an important secondary status. People once officially and now culturally classified as Coloured regard themselves as South African, as they are a residual social category and their heritage is a blend of all the other cultural backgrounds. Overall, national identity has been forged through a struggle among peoples who have become compatriots. Since 1994, the democratic majority government has avoided imposing a unified national identity from above instead of encouraging social integration through commitment to a common national future.

Ethnic Relations. A strong sense of ethnic separateness or distinctiveness coincides with well-established practical forms of cooperation and common identification. The diversity and fragmentation within ethnic groupings and the balance of

tensions between those groups during the twentieth century prevented interethnic civil conflict. While intergroup tensions over resources, entitlements, and political dominance remain, those conflicts are as likely to pit Zulu against Zulu as Zulu against Xhosa or African against Afrikaner.

URBANISM, ARCHITECTURE, AND THE USE OF SPACE

Architecture in the European sense began with the construction of Cape Town by the Dutch late in the seventeenth century. Monumental public buildings, houses of commerce, private dwellings, churches, and rural estates of that period reflect the ornamented but severe style of colonial Dutch architecture, which was influenced by traditions from the Dutch East Indies. Many of the Cape's most stately buildings were constructed with masonry hand carved by Muslim "Malay" artisans brought as slaves from Indonesia. After the British took over the Cape in 1806, buildings in the British colonial style modified the Cape Town architectural style. From colonial India, British merchants and administrators brought the curved metal ornamental roofs and slender lace work pillars that still typify the verandas of cottages in towns and cities throughout the nation. Houses of worship contribute an important architectural aspect even in the smallest towns. In addition to the soaring steeples and classic stonework of Afrikaans Dutch Reformed churches, Anglican churches, synagogues, mosques, and Hindu shrines provide variety to the religious architectural scene.

The domestic architecture of the Khoi and Bantu speaking peoples was simple but strong and serviceable, in harmony with a migratory horticultural and pastoral economy. Precolonial multiple dwelling homesteads, which still exist in rural areas, tended to group lineage clusters or extended families in a semicircular grouping of round or oval one-room dwellings. The term "village" applies most accurately to the closer, multifamily settlements of the Sotho and Tswana peoples, ruled by a local chief, than to the widely scattered family homesteads of the Zulu, Swazi, and Xhosa. Both Sotho-Tswana and Nguni-speaking communities were centered spatially and socially around the dwelling and cattle enclosure of the subchief, which served as a court and assembly for the exercise of authority in local affairs.

Missionaries and the white civil authorities introduced simple European-style square houses along lined streets in "native locations" for Chris-

Post Office Clock Tower in Durban. South Africa's architecture reflects the influence of Dutch and British colonists.

whites lived in town centers and near suburbs, while black workers were housed in more distant "townships" to serve the white economy. The current government does not have the resources to transform this pattern, but economic freedom and opportunity may enable citizens to create a more integrated built environment. In the meantime, the old townships remain with their black population, augmented by miles of new shack settlements containing impoverished rural migrants hoping for a better life in the environmentally overstressed urban areas.

FOOD AND ECONOMY

Food in Daily Life. The consists of the traditionally simple fare of starches and meats characteristic of a farming and frontier society. Early Afrikaner pioneer farmers sometimes subsisted entirely on meat when conditions for trade in cereals were not favorable. A specialized cuisine exists only in the Cape, with its blend of Dutch, English, and Southeast Asian cooking. Food plays a central role in the family and community life of all groups except perhaps the British.

Food Customs at Ceremonial Occasions. The gift and provision of food, centering on the ritual slaughtering of livestock, are central to all rites of passage and notable occasions in black communities. Slaughtering and the brewing of traditional cereal beer are essential in securing the participation and goodwill of the ancestors who are considered the guardians of good fortune, prosperity, and well-being. Indian communities maintain their native culinary traditions and apply them on Islamic and Hindu ritual and ceremonial occasions. Afrikaners and Coloured people gather at weekends and special occasions at multifamily barbecues called *braais*, where community bonds are strengthened.

Basic Economy. South Africa accounts for forty percent of the gross national product of sub-Saharan Africa, but until the late nineteenth century, it had a primarily agricultural economy that had much marginally productive land and was dependent on livestock farming. Because this was the primary economic enterprise of both black Africans and white colonists, conflict between those groups centered on the possession of grazing land and livestock. In 1867, the largest diamond deposits in the world were discovered at Kimberley in the west central area. The wealth from those fields helped finance the exploitation of the greatest gold reef in the world, which was discovered on the

tianized black people, beginning the architectural history of racial segregation. That history culminated in the 1950s in the rearrangement of the landscape to separate Bantu African, Coloured, Indian, and white population groups from one another in "Group Areas." In 1936, the final boundaries of Bantu African reserves limited the rights of residence of those groups to rural homelands scattered over thirteen percent of the country. In the eighty-seven percent of the land proclaimed "White areas,"

Witwatersrand in 1886. Above this gold vein rose the city of Johannesburg. Diamond and gold magnates such as Cecil Rhodes used their riches to finance political ambitions and the extension of the British Empire. On the strength of mining, the country underwent an industrial revolution at the turn of the twentieth century and became a major manufacturing economy by the 1930s. Despite the discovery of new gold deposits in the Orange Free State in the early 1950s, the mining industry is now in decline and South Africa is searching for new means to participate in the global economy.

Land Tenure and Property. African communal notions of territory, land usage, and tenure differ fundamentally from European concepts of land as private or public property. This led to misunderstandings and deliberate misrepresentation in the dealings of white settlers and government officials with African chiefs during the colonial period. In the establishment of African reserves, some aspects of communal and chiefly "tribal trust" land tenure were preserved, and even in white rural areas, forms of communal tenure were still practiced in areas with African communities. African Christian mission communities in some areas drew together to purchase land after colonial conquest and dispossession, only to have that land expropriated again by the Land Acts of 1913 and 1936, which confined black Africans to thirteen percent of the land area.

After the democratic transformation of 1994, programs for land restitution, redistribution, and reform were instituted, but progress has been slow. The white minority still controls eighty percent of the land. In the wake of agricultural land invasions in Zimbabwe, the Department of Land Affairs has pledged to speed land redistribution. However, it is not certain whether dispossessed people who qualify for land redistribution can make profitable economic use of the land.

Commercial Activities. Since Cape Town was founded in 1652 as a refreshment, refitting, and trading station of the Dutch East India Company, international commerce has played a central role in the development of the nation. Local black societies did not engage in significant trade, being self-sufficient mixed pastoral economies, and there were no local market centers or long distance trading systems. With the advent of colonial forms of production, black Africans quickly adapted to commercial agricultural production. Their ability to outproduce white settler farms that employed European technology and an African family labor system was a factor in colonial dispossession and enforced wage

Cape Town harbor. The city was formed in 1652 as a trading station of the Dutch East India Company.

labor in rural areas. Until the 1920s, itinerant traders sold manufactured items to African communities and isolated white farms and small farming towns. After 1910, formerly indentured sugar workers from India left these plantations and formed wealthy trading communities. Industries grew after the South African War, and during World War I South Africa supplied weapons to both sides. By the start of the World War II, South Africa had become the only industrialized economy in Africa south of the Sahara. The legal enforcement of white commercial domination until the 1990s has left the majority of private economic and financial resources under the control of the white minority, but this imbalance is being addressed.

Major Industries. Mining is still the largest industry, with profits from diamonds, gold, platinum, coal, and rare metals accounting for the majority of foreign exchange earnings. Currently, a significant portion of those earnings comes from the ownership and management of mines in other countries, particularly in Africa. With the decline in the mining sector, other industries have emerged, including automobile assembly, heavy equipment, wine, fruit and other produce, armaments, tourism, communications and financial services.

Trade. The most important trading partners are the United States and the European Union, particularly Great Britain and Germany, followed by Malaysia, Indonesia, India, and African neighbors such as Zimbabwe, Mozambique, and the Democratic Republic of the Congo. Exports have surged since 1991, and the country has a trade surplus. South Africa is attempting to expand trade with its neighbors by extending its world-class urban infrastructure and industrial, communications, and financial services technologies. Political chaos and economic decline in sub-Saharan Africa, however, have delayed many of these initiatives.

Division of Labor. In precolonial times, division of labor between the sexes and the generations was well defined, and this is still the case in many rural black communities. Before the introduction of the plow, women and girls did most forms of agricultural labor, while men and boys attended to the livestock. Ritual taboos barred women from work involving cattle. Men also dominated law, politics, cattle raiding, and warfare. Some chieftaincies, however, were ruled by women, with women accounting for a significant minority of chiefs today. With the introduction of European agricultural methods in the nineteenth century, men undertook the heavy work of plowing, loading, and transport. That period saw the beginnings of African male labor migration to mines, farms, and commercial and industrial centers. The resultant loss of family labor power was compensated for by the flow of wages to rural communities, but the political and organizational life of rural African communities suffered. As the small towns and urban centers grew, black labor was drawn permanently away from rural communities and toward residence in poorly constructed and overcrowded "locations" attached to the towns. The Indian population also centered in urban areas, especially in Natal, as did Coloured communities other than farm workers in the western and northern Cape. Today there is a crisis in the rural economy, and the pattern of movement of black people off farms and into the urban labor force continues at an accelerated pace.

As educational opportunity has expanded for black citizens, a gradual shift from a racial to a class-based division of labor has begun, and there is now a growing black middle class. Employment is still skewed by racial identity, however, with black unemployment levels that are double those of whites.

SOCIAL STRATIFICATION

Classes and Castes. After the founding of Cape Town in 1652, physical indicators of racial origin served as the basis of a color caste system. That system did not prevent interracial sex and procreation, as the shortage of European women was compensated for by the availability of slave women. Slaves, particularly those of mixed parentage, rated higher than free black Africans, and Cape Town soon developed a creole population of free people of color. Over three centuries, the system of racial segregation gradually attained a formal legal status, culminating in the disenfranchisement and dispossession of people of color in the 1960s. In that process, color and class came to be closely identified, with darker peoples legally confined to a lower social and economic status. Despite the color bar in all economic areas, some Africans, Coloureds, and Indians obtained a formal education and a European-style middle class cultural and economic identity as merchants, farmers, colonial civil servants, clerks, teachers, and clergy. It was from this class, educated at mission "Native colleges," that black nationalism and the movement for racial equality recruited many prominent leaders, including Nelson Mandela. Since 1994, people of color have assumed positions in the leading sectors and higher levels of society. Some redistribution of wealth has occurred, with a steady rise in the incomes and assets of black people, while whites have remained at their previous levels. Wealth is still very unevenly distributed by race. Indians and Coloureds have profited the most from the new dispensation, with the middle classes in those groups growing in numbers and wealth.

Symbols of Social Stratification. Before colonialism, the aristocratic chiefs symbolized their authority by wearing special animal-skin clothing, ornaments, and the accoutrements of power, and expressed it through the functioning of chiefly courts and assemblies. Chiefs were entitled by custom to display, mobilize, and increase their wealth through the acquisition of many wives and large herds of cattle. Concentrating their wealth in livestock and people, chiefs of even the highest degree did not live a life materially much better than that of their subjects. Only with the spread of colonial capitalism did luxury goods, high-status manufactured items, and a European education become symbols of social status. European fashions in dress, housing and household utensils, worship, and transport became general status symbols among all groups except rural traditional Africans by the mid-nineteenth century. Since that time, transport has

Inkhatha march.

served as a status symbol, with fine horses, pioneer wagons, and horse-drawn carts giving way to imported luxury automobiles.

POLITICAL LIFE

Government. Political life in black African communities centered on the hereditary chieftaincy, in which the senior son of the highest or "great wife" of a chief succeeded his father. In practice, succession was not straightforward, and brothers, older sons of other wives, and widow regents all competed for power. Building large states or polities was difficult under those political conditions, but a number of African chiefs founded national kingdoms, including King Shaka of the Zulu.

European political life began with the Dutch East India Company in the Cape; this was more a mercantile administration than a government. With the transfer of the Cape to Britain in 1806, a true colonial government headed by an imperial governor and a parliamentary prime minister was installed. The legal system evolved as a blend of English common law and European Roman-Dutch law, and people of color, except for the few who attained the status of "free burgers," had few legal rights or opportunities to participate in political life. In the 1830s, the British Crown Colony of Natal was founded on the coast of Zululand in the east. A decade later, Afrikaner emigrants from the Cape (*voortrekkers*), established the independent republics of the Orange Free State and the Transvaal, ruled by an elected president and a popular assembly called a *volksraad*. The founding and development of European colonies and republics began the long and bitter conflicts between African chiefs, British and Afrikaners, and whites and black Africans that have shaped the nation's history. Since 1994, the country has had universal voting rights and a multiparty nonconstituency "party list" parliamentary system, with executive powers vested in a state president and a ministerial cabinet.

Leadership and Political Officials. The first democratically elected president, Nelson R. Mandela, remains one of the most admired political figures in the world. There are nine provinces, each with a premier selected by the local ruling party and provincial ministerial executives. The party in power since 1994 has been the African National Congress, but other parties currently control two of the provinces.

Social Problems and Control. White minority rule and the policy of racial segregation, disempowerment, and suppression left the government a legacy of problems that amount to a social crisis.

Unrepresentative government and repressive racial regulations created mistrust of the law among the black majority. Unemployment is high and rapidly increasing, with the economy losing over a million jobs since 1994. Accompanying this situation are some of the highest crime rates in the world. The education and health care systems are failing in economically depressed communities. The collapse of family farming and the dismissal of thousands of black farm workers have created a rural crisis that has forced dispossessed and unemployed rural people to flock to the cities. Shantytowns ("informal areas") have mushroomed as the government has struggled to provide housing for migrants in a situation of rapid inner-city commercial decline and physical decay. The established black townships also are plagued by unemployment, crime, and insecurity, including drug dealings, alcoholism, rape, domestic violence, and child abuse. The government has imposed high taxes to transfer resources from the wealthy formerly white but now racially mixed suburbs to pay for services and upgrading in the poorer, economically unproductive areas. Although considerable progress has been made, the government and the private sector have been hampered by endemic corruption and white-collar crime. The interracial conflict that could have presented a major difficulty after centuries of colonial and white minority domination has proved to be a manageable aspect of postapartheid political culture, partly as a result of the work of the Truth and Reconciliation Commission between 1997 and 1999.

Military Activity. The South African Defense Force was notorious for its destabilization of neighboring countries in the 1970s and 1980s and its intervention in the civil war in Angola in the mid-1970s. Since 1994, the army has been renamed the South African National Defense Force (SANDF) and has achieved progress toward racial integration under the command of recently promoted black officers drawn from the armed wing of the ANC, *Umkhonto we Sizwe,* who serve alongside the white officer corps. The military budget has, however, experienced severe reductions that have limited the ability of the SANDF to respond to military emergencies. The SANDF's major military venture since 1994, the leading of an invasion force to save Lesotho's elected government from a threatened coup, was poorly planned and executed. South Africa has found it difficult to back up its foreign policy objectives with the threat of force. Participation in United Nations peacekeeping missions has been made questionable by high rates of HIV infection in some units.

SOCIAL WELFARE AND CHANGE PROGRAMS

The government has not pursued socialistic economic policies, but the socialist principles once espoused by the ANC have influenced social policy. Strong legislation and political rhetoric mandating and advocating programs to aid the formerly dispossessed majority (women, children, and homosexuals), play a prominent role in the government's interventions in society. Land restitution and reform, judicial reform, pro-employee labor regulations, welfare grants, free primary schooling, prenatal and natal medical care, tough penalties for crimes and child abuse, and high taxes and social spending are all part of the ruling party's efforts to address the social crisis. These problems have been difficult to deal with because only thirty percent of the population contributes to national revenue and because poverty is widespread and deeply rooted. This effort has been made more difficult by restrictions on the level of deficit spending the government can afford without deterring local and foreign investment. A high level of social spending, however, has eased social tension and unrest and helped stabilize the democratic transformation.

NONGOVERNMENTAL ORGANIZATIONS AND OTHER ASSOCIATIONS

Despite government interference, nongovernmental organizations working to ameliorate the plight of the dispossessed majority, advance democratic ideals, and monitor human rights violations flourished in the 1970s and 1980s. Many of those groups were funded by foreign governmental and private antiapartheid movement donors. With the fall of apartheid and the move toward a nonracial democracy in the 1990s, much of their funding dried up. Also, the new government has been unreceptive to the independent and often socially critical attitude of these organizations. The ANC insists that all foreign funding for social amelioration and development be channeled through governmental departments and agencies. However, bureaucratic obstruction and administrative incapacity have caused some donors to renew their connection with private organizations to implement new and more effective approaches to social problems.

GENDER ROLES AND STATUSES

Division of Labor by Gender. In rural African communities, women historically were assigned to agricultural tasks (with the exception of herding

A shantytown in Cape Town. Poverty and segregation are persistent legacies of South Africa's former policy of apartheid.

and plowing), and to domestic work and child care. Men tended livestock, did heavy agricultural labor, and ran local political affairs. With the dispossession of the African peasantry, many men have become migrant laborers in distant employment centers, leaving women to manage rural households. In cases where men have not sent their wages to rural families, women have become labor migrants. This pattern of female labor migration has increased as unemployment has risen among unskilled and semiskilled African men. In urban areas, both women and men work outside the home, but women are still responsible for household chores and child care. These domestic responsibilities usually fall to older female children, who have to balance housework and schoolwork.

The Relative Status of Women and Men. Male dominance is a feature of the domestic and working life of all the nation's ethnic groups. Men are by custom the head of the household and control social resources. The disabilities of women are compounded when a household is headed by a female single parent and does not include an adult male. The new democratic constitution is based on global humanitarian principles and has fostered gender equality and other human rights. Although not widely practiced, gender equality is enshrined in the legal system and the official discourse of public culture. Slow but visible progress is occurring in the advancement of women in the domestic and pubic spheres, assisted by the active engagement of the many women in the top levels of government and the private sector.

MARRIAGE, FAMILY, AND KINSHIP

Marriage. Pre-Christian marriage in black communities was based on polygyny and bridewealth, which involved the transfer of wealth in the form of livestock to the family of the bride in return for her productive and reproductive services in the husband's homestead. Christianity and changing economic and social conditions have dramatically reduced the number of men who have more than one wife, although this practice is still legal. Monogamy is the norm in all the other groups, but divorce rates are above fifty percent and cohabitation without marriage is the most common domestic living arrangement in black and Coloured communities. Despite the fragility of marital bonds, marriage ceremonies are among the most visible and important occasions for sociability and often take the form of an elaborate multisited and lengthy communal feast involving considerable expense.

Domestic Unit. In rural African communities, the domestic unit was historically the homestead,

Women and children sit alongside a road with food. Women are responsible for the care of infants, and they typically carry their babies on their backs.

which consisted of a senior man and his wives and their children, each housed in a small dwelling. By the mid-twentieth century, the typical homestead consisted more often of small kindreds composed of an older couple and the younger survivors of broken marriages. The multiroom family house has largely replaced or augmented the multidwelling homestead, just as nuclear and single-parent families have supplanted polygynous homesteads. The nuclear family model is approximated in practice primarily in white families, whereas black, Coloured, and Indian households tend to follow the wider "extended family" model. A new pattern characteristic of the black shantytowns at the margins of established black townships and suburbs consists of households in which unrelated people gather around a core of two or more residents connected by kinship.

Inheritance. Inheritance among white, Coloured, and Indian residents is bilateral, with property passing from parents to children or to siblings of both sexes, with a bias toward male heirs in practice. Among black Africans, the senior son inherited in trust for all the heirs of his father and was responsible for supporting his mother, his junior siblings, and his father's other wives and their children. This system has largely given way to European bilateral

inheritance within the extended family, but the older mode of inheritance survives in the responsibility assumed by uncles, aunts, grandparents, and in-laws for the welfare of a deceased child or sibling's immediate family members.

Kin Groups. Recognition of lengthy family lines and extended family relationships are common to all the population groups, most formally among Indians and blacks. For Africans, the clan, a group of people descended from a single remote male ancestor, symbolized by a totemic animal and organized politically around a chiefly title, is the largest kinship unit. These clans often include hundreds of thousands of people and apply their names to branches extending across ethnic boundaries, so that a blood relationship is not an organizing feature of clanship. Among the Nguni-speaking groups, it is against custom for people to marry anyone with their own, their mother's, or grandparents' clan name or clan praise name. Among the Basotho, it is customary for aristocrats to marry within the clan. A smaller unit is the lineage, a kin group of four or five generations descended from a male ancestor traced though the male line. Extended families are the most effective kin units of mutual obligation and assistance and are based on the most recent generations of lineal relationships.

SOCIALIZATION

Infant Care. Infant care is traditionally the sphere of mothers, grandmothers, and older sisters in black and Coloured communities, and females of all ages carry infants tied with blankets on their backs. Among the social problems affecting the very young in these communities is the high incidence of early teenage pregnancy. Many whites and middle-class families in other ethnic groups have part-time or full-time servants who assist with child care, including the care of infants. The employment of servants to rear children exposes children to adult caregivers of other cultures and allows unskilled women to support their own absent children.

Child Rearing and Education. The family in its varied forms and systems of membership is the primary context for the socialization of the young. The African extended family system provides a range of adult caregivers and role models for children within the kinship network. African families have shown resilience as a socializing agency, but repression and poverty have damaged family structure among the poor despite aid from churches and schools. Middle-class families of all races socialize their children in the manner of suburban Europeans.

Historically, rural African communities organized the formal education of the young around rites of initiation into adulthood. Among the Zulu, King Shaka abolished initiation and substituted military induction for males. These ceremonies, which lasted for several months, taught boys and girls the disciplines and knowledge of manhood and womanhood and culminated in circumcision for children of both sexes. Boys initiated together were led by a son of the chief under whom those age mates formed a military regiment. Girls became marriageable after graduation from the bush initiation school.

Christian missionaries opposed rites of circumcision, but after a long period of decline, traditional initiation has been increasing in popularity as a way of dealing with youth delinquency. Christian and Muslim (Coloured and Indian) clergy introduced formal schools with a religious basis in the eighteenth and nineteenth centuries. Apartheid policies attempted to segregate and limit the training, opportunities, and aspirations of black pupils. Today a unified system of formal Western schooling includes the entire population, but the damage done by the previous educational structure has been difficult to overcome. Schools in black areas have few resources, and educational privilege still exists in the wealthier formerly white suburbs. Expensive private academies and schools maintained by the relatively wealthy Jewish community are among the country's best. Rates of functional illiteracy remain high.

Higher Education. There are more than twenty universities and numerous technical training institutes. These institutions are of varying quality, and many designated as black ethnic universities under apartheid have continued to experience political disturbances and financial crises. Formerly white but now racially mixed universities are also experiencing financial difficulties in the face of a declining pool of qualified entrants and a slow rate of economic growth.

ETIQUETTE

South Africans are by custom polite and circumspect in their speech, although residents of the major urban centers may bemoan the decline of once-common courtesies. Each of the quite different culture groups—corresponding to home language speakers of English, Afrikaans, Tamil and Urdu, and the southern Bantu Languages, cross-cut by religion and country of original origin—has its own specific expressive forms of social propriety and respect.

Black Africans strongly mark social categories of age, gender, kinship, and status in their etiquette. Particular honor and pride of place are granted to age, genealogical seniority, male adulthood, and political position. Rural Africans still practice formal and even elaborate forms of social greeting and respect, even though such forms are paralleled by a high incidence of severe interpersonal and social violence. While the more westernized or cosmopolitan Africans are less formal in the language and gesture of etiquette, the categories of social status are no less clearly marked, whether in the homes of wealthy university graduates or in cramped and crowded working-class bungalows. The guest who does not greet the parents of a household by the name of their senior child preceded by *ma* or *ra* (Sesotho: ''mother/father of . . . '') or at least an with an emphatic *'me* or *ntate* (Sesotho: mother/father [of the house]) will be thought rude. The youngster who does not scramble from a chair to make way for an adult will draw a sharp reproof.

Comparable forms with cognate emphasis on age, gender, and seniority are practiced in Muslim, Hindu, and Jewish communities according to religious prescriptions and places of original family origin. South Africans of British origin insist on a

Voters wait in line in the first all-race elections, 1994. All South Africans have had the right to vote since this landmark year.

calm, distanced reserve mixed with a pleasant humor in social interactions, regardless of their private opinions of others. Afrikaners are rather more direct and sharp in their encounters, more quick to express their thoughts and feelings towards others, and not given to social legerdemain. In general, despite the aggressive rudeness that afflicts stressful modern urban life everywhere, South Africans are by custom hospitable, helpful, sympathetic, and most anxious to avoid verbal conflict or unsociable manners. Even among strangers, one of the strongest criticisms one can make in South Africa of another is that the person is "rude."

RELIGION

Religious Beliefs. Despite the socialist roots of the ruling ANC, South Africa is traditionally a deeply religious country with high rates of participation in religious life among all groups. The population is overwhelmingly Christian with only very small Jewish, Muslim, and Hindu minorities. Among Christian denominations, the Calvinist Dutch Reformed Church is by far the largest as most White and some Coloured Afrikaners belong to it. Other important denominations include Roman Catholics,

Methodists, Lutherans, Presbyterians, and Anglicans, the last led by Nobel Peace Prize winner Bishop Desmond Tutu. Apostolic and Pentacostal churches also have a large Black membership. Indigenous Black African religion centered on veneration of and guidance from the ancestors, belief in various minor spirits, spiritual modes of healing, and seasonal agricultural rites. The drinking of cereal beer and the ritual slaughter of livestock accompanied the many occasions for family and communal ritual feasting. The most important ceremonies involved rites of the life cycle such as births, initiation, marriage, and funerals.

Religious Practitioners. Indigenous African religious practitioners included herbalists and diviners who attended to the spiritual needs and maladies of both individuals and communities. In some cases their clairvoyant powers were employed by chiefs for advice and prophesy. Historically, Christian missionaries and traditional diviners have been enemies, but this has not prevented the dramatic growth of hybrid Afro-Christian churches, religious movements, prophetism, and spiritual healing alongside mainstream Christianity. Other important religions include Judaism, Islam, and Hinduism. For the Afrikaners, the Dutch Reformed Church has provided a spiritual and organizational foundation for their nationalist cultural politics and ideology.

Rituals and Holy Places. All religions and ethnic subnational groups have founded shrines to their tradition where momentous events have occurred, their leaders are buried, or miracles are believed to have happened. The grave of Sheikh Omar, for example, a seventeenth-century leader of resistance to Dutch rule in the East Indies who was transported to the Cape and became an early leader of the "Malay" community, is sacred to Cape Muslims. Afrikaners regard the site of the Battle of Blood River (Ncome) in 1838 as sacred because their leader Andries Pretorius made a covenant with their God promising perpetual devotion if victory over the vastly more numerous Zulu army were achieved. The long intergroup conflict over the land itself has led to the sacralization of many sites that are well remembered and frequently visited by a great many South Africans of all backgrounds.

Death and the Afterlife. In addition to the beliefs in the soul and afterlife of the varying world religions in South Africa, continued belief in and consultation with family ancestors remains strong among Black Africans. Among the important shrines where the ancestors are said to have caused

People at a Zulu market. Zulu is the largest South African language group, with about nine million speakers, but it does not represent a dominant ethnic grouping.

miracles are the caves of Nkokomohi and Matuoleng in the eastern Free State, both sites of healing sacred to the Basotho, and the holy city of Ekuphakameni in KwaZulu-Natal, built by Zulu Afro-Christian prophet and founder of the Nazarite Jerusalem Church, Isaiah Shembe in 1916. Formal communal graveyards, not a feature of pre-colonial African culture, have since become a focus of ancestral veneration and rootedness in the land. Disused graves and ancestral shrines have most recently figured in the land restitution claims of expropriated African communities lacking formal deeds of title to their former homes.

MEDICINE AND HEALTH CARE

There is a first class but limited modern health care sector for those with medical coverage or the money to pay for the treatment. Government-subsidized public hospitals and clinics are overstressed, understaffed, and are struggling to deal with the needs of a majority of the population that was underserved during white minority rule. A highly developed traditional medical sector of herbalists and diviners provides treatment for physical and psycho-spiritual illnesses to millions in the black population, including some people who also receive

treatment from modern health professionals and facilities. South Africa has a high HIV infection rate, and if successful strategies for AIDS prevention and care are not implemented, twenty-five percent of the country's young women will die before age thirty.

SECULAR CELEBRATIONS

Secular celebrations and public holidays are much more numerous than religious celebrations. The old holiday calendar consisting of commemorations of milestones in the history of colonial settlement, conquest, and political dominance has not been abandoned. In the service of political reconciliation, old holidays such as 16 December, which commemorates the victory of eight hundred Afrikaner settlers and their black servants over four thousand Zulu at the Battle of Blood River in 1838, is now celebrated as Reconciliation Day. Holidays commemorating significant events in the black struggle for political liberation include Human Rights Day, marking the shooting to death of sixty-one black pass-law protesters by the police in Sharpeville on 21 March 1961, and Youth Day, recalling the beginning of the Soweto uprising, when police opened fire on black schoolchildren protesting the use of

Afrikaans as a medium of instruction in township schools on 16 June 1976. Other holidays emphasize social advancements guaranteed by the new constitution, such as Women's Day, which also commemorates the march by women of all groups to protest the extension of the pass laws to women in Pretoria on 9 August 1956.

THE ARTS AND HUMANITIES

Support for the Arts. Pre-colonial African cultures produced a wide range of artistic artifacts for both use and beauty as clothing and personal adornment, beadwork, basketry, pottery, and external house decoration and design. Today these traditions are not only continued but have been developed in new as well as established forms in exquisitely fashioned folk and popular craft work and even painting. Among the most famous of these is the geometric house painting design of the Ndebele people.

Urban South Africa has highly developed traditions in the full range of arts and humanities genres and disciplines, long supported by government and the liberal universities, among the most prominent in Africa. During the colonial period these traditions spread to the non-European population groups who also produced artists, scholars, and public intellectuals of renown despite the obstacles deliberately placed in their path by the White apartheid cultural authorities. Building on the work of artists in exile such as painter Gerald Sekoto, painters and graphic artists vividly expressed the struggles and sufferings of black South Africans during the 1960s, 1970s, and 1980s. Social dislocation and poverty along with rich evocations of a regenerated African folk culture have inspired graphic artists of all backgrounds in the transformational 1990s.

Most recently other pressing social concerns have taken priority over the arts and humanities and both public and private support have dwindled. While the government struggles to make the once racially exclusive arts and educational facilities accessible to all, arts councils have experienced severe reductions in funding and many once-vibrant arts institutions are closed or threatened with closure. The government-sponsored Johannesburg Bienniale arts festival has yet to attract a significant audience.

Literature. The country has long had important writers of different cultural and ethnic backgrounds. Black literature thrived under the adverse conditions of apartheid, but today there is no black writer, playwright, or journalist with the stature of E'skia Mphahlele and Alex la Guma from the 1950s

through the 1970s. The White population continues to produce world-class literary artists, however, including Nobel Prize winner Nadine Gordimer, twice Booker Prize winner J. M. Coetzee, and distinguished bilingual Afrikaans novelist André Brink.

Graphic Arts. Graphic artists with a rural folk background who have made the transition to the contemporary art world, such as renowned painter Helen Sibidi, have found a ready international market. South Africa too produced a number of world-class art and documentary photographers in the second half of the twentieth century, whose works vividly evoke all aspects of this diverse, powerful conflictual and divided society. Among such photographers are elders Ernest Cole, David Goldblatt, and Peter Magubane, followed by new talents such as Santu Mofokeng.

Performance Arts. Theater, during the 1960s, 1970s, and 1980s a thriving formal elite and informal popular performing art, has recently fallen on hard times. Even Johannesburg, the urban cultural center of the country, has witnessed the closure of several major downtown theatre complexes that are now surrounded by urban decay, and the virtual disappearance of popular Black township theatre. The grand State Theatre complex in Pretoria has recently been closed due to insolvency and mismanagement.

New opportunities and interesting choreographers are appearing in the field of contemporary Black dance, but audiences and budgets are still painfully small. South Africa's four great symphony orchestras too have either dissolved or are threatened with dissolution. Alternatively popular music, particularly among Black South African musicians and audiences whether in live performances, recordings, or the increasingly varied broadcast industry, is thriving in the new era and holds out great potential for both artistic and financial expansion. South Africa is possessed of video and digital artists with excellent professional training and great talent, but there is only a limited market for their works within the country. Local television production provides them with some employment, but the South African film industry is moribund.

The very slow pace of economic growth and the high and increasing levels of unemployment and taxation have created an unfavorable environment for artistic and intellectual development in the new nonracial society. One sector in which both artistic and financial progress is occurring is in the growth of arts and performance festivals. The greatest of these is the National Arts Festival held every year in Grahamstown, Eastern Cape, drawing large audiences to a feast of the best new work in theatre, film, serious music, lecture programs, and visual arts and crafts. Other local festivals have sprung up after the example of Grahamstown, and all have achieved some measure of success and permanence in the national cultural calendar.

THE STATE OF THE PHYSICAL AND SOCIAL SCIENCES

Since the 1920s, the universities have graduated world-class professionals in the physical and social sciences. Rapid democratization has stressed the higher education system, and public and private funding for the social sciences has declined at a time when the society is facing a social and economic crisis. The physical sciences have fared better, with the opening of new technical institutions and the expansion of professionally oriented science education programs at the universities. The crisis in primary and secondary education has lowered the quality and quantity of entrants to institutions of higher education, and a lack of economic growth has created an inability to absorb highly trained graduates and a skills shortage as those graduates are attracted by better opportunities abroad.

BIBLIOGRAPHY

Adam, Heribert, F. van Zyl Slabbert, and K. Moodley. *Comrades in Business: Post-Liberation Politics in South Africa*, 1997.

Allen, V. L. *The History of Black Mineworkers in South Africa*, 1992.

Atkinson, Brenda, and Candice Breitz, eds. *Grey Areas: Representation, Identity and Politics in Contemporary South African Art*, 1999.

Bhana, Surendra, and Bridglal Pachai, eds. *A Documentary History of Indian South Africans*, 1984.

Bickford-Smith, Vivian, E. van Heyningen, and N. Worden. *Cape Town in the Twentieth Century: An Illustrated Social History*, 1999.

Bonner, Philip, and Lauren Segal. *Soweto: A History*, 1998.

Boonzaier, Emile, and John Sharp, eds. *South African Keywords*, 1988.

Butler, Jeffrey. *The Black Homelands of South Africa: The Political and Economic Development of Bophuthatswana and Kwazulu*, 1977.

Christopher, A. J. *The Atlas of Apartheid*, 1994.

Coetzee, J. M. *Doubling the Point: Essays and Interviews*, 1992.

Coplan, David B. *In Township Tonight! South Africa's Black City Music and Theatre*, 1985.

Elphick, Richard, and Rodney Davenport, eds. *Christianity in South Africa: A Political, Social and Cultural History*, 1977.

Fine, Ben, and Zavareh Rustomjee. *The Political Economy Of South Africa: From Minerals–Energy Complex to Industrialization*, 1996.

Fox, Roddy, and Kate Rowntree, eds. *The Geography of South Africa in a Changing World*, 2000.

Gerhart, Gail. *Black Power in South Africa*, 1978.

Gordimer, Nadine. *Living in Hope and History: Notes from Our Century*, 1999.

Hammond-Tooke, W. D., ed. *The Bantu-Speaking Peoples of Southern Africa*, 1974.

Harker, John, et al. *Beyond Apartheid: Human Resources for a New South Africa*, 1991.

Hugo, Pierre, ed. *Redistribution and Affirmative Action: Working on the South African Political Economy*, 1992.

Human, Linda, ed. *Educating and Developing Managers for a Changing South Africa: Selected Essays*, 1992.

Kuper, Adam. *Wives for Cattle: Bridewealth and Marriage in Southern Africa*, 1975.

Mahida, Ebrahim M. *History of Muslims in South Africa: A Chronology*, 1993.

Mesthrie, Rajend, ed. *Language and Social History: Studies in South African Sociolinguistics*, 1995.

Muller, Andre L. *Minority Interests: The Political Economy of the Coloured and Indian Communities in South Africa*, 1968.

Nelson, Harold D. *South Africa: A Country Study*, 1981.

Pampallis, John. *Foundations of the New South Africa*, 1991.

———. *The Political Directory of South Africa*, 1996.

Powell, Ivor. *Ndebele: A People and Their Art*, 1995.

Reader's Digest Illustrated History of South Africa: The Real Story, 1994.

Sachs, Albie. *Advancing Human Rights in South Africa*, 1992.

Sampson, Anthony. *Mandela: The Authorized Biography*, 1999.

South Africa through the Lens: Social Documentary Photography, 1983.

Thompson, Leonard Monteath. *A History of South Africa*, 1995.

———. *The Political Mythology of Apartheid*, 1985.

Townsend, R. F. *Policy Distortions and Agricultural Performance in the South African Economy*, 1997.

Truluck, Anne. *No Blood on Our Hands: Political Violence in the Natal Midlands 1987–Mid-1992*, 1992.

Unterhalter, Elaine, et al. *Apartheid Education and Popular Struggles*, 1991.

Van Graan, Mike, and Nicky du Plessis, eds. *The South African Handbook on Arts and Culture*, 1998.

Van Wyk, Gary. *African Painted Houses*, 1998.

Western, John. *Outcast Cape Town*, 1981.

Wilmsen, Edwin N., and Patrick McAllister, eds. *The Politics of Difference: Ethnic Premises in a World of Power*, 1996.

—DAVID COPLAN

SPAIN

CULTURE NAME

Spanish

ALTERNATIVE NAMES

Los españoles

ORIENTATION

Identification. The name España is of uncertain origin; from it derived the Hispania of the roman Empire. Important regions within the modern nation are the Basque Country (País Vasco), the Catalan-Valencian-Balearic area, and Galicia—each of which has its own language and a strong regional identity. Others are Andalucía and the Canary Islands; Aragón; Asturias; Castile; Extremadura; León; Murcia; and Navarra, whose regional identities are strong but whose language, if in some places dialectic, is mutually intelligible with the official Castilian Spanish. The national territory is divided into fifty provinces, which date from 1833 and are grouped into seventeen autonomous regions, or *comunidades autónomas*.

Location and Geography. Spain occupies about 85 percent of the Iberian peninsula, with Portugal on its western border. Other entities in Iberia are the Principality of Andorra in the Pyrenees and Gibraltar, which is under British sovereignty and is located on the south coast. The Pyrenees range separates Spain from France. The Atlantic Ocean washes Spain's north coast, the far northwest corner adjacent to Portugal, and the far southwestern zone between the Portuguese border and the Strait of Gibraltar. Spain is separated from North Africa on the south by the Strait of Gibraltar and the Mediterranean Sea, which also washes Spain's entire east coast. The Balearic Islands lie in the Mediterranean and the Canary Islands in the Atlantic, off the coast of Africa. Spain also holds two cities, Ceuta and Melilla, on the Mediterranean coast of Morocco.

Spain's perimeter is mountainous, the mountains generally rising from relatively narrow coastal plains. The country's interior, while transected by various mountain ranges, is high plateau, or *meseta*, generally divided into the northern and southern mesetas.

Such general geographic distinctions as north/south, coastal/interior, mountain/lowland/plateau, and Mediterranean/Atlantic are overwhelmed by the variety of local geographies that exist within all of the larger natural and historical regions. Great local diversity flourishes on Spanish terrain and is part of Spain's essence. The people of hamlets, villages, towns, and cities—the basic political units of the Spanish population—and sometimes even neighborhoods (*barrios*) hold local identities that are rooted not only in differences of local geography and microclimate but also in perceived cultural differences made concrete in folklore and symbolic usages. Throughout rural Spain, despite the strength of localism, there is also a perception of shared culture in rural zones called *comarcas*. The comarca is a purely cultural and economic unit, without political or any other official identity. In what are known as market communities in other parts of the world, villages or towns in a Spanish comarca patronize the same markets and fairs, worship at the same regional shrines in times of shared need (such as drought), wear similar traditional dress, speak the language similarly, intermarry, and celebrate some of the same festivals at places commonly regarded as central or important.

The comarca is a community of concrete relationships; larger regional identities are more easily characterized as imagined but emerge from a tradition of local difference and acquire some of their strength from that tradition. A recognition of difference among Spaniards is woven into the very fabric of Spanish identity; most Spaniards begin any discussion of their country with a recitation of Spain's diversity, and this is generally a matter of pride. Spaniards' commitment to Spain's essential

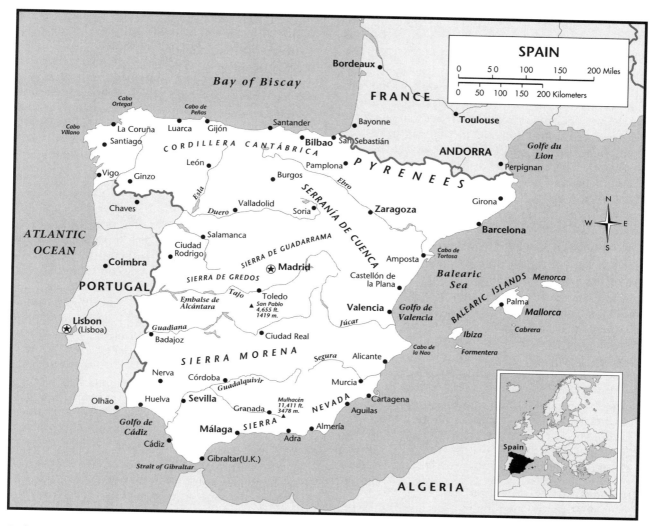

Spain

diversity is the benchmark from which any student of things Spanish must depart. It is essential to realize that outsiders can legitimately consider some of Spain's diversity as imagined every bit as much as its unity might be—that is, Spaniards sort their differences with a fine-toothed comb and create measures of local and regional differences which might fail tests of general significance by other measures. The majority of Spaniards endorse the significance of local differences together with an overarching unity, which makes them regard Spain's inhabitants as Spanish despite their variety. This image of variety is itself a shared element of Spanish identity.

The populations least likely to feel Spanish are Catalans and Basques, although these large, complex regional populations are by no means unanimous in their views. The Basque language is unrelated to any living language or known extinct ones;

this fact is the principal touchstone of a Basque sense of separateness. Even though many other measures of difference can be questioned, Basque separatism, where it is endorsed, is fueled by the experience of political repression in the twentieth century in particular. There has never been an independent Basque state apart from Spain or France.

Cataluña has had greater autonomy in the past and had, at different times, as close ties with southwestern France as with Spain. The Catalan language, like Spanish, is a Romance language, lacking the mysterious distinction that Basque has. But other measures of difference, in addition to a separate language, distinguish Cataluña from the rest of Spain. Among these is Cataluña's deeply commercial and mercantile bent, which has underlain Catalan economic development and power in both past and present. Perhaps because of this power, Cataluña has suffered longer from periodic repression at the hands of the central Castilian state than has any other of modern Spain's regions; this underlies a separatist movement of note in contemporary Cataluña.

The state now known as Spanish has long been dominated by Castile, the region that covers much of the Spanish meseta and the marriage of whose future queen, Isabel, to Fernando of Aragón in 1469 brought about the consolidation of powers that underlay the development of modern Spain. This growing power was soon to be enhanced by the Crown's monopoly (vis-a-vis other regions and the rest of Europe) on all that accrued from Christopher Columbus's discovery of the New World, which occurred under Crown sponsorship.

Madrid, already at the time an ancient Castilian town, was selected as Spain's capital in 1561, replacing the court's former home, Valladolid. The motive of this move was Madrid's centrality: it lies at Spain's geographic center and thus embodies the central power of the Crown and gives the court geographic centrality in relation to its realm as a whole. At the plaza known as Puerta del Sol in the heart of Madrid stand not only Madrid's legendary symbol—a sculpted bear under a strawberry tree (madroño)—but also a signpost pointing in all directions to various of Spain's provincial capitals, a further statement of Madrid's centrality. The Puerta del Sol is at kilometer zero for Spain's road system.

Demography. Spain's population of 39,852,651 in early 1999 represented a slight decline from levels earlier in the decade. The population had increased significantly in every previous decade of the twentieth century, rising from under nineteen million in 1900. Spain's declining birthrate, which in 1999 was the lowest in the world, has been the cause of official concern. The bulk of Spain's population is in the Castilian provinces (including Madrid), the Andalusian provinces, and the other, smaller regions of generalized Castilian culture and speech. The Catalan and Valencian provinces (including the major cities of Barcelona and Valencia), along with the Balearic Islands, account for about 30 percent of the population, Galicia for about 7 percent, and Basque Country for about 5 percent. These are not numbers of speakers of the minority languages, however, as the Catalan, Gallego, and Basque provinces all hold diverse populations and speech communities.

Linguistic Affiliation. Spain's national language is Spanish, or Castilian Spanish, a Romance language derived from the Latin implanted in Iberia following the conquest by Rome at the end of the

third century B.C.E. Two of the minority languages of the nation—Gallego and Catalan—are also Romance languages, derived from Latin in their respective regions just as Castilian Spanish (hereafter "Spanish") was. These Romance languages supplanted earlier tribal ones which, except for Basque, have not survived. The Basque language was spoken in Spain prior to the colonization by Rome and has remained in use into the twenty-first century. It is, as noted earlier, unique among known languages.

Virtually everyone in the nation today speaks Spanish, most as a first but some as a second language. The regions with native non-Spanish languages are also internally the most linguistically diverse of Spain's regions. In them, people who do not speak Spanish even as a second language are predictably older and live in remote areas. Most adults with even modest schooling are trained in Spanish, especially as the official use of the Catalan and Basque languages has suffered repression by centrist interests as recently as Francisco Franco's régime (1939–1975), as well as in earlier periods. None of the regional languages has ever been in official use outside its home region and their speakers have used Spanish in national-level exchanges and in wide-scale commerce throughout modern times.

Under the democratic government that followed Franco's death in 1975, Gallego, Basque, and Catalan have come into official use in their respective regions and are therefore experiencing a renaissance at home as well as enhanced recognition in the rest of the nation. Proper names, place-names, and street names are no longer translated automatically into Spanish. The unique nature of Basque has always brought personal, family, and place-names into the general consciousness, but Gallego and Catalan words had been easily rendered in Spanish and their native versions left unannounced. This is no longer so. There is evidence now—as has long been the case in Cataluña—that speakers of the regional languages are increasing in number. In Cataluña, where Catalan is spoken by Catalans up and down the social structure and in urban and rural areas alike, immigrants and their children become Catalan speakers, Spanish even falling to second place among the young. In Basque Country, the easy use of Basque is increasing among Basques themselves as the language regains status in official use. The same is true in Galicia in circles whose language of choice might until recently have been Spanish. An important literary renaissance expectedly accompanies these developments.

In those parts of Spain in which Spanish is the only language, dialectical patterns can remain significant. As with monolingualism in Basque, Catalan, or Gallego, deeply dialectic speech varies with age, formal schooling, and remoteness from major population centers. However, in some regions—Asturias is one—there has been a revival of traditional language forms and these are a focus of local pride and historical consciousness. Asturias, which in pre-modern times covered a wider area of the Atlantic north than the modern province of Asturias, was a major seat of early Christian uprising against Islam, which was established in southern Spain in 711 C.E. Events in Asturian history are thus emblematic of the persistence and re-emergence of the Christian Spanish nation; the heir to the Spanish throne bears the title of Prince of Asturias. The Asturian dialect belongs to the Old Leonese (*Antiguo Leonés*) dialect area; this dialect was spoken and written by the kings of the early Christian kingdoms of the north (Asturias, León, Castile) and is ancestral to modern Spanish. Thus the Asturian dialect, like the province itself, is emblematic of the birth of the modern nation.

Symbolism. Spain's different regions, or smaller entities within them, depict themselves richly through references to local legend and custom; classical references to places and their character; Christian heroic tales and events; and the regions' roles in Spain's complex history, especially during the eight-century presence of Islam. Examples already cited here are the association of Madrid with a site at which a bear and a strawberry tree were found together, of Asturias with tales of local Christian resistance early in the Islamic period, and of Basque country with a pre-Roman language and a defiant resistance to Rome. Many such images are stable in time; others less so as new touchstones of identity emerge.

Current symbolism at the national level respects the mosaic of more local depictions of identity and joins Spain's regions in a flag that bears the fleurs-de-lis of the Bourbon Crown and the arms or emblems of the several historical kingdoms that covered the present nation in its entirety. The colors, yellow and red, of what was to become the national flag were first adopted in 1785 for their high visibility at sea. The presence of an eagle, either double- or single-headed, has been historically variable. So has the legend (under the crowned columns that represent the pillars of Hercules) based on the older motto *nec* plus *ultra* ("nothing beyond") that now reads *plus ultra* in recognition of Spain's discovery of new lands. The presence of a crown symbol, of course, has been absent in republican periods. The national flag is thus quite recent—it has only been displayed on public buildings since 1908—and its iconography much manipulated, as is that on the coins of the realm. Many regional and local symbols have been more stable in time. This in itself suggests the depth of localism and regionalism and the seriousness of giving them due weight in symbolizing the nation as a whole. In some instances the iconography or language of monarchy and the use of the adjective "royal" (*real*) takes precedence over the term "national." The national anthem is called the *Marcha real*, or Royal March, and has no words; at least one attempt to attach words met with public apathy.

Some of the most compelling and widespread national symbols and events are those rooted in the religious calendar. The patron saint of Spain is Santiago, the Apostle Saint James the Greater, with his shrine at Santiago de Compostela in Galicia, the focus of medieval pilgrimages that connected Christian Spain to the rest of Christian Europe. The feast of Santiago on 25 July is a national holiday, as is the feast of the Immaculate Conception, 8 December, which is also Spain's Mother's Day. Other national holidays include Christmas, New Year's Day, Epiphany, and Easter. The feast of Saint Joseph, 19 March, is Father's Day. The ancient folk festival of Midsummer's Eve, 21 June, is conflated with the feast of Saint John (San Juan) on 24 June and is also the current king's name day. Our Columbus Day, 12 October, is the *Día de Hispanidad*, also a national holiday.

There are also secular figures that transcend place and have become iconic of Spain as a whole. The most important are the bull, from the complex of bullfighting traditions across Spain, and the figures of Don Quixote and Sancho Panza, from Miguel de Cervantes's novel of 1605. These share a place in Spaniards' consciousness along with the Holy Family, emblems of locality (including locally celebrated saints), and a deep sense of participation in a history that has set Spain apart from the rest of Europe.

HISTORY AND ETHNIC RELATIONS

Emergence of the Nation. Early unification of Spain's tribal groups occurred under Roman rule (circa 200 B.C.E. to circa 475 C.E.) when the Latin ancestral language was implanted, eventually giving rise to all of the Iberian languages except Basque. Other aspects of administration, military and legal organization, and sundry cultural and social processes and institutions derived from the Roman presence. Christianity was introduced to Spain in Roman times, and the Christianization of the populace continued into the Visigothic period (475 to 711 C.E.). Spain's major contacts were Mediterranean (Phoenician, Greek, Roman, and North African) until the entry of the Visigoths from across the Pyrenees. The Visigoths were the first foreign power to establish their centers in the northern rather than the southern half of the peninsula. Visigothic rule saw the implantation of new forms of local governance, new legal codes, and the Christianization of the peoples of Spain's mountainous north. A Jewish population was present in Spain from about 300 B.C.E., before Roman colonization, and throughout Spain's subsequent history until the expulsion in 1492 of those Jews who did not choose to convert to Christianity.

The Visigoths fell to Muslim invasion from North Africa in 711 C.E. and subsequently took refuge in the far north, while the south came under Islamic rule, most notably from the caliphate established at the southern city of Córdoba and ruling from 969 until 1031. The presence of Islam inspired from the beginning a Christian insurgency from the northern refuge areas, and this built over the centuries. Much of the northern meseta was a frontier between Christian kingdoms and the caliphate—or smaller Muslim kingdoms (*taifas*) after the caliphate's fall. Christians pushed this frontier increasingly southward until their final victory over the last Islamic stronghold, Granada, in 1492. During this period, Christian power was continually consolidated with Castile at its center. Also in 1492, under the sponsorship of the Catholic Kings, Fernando and Isabel, Columbus encountered the New World. Thus began the formation of Spain's great overseas empire at exactly the time at which Christian Spain triumphed over Islam and expelled unconverted Muslims and Jews from Spanish soil.

Spain has been a committed Roman Catholic nation throughout modern times. This commitment has informed many of Spain's relations with other nations. Internally, while the populace is almost wholly Catholic, there has been much philosophical, social-class, and regional variance over time regarding the position of the church and clergy. These issues have joined other secular ones, some regarding succession to the Crown, to produce a dynamic national political history. Twice the monarchy has given way to a republic—the first from 1873 to 1875, the second from 1931 to 1936. The Second Republic was overthrown in 1936 by a military uprising. Following a bloody civil war, General Francisco Franco, in 1939, established a conservative, Catholic, and fascist dictatorship that lasted until his death in 1975. Franco regarded himself as a regent for a future king and selected the grandson of the last ruler (Alfonso XIII, who left Spain in 1931) as the king to succeed him. Franco died in 1975 and King Juan Carlos I then gained the helm of a constitutional monarchy, which took a democratic Spain into the twenty-first century.

National Identity. Spanish national sentiment and a sense of unity rest on shared experience and institutions and have been strengthened by Spain's relative separation from the rest of Europe by the forbidding barrier of the Pyrenees range. Processes promoting unification were begun under Rome and the Visigoths, and the Christianization of the populace was particularly important. Christian identity was strengthened in the centuries of confrontation with Islam and again with the Spaniards' establishment of Christianity in the New World. The events of 1492 brought senses of both a renewed and an emergent nation through the reestablishment of Christian hegemony on Spanish soil and the achievement of new power in the New World, which placed Spain in the avant garde of all Europe.

Ethnic Relations. One legacy of Spain's medieval *convivencia* (living together) of Christians, Jews, and Muslims is a universal consciousness of that history and the presence in folklore, language, and popular thought of images of Jews and "Moors" and of characteristics and activities imputed to or associated with them. The notion of cultural difference or ethnicity is often submerged by facts of religious difference (except in the case of Spanish Gypsies, who are Catholics). Through most of the twentieth century, Spanish society (unlike Spain's former colonies in the New World, Africa, and Asia) was not ethnically diverse, except for the presence of Gypsies, who arrived in Spain in the fifteenth century. Other non-European presences were relatively few, except for growing tourism in the last decades of the century, a United States military presence at a small number of bases in Spain, a modest Latin American presence, and the beginning of the passage through Spain of North African workers, especially Moroccans (who by late in the century would become a labor presence in Spain itself). Small communities of Jews, mostly European and not necessarily of Sephardic origin, were reestablished in Spain following World War II, particularly in Madrid and Barcelona. Despite these late twentieth century trends, Spaniards' most consistent and abiding sense of difference between themselves and others on their own soil is in regard to

Spanish families tend to consist of nuclear family only, with older couples or unmarried adults living on their own rather than with kin.

Gypsies, who occupy the same marginal place in Spanish society to which they are relegated in most European countries.

URBANISM, ARCHITECTURE, AND THE USE OF SPACE

Spanish settlements are typically tightly clustered. The concentration of structures in space lends an urban quality even to small villages. The Spanish word *pueblo*, often narrowly translated as ''village,'' actually refers equally to a populace, a people, or a populated place, either large or small, so a pueblo can be a village, a city, or a national populace. Size, once again, is secondary to the fact of a concentration of people. In most rural areas, dwellings, barns, storage houses, businesses, schoolhouses, town halls, and churches are close to one another, with fields, orchards, gardens, woods, meadows, and pastures lying outside the inhabited center. These latter are ''the countryside'' (*campo*), but the built center, no matter how large or small, is a distinct space: the urban center with a populace. Campo and pueblo are essentially separate kinds of space.

In some areas, human habitation is dispersed in the countryside; this is not the norm, and many Spaniards express pity for those who live isolated in the countryside. Dispersed settlement is most systematically associated with areas of mixed cultivation and cattle breeding, mostly in humid Spain along the Atlantic north coast. The *latifundios* (extensive estates) of the south also see some isolated complexes of dwelling and out-buildings (*cortijos*), and the Catalan *masía* is an isolated farmstead outside pueblo limits, but by and large, rural Spain is a place of multi-family pueblos.

Spain's major cities—Madrid, Barcelona, Valencia, Seville, and Zaragoza—and the many lesser cities, mostly provincial capitals, are major attractions for the rural populace. The qualities of urban life are sought after; in addition, nonagrarian work, market opportunities, and numerous important services are heavily concentrated in cities.

Dwelling types are varied, and what are sometimes called regional types are often in reality associated with local geographies or, within a single zone, with rustic versus more modern styles. Many parts of rural Spain display dwelling types that are rapidly becoming archaic and in which people and animals share space in ways that most Spaniards view with distaste. Most houses that meet with wider approval relegate animals to well-insulated stables within the dwelling structures, but with separate entries. Increasingly, however, animals are stalled entirely in outbuildings, and motor transport and the mechanization of agriculture have, of course, caused a significant decrease in the number and kinds of animals kept by rural families.

Houses themselves are usually sturdily built, often with meter-thick walls to insure stability, insulation, and privacy. Preferred materials are stone and adobe brick fortified by heavy timbers. Privacy is crucial because dwellings are closely clustered and often abut, even if their walls are structurally separate. Southern Spain, in particular, is home to houses built around off-street patios that may show mostly windowless walls to the public street. Urban apartment buildings throughout Spain may use the patio principle to create inner, off-street spaces for such domestic uses as hanging laundry. Building patios also constitute informal social space for exchange between neighbors.

Outside of dwellings and within a population center, most spaces are very public, particularly those areas that are used for public events. Village, town, and city streets, plazas, and open spaces are common property and subject to regulation by civic authority. The very public nature of outdoor space heightens the concern with the separation of domestic from public space and the maintenance of domestic privacy. Yet family members who share dwelling space may enjoy less privacy from one another than their American counterparts: most urban families, in particular, live in fairly cramped spaces in which the sharing of bedrooms and the multifunctional uses of common rooms are frequent.

Beyond the homes of rural or middle-class urban Spaniards, there are palaces, mansions, and monuments of both civil and sacred architecture that display some distinctions but much similarity to comparable structures in other parts of Europe. Spain also boasts such unique monuments of Islamic architecture as the Alhambra in Granada and the great Mosque of Córdoba; monuments of Roman building such as the aqueduct of Segovia and the tripartite arch at Medinaceli; and religious architecture of early Christian through Renaissance times. These—along with prehistoric art and sites—are important in the array of emblems of local and regional identities.

FOOD AND ECONOMY

Food in Daily Life. The traditional Spanish diet is rooted in the products of an agrarian, pastoral, and horticultural society. Principal staples are bread (wheat is preferred); legumes (chickpeas, Old and New World beans, lentils); rice; garden vegetables; cured pork products; lamb and veal (and beef, in many regions only recently sought after); eggs; barnyard animals (chickens, rabbits, squabs); locally available wild herbs, game, fish, and shellfish; saltfish (especially cod and congereel); olives and olive oil; orchard fruits and nuts; grapes and wine made from grapes; milk of cows, sheep, and/or goats and cured milk products and dishes (cured cheeses and fresh curd); honey and Spanish-grown condiments (parsley, thyme, oregano, paprika, saffron, onions, garlic). Home production of honey is today mostly eclipsed by use of sugarcane and sugar-beet products, which have been commercialized in a few areas.

Most important among the garden vegetables are potatoes, peppers, tomatoes, carrots, cabbages and chard, green peas, asparagus, artichokes and vegetable thistle (*cardo*), zucchini squash, and eggplant. Most of these are ubiquitous but some, like artichokes and asparagus, are also highly commercialized, especially in conserve. Important orchard fruits besides olives are oranges and lemons, quinces, figs, cherries, peaches, apricots, plums, pears, apples, almonds, and walnuts. Of these, oranges, almonds, and quinces, in particular, are commercialized, as are olives and their oil. The most important vine fruits are grapes and melons, and in some regions there is caper cultivation. The heavily commercialized herbs are paprika and saffron, both of which are in heavy use in Spanish cookery.

The Spanish midday stew, of which every region has at least one version, is a brothy dish of legumes with potatoes, condimented with cured pork products and fresh meat(s) in small quantity, and with greens in season at the side or in the stew. This is known as a *cocido* or *olla* (or *olla podrida*) and in some homes is eaten, in one or another version, every day. On days of abstinence from meat, cocido will be made with saltcod (*bacalao*) or salted congereel (*cóngrio*). In the eastern rice-producing areas around Valencia and Murcia, the midday meal may instead be one of the *paella* family of dishes (rice with vegetables, meat, poultry, and/or seafood). These rice dishes are eaten everywhere but in some areas are often reserved for Sundays.

The midday meal (*comida*) around 2:00 P.M. is the day's principal meal, usually taken by families together at home. This follows a small breakfast (*desayuno*) of coffee or chocolate and bread or other dough products—purchased breakfast cakes, packaged cookies, or dough fritters (*churros*). Family members may breakfast at different times. A mid-

A flamenco dancer in Madrid. This idiom of song, dance, and musical accompaniment is regarded as uniquely Spanish.

morning snack (*almuerzo*)—which is a heavy one for farmers in the fields or physical laborers—may also be taken more individually. In the late afternoon, between 6:00 and 8:00 P.M., people may eat a substantial snack (*merienda*) at or away from home—or snack on *tapas* (appetizers) with a drink at a bar; for some families the *merienda* replaces the later supper. When taken, the supper (*cena*) is a light meal—often of soup, eggs, fish, or cold meats—and is eaten by families together around 10:00 P.M. This meal pattern is national except that in the Catalan area main meal hours are earlier, somewhat as in France (1:00 P.M. and 8:00 P.M.).

The family meals, comida and cena, are important gathering times. Even in congested urban areas, most working people travel home to the comida and return to work afterwards. Commercial and office hours are designed around the comida hours: most businesses are closed by 1:00 or 2:00 P.M. and do not reopen for afternoon business until 4:00 or 5:00 P.M. at the earliest, depending upon the season—winter bringing earlier afternoon hours than summer. Banks and many offices have no afternoon hours. Food stores, butchers, and fishmongers may remain open longer in the mornings and not reopen until at least 6:00 (or not reopen at all) and then remain open until about 9:00

P.M. to accommodate late shoppers. Virtually all commerce is closed by the family supper hour of 10:00 P.M., except of course taverns, bars, and restaurants.

Restaurant dining has become common in the urban middle, professional, and upper classes, where restaurants have made a few inroads on the home meals of some families; in general, however, family comida and cena hours are crucial aspects of family life throughout the nation. Restaurants in urban areas date only from the mid-nineteenth century: the Swiss restaurateur opened his eponymous Lhardy in Madrid in 1839. Other kinds of establishments—taverns, houses specializing in specific kinds of drinks (such as chocolate), and inns (*fondas*) offering meals to travelers are of course much older. But urban restaurants offering meals to those who could eat at home instead represented a new kind of social activity to those who could afford the price. Into the 1970s, Spaniards who ate in restaurants did so mostly in families and mostly to eat together, at leisure and in public, and not to try new foods. Menus were mostly of Spanish dishes from the same inventory home cooks also produced.

Spain's principal national dishes and foodstuffs are the various cocidos and the *paella* family of dishes, stuffed peppers, the *tortilla española* or Spanish omelette (a thick cake of eggs and sliced potatoes), and cured hams and sausages. A dish like gazpacho is most closely associated with Andalucía and is usually seasonal but today has national recognition, even though most of its varieties are little known outside their home zones. Tomato gazpacho is one of the Spanish dishes that has an international presence, as do *paellas* and mountain (*serrano*) hams.

Spain's contemporary version of the ancient refreshments barley-water (French *orgeat*) or almond-water is made from the tuber *chufa* and is called *horchata*. This beverage is produced mostly for Spanish consumption. Another beverage, sherry wine, which is produced around the southern town of Jerez de la Frontera, has international fame. And it was Spaniards who first introduced Europeans to drinking chocolate. Chocolate parlors, like coffee-houses and wine cellars, are public gathering places that purvey and attract customers to drink specific beverages. In the apple country of the north, especially in Asturias, *sidrerías*, or cider lagers, are important gathering places. Their product, hard cider, is also bottled and exported to other regions and abroad. Wine, however, is the most common accompaniment to meals in most of the nation, and beer is drunk mostly before or between meals.

A number of desserts and sweets have a national presence, principally a group of milk desserts of the flan or caramel custard family. Cheese figures strongly as a dessert and is often served with quince paste. Almond or almond-paste confections made with honey and egg whites (*turrón*, almond nougat or brittle) and marzipan (*mazapán*) are eaten everywhere during the Christmas season and are shipped across the nation and abroad from eastern almond-growing centers around Alicante (especially the town of Jijona).

Food Customs at Ceremonial Occasions. Eating and drinking together are Spaniards' principal ways of spending time together, either at everyday leisure moments, weekly on Sundays, or on special occasions. Special occasions include both general religious feast days such as Easter and Christmas and such family celebrations as birthdays, personal saints' days, baptisms, First Communions, and weddings. Many of these involve invited guests, and in small villages there may be at least token food offerings to the whole populace. Food is the principal currency of social exchange. Everywhere people with enough leisure form groups whose main purpose is the periodic enjoyment together of food and/or drink. These sociable groups of friends are called *cuadrillas*, *peñas*, or by other terms, and their number is by no means confined to the well-known men's eating societies of Basque Country.

The contents of special meals vary. Some feature dishes from the daily inventory at their most elaborate and numerous, with the most select ingredients. Some respond to the Church's required abstentions (principally from meat) on particular days such as Christmas Eve and during Lent. Salt cod and eel are especially important in meatless dishes. Some purely secular festivals of rural families accompany the execution of major tasks: the sheepshearing, the pig slaughter, or the threshing of the grain harvest. In some regions, a funeral meal follows a burial; this is hosted by the family of the deceased for their kin and other invited guests. This (meatless) meal is in most places a thing of the past, and the Church has discouraged funeral banquets, but it was an important tradition in the north, in Basque, and in other regions.

Basic Economy. Spain has been a heavily agrarian, pastoral, and mercantile nation. As of the middle of the twentieth century the nation was principally rural. Today, industry is more highly developed, and Spain is a member of the European Economic Community and participates substantially in the global economy. Farmers' voluntary reorganiza-

tion of the land base and the mechanization of agriculture (both accomplished with government assistance) have combined to modernize farming in much of the nation; these developments have in turn promoted migration from rural areas into Spain's cities, which grew significantly in the twentieth century. With the development of industry following World War II, cities offer industrial and other blue- and white-collar employment to the descendants of farm families.

The Spanish countryside as a whole has been largely self-sufficient. Local production varies greatly, even within regions, so regional and interregional markets are important vehicles of exchange, as has been a long tradition of interregional peddling by rural groups who came to specialize in purveying goods of different kinds away from their homes.

Land Tenure and Property. The chief factors that differentiate Spanish property and land tenure regimes are estate size and their partibility or impartibility.

Much of the southern half of Spain, roughly south of the River Tajo, is characterized by *latifundios*, or large estates, on which a single owner employs farm laborers who have little or no property of their own. Large estates date at least from Roman times and have given rise to a significant separation of social classes: one class consisting of the relatively leisured latifundio owners and the other class comprising the landless agrarian laborers who work for them, usually on short-term contracts, and live most of the time in the fairly large centers known as agro-towns. In the north, by contrast, properties are small (*minifundios*) and are lived on—usually in pueblo communities—and worked principally by the families of their owners or secondarily by families who live on and work the estates on long-term leases.

The north of Spain, dominated by minifundios, is crosscut by a difference in inheritance laws whereby in some areas estates are impartible and in others are divisible among heirs. Most of the nation is governed by Castilian law, which fosters the division of the bulk of an estate among all heirs, male and female, with a general (though variable) stress on equality of shares. There is a deep tradition in the northeast, however, whereby estates are passed undivided to a single heir (not everywhere or always necessarily a male or the firstborn), while other heirs receive only some settlement at marriage or have to remain single in order to stay on the familial property. This tradition characterizes the entire Pyrenean region, both Basque and Catalan, and adjacent zones of Cataluña, Navarra, and Aragón. The passage of estates undivided down the generations is a touchstone of cultural identity where it is practiced (just as estate division is deeply valued elsewhere), and as part of a separate and ancient legal system, the protection of impartibility has been central to these regions' contentions with Castile over the centuries. Spanish civil law recognizes stem-family succession in the regions where it is traditional through codified exceptions to the Castilian law followed in the rest of the nation. Nonetheless, the tradition of estate impartibility along the linguistic distinctions of the Basque and Catalan regions have long combined with other issues to make the political union of these two regions with the rest of Spain the most fragile seam in the national fabric.

Commercial Activities. Among Spain's traditional export products are olive oil, canned artichokes and asparagus, conserved fish (sardines, anchovies, tuna, saltcod), oranges (including the bitter or "Seville" oranges used in marmalade), wines (including sherry), paprika made from peppers in various regions, almonds, saffron, and cured pork products. Cured *serrano* ham and the paprika-and-garlic sausage called *chorizo* have particular renown in Europe.

Historically, Spain held a world monopoly on merino sheep and their wool; Spain's wool and textile production (including cotton) is still important, as is that of lumber, cork, and the age-old work of shipbuilding. There is coal mining in the north, especially in the region of Asturias, and metal and other mineral extraction in different regions. The Canary Islands' production of tobacco and bananas is important, as is that of esparto grass on the eastern meseta for the manufacture of traditional footgear and other items. Even though Spain no longer participates in Atlantic cod fishery, Spain's fisheries are nonetheless important for both national consumption and for export, and canneries are present in coastal areas. There is increasingly rapid transport of seafood to the nation's interior to satisfy Spaniards' high demand for quality fresh fish and shellfish.

Leather and leather goods have longstanding and continuing importance, as do furniture and paper manufacture. Several different regions supply both utilitarian and decorative ceramics and ceramic tiles, along with art ceramics; others supply traditional cloth handiwork, both lace and embroidery, while others are known for specific metal crafts—such as the knife manufacture associated with Albacete and the decorative damascene work on metal for which Toledo is famed.

Major Industries. Spain's heavy industry has developed since the end of the Civil War, with investments by Germany and Italy, and after the middle of the twentieth century with investments by the United States. The basis for these developments is old, however: iron mining and arms and munitions manufacture have been important for centuries, principally in the north. Spain's arms and munitions production is still important today, along with the manufacture of agricultural machinery, automobiles, and other kinds of equipment. Most industry is concentrated around major cities in the north and east—Bilbao, Barcelona, Valencia, Madrid, and Zaragoza. These industries have attracted migrants from the largely agrarian south, where there are sharp inequalities in land ownership not characteristic of the north, while other landless southerners have made systematic labor migrations into industrial areas of Europe—France, Belgium, Germany, Switzerland.

The most far-reaching development in Spain's economy since the 1950s has been in the multifaceted tourist industry. The number of tourists who visit Spain each year is roughly equal to Spain's resident population. Much of the influx is seasonal, between March and October, but the winter season is important in a number of areas—for winter sports in mountain zones and for the warmth of the southern coasts and the Balearic and Canary Islands. The hotel, restaurant, and other service sectors related to tourism constitute Spain's most significant industry, and it is one whose effects are felt in every corner of the nation. This has to do not only with the actual presence of tourists and the opening of areas of touristic interest, but also with expanded markets for Spanish products abroad as well as at home. A growing international acquaintance with Spanish foodways has enhanced the demand for certain Spanish foodstuffs and wines. Spanish leather goods, ceramics, and other crafts have a heightened and increasingly global market. Additionally, the consciousness of touristic interest even in remote regions (and not always with the help of professional promoters) has broadened local people's awareness of the interest in their own cultural heritage. Consequently, a variety of festivals and local products now enjoy expanded markets that often make real differences in local economies. The market for Spain's local and regional folk culture is not dependent just on international tourism; internal tourism, once reserved for the wealthy, is now promoted by television and the growth of au-

A cart outside a rural building in Castillo. Stone is a popular building material in Spain, providing strength, insulation, and privacy.

tomobile travel since the 1960s and has added Spaniards to the mass of foreign tourists spending their vacation money in Spain.

Trade. Spain is a member of the European Economic Community (Common Market) and has its heaviest trading relationship there, especially with Britain, and with the United States, Japan and the Ibero–American nations with which Spain also has deep historical ties and some trade relationships which date from the period of her New World empire. Among Spain's major exports are leather and textile goods; the commercialized foodstuffs named earlier; items of stone, ceramic, and tile; metals; and various kinds of manufactured equipment. Probably Spain's most significant dependence on outside sources is for crude oil, and energy costs are high for Spanish consumers.

Division of Labor. Once a predominantly agrarian and commercial nation, Spain was transformed during the twentieth century into a modern, industrial member of the global economic community. With land reform and mechanization, the agrarian sector has shrunk and the commercial, industrial, and service sectors of the economy have grown in size, significance, and global interconnection. Because the tourist industry is Spain's greatest and

this rests on various forms of services, the service sector of the economy has seen particular growth since the 1950s.

SOCIAL STRATIFICATION

Classes and Castes. The apex of Spain's social pyramid is occupied by the royal family, followed by the titled nobility and aristocratic families. The Franco régime maintained a conservative appearance in this respect, even in the absence of a royal family (for which Franco substituted his own). But through history, Spaniards have been critical of their rulers. The anonymous medieval poet said of the soldier-hero El Cid, (Ruy Díaz de Vivar), "God, what a good vassal! If only he had a good lord!" and the populations of large territories in the north known in the Middle Ages as *behetrías* had the right to shift their collective allegiance from one lord to another if the first was found wanting.

In today's modern and democratic Spain, the circles around the royal family, titled nobility, and old aristocrats are ever widened by individuals who are endowed with social standing by virtue of achievements in business, public life, or cultural activity. Wealth, including new wealth, and family connections to contemporary forms of power count for a great deal, but so do older concepts of family eminence. Spain's middle class has burgeoned, its development having not suffered under Franco, and because the disdain for commercial activity that marked the *ancien regime,* and made nobles who kept their titles refrain from manual labor and most kinds of commerce, is long gone. Many heirs to noble titles choose not to pay the cost of claiming and maintaining them, but this does not deny them social esteem. Many titled nobles make their livings in middle-class professions without loss of social esteem. The bases on which Spaniards accord esteem have expanded enormously since the demise of the feudal regime in the mid-nineteenth century. Entrepreneurial and professional success are admired, as are new and old money, rags-to-riches success, and descent from and connection to eminent families.

Spain's class system is marked by modern Euro-American models of success; upward mobility is possible for most aspirants. Education through at least the lowest levels of university training are today a principal vehicle of mobility, and Spain's national system of public universities expanded greatly to accommodate demand in the last third of the twentieth century. After family eminence combined with some level of inherited wealth, education is increasingly the sine qua non of social advancement. The models of social success that are emulated are various, but all involve the trappings of material comfort and leisure as well as styles that are urbane and sometimes have global referents rather than simply Spanish ones. While Spain has a landed gentry—particularly in the southern latifundio regions where landlords are leisured employers rather than farmers themselves—the gentry itself values urbanity; increasingly these families have removed themselves to the urban settings of provincial or national capitals.

The wide base of the social pyramid is composed, as in western societies generally, of manual laborers, rural or urban workers in the lower echelons of the service sector, and petty tradesmen. The rural-urban difference is important here. Self-employed farming has always been an honored trade (others that do not involve food production were once seen as more dubious), but rusticity is not highly valued. Therefore, Spanish farmers, along with country tradesmen, share the disadvantage of having a rustic rather than an urbane image; urbanity must be gained with some effort (through education and emulative self-styling) if one is to move upward in society from rural beginnings.

At the margins of Spanish society are individuals and groups whose trades involve itinerancy, proximity to animals, and the lack of a fixed base in a pueblo community. Chief in this category are Spain's Roma or Gypsies (though some settle permanently) and other groups who are not necessarily of foreign origin but who shun the values Spaniards cherish and follow more of the model that contemporary Spaniards associate with Gypsies.

Symbols of Social Stratification. The outward signs of social differences are embodied in the degrees to which people can display their material worth through their homes (especially fashionable addresses) and furnishings, dress, jewelry and other possessions, fashionable forms of leisure, and the degrees to which their behavior reflects education, urbane sophistication, and travel. A Spanish family's ability to take a month's vacation is famously important as a sign of economic well-being and social status. Comfortable, even luxurious, modes of travel—not necessarily by one's own automobile—also enhance people's social images.

POLITICAL LIFE

Government. Spain is a parliamentary monarchy with a bicameral legislature. The current king, Juan Carlos I (the grandson of Alfonso XIII, who was displaced by the Second Republic) is the first monarch to reign following the Franco period. His succession (rather than that of his father, Juan de Borbón) was determined by Franco: Juan Carlos ascended to the throne in 1975 following Franco's death. In 1978 the constitution that would govern Spain in its new era took effect. While organizing a parliamentary democracy, it also holds the king inviolable at the pinnacle of Spain's distribution of powers. In 1981 the king helped to maintain the constitution in force in the face of an attempted right-wing coup; this promoted the continuance of orderly governance under the constitution despite other kinds of disruptions—separatist terrorism in the Basque and Catalan areas and a variety of political scandals involving government corruption. Spain has repeatedly seen orderly elections and changes of government and ruling party. The head of state, the prime minister, is a member of the majority party in a multiparty system. The years under the constitutional regime have brought Spain into the North Atlantic Treaty Organization (NATO) and the European Community—and therefore, politically and economically closer to Europe—as well as into ever wider circles of global involvement.

The major change that has come about in Spain's political organization under the modern

Apartments next to a marina in Malaga. Urban families often share bedrooms, and common rooms may be used for multiple purposes.

constitution is the creation of seventeen "autonomous regions" into which the fifty provinces are distributed. Each of the autonomous regions has its own regional government, budget, and ministries; these replicate those at the national level. Some provinces are now separated from or grouped differently from their groupings in the historical kingdoms of traditional reference and so regional identities are in many cases being newly forged. This process has its only parallel in modern times in the original formation of the provinces themselves in 1833.

Leadership and Political Officials. Leadership is a personal achievement but can be aided by family connections. In Spain's multiparty system, shifts in party governance tend to bring about changes in officialdom at deeper levels in official entities and agencies than occur in the United States; that is, party membership is a correlate of government employment at deeper levels and in a greater number of spheres in Spain than in the United States. Spain's political culture in the post-Franco period, however, is still developing.

The most local representative of national government is the *secretario local*, or civil recorder, in each municipality. Municipalities might cover one or more villages, depending on local geography, and there is a recent trend toward consolidation. Every locality as well has its municipal head of government, its *alcalde* (mayor), or—where a village has become a dependency of a larger seat in the municipality—an *alcalde pedáneo* (dependent mayor). *Alcaldes* are local residents who are elected locally while the *secretarios* are government appointees who have undergone training and passed civil service examinations. The secretario is the local recorder of property transactions and keeper of the population rolls that feed the nation's decennial census.

Social Problems and Control. Spain's justice system serves citizens from local levels, with justices of the peace and district courts, through the level of the nation's Supreme Court (and a separate Supreme Court for constitutional interpretations). The system is governed by civil and criminal law codes.

Every Spanish locality is served by one or another police force. Urban areas have municipal police forces, while rural areas and small pueblos are covered by the *Guardia Civil*, or Civil Guard. The Civil Guard, which is a national police corps, also handles the policing of highway and other transit systems and deals with national security, smuggling and customs, national boundary security, and terrorism.

Informal social controls are powerful forces in Spanish communities of all sizes. In tightly clustered villages, residents are always under their neighbors' observation, and potential criticism is a strong deterrent against culturally defined misconduct and the failure to adhere to expected standards. Many village communities rarely if ever activate the official systems of justice and law enforcement; gossip and censure within the community, and surveillance of all by all, are often sufficient. This is true even in urban neighborhoods (though not in entire large towns and cities) because Spaniards are socialized to observe and comment upon one another and to establish neighborly consciousness and relationships wherever they live. The anonymity of an American high-rise community, for example, is relatively foreign to Spain. But it is also true that larger Spanish populations resort to their police forces frequently and, today, are additionally plagued by the increased street crime and burglary that characterize modern times in much of the world.

Military Activity. Spain's armed forces—trained for land, sea, and air—are today engaged primarily in peacetime duties and internationally in such peacekeeping forces as those of the United Nations and in NATO actions.

Spain entered the twentieth century having lost its colonies in the New World and the Pacific in the Spanish-American War or, as it is known in Spain, the War of 1898. Troubles in Morocco and deep unrest at home engaged the military from 1909 into the 1920s. Spain did not enter World War I. The Civil War raged from 1936 to 1939. Exhausted and depleted, Spain did not enter World War II, although its Blue Division (*División Azul*) joined Hitler's campaign in Russia. The remainder of the twentieth century has seen years of recovery, rebuilding, the maintenance by Franco of a strong military presence at home, and—after his death— of the increasing internationalization of Spain's involvements and cooperation, military and otherwise, with the rest of western Europe.

Military officers have enjoyed high social status in Spain and, indeed, are usually drawn from the higher social classes, while the countryside and lower classes give their men to service when drafted. In many places, men who reach draft age together form recognized social groups in their hometowns. At the end of the twentieth century, although young men are still subject to the draft, military service is open to women as well, and the armed forces are becoming increasingly voluntary. Spain's final draft lottery was held in the year 2000.

SOCIAL WELFARE AND CHANGE PROGRAMS

Most of Spain's programs of social welfare, service, and development are in the hands of the state— including agencies of the regional governments— and of the Roman Catholic Church. Church and state are separate today, but Catholicism is the religion of the great majority. The Church itself—and Catholic agencies—have a weighty presence in organizing social welfare and in sponsoring hospitals, schools, and aid projects of all sorts. Local, national, and international secular agencies are active as well, but none covers the spectrum of activities covered by the Church and the religious orders. The state offers social security, extensive health care, and disability benefits to most Spaniards. Actual ministration to the sick and disadvantaged, however, often falls to Church agencies or institutions staffed by religious personnel.

NONGOVERNMENTAL ORGANIZATIONS AND OTHER ASSOCIATIONS

The importance of the Catholic Church in the spectrum of nongovernmental associations is great, both at parish levels and above. A hallmark of Spanish social organization in purely secular as well as in religious matters, however, is the formation of small groups on the basis of shared locality and/or other interests—sometimes in a guildlike manner— to pool resources, extend mutual aid, complete large tasks, or simply to share sociability. When based on shared locality, these groups are found from small villages to neighborhoods of large cities; nonlocal groups are based on common occupations or other shared experiences and interests. They offer intimacy beyond the family and join individuals within or between neighborhoods and localities. The spectrum of secular groups of this kind is extended— but by no means dominated—by such religious groups as saints' confraternities, other kinds of brotherhoods, and voluntary church-based associations dedicated to a variety of social as well as devotional ends. In addition, large-scale regional, national, and international organizations have an increasing importance in Spanish society in the field of nongovernmental associations, an area that was once more completely dominated by Church-related organizations.

GENDER ROLES AND STATUSES

Division of Labor by Gender. The sexual division of labor varies by region and social class. In rural areas with a plow culture, men do most of the

Tightly clustered towns are typical in Spain, where isolation in the countryside is often pitied.

agricultural tasks, and women garden and keep house. In areas such as the humid north coast, where one finds a greater emphasis on animal husbandry and horticulture, both sexes garden and tend cattle, sheep, and goats. Professional herding (i.e., for hire), however, normally falls to men, and in regions of sheep—rather than cattle—herding, men do most of the herding. Women perform men's tasks when necessary but are least likely to drive a plow or tractor. Men do women's tasks when necessary—and many men like to cook—but are least likely to do mending and, above all, laundry. Married men and women run their domestic economies and raise their children in partnership. It is traditional throughout Spain, however, that men and women pursue leisure separately, particularly in public places, where they gather with friends and neighbors of like sex and the same general age. The kinds of groups that enjoy leisure together form early in life.

The separation of the sexes in leisure establishes the pattern on which the division of labor is enacted among the elite. Where economic circumstances permit, men and women lead more separate lives than occurs among the peasantry, and then the traditional divisions of male from female tasks are less often breached. In public life, men more often pursue politics, and women maintain the family's religious observance and spend more time in child rearing and household management than men do. Where they have hired household help, the servants are likely women, and these are an old part of the nation's female work force, which is now expanding in new directions. The traditional ideal of a sexual division of labor is best achieved by the leisured classes, whom peasants emulate when they can. Domestic servants have always played a vital role in communicating élite models to the peasantry and working classes.

The Relative Status of Women and Men. Spanish women under Castilian law inherit property equally with their brothers. They may also manage and dispose of it freely. This independence of control was traditionally relinquished to the husband upon marriage, but unmarried women or widows could wield the power of their properties independently. Today spouses are absolutely equal under the law.

Royal and noble women succeed to family titles if they have no brothers. In some areas of Spain, a woman may be heir to the family estate, but if she is not and instead marries an heir, she lives under the roof and rule of her husband and his parents. Nonetheless, women do not change their birth surnames at marriage in any part of Spain and can have public identities quite separate from those of their husbands.

Women were traditionally homemakers. Today they are found throughout the business, professional, and political worlds. In rural and working-class families, too, married women now often work outside the home and so experience both the independence and the frustrations of working women in countries where the female workforce emerged earlier. Spanish couples began controlling their family size long ago, and Spain now permits divorce, so more Spanish women are finding new kinds of freedom from their traditional roles as wives and mothers of large families. There seem to be relatively few barriers to their advancement in most kinds of work. Despite women's traditional association with home-making, Spaniards have long accepted the independence of women and the prominence of some of them (including their queens and noble women). Women's present emergence in the workforce, in the professions, and in government occurred in Spain without a marked feminist rebellion.

MARRIAGE, FAMILY, AND KINSHIP

Marriage. Spaniards today marry for mutual attraction and shun the idea of arranged marriages.

Class consciousness and material self-interest, however, lead people to socialize and marry largely within their own social classes or to aim for a match with a spouse who is better off. Traditionally, access to property was an important concern for farmers, with well-being often counting for more than love. But marriage ties traditionally could not be broken and long courtships helped couples find compatibility before they took their marriage vows. Marriage is a partnership, although different input is expected of the two sexes, and the rearing of a family is regarded as central to it. Remarriage for widowed individuals beyond childbearing age was traditionally greeted with community ribaldry, since a sexual relationship was being entered into without the end of family-building. These views and customs are becoming archaic. Divorce is now permitted; liaisons outside of marriage are increasingly common and accepted; and the economics of marriage for most people are freed from the ties to landed property that obtained when Spain was more heavily rural and agrarian.

Domestic Unit. Most Spaniards live in nuclear-family households of parents and unmarried children, and this is widely held as ideal. A Spanish saying goes "*casado casa quiere*" ("a married person wants a house"). Older couples or unmarried adults tend to live on their own.

Two kinds of household formations produce stem families. Where estates are impartible, the married heir lives and raises his children on the parental estate and expects his heir to do likewise. In areas where estates are divided, an adult heir may nonetheless stay on with his or her parents on their house site. This is often the youngest child, who agrees to stay on in the aging parents' household, but such arrangements are not necessarily replicated generation after generation. Where two generations of married adults co-reside, it is often on impartible farms, and many heirs forsake farming these days in order to live independently and earn a salaried living in urban comfort. The acknowledged strains between co-resident married couples suggest that indeed casado casa quiere, and demographers find the stem-family régime to be waning. This does not mean that the philosophy of estate impartibility is any weaker, however, in areas where it is traditional.

Inheritance. In addition to land, rural estates include houses and outbuildings; animals; farm machinery; household goods, utensils, and tools; larder contents; furniture and clothing; jewelry; and cash. Nonfarm estates might include fewer types of property. Where estates go to a single heir, this usually includes animals, equipment, house and outbuildings, and most furnishings—the things that are essential for the farm effort. Some amounts of other types of property, especially liquid cash, can be separated and go to noninheriting children. This kind of settlement with nonheirs is ordinary when a young heir takes over an estate at his parents' death. Sometimes—in any part of Spain—parents make premortem donations to their heirs, dividing estates according to custom and either keeping enough for their own maintenance or contracting for maintenance with the heirs. Maintenance is less a question in stem family households in which aging parents continue to live. Where there are multiple heirs, as in most of Spain, the majority of an estate is divided equally among them. This may involve lots containing very different types of property—some with more land and animals, others with more cash or other goods—all items are assigned a cash value so that lots are of equal value even if their contents differ. In other local traditions, every kind of item, including a house, is divided equally. Castilian law allows for the free disposition of a portion of estates: some families use this to benefit disabled children, for example, but regions differ (as do families) as to how willing people are to dispense with the equal division of the entire estate. Some are meticulous about equal shares down to the last cent.

Kin Groups. All Spaniards, including Basques, reckon kinship in effectively the same way: bilaterally and using an Eskimo-type terminology—the same as most Europeans and Americans. Basques, however, have a concept of the kindred that joins certain relatives (including some in-laws) beyond the nuclear or extended family for particular purposes, notably funerary observances. This notion of the kindred is lacking elsewhere in Spain, where kinship relations beyond the household are nonetheless supremely important in social life.

Family (*familia*) and relatives (*parientes*) are defined broadly (without genealogical limits) and inclusively (embracing in-laws as well as blood relatives) to create a large pool of relations beyond the limits of any single household or locality. Within this pool, people socialize as much by choice as by obligation, and obligations to relatives beyond the nuclear family are more moral than legal ones. Although this field of relations is at best loosely structured and relations between kinsmen from different households must be viewed as voluntary, kinship networks are extraordinarily important in Spaniards' lives and serve as vital connectors in many realms, influencing such choices as those of residence, occupation, migration, and even marriage. Despite diminishing family size, the Spanish family as an instituted set of relationships remains extremely strong.

SOCIALIZATION

Infant Care. Infants are breast- or bottle fed and weaned on cereal pap and other soft or mashed solid foods. Neither feeding patterns nor weaning and toilet training are rigid. Infants are treated with affection and good humor and scoldings are often accompanied by kisses. The threat of social shame is a tool in teaching desirable conduct, but adults do not actually shame children in public. Teasing and taunting are not normal parts of adults' exchange with children. men and women alike hold and shower affection on babies, although in the urban middle classes fathers may—or once did—treat their growing children more formally than their mothers do.

Infants of both sexes are carefully, even ornately, dressed. Sometimes strangers can detect their sex only by the presence of earrings on girl babies, whose ears are usually pierced in their first weeks of life. As they become toddlers, babies' clothes come to reflect their sex, as boys wear short pants and girls wear dresses. Toddlers of both sexes may sleep together at home and in public form mixed play groups. Their play becomes separate as they reach the ages of five or six, and they are also likely then to sleep in separate rooms or with older siblings of the same sex. At this stage, sex-appropriate behavior models are presented to them.

Child Rearing and Education. The birth of children is seen as the chief purpose of marriage. Children of both sexes are valued and raised with affection, even adoration, by parents, grandparents, aunts and uncles, and older siblings. Children are expected to be loving in return; a modicum of obedience is expected, but displays of obstinacy or temper are not sternly punished. Upbringing is not rigid, but as they grow children are expected to understand the constraints upon the adults around them and to learn respect and helpfulness as they approach the age at which they begin school (six). Children's environments are intensely social, not usually enhanced by large numbers of toys or children's furniture. Children are expected to take their pleasures (and also learn) from inclusion in the adult world, where they are involved in and witness to interactions from their earliest days. They are almost constantly surrounded by others and often also sleep as infants with their parents and later with older siblings. Parents may depend on schoolteachers for discipline and use teachers' judgments—or those of priests—as part of their own approach to child training once children are of school age. Most Spaniards see schooling as crucial to their children's life chances, particularly if they are to leave traditional rural occupations as most do. The urban working classes, like most rural food producers, place high value on basic literacy and on schooling beyond the obligatory age of fourteen to ensure entry into the world of employed or self-employed modern Spaniards.

Higher Education. For most Spaniards, vocational and academic secondary schooling is crucial, but they also hope to send their children to college if not for higher degrees as well. The professions are much admired, as is knowledge in general. Most of Spain's university system is public and governed in accord with nationwide regulations; it is heavily enrolled and was vastly expanded in the last decades of the twentieth century.

ETIQUETTE

Basic norms of civility and propriety, such as definitions of accepted levels of dress or undress, are comparable to the rest of Europe and the West in general. A crucial aspect of spoken exchange in Spanish is selective use of the formal you (*usted*, pl. *ustedes*) or the familiar *tú* (pl. *vosotros*). The formal form was once used by the young to their seniors even in the family but this is now uncommon. Outside of the family, the formal is used in situations of social distance and inequality, including age inequalities, and it is often used reciprocally by both parties as a sign of respect for social distance rather than a mark of one party's superiority. There is some regional and social-class variance in patterns of formal versus familiar address and the ease or rapidity with which people who are no longer strangers shift to the familiar *tú*.

Table etiquette for most occasions is informal by many European standards. People who eat together do so with relative intimacy and unpretension. Even in many restaurants, but especially at home, diners share certain kinds of dishes from a common platter: certain appetizers, salads, and traditionally *paella*. Verbal etiquette—to say to others "*que aproveche*" ("may it benefit you")—is reserved for people who are not sharing food at the same table: it is an etiquette of separation rather than inclusion. Eaters may say to an outsider "*Si le guste*" ("would you like some?"), to which the re-

Several women in the flower section of the Rastro Market in Madrid. Spaniards have long accepted the independence of women.

sponse is *"que aproveche,"* but this exchange does not occur when the outsider is expected to join the table. Instead, in the latter case, the outsider would simply be told, *"come and eat."*

RELIGION

Religious Beliefs. Spain has been a profoundly Catholic country for centuries, and Catholicism was the official religion for most of recent history until after the death of Franco. Church and state were separated briefly under both the First and Sec-

ond Republics, but their lasting separation did not begin until the 1978 constitution took effect. Even though their numbers have grown, non-Catholics in Spain today probably number less than 2 percent of the populace. Under Franco, regulations concerning the practice of other religions relegated them to near invisibility even while they were not outlawed. Today non-Catholics practice openly.

Although the vast majority of Spaniards are Catholics, there is great variance in the degree to which baptized Spaniards are observant and in the style of their devotions. The economic and political powers of the Church have promoted deep anticlericalism among many believing Catholics, often setting regions, smaller localities, or households, as well as different social classes, against one another. The differing politics of Spanish Catholicism give different sectors of the population different profiles even when basic religiosity itself is not at issue. The complex Catholic tradition admits private forms of devotion along with the more public and collective forms, so that even small populations see and tolerate some internal diversity in religious practice.

There are also nonbelievers. The current environment encourages a freer expression of nonbelief than has been usual except briefly in the last centuries, and some young parents do not baptize their children. This is not necessarily very common; the number of baptisms performed in Spain has shown some decline, but so has the birthrate.

All Spaniards of whatever faith live in a Catholic environment—a landscape filled with shrines and churches; an artistic heritage rich in religious reference; language and customs in which folklore and religious lore converge; chiefly secular festivals that are enacted on a religious calendar; and a national history accurately construed as the defense of Christianity, with the Catholic Church a central presence from century to century. Students of Spain, visitors, and practitioners of other faiths must all understand this Catholic environment if they are to understand Spanish national culture.

Religious Practitioners. In an overwhelmingly Catholic country, the religious practitioners are members of the Church hierarchy, the ordinary clergy, and members of the monastic orders (both monks and nuns). The monastic orders are very important in sponsoring institutions of primary and secondary education. The clergy, of course, serve the entire population beginning at parish level. The hierarchy of religious officialdom has its pinnacle in the Vatican and the office of Pope. The clergy and officialdom of minority religions—Jewish, Muslim, various Protestant denominations, and others—are also present to openly serve their adherents. They are, however, very few in number.

Rituals and Holy Places. Spanish pueblos, from hamlets to large cities, and many neighborhoods within population centers, all have patron saints each of whose days occasions a public festival, or fiesta. These fiestas punctuate the year and, along with weddings, comprised the principal events of traditional social life, especially in rural areas. Fiestas are both religious and secular in nature and usually involve feasting on both public and house-hold levels as well as the celebration of masses. Some populations sponsor bullfights or other public entertainments on major fiestas. Shrines, which are associated with miracles, are often located outside of population centers and are visited (as are churches) by individual devotés or by large groups on the days associated with the holy figures to whom they are dedicated. Collective pilgrimages to shrines in the countryside on their special days are called *romerías* and typically involve picnicking as well as masses and prayer.

Shrines, from caves or country huts to elaborate structures, and churches, from village parish churches to cathedrals, are the holy places of Spanish Catholicism. Their fiestas are scattered through the year and do not involve the nation or necessarily even a whole town or region. Overarching Church fiestas that engage the whole populace are such official Church holidays as Easter, Christmas, or Corpus Cristi, for a few examples, and the day of Santiago (the Apostle Saint James the Greater), the national patron, on 25 July. These national religious holidays are celebrated by formal masses but also with varied local traditions throughout the nation. Catholic masses themselves are largely universal rituals not subject to significant local variance.

MEDICINE AND HEALTH CARE

Spaniards are covered by a national health care system which today serves virtually the entire population. Folklorists and ethnographers have studied a wealth of folk beliefs regarding causes and cures of illness, but it is rare that people in any corner of the nation forego their free medical coverage to depend solely on folk cures or curers. The use of herbal remedies and knowledgeable but medically untrained midwives or bonesetters may persist, but only alongside the widespread patronage of pharmacies and medical practitioners. Scholars of folk medical systems and beliefs can find rich material in Spain, but this in no way marks Spaniards as primitive users unaware of the benefits of mainstream modern medicine.

SECULAR CELEBRATIONS

Many of Spain's major festivals have a dual quality whereby essentially secular festivals are enacted at times that have religious meaning as well. Every day of the year is associated with one or more saints or holy meanings in the Catholic calendar, yet some of the events that take place on specified religious holidays have a distinctly secular quality—bullfights on fiesta days; the king's official birthday

A family enjoys vin cau, or mulled wine, after a large family meal. Meals, especially the midday comida and late-evening cena, are important gathering times in Spain.

(a national holiday) on 24 June, the Feast of San Juan (Saint John); village business accounting meetings held after mass on designated days. Spain's most secular national holiday is 12 October, the celebration of *Hispanidad*, or the Hispanization of the New World following Columbus's landfall on that day in 1492. But true to form, many Spaniards also celebrate the very popular Virgin of El Pilar on 12 October, either because they are named for her, live around Zaragoza (of which she is patroness), or belong to a guild or other group (such as the Civil Guard) of which she is the designated patroness.

THE ARTS AND HUMANITIES

Support for the Arts. Spain's artistic production has recovered rapidly from the stultifying Franco years when many artists, writers, and musicians worked in exile. There is enormous public interest in works of art and architecture (where Antoni Gaudí's name must be listed), in Spain's art museums, as well as in its architectural monuments of various periods and in its important archeological sites, widely visited by Spaniards along with foreign tourists. Madrid and Barcelona both count among Europe's stellar museum cities. The arts receive both government and private support; major artists are treated as celebrities, and the humanities and fine arts are all firmly instituted in universities and professional academies, along with a multitude of local, regional, and national museums.

Literature. Spanish writers from the Middle Ages to the present have contributed to the inventory of literary masterpieces of the West. Cervantes's (1547–1616) *Don Quixote*; the works of Lope de Vega Carpio (1562–1635) and Pedro Calderón de la Barca (1600–1681); the poetry and plays of Federico García Lorca (1898–1936); and the works of five Nobel laureates in literature are but a few from different periods. There are early monuments of vernacular literature from the Middle Ages, as well, that enlighten the study of medieval Europe as a whole.

Graphic Arts. Spain's graphic artists are also world renowned and also span centuries—El Greco (Doménikos Theotokópoulos; 1541–1614), Diego de Velázquez (1599–1660), Francisco de Goya (1746–1828), Joaquín Sorolla (1863–1923), Joan Miró (1893–1983), Salvador Dalí (1904–1989), and Pablo Picasso (1881–1973), among many others, can be studied in museums and universities anywhere. Contemporary painters and sculptors have an avid following in Spain and elsewhere.

The decorative arts also form a rich part of Spain's national heritage and are well displayed in museums in Spain and elsewhere. Ceramic tile, other ceramic forms, lace work, weavings, embroidery, and other craft art often form the chief adornments in Spanish homes, are part of the traditional trousseau (personal possessions of a bride), and are the treasures passed down the generations. More than painting and sculpture, these are forms to which even humble Spaniards have intense attachments and whose style and motifs often serve as emblems of national or regional identity.

Performance Arts. The *flamenco* idiom of song, dance, and musical accompaniment is generally seen as uniquely Spanish and, while appreciated everywhere, is most closely associated with Andalucía. The elevation of the classical guitar to wide recognition as a concert instrument in the twentieth century is also closely identified with Spain and with Spanish composers and performers (for example, Joaquín Rodrigo [1901–1999] and Andrés Segovia [1893?–1987] respectively). Spanish composers generally—such as Enrique Granados (1867–1916), Isaac Albéniz (1860–1909), and Manuel de Falla (1876–1946)—have brought the Spanish folk musical idiom onto world concert stages. Appreciation of Spanish light opera, the *zarzuela*, is more dependent on Spanish-language competence. Nevertheless, the zarzuela has recognition beyond the Spanish-speaking world, especially through the person of such a performer as Plácido Domingo (1941–).

Spain has had an active film industry since the 1890s. The great popularity in Spain of the film medium has made it a vehicle of social and political commentary and, therefore, opened it to the censorship under which film production has labored in some periods. Movie makers worked under restrictive censureship during different periods between about 1913 and 1978, and therefore some Spaniards produced their films clandestinely or outside of Spain. Luís Buñuel is one example who gained international renown. Others, like Luís García Berlanga managed to gain wide recognition with films made in Spain. Contemporary Spanish directors whose names are familiar to Americans are Carlos Saura and Pedro Almodóvar. Almodóvar won the 1999 Oscar for best foreign film for his ''All About My Mother.'' Spaniards are avid movie-goers and the history of their film industry has been the subject of serious study by cultural analysts.

THE STATE OF THE PHYSICAL AND SOCIAL SCIENCES

The physical sciences, along with the engineering sciences, have all long been instituted in the Spanish educational system. Some of the social sciences as they are instituted in the United States are younger in Spain. Social-cultural anthropology is one of these, dating from the 1960s, although ethnography, folklore, archaeology, philology, and physical anthropology are older, and there are national, regional, and local museums dedicated to these topics as well. Today, such younger fields as cultural anthropology and psychology are thriving and are taught throughout the university system. Sociologists are importantly engaged in the self-study of Spain as well as the study of other societies.

Spanish researchers are in active and increasing exchange with their counterparts around the world. Professional journals abound. The most important establishment that publishes books and journals, funds research, and employs scholars in research positions across the entire span of academic disciplines, including the humanities, is the Consejo Superior de Investigaciones Científicas (the Higher Council for Scientific Research), founded in 1939. The Consejo has its seat in Madrid but its various sections and institutes sponsor research and publication of books and journals in and about the various regions and provinces and on a wide range of topics.

In all fields of scientific endeavor, funding is from both governmental and private sources, and also from Spain's major banks, but with an emphasis on the governmental.

BIBLIOGRAPHY

Aceves, Joseph B., and William A. Douglass, eds. *The Changing Faces of Rural Spain*, 1976.

Amador de los Ríos, José. *Historia social, política, y religiosa de los Judíos de España y Portugal*, 1875–1876, reprinted 1960.

Anonymous. *Poema del Cid.* Edition of Ramón Menéndez Pidal and Alfonso Reyes, 1960.

Bettagno, Alessandro, et al. *The Prado Museum*, 1996.

Boyd, Carolyn P. *Historia Patria: Politics, History, and National Identity in Spain, 1875–1975*, 1997.

Brenan, Gerald. *The Spanish Labyrinth: An Account of the Social and Political Background of the Spanish Civil War*, 1943.

Callahan, William J. *Honor, Commerce, and Industry in Eighteenth-Century Spain*, 1972.

Caro Baroja, Julio. *Los pueblos de España*, 1946.

Chase, Gilbert. *The Music of Spain*, 1941, 2nd ed., 1959.

Christian, William A., Jr. *Person and God in a Spanish Valley*, 1972.

Collier, Jane Fishburne. *From Duty to Desire: Remaking Families in a Spanish Village*, 1997.

Douglass, Carrie B. *Bulls, Bullfighting, and Spanish Identities*, 1997.

Douglass, William A. *Death in Murélaga: Funerary Ritual in a Spanish Basque Village*, 1969.

Flores, Carlos. *Arquitectura popular española*, 5 vols, 1977–1981.

Freeman, Susan Tax. *Neighbors: The Social Contract in a Castilian Hamlet*, 1970.

———. *The Pasiegos: Spaniards in No Man's Land*, 1979.

Glick, Thomas F. *Islamic and Christian Spain in the Early Middle Ages: Comparative Perspectives on Social and Cultural Formation*, 1979.

Greenwood, Davydd J. "Continuity in Change: Spanish Basque Ethnicity as a Historical Process." In Milton J. Esman, ed., *Ethnic Conflict in the Western World*, 1977.

———. *Unrewarding Wealth: The Commercialization and Collapse of Agriculture in a Spanish Basque Town*, 1976.

Herr, Richard. *An Historical Essay on Modern Spain*, 1971.

Hooper, John. *The New Spaniards*, 1995.

Instituto Nacional de Estadística. *España: Anuario Estadístico*, 1997, 1998.

Kaprow, Miriam Lee. "Gitanos." *Encyclopedia of World Cultures*, 4: 127–130. Boston, 1992.

Linz, Juan, and Amando de Miguel. "Within-Nation Differences and Comparisons: The Eight Spains." In Richard L. Merritt and Stein Rokkan, eds., *Comparing Nations: The Use of Quantitative Data in Cross-National Research*, 1966.

Liss, Peggy K. *Isabel the Queen: Life and Times*, 1992.

Payne, Stanley G. *Falange: A History of Spanish Fascism*, 1961.

Pitt-Rivers, Julian A. *The People of the Sierra*, 1954.

Press, Irwin. *The City as Context: Urbanism and Behavioral Constraints in Seville*, 1979.

Reher, David S. *Perspectives on the Family in Spain Past and Present*, 1997.

Terán, Manuel de, L. Solé Sabarís, et al. *Geografía regional de España*, 1969.

Torres, Augusto M., supervisor. *Spanish Cinema 1896–1983*, 1986.

Thomas, Hugh. *The Spanish Civil War*, rev. ed., 1977.

Ullman, Joan Connelly. *The Tragic Week: A Study of Anticlericalism in Spain, 1875–1912*, 1968.

—SUSAN TAX FREEMAN

SRI LANKA

CULTURE NAME
Sri Lankan

ALTERNATIVE NAMES
Ceylonese, Lankan

ORIENTATION

Identification. The official name of the nation is the Democratic Socialist Republic of Sri Lanka. In 1972, the national constitution discarded the name Ceylon and adopted the name of Sri Lanka. In Sinhala, the language of the majority, *Sri* means "blessed" and Lanka is the name of the island.

The island's history of immigration, trade, and colonial invasion has led to the formation of a variety of ethnic groups, each with its own language and religious traditions. Besides the majority Sinhala Buddhists, the nation also includes Sri Lankan Tamils, Tamils of recent Indian origin, Muslims, semitribal Väddas, and Burghers, descendants of intermarriages between Sri Lankans and Europeans. Although the members of these groups share many cultural practices, beliefs, and values, ethnic differences have become especially marked since the nation's independence in 1948. These differences and the exclusive policies of the Sinhala-dominated central government have led to escalating ethnic conflicts, including the current civil war in which Sri Lankan Tamil rebels are fighting for an independent nation in the northern and eastern regions of the island to be called *Eelam*.

Location and Geography. Sri Lanka is a small tropical island off the southern tip of India. The island nation covers approximately 25,332 square miles (65,610 square kilometers) and is divided ecologically into a dry zone stretching from the north to the southeast and a wet zone in the south, west, and central regions. This contrast in rainfall combined with topographical differences has fostered the development of regional variation in economy and culture. The north-central plains are dotted by the ruins of ancient kingdoms built around man-made lakes. The northern tip of the island is the traditional home to the Sri Lankan Tamils who consider Jaffna, its principal city, their cultural and political center. The dry lowlands of the eastern coast, site of fishing and rice cultivation, are particularly diverse both ethnically and culturally, with Muslims, Tamils, and Sinhalas composing almost equal portions of the population in some areas. The central highlands are famous for tea plantations and, in the southwestern part, gem mines. Kandy, the principal city of this central "Hill Country," was the seat of the last of the indigenous kingdoms and continues to be an important ritual, administrative, and tourist center. The southern coastal lowlands are the site of coconut, rubber, and cinnamon estates, an active fishing industry, and beautiful beaches. Located on the west coast is the island's largest city, Colombo, a hub of international commerce as well as the seat of government administration located on its outskirts in Sri Jayawardenepura.

Demography. According to the islandwide census in 1981, there were nearly 15 million inhabitants of Sri Lanka. This population was concentrated in the wet zone and around the principal cities, although barely three million people were considered to live in urban areas. At that time, there were approximately eleven million Sinhalas, two million Sri Lankan Tamils, one million Tamils of recent Indian origin, 1.5 million Muslims, and less than seventy thousand people of other ethnicities. Although the civil war in the north and east of the island has thwarted subsequent census plans, it was estimated that the population in 2000 stood near nineteen million.

Linguistic Affiliation. There are three official languages in Sri Lanka: Sinhala, Tamil, and English. Sinhala, the language of the majority, and Tamil, spoken by Muslims as well as ethnic Tamils, are the

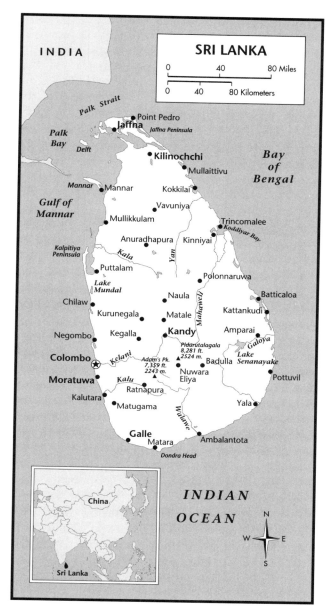

Sri Lanka

Also pictured on the flag and other emblems of national culture are the leaves of the sacred Bo Tree under which the Buddha found enlightenment. Other symbols central to Sri Lankan Buddhism and Sinhala mythology have also become icons of national identity, such as the Tooth Relic of the Buddha, the possession of which has provided legitimacy to Sinhala rulers for thousands of years.

There are also symbols of national culture that reflect a more integrated national identity. For instance, the color blocks on the nation's flag represent each of Sri Lanka's three major ethnic groups. The Sri Lankan elephant is a symbol of national heritage and of prosperity, both for its long association with wealth and royalty and for its association with Ganesh, the elephant-headed Hindu god of wealth. The betel leaf and oil lamp are used to mark special occasions. Images of the island's natural resources, such as palm trees, gems, and beaches, are promoted as part of the tourist industry and other international commercial enterprises. The players and events that are part of the wildly popular national cricket team serve as symbolic foci of national culture. Further, the performance of certain islandwide customs, such as bowing in respect, serve as symbolic enactments of a national cultural identity.

HISTORY AND ETHNIC RELATIONS

Emergence of the Nation. There is archaeological evidence that the island was inhabited as early as 10,000 B.C.E. The present-day Väddas, who live in remote areas of Sri Lanka and use a simple technology, are apparently descended from these early inhabitants mixed with the later arriving Tamils and Sinhalas, who were both well established on the island by the third century B.C.E. It is widely believed that the Sinhala people migrated to the island from north India, bringing their Indo-Aryan language and some version of Brahmanism with them, although Buddhism was introduced in their principal areas of settlement during the third century B.C.E. The Tamils emigrated to the north of the island from southern India, bringing Hinduism and their Dravidian language with them. The Sinhalas, the Tamils, and various south Indian invaders built powerful kingdoms with advanced agricultural projects and elaborate religious institutions, kingdoms that periodically brought the island under the authority of a single regime.

Because of its important ports along the East-West trade routes and desirable goods, traders were drawn to the island. Some of these Arab traders

primary languages of the island. English was introduced during British rule and continues to be the language of commerce and the higher levels of both public and private sector administration. Language has been a volatile issue in Sri Lanka, particularly following independence when the "Sinhala Only" campaign came to the political fore, provoking resistance from the Sri Lankan Tamils in particular, and thus paving the way toward the civil war.

Symbolism. The official symbols of Sri Lanka are largely drawn from those representing the Sinhala Buddhist majority. *Sinhala* means "lion's blood" and the lion is the central image on the national flag.

made Sri Lanka their permanent home, adding Islam to the island's religions. In the early sixteenth century Portuguese traders introduced Christianity as they began to make use of the island, eventually gaining control over productive portions of it.

In 1638 the king of Kandy drove out the Portuguese with the help of the Dutch. The Dutch then kept the land for themselves, controlling all but the kingdom of Kandy until they were driven out by the British in 1796. In 1815 the British ousted the last king of Kandy, gaining control over all of Sri Lanka, which remained a British colony until 1948.

On 4 February 1948, Ceylon, as the nation was then known, became politically independent of Great Britain, though it remained part of the Commonwealth.

National Identity. The current Sri Lankan national identity is dominated by the Sinhala majority, although this identity is resisted by the minority ethnic groups. Since independence, national leadership has consistently appealed to the Sinhala majority and the strength of the Buddhist monastic orders, marginalizing the non-Sinhala, non-Buddhists from the Sri Lankan identity and limiting access to state-controlled benefits. Despite the politicization of separate ethnic identities, there is a core of cultural beliefs, practices, and values that are largely shared among the people of Sri Lanka, particularly in the domains of the economy, social stratification, gender, family, and etiquette.

Ethnic Relations. Sri Lanka has always been home to a multiethnic and multireligious society. Because of the historic fluidity in migration and marriage patterns, the physical attributes of the principal ethnic groups are widely distributed. While conflicts between various groups have periodically flared up, beginning in 1956 the ethnic rivalry between the Sinhala-Buddhist majority and the Sri Lankan Tamil minority has intensified to an unprecedented level and led to the eruption of civil war in 1983. Since that time, the Liberation Tigers of Tamil Eelam, a militant organization of Sri Lankan Tamils, have been fighting for an independent Tamil state in the north and east.

URBANISM, ARCHITECTURE, AND THE USE OF SPACE

In the precolonial period, only the ruling elite and religious establishments were permitted to have permanent buildings. As a result, most of the archaeological ruins represent the heritage of elite culture, the ancient states, and the temple complexes,

many of which are still in use today. The most elaborate of Sri Lanka's architecture continues to be dedicated to religious purposes, ranging from the imposing domes of the mosques to the graceful spires of the Portuguese churches to the ornate and colorful figures covering the Hindu temples to the white, bell-shaped *dagobas* that house the relics of the Buddha. The influences from these religious traditions have combined with the influences of the colonists and more modern designs to produce a diverse architectural landscape in the urban areas as well as the rural, where 70–80 percent of the population continues to live.

Residential buildings vary widely according to the socioeconomic status of their inhabitants. Rural peasants live in small temporary wattle and daub (stick and mud), thatched houses whose style has remained unchanged since ancient times. In the urban area of Colombo, half of the residents are estimated to live in "low income" areas characterized by crowded dilapidated buildings and adjoining *watte*, built of a hodgepodge of thatch, wooden planks, and corrugated metal sheets along railways and roadways, beaches, rivers, and canal banks. In this same city are modern apartment buildings and colonial-era gated compounds with attached servants' quarters.

All over the island, there is a preference for whitewashed cement houses with polished cement floors and windows designed to keep out the heat and light but let in the air through built-in vents. The front of the house with its sitting room, bedrooms, dining area, and veranda is typically separated from the back of the house in which the kitchen and washing areas are located, a division that reflects notions of the danger of pollution by outsiders. Buddhist, Hindu, or even Christian shrines are often located within the house or the garden areas that surround it.

Public spaces provide the setting for a variety of valued activities. Each community, no matter how small, contains a public school, a place of worship, and a shop or two where people can buy daily necessities as well as exchange gossip. Wells, rivers, and other bathing places are also important social gathering places.

FOOD AND ECONOMY

Food in Daily Life. Sri Lanka's staple meal is a large serving of rice accompanied by up to twelve different side dishes of vegetables, egg, meat, or fish stewed together with peppers, spices, and often coconut milk. This rice and curry meal is traditionally eaten at midday, although it may also be served in the evening. The traditional morning and evening meals are usually composed of a traditional starchy staple, such as *string hoppers* (fresh rice noodles), *hoppers* (cup-shaped pancakes), *roti* (coconut flat bread), or *thosai* (sourdough pancakes), served with a *sambol* (a mixture of hot peppers and other vegetables, served cool) and one or two curries.

A variety of snacks and beverages are also eaten periodically throughout the day. Strong, sweat tea, usually with milk, is drunk alone or following a small serving of finger food or sweets, especially at mid-morning and late afternoon. *Curd*, a yogurt made from the milk of water buffaloes or cows, is often served as a dessert with palm syrup or sugar. A rich variety of fruits is available year-round.

Eating outside of the home has not been very common, although it is becoming more so. In almost every town there is at least one Chinese-style restaurant where alcohol is also served, as well as Sinhala, Muslim, and Tamil restaurants and traditional snack booths. In the capital, Western chain restaurants as well as other foreign-style foods are increasingly available.

There is some ethnic variation in foods and customs, as well as food taboos. For instance, Muslims avoid pork while Hindus are often vegetarian. Sinhala and Tamil people tend to take care that the foods served together create a balance of hot and cold energies. They also typically will not accept food prepared by those of relatively lower caste status.

Food Customs at Ceremonial Occasions. *Kiribath*, rice cooked in coconut milk, is part of nearly every ceremonial occasion in Sri Lanka. *Kawum* (sweet oil cakes) and other special snacks are also popular at special events. Alcoholic beverages do not play a role in the formal rituals of Sri Lanka, being condemned by Islam, Buddhism, and Hinduism alike. Alcohol is, however, a ubiquitous part of men's social gatherings, where beer, *toddy* (fermented palm nectar), *arrack* (distilled palm nectar), and *kassipu* (an illegally distilled beverage), are consumed in great quantities.

Basic Economy. Sri Lanka's economy is shifting away from its traditional agricultural base to include production for an international market, a shift accelerated by a major policy change in the 1977 transition from a socialist-style, state controlled economy to a free market economy lead by the private sector. By the mid-1990s, roughly one-quarter of the population was employed as skilled workers in agriculture, fishing, or animal hus-

bandry; one-quarter in skilled craft or factory production; one-quarter in administration, medicine, law, education, accounting, sales, services, or clerical work; and one-quarter as unskilled laborers. In spite of this shift away from agriculture, Sri Lanka has recently achieved near self-sufficiency in rice production and other staple foods.

Land Tenure and Property. Although private ownership of land has been well established in Sri Lanka since the precolonial period, most of the land is currently owned by the state and leased to private individuals and companies. Religious establishments also own substantial tracts of land. Today as in the past, private property is passed from parents to children, with the bulk of landholdings going to sons. Although the sale of housing lots is a growing industry, the sale of agricultural land is relatively uncommon. This, in combination with the subdivision of property with each generation, has created very small holdings of paddy land, which are inefficient to farm, something that the World Bank has identified as the primary cause of poverty in Sri Lanka.

Commercial Activities. Sri Lanka's towns and villages as well as its urban centers are typically active sites of commercial exchange. Most of the nonplantation agricultural crops that are not consumed in the home are sold at local markets, along with traditional craft products such as brass, pottery, and baskets, which are largely produced by hereditary caste groups. Repair, construction, tailoring, printing, and other services are always in demand, as is private tutoring. Tourists are also the focus of a range of commercial activity.

Major Industries. The major industries in Sri Lanka are involved with agricultural production and manufacturing. Nearly one-third of the agricultural production of the island is from the tea and rubber estates, products that are partially processed locally. The production of textiles and apparel; food, beverages, and tobacco; and wood and wood products together account for a quarter of all manufacturing. Heavy industry is largely confined to government-controlled steel, tire, and cement manufacturing, oil refining, mining, and quarrying. Transportation, construction, and energy production are also important locally oriented industries. In addition, the ongoing war effort, the education system, and the tourism industry comprise significant sectors of the economy.

Trade. In recent years, the sale of garments manufactured in Sri Lanka has outstripped the more tra-

Modern office buildings often share space with older religious structures, forming a diverse architectural landscape in cities such as Colombo.

ditional exports of tea, rubber, and coconut products, although the latter continue to be among the largest exports, along with locally mined gems. Textiles, machinery and equipment, foodstuffs, chemicals, pharmaceuticals, and metals, and other raw materials are among the principal imports. In 1996, Sri Lanka exported nearly $5 billion (U.S.) worth of goods, with nearly $1.5 billion (U.S.) worth of products going to the United States, three times more than any other country. In the same year, over $5 billion (U.S.) worth of goods were imported from other countries, over half a billion each from Japan and India.

Division of Labor. Traditionally, the division of labor in Sri Lanka has been largely based on caste, gender, and ethnicity. Although members of all ethnic groups participate to some degree across the range of occupations, particular ethnic groups are thought to predominate in certain occupations, for instance, the Sinhala in rice cultivation and the public sector, and the Muslims, Tamils, and recent immigrants in trade. Different castes are also associated with particular occupations, which is not necessarily reflected in the actual work that people do. Symbolically associated with occupations such as rice farming, the largest and highest status Sinhala castes are typically land holders and recipients of service obligations from the lower castes. The lower status service castes are associated with hereditary crafts such as mat weaving, jewelry making, and clothes washing. Increasingly, these hereditary statuses are being replaced by education and command of English as the most important determinants of employment.

SOCIAL STRATIFICATION

Classes and Castes. Even though the ideal of social equality is widely diffused in contemporary Sri Lanka, stratification according to caste and class, as well as gender and ethnicity, continues to be very important. Class is determined by attributes such as wealth and education while caste, a traditional part of Hindu and Buddhist society in Sri Lanka, is determined by birth into a predetermined status hierarchy, typically understood as a matter of reward or retribution for one's deeds in previous lives. The traditional correspondence between these statuses was upset by 450 years of colonial rulers who often privileged members of certain, relatively low-status castes, effectively raising their class status and that of their offspring. The importance and legitimacy of caste continues to be undermined by political and economic developments. Class differentiation, on the other hand, is increasing both in day-to-day social interaction and manifestations of disparities.

Symbols of Social Stratification. Traditionally, caste identity was extensively marked by ritual roles and occupations, names of individuals and places, networks of social relations, and regulations of dress and housing. Degrees of difference within the caste hierarchy were also marked by forms of address, seating arrangements, and other practices of deference and superiority. Today, where these hierarchical relations continue, there is a degree of uneasiness or even resentment toward them, particularly among the educated younger generations. Class status, in contrast, is increasingly manifested in speech, dress, employment, education, and housing. In general, elite classes can be identified by their command of English, education in exclusive schools, executive-level employment, possession of valued commodities, and access to international networks, whereas the lower classes are associated with manual labor, minimal comforts, and a lack of social contacts with the elite.

POLITICAL LIFE

Government. Sri Lanka is governed by a democratically elected president and a 225-member parliament. The president serves for a term of six years and has the power to dismiss the parliament, out of which the president selects cabinet members, a prime minister, and a chief justice. Although regular elections at all levels of government have been held since independence, there are increasing allegations of tampering and violence. The current leadership is considering a new constitution in which greater powers would be reserved for the provincial governments, a move calculated to address the ethnic conflicts and end the nation's civil war.

Leadership and Political Officials. Although a spectrum of political parties campaign within Sri Lanka, political leadership is almost exclusively drawn from the traditional, propertied elite. Family lineage and caste affiliation figure prominently in selection of candidates at all levels. Since independence, only two parties have drawn the majority of their leadership from the lower classes and challenged the control of the elite: the ultraleft Janatha Vimukthi Peramuna, who staged armed insurrections that posed a significant threat to the stability of the nation in 1971 and again between 1987 and 1989, and the Liberation Tigers of Tamil Eelam (LTTE).

Since political leaders distribute state-controlled benefits and resources, such as access to employment, quality schools, and even passports, their constituents work to stay in their good graces. These elected leaders, who typically distribute resources preferentially to their supporters, make an effort to be seen as benefactors and are often more personally accessible than many bureaucrats.

Social Problems and Control. Although crime rates are rising, Sri Lanka's citizens are generally respectful of both formal and informal laws, as well as of each other. Throughout the nation's history, however, there have been periodic explosions of violence and lawlessness. Since the 1980s, there have been massive riots, bombings, and insurrections that have effectively challenged the authority of the state and resulted in massive bloodletting. Large portions of the island are not under the control of the state but are in the hands of the LTTE rebels. In response to these challenges, the government has periodically declared states of "emergency rule" that extend its constitutional authority.

The police, the military, and the judiciary system are in place to maintain government control. Imprisonment is the main legal sanction for those who are convicted of violations of the law. The death penalty, suspended for many years, is being considered for re-introduction in response to the perceived rise in crime and violence.

Informal sanctions also provide strong deterrents against socially unacceptable behavior. Rumor and gossip are particularly feared, whether these take the form of village talk, anonymous petitions to the newspapers, or posters mounted in public spaces. Acceptance in the family and other important social groups to which one belongs and how one's behavior reflects on the reputation of these groups are among the most powerful motivators of social compliance. The threat of sorcery or divine retribution on an injured party's behalf, as well as more earthly threats of violence and revenge, also act to ensure good behavior.

Military Activity. There are three branches of the all-volunteer national military: the army, the navy, and the air force. Since independence, Sri Lanka's military, once largely ceremonial, has been called on to counter civil violence and terrorist activities, as well as provide more peaceable services, such as coastal supervision and surveying. Since 1983, they have been fighting a full-scale civil war against the LTTE army which is reportedly well-trained and internationally funded. Between 1990 and 1995, defense spending made up the largest portion of the national budget, comprising over 20 percent of annual expenditures.

A man operates a Heidelburg printing press at a printer shop in Sri Lanka.

SOCIAL WELFARE AND CHANGE PROGRAMS

Sri Lanka has often been referred to as the model welfare state. With free and universal education and health care, subsidized transportation, and a wide range of public sector programs to assist the poor, the quality of life is high in comparison with other developing countries. Since the change in economic policies of 1977 which emphasize private sector growth, however, the quality and availability of these government services have been eroding and have been increasingly replaced by private resources accessed by the middle and elite classes. Besides the difficulty posed by reductions in state funding, the civil war has created additional challenges to the welfare system as up to 1.5 million people have been displaced, a group that has been targeted for relief and resettlement by nongovernmental organizations and private donors.

NONGOVERNMENTAL ORGANIZATIONS AND OTHER ASSOCIATIONS

Since 1977, foreign-supported nongovernmental organizations have proliferated, providing welfare services and promoting social agendas such as human rights, fair elections, conflict resolution, and peace initiatives. Other civil organizations that are more locally led and membership-based, such as trade unions and cooperatives, are largely dependant on or part of the political sector of Sri Lankan society. Religious organizations are the primary exception to this, and are independent from political society, which tends to regard them with fear and respect. Another notable exception is the Sarvodaya Movement which has been active since 1958, mobilizing volunteer labor for community service.

GENDER ROLES AND STATUSES

Division of Labor by Gender. In Sri Lanka, there is a strong tradition of both men and women working, with men focusing more on income opportunities and women focusing on the household. Currently, women's participation in the paid labor force is significant, although not evenly distributed, concentrated in professions such as nursing, teaching, tea picking, and garment construction. In manufacture and agricultural work, men are typically assigned tasks considered more physically demanding, while women are assigned the more repetitive, detail-oriented work at which they are thought to be better than men. Opportunity for foreign employment for women, while relatively available and well-paying, is restricted to domestic work, whereas opportunities for men are more varied, ranging from manual labor to engineering. Within the home, regardless of their engagement in paid labor, women and girls do all food preparation and most other domestic work.

Although most schools are segregated by gender, education has always been important for both boys and girls in Sri Lanka. The literacy rates for men and women are similarly high; the last census in 1981 found that 87 percent of females over the age of ten years were literate, compared to 91 percent of males.

Leadership roles in Sri Lanka are largely held by men, with some important exceptions. Sri Lanka elected the world's first female prime minister in 1960, Sirimavo Bandaranaike, whose daughter is the current president of the nation. While this is not indicative of the political power of women in general, it is true that Sri Lankan women have held voting rights since they were instituted in 1931 and have long held certain property rights. The large majority of religious leaders and officiants are also male, while women tend to be overrepresented among their followers.

The Relative Status of Women and Men. It is a widely held position among social scientists as well as lay people that the status of women is relatively high in Sri Lanka, especially in comparison to other South Asian nations. There has never been the practice of child marriage or the burning of widows in Sri Lanka. Even though most groups on the island prefer for new brides to move into their husbands' homes, women traditionally retain strong ties with their own natal families. Additionally, although it is expected among most groups for the bride's family to give the groom a dowry, in practice this property commonly remains in the possession of the wife until she passes it on, typically to her daughters.

Despite these traditional practices and the full rights of citizenship that women in Sri Lanka enjoy today, women consistently defer to men across all domains of life, including the workplace and the home. Women also bear the greater weight of social expectations and sanctions for noncompliance. In addition, sexual harassment and assault, while seldom reported to the authorities, are common experiences.

MARRIAGE, FAMILY, AND KINSHIP

Marriage. In all ethnic groups, marriages are traditionally arranged by the families of the couple. "Love marriages" initiated by the couples themselves are, however, increasingly common. Regard-less of who initiates the marriage, the bride and groom are expected to be of the same socioeconomic status, ethnicity, and, for Buddhists and Hindus, caste status, although the groom is expected to be slightly older, taller, and educationally and professionally more qualified than the bride. Additionally, there is a preference among Tamil and Sinhala groups for cross-cousin marriage, which is marriage with the child of one's father's sister or one's mother's brother. Among Muslims, the preferred match is between parallel cousins, the children of two brothers. It is also considered best if the couple are of similar ages.

The age at which people marry is on the rise, especially for women. According to the 1981 census, over a quarter of those over twenty have never been married. Divorce, while increasingly common, still occurs in less than 1 percent of marriages. Remarriage following divorce or the death of a spouse is possible for both men and women, although it is uncommon for previously married women to marry never-married men.

Domestic Unit. Ideally, a husband and wife live in their own household with their unmarried children, even if that household is actually a small section of an extended family home. In Sri Lanka, individual households are identified by cooking practices, so that, even within a larger house, a wife will cook for her husband and children independently from others who may live within the structure, perhaps sharing the same kitchen.

While women may have a great deal of power within a family, ultimate authority belongs to the oldest male member of a household, whether that is the father, husband, brother, or son. Sri Lankans express a preference that their first child be a girl, whom they believe will help care for and be a disciplining influence on younger siblings. While overall there is a preference for sons, this is not as strong as in other South Asian countries.

Inheritance. The majority of Sri Lankan families practice bilateral inheritance, giving a portion of the family possessions to all children in the family. In practice, fixed property such as land and the family home go to sons and mobile property such as cash and jewelry go to daughters, usually in the form of her dowry.

Kin Groups. In Sri Lanka, the notion of ancestral place and the kin group associated with it is very important, even as people move to other areas because of employment opportunities or displacement. This hereditary home is the site of life-cycle

A woman picking tea at a plantation in Sri Lanka. Approximately one-quarter of the workforce is employed in the agricultural sector.

rituals as well as day-to-day interaction with extended kin. It is most common for this kin group to belong to the father's family, as there is a preference for women to move to the homes of their husband, raising their children among his relatives. It also happens, however, that husbands join wives' families instead, particularly among the matrilineal people of the island's east.

SOCIALIZATION

Infant Care. In Sri Lanka, young children are highly adored, fondled, and indulged by everyone, both male and female. Infants are traditionally kept with their mothers or female relatives. Babies are carried until they can walk and sleep with mothers until they are school-aged, at which time they are encouraged to move into a bed with their siblings. Nearly all mothers breast-feed their children, commonly through the first year.

Child Rearing and Education. Throughout childhood, important rituals are conducted around culturally significant milestones, such as the first feeding of solid food and the introduction of the letters of the alphabet. The coming of age ritual following a girl's first menstruation is an important marker of her entrance into the adult world, although there is no such similar rite of passage for boys.

As children grow, they are expected to develop a sense of *lajjawa*, a feeling that combines shyness, shame, modesty, and fear. It is cultivated early in childhood and used to teach self-control, beginning with bowel-control training, which starts at one year, then with weaning and nudity, and later with school performance.

Although mothers perform most of the child rearing, they are more responsible for their daughters' discipline and tend to be more indulgent with their sons. Fathers tend to indulge all of their children under five, at which point they take on a stricter disciplinary role, particularly with their sons whom they are responsible for controlling. Corporal punishment is quite common, especially from older males to boys.

In Sri Lanka, education has always been highly valued and encouraged. School attendance is compulsory between the ages of six and fourteen, although children often attend preschool and typically continue until the completion of the secondary level. Academic competition starts early, as parents scramble to place their children in the better primary schools, and continues with three sets of standardized exams that determine access to subsequent

Stilt fishermen in the waters near Weligama, Sri Lanka. Fish are a large part of the Sri Lankan diet.

educational privileges. To prepare for these exams and other academic challenges, almost all children attend private tutorial sessions in addition to their regular schooling.

Higher Education. All of Sri Lanka's universities are government sponsored and attendance is free. Admission is determined by exam, so that only 2 percent of Sri Lanka's children eventually are enrolled in the universities, although children from affluent families frequently gain admittance to foreign universities. Of those who enter the Sri Lankan university system, the majority go into the arts, which includes humanities and social sciences, a course of study taught in the vernacular languages. Unemployment following graduation is high for these students, reflecting a disjuncture between market needs and university education. Those who attend the technical/professional schools, which are taught in English, tend to be more employable. Opportunities for postgraduate education are quite limited within the country.

Protests against authorities are well established among university students at all levels. New entrants to the university student community are routinely subjected to "ragging," a form of collective harassment by the senior students in an effort to create a sense of common identity and an anti-establishment consciousness.

ETIQUETTE

Many of the most important rules of etiquette serve to mark differences in social rank. Both Sinhala and Tamil contain a range of linguistic markers for status as well as relative social distance and intimacy. In routine social interactions, personal names are avoided in preference to nicknames, relationship terms, or other titles.

Gender is also an important factor in determining appropriate conduct. Among all but the most urbanized, women are expected to defer to men of relatively equal status and to avoid all implication of sexual impropriety by keeping themselves well covered at all times. They are also expected to refuse all alcohol and tobacco and to refrain from direct physical contact with men. Between members of the same gender and with children, however, there is a great deal of physical contact that emphasizes closeness.

At meals, women usually eat last, after they have served the men and the children of the household, although visitors are served first, regardless of gender. While the more Westernized may use silverware, food is commonly eaten with the right hand, a preference that extends to other domains as well.

In public, people tend to speak in hushed tones if at all, although leaders and sellers are expected to shout. Large emotional displays of any type are uncommon in public. Greetings are often unvocalized, with broad smiles exchanged between strangers and a friendly raised eyebrow to frequent acquaintances. When new people are involved in a conversation, the mutual acquaintance is asked questions about the stranger. Seldom does direct self-introduction occur. Unusual behavior of any kind draws unconcealed observation.

RELIGION

Religious Beliefs. Buddhism, the religion of the majority of people in Sri Lanka, is given a place of preference in the national constitution and public life, although Hinduism, Islam, and Christianity are also practiced by significant portions of the population. Except in the case of Christians, who are drawn from a variety of ethnic groups, these religious traditions map directly onto the three major ethnic groups: Sinhala/Buddhist, Tamil/Hindu, and Muslims.

The 1981 census reported that 69 percent of the population considered themselves Buddhists, 15 percent Hindus, 8 percent Muslims, and 8 percent Christians. In practice, however, there is a degree of blending between these practices as well as an incorporation of ancient indigenous and astrological beliefs.

Sri Lankan Buddhists and Hindus, in particular, share a number of foundational beliefs and ritual practices. The moral codes of both of these religious traditions recommend moderation and restraint, Hindus stressing the discipline of one's behavior and Buddhists advocating "the middle path." In both, the concept of karma and rebirth are central, ideas that posit that one's actions in this lifetime determine the kind of life into which one will be reborn through the quantity of merit that one earns. While both Buddhism and Hinduism also propose that one can escape the cycle of rebirth, a goal that is highly elaborated within Buddhism, the acquisition of spiritual merit to gain a better rebirth either for one's self or one's loved ones generates much of the religious activity of the laity. Among the participants in both of these religions, there is also a belief in a broad pantheon of gods, spirits, and demons, into which many local deities have been absorbed. These beings may be male or female, benevolent or malevolent, moral or amoral, but they are all considered subject to the same laws of death and rebirth as other beings. Devotees, including some Muslims and Christians, appeal to these gods to assist them with a variety of (mostly worldly) concerns.

Religious Practitioners. In Sri Lanka, each of the four major religions are served by native religious leaders, although not exclusively; the island is home to training institutions for specialists in each of its organized religions.

The largest and most active group of religious specialists are the members of the Buddhist monkhood, or *Sangha*, who are ordained for life to follow a path of celibacy committed to the disattachment from worldly life. As temple monks, they provide spiritual guidance to the laity, serve as role models, and act as a source of merit acquisition for those who support them. They do not, however, traditionally play a role in secular matters or life-cycle rituals, except the death rites. Well organized and often in control of fair amounts of property, the Sangha have considerable influence in society, both historically and today.

The priests of the various gods are more independently organized. The ethnicity of the priests depends on their clientele more than the origin of the gods they serve. Tamil Hindu priests are born into their roles, almost traditionally but not exclusively coming from the Brahman caste. Sinhala Buddhist priests, who serve many of the same gods, are drawn from the laity and are increasingly likely to be women.

Members of both the Buddhist and Hindu laity also play a variety of specialized religious roles as mediators, renunciates who withdraw from worldly pursuits, and other kinds of adepts.

Rituals and Holy Places. Sri Lanka is home to many sacred sites visited by foreigners and locals alike. Kandy's Sri Dalada Maligawa, which houses the Tooth Relic of the Buddha, is an active temple complex that is the ritual center of Buddhism in Sri Lanka. During this temple's annual *perahera* season, the Tooth Relic is paraded through the torch-lit streets, accompanied by dancers, drummers, and elephants. While this is the island's largest perahera, or religious procession, other temples around the island host their own at different times of the year.

Pilgrimage is an important religious activity for many Sri Lankans. Kataragama, the most popular and elaborate of the pilgrimage centers, is primarily dedicated to the deity, although it is visited by members of all four of the island's religions. The summit of *Sri Pada*, or Adam's Peak, another important

Wading in a pool of brackish water, a man pans for rubies, sapphires and other gems using a basket at one of Sri Lanka's many pit mines.

pilgrimage destination, is the traditional home of Saman, a Sinhala guardian deity common to both Sri Lankan Buddhists and Hindus. A large rock at the top is believed by Buddhists to have been imprinted with the footprint of the Buddha during one of his legendary visits to Sri Lanka and by Muslims to hold the footprint made by Adam as he was cast out of paradise. The ancient temples, especially of Anuradhapura and Polonnaruwa, are also important pilgrimage sites.

Death and the Afterlife. Death ceremonies are quite elaborate in Sri Lanka, usually conducted by the families of the deceased in conjunction with religious officiants. Bodies are first embalmed in a secular, medical process and then returned to the families for funeral rites involving the gathering of extended family and the sharing of food, followed by either burial or cremation. Among Buddhists and Hindus the body is kept in the ancestral home for as long as a week while a variety of rituals are performed to give merit to the deceased in order to ensure a good rebirth. A series of purification rituals are also performed to protect the family members from the pollution from the body. White is the color associated with funerals, except for monks whose death is marked with yellow. Following a death, white banners, flags, and other decorations are put up according to the status of the deceased. Anniversaries of a death are also marked by rituals performed by family members.

MEDICINE AND HEALTH CARE

The quality of life in Sri Lanka is among the highest in the developing world based on indicators such as its average life expectancy of seventy years, a relatively low infant mortality rate, and a well-developed infrastructure that provides safe drinking water and latrines to at least two-thirds of its inhabitants, an adequate food supply, and an extensive network of health-care providers.

In Sri Lanka, several different types of health systems are available. The state's free and universal health-care system includes Western allopathic medicine as well as South Asian Ayurvedic treatments. In addition, there are a variety of private clinics offering Western and Ayurvedic services, indigenous herbal specialists, and ritual healers. In general, people do not see these various health systems as mutually exclusive or contradictory, simultaneously accessing different systems for the same or different types of ailments.

Dosha, which loosely translates as "troubles," is the central concept that integrates these various health systems. Within Ayurveda, the concept refers to the physical and emotional problems resulting from imbalances in the body humors of heat, coolness, and wind. But the concept of Dosha is much broader in the folk system, referring to all kinds of problems including financial, academic, and social difficulties. Imbalances may result from food, spirit attack, or contact with some other extreme and may require different treatment approaches available from the different health systems.

Although there is a certain amount of popular knowledge about illness prevention, diagnosis, and treatment derived from these different systems, each is primarily administered by trained practitioners. Doctors, nurses, and other health-care workers are trained in modern Western allopathic medicine through Sri Lanka's university system as well as in foreign institutions. Ayurvedic doctors are trained in university-affiliated colleges in Sri Lanka and India. Indigenous herbal medical training is passed through apprenticeship from father to son. Different types of healing rituals are also conducted by experts—such as exorcists, drummers and other caste-based professionals, and priests and priestess of the gods—sometimes in consultation with astrologers.

SECULAR CELEBRATIONS

All Saturdays and Sundays are public holidays, as is the Poya Day of each month which marks the full moon. Independence Day on 4 February and May Day on 1 May are also public holidays. During April, the island largely shuts down for a week as its Sinhala and Tamil residents celebrate the traditional new year, the exact day of which is determined by astrologers. In addition, the major Buddhist, Hindu, Muslim, and Christian days are also reserved as public holidays.

THE ARTS AND HUMANITIES

Support for the Arts. Whether nationally acclaimed or only locally recognized, Sri Lankan artists are primarily supported by the clients who commission or purchase their work. In addition, some larger corporations sponsor particular projects and the government gives some small stipends and positions of honor to notable artists.

Literature. Sri Lanka has a long and prolific history of written as well as oral literature. As early as the fifth century C.E., both Sinhala and Tamil writers were recording histories and religious stories, as well as writing on more secular topics. This tradition continues today as fiction writers, poets, playwrights, and journalists write in all three of the nation's languages; some of their works have been translated into other languages as well. However, Sri Lanka's university and public libraries, once reputed to be the best in South Asia, are underfunded and poorly maintained as a result of increased budgetary constraints since 1977.

Graphic Arts. Religious topics and institutions heavily influence Sri Lanka's statuary and pictorial art. Local handicrafts, encouraged during the socialist days, have been challenged by less expensive imports since 1977. Some of these traditional handicrafts, such as pottery and basket weaving, are caste-based activities and tend to be more utilitarian than decorative. Others, such as wood carving, are highly ornate and well respected in international as well as local markets.

Performance Arts. Performance is the most vibrant of all art forms in Sri Lanka, particularly drumming and dancing. All fully professional theater productions are performed in a ritual context, although there is also modern, secular theater which is semiprofessional. There are also numerous forms of music produced and appreciated on the island including traditional drumming, religious chanting, work songs, South Asian and Western classical music, as well as contemporary popular music and film songs from national artists and abroad. Although appealing to different sections of the community, performances of all types are typically well-attended in Sri Lanka.

THE STATE OF THE PHYSICAL AND SOCIAL SCIENCES

Sri Lanka's medical, engineering, and sociological fields are internationally respected although they are challenged by lack of funding and the loss of many of the best researchers to foreign institutions. Additionally, the switch from English to the vernacular languages in the social science departments of the universities has made it difficult for scholars to participate in an international exchange of ideas.

BIBLIOGRAPHY

Alexander, Paul. *Sri Lankan Fisherman: Rural Capitalism and Peasant Society*, 1982.

Arachchige-Don, Neville S. *Patterns of Community Structure in Colombo, Sri Lanka: An Investigation of Contemporary Urban Life in South Asia*, 1994.

Baker, Victoria J. *A Sinhalese Village in Sri Lanka: Coping with Uncertainty*, 1998.

Brow, James. "The Incorporation of a Marginal Community within the Sinhalese Nation." *Anthropological Quarterly* 63 (1): 7–17, 1990.

Daniel, E. Valentine. *Charred Lullabies: Chapters in an Anthropography of Violence*, 1996.

David, K. A. "Until Marriage Do Us Part: A Cultural Account of Jaffna Tamil Categories for Kinsmen." *Man* 8 (4): 521–535, 1973.

de Munck, Victor C. *Seasonal Cycles: A Study of Social Change and Continuity in a Sri Lankan Village*, 1993.

de Silva, K. M. *A History of Sri Lanka*, 1981.

Dissanayake, Wimal. "Newspapers as Matchmakers: A Sri Lankan Illustration." *Journal of Comparative Family Studies*, 13 (1): 97–108, 1982.

Gombrich, Richand F. *Precept and Practice: Traditional Buddhism in the Rural Highlands of Ceylon*, 1971.

———, and Gananath Obeyesekere. *Buddhism Transformed: Religious Change in Sri Lanka*, 1988.

Good, Anthony. *The Female Bridegroom: A Comparative Study of Life-Crisis Rituals in South India and Sri Lanka*, 1991.

Kapferer, Bruce. *Legends of People, Myths of State: Violence, Intolerance, and Political Culture in Sri Lanka and Australia*, 1988.

Kearney, R. N., and D. B. Miler. "The Spiral of Suicide and Social Change in Sri Lanka." *Journal of Asian Studies*, 2 (1): 81–101, 1985.

Knox, Robert. *An Historical Relation of Ceylon*, 1681, reprinted, 1966.

Leach, E. R. "Introduction: What Should We Mean by Caste?" In E. R. Leach, ed., *Aspects of Caste in South India, Ceylon, and Northwest Pakistan*, 1960.

McGowan, William. *Only Man Is Vile: The Tragedy of Sri Lanka*, 1992.

Obeyesekere, Gananath. *Medusa's Hair: An Essay on Personal Symbols and Religious Experience*, 1981.

Rahula, Walpola. *What the Buddha Taught*, 1974.

Roberts, M. "Filial Devotion in Tamil Culture and the Tiger Cult of Martyrdom." *Contributions to Indian Sociology*, 31 (2): 245–272, 1996.

Ryan, Bryce F. *Caste in Modern Ceylon: The Sinhalese System in Transition*, 1953.

Schalk, P. "Women Fighters of Liberation Tigers in Tamil Ilam: The Martial Feminism of Atel Palacinkam." *South Asia Research*, 14 (2): 163–183, 1994.

Silva, Kalinga Tudor. "Caste Ethnicity and the Problem of National Identity in Sri Lanka." *Sociological Bulletin* 48 (1 and 2):201–215, 1999.

———, and Karunatissa Athukorala. *The Watte-dwellers: A Sociological Study of Selected Urban Low-income Communities in Sri Lanka*, 1991.

Spencer, Jonathan. *A Sinhala Village in a Time of Trouble: Politics and Change in Rural Sri Lanka*, 1990.

———, ed. *Sri Lanka: History and Roots of the Conflict*, 1990.

Tambiah, S. J. *Buddhism Betrayed? Religion, Politics, and Violence in Sri Lanka*, 1992.

Yalman, Nur. *Under the Bo Tree: Studies in Caste, Kinship, and Marriage in the Interior of Ceylon*, 1967.

—Bambi L. Chapin
and Kalinga Tudor Silva

SUDAN

CULTURE NAME

Sudanese

ALTERNATIVE NAMES

In Arabic, it is called Jumhuriyat as-Sudan, or simply as-Sudan.

ORIENTATION

Identification. In the Middle Ages, Arabs named the area that is present-day Sudan "Bilad al-Sudan," or "land of the black people." The north is primarily Arab Muslims, whereas the south is largely black African, and not Muslim. There is strong animosity between the two groups and each has its own culture and traditions. While there is more than one group in the south, their common dislike for the northern Arabs has proved a uniting force among these groups.

Location and Geography. Sudan is in Africa, south of Egypt. It shares borders with Egypt, Libya, Chad, the Central African Republic, the Democratic Republic of the Congo, Uganda, Kenya, and Ethiopia. It is the largest country in Africa and the ninth largest in the world, covering one million square miles (2.59 million square kilometers). The White Nile flows though the country, emptying into Lake Nubia in the north, the largest manmade lake in the world. The northern part of the country is desert, spotted with oases, where most of the population is concentrated. To the east, the Red Sea Hills support some vegetation. The central region is mainly high, sandy plains. The southern region includes grasslands, and along the border with Uganda the Democratic Republic of the Congo, dense forests. The southern part of the country consists of a basin drained by the Nile, as well as a plateau, and mountains, which mark the southern border. These include Mount Kinyeti, the highest peak in Sudan. Rainfall is extremely rare in the north but profuse in the south, which has a wet season lasting six to nine months. The central region of the country generally gets enough rain to support agriculture, but it experienced droughts in the 1980s and 1990s. The country supports a variety of wildlife, including crocodiles and hippopotamuses in the rivers, elephants (mainly in the south), giraffes, lions, leopards, tropical birds, and several species of poisonous reptiles.

The capital, Khartoum, lies at the meeting point of the White and Blue Niles, and together with Khartoum North and Omdurman forms an urban center known as "the three towns," with a combined population of 2.5 million people. Khartoum is the center for commerce and government; Omdurman is the official capital; and North Khartoum is the industrial center, home to 70 percent of Sudan's industry.

Demography. Sudan has a population of 33.5 million. Fifty-two percent of the population are black and 39 percent are Arab. Six percent are Beja, 2 percent are foreign, and the remaining 1 percent are composed of other ethnicities. There are more than fifty different tribes. These include the Jamala and the Nubians in the north; the Beja in the Red Sea Hills; and several Nilotic peoples in the south, including the Azande, Dinka, Nuer, and Shilluk. Despite a devastating civil war and a number of natural disasters, the population has an average growth rate of 3 percent. There is also a steady rural-urban migration.

Linguistic Affiliation. There are more than one hundred different indigenous languages spoken in Sudan, including Nubian, Ta Bedawie, and dialects of Nilotic and Nilo-Hamitic languages. Arabic is the official language, spoken by more than half of the population. English is being phased out as a foreign language taught in the schools, although it is still spoken by some people.

Symbolism. The flag adopted at independence had three horizontal stripes: blue, symbolizing the Nile

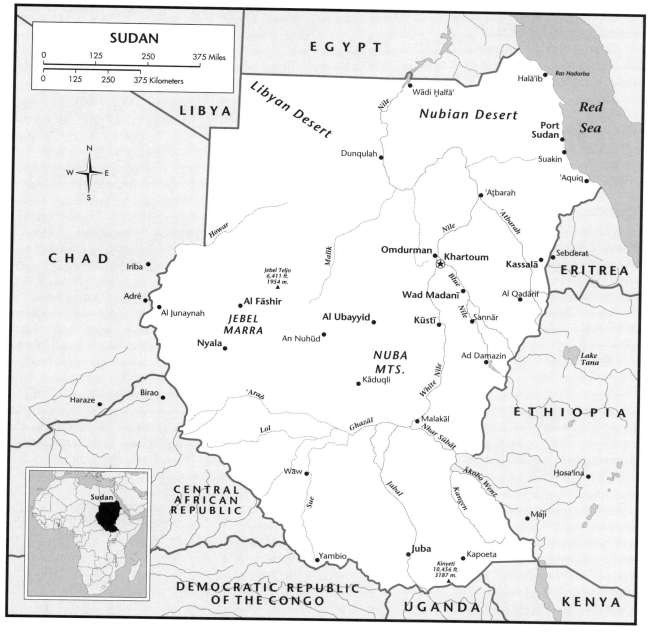

Sudan

River; yellow, for the desert; and green, for the forests and vegetation. This flag was replaced in 1970 with one more explicitly Islamic in its symbolism. It consists of three horizontal stripes: red, representing the blood of Muslim martyrs; white, which stands for peace and optimism; and black, which represents the people of Sudan and recalls the flag flown by the Mahdi during the 1800s. It has a green triangle at the left border, which symbolizes both agriculture and the Islamic faith.

HISTORY AND ETHNIC RELATIONS

Emergence of the Nation. The first known civilization to inhabit the region of present-day Sudan were the Meroitic people, who lived in the area between the Atbara and Nile Rivers from 590 B.C.E. until 350 B.C.E., when the city of Meroe was ransacked by the Ethiopians. At about this time, three Christian kingdoms—Nobatia, Makurra, and Alwa—came into power in the area. Several hundred years later, in 641, the Arabs arrived, bringing the Islamic faith with them. They signed a treaty with the Christians to coexist in peace, but throughout the next seven centuries, Christianity gradually died out as more Arabs immigrated to the area and gained converts. In 1504 the Funj people arrived, initiating a rule that would last for nearly three centuries. This was known as the Black Sultanate. Little is known about the origins of the Funj; it is speculated that perhaps they were part of the Shilluk or some other southern tribe that migrated north. Funj rulers converted to Islam, and their dynasty saw the spread of the religion throughout the area.

During the 1800s, the slave trade became a growing business in the region. There had long been a system of domestic slavery, but in the nineteenth century, the Egyptians began taking Sudanese slaves to work as soldiers. Also, European and Arab traders who came to the area looking for ivory established a slave-trade market. This tore apart tribal and family structures and almost entirely eliminated several of the weaker tribes. It was not until the twentieth century that the slave trade was finally abolished.

In 1820, Egypt, at the time part of the Ottoman Empire, invaded the Sudan, and ruled for sixty years until the Sudanese leader Muhammad Ahmed, known as the Mahdi, or ''promised one,'' took over in 1881.

When the British took control of Egypt in 1882, they were wary of the Mahdi's increasing power. In the Battle of Shaykan in 1883, followers of the Sudanese leader defeated the Egyptians and their British supporting troops. In 1885 the Mahdi's troops defeated the Egyptians and the British in the city of Khartoum. The Mahdi died in 1885 and was succeeded by Khalifa Abdullahi.

In 1896 the British and the Egyptians again invaded Sudan, defeating the Sudanese in 1898 at the Battle of Omdurman. Their control of the area would last until 1956. In 1922 the British adopted a policy of indirect rule in which tribal leaders were invested with the responsibility of local administration and tax collection. This allowed the British to ensure their dominion over the region as a whole, by preventing the rise of a national figure and limiting the power of educated urban Sudanese.

Throughout the 1940s an independence movement in the country gained momentum. The Graduates' Congress was formed, a body representing all Sudanese with more than a primary education and whose goal was an independent Sudan.

In 1952 Egypt's King Farouk was dethroned and replaced by the pro-Sudanese General Neguib. In 1953 the British-Egyptian rulers agreed to sign a three-year preparation for independence, and on 1 January 1956 Sudan officially became independent.

Over the next two years the government changed hands several times, and the economy floundered after two poor cotton harvests. Additionally, rancor in the south grew; the region resented its under representation in the new government. (Of eight hundred positions, only six were held by southerners.) Rebels organized a guerrilla army called the Anya Nya, meaning ''snake venom.''

In November 1958 General Ibrahim Abboud seized control of the government, banning all political parties and trade unions and instituting a military dictatorship. During his reign, opposition grew, and the outlawed political parties joined to form the United Front. This group, along with the Professional Front, composed of doctors, teachers, and lawyers, forced Abboud to resign in 1964. His regime was replaced by a parliamentary system, but this government was poorly organized, and weakened by the ongoing civil war in the south.

In May 1969 the military again took control, this time under Jaafar Nimeiri. Throughout the 1970s, Sudan's economy grew, thanks to agricultural projects, new roads, and an oil pipeline, but foreign debts also mounted. The following decade saw a decline in Sudan's economic situation when the 1984 droughts and wars in Chad and Ethiopia sent thousands of refugees into the country, taxing the nation's already scarce resources. Nimeiri was originally open to negotiating with southern rebels, and in 1972 the Addis Ababa Peace Agreement declared the Southern Region a separate entity. However, in 1985 he revoked that independence, and instituted new laws based on severe interpretations of the Islamic code.

The army deposed Nimeiri in 1985 and ruled for the following four years, until the Revolutionary Command Council (RCC), under the leadership of General Omar Hassan Ahmed al-Bashir, took control. The RCC immediately declared a state of emergency. They did away with the National Assembly, banned political parties, trade unions, and newspapers, and forbade strikes, demonstrations, and all other public gatherings. These measures prompted the United Nations to pass a resolution in 1992 expressing concern over human rights violations. The following year, the military government was disbanded, but General Bashir remained in power as Sudan's president.

Internal conflict between the north and the south continued, and in 1994 the government initiated an offensive by cutting off relief to the south from Kenya and Uganda, causing thousands of Sudanese to flee the country. A peace treaty between the government and two rebel groups in the south was signed in 1996, but fighting continued. In 1998 peace talks, the government agreed to an internationally supervised vote for self-rule in the south, but a date was not specified, and the talks did not result in a cease-fire. As of the late 1990s, the Sudanese People's Liberation Army (SPLA) controlled most of southern Sudan.

In 1996 the country held its first elections in seven years. President Bashir won, but his victory was protested by opposition groups. Hassan al-Turabi, the head of the fundamentalist National Islamic Front (NIF), which has ties with President Bashir, was elected president of the National Assembly. In 1998 a new constitution was introduced, that allowed for a multiparty system and freedom of religion. However, when the National Assembly began to reduce the power of the president, Bashir declared a state of emergency, and rights were again revoked.

National Identity. Sudanese tend to identify with their tribes rather than their nation. The country's borders do not follow the geographical divisions of its various tribes, which in many cases spill over into neighboring countries. Since independence, Muslims in the north have attempted to forge a national Sudanese identity based on Arabic culture and language, at the expense of southern cultures. This has angered many southerners and has proved more divisive than unifying. Within the south, however, the common fight against the north has served to bring together a number of different tribes.

Ethnic Relations. More than one hundred of Sudan's tribes coexist peacefully. However, relations between the north and the south have a history of animosity that dates to independence. The north is largely Arab, and the south has resented their movement to "Arabize" the country, replacing indigenous languages and culture with Arabic. This conflict has led to bloodshed and an ongoing civil war.

URBANISM, ARCHITECTURE, AND THE USE OF SPACE

Only 25 percent of the population live in cities or towns; the remaining 75 percent are rural.

Khartoum boasts beautiful, tree-lined streets and gardens. It is also home to a large number of immigrants from rural areas, who come looking for work and who have erected shantytowns on the city's fringes.

The biggest town in the south is Juba, near the borders with Uganda, Kenya, and the Democratic Republic of the Congo. It has wide, dusty streets and is surrounded by expanses of grassland. The town has a hospital, a day school, and a new university.

Other cities include Kassala, the country's largest market town, in the east; Nyala, in the west; Port Sudan, through which most international trade passes; Atbara, in the north; and Wad Medani in the central region, where the independence movement originated.

Architecture is varied, and reflects regional climatic and cultural differences. In the northern desert regions, houses are thick-walled mud structures with flat roofs and elaborately decorated doorways (reflecting Arabic influence). In much of the country, houses are made of baked bricks and are surrounded by courtyards. In the south, typical houses are round straw huts with conical roofs, called *ghotiya*. Nomads, who live throughout Sudan, sleep in tents. The style and material of the tents vary, depending on the tribe; the Rashiaida, for example, use goat hair, whereas the Hadendowa weave their homes from palm fiber.

FOOD AND ECONOMY

Food in Daily Life. The day usually begins with a cup of tea. Breakfast is eaten in the mid- to late morning, generally consisting of beans, salad, liver, and bread. Millet is the staple food, and is prepared as a porridge called *asida* or a flat bread called *kisra*. Vegetables are prepared in stews or salads. *Ful*, a dish of broad beans cooked in oil, is common, as are cassavas and sweet potatoes. Nomads in the north rely on dairy products and meat from camels. In general, meat is expensive and not often consumed. Sheep are killed for feasts or to honor a special guest. The intestines, lungs, and liver of the animal are prepared with chili pepper in a special dish called *marara*.

Cooking is done in the courtyards outside the house on a tin grill called a *kanoon*, which uses charcoal as fuel.

Tea and coffee are both popular drinks. Coffee beans are fried, then ground with cloves and spices. The liquid is strained through a grass sieve and served in tiny cups.

A Rasheida resident employs a worker to mud-plaster his house. These mud structures are common in the northern region of the Sudan.

Food Customs at Ceremonial Occasions. At the *Eid al-Adha*, the Feast of the Great Sacrifice, it is customary to kill a sheep, and to give part of the meat to people who cannot afford it themselves. The *Eid al-Fitr*, or Breaking of the Ramadan Fast, is another joyous occasion, and involves a large family meal. The birthday of the Prophet Muhammad is primarily a children's holiday, celebrated with special desserts: pink sugar dolls and sticky sweets made from nuts and sesame seeds.

Basic Economy. Sudan is one of the twenty-five poorest countries in the world. It has been afflicted by drought and famine and by staggering foreign debt, which nearly caused the country to be expelled from the International Monetary Fund in 1990. Eighty percent of the labor force works in agriculture. Yields have suffered in recent years from decreased rainfall, desertification, and lack of sufficient irrigation systems; currently only 10 percent of arable land is cultivated. Major crops include millet, groundnuts, sesame seed, corn, wheat, and fruits (dates, mangoes, guavas, bananas, and citrus). In areas not conducive to farming, people (many of them nomads) support themselves by raising cattle, sheep, goats, or camels. Ten percent of the labor force is employed in industry and commerce, and 6 percent in the government. There is a shortage of skilled workers, many of whom emigrate to find better work elsewhere. There also is a 30 percent unemployment rate.

Land Tenure and Property. The government owns and operates the country's largest farm, a cotton plantation in the central El Gezira region. Otherwise, much of the land is owned by the different tribes. The various nomadic tribes do not make a claim to any particular territory. Other groups have their own systems for landownership. Among the Otoro in the east-central region, for example, land can be bought, inherited, or claimed by clearing a new area; among the Muslim Fur people in the west, land is administered jointly by kin groups.

Commercial Activities. *Souks*, or markets, are the centers of commercial activity in the cities and villages. One can buy agricultural products (fruits and vegetables, meat, millet) there, as well as handicrafts produced by local artisans.

Major Industries. Industries include cotton ginning, textiles, cement, edible oils, sugar, soap distilling, and petroleum refining.

The town of Omdurman, situated on the left bank of the White Nile. Together with Khartoum and North Khartoum, the city forms the vast urban region known as "the three towns."

Trade. Cotton is Sudan's primary export, accounting for more than a quarter of foreign currency that enters the country. However, production is vulnerable to climatic fluctuations, and the crop is often hurt by drought. Livestock, sesame, groundnuts, oil, and gum arabic also are exported. These products go to Saudi Arabia, Italy, Germany, Egypt, and France. Sudan imports large quantities of goods, including foodstuffs, petroleum products, textiles, machinery, vehicles, iron, and steel. These products come from China, France, Britain, Germany, and Japan.

Division of Labor. It is traditional for children to follow in the professions of their parents; for the majority of the population, this means continuing in the farming lifestyle; 80 percent of the workforce is in agriculture; 10 percent is in industry and commerce; 6 percent is in government; and 4 percent is unemployed (without a permanent job). In many tribes, political positions, as well as trades and livelihoods, also are hereditary. It is possible nowadays for children to choose professions different from their parents', but most people are constrained by financial considerations. There are facilities for training in a variety of professions, but Sudan still suffers from a shortage of skilled workers.

SOCIAL STRATIFICATION

Classes and Castes. Northern Sudanese have more access to education and economic opportunities and generally are better off than southerners. In the south, many of the upper class and politically powerful are Christian and attended missionary schools. In many Sudanese tribes, class and social status are traditionally determined by birth, although in some cases it took a good deal of savvy by the upper classes to maintain their positions. Among the Fur group, ironworkers formed the lowest rung of the social ladder and were not allowed to intermarry with those of other classes.

Symbols of Social Stratification. Among some southern tribes, the number of cattle a family owns is a sign of wealth and status.

Western clothing is common in the cities. Muslim women in the north follow the tradition of covering their heads and entire bodies to the ankles. They wrap themselves in a *tobe*, a length of semi-transparent fabric which goes over other clothing. Men often wear a long white robe called a *jallabiyah*, with either a small cap or a turban as a head covering. In rural areas people wear little clothing, or even none at all.

Facial scarring is an ancient Sudanese custom. While it is becoming less common today, it still is practiced. Different tribes have different markings. It is a sign of bravery among men, and beauty in women. The Shilluk have a line of bumps along the forehead. The Nuer have six parallel lines on the forehead, and the Ja'aliin mark lines on their cheeks. In the south, women sometimes have their entire bodies scarred in patterns that reveal their marital status and the number of children they have had. In the north, women often have their lower lips tattooed.

POLITICAL LIFE

Government. Sudan has a transitional government, as it is supposedly moving from a military junta to a presidential system. The new constitution went into effect after being passed by a national referendum in June 1998. The president is both chief of state and head of government. He appoints a cabinet (which is currently dominated by members of the NIF). There is a unicameral legislature, the National Assembly, which consists of 400 members: 275 elected by the populace, 125 chosen by an assembly of interests called the National Congress (also dominated by the NIF). However, on 12 December 1999, uneasy about recent reductions in his powers, President Bashir sent the military to take over the National Assembly.

The country is divided into twenty-six states, or wilayat. Each is administered by an appointed governor.

Leadership and Political Officials. Government officials are somewhat removed from the people; on the local level, governors are appointed rather than elected. A military coup in 1989 reinforced the general feeling of distance between the government and much of the populace. All political parties were banned by the military government. The new constitution legalized them, but this law is under review. The most powerful political organization is the NIF, which has a strong hand in government operations. In the south, the SPLA is the most visible political/military organization, with the goal of self-determination for the region.

Social Problems and Control. There is a two-tiered legal system, of civil courts and religious courts. Previously, only Muslims were subject to religious rulings, but Bashir's fundamentalist government holds all citizens to its strict interpretation of *Shari'a*, or Islamic law. Separate courts handle offenses against the state. Political instability has resulted in high crime rates, and the country is unable to prosecute many of its criminals. The most common crimes are related to the ongoing civil war in the country. Religion and a sense of responsibility to the community are powerful informal social control mechanisms.

Military Activity. The military is composed of 92,000 troops: an army of 90,000, a navy of 1,700, and an air force of 300. The age of service is eighteen. A draft was instituted in 1990 to supply the government with soldiers for the civil war. It is estimated that Sudan spends 7.2 percent of its GNP on military expenses. The Sudanese government estimates that the civil war costs the country one million dollars a day.

SOCIAL WELFARE AND CHANGE PROGRAMS

The government supports limited health and welfare programs. Health initiatives concentrate primarily on preventive medicine.

NONGOVERNMENTAL ORGANIZATIONS AND OTHER ASSOCIATIONS

Various aid organizations have played a role in helping Sudan deal with its significant economic and social problems, including the World Food Program, Save the Children Fund, Oxford Committee for Famine Relief, and Doctors without Borders. The World Health Organization has been instrumental in eliminating smallpox and other diseases.

GENDER ROLES AND STATUSES

Division of Labor by Gender. Women take care of all domestic tasks and child rearing. In rural areas it is traditional for women to work in the fields as well. While a woman's life in town was traditionally more restricted, it is increasingly common to see females employed outside the home in urban areas. However, it is still the case that only 29 percent of the paid workforce is female.

The Relative Status of Women and Men. Sudan is a patriarchal society, in which women are generally accorded a lesser status than men. However, after age forty, women's lives become less constrained. Men and women live largely separate lives, and tend to socialize primarily with members of their own sex. Men often meet in clubs to talk and play cards, while women usually gather in the home.

Several people gather at an irrigation canal in Gezira. The northern part of the country is desert.

MARRIAGE, FAMILY, AND KINSHIP

Marriage. Marriages are traditionally arranged by the parents of the couple. This is still the case today, even among wealthier and more educated Sudanese. Matches are often made between cousins, second cousins, or other family members, or if not, at least between members of the same tribe and social class. Parents conduct the negotiations, and it is common for a bride and groom not to have seen each other before the wedding. There is generally a significant age difference between husband and wife. A man must be economically self-sufficient and able to provide for a family before he can marry. He has to be able to furnish an acceptable bride-price of jewelry, clothes, furniture, and among some tribes, cattle. Among the middle class, women usually are married after they finish school, at age nineteen or twenty; in poorer families or in rural areas, the age is younger. Polygyny was a common practice in the past. Divorce, although still considered shameful, is more common today than it once was. Upon dissolution of a marriage, the bride-price is returned to the husband.

Domestic Unit. Extended families often live together under the same roof, or at least nearby. Husband and wife typically move in with the wife's

family for at least a year after marriage, or until they have their first child, at which point they move out on their own (although usually to a house in close proximity to the wife's parents).

Inheritance. Islamic law has a provision for inheritance by the oldest male son. Other inheritance traditions vary from tribe to tribe. In the north, among the Arab population, property goes to the eldest son. Among the Azande, a man's property (which consisted primarily of agricultural goods) was generally destroyed upon his death to prevent the accumulation of wealth. Among the Fur, property is usually sold upon the death of its owner; land is owned jointly by kin groups and therefore not divided upon death.

Kin Groups. In different regions of Sudan, traditional clan structures function differently. In some regions, one clan holds all positions of leadership; in others, authority is delegated among various clans and subclans. Kinship ties are reckoned through connections on both the mother's and the father's side, although the paternal line is given stronger consideration.

SOCIALIZATION

Infant Care. There are several practices to protect newborn babies. For example, Muslims whisper Allah's name in the baby's ear, and Christians make the sign of the cross in water on his or her forehead. An indigenous tradition is to tie an amulet of a fish bone from the Nile around the child's neck or arm. Women carry their babies tied to their sides or backs with cloth. They often bring them along to work in the fields.

Child Rearing and Education. Boys and girls are raised fairly separately. Both are divided into age-specific groups. There are celebrations to mark a group's graduation from one stage to the next. For boys, the transition from childhood to manhood is marked by a circumcision ceremony.

The literacy rate is only 46 percent overall (58% for men and 36% for women), but the overall education level of the population has increased since independence. In the mid-1950s fewer than 150,000 children were enrolled in primary school, compared with more than 2 million today. However, the south still has fewer schools than the north. Most of the schools in the south were established by Christian missionaries during colonial times, but the government closed these schools in 1962. In villages, children usually attend Islamic

Three men sit by the river in the Ali-Abu region of Sudan. Seventy percent of Sudanese are Sunni Muslim.

schools known as *khalwa*. They learn to read and write, to memorize parts of the Qur'an, and to become members of an Islamic community—boys usually attend between ages five and nineteen, and girls generally stop attending after age ten. (Girls generally receive less education than boys, as families often consider it more valuable for their daughters to learn domestic skills and to work at home.) As payment at the khalwa, students or their parents contribute labor or gifts to the school. There also is a state-run school system, which includes six years of primary school, three years of secondary school, and either a three-year college preparatory program or four years of vocational training.

Higher Education. Early in the twentieth century, under Anglo-Egyptian rule, the only educational institution beyond the primary level was Grodon Memorial College, established in 1902 in Khartoum. The original buildings of this school are today part of the University of Khartoum, which was founded in 1956. The Kitchener School of Medicine, opened in 1924, the School of Law, and the Schools of Agriculture, Veterinary Science, and Engineering are all part of the university. The capital city alone has three universities. There also is one in Wad Medani and another in the southern city of Juba. The first teacher training school, Bakht er Ruda, opened in 1934, in the small town of Ed Dueim. In addition, a number of technical and vocational schools throughout the country offer training in nursing, agriculture, and other skilled professions. Ahfad University College, which opened in 1920 in Omdurman, as a girls' primary school, has done a great deal to promote women's education and currently enrolls about eighteen hundred students, all female.

ETIQUETTE

Greetings and leave-takings are interactions with religious overtones; the common expressions all have references to Allah, which are taken not just metaphorically but also literally. *"Insha Allah"* (*"if Allah wills"*) is often heard, as is *"alhamdu lillah"* (*"may Allah be praised"*).

Food is an important part of many social interactions. Visits typically include tea, coffee, or soda, if not a full meal. It is customary to eat from a common serving bowl, using the right hand rather than utensils. In Muslim households, people sit on pillows around a low table. Before the meal, towels and a pitcher of water are passed around for hand washing.

RELIGION

Religious Beliefs. Seventy percent of the population are Sunni Muslim, 25 percent follow traditional indigenous beliefs, and 5 percent are Christian.

The word "Islam" means "submission to God." It shares certain prophets, traditions, and beliefs with Judaism and Christianity, the main difference being the Muslim belief that Muhammad is the final prophet and the embodiment of God, or Allah. The foundation of Islamic belief is called the Five Pillars. The first, Shahada, is profession of faith. The second is prayer, or *Salat*. Muslims pray five times a day; it is not necessary to go to the mosque, but the call to prayer echoes out over each city or town from the minarets of the holy buildings. The third pillar, *Zakat*, is the principle of almsgiving. The fourth is fasting, which is observed during the month of Ramadan each year, when Muslims abstain from food and drink during the daylight hours. The fifth Pillar is the Hajj, the pilgrimage to the holy city of Mecca in Saudi Arabia, which every Muslim must make at some time in his or her life.

The indigenous religion is animist, ascribing spirits to natural objects such as trees, rivers, and rocks. Often an individual clan will have its own totem, which embodies the clan's first ancestor. The spirits of ancestors are worshiped and are believed to exercise an influence in everyday life. There are multiple gods who serve different purposes. Specific beliefs and practices vary widely from tribe to tribe and from region to region. Certain cattle-herding tribes in the south place great symbolic and spiritual value on cows, which sometimes are sacrificed in religious rituals.

Christianity is more common in the south than in the north, where Christian missionaries concentrated their efforts prior to independence. Most of the Christians are of the wealthier educated class, as much of the conversion is done through the schools. Many Sudanese, regardless of religion, hold certain superstitions, such as belief in the evil eye. It is common to wear an amulet or a charm as protection against its powers.

Religious Practitioners. There are no priests or clergy in Islam. *Fakis* and *sheiks* are holy men who dedicate themselves to the study and teaching of the Qur'an, the Muslim holy book. The Qur'an, rather than any religious leader, is considered to be the ultimate authority and to hold the answer to any question or dilemma one might have. *Muezzins* give the call to prayer and also are scholars of the Qur'an. In the indigenous religion of the Shilluk, kings are considered holy men and are thought to embody the spirit of the god Nyikang.

Rituals and Holy Places. The most important observation in the Islamic calendar is that of Ramadan. This month of fasting is followed by the joyous feast of Eid al Fitr, during which families visit and exchange gifts. Eid al-Adha commemorates the end of Muhammad's Hajj. Other celebrations include the return of a pilgrim from Mecca, and the circumcision of a child.

Weddings also involve important and elaborate rituals, including hundreds of guests and several days of celebration. The festivities begin with the henna night, at which the groom's hands and feet are dyed. This is followed the next day with the bride's preparation, in which all her body hair is removed, and she, too, is decorated with henna. She also takes a smoke bath to perfume her body. The religious ceremony is relatively simple; in fact, the bride and groom themselves are often not present, but are represented by male relatives who sign the marriage contract for them. Festivities continue for several days. On the third morning, the bride's and groom's hands are tied together with silk thread, signifying their union. Many of the indigenous ceremonies focus on agricultural events: two of the most important occasions are the rainmaking ceremony, to encourage a good growing season, and the harvest festival, after the crops are brought in.

The mosque is the Muslim house of worship. Outside the door there are washing facilities, as cleanliness is a necessary prerequisite to prayer, which demonstrates humility before God. One also must remove one's shoes before entering the mosque. According to Islamic tradition, women are not allowed inside. The interior has no altar; it is simply an open carpeted space. Because Muslims are supposed to pray facing Mecca, there is a small niche carved into the wall pointing out in which direction the city lies.

Among the Dinka and other Nilotic peoples, cattle sheds serve as shrines and gathering places.

Death and the Afterlife. In the Muslim tradition, death is followed by several days of mourning when friends, relatives, and neighbors pay their respects to the family. Female relatives of the deceased wear black for several months to up to a year or more after the death. Widows generally do not remarry, and often dress in mourning for the rest of their lives. Muslims do believe in the afterlife.

MEDICINE AND HEALTH CARE

Technically, medical care is provided free of charge by the government, but in actuality few people have access to such care because of the shortage of doctors and other health care personnel. Most trained health workers are concentrated in Khartoum and other parts of the north. Health conditions in most of the country are extremely poor. Malnutrition is common, and increases people's vulnerability to diseases. It is especially pernicious in children. Access to safe drinking water and adequate sanitation also are problems, which allow disease to spread rapidly among the population. Malaria, dysentery, hepatitis, and bilharizia are widespread, particularly in poor and rural areas. Bilharzia is transmitted by bathing in water infected with bilharzia larvae. It causes fatigue and liver damage, but once detected can be treated. Schistosomiasis (snail fever) and trypanosomiasis (sleeping sickness) affect significant numbers of people in the south. Other diseases include measles, whooping cough, syphilis, and gonorrhea.

AIDS is a growing problem in Sudan, particularly in the south, near the borders with Uganda and the Democratic Republic of the Congo. Khartoum also has a high infection rate, due in part

A fellani woman eats at a market. Food is a large part of many social interactions.

to emigration from the south. The spread of the disease has been exacerbated by uninformed health care workers transmitting it through syringes and infected blood. The government currently has no policy for dealing with the problem.

SECULAR CELEBRATIONS

The principal secular celebrations are on 1 January, Independence Day, and 3 March, National Unity Day

THE ARTS AND HUMANITIES

Support for the Arts. There is a National Theater in Khartoum, which hosts plays and other performances. The College of Fine and Applied Arts, also in the capital, has produced a number of well-regarded graphic artists.

Literature. The indigenous Sudanese literary tradition is oral rather than written and includes a variety of stories, myths, and proverbs. The written tradition is based in the Arab north. Sudanese writers of this tradition are known throughout the Arab world.

The country's most popular writer, Tayeb Salih, is author of two novels, *The Wedding of Zein* and *Season of Migration to the North*, which have been translated into English. Contemporary Sudanese poetry blends African and Arab influences. The form's best-known practitioner is Muhammad al-Madhi al-Majdhub.

Graphic Arts. Northern Sudan, and Omdurman in particular, are known for silver work, ivory carvings, and leatherwork. In the south, artisans produce carved wooden figures. In the deserts in the eastern and western regions of the country, most of the artwork is also functional, including such weapons as swords and spears.

Among contemporary artists, the most popular media are printmaking, calligraphy, and photography. Ibrahim as-Salahi, one of Sudan's best-known artists, has attained recognition in all three forms.

Performance Arts. Music and dance are central to Sudanese culture and serve many purposes, both recreational and religious. In the north, music reveals strong Arabic influence, and often involves dramatic recitations of verses from the Qur'an. In the south, the indigenous music relies heavily on drums and complex rhythms.

One ritual in which music plays a large part is the *zar*, a ceremony intended to cure a woman of possession by spirits; it is a uniquely female ritual that can last up to seven days. A group of women play drums and rattles, to which the possessed woman dances, using a prop as an object associated with her particular spirit.

THE STATE OF THE PHYSICAL AND SOCIAL SCIENCES

Because of its extreme poverty and political problems, Sudan cannot afford to allocate resources to programs in the physical and social sciences. The country does have several museums in Khartoum, including the National History Museum; the Ethnographical Museum; and the Sudanese National Museum, which houses a number of ancient artifacts.

BIBLIOGRAPHY

Anderson, G. Norman. *Sudan in Crisis: The Failure of Democracy,* 1999.

Dowell, William. "Rescue in Sudan." *Time,* 1997.

Haumann, Mathew. *Long Road to Peace: Encounters with the People of Southern Sudan,* 2000.

Holt, P. M., and Daly, M. W. *A History of Sudan: From the Coming of Islam to the Present Day,* 2000.

Johnson, Douglas H., ed. *Sudan,* 1998.

Jok, Jok Madut. *Militarization, Gender, and Reproductive Health in Southern Sudan,* 1998.

Kebbede, Girma, ed. *Sudan's Predicament: Civil War, Displacement, and Ecological Degradation,* 1999.

Macleod, Scott. "The Nile's Other Kingdom." *Time,* 1997.

Nelan, Bruce W., et al. "Sudan: Why Is This Happening Again?" *Time,* 1998.

Peterson, Scott. *Me Against My Brother: At War in Somalia, Sudan, and Rwanda,* 2000.

Petterson, Donald. *Inside Sudan: Political Islam, Conflict, and Catastrophe,* 1999.

Roddis, Ingrid and Miles. *Sudan,* 2000.

"Southern Sudan's Starvation." *The Economist,* 1999.

"Sudan." *U.N. Chronicle,* 1999.

"Sudan's Chance for Peace." *The Economist,* 2000.

"Sudan Loses Its Chains." *The Economist,* 1999.

"Terrorist State." *The Progressive,* 1998.

"Through the Looking Glass." *The Economist,* 1999.

Woodbury, Richard, et al. "The Children's Crusade." *Time,* 1998.

Zimmer, Carl. "A Sleeping Storm." *Discover,* 1998.

Web Sites

"Sudan." *CIA World Factbook 2000,* http://www.odci.gov/cia/publications/factbook/geos/su

—ELEANOR STANFORD

SURINAME

CULTURE NAME
Surinamese

ORIENTATION

Identification. The name "Suriname" (Sranan, Surinam) may be of Amerindian origin. Suriname is a multiethnic, multicultural, multilingual, and multireligious country without a true national culture.

Location and Geography. Suriname is in South America but is considered a Caribbean country. The total area is 63,250 square miles (163,820 square kilometers). The majority of the inhabitants live in the narrow coastal zone. More than 90 percent of the national territory is covered by rain forest. Suriname is a tropical country with alternating dry and rainy seasons. Since the early colonial days, Paramaribo has been the capital.

Demography. The official population estimate in 2000 was 435,000. Approximately 35 to 40 percent of the population is of British Indian descent (the so-called Hindostani), 30 to 35 percent is Creole or Afro-Surinamese, 15 percent is of Javanese descent, 10 percent is Maroon (descended from runaway slaves), and there are six thousand to seven thousand Amerindians. Other minorities include Chinese and Lebanese/Syrians. Since 1870, the population has increased, but with many fluctuations. In the 1970s, mass emigration to the Netherlands led to a population decrease; an estimated 300,000 Surinamers now live in the Netherlands.

Linguistic Affiliation. The official language and medium of instruction is Dutch, but some twenty languages are spoken. The major creole language and lingua franca is Sranantongo, which developed at the plantations, where it was spoken between masters and slaves. Sranantongo is an English-based creole language that has African, Portuguese, and Dutch elements. Attempts to make Sranan-tongo the official language have met with resistance from the non-Creole population. Other major languages are Sarnami-Hindustani and Surinamese-Javanese. The Chinese are Hakka-speaking. The Maroon languages are all English-based. Eight Amerindian languages are spoken.

Symbolism. The major symbols of the "imagined community" are the national flag, the coat of arms, and the national anthem. The flag was unveiled at independence. It consists of bands in green, white, red, white, and green. Green is the symbol of fertility, white of justice and peace, and red of patriotism. In the center of the red band is a yellow five-pointed star that stands for national unity and a "golden future." The five points refer to the five continents and the five major population groups. The national coat of arms shows two Amerindians holding a shield and has the motto Justitia-Pietas-Fides ("Justice-Love-Fidelity"). The left part of the shield shows a ship; the palm tree on the right represents the future and is the symbol of the righteous man. The national anthem is based on a late nineteenth-century Dutch composition. In the 1950s, a text in Sranantongo was added. In the first lines, Surinamers are encouraged to rise because *Sranangron* (Suriname soil or territory) is calling them from wherever they originally come.

Independence Day has lost its meaning for many people because of the political and socioeconomic problems since independence. The *mamio*, a patchwork quilt, is often used as an unofficial symbol of Suriname's variety of population groups and cultures. It reflects a sense of pride and a belief in interethnic cooperation. The country's potential richness and fertility are captured in the saying "If you put a stick in the ground, it will grow."

HISTORY AND ETHNIC RELATIONS

Emergence of the Nation. Suriname was a classical Caribbean plantation society. In the 1650s, En-

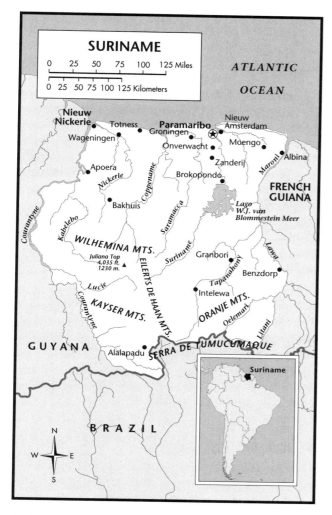

Suriname

to perform paid work on the plantations, contract laborers from Asia were imported to replace them. Between 1873 and the end of World War I, 34,304 immigrants from British India (the Hindostani) arrived. A second flow of immigrants came from the Dutch East Indies, bringing almost 33,000 Javanese contract laborers between 1890 and 1939. The idea was that the Asian immigrants would return to their homelands as soon as their contracts had expired, but most remained.

The policy of the Dutch colonial administration was one of assimilation: Native customs, traditions, languages, and laws had to give way to Dutch language, law, and culture. The introduction of compulsory education in 1876 was an important aspect of this policy. Javanese and Hindostani traditions proved so strong, however, that in the 1930s assimilation was replaced by overt ethnic diversity. Against the will of the influential light-skinned Creole elite, the governor recognized so-called Asian marriages and other Asian cultural traditions.

The Creole elite increased its influence in the wake of a political process that started in 1942, when the Dutch promised their colonies more autonomy. The Creole slogan "Boss in our own home" expressed the prevailing feeling. Before the first general elections in 1949, number of political parties were formed, mostly on an ethnic basis. In 1954, Suriname became an autonomous part of the Kingdom of the Netherlands.

World War II had a profound effect on the nation's socioeconomic structure. The presence of U.S. troops to protect bauxite mines and transport routes led to an increase in employment and migration from the rural districts to Paramaribo and the mining centers. This urbanization gradually made Paramaribo a multiethnic city, and the proportion of Creoles in the urban population dwindled.

The position of the light-skinned Creole elite was challenged by the so-called fraternization policy, which involved political cooperation among nonelite Creoles and Hindostani. Creole nationalism later led to Hindostani opposition. Despite the strong resistance of the Hindostani party and the fact that the cabinet had only small majority in the parliament, a Creole-Javanese coalition led the nation to independence on 25 November 1975.

National Identity. After independence, Suriname attempted to bring about a process of integration that would transcend ethnic, social, and geographic barriers. That process was accelerated by the military regime that gained power on 25 February 1980, but lost popular backing when it committed

glish colonists and Sephardi Jewish refugees from Brazil introduced the cultivation of sugar. When the Dutch took over from the British in 1667, fifty sugar plantations were operating. After a decrease in the number of estates, Suriname developed into a prosperous colony producing sugar and later coffee, cacao, and cotton. In the nineteenth century, the value of these products dropped sharply, although sugar exports were more stable.

In 1788, slaves numbered fifty thousand out of a total population of fifty-five thousand, yet there were not many slave rebellions. By 1770, five thousand to six thousand Maroons or runaway slaves were living in the jungle. After waging protracted guerrilla wars, they established independent societies in the interior. Between 215,000 and 250,000 slaves were shipped to Suriname, mostly from West Africa. Slavery was not abolished until 1863. After a ten-year transition period in which ex-slaves had

gross violations of human rights during the so-called December murders of 1982. In 1987, the transition to democracy restored the "old political parties" to power. Race, class, and ethnicity continue to play an overwhelming role in national life.

URBANISM, ARCHITECTURE, AND THE USE OF SPACE

Greater Paramaribo, with 280,000 inhabitants, is the only city and the traditional commercial center. Paramaribo is multiethnic, but the rest of the coastal population lives in often ethnically divided villages.

Paramaribo is a three hundred-year-old colonial town with many wooden buildings in the old center. A distinctive national architectural style has developed whose most important characteristics are houses with a square brick foundation, white wooden walls, a high gabled roof, and green shutters. Multiethnicity is demonstrated by the many churches, synagogues, Hindu temples, and mosques.

FOOD AND ECONOMY

Food in Daily Life. The nation's many immigrants have left culinary traces. The only truly national dish is chicken and rice. In Paramaribo, Javanese and Chinese cuisine and restaurants are popular. In the countryside, breakfast consists of rice (for the Javanese), roti (Hindostani), or bread (Creoles). The main meal is eaten at 3 P.M., after offices have closed. After a siesta, sandwiches and leftovers are eaten. Drinking water and street food are generally safe.

Food Customs at Ceremonial Occasions. At weddings and birthday parties, especially those celebrating a jubilee year, the so-called *Bigi Yari*, huge amounts of food are served. In Javanese religious life, ritual meals called *slametans* commemorate events such as birth, circumcision, marriage, and death.

Basic Economy. Commercial agriculture is limited to the narrow alluvial coastal zone. Smallholders are mostly Javanese and Hindostani. The largest rice farms are government-owned. The country is self-sufficient in rice, some tropical fruits, and vegetables, which also are exported. In 1996, agriculture contributed 7 percent to the national economy and employed 15 percent of the workforce. There is a small fishing industry. Overall, the country is a net importer of food.

Land Tenure and Property. Provisions for collective landholding are part of the legal system. Collective holding of agricultural lands can be found among Maroons, Amerindians, and Javanese.

Commercial Activities and Major Industries. The most important sector is mining, with bauxite and gold the leading products. Most of the bauxite is processed within the country produce alumina. Alumina and aluminium account for three-fourths of exports. Gold production is difficult to estimate.

Trade. In the 1990s, the main trading partners were Norway, the United States, the Netherlands, and the Netherlands Antilles. Besides mining products, exports include rice, bananas, shrimp, and timber. Imports come mainly from the United States, the Netherlands, and Trinidad and Tobago and include capital goods, basic manufactured goods, and chemicals.

Division of Labor. More than half the labor force is employed by the state. Those jobs are officially assigned on the basis of education, experience, and competence, but unofficially, ethnicity and political affiliation often play a role.

SOCIAL STRATIFICATION

Classes and Castes. Classes are increasingly multiethnic as a result of the social mobility of all population groups. The class structure is based on income and, to a lesser degree, social position. The elite includes import–export merchants, entrepreneurs, politicians, and military officers. Devaluation of the currency has squeezed a traditional middle class that is dependent on fixed incomes (civil servants, pensioners, teachers, paramedics). The gap between rich and poor is widening. The Hindostani could not maintain their caste system once they left India, but some notion of caste persists.

POLITICAL LIFE

Government. Suriname has been an independent republic since 1975. Its political institutions are defined by the constitution of 1987. The National Assembly has fifty-one members who are elected for a five-year term by proportional representation. The president is elected by a two-thirds majority in the Assembly. The president appoints the cabinet ministers. The Council of State, chaired by the president and including representatives of the military, trade unions, business, and political parties, can veto legislation that violates the constitution.

The decorative façade of a house in a Djuka village. Commercial oil paints are applied to the wood with a length of a cut plant stem.

Leadership and Political Officials. Most political parties are based on ethnicity. Party politics are characterized by fragmentation and the frequent splitting up of parties. Since the elections of 1955, no party has had majority in the National Assembly, and so coalitions of are always necessary to form a government. Many party leaders are authoritarian. Clientelism, a patron–client relationship between a politician and voters in which the politician delivers socioeconomic assistance (e.g., jobs) in exchange for a vote, is an important feature of politics.

Social Problems and Control. The administration of justice is entrusted to a six-member Court of Justice and three cantonal courts. The crime rate has increased since the 1980s because of socioeconomic regression; crimes against property accounted for nearly 80 percent of all crimes in 1995. Formal punishments include jail sentences and fines; no death penalty has been enacted since World War II, but the law is still on the books. So far, human rights violations have not been prosecuted. Informal control is still fairly high but has eroded since a military coup in 1980.

Military Activity. The National Army played a major role in domestic (political) affairs from 1980 to 1992. It was involved in a civil war in the interior in the 1980s and in a United Nations mission in Haiti.

SOCIAL WELFARE AND CHANGE PROGRAMS

There is a limited social welfare system funded by the state. Assistance by social organizations and benevolent societies to the elderly, poor, and infirm remains indispensable, as do remittances and care packages sent by emigrants.

NONGOVERNMENTAL ORGANIZATIONS AND OTHER ASSOCIATIONS

Labor unions traditionally play an important political role. The number and significance of human rights, women's, and social welfare organizations has grown. Suriname is a member of several major global and regional organizations.

GENDER ROLES AND STATUSES

The Relative Status of Women and Men. Official labor force figures underestimate the participation of women, many of whom are employed in the informal sector. Women also work in subsistence agriculture.

Despite the economically independent position of many women within their households, in society in general women cannot claim equal status. The domestic status of women varies. Women are the emotional and economic center of the household (matrifocality) in many Creole groups but are subordinated in traditional, patriarchal Hindostani circles.

Carrying bundles balanced on the head is common in Djuka villages in Suriname.

MARRIAGE, FAMILY, AND KINSHIP

Marriage. Although many marriage partners are of the same ethnic group, mixed marriages do take place in Paramaribo. In traditional Hindostani families in the agricultural districts, parents still select partners for their children. Weddings can be very lavish. Living together without being married is common but is not acceptable to traditional Hindostani, among whom the bride is expected to be a virgin. In the Caribbean family system, female-headed households and the fact that women have children from different partners are accepted. Some women practice serial monogamy; it is more common for men to have several partners simultaneously. Having a mistress (*buitenvrouw*) is accepted and usually is not shrouded in secrecy. Maroon men often have different wives in different villages; those men do, however, have the responsibility to supply each wife with a hut, a boat, and a cleared plot for subsistence agriculture.

Domestic Unit. Domestic units vary in type, size, and composition, ranging from female-headed households to extended families. Among the Hindostani, the institution of the joint family has given way to the nuclear family, and the authority of the man is eroding.

Kin Groups. The clan system among the Maroons is based on a shared belief in a common matrilineal descent. The population of a village can overlap considerably with a matrilineal clan (*lo*).

SOCIALIZATION

Infant Care. Babies usually sleep in cribs near the mother and are moved to a separate room when they are older. In the interior, mothers carry their babies during the day; at night, babies sleep in a hammock. In contrast to Maroon women, Amerindian women are reluctant to let anybody touch their babies.

Child Rearing and Education. Education and diplomas are considered exceedingly important by all population groups.

The Maroons and Amerindians have rites of passage. Among the Wayana, boys undergo an initiation rite, *eputop*, in which wasps are woven into a rush mat in the form of an animal that symbolizes power and courage. The mats are tied to the boys, who must withstand the stinging without a whimper. Among the Caribs, the girls undergo a similar ritual, except that stinging ants rather than wasps are used. The circumcision of Muslim boys is considered a rite of passage.

Higher Education. Despite economic constraints, public expenditure on education remains relatively high. Higher education is free. Education is compulsory between ages six and twelve. Between ages six and seventeen, school enrollment ratio is officially about 85 percent but the dropout rate is high. The adult literacy rate was 93 percent in 1995.

Paramaribo is the only city in Suriname and, as such, serves as the country's commercial center.

ETIQUETTE

A typical, mainly urban Creole, expression is "no span" ("Keep cool; don't worry"), symbolizing the generally relaxed atmosphere. The population has a reputation for being hospitable, and most houses do not have a knocker or a bell. Shoes often are taken off when one goes inside. Guests usually are expected to partake in a meal. A casual conversation is initiated by a handshake, and good friends are greeted with a *brasa* (hug). Children are expected to respect adults, use the formal form of address when speaking to them, and be silent when adults speak.

RELIGION

Religious Beliefs. The three major religions are Hinduism, Christianity, and Islam. About 80 percent of the Hindostani are Hindus, 15 percent are Muslims, and 5 percent are Christians. Most Creoles are Christians: the largest denominations are Roman Catholicism and the Moravian Church (Evangelische Broedergemeente); the Pentecostal Church has been growing. Most Javanese are Muslims. Officially most Amerindians are baptized, as are many Maroons. However, many of these groups also adhere to their traditional religious beliefs. The most important alternative system for Maroons and Creoles is Winti, a traditional African religion that was forbidden until the 1970s.

Religious Practitioners. Religious practitioners of all beliefs are paid by the Ministry of the Interior.

MEDICINE AND HEALTH CARE

Despite a lack of public funding, health care indicators are comparable with those in other Caribbean countries. Life expectancy at birth was 70.5 years in 1996 compared with 64.8 years in 1980. Infant mortality was 28 per 1,000 live births in 1996 (46.6 in 1980). Specialized care is available at the University Hospital in Paramaribo. There are medical posts throughout the interior. In all population groups, traditional healers are often consulted.

SECULAR CELEBRATIONS

Holidays include 1 January (New Year's Day), Id al-Fitr (end of Ramadan), Holi Phagwa (Hindu New Year, March/April), Good Friday and Easter Monday (March/April), 1 May (Labor Day), 1 July (Keti Koti, Emancipation Day, previously Day of Freedoms), 25 November (Independence Day), and 25–26 December (Christmas).

THE ARTS AND HUMANITIES

Support for the Arts. Government and private, support for the arts is virtually nonexistent. Most artists and writers are amateurs. A lack of publishers and money makes writing and selling literature a difficult enterprise. Most authors try to sell their publications to friends or on the street. The great majority of established authors live and work in the Netherlands. Oral literature has always been important to all the population groups.

Painting is the most fully developed graphic art. The most popular art form is music. Popular among Creoles are kaseko and kawina music, originally sung and played at the plantations. Among Hindostani, the songs from Hindi movies and videos are favorites. A few traditional Javanese gamelan orchestras perform traditional Javanese songs.

THE STATE OF THE PHYSICAL AND SOCIAL SCIENCES

The University of Suriname in Paramaribo has faculties of law, economics, medicine, and social sciences. There are also a number of technical and vocational schools.

BIBLIOGRAPHY

Bakker, Eveline, et al., eds. *Geschiedenis van Suriname: Van stam tot staat*, 2nd ed., 1998.

Binnendijk, Chandra van, and Paul Faber, eds. *Sranan: Cultuur in Suriname*, 1992.

Bruijning, C. F. A., and J. Voorhoeve, eds. *Encyclopedie van Suriname*, 1978.

Buddingh', Hans. *Geschiedenis van Suriname*, 2nd ed., 1995.

Colchester, Marcus. *Forest Politics in Suriname*, 1995.

Dew, Edward M. *The Difficult Flowering of Surinam: Ethnicity and Politics in a Plural Society*, 1978.

Economist Intelligence Unit. *Country Profile Suriname 1998–99*, 1999.

Hoefte, Rosemarijn. *Suriname*, 1990.

Lier, R. A. J. van. *Frontier Society: A Social Analysis of the History of Surinam*, 1971.

Meel, Peter. "Towards a Typology of Suriname Nationalism." *New West Indian Guide* 72 (3/4): 257–281, 1998.

Oostindie, Gert. *Het paradijs overzee: De 'Nederlandse' Caraiben en Nederland*, 1997.

Plotkin, Mark. J. *Tales of a Shaman's Apprentice: An Ethnobotanist Searches for New Medicines in the Amazon Rain Forest*, 1993.

Price, Richard. *First-Time: The Historical Vision of an Afro-American People*, 1983.

Sedoc-Dahlberg, Betty, ed. *The Dutch Caribbean: Prospects for Democracy*, 1990.

Szulc-Krzyzanowski, Michel, and Michiel van Kempen. *Deep-Rooted Words: Ten Storytellers and Writers from Surinam (South America)*, 1992.

—ROSEMARIJN HOEFTE

SWAZILAND

CULTURE NAME

Swazi

ALTERNATIVE NAMES

Swati, abakwaNgwane

ORIENTATION

Identification. The Swazi nation is named for Mswati II, who became king in 1839. The royal lineage can be traced to a chief named Dlamini; this is still the royal clan name. About three-quarters of the clan groups are Nguni; the remainder are Sotho and Tsonga. These groups have intermarried freely. There are slight differences among Swazi groups, but Swazi identity extends to all those with allegiance to the twin monarchs Ngwenyama "the Lion" (the king) and Ndlovukati "the She-Elephant" (the queen mother).

Location and Geography. Swaziland, in southern Africa between Mozambique and South Africa, is a landlocked country of 6,074 square miles (17,360 square kilometers). The terrain is mostly mountainous with moderately sloping plains. The legislative capital is Lobamba, one of the traditional royal seats. The administrative capital is the nearby city of Mbabane. Manzini is the business hub.

Demography. The population in 2000 is about 980,000. A small European population (about 3 percent) sometimes is called "White Swazi."

Linguistic Affiliation. The official languages are siSwati and English. SiSwati, a Southern Bantu language, is a member of the Nguni subgroup.

Symbolism. The primary national symbol is the monarchy. King Sobhuza II (died 1982) oversaw the transition from colony to protectorate to independent country. The symbolic relationship between the king and his people is evident at the *incwala*, the most sacred ceremony, which may not be held when there is no king. The full ritual, which takes several weeks, symbolizes the acceptance of traditional rulers, the unity of the state, the agricultural cycle, fertility, and potency.

HISTORY AND ETHNIC RELATIONS

Emergence of the Nation. The Nguni clans, which originated in East Africa in the fifteenth century, moved into southern Mozambique and then into present-day Swaziland; the term *abakwaNgwane* ("Ngwane's people") is still used as an alternative to *emaSwati*. Sobhuza I ruled during a period of chaos, resulting from the expansion of the Zulu state under Shaka. Under Sobhuza's leadership, the Nguni and Sotho peoples as well as remnant San groups were integrated into the Swazi nation. "Swazi" eventually was applied to all the peoples who gave allegiance to the Ngwenyama.

National Identity. In the late 1830s, initial contact occurred among the Swazi, the Boers, and the British. A substantial portion of Swazi territory was ceded to the Transvaal Boers, the first of many concessions to European interests. The Pretoria Convention for the Settlement of the Transvaal in 1881 recognized the independence of Swaziland and defined its boundaries. The Ngwenyama was not a signatory, and the Swazi claim that their territory extends in all directions from the present state. More than a million ethnic Swazi reside in South Africa. Britain claimed authority over Swaziland in 1903, and independence was achieved in 1968.

Ethnic Relations. Relations among the Swazi peoples have generally been peaceful. Relations with Europeans historically were strained as a result of land concessions and tension caused by the administrative domination of Great Britain.

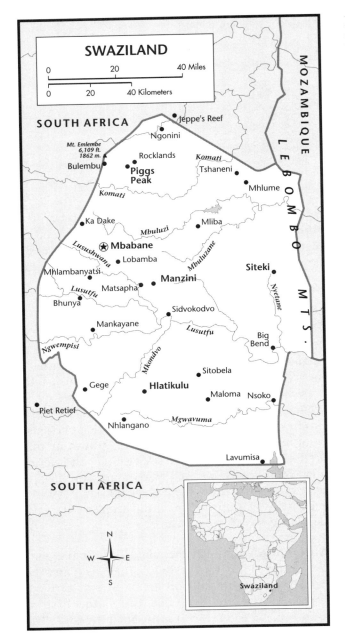

Swaziland

pean architectural styles. Traditional homestead organization follows the "central cattle pattern." In the center of the homestead is an unroofed, fenced cattle pen, the *sibaya*, from which women are barred. Residential huts are grouped around the western side. The "great hut," *indlunkulu* is used as the family shrine, dedicated to the senior patrilineal ancestors. Other huts are occupied by individual wives.

FOOD AND ECONOMY

Food in Daily Life. The traditional food supply fluctuated seasonally. Between winter and the new crops of summer, shortages were common. Maize and millet were the main staples. Dairy products, especially soured milk, were reserved for children. Cattle were slaughtered mainly for ritual purposes, and meat was in short supply. Leafy vegetables, roots, and fruits completed the traditional diet. The introduction of supermarkets means that meat and other products are available throughout the year. The Swazi typically observed a fish taboo, along with a taboo on egg consumption for females and a dairy taboo for wives. There were also clan-specific food taboos on particular birds and wild animals.

Basic Economy. Subsistence agriculture is engaged in by more than half the population. Manufacturing includes a number of agroprocessing factories. Exports of soft drink concentrate, sugar, and wood pulp are sources of hard currency; most of these products go to South Africa. High-grade iron ore deposits were depleted in the 1970s and the demand for asbestos has fallen. Badly overgrazed pastureland, soil depletion, and drought are persistent problems. Swaziland has an unemployment rate of 22 percent.

Land Tenure and Property. All land was owned and allocated by the king through chiefs and headmen. Land not allocated to individuals remained under the control of the political authority and was reserved for common use, such as for firewood, reed collection, and hunting. Vast tracts of land that were under foreign control at independence have been purchased "for the nation." Sons can inherit from their male kin.

Commercial Activities. The major agricultural products are sugarcane, cotton, maize, tobacco, rice, citrus fruits, pineapples, corn, sorghum, and peanuts.

Trade. Soft drink concentrates, sugar, wood pulp, and cotton yarn are the major export commodities.

URBANISM, ARCHITECTURE, AND THE USE OF SPACE

The predominant home style is the Nguni "beehive" hut, in which a rounded frame made of poles is covered with thatch bound with plaited ropes. Sotho huts, which have pointed, detachable roofs on walls of mud and wattle, are found throughout the country; these huts have window frames and full doorways. Both types can be found within a single homestead, which may also include Euro-

A village along the Drakensberg Mountains. Most of the country is made up of mountainous terrain.

Most exports go to South Africa, and 20 percent are sent to the European Union. Motor vehicles, machinery, transport equipment, foodstuffs, petroleum products, and chemicals are imported, mostly from South Africa.

SOCIAL STRATIFICATION

Classes and Castes. There is a sharp social division between rural and urban residents, reflecting the growth of the middle class. Clans are ranked by their relationship to the king and heads of state. The Nkosi Dlamini clan, the royal clan, is the highest, followed by clans traditionally described as "Bearers of Kings" (clans that have provided queen mothers). Among co-wives, the ranking wife is usually determined by clan memberships rather than by order of marriage. Interclan contact is free.

Symbols of Social Stratification. Apart from dress, knowledge of English is the main marker of education and status.

POLITICAL LIFE

Government. The government is a monarchy, with the Ngwenyama functioning as the head of state. The prime minister is appointed by the king. The "Westminster Constitution" of 1968 was suspended by royal decree in 1973. A new constitution was written in 1978 but has not been ratified. A bicameral parliament with a Senate and a House of Assembly has only advisory functions. The judiciary includes a high court and a court of appeals whose judges are appointed. As a result of growing pressure from student and labor groups in late 2000, King Mswati III has promised to introduce democratic reforms.

Leadership and Political Officials. Political parties are illegal, though some operate domestically and in exile. The most important is the People's United Democratic Movement, which calls for a peaceful transition to democracy and abandonment of the advisory system.

Social Problems and Control. The legal system is based on South African law in statutory courts and Swazi traditional law and custom in traditional courts.

Military Activity. The separation of the armed forces and the police is a modern distinction. Traditionally, both functions were performed by regiments in which every man was required to serve. The Umbutfo Swaziland Defense Force and the Royal Swaziland Police are under civilian control.

GENDER ROLES AND STATUSES

Division of Labor by Gender. The queen mother serves as a check on the power of the king. In part, the selection of the royal heir is a selection of the next king's mother. Traditionally, men and women cooperated in the agricultural cycle, though only men were responsible for plowing. Women receive gardens from their husbands, but the cultivation of cash crops involves both men and women. Herding is exclusively a male domain. Cattle have important economic and symbolic value. Sex-based stratification characterizes the workforce, though a few women hold important civil service positions.

The Relative Status of Men and Women. The traditional culture was patriarchal. Within the homestead, the only females related by blood to the patriarch were minor children. Their economic value was measured in *lobolo* (brideprice), usually in the form of cattle. Sons are valued more highly than daughters. Human rights groups have cited legal and cultural discrimination against women and abuse of children as social problems.

MARRIAGE, FAMILY, AND KINSHIP

Marriage. Marriage is defined as the union of two families. Polygynous marriages were once common, but the spread of Christianity and economic considerations have made them much less common today. The production of children is seen as an essential part of the marriage contract. Marriage between members of the same clan is forbidden; this practice extends and maintains social ties. Subclans occasionally are created to facilitate marriage between members of the same clan. Divorce has increased as a result of urbanization. Since traditional marriage is governed by uncodified law and custom, women's rights are interpreted differently by different parties. Under civil law, a man is technically restricted to a single wife.

Domestic Unit. In rural areas, patrilocal residence traditionally was the norm, and a homestead would include the headman, his wives, unmarried siblings, and married sons with their wives and children. With the exception of minor children, all females within the homestead are considered "outsiders." Nuclear family residence is the norm in towns.

Inheritance. Only males can inherit. The heir usually is not appointed until the father's death. In traditional polygynous households, the main heir is rarely the oldest son. The rank of the mother, not the order of marriage, plays an important role in the selection of the main heir.

Kin Groups. The clan is the major kin group. Every Swazi bears the clan name of the father, which also serves as a surname. Women retain membership in their paternal clan, though it is common for wives to use the husband's clan name as a surname. Each clan contains a number of lineages.

SOCIALIZATION

Infant Care. Traditionally, infants were not recognized as "persons" until the third month of life. Before that age they were described as "things," had no names, and could not be touched by men. After the achievement of personhood, a child remained closely attached to the mother. It was carried in a sling on her back and fed upon demand. Weaning occurred between two and three years of age.

Child Rearing and Education. A child began to associate with peers at age three. The mother left the

A Swazi warrior dressed in traditional costume. Males are very dominant in all aspects of Swazi society.

child in the care of other children. Discipline was introduced later. Young children "played house" and acted out adult kin roles. Today boys play with toy cars and motorbikes, and girls pretend to cook and groom each other's hair. The traditional training of boys and girls required them to be separated from about age six. Boys needed to be hardened for public life, and so they were socialized by older youths and took care of livestock. Girls had greater freedom of movement, though much of their time was spent in domestic chores.

Almost all children receive primary education today, although there is a significant dropout rate before age thirteen. Only about half the children of secondary school age attend school. Agricultural activities are a national priority, and relevant subjects are taught at many secondary schools.

Higher Education. Several institutions provide technical, commercial, and vocational training. About three thousand students are enrolled at the University of Swaziland (UNISWA), which has three campuses. UNISWA has established a program of distance learning. Students seeking a postgraduate education often enroll in South Africa.

ETIQUETTE

Respect is due to one's elders. Traditionally, greeting all persons, including strangers, was a normal event; this is no longer the case in towns.

RELIGION

Religious Beliefs. Christianity is the predominant religion. In addition to the traditional Western forms, there are numerous syncretist churches, and indigenous beliefs about the supernatural, particularly regarding ancestors, are still important. Many people consult *tinyanga* (traditional healers), who employ natural medicine and ritual in their cures. There is a widespread belief in witchcraft and sorcery. "*Muti* (medicine) murders" in which persons are killed so that their body parts can be used for medicine are now uncommon.

Religious Practitioners. Traditional religion has no class of ordained priests. The senior male in each family maintains communication with the ancestors. Diviners known as *tangoma* are considered more powerful than healers and are often possessed by spirits. Traditional healers are typically male.

Silkscreens lean against the walls of a cloth-printing factory in Swaziland.

Rituals and Holy Places. The *incwala* is the major sacred ritual. Certain parts of the homestead are ritually protected; the royal burial sites in the southern mountains are considered sacred.

Death and the Afterlife. Swazi believe that the spirit of a person has a distinct existence. One's social place is demonstrated through the elaborateness of funeral rituals. A head of household is buried at the *sibaya*; his widow shaves her head and undertakes a long period of mourning.

MEDICINE AND HEALTH CARE

Western medical care is available throughout the country. Many individuals seek treatment from both Western and indigenous practitioners. There is an extensive AIDS education campaign.

SECULAR CELEBRATIONS

The king's birthday is celebrated on 19 April, National Flag Day on 25 April, and Independence Day (Somhlolo Day) on 6 September.

THE ARTS AND HUMANITIES

Literature. Oral literature continues to flourish, and there is a small body of written literature in siSwati.

STATE OF THE PHYSICAL AND SOCIAL SCIENCES

Little advanced work is done in the sciences, although several scientists work at UNISWA, which has established a research center.

BIBLIOGRAPHY

Booth, Alan R. *Swaziland: Tradition and Change in a Southern African Kingdom,* 1983.

De Vletter, Fion, ed. *The Swazi Rural Homestead,* 1983.

Hall, James. *Sangoma: My Odyssey into the Spirit World of Africa,* 1994.

Harrison, David. "Tradition, Modernity and Tourism in Swaziland." In David Harrison, ed., *Tourism and the Less Developed Countries,* 1992.

Kasenene, Peter. *Religion in Swaziland,* 1992.

Kuper, Hilda. *An African Aristocracy: Rank among the Swazi,* 1947.

———. *The Swazi: A South African Kingdom*, 2nd ed., 1986.

Marwick, Brian A. *The Swazi*, 1940.

Matsebula, J. S. M. *A History of Swaziland*, 1987.

McFadden, Patricia. "The Condition of Women in Southern Africa: Challenges for the 1990s." *Southern African Political and Economic Monthly* 3 (10): 3–9, 1990.

Nyeko, Balam. *Swaziland*, 1994.

Rose, Laurel L. *The Politics of Harmony: Land Dispute Strategies in Swaziland*, 1992.

Simelane, Nomthetho G., ed. *Social Transformation: The Swaziland Case*, 1995.

—ROBERT K. HERBERT

SWEDEN

CULTURE NAME
Swedish

ORIENTATION

Identification. The people who came to be called Swedes were mentioned by the Roman historian Tacitus in 98 C.E. The names given to these people— *Sviones, Svear, swaensker*—led to the modern English term. Sweden has been a sovereign state for more than a millennium, and this has fostered cultural cohesion.

Centuries of relative ethnic, religious, and linguistic homogeneity were followed by substantial immigration during the last sixty years, creating a multicultural society. The indigenous Sami (sometimes called Lapp) people live in the northernmost part of the country and the neighboring states.

Location and Geography. The land area is 173,732 square miles (449,964 square kilometers). Except for mountain chains in the north and west along the Norwegian border, the land is relatively flat. Half is blanketed by forests, while just under a tenth is farmed. There are nearly 100,000 lakes, and a long, rocky coastline on the Baltic Sea. These diverse landscapes are warmed by the Gulf Stream, creating a temperate climate.

Despite Swedes' love of long summer days at waterside cottages, there has been a continuing movement of the population from rural areas to urban centers for more than a century. The largest city is Stockholm, the political, economic, and cultural hub. This port city is in the southernmost third of the country, where a large majority of the population lives; it has been the capital since 1523.

Demography. The population is about 8.9 million people as of 2000. A land of relative ethnic homogeneity has been transformed into a multiethnic society, by immigration in the second half of the twentieth century. Today, about a tenth of the inhabitants are foreign-born, and an additional one-tenth were born in Sweden but have at least one foreign-born parent. These include persons from the rest of Scandinavia and Finland. Immigrants from non-Nordic countries are concentrated largely in urban areas, particularly Stockholm, despite government efforts to promote a more even distribution. The indigenous Sami people number between 17,000 and 20,000.

Linguistic Affiliation. Most citizens speak Swedish as their first language and English as their second. Swedish is a north Germanic language related to Norwegian, Danish, Icelandic, and Faeroese; it has incorporated elements of German, French, English, and Finnish. The language has been nationally standardized for more than a century, but regional variations in pronunciation persist. English is a required second language in school. The many immigrant groups speak roughly two hundred languages, of which the largest first language is Finnish, which is spoken by about 200,000 persons. The public school system allows immigrant children to continue studying their first languages as a supplement to their other studies.

Symbolism. In 1928, Prime Minister Per Albin Hansson described Sweden as *folkhemmet*, ''the people's home.'' This metaphor of the nation as a great family household helped nourish the general-welfare society for the remainder of the century. *Folkhemmet* stood at the center of a cluster of institutions symbolizing social democratic ideals of equality and mutual care. Day-care centers, hospitals, old-age homes, communal music schools, municipal meeting centers (*folkets hus*), labor unions, and First of May parades were symbols of the new society.

Another significant set of symbols is linked to Sweden's agrarian past. Examples include mid summer dances, Maypoles, painted wooden horses from the province of Dalarna, and Christmas feasts. Industrialization and urbanization came late, helping

Sweden

in the 1960s and 1970s led many foreigners to view Sweden as a forerunner of the future.

The flag was often downplayed as a symbol. In the decades after World War II, internationalist ideals made it embarrassing to exhibit the flag to a degree that would be normal in other countries. By the early 1990s, the flag had become popular in the small subculture of anti-immigrant, right-wing extremists. This made it unattractive to the rest of the population. Only recently has this blue and yellow flag been employed more widely. The partial relinquishment of sovereignty to the European Union (EU) is seen by many people as jeopardizing national integrity; renewed interest in the flag is one response to that situation.

HISTORY AND ETHNIC RELATIONS

Emergence of the Nation. The first people arrived as an ice age ended between 12,000 and 10,000 B.C.E. They were tribes of reindeer hunters. Stone, bronze, and iron tools were developed, and by the time of Tacitus there was trade with the Roman empire. Bands of Vikings pursued plunder and commerce as they traveled by ship over the Baltic Sea and up Russian rivers, as well as into Western Europe, between 800 and 1050 C.E. Around 1000 C.E. the many independent provinces began to be united into a single, loosely federated kingdom. Monarchs were able to impose increasing degrees of national power in succeeding centuries. State building advanced rapidly under Gustav Vasa, who was elected king in 1523 C.E. He confiscated lands from the Roman Catholic Church and the nobility, promoted the Lutheran Reformation, built a German-inspired central administration, imposed taxes, suppressed dissent, and established a hereditary monarchy. By the end of his reign in 1560 C.E., Sweden was a relatively consolidated kingdom. The economy was predominantly agricultural, supplemented by iron and copper mining. During the next 250 years, Sweden fought wars against Denmark, Russia, Poland, and Norway. The nineteenth century brought peace, but poverty prompted mass emigration, particularly to North America.

National Identity. Sweden's egalitarian society builds on historical circumstances that favor a sense of solidarity. More than a thousand years of continuous existence as a sovereign state allowed for the gradual development of strong national institutions. During the medieval period, the practice of serfdom was never established, and the preponderance of independent farmers helped minimize social class differences and nurture an ethic of equality.

to fuel a twentieth-century cultural emphasis on modernity. Rational planning and high technology became important collective orientations, as seen in meticulously designed suburbs and in corporations that project an aura of acute rationality. The image of a supermodern nation also drew support from pioneering policies and practices in child care, gender equality, and sexual freedom. Social innovation

Relative ethnic, religious, and linguistic homogeneity facilitated the establishment of a national community. Wars with neighboring states sharpened consciousness of Swedishness in contrast to opposing national identities.

Ethnic Relations. Between the late 1940s and late 1960s, the booming economy attracted skilled workers from southern Europe. Those workers were allowed to immigrate freely and gain full citizenship. Norway, Denmark, and Finland also provided large numbers of immigrants.

No other affluent nation in recent decades has accepted as many political refugees, per capita, as Sweden has. People fleeing wars and repression from such places as Hungary, Vietnam, Chile, and Kurdistan have been granted a safe haven. In the 1990s, Sweden was the leading industrialized nation, in relation to population, in accepting those uprooted by wars in the former Yugoslavia. Foreigners enjoy full access to the welfare system, can vote in local elections, and can become citizens in five years.

Today it is common to hear a distinction made between "Swedes" (*svenskar*) and "immigrants" *(invandrare)*. This distinction is linked to physical appearance, imputed cultural affiliation, and social class. A person who bears a Swedish passport, speaks Swedish fluently, and is the daughter of two Swedish citizens may still be classified by some as an immigrant if she appears to be of African or Asian descent. Socially concerned citizens avoid this dichotomy, and the legal system makes no distinction. Official public documents that deal with immigration often use alternative formulations such as "new Swedes."

URBANISM, ARCHITECTURE, AND THE USE OF SPACE

The country is renowned for its urban planning. Through most of the twentieth century, close cooperation between municipalities and private firms was the usual form for urban planning. One goal was to design vibrant neighborhoods, complete with schools, workplaces, community buildings, parks, health clinics, and shops; a successful example is Vällingby, a Stockholm suburb that attracted international attention upon its completion in 1954. Traffic safety has been an ongoing preoccupation of planners, and that effort, combined with campaigns against drunk driving, has given the country the world's lowest rate of traffic deaths.

In 1965, the parliament decided to promote the building of a million new housing units in the succeeding ten years. As a result, even working-class residents have one of the highest housing standards in the world. A majority of the people live in apartments in towns and cities, while a substantial minority own their own houses. Summer cottages are popular, and cooperative communal gardens provide opportunities for city dwellers to grow their own vegetables.

Swedish functionalism, in architecture as well as furniture design, is a modernist style that emphasizes practical utility. In architecture, functionalism has often involved standardization as a way to lower costs and ensure high levels of hygiene and safety. The displacement of historic city centers by glass and steel commercial buildings has provoked a backlash against functionalism in the last thirty years. The style has fared better in furniture design, which features simplicity, practicality, and the use of wood and other natural materials.

A diffident respect for other people's privacy is typical in public spaces, where voices are kept low, bus passengers converse minimally, and well-known individuals are rarely accosted. The custom of removing one's shoes before entering a home marks a sharp conceptual separation between the public and private realms.

FOOD AND ECONOMY

Food in Daily Life. There is a wide array of culinary choices, including pizza, kebabs, falafel, hamburgers, and Chinese cuisine. Nonetheless, it is customary to identify certain items as particularly Swedish because of their association with the agricultural or early industrial past. The term *husmanskost*, or homely fare, refers to a basic diet of potatoes, meat or fish, and a hearty sauce. A less agrarian dinner alternative is the *smörgåsbord*. This buffet meal of cold and hot hors d'oeuvres often includes various forms of herring, meats, cheeses, and vegetables.

Breakfast typically includes bread with butter or cheese; muesli or cornflakes with *filmjölk*, a yogurtlike milk product; and coffee. Relatively light hot or cold lunches at midday customarily are followed by early-evening suppers. Common components of these two meals include bread, pasta, potatoes, carrots, cabbage, peas, herring, salmon, and meat. Immigration has enriched the range of restaurants, and restaurant patronage is rising.

Effective regulation has made Swedish food perhaps the safest in the world; standardized symbols identify foods that are low-fat, ecologically certified, or produced abroad under humane working conditions. Vegetarian, vegan, and animal-rights movements have prompted Sweden to become the first E.U. member to outlaw battery cages for hens.

Food Customs at Ceremonial Occasions. The smörgåsbord is well adapted to festive meals such as Christmas, Easter, Midsummer, and wedding banquets. Meat and fish dishes have greater prominence at these times, as do schnapps and other alcoholic beverages. Certain holidays have trademark dishes: The feast of Saint Lucia (13 December) calls for saffron buns, Midsummer revelers eat pickled herring and new potatoes, and late summer is a time for crayfish parties (*kräftskivor*) and, in the north, gatherings for the ingestion of fermented herring (*surströmming*).

Basic Economy. The economy is unusually diversified for a small country. Sweden is home to several giant transnational corporations, which dominate foreign trade. Their economic and political might is counterbalanced by large labor unions and a strong public sector.

Exports account for 36 percent of the gross domestic product in a nation that has been open to the globalization of its economy. Sweden was early in opening its telecommunications and other key domestic markets to foreign competition. European Union membership has forced the country to become less liberal in its trade policy. Sweden has not joined the European Monetary Union; its currency remains the *krona*.

Land Tenure and Property. Less than a tenth of the land is devoted to agriculture, mostly in the form of family farms. Forested land is held largely by individuals and corporations; the state owns less than 5 percent. Access to nature is protected by *allemansrätten*, the right of common access to land. This law makes it permissible for anyone to walk and camp on almost all private property; landowners are not permitted to barricade their estates. Strict building codes safeguard the quality of publicly accessible spaces. Urban apartment units are often owned by national renters' associations rather than by private landlords, an arrangement that makes it possible for working-class people to obtain desirable addresses.

Commercial Activities. Forests and iron ore have enriched the economy since medieval times, and those natural resources remain important. The largest export industries today are in the engineering and high-technology sectors. These knowledge-based fields benefit from the country's massive public investment in schools and universities, which has produced a highly skilled workforce. The public-sector activities of child care, education and health care account for a significant proportion of employment.

Major Industries. The country's greatest industrial strength is in engineering and related high-technology manufacturing. Major products include telecommunications equipment, cars and trucks, airplanes, household appliances, industrial machinery, electricity generation and transmission systems, steel and high-grade steel products, armaments, paper and pulp, furniture, chemicals, and pharmaceuticals.

Trade. All the major industries are export-oriented and depend on economies of scale created by sales beyond the small domestic market. Pop music in English is another notable export. Major trading partners include Germany, Britain, the United States, and the Nordic neighbors. Significant imports include computers and telecommunications equipment, industrial machinery, motor vehicles, food, clothing, chemicals, and fossil fuels. Trade with developing countries has been encouraged by social democratic aid policies and, during the Cold War, by political neutrality.

Division of Labor. Career paths depend to a great extent on educational attainment. Public funding of education, including universities, has made it possible for the children of manual laborers to prepare for and obtain executive and professional positions. Opportunities for achieving high status are thus relatively equal, but persons with affluent and well-educated parents are overrepresented in elite occupations.

The Security of Employment Act of 1974 and subsequent laws limit the power of employers to fire workers at will; legislation also sets minimum periods of notice before layoffs. Adult education and retraining are widespread, encouraged by active labor-market policies that promote full employment. There is a high level of employee participation in workplace decision making, particularly in health and safety matters. More than 80 percent of workers belong to trade unions.

SOCIAL STRATIFICATION

Classes and Castes. The distribution of income is among the most equal in the industrialized world, although inequality rose rapidly in the 1990s. The

A mid-summer festival featuring traditional Swedish dress and activities.

extremes of wealth and poverty have been reduced through the efforts of social democratic governments and trade unions. Manual labor is well paid, and higher education leads to relatively small monetary dividends.

Symbols of Social Stratification. Many traditional markers of social class affiliation have faded in recent decades: language reform in the early 1970s discouraged the use of the formal second-person pronoun to address persons of high standing; typically white-collar jobs in the office and service sectors have displaced much employment in traditionally working-class sectors such as factories and mines; dress standards have become less class-differentiated and more relaxed; and regional accents have been muted by a national media culture.

The one significant caste distinction is that of "Swedes" versus "immigrants," usually those from less affluent lands. This division is particularly notable in housing, as certain satellite suburbs of major cities have come to be seen as immigrant domains characterized by disorder and danger. Residents of these communities often experience a sense of exclusion, and their unemployment rates are higher. But even in the most notorious of these suburbs—Stockholm's Rinkeby—the rates of poverty and crime are relatively low.

POLITICAL LIFE

Government. Sweden is a parliamentary democracy with a ceremonial monarch. Four constitutional laws define the form of government and guarantee freedom of the press and of expression as well as open access to public documents. A unicameral parliament is elected by universal adult suffrage in a proportional representation system. During the current four-year term (1998–2002), seven parties share the 349 parliamentary seats. Parties typically divide into a left-leaning "socialist" bloc and a right-leaning "bourgeois" bloc; a party or coalition of parties in the more successful bloc forms an administration consisting of a prime minister and about twenty other cabinet members. Local government consists of elected county and municipal councils.

Leadership and Political Officials. Political parties are stable; five of the current seven have been represented in the parliament since 1921. The largest party, the Social Democrats, won 36 percent of the vote in the 1998 election. Closely allied with the labor movement, the Social Democrats have been in power, singly or in a coalition, for sixty of the last sixty-nine years. The current administration depends on the support of the Left Party—a democratic-socialist, eco-feminist party—and the environmentalist Green Party. The rival of this alliance is the Moderate Party, which received 23 percent of the vote in 1998. Supported by the well-to-do and by industry, the Moderates work for tax cuts, welfare-state retrenchment, and increased military expenditure. Three smaller parties—Christian Democratic, Center, and Liberal—join the Moderates in the bourgeois bloc.

Elections are noted for high voter turnout, effective shielding against corruption by monied interests, and a focus on contested issues rather than personalities. A demanding standard of financial honesty is expected of politicians, and even small-scale tax evasion or misuse of an expense account can lead to removal from office. An elected official may be unfaithful in marriage, but to get caught driving while intoxicated could mean the end of a political career.

A tradition of public access to official documents dates back to the Freedom of the Press Act of 1766. Any individual has a right to see almost any document in national or local government files. There are exceptions to protect the privacy of individuals, but the state's power to classify documents as national-security secrets is strictly limited.

Social Problems and Control. The legal system is less elaborately codified than continental European systems but less reliant on case-law precedents than is Anglo-American law. New legislation is prepared with the help of official commissions of inquiry that produce exhaustive published reports. Judges, administrators, and lawyers later refer to these reports when interpreting the law. Civil and criminal cases are tried in a three-tiered court system, and a parallel system exists for proceedings concerning public administration. In certain kinds of cases, professional judges are joined on the bench by elected lay assessors (*nämndemän*) who participate in deliberations with the judges. There are no executions, and prison is reserved principally for those who commit violent crimes. Fines are issued in proportion to the income of the guilty party.

Sweden invented the ombudsman in 1809. An ombudsman is an independent public official who hears complaints from citizens, investigates abuses, and seeks to ensure that authorities follow the law and that citizens' rights are protected. In addition to four general ombudsmen appointed by the parliament, there are specialized ombudsmen for children's rights, disabled persons' rights, consumer issues, journalistic ethics, equal opportunities for women and men, prevention of ethnic discrimination, and prevention of discrimination on the basis of sexual orientation.

Scrupulous compliance with laws and social conventions is widespread because of moral pressure from fellow citizens. Considerable conscientiousness is generated by conversations between adults and children concerning moral and social issues. Violence is condemned, gun ownership is carefully regulated, and the media describes with horror the massacres that occur in other countries.

A vexing social problem during the last decade has been racist violence by right-wing extremists. A small number of young men, often from troubled homes, become "skinheads," neo-Nazis, or motorcycle-gang members. Their attacks on nonwhite immigrants and proimmigrant journalists and public servants have provoked public outrage. Antiracist sentiments are expressed in marches and rallies, journalistic reports, educational campaigns, and government investigations.

Military Activity. The nation has not been at war since 1814. An official policy of "nonalignment in peace aiming at neutrality in war" enabled the country to avoid being drawn into the twentieth century's world wars. During the Cold War, Sweden had the ability to make an atomic bomb but chose not to do so. Situated between the two antagonistic superpower blocs, the country preserved its independence by means of technologically sophisticated conventional armed forces, civilian-based defense programs, and diplomatic efforts to build solidarity among nonaligned nations as a counterbalance to the superpowers. These policies have continued, with a reduction in military expenditure, since the end of the Cold War.

Current debates concern arms manufacture and conscription. To facilitate nonalignment by avoiding dependence on foreign suppliers, the country has a robust weapons industry. It accounts for less than 1 percent of exports but is strongly opposed by the thousands of residents who engage in international peacemaking efforts. The key questions about conscription are whether to extend it to women or to abolish it in favor of professional, voluntary armed services.

SOCIAL WELFARE AND CHANGE PROGRAMS

In Sweden's advanced general welfare state, communal institutions ensure the well-being and economic security of all citizens. No other country has as low a rate of poverty and social exclusion.

Health, education, and social-welfare programs are comprehensive and universal. Coverage for all citizens prevents the development of an underclass.

Pedestrians walk down a busy street in a shopping district in Göteborg.

Education is free from preschool through the university level, and most medical care is free or available for negligible fees. The costs of these services are covered by a system of progressive taxation.

The combination of strong popular organizations (labor unions, political parties, and social movements) and activist state agencies provides institutional means to define and respond to social problems. Typically, debates in the media are followed by the appointment of an expert investigative commission, whose findings prompt new legislation. This approach is particularly evident in matters of health and safety.

NONGOVERNMENTAL ORGANIZATIONS AND OTHER ASSOCIATIONS

The labor movement has organized more than 80 percent of the nation's workers. A child of that movement and of independent evangelical churches and temperance campaigns in the early twentieth century is adult education. Roughly one-third of adults participate, most often through study circles sponsored by nonprofit organizations. Other popular associations are devoted to amateur sports, music, and the enjoyment and protection of nature.

There is a network of popular organizations concerned with international peace and justice. The country consistently has supported the United Nations and has been one of the largest providers of personnel for peacekeeping operations. Stockholm has hosted many international conferences, such as the 1996 World Congress against Commercial Sexual Exploitation of Children. These activities foster former prime minister Olof Palme's vision of "common security," a commitment to international development and disarmament as a strategy for easing global tensions.

GENDER ROLES AND STATUSES

Division of Labor by Gender. No other country has a higher proportion of women as parliamentarians (43 percent) and cabinet ministers (50 percent), and Sweden leads the developed world in the percentage of professional and technical workers who are women. The proportion of women in the labor force is the highest worldwide. This is due both to job opportunities in the public sector, and to the support that sector provides to women in private firms. Public child-care institutions make it easier for women to work outside the home. Nonetheless, some occupational segregation still exists; corporate chief executives tend to be male, for example, and primary school teachers female. However, the traditionally gender professions (female child-care workers, male doctors and police officers) are becoming more equally shared.

The Relative Status of Women and Men. With a robust feminist movement, comprehensive publicly supported child care, and an unparalleled percentage of women in government, Sweden is considered a leader in gender equality. Advancement in this arena is a significant national self-stereotype, a symbol of what distinguishes Swedes from others.

Two pieces of recent legislation reflect gender attitudes. In 1995, Sweden began reserving one month of parental leave for fathers. After the birth of a child, a couple receives fifteen months of paid leave to divide between them, with one month set aside for each parent; a father who chooses not to participate forfeits the couple's parental benefit payment for that month. This policy has increased the rates of paternal participation in child care.

In 1999, Sweden became the first nation to criminalize the buyer, not the seller, of sexual services. The law's authors noted their aim of prosecuting only those they considered the exploiters (normally men), not the exploited (normally women). The sexual liberalism of the 1960s and

1970s has been replaced by laws, attitudes, and enforcement regimes that are among the most stringent in the European Union.

MARRIAGE, FAMILY, AND KINSHIP

Marriage. The selection of romantic, sexual, and conjugal partners is a matter of individual choice. A prospective mate's personal character and appearance are important criteria, while family approval is not. Marrying for money and security is rare; the general welfare society frees individuals to base marriage on affection, not economic need.

Public schools inaugurated modern sex education in 1955. Today free or subsidized contraception allows women to postpone or limit childbearing. Abortion is permitted through the eighteenth week of pregnancy, but 93 percent of abortions are performed before the twelfth week. Roughly one of four couples consists of unmarried partners. Such nonmarital cohabitation (called *sambo*, or "living with") is socially accepted and has since 1988 entailed nearly the same legal rights and responsibilities as marriage.

Many *sambo* partners eventually marry, particularly if a child is expected or has arrived, but illegitimacy is not stigmatized. If a couple does not specify a newborn's surname, the child automatically receives the mother's surname. The divorce rate has doubled in the last thirty years. Lesbian and gay couples can have a sambo relationship or can establish a registered partnership with the same legal consequences as matrimony.

Domestic Unit. Families are predominantly nuclear rather than extended. While the two-parent household with children remains normative, the rate of single-parent households is high. No industrialized nation has a higher frequency of one-person households, which are particularly common among young adults in urban areas and among the elderly.

Women are the chief providers of social support for the young and the aged. This burden has been mitigated as women's unpaid work has been partially displaced by state-supported professional child-care and elder-care services. Patriarchal family structures have declined as traditional patterns of male authority and female economic dependency have been supplanted by a reliance on communal institutions.

Inheritance. Since 1845, sons and daughters have had equal rights to inherit. Today the law seeks an equitable balance between potential claimants. A single or widowed person's estate is divided evenly between his or her children or between other relatives. One cannot disinherit one's children: the law overrides wills and sets aside half of an estate for the descendants. Upon a married person's death, the estate belongs to the surviving spouse; when that spouse dies, the couple's children can inherit. If the deceased had children by a former marriage or relationship, they may claim a partial inheritance. Sambo relationships do not entail the same rights of survivorship.

Kin Groups. Kin solidarity is weak beyond the level of the nuclear family. Only 3 to 4 percent of elderly persons live with family members other than their spouses. Working adults typically spend time with their parents at Christmas, on birthdays and anniversaries, and during vacations; those who live in the same city as their parents may have some meals together. Detailed population records kept by the Church of Sweden make it possible for people to trace their kin over many generations.

SOCIALIZATION

Infant Care. Expectant mothers are entitled to paid leave from work during the last months of pregnancy. Both parents normally attend free childbirth-education classes; most mothers and some fathers continue with parenting classes. Fathers are usually present at birth. Nearly all mothers breast-feed their babies, a practice made feasible by the fifteen months of paid parental leave per child. Breast-feeding can be done in public places without embarrassment. Parent-child cosleeping is relatively prevalent. Infants are allowed to develop at their own pace; to attempt to "discipline" them in matters that they cannot understand is considered a mark of parental ignorance.

Child Rearing and Education. Most young children spend some of their time in professional child-care settings. These institutions are publicly funded and are available to all children. Parents may choose between day-care centers, part-time children's groups, drop-in preschool activity centers, and child minders in private homes. Most of these services are municipally organized, but some take the form of nonprofit foundations, private companies, and parent cooperatives. User fees cover about 14 percent of the total costs, with tax revenues covering the rest.

Schools are well funded and of high quality. Until the late 1990s there were few private schools. The public school system emphasizes inclusive values such as aiding children with special difficulties

A worker assembles parts in an automobile plant in Göteborg. Automobile manufacturing is just one part of Sweden's highly diverse industrial base.

rather than targeting resources toward the most talented pupils. Much school activity cultivates independence and self-sufficiency. At the same time, cooperative social skills are of central importance and are nurtured in after-school activities, leisure-time centers, clubs, and sports leagues.

In 1979, the parliament passed a law forbidding corporal punishment, making Sweden the first nation in which parents were forbidden to strike their children. The law is widely known and accepted.

Literature written for children is frank, open, and nonpatronizing. This sensibility was visible in the critical social realism of many 1960s and early-1970s works, and is equally present in the more fantasy-oriented children's books of the decades before and after that period. Strong, self-reliant female characters have been a specialty; the most celebrated is Astrid Lindgren's Pippi Longstocking.

The frankness that characterizes children's literature is typical of conversations between adults and children, and parents engage in serious discussions with their children on morally charged topics ranging from fair play to drugs to sexuality (sex education begins at the age of seven). Taking children seriously is seen as a matter of basic respect for persons who exist in their own right.

Higher Education. About one in three students begins some form of higher education within five years after completing upper secondary school. Half of these students are women. Most universities and colleges are state-financed but locally administered. Free tuition and grants and loans for living expenses make higher learning available without regard to social class.

In regard to adult education, individuals have a right to continue their education in municipally organized programs, which have expanded significantly since 1997. In addition, 150 folk colleges (*folkhögskolor*) offer a wide range of state-subsidized courses for adults. Local governments, unions, churches, and voluntary associations run the folk colleges, which are usually residential and are situated in bucolic settings.

ETIQUETTE

Much etiquette involves the ritual enactment of equality. Thanking occurs frequently, and it is common for the person being thanked to offer thanks in return. People seek to repay debts of gratitude and thus restore symmetrical relations. Conversation partners rarely interrupt one another. Politeness requires attentive listening, which is often made evident by affirmative murmurs. When people disagree, they avoid open expression of conflict.

Rigorous codes of modesty prevent interpersonal competition from sabotaging collective life. All forms of boastfulness are proscribed. Academic and corporate titles are seldom used, and conspicuous consumption is condemned. These norms are beginning to erode, however, particularly among businesspeople who participate in a transnational corporate world in which self-promotion is seen as a virtue.

RELIGION

Religious Beliefs. The Church of Sweden emerged as a national church during the Protestant Reformation. For centuries, this evangelical Lutheran institution had state support and cultural hegemony, although it faced competition from nonconformist churches born of nineteenth-century revival movements. In the year 2000, state and church divorced amicably, leaving the church with increased autonomy.

Eighty-five percent of the people are members of the Church of Sweden. There is considerable religious pluralism, as a result of immigration. There are an estimated 250,000 Muslims and 166,000 Roman Catholics as well as significant numbers of adherents of other religious movements. Freedom of religion is constitutionally guaranteed.

Members of the Church of Sweden often say that they are Christian ''in their own way,'' and are uninterested in dogma. The deepest spiritual emotions are often experienced while one is alone in nature. Lutheran ideals and Renaissance humanism have engendered a demanding social morality with an openness to scientific modernity. Boasting about one's faith is considered distasteful.

Religious Practitioners. Recent reforms have made the Church of Sweden a more democratic religious organization. Members elect a General Synod that decides questions of doctrine as well as administrative matters. Women make up 30 percent of the priesthood, a proportion that is rising. Church workers often combine pastoral labors with civic engagement, particularly in support of refugees and international aid. Pastors' presence as community leaders is most evident after collective tragedies such as fatal accidents and violent crimes.

Rituals and Holy Places. Church attendance is low except on special occasions; less than 5 percent of the members regularly attend Sunday services in the Church of Sweden. Holiday observances are more popular. Three of four infants are baptized, of whom half are later confirmed. Three of five marriages are performed by the Church of Sweden.

Death and the Afterlife. Ninety percent of funerals take place in the Church of Sweden. The practical arrangements usually are handled by a national organization that is part of the cooperative movement. Autopsies are common to determine the cause of death, embalming is rare, and cremation is prevalent. Graveyards are noted for their natural beauty. Many individuals believe that death involves losing one's individual existence while becoming part of something greater.

MEDICINE AND HEALTH CARE

Sweden's health- and safety-conscious society invests heavily in preventive public-health measures. Educational campaigns promote healthy lifestyles. Individuals can choose their own physicians, and medical visits are free or subject to a nominal charge. As a result of this egalitarian system, social-class differences in health are small. Nonetheless, these differences have grown in the past decade, because of rising income inequality and cutbacks in public budgets. Health care accounts for 7 to 8 percent of the gross national product, not counting the country's massive investments in medical research.

SECULAR CELEBRATIONS

New Year's Day (1 January) is welcomed at midnight by ships' horns and civil-defense sirens. Public bonfires illuminate Walpurgis Night (30 April), a celebration popular among university students. On 1 May, trade unionists, Social Democrats, and their allies march through the cities to express solidarity and protest injustices. The National Day is observed on 6 June. Midsummer (near the summer solstice in June) is a long-awaited holiday of eating, drinking, and dancing, rivaled in importance only by Christmas. August brings crayfish parties. United Nations Day (24 October) is marked mainly in schools. Halloween (31 October) is a recent import. The world's most prestigious scientific and literary prizes are presented by the king on Nobel Day (10 December). Candle-lit pageants break the winter darkness on Lucia Day (13 December). Other significant observances include birthdays (with a special jubilee at age fifty), name days, secondary-school graduation, royal fetes, and the long summer vacation. Widely celebrated religious holidays include Easter, Pentecost, Advent, and Christmas.

A ship on the Göta Canal, which travels the entire width of Sweden between Stockholm and Göteborg.

THE ARTS AND HUMANITIES

Support for the Arts. Artists are not completely dependent on commercial sales and wealthy patrons. Public funding encourages their work, and the security provided by the general welfare society frees them to take aesthetic risks without fear of destitution. One result is an artistic community known for avant-garde innovation.

Support is channeled through various public and partially public institutions. Recipients range from preeminent national museums to small literary magazines that could not survive without subsidies. Popular participation is also promoted: cultural centers, public libraries, and communal music schools give citizens an opportunity to exercise their creativity.

Literature. Among the most eminent modern authors are August Strindberg, Selma Lagerlöf, Pär Lagerkvist, and Harry Martinson. The most influential living writer is Astrid Lindgren, whose stories are familiar to children in many countries. A genre of particular note is the literary documentary tradition, in which authors since the 1960s have reported on the lives of ordinary people. The common elements of the national literature include a brooding seriousness about social and existential questions, an appreciation of nature, and an avoidance of psychoanalytic speculation.

Graphic Arts. A 1934 parliamentary act stipulated that 1 percent of the expenditure on new public buildings be devoted to works of art. The country's most famous sculptor was Carl Milles, who produced gravity-defying forms. The loving depictions of children and domestic life by the painter Carl Larsson are popular with Swedes and tourists nostalgic for a rural past. It is for design that Sweden is most famous, particularly in wood and glass but also in other media. The interplay of handicraft traditions and social democratic ideals has led to world-renowned work in industrial design, ergonomics, child safety, and products for the disabled.

Performance Arts. Celebrated performers include the soprano Jenny Lind, the film and theater director Ingmar Bergman, and the pop musicians ABBA. The country seldom produces superstars with astronomical incomes. Resources are instead used to provide steady salaries and benefits to ordinary actors, dancers, and musicians, giving them a basic level of security. State subsidies make possible a similar egalitarianism in ticket prices: traditionally upper-class pleasures such as opera, ballet, and theater are affordable to all.

THE STATE OF THE PHYSICAL AND SOCIAL SCIENCES

A tradition of technocratic planning, widespread respect for professional expertise, and an increasingly high-technology economy encourage investment in research. Public funding is crucial, and it is administered through national research councils, universities, and specialized institutes. Natural science is quite advanced, particularly as applied in engineering and medicine. Swedish social scientists are noted for their positivistic methodologies, which demand meticulous data collection. Thanks to the Nobel Prizes, foreign laureates and hopefuls maintain ties with their colleagues in Sweden. The Right Livelihood Award, or ''Alternative Nobel Prize,'' honors work that grapples with pressing human problems. In science as in politics, solving such problems is a national preoccupation.

BIBLIOGRAPHY

Arter, David. *Scandinavian Politics Today*, 1999.

Boli, John. *New Citizens for a New Society: The Institutional Origins of Mass Schooling in Sweden*, 1989.

Bråkenhielm, Carl Reinhold. ''Christian Tradition and Contemporary Society.'' *Concilium* 256: 23–34, 1994.

Croall, Stephen. ''A New Swedish Model: Safe, Clean Food.'' *Scandinavian Review* 87 (3): 25–32, 2000.

Daun, Åke. *Swedish Mentality*, Jan Teeland, trans., 1996.

Frykman, Jonas, and Orvar Löfgren. *Culture Builders: A Historical Anthropology of Middle-Class Life*, Alan Crozier, trans., 1987.

Hall, Peter. *Cities in Civilization: Culture, Innovation, and Urban Order*, 1998.

Hannerz, Ulf. *Transnational Connections: Culture, People, Places*, 1996.

Herlitz, Gilles. *Swedes: What We Are Like and Why We Are as We Are*, 1995.

Löfgren, Orvar. *On Holiday: A History of Vacationing*, 1999.

Misgeld, Klaus, Karl Molin, and Klas Åmark, eds. *Creating Social Democracy: A Century of the Social Democratic Labor Party in Sweden*, 1993.

Orfali, Kristina. ''The Rise and Fall of the Swedish Model.'' Arthur Goldhammer, trans. In Antoine Prost and Gérard Vincent, eds., *A History of Private Life*, 1991.

Palmer, Brian. ''Wolves at the Door: Existential Solidarity in a Globalizing Sweden.'' Ph.D. dissertation. Harvard University, Cambridge, MA, 2000.

Popenoe, David. ''Family Decline in the Swedish Welfare State.'' *The Public Interest*, 102: 65–77, 1991.

Pred, Allan. *Even in Sweden: Racisms, Racialized Spaces, and the Popular Geographical Imagination*, Berkeley: University of California Press, 2000.

Rothstein, Bo. *Just Institutions Matter: The Moral and Political Logic of the Universal Welfare State*, 1998.

Ruth, Arne. ''The Second New Nation: The Mythology of Modern Sweden.'' In Stephen R. Graubard, ed., *Norden—The Passion for Equality*, 1986.

Scott, Franklin D. *Sweden: The Nation's History*, 1988.

Sontag, Susan. ''Letter from Sweden.'' *Ramparts*, July 1969.

Stromberg, Peter. *Symbols of Community: The Cultural System of a Swedish Church*, 1986.

Sverne, Tor. ''Children's Rights in Scandinavia in a Legal and Historical Perspective.'' *Family and Conciliation Courts Review* 31 (3): 299–312, 1993.

Trägårdh, Lars. ''Welfare State Nationalism: Sweden and the Specter of the European Union.'' *Scandinavian Review* 87 (1): 18–23, 1999.

Web Sites

Nordic News Network. http://www.nnn.se

Statistics Sweden. *Sweden in Figures 2000*, http://www.scb.se/indexeng.htm

Swedish Institute. *Factsheets on Sweden* series. http://www.si.se/infosweden

—BRIAN C. W. PALMER

SWITZERLAND

CULTURE NAME

Swiss

ALTERNATIVE NAMES

Schweiz (German), Suisse (French), Svizzera (Italian), Svizzra (Romansh)

ORIENTATION

Identification. Switzerland's name originates from Schwyz, one of the three founder cantons. The name Helvetia derives from a Celtic tribe called Helvetians that settled in the region in the second century B.C.

Switzerland is a federation of twenty-six states called cantons (six are considered half cantons). There are four linguistic regions: German-speaking (in the north, center, and east), French-speaking (in the west), Italian-speaking (in the south), and Romansh-speaking (a small area in the southeast). This diversity makes the question of a national culture a recurring issue.

Location and Geography. Covering 15,950 square miles (41,290 square kilometers), Switzerland is a transition point between northern and southern Europe and between Germanic and Latin cultures. The physical environment is characterized by a chain of mountains (the Jura), a densely urbanized plateau, and the Alps range, which forms a barrier to the south. The capital, Bern, is in the center of the country. It was chosen over Zurich and Lucerne because of its proximity to the French-speaking region. It is also the capital of the German-speaking canton of Bern, which includes a French-speaking district. Bern had 127,469 inhabitants in 1996, whereas Zurich, the economic capital, had 343,869.

Demography. The population in 1998 was 7,118,000; it has increased more than threefold since 1815, when the borders were established. The birth-

rate has been decreasing since the end of the nineteenth century, but immigration plays a major role in increasing the population. Since World War II and after a long tradition of emigration, Switzerland became an immigration destination because of its rapid economic development, and has one of the highest rates of foreigners in Europe (19.4 percent of the population in 1998). However, 37 percent of the foreigners have been in the country for more than ten years and 22 percent were born in Switzerland.

According to the 1990 census, 71.6 percent of the population lives in the German-speaking region, 23.2 percent in the French-speaking region, over 4 percent in the Italian-speaking region, and just under one percent in the Romansh-speaking region.

Linguistic Affiliation. The use of the German language goes back to the early Middle Ages, when the Alamans invaded lands where Romance languages were developing. The dominance of German in Switzerland has been lessened by the bilingualism of the German-speaking region, where both standard German and Swiss German dialects are used. These dialects have a high social prestige among Swiss Germans regardless of education level or social class because they differentiate Swiss Germans from Germans. Swiss Germans often do not feel comfortable speaking standard German; they often prefer to speak French when interacting with members of the French-speaking minority.

In the French-speaking region, the original Franco-Provencal dialects have almost disappeared in favor of a standard French colored by regional accents and some lexical features.

The Italian-speaking region is bilingual, and people speak standard Italian as well as different regional dialects, although the social status of the dialects is low. More than half the Italian-speaking population living in Switzerland is not from Ticino but of Italian origin. Romansh, a Romance language of the Rhaetian group, is the only language specific to Switzerland except for two parent languages

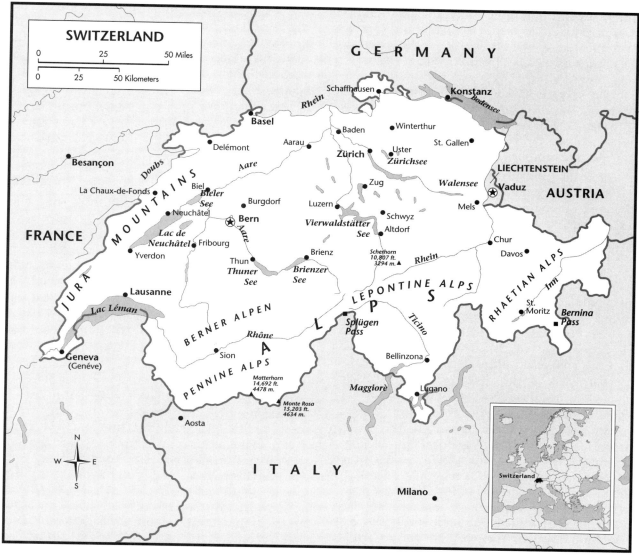

Switzerland

spoken in southeastern Italy. Very few people speak Romansh, and many of those people live outside the Romansh linguistic area in parts of the alpine canton of Graubünden. Cantonal and federal authorities have taken measures to preserve this language but success in the long term is threatened by the vitality of Romansh speakers.

Because the founding cantons were German-speaking, the question of multilingualism appeared only in the nineteenth century, when French-speaking cantons and the Italian-speaking Ticino joined the confederation. In 1848, the federal constitution stated, ''German, French, Italian and Romansh are the national languages of Switzerland. German, French, and Italian are the official languages of the Confederation.'' Not until 1998 did the confederation establish a linguistic policy, reaffirming the principle of quadrilinguism (four languages) and the need to promote Romansh and Italian. Despite the cantonal differences in the educational system, all students learn at least one of the other national languages. However, multilingualism is a reality for only a minority of the population (28 percent in 1990).

Symbolism. The national symbols mirror the attempt to achieve unity while maintaining diversity. The stained-glass windows of the House of Parliament's dome show the cantonal flags brought together around the national emblem of a white cross on a red background, surrounded by the motto *Unus pro omnibus, omnes pro uno* (''One for all, all for one''). The national flag, officially adopted in 1848, originated in the fourteenth century, as the first confederate cantons needed a common sign for recognition among their armies. The white cross on a red background comes from the flag of the canton of Schwyz, which has a red background symbolizing holy justice and a small representation of Christ on the cross at the upper left corner. Because of the ferocity of the Schwyz soldiers, their enemies used the name of this canton to designate all the confederated cantons.

After the formation of the federal state, efforts were made to promote national symbols that would strengthen a common national identity. However, the cantonal sense of identity never lost its significance and the national symbols often are considered artificial. The national day (1 August) did not become an official holiday until the end of the twentieth century. The celebration of the national day is often awkward, as very few people know the national anthem. One song served as the national anthem for a century but was criticized because of its warlike words and because its melody was identical to that of the British national anthem. This led the Federal Government to declare the "Swiss Psalm," another popular song, the official national anthem in 1961, although this did not become official until 1981.

William Tell is widely known as the national hero. He is presented as a historical figure living in central Switzerland during the fourteen century, but his existence has never been proved. After refusing to bow to the symbol of the Hapsburg power, Tell was forced to shoot an arrow at an apple placed on the head of his son. He succeeded but was arrested for rebellion. The story of William Tell is a symbol for the bravery of an alpine people who reject the authority of foreign judges and are eager for independence and freedom, perpetuating the tradition of the first "Three Swiss" who took the original oath of alliance in 1291.

Helvetia is a feminine national icon. Symbolizing the federal state bringing together the cantons, she often is represented (for example, on coins) as a reassuring middle-aged woman, an impartial mother creating harmony among her children. Helvetia appeared with the creation of the confederation in 1848. Both symbolic figures are still used: Tell for the independence and freedom of the Swiss people and Helvetia for the unity and harmony in the confederation.

HISTORY AND ETHNIC RELATIONS

Emergence of the Nation. The construction of the nation lasted six centuries, after the original oath in 1291, when the cantons of Uri, Schwyz, and Unterwald concluded an alliance. The different circumstances under which the cantons joined the confederation account for differences in the degree of attachment to the "nation," a term rarely used in Switzerland.

The model of a united nation was tested by the Helvetian Republic (1798–1803) imposed by Napoleon Bonaparte, who tried to make Switzerland a centralized nation. The republic abolished the domination of some cantons by others, all cantons became full partners in the confederation, and the first democratic parliament was established. The inadequacy of the centralized model rapidly became evident, and in 1803 Napoleon reestablished the federal organization. After the collapse of his empire in 1814, the twenty-two cantons signed a new federal pact (1815), and the neutrality of Switzerland was recognized by the European powers.

Tension among the cantons took the form of conflict between liberals and conservatives, between industrialized and rural cantons, and between Protestant and Catholic cantons. The liberals struggled for popular political rights and the creation of federal institutions that would allow Switzerland to become a modern state. The conservative cantons refused to revise the 1815 Pact, which guaranteed their sovereignty and gave them more power within the confederation than their population and economy warranted. This tension resulted in the civil war of the Sonderbund (1847), in which the seven Catholics cantons were defeated by federal troops. The constitution of the federal state provided a better means of integration for the cantons. The constitution of 1848 gave the country its present shape except for the creation of the canton of Jura, which separated from the canton of Bern in 1978.

National Identity. Switzerland is a patchwork of small regions that gradually joined the confederation not because of a shared identity but because the confederation appeared to guarantee their independence. The existence of a national identity that would transcend cantonal, linguistic, and religious differences is still debated. There has been oscillation between a self-satisfied discourse about a blessed people that considers itself a model for others and a self-deprecating discourse that questions the existence of the nation: The slogan "Suiza no existe," used at the Swiss pavilion at the Seville universal fair in 1992, reflects the identity crisis Switzerland faced in 1991 when it celebrated seven hundred years of existence.

A reexamination of the national image has resulted from the country's banks' treatment of Jew-

Traditional-style buildings in the old part of Geneva. Preserving the country's architectural heritage is an important consideration throughout Switzerland.

ish funds during World War II. In 1995, public revelations started to be made about "sleeping" accounts in Swiss banks whose holders had disappeared during the Nazi genocide. Historians had already published critical analyses of the behavior of banks and the Swiss federal authorities during a period when thousands of refugees were accepted but thousands of others were sent back to probable death. The authors of these analyses were accused of denigrating their country. It took fifty years for internal maturation and the international accusations for a critical reexamination of the country's recent history to occur and it is too early to assess how this self-examination has affected the national identity. However, it probably represents the acme of a period of collective doubt that has marked the last decades of the twentieth century.

Ethnic Relations. The notion of ethnic groups is rarely used in a nation where the concept of a linguistic or cultural group is preferred. Reference to ethnicity is very rare in regard to the four national linguistic groups. Ethnicity emphasizes a sense of a common identity that is based on a shared history and shared roots transmitted from generation to generation. In Switzerland, membership in a linguistic group depends as much on the establishment in a linguistically defined territory as on the cultural and linguistical heritage of the individual. According to the principle of the territoriality of languages, internal migrants are forced to use the language of the new territory in their contacts with the authorities, and there are no public schools where their children can receive an education in the parents' original language. The composition of the population in the different linguistic regions is a result of a long history of intermarriage and internal migrations, and it would be difficult to determine the inhabitants' "ethnicity." In addition, many people feel that ethnic differences among the Swiss pose a threat to national unity. Even the concept of culture is looked at with distrust, and differences between regions often are presented as being only linguistic in nature.

Tensions between the linguistic, cultural, and religious groups have always generated a fear that intergroup differences would endanger the national unity. The most difficult relations are those between the German-speaking majority and the French-speaking minority. Fortunately, in Switzerland the religious dimension crosses the linguistic dimension; for example, areas of Catholic tradition exist in the German-speaking region as well as the French-speaking region. However, with the decrease in social importance of the religious dimen-

A Swiss alpine village in the Jungfrau Region of Switzerland.

sion, the risk of focusing on the linguistic and cultural dimensions cannot be ignored.

URBANISM, ARCHITECTURE AND THE USE OF SPACE

Switzerland is a dense network of towns of various sizes, linked by an extensive network of public transportation and roads. There is no megalopolis, and even Zurich is a small city by international criteria. In 1990, the five main urban centers (Zurich, Basel, Geneva, Bern, Lausanne) contained only 15 percent of the population. There are strict regulations on construction, and the preservation of the architectural heritage and landscape preservation are taken very seriously.

The architectural styles of traditional regional houses have great diversity. A common neo-classical architectural style can be seen in national public and private institutions such as the railway company, the post office, and the banks.

FOOD AND ECONOMY

Food in Daily Life. Regional and local culinary specialties generally are based on a traditional type of cooking, rich in calories and fat, that is more suited to outdoor activity than to a sedentary way of life. Dairy products such as butter, cream, and cheese are important parts of the diet, along with pork. More recent eating habits show a growing concern for healthy food and a growing taste for exotic food.

Basic Economy. A lack of raw materials and limited agricultural production (one-fourth of the territory is unproductive because of mountains, lakes, and rivers) caused Switzerland to develop an economy based on the transformation of imported raw materials into high-added-value finished products mainly destined for exportation. The economy is highly specialized and dependent on international trade (40 percent of the gross domestic product [GDP] in 1998). The per capita gross domestic product is the second highest among the Organization for Economic Cooperation and Development countries.

Land Tenure and Property. Land can be acquired and used like any other goods, but a distinction is made between agricultural and nonagricultural land to prevent the disappearance of agricultural plots. Land speculation flourished in the 1980s. In reaction to that speculation, measures have been taken to limit the free use of privately owned land. Precise land planning was established to specify the possible uses of plots. Since 1983, nonresident foreigners have faced limitations in buying land or buildings.

Commercial Activities. In the last decades of the twentieth century, the Swiss economic structure was deeply transformed. Core economic sectors such as machine production declined considerably, while the tertiary sector experienced considerable growth and became the most important employer and contributor to the economy.

Trade. The most important exported industrial products are machines and electronic instruments (28 percent of exports in 1998), chemicals (27 percent), and watches, jewelry, and precision instruments (15 percent). Due to the lack of natural resources, raw materials are an important part of the imports and are vital to industry, but Switzerland also imports all kinds of goods, from food products to cars and other equipment goods. The major trading partners are Germany, the United States, and France. Without being formally part of the European Union or the European Economic Area, economically, Switzerland is highly integrated in the European Union.

Swiss cities, such as Bern (shown here) are densely populated but fairly small.

Division of Labor. In 1991, over 63 percent of the GDP consisted of services (wholesale and retail trade, restaurants and hotels, finance, insurance, real estate, and business services), over 33 percent was accounted for by industry, and 3 percent by agriculture. The historically very low unemployment rate rose to over 5 percent during the economic crisis of the 1990s with important differences between the regions and between nationals and foreigners. The economic recovery of the last years of the decade reduced the unemployment rate to 2.1 percent in the year 2000, but many workers in their fifties and workers with low qualifications have been excluded from the labor market. The level of qualification determines access to employment and thus to participation in a society that values work highly.

SOCIAL STRATIFICATION

Classes and Castes. In one of the wealthiest countries in the world, the richest 20 percent of the population owns 80 percent of total private assets. Yet the class structure is not particularly visible. The middle class is large and for its members, upward or downward social mobility is rather easy.

Symbols of Social Stratification. The cultural norm is for wealth to remain discreet. Too manifest a demonstration of wealth is negatively valued, but poverty is perceived as shameful, and many people hide their economic situation.

POLITICAL LIFE

Government. Switzerland is a "concordance democracy" in which cooperation and consensus between political, social, and economic groups is valved. Federalism ensures considerable autonomy for communes and cantons, which have their own governments and parliaments. The Federal Assembly has two chambers with equal powers: the National Council (two hundred members elected by proportional representation of the cantons) and the Council of States (forty-six members, or two per canton). Members of both chambers are elected for a four-year term. Laws are subject to referendum or obligatory referendum (for constitutional changes). The people also can submit demands by means of a "popular initiative."

The Federal Assembly elects the seven members of the executive branch, known as the Federal Council. They form a collective government with a rotating one-year presidency mainly for ceremonial tasks. Several criteria are taken into account in electing members of the Federal Council, including political party membership (since the late 1950s, the political composition follows the "magic formula," which gives two representatives to each of the three main parties and one representative to the fourth one), linguistic and cantonal origin, religious affiliation, and gender.

Leadership and Political Officials. Leadership positions can be achieved by being a militant (usually starting at the communal level) in one of the four governmental parties: FDP/PRD (Liberal-Radicals), CVP/PDC (Christian Democrats), SPS/PSS (Social Democrats), and SVP/UDC (a former farmers' party but since 1971 the Swiss People's Party in the German-speaking region and the Democratic Union of the Center in the French-speaking region). Contact with political officials can be relatively easy, but a cultural norm states that well-known persons should be left in peace. The numerous activities of a highly participatory society are considered more appropriate opportunities to meet political officials.

Social Problems and Control. Civil and criminal law are powers of the confederation, while legal procedure and the administration of justice are

The Matterhorn towers beyond a railway as it ascends toward Gornergrat. Skiing and tourism are an important part of the Swiss economy.

cantonal responsibilities. Each canton has its own police system and the powers of the federal police are limited. Fighting modern crime such as money laundering revealed the inadequacy of those fragmented justice and police systems, and reforms are under way to develop coordination among the cantons and give more authority to the Confederation.

Switzerland is safe, with a low rate of homicide. The most common crimes are infractions of the traffic code, infractions of drug laws, and theft. The trust of the population in the judiciary system and the observance of laws are high, largely because the majority of the population lives in communities where informal social control is powerful.

Military Activity. In a neutral country, the army is purely defensive. It is a militia based on obligatory service for all men between ages eighteen and forty-two and represents for many people a unique opportunity to relate to compatriots from other linguistic regions and social classes. Therefore, the army is often considered an important factor in national identity. Since 1990, a few Swiss soldiers have been active in international conflict sites in support activities such as logistics.

SOCIAL WELFARE AND CHANGE PROGRAMS

Social welfare is mainly a public system, organized at the federal level and partially financed by an insurance system involving direct contributions by residents. An exception is health coverage, which is obligatory but decentralized among hundreds of insurance companies. Federal regulation of health coverage is minimal and contributions are not proportional to one's salary. Parental leave depends on sector-based agreements between employees and unions. During the last twenty-five years, public spending for social welfare increased more rapidly than the GDP because of the economic recession and increasing unemployment, as well as the extension of the social welfare system. The aging of the population is expected to increase the pressure on social welfare in the future. Nongovernmental organizations often are subsidized and provide complementary services notably in supporting the poor.

NONGOVERNMENTAL ORGANIZATIONS AND OTHER ASSOCIATIONS

Associative life ranges from the local level to the federal level. The rights of referendum and initiative foster active participation by citizens in numerous associations and movements, which are widely

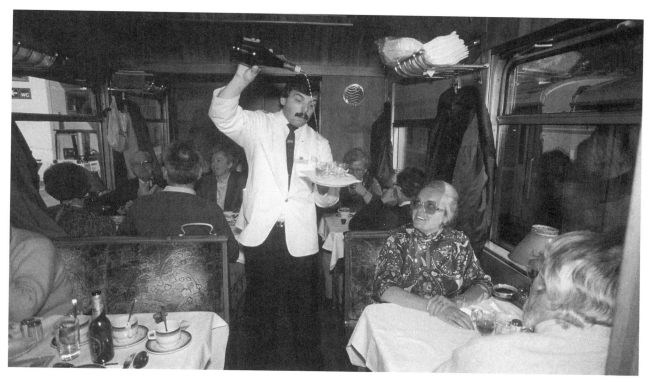

A waiter pours drinks on the Glacier Express, a famous mountain railway that makes a nearly eight-hour journey between Saint Moritz and Zermatt.

consulted by the political authorities. The authorities' search for a social consensus results in a kind of institutionalization of these movements, which are rapidly integrated into the social system. This gives them a chance to propagate their ideas and concerns but also results in a certain loss of pugnacity and originality.

GENDER ROLES AND STATUSES

Division of Labor by Gender. Although women's situation has improved since the 1970s, the constitutional article dealing with equality between the sexes has not been effective in many fields. The dominant model of sex roles is traditional, reserving the private sphere for women (in 1997, 90 percent of women in couples with young children were responsible for all housework) and the public sphere for men (79 percent of the men had a job, whereas the proportion was only 57 percent for women, whose jobs are often part-time). The vocational choices of women and men are still influenced by traditional conceptions of sex roles.

The Relative Status of Women and Men. Switzerland has long been a patriarchal society where women submit to the authority of their fathers and then to that of their husbands. Equal rights for women and men are relatively recent: only in 1971 was women's right to vote at the federal level established. Women are still disadvantaged in many fields: there are proportionally twice as many women as men without post-secondary education; even with a comparable level of education, women hold less important positions than do men; and with a comparable level of training, women earn less than men (26 percent less for middle and senior managers). Women's participation in political institutions also shows inequality: On the communal, cantonal, and federal levels, women represent one-third of candidates and only one-quarter of those elected.

MARRIAGE, FAMILY, AND KINSHIP

Marriage. Marriages are not arranged anymore, but there has been a persistence of endogamy in terms of social class. Binational marriages represent a growing trend. After a loss of popularity in the 1970s and 1980s, the marriage rate increased in the 1990s. Marriage frequently is preceded by a period of cohabitation. Couples get married late in life, and divorce and remarriage are common. There are no longer any dowry obligations. The possibility of a legal partnership status for homosexual couples is being investigated.

Domestic Unit. Households made of one or two persons represented only one-quarter of households in the 1920s but accounted for two-thirds in the 1990s. The extended family of the beginning of the twentieth century, with three or more generations living together, has been replaced by the nuclear family. Both parents share family responsibility. Since the 1980s, other family models have become more common, such as single-parent families and blended families in which couples form a new family with the children from their former marriages.

Inheritance. The law restricts a testator's freedom to distribute property, since a proportion of it is reserved for the legal heirs, who are difficult to disinherit. The order of precedence among legal heirs is defined by the degree of proximity of kinship. The children and the surviving spouse have priority. Children inherit equal shares.

Kin Groups. Although kin groups no longer live under the same roof, they have not lost their social function. Mutual support among kin groups is still important, especially in critical situations such as unemployment and illness. With increased life expectancy recently retired persons may take care of their parents and grandchildren simultaneously.

SOCIALIZATION

Infant Care. Although the second half of the twentieth century saw the appearance of fathers who take an active part in their children's education, child care is still seen mainly as the mother's responsibility. Women often face this responsibility while being professionally active, and the demand for day care centers is far beyond their availability. Customary practices teach infants both autonomy and docility. Newborns are expected to learn rapidly to sleep alone in a separate room, submitting to a schedule of feeding and sleep that is set by adults.

Child Rearing and Education. Traditional conceptions of child rearing are still strong. This often is seen as a natural process that takes place primarily in the family, especially between a child and his or her mother. Day care centers often are seen as institutions for children whose mothers are forced to work. These conceptions are still prominent in the German-speaking region and led to the rejection in 1999 of an initiative to institutionalize a generalized social insurance system for maternity. Kindergarten is not mandatory, and attendance is particularly low in the German-speaking region. In kindergarten, in the German-speaking region, play and a family-like structure are favored, whereas in those in the French-speaking region, more attention is given to the development of cognitive abilities.

Higher Education. Education and training are highly valued in a country with few natural resources. The emphasis has traditionally been on vocational training through a system of apprenticeship. The most popular areas are the clerical professions (24 percent of the apprentices) and professions in the machine industry (23 percent). Apprenticeship is more popular in the German-speaking region than in the French and Italian-speaking regions. In 1998, only 9 percent of the population age twenty-seven had an academic diploma. Education is mostly state subsidized, even if uniersity fees have been significantly increased recently. Humanities and social sciences are by far the most popular fields for study (27 percent of the diplomas), especially for women, as 40 percent of the female student population chooses these fields. Only 6 percent of the female student population studies technical sciences. Regional differences exist, with more French-speaking students attending a university.

ETIQUETTE

Respect for privacy and discretion are key values in social interaction. In public spaces such as trains, strangers normally do not speak to each other. Kindness and politeness in social interaction are expected; in smaller shops, clients and vendors thank each other several times. Cultural differences between the linguistic regions include the more frequent use of titles and professional functions in the German-speaking region, and the use of a kiss rather than a handshake in the French-speaking region.

RELIGION

Religious Beliefs. Catholicism and Protestantism are the major religions. For centuries, Catholics were a minority, but in 1990 there were more Catholics (46 percent) than Protestants (40 percent). The proportion of people belonging to other churches has risen since 1980. The Muslim community, representing over 2 percent of the population in 1990, is the largest religious minority. The Jewish community has always been very small and experienced discrimination; in 1866, Swiss Jews received the constitutional rights held by their Christian fellow citizens.

Church attendance is decreasing, but the practice of prayer has not disappeared.

Religious Practitioners. Although the Constitution calls for separation of church and state, churches are still dependent on the state. In many cantons, pastors and priests receive salaries as civil servants, and the state collects ecclesiastical church taxes. Theses taxes are mandatory for persons who are registered as members of publicly recognized religion unless they officially resign from a church. In some cantons, the churches have sought independence from the state and are now faced with important economic difficulties.

Death and the Afterlife. In the past death was part of the social life of a community and involved a precise set of rituals, but the modern tendency has been to minimize the social visibility of death. More people die in the hospital than at home, funeral homes organize funerals, and there are no more funeral processions or mourning clothing.

MEDICINE AND HEALTH CARE

In the twentieth century, life expectancy increased, and health expenditures have been increasing. As a consequence, the health system is confronted by the ethical dilemma of rationalizing health services. The western biomedical model is dominant among the medical authorities and most of the population, and the use of natural or complementary medicines (new alternative therapies, exotic therapies, and indigenous traditional therapies) is limited.

SECULAR CELEBRATIONS

Celebrations and official holidays differ from canton to canton. Common to the whole country are National Day (1 August) and New Year's Day (1 January); religious celebrations shared by Protestants and Catholics include Christmas (25 December), Good Friday, Easter, Ascension, and Pentecost.

THE ARTS AND HUMANITIES

Support for the Arts. Several institutions support cultural activities including cantons and communes, the confederation, foundations, corporations, and private donors. At the national level, this is the task of the Federal Office for Culture and Pro Helvetia, an autonomous foundation financed by the confederation. To support artists, the Federal Office for Culture is advised by experts who represent the linguistic regions and are often artists themselves. Pro Helvetia supports or organizes cultural activities in foreign countries; within the nation, it supports literary and musical work as well as cultural ex-

changes between linguistic regions. These interregional cultural exchanges are particularly difficult for literature, as the different regional literatures are oriented toward their same-language neighboring countries. A foundation called the *ch*-Stiftung, which is subsidized by the cantons, supports the translation of literary works into the other national languages.

Literature. Literature reflects the national linguistic situation: very few authors reach a national audience because of the language but also because of the cultural differences between the linguistic regions. French-speaking Swiss literature is oriented towards France, and German-speaking Swiss literature towards Germany; both are engaged in a love–hate relationship with their imposting neighbors and try to create a distinctive identity.

Graphic Arts. Switzerland possesses a rich tradition in graphic arts; several Swiss painters and graphists are internationally well-known for their work, principally for the creation of posters, banknotes, and fonts for printing (for example, Albrecht Dürer, hans Erni, Adrian Frutiger, Urs Graf, Ferdinand Hodler, and Roger Pfund).

Performance Arts. Besides the subsidized theatres (subsidized most frequently by towns), numerous partially subsidized theatres and amateur companies offer rich programs to their audiences, with both local and international productions. The history of dancing in Switzerland really started at the beginning of the twentieth century, when well-known international dancers and choreographers sought asylum in Switzerland.

THE STATE OF THE PHYSICAL AND SOCIAL SCIENCES

The physical sciences receive a high level of funding because they are considered crucial for maintaining and strengthening the country's technological and economic position. Swiss research in physical sciences has an excellent international reputation. A growing source of concern is that many young researchers trained in Switzerland move to other countries to find better opportunities to continue their research activities or develop applications of their findings.

The situation of the social sciences is less positive as a result of low level of funding and a lack of status and public attention.

BIBLIOGRAPHY

Bergier, J.-F. *Guillaume Tell*, 1988.

———. *Switzerland and Refugees in the Nazi Era*, 1999.

Bickel, H., and R. Schläpfer. *Mehrsprachigkeit – eine Herausforderung*, 1984.

Blanc, O., C. Cuénoud, M. Diserens, et al. *Les Suisses Vont-ils Disparaître? La Population de la Suisse: Problèmes, Perspectives, Politiques*, 1985.

Bovay, C., and F. Rais. *L'Evolution de l'Appartenance Religieuse et Confessionnelle en Suisse*, 1997.

Campiche, R. J., et al. *Croire en Suisse(s): Analyse des Résultats de l'Enquête Menée en 1988/1989 sur la Religion des Suisses*, 1992.

Commissions de la Compréhension du Conseil National et du Conseil des Etats. "*Nous Soucier de nos Incompréhensions*": *Rapport des Commissions de la Compréhension*, 1993.

Conférence Suisse des Directeurs Cantonaux de l'Instruction Publique. *Quelles Langues Apprendre en Suisse Pendant la Scolarité Obligatoire? Rapport d'un Groupe d'Expers Mandatés par la Commission Formation Générale pour Elaborer un "Concept Général pour l'Enseignement des Langues,"* 1998.

Cunha, A., J.-P. Leresche, I. Vez. *Pauvreté Urbaine: le Lien et les Lieux*, 1998.

Département Fédéral de l'Intérieur. *Le Quadrilinguisme en Suisse – Présent et Futur: Analyse, Propositions et Recommandations d'un Groupe de Travail du DFI*, 1989.

du Bois, P. *Alémaniques et Romands, entre Unité et Discorde: Histoire et Actualité*, 1999.

Fluder, R., et al. *Armut verstehen – Armut Bekämpfen: Armutberichterstattung aus der Sicht der Statistik*, 1999.

Flüeler, N., S. Stiefel, M. E. Wettstein, and R.Widmer. *La Suisse: De la Formation des Alpes à la Quête du Futur*, 1975.

Giugni, M., and F. Passy. *Histoires de Mobilisation Politique en Suisse: De la Contestation à l'Intégration*, 1997.

Gonseth, M.-O. *Images de la Suisse: Schauplatz Schweiz*, 1990.

Haas, W. "Schweiz." In U. Ammon, N. Dittmar, K. J. Mattheier, eds., *Sociolinguistics: S. An International Handbook of the Science of Language and Society*, 1988.

Haug, W. *La Suisse: Terre d'Immigration, Société Multiculturelle: Eléments pour une Politique de Migration* 1995.

Hogg, M., N. Joyce, D. Abrams. "Diglossia in Switzerland? A Social Identity Analysis of Speaker Evaluations." *Journal of Language and Social Psychology*, 3: 185–196, 1984.

Hugger, P., ed. *Les Suisses: Modes de Vie, Traditions, Mentalités*, 1992.

Im Hof, U. *Mythos Schweiz: Identität – Nation – Geschichte 1291–1991*, 1991.

Jost, H. U. "Der Helvetische Nationalismus: Nationale Lentität, Patriotismus, Rassismus und Ausgrenzungen in der Schweiz des 20. Jahrhunderts." In H.-R. Wicker, Ed., *Nationalismus, Multikulturalismus und Ethnizität: Beiträge zur Deutung von Sozialer und Politischer Einbindung und Ausgrenzung*, 1998.

Kieser, R., and K. R. Spillmann, eds. *The New Switzerland: Problems and Policies*, 1996.

Kreis, G. *Helvetia im Wandel der Zeiten: Die Geschichte einer Nationalen Repräsentationsfigur*, 1991.

———. *La Suisse Chemin Faisant: Rapport de Synthèse du Programme National de Recherche 21 "Pluralisme Culturel et Identité nationale,"* 1994.

———. *La Suisse dans l'Histoire, de 1700 à nos Jours*, 1997.

Kriesi, H., B. Wernli, P. Sciarini, and M. Gianni. *Le Clivage Linguistique: Problèmes de Compréhension entre les Communautés Linguistiques en Suisse*, 1996.

Lüdi, G., B. Py, J.-F. de Pietro, R. Franceschini, M. Matthey, C. Oesch-Serra, and C. Quiroga. *Changement de Langage et Langage du Changement: Aspects Linguistiques de la Migration Interne en Suisse*, 1995.

———. I. Werlen, and R. Franceschini, eds. *Le Paysage Linguistique de la Suisse: Recensement Fédéral de la Population 1990*, 1997.

Office Fédéral de la Statistique. *Le Défi Démographique: Perspectives pour la Suisse: Rapport de l'Etat-Major de Propsective de l'Administration Fédérale: Incidences des Changements Démographiques sur Différentes Politiques Sectorielles*, 1996.

———. *Enquête Suisse sur la Santé: Santé et Comportement vis-á-vis de la Santé en Suisse: Résultats Détaillés de la Première Enquête Suisse sur la Santé 1992/93*, 1998.

Racine, J.-B., and C. Raffestin. *Nouvelle Géographie de la Suisse et des Suisses*, 1990.

Steinberg, J. *Why Switzerland?* 2d ed., 1996.

Swiss Science Council. "Revitalising Swiss Social Science: Evaluation Report." *Research Policy FOP*, vol. 13, 1993.

Weiss, W., ed. *La Santé en Suisse*, 1993.

Windisch, U. *Les Relations Quotidiennes entre Romands et Suisses Allemands: Les Cantons Bilingues de Fribourg et du Valais*, 1992.

—TANIA OGAY

SYRIA

CULTURE NAME

Syrian

ORIENTATION

Identification. Syria is the name that was given to the region by the Greeks and Romans and probably derives from the Babylonian *suri*. Arabs traditionally referred to Syria and a large, vaguely defined surrounding area as *Sham*, which translates as "the northern region," "the north," "Syria," or "Damascus." Arabs continued to refer to the area as *Sham* up until the twentieth century. That name still is used to refer to the entire area of Jordan, Syria, Lebanon, Israel, and the West Bank and has become a symbol of Arab unity.

Location and Geography. Syria borders Turkey to the north, Iraq to the east, Israel and Jordan to the south, and Lebanon and the Mediterranean Sea to the west. It is 71,000 square miles (183,900 square kilometers) in area. One-third of the land is arable, and one-third is pasturable. The terrain is mostly desert, and home to drought resistant plants such as myrtle, boxwood, and wild olive. There is little wildlife. Remote areas have wolves, hyenas, and foxes; the desert has lizards, eagles, and buzzards. Most of the population is concentrated in the western region of the country, near the Mediterranean. Damascus, the capital and the largest city, is located at the foot of the Anti-Lebanon Mountains along the small Barada River. It has a favorable location in a fertile area close to the desert and has historically served as a refueling stop and commercial center for traders making trips through the desert. Inland of this area is a range of limestone mountains, the Jabal al-Nusayriya. The Gharb Depression, a dry but fertile valley, lies between this range and other mountains to the east. The Euphrates River and several of its tributaries pass through Syria, supplying more than 80 percent of the country's water. There are two natural lakes:

Arram in the crater of an extinct volcano in the Golan Heights and Daraa along the Jordanian border. There are several artificial lakes created by dams that supply irrigation and electrical power. Most of the country has a desertlike climate, with hot, dry summers and milder winters. What little rain there is falls in the winter, mainly along the coast.

Demography. The population in 2000 was 16,673,282 (not including the 35,150 people living in the Israeli-occupied Golan Heights, of whom 18,150 are Arabs and 17,000 are Israelis). The country is 90.3 percent Arab. Kurds are estimated to constitute between 3 and 9 percent of the population. Also represented are Turks; Armenians, most of whom fled Turkey between 1925 and 1945; and small numbers of Circassians, Assyrians, and Jews. The Bedoins are Arabs, but form a distinct group. They were originally nomadic, but many have been forced to settle in towns and villages.

Linguistic Affiliation. Arabic is the official language, and 90 percent of the population speaks it. The Syrian dialect is very similar to Jordanian and Egyptian and varies little from Modern Standard Arabic, the standardized form used in communications throughout the Arab world. Kurdish, Armenian, and Circassian also are spoken. Kurdish is spoken mostly in the northeast, but even there it is rarely heard, as speaking it is viewed as a gesture of dissent. Some ancient languages are still spoken in parts of the country, including Maalua, Aramaic, and Syriac. As a result of colonial influence, French and English (French in particular) are understood and used in interactions with tourists and other foreigners.

Symbolism. The coat of arms displays a hawk, which is the emblem of Muhammad, the founder of the Islamic faith. The flag consists of three horizontal stripes: red on top, white in the middle, and black on the bottom. In the white section are two green stars, symbolizing Islam.

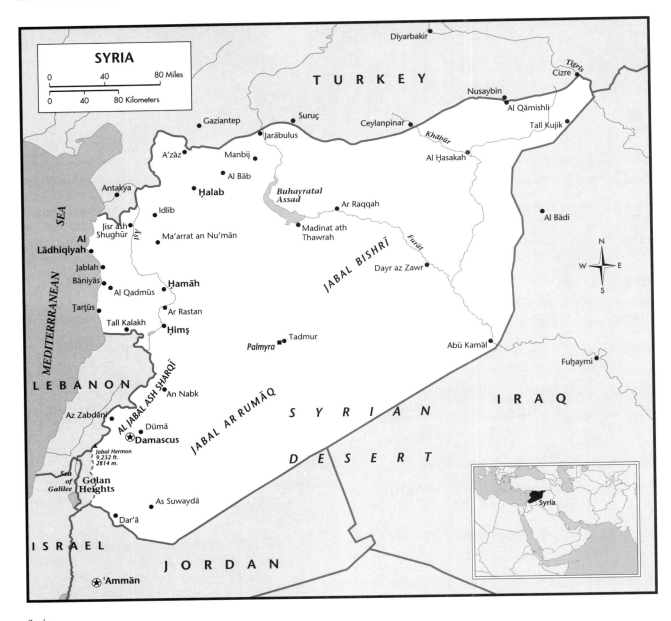

Syria

HISTORY AND ETHNIC RELATIONS

Emergence of the Nation. The modern-day nation emerged from *Sham*, an area that historically included Jordan, Israel, and Lebanon. Between 2700 and 2200 B.C.E., this area was home to the Ebla kingdom. Later, the country's strategic location helped its coastal towns rise to prominence as Phoenician trading posts. It was conquered by the Persians around 500 B.C.E., and by the Greeks in 333 B.C.E. The Romans took over in 64 B.C.E., and established a fortress at Palmyra whose remains still stand in the desert. Muslim Arabs conquered Damascus in 635 C.E. Beginning in 1095, Syria was a target of the Crusades, but the Arabs ultimately defeated the Christian invaders. The Turkish Ottoman Empire took control in 1516 and ruled the area for four hundred years. That era came to an end in 1920 with the end of World War I, when the French took control of Syria and Lebanon. The French drew a straight-line border to separate this territory from British-ruled Transjordan. Syria had experienced a brief period of independence from 1918–1920, and was dissatisfied with French rule, which ignored the will of the people and did little for the country as a whole. There was a brief insurrection in 1925 and 1926, which the French put down by bombing Damascus.

Syria held its first parliamentary elections in 1932. All the candidates were hand-picked by the French, but once elected, they declined the constitution France had proposed for the country. Anti-French sentiment grew when France turned over control of the Syrian province of Alexandretta to Turkey. It was exacerbated by the promise of independence in 1941, which was not delivered until five years later. After independence, civilian rule was short-lived, and the early 1950s saw a succession of coups, after which Syria formed the United Arab Republic with Egypt in 1958. This represented an effort to keep the Arab states more powerful than Israel, but it disintegrated in 1961, when Syria came to resent the concentration of power in Egypt. The disbanding was followed by further political instability. The situation was worsened by the Six Day War against Israel in 1967 and the Black September disagreement with Jordan in 1970.

Hafez al-Assad, the leader of a radical wing of the Arab Socialist party, the Baath, seized control in 1971. He cracked down hard on dissent and in 1982 killed thousands of members of the the Muslim Brotherhood opposition organization. However, his tight-reined rule averted the civil war and political anarchy that plagued Middle Eastern countries such as Lebanon. In 1992, he won his fourth consecutive bid for election with 99.9 percent of the vote. During the Gulf War in the early 1990s, the country aligned itself with the anti-Iraq coalition, thus winning the approval of the United States and removing itself from the United States' government's list of nations supporting international terrorism. Hafez al-Assad died in June 2000. The younger of his two sons, Bashar, assumed his father's position.

National Identity. Syrians tend to identify primarily with their religious group or sect; however, as the majority of the country is Sunni Muslim, this creates a strong feeling of cultural unity. Modern-day Syria is in part the result of geographic lines drawn by the French in 1920, and there is still a strong pan-Arab sympathy that defines national identity beyond the current borders. The current map was also redrawn in 1967, when Israel took the Golan Heights, a previously Syrian territory, and the national identity is based in part on the concept of defending and reclaiming this land.

Ethnic Relations. Syria is ethnically fairly homogeneous (80 percent of the population is Arab). Religious differences are tolerated, and minorities tend to retain distinct ethnic, cultural, and religious identities. The Alawite Muslims (about a half-million people) live in the area of Latakia. The Druze, a smaller group that resides in the mountainous region of Jebel Druze, are known as fierce soldiers. The Ismailis are an even smaller sect, that originated in Asia. The Armenians from Turkey are Christian. The Kurds are Muslim but have a distinct culture and language, for which they have been persecuted throughout the Middle East. The Circassians, who are Muslim, are of Russian origin and generally have fair hair and skin. The nomadic Beduoin lead a lifestyle that keeps them largely separated from the rest of society, herding sheep and moving through the desert, although some have settled in towns and villages. Another group that remains on the outside of society both politically and socially, is the roughly 100,000 Palestinian refugees, who left their homeland in 1948 after the founding of Israel.

URBANISM, ARCHITECTURE, AND THE USE OF SPACE

The focal point of any Middle Eastern city is the *souk*, or marketplace, a labyrinthine space of alleys, stalls, and tiny shops that also include ancient mosques and shrines. Traditionally, the residential quarters of a city were divided along ethnic and religious lines. Today, this system has been largely replaced by divisions along class lines, with some wealthier neighborhoods and some poorer ones. Damascus is an ancient city, and along with Aleppo, one of the oldest continuously inhabited places in the world. The Great Omayyad Mosque, which dates back to the early days of Islam, is one of its oldest and most famous buildings. It formerly served as a Byzantine church honoring Saint John the Baptist and was constructed on the site of an old temple to pre-Islamic gods. The walls are lined with marble and overlaid with golden vines. Six hundred gold lamps hang from the ceiling. The city is home to ruins as well as intact buildings that date back thousands of years. These structures are located in the area called the Old City. Damascus is also a city of cars, highways, and tall modern buildings made of reinforced concrete.

Aleppo, although smaller, is equally ancient. It is geographically protected by its elevation and rocky terrain, and traces its history back to its days as a fort. Today Aleppo is the nation's second largest urban center and most industrialized city. It engages in silk weaving and cotton printing as well as the tanning of animal hides and the processing of produce. Other cities include Latakia, the country's main port, and Homs and Tartus, both of which have oil refineries.

In villages, houses present a closed front to the outside world, symbolizing the self-contained family unit. They are small, usually with one to three rooms, and are built around an enclosed central courtyard. Traditional rural houses in the northwest are mud structures that are shaped like beehives. In the south and east, most houses are made of stone. The nomadic Bedouin, who live mainly in the south and east, sleep in tents that are easily transportable.

In 1960, 30 percent of the population lived in cities; in 1970, that proportion was 46 percent; and by 1988, the number had climbed to half. Most of this growth has been concentrated in Damascus. The rapid spread of that city into nearby farmland has resulted in traffic congestion, overtaxed water supplies, pollution, and housing shortages. Many older buildings have been taken down to make room for roads and newer structures. The outskirts of the city have become overrun with quickly and shoddily constructed homes that sometimes have electricity but rarely have running water or sewage facilities.

FOOD AND ECONOMY

Food in Daily Life. Wheat is the main crop and one of the staple foods. Vegetables, fruits, and dairy products also are eaten. Lamb is popular, but most people cannot afford to eat meat on a regular basis. Islam proscribes the consumption of pork, and other meats must be specially prepared in a method called *halal* cooking. In middle-class and wealthier homes, meals are like those eaten in other Middle Eastern countries: roast or grilled chicken or lamb with side dishes of rice, chickpeas, yogurt, and vegetables. A *mezzeh* is a midday meal composed of up to twenty or thirty small dishes. These dishes can include *hummous*, a puree of chickpeas and *tahini* (ground sesame paste); *baba ganouj*, an eggplant puree; meat rissoles; stuffed grape leaves; *tabouleh* (a salad of cracked wheat and vegetables); *falafel* (deep-fried balls of mashed chickpeas); and pita bread. Olives, lemon, parsley, onion, and garlic are used for flavoring. Popular fruits that are grown in the region include dates, figs, plums, and watermelons. Damascus has a number of French restaurants remaining from the time of colonial rule.

Tea is the ubiquitous drink and is often consumed at social gatherings. Soda is also very popular, as is milk and a drink made by mixing yogurt with water, salt, and garlic. Alcohol consumption is rare, as it is forbidden by the Islamic religion, but beer and wine are available, as is arak, an aniseed drink that also is popular in other Middle Eastern countries.

Food Customs at Ceremonial Occasions. Food is an important part of many celebrations. During Ramadan, each day's fast is broken with an evening meal called *iftar*. This meal begins in silence and is consumed rapidly. *Eid al-Fitr*, the final breaking of the Ramadan fast, entails the consumption of large quantities of food, sweets in particular. Food is also a central element at weddings, parties, and other festivities.

Basic Economy. The country supplies almost all of its own food needs. The proportion of the population working in agriculture has decreased significantly from 50 percent in 1970, to 30 percent in the 1980s, to 23 percent today. Despite this decline, production has increased, thanks in large part to the dam at Tabqa, which has allowed for increased irrigation. Half of the workforce is employed in industry and mining. There is less of a gap between the rich and the poor in Syria than there is in many other countries, and as more of the population gains access to education, the middle class continues to expand.

The basic unit of currency is the pound.

Land Tenure and Property. Before independence, urban landlords controlled the countryside, often mistreating the peasants and denying them any rights. The majority of peasants worked as sharecroppers and were economically and politically powerless. When the socialist Baath Party took control, it introduced measures to limit and redistribute land ownership and establish peasant unions. It also set up local governing organizations and cooperatives, that have allowed the peasants to attain more control of their lives and livelihood.

Commercial Activities. The center of commercial activity in each town or city is the souk. People from all walks of life and all ethnic and religious backgrounds come together to buy and sell a wide variety of goods. Spices, meats, vegetables, cloth, traditional handicrafts, and imported products jostle for space in the crowded booths and alleyways. Souks are not just commercial centers but gathering places as well, and haggling is a necessary part of social interactions. Shopping centers and supermarkets exist but have not supplanted this uniquely Arab institution.

Major Industries. The main industries are oil, agriculture, and textiles. Wheat is the largest crop, followed by cotton. Vegetables, beans, and fruits

The busy Liberation Square in Damascus. The city is one of the oldest inhabited places in the world, but now it is also a very modern city.

also are grown. There is some heavy industry (metallurgy and aluminum) as well as pharmaceuticals and petrochemicals. The oil industry is controlled by the government. Other manufactures include cement, glass, soap, and tobacco.

Trade. Syria's primary trading partners are Germany, Italy, and France. Although Syria is not as rich in oil as other Middle Eastern nations, oil is the main export, and the exploration for deposits continues. Other exports are cotton, fruits and vegetables, and textiles. Imports include industrial and agricultural machinery, vehicles and automotive accessories, pharmaceuticals, foodstuffs, and fabric.

Division of Labor. Syrians are legally entitled to pursue the career of their choice; however, those choices are often limited by gender, family, social pressure, and economic hardship. There is often relatively little difference in the salaries of the working class and those of the professional class.

SOCIAL STRATIFICATION

Classes and Castes. Syrian society was traditionally extremely stratified. People from different classes generally do not socialize with one another, and people in the lower classes often adopt a humble attitude and an acceptance of their position. Class lines tend to coincide with racial differences, as lighter-skinned people hold higher economic and political positions and most of the people in the lower-ranked professions are darker-skinned.

The families of landholders and merchants traditionally occupied the highest position socially and politically. They usually lived in Damascus or Aleppo and managed their land from afar. Religious teachers known as *ulama* were also influential. They served as judges, teachers, and political officials as well as advisers to the government. In this role, the ulama generally supported the status quo. The towns and cities also housed artisans, small merchants, and a small working class.

The Baath government has created some shifts in that pattern. Some peasants are moving to the cities and joining the middle class; others now own land. However, there are still large numbers of indigent and landless peasants. Since the Baath takeover, the army officers who participated in the coup have succeeded the landowners as the new elite. There is also a growing middle class as a result of the spread of education.

Symbols of Social Stratification. The wealthy and well educated have a fairly modern lifestyle with many of the trappings of Western life. Televisions and radios are common except among the extremely poor. Appliances such as air conditioners, dishwashers, and microwaves are only for the very wealthy.

Dress is another indicator of social class. Different tribes and villages have their own distinctive patterns, designs, and colors of clothing. Men traditionally wear long gowns called kaftans, and women wear long robes that leave only their hands and feet exposed. Both men and women wear head wraps. The educated upper classes, particularly the young, tend to prefer modern Western attire. These women favor bright colors, jewelry, makeup, and high heels; men wear dressy slacks and shirts. Blue jeans and T-shirts are rare, as are shorts and miniskirts and bare shoulders or upper arms for women. Traditionally, it is a sign of wealth and status in a family for its women to dress in long robes with their faces veiled.

POLITICAL LIFE

Government. Syria adopted its current constitution in 1973. There is universal suffrage. The unicameral legislative branch is composed of the People's Council, or *Majlis al shaab*, whose 195 members are elected for four-year terms. This body proposes laws, discusses cabinet programs, and approves the national budget. The president, who serves as the head of state and is required by the constitution to be a Muslim, is elected every seven years by popular vote. The president appoints a vice president, a prime minister who serves as head of government, a cabinet, and deputy prime ministers. The president has wide-reaching powers, including serving on the supreme court. Despite the distribution of political power, in practice, the military government has the ability to overrule all decisions.

Leadership and Political Officials. The importance placed on the family as the central structure in society has ramifications in politics and government. Family loyalty is a primary consideration, and there is a general sentiment that family members (even distant relatives) can be trusted more than other people. The best jobs in the government generally are held by people related to the president, either of the same religious group or the same regional background or part of his extended family.

While residents generally are interested in politics both at a local level and as a part of the larger Arab world and are critical of leaders, they tend not to join political parties. Even the ruling Baath Party has relatively small numbers of members. It is more

Women outside a mosque in Damascus. Religion is an important part of daily life in Syria.

common to belong to a labor, farm, or professional union or another organization based on family and religion that may have political goals. Within these groups, leadership positions are often hotly contested.

Social Problems and Control. The legal system is based on the French model, with both civil and criminal courts. There is also a State Security Court that tries political opponents of the government. The proceedings of this court violate many international standards for fair trials. There are large numbers of political prisoners in the jails. In 1992, the government announced that it would free 2,864 of these prisoners, perhaps signaling a loosening of its autocratic policies.

For cases dealing with issues such as birth, marriage, and inheritance, the system has different courts for people of different religions. The Muslim courts are called *Sharia*. There are other ciyrts for Druze, Roman Catholics, Protestants, and Jews.

Military Activity. Syria has armed forces with 408,000 members. This includes an army and an air force but no navy. It spends 30 percent of the national budget on defense as a result of the state of war that has existed between Syria and Israel since the founding of Israel. Syria also has thirty thousand troops stationed in Lebanon to maintain the peace. All men are required to serve thirty months in the armed forces, with the exception of only sons, who are exempt. It is possible to buy exemption from service for a very large sum of money. Women are allowed to serve voluntarily.

SOCIAL WELFARE AND CHANGE PROGRAMS

The government strictly enforces price controls on basic items as well as rent control laws, that help low-income people get by. Medical fees are covered by the state for those who cannot afford private care. The government also provides assistance to the elderly, invalids, and those suffering from work injuries. Most assistance comes from within the family structure; young people often live with their parents until and even after marriage, and children are expected to take in and care for their elderly parents.

GENDER ROLES AND STATUSES

Division of Labor by Gender. Traditionally, wives in towns are responsible for running the household and are restricted to the home. Rural women often work in the fields in addition to performing domestic tasks. While women are legally allowed to work outside the home, there are significant obstacles. For example, the government's Moral Intelligence Department investigates women before allowing them to hold federal jobs. Only 11 percent of women of working age are employed outside the home; among those women, 80 percent work in agriculture. They also are represented in textiles and the tobacco industry, but only 1 percent of employed women have administrative or managerial positions. There are women in the national government, and in the capital a few women work in metal or electrical workshops. It is not uncommon for women to do piecework in their homes.

The Relative Status of Women and Men. The Baath Party was one of the first in the Arab world to declare as one of its goals the emancipation and equal treatment of women; its constitution of 1964 states that all citizens have equal rights. While women are now entitled to receive the same education as men and to seek employment, the traditional attitude that views females as inferior beings prevails. A woman is considered the possession of a man rather than her own person. She is identified as her father's daughter until marriage; after the birth of a male child, her identity is transferred from the wife of her husband to the mother of her son.

MARRIAGE, FAMILY, AND KINSHIP

Marriage. By Muslim tradition, marriage is arranged by the couple's families. While more leniency is now allowed, particularly in cities and among the upper classes, it is still extremely rare for a couple to marry against their family's wishes. According to the constitution, the state has assumed the duty of protecting and encouraging the institution of marriage. Nonetheless, the marriage rate has declined because of housing shortages, inflation, rising levels of education, bride money, and the prohibitive cost of weddings.

Although the state and the Muslim religion both oppose the current dowry system, it is deeply entrenched in the family structure. It places immense pressure on the husband and his family, who have to raise large sums of money, and on the bride, who often is forced to marry the suitor who can provide the biggest dowry. Syria was the first Arab country to pass laws concerning polygamy. In 1953, it passed the Law of Personal Status, under which a man was bound to demonstrate that he could financially support two wives before marrying the second one. Whereas divorce laws used to follow the Arabic tradition that a man had only to repeat three times "I divorce you" (in his wife's presence or not), court proceedings are now required.

Domestic Unit. The family is the primary social unit. An older male, usually the father or grandfather, has the ultimate authority and is responsible for providing for the other family members. It is customary for several generations to live together in the same house. Particularly for women, who are not allowed to leave the home, family provides the primary or only social outlet and relationships with other people.

Inheritance. An estate passes from the father to the oldest son in a family. Traditionally, not only property is bequeathed, but social and political position as well.

Kin Groups. Syrians identify very strongly with their families, both immediate and extended. While kinship ties have weakened somewhat with urbanization and modernization, the clan mentality is still a strong influence in the nation's political system.

SOCIALIZATION

Child Rearing and Education. Children are highly valued as a blessing from God. The more children one has, the more fortunate one is consid-

A Bedouin family in their tent in the Syrian Desert. The nomadic people live primarily in southern and eastern Syria.

ered, as children provide extra hands to work in the fields and ensure that their parents will be taken care of in old age. Children are treated with a great deal of affection. The bond between mother and son (especially the oldest son) is particularly strong.

The literacy rate is 64 percent—78 percent for men and 51 percent for women. Primary education is mandatory and free for six years. Middle school, which begins at age thirteen, marks the end of mixed-sex education. Most schools are run by the state, which combines a French structure with the rigid discipline and rote learning of the Islamic tradition. There are a few religious schools, some schools that are run by the United Nation relief program, and some that are run by the Works Agency for Palestinian Refugees.

Higher Education. Syria has vocational and teacher-training education as well as universities in Damascus, Aleppo, and Latakia. About 165,000 students (40 percent of them women) are enrolled in the universities. The learning situation is less than ideal, with large class sizes and outdated teaching and testing techniques. Students who can afford to obtain visas often prefer to study abroad.

ETIQUETTE

Men and women socialize separately except on occasions when the whole family is involved. Talking is a favorite pastime, and the art of conversation is a prized skill. Men often engage in a sort of banter in which they try to one up each other with witty and eloquent insults.

In social interactions, people stand close together, speak loudly, and gesture widely with their hands and heads. Greetings hold great social significance. They are often lengthy, including questions about health. They usually are accompanied by a handshake and sometimes by a hug and a kiss on each cheek. Placing the right hand on the heart when meeting someone is a signal of affection.

Syrians are very affectionate people. Men walk linking arms or holding hands and hug and kiss a great deal, as do women. Close physical contact in public is more common between people of the same gender than it is between girlfriend and boyfriend or husband and wife.

RELIGION

Religious Beliefs. Seventy-four percent of the population is Sunni Muslim. Sixteen percent be-

People walking along a street in Aleppo, the nation's second largest city. Protected by rocky terrain, Aleppo was once a fort.

longs to Alawite, Druze, and other Muslim sects, and 10 percent is Christian. There are small Jewish communities in Damascus, Al Qamishli, and Aleppo. As in many Arabic countries, religion is an integral part of the culture and daily life. The word ''Islam'' means ''submission to God.'' The religion shares certain prophets, traditions, and beliefs with Judaism and Christianity. The foundation of Islamic belief is called the Five Pillars.

It is speculated, although not certain, that Alawite Muslims do not observe the holy month of Ramadan or make a pilgrimage to Mecca as other Muslims do and celebrate some Christian holidays. The practices of the Druze are also somewhat mysterious. A smaller group known as the Ismailis recognizes a living person, the Aga Khan, as their sacred leader.

The mystical branch of Islam called *sufi*, has a small presence in Syria, although the government sees this sect as subversive and disapproves of its practice. Sufi rituals involve chanting and dancing while moving in a circular formation.

Despite the powerful influence of Islam in people's lives, some elements of folk religion persist. Particularly in rural areas, there is a strong belief in the evil eye as well as in *jinn* (spirits). There is also a tradition of local saints to whom people pray.

Religious Practitioners. There are no priests or clergy in Islam. Instead, there are people with the job of leading prayers and reading from the Qur'an, the Muslim holy book. The Qur'an, rather than a religious leader, is considered the ultimate authority and holds the answer to any question or dilemma one might have. There are also *muezzins* who give the call to prayer and are scholars of the Qur'an and spend their lives studying and interpreting the text.

Rituals and Holy Places. The most important observation in the Islamic calendar is Ramadan. This month of fasting is followed by the joyous feast of *Eid al Fitr*, during which families visit and exchange gifts. *Eid al-Adha* commemorates the end of Muhammod's Hajj. The mosque is the Muslim house of worship. Outside the door, there are washing facilities, as cleanliness is a prerequisite to prayer, demonstrating humility before God. One also must remove one's shoes before entering the mosque. According to Islamic tradition, women are not allowed inside. The interior has no altar; it is simply an open carpeted space. Because Muslims are supposed to pray facing Mecca, there is a small niche carved into the wall that points to the direction in which that city lies.

Death and the Afterlife. A death is followed by three days of mourning during which friends, rela-

People walk around the bazaar in Damascus. The marketplace is the focal point of every Syrian city.

tives, and neighbors pay their respects to the family. Female relatives of the deceased wear black for several months to up to one year or more after the death. Widows generally do not remarry and often dress in mourning for the rest of their lives.

MEDICINE AND HEALTH CARE

There are private medical practices, in addition to the free medical care provided by the state. The health care system is poor but improving. Infectious diseases are a major health threat, especially in rural areas, where water quality is poor and sewage disposal systems are not well developed. There is a high child mortality rate that is due mainly to measles and digestive and respiratory diseases.

SECULAR CELEBRATIONS

The major secular holidays are New Year's Day on 1 January, Revolution Day on 8 March, and the anniversary of the formation of the Arab League, 22 March. Syrians celebrate Martyrs Day in memory of the nation's heroes on 6 April; National Day (also known as Evacuation Day, celebrating independence), on 17 April; and the Day of Mourning on 29 November.

THE ARTS AND HUMANITIES

Support for the Arts. The Ministry of Culture and National Guidance promotes the national culture. Most publishing houses are owned by the state, and writers tend to be government employees. Censorship is enforced strictly, and foreign books about politics and contemporary Syrian or Middle Eastern history are banned. The National Film Centre, established in 1966, oversees the production of most films.

Literature. There is a long literary tradition that dates back to poets such as al-Mutanabbi in the 900s and al-Maarri in the 1000s. Writers must contend with government censorship, but fiction writing is not as tightly monitored as is nonfiction. Whereas the punishment for breaking laws concerning nonfiction is usually imprisonment, fiction writers generally are reprimanded. Perhaps for this reason, poetry and the short story are widely read and appreciated, represented by writers such as Nizar Qabbani, Shawqi Baghdadi, and 'Ali Ahmad Sa'id. There are few women in the ranks of well-known Arab writers, but one of them is Ghada al-Samman, who was born in 1942. She writes on many of the same issues as her male contemporaries, including cultural identity and the clash between tradition and progress as well as issues specific to being a woman and writer in a male dominated society.

Graphic Arts. Islam forbids the artistic depiction of animals or human beings. Therefore, Syrian art until World War I consisted mainly of geometric designs in arabesque and calligraphy. These works can be seen in many palaces and mosques. After World War I, Western drawing techniques began to be taught, and fine arts was introduced as a discipline at the University of Damascus. Most sculpture is carved in white marble and often is displayed in palaces and public buildings.

There is a lively tradition of handicraft production. Jewelry, particularly in gold and silver, is popular, as is other metalwork, such as brass and copper plates and bowls. These items traditionally were produced by Syrian Jews, and as their population has diminished, so has this art form. Mosaic woodworking is also practiced and is used in the construction of boxes, trays, tables, desks, and game boards. Damascus is a center of glassblowing and fabric production, including the silk brocade called damask, which was named for the city. The Bedouins are known for their weaving of fabrics, including carpets and prayer rugs made on hand-built looms, and traditional clothing that is painstakingly embroidered.

Films have been produced in Syria since the 1920s. Musicals and light comedies were popular through the late 1940s. During the 1970s, film clubs were important in the resistance to the government, and for this reason they were shut down in 1980. Syria has spawned several internationally regarded filmmakers, including Omar Amirallay and Usama Muhammed, but their films, which deal with social issues, have been banned in the country, or ignored by distribution companies.

Performance Arts. Memorizing and reciting from the Qur'an and from secular poetry is a popular form of entertainment. There is a rich tradition of storytelling that dates back thousands of years. Even today there are coffee shops where men go to drink tea and hear nightly installments of an on-going saga recited by a professional storyteller.

Arabic music is tied to the storytelling tradition and often recounts tales of love, honor, and family. Technically, it is repetitive and subtle. It uses quarter notes with small jumps in the scale. Classical Arabic music makes use of the oud, an ancient stringed instrument similar to the lute; small drums held in the lap; and flutes. Contemporary music is played by an orchestra that mainly uses European instruments with a lead singer and chorus.

THE STATE OF THE PHYSICAL AND SOCIAL SCIENCES

Damascus has a museum for agriculture and one for military history. Aleppo and other important sites have museums of archaeology.

The main challenge in the area of the sciences is that most Syrians study abroad, and many do not return to Syria to work.

BIBLIOGRAPHY

Ball, Warwick. *Syria: A Historical and Archaeological Guide*, 1998.

Beaton, Margaret. *Syria*, 1988.

Beattie, Andrew, and Timothy Pepper. *Syria: The Rough Guide*, 1998.

Galvin, James. *Divided Loyalties: Nationalism and Mass Politics in Syria at the Close of Empire*, 1998.

Hopwood, Derek. *Syria, 1945–1986*, 1988.

Lye, Keith. *Take a Trip to Syria*, 1988.

Mulloy, Martin. *Syria*, 1988.

Quilliam, Neil. *Syria and the New World Order*, 1999.

Sinai, Anne, and Allen Pollack, eds. *The Syrian Arab Republic*, 1976.

South, Coleman. *Syria*, 1995.

Tareq, Ismael Y., and Jacqueline S. Tareq. *Communist Movement in Syria and Lebanon*, 1998.

Wedeen, Lisa. *Ambiguities of Domination: Politics, Rhetoric, and Symbols in Contemporary Syria*, 1999.

Winkler, Onn. *Demographic Developments and Population Policies in Ba'athist Syria*, 1998.

Web Sites

Destination Syria, www.lonelyplanet.com/dest/mea/syr

Guide to Syria, www.middleeastnews.com/syria

Syria: A Country Study, www.lcweb2.loc/gov/frd/cs/sytoc

Syria—The Cradle of Civilizations, www.arabicnet.com

U.S. Government, Department of State, Central Intelligence Agency. *World Factbook: Syria*, www.odci.gov/cia/publications/factbook/geos/sy

—ELEANOR STANFORD

TAIWAN

CULTURE NAME

Taiwanese; Formosan

ALTERNATIVE NAME

Republic of China

ORIENTATION

Identification. Over four-fifths of the people are descendants of Han Chinese settlers who came to the island in the seventeenth through nineteenth centuries from southeastern China. They were joined in 1949 by remnants of the Nationalist party and army that left China after their defeat in the Chinese Civil War (1927–1949). The island's original inhabitants (*Yuanzhumin*), who are related to Malayo-Polynesian peoples of Southeast Asia, have lived on the island for thousands of years. The culture is a blend of aboriginal cultures, Taiwanese folk cultures, Chinese classical culture, and Western-influenced modern culture. The Nationalists have failed to impose a Chinese national culture on the island, and the potential for a Taiwanese national culture is held in check by both the Nationalists and the People's Republic of China (PRC) as they contest the country's sovereignty.

Location and Geography. Taiwan lies between Japan and Philippines, off the southeastern coast of China. The total area is 13,800 square miles, (32,260 square kilometers). A massive mountain range covers two-thirds of the island and includes East Asia's highest peak, Yü Shan. The subtropical climate is affected by two weather patterns: a continental monsoon that brings cool, wet weather to the northern half of the island between October and March and an ocean monsoon that brings rain to the southern half between April and September. The monsoons can bring devastating typhoons. Most mainlanders live in the north, Taiwanese live along the western coast, and aborigines live in the mountains and on the eastern coast.

Demography. With an estimated population of 22,113,250 in 1999, Taiwan is the second most densely populated country in the world. Seventy percent of the population is Hokkien, 14 percent is Hakka, 14 percent is Mainlander, and two percent is aboriginal. The population is 56 percent urban.

Linguistic Affiliation. Mandarin Chinese is the national language and the language of education, government, and culture. Taiwanese speak *Taiyu*, a southern Min dialect (*nanminhua*), or Hakka. There are seven distinct aboriginal languages, which are grouped into three language families. Most Taiwanese and aborigines speak both a local language and the national language. Mainlanders are monolingual, although some second-generation mainlanders speak Taiwanese.

Symbolism. The symbols of the national culture are conspicuous on the Double Ten (10 October), a national holiday that commemorates the founding of the Republic of China (ROC) in 1911. In Taipei, the Presidential Office Building is lit up and covered with a colossal portrait of Sun Yat-sen, the ROC's founding father. The highlight of the parade is a city-block-long dragon, a symbol of imperial China and the ROC's recently abandoned claim to be the legitimate government of all of China and the preserver of the Chinese cultural heritage. A large military presence reminds onlookers of the government's determination to defend the homeland against communist aggression. High school marching bands in brightly colored uniforms are symbols of the modern educational system and modernity in general. Students from the eastern coast dress in aboriginal costumes to symbolize the government's paternalistic benevolence. Missing from the parade are aborigines who advocate self-determination and the Taiwanese goddess and protector Mazu, who is a potent symbol of popular culture, a local variant

northern origin. A third theory proposes that Taiwan is the homeland of Austronesian culture and language and the source of migrations throughout the region. These theories have become politically charged, with aborigines and opposition party members favoring either the southern origin or homeland theory, and mainlanders favoring the northern origin theory.

Most of the Han settlers came from southern Fujian Province and eastern Guangdong Province, beginning in the seventeenth century. The pioneer era can be divided into three stages marked by different agendas and ethnic tensions. In the early stage (1683–1787), settlers reclaimed land and established farming communities. This period was relatively peaceful except for conflict between Han settlers and the aborigines. The second historical period (1788–1862) saw growth in agricultural production and markets, and leaders representing dominant surname groups competed for control of agricultural production and the lucrative market in grain and sugar. This was a violent period, with numerous uprisings and rebellions that pitted groups identifying with different homelands against one another. This fighting fortified ethnic identities and divisions as refugees sought protection within larger ethnic enclaves. The Lin Shuang-wen Rebellion in 1786 engulfed the island and took two years to suppress. A few families rose out of the struggles of this intermediate period to form an island-wide elite that controlled the trade in the major export commodities. The third stage (1863–1895) was marked by the growth of cities and the conflict between occupational groups.

Various incidents between China and foreign powers, including Japan, raised concerns about Taiwan's sovereignty. The imperial court granted the island provincial status in 1886, and strenuous efforts were made to develop the infrastructure and defensive capabilities. Taiwan was ceded to Japan after China's defeat in the Sino-Japanese War in 1895. Communication with the mainland was cut off, and Taiwan was incorporated into the Japanese Empire as a supplier of grain and sugar and a consumer of manufactured goods. Japan brought order and peace to the island at the cost of political and economic subjugation. While rice yields outpaced population growth, per capita consumption of rice decreased. Taiwan became a nation of sweet potato eaters, and the sweet potato became a symbol of the hardships the people suffered under colonial rule.

Japan's defeat in World War II led to the return of Taiwan to China. The Taiwanese were hopeful about the new political relationship but soon were

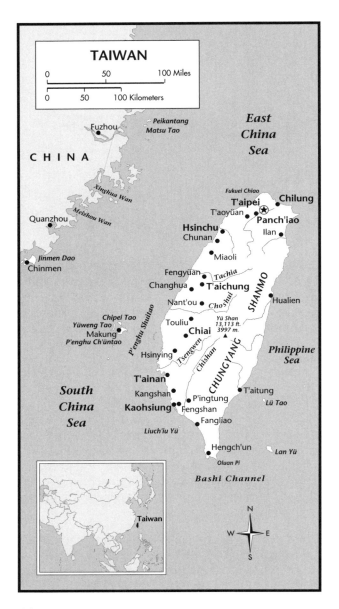

Taiwan

of China's Little Tradition that resists the inculcation of an elite Chinese national culture.

HISTORY AND ETHNIC RELATIONS

Emergence of the Nation. The earliest record of human habitation on Taiwan dates back ten thousand to twenty thousand years. The origin of the first inhabitants is open to debate. Linguistically, the aborigines are related to the Austronesian language family, which points to a southern origin in Southeast Asia. Early stone tool and ceramic styles have been placed in the same traditions as those of Fujian and other mainland sites and suggest a

disappointed. After losing in the Chinese Civil War, the Nationalists (Cementing [KMT]) were concerned about the security of their future island refuge and imposed severe restrictions on the population. An incident in 1947 erupted into an islandwide demonstration against Nationalist rule. The Nationalists killed thousands and wiped out the Taiwanese leadership. Forty years of martial law and authoritarian rule followed. The repressive regimes of Japan and China helped forge a common identity from multiple identities based on homeland, religious sect, and surname group.

The Korean War (1950–1953) made clear to the United States the significant role of Taiwan as a model of capitalist development and a military bulwark against socialist expansion. The country experienced a forty-year period of phenomenal economic growth based on the production and exportation of light consumer goods, but this came at the cost of political oppression, including unlawful detentions, torture, and murder.

In 1975, Chiang Kai-shek died and Taiwan lost its seat in the United Nations. In 1977, an antigovernment riot in Chungli sent a message to the KMT that it had to relax its control of society. In 1978, the KMT's dream of retaking the mainland was shattered when the United States recognized the PRC and closed its embassy in Taipei. Other countries followed suit, leaving Taiwan in international limbo. In that year, President Chiang Ching-Kuo, Chiang Kai-shek's son, set in motion a series of reforms that resulted in the lifting of martial law in 1987 and emergency rule in 1991. The reforms also included the Taiwanization of the KMT. Lee Teng-hui won the first national presidential election in 1996. Lee has played the independence card to the chagrin of the mainland and KMT stalwarts, who broke away from the KMT to form their own party (New Party).

A three-party race in the 2000 presidential elections resulted in the election of the main opposition party's (the Democratic Progressive Party—DPP) candidate and former mayor of Taipei, Chen Shui-bian. Elected with only 39 percent of the vote, Chen and the DPP must carry on the difficult role of governing and negotiating with the PRC. Chen Shui-bian's election symbolizes the determination of the people to control their own destiny.

National Identity. The DPP rise to power has signaled an end to the KMT's futile effort to forge a common Chinese national identity through its control of government, education, and the media. The project was doomed from the start as long as China

remained divided and Taiwanese were free to participate in the postwar economic boom that fueled a revival of their own culture and identity. Taiwan's national identity remains an open question.

Ethnic Relations. In spite of their cultural and linguistic differences, aborigines have found a common cause in their struggle for land rights and self-determination. The Alliance of Taiwan Aborigines (ATA) was founded in 1985. In 1988, the ATA issued a Manifesto of the Rights of the Taiwan Aborigines, and in 1991, it established the Taiwan Aboriginal Autonomous Area Assembly, a failed attempt at self-government. In 1994, President Lee Teng-hui met with aboriginal leaders to discuss their demands but rejected self-government. In 1996, the Legislative Yuan established an Aboriginal Affairs Commission chaired by a Paiwan leader from the National Assembly. The aborigines continue to press for self-government in their struggle for recognition and a place in society. Mainlander-Taiwanese tensions continue to exist but have been ameliorated by a broad dispersal of economic and political power as democracy takes root.

Today little animosity exists among Hokkien Taiwanese, but Hakka-speaking Taiwanese, who are originally from eastern Guangdong Province, have maintained a separate identity and political voice.

URBANISM, ARCHITECTURE, AND THE USE OF SPACE

According to tradition, the landscape includes imaginary flows of cosmic energy (*qi*). The divination practice of *fengshui* taps into pools of *qi* that are concentrated at points (*xue*) in the landscape. The proper location and orientation of a house or grave can bring a family good fortune. Charms strategically placed in the house also achieve this end, as do the characters for longevity, happiness, and prosperity that are carved into wood screens and windows or painted on paper to adorn interior walls.

Good fortune also is tied to the moral order of the family, and the building plan of the traditional country house reflects and reinforces that order. The relative statuses of the different generations are evident in the floor plan and dimensions of a building and its rooms. At the center of a home is the all-purpose main hall where the family rests, eats, and receives guests, and that contains the family altars, ancestral tablets, and god. On both sides of the main hall are bedrooms. The parents occupy the room immediately to the left, and the oldest son and his wife the one to the right. Unmarried children sleep in

A busy street in downtown Taipei, Taiwan. Taiwan is the second most heavily populated city in the world.

the outermost rooms on each side, usually separated by sex. After the marriage of the second son, wings are built perpendicular to the main house, creating the U shape found not only in domestic architecture but also in palace and temple construction.

Towns and cities have the *yanglou*, a foreign-style town house in which hierarchical elements are arranged vertically instead of horizontally; stories instead of wings are added as the family expands. On commercial streets, the ground floor is the family shop and the domestic quarters are upstairs. During the heyday of rural industry in the 1980s, family-operated workshops were located on the ground floor and whole streets became production lines.

Urban architecture, especially in Taipei, is a mix of the classical, modern, and postmodern. There are walled single-story residences and temples, such as the Lungshan and Hsingtien temples, in the city's older quarters. A Western–Japanese hybrid architecture from the Japanese colonial period is found in the Presidential Office Building and National Taiwan University. The cantilevered concrete boxes and plate glass windows of the Taipei Fine Arts Museum and the corporate modernism of the Taipei World Trade Center express varying forms of modernity. The steel, concrete, and glass edifices that face Tunhwa Road are typical of the world's major metropolitan centers. The new Taipei Railway Sta-

tion is a postmodern mix of classic and modern forms, a geometric concrete structure covered by a massive ceramic-tiled roof.

The KMT has inscribed its political ideology on the urban landscape. Every city has a Sun Yat-sen memorial and a Chungshan Road. The names of major avenues echo the philosophy of Confucius and Sun Yat-Sen, with names such as Jenai Lu (Benevolence Road) and Hoping Lu (Peace Road). As the claimant to China's political and cultural heritage, the KMT has built in a grandiose classical style. The Ming-style Chiang Kai-shek Memorial with its distinctive blue-tiled roof and the new opera and concert halls occupy a common plaza in downtown Taipei that rivals Beijing's Forbidden City in scale.

FOOD AND ECONOMY

Food in Daily Life. Food brings people together, and the eating and exchange of food define social groups. The family is identified as people who eat together, and dinner is a secular ritual that reinforces family relationships. Sharing food in the home signifies equality, and people of higher rank are never invited to dine in one's home. Larger groups of kin, neighbors, and temple members come together less frequently to share meals and reinforce their social connections.

Farm workers carrying and sifting rice on a street in Taiwan. Rice is a major agricultural product.

Taiwan is a country of fish eaters. Food is cooked slowly in soups and stews or quickly by deep frying. Favorite dishes include oysters with black bean sauce, prawns wrapped in seaweed, abalone, cucumber crab rolls, and clam and winter melon soup. Small restaurants display fresh produce on the street so that customers can choose their evening meal. Fruit drinks are prepared in special beverage shops. Prosperity has produced a business culture that stresses entertaining, which supports restaurants that offer food from all the culinary regions of China. Western influences are found in bakeries and coffee shops in towns and cities. Buddhist food restrictions have produced a vegetarian cuisine in which bean curd, wheat gluten, and mushrooms are transformed into renditions of standard cuisine, sometimes being molded into the shape of ducks, chickens, and fish.

Taiwan is famous for tea, especially the lightly roasted oolong tea. Teahouses exist in almost every town, and most households have a tea cart to serve guests. Tea is brewed in a small pot and served in one-ounce cups. It is considered stimulating, conducive to conversation, and beneficial to health.

Food Customs at Ceremonial Occasions. Food is served as offerings to gods, ancestors, and ghosts. A cup of tea or wine is placed on the family altar for the ancestors and gods, along with incense. More elaborate offerings are made on special days, including New Year's, gods' birthdays, and the Ghost Festival. Food offerings to ancestors are made in the form of a family dinner with seasoned dishes and rice. The altar table is set with chopsticks, bowls, soup spoons, soy sauce, vinegar, and condiments. The gods are offered cooked but not seasoned or sliced meats. Ghosts are offered cooked meals, but outside the house, where one would feed beggars.

Basic Economy. The Taiwanese have long been traders. Before the first Han settlers arrived, aborigines traded dried deer meat and hides with Chinese and Japanese merchants. When the Dutch arrived at the beginning of the seventeenth century, they developed markets in grain and sugar. In the second half of the nineteenth century, camphor and tea became major exports. The Japanese developed the island's economic infrastructure and agricultural capacity, making Taiwan a major producer and exporter of sugar. During World War II, the Japanese began to industrialize Taiwan, but this initiative was cut short by the bombing that destroyed a large portion of the island's industry and transportation infrastructure. Significant amounts of U.S. aid were received in the postwar years. The government used that money to develop key industries, especially petrochemicals, which produced human-made raw materials such as plastic. When U.S. aid was phased out in the early 1960s, the government was forced to find other sources of revenue. After a brief period of import substitution that allowed the building of industries, the government encouraged export production, which could utilize the cheap and educated labor force. Japan's large trading companies provided second hand machinery to manufacturers. The Cold War sharply divided world markets, and both Japan and Taiwan benefitted from their close connection to the U.S. market. Real growth in the gross domestic product (GDP) averaged over 9 percent per year between 1952 and 1980. In that period, Taiwan transformed itself from an agrarian economy in which farming constituted 35 percent of GDP in 1952 to an industrial economy in which industry accounted for by 35 percent of GDP and agriculture. Taiwan's 1997 GDP made it the twentieth largest economy in the world. The real motor of expansion has been accounted for by small and mediums size companies, which in 1998 made up over 98 percent of all companies, 75-80 percent of employment, and was responsible for 47 percent of economic production.

Land Tenure and Property. The country's indigenous people hunted and gathered for food and cultivated slash-and-burn plots. Neither practice encouraged permanent forms of property. Chinese immigrant farmers regarded fallow plots as unproductive wasteland and worked out arrangements for their use with aboriginal leaders, to whom they paid a nominal fee. Land tenure evolved into a three-tier system of patent holder, landowner, and tenant. The patent holder held the subsurface rights, or "bones," of the field in "perpetuity"; the landowner owned the surface rights, or "skin," of the field; and the tenant worked the field. One of the first programs instituted by the Japanese was land reform that made the landowner the sole owner. The Nationalists reduced taxes and returned land to the tiller. Today, full rights to private property are protected by the constitution.

Commercial Activities. Taiwan has a modern market economy with a large service sector, which comprises two-thirds of GDP. In July 2000, the Taipei Stock Exchange Corporation listed 473 companies with a total capitalization of NT $910 billion (U.S. $30.33 billion). The exchange rate for the New Taiwanese dollar (NT$) on 23 February 2001 was NT $33 to U.S. $1.00 (NT $1.00 = U.S. $0.031).

Major Industries. The major agricultural products are pork, rice, betel nuts, sugarcane, poultry,

shrimp, and eel. The major industries are electronics, textiles, chemicals, clothing, food processing, plywood, sugar milling, cement, shipbuilding, and petroleum refining.

Trade. In 1997, the major exports were electronics and computer products, textile products, basic metals, and plastic and rubber products. The United States, Hong Kong (including indirect trade with the PRC), and Japan account for 60 percent of exports, and the United States and Japan provide over half the imports. The country also exports capital to Southeast Asian countries such as Thailand, Indonesia, the Philippines, Malaysia, and Vietnam. Taiwan has become a major investor in China. In the year 2000, 250,000 Taiwanese worked on the mainland in forty-thousand companies owned or partly owned by Taiwanese, representing an investment of $40 billion (U.S.) and accounting for 12 percent of China's export earnings.

Division of Labor. In 1991, the seven major urban occupational classifications were (1) Professional, technical, and administrative (32 percent), such as teachers, physicians, engineers, architects, artists, actors, accountants, reporters, managers, and government officials; (2) large business owners (20 percent) and private business firms employing ten or more people; (3) lower white-collar clerical employees (12 percent) such as clerks, secretaries, sales personnel, and bookkeepers; (4) small business owners (24 percent) of firms employing fewer than ten workers; (5) skilled blue-collar workers (6 percent) such as carpenters, auto mechanics, electricians, lathe operators, printers, shoemakers, tailors, ironworkers, textile workers, and drivers; (6) farmers (1 percent); and (7) semi skilled and unskilled blue-collar workers (7 percent) such as bricklayers, cooks, factory workers, construction workers, railroad firemen, janitors, laborers, street cleaners, temple keepers, barbers, security guards, police officers, and masseurs.

SOCIAL STRATIFICATION

Classes and Castes. The class system includes the chronically unemployed poor, beggars, and the underworld; the upper and lower bourgeoisie; and the working and middle classes. The upper bourgeoisie constitutes 5 percent of the population and include high-ranking government officials, officials who run large state-owned companies, and the owners of companies that employ more than two hundred people. The petty bourgeoisie makes up half the population and includes farmers, small

A family rides a motorcycle in Taipei, Taiwan, which is a common mode of transportation.

businesspeople, and artisans. The working class makes up a fifth of the population, and the middle class another fifth. The middle class is composed of more educated persons who engaged in nonmanual work in government, education, the military, and large companies. In the past, class coincided with ethnic group. Mainlanders constituted the bulk of the upper bourgeoisie and the middle class, and Taiwanese and aborigines accounted for most of the chronically poor, the working class, and the lower bourgeoisie. However, Taiwan's economic miracle and the Taiwanization of the government have lifted many residents into the upper bourgeoisie and the middle class.

Symbols of Social Stratification. Taiwan is a modern consumer society in which status is measured by wealth and marked by the commodities one can afford to buy, such as automobiles, clothes, and homes, as well as one's lifestyle. A person can live very cheaply in the countryside in a modest apartment, buying produce from an outdoor market, eating at street stands, and transporting a family of five on a scooter. One also can own a large condominium on a prestigious avenue in Taipei, eat in expensive restaurants, wear Western brand-name clothes, and ride in cabs or a chauffeured Mercedes.

POLITICAL LIFE

Government. The territory of the ROC includes the islands of Taiwan, Kinmen, Matsu, and the Penghus (Pescadores), along with several smaller islands. Taiwan and the Penghu Islands are administered together as the Province of Taiwan. Kinmen, Matsu, and the smaller nearby islands are administered by the government as counties of Fujian Province. The seat of the provincial government is in central Taiwan. The two largest cities, Taipei and Kaohsiung, are centrally administered municipalities. In 1998, the legislative Yuan eliminated the position of governor and many other administrative functions of the Taiwan Provincial Government.

From 1949 to 1991, the ROC on Taiwan claimed to be the sole legitimate government of all of China, and the Nationalists (KMT) reestablished on the island the full state apparatus that had existed on the mainland. The first National Assembly was elected on the mainland in 1947. Because elections were no longer possible on the mainland, representatives of mainland constituencies held their seats for nearly forty-five years. In 1991, the Council of Grand Justices mandated the retirement of all members of the National Assembly who had been elected in 1947 and 1948.

The second National Assembly, which was elected in 1991, amended the constitution to allow for the direct election of the president and vice president. The president is both the political leader and the commander in chief of the armed forces and presides over the five administrative branches, or Yuan: executive, legislative, control, judicial, and examination. The legislative Yuan is the main law-making body; its members are elected directly by the people and serve three-year terms. The control Yuan oversees public servants and investigates corruption. The twenty-nine control Yuan members are appointed by the president and approved by the National Assembly; they serve six-year terms. The judicial Yuan administers the court system and includes a sixteen-member Council of Grand Justices that interprets the constitution. Grand justices are appointed by the president with the consent of the National Assembly and serve nine-year terms. The examination Yuan recruits and manages the civil service through the Ministry of Examination and the Ministry of Personnel.

Leadership and Political Officials.
Before 1987, Taiwan had a one-party system with the KMT firmly in control. Although "outside the party" candidates sometimes won local elections, opposition parties were banned. Mainlanders dominated the government at the upper level and controlled the lower level of local Taiwanese leaders through a patronage system. To ensure that no leader or faction became too strong, the KMT supported rivalries between local leaders and factions. Vote buying was prevalent.

In the 1998 elections, the DPP won 31 percent of the 176 seats and the KMT won 55 percent. In other elections, the DPP won twelve of the twenty-three county magistrate and city mayor contests compared to the KMT's eight. Aboriginal representatives hold six reserved seats in the National Assembly and the legislative Yuan. The chairman of the Aboriginal Affairs Commission is an aborigine, as is the magistrate of Taitung County. An increasing number of women are involved in politics, and some hold key positions. Women sit in the cabinet and head several agencies and commissions, and three women are members of the KMT's Central Standing Committee. A fifth of legislative Yuan and National Assembly members and two of twenty-nine control Yuan members are women.

Social Problems and Control.
In 1990, the most serious social problems were juvenile delinquency, transportation, public security, environmental pollution, vice and prostitution, bribery, speculation, the poor-rich discrepancy, rising prices, and gambling. Juvenile crime tripled between 1980 and

Small and medium companies account for 98 percent of all businesses in Taiwan.

1995. In 1995, over a third of drug-related offenses were committed by youth, prompting the government to declare a war on drugs. The rise in juvenile delinquency has been attributed to the deterioration of the family system and the competitive education system. Fathers spend more time away from the home, and single-parent homes have increased. Many fifteen-year-olds have nowhere to go after finishing their nine years of compulsory education. Petty crime, drug dependency and suicides have risen dramatically in this age group.

Affluence has transformed Taiwan from a country of scooters to one of automobiles, creating traffic congestion and air pollution in the cities and a high death toll on the highways.

Murder, rape, robbery, and other violent crimes have doubled in the last ten years. Organized crime is involved in extortion, kidnaping, murder, fixing bids for public works, and gunrunning. The 1997 slaying of a prominent opposition feminist underscored the fact that 54 percent of the victims of violent crime that year were women. In 1992, 225,500 women were engaged in prostitution, including 61,400 teenagers.

Authoritarian rule in the past led to many human rights abuses. A 1997 reform has strengthened human rights protections in several ways. Prosecutors and police officers must release suspects within twenty-four hours unless a warrant is obtained from a court. Also, suspects must be informed of their right to remain silent, lawyers may be present during interrogation, and overnight interrogation is prohibited. The Council of Grand Justices has eliminated restrictions on freedom of association.

The judicial system has three levels: district courts, high courts, and the supreme court. District courts hear civil and criminal cases, high courts hear appeals, and the supreme court reviews judgments by lower courts. Criminal cases that involve rebellion, treason, and offenses against friendly relations with foreign states are handled by the high court.

Many social problems stem from lax enforcement of strict legal code. Business licenses are difficult to obtain, but once they are gotten, there is little monitoring of business. Companies, both legal and illegal, easily skirt tax, labor, environmental protection, and zoning laws. Thousands of businesses operate underground in an informal economy that may account for 25–50 percent of the GDP. Social order is maintained through personal connections and informal relationships in which the sanctions of face apply. However, this "Confucian" order requires enforcement, and businesses rely on gangsters to collect debts and enforce agreements.

Military Activity. Throughout the Chiang years (1949–1988), the KMT was fixated on retaking the mainland and maintaining its large military force that was partly sponsored by the United States. In 1979, Taiwan and the United States signed the Taiwan Relations Act, which defined the country's military mission as primarily a defensive one against the PRC and banned the sale of offensive weapons such as submarines, missiles, and bombers to Taiwan. The country maintains a large military force of 376,000 active and 1,657,000 reserve personnel. The People's Liberation Army (PLA) of China has deployed hundreds of short-range ballistic missiles on the mainland opposite Taiwan and in 1996, during the presidential election campaign, "test" fired several missiles outside the harbors of the two largest ports. This demonstration produced the intended effect on Taiwan's export-dependent economy as the stock market fell and large sums of money left the island. The latest PLA threat is electronic and informational warfare, which is aimed at overloading and jamming the country's communications systems.

SOCIAL WELFARE AND CHANGE PROGRAMS

The family has long provided welfare services to its older members. Letting the elderly live by themselves was considered unconscionable, and brothers often looked after their aging parents on a rotating basis. Older family members provided useful services such as looking after children and house sitting. While families continue to be responsible for the aged, there are holes in the system. In 1997, one third of the population sixty-five years old and above did not receive assistance from their children, 10 percent lived alone, and one-quarter experienced economic difficulties. Benevolent homes provide care for people over seventy years old. The state also provides some home care and day care services. Since 1950, labor laws have mandated that companies provide labor insurance, but this applies only to companies that employ more than fifteen workers, leaving a majority of workers unprotected.

NONGOVERNMENTAL ORGANIZATIONS AND OTHER ASSOCIATIONS

Taiwan participates in few international nongovernmental organizations (NGOs), but the recent change in government has opened the way for more involvement. The government views working with NGOs as an alternative to being a member of the United Nations or having full diplomatic relations with most countries. Eighty-one Taiwanese NGOS aid children, teenagers, women, the handicapped, and aboriginal organizations. Human rights NGOs include the Taipei Women's Resource Foundation, the Garden of Hope Foundation, and the Taiwanese Foundation for Human Rights. After a devastating earthquake in 1999, the country received aid from several world relief agencies. Taiwanese disaster relief organizations include the Overseas Aid Council of Taiwan, World Vision Taiwan, the Tzu-chi Compassion Relief Foundation (Buddhist), the Red Cross of ROC, and the Eden Social Welfare Foundation (Christian).

GENDER ROLES AND STATUSES

Division of Labor by Gender. A universal educational system and a modern industrial economy have not changed the nation's patriarchal culture. Although women work in every industry, they tend to have poorly paid menial jobs. In the office, they occupy the lower tier of managerial jobs. Women's wages and salaries are generally lower than men's and women earn only 72 percent of men's income for equivalent work. In the heyday of

Fish is the primary food consumed in Taiwan.

rural industry, factories accommodated young mothers by bringing work to their homes. Some women run their own businesses and occupy positions of power in the government.

The Relative Status of Women and Men. Filial piety, fraternal loyalty, lineage solidarity, and family are the pillars of this patriarchal society. Although women were vital to the reproduction of the patrilineage, that role translated into few rights for women. However, the domestic notions of prosperity, happiness, and peace constituted a parallel set of values that was tied to household productivity and well-being. Insofar as women's hard work and organizing skills contributed to a household's prosperity, women gained respect in the home. Women's organizing skills and adeptness at relationship building have to been important assets in small-scale industries, in which many successful women manage businesses and supervise workers in small factories and workshops. The network building required in the rural and export industries has favored relationships with relatives on both sides of the family, increasing the importance of women. Women have gone to college and joined professional ranks, and some have entered politics. Recent trends reflect an increase in women's power and status, such as delayed marriages, higher divorce rates, fewer children, and higher educational attainment among women. A growing feminist movement actively promotes women's rights. Legislation has been enacted that recognizes women's rights to child custody and inheritance of property. However, men continue to hold most material wealth and political power and strongly resist the women's movement. Women leaders have been vilified and jailed.

MARRIAGE, FAMILY, AND KINSHIP

Marriage. Historically, there were three ways to marry. Major marriage was the standard and most common form. It was an arrangement between families involving the use of a matchmaker. Often, the bride and groom met for the first time on the day of the wedding. Each family would sponsor its own wedding feasts on different days. Both a brideprice and a dowry were exchanged. The wife left her natal family to take up residence in her father-in-law's household. The second most common form of marriage was called *sim pua*. It involved adopting an infant girl and raising her as daughter and future daughter-in-law. Although this form was affordable for poorer families, it was also the choice of mothers because it allowed them exercise authority over their daughters and daughter-in-law from an early age. Often this meant that the adopted daughter was treated very poorly. Minor marriages were the type of marriage most likely to end in divorce. The third form of marriage was uxorilocal marriage, which involved a man marrying into his wife's family. The groom entered into to this form because he had no property, and the bride because her family had no male heir. Sim pua and uxorilocal marriages are far less common today. Young men and women now have more of a say about who they want to marry but still need their parents' blessings and the mediation of a matchmaker.

Domestic Unit. The ideal family type is the grand or joint family, a multigenerational family that includes a father, a mother, single children, and married brothers and their families living together under one roof. However, for this form of family to succeed, it must be wealthy and have a strong patriarch, diverse business interests, compliant daughters-in-law, and lineage support. The most common family unit is the stem family, consisting of the parents and a married son, a daughter-in-law, and their children. In a modern society, increased opportunities for employment outside the family and village, larger incomes, and universal education have favored smaller households. Nuclear families have become more common as the role of the family as a productive unit has diminished.

Inheritance. In spite of amendments to the constitution that guarantee equal rights of inheritance for women, men inherit most property, especially land. In this patrilineal society, property is a male birthright. Traditionally, the property a woman inherited was obtained at her marriage, in the form of a dowry, when she left her family. Also, at that time women inherited pocket money that was theirs to spend.

Kin Groups. After the family, the most important kin group used to be the surname group. Historically, in a frontier society, the surname group was an important source of security and protection. Many surname groups were made up of the broken remnants of lineages that were casualties of clan wars on the mainland. Members of surname groups might not have been able to demonstrate a genealogical connection, but they shared a name and could point to a common place of origin on the mainland; this constituted sufficient criteria to claim a blood tie. Most surname groups worshiped a common god and centered their collective activities at temples. The modern state has replaced many of the functions of the surname group.

SOCIALIZATION

Infant Care. Infants and small children sleep with their mothers and are fed on demand. They are carried and entertained by adults and older children. Weaning is done abruptly at about age two. Little is expected of young children, who are seldom punished. By the time they begin primary school, children start doing chores. Girls help care for younger siblings and do household tasks, and boys run errands. Children are expected to be obedient, avoid fighting, and work hard. Threats and scolding are used to discipline children, but physical punishment is rare. Rewards also are used to motivate children. The mother is primarily responsible for child care, and the mother-child relationship is usually close. Fathers play with younger children and punish children for misbehavior; their aloofness often causes children to fear their fathers. Girls generally are treated more strictly than boys, but fathers often are more affectionate toward their daughters.

Child Rearing and Education. The Japanese instituted a system of universal primary education for grades one through six. The Nationalists extended the educational system to the ninth grade in 1968 and made it compulsory in 1982. In 1993,

A boy holds onto a handful of lanterns for celebrating the New Year Lantern Festival at Chiang Kaishek Memorial in Taipei, Taiwan.

they extended free education to the twelfth grade. In 1997, about 90 percent of junior high graduates continued their studies in a senior high school or a vocational school. Children enter kindergarten at age six. After junior high school (grade nine), students take a competitive examination to determine the school they will attend. There are three routes: an academic high school, a secondary vocational school, or a vocational junior college.

Higher Education. The academic route leads to the best colleges and universities, of which National Taiwan University is the most prestigious. There are over one hundred institutions of higher learning, which admit sixty thousand students a year. For graduate education, many students go abroad, including thirteen thousand who study in the United States each year. The premier research institution is the Academia Sinica.

ETIQUETTE

Because social relationships and the cultivation of social relationships are considered important, Taiwanese people are friendly and courteous. Social relationships derive importance from the belief that one cannot do anything alone and everyone requires the help and cooperation of others. The exchange of cigarettes, business cards, or small gifts is a quick and easy way to overcome initial shyness in forming a personal connection. Introductions are important in initiating a relationship. One's name and reputation have currency, as is demonstrated by the exchanging of business cards. Initial friendliness is only an overture to friendship and can quickly turn cold if one's intentions are suspected. As cordial as Taiwanese can be in a personal setting, on the street with strangers, it is a free-for-all; one fights for every inch of space on the streets of Taipei, and holding one's place in a line is a contest. It takes time to build relationships of trust. Teahouses, restaurants, and homes are places where people cultivate relationships. The object of these encounters is to relax, let down one's guard, and connect in a genuine and open way. Although people are interested in friendship, they understand that friendship has utilitarian benefits, as friends are expected do each other favors and help each other get things done. In spite of their openness and friendly demeanor, people pay close attention to status and authority as defined by age, education, occupation, and gender. Although it is difficult for people of different statuses to be friends, they still can form a relationship of mutual benefit (*guanxi*). Much of the work of government and business gets done through these relationships.

RELIGION

Religious Beliefs. Most of the people are followers of China's three religious traditions; Confucianism, Taoism, and Buddhism, collectively referred to as the "three teachings," or *sanjiao*. Each religion has a long history and its own temples, priests, and sacred texts. Although the elite make distinctions between the *sanjiao*, most people practice a syncretic blend referred to as popular or folk religion. Popular religion includes elements of these three sets of teachings, along with beliefs in ancestors, ghosts, magic, and the efficacy of religious mediums. Popular religion is based on localized cults of nearly two hundred gods. The cults are centered in thousands of temples throughout the island. Many of the gods were originally historical figures who founded communities in Fujian during the Song Dynasty and were brought to Taiwan by Han immigrants. The gods were a source of magical power, or *ling*, which could be tapped through ritual. They were also the focal point of the community, bringing people together to form new social groupings. If families left to form a new community, they brought a newly carved statue of their god with them. In a ritual called dividing incense (*fenxiang,*) they formed a new temple, which remained linked to the mother temple. On a god's birthday, pilgrims pay their respects to the temples from which their own temples are descended. Through their travel, they retrace their region's history and reconfirm their subethnic ties. Rural industrialization brought prosperity to many communities, which rebuilt their temples or constructed new ones. The gods continue to play a role in mediating community and regional relationships in an industrial society.

Two percent of the population is Protestant. The Canadian Presbyterian missionary George Leslie MacKay came to the country in the 1870s and established sixty churches and trained native missionaries until the Japanese undid much of his work. Protestantism has remained strong among the aborigines and Hakka. In the postwar period, Taiwanese Protestant leaders played a leading role in the opposition movement for human rights and democracy and suffered the consequences of defying the government's authority with detention, prison, and self-exile.

Rapid modernization has spawned many new religions, which have their roots in popular religion but address the social and psychological dislocations caused by modernity. One popular new religion, *Yiguandao*, states that the Maitreya Buddha has returned to the world to spread the Tao and save the world from destruction.

Religious Practitioners. Each of the three great religions has priests who are responsible for observing the religious calendar and carrying out the prescribed rituals. The most colorful are the spirit mediums *tongqi*. Gods possess a *tongqi* and through him or her communicate to cult followers verbally or in the form of "spirit writing." The *tongqi* also dispenses charms in response to personal requests for aid, holding office hours certain days of the week.

Rituals and Holy Places. The gods are honored on their birthdays in a public demonstration of popular religion. The gods are brought out of their temples and paraded down the streets in elaborately carved palanquins rolled along by four men. Two men carry a litter on which the god's spirit descends violently, shaking and rocking the chair. The procession is led by the *tongqi* who falls into a trance while possessed by the god's spirit and practices self-mortification, by piercing his cheek with a skewer, slashing his chest with a sword, or banging his forehead with a ball of nails. The entourage visits each follower's household, which displays an offering of food on a table outside the front gate. Afterward, tables are set up in the street and a banquet is held for all temple members. The more faithful go on a pilgrimage that includes visits to other temples dedicated to their god and eventually arrive at the god's home temple, which usually is in the south, where the first immigrants arrived. The birthday of Mazu, Taiwan's most popular god, is celebrated on 23 May.

The main ritual honoring ancestors occurs during the *Qingming* festival on 5 and 6 April. Family members gather and visit the graves of their ancestors to burn offerings of paper money and incense. The offerings are preceded by a flurry of activity to clear the overgrown gravesite. The Ghost Festival on 15 July is a three-day affair in which ghosts of all stripes are propitiated. The 15 August Mid-Autumn Festival rounds out the ceremonial calendar as families worship the moon god and ask for protection, fortune, and family unity.

Death and Afterlife. Taiwanese believe in the Buddhist heaven and hell and reincarnation. A good life is rewarded in heaven, and a bad life in hell, before reincarnation. A person's fate is determined by past lives. One can improve one's fortunes after death by performing good deeds while one is alive. Through special prayers and offerings, the living can improve the afterworld conditions of the deceased and their chances in the afterlife.

MEDICINE AND HEALTH CARE

Taiwan has a legacy of both Western and Chinese medicine. The missionary George MacKay opened a clinic in the northern port of Tan-shui in 1880, treating patients and training indigenous practitioners in Western medical science. In the colonial period, the Japanese implemented an islandwide program of public health and sanitation, that brought under control infectious diseases such as cholera, smallpox, and bubonic plague. They also built a Western hospital and medical college in Taipei and charity hospitals and treatment centers around the island. Medicine became one of the only professional occupations open to the Taiwanese. Today the National Health Insurance program covers all citizens and provides free medical care for children up to four years old and people over seventy.

Chinese medicine also is practiced. It is a system of health care based on ancient Chinese philosophy and thousands of years of clinical practice. Traditional doctors understand the body in terms of dynamic forces and consider each patient's illness unique. Examination of the patient's pulse and tongue is the principal diagnostic tool. Doctors also consider weather conditions and the patient's emotional state. Sickness is regarded as the result of a disturbance in the polarity of one or more of the body's systems that affects the flow of *qi*, or life force. Doctors prescribe a concoction of herbs and other natural pharmaceuticals to reset the polarity or use acupuncture to adjust the flow of *qi*.

SECULAR CELEBRATIONS

Traditional Chinese festivals mark an agricultural cycle based on the lunar calendar. The first day of Chinese New Year, called the Spring Festival (*Chunjie*), is the most important festival. Families whose members are dispersed throughout the island usually come home to celebrate it. The night before New Year's Day is devoted to feasting. Parents give their children red envelopes with money inside. On New Year's Day, the family pays its respect to ancestors, gods, and elders. It visits the local temple to worship and burn incense, followed by visit to friends. The fifteenth and last day of the New Year celebrations is the Lantern Festival (*yuanxiaojie*). Children carry lanterns to the temple, watch fireworks, and eat round dumplings (*yuanxiao*), a symbol of unity. The Dragon Boat Festival (7 May), or Poets' Festival, commemorates the poet Ch'u Yuan, who threw himself into a river after an altercation with the emperor. Glutinous rice cakes are thrown into the water to prevent sea creatures from eating the poet's body.

THE ARTS AND HUMANITIES

Support for the Arts. The arts have not received general support in this poor and politically

In Taiwan, women earn only 72 percent of men's income for equivalent work.

oppressed country, and some of the most prominent painters and writers have been imprisoned and killed. During the Japanese era (1895–1945), Taiwanese painters studied at the Tokyo Fine Arts Institute and showed their work at annual exhibitions in Taipei. In the postwar period, the U.S. Information Service provided one of the first public spaces for fine arts, to promote Western-style modern art. A National Arts Academy was established in 1982, and a year later the Taipei Fine Arts Museum, the country's first museum of modern art, opened. At that time, the Ministry of Culture and the Council for Cultural Planning and Development began to sponsor native and international exhibitions. The 1980s witnessed a surge in art collecting and a proliferation of art galleries. Literary magazines have been a source of support for writers and were a forum for lively debates throughout the Japanese and Nationalist periods. In the mid-1970s, newspapers began to sponsor annual fiction contests.

Literature. Living in Japan in the 1920s, the first generation of modern Taiwanese writers wrote in Japanese, embraced modernity, and denounced

China's cultural heritage. This generation of authors included Lai He (1894–1943), the father of the Taiwanese New Culture Movement and the founder of the magazine *Taiwanese New Literature*. The next decade saw the younger generation of writers react against modernism, which had become identified with Japanese colonialism. The chief spokesman in the Nativist Literary debate was Huang Shih-hui, who advocated a class-oriented perspective and the of vernacular language to express a national consciousness. Beginning in the 1930s, the Nativist movement suffered under the general crackdown on leftists by the Japanese and later the Nationalists. The 1960s modernist fiction writers Pai Hsien-yung and Wang Wen-hsing wrote about the conflict between bourgeois individualism and filial piety. Ch'en Ying-chen wrote about the lives of native Taiwanese and the hardships they experienced under the Japanese and the KMT, presaging the modernist-nativist literary debates that raged in the 1970s. Interest in modernist and nativist writers declined in the late 1970s and 1980s as the new urban middle class found their work too formal or too political. Writers in the 1980s and 1990s experimented with postmodern literary forms and more eclectic subject matter, including sexual liberation, political complacency, and corporate life.

Graphic Arts. During the Japanese era, painters were influenced by Impressionism and painted native scenes in oils. After World War II, the Nationalists revived classic Chinese ink painting and persecuted nativist painters, including Taiwan's best known painter at the time, Chen Cheng-po. Li Chung-sheng was a pioneer of abstract painting in the 1950s. Other modernist movements, such as surrealism, dadaism, pop art, minimalism, and op art, influenced artists in the 1960s and 1970s. A new nativist movement (*xiangtu*) emerged in the late 1960s with the work of Hsi Te-chin, who painted local scenery and architecture and experimented with folk art. The lifting of martial law in 1987 generated a second wave of nativist consciousness (*bentu*), this time with an urban and modernist outlook. In the 1990s, postmodern artists explored the symbolism of the body and the tensions between individual existence and collective values.

Performance Arts. Liu Feng-hsueh introduced modern dance to Taiwan in 1967 after studying in Germany. Her work combines structured modern choreography with the movement styles of Chinese opera, martial arts, and more recently aboriginal folk dance. Lin Hwai-min was a student of Martha Graham and the founder of the Cloud Gate Dance Theater, the country's premier dance company. His dances explore Chinese and Taiwanese identity, combining modern dance techniques and Chinese opera movements. Students of Lin Hwai-min have opened their own studios, performing dances that incorporate modern dance technique with Chinese and Taiwanese narratives. The Taipei Folk Dance Theatre and the Formosan Aboriginal Song and Dance Troupe are among several new dance companies that have formed to reconstruct and preserve traditional dances.

THE STATE OF THE PHYSICAL AND SOCIAL SCIENCES

Continued economic prosperity is dependent on progress in telecommunications, computer, and electronic technologies. Sizable amounts of public and private resources have been mobilized toward this effort. The National Science Council is funding scientific research for fiscal year 2000. The Industrial Technology Research Institute (ITRI), the largest nonprofit research institute, was founded in 1973 by the Ministry of Economic Affairs and helps develop industrial technologies and transfer them to domestic private enterprises to improve their competitive position in international markets. The social sciences constitute major university departments, research institutes, associations, and organizations, including anthropology, archaeology, business and management, economics, law, political science, sociology, and women's studies.

BIBLIOGRAPHY

Ahern, Emily. *The Cult of the Dead in a Chinese Village*, 1973.

———, and Hill Gates, eds. *The Anthropology of Taiwanese Society*, 1981.

Baity, Philip Chesley. *Religion in a Chinese Town*, 1975.

Cohen, Myron L. *House United, House Divided: The Chinese Family in Transition*, 1976.

Davidson, James W. *The Island of Formosa: Past and Present*, 1903, rev. ed. 1988.

Davison, Gary Marvin, and Barbara E. Reed. *Culture and Customs of Taiwan*, 1998.

Gallin, Bernard. *Hsin Hsing, Taiwan: A Chinese Village in Change*, 1966.

Gates, Hill. *China's Motor: A Thousand Years of Petty Capitalism*, 1996.

Gold, Thomas. *State and Society in the Taiwanese Miracle*, 1986.

Harrell, Stevan. *Ploughshare Village: Culture and Context in Taiwan*, 1974.

Ho, Samuel P. S. *Economic Development of Taiwan 1860–1970*, 1978.

Hsiung, Ping-chun. *Living Rooms as Factories: Class, Gender, and the Satellite Factory System in Taiwan*, 1996.

Hu, Tai-li. *My Mother-in-Law's Village: Rural Industrialization and Change in Taiwan*, 1983.

Kerr, George H. *Formosa Betrayed*, 1965.

Knapp, Ronald G. *China's Living Houses: Folk Beliefs, Symbols, and Household Ornamentation*, 1999.

Kung, Lydia. *Factory Women in Taiwan*, 1978, rev. ed 1994.

Marsh, Robert M. *The Great Transformation: Social Change in Taipei, Taiwan since the 1960s*, 1996.

Meskill, Johanna Menzel. *A Chinese Pioneer Family: The Lins of Wu-feng, Taiwan 1729–1895*, 1979.

Olsen, Nancy Johnston. *The Effect of Household Composition on the Child Rearing Practices of Taiwanese Families*, 1971.

Pasternak, Burton. *Kinship and Community in Two Chinese Villages*, 1969.

Rubinstein, Murray R., ed. *The Other Taiwan: 1945 to the Present*, 1994.

———. *Taiwan: A New History*, 1999.

Sangren, P. Steven. *History and Magical Power in a Chinese Community*, 1987.

Seaman, Gary. *Temple Organization in a Chinese Village*, 1978.

Shepherd, John Robert. *Statecraft and Political Economy on the Taiwan Frontier 1600–1800*, 1993.

Skoggard, Ian A. *The Indigenous Dynamic in Taiwan's Postwar Development: The Religious and Historical Roots of Entrepreneurship*, 1996.

Thorton, Arland, and Hui-Sheng Lin, eds. *Social Change and the Family in Taiwan*, 1994.

Weller, Robert P. *Unity and Diversities in Chinese Religion*, 1987.

Winkler, Edwin A., and Susan Greenhalgh, eds. *Contending Approaches to the Political Economy of Taiwan*, 1990.

Wolf, Arthur, ed. *Studies in Chinese Society*, 1978.

Wolf, Margery. *Women and Family in Rural Taiwan*, 1972.

—IAN SKOGGARD

TAJIKISTAN

CULTURE NAME

Tajik; Tajikistani; Tajiki

ORIENTATION

Identification. The name "Tajik" may derive from the name of a pre-Islamic tribe, perhaps of Zoroastrian origin, and means "crown" or "royalty."

The Tajik people are of ethnic Persian descent and constitute the largest indigenous group in the country (about 65 percent of the population). Within this group are the Pamiris, who live in the Gorno-Badakhshan Autonomous Province and number nearly forty thousand. The Pamiris speak a different language and belong to the Ismaili Shiite sect of Islam, while Tajiks are Sunni. Gorno-Badakhshon is surrounded by mountains, and is isolated for most of the year.

Other ethnic groups that were caught within the country as the borders in Central Asia were redrawn during the Soviet era include Uzbeks, Kyrgyz, Turkmen, Kazakhs, Uyghur, and Bukharan and European Jews. Beginning in the eighteenth century, many Russians migrated to the area as soldiers and laborers. Other nonindigenous ethnic groups include Crimean Tartars, Ukrainians, Belorussians, Georgians, Osetians, Koreans, and Armenians.

When Tajikistan won independence in 1991, a struggle for power between the clans developed into a civil war. At that time, Islamic fundamentalists wanted to create an Islamic state. Political instability led to a collapsing infrastructure, corruption, and extreme poverty.

Location and Geography. Tajikistan borders Afghanistan to the south, China to the east, Kyrgystan to the north, and Uzbekistan to the west and has a land area of 58,809 square miles (143,100 square kilometers). There are numerous glaciers.

The Fergana Valley in the northern region is densely populated. It is separated from the rest of the country by mountains from which the Syrdariya and Amu Darya rivers bring rich soil deposits. In the Soviet era, the Vakhsh River was dammed for irrigation and electric power, and factories were built along its banks. Hot summers and frigid winters characterize the climate. The high mountain ridges protect the Fergana Valley and other lowlands from Arctic air masses, but temperatures drop below freezing more than one-hundred days a year.

The isolation of the Pamiri has kept them close to their ancient traditions. Although the people of the Khujand (Leninobad) region also are isolated, they are more accessible to the other republics. They were the ruling clan in the Soviet era.

Dushanbe (Stalinobod from 1929 to 1961), the capital, is in the west-central region and is the largest city. In 1924, it was chosen to be the capital of the new autonomous republic because of its low population and central location.

Demography. In 2000, the population was estimated to be 6,213,000. In the first years after independence many non-Central Asian peoples emigrated because of the establishment of Tajiki as the official language, dissatisfaction with the standard of living, and fear of political violence.

Linguistic Affiliation. Tajiki, which is closely related to Farsi, is the most widely used language. Villagers who have developed regional dialects have only a rudimentary understanding of the official language. In the Pamiri mountain regions, various languages have kept many characteristics of ancient Iranian. Russian is preferred in government and business transactions, and Uzbeki is used widely in the Khujand region.

Symbolism. The flag has a horizontal red stripe on top, a wider white stripe with a gold crown surmounted by seven stars in the middle, and a

Tajikistan

green stripe at the bottom. Those colors represent sunshine and health, chastity, the journey on the right path of life, peace and stability, agriculture, the mountains, and the spring. The crown shows a royal house, and the stars represent friendship between nationalities, class, unity, and Islam.

HISTORY AND ETHNIC RELATIONS

Emergence of the Nation. Before the Soviet era, the Republic of Tajikistan experienced population changes that brought political and cultural influences from Asia and the Middle East. The conquests of Alexander the Great in the fourth century B.C.E., led to the founding of Khujand and Panjakent. Un-

der the Sassanians (third century C.E.), the Persian language and culture and the Zoroastrian religion spread throughout the region. Conversion to Islam began in the seventh century. By the ninth century, it was the prevalent religion.

After the Uzbeki nomadic tribes conquered Central Asia, the future Tajikistan was divided into three states: the Uzbek–ruled Bukhara Khanate, the Kokand Khanate, in the Fergana Valley, and the kingdom of Afghanistan. These states lasted until the nineteenth century, when they were gradually overtaken by traders and settlers from the Russian Empire. In 1925, Tajikistan became an autonomous republic within Uzbekistan. In 1929, it was detached from Uzbekistan and given full status as a republic.

In 1991, Tajikistan declared independence from the Soviet Union, and Nabiyev was installed as president after a coup. Nationalism and anti-Russian feeling intensified, leading to a state of emergency and the suppression of opposition parties. Civil war broke out in 1992.

National Identity. Although the Soviet Union arbitrarily redefined the nation's borders, many Tajik intellectuals and nationalists believed that communism brought progress to their people and joined the Communist Party. During this period, Islam was the defining cultural element and helped consolidate the clans and reinforce ethnic solidarity.

Although the Soviet era brought stability, education, and an economic infrastructure, social integration among the ethnic groups has never been achieved. Today, people look to their history in developing a national idea, identifying with the Persian-speaking Samanids of Bukhara, who supported the revival of the written Persian language and the cultural ideals of the Zorastrians.

Ethnic Relations. The leaders of clans manipulate events to serve their own ethnoregional views. The Khojand clan in the north is identified with hardline communism; the Kulab clan, also pro-Russian, gained control of the government after a power struggle in 1994; and the Garm clan of the Gorno-Badakhshn region is a stronghold of the Islamic Renaissance movement.

Although Sunni Islam is the most important cultural commonality, it has become a dividing force. The lack of leadership from the Islamic hierarchy allowed fundamentalists to proliferate after independence, and the revival of ancient traditions in the Fergana Valley could lead to conflict with the neighboring countries. However, tribal loyalties, Western cultural influences, and the growth of a free-market economy have militated against such movements. The hardships caused by the civil war and the economic transition have created a negative attitude toward sovereignty and a desire among many people to return to Soviet statehood.

URBANISM, ARCHITECTURE, AND THE USE OF SPACE

Railroads do not link the northwest and the southwest, and only one highway connects Dushanbe in the southwest with Khujand in the northwest. In 1991, the five largest cities accounted for only 17 percent of the total population.

During the Soviet era, a purely functional architectural style developed in the form of centrally planned development projects, government office buildings, and cultural facilities. More recent architecture emphasizes the revival of the Samanid and Timurid periods.

During the Samanid period, baked brick was used in the construction of mosques, minarets, and mausoleums; calligraphic inscriptions were used to decorate walls. In the fourteenth century, the Timurids introduced the use of mosaic tile.

Today, communities are divided into *mahallas*, or neighborhoods, which are governed by responsible and respected elderly persons.

FOOD AND ECONOMY

Food in Daily Life. With over 80 percent of the population living below the poverty line, food is scarce. A basic breakfast consists of tea and bread. A wealthy family may eat butter and jam and perhaps eggs or porridge. Soup often is served for dinner; it may contain a soup bone with meat, carrots, onions, and potatoes. *Osh*, a rice dish made with carrots, onions and meat, is served two or three times a week. At other times pasta, meat- and onion-filled pastries, and tomato and cucumber salads may be served. All meals are accompanied with large rounds of flat bread.

Restaurants usually offer Western and Russian food, and *choihonas* (teahouses) serve traditional foods. Guests often sit on a platform with a low table surrounded by thin mats.

Pork is never eaten. Bread may not be placed upside down; the crumbs are collected and disposed of ceremoniously. Tea is served to the host first to show that it is safe to drink. Islamic law forbids the consumption of alcoholic beverages, but this prohibition often is ignored.

Food Customs at Ceremonial Occasions. On holidays and ceremonial occasions, the table is covered with small plates containing delicacies that represent the pride and wealth of the host. *Osh* usually is served. *Sumalak*, a dish made from the juice of wheat sprouts, is served during the Islamic New Year. The making of *sumalak* is a ceremony, as the women recite poetry, sing, and dance.

Basic Economy. Rural people depend almost entirely on what they produce themselves. Seventy-five percent of households grow food for their own use, and people in the cities plant gardens in vacant lots. Farmers have difficulty gaining access to land,

A man cooking lunch at a café in Dushanbe, Tajikistan. Restaurants in Tajikistan usually offer Western and Russian food.

and farm implements are in disrepair. Millions face hunger as grain production has plummeted.

Most people have no specialized skills; most specialists were from the Russian-speaking sector and left after independence. This resulted in the closing of most factories. The country depends on international assistance for its basic needs. However, the civil war and geographic isolation have hampered international trade.

The government encourages foreign investment, but registration procedures are unclear and the laws are contradictory. In the 1990s, firms from the United States, Israel, Austria, Italy, and Canada constructed factories and mining projects.

Land Tenure and Property. In 1992, legislation was passed that protected personal property and gave citizens the right to own, lease, and inherit land. Agricultural land remains under state ownership but can be leased. Leases can be sold and inherited.

In the Soviet era, the government owned all businesses. After independence, the parliament adopted a privatization law, to transfer ownership of businesses to the public. However, no enterprise is privatized without the approval of a committee or ministry, and officials frequently refuse to cooperate. In 1997, the government created a Higher Eco-

nomic Court, to handle economic disputes. Judges are subject to pressure from the executive branch, local warlords, and criminal syndicates.

Commercial Activities. The dominance of cotton has limited the growth of food products. The country cannot meet basic domestic consumption requirements, especially for meat and dairy products. Although factories produce thread, most cotton is sent abroad for processing. There are small, obsolete factories for weaving and food processing. Drug traffickers control a large proportion of the economic activity.

Major Industries. After the damming of the Vakhsh River in the 1930s, Tajikistan became the third largest producer of hydroelectric power in the world. The dams also enhanced agricultural production through irrigation and provided energy for industries. The aluminum-processing plant at Regar has the largest smelter in the world. Other industries include mining, chemicals, metal processing, and building materials. All industries are constrained by outmoded equipment, low world prices, emigration of the skilled labor force, and civil war.

Trade. Exports to the United States include aluminum, textiles, machinery, and cereals. Imports from the United States include grain, dairy products, eggs, honey, machinery, and preserved foods. An Afghani company opened shops in Dushanbe to sell clothing, textiles, fruits, and nuts. In 1992, 36 percent of imports came from Russia and 21 percent of its exports went to that country. Fruits and vegetables, textiles, and paint were exported in return for automobiles, televisions, and other consumer goods. Tajikistan exports electricity to Uzbekistan in exchange for natural gas. Other trading partners include countries in Central Asia and Europe.

Division of Labor. Jobs are assigned according to education and specialization or they are regionally determined. Political leaders and people in law enforcement usually come from the ruling clan, farmers come from the Garm area, and the Pamiris dominate the fine arts. Technical and professional jobs often go unfilled, but the most pressing economic problem is unemployment, particularly among young people. Approximately three-fourths of graduates of middle schools do not go on to receive higher education and cannot find employment. Wages are so low that even professionals take low-skill jobs to supplement their incomes.

SOCIAL STRATIFICATION

Classes and Castes. Most class variation involves the distribution of wealth. People from different classes attend the same parties and celebrations, but the wealthy usually host a party in a restaurant. Urban residents have the highest social status, especially those who work in the national government and international organizations. Bankers, directors of enterprises, intellectuals, and professionals follow; at the lowest level are workers and peasants. Military and religious leaders have high status, although they may not be wealthy.

Symbols of Social Stratification. People are distinguished more by region than by class. People in the cities wear Western fashions, while villagers dress more traditionally. Traditionally, when a man holds a religious office, or becomes a grandfather, he grows a beard. Before the civil war, a beard was a symbol of political support for the Islamic opposition. People who work for the government often are imitated by lower classes in their speech and mannerisms.

POLITICAL LIFE

Government. After independence, a system based on civil law was developed. The office of president

One of Tajikistan's major exports to the United States is textiles.

was abolished in November 1992 and reestablished in 1994.

The Council of Ministers and the prime minister manage government activities in accordance with the laws and decrees of the president and the Supreme Assembly. The judiciary includes the Supreme Court, the Constitutional Court, the Supreme Economic Court, and the Military Court as well as subordinate courts. Judges are appointed by the president. The office of the procurator general investigates and prosecutes crimes. The president appoints the heads of regional governments.

Leadership and Political Officials. After independence, politics was characterized by a long struggle for political power between cliques that sought Soviet-style dominance and opposition forces seeking to establish a new government. Opposition parties were banned in 1993 and operate from abroad. The Communist Party dominates politics, although the People's Party, the Party of People's Unity, and the Party of Economic and Political Renewal are recognized.

In dealings with government officials, a bribe usually is offered. The payer must be polite or the price may increase, and the size of the bribe is never discussed. A mediator usually conducts the transaction.

Social Problems and Control. Although the constitution guarantees human rights, governance amounts to one-man rule based on emergency executive powers. The result has been imprisonment, exile, and assassination of political figures.

The police and the procurator's office may legally detain a suspect without a warrant. Security officials use beatings to extort confessions. Most citizens fear retaliation by the police. Many judges are poorly trained. Bribery of judges is common, as is political and paramilitary pressure.

The constitution provides for freedom of religion, but the Council of Ministers registers religious communities and monitors the religious establishments to observe political activity.

The way in which people conduct their lives is affected by the opinion of others. When a crime is committed, the authorities are usually contacted and the rule of law is invoked. However, when a social rule is broken, the clan will deny privileges to the offender, who may be beaten or ostracized.

One of the most widespread crimes is the smuggling of narcotics. There has been an increase in violent crime as a result of unregistered weapons remaining in private hands after the civil war. Official corruption and white-collar crime have increased. Wife beating is a common problem, as is the abduction of young women, who are raped or forced to marry.

Military Activity. In 1992, an informal coalition of political and Islamic groups seized power after two months of demonstrations, and a civil war began. By 1993 an estimated 50,000 people had been killed, and 660,000 had been displaced. This was followed by a military rebellion in 1996. In 1997, the peace process again erupted in violence. During this time there was heavy reliance on Russian equipment, arms and air power, and Russians made up almost three-quarters of the officer corps.

By the end of the decade conflict increased between Tajikistan and Uzbekistan, which fears that Islamic radicalism will spill over the border. In 2000, Uzbekistan planted mines along the border. There is military tension with China over the Gorno-Badakhshan region.

SOCIAL WELFARE AND CHANGE PROGRAMS

Poverty has been targeted by humanitarian assistance and income-generating microprojects. With financing from the World Bank, people are implementing programs that provide job opportunities. The Women in Development Bureau and the Reconstruction, Rehabilitation, and Development Program work in the areas most affected by the civil war. Some organizations are active in cultural affairs and welfare, and others represent businesswomen, teachers, and other professionals. Most have limited funding and are dependent on foreign contributions.

NONGOVERNMENTAL ORGANIZATIONS AND OTHER ASSOCIATIONS

Tajikistan is a member of the United Nations, the Organization for Security and Cooperation in Europe, the Confederation of Independent States, and the Economic Cooperation Organization. All state workers belong to the Confederation of Trade Unions, which controls access to pension funds, health care benefits, housing, and other social services. Many United States and multilateral institutions promote business by lowering tariffs and offering loans and consultations.

Some of the most important organizations active in the development of new businesses are the Khujand Association of Business Women, the National Association of Small and Medium-Sized Businesses of Tajikistan, the Dilafruz Association of Businesswomen, and the Tajik Center for Entrepreneurship and Management. Humanitarian organizations include the Aga Khan Foundation, Relief International, Humanitarian Health Assistance, and Medicine sans Frontieres.

GENDER ROLES AND STATUSES

Division of Labor by Gender. Islamic law assigns all authority and power to men, but the constitution gives men and women equal rights. There is no formal discrimination in the employment of women, who work in government, academic institutes, and enterprises. However, only 27 percent of women workers are leaders or directors. In general women earn about two-thirds the salary of men doing the same work. In rural areas, husbands frequently do not allow their wives to study or work outside the home. Men control the political arena and hold the leadership positions in religion.

The Relative Status of Women and Men. While men control leadership and decision making, societal pressure encourages them to make the right decisions. They often seek the advice and council of respected elders in the community. Women raise the

Men wearing traditional Tajikistani clothing sit in front of a Soviet-constructed theater.

children, and are responsible for household management. Women are seen as the compassionate force within the home, while men are the breadwinners and the protectors of their wives, mothers, and daughters. Traditional men believe that women have the right to be taken care of by men.

MARRIAGE, FAMILY, AND KINSHIP

Marriage. Building a family through a marriage sanctified by a religious ceremony is considered one of the most sacred aspects of life. It is also a way to develop a social structure with the blessings and support of the community. Often a matchmaker is involved in choosing a bride. A daughter will move to the home of her husband's family, and her parents want to be sure that she will be provided for. They pay close attention to the groom's education and lifestyle, and the economic situation of his family.

The wedding feast or *tui* involves friends and relatives. The celebration includes music, dancing, and the recitation of poems. A representative of the bride brings an iron tray filled with burning herbs to chase away illness and the evil eye. The wedding bed is prepared ceremoniously for the first conjugal night. The next morning the purity of the bride must be proved to her mother-in-law.

Children may be promised in infancy, or a daughter may marry the son of her uncle. A marriage between the children of brothers is considered economically disadvantageous. Although illegal, polygyny has become common. These marriages are not officially recorded but may account for 20 percent of all marriages. After age 23, a young woman is considered unmarketable for marriage except as a second wife. Divorce is rare, and a first wife usually does not leave when her husband takes a second wife. Marriage to a non-Muslim is frowned upon.

Domestic Unit. Family size has been declining, but large families are still common. Usually the nuclear family includes the parents of the husband. Traditionally, the youngest son, with his wife and children, stays with his parents. The head of the house is the elderly father or the patriarch of the family, and the mother has authority over her daughter-in-law.

Inheritance. Because he takes responsibility for his parents in their old age, the youngest son is traditionally the heir to family property. Parents will try to provide a house for each of their sons to improve their prospects of marrying women from a higher economic class. The personal belongings of the mother-in-law go to the wife of the youngest son.

Kin Groups. A kin group extends far beyond the nuclear family, including the grandchildren of a great-uncle. These ties help develop support throughout the community. The oldest and wisest men are the leaders of the kin group. Most people in a kin group live in close proximity. Many household items are shared with the members of the group.

SOCIALIZATION

Infant Care. Because a baby is thought to be subject to infection, it cannot be shown until forty days after it is born, when a cradle ceremony with a feast may be celebrated. This may include a coming of age ceremony for the mother, who is not considered a woman until she gives birth to a child. Infants and children are not exposed to drafts or cold water to prevent illness. A baby is discouraged from fussing or moving about and is trained to be modest, quiet, and shy. The mother often nurses an infant until the age of two.

Child Rearing and Education. The mother trains children in the traditions of the culture. Daughters are taught how to cook, clean, and sew. A son must prepare himself to take care of his parents in their old age, work in the fields, and provide for a family. Religious training is done through participation in ceremonial events. The most important qualities of a good child are respect for the elderly and obedience to parental authority.

According to Islamic custom, boys must be circumcised between the ages of one and seven. This involves a ceremony, and a religious leader may perform the circumcision.

Soviet social policy created a modern educational system and a high degree of literacy. After independence, the education completion rate fell. The curriculum includes the Tajik language and classical Persian literature. Many people do not consider formal education important. A child's responsibility to the family takes precedence over formal schooling.

Higher Education. The facilities for higher education include Tajikistan State University in Dushanbe, which emphasizes history, philology, and economic planning, and the Polytechnic Institute in Dushanbe, which offers training in energy, architecture, and mechanical engineering. There is a shortage of textbooks in all fields of study.

The education of a son is a priority, but parents train and educate their daughters to make them marketable for marriage. A wealthy family is able to pay for a personal tutor and the contracts and bribes required to get a child into an institute of higher learning.

ETIQUETTE

Hospitality, humility, and respect are considered essential for successful interaction in the culture. The elderly are always given the place of honor. A man must never enter a home where there are only women, and a girl must never be left alone with a boy. At large social gatherings, men and women often are separated. Everyone stands when another guest enters. When shaking hands in greeting, it is a demonstration of good manners and respect to place the left hand over the heart and bow slightly.

Bargaining is accepted in the marketplace. Personal space is not respected in either private or public places. When cultural rules are violated, gossip or ostracism may result.

RELIGION

Religious Beliefs. The Muslim communities are divided into two primary sects: Hanafi Sunnis and Ismaili Shiites. The Hanafi Sunnis are the largest group, with about 90 percent of the Islamic population.

The Zorastrian religion has influenced the traditions and superstitions of the people. Many people believe that supernatural forces affect their daily lives, and they wear amulets to protect themselves from evil. They may seek out fortune-tellers, or consult a witch to ward off illness or cast a spell on a potential lover.

Bukharan and Ashkenazi minorities constitute the tiny Jewish community. Bukharan Jews have lived in the country since the Middle Ages; Ashkenazi Jews arrived after World War II, and worked mainly as engineers and in specialized occupations. In 1989, there were approximately twenty thousand Jews; after the civil war, all but two thousand emigrated. Other religious groups include Russian Orthodox, Seventh Day Adventists, Catholics, and Baptists.

Religious Practitioners. For many people, Islam is more important as a cultural heritage than as a religion. When Islamic practices were curtailed during the Soviet era, folk Islam gained strength. Sufism, which emphasizes the spiritual side of the religion, grew during that period. An individual whose knowledge or personal qualities have made him influential becomes the religious specialist and the most respected member of the community.

Rituals and Holy Places. Religious ceremonies include funerals, periods of fasting, and weekly visits to the local mosque by men. During Ramadan, believers fast during the day. The fast is broken at sunset, when an evening feast begins.

A man stands in the doorway of a yurt in a desolate area in the western Pamirs.

Ismaili Shiites in Badakhshan recite religious poetry called *madah*; these poems are sung in Persian.

Death and the Afterlife. A deceased person is prepared for burial on the day of death. Islamic law forbids autopsies. The body is washed and wrapped in white material and placed in a box. It is carried in a procession to the cemetery, where it is removed from the box and placed in the ground. Mourners wearing traditional clothing wail and lament and sometimes dance in a slow, solemn rhythm. *Osh* is served to guests after three days, and memorials are held after seven days, forty days, six months, and one year.

MEDICINE AND HEALTH CARE

Traditional medical beliefs are based on the works of Avicenna (980–1037), a Persian philosopher and physician. His system of medicine was followed in Central Asia until the fifteenth century, after which many superstitions about cures and diseases became prevalent.

It is believed that burning herbs wards off illness, kills infection and cures a fever while bringing good luck. To stave off stomach ailments, one boils a pomegranate rind and drinks the broth; it is believed that mint cures fever, sore throat, and pleurisy.

Many medical professionals have left the country, and those who have remained lack the skills and technology to administer adequate health care. Medicine is officially socialized, but there is no treatment without money, and the family of a hospitalized patient must provide the patient's food. Hospitals often lack drugs, clean water, and sanitation facilities. As a result, the risk of diseases such as typhoid fever and cholera has increased. Environmental problems are believed to contribute to maternal and child mortality and birth defects.

In the 1980s, the Soviet government encouraged family planning, but its efforts failed because of poor promotion, inadequate birth control, and the traditional desire to have a large family.

SECULAR CELEBRATIONS

In 1999, the government created Consolidation Day (17 June) to celebrate the Saminid era, in an attempt to unify the people and promote the idea of the state. New Year's Day is celebrated on 1 January. International Women's Day is celebrated on 8 March. Navruz (21 March), a Zoroastrian feast is the traditional New Year's celebration. On this day one must think good thoughts, speak good words,

A Tajik girl watching over goats in the Pamir Mountains.

and perform good deeds. International Labor Day is celebrated on 1 May. Victory Day on 10 May celebrates the triumph of the allied forces in World War II. Independence Day is celebrated on 9 September, and Constitution Day on 6 November.

THE ARTS AND HUMANITIES

Support for the Arts. The Soviet Union supported opera, symphony orchestras, literature, painting, and sculpture, all of which attracted support from the public. In 1990, the country had twenty-seven museums, fourteen theaters, and a film studio.

Literature. Tajikistan claims ancient poets Omar Khayyám and Alisher Navoi as part of its literary tradition. Firdowsī is appreciated for creating epic poetry as a way to educate the people.

Under Soviet rule, writing had to correspond closely to official views. The main topics were the civil war in Central Asia, collectivization and industrialization, and Communist Party politics. Very little Persian literature was published in the Cyrillic alphabet.

Sadriddin Aini (1878–1954) witnessed most of the upheavals of the Soviet era, including the fall of the Khanate of Bukhara. Abdulqosim Lohuti (1887–1957) wrote both lyric poetry and ''socialist realist'' verse. Mirzo Tursunzoda (1911–1977) collected Tajik literature and wrote poetry about social change.

Graphic Arts. The great epic of Firdowsī, *Shahname*, influenced all genres, including painting, carpet making, and commemorative and graphic art. The trend in modern art has been to recreate the philosophical thought of the earlier civilization in order to bring about a cultural revival. This theme can be seen in all genres, including stage decoration.

Performing Arts. Women founded a classical national dance that has become a feature of family celebrations and festivities. The dances begin slowly, becoming faster and more intense as they progress. The movements are harmonious and subtle, and the costumes colorful and bright. The performers dance according to the emotions of the moment.

Folk music is characterized by solo playing and singing in small ensembles. The songs are monophonic, with harmony taking the form of a drone. Some of the most commonly used instruments are the *rubob*, a stringed instrument, and the *karnai*, a long trumpet. The *daf* is the most important percussion instrument, and can be traced back to the fourteenth century. Traditionally, the *daf* is one of the few instruments allowed in Muslim ceremonies.

THE STATE OF THE PHYSICAL AND SOCIAL SCIENCES

The social and physical sciences are strong in the areas of environmental studies, telecommunications, social policies of the state, geology, seismology, and archeology. Research involves cooperation among universities, technical institutes, and academies. All programs are government-financed, with contracts from the United Nations, the World Bank, and the International Monetary Fund as well as other international organizations.

BIBLIOGRAPHY

Center for Post-Soviet Studies. *Regionalism in Tajikistan: Its Impact on the Fergana Valley*, 2000.

Central Intelligence Agency. *World Fact Book, Tajikistan*, 2000.

Dodkhoudoeva, L., and M. Sharif. *Firdowsī and His Shahname in Tajik Representational Art*, translated by Iraj Bashiri, 1994.

Eurasianet. *Tajikistan Daily Digest*, 2000.

Grimes, Barbara F., ed. *Ethnologue*, 1996.

Imperial and Asiatic Quarterly Review and Oriental and Colonial Record. *Revelations Regarding Badakhshan*, 1895.

Kayumova, Gulsara. *Forgotten Traditions*, 1993–1999.

Khoshmukhamedov, Sukhrob. *Problems of Poverty and Economic Development during Tranistion in Tajikistan*, 2000.

——. *Revival of Islam and Nationalism in Central Asia: Problems and Prospects*, 2000.

Library of Congress. *Tajikistan, a Country Study*, ed. by Glenn E. Curtis, 1996.

Massoume. *Iranian New Year No Ruz*, 1999.

Nations in Transit. *Tajikistan*, 1998.

Nurjanov, Nizam. *Constructive Customs in the Music and Dance of the Tajiks*, translated by Iraj Bashiri, 1995.

Rahmatullaeva, Sulhiniso. *Architectural Decoration in MaWara' al-Nahr During the Khujandi Era*, translated by Iraj Bashire, 1995.

——. *The Peculiarities of Samanid Decorative Architecture*, translated by Iraj Bashiri, 1994.

Straub, David. *The Culture of Tajikistan*, 1999.

Tadjbakhsh, Shahrbanou. *Women and War in Tajikistan*, 1994.

Tajikistan Privatization Agency. *Current Situation in Privatization: Problems and Recommendations*, 1999.

Union of Councils for Soviet Jews. *Tajikistan*, 1998.

United Nations Security Council. *Report of the Secretary-General of the Situation in Tajikistan*, 2000.

U.S. Bureau of the Census. *Economic Overview of Tajikistan*, 1999.

Van Belle, Jan. *Dafsaz in Tajik Badaxshan; Musical Genre and Rhythmic Pattern*, 1998.

Van den Berg, Gabrielle. *Religious Poetry in Tajik Badakhshan*, 1998.

Ya'qubshah, Yusefshah. *The Image of Funerary Dances on Sughdian Ossuaries*, translated by Iraj Bashiri, 1995.

Yunusova, Eleonora. *The Activities of the Aga Khan Foundation in Tajikistan*, 1998.

—MARILYN F. PETERSEN

TANZANIA

CULTURE NAME

Tanzanian

ORIENTATION

Identification. It is said that the mainland portion of what is now Tanzania was named by a British civil servant in 1920, from the Swahili words *tanga* (sail) and *nyika* (bright arid plain). Thus what was known formerly as German East Africa became Tanganyika Territory. In 1964, Tanganyika was joined with Zanzibar, an offshore archipelago of islands, to form the present United Republic of Tanzania. Because of a unique combination of historic and cultural factors, Tanzanians share strong feelings of national pride and cohesion. This sense of nationalism has served to keep the country at peace for over two decades, while most of its neighbors have been involved intermittently in catastrophically destructive civil and cross-border wars. Tanzanians have been able to resolve most internal problems without resorting to violence because of a shared language, the lack of political or economic dominance by any ethnic group, and the strong leadership provided by Julius Nyerere (1922–1999), the first president of Tanzania. At the same time, however, repressive, corrupting influences emanating from the colonial, socialist, and capitalist eras have fostered among many Tanzanians an attitude of dependency and fatalistic resignation that helps keep the country one of the poorest in the world.

Location and Geography. Covering approximately 365,000 square miles (945,000 square kilometers)—an area about one and one-half times the size of Texas, Tanzania lies on the east coast of Africa, just south of the equator. It shares borders with Kenya, Uganda, the Democratic Republic of the Congo, Rwanda, Burundi, Zambia, Malawi, Mozambique, and the Indian Ocean. Tanzania also shares three great lakes—Victoria, Tanganyika, and Malawi—with its neighbors. The country is comprised of a wide variety of agro-ecological zones: low-lying coastal plains, a dry highland plateau, northern savannas, and cool, well-watered regions in the northwest and south. The 120 ethnic groups that inhabit Tanzania have adapted to a wide range of geophysical and climatic conditions. The specific habits, customs, and life-views of each group have been influenced by tribal traditions and alliances, European invasions, population movements over the centuries, and introduced and endemic diseases. In the late 1990s, the central political administration was moved from Dar es Salaam on the Indian Ocean coast to the more centrally located city of Dodoma, which lies in the middle of the central plateau. Because of Dodoma's dry climate, relative lack of economic development, and small size, however, the port of Dar es Salaam remains the urban center of national importance.

Demography. The current population in Tanzania is approximately 30 million, comprised of indigenous peoples and Pakistani, Indian, Arab, and European subpopulations. There are heavy population concentrations in the urban centers (including Dar es Salaam, Mwanza, Tabora, and Mbeya), in the foothills of Mount Kilimanjaro, and along the coast of Lake Malawi.

Linguistic Affiliation. While each ethnic group speaks its own local language, almost all Tanzanians are also fluent in the national language, Swahili (*Kiswahili* in Swahili), a coastal Bantu language strongly influenced by Arabic. The second official language is English, a vestige of the British colonial period. Most Tanzanians with postsecondary educations speak both official languages fluently in addition to their tribal language. Nyerere encouraged the adoption of Swahili for all Tanzanians in a concerted and successful effort to enable people from different parts of the country to communicate with one another and to encourage them to identify themselves as one people. The use of a single common language has greatly facilitated

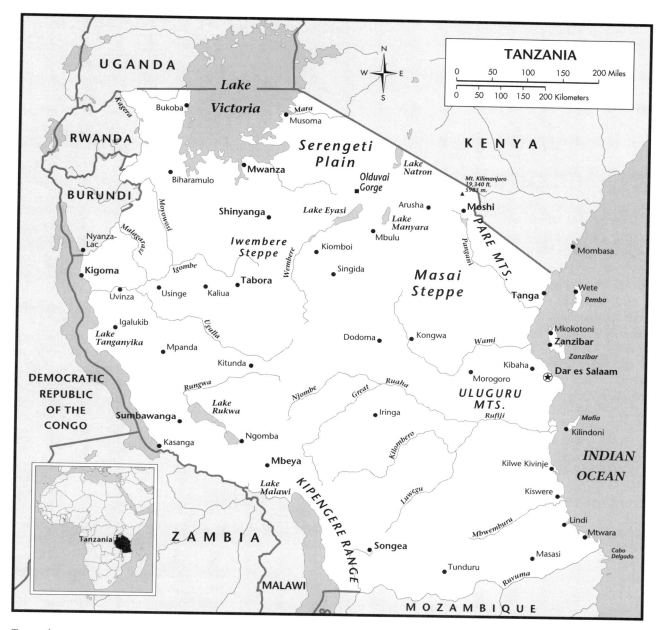

Tanzania

trade, political debate, nationalism, information dissemination, and conflict resolution.

Symbolism. Mount Kilimanjaro, the highest peak in Africa, and the magnificent wild animals (including lions, elephants, rhinoceros, giraffes, leopards, and cheetahs, to name only a few) draw millions of tourists to the country every year. The landscape and animals are valued national treasures, symbolized on coins and as brand names for manufactured products. Severe depredations by poachers from both inside and outside the country, however, continue to threaten the survival of many species.

The torch of freedom (*uhuru*) and the figure of a soldier (representing the sacrifice of veterans and the war dead) are also common symbols throughout the country. Elegant ebony carvings of both representational and modern design, a specialty of the Makonde people of southeast Tanzania, are prized by collectors around the world.

HISTORY AND ETHNIC RELATIONS

Tanzania was cradle to some of the earliest hominids on earth, made famous by the discoveries of Louis and Mary Leakey at Olduvai Gorge. Bantu–

speaking peoples migrated to eastern Africa at the same time that trade between Arabic-speaking peoples and coastal populations was initiated in the first century B.C.E. By the twelfth century, Arab trading posts were well established along the coast and on some islands.

Although Vasco da Gama landed on the East African coast in 1498, it was not until 1506 that the Portuguese fully controlled trade on the Indian Ocean. The Arabs had been trading along the coastline for centuries when Sa'id ibn Suttan moved his capital from Oman to Zanzibar in 1840 to take advantage of the slave markets. During the early nineteenth century, Arab slave and ivory traders began to penetrate deeper into the interior of what was to become Tanzania.

In 1890, Zanzibar became a British protectorate while the mainland became part of German East Africa. The period of German rule was extremely heavy-handed; when the Africans fought back during the Maji-Maji rebellion of 1905, tens of thousands were killed. After the defeat of Germany in World War I (1914–1918), German East Africa was made a League of Nations Mandated Territory, called Tanganyika, controlled by the British. Following World War II, Tanganyika became a United Nations trusteeship of Great Britain. Adhering to a policy of ''indirect rule,'' the British government used indigenous political systems to implement their control, thereby resulting in much less open hostility than occurred during the time of German rule.

Emergence of the Nation. The birth of nationhood may be attributed to the earlier independence of other African nations along with a growing sense of unity and a need to become independent from the British colonial government. Independence was achieved without bloodshed. Julius Nyerere was elected president of the Tanganyika African Association, later renamed the Tanganyika African National Union (TANU), in 1953. African officials elected to TANU in 1958 and 1959 constituted the administration for internal self-government in May 1961. On 9 December 1961, Tanganyika was proclaimed an independent nation. In 1963, Zanzibar was granted independence from Great Britain, and in 1964 an Act of Union was signed between Tanganyika and Zanzibar to form the United Republic of Tanzania.

National Identity. The national identity is influenced by several factors. One of the most important integrating forces is the use of the national lingua franca—Swahili, a language spoken and revered by nearly all Tanzanians. Swahili is a compulsory subject in schools, and some 83 percent of the population are literate. Equally important, of course, is Tanganyika's independence and subsequent unification with Zanzibar to form the United Republic. Perhaps the most important influence on a sense of national identity was the development of Tanzanian socialism. The creation of Nyerere, Tanzanian socialism was codified in the Arusha Declaration of 1967.

Both the symbolic and practical cornerstone of Tanzanian socialism was *ujamaa*, a Swahili word meaning ''family'' or ''familyhood.'' The core structure of *ujamaa* is the traditional extended family and clan structure of most ethnic groups, which provides a framework for mutual assistance and cooperation. It was believed this structure would provide the foundation for socialist production. In practice, the forced resettlement of rural populations into *ujamaa* villages was met with great local opposition, and Tanzanian socialism has largely proven to be an economic failure. The concept of *ujamaa* and mutual assistance, however, did infiltrate the national ethos; they are represented, for example, in elaborate ebony carvings of intertwined figures, standing upon or grasping one another in expression of mutual support and social collectivity.

National resources also contribute to a sense of national identity. For example, at 19,340 feet (5,895 meters), Mount Kilimanjaro is the highest point on the African continent. This beautiful, now quiet volcano is located near Arusha, the major tourist city in the nation. Wildlife safaris to the Serengeti Plain and the world's largest caldera, Ngorongoro Crater, are initiated from this city. Few Tanzanians, however, are wealthy enough to afford such luxuries, and many never see the wildlife Westerners associate so closely with Africa. Finally, Lake Victoria, the second largest freshwater lake in the world and source of the Nile, is an important symbolic and natural resource—although it is shared with Uganda and Kenya.

Ethnic Relations. Within the borders of Tanzania co-exist approximately 120 ethnic groups speaking languages representing all four major African language groups. These include Khoisan, or ''click''-speaking hunter-gatherers, Nilotic-speaking pastoralists (such as the Maasai), Cushitic speakers, and Bantu speakers; the latter predominate in terms of population size. The largest ethnic groups include the Sukuma (over three million), and the Chagga, Haya, and Nyamwezi (over one million each). Despite the tremendous cultural and linguistic diversity among Tanzanians, ethnic groups are united by the use of a common language—Swahili—and a sense of national identity. The growing number of refugees (from neighboring Rwanda, Burundi, and Uganda in particular) do not appear to have caused serious ethnic tensions, but they have become a serious strain on the economy and the local environment.

URBANISM, ARCHITECTURE, AND THE USE OF SPACE

The architecture of urban coastal centers reflects the long, rich history of Tanzania. Ruins of Arab mosques, cemeteries, and house structures can be found at sites such as Kaole, just south of Bagamoyo. Tombs embedded with Chinese ceramics dating to the twelfth century reflect the trade between distant civilizations. Nineteenth-century stone houses on narrow streets characterize Bagamoyo, which was one of the main endpoints of the East African slave trade.

Founded in the 1860s by Sultan Seyyid Majid of Zanzibar, Dar es Salaam, which most likely means ''house of peace or salvation,'' is the main commercial center. Looking out over the Indian Ocean, the sails of dhow fishing vessels are dwarfed by transoceanic cargo ships gliding into the port. Architectural styles reflect Arab, German, and British influence and occupation. Major buildings include elaborate mosques and churches, such as the German-style Lutheran Church. One of the largest public gathering locations in all Tanzanian cities and towns is the marketplace, where meat, produce, housewares, and a variety of miscellaneous items are sold. In addition, football (soccer) stadiums are important areas where people convene in Dar es Salaam and in all large urban areas. One of the most visible monuments in the center of Dar es Salaam is the *Askari*, or ''soldier,'' which was unveiled in 1927 and commemorates the loss of African troops during World War I. The most significant monument is the *Uhuru*, or ''freedom,'' torch commemorating Tanganyika's independence from Great Britain in 1961.

Suburban dwellings, most of which are built along a grid pattern, include the *swahili* house, a rectangular structure made of either stone with a corrugated roof or earth on a wooden frame with a thatch roof. This type of house is found all along the coast.

About 90 percent of Tanzania's people live in rural settings. Each ethnic group has a unique traditional house structure, ranging from the round,

Only about 10 percent of Tanzania's people live in urban areas.

beehive-shaped house of the Haya, who live on the western shore of Lake Victoria, to the long, rectangular houses made of wood and thatch of the Gogo people in central Tanzania. Each ethnic group's traditional house structure has a corresponding cultural logic that determines the use of space. For example, the Haya traditional house is surrounded by a banana plantation; an area in front of the house used for relaxation and food drying is kept free of debris by daily sweeping. The interior of the house is divided into separate use areas, some reserved for men; some for women, children, and cooking; some for animals; and one for honoring ancestors.

Traditional houses are being replaced increasingly by rectangular, ''European''-style houses made from a variety of materials, including brick, wood, earth, and thatch. Unlike in traditional houses, cooking areas have been moved outside.

FOOD AND ECONOMY

Food in Daily Life. For most Tanzanians, including those who live in urban areas, no meal is complete without a preferred staple carbohydrate—corn, rice, cassava, sorghum, or plantains, for example. Plantains are preferred in the northwest, *ugali* (a thick mash of corn or sorghum) in the central and southwestern regions, and rice in the south and along the coast. The staple is accompanied by a fish, beef, goat, chicken, or mutton stew or fried pieces of meat, along with several types of vegetables or condiments, commonly including beans, leafy greens resembling spinach, manioc leaves, chunks of pumpkin, or sweet potatoes. Indian food (such as *chapatis*, a flat bread; *samosas*, vegetable or meat-filled pastries; and *masala*, a spiced rice dish), is widely available in all urban areas.

Breakfast preferences depend on income levels and local tradition: bread, sweet rolls or biscuits (*mandazi*), coffee or tea (sometimes with spices, sugar, and/or milk), buttermilk, and chicken broth are the most common foods. Finger foods sold on the streets include fried plantains and sweet potatoes, charcoal-roasted corn on the cob (with no butter or salt), small bags of peanuts and popcorn, pieces of dried or fried fish, *samosas*, bread, fruit, dates, hard candy, gum, and *mishikaki*, or shish kebabs of beef or goat grilled over a charcoal fire. In local bars selling homemade brews or bottled spirits and pop, it is common to eat roasted meat—beef or goat; often the meat will be flavored with hot peppers, salt, and fresh lime juice.

Food Customs at Ceremonial Occasions. Without exception, all ceremonial occasions demand the preparation of enormous platters of food, such as *pilau*, a spiced rice, potato, and meat dish that caters to local tastes and culinary traditions. It is considered very shameful for guests to leave hungry from a ceremonial meal or dinner party. Except among religions that forbid it, alcohol is also an integral— and sometimes highly symbolic—part of ceremonies. Local beers and spirits derived from bananas, corn, rice, honey, or sorghum are served alone or alongside manufactured alcoholic beverages. Konyagi, a ginlike spirit, is brewed commercially in Tanzania as are a variety of beers and soft drinks. Certain beers produced in neighboring countries— Primus, from Burundi, for example—are also popular.

Basic Economy. Agriculture provides the mainstay of the Tanzanian economy, still employing close to four-fifths of the economically active population. Farmers grow food for subsistence and for sale. Minerals, precious metals, fish, timber, and meat are also important products.

Land Tenure and Property. Although Tanzania is one of the least densely populated countries in eastern Africa, control and access to productive lands has become an increasingly contentious issue. Following independence, national laws were enacted to provide the state with ownership of all lands, granting citizens use rights only through short- and long-term leases. At the local level, however, different sets of traditional tribal laws pertain. Since the demise of socialism and the penetration of the market economy, customary or tribal claims to land have clashed with the national laws. Throughout Tanzanian history, few customary laws have permitted women, who perform the bulk of agricultural labor in the country, to own land. While national laws have been modified to enable women to buy or inherit property, these changes challenge— and are often overruled at the local level—by customary laws. Many analysts believe that enhanced access to and control of land by women would result in significant increases in agricultural production.

Commercial Activities. Agricultural and manufactured products are sold both retail and wholesale. The informal economy in Tanzania is significant, petty hawkers making up the bulk of traders. Second hand clothing, household goods, cloth, and foodstuffs dominate the informal trade. Forced licensing and taxation of small-scale businesspeople has caused some friction between the government and citizens, leading on multiple occasions to demonstrations and local resistance.

Major Industries. Most of the industrial production is geared toward local commodities. Important industries include food processing and the manufacture of textiles, alcoholic beverages, and cigarettes. Other industrial activities include oil refining, and the manufacture of cement, gunnysacks, fertilizer, paper, glass, ceramics, and agricultural implements. Because of the relatively unspoiled game parks and only rare incidents of insecurity, tourism is a growing industry.

Trade. The most important commodities include cotton, fish and shrimp, coffee, cashew nuts, cloves (grown mainly on the offshore islands), tea, beans, precious stones, timber, sisal, sugar, pyrethrum, coconuts, and peanuts. Textiles, clothing, shoes, batteries, paper, and cement are examples of products commonly sold to neighboring countries. Throughout most of the country, however, production and marketing are severely constrained by very poor infrastructure, from roads and railroads to communication and power networks. During the socialist period, many products of inferior quality—from hardware to bicycles—were imported from China and other socialist countries. Today, a much wider variety of higher quality items from many countries around the world are available in shops and markets, although their high prices often prohibit all but the wealthy from purchasing them.

Division of Labor. Customary divisions of labor generally relegate the heaviest physical labors (for example, clearing of fields, cutting trees) to men and lighter tasks to women. Similarly, few women work with machines and other highly valued productive assets. Children as young as three or four learn to help their parents with household and field chores, although girls often shoulder a much greater work burden than boys, a pattern that often repeats itself as children grow into adulthood.

Professional positions are usually occupied by individuals who have had post secondary school education. Successful businesspeople may or may not have formal education, but often have relatives, friends, or patrons who helped finance the establishment of their business.

SOCIAL STRATIFICATION

Classes and Castes. Tanzanian society is divided along many lines. The traditional elite includes descendants of kings and paramount chiefs, who, after independence, lost their traditional titles. The modern elite includes many individuals in the government, successful businesspeople, and highly educated individuals. With the advent of the HIV-AIDS epidemic and the decrease in social services, the poorest families are no longer able to care for all of their children and relatives. Beggars in urban areas and street children have become more visible and are often victims of police brutality.

Symbols of Social Stratification. Economic stratification became more pronounced during the German and British colonial periods, when certain ethnic groups or individuals who were favored for particular physical traits or skills were able to profit from a special relationship with the colonial hierarchy. Ownership of one or more automobiles, expensive hairstyles and Western clothing, large, Western-style houses with modern amenities, perfect command of English and/or other nonnative languages, and frequent travel are all markers of the upper classes. At the other extreme, many of the poorest Tanzanians are severely malnourished and clothed in rags, living constantly on the edge. The market economy has encouraged individual success, proliferation of Western goods, and systemic corruption, causing the gap between the rich and the poor to widen even further.

A Tanzanian fisherman mends his net in Nungwi, Zanzibar, Tanzania. Dried or fried fish is a staple food.

POLITICAL LIFE

Government. Modeled after the government of Great Britain, the United Republic of Tanzania developed a parliamentary system of government soon after independence. The highest positions include the president, prime minister, and chief justice. A term limit for the presidency was set at five years in 1984. In addition, two vice presidents were established to balance power between the mainland and Zanzibar. If the president is from the mainland, for example, one of the vice presidents must be from Zanzibar to help minimize the excessive influence of individuals.

Leadership and Political Officials. Called *Mwalimu* or "respected teacher," Julius Nyerere was president of Tanzania for more than two decades (1964–1985). Widely revered throughout Africa and the world for his honesty, integrity, and wisdom, *Mwalimu* Nyerere was largely responsible for the enduring stability of the new nation. He is perhaps most noted for his attempts to help negotiate an end to violence in other African nations, including South Africa and Burundi. The former president and father of the nation died on October 14, 1999, at the age of 77. The impact of his loss to the nation and the continent is just beginning to be felt.

Nyerere was succeeded by Ali Hassan Mwinyi, a Zanzibari native, who served two terms (1985–1995).

Tanzania implemented a one-party political system for many years after independence. In 1977, the Tanganyika African National Union was merged with representatives of the Zanzibari Afro-Shirazi Party to form the *Chama cha Mapinduzi* (CCM) or the ''Party of Revolution,'' with Nyerere as chairman. The CCM ruled unopposed until the first multiparty elections were held in 1995 when Benjamin William Mkapa was elected president.

Many Tanzanian government officials are noted for their dedication and austerity, although corrupting influences of the market economy have become more prevalent over time. In a general sense, the authority of government officials at all levels is respected by local citizens, regardless of ethnic affiliation. This respect is demonstrated by greeting officials with a shaking of right hands, often while laying the left hand under one's right arm. This is also the proper way to receive a gift. Women and girls often bend down slightly on one knee (a modified curtsy) to greet officials and elders.

Social Problems and Control. Tanzania has been less afflicted by large-scale social problems than its neighbors. Social conflicts due to religious differences have been relatively minor, although recent tensions between Muslims and Christians threaten to destabilize the unity between Zanzibar and the mainland. On 7 August 1998, terrorist bombings of the American Embassies in Dar es Salaam and Nairobi, Kenya, killed 81 people and injured hundreds more. Although the individuals responsible have not yet been identified, it has been suggested that organized Muslim fundamentalists outside of Tanzania may have planned the attack. In addition, there is long-standing tension between Asians (e.g., Indians and Pakistanis), who own most of the businesses in Tanzania, and indigenous Tanzanians.

Theft is a serious social problem, especially in larger cities and towns. If a criminal act is witnessed by the public, often a crowd will punish the thief with a beating. With the exception of the military and police, very few people have access to guns. There is some evidence that Tanzanian ports are assuming an increased role in the shipment of illegal drugs destined for American and European markets. Some use of illegal drugs among the local population has surfaced, but the full extent is unknown.

Military Activity. The Tanzanian People's Defense Force includes the army, navy, and air force; in 1998/1999, military expenditures were about $21 million. The most important military activity occurred in 1978–1979, after Uganda attempted to annex part of the Kagera Region in northwest Tanzania. Under the direction of Idi Amin Dada, Ugandan troops invaded the region, but were repelled by the Tanzanian army—at great expense to the nation. The war is vividly portrayed in local songs, and a monument commemorating the loss of Tanzanians stands in Bukoba, the Kagera Region's administrative headquarters.

SOCIAL WELFARE AND CHANGE PROGRAMS

The dismal economic failure of Nyerere's socialist system in Tanzania opened up the country to the influences of international banking organizations that intervened—ostensibly to save the economy. Loans to rebuild the economy after the socialist period were conditioned upon cost-cutting structural adjustment programs that severely reduced the size of the government as well as the number and quality of social support systems. As a result, many Tanzanians have resorted to basic survival strategies, assisted in many parts of the country by foreign aid programs and church organizations.

NONGOVERNMENTAL ORGANIZATIONS AND OTHER ASSOCIATIONS

With the support of several Scandinavian countries, the high level of development assistance in Tanzania began in the 1970s and 1980s, and spawned a dramatic growth of nongovernmental organizations (NGOs). Many of these NGOs collaborate with international organizations (the United Nations and the International Committee of the Red Cross, for instance) and U.S. and European private voluntary organizations (CARE, Catholic Relief Services, Save the Children, and Doctors without Borders, for example) to implement a wide variety of projects in health, water and sanitation, agriculture, and microenterprise. Dozens of humanitarian aid programs—which rely on the availability and expertise of local NGOs—support an estimated 800,000 refugees currently in Tanzania who have fled conflict and political instability in the Democratic Republic of the Congo, Rwanda, and Burundi. NGO staff positions provide a very important avenue of employment for highly educated Tanzanians who are finding it difficult to secure civil service positions in a government downsized by structural adjustment. Increasingly, NGOs are competing with one another for limited development and relief funds.

Most women in Tanzania have a lower standard of living than men.

GENDER ROLES AND STATUSES

Division of Labor by Gender. In many rural areas of Tanzania, tribal customs advocate a gender division of labor: women and girls take care of the household chores, small children, and livestock, and plant and weed the agricultural fields. Men prepare land for cultivation, care for large livestock, market produce, and make the important financial and political decisions for the family. As girls and women throughout the country have gained access to more formal education, however, they are challenging the customary division of labor. Similarly, where conditions of extreme poverty obligate male heads of households to migrate in search of work, women in these communities have taken over some of the hard physical labor. In many modern households in Tanzania, wives and husbands are challenging and questioning one another's changing roles. The disruptive effects of alcohol abuse, AIDS, and materialism have also placed great strains on relationships within and among families.

The Relative Status of Women and Men. Among the lower socioeconomic strata, with few exceptions, women have a lower standard of living than do men. Generally speaking, boys are valued more than girls. Only women descended from ruling tribal families, successful businesswomen, or women politicians enjoy privileges equal to that of men. Among the formally educated there are conflicts between husbands and wives regarding the appropriate roles and responsibilities of each. When an activity undertaken by a woman becomes successful, her husband or a male relative will try to take control of the activity or the money it has generated, especially in rural areas.

MARRIAGE, FAMILY AND KINSHIP

Traditional systems of social organization are still of great significance in the daily lives of Tanzanians. Kinship systems provide networks for support and become visible during all major life-cycle ceremonies.

Marriage. In general, traditional marriage customs vary by ethnic group. The practice of clan exogamy—or marriage outside of the clan or group—is typical, however, of almost all ethnic groups. Traditional customs call for marriages to be arranged by the parents of the bride and groom, although such arrangements are becoming less common, particularly in urban settings. In patrilineal ethnic groups (those in which descent is traced through males), traditional marriage customs often include the presentation of a dowry or bride price to the wife's family by the bridegroom. The dowry may include livestock, money, clothing, locally brewed beer, and other items. The amount of the dowry is determined through negotiations between the families of the engaged. Preparations for marriage may take months. For those wealthy enough to afford it, marriage may include a separate dowry ceremony and, several months later, a church wedding followed by traditional ceremonies. Although many ethnic groups and Muslims allow polygyny (having more than one wife), the practice is decreasing in popularity, in part because of the influence of Christianity and the expense of maintaining several households.

Domestic Unit. The basic family structure is extended, although the pressures of development have led increasingly to nuclear family units, particularly in urban areas. In most cases, the man is the supreme head of the household in all major decisions. A wife earns respect through her children and, indeed, is not considered to be a fully mature woman until she has given birth to a healthy child. In most ethnic groups, she is recognized by her eldest child's name and called, for example, "Mama

Kyaruzi,'' after her eldest child of the same name. Children eat separately, often with their mothers.

The market economy has placed significant pressure on the stability of the domestic unit and the extended family. Educated, wealthy family members are often called upon to provide resources to other family members for their education and general welfare. In many areas deaths due to AIDS have placed additional strain on the extended family.

Inheritance. Tanzanian laws of inheritance vary according to ethnic group. There are also significant differences between national and customary laws of inheritance, which are settled in the court system. Generally speaking, boys and men are favored over girls and women in customary ethnic laws, in part to keep clan holdings together. (When women in patrilineal ethnic groups marry in Tanzania, they tend to live with or near their husband's family.) Nevertheless, the customary subdivision of land holdings—even just among sons—has already led to serious fragmentation of land in areas where arable land is scarce.

In some groups, widows and divorcees are not adequately provided for through customary laws and must fend for themselves or be cared for by their children. This discrimination is being challenged by lawyers, affected individuals, and organized groups.

Kin Groups. Clanship systems are common in most ethnic groups. While the majority of ethnic groups are patrilineal, recognizing descent through male ancestors, there are some matrilineal groups (where descent is traced through females) in Tanzania: the Kaguru in the east-central part of the country, for example. In practice the structure and function of clans differs significantly from one ethnic group to another. In some cases, they form well-recognized groups while in others they are dispersed. In general, an elder, or group of elders, is often responsible for settling disputes within the clan and for conducting various ceremonies to venerate the ancestors.

SOCIALIZATION

Infant Care. Throughout the nation, children are raised with the strong influence of parents as well as close relatives, friends, and neighbors. Using a *kanga*, a brightly colored rectangular cloth with elaborate designs, mothers carry babies close to their bodies in a sling, even while working in the fields, at home, or in shops. An essential multipurpose item of women's apparel, the *kanga* can also be used as a shawl, head cover, skirt, or dress. Daughters at very young ages begin helping their mothers care for their younger siblings.

Child Rearing and Education. Until the age of five or so for boys, and until adolescence for girls, children have the most contact with their mothers, sisters, and other female relatives. Both boys and girls attend school if the parents can afford the fees. If there is not sufficient money for both to attend, the boy is usually favored, and the girl remains home to help her mother until she gets married and moves away. Students are supposed to respect their teachers, and corporal punishment is still practiced in Tanzanian schools.

Among some ethnic groups, puberty ceremonies for boys and girls are practiced. Marking the transition to adulthood, such elaborate ceremonies may involve circumcision of boys and several kinds of genital surgery on girls. Unsterile surgical procedures performed on girls may have severe health consequences.

Development programs have recently begun to make more use of the performing arts to deliver public service messages (about AIDS prevention and the importance of breast-feeding, for example).

Higher Education. As fees for schooling have risen, families are finding it difficult to send their children to secondary schools. The wealthy send their older children to boarding schools both within and outside the country, although they worry that the materialistic influences of the modern world and lack of family supervision will negatively influence their children.

ETIQUETTE

Tanzanians are proud of their disciplined upbringing. The ability to keep control of one's temper and emotions in public is highly valued. Young men and women in rural areas are not supposed to show mutual affection in public in daylight, although this rule is often broken in urban centers. Boys and men, however, are commonly seen in public holding hands as a sign of friendship or camradarie. In many rural areas, women are not supposed to smoke, talk in a raised voice, or cross their legs while sitting or standing. Traditionally, elders are honored and respected by the rest of the community, although youth are increasingly challenging such customs as arranged marriages.

Although the use of silverware is increasing, traditional customs prescribe eating all foods, in-

Three women relax in Tanzania. Successful women from ruling families enjoy many of the same privileges as men.

cluding rice and meat sauces, with the right hand. Children who attempt to eat with their left hands are disciplined appropriately at very early ages. This custom is related to the perceived symbolic purity of the right hand, compared to the left hand which is often used for cleaning after using the toilet.

RELIGION

Religious Beliefs. Religious freedom is a virtue that has contributed to Tanzania's long, relatively peaceful history since the nation's independence. All

religious holidays receive equal public recognition. Many world religions played a part in the nation's history.

Islam began to be practiced as early as the twelfth century when Arab traders set up posts along the coast and on Zanzibar and Pemba Islands. The influence of Islam and Arab culture is strongly reflected in the Swahili language. Arab traders brought their religion to some interior settlements, but their proselytizing did not match the impact of the Christian missionaries during the German and British colonial periods in the first half of the twentieth century. Long before the influence of Islam or Christianity, indigenous belief systems shaped the cosmology of each ethnic group. The influence of these beliefs is still very strong; they are often practiced alone or alongside of the major religions.

Virtually 100 percent of the people in Zanzibar are Muslim; on the mainland, about 40 percent are Christian, 35 percent are Muslim, and 20 percent follow indigenous religions. Among Asian minorities, the Hindu, Sikh, and Buddhist faiths are practiced. Christian sects include Catholics, Lutherans, Anglicans, Baptists, Presbyterians, and Orthodox. Both Christian and Islamic religions provide access to educational opportunities and often to some of the best medical care. Wealthy Muslims make their pilgrimage to Mecca, but this is a minority of the overall Muslim population.

Religious holidays include Christmas (25 December); and Good Friday, Easter Monday, Idd-ul-Fitr, Islamic New Year, and the Prophet's Birthday (all of which fall on different dates every year). Idd-ul-Fitr is a Muslim festival and public holiday that is celebrated on the sighting of the new moon at the end of the calendar year. The exact date varies according to the new moon's position.

Religious Practitioners. Native Tanzanians preside in all positions in major religions. In indigenous belief systems among some ethnic groups, certain people assume religious functions that often include healing. These indigenous religious practitioners differ significantly according to ethnic group. For example, in some cases among the Haya, the *omufumu* ("healer" in the Kihaya language) uses herbs and spiritual power to diagnose and cure illnesses. Acting spirit mediums, the *Wazee* ("Ancestors" or "Old ones" in Swahili) "come in to the *omufumu's* head" and speak through him or her. The *Wazee* have the ability to travel great distances and bring about a therapeutic cure, such as the recovery of stolen objects or even success in soccer matches. In some parts of the country, an indigenous religious practitioner, such as the *omufumu* in parts of northwest Tanzania, will survey a "football" or soccer field before a match to remove any object placed there to influence the course of the game by an opposing team.

Death and the Afterlife. Death is a part of daily life for Tanzanians. In regions hit hard by the AIDS epidemic, families are often not able to afford the time or resources to follow traditional mourning and burial customs, which differ by religion and ethnic group.

Among many ethnic groups, the "ancestors" assume an extremely important role. Ancestor spirits are remembered through various rituals and are believed to exert significant influence on daily life. For example, at drinking occasions, some people pour a small libation of beer onto the ground in respect of the ancestors. In other cases, a small vessel of beer is left in a special location as an offering to the ancestors. In still other cases, sacrifices of a chicken or goat, for example, are made to the ancestors in ceremonies that vary according to ethnicity.

MEDICINE AND HEALTH CARE

Similar to people in other poor, tropical nations, Tanzanians are challenged by numerous health problems, including parasitic, intestinal, nutritional, venereal, and respiratory diseases. In the mid-1990s, life expectancy at birth was forty-two years for men and forty-five years for women.

Malaria, commonly referred to as the "Tanzanian flu," remains the leading cause of illness and death. Transmitted by the Anopheles mosquito, the parasite *Plasmodium falciparum* has become increasingly resistant to treatment. It is especially severe among children, the elderly, and people with compromised immune systems. Other common diseases include schistosomiasis, sleeping sickness, poliomyelitis, tuberculosis, and pneumonia. There are an estimated 150,000 cases of leprosy.

Public health problems are further exacerbated by the nation's poverty, which makes proper food storage and the provision of adequate waste disposal and safe drinking water difficult to achieve. Nevertheless, technologically appropriate solutions to these and other public health problems, such as improved ventilated pit latrines, are increasingly being implemented.

The Arusha Declaration for Tanzanian Socialism prepared the way to extend primary health care to the rural population. This led to the establishment of some three thousand rural health facilities and seventeen regional government hospitals. Although community health workers have been somewhat successful in alleviating health problems, the lack of medical supplies, facilities, and physicians continues to make confronting illness a primary survival issue.

The third poorest nation in the world, Tanzania has decreased its spending on health care significantly in recent years, largely because of higher levels of foreign debt repayment. The measles im-

Manufacturing sisal at the Amboni Estate in Tanzania.

munization rate, for example, has fallen from an estimated 86 percent to about 60 percent in recent years.

Health problems have been exacerbated by AIDS which emerged in Tanzania in the mid-1980s. In 1998, the estimated HIV seroprevalence rate was 49.5 percent among high-risk populations in major cities and 13.7 percent among low-risk groups. In rural areas, the estimated HIV seroprevalence was 34.3 percent and 16.6 percent among high- and low-risk groups, respectively. AIDS has placed tremendous strain on an already challenged health care system; in some parts of the country, underlying HIV infection may be the primary reason for hospital admissions.

It has been projected that Tanzania's economy will decrease 15–25 percent by 2010 as a result of the AIDS epidemic. The number of children orphaned due to deaths associated with AIDS is very high. The staggering number of AIDS-related deaths among young adults has placed serious strain on the extended family and the elderly, who are often called upon to care for the resulting orphans.

All Tanzanian ethnic groups have highly so-phisticated indigenous healing systems that help circumvent the inadequate supply of Western drugs and biomedical health services. The *mganga*, or "traditional healer" in Swahili, plays an extremely important role in health care, and treats chronic and infectious illnesses. In many cases, herbal remedies have established pharmaceutical efficacy. In addi-tion, the *mganga* may also be called upon to treat social and "psychological" problems as well as problems not commonly perceived as "illnesses" by people outside of Africa, such as difficulty finding a lover, difficulty conceiving a child, or lack of success in business affairs. Predicated on a holistic approach to health, traditional healers treat body, mind, and spirit as an integrated system, often in the commu-nal sense of the "social body." Faith healing among some Christian sects as well as various Islamic heal-ing practices are also common.

Although infectious diseases are the most visi-ble health problems in Tanzania, social problems related to alcohol abuse are increasingly being rec-ognized. Low-alcohol-content (approximately 5 percent) beers made from grains, fruits, palm sap, and honey play a vital role in almost all ethnic groups. Traditional beers are commonly consumed as part of nearly all ceremonies as well as being used in offerings to ancestors. While still used for these purposes, beer and other alcoholic beverages began to be sold as commodities in the postcolonial period, contributing greatly to social problems.

SECULAR CELEBRATIONS

The major state holidays are New Year's Day (1 January); Zanzibar Revolution Day (12 January); Union Day (26 April); International Workers' Day (1 May); Saba Saba (7 July, commemorating the establishment of TANU); Peasants' Day (8 August); and Independence Day (9 December). All holidays are celebrated with large amounts of food and alco-hol at the appropriate time. The middle classes use days off to take outings with their families, watch soccer matches, or travel to see relatives.

THE ARTS AND HUMANITIES

The formal development of the humanities and arts in Tanzania has been constrained by a severe lack of government and private funding. Tourists, the local elite, and expatriates support most of the fine art-ists, foremost among them the Makonde ebony carvers. While not as well known as Congolese or Senegalese singers, Tanzanian musicians are begin-ning to make their mark in the music world.

Literature. Because most of the local languages in Tanzania are expressed orally rather than in writ-ten form, little other than dictionaries and collec-tions of idioms and fables collected by missionaries or local and foreign researchers have been pub-lished. The national language of Kiswahili, how-ever, has a very old and rich history. Stories, novels, poetry, epics, textbooks, children's litera-ture, and historical treatises are widely available around the country.

Graphic Arts. A thriving tourist industry sup-ports thousands of artisans in Tanzania, the most famous being the Makonde carvers of ebony from the extreme southeast corner of the country. Other tourist items include paintings and greeting cards of landscapes, local peoples, and wildlife; intricately woven baskets; soapstone, ceramic, and malachite carvings and jewelry; woven or printed wall hang-ings, and decorative and functional objects formed from banana leaves and coconut hulls.

Performance Arts. Individual tribes are character-ized in part by distinctive theatrical performances, dances, and music—for example, the Snake Dance performed by the Sukuma people in the north-cen-tral part of the country. Some of these groups are invited to Dar es Salaam to honor the president, ministers, or foreign dignitaries. Occasionally, pri-vate or state funding is found to send them to for-eign capitals to perform. While not as well known as Congolese, Malian, or Senegalese singers, Tanza-nian musicians are beginning to make their mark in the music world. Theater, dance, and music skits on radio and television are also being used by churches, state agencies, and development organizations to relay public service messages about such topics as AIDS, corruption, vaccination campaigns, and con-traception.

THE STATE OF THE PHYSICAL AND SOCIAL SCIENCES

Lack of funding has also constrained the develop-ment of the physical and social sciences in Tanzania. Like Makerere University in Uganda, the University of Dar es Salaam was once one of the leading centers of critical socialist thought in Africa. While it still attracts some of the world's foremost thinkers and philosophers, the university currently suffers from substandard infrastructure, an inadequate library, and poorly paid but internationally recognized pro-fessors.

BIBLIOGRAPHY

Airhihenbuwa, Collins O. "Perspectives on AIDS in Africa: Strategies for Prevention and Control." *AIDS Education and Prevention* 1 (1): 57–69, 1989.

Beidelman, T. O. *The Matrilineal Peoples of Eastern Tanzania*, 1967.

Briggs, Philip. *Guide to Tanzania*, 1967.

Carlson, Robert G. "Haya Worldview and Ethos: An Ethnography of Alcohol Production and Consumption in Bukoba, Tanzania." Ph.D. thesis, University of Illinois at Urbana-Champaign, 1989.

———. "Symbolic Mediation and Commoditization: A Critical Examination of Alcohol Use among the Haya of Bukoba, Tanzania." *Medical Anthropology* 15: 41–62, 1992.

Coulson, Andrew, ed. *African Socialism in Practice: The Tanzanian Experience*, 1979.

Duggan, William Redman and John R. Civille. *Tanzania and Nyerere: A Study of Ujamaa and Nationhood*, 1976.

Eriksen, Stein Sundstol. "Between a Rock and a Hard Place: Development Planning in Tanzanian Local Governments." *Third World Planning Review* 19 (3): 251–269, 1997.

Fivawo, Margaret. "Community Response to Malaria: Muhezae District, Tanzania 1983–1984: A Study in Cultural Adaptation." *Journal of the Steward Anthropological Society* 21: 1–151, 1993.

Goodall, Jane. *The Chimpanzees of Gombe: Patterns of Behavior*, 1986.

Heggenhougen, Kris, Patrick Vaughan, Eustace P. Y. Muhondwa, and J. Rutabanzibwa-Ngaiza. *Community Health Workers: The Tanzanian Experience*, 1987.

Heilman, Bruce. "Who Are the Indigenous Tanzanians? Competing Conceptions of Tanzanian Citizenship in the Business Community." *Africa Today* 45 (3–4): 369–387, 1998.

Kimambo, I. N., and A. J. Temu, eds. *A History of Tanzania*, 1969.

Knappert, Jan. *East Africa: Kenya, Tanzania & Uganda*, 1987.

Lugalla, Joe L. P. "Development, Change, and Poverty in the Informal Sector during the Era of Structural Adjustments in Tanzania." *Canadian Journal of African Studies* 31: 3, 1997.

Kwesigabo, G., J. Z. J. Killewo, A. Sandstrom, S. Winani, F. S. Mhalu, G. Biberfeld, and S. Wali. "Prevalence of HIV Infection among Hospital Patients in North West Tanzania." *AIDS CARE* 11 (1): 87–93, 1999.

Mlozi, Malongo. "Urban Agriculture: Ethnicity, Cattle Raising, and Some Environmental Implications in the City of Dar es Salaam, Tanzania." *African Studies Review* 40 (3): 1–28, 1997.

Ofcansky, Thomas P., and Rodger Yeager, eds. *Historical Dictionary of Tanzania*, 1997.

Nyoni, Timothy S. "Foreign Aid and Economic Performance in Tanzania." *World Development* 26 (7): 1235–1240, 1998.

Phillipson, D. W. *The Later Prehistory of Eastern and Southern Africa*, 1977.

Polomé, Edgar, and C. P. Hill, eds. *Language in Tanzania*, 1980.

Pratt, Marion. "Useful Disasters: The Complexity of Response to Stress in Tropical Lake Ecosystems." *Anthropologica* (special issue), winter 1998.

Rugumamu, Severine M. *Lethal Aid: The Illusion of Socialism and Self-Reliance in Tanzania*, 1997.

Rutayuga, John B. K. "Assistance to AIDS Orphans within the Family/Kinship System and Local Institutions: A Program for East Africa." *AIDS Education and Prevention*, fall 1992 supplement, 57–68.

Seppala, Pekka, and Bertha Koda. *The Making of a Periphery: Economic Development and Cultural Encounters in Southern Tanzania*, 1998.

Sofoluwe, G. O., R. Schram, and D. A. Ogunmekan. *Principles and Practice of Public Health in Africa*, vol. 1, 1996.

Tripp, Aili Mari. *Changing the Rules: The Politics of Liberalization and the Urban Informal Economy in Tanzania*, 1997.

Waters, Tony. "Beyond Structural Adjustment: State and Market in a Rural Tanzanian Village." *African Studies Review* 40 (2): 59–89, 1997.

Yeager, Rodger. *Tanzania: An African Experiment*, 2nd ed., 1989.

Yudkin, John S. "Tanzania: Still Optimistic after All These Years?" *Lancet* 353: 1519–1521, 1999.

—ROBERT G. CARLSON
AND MARION PRATT

THAILAND

CULTURE NAME
Thai

ALTERNATIVE NAMES
Siamese, Central Tai

ORIENTATION

Identification. The name ''Thailand'' is associated with the dominant ethnic group, Thai. Thailand was never under European colonial rule. It was an absolute monarchy until 1932, when it became a constitutional monarchy. In 1939 the country's name was changed from Siam to Thailand. Military dictators ruled the nation until the early 1970s; the military remained a powerful force in national politics into the early 1990s. Since that time, its role has diminished, and a new constitution was adopted in 1997. The military governments after World War II promoted rapid economic development and attempted to assimilate ethnic minorities. Rapid economic growth continued until the late 1990s, when the economic boom of the early part of the decade came to an abrupt end. As part of a trend toward devolution of authority, the democratic governments of the 1990s adopted more liberal policies with regard to ethnic minorities. However, members of ethnic minorities continue to face many problems in regard to political rights and economic security.

Location and Geography. The Kingdom of Thailand has an area of 198,114 square miles (513,115 square kilometers). The country is commonly divided into four main regions and borders Burma, Laos, Cambodia, and Malaysia. The northern region is hilly, with much of its population concentrated in upland valleys and the flood plains of rivers; the dominant geographic feature is the Khorat Plateau. The southern region is a narrow isthmus with hills running down the center.

The Thai (also known as the Central Tai) live mainly in the central region, with closely related groups of Tai-speaking peoples occupying most of the remainder of the nation. Smaller ethnic groups are scattered throughout the country, especially in the north and the northeast. Bangkok has been the capital since the late eighteenth century, when it replaced the earlier capital of Ayutthaya, which was sacked by Burmese invaders in 1767. With a population of almost 10 million, Bangkok is the most important city politically and economically. About twenty smaller regional cities have populations of two hundred to three hundred thousand.

Demography. The population estimate for 2000 is approximately 62 million. There are about 75 ethnic groups, and approximately 84 percent of the population is Thai, including people from other Tai-speaking ethnic groups; the Thai, constitute about 36 percent of the population. The Thai-Lao account for about 32 percent of the population; their territory formerly was part of the Lao kingdom. The Lanna Thai account for about 8 percent of the national population. The Pak Thai constitute about 8 percent of the population. Other major ethnic groups include Chinese (about 12 percent of the population), Malay-speaking Muslims (about 3 percent), and Khmer (about 2 percent). The majority of the Chinese live in central Thailand, especially in urban areas. The Malay-speaking Muslims live near to the border with Malaysia. The Khmer live near the Cambodian border.

There are communities of Korean- and Urdu-speaking peoples in Bangkok, and there is a small population of Mon in central Thailand. Various peoples, commonly designated as hill tribes, inhabit the northern mountain areas. The total hill tribe population is about 500,000, with the Karen being the largest group (about 350,000). There are several settlements of Palaung (about 5,000 people) near the Burmese border and several communities of Khmu, Phai, Mal, and Mlabri (about 75,000 in

Thailand

total) near the border with Laos. Several small ethnic groups in the northeast speak Mon-Khmer languages; the largest of these groups is the Kuy (about 235,000). These groups have been largely assimilated into the Tai-speaking populations. In the south, there are small groups of so-called sea gypsies and aboriginal Malays (about 6,000 people). In the isolated inland areas of the south, there are about 1,000 forest-dwelling peoples referred to as Orang Asli in Malay.

Linguistic Affiliation. Thai is a Daic language in the southwestern Tai group. Other Thai groups speak related southern and east-central Thai languages. Large-scale Chinese migration took place in the nineteenth century. Most of the Chinese in the country speak dialects of Min Nan Chinese. There are twenty-four Mon-Khmer-speaking groups, whose languages can be subdivided into four groups: Monic, Aslian, Eastern Mon-Khmer, and Northern Mon-Khmer.

Seven Austronesian languages are spoken, all of which belong to the Malayic Malayo-Polynesian group. The main Austronesian language is Pattani Malay, which is spoken by about 2.5 million people in the southern region. The Pattani Malay, Malay, and Kedah Malay populations live in an area associated with the kingdom of Patani, which fell under Thai control in 1786.

The nineteen Tibeto-Burman-speaking groups include nine groups that speak Karen languages. Three Hmong-Mien languages are spoken in the north. Various migrant communities speak Korean, Japanese, Tamil, and Urdu.

Thai is the national language and the medium for education and mass communication. It is widely used by speakers of other Tai languages and is a second language for most other people.

Symbolism. The most potent national symbols are the king and images associated with Buddhism. The monarch serves as the most important symbol of national identity and unity. Images of the king appear frequently in public and in people's homes, and he is featured often on television and the other mass media. His image is on all banknotes and coins. Showing disrespect for the king is a serious legal offense. Images of the Buddha and shrines are found in public buildings (including schools and government offices) and homes as well as temples. The promotion of Buddhism as a symbol of national identity has met with opposition from the Muslim minority.

HISTORY AND ETHNIC RELATIONS

Emergence of the Nation. Evidence of an agricultural civilization with metallurgical capabilities has been found in northeastern Thailand; the earliest bronze artifacts date back to approximately 3,000 years ago. In the eighth and ninth centuries C.E., Mon states influenced by Indian civilization occupied portions of central and northern Thailand, where they were referred to as Dvaravati. In Thailand, the most important Mon center was Nakhon Pathom west of Bangkok. Mon influence declined in the eleventh century as the Khmer invaded the area from the east. The Khmer occupied not only the Mon areas, but part of northeastern Thailand.

As early as the fifth or sixth century, Tai-speaking peoples began migrating from northern Vietnam and southern Yunnan into areas adjacent to the Mekong River. The Tai in northern Thailand came into contact with the Mon, who converted many of them to Theravada Buddhism. Tai-speaking peoples gradually migrated southward and by the early eleventh century had moved into Mon territory. Tai peoples living in central Thailand came under Khmer control as the Khmer empire expanded. The Khmer referred to the Tai as Siams. The Tai in the vicinity of Sukhothai revolted against the Khmer rulers in 1238 and established a kingdom that promoted a writing system that formed the basis of modern Thai. In the wake of declining Khmer power, the center of Thai power shifted south to Ayutthaya, which was founded in 1351. In the north, the kingdom of Lan Na was founded in 1259. The Lao kingdom of Lan Sang was founded in 1353 and came to include much of northeastern Thailand.

The founder of the kingdom of Ayutthaya, Rama Thibodi, promoted Theravada Buddhism and compiled a legal code based on Hindu sources and Thai customs that remained important until the late nineteenth century. Ayutthaya pushed into Khmer territory and sacked the capital of Angkor. Both Ayutthaya and Lan Na became strong and prosperous states during the latter part of the fifteenth century. After the deaths of the two rulers both kingdoms degenerated. Lan Na witnessed several civil wars and came under Burmese control. Ayutthaya was attacked by the Khmer and Burmese in the sixteenth century briefly came under Burmese control. In 1585, Ayutthaya began a period of rejuvenation. Starting with the establishment of a Portuguese embassy in 1511, there was a growing European presence in Ayutthaya. In 1765, the kingdom was invaded again by the Burmese; in 1767, the Burmese captured and destroyed the city.

Thailand is a major producer of agricultural products.

After pushing the Burmese back, the Thai established a new capital at Thonburi. Chao Phraya Chakkri became king in 1782 and founded Bangkok. The third Chakkri ruler established a system of royal titles, and named himself Rama III. During his reign, treaties were signed with the United States and some European countries, and Christian missionaries were allowed into the kingdom. Rama V (ruled 1868–1910) successfully resisted European colonization and introduced modernizing reforms.

A group of young Thais who had studied abroad staged a coup in 1932 and transformed the country into a constitutional monarchy. From 1935 to 1945, a military dictator, Phibun Songkhram (commonly known as Phibun), ruled the country. Phibun changed the name of Siam to Thailand. In 1945, there was a brief return to civilian government, and the country's name was changed back to Siam. Between 1947 and 1973, the country was ruled by military dictators. After the brutal suppression of antigovernment demonstrators in 1973, military was forced out of office, but in 1976 it again seized power.

In 1980, a more moderate government headed by Prem Tinsulanonda assumed office. Prem is credited with achieving political and economic stability. This period saw the end of a communist insurgency in the countryside, a gradual transition to democracy and economic growth. An election was held in 1988, but the elected government was overthrown by a military coup in 1991. Those who staged the coup appointed a civilian prime minister and a cabinet of civilian technocrats. A new constitution was passed in 1991, and an election was held in 1992, returning the country to civilian rule. After a subsequent period of political and economic instability a far more democratically reformist constitution was promulgated in late 1997. National elections were held under this constitution in early 2001.

National Identity. In the twentieth century, the culture of the Central Tai came to dominate the national culture. The military dictator, Phibun, passed a number of Cultural Mandates that promoted a centralized national culture and identity. Other mandates promoted the use of the national dress and the national language.

The term "Thai identity" was coined in the late 1950s. The Ministry of Education played an important role in expanding the national culture. The military government that seized power in 1976 viewed the national identity as something that had to be defended against Western cultural influences. A National Culture Commission was established in 1979 to coordinate efforts to defend the national culture. Those efforts were closely linked to national security and occurred against the backdrop of a communist insurgency that involved members of ethnic minorities.

In the 1980s, a revival of regional and local identities began, especially in the northern and northeastern regions where there was a resurgence of local foods, celebrations, and styles of traditional dress. Democratic reforms and moves to devolve power since the early 1990s have allowed this process to accelerate. The sense of national identity is no longer viewed as precluding local and regional identities.

Ethnic Relations. Thailand often is portrayed as a culturally homogeneous country, but there are approximately seventy-five distinct ethnolinguistic groups. The Central Tai is the dominant ethnic group and accounts for 36 percent of the population. The Thai-Lao and Lanna Tai, who together account for about 40 percent of the population, were not assimilated into the national culture until the twentieth century.

There have been Chinese in Thailand for centuries. In the nineteenth century, their numbers more than doubled until they constituted about 10 percent of the population. Along with Westerners, the Chinese merchant class dominated the economy in the nineteenth century, especially with the exportation of rice. In the early twentieth century, the Chinese established their own educational institutions, resulting in antipathy toward them under the nationalistic Phibun regime, which blamed the Chinese for the country's economic problems. In 1938, the Phibun government taxed the Chinese, limited the use of their language in schools, and closed most Chinese-language newspapers. Chinese immigration came to a virtual halt. While anti-Chinese sentiment remained strong, by the 1970s virtually all the Chinese had Thai citizenship. With the growth of a more open and democratic society in the 1990s, the Chinese began to express their culture openly.

Since it came under Thai control in 1786, the Malay Muslim population has posed difficulties for the Thai state. This region has mounted numerous rebellions against central authority over the past two centuries. In 1948, the Phibun regime banned Malay and Islamic organizations, sparking a rebellion that was violently crushed. Education has been a point of conflict between Thai authorities and the Malay Muslims since the government introduced compulsory education in 1921. As a result, many Muslims sent their children to Malaysia and other Muslim countries to be educated. In the 1960s, returning students joined various independence movements. Guerrilla activities in the south reached their height between 1970 and 1975. Counterinsurgency operations failed to end support for the separatists. In the late 1980s, the national political environment changed with greater sensitivity to the Muslim religion and culture. The civilian government elected in 1992 initiated reforms to ease tension in the Muslim south.

The Thai government treats the Khmer as part of a generic northeastern Thai ethnic category called Isan. Efforts to assimilate the Khmer into the national culture in the 1960s and 1970s were spurred by concern over their support for communist insurgents in the northeast. In the 1990s there was a cultural revival among the Khmer in the northeast that included the formation of dance and music groups to promote Khmer culture. The hill tribes in the north, with the exception of the Lawa and Karen, are relatively recent immigrants. The majority of hill tribe members did not become citizens until recently and lacked political rights. These hill tribes have faced economic difficulties related to their lack of land rights. The authorities generally have viewed them as primitive peoples. In the 1980s and 1990s, there was encroachment on their land by lowlanders, who believed that their presence was a key factor in environmental degradation in highland areas. Proponents of rights for the tribes in the 1990s led to the granting of citizenship for the hill tribes. Nevertheless, there are many conflicts, including those involving corrupt government officials and business interests that are attempting to exploit highland resources.

URBANISM, ARCHITECTURE, AND THE USE OF SPACE

A little over 20 percent of the population lives in urban areas, including about ten million residents of the Bangkok metropolitan area. Over the last decade, regional towns have undergone rapid growth. Thailand's second largest city, with a population of around 300,000, is Nakon Ratchasima (also known as Korat). Until the early 1980s it was a relatively small country town, but industrialization has resulted in rapid growth. Other northeastern towns also have experienced rapid growth. Economic growth in the southern region (in part associated with the rubber, shrimp, and fishing industries) in the late 1980s and 1990s also resulted in sharp population increases.

In the past, towns were centers of government administration, Chinese business, and the Buddhist religion, featuring government offices and housing for civil servants, Chinese shops and storage facilities, and Buddhist temples. The growth of the cities is reflected in a lack of planning and growing congestion, but the core features of the cities have not changed. Wood has given way to cement as the main building material, and new forms of architecture include high-rise buildings for offices and residences, and air-conditioned shopping malls. The 1980s witnessed the emergence of suburban housing developments and shopping complexes. There are few public parks, and urban planning is focused on building roads. The use of waterways for transportation is waning.

Modern government offices are highly standardized to instill a sense of national unity, and even Buddhist religious architecture has become uniform. There were regional differences in houses, especially in rural areas, but these differences are disappearing. The traditional house is raised on a framework of wooden posts to provide protection from floods and intruders, and to create a multipurpose space under the house. This underpart served as a place for women to work, a place to sleep during the hot season, a storage space, and a place to keep domestic animals. The size and complexity of the raised area varied with the wealth and status of the family. The house is constructed of prefabricated units that fit together with wooden pegs. The raised part can be divided into an open area and an enclosed area. The open area includes a front veranda that is partially shaded. People usually sit on mats on the veranda. The rear of the house has an open balcony for washing clothes, doing laundry, and performing other domestic chores. This area also is used to lie out food to dry, and for spinning and sewing. The interior includes a living room and a sleeping space. People usually sit on mats, and there is little furniture. There may be a cooking area in the living room in smaller houses, but usually there is a separate space for cooking. In larger houses, there is a separate kitchen and granary.

FOOD AND ECONOMY

Food in Daily Life. Rice is the staple food at every meal for most people. All food is brought to the table at once rather than being served in courses. A meal will include rice, dishes with gravy, side dishes, soup, and a salad. Whereas in central and southern Thailand polished white rice is eaten, in the north and northeast people eat glutinous or sticky rice. Fish and shellfish are popular. Curries are eaten throughout the country, but there are regional varieties. Northern and northeastern food is similar to that of Laos and consists of more meat, including meat served as sausages, or as *larb* (a salad is usually made of raw meat). Chinese food has influenced the national cuisine, especially in regard to noodle dishes. Sweets are eaten as snacks. A popular snack is green papaya salad. In the past, there were marked differences between the food of the common people and that of the nobility. Women in noble households were proficient at decorative carving of vegetables and fruits. In recent decades, this practice has become popular among the middle classes. Whereas commercial alcoholic drinks are common throughout the country, noncommercial alcohol made from rice is still drunk.

Basic Economy. Thailand has a relatively diversified export-oriented economy that grew rapidly in the latter part of the twentieth century until the crash of 1997. Manufacturing and tourism led its growth, but agriculture continued to play an important role—employing over 60 percent of the workforce. The country remains a major producer and exporter of agricultural products, including rice, rubber, and tapioca. Thailand's currency is called the *baht*.

People observe a vegetarian festival. Eighty-five percent of Thais are Theravada Buddhists.

Land Tenure and Property. In the past, all land was owned by the crown in theory, but individuals had use rights if they paid taxes on the land that they occupied. Because of the low population density, land ownership in rural areas was not a matter of concern. Large agricultural estates were rare. The commercial buying and selling of land took place in the main towns, where commercial life was concentrated. Urban land was often owned by Sino-Thais. In the 1950s, around 90 percent of farmers owned their own land. Strong nationalist sentiments influenced the 1941 Land Act, which made it difficult for non-Thais to own land. Informal means of circumventing these restrictions on land ownership helped create a chaotic system in which the title to land was difficult to determine. Under the new constitution and after the economic collapse, efforts were made to reform land ownership. Many restrictions on foreign ownership were removed, including those placed on Thais married to foreigners and their children.

Commercial Activities. Thailand has a large and relatively modern commercial sector, with domestic and foreign commercial banks and a stock exchange. The 1997 crash resulted in the closing of some financial institutions and the consolidation of others. Producers of agricultural products traditionally sold their products through local brokers, but since the 1980s there has been a trend toward contract production for sale to large firms. Most towns and cities have small shops and traditional markets with small-scale traders who sell food, consumer goods, hardware, and medicines. In larger towns, shopping malls and large multipurpose stores have assumed a significant role since the 1980s.

Major Industries. Major manufacturing industries include motor vehicle and motorcycle units and parts, computers, garments and footwear, electrical appliances, and plastic products. There also are large commercial farming and fishing industries. The main agricultural products are rice, tapioca, sugar, corn, and fruits. In addition to fresh and frozen agricultural products, food-processing industries produce canned and frozen products. Thailand has a large fishing industry and is a major producer of farmed shrimp. The country is one of the world's leading producers of rubber. Cement production is also important. Mining has declined in recent decades. The country produces some oil and natural gas but must import gas and petroleum products to meet domestic demand. It is a major center for cutting and selling gems. Thailand is Southeast Asia's top tourist destination, and that industry is the largest earner of foreign exchange.

Japan is the largest foreign investor; the United States is also a major source of foreign investment.

Trade. In the mid-1990s, exports were equal in value to about 25 percent of the gross domestic product. The most important exports are computers, integrated circuits, and related parts. Other major exports include electric appliances, garments, rubber, plastic products, shrimp, footwear, gems and jewelry, rice, and canned seafood. Major imports include nonelectric machinery and parts, electrical machinery and parts, chemicals, vehicle parts, iron and steel, crude oil, computers and parts, metal products, and integrated circuits. After the 1997 crash, the manufacturing sector declined sharply, especially the sectors that were highly dependent on imports, such as garments. By late 1998, however, manufacturing had begun to recover. The United States and Japan are the largest markets for the country's exports and suppliers of its imports. Neighboring countries, especially China, have become increasingly trading important partners.

Division of Labor. The division of labor in the agricultural sector is based on gender, with little specialization by ethnicity. Ethnic Chinese have long played a major role in commerce and industry, but few jobs or professions are the monopoly of a single ethnic group. Traditional craft specialization is sometimes associated with specific villages or communities. Primarily ethnic minorities produce hand-woven textiles. Positions in modern technical professions such as medicine and engineering are related to education and specialized training and thus exclude members of the smaller rural ethnic minorities.

SOCIAL STRATIFICATION

Classes and Castes. In the nineteenth and early twentieth centuries, the social strata included an elite of Thai nobles, a small commercial middle class of Chinese and Europeans, and a lower class that included mostly rural farmers. With the development of a more modern economy, the structure of social stratification has become more complex. Noble birth continues to have some bearing on status, but the modern class system is based primarily on wealth. There now is a much larger middle class. The growth of towns and cities has given rise to a class of urban poor in addition to the traditional rural poor. In addition to regional differences in income, there are regional differences in income distribution: Income is distributed more equally in the center and south than it is in the north and northeast.

POLITICAL LIFE

Government. Thailand is a constitutional monarchy. The king, on occasion, involves himself directly in political affairs when national stability is threatened. Between 1932 and the early 1990s, the government was dominated by a military and bureaucratic elite. After the elections in 1992, political parties opposed to military intervention formed a coalition government, with the leader of the Democratic Party becoming prime minister. Parliament was dissolved in 1995, and the Democratic Party lost to the Thai Nation Party. That government lasted only until 1996, when a former military commander formed a coalition government and became prime minister. The economic collapse of 1997 led to the fall of that government and the eventual assumption of power by a coalition government led by the Democratic Party with its leader, Chuan Leekpai, as prime minister.

A reformist constitution was promulgated in late 1997 with the intent to enhance participatory democracy. Attention has focused on eliminating corrupt political practices and devolving power. Devolution has included holding elections to a wider range of local offices. A National Counter-Corruption Commission was formed and given some powers to monitor electoral fraud.

Thailand held its first national election under the 1997 constitution in January 2001. The newly formed Thai Rak Thai party led by Taksin Shinawatra, one of Thailand's richest men, defeated the Democrats and won 248 of parliament's 500 seats. The Thai Rak Thai party was joined by the smaller New Aspiration party to form a coalition with 325 seats. Voters appeared to have grown tired of Chuan Leekpai's six-party coalition government. They were lured by Taksin Shinawatra's promises of expansive economic policies, including his pledge to give every one of the country's 70,000 villages 1 million *baht* (about U.S. $25,000) in development funds. The election was fraught with corruption, which the National Counter-Corruption Commission proved to have only limited influence in curtailing.

Leadership and Political Officials. The kings of the Chakri dynasty had numerous wives and concubines, resulting in the existence of a large number of nobles who were related to the king; in addition, some commoners were given high positions. In central Thailand, administration was directly linked to Bangkok and the king; in more remote areas, there were vassal princes. Below the government officials were freemen and slaves. The system was stratified, but social mobility was possible.

People harvesting garlic in Mae Hong Song. Thailand has a largely export-based economy.

After the advent of military rule and the end of the absolute monarchy in the 1930s, the state remained highly centralized, with government officials being appointed by those in power in Bangkok, primarily military officers and former officers. In the new system, power was gained through factional struggles within the military. The 1980s and 1990s witnessed the rise of "money politics," as wealthy civilians came to play an increasingly important role in politics. Increased democratization in the 1990s resulted in a much more complex political system. While wealth continued to be important, many major political figures claimed to speak for the poor, especially the rural poor. The newly formed government of Taksin Shinawatra is seen by some observers as a return to the old politics of wealth and patronage. Taksin is one of the country's wealthiest men and his party is held together mainly through an extensive patronage network. In the 1990s, a growing number of Muslims from the south attained elected political positions. Similar political gains have not occurred among the smaller ethnic minorities.

Social Problems and Control. The government generally respects the human rights of its citizens. There is considerable freedom of expression, but there are laws that prohibit criticism of the royal family, threats to national security, and speech that

may incite disturbances or insult Buddhism. The constitution makes it unlawful for the government to censor, ban, license, or restrict print or broadcast media except in times of crisis. While newspapers and periodicals practice some self-censorship, media criticism of public figures, political parties, and the government is widespread. Freedom of religion is protected by law.

Thailand is no longer a significant producer of narcotics, but is still an important route for international heroin trafficking, and domestic consumption of narcotics has increased dramatically. Social problems associated with narcotics trafficking include money laundering, police and military corruption, and criminal activity by addicts. Political corruption is widely viewed as a serious problem.

The National Police Department, with over one-hundred thousand personnel, includes the provincial police, metropolitan police, Border Patrol Police (BPP), and Central Investigation Bureau. The police force has a culture of corruption, and demands for bribes are routine. This corruption encourages illegal activities such as income tax evasion, gambling, drug trafficking, smuggling, and prostitution. Enforcement of the law is lax, but in many respects the police force works well. In general, the law requires that police officers making an arrest have warrants, and it is rare for police officers to be tried for extrajudicial killings or the use of excessive force.

The legal system blends principles of traditional Thai and Western laws. In the Muslim south, Koranic law is applied. There are courts of the first instance, courts of appeal, and the supreme court, along with a separate military court. A constitutional court was created in 1998 to interpret the new constitution. There is no trial by jury. Career civil service judges preside over the courts, and supreme court judges are appointed by the king. Judicial appointments and structures are not subject to parliamentary review, and judges have a reputation for venality.

Conditions in prisons are poor because of overcrowding, and medical care in prisons does not meet minimum international standards. Access to prisons is not restricted, and the government permits visits by human rights monitors and the Thai International Red Cross.

Military Activity. Since 1992, the military's role in political affairs has been reduced. Responsibility for internal security and law enforcement is mainly in the hands of the police. The military's primary role is national defense, especially problems along the border with Burma. However, former senior military officers still account for a large percentage of the elected members of parliament and the military retains wide-ranging legal powers.

The total strength of the military is around 270,000, including the army, navy, and the air force. In addition, there are about five-hundred thousand reserves. Male citizens between ages twenty-one and thirty are required to serve in the military for two years. Under civilian governments, defense spending has declined. Although there is a domestic arms industry, most military supplies are provided by the United States and Great Britain.

NONGOVERNMENTAL ORGANIZATIONS AND OTHER ASSOCIATIONS

Local, domestic, and international nongovernmental organizations are active in social welfare, heath, political reform, the status of women, the environment, religion, and business. Those organizations face few restrictions and are relatively free to publish their findings. Government officials generally are cooperative with such organizations.

There continues to be discrimination against the hill tribes, which are widely viewed as being involved in narcotics trafficking. The Tribal Assembly of Thailand has lobbied the government for greater transparency in decisions affecting those tribes, especially in regard to the granting of citizenship and land issues.

GENDER ROLES AND STATUSES

Division of Labor by Gender. Both men and women do agricultural work, and although some tasks tend to be assigned mainly to men or women, that division of labor is not adhered to rigidly. There is also some variation in the allotment of tasks according to region. In the north it is traditional for men alone to prepare land for planting and sow seeds, but in central Thailand, women sometimes perform those tasks. Women transplant rice seedlings in all areas, but sometimes men do that job as well. Harvesting is done by both men and women. Domestic work is done mostly by women. Weaving usually is done by women. Pottery, basketry, plaiting, making lacquerware, and making umbrellas can be done by men or women. Small-scale market selling and itinerant trading are conducted by both men and women. Transportation of goods and people by animal, carts, boats, and motor vehicles is done mainly by men. Religious specialists and traditional healers generally are male. Traditional theatrical and musical performances involve both genders. In the modern professions, women work mainly in teaching and nursing.

The Relative Status of Women and Men. Gender inequality is manifest in violence against women, societal discrimination against women, and trafficking in women for prostitution. Efforts to improve the status of women have increased, and the 1997 constitution provides women with equal rights and protections, although, some inequalities in the law remain. Domestic abuse affects women in all social classes. Specific laws concerning domestic violence have not been enacted, and the rules of evidence make prosecuting such cases difficult. Domestic violence often is not reported, since many victims and the police view it as a private matter. Sexual harassment in the workplace was made illegal in 1998, but only in the private sector, and no cases have been prosecuted. Thailand serves as a source, place of transit, and destination for trafficking in women for prostitution. Prosecutions for such activities are rare.

Women constitute forty-four percent of the labor force. Laws require employers to give women equal wages and benefits for equal work, and there are no legal restrictions on women owning and managing businesses. An increasing number of women hold professional positions, and women's

A Thai woman hand spinning wool. Though women have made many advancements in Thailand, they are concentrated in lower-paying jobs.

access to higher education has grown. More than half the university graduates are women. Police and military academies do not accept female students. There is still a gap between the average salaries of men and women since women are concentrated in lower-paying jobs. There are no legal restrictions on women's participation in politics. While there have been improvements at the lower levels, women remain underrepresented in national politics.

MARRIAGE, FAMILY, AND KINSHIP

Marriage. In general, individuals find their own marriage partners, although the choice of a spouse may be influenced by one's family among the wealthy. The value of goods provided to the couple and elaborateness of the wedding ceremony vary with the wealth of the families of the couple. Polygyny was common among the elite in the past but is now rare, although wealthy and powerful men often have a de facto second wife known as a minor wife. Divorce is not difficult and is usually a matter of a couple ceasing to live together and dividing their property.

Domestic Unit. The ideal is for a married couple to establish its own household as soon as possible. However, especially among poorer couples, resi-

dence with the parents of the husband or wife is common. The nuclear family is the core of the domestic unit, but it often includes members of the extended family. Including unmarried siblings, widowed parents, and more distant unmarried or widowed male and female relatives. The husband is nominally the head of the household, but the wife has considerable authority. Female members of the household are responsible for most domestic chores.

Inheritance. Property generally is divided equally among the children after the parents die. However, it is common practice for one child, usually the youngest daughter, to assume primary responsibility for looking after the parents in their old age, and this person inherits the family home.

Kin Groups. The Central Tai reckon descent bilaterally. Various forms of kin groups may be formed. The most common type is formed by siblings, married children, and sometimes more distant relatives living in a multihousehold compound. Members of these groups may share domestic and other tasks. Sometimes larger kin groups encompass several compounds to form a hamlet cluster. In some instances, a hamlet cluster forms around a wealthy and powerful individual.

Footwear is removed when attending a ceremony near the Mae Nam Noi River, Thailand.

SOCIALIZATION

Infant Care. Adults take a great deal of interest in children, including the children of other people. A mother keeps her baby with her whenever she leaves the house. Young children are pampered and given considerable freedom of movement and are allowed to handle almost anything that catches their attention. Weaning usually takes place when a child is two or three years old.

Child Rearing and Education. Children in rural areas grow up surrounded by the implements that they will later use and see adults performing domestic, agricultural, and artisanal tasks. In the past, young boys attended school in a nearby Buddhist monastery, where they would be taught to read and write. Girl's education took place mainly at home as they learned to perform domestic tasks. After 1932, the government secularized the public school system by replacing monks with trained teachers. In the late 1990s, eighty-eight percent of children of primary school age were enrolled in schools and ninety-three percent of the adult population was literate. However, the economic crisis of the late 1990s resulted in an increase in the number of children leaving school. The government raised compulsory education requirements from six to nine years in 1999 and is attempting to improve educational standards.

Higher Education. Institutes of higher education include comprehensive universities, technical institutes, and religious universities. Traditionally, education was handled by religious bodies. In the nineteenth and early twentieth centuries, a growing number of people went abroad for higher education. The first university, Chulalongkorn University, was founded in 1916. That university initially served mainly to train civil servants. An Arts and Crafts School was established in the 1920s. After the 1932 revolution, Thammasat University was founded. This was an open university with unrestricted admission and an emphasis on legal training. Chulalongkorn University tended to cater to the elite, while Thammasat University was more populist. In 1942, the Arts and Crafts School attained the status of a university, Silpakorn University. All three of these institutes are in Bangkok. A fourth institute was added in 1948 after the reorganization of advanced military education at the Chulalongkorn Royal Military Academy, whose graduates came to dominate not only the military but also politics. Admission to the military academy was restricted to "native Thai" until 1973, mainly to keep out ethnic Chinese.

In 1960, less than one percent of the population had completed a higher education. In the 1960s and 1970s, new universities were founded, including the first regional university and a number of technical colleges and teacher training colleges.

Buddhist educational bodies continue to play a role in education, offering not only religious education but a wide range of other subjects. There are also private universities which tend to focus on business education. There has been a boom in the growth of private higher educational institutes since the early 1990s, and plans are in place for the privatization of public universities.

ETIQUETTE

The Thai and other Buddhists follow the widespread Buddhist custom of not touching a person on the head, which is considered the highest part of the body. Patting a child on the head is thought to be dangerous to the well-being of the child. A person should not point the feet at anyone or at an image of Buddha. Footwear is removed when entering temple complexes, and it is polite to remove footwear when entering a house. Buddhist monks are not supposed to come into contact with women. It is traditional to greet a person with a prayerlike gesture called a *wai*. It is considered improper to lose one's temper or show too much emotion in public.

RELIGION

Religious Beliefs. About eighty-five percent of the people are Theravada Buddhists, and the monarch must be a Buddhist. Virtually all Tai-speaking peoples are Theravada Buddhists, as are members of many of the ethnic minorities. The Buddhism of Central Tais often is referred to as Lankavamsa, reflecting its origins in Sri Lanka. Thai Buddhism, however, is a syncretic religion that borrows from earlier animistic beliefs, Hinduism, and Christianity. A noticeable manifestation of animism in Thai Buddhism are the spirit houses associated with almost all houses and buildings. These usually are small model houses placed on a pedestal, that serve as a home for the spirits associated with the site. These houses are decorated and presented with daily offerings. Many large trees also are considered to serve as the home of spirits and are decorated and given offerings.

Approximately ten percent of the population is Muslim, primarily ethnic Malays in the south. Although Christian missionaries have been active in the country since the nineteenth century, only about one percent of the population is Christian. The Christian population consists primarily of non-Tai ethnic minorities in the north and ethnic Vietnamese and Chinese. There are small numbers of animists, Confucianists, Taoists, Mahayana Buddhists, and Hindus.

Religious Practitioners. The majority of religious practitioners are Buddhist monks. Most young men become Buddhist novices and go to live in a monastery. While most young men remain at the monastery for a short time before returning to the secular life, some become ordained monks. A person who wants to become a monk is expected to be free of debt and certain diseases, have the permission of his parents or spouse, to agree to follow the disciplinary rules of the monkhood, and not become involved in secular life. Monks are expected to lead a life of aestheticism but commonly perform important functions in the community, especially as counselors. A variety of religious practitioners are associated with the animistic side of the religious beliefs of most Buddhists, including exorcists, spirit doctors, astrologers, and diviners.

Rituals and Holy Places. A number of Buddhist religious festivals are held throughout of the country, and there are local events related to particular places and individuals. The Buddhist religious calendar begins with Songkran, in mid-April when images of Buddha are washed and monks are offered special alms. This celebration is marked by dousing people with water and festive behavior including dancing, singing, and theatrical performances. Visakha Puja in May celebrates Buddha's birth, enlightenment, and entrance into nirvana. The day includes the ceremonial watering of the banyan trees that represent the tree under which Buddha sat when he attained enlightenment. Asanha Puja celebrates a sermon given by Buddha. Khao Phansaa in July marks the start of the three-month lenten period. It is at this time that young males become novices. Lent is considered a period of spiritual retreat for monks, who are expected to remain in the monasteries. Thawt Kathin from mid-October to mid-November marks the end of lent. During this period, monastic robes and other paraphernalia are given to monks. In some communities, there is a celebration to produce new garments for monks and images of Buddha in which members of the community work together to produce the cloth in a single day. Magha Puja in February commemorates Buddha's preaching to enlightened monks. It culminates in a candlelit procession at temples.

Death and the Afterlife. Buddhists believe that those who die are reborn in a form that is appropriate to the amount of merit they accumulated while alive. The cycle of death and rebirth is believed to continue as long as ignorance and craving remain. The cycle can be broken only through enhanced personal wisdom and the elimination of desire. Funerals involve either burial or cremation. The funeral ceremony includes a procession of monks and mourners who accompany the coffin to the cemetery or crematorium, with monks chanting and performing rites along the way. Funerals for monks tend to be very elaborate, while people who have died a violent death are buried quickly, with very little ceremony, since their spirits are believed to linger after death as malevolent ghosts.

MEDICINE AND HEALTH CARE

The health of the population has improved over the last few decades, with increased life expectancy and lower rates of major diseases. An exception to this trend is the AIDS epidemic. The spread of AIDS is related to both sexual practices and narcotics use. The government has devoted substantial resources toward AIDS education and awareness programs and AIDS-related research.

Buddhist monks walk down a street in Thailand. Most young men become Buddhist novices.

The health infrastructure includes facilities and programs provided by the public sector, nongovernmental organizations, and the private sector. The majority of health resources are concentrated in urban areas, where a marked difference in access to health facilities depends on wealth. Private sector facilities exist almost exclusively in urban areas. Public health facilities in rural areas include district hospitals and community health centers. In small towns and villages, health care is provided mainly by village health communicators and village health volunteers who receive little training. In urban areas, private hospitals are becoming important providers for the wealthy and the middle class. In the 1990s, the government adopted a policy of self-reliance that included greater attention to classical traditional medicine and herbal folk medicine. A government sponsored, codified system of traditional medicine draws on elements of Chinese and Indian medicine. Many unlicensed healers practice folk medicine.

SECULAR CELEBRATIONS

Most celebrations are associated with the Buddhism or other religions. The most important secular holidays are related to the monarchy. Celebrations include Chakkri Day (6 April), commemorating Rama I, the founder of the Chakri Dynasty; Coronation Day (5 May), commemorating the coronation of the current king; the Royal Plowing Ceremony (second week in May), an ancient ritual held near the Royal Palace in Bangkok to start the rice-planting season; the queen's birthday (12 August); Chulalongkorn Day (23 October), held in commemoration of King Chulalongkorn (Rama V); and the current king's birthday (5 December). Other secular celebrations include Constitution Day (10 December) and New Year's Day.

THE ARTS AND HUMANITIES

Support for the Arts. Support for the arts comes from both the public and private sectors. The Department of Fine Arts underwrites programs throughout the country, and there a national theater. Silpakorn University is the main public educational institution for the arts, and there is a national College of Dance and Music. The Foundation for the Promotion of Supplementary Occupational and Supplementary Techniques, founded in 1976, is associated with the queen and runs projects throughout the country for traditional artisans. There are private art galleries, mainly in Bangkok, and private auction houses have become a commercial outlet for paintings.

Muslim fishing village on Koh Pannyi in southern Thailand.

Literature. Written literature dates back to the Sukhothai period (1250–1350), and earlier traditions. The oldest known poem, the *Suphasit Phra Ruong*, was written in the late 1200s. The Traiphum Khatha (1345), is a treatise on Buddhist cosmology.

Poetry from the fifteenth century includes epics, poems based on the life of Buddha, and the *Lilit Phra Lo*, Thailand's first love story. The reign of King Narai in the seventeenth century is considered the golden age of Thai literature. Most of this literary work consisted of epics and love stories written in poetic form. Cau Fa Thamathibet (1715–1755) is famous for so-called boat songs, which abound in mythical allusions. The eighteenth century saw the emergence of a new genre of poetry, *lakhon*. This was a type of theatrical poetry in which players positioned themselves before an audience and recited texts derived from the *Ramakien* (the Thai version of the *Ramayana*), *Inau* (an epic of Javanese origin), and *Anirut* tales (which were more local in origin).

King Rama II was a poet, and during his reign epics expanded in scale and in performance. There were some famous female poets during this period, including Khun Phum, who wrote a poetic eulogy for Rama IV. During the reign of King Chulalongkorn (Rama V), prose writing emerged and poetry became more realistic. Prince Damrong Ratchanuphap (1861–1947) compiled histories of Thai literature.

The modern period has witnessed the emergence of many new forms of poetry and popular fiction. This fiction is realistic, often portraying the lives of common people and the underclass in the face of adversity. While most of the stories are set in central Thailand, there has also been regional literature, such as the novels of Khamphun Bunthami, which are set in the northeast. Since the 1970s a good deal of fiction and poetry has focused on social criticism.

Graphic Arts. The graphic arts include art forms associated with Buddhist temples such as sculpture in wood, stucco, and stone; mural painting; and bronze castings of images of Buddha. Other forms of graphic arts include lacquerware, mother-of-pearl inlay, gold work, nielloware, silverware, wood carving, ceramics, basketry and plaiting, weaving, and painting on paper or canvas.

In the Ayutthaya and Bangkok periods, there were distinct royal and common textile traditions. The nobility imported textiles from China, India, and Persia and received special textiles as tribute from neighboring regions. Commoners produced clothing for themselves until the nineteenth century, when imported cloth became widely available. There are still distinct regional styles of weaving that include the production of special hand-woven cloth for sale to elite customers in urban areas. There are many local, regional, and national weaving competitions and fairs to promote textiles.

Painting traditionally was done in tempera in the form of murals on temple walls as well as on cloth and paper. While Buddhist themes were predominant, temple murals often included depictions of secular objects. Artistic styles initially were influenced by Sri Lanka and southern India and later were influenced by China and the West. King Chulalongkorn (Rama V) imported Western works of art and Western artists. Especially noteworthy were realistic painted portraits and statues of prominent individuals. In 1910, King Vajiravudh tried to revive traditional art, by creating the Department of Fine Arts in 1912 and the Arts and Crafts School in 1913. The Italian-born sculpture Corrado Feroci became a central figure in creating modern art in Thailand. As director of the Fine Arts University (Silpakorn University), he is widely viewed as the father of modern art in the country. The university held the first National Exhibition of Art in 1949, and this annual event became central in defining the state of contemporary art.

Much of the work of modern Thai artists has mirrored trends in Europe and North America, but many artists have mixed imported styles with subjects associated with the national culture.

Performance Arts. Classical dance developed from folk dances and incorporated elaborate Indian hand gestures and arm and leg movements, probably through the Mon and Khmer cultures. Various forms of dance, including masked dance dramas, are shown on Sukhôtâi stone inscriptions. The eighteenth century is considered the golden age of classical dance and dance drama. Although many musicians and dancers of Ayutthaya were taken by force to the Burmese royal court in 1767, those who remained behind taught their traditions to others during the early Bangkok period.

Classical dance and drama were attacked by leftists in the 1970s because of their links to the aristocracy. When the military returned to power in 1976, it promoted classical art forms. In 1977, the military regime held a national festival of dance and drama that included classical forms and patriotic plays glorifying the country's past. In recent years, classical, folk, and modern dance and drama have been popular. Folk dances are regional in character. Each dance style is accompanied by different musical instruments. Dances in the central region have been influenced by courtly traditions. Southern dances have been influenced by Sri Lankan and southern Indian styles. Individual dance styles are associated with many of the ethnic minorities.

THE STATE OF THE PHYSICAL AND SOCIAL SCIENCES

Teaching, training, research, and publishing in the physical and social sciences are well developed. Most higher educational institutions offer courses in the physical and social sciences, and a number of government and government-sponsored institutes and agencies work in those fields. However, an insufficient number of university students are pursuing degrees in the physical sciences. The government has launched a number of programs to encourage students to go into the physical sciences.

BIBLIOGRAPHY

Askew, Mark. *Interpreting Bangkok: The Urban Question in Thai Studies*, 1994.

Che Man, W. K. *Muslim Separatism: The Moros of Southern Philippines and the Malays of Southern Thailand*, 1990.

Cohen, Erik. *Thai Society in Comparative Perspective*, 1991.

———. *Thai Tourism: Hill Tribes, Islands and Open-Ended Prostitution*, 1996.

Gittinger, Mattiebelle, and H. Leedom, Jr. *Textiles and the Tai Experience in Southeast Asia*, 1992.

Howard, Michael C., Wattana Wattanapun, and Alec Gordon. eds. *Traditional T'ai Arts in Contemporary Perspective*, 1998.

Kemp, Jeremy. *Hua Kok: Social Organization in North-Central Thailand*, 1992.

Keyes, Charles F. *Thailand: Buddhist Kingdom as a Modern Nation-State*, 1987.

Kingshill, Konrad. *Ku Daeng: Thirty Years Later: A Village Study in Northern Thailand 1954–1984*, 1991.

Komin, Suntaree. *Psychology of the Thai People: Values and Behavior Patterns*, 1990.

Lewis, Paul, and Elaine Lewis. *Peoples of the Golden Triangle: Six Tribes in Thailand*, 1984.

Phanichphant, Vithi, Songsak Prangwatthanakun, and Patricia Naenna. *Thai Textiles: Threads of a Cultural Heritage*, 1994.

Phillips, Herbert. *The Integrative Art of Modern Thailand*, 1992.

Pitsuwan, Surin. *Islam and Malay Nationalism: A Case Study of the Malay-Muslims of Southern Thailand*, 1985.

Poshyananda, Apinan. *Modern Art in Thailand: Nineteenth and Twentieth Centuries*, 1992.

Reynolds, Craig J., ed. *National Identity and Its Defenders: Thailand, 1939–1989*, 1991.

Rhum, Michael R. *The Ancestral Lords: Gender, Descent, and Spirits in a Northern Thai Village*, 1994,

Rigg, Jonathan, ed. *Counting the Costs: Economic Growth and Environmental Change in Thailand*, 1995.

Rutnin, Mattani Mojdara. *Dance, Drama, and Theatre in Thailand: The Process of Development and Modernization*, 1993.

Skinner, G. William. *Chinese Society in Thailand: An Analytical History*, 1957.

Tambiah, Stanley Jeyaraja. *The Buddhist Saints of the Forest and the Cult of Amulets*, 1984.

Taylor, J. L. *Forest Monks and the Nation–State: An Anthropological and Historical Study in Northeastern Thailand*, 1993.

Walker, Anthony R., ed. *The Highland Heritage: Collected Essays on Upland North Thailand*, 1992.

Warren, William, and Luca Invernizzi Tettoni. *Arts and Crafts of Thailand*, 1994.

Wenk, Klaus. *Thai Literature: An Introduction*, 1995.

Wyatt, David. *Thailand: A Short History*, 1984.

—MICHAEL C. HOWARD

TOBAGO SEE TRINIDAD AND TOBAGO

TOGO

CULTURE NAME

Togolese; Togolais

ALTERNATIVE NAMES

Republic of Togo; Republique du Togo; Togoland

ORIENTATION

Identification. Togo is named after the town of Togoville, where Gustav Nachtigal signed a treaty with Mlapa III in 1884, establishing a German protectorate. Togo is an Ewe (pronounced Ev'hé) word meaning "lake" or "lagoon." Since 1884, Togoland and later Togo became synonymous for the entire region under colonial control. The term Togolese first appeared after World War I, and the population increasingly identified with this term, culminating in 1960 with the choice of the Republic of Togo as the official name.

Location and Geography. Covering a total area (land and inland water) of 21,925 square miles (56,785 square kilometers), Togo extends 365 miles (587 kilometers) inland, 40 miles (64 kilometers) wide at the coast and 90 miles (145 kilometers) wide at its widest point. It is bordered by Ghana, Burkina Faso, and Benin.

Togo consists of six geographical regions. The coastal region is low-lying, sandy beach backed by the Tokoin plateau, a marsh, and the Lake Togo lagoon. The Tokoin (Ouatchi) Plateau extends about 20 miles (32 kilometers) inland at an elevation of 200 to 300 feet (61 to 91 meters). To the northeast, a higher tableland is drained by the Mono, Haho, Sio, and tributaries. The Atakora massif stretches diagonally across Togo from the town of Kpalime northeast; at different points it is known as the Danyi and Akposso Plateau, Fetish massif, Fazao mountain, Tchaoudjo massif, and Kabye mountains. The highest point is the Pic d'Agou at 3,937 feet (986 meters). North of the mountain range is the Oti plateau, a savanna land drained by the river of the same name. A higher, semi-arid region extends to the northern border.

The climate is tropical and humid for seven months, while the dry, desert winds of the Harmattan blow south from November to March, bringing cooler weather though little moisture. Annual temperatures vary between 75 and 98 degrees Fahrenheit (23 and 35 degrees Celsius) in the south and 65 to 100 degrees Fahrenheit (18 to 38 degrees Celsius) in the north.

The thirty Togolese ethnic groups are now found in all parts of the country, most notably in the capital Lomé, which is situated on the border with Ghana.

Demography. The population of Togo is estimated by the United Nations to be 5 million in 2000, with growth at approximately 3.5 percent per annum (though the last government census dates from 1981). One fifth of the population lives in Lomé, the capital. Kara, the second largest city, has approximately two hundred thousand inhabitants. Population density reached 42 per square mile (67 per square kilometer) in 1991, with 75 percent in rural villages.

Linguistic Affiliation. French is the official language of government, but both Ewe of the Kwa and Kabye of the Gur language families have semi-official status. Ewe has a much wider use than its ethnic boundaries, partly as a consequence of German colonial education policies. Mina—a constantly evolving melange of Ewe, French, English, and other languages—is the lingua franca of Lomé, of the coastal zone, and of commerce in general.

Symbolism. National symbols include *Ablodé* (an Ewe word meaning freedom and independence), immortalized in the national monument to independence; the African lion on the coat of arms (though long since extinct in Togo); and colorful Kente cloth,

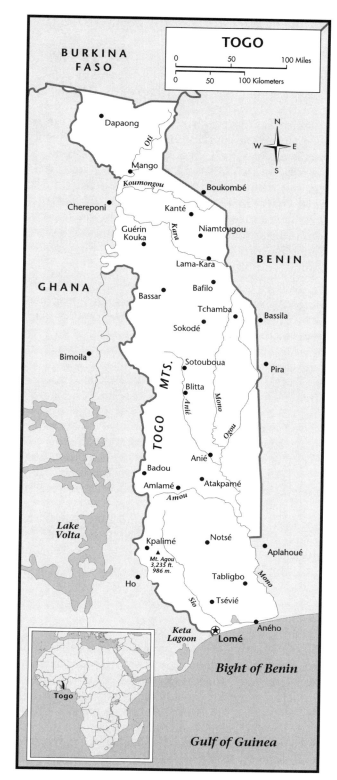

Togo

originating in the Awatime region shared with neighboring Ghana.

HISTORY AND ETHNIC RELATIONS

The population of the central mountains is perhaps the oldest in Togo, with recent archeological research dating the presence of the Tchamba, Bogou, and Bassar people as far back as the ninth century. Northern Mossi kingdoms date back to the thirteenth century. Ewe migration narratives from Nigeria and archaeological finds in the region of Notse put the earliest appearance of Ewe speakers at c. 1600. Other research suggests the Kabye and others were the last to settle in the Kara region coming from Kete-Krachi in Ghana as recently as two hundred fifty years ago. Parts of north Togo were for a long time under the influence of Islamic kingdoms, such as that of Umar Tal of the nineteenth century.

European presence began in the fifteenth century and became permanent from the sixteenth. Though the Danish, Dutch, Spanish, British, German, and French all sailed the coastal region, the Portuguese were the first to establish local economic control. For the next three centuries the area that is Togo today was sandwiched between the two powerful slave trading kingdoms of Ashanti and Dahomey. Consequently the Togolese population was overrepresented among those unfortunates sold into the trans–Atlantic slave trade. During the same period a growing Arab controlled trans-Saharan trade in slaves, kola, and gold passed through Togo.

Missionaries arrived in the mid–1800s and set up schools and churches in the regions of Ho (present-day Ghana), Kpalimé, and Agou. The Berlin Conference led to the annexation of Togo as a *Schutzgebiet* (protectorate) by the German Empire in 1884, under the leadership of Captain Gustav Nachtigal. Initially the treaty negotiated covered only the coastal region of about fifteen miles, though over the next fifteen years the German colonial administrators moved their capital from Zebe to Lomé and extended control north as far as present day Burkina Faso. The borders were finalized in treaties with France (1897) and Britain (1899).

German colonial rule consisted largely of export-oriented agricultural and infrastructural development, and frequent accounts of barbarity reached international attention. The most significant contribution was an system of roads and railroads built by German money and Togolese forced labor.

British and French troops invaded and captured German Togoland in 1914. For the duration of World War I, British troops controlled much of the region, including the capital, but with the Treaty of Versailles and the creation of the League of Nations Mandate system, Togoland was repartitioned. Officially in 1922, one third came under British control, and two-thirds under the administration of France (modern-day Togo), including the capital Lomé. After World War II, the mandates passed to the control of the United Nations (UN) Trusteeship in 1946. In 1956, in a UN-sponsored plebiscite, the British section voted to join the Gold Coast Colony as independent Ghana in 1957.

Emergence of the Nation. During the interwar period, several organizations—including the *Cercle des Amitiés Françaises*, the Duawo, and the Bund der deutschen Togoländer—organized and militated in public and private against French rule. The Cercle became the Committee for Togolese Unity Party (CUT), under the leadership of Sylvanus Olympio. The Togolese Party for Progress, led by Nicolas Grunitzky, offered a more conservative message. In 1956 France made French Togoland a republic within the French Union, with internal self-government. Grunitzky was made prime minister and against the wishes of the UN, France attempted to terminate the trusteeship. In a UN-sponsored election, the CUT won control of the legislature and Olympio became the country's first president on 27 April 1960. In 1963 Togo gained the dubious distinction of being the first country in sub-Saharan Africa to experience a military coup d'état.

National Identity. Until the dictatorship of Gnassingbé Eyadema, the southern Ewe culture predominated in all realms of life and was second only to the influence of French. After 1967, however, the president deigned to redress the southern bias in cultural, political, and social life, and to this end created *authenticité*, modeled on the same program of the Zaire dictator Mobutu. This movement attempted to highlight the many and diverse cultures of Togo, but resulted in reducing them to two only: that of the north and south. More recently, the idea of Togolese nationhood has become submerged to that of Kabye ethnicity.

Ethnic Relations. Ethnic tensions are minimal, despite the persistent murmurings of certain politicians. Political strife came to a head in 1991–1994 and did result in south against north violence and the reverse, with its concomitant refugees and resettlement, but Togo's thirty ethnic groups continue to mix and intermarry throughout the country.

URBANISM, ARCHITECTURE, AND THE USE OF SPACE

The city of Lomé and the coastal region are deeply influenced by the architectural programs of the successive colonial regimes. Vestiges of the German administrative buildings, several cathedrals and many churches, as well as private houses can be found throughout the country, though German influence was less pervasive in the north. The British period featured no architectural innovation, but more than forty years of French administration left its mark, most prominently in the work of Georges Coustereau. The works of this Frenchman are to be found throughout the country and include the national independence monument and an unusual church in the small town of Kpele-Ele.

During the prosperous 1960s and 1970s, the president inaugurated an extravagant program, lavishing upon Lomé and his home town of Kara five-star hotels, a new port, and sports and government buildings. The skyline of Lomé is broken by four enormous skyscrapers, most prominently the five-star Hotel Deux Février. Since the economic decline of the 1980s and indebtedness, few new projects have succeeded. The Chinese government, however, funded the building of a forty-thousand-seat stadium, which opened in 2000. In the dire economic climate at the end of the twentieth century, private Togolese citizens invest their small incomes in private building, usually constructed by homemade concrete bricks. The vast majority, however, live in rural settings in a variety of traditional village designs: centralized, dispersed, on stilts, or in two-story conical mud huts like those of the Tamberma. Enclosures are gendered spaces, with the external kitchen area a female realm.

FOOD AND ECONOMY

Food in Daily Life. Togolese usually have two or three meals per day, each consisting largely of a starch product, such as cassava, maize, rice, yams, or plantains. A hot, spicy sauce is served with midday or evening meals, consisting of a protein—fish, goat, beans, or beef—and often rich in palm (red) oil or peanut paste. Fruits and vegetables, though readily available, are eaten more by the bourgeoisie. Traditional French staples, including baguettes, are mainstream in the cities.

Food Customs at Ceremonial Occasions. Food does not serve a significant ceremonial function, except perhaps in terms of animist rituals, when the sacrificed animals are prepared, cooked, and served.

Hair hangs from poles, and skulls lay on the ground in a fetish market. Traditional vodou cults are popular.

Beer, gin, and *sodabi* (distilled palm wine) are, however, essential. Among wealthy middle-class Togolese, the usual French three- or four-course meals are always served at functions.

Basic Economy. Agriculture provides the mainstay of the economy, employing close to four-fifths of the active population. Farmers grow food for subsistence and for sale.

Land Tenure and Property. Private property exists in Togo alongside traditional community custodianship, and land is bought and sold under both systems. Private ownership of land began during the German period, as small parcels were purchased for commerce and for missions. The French continued this policy of gentle aggrandizement, but post-independence this was complicated by the president's illegal seizure and redistribution of plantations owned by his opponents. Thus, much land in the south, and particularly in the capital Lomé, remains the site of intense litigation, which takes place in the civil courts. Warnings are often written in red on the walls of land parcels to deter sale or deception.

Commercial Activities. Agricultural and manufactured products are sold both retail and wholesale in shops and markets. The informal economy is significant and is found in every town and village market, including the Assigamé (Grand Marché) in Lomé.

Major Industries. The 1990s saw most government industries privatized. Phosphates, run as a monopoly, remain Togo's largest industry, with electricity production a distant second. The once highly favored banking sector is in permanent decline, and tourism is insignificant. Togo has a small oil refinery, and animal husbandry, telecommunications, and information technology are growth industries. Togo has possibly the highest use of Internet and email services per capita in West Africa.

Trade. Togo's stagnant, underdeveloped economy is largely dependent on agricultural exports. In the mid 1990s, over 50 percent of Togo's exports were of four primary products—coffee, cocoa, cotton, and phosphates. Until the relaunching of ports in Cotonou and Lagos, Lomé was one of the busiest on the coast. The roads and rail infrastructure are rapidly declining, however, despite the launching of the Free Trade Zone in 1989.

France is by far Togo's largest trading partner. Fifty percent of imports from France are consumption goods, of which a minority are re-exported to

Burkina and Niger. Forty-two percent of imports are of equipment, building, and agricultural supplies. Togo imports all its petroleum needs.

Division of Labor. Child labor has been ubiquitous, and in 1996 and 1998 several incidents of child slavery were exposed. Girls are more likely to work than go to school in much of Togo.

Professional positions are usually occupied by individuals who have had post-secondary school education. Successful business people may or may not have formal educations, but often they have relatives, friends, or patrons who helped finance their establishment.

SOCIAL STRATIFICATION

Classes and Castes. Society is divided along traditional and nontraditional lines. The elite includes kings, paramount chiefs, and vodou priests. The modern elite includes government functionaries, business professionals, and the educated. Poor rural families often send their children to city-living relatives for schooling or employment.

Symbols of Social Stratification. During the colonial period, all but the simplest clothing was considered a social distinguishing factor in villages, while brick houses and cars were in towns. During the last decades of the twentieth century, wealthy villagers could afford tin roofs and some even telephones, while in the cities, large houses, cable television, western dress, and restaurant dining were hallmarks of success.

POLITICAL LIFE

Government. The Fourth Republic provides for a constitution modeled on that of the Fifth French Republic, with the president, the prime minister, and the president of the National Assembly being the three chief posts. The constitution limits the president to two successive five-year terms, although he has amended the constitution frequently in the past.

Leadership and Political Officials. President Gnassingbe Eyadema came to power by force in 1967, though he was implicated in the assassination of the first president, Sylvanus Olympio, and played kingmaker from 1961 until coming to power. There were no obvious successors within his party—the *Rassemblement du Peuple Togolais* (RPT)—at the end of the twentieth century. After the 1991 national conference, Eyadema made the transition to being a democratically elected leader, though the 1998 presidential election was condemned internationally as flawed and fraudulent.

A one-party state from 1961 until 1991, Togo experienced a renaissance in multiparty politics, though political in-fighting beleaguer the chances of the Committee for Action and Renewal and the Union for Democratic Change (UDC). The leader of the UDC, Gilchrist Olympio, widely considered to have won the 1998 presidential election, lives in voluntary exile in Ghana.

Social Problems and Control. Large-scale social upheaval followed the political violence of 1992–1993 and approximately one-third of the population moved to neighboring countries. With the political deadlock, relative calm returned. The cancellation of all international aid projects and withdrawal of most nongovernmental organizations, however, put strain on the economy. Unemployment, unsustainable wages, and poverty rose rapidly. Crime increased, particularly violent robberies and carjackings. Most educational institutions were on strike throughout much of 1999–2000.

Military Activity. Togo has a small army and minimal naval and air forces. Eighty percent of the gendarmerie and 90 percent of the military are of the Kabye ethnic group. Most regularly go unpaid and set up ad hoc roadblocks to extort money. The French and Chinese were the leading suppliers of military hardware to Togo from the latter portion of the twentieth century to the present day.

SOCIAL WELFARE AND CHANGE PROGRAMS

Welfare is almost nonexistent, though pensioners who paid contributions to the Francophone cooperative system continue to receive payments. Structural readjustment is hardly a success story, but a great number of state industries have been privatized under the guidance of the IMF/World Bank.

NONGOVERNMENTAL ORGANIZATIONS AND OTHER ASSOCIATIONS

Most nongovernmental and aid organizations quit Togo in the 1990s, with only Population Services International and *Organizacion Ibero Americana de Cooperacion Inter Municipal* (OICI) still operating throughout the country. Voluntary service organizations, such as Rotary, Lions, and Zonta continue to operate.

The Bank of Africa in Togo was constructed during a period of architectural innovation.

GENDER ROLES AND STATUSES

Division of Labor by Gender. Customary divisions of labor generally do not still hold in Togo, though men do most heavy construction work. Women perform almost all other manual labor in towns and villages, though less machine work, and control small market commerce.

The Relative Status of Women and Men. Women, though having attained legal equality, remain unequal in all walks of life. Women and men are kept apart in most social gatherings. Women usually eat after men but before children. Discrimination against women in employment is common practice and widespread. Women have little place in political life and less in government programs, though there is a ministry allocated to women's and family affairs. Only women descended from ruling tribal families, successful businesswomen, or women politicians enjoy privileges equal to that of men, more won than granted. Togo recently banned the practice of female genital mutilation.

Marriage, Family, and Kinship. Traditional systems of social organization are significant in the daily lives of Togolese. Kinship systems provide networks for support and are visible during all major life–cycle ceremonies.

Marriage. Marriage practices vary throughout Togo according to the ethnic group, though organized religions and the State have altered the ceremonies of even the most secluded villages. Social disapproval of ethnic exogamy is lessening, though the government unofficially discourages it. Marriage law follows French legal statutes and requires an appearance before a magistrate for all state apparatuses to be in effect. Customary marriages, without state sanction, are still widespread. A bride-wealth, but not a dowry, remains important throughout Togo. Polygyny is officially decreasing, though unofficial relationships uphold its role.

Domestic Unit. The basic family structure is extended, although nuclear family units are increasingly commonplace, particularly in urban areas. In most cases, the man is the supreme head of the household in all major decisions. In the absence of the husband, the wife's senior brother holds sway. The extended family has a redistributive economic base.

Inheritance. Inheritance laws follow French legal statutes in the case of a legal marriage. In the event of a customary marriage only, customary inheritance laws are enforced. Most ethnic groups in Togo are patrilineal by tradition or have become so as a consequence of colonization.

Kin Groups. Kinship is largely patrilineal throughout Togo and remains powerful even among Westernized, urban populations. Village and neighborhood chiefs remain integral to local dispute resolution.

SOCIALIZATION

Infant Care. Infants are cared for by their mothers and female members of their households, including servants. Among some ethnic groups, infants are often only exposed to the father eight days after birth. Vaccination against all childhood diseases has been strongly encouraged by the government.

Child Rearing and Education. Until the age of five, children remain at home. Initiation ceremonies occur from this age and throughout adolescence. After the age of five, all children can commence school, providing they can pay the school fees. On average, boys are three times more likely to complete primary schooling than girls. This discrepancy increases into secondary schooling and is most marked in the rural central and northern regions.

Higher Education. Secondary schooling is more common in the south, and numerous private and public schools offer the French baccalaureate system. Often children are sent abroad during strikes. Togo has one university, located in the capital, and it offers first- and second-level degrees in the arts and sciences, as well as in medicine and law.

ETIQUETTE

Public displays of affection are seldom. Men and boys hold hands, but not boys and girls. Courting remains private and is not generally arranged by parents except among some ethnic groups; for example, the Tchamba. Old people and village elders are highly esteemed, though the climate of political fear has brought the undue influence of youths. Eating is done most often with the right hand, though among the bourgeoisie flatware is prevalent. When guests arrive, water is offered and the traditional greeting—asking about the family and their health—ensues.

RELIGION

Religious Beliefs. Since the inception of the mandate, freedom of religious worship has been protected by law. The French interpreted this to include animistic African religions, and this perhaps partly accounts for the popularity of traditional vodou cults and rituals.

Throughout the country, many different forms of Christianity and Islam are practiced. Roman Catholicism is the most prevalent form of Christianity. Various American Baptist sects, the Assemblies of God, Mormons, Jehovah's Witnesses, and Eckankar have been making inroads among urban and rural populations alike. Islam is virtually paramount in the north.

Religious Practitioners. Religious officials, whether Catholic priests or vodou *sofo*, are held in the highest esteem in both rural and urban settings. They are always invited to bless traditional ceremonies as well as building projects or any new initiative. Traditional healers also hold sway, and—in the wake of the AIDS epidemic—are regaining popularity.

Death and the Afterlife. A Togolese funeral is a most important event. Wildly extravagant (by Western standards), funeral celebrations are a daily occurrence. Marching bands, choirs, football tournaments, banquets, and stately services are as fundamental as an expensively decorated coffin. Funerals often take place over a month or more, and families frequently sell or mortgage land or homes to pay for the funeral of a beloved and elderly relative. If the person dies in an accident, however, or some other sudden tragedy (AIDS, for example), this is considered a ''hot death,'' and the funeral services are concluded more quickly, with little circumstance.

MEDICINE AND HEALTH CARE

Similar to other underdeveloped, tropical nations, Togo's population is challenged by numerous health problems, including parasitic, intestinal, nutritional, venereal, and respiratory diseases.

Public health problems are exacerbated by inadequate waste disposal, sewerage, drinking water, and food storage.

In the 1990s, life expectancy at birth was fifty-one years, though this is declining steeply with the onset of AIDS. Malaria, commonly referred to as *palu*, remains the leading cause of illness and death. Other common diseases include schistosomiasis, meningitis, tuberculosis, pneumonia, and HIV/AIDS.

Traditional healing methods and preparations continue to be the most widely used form of health

Houses like these in Tata village house a large number of Togolese citizens.

care in Togo. Every small town has an herbalist, and one market in Lomé specializes in the sale of medicinal herbs. Frequently medical treatments are coupled with visits to the local vodou house or fetish priest.

SECULAR CELEBRATIONS

Major state holidays are 1 January; the Fête Nationale, 13 January; Fête de la Libération Economique, 24 January; Fête de la Victoire, 24 April; May Day, 1 May; Day of the Martyrs, 21 June; and Day of Struggle, 23 September. 27 April, Independence Day, is not officially celebrated by President Eyadema and is frequently a day of opposition activity.

THE ARTS AND HUMANITIES

There is little government support for the arts in Togo, beyond the rudimentary presence of a Ministry of Culture and the poorly funded and maintained departments of the university. Private organizations include the Centre Culturel Français, the American Cultural Center, and the Goethe Institut.

THE STATE OF THE PHYSICAL AND SOCIAL SCIENCES

There is little government support for the physical and social sciences in Togo, beyond the existence of a Ministry for Scientific Research and Education. Private organizations and nongovernmental organizations provide various services, and a private academy of social sciences was created.

BIBLIOGRAPHY

Agier, Michel. *Commerce et sociabilité: les négociants soudanais du quartier zongo de Lomé (Togo)*, 1983.

Comhaire-Sylvain, Suzanne. *Femmes de Lomé*, 1982.

Cornevin, Robert. *Histoire du Togo*. 3d ed., 1969.

Decalo, Samuel. *Historical Dictionary of Togo*. 3d ed., 1996.

Delval, Raymond. *Les Musulmans au Togo*, 1980.

Gérard, Bernard. *Lomé: capital du Togo*, 1975.

Greene, Sandra. "Gender, Ethnicity, and Social Change on the Upper Slave Coast: A History of the Anlo-Ewe," in *Cahiers d'Etudes African*, 169:489–524, 1996.

Lawrance, Benjamin Nicholas. *Most Obedient Servants: The Politics of Language in German Colonial Togo*, 2000.

Marguerat, Yves. *Lomé, les étapes de la croissance: Une Brève Histoire de la capitale du Togo*, 1992.

————, et al. *''Si Lomé m'etait contée . . . '': dialogues avec les vieux Loméens*, 1992.

Piot, Charles. *Remotely Global: Village Modernity in West Africa*, 1999.

Prigent, Françoise. *Encyclopédie nationale du Togo*, 1979.

Rosenthal, Judy. *Possession, Ecstasy and the Law: Spirit Possession in Ewe Vodou*, 1998.

Sebald, Peter. *Togo 1884–1914: Eine Geschichte der deutschen ''Musterkolonie'' auf der Grundlage amtlicher Quellen*, 1987.

Spieth, Jakob. *Die Ewe-Stmme: Material zur Kunde des Ewe Volkes in Deutsch-Togo*, 1906.

Viering, Erich. *Togo Singt ein neues Lied*, 1967.

Winslow, Zachery. *Togo*, 1988.

Westermann, Dietrich. *Die Glidyi-Ewe in Togo*, 1935.

—BENJAMIN NICHOLAS LAWRANCE

TOKELAU

CULTURE NAME
Tokelauan

ORIENTATION

Identification. "Tokelau" means "north-north-east." Its people also identify themselves by their atoll villages: Atafu, Fakaofo, and Nukunonu.

Location and Geography. Three unbroken rings of coral with a combined land area of somewhat over four square miles (ten square kilometers) lie along a 93 mile (150 kilometers) northwest–southeast axis, separated from each other by 37 to 56 miles (60 to 90 kilometers) of open sea.

Demography. The population is about 1,700. An additional estimated five thousand reside overseas, mainly in New Zealand.

Linguistic Affiliation. Tokelauan is a Polynesian language. Older people are bilingual in Samoan, which was introduced with Christianity in the 1860s; younger people are more apt to be bilingual in English through their schooling.

Symbolism. Homeland atolls are the preeminent symbols, denoting both place and ancestry.

HISTORY AND ETHNIC RELATIONS

Emergence of the Nation and National Identity. As a culturally distinctive dependency of New Zealand, Tokelau is a nation. After sixty years as a British protectorate and then a colony ruled with "benign neglect," in 1948 Tokelau became "a part of New Zealand" and its people became New Zealand citizens. Most people want to retain that status, which combines considerable local political autonomy with substantial external support.

Ethnic Relations. Virtually all residents are of Tokelauan ancestry. In New Zealand, Tokelauans are a minority population among other Pacific Islanders, Maori, and persons of Asian and European ancestry. Many conscientiously maintain aspects of their culture.

URBANISM, ARCHITECTURE, AND THE USE OF SPACE

The villages are densely peopled and like small rural towns in character. Public buildings under the aegis of the village are the meeting house and the church. Public amenities under the control of the administration/public service are the dispensary/hospital, school, and administration compound that houses the communications center (formerly the two-way radio), the village cooperative store, and offices for administrative and elected officers. Dwelling houses are rectangular single-room structures on raised coral-filled foundations and aligned with the straight heavily traveled footpaths. Until the 1970s, the houses were open constructions of local timber and pandanus-leave thatch, with plaited coconut frond blinds that could be lowered against wind and rain. Now the houses are more closed, built of imported lumber, concrete, and corrugated iron, sometimes with louvered glass windows. They are still, however, carpeted with mats plaited from pandanus and/or coconut leaves, upon which the occupants sit and lounge. Other furnishings are rolled-up sleeping mats, locked wooden boxes containing clothing and other personal belongings, and miscellaneous chairs, tables, and bedsteads. Separate cookhouses, still constructed of local materials, may be adjacent to, or more likely, distant from dwelling houses.

FOOD AND ECONOMY

Food in Daily Life. Fish and coconuts are abundant; other local foods are seasonal or scarce. Stores stock imported food, mainly rice, flour, and sugar.

Basic Economy. Traditional economic activities center on the land, reef, lagoon, and sea. Fishing is

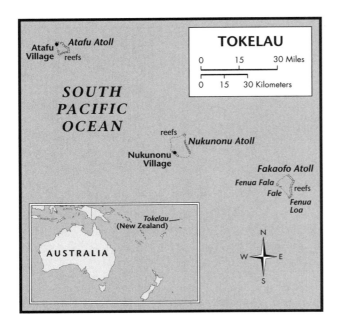

Tokelau

strictly a subsistence activity, pursued with ingenuity backed by extensive knowledge. Coconuts rarely are harvested for uses other than subsistence since public service employment became the main source of cash. Handicrafts are more often produced as gifts than for cash.

Land Tenure and Property. Aside from a small portion of land used for communal purposes, all land is held by cognatic kin groups and managed by persons with recognized positions within those groups. Village houses are occupied and managed by kin group women; men manage and harvest plantation lands. Virtually everyone has rights to land and to a share of the produce from the land. Most people are members of more than one kin group and many receive produce from four or more.

Commercial Activities. All entrepreneurial activities are closely scrutinized by the Councils in each village.

Division of Labor. A major division exists between salaried public service employees who have job qualifications and wage-earning public service employees who do not. The distinction between paid and unpaid work has been partially eroded by village management of aid projects, for which all village workers are paid. Age determines who does what, who directs, and who labors.

SOCIAL STRATIFICATION

Classes and Castes. An egalitarian ethic overrides differentials in wealth among a growing elite whose education and experience qualify them for better-paid employment or positions. They contribute generously to village and family enterprises and avoid ostentatious displays of affluence.

POLITICAL LIFE

Government. The New Zealand Ministry of Foreign Affairs administers Tokelau, delegating certain powers to the three village-elected Faipule, who rotate as "head" of Tokelau during their three-year terms.

Leadership and Political Officials. Councils of elderly men and/or representatives of kin groups control the villages and direct village activities through the elected Pulenuku ("mayor").

Social Problems and Control. Persons are reprimanded in communal venues by their elders and peers for minor misdemeanors and are brought before local courts for more serious ones.

SOCIAL WELFARE AND CHANGE PROGRAMS

Development programs proliferate, supported by New Zealand and by international, regional, and other aid.

NONGOVERNMENTAL ORGANIZATIONS AND OTHER ASSOCIATIONS

Organizations of able-bodied men, adult women, and competing "sides" are long-standing village institutions, as are several church associations. Clubs and youth groups are less permanent.

GENDER ROLES AND STATUSES

Division of Labor by Gender. The adage that men "go"—fishing and harvesting—and women "stay"—managing the family—has been compromised by widespread public service employment. Both men and women work in skilled jobs; most unskilled workers are men.

Relative Status of Women and Men. Complementary equity predicated on sister-brother relationships has been compromised by Christian ideology and money.

Performers from the Tokelau Islands wear traditional dress as they attend the South Pacific Arts Festival.

MARRIAGE, FAMILY, AND KINSHIP

Marriage. Virtually all residents enter into sanctified, lifelong monogamous unions. Individual choice is constrained by kin group exogamy.

Domestic Unit. The pattern is an uxorilocal, often expanded nuclear family, in line with the adage that women "stay" and men "go."

Inheritance. All offspring inherit rights from both parents.

Kin Groups. Members of each cognatic kin group reside throughout the village and interact regularly.

SOCIALIZATION

Child Rearing and Education. Infant care is indulgent. Children are closely disciplined and precisely instructed in increasingly complex tasks.

Higher Education. All children attend village primary and secondary schools; many continue their schooling abroad.

ETIQUETTE

Deference and obedience to one's elders and restraint between cross-sex siblings is expected. Physical aggression is abhorred.

RELIGION

Religious Beliefs. Protestant and Catholic congregations practice a fundamentalist, puritanical form of Christianity.

Religious Practitioners. Protestant pastors, deacons, and lay preachers and Catholic priests, catechists, and elders direct their respective congregations.

Rituals and Holy Places. Churches are cherished sites with frequent masses and services.

Death and the Afterlife. A short wake, church service, and burial are followed by evenings of mourning and ended by a feast. Unusual events and encounters may be attributed to ghost spirits. The dead are fondly remembered.

MEDICINE AND HEALTH CARE

Western curative and preventive medicine has long been available. The hospital is normally the first resort. Local therapists mainly use massage.

SECULAR CELEBRATIONS

Numerous commemorative days and other celebrations feature feasts, competitions, parades, and entertainment.

THE ARTS AND HUMANITIES

Literature. Oral narratives may be fictional stories or recountings of the past.

Graphic Arts. Women work in fiber, and men work in wood.

Performance Arts. Poetry, music, and dance are combined in old and new group compositions.

BIBLIOGRAPHY

Angelo, A. H. "Tokelau." In M. A. Ntumy, ed., *South Pacific Legal Systems*, 1993.

Angelo, T. "The Last of the Island Territories? The Evolving Constitutional Relationship with Tokelau." *Stout Centre Journal*, 1996.

Hooper, Antony. "The MIRAB transition in Fakaofo, Tokelau." *Pacific Viewpoint* 34 (2): 241–264, 1997.

Huntsman, J., and A. Hooper. "Male and Female in Tokelau Culture." *Journal of the Polynesian Society* 84: 415–430, 1975.

———. *Tokelau: A Historical Ethnography*, 1996.

Matagi Tokelau. *Tokelau History and Traditions*, 1991.

Simona, R. *Tokelau Dictionary*, 1986.

Wessen, A. F., A. Hooper, J. Huntsman, I. A. M. Prior, and C. E. Salmond, eds. *Migration and Health in a Small Society: The Case of Tokelau*, 1992.

—JUDITH HUNTSMAN

TONGA

CULTURE NAME
Tongan

ALTERNATIVE NAMES
Friendly Islands

ORIENTATION

Identification. The name "Tonga" is composed of *to* (to plant) and *nga* (a place). It also means "south." According to the most recent archaeological findings, people arrived in the archipelago from Fiji around 1500 B.C.E. Thus, it is appropriate to translate the nation's name as "land lying in the south."

Location and Geography. Tonga is an archipelago of one hundred fifty islands, thirty-six of which are inhabited. There are four major groups of islands: the Tongatapu, Ha'apai, Vava'u, and Niua groups. Most of the islands are raised coral islands, some are volcanic, and a few are atolls. Coral beaches lined with palm trees and emerald lagoons with luxuriant tropical vegetation are characteristic features. The capital, Nuku'alofa, is on Tongatapu.

Demography. The population was 97,784 according to the 1996 census. Since 1891, the growth rate has increased steadily, peaking in the 1950s and 1960s. Migration to New Zealand, Australia, and the United States in the 1970s and 1980s resulted in slower growth. Internal migration has been from the outer, northern, and central islands toward the southern island of Tongatapu. A third of the population (31,404) lives in the capital.

Linguistic Affiliation. Tongan is an Austronesian language of the Oceanic subgroup. It belongs to the Western Polynesian languages, specifically the Tongic group. There are three social dialects: one for talking to the king, one for chiefs and nobles, and one for the common people. "Talking chiefs" are among the few who know all three dialects; they mediate in official ceremonies and in encounters between the king, the nobility, and the commoners.

Seventy years as a British protectorate (until 1970) resulted in widespread knowledge of English. Though much of the village population knows little English, in Nuku'alofa and other major towns, most business transactions are conducted in it. English is taught in elementary schools and is the language of most high school instruction. However, Tongan is the language commonly spoken in the streets, shops, markets, schools, offices, and churches.

HISTORY AND ETHNIC RELATIONS

Emergence of the Nation. The Tongan creation myth describes how the islands were fished from the ocean by Maui, one of the three major gods. Another myth explains how 'Aho'eitu became the first *Tu'i Tonga* (king). He was the son of a human female and the god Tangaloa. Human and divine at the same time, the Tu'i Tonga was the embodiment of the Tongan people, and this is still a powerful metaphor.

Tongans were fierce warriors and skilled navigators whose outrigger canoes could carry up to two hundred people. For centuries they exercised political and cultural influence over several neighboring islands. By the time of the first European contact in late 1700s and early 1800s, the empire had collapsed, and the authority of the Tu'i Tonga was restricted mostly to the religious realm.

National Identity. King George Tupou I, the first king of modern Tonga, introduced the constitution in 1875 after unifying the four island groups. He had previously converted to Christianity and opportunistically waged expansionist wars from Ha'apai to Vava'u and then to Tongatapu. Christian principles characterize the constitution, which very likely was prepared under the influence of Wesleyan

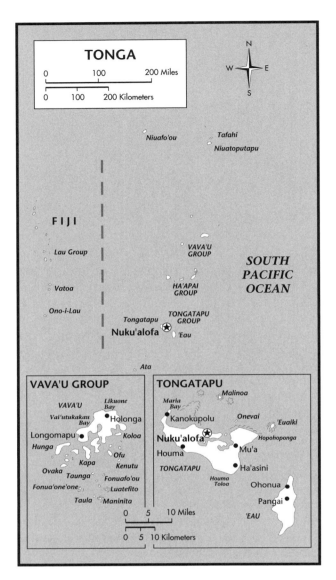

Tonga

missionaries. George Tupou I transformed Tonga into a modern state, abolishing slavery and the absolute power of chiefs. Since the last Tu'i Tonga had no official heir, as the head of the other two royal lines, King George became the only king of Tonga. The 1875 constitution recognizes only his royal line.

In 1900, the British granted Tonga's request for protectorate status. In 1970, all powers were restored to the Tongan monarchy. The British protectorate shielded Tonga from other colonizing powers. A spirit of independence and pride was nurtured during the long reign of Queen Salote (1918–1965), who led the nation into the twentieth century, paying special attention to preserving its heritage. Because of her vision, Tongan culture is an integral part of the school curriculum. Students learn Tongan history, traditional poetry, music, and dancing, along with wood carving, mat weaving, and bark cloth making.

URBANISM, ARCHITECTURE, AND THE USE OF SPACE

The first European visitors spoke of a population scattered throughout a densely cultivated land. Now Tongans are concentrated in villages and small towns. Most villages lie around an empty area, called *mala'e*, that is used for social gatherings and games. A traditional house stands on a raised platform of stones and sand. It is oval in shape with a thatched roof and walls of woven palm tree panels. The toilet and the kitchen are in separate huts. Contemporary houses are usually bigger and made of timber with corrugated iron roofs. Little furniture is used.

The simplicity of house architecture contrasts with the monumentality of earlier royal buildings and tombs. The royal tombs are layered pyramidal structures built of massive stone slabs. The huge *Ha'amonga* trilithon, made of two stone columns topped with a notched column, was built around 1200 C.E. One hypothesis suggests that it was the door to the royal compound, and another that it was used for astronomical purposes. These monuments bear witness to the power of the Tu'i Tonga. They also indicate the sophisticated stone-cutting technology and skills of the ancient craftsmen.

FOOD AND ECONOMY

Food in Daily Life. Both in villages and in the main towns, food is the occasion for a family gathering only at the end of the day. Otherwise, food is consumed freely at any time. The basic staples are root crops like taro accompanied by fried or roasted meat or fish. Taro leaves are one of the various green vegetables used together with a variety of tropical fruits like bananas, pineapples, and mangoes.

Food Customs at Ceremonial Occasions. The ritual of kava drinking characterizes both formal and daily events. Kava is prepared by grinding dried roots and mixing the powder with water in a ceremonial bowl. It is nonalcoholic but slightly narcotic. People sit cross-legged in an elliptical pattern whose long axis is headed by the bowl on one side and by the highest-ranked participant on the other. The preparation and serving of the drink are done by a young woman, usually but not always the only female participant, or by male specialists. The

The royal palace in Nukualofa. Tonga is a constitutional monarchy.

formal coronation of a ruler and formal receptions for foreign delegations are marked by a kava ceremony. Kava clubs are found in the towns, and kava drinking gatherings take place almost daily in the villages.

Basic Economy. The economy centers on agriculture and fishing. Major exports are vanilla, fish, handicrafts, and pumpkins grown for export to Japan. King Taufa'ahau Tupou IV has modernized the country's economy. Based largely on foreign aid from New Zealand, Australia, the United States, and the European Community and on imports, this process has created a widespread presence of Western products. The agricultural base of the economy remains. The tourist industry is growing, and revenues from Tongans working abroad are one of the largest sources of income.

Typical agricultural produce are root crops such as taro, tapioca, sweet potatoes, and yams. Coconuts, bananas, mangoes, papayas, pineapples, watermelons, peanuts, and vegetables are grown. Pigs and fowl are abundant and free ranging. Cows, sheep, and goats also are present. Intensive shellfishing is conducted along the shores, and there is an abundant fish supply.

Royal visits and funerals call for the preparation of large amounts of food. Roasted piglets are laid in the center of a *pola* (tray) made of woven palm tree leaves. Root crops, meats, and shellfish prepared in the *'umu* (underground oven) are added and garnished with fresh fruits, decorative flowers, ribbons, and balloons. In villages, food is consumed while one sits on a mat; in towns, tables are used.

Land Tenure and Property. All land is owned by the king, the nobles, and the government. Foreigners cannot own land by constitutional decree. Owners have the right to sublet land to people who pay a tribute, traditionally food. Every citizen above age 16 is entitled to lease eight and a quarter acres of land from the government for a small sum, but the growing population and its concentration in the capital make it increasingly difficult to exercise this right.

SOCIAL STRATIFICATION

Classes and Castes. Traditional society had at its top the *ha'a tu'i* (kings), followed by the *hou'eiki* (chiefs), *ha'a matapule* (talking chiefs), *kau mu'a* (would-be talking chiefs), and *kau tu'a* (commoners). All titles were heritable and followed the male line of descent almost exclusively. This hierarchical social structure is still essentially in place.

Tribute to the chiefs was paid twice a year. Agricultural produce and gifts such as butchered animals, bark cloth, and mats were formally offered to the Tu'i Tonga and, through him, to the gods in an elaborate ceremony called 'inasi. The king now visits all the major islands at least once a year on the occasion of the Royal Agriculture Show. The gift giving and formalities at the show closely resemble those of the 'inasi.

The 1875 constitution eliminated the title of chief and introduced the title of nopele (noble), which was given to thirty-three traditional chiefs. Only nobles and the king are now entitled to own and distribute land. An increasingly market-oriented economy and an expanding bureaucracy have recently added a middle class that runs the gamut from commoners to chiefs. Newly acquired wealth, however, does not easily overcome social barriers rooted in history. Often claims to higher social status are established by claiming kinship to holders of aristocratic titles.

POLITICAL LIFE

Government. The Kingdom of Tonga is a constitutional monarchy. The constitution prescribes a legislative assembly with twenty members representing the thirty-three nobles and twenty members elected as people's representatives. In 1984, both groups were reduced to nine each. Twelve other members are appointed by the king: ten Cabinet members including the prime minister, who is also the governor of Tongatapu, and the governors of Ha'apai and Vava'u. In the 1993 election, six of the people's representatives belonged to the new Pro-Democracy Movement that in 1994 became the Democratic Party founded by 'Akilisi Pohiva.

The kingdom is divided into districts, each headed by a district officer. Every three years, each village elects a town officer who represents the government and holds village meetings (fono) where government regulations are made known. Every villager above 16 years of age is entitled to attend. People do not take part in the decision-making process but show approval or dissent through their implementation of the instructions.

SOCIAL WELFARE AND CHANGE PROGRAMS

Every citizen is entitled to free primary education, a plot of land at age 16, and free medical care. Hospitals, dispensaries, and pharmacies are distributed over the territory. Smaller government clinics are present in some villages in the outer islands.

To support the modernization of the country, in 1977 the Tongan Development Bank was estab-

lished. Financed by the World Bank and contributions from New Zealand and Australia, it provides low-interest loans for entrepreneurs. Foreigners who want to invest in the country need a Tongan partner for any economic venture.

NONGOVERNMENTAL ORGANIZATIONS AND OTHER ASSOCIATIONS

The U.S. Peace Corps, the Japanese Overseas Cooperation Volunteers, and development organizations connected with the British, New Zealand, and Australian governments are among the active aid agencies. They work in the fields of education, health, agriculture, and entrepreneurship.

GENDER ROLES AND STATUSES

Division of Labor by Gender. The introduction of wage labor in twentieth century privileged men, altering an equilibrium between genders that had lasted for centuries. Cash is now an element of wealth, and wage-earning men have easier access to it. However, the old egalitarian attitude toward the two sexes has not been altered by economic and technological changes. In contemporary offices, shops, and banks, working women are prominent. In villages, most men take care of the land or tend animals. Women weave mats and make bark cloth.

Both women and men actively participate in parenting. Food preparation is shared between the male and female members of a family. The preparation of the 'umu (underground oven), now restricted to Sundays and special occasions, is an almost exclusive male activity. Older children help with activities and household chores.

The Relative Status of Women and Men. The hierarchical system's emphasis on the higher status of females guarantees an equal role in society for females and males in spite of the fact that men usually inherit titles and land.

MARRIAGE, FAMILY, AND KINSHIP

Marriage. There are no explicit rules for marriage, and couples are formed through reciprocal free choice. Pronounced social stratification discourages marriages between people of vastly different social status. Divorce is legal and not uncommon. During a wedding, the two kainga involved exchange mats, bark cloth, and food. On the day of the ceremony, the bride and groom ''wear their wealth.'' They are wrapped in their best mats and bark cloth, their

Tongan students use microscopes as part of a science experiment. Tonga has an almost universal rate of literacy.

bodies shine with precious oils, and they wear flower necklaces and hair adornments.

Kin Groups. Kinship ties are of paramount importance. The two major kin groups are *famili* (family) and *kainga* (extended family). A *famili* consists of a married couple and their children living in the same house and usually includes male and/or female collaterals and affinals. The *'ulumotu'a* (head of the family) presides over this group. A *kainga* consists of relatives living in different households in the same village or in several villages. They are related by bilateral relationships of consanguinity in a cognatic system. Membership in kin groups is restricted to fewer and closer relatives than it was in the past.

The parameters in establishing hierarchy at any level of society are gender and age. A female is always considered higher in rank than a male. Inheritance of land and titles goes through the male line, and primogeniture rule usually is enforced. Because of traditional brother-sister avoidance, 10-year-old boys sleep in a separate house. Though avoidance is less strictly enforced now, it still affects daily life. Topics such as sex and activities such as watching videos are not shared between brothers and sisters.

SOCIALIZATION

Infant Care and Child Rearing. The birth of a child is among the most important events, but the official social introduction of a child to the community is celebrated only at the end of a child's first year. Mothers increasingly give birth in modern hospitals, and infant mortality has decreased. Infants typically are breast-fed and sleep in their parents' bed until age 5 to 8 years. Parents are the main caretakers, but in an extended family everybody contributes to parenting. This feeling of shared parenting extends as far as the village and even further. Older siblings often care for younger ones, but compulsory education has made this practice less common.

Tongans are proud of their almost 100 percent level of literacy. Government high schools limit enrollment by using a competitive examination and charging fees. Those who are not admitted can attend private religious high schools. There is a branch of the University of the South Pacific on Tongatapu. Sia'atoutai Theological College trains teachers. 'Atenisi University, a private institution in Nuku'alofa, offers degrees in the humanities.

Adoption is common. An older couple whose children have left to form their own families may

In rural Tongan villages, many women like this one make bank cloth. Women and men are treated equally.

adopt from a younger couple with many children. A couple may decide to give a child to a relative of higher social or economic status, and many parents who work abroad leave their children with relatives. Children are present in private or public events and are almost never forbidden to look, observe, and learn.

The most important life events are celebrated with elaborate ceremonies that may last weeks in the case of weddings or funerals of royalty or nobles. These events include a complex pattern of gift exchanges; the preparation, consumption, and distribution of a large quantity of food; and speech giving. Pieces of bark cloth, mats, kava roots, and food are exchanged. Speakers use an elaborate figurative language.

ETIQUETTE

Formal attire for men includes a *tupenu* (skirt) and a *ta'ovala* (mat) worn around one's waist and kept in place by a belt of coconut fiber. Prestigious old belts made of human hair also are used. A shirt with a tie and a jacket complete the attire. Women wear long dresses and *ta'ovala* as well. The softness, color, and decorations of a *ta'ovala* indicate status and wealth.

People shake hands when they meet, and relatives kiss by pressing each other's noses against their faces and soundly inhaling through the nose. The men preparing the *'umu* or roasting for a big feast do not eat with the guests and are allowed at the table only when the first round of people has finished eating and left. Most food is eaten with the hands, although silverware also is used. It is customary to wash one's hands at the beginning and end of a meal.

The gesture of raising the eyebrows in conversation expresses one's understanding of the speaker's speech and is an invitation to continue. It is difficult for people to admit failure in understanding or to respond negatively to requests.

RELIGION

Religious Beliefs. Christian churches exist in even the most remote villages. Bells or log drums call people for services at the crack of dawn. After a failed attempt by Wesleyan missionaries to Christianize the islands in 1797, they and other Christian missionaries were more successful in the mid-nineteenth century. Forty-four percent of Tongans belong to the Free Wesleyan Church. Wesleyanism is also the official religion of the state and the monarchy. Among the other major churches are the Roman Catholic Church (16.3 percent), the Church of Latter Day Saints (12.3 percent), the Free Church of

Tonga (11.4 percent), the Church of Tonga (7.5 percent), Seventh-Day Adventist Church (2.3 percent), and Anglican Church (0.6 percent).

MEDICINE AND HEALTH CARE

Traditional medicine exists alongside Western medicine in the person of the *faito'o* (native doctor). Knowledge about medicine is passed on from parent to child. The *faito'o* uses mainly herbal medicines. No payment is required for treatment, but gifts are given at the beginning or end of the cure. Massage is also used. Sometimes in the outer islands traditional medicine is the only defense against a number of diseases. Although people recognize the effectiveness of Western medicine, traditional medicine is highly respected.

SECULAR CELEBRATIONS

Besides Constitution Day (4 November) and Emancipation Day (4 June), the major secular holiday is the king's birthday on 4 July. Nobles and chiefs from all over the kingdom present gifts to the king in a ceremony adjacent to the royal palace. The capital is adorned with festive arches covered with fragrant flowers under which floats parade. After the parade, people feast and light bonfires.

THE ARTS AND HUMANITIES

Graphic Arts. Women make bark cloth that can reach fifty feet in length and fifteen feet in width. The design of the carved tablets used to decorate bark cloth is traditionally purely geometrical. Naturalistic figures such as trees, flowers, and animals are also used. Women also weave mats and make flax baskets. Color, thinness, and the number of threads used determine the quality of a mat. The uniformity and consistency of the patterns reveal a weaver's skill. These activities are always conducted in groups while talking, gossiping, or singing.

Men carve wood, black coral jewelry, and objects made of turtle shell or whalebone. Seeds, shells, and fresh flowers are woven into necklaces by both sexes.

Performance Arts. Choral singing is done in churches and kava clubs. Singing is part of the more holistic traditional art of *faiva*, the blending of dance, music, and poetry. The *punake* (master poet) composes pieces that combine music, text, and body movements. Traditional dances include the *Me'etu'upaki* (paddle dance), the *Tau'olunga* (solo dance), and the *Lakalaka* (line dance).

BIBLIOGRAPHY

Barrow, John. *Captain Cook: Voyages of Discovery*, 1993.

Benguigui, G. "The Middle Classes in Tonga." *The Journal of the Polynesian Society* 98(4): 451–463, 1989.

Bennardo, G. *A Computational Approach to Spatial Cognition: Representing Spatial Relationships in Tongan Language and Culture*, 1996.

Campbell, I. C. *Island Kingdom: Tongan Ancient and Modern*, 1992.

Ferdon, E. N. *Early Tonga: As the Explorers Saw It 1616–1810*, 1987.

Gailey, C. W. *Kinship to Kinship: Gender Hierarchy and State Formation in the Tongan Islands*, 1987.

Gifford, E. W. *Tongan Myths and Tales*, 1924.

———. *Tongan Society*, 1929.

Hoponoa, Leonaitasi. *The Aesthetic of Haka as a Component of the "Art" of Faiva: Differences between Referential and Non-Referential Constructions*, 1996.

James, K. "Gender Relations in Tonga 1780 to 1984." *The Journal of the Polynesian Society* 92(2): 233–243, 1985.

Kaeppler, A. L. *Poetry in Motion: Studies of Tongan Dance*, 1993.

Kingdom of Tonga. *Sixth Development Plan: 1991–1995*, 1999.

Kirch, P. V. "A Brief History of Lapita Archaeology." In P. V. Kirch and T. L. Hunt, eds. *Archaeology of the Lapita Cultural Complex: A Critical Review*, 1988.

Latukefu, S. *Church and State in Tonga*, 1974.

Law of Tonga, The, rev. ed., 1985.

Morton, Helen. *Becoming Tongan: An Ethnography of Childhood*, 1996.

Pawley, A. "Austronesian Languages." In *Encyclopedia Britannica*, 13th ed., 1974.

van der Grijp, Paul. *Islanders of the South: Production, Kinship, and Ideology in the Polynesian Kingdom of Tonga*, 1993.

Whistler, W. Arthur. *Tongan Herbal Medicine*, 1992.

Wood-Ellem, Elizabeth. *Queen Salote of Tonga: The Story of an Era 1900–1965*, 1999.

Web Sites

"Tonga on the Net." http://www.tongatapu.net.to/

"Tonga Online." http://www.tongaonline.com/

"UN System-Wide Earthwatch Web Site: Island Directory—Tonga." http://www.unep.ch/islands/CKY.htm

—GIOVANNI BENNARDO

TRINIDAD AND TOBAGO

CULTURE NAME

Depending upon which island in this twin–island state is being discussed, the culture name is "Trinidadian" or "Tobagonian."

ALTERNATIVE NAMES

Trinidadians, but not Tobagonians, often refer to citizens of the Republic of Trinidad and Tobago as "Trinidadians" or "Trinis," or occasionally in an effort to be inclusive, as "Trinbagonians."

ORIENTATION

Identification. Trinidad was named by Christopher Columbus on his third voyage to the New World. On the morning of 31 July 1498, he saw what appeared to him as a trinity of hills along the southeastern coast. The island was called Iere, meaning "the land of the hummingbird," by its native Amerindian inhabitants. Tobago's name probably derived from *tabaco* (tobacco in Spanish).

Trinidad (but not Tobago) is ethnically heterogeneous. Trinidadians and Tobagonians of African descent are called "Negro," "Black," or "African." Trinidadians of Indian descent are called "East Indian" (to differentiate them from Amerindians) or "Indian." More recently the terms "Afro-Trinidadian" (or "Afro-Tobagonian") and "Indo-Trinidadian" have gained currency, reflecting heightened ethnic claims to national status. Trinidadians of European ancestry are called "White" or "French Creole." There are a number of designations for those of black–white ancestry, including "Mixed," "Colored," "Brown," and "Red" among other terms. The term Creole, from the Spanish *criollo*, meaning "of local origin," refers to Blacks, Whites, and mixed individuals who are presumed to share significant elements of a common culture as well as biogenetic properties because most claim these designations do not represent "pure races." The term Creole thus tends to relegate non-Creoles like East Indians to a somewhat foreign status. Creole also serves to modify whiteness. The term "French Creole" refers to white families of long standing whether their surname is French-derived or not. The terms "Trinidad White" and "Pass as White" are sometimes used to deride those who are considered White in Trinidad but would not be so considered elsewhere. Trinidadians and Tobagonians (the population of Tobago is almost 100 percent of African descent) identify strongly with their home island and believe each other to be different culturally.

Location and Geography. Trinidad and Tobago are the southernmost islands in the Caribbean Sea. Trinidad is 1,864 square miles in area (4,828 square kilometers), and Tobago is 116 square miles (300 square kilometers). At its closest point, Trinidad is some seven miles from the coast of Venezuela on the South American mainland. Trinidad is diverse geographically. It has three mountain ranges, roughly parallel to each other, running east to west in the north, central, and south parts of the island. The mountainous north coast is heavily wooded. The central part of the island is more flat and is where sugar cane is grown. The East–West corridor is an urban–industrial conurbation from Port of Spain, the capital, in the west to Arima in the east. San Fernando in the south is Trinidad's second city. The Point Lisas industrial park is nearby. Scarborough is the capital of Tobago. Afro-Trinidadians and other Creoles predominate in urban areas and in the north of Trinidad; Indo-Trinidadians live mostly in the central and south parts of the island.

Demography. According to the 1990 census, the total population was 1,234,400. The two major ethnic groups are Blacks (39.59 percent of the population) and East Indians (40.27 percent). The remainder of the population in 1990 included Mixed, White, and Chinese.

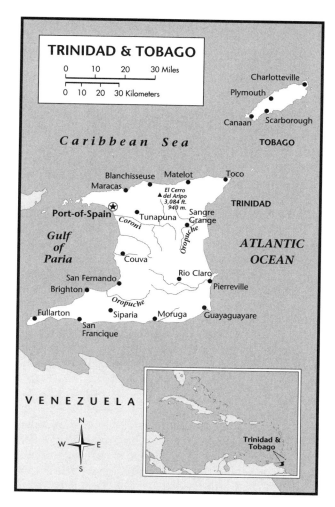

TRINIDAD & TOBAGO

Trinidad and Tobago

Linguistic Affiliation.

Linguistic Affiliation. The official language is English. At present, Trinidad is multilingual, with inhabitants speaking standard and nonstandard forms of English, a French-based creole, nonstandard Spanish, and Bhojpuri. Urdu is spoken in some rural areas. Arabic, Yoruba, Bhojpuri, Urdu and other languages are used in religious contexts, and the traditional Christmas music called *parang* is sung in Spanish. Trinidadians delight in their colorful speech and like to emphasize its distinctive use and development as a marker of identity. Standard and nonstandard English are spoken in Tobago.

Symbolism. The public symbols of the nation tend to evoke the themes of multiculturalism, unity in diversity, and tolerance. The national motto is "Together we aspire, together we achieve." The national anthem features the line "Here every creed and race find an equal place," which is sung twice for emphasis. Some public holidays and celebrations emphasize group contributions to the nation, in-

cluding Independence Day (31 August), Emancipation Day (1 August; commemorating the ending of slavery), and Indian Arrival Day (30 May).

HISTORY AND ETHNIC RELATIONS

Emergence of the Nation. Claimed by Columbus for Spain, Trinidad was a forgotten Spanish colony for three hundred years. Native Amerindians died upon contact with European diseases, were forcibly exported to the mainland to work in mines, and those who survived were subject to Spanish missions and labor schemes. The African slave population was small during Spanish rule. The Spanish *Cedula de Población* of 1783 was designed to convert Trinidad into a plantation colony. It attracted white and colored French planters who brought their African and African-descended slaves to cultivate sugar and cocoa. While controlled by Spain, Trinidad became French in orientation and dominant language use. Captured by the British in 1797, the island was formally ceded to Britain in 1802. British administrators, British planters, and their slaves added to the island's ethnic, national, and linguistic diversity. Enslaved Africans arrived from varied ethnic, cultural, linguistic, and religious groups from along the West African coast, while Creole slaves spoke a French or English creole, depending on their islands of origin. Spanish-speaking *peon* laborers from Venezuela arrived in the nineteenth century to clear forests and work in cocoa cultivation. Even before the abolition of slavery in 1834 and the end of the apprenticeship system for ex-slaves in 1838, free Africans arrived. Blacks from the United States also settled in Trinidad. From 1845 to 1917, about 144,000 indentured Indians were brought to the island. The majority were from the north of India and were drawn from a multiplicity of castes. The vast majority were Hindus, but there was a significant Muslim minority. Planters were encouraging Portuguese speakers from Madeira and Chinese from the Cantonese ports of Whampoa and Namoa to come as indentured laborers.

Tobago developed separately, with the Spanish, French, Dutch, English, and Courlanders all laying claim to the island at different times. Plantation agriculture based on enslaved labor existed alongside a significant peasant sector. The British colonies of Trinidad and Tobago were united administratively in 1889.

Under British colonialism there was a clear ethnic division of labor, with Whites as plantation owners, Chinese and Portuguese in trading occupations, Blacks and Coloreds moving into the professions and skilled manual occupations, and East Indians almost completely in agricultural pursuits. Blacks and East Indians were separated geographically, as many Blacks were urban-based and East Indians were more numerous in the agricultural central and south parts of the island. There was little if any intermarriage and little intermating between the two groups. These divisions dictated the course of national identity and nationalist politics.

National Identity. The political process has molded ethnic relations. Colonial discourses on African and Indian ancestral culture depicted Blacks as culturally "naked" and Indians possessing a culture, albeit an inferior one to European culture. Perhaps for this reason, Blacks have emphasized Western learning and culture and Indians have emphasized the glories of their subcontinental past. Despite imposed divisions, Blacks and East Indians united in the nationalist labor movements of the 1930s. However, politics quickly became contested terrain. Political parties and candidates appealed to ethnicity. Oxford-trained historian Eric Williams (1911–1981) started the People's National Movement (PNM) in 1955 with other middle-class Blacks and Creoles. Williams maintained that the PNM was a multi-ethnic party, but its interests were soon identified with Blacks. The PNM held power from 1956 until 1986, leading the country to independence in 1962. Its perpetual opposition parties were identified as "Indian," given the composition of their leaders and followers. Politics became an ethnic zero-sum game.

With independence, symbols of the state and nation were conflated with what was taken to be Afro-Trinidadian culture, such as Carnival, the steel band, and calypso music—turning the colonial hierarchy on its head. Deviating cultural practices, such as "East Indian culture," were labeled as unpatriotic and even racist. The country was depicted as a melting pot where races mixed under the rubric of "creolization." Those who did not were less than Trinidadian. A discourse of the past entered, centering on arguments over which group historically contributed most substantially to building the nation, which therefore is construed as legitimately belonging to that group. There were two opposing but related processes at work. First, an identification of nation, state, and ethnicity to construct a "non-ethnicity" where there are "Trinidadians" and then there are "others," that is, "ethnics." There is also the construction of ethnic and cultural difference to prove and justify contribution, authenticity, and citizenship. Through the mid-1990s, Afro-Trinidadians and Creoles were

able to command this discourse, but East Indians began to mount a serious challenge. At the same time, there was even a small group claiming "Carib" Amerindian identity.

Ethnic Relations. Post-independence ethnic relations have involved contests to control the state and the allocation of resources. The PNM maintained dominance through a patronage network targeted at urban Blacks as recipients. This was accomplished by a tremendous state expansion facilitated by the oil boom of the 1970s, which led to one of the highest standards of living in Latin America. Indo-Trinidadians were also able to take advantage of gains in education and fill lower-level state jobs. The government nationalized many industries, including sugar, which employed mainly Indians. A downturn in oil income severely limited state patronage opportunities. Albeit absent from formal politics, Whites, Chinese, Syrian, and some Indo-Trinidadian entrepreneurs control significant sectors of the economy. By 1986, several forces led to the formation of a black-Indian coalition party, the National Alliance for Reconstruction (NAR), that toppled the PNM. However, ethnic and personality strife broke the NAR apart, and the PNM won the next election. But by 1995, an Indian-based party, the United National Congress, barely prevailed, bringing to power the country's first Indo-Trinidadian prime minister, Basdeo Panday. While symbolic ethnic conflict seems to permeate daily life, it must be emphasized that Trinidad has never exploded in ethnic violence, as has its neighbor Guyana which has a similar demographic profile.

URBANISM, ARCHITECTURE, AND THE USE OF SPACE

In cities, glass and steel high rise office buildings mingle with colonial houses with gingerbread fretwork. The colonial Red House is the parliament building, and Woodford Square, the site of political rallies, sits opposite. Exclusive neighborhoods feature modern and colonial mansions with satellite dishes. Concrete public housing projects evoke their counterparts elsewhere and shanty towns exist on the urban periphery. Suburban developments are reminiscent of American ranch-style houses. The ever-present cacophony in urban areas is the result of cars, taxis, "maxi-taxi" minibuses, street vendors, pedestrians, and the homeless jamming the streets. Women develop stock responses to men's "sooting" (cat calls). Development in rural areas means concrete houses built on pilings to allow a breezeway and carport underneath.

Iron lacing decorates a colonial style mansion in Port of Spain, Trinidad and Tobago.

FOOD AND ECONOMY

Food in Daily Life. Cuisine is ethnically marked. A typical Creole dish is stewed chicken, white rice, red beans, fried plantains, and homemade ginger beer. Indian food consists of curried chicken, potatoes, *channa* (chick peas), white rice, and *roti*, an Indian flatbread. Chinese food is typically chow mein. However, all of these are simultaneously regarded as national dishes and food metaphors are made to stand for the nation. Trinidadians are said by Creoles to be ethnically "mixed-up" like *callaloo*, a kind of soup made from dasheen leaves and containing crab. Crab and dumplings is said to be the typical Tobago meal. A society-wide concern for cleanliness is revealed when concerns over food preparation are voiced.

Food Customs at Ceremonial Occasions. Indian food taboos and customs remain in some areas, while in others, the food customs are reinterpreted and take new form or are not relevant. A society-wide ethos valorizing generosity with food prevails, especially at ceremonial occasions. Trinidadian novelist V.S. Naipaul wrote in his travelogue *The Middle Passage* about Creoles that "Nothing is known about Hinduism or Islam. The Muslim festival of Hosein, with its drum-beating and in the old days stick-fighting is the only festival which is known; Negroes sometimes beat the drums. Indian weddings are also known. There is little interest in the ritual; it is known only that food is given to all comers." Creole knowledge of Indian rites is now considerable, as is their participation as guests at these events. Food is important in both Hindu and Muslim celebrations. In Christian families, sorrel, made from a flower, and ponche de creme, a kind of eggnog with rum, are typical Christmas drinks. Ham and pastelles are Christmas fare.

Basic Economy. Upon independence the PNM followed the colonial "industrialization by invitation" import substitution strategies to lure foreign capital and protect local manufacturers. The oil boom of 1974–1982 saw continuous real Gross Domestic Product growth averaging 6.1 percent a year, and during this time the government acquired and established a number of state enterprises, including oil and sugar companies. Government and private spending accelerated. Members of the expanding middle-class made frequent shopping trips to Miami and Caracas. The subsequent fall in oil prices meant losses in savings and foreign exchange, disinvestment, privatization, International Monetary Fund-directed trade liberalization policies, and general austerity. In the 1990s unemployment ran at more than 20 percent. Imported food and consumer goods are still prized. Agriculture occupations continued to decline as service industry occupations grew. By the end of the 1990s there was reason for optimism. In 1997, the economy grew by 4 percent, compared with a 1.5 percent contraction in 1993. Over the same period, inflation dropped to 3.8 percent from 13 percent. Income per capita (in 1990 dollars) rose from $3,920 to $4,290.

Land Tenure and Property. Land ownership is thoroughly commoditized and the government maintains significant holdings. The Sou-Sou Lands organization, named after a rotating credit association, redistributed land. Squatters remain in a number of areas. The Afro-Caribbean institution of "family land" exists in Tobago. A rural cooperative institution known as *gayap* is a means whereby some lands are cultivated and houses constructed.

Commercial Activities. There is considerable formal and informal market commercial activity in the sale of imported and locally-produced consumer goods. Towns like Chaguanas in central Trinidad have impressive high streets devoted to shopping. There are air-conditioned shopping malls around the country, supermarket chains, and small "mom and pop" shops ("arlors") with the owners living upstairs. Sales are fueled by a well-developed advertising industry and communications network. There are a number of regional open-air produce markets.

Major Industries. Government- and foreign-owned oil, natural gas, and iron and steel industries are the most important industries. A number of international goods are manufactured locally under license. Sugar is exported by the state firm. International tourism is underdeveloped in Trinidad, but government has taken steps for its promotion. Tobago is a growing international tourist destination.

Trade. Commodities sold on the international market include oil, steel, urea, natural gas, cocoa, sugar, and Angostura bitters. It is the world's second-largest exporter of ammonia and methanol. The major trading partner is the United States, but inroads were made in the late 1990s into Latin American markets.

Division of Labor. The traditional ethnic division of labor has tended to break down somewhat with time, but whites and other minorities have retained significant control of the economy. Firms owned by one ethnic group tend to have members of that group in management and as employees. State hiring is more credentials-based, despite the feeling among Blacks and Indians that certain sections of the public service are one or the other's preserve.

SOCIAL STRATIFICATION

Classes and Castes. Given ethnic diversity and ethnic politics, the salience of class is often overlooked or even actively denied. In fact, ethnicity and class work in tandem. Blacks and Indians have lagged behind other racial groups in earning power. Caste for Indians broke down with migration, but informal claims to high caste ancestry are still made at times.

Symbols of Social Stratification. Status symbols tend to be Western symbols—material possessions such as cars, the year model of which are designated by their license plates, houses, television sets, and dress. Education and use of standard English are key symbols of middle-class status. A tension exists between individualism and expectations of generosity. Upward mobility exposes one to community sanctions, captured by the proverb "The higher monkey climb, the more he show his tail."

POLITICAL LIFE

Government. The government of Trinidad and Tobago consists of a parliamentary democracy with an elected lower house and an appointed upper house. The prime minister—the leader of the party with the most seats in parliament—holds political power. The appointed president is the official head of state. The Tobago House of Assembly retains some autonomy.

Leadership and Political Officials. Political parties have for the most part made their appeals on the basis of ethnicity, even if not overtly, and nationalism, rather than on class or ideology. Cases of corruption have been highly publicized. The media, including tabloid newspapers, is particularly aggressive in making corruption allegations.

Social Problems and Control. High unemployment, especially for youth, is a central problem, spawning others. Since the 1980s, crime is seen as a serious problem, especially violent property crimes connected to the sale and transhipment of illegal drugs. Some also blame cable television and the Internet for inculcating North American values and aspirations. In neighborhoods and villages, gossip exerts control, although one loses status for being "long eye" (envious) or a *maco*, someone who minds the business of others.

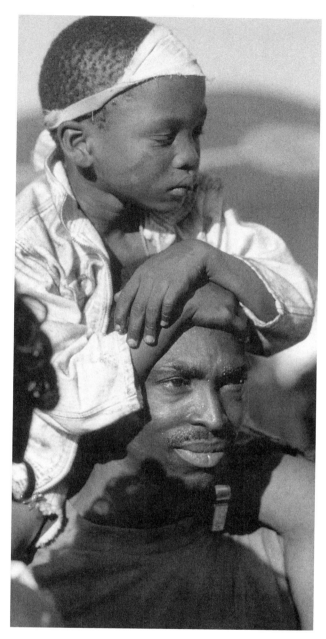

A boy sits on his father's shoulders during a Carnival procession. Carnival is a major celebration.

Military Activity. There is a small Defense Force and Coast Guard. These forces cooperate with the United States and other countries in drug interdiction.

SOCIAL WELFARE AND CHANGE PROGRAMS

A number of programs exist with specific areas of interest. For instance, women's groups include Concerned Women for Progress, The Group, and Working Women. Servol is a Catholic organization based in Laventille, a slum area, that teaches job skills to youth. The Society of Saint Vincent de Paul is also active.

NONGOVERNMENTAL ORGANIZATIONS AND OTHER ASSOCIATIONS

Nongovernmental organizations range from influential religious groups, such as the Sanatan Dharma Maha Sabha, a Hindu organization, to FundAid, an NGO that funds small businesses. Fraternal and civic organizations are very popular among the middle classes. Trade unions are very organized and influential.

GENDER ROLES AND STATUSES

Division of Labor by Gender. Women have made many gains in the last three decades: they now join men as lawyers, judges, politicians, civil servants, journalists, and even calypsonians. However, despite generally better educational levels, women earn less than men, especially in private industry. Men dominate as artisans, mechanics, and oilfield riggers. Many occupations are dominated by women, such as domestic service, sales, and some light manufacturing. Many women are microenterprise owners. Sexual harassment has been a societal issue since the 1980s.

The Relative Status of Women and Men. Power differentials remain salient in different contexts. Afro-Trinidadian women enjoy some autonomy and power within domestic domains and are often heads of households. Women are said to dominate in "playin' mas'," participating in Carnival, where they demonstrate an assertive sexuality. Women are marginalized from leadership positions in the established churches, Hinduism, and Islam, but are influential in the Afro-Christian sects. Women run the *sou-sou* informal rotating credit associations. An active women's movement has put domestic violence, rape, and workplace sexual harassment on the public agenda.

MARRIAGE, FAMILY, AND KINSHIP

Marriage. Marriage practices differ according to ethnicity and class, although for both blacks and Indians kinship is bilateral in structure. For the middle and upper classes, formal marriage with religious sanction is the norm. Legal recognition for Hindu and Muslim marriages came very late in the colonial period. In the past, East Indian women were betrothed in arranged marriages at young ages.

Children marching in the Junior Parade of the Bands in Queen's Park Savannah. Port of Spain, Trinidad and Tobago.

Many Afro-Trinidadians entered into non-coresidential relationships, then common-law marriages, and then, later in life, formal marriage. There is evidence that this is changing, with the age of marriage for Indian women increasing along with their propensity to enter non-coresidential relationships, and the importance of arranged marriages greatly diminished. The prevalence of non-coresidential relationships is increasing for the upper classes as well. Many Indo-Trinidadians see creolization as tantamount to miscegenation. Given the persistence of colonial stereotypes of Blacks, there has generally been strong Indian resistance to intermarriage with Blacks.

Domestic Unit. As with marriage patterns, the domestic unit has historically varied with class and ethnicity. Upper class families are often multi-generational. Many working-class Afro-Trinidadian households are female-headed, and multi-generational. In the past, a married Indian couple lived with the husband's extended family; however, neolocal residence is increasingly seen as the preferred form.

Inheritance. Among East Indians and upper class others, inheritance was patrilineal. This has become more egalitarian in terms of gender. Among Afro-

Trinidadians, inheritance patterns have not necessarily favored males. There are often disputes over the inheritance of land.

Kin Groups. Fictive kinship and godparenthood are important institutions. Most families have migrant kin abroad, some who play significant roles with visits and remittances.

SOCIALIZATION

Infant Care. Practices vary somewhat significantly according to ethnicity, class, and the age and education of the parents and/or caretakers. Middle class parents read North American child care books and often are knowledgeable of the latest trends. Still, there are some commonalities. For all groups, older siblings, kin, and neighbors often play significant roles. Infants are not confined to separate spaces or playpens and often sleep in the same bed as the caretaker. Infants are carried in arms from place to place. Strollers or prams are not used. Car seats for safety are becoming popular. Many toddlers are sent to pre-schools and nurseries by age two. Corporal punishment in public for toddlers is common.

Child Rearing and Education. Values inculcated vary by ethnicity, class, and the sex of the child. In general, caretakers, be they parents, grandparents, or other kin or fictive kin, are quick to discipline children. "Back chat" to an adult is not permitted. Children are expected to show that they are "broughtupsy" having decorum, but not to the point of being "social" (pretentious). A "harden" (disobedient) child or a *wajang* (rowdy, uncouth) youth involved in *commesse* (scandal, acrimony) is an embarrassment to the family. Boys are expected to be aggressive and, as they get older, sexually aware, but respectful to adults. Ideally, girls do not have free reign. Most girls are encouraged to emphasize physical beauty.

Higher Education. The society places a high value on higher education and many parents and kin make great sacrifices to enable students to reach their educational goals. In the past, training for white-collar professions was favored and emphasized, and titles and diplomas were fetishized. Status is attached to better secondary schools, such as Queen's Royal College (state) and Catholic Church-affiliated Saint Mary's College for boys and Saint Joseph's Convent for girls. The Trinidad campus of the regional, comprehensive University of the West Indies (UWI) is in Saint Augustine (other sites are in Barbados and Jamaica). UWI in Trinidad began in 1960 when the Imperial College of Tropical Agriculture became the Faculty of Agriculture of the University College of the West Indies, University of London. Many citizens with higher education were trained abroad and they often emigrate permanently.

ETIQUETTE

While class and ethnic differences matter, as do contexts, sociability and gregariousness are generally highly valued. Business settings require more subdued behavior, but it is not considered good form to talk about one's work endlessly at cocktail parties. Middle-class men receive status for offering their comrades imported Scotch whiskey. In general, punctuality is not expected. "Trinidad time" refers to habitual lateness and "jus' now" means "in a little while" but in practice can mean hours. On city streets it is common for men to verbally harass women and women generally lose status if they reply. In country districts, it is expected that one salutes passers by with a "good morning" or "good aftimiernoon." Slarly, one should begin phone conversations, address fellow passengers upon entering a taxi, and address occupants when entering a room or a home with a "good morning," "good afternoon," or "good night."

Women are often heads of households.

RELIGION

Religious Beliefs. The country is noted for its religiosity and religious diversity. In 1990, the majority religion was Roman Catholic, encompassing 29 percent of the population. The majority of Indians are Hindu, but many are Christians, resulting from Canadian Presbyterian missions in the nineteenth century. Evangelical Christian sects from North America are growing rapidly. American Muslim groups claim adherents. There are followers of Sai Baba and Rastafarians. Afro-Christian forms of worship are prevalent, such as the Orisha religion and the Spiritual Baptists, and worship in these is not exclusive of membership in established churches. There are folk beliefs in *jumbies* (ghosts, spirits). Official religious holidays include Divali (called Holi in India; Hindu), Eid (Muslim), Spiritual Baptist Liberation Day (30 March), Good Friday, Corpus Christi, and Christmas Day. The two days before Ash Wednesday, when Carnival is held, and Phagwa (Hindu) and Hosay (Muslim) are holidays for all intents and purposes.

Religious Practitioners. Religious leaders include imams (Muslim), pundits (Hindu), priests (Anglican and Catholic), Orisha and Spiritual Baptist leaders. There is a hierarchy in established churches, with a Catholic archbishop and an Anglican bishop at the head of those communities.

Ritual and Holy Places. On Holy Thursday night, thousands of Hindus pay homage to a carved wood statue of the Madonna at the Catholic church at Siparia. Weeks later, Catholics parade the same statue through the streets. In the past, Chinese came to honor the statue when it passed on the street. Places of worship, such as the Holy Trinity Cathedral in Port of Spain and the Abbey of Mount Saint Benedict, a functioning monastery, are seen as holy places. The Caroni River, where Hindu cremations are held, is an important ritual and holy place.

Death and the Afterlife. Funerals and all-night wakes, called "sit-ups," are important social occasions. Obituaries are read on the radio. Cremation at the Caroni River is practiced for Hindu Trinidadians.

MEDICINE AND HEALTH CARE

There is a national health service, but private medicine serves a large share of the population. Both are based on the Western bio-medical model. There are traditional healers, some related to Afro-Christian forms of worship. Many ordinary citizens use herbal teas and bush medicine for everyday ailments. Drug addiction and AIDS are seen as serious problems and the country has one of the highest AIDS rates in the world.

SECULAR CELEBRATIONS

Besides Emancipation, Independence, and Indian Arrival days, official secular holidays include New Year's Day, Easter Monday, Labour Day (19 June), when 1930s labor leader T.U.B. Butler and the trade union/nationalist movement are commemorated, and Boxing Day (26 December). The pre-Lenten Carnival is the biggest secular celebration.

THE ARTS AND HUMANITIES

Support for the Arts. The government supports Carnival, the Best Village competition (which includes dance, music, and drama), the National Youth Orchestra, the biennial Music Festival, and the National Museum.

Literature. An impressive literary tradition exists among writers who have mainly made their names and reputations abroad, including C.L.R. James, Ralph de Boissière, V.S. Naipaul, Shiva Naipaul, Samuel Selvon, Earl Lovelace, Ismith Khan, Ramabai Espinet, and Michael Anthony. Calypso must count

as oral literature. Contemporary calypsonians include the Mighty Sparrow, Lord Kitchener, the Mighty Chalkdust, Gypsy, Black Stalin, Drupatee, Cro Cro, Calypso Rose, Super Blue, David Rudder, Crazy, Baron, Explainer, Sugar Aloes, and Denyse Plummer among many others. Relatively new music forms are Indian music-influenced "chutney" and "pitchakaree," performed by well-known singers such as Sundar Popo, Anand Yankaran, Heeralal Rampartap, Savitri Jagdeo, Vinti Mohip, Jagdeo Phagoo, and Ramraajee Prabhoo.

Graphic Arts. Trinidad's best known artist is perhaps the painter Michel Jean Cazabon (1813–1888). Some of the better-known artists of the past few decades are Dermot Louison, M.P. Alladin, Sybil Attek, Amy Leong Pang, Pat Chu Foon, and the sculptor Ralph Baney. Active living artists include Carlisle Chang, LeRoy Clarke, Boscoe Holder, Francisco Cabral, Pat Bishop, Isaiah Boodhoo, Ken Crichlow, Wendy Naran, and Jackie Hinkson. A younger generation includes Eddie Bowen, Kathryn Chang, Chris Cozier, and Che Lovelace. A recent appreciation of untrained artists has resulted in the establishment of the Museum of Popular and Folk Art.

Performance Arts. Carnival is Trinidad's most noteworthy performance art, attracting tourists, emigrated Trinidadians, and scholars from abroad. Masquerade designer Peter Minshall is one of the best known internationally. He was artistic director for the opening and closing ceremonies of the 1992 Olympics in Barcelona, the 1996 Olympics in Atlanta, and the 1994 World Cup opening ceremony in the United States. Live calypso and steelband performances occur in the Carnival season (Christmas through Lent). A dance performance tradition centers around Beryl McBurnie and the Little Carib Theatre.

THE STATE OF THE PHYSICAL AND SOCIAL SCIENCES

In 1961, the UWI Faculty of Engineering opened. In 1963, teaching in the arts, natural, and social sciences began. There are a number of research institutes, such as the Centre for Ethnic Studies, the Centre for Gender and Development Studies, and the Institute of Social and Economic Research. In Tobago the government-run Hospitality and Tourism Institute offers tourism training. Some locally-based social scientists are very visible as pollsters, newspaper columnists, and television analysts.

BIBLIOGRAPHY

Braithwaite, Lloyd. *Social Stratification in Trinidad*, 1975 [1953].

Brereton, Bridget. *A History of Modern Trinidad 1783–1962*, 1981.

Harewood, Jack, and Ralph Henry. *Inequality in a Post-Colonial Society: Trinidad and Tobago*, 1985.

Hill, Errol. *The Trinidad Carnival: Mandate for a National Theatre*, 1972.

LaGuerre, John G., ed. *Calcutta to Caroni: The East Indians of Trinidad*, 1985 [1974].

Mendes, John. *Cote ce Cote la: Trinidad and Tobago Dictionary*, 1986.

Miller, Daniel. *Modernity—An Ethnographic Approach: Dualism and Mass Consumption in Trinidad*, 1994.

Oxaal, Ivar. *Black Intellectuals and the Dilemmas of Race and Class in Trinidad*, 1982.

Reddock, Rhoda E. *Women, Labour and Politics in Trinidad and Tobago: A History*, 1994.

Rohlehr, Gordon. *Calypso and Society in Pre-Independence Trinidad*, 1990.

Ryan, Selwyn, ed., *Trinidad and Tobago: The Independence Experience 1962–1987*, 1988.

Stuempfle, Stephen. *The Steelband Movement: The Forging of a National Art in Trinidad and Tobago*, 1995.

Vertovec, Steven. *Hindu Trinidad: Religion, Ethnicity and Socio-Economic Change*, 1992.

Wood, Donald. *Trinidad in Transition: The Years After Slavery*, 1968.

Yelvington, Kevin A., ed. *Trinidad Ethnicity*, 1993.

———. *Producing Power: Ethnicity, Gender, and Class in a Caribbean Workplace*, 1995.

—KEVIN A. YELVINGTON

TUNISIA

CULTURE NAME

Tunisian

ALTERNATIVE NAMES

Republic of Tunisia or Tunisian Republic. In Arabic the name of the capital, Tunis, includes the whole country. The old Roman province of Africa under the Arabs became first Ifriqiya, then later Tunisia.

ORIENTATION

Identification. Originally Tunis was a satellite town of Carthage, located about 6.2 miles (10 kilometers) inland from the Mediterranean Sea. Carthage with its port was the historic urban center in the region from the ninth century B.C.E. through the eighth century C.E. Since Carthaginian times the rural hinterland around Carthage, later Tunis, has approximately corresponded to the contemporary boundaries of Tunisia. It has sometimes been part of a larger empire, as when it was the Roman province of Africa, sometimes an independent unit, as under the medieval Hafsid dynasty, but always distinct. Today Tunisia is part of the larger Arab world, with which it shares a language and many cultural elements, including a political identification. Within this broader identity, the sense of Tunisian uniqueness remains strong.

Location and Geography. Tunisia is located in north-central Africa, between Algeria and Libya, with an area of 63,200 square miles (164,000 square kilometers). It has a lengthy Mediterranean coast and is very open to Mediterranean influences. Tunisians are a maritime people and have always maintained extensive contacts by sea with other Mediterranean countries. The main cities are all on the coast, and contemporary development, including tourism, is also concentrated on the coast. Some ecologically significant wetlands are found along the coast. From a physical and economic point of view, there is considerable variety in the country, from cork oak forests in the north to open desert in the south, but this physical variety has not produced cultural variety.

Mountains play a role in Tunisia as determiners of climatic variation and refuge for political outsiders. A chain of mountains separates the grain-producing areas of northern Tunisia from the high, dry plateau to the south, where animal husbandry dominates, and the semiarid coastal plains where olive cultivation is common. The highest point is Mount Ash-Sha'nabi, near Al-Qasrayn (Kasserine), at 5,050 feet (1,544 meters). The country is heavily dependent on rainfall, which falls mostly between September and May, and in northern Tunisia averages around 20 inches (50 centimeters) a year. The mountains in the northwest attract heavier rain and even snow in the winter. The longest river in the country is the Medjerda, which rises in Algeria and flows through Tunisia to the sea. Many drainage systems end in saline lakes. Southern Tunisia extends into the Saharan desert, and includes some notable oases; people live wherever there is water.

Demography. In the 1994 census, Tunisia's population was 8,785,711. In 2000 the population was estimated at 9.6 million with a natural increase rate of 1.6 percent. The urban population is 64 percent and tending higher. About 19 percent of the population lives in Greater Tunis. The adult literacy rate is 69 percent (58 percent for women, 80 percent for men), and the life expectancy is 70 years (69 for men, 71 for women). The per capita gross domestic product (GDP) was $2,283 (U.S.) in 1998. The United Nations Development Program's report for 2000 placed Tunisia in the middle rung of development, ranking 101st out of 174 countries.

Almost all Tunisians are Arabic-speaking Muslims. Berber languages are spoken in a few villages in southern Tunisia, and there is a small remnant of the historic Jewish population, now concentrated in Tunis and on the island of Jerba off the southern

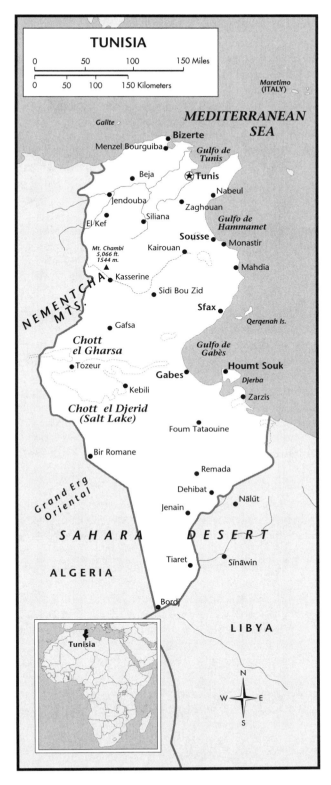

TUNISIA

| 0 | 50 | 100 | 150 Miles |
| 0 | 50 | 100 | 150 Kilometers |

Tunisia

coast. Before the migration of Jews to Israel and France, most towns had a small Jewish community, and Tunis itself was 10–15 percent Jewish. Neither of these minorities now reaches 1 percent.

Linguistic Affiliation. The language of Tunisia is Arabic. As elsewhere, the spoken language differs considerably from the written language. The regional dialects are tending to disappear under pressure from mass media centered in Tunis. The main second language is French. The educational system is geared to produce bilingualism in French and Arabic, with a few elite schools now focusing on English. Only a minority of Tunisians, however, are comfortable in French. Fluency in French is a status marker, and so social considerations, as well as the practical ones of an opening to the world, have impeded full Arabization. Knowledge of other European languages is largely a function of television exposure and tourism.

Symbolism. Perhaps because Tunisia is a relatively small and homogeneous country, the sense of national identity is strong. It is constantly maintained by reference to recent national history, particularly the struggle against French colonialism (1881–1956) and the subsequent efforts to create a modern society. The struggle was more political and tactical than violent, though there were some violent outbursts. This narrative is constantly rehearsed, in the sequence of public holidays, in the names of streets, and in the subject matter of films and television shows. The sense of difference is also reinforced by the achievements of the national football (soccer) team in international competitions.

The Tunisian flag did not change during or after the colonial period. The flag has a red star and crescent, symbolizing Islam, in a white circle in a red field. It derives from the Ottoman flag, reflecting Ottoman suzerainty over Tunisia from the sixteenth through the nineteenth centuries.

HISTORY AND ETHNIC RELATIONS

Emergence of the Nation. Tunisia's geographical location has meant that many different peoples have entered and dominated the country. Probably the original population was Berber speaking. The parade of invaders began with the Phoenicians, who settled Carthage, used it as a trading base, and eventually entered into a losing conflict with Rome. Under the Romans, who dominated Tunisia for several centuries, Christianity also entered the country. After the decline of the Romans, the Vandals invaded from the west, followed by a Byzantine reconquest from the east. The Byzantines were replaced by Muslim Arabs from the east, but by land, in the seventh century. Tunisia has been predominantly Arabic-speaking and Muslim since then, though dynasties have come and gone. After 1574, Tunisia was incorporated into the Ottoman Empire. The Spanish held parts of Tunisia briefly before the Ottomans, and the French ruled Tunisia during the colonial period from 1881 to 1956.

Tunisia was ruled by the Husseini dynasty of beys from 1705 to 1957. The beys of Tunis and their government tried to construct a modern Tunisia during the nineteenth century to fend off stronger European powers. After France took over Algeria in 1830, pressure on Tunisia grew. In 1881, the bey of Tunis accepted a French protectorate over the country. France set up a colonial administration, and facilitated the settlement in Tunisia of many French and other Europeans, mainly Italians. About a generation after the establishment of the protectorate, a nationalist movement emerged, seeking a modern and independent Tunisia. The Destour (Constitution) Party was founded about 1920, and in 1934 an offshoot known as the Neo-Destour Party became dominant under the leadership of Habib Bourguiba (1903–2000).

Parallel to the political movement, a strong labor movement also emerged. Usually working together, the political and labor wings struggled against French colonialism until independence in 1956. A republic was declared in 1957, with Bourguiba as the first president. The independent government carried out many social reforms in the country, with regard to education, women's status, and economic structures. During the 1960s the government followed a socialist policy, then reverted to liberalism while retaining a substantial state involvement. In 1987 Bourguiba was declared senile and replaced by Zine El Abidine Ben Ali (1936–), but without a major shift in policy. Contemporary policy is pragmatic rather than ideological.

National Identity. By the end of the nineteenth century, Tunisians distinguished between Moors, Turks, Jews, Berbers, Andalusians, Arabs, and various sorts of Europeans. Few of these distinctions are relevant today. Some groups were assimilated, others such as the colonial Europeans eventually retreated. None of the invasions and population movements left traces in the ethnic structure of the country. The geography of the city of Tunis and its hinterland, and the effort to create a national culture, have proved stronger than diverse ethnic origins in shaping Tunisian identity.

URBANISM, ARCHITECTURE, AND THE USE OF SPACE

Tunisia is dominated by its capital city, Tunis. The other main cities are along the coast, and include Bizerte, Sousse, Sfax, and Gabès. These precolonial towns have an older nucleus, or medina, surrounded by modern administrative and residential neighborhoods and by slums. The classical town in Tunisia includes a main mosque, a market, and a public bath. All three are sites for interaction. Friday prayers are essentially linked with urbanity, the market attracts people for trade and exchange, and the public bath expresses a certain concern with personal cleanliness from a time when houses did not have their own bathrooms. The cities are well supplied with water, electricity, and other public services. Garbage and sewage, formerly just dumped, are now treated and sometimes recycled.

The old urban neighborhoods contain magnificent examples of traditional Islamic urban architecture, both public buildings such as mosques and markets as well as elite residences. Houses rich and poor are built around a courtyard, which serves as a family work space away from strange eyes. Entrances are designed to prevent passersby from seeing into the building. The older pedestrian neighborhoods are often not readily accessible to automobiles, while the newer suburbs are built with cars in mind. Generally, buildings in Tunisia are painted white with blue trim.

Some rural people live in villages, but away from the coast many live in scattered homesteads, near their fields. People seek privacy by distancing themselves from neighbors. Formerly, Tunisia had a substantial nomadic population, which lived in tents, but this is now exceptional. Water scarcity is a problem for Tunisia. The annual per capita availability of renewable water is low and puts Tunisia in the water-scarce category. Tunisia has managed to tap all its water resources and to provide for all urban areas and some rural areas, but the system is stretched to its limit. Rural people may have to haul water from a distance, and with considerable effort. City water is brought from distant mountains, since the coastal areas rely heavily on rainfall alone.

FOOD AND ECONOMY

Food in Daily Life. Traditional Tunisian cuisine reflects local agriculture. It stresses wheat, in the form of bread or couscous, olives and olive oil, meat (above all, mutton), fruit, and vegetables. Couscous (semolina wheat prepared with a stew of meat and vegetables) is the national dish, and most people eat

Tunisian mourners wear traditional bright red costumes at funerals. Corpses are laid on the left side, facing Mecca.

it daily in simple forms, and in more complex forms for celebrations. Bread with stew is a growing alternative. Tunisians near the coast eat a lot of seafood, and eggs are also common. Tunisians tend to eat in family groups at home, and restaurants are common in tourist areas and for travelers. In the countryside, tea is served in preference to the urban coffee. Tunisians also fast from dawn to dark during the month of Ramadan.

Food Customs at Ceremonial Occasions. Sweet or colorful dishes symbolize religious holidays, usually in addition to couscous. For weddings and other happy occasions, sweets are added to the couscous. Animals are slaughtered for religious gatherings, and the meat is shared among the participants as a way of symbolizing the togetherness.

Basic Economy. Tunisia is historically an agricultural country, and agriculture now absorbs 22 percent of the labor force; about 20 percent of the country is farmland. Rain-fed agriculture dominates and concentrates on wheat, olives, and animal husbandry. Wheat is mostly used domestically, and Tunisia is a major world producer of olive oil. Animal husbandry for domestic consumption is significant, especially sheep and goats, but also cattle in the north and camels in the south. Citrus and other tree crops are produced both under rain-fed and irrigated conditions, and are often exported. About 6 percent of the arable land is irrigated and is used to grow the full range of crops, but perhaps is most typically used for vegetables and other garden crops. Dates are grown in irrigated oases. The long coastline orients Tunisians toward the sea and toward fishing.

Land Tenure and Property. Traditionally, much agricultural land and urban property was held as collective property, either undivided inheritances or endowed land. From the mid-nineteenth century this system has been giving way to the predominance of individual land and property ownership. The state itself is a major property owner.

Commercial Activities. Most aspects of life in Tunisia have been monetized, apart from some subsistence farming. Subsistence farmers can be recognized because they cultivate a variety of crops, while market-oriented farmers concentrate on a few. Most Tunisian farmers expect to sell their crops and buy their needs. The same applies to craftsmen and other occupations. Rural Tunisia is covered by an interlocking network of weekly markets that provide basic consumption goods to the rural population and serve as collecting points for animals and other produce. Among the very poor in

Tunisia are self-employed street vendors, market traders, and others in the lower levels of the informal sector.

Major Industries. The national government after independence continued to develop phosphate and other mines, and to develop processing factories near the mines or along the coast. There is some oil in the far south and in the center. Efforts to develop heavy industry (such as steel and shipbuilding) are limited. More recently light industry has expanded in the clothing, household goods, food processing, and diamond-cutting sectors. Some of this is done in customs-free zones for export to Europe.

Considerable small-scale manufacturing is done in artisanal workshops for the local market. These workshops, often with fewer than ten workers including the owner, are the upper level of the informal sector. Overall, manufacturing accounts for 23 percent of the labor force.

The service sector is also substantial in Tunisia. Employment in services is about 55 percent of the labor force. A major service industry is tourism, mostly along the coast and oriented toward Europeans on beach holidays with excursions to historical sites. Contact with tourists has been a major source of new ideas. Banking and trade are also well developed, both internationally and in terms of a network of markets and traders in the country.

Trade. Exports include light industry products and agricultural products, such as wheat, citrus, and olive oil. Imports include a variety of consumer goods and machinery for industry.

Division of Labor. The national division of labor reflects education and gender. There are many relatively complex jobs, whether for the government or not, that require specific educational skills and background. Thus the educational system provides a major input into the division of labor.

Many Tunisian men, and some families, now live and work abroad. This began with migration to France in the early twentieth century. Tunisians now also migrate to various European countries, and to oil countries such as neighboring Libya or the more distant Persian Gulf nations. Remittances and other forms of investment at home are significant, and returned migrants play a role in many communities. Since many men from the marginal agricultural areas have migrated in search of work, agricultural labor has been feminized. Intellectual and professional Tunisians also migrate, but the paths are more individual.

SOCIAL STRATIFICATION

Classes and Castes. Tunisian society is marked by class distinctions, with considerable upward mobility and fuzzy class awareness. Class distinctions based on wealth are the most apparent, with enormous differences between the wealthy bourgeoisie living in the affluent suburbs of Tunis and the rural and urban poor. Wealth in one generation leads to improved education in the next. Status through ancestry is relatively unimportant.

Symbols of Social Stratification. The symbols of social stratification are basically in style and level of consumption.

POLITICAL LIFE

Government. Tunisia is a republic headed by a president. There is a prime minister, a council of ministers, and an elected national assembly. Local administration works through officials appointed by the minister of interior. Urban areas organized in municipalities also have a town council.

Leadership and Political Officials. The political party that took the lead in the nationalist movement from 1934 to 1956 has essentially been a single party since independence in 1956. This party was initially known as the Neo-Destour Party, then in the 1960s was called the Destour Socialist Party, and since the deposition of Bourguiba in 1987 is named the Democratic Constitutional Rally. The word that has remained in its name is "constitution" (*destour* in Arabic), which implies a concern with legality. This party has historically been relatively well structured with active local branches organized in a rational hierarchy. There is a parallel structure for women. The formerly autonomous labor union movement has now essentially been coopted. Successful political careers involve slow advance in the party hierarchy.

Some opposition parties are allowed to operate legally, but have little influence. In the 1999 elections, the government introduced a form of proportional representation to allow opposition parties to enter parliament despite relatively low voting scores. The twenty-one women in parliament represent 11.5 percent of the membership.

Social Problems and Control. Crime is low, and public order is generally quite peaceful in Tunisia, though there have been one or two outbreaks of rioting around economic issues in different parts of the country. The concern of the government to maintain order is reflected in the growth of police

A bedouin family drink tea in Matmata. Tunisian families are patriarchal.

forces in recent years. Political dissidents of all kinds are given very little freedom to act. Even traffic police are severe.

Military Activity. Tunisia's relatively small army has seen little action.

SOCIAL WELFARE AND CHANGE PROGRAMS

Part of the contract between government and people is that government officials take the lead in promoting welfare and development. These programs are done either with foreign bilateral assistance or through the government's own resources. They include programs in the areas of health, family planning, environment, agricultural and regional development, and major infrastructure construction, such as dams and irrigation projects.

NONGOVERNMENTAL ORGANIZATIONS AND OTHER ASSOCIATIONS

Since independence, the government has worked to create a sense of individual citizenship, with citizens dealing individually with the state. Thus in practice it restricts the activities of nongovernmental organizations. The more political organizations, such as human rights, women's rights, or environmental

organizations, are either coopted or suppressed. The government and the party themselves offer a range of associations for women, youth, and labor, and it is difficult to compete. After independence, the labor union organization entered into a long struggle to maintain its independence of government control, but eventually succumbed. Efforts to create water user associations in rural areas were limited by laws restricting their right to collect and spend their own money. An important form of nongovernmental organization is the sports clubs, essentially football clubs, which are usually dominated by figures from the national elite.

GENDER ROLES AND STATUSES

Division of Labor by Gender. In family and household settings, the men are responsible for producing an income, whether through self-employment in agriculture or through a job, while women are responsible for managing the household. In agricultural households, this may involve transforming the raw material of agriculture into useful items—spinning and weaving wool from family sheep, preparing the wheat into couscous, or preserving fruit and vegetables. Women work in agriculture either in a family context, especially when

The architecture in Ksar Ouled Soultane reflects the influence of Islamic design.

men are absent, or sometimes as wage labor on the large farms in northern Tunisia. Women who work for wages in agriculture are paid about half the rate for men. This rate is sometimes justified on the grounds that they do not produce as much, but this is also a strategy to maintain low overall wages. In the wider community, the division of labor is less strict, and there are many women who now occupy jobs in government, industry, and the private sector. In the late 1990s, women were 36 percent of professional and technical workers, and 13 percent of administrators and managers. Their per capita share of GDP, however, was about half the national average.

The Relative Status of Women and Men. Independent Tunisia under Bourguiba made a major effort to improve women's status by encouraging education and employment, improving the conditions of marriage, and encouraging family planning. This has reduced rather than eliminated the gap between the status of women and men. Women still endure a lot of stress trying to follow a career or enter public life in a male-dominated society. Some men resent the formal employment of women when unemployment of educated men remains high, and also scorn the idea of women in public life.

MARRIAGE, FAMILY, AND KINSHIP

Marriage. Choice of marriage partners may be by arrangement between families or the result of individual selection based on acquaintances made at school or work. There is some preference for cousins, in part because cousins are considered to be of equal status. Girls are not supposed to marry beneath them. Mothers search for brides for their sons, and may scrutinize possible candidates during the women's periods in the public baths. Once an engagement is settled on there is a complex series of visits between the two families. Sometimes disputes over gifts or etiquette leads to a collapse of the engagement, or one or the other of the partners may back out. The marriage ceremony itself involves the shift of the bride from her house to her groom's house, while the groom waits outside, so that he may enter into the bridal chamber where she is waiting. After the consummation of the marriage, there is a period of seclusion until the young couple reenters society.

The legal aspects of marriage are covered by the Personal Status Code, introduced right after independence (1956) by Bourguiba. This code generally had the effect of protecting women's rights and encouraging companionate marriage. The code prohibited polygamous marriages and forced marriage for girls, established a minimum age for marriage, and required judicial divorce rather than repudiation. Later amendments allowed women to initiate divorce.

Domestic Unit. The household in Tunisia is based on the patriarchal family. Beliefs and practices sustain the notion of the dominant male head. Most households are based on the nuclear family. Apart from the urban poor in the old city of Tunis, most households at all income levels consist of a separate house, together with its courtyard and annexes. Within the household, tasks are assigned on the basis of age and gender, as well as personal skills. Changes in educational and employment patterns have made the companionate marriage between equals more common.

Inheritance. Inheritance, following Islam, is partible, with male heirs receiving twice the share of equivalent female heirs. Bequests are allowed only to those who would not otherwise inherit. Certain kinds of property, such as farmland, may not actually be divided in use, though a record of the inheritance situation is maintained. Formerly, property could be kept as a unit by making it endowed for the family, but this is now rare.

Kin Groups. Tunisians recognize the extension of kinship beyond the nuclear family, and maintain the network of connections. As elsewhere, these links are more alive among the wealthy and powerful, where the stakes are higher, and among the very poor, where they are a major resource.

Where a family retains a connection with an ancestral "saint," the annual festival of this saint serves as a family reunion, and sacralizes the group, meaning those descended in the male line from the ancestor. In the parts of interior Tunisia where pastoralism once dominated, these connections extend to a "tribe" (here called an *arsh*) such as the Zlass around Al-Qayrawan (Kairouan) or the Freshish and Mateur around Al-Qasrayn and Sbetla. This is a larger identity based on extension of kin ties. These units and their chiefs were recognized in the colonial system, but were rejected by the independent government. The ties are now only occasionally activated, for instance in elections and marriages.

SOCIALIZATION

Infant Care. Infants are cared for by their mothers or older siblings in a family setting. Most newborns are breastfed.

Child Rearing and Education. Once children can walk, their fathers may play more of a role in their

Women's responsibilities can include spinning and weaving wool.

upbringing, especially for boys. At age six, the state takes over socialization for both boys and girls through virtually universal primary school. The schools are well-organized and managed, though perhaps underequipped.

Higher Education. The paths of children begin to diverge after primary school. Some remain on an academic track, while others undertake vocational education. Child labor is relatively uncommon, but boys may begin to work as apprentices when they are teenagers. Those who remain on an academic track eventually pass a "baccalaureate" type of examination, which governs their subsequent career. The academic elite continue on to one of the university faculties in Tunis or elsewhere.

ETIQUETTE

Tunisians are relatively egalitarian in their interpersonal relations, but there is a strong sense of etiquette. People should be addressed respectfully. A man should not show too much curiosity towards the women in his friend's family, and may not even know their names. In some cases, men do not visit each other's homes because the women would inevitably be present. Some people with a sense of their own status do not visit those they consider lower in rank. These rules are relaxed in the urbanized upper classes.

Modesty codes for women prevail in some areas. In traditional urban society, women were supposed to be circumspect in their behavior. They were supposed to limit trips outside the house to certain culturally approved destinations, such as the public bath or the tombs of their relatives in the cemetery. In certain sectors of Tunisian urban society, women cover head and body in public with a rectangular white cloth, the *safsari*. Rural women follow different dress practices, but may adopt urban forms on visits to the city. These older practices are rarer now, and the "modern" veil has been officially discouraged, so there is no common dress code.

Men are also supposed to show respect for each other. A man is not supposed to smoke in front of his father, and he is not supposed to carry his own child in the presence of his father. Brothers might frequent different cafs so that the presence of a brother would not inhibit relaxation. Traditional male dress included loose trousers and shirt, with perhaps a robe over that, and a red-felt skullcap. Again, practices are now less uniform than in the past, with the differences reflecting degrees of modernity, or level of education and income.

RELIGION

Religious Beliefs. As Muslims, Tunisians accept the oneness of God and the power of his word as expressed in the Koran. For many purposes, people refer to the texts of the Koran and of certain related texts such as the Hadith (authentic traditions). The Shari'ah, or Islamic law, is central to people's understanding of what is proper. Together these texts lay down correct behavior and lead to certain everyday rituals. In practice there is a certain amount of variation in belief and practice. The variation corresponds broadly to the social position of families and individuals.

The religious calendar provides the main occasions for the expression of these beliefs. The five daily prayers, the weekly cycle organized around the Friday midday prayer, and the yearly festivals structure time. The annual cycle includes the fasting month of Ramadan. There is also the Feast of the Sacrifice, which coincides with the annual pilgrimage to the holy places of Mecca and Medina. On this feast, every householder must sacrifice a ram in emulation of Abraham's willingness to express his faith by sacrificing his son, who was then miraculously replaced on the altar by a ram. Another festi-

val, traditionally more associated with sufi orders, is the Prophet's Birthday. The feast of Ashura, commemorating the martyrdom of the grandson of the prophet Muhammad at the battle of Kerbala, may be celebrated in Tunisia by visits to tombs and bonfires. The dates of these celebrations are all set according to the Islamic lunar calendar, which does not follow the seasons.

Religious Practitioners. Islam does not recognize a sacerdotal priesthood. The formal religious specialists are experts in Islamic law and practice, including religious judges, prayer leaders and others who care for mosques, and traditional teachers of Arabic and religious texts. These posts are limited to men. Informal religious specialists also include men (and sometimes women) who are seen as the vessels of divine grace (*baraka*) and who thus have the power to heal, foresee the future, interpret dreams, or mediate with God on behalf of petitioners. This divine grace may be attributed because of the individual's actions or it may be inherited. Between the formal and the informal are the leaders of Sufi orders. Since the 1970s a reform movement has grown up in Tunisia. This movement is based on a close adherence to the Koran and other sacred texts, and is opposed to some of the heterodox practices described below. It also has political implications, and at times functions as an opposition party. Thus its prominent leaders are more political than religious. Most are now in exile or prison.

Rituals and Holy Places. The main life-crisis rites are ritualized through Islam—birth, naming, circumcision (for boys), marriage, pilgrimage, and death. Muslims are enjoined to make the pilgrimage to the holy places of Mecca and Medina, located in Saudi Arabia. For Tunisians, as for most Muslims, the holy places are a "center out there." Both the departure on pilgrimage and the return are ceremonialized by visits to mosques, family gatherings, and gifts. Of course, the stay in the holy places is also part of this rite of passage. To reflect the new status, a returned pilgrim should be addressed as "hajj," meaning pilgrim.

Tunisia is also a land of wonder as expressed in the numerous holy places scattered in rural and urban areas. These shrines in principle contain the tomb of a holy person, often male, and serve as key points for links between the human and the divine. Some shrines are the object of an annual festival that draws together people from a particular community (such as a village, extended family, or tribe) to honor the saint. These festivals intensify and reinforce the solidarity of that group. Each town or community is likely to have one shrine that serves as the symbolic focal point for that group. People make individual visits to a shrine for many other reasons, including a specific request for help from the shrine's "saint," or to thank the saint for favors granted. Thanking the saint may turn into an annual ritual of reconnection between the individual and the saint, and through the saint with God. Properly, only God can grant favors, and the saint is merely the intermediary, but there is some slippage toward the idea of the power of the saint to help directly.

An examination of these shrines shows that many reflect unusual features in the landscape, such as caves, hilltops, springs, unusual trees, or points on the coastline. Presumably this saint cult incorporates certain features of an older nature cult.

Some people believe that saints, those connected with spirits or jinns, may also be angry if they feel slighted, because, for instance, people overlooked an annual visit of reconnection. Thus they send their jinns to afflict those who slight them. Cure for the affliction consists of diagnosing the source and placating the saint so that the affliction is reversed. The curing usually also involves a reaffirmation of family ties, since it is effective only if it takes place in a group context. Although heterodox in Islamic terms, this complex serves as a folk explanation for illness or misfortune. While formal Islam is heavily male oriented, this "saint cult" allows more scope for women to take initiatives or even to display divine grace themselves. Conceptually linked with the complex of beliefs in saints are the mystical associations, known as "Sufi ways" or "orders." Here the stress is rather on a mystical loss of self in the divine, with the help of the teachings of a saintly individual. These Sufi orders are less evident in Tunisia than they used to be. Until the early twentieth century, their national leaders were often linked to the court of the bey of Tunis, they often had political roles, and their prestige was high. Later they suffered from their association with colonial power. The shrines associated with key figures in the history of these associations also often function as "saints" shrines, and often also as the centers of curing cults.

Death and the Afterlife. Muslims believe that the soul lives on after physical death. Corpses are buried quickly, the same day or early the next morning, in cemeteries reflecting the social identity of the dead person. The corpse is washed, wrapped in a shroud, carried to the cemetery by a group of mourners, and buried in a tomb. The body is laid on its left side facing Mecca. There are periodic commemorations

Side street stores on Kerkenna Island are packed with local shoppers on a Tunisian afternoon.

of the death, after seven and forty days, and sometimes after a year. Survivors also make visits to the tomb, men and women separately, and leave offerings for the soul of the dead person.

MEDICINE AND HEALTH CARE

Tunisia has a modern system of health care with hospitals and clinics well distributed in the country. In addition, there are private doctors and hospitals. The University of Tunis has a medical school. Some doctors in the capital have formed associations to promote public health awareness, notably around the question of preventing pollution.

Traditional healers include bonesetters, dream interpreters, herbalists, and other specialists. Tunisians often seek mystical healing in a religious context. Modern alternative medicine, including acupuncture, is also found in cities.

SECULAR CELEBRATIONS

The national holidays are all evocations of the recent past of the country, and celebrate the markers of the nationalist history. They include independence from France (20 March 1956), the proclamation of the republic (25 July 1957), the adoption of the first constitution of the republic (1 June 1959), the final evacuation of the French military from Tunisia (15 October 1963), and the "change-over" when President Ben Ali was sworn in to replace Bourguiba (7 November 1987). These days are generally holidays from work.

THE ARTS AND HUMANITIES

Support for the Arts. The government and some wealthy benefactors support the arts. One way of doing so is through national and local festivals devoted to one form or another of music, poetry, or folklore. These festivals include competitions, with prizes for the winner.

Literature. Tunisia has produced some fine writers, more in Arabic than in French.

Graphic Arts. Paintings, mosaics, and murals by Tunisian artists are commonly seen.

Performance Arts. Music plays a major role in everyday life in Tunisia, and many people are amateur musicians who perform in a circle of friends and neighbors. Professional performers appear in restaurants and nightclubs as well as in festivals. Tunisian drama is especially known for experimental theater, as well as for classical plays. Tunisian filmmakers have established a collective reputation for solid films, many of which deal with a coming-of-age in the recent historical past, so they are both psychological dramas and re-creations of the national narrative.

THE STATE OF THE PHYSICAL AND SOCIAL SCIENCES

The physical and social sciences are both concentrated in the University of Tunis. Also affiliated with the University of Tunis is the Centre d'Etudes et de Recherches conomiques et Sociales. There are other scientific research institutes, such as the Oceanographic Research Institute on the coast at Salammbo, near Tunis. Also attached to the University of Tunis is a center focusing on the national independence movement. Research quality is high, and many Tunisian scholars in these areas publish in Tunisian and non-Tunisian journals, usually in French.

BIBLIOGRAPHY

Abdelkafi, Jellal. *La Médina de Tunis*, 1989.

Abu, Zahra, Nadia. *Sidi Ameur, a Tunisian Village*, 1982.

Allman, James. *Social Mobility, Education, and Development in Tunisia*, 1979.

Anderson, Lisa. *The State and Social Transformation in Tunisia and Libya, 1830–1980*, 1986.

Duvignaud, Jean. *Change at Shebika: Report from a North African Village*, 1970.

Dwyer, Kevin. *Arab Voices: The Human Rights Debate in the Middle East*, 1991.

Ferchiou, Sophie, ed. *Hasab wa nasab: Parenté, alliance et patrimoine en Tunisie*, 1992.

Green, Arnold. *The Tunisian Ulama, 1873–1915: Social Structure and Response to Ideological Currents*, 1978.

Hejaiej, Monia. *Behind Closed Doors: Women's Oral Narratives in Tunis*, 1996.

Hermassi, Elbaki. *Leadership and National Development in North Africa: A Comparative Study*, 1972.

Hopkins, Nicholas S. "The Emergence of Class in a Tunisian Town." *International Journal of Middle East Studies* 8: 453–491, 1977.

———. "The Articulation of the Modes of Production: Tailoring in Tunisia." *American Ethnologist* 5: 468–483, 1978.

Labidi Lilia, Çiabra. *Hachma: Sexualité et tradition*, 1989.

Murphy, Emma C. *Economic and Political Change in Tunisia: From Bourguiba to Ben Ali*, 1999.

Pierre, Amor Belhadi, Jean-Marie Miossec, and Habib Dlala. *Tunis: Evolution et fonctionnement de l'espace urbain*, 1980.

Salem, Norma. *Habib Bourguiba, Islam, and the Creation of Tunisia*, 1984.

Stone, Russell A., and John Simmons, eds. *Change in Tunisia: Studies in the Social Sciences*, 1976.

Udovich, Abraham L., and Lucette Valensi. *The Last Arab Jews: The Communities of Jerba, Tunisia*, 1984.

Waltz, Susan. *Human Rights and Reform: Changing the Face of North African Politics*, 1995.

Webber, Sabra J. *Romancing the Real: Folklore and Ethnographic Representation in North Africa*, 1991.

Weingrod, Alex. *The Saint of Beersheba*, 1990.

Zartman, William, ed. *Tunisia: The Political Economy of Reform*, 1991.

Zghal, Abdelkader. *Modernisation de l'agriculture et populations semi-nomades*, 1967.

Zussman, Mira. *Development and Disenchantment in Rural Tunisia: The Bourguiba Years*, 1992.

—NICHOLAS S. HOPKINS

TURKEY

CULTURE NAME

Turkish

ORIENTATION

Identification. The English word "Turkish" comes from the ancient Turkish word *Türk*, which can be used as an adjective or a proper noun. In Turkish, the name of the country is *Türkiye*. After decades of nationalistic indoctrination, most citizens self-identify as Turks regardless of ethnic background. Some of the major non-Turkish ethnic groups—the Kurds in the southeast, the Arabs in the south, the Laz of the western Black Sea coast, and the Georgians in the northeast and northwest—express double identities.

Location and Geography. Turkey occupies Asia Minor and a small portion of Europe. Its area is 301,382 square miles (814,578 square kilometers). It is bounded on the west by the Aegean Sea; on the northwest by the Sea of Marmara, Greece, and Bulgaria; on the north by the Black Sea; on the east by Georgia, Armenia, Azerbaijan, and Iran; and on the south by Iraq, Syria, and the Mediterranean. Although Istanbul (formerly Constantinople) is the major city and was the capital of the Ottoman Empire, the first president—Mustafa Kemal Atatürk—chose Ankara, an interior Anatolian city, as the capital in 1923. Militarily Ankara was less exposed and more easily defended than Istanbul. The choice also symbolized Atatürk's policy of nationalism, because Ankara was more Turkish and less cosmopolitan than the old capital.

Turkey has 4,454 miles of coastline. The interior consists of mountains, hills, valleys, and a high central plateau. The western coastal plains are generally more densely populated and industrial than are the central and eastern regions, except for Ankara on the central Anatolian plateau. Because Asia Minor had been home to Lydians, Hittites, Greeks, Romans, Byzantines, Seljuks, and Ottomans over the centuries, it is dotted with historic monuments.

Physiographically, the country may be divided into five regions. The Black Sea region has a moderate climate and higher than average rainfall. It is dominated by the Pontic mountain range. The west is noted for agriculture, including grains, vegetables, fruits, nuts, and tobacco. In the more humid east, the mountains leave a narrow coastal plain rarely exceeding twenty miles wide. The Black Sea peoples settled and farmed the valleys and narrow alluvial fans of the area's rivers, developing a form of steep slope agriculture to grow vegetables and fruits. Tea, the major cash crop, did not become popular until the 1960s. Some villagers combined gardening with transhumant pastoralism, which involves grazing small herds of sheep, goats, and cattle on the lowlands in the winter and in the high Pontic pastures in the summer.

Until recently, the rugged topography limited agriculture, and alternative land-based industries were virtually absent. Thus, many western Black Sea men sought work outside the region in the navy and merchant marine or in major cities, later returning home to retire. While the men worked away, the women kept up the home, farmed the land, and cared for the livestock.

The central Anatolian plateau region is dotted with mountains and denuded of trees. It has a semiarid climate with high temperatures in summer and low ones in winter. Villagers engage in animal husbandry and cultivate wheat, barley, and sugar beets. Areas unsuited for cultivation are used to graze large herds of sheep, cattle, and goats.

Eastern Anatolia is the most mountainous, remote, undeveloped, and sparsely populated region. Its elevation and cold temperatures make it less suitable for crop cultivation than the rest of Anatolia. Historically, its people engaged predominantly in animal husbandry, especially transhumant nomadism with herds of sheep, cattle, and

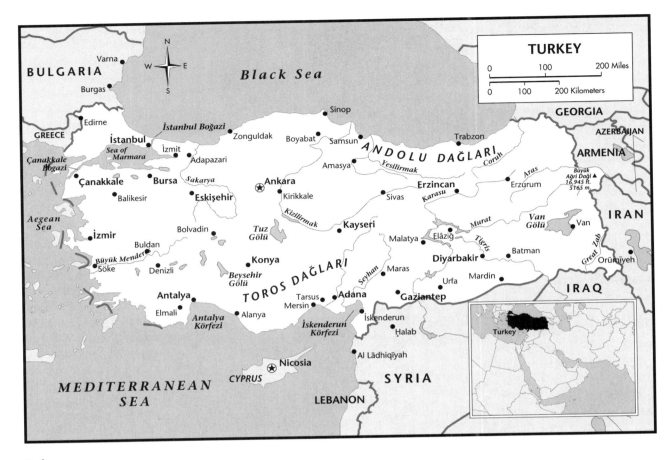

Turkey

goats. A tribal social organization survived longer in this area among the Turkish and Kurdish peoples.

The Mediterranean coastal region is lined by the Taurus Mountains. It has a Mediterranean climate with hot, dry summers and mild, humid winters. The eastern part, around Mersin and Adana, is known for extensive cotton production by wealthy landowners. Mersin is an important seaport and oil-refining center. The western region is noted for citrus and banana groves. Seminomadic peoples traditionally utilized the Taurus Mountains to graze sheep, goats, cattle, and camels. Women among the Turkish Yürük pastoralists made woolen kilims, rugs, and saddlebags. Tourism is now a major industry.

The Aegean region also has a Mediterranean climate. It contains rich valleys and alluvial plains as well as rolling hills and mountains. A wide variety of crops are produced, including citrus fruits, olives, nuts, sunflowers, tobacco, sugar beets, grains, fruits, and vegetables. The area contains most of Turkey's prosperous small farmers and food-processing plants. Izmir is the region's major

commercial and industrial center; it is the third largest city and second major port.

The Marmara–Istanbul region, a crossroads of Europe and Asia, is the most densely settled, commercial, industrial, and touristic region. It has a moderate climate, rich soil, and extensive coastlines. As a result of modern development, it has the highest percentage of the population engaged in nonagricultural pursuits of any region in the country. Istanbul, the largest and most cosmopolitan city, leads the country in commerce, shipping, fashion, literature, arts, and entertainment. Over the decades, it has attracted a steady stream of migrants from all parts of the country.

Demography. The annual population increase fell to 1.6 percent in 1998 after decades of annual growth over 2.5 percent. The 1998 population was estimated at 64,566,511, with 65 percent of the people living in urban areas and 35 percent in some thirty-five thousand villages. Turkey does not categorize its population by ethnicity, and the sizes of ethnic groups must be estimated. There are at least thirty-five non-Turkish ethnic groups, including other Turkic peoples who speak different Turkic languages, such as the Uygurs, Kirgiz, Kazaks, Uzbeks, Balkar, and Azerbaijanis. Those who speak non-Turkic languages include Kurds, Armenians, Greeks, Circassians, Georgians, Laz, Arabs, Rom (Gypsies), Ossetes, Albanians, and Chechens. The Kurds are the largest of these groups, probably numbering over ten million. The next largest may be the Arabs concentrated along the Syrian border at about one million and the Laz of the Eastern Black Sea coastal region, who may number about three hundred thousand.

Linguistic Affiliation. The Turks originated in inner Asia. Their language belongs to the Altaic family. The earliest evidence of Turkish writing dates to eighth-century C.E. runic inscriptions on steles along the Orkhon River near present-day Ulan Bator, Mongolia. The language was influenced by Persian and Arabic after the ninth century, when Turks began moving into the Middle East and converting to Islam. After the establishment of the Turkish Republic, many Arabic and Persian words were replaced with words derived from ancient Turkish. As part of Atatürk's Turkification program, all Muslim citizens were legally required to speak and write in Turkish. Until 1991, publications, radio broadcasts, and public speaking in many non-Turkish languages were legally prohibited. Today the vast majority of young people speak only Turkish. However, most Kurds raised in southeastern Turkey speak Kurdish as well as Turkish.

HISTORY AND ETHNIC RELATIONS

Emergence of the Nation. Present-day Turkey was founded in 1923 as an offspring of the multiethnic and multilingual Ottoman Empire, which existed between the fourteenth and early twentieth centuries and embraced much of the Middle East along with parts of southeastern Europe and North Africa in the sixteenth century. In the nineteenth century, when the Balkans and the Trans-Caspian regions were separated from the empire, many non-Turkish Ottoman citizens fled or migrated to Anatolia and Turkish Thrace to resettle.

With the Ottoman Empire's demise in World War I, the heartland of the old empire—Istanbul and Asia Minor—was reconstituted as the Republic of Turkey under the leadership of Mustafa Kemal (later called Mustafa Kemal Atatürk). To make Turkey a modern, Western-style, secular nation-state, Atatürk disestablished Islam as the state religion, adopted Western legal codes, and established a compulsory secular educational system in which all young Muslim citizens, regardless of ethnicity, were taught that they were ethnically Turkish and citizens of a Turkish nation-state. After centuries of intermarriage with Mediterranean and Balkan peoples and the assimilation of those peoples into the Ottoman Empire and the Turkish state, the vast majority of today's Turks physically resemble southern Europeans rather than central Asiatics.

National Identity. The government founded and supported historical and linguistic societies that researched and, if necessary, invented a glorious Turkish past that would instill pride in the country's citizens. The official policy of Turkish nationalistic indoctrination has been largely effective. Most citizens, regardless of their non-Turkish ancestry, self-identify as Turks both ethnically and nationally, with the exception of some Kurds.

Ethnic Relations. After the post-World War I Treaty of Laussane, only Christian Armenians, Orthodox Greeks, and Jews were allowed to maintain their religious and educational institutions. Since 1999, the only non-Turkish languages taught in public schools have been western European languages and Arabic.

About half the Kurds reside in southeastern Turkey, their traditional homeland. Most of those in other regions have become Turkified though education, work, military service, and intermarriage. Since the 1970s, a growing number of Kurds have rediscovered their non-Turkish roots, based in part on Kurdish, an Indo-European language related to Persian.

Although the use of Kurdish in public speech and print has been legal since 1991, prosecutors often arrest Kurdish speakers and confiscate Kurdish publications under the Anti-Terror Law, which prohibits the dissemination of separatist propaganda. Prosecutors also have used other parts of the criminal code to limit ethnic expression. As of 1999, Kurdish-language broadcasts remained illegal. The Sanliurfa (southeastern Turkey) branch of the Mesopotamian Cultural Center, a corporation established to promote the Kurdish language and culture, was banned in 1997 by the provincial governor. In 1997, the governor's office in Istanbul refused the Kurdish Culture and Research Foundation permission to offer Kurdish-language classes.

Some Kurds are demanding cultural rights and even independence or regional autonomy for the southeast. Since 1984, the Kurdish Workers Party (PKK), a secessionist and sometimes terrorist organization, has been fighting the Turkish military in that area. Up to March 1999, about thirty thou-

Workers from the Dobag Project wash a traditional hand-knotted carpet. Turkish carpets are prized for their quality and intricate design.

sand people, mostly PKK members, had been killed in the fighting. The Turkish military's actions have engendered support for the PKK, which occasionally carries out cross-border raids from northern Iraq. Turkish armed forces have compelled the evacuation of over a million civilians from the southeast and destroyed over two thousand villages.

In June 2000, a Turkish court convicted Abdullah Ocalan, the leader of the PKK, of murder and sentenced him to death. Kurds in Turkey, Europe, and other countries demonstrated in support of him. Ocalan has appealed the sentence to the European Court of Human Rights. Should Turkey impose the death penalty on Ocalan, its relations with its Kurdish citizens will become severely strained.

In recent years, Georgians, Circassians, and Laz have been attempting to revive their non-Turkish languages and cultural traditions within the limits allowed by Turkish law. In the early 1990s, a group of Georgian Turks began publishing *Çveneburi*, a cultural journal devoted to Georgian poetry, literature, and folklore. These peoples consider themselves Muslims and Turkish citizens with non-Turkish Ottoman ancestries.

The vast majority of citizens, however, share a common Turkish culture with some regional, urban–rural, social class, and ethnic variations.

There has been a good deal of intermarriage, especially among Sunni Muslims with different ethnic backgrounds. The state accepts all citizens as Turks. There are no official legal, educational, or employment disabilities associated with ethnicity and no system of ethnic identity cards.

Turkey has expressed concern for the treatment of Turkic peoples in neighboring countries, such as Bulgaria, Iraq, and Iran. However, Turkey is concerned primarily with the rights of Turks in Europe. Turkey is an associate member of the European Union. Since the 1960s, millions of its citizens have immigrated to western European countries to work, and only a small percentage have received European citizenship. Consequently, Turkey has about three million citizens living in Europe.

For Ankara, this overseas workforce has been a mixed blessing. While many send back hard currency to their relatives, many are exposed to political and religious ideas that are prohibited in Turkey. For example, about 20 to 25 percent of Turkish citizens in Europe are Kurds; many were not aware of their ethnic roots until they were educated by Kurdish nationalists there. Kurdish nationalists have also won the sympathy of many Europeans. The forms of cultural suppression exercised by the Turkish government violate the European Convention for the Protection of Human Rights and Fundamental Freedoms, a treaty that Ankara has ratified and is obligated to respect.

Urbanism, Architecture, and the Use of Space. Architecture and the use of space have been influenced by economic factors, political ideology, environment, tradition, and foreign ideas. Ottoman architecture with its Byzantine and Islamic elements represented a clear cultural expression of the imperial past. Leaders of the new republic wanted a different architecture that would proclaim their new vision of a Western, secular nation-state. One goal of the republic was to catch up with the material culture and technology of the West. Hence, they turned to western Europe to help create a new capital in Ankara.

Ankara represented a *tabula rasa* on which a new Turkish order could be constructed. In the early 1920s, it was an insignificant town of 20,000 people, with narrow winding streets and simple mud-brick houses. During the early years of the republic, Ankara was transformed with monumental government buildings symbolizing the ambitions and power of the new state.

Although some early building designs maintained a nostalgic association with the Ottoman past, modern architects and government officials regarded that style as inappropriate. Contemporary architectural styles, inspired by Europe, began to replace Ottoman revivalism in institutional building after 1927. In the late 1920s and early 1930s in part as a result of an economic crisis, the government favored drab forms of international architecture influenced by the Bauhaus school.

In the pre–World War II period, the monumental official architecture of the German and Italian regimes became dominant. Ankara's Grand National Assembly building (1938–1960) manifested the spirit of National Socialist architecture. In the area of housing, a "Republican Bourgeoisie" consisting of highly paid military and civilian officials played an important role in the acceptance of modern architecture. Western buildings with indoor plumbing and electricity fit their search for a contemporary lifestyle without ties to the past.

After World War II, the International Style became more common. Its site plans were typified by functional geometric elements, and its building facades employed grid systems. The Istanbul Hilton Hotel (1952) became an influential and highly copied example of this style.

In the 1960s, the Bauhaus school with its emphasis on mass production influenced the construction of middle-class urban housing in Ankara and some other cities. Turkey's first skyscraper, a commercial office building, was constructed in 1959 in Ankara. Since that time, modern skyscrapers and high-rise government, commercial, and apartment buildings have transformed most major cities. Since the 1950s, modern urban centers have been ringed by expanding squatter settlements (*gecekondus*) of substandard housing constructed quickly by peasants from rural areas. Today between 50 and 60 percent of Turkey's urban population consists of *gecekondu* residents.

Housing styles in small towns and villages are determined by tradition, family structure, environment, local building materials, and income. There is considerable variety in external appearance by region.

Most homes are divided in a *selamlîk* (a public reception room) and a *harem* (private family quarters). In traditional households, male guests are confined to the *selamlîk*, where they converse with the male members of the household, while women stay in the *harem*. Many traditional homes also have an enclosed garden or courtyard where females can perform some of their domestic duties and chat with neighbors.

In small towns and villages, males dominate public space while females dominate the private space of the home. In the mosque, females pray in an area apart from and outside the view of males. It is not uncommon for movie theaters, restaurants, beaches, and public parks to have a "bachelors" section for males and a "family" section for families and single females. In public transportation conveyances, it is not considered proper for a male to take a seat next to an unrelated female. In recent years, many of these restrictions have been eased in major cities, but coffeehouses and some bars remain exclusively male domains.

FOOD AND ECONOMY

Food in Daily Life. Turkish cuisine includes many different stews of vegetables and meat (lamb and beef primarily); *borek*, *kebab*, and *dolma* dishes; and a sourdough bread eaten with almost every meal. *Borek* is a pastry made of many thin layers of dough interspersed with cheese, spinach, and/or ground meat. *Kebab* is the common word for meat roasted in pieces or slices on a skewer or as meatballs on a grill. *Dolma* is the generic name for dishes made of vegetables (e.g., tomatoes and peppers) and leaves (e.g., grape, cabbage, and eggplant) that are stuffed with or wrapped around rice or bulgur pilaf,

The Lycian Rock Tombs of Myra, Turkey.

ground meat, and spices. Turks are especially fond of eggplant.

In the winter, many Turks eat a breakfast of bread with hot soup. In the warmer seasons, they commonly eat bread and jam, hard- or soft-boiled eggs, a white cheese made from sheep's milk, salty olives, and warm milk or hot tea with milk. A typical noon meal consists of vegetable and meat stew with a side dish of rice or bulgar pilaf and salad, with fruit for desert. *Borek* or *dolma* may substitute for the stew. Sweet deserts, such as baklava, are served on special occasions. The evening meal is usually lighter, consisting of leftovers from noon or a *kebab* with salad. Ordinarily, only water is drunk with the noon and evening meals.

Food preferences and preparations vary by region and ethnicity. For example, the Black Sea is noted for fish, especially anchovy, dishes, while the eastern region is noted for spicy foods. Circassians are famous for preparing chicken in a walnut sauce, while Georgian cuisine is typified by thick corn bread and corn soup. *Lahmacun*, or Armenian pizza, originated in the southeastern provinces once occupied by Armenians.

All cities have numerous restaurants and snack stands. Many specialize in a limited number of foods, such as kebabs, soups, meat wraps made with *pide* (a flat bread), pastries, and fish. Others offer a variety of meals, including stews, pilafs, vegetables, and deserts. Inexpensive restaurants cater to workingmen, who commonly eat only breakfast and the evening meal at home. Higher-class restaurants generally set aside a section for females and families. American fast-food chains have become popular in the large cities.

The major food taboo in Turkey is pork, which is forbidden to Muslims. Although the Koran also forbids alcoholic beverages, many Turks drink beer, wine, and liquors. Certain segments of the Muslim population regard other foods as taboo even though their religion does not prohibit them. For example, Yürüks, a formerly nomadic Turkish people, avoid all seafood with the exception of fish. Members of the Alevi sect of Islam do not eat rabbit because it menstruates. Turks in the northwestern province of Balikesir avoid snails, claiming incorrectly that the Koran forbids their consumption.

Food Customs at Ceremonial Occasions. Special dishes are associated with holy days and celebrations. In Gaziantep, *yuvarlama* (a blend of ground meat, rice, chickpeas, onions, and spices served with yogurt) is a special dish for the Feast of Ramadan at the end of the Islamic month of fasting. In some of the southern provinces the special meal for that

Fishing is an important facet of the Turkish economy.

feast consists of lamb *kebab* served with tomatoes and *borek*.

For the holy month of *Ashure*, which comes after the Feast of Ramadan, many households prepare a pudding called *Ashure* to share with guests, friends, and neighbors. According to tradition, *Ashure* must contain at least fifteen different ingredients, such as peas, beans, almonds, cereals, rice, raisins, rosewater, pomegranate seeds, orange peels, figs, and cinnamon. Throughout much of Turkey, wedding soup, a preparation of lamb meat with bone, egg, lemon juice, flour, butter, and red pepper, is served at wedding celebrations.

Turkish beverages include tea drunk throughout the day, thick coffee usually taken after a meal, *ayran* (buttermilk), *boza* (a fermented bulgur drink taken in the winter), and *rakî* (an aniseed-flavored brandy usually mixed with water). Carbonated drinks have become popular with young people, and beer gardens in major cities have become hangouts for men.

Basic Economy. Turkey is self-sufficient in food production. Fishers, farmers, and animal husbandry workers produce a wide variety of fish, vegetables, fruits, nuts, and meat for consumers. However, malnutrition affects some of the urban poor

and small segments of the rural population in the southeastern region.

In 1996, agriculture contributed 15 percent to the gross national product and 43.1 percent of the labor force was engaged in agriculture. Turkey exports cereals, pulses, industrial crops, sugar, nuts, fresh and dried fruits, vegetables, olive oil, and livestock products. In the early 1990s agricultural products accounted for 15 percent of total exports. However, if one includes cotton and wool, agriculture's contribution to total exports is even greater.

Since 1984, Turkey has liberalized its policy on food imports. Daily products and luxury food items, especially from European Union countries, are available in most large cities.

Most farmers produce for both domestic consumption and sale. Very few are self-sufficient. The vast majority rely on a well-established network of local and regional markets as well as large wholesalers to sell their surplus product. They then buy food and manufactured items from the proceeds.

Land Tenure and Property. Between the 1920s and 1970, the government distributed more than three million hectares of mostly state land to landless peasants. Although no comprehensive property surveys have been conducted, it is believed that most farm families own some land. According to the data in a 1980 agricultural census, 78 percent of farms had five hectares or less and together accounted for 60 percent of all farmland. Twenty-three percent of farms were between five and twenty hectares and accounted for 18 percent of all farmland. Fewer than 4 percent exceeded a hundred hectares, but they amounted to 15 percent of the farmland.

Less than one-fifth of farmers lease or sharecrop the land they till. Sharecroppers generally receive half the crop, with the remainder going to landlords, who supply seed and fertilizer. Most villages have common pastures for the residents' herd animals. In the past, southeastern Anatolia had feudal landlords who owned entire villages.

Many large farms have been converted into modern agricultural enterprises that employ machinery, irrigation, and chemical fertilizers. Such farms concentrate on high-value fruits and industrial crops and employ land-poor farmers. Since the 1950s, the mechanization of agriculture has reduced the need for farm labor, causing many villagers to migrate to the cities.

Major Industries. Turkey's economy is a mix of private and state economic enterprises (SEEs). From

A view of the ancient city wall surrounding the Midterranean city of Anlanya, Turkey.

the 1920s to the 1980s, the state owned many of the major manufacturing, banking, and communications companies. Since that time, a policy of privatization of SEEs has been followed. Currently, factories produce a wide variety of products, including processed foods, textiles and footwear, iron and steel, chemicals, cement, fertilizers, kitchen appliances, radios, and television sets. Montage industries that utilize a combination of imported and domestic parts assemble cars, trucks, and buses as well as aircraft.

Trade. Since the 1980s, trade has played an increasingly important role in the economy. Turkey's entrance into a customs union agreement with the European Union (EU) in 1995 facilitated trade with EU countries. In 1997, recorded exports amounted to $26 billion (U.S.), with unrecorded exports estimated at $5.8 billion. The major export commodities were textiles and apparel (37 percent), iron and steel products (10 percent), and foodstuffs (17 percent). The major export partners were Germany (20 percent), the United States (8 percent), Russia (8 percent), the United Kingdom (6 percent), and Italy (5 percent).

Imports were valued at $46.7 billion (U.S.) in 1997. Import commodities included machinery (26 percent), fuels (13 percent), raw materials (10 percent), and foodstuffs (4 percent). The primary import partners were Germany (16 percent), Italy (9 percent), the United States (9 percent), France (6 percent), and the United Kingdom (6 percent).

Division of Labor. Most jobs are assigned on the basis of age, skill, education, gender, and in some cases kinship. There are many small family-owned and -operated businesses in towns and cities. In those businesses, young people, especially sons, are trained from an early age to operate the enterprise. Until the 1960s, many young people, especially males, learned their skills in the traditional apprentice system. Today the Ministry of Education operates thousands of basic and advanced vocational and technical schools for males and females.

Turkey has numerous universities where students of both sexes study to become businesspersons, doctors, engineers, lawyers, teachers, accountants, bankers, and architects. Civil service jobs require applicants to meet educational requirements and pass a written examination.

Turkish law generally prohibits the employment of children under 15 years of age, except that those who are 13 and 14 may do light, part-time work if they are enrolled in school or vocational training. In practice, the children of poor families work to earn needed income. Aside from farm labor, underage boys work in tea gardens as waiters, auto repair shops, and small wood and metal craft industries. Underage girls generally work at home at handicrafts.

SOCIAL STRATIFICATION

Classes and Castes. The most important determinants of social status are wealth and education. The basic categories include the wealthy urban educated class, the urban middle class, the urban lower class, the large rural landowner class, and the general rural population. A university education is the minimum qualification for entry into the urban educated class, in which there are numerous substrata.

Distinctions can be drawn between the urban upper and urban middle classes. The urban upper class includes several groups with high status determined by education, political influence, and wealth. Wealthy businessmen are accorded very high status, as are successful physicians, cabinet ministers, and many members of the assembly, directors of important government departments, and other high-level officials. Since World War II, businessmen have challenged the old military–bureaucratic elite for power and social prestige. Members of the urban upper class are generally westernized; most speak at least one Western language, are well acquainted with European or American life and culture, and have close contact with the diplomatic and foreign business communities.

The urban middle class includes most civil servants, proprietors of medium-size businesses and industries, many persons in service occupations, some skilled workers, and university students. These groups usually are less westernized than the upper class and more oriented to Turkish culture. The urban middle class also includes virtually the entire upper strata of the provincial cities. There is considerable mobility within the urban educated class.

The urban lower class includes semiskilled and unskilled laborers, low-paid service workers, and the urban unemployed. The high rate of migration of young villagers to urban areas makes this the most rapidly growing class. Many migrants have difficulty finding jobs, and others work only seasonally. Many live in poverty in the shantytowns that ring the major cities. Urbanization continues as the rural population grows and urban industry offers better incomes.

Some 30 percent of the population are rural farmers, often referred to as peasants. Improved communications and transportation have brought them into closer contact with towns and cities. Educational efforts since 1923 succeeded in bringing the national literacy level up to 82.3 percent by 1995, although the rural literacy level is lower. Some eastern rural areas are still dominated by large landowners, traditional clan heads, and religious leaders. Young villagers who migrate to towns and cities cannot find their way into the middle class unless they receive further education.

Symbols of Social Stratification. Most men of all social classes have adopted Western styles of dress, including trousers, shirts, and jackets. Men and women in the upper and middle urban classes pay attention to Western fashions. They also live in high-priced apartments and try to possess Western luxury items, such as cars, electronic devices, cell phones, and computers. They have developed a taste for Western literature and music and attend musical events and plays. The upper class favors European-language high schools and universities; the middle class is more satisfied with standard Turkish educational institutions. Both classes prefer to speak an educated Istanbul style of standard Turkish.

Ankara, Turkey is a fast-paced city.

Most members of the lower urban classes live in shantytowns. Only a small proportion have graduated from high school (*lise*). The women tend to wear traditional conservative clothing, including head scarves and long coats, even in the summer. They favor Turkish and Middle Eastern music. The peasant and rural classes are the least exposed to Western and urban influences in dress, styles, language, and music. They, like the lower urban class, tend to speak Turkish with regional accents and grammatical peculiarities. The women wear conservative peasant dress consisting of baggy pantaloons and head scarves.

POLITICAL LIFE

Government. The government operates under the 1982 constitution. All the constitutions (1924, 1961, and 1982) were written and adopted while military leaders were in control. The 1982 constitution states that "Turkey is a democratic, secular and social State . . . loyal to the nationalism of Atatürk" (Article 2). "The Turkish State, with its territory and nation, is an indivisible entity. Its language is Turkish" (Article 3).

The constitution enumerates a long list of civil and political rights but subordinates them to considerations of "national security," "national unity," and "public morality." It also allows the government to impose emergency rule or martial law. The constitution establishes a popularly elected single-chamber national assembly with full legislative powers, a prime minister and cabinet responsible to the national assembly, and a constitutional court with the power of judicial review. It provides for a president with extensive executive powers and legislative veto authority who is elected by the assembly for a seven-year term.

There is a wide array of political parties. It is illegal for parties to appeal to religion, advocate the establishment of a religious state, or claim to represent a class or ethnic group. In recent elections, no party has been able to win more than 22 percent of the vote, leading to coalition governments.

Turkey is divided administratively into eighty provinces (iller), which are subdivided into sub-provinces (ilçeler), which in turn are divided into districts (bucaklar). A governor (vali) appointed by the minister of the interior heads each province and represents the state. Locally elected representative bodies at the village, city, and provincial levels also play governing roles.

Leadership and Political Officials.

Most of Turkey's political leaders have been high-ranking military officers, university professors, or successful businessmen. Many provincial governors are former generals or career civil servants who graduated from Ankara University's public administration program. The military elite sees itself as the protector of the constitution and Atatürk's principles. It has formal influence over governmental matters through the National Security Council, which is composed of the prime minister; the chief of the general staff; the ministers of national defense, the interior, and foreign affairs; and the commanders of the armed forces and the gendarmerie. This body sets national security policy.

Military leaders have been especially concerned about threats to secularism and the unity of the state and nation. In 1997, the militarily dominated National Security Council presented the prime minister, Necmettin Erbakan, with twenty demands, including closing religious lodges, enforcing laws prohibiting religious dress in public, closing some state-supported religious schools, cooling relations with Iran, and curtailing the activities of religious organizations.

Citizens often petition elected officials for favors or aid. Unless they are personally acquainted with an official, they convey a petition through a friend or sponsor who knows an official, a member of his or her family, or one of his or her friends.

Turkish law prohibits communist and religious parties. The parties range from socialist (Democratic Left Party), to moderately conservative and free enterprise (Motherland Party), to right-wing ultranationalistic (Nationalist Action Party), to near-religious (Virtue Party).

Social Problems and Control.

Internal security and law enforcement are handled primarily by the national police in urban areas and the gendarmerie in rural areas. However, in areas under a state of emergency or martial law, the gendarmerie functions under the military. The national police are armed and authoritarian in demeanor. They have been accused of treating arrested persons roughly to obtain information or confessions during incommunicado detention. The government has instituted human rights training for the police.

The gendarmerie maintains security outside municipal boundaries and guards land borders against illegal entry and smuggling. Recruits are supplied through military conscription. Gendarmes have been subject to the same criticisms as the national police.

Turkey abandoned Islamic law and adopted the Italian penal code in 1926. Serious crimes include premeditated homicide, theft, arson, armed robbery, embezzlement of state property, perjury, and rape. Political speech insulting the president, the military, and parliament has been criminalized. The antiterror law criminalizes written and oral propaganda, meetings, and demonstrations aimed at damaging the unity of the state.

The death penalty can be imposed for certain crimes against the state and premeditated murder, but there have been no executions since 1984. Conviction for a serious felony can disqualify one from holding public office, voting, and practicing certain professions.

Compared to other Middle Eastern countries, the incidence of ordinary crime is low. The most common felonies resulting in incarceration in 1991 were crimes against property (8,360), crimes against individuals (5,879), and crimes against "public decency and family order" (2,681). Every year an unknown number of people are incarcerated for illegal political activity and thought crimes, such as advocating an Islamic state or cultural rights for an ethnic minority.

In addition to Kurdish nationalism, Turkey's security forces are concerned with narcotics trafficking, since Turkey is a route for the transfer of

Coffeehouses are male domains.

hashish from Pakistan, Afghanistan, and Iran to Europe.

Military Activity. The Turkish military plays political, cultural, and security roles. Military leaders created the republic in 1923, replaced civilian governments in 1960 and 1980, and forced a civilian government out of office in 1971. Because of universal male conscription, the military is a major national socialization agent for young men of different regions, classes, and ethnicities.

Since joining the North Atlantic Treaty Organization in 1952, Turkey has maintained a large military consisting of land forces, navy, air force, coast guard, and gendarmerie. In 1994, it had 503,800 officers and enlisted men on active duty. Defense is usually the largest category in the national budget; from 1981 to 1991, it averaged 20 percent of total government expenditures.

SOCIAL WELFARE AND CHANGE PROGRAMS

In 1998, the government estimated that 81.3 percent of the population were covered by state social security and retirement services. Employers pay insurance premiums for work-related injuries, occupational diseases, and maternity leave; employers and employees pay premiums to cover illness, disa-

bility, retirement, and death benefits. The government also offers social security insurance to the self-employed and operates orphanages. Local associations or nongovernmental organizations (NGOs) associated with mosques and crafts also provide welfare to the needy.

NONGOVERNMENTAL ORGANIZATIONS AND OTHER ASSOCIATIONS

One of the most important NGOs is the Army Mutual Assistance Foundation (OYAK), created in 1962. It controls a huge investment fund of obligatory and voluntary contributions from military personnel and investment profits. It has invested substantially in the auto, truck, tractor, and tire industries; the petrochemical, cement, and food processing industries; and retail and service enterprises. Through OYAK, the Turkish military became partners with foreign and domestic investors and shares their economic interests. Because of OYAK's investments, the economic security of thousands of active and retired armed forces personnel became dependent on the profitability of large capitalistic enterprises. Consequently, military corporate interests expanded into the areas of labor law, trade unionism, trade and monetary policy, corporate taxation, tariffs, investment banking, and related matters.

Other major NGOs include the Turkish Trade Association, representing the interests of merchants, industrialists, and commodity brokers; the Turkish Confederation of Employers' Unions, representing employers; and the Confederation of Turkish Trade Unions, representing labor. In addition, NGOs exist for practically every interest group in crafts, sports, social issues, education, religion, and the arts.

GENDER ROLES AND STATUSES

Division of Labor by Gender. Turkish law guarantees equal pay for equal work and has opened practically all educational programs and occupations to women. Exceptions are the religious schools that train imams (Islamic prayer leaders) and the job of imam itself. In general, men dominate the high-status occupations in business, the military, government, the professions, and academia. According to traditional values, women should do domestic work and not work in the public arena or with unrelated men. However, women have begun to work more in public.

Lower-class women generally have worked as maids, house cleaners, women's tailors, seamstresses, child care givers, agricultural laborers, and nurses, but in the early 1990s, about 20 percent of factory employees and many store clerks were women. Middle-class women commonly are employed as teachers and bank tellers, while upper-class women work as doctors, lawyers, engineers, and university teachers. Only a small percentage of women are politicians.

Men work in all these fields but avoid the traditional nonagricultural occupations of lower-class women. Men monopolize the officer ranks in the military and the transportation occupations of pilot and taxi, truck, and bus driver. In urban areas, lower-class men work in crafts, manufacturing, and low-paid service industries. Middle-class men work as teachers, accountants, businessmen, and middle-level managers. Upper-class men work as university teachers, professionals, upper-level managers, businessmen, and entrepreneurs.

MARRIAGE, FAMILY, AND KINSHIP

Marriage. Turks expect adults to marry and have children, and the vast majority do. Because men should not lower their wives' standard of living, they are not supposed to marry women of a higher economic class. People generally marry within their own religious sect and ethnic group, although interethnic marriages among Sunni Muslims are not uncommon. In traditional Turkish society, the selection of spouses and the marriage ceremony were controlled by kin groups. During the premarital process, the individuals to be married played minor roles. The rituals, especially the imam marriage ceremony, were essential for a morally and socially acceptable marriage.

In 1926, the revolutionary Turkish government abolished Islamic family law and adopted a slightly modified version of the family law in the Swiss civil code. The new Family Law requires and recognizes civil marriage ceremonies only. It requires the consent of mature individuals for a binding marriage contract and prescribes monogamy only. Even though the law prohibits parents from entering into engagement or marital agreements on behalf of their children, arranged marriages without the consent of the brides have been somewhat common. In a 1968 survey, 11.4 percent of women said their marriages had been arranged by their families without their consent, while 67 percent said they had had family-arranged marriages with their consent. The figures for the unconsented arranged marriages ranged from 7.7 percent for women living in Istanbul, Ankara, and Izmir to 11.3 percent to 12.5 percent for women living in smaller cities, towns, and villages. An impressive 49.9 percent of the husbands surveyed said their fathers or other relatives had made the final decision about their marriages. This response category ranged from 59.1 percent for village men to 15.3 percent for men in Istanbul, Ankara, and Izmir. Today the vast majority of marriages occur with the couple's consent, but families still play a role recommending and screening potential spouses, especially for their daughters.

Even though divorce is not considered an Islamic sin, it occurs infrequently. Divorcees, especially men with children, quickly remarry, usually to divorced women. The new code eliminated a husband's Islamic prerogative of verbal and unilateral divorce and prescribed a court proceeding. The law recognizes only six grounds for divorce: adultery; plot against life, grave assaults, and insults; crime or a dishonorable life; desertion; mental infirmity; and incompatibility. The evidentiary requirements are so substantial that establishing one of these grounds has proved difficult. A couple cannot divorce by mutual consent.

Domestic Unit, Inheritance, and Kin Groups. Traditionally, most Turks traced their descent and passed on property, especially homes and land, through the male line. Even though most households have always contained only one nuclear family, the ideal household, especially among the rural and urban wealthy, was patrilocal extended, in which a son and his bride lived in his parents' home after marriage. The basic kinship units are the family (*aile*) and the household (*hane*). Household members normally eat together and share income and expenses. The next larger unit is the patrilineage (*sulale*), consisting of relatives connected intergenerationally by a common male ancestor. While patrilineage is important to old, noble Ottoman families and tribal peoples, it is of little significance to most Turks.

The traditional Turkish household is characterized by male dominance, respect for elders, and female subservience. The father or oldest male is the head, an authority figure who demands respect and obedience. The mother is also respected, but her relationship with her children is warm and informal.

Although supreme authority ordinarily rests with the father, the household is usually mother-centered. The mother, being largely confined to the home, manages and directs its internal affairs. The division of labor has traditionally been clear-cut, with women having responsibility for the internal home, and men providing the income and representing the household to the outside world. Before the 1960s, even grocery shopping was a male duty.

In recent decades, much of this has changed. The new Family Law grants women equal rights to private property and inheritance. A larger percentage of women work outside the home, and educated women demand more equal rights.

SOCIALIZATION

Women are very protective of their children. Breast-feeding for a year or more is common. The child commonly sleeps in a hammock or crib near the parents. Boys are socialized to be courageous, assertive, proud, and respectful of elders. When they undergo a painful circumcision ceremony between ages 9 and 12, they are told to be as brave as lions. Girls are socialized to be modest, compliant, supportive of males, virtuous, and skilled in domestic tasks. Fathers are authoritarian disciplinarians; mothers are generally loving and nurturing.

Every woman rejoices when giving birth to a son, because that event increases her status in the eyes of her husband, in-laws, and community. She usually pampers her son, who remains close to her until age 10 or 11, after which he spends most of his time with other males and identifies more closely

with men. Mothers and daughters are especially close, as daughters usually spend much of their premarital lives close to their mothers, learning domestic skills: Generally, the father–daughter relationship is rather formal, with little public displaying of affection. Although a daughter or son may argue or joke with the mother, they are respectful and subdued in the father's presence.

During prepubescence, relations between brothers and sisters are free and easy. Later, their statuses change as the older sibling takes on some of the rights and duties of a parent. The older sister (*abla*) becomes like a second mother, loved for her warmth and affection. The older brother (*agabey*) assumes the helpful but authoritarian status of a minor father. In extended families, grandparents, especially grandmothers, provide a good deal of child care.

School attendance is compulsory to age 14. The first day of class constitutes an important rite of passage. The children are dressed in black smocks with white collars and taken to school with pomp and ceremony. Most families that can afford it, keep their children in school beyond age 14. Most would like to see their children, especially their sons, complete university, but this is rarely possible for poor families.

ETIQUETTE

Formal etiquette is central to Turkish culture, governing most social interactions and the use of space. Turkish culture has an exact verbal formula for practically every occasion. Etiquette requires the pronouncement of the proper formulas for these occasions.

Strict etiquette governs intergenerational and heterosexual interactions. Unless they are close friends or relatives, older people are addressed formally. For example, older men should be addressed with the title "Bey" (Mister) and women with the title "Hanim" (Lady). Younger people are expected to be reserved in their presence. Adults of the opposite sex are expected not to act casually or show affection toward each other in public. Friends of the same sex may hold hands and greet each other with kisses on the cheek. Upon meeting, men shake hands, but a man does not shake a woman's hand unless she extends it to him.

People are not criticized for being late. Business meetings usually are preceded by tea and unrelated conversation. Consideration for companions is important. One does not drink, smoke, or eat something without first offering to share it with one's companions.

Ninety-eight percent of Turks are nominally Muslim.

Homes are divided into guest and private areas, and it is improper to ask for a tour of the house. The soles of shoes are considered dirty, and shoes are removed when one enters a home or mosque.

RELIGION

Religious Beliefs. Islamic tradition, ideology, and ritual are very important. About 98 percent of Turkey's citizens are nominally Muslims, of whom about 80 to 85 percent are Sunnis of the Hanafi school and 15 to 20 percent are members of Shiite sects (mostly Alevi). Turkish Muslims recognize the standard Islamic creed and duties, but only the most religious fast or make a pilgrimage to Mecca. Four percent of Turks identify themselves as atheists, and 4 percent as agnostics.

For most Turks, Islam plays an important role in rites of passage: naming shortly after birth, circumcision for boys, marriage, and funerals. The state controls religious education and most religious personnel by supervising the schools that train Sunni imams and certifying imams as state employees who work in community mosques.

In recent decades, a revival of fundamental Islam has been supported by about 20 percent of the population. A small proportion of the population participates in Sufi orders and brotherhoods.

The most important events in the Turkey's Islamic calendar are *Ramazan*, the lunar month of fast; *Kadir Gecesi* (Night of Power), the twenty-seventh day of *Ramazan*, when Mohammad was appointed the messenger of Allah; *Sheker Bayram* a three-day national holiday at the end of *Ramazan* in which people exchange visits and candy; and *Kurban Bayram* (Feast of Sacrifice), a four-day national holiday held during the lunar month of *Hajj* (Pilgrimage) to commemorate Abraham's willingness to sacrifice Isaac. As many as 2.5 million sheep have been sacrificed in Turkey on this holiday; most of the meat is shared with neighbors and donated to the poor.

Medicine and Health Care. Modern Western medical services have expanded significantly over the past two decades. The Ministry of Health is authorized to provide medical care and preventive health services, train health personnel, establish and operate hospitals and clinics, inspect private health facilities, and regulate pharmacies. In 1995, Turkey had 12,500 health facilities and a doctor for every 1,200 persons. The incidence of measles, pertussis, typhoid fever, and diphtheria has declined markedly since the 1970s. Infant mortality declined from 120 per 1,000 in 1980 to 55 per 1,000 in 1992. In rural areas, midwives deliver most babies.

Most urban dwellers have access to public health facilities, but many rural citizens do not. In the countryside and among recent migrants to the cities, folk medicine is still practiced. Peasant women learn folk medicine involving herbs, spices, prayers, and rituals from their mothers and apply it to family members instead of or in addition to modern medicine. Traditionally, some men specialized in folk medicine as well.

SECULAR CELEBRATIONS

The major secular celebrations and official holidays begin with New Year's Day on 1 January, an adoption from the West. Many people exchange greetings cards, and some celebrate in a Western fashion. National Sovereignty Day on 23 April commemorates the first meeting of the Grand National Assembly. Because 23 April is also National Children's Day, much of the day is devoted to children's activities such as dances and music recitals. Youth and Sport Day, commemorating Atatürk's birth, is celebrated on 19 May. Victory Day, celebrating victorious battles during Turkey's War of Independence, is observed on 30 August. Republic Day, 29 October, commemorates Atatürk's proclamation of the republic in 1923. Both Victory Day and Republic Day are celebrated with patriotic parades, music, and speeches.

THE ARTS AND HUMANITIES

Support for the Arts. The Ministry of Culture has implemented a policy of promoting nonreligious Turkish and Western art. It provides a limited number of scholarships for the study of art and music in Europe, especially France. The ministry also supports the Academy of Fine Arts and art museums in the major cities. Most artists come from the middle and upper classes in major cities. Graphic artists rely primarily on major corporations and the upper class to buy their work. They sell through private exhibition and a limited number of art shops. Traditional craft artists who produce ceramics, rugs and kilims, brass and copper ornaments, and embroidery have a broader market for their work. Most sculptors rely largely on state commissions.

Literature. Until the middle of the nineteenth century, Turkish literature centered on the Ottoman court, which produced poetry and some prose. This literature represented a fusion of Persian, Arabic, and Turkish classical styles. Western influences were introduced in the 1860s by a group of intellectuals who attempted to combine Western cultural forms with a more simple form of the Turkish language. This westernizing trend continued throughout the nineteenth century and became more pronounced just before World War I. After 1923, the republic produced an impressive number of novelists, poets, singers, musicians, and artists. Novelists who gained international fame include Halide Edib, Resat Nuri Güntekin, and, more recently, Orhan Pamuk. Several important works dealt with village life, ranging from Yakup Kadri Karaosmanoglu's *Yaban* (*The Stranger*) in the 1930s to Mahmut Makal's *A Village in Anatolia*, and Yasar Kemal's *Mehmet My Hawk*, which won world recognition in 1961.

Orhan Veli generally is considered the father of modern Turkish poetry, which has been characterized by a rebellion against rigidly prescribed forms and a preoccupation with immediate perception. Some poets have experimented with obscurantist forms and ideas; many others have expressed concern for social democratic issues.

Graphic Arts. Western influence in the graphic arts began in the late Ottoman period with the founding of the Fine Arts Academy in Istanbul, which continues to be staffed by European and European-educated Turkish artists. In the republican periods, Turkish art has involved a mixture of Western and indigenous styles. Practically all artists of note have studied at the academy or in Europe. Some have imitated European forms, while others have searched for a Turkish style and portray Turkish themes such as village and urban scenes in a representational manner. Many sculptors receive state commissions to create monumental works depicting Atatürk and other patriotic themes.

Performance Arts. Foreign plays outnumber Turkish works in the theater, but theater attendance has grown in recent decades and many Turkish playwrights who combine Western techniques with Turkish social issues have had an opportunity to present their works.

Both Ankara and Istanbul have well-respected opera companies. The Presidential Symphony Orchestra gives concerts both in Ankara and on tour. Ankara and Istanbul have music conservatories that include schools of ballet. Several Turkish composers, of whom the best known is Adnan Saygun, have won acclaim in Europe and America for fusing Turkish folk themes with Western forms.

The Istanbul Music Conservatory has taken steps to preserve authentic folk music by recording it in all parts of the country. Annual folk arts festivals in Istanbul present a wide variety of Turkish music and dance.

THE STATE OF THE PHYSICAL AND SOCIAL SCIENCES

Most scientific research is carried out at a few universities in Ankara, Istanbul, and Izmir. The government funds two-thirds of it. The Technology Development Foundation of Turkey provides grants for industrial research and development (R&D) activities, mostly in electronics, telecommunications, and environmental technologies. The Ministry of Rural Affairs and the Ministry of Housing and Settlement provide funds for social scientific research.

Practically all Turkish leaders in the natural, social, and engineering sciences have received some education abroad, particularly in the United States. Turkey obtains much of its technology for the food-processing, metals, and textiles sectors from abroad. The Supreme Council for Science and Technology, the science and technology policy-making body, sets R&D targets for high-priority activities: information, advanced materials, biotechnology, space, and nuclear technology.

The number of scientific researchers was estimated at 8 per 10,000 members of the labor force in 1992. Almost three-quarters, or 30,172, of those researchers were in universities; basic science (10 percent), engineering (20 percent), health science (34 percent), agriculture (7 percent), social science and humanities (29 percent). Turkey's only school of social work and research is at Ankara's Hacettepe University.

BIBLIOGRAPHY

Abadan-Unat, Nermin, ed. *Women in Turkish Society*, 1981.

Ahmad, Feroz. *The Turkish Experiment in Democracy, 1950–1975*, 1997.

Anderson, June. *Return to Tradition: The Revitalization of Turkish Village Carpets*, 1998.

Andrews, Peter A. *Ethnic Groups in the Republic of Turkey*, 1989.

Ansay, Tugrul, and Don Wallace. *Introduction to Turkish Law*, 1996.

Arat, Yesim. *The Patriarchal Paradox: Women Politicians in Turkey*, 1989.

Balim, Cigdem, ed. *Turkey: Political, Social and Economic Challenges in the 1990s*, 1995.

Baysal, Ayse, et al. *Samples from Turkish Cuisine*, 1993.

Birand, Mehmet Ali. *The Generals' Coup in Turkey*, 1991.

Erder, Türkoz. *Family in Turkish Society: Sociological and Legal Studies*, 1985.

Gole, Nilufer. *The Forbidden Modern: Civilization and Veiling*, 1996.

Gunter, Michael M. *The Kurds and the Future of Turkey*, 1997.

Heper, Metin, and Jacob M. Landau, eds. *Political Parties and Democracy in Turkey*, 1991.

Holod, Renata, and Ahmet Evin. *Modern Turkish Architecture*, 1984.

Inalcik, Halil, ed. *From Empire to Republic: Essays on Ottoman and Turkish Social History*, 1995.

Kagîtçîbasî, Çigdem, ed. *Sex Roles. Family and Community in Turkey*, 1982.

Karpat, Kemal H. *Turkey's Politics*, 1959.

Lewis, Bernard. *The Emergence of Modern Turkey*, 1968.

Magnarella, Paul J. *Tradition and Change in a Turkish Town*, 1974 (rev. ed. 1981).

———. *The Peasant Venture: Tradition, Migration and Change among Georgian Peasants in Turkey*, 1979.

———. *Anatolia's Loom: Studies in Turkish Culture, Society, Politics and Law*, 1998.

Mango, Andrew. *Turkey: The Challenge of a New Role*, 1994.

McDowall, David. *A Modern History of the Kurds*, 1997.

Metz, Helen Chapin. *Turkey: A Country Study*, 1996.

Olson, Robert. *The Emergence of Kurdish Nationalism and the Sheikh Said Rebellion*, 1989.

Ozbay, Ferhunde, ed. *Women, Family and Social Change in Turkey*, 1990.

Pînar, Selman. *A History of Turkish Painting*, 1990.

Pope, Nicole, and Hugh Pope. *Turkey Unveiled*, 1997.

Rittenberg, Libby, ed. *The Political Economy of Turkey in the Post-Soviet Era*, 1998.

Rugman, Jonathan. *Atatürk's Children: Turkey and the Kurds*, 1996.

Shaw, Stanford J., and Ezel Kural Shaw. *History of the Ottoman Empire and Modern Turkey*, 1976.

Stone, Frank A. *The Rub of Cultures in Modern Turkey*, 1973.

Tapper, Richard, ed. *Islam in Modern Turkey; Religion, Politics, and Literature in a Secular State*, 1991.

Tekeli, Sirin, ed. *Women in Modern Turkish Society*, 1995.

Turkish Daily News. Turkey 1989 Almanac, 1990.

U.S. Department of State. *Turkey: Country Report on Human Rights Practices for 1998*, 1999.

Van Bruinessen, Martin. *Agha, Shaikh, and State: The Social and Political Structure of Kurdistan*, 1992.

White, Jenny B. *Money Makes Us Relatives: Women's Labor in Urban Turkey*, 1994.

World Bank. *Turkey: Women in Development*, 1993.

Zürcher, Erik J. *Turkey: A Modern History*, 1994.

—PAUL J. MAGNARELLA

TÜRKMENISTAN

CULTURE NAME
Türkmen

ALTERNATIVE NAMES
Turkmenia (Russian), Turcoman (Persian)

ORIENTATION

Identification. "Türkmenistan," with the Persian suffix "-istan" to indicate "land of the Türkmen," has been home to the Turkic people today known as Türkmen since about the tenth century. Türkmen descend from the Oguz, a confederation of tribes which migrated out of the Gök Türk empire (c. fifth–eighth centuries) near Mongolia. It is thought that the term "Türkmen" was used to classify the Oguz who had adopted Islam, although this is not conclusive; the designation had earlier held political significance. The name "Türkmen" eventually replaced "Oguz."

The majority of Türkmen live in the country Türkmenistan, formerly the Türkmen Soviet Socialist Republic (SSR) of the Soviet Union. Significant Türkmen communities live in Iran, Afghanistan, Iraq and Turkey. There are also groups in Azerbaijan called Trukhman.

Location and Geography. Türkmenistan lies east of the Caspian Sea, north of Iran and Afghanistan. It shares a short northwestern border with Kazakhstan and its eastern border with Uzbekistan.

Ninety percent of Türkmenistan consists of the Gara Gum and Gyzyl Gum deserts, which are largely uninhabited. The Garagum canal irrigates much of the country.

Summers are hot and dry; winters bring freezing temperatures, but snowfall is infrequent. Türkmen have adapted their lifestyle to the desert environment. They drink hot green tea to keep the body cool during summer and have used the desert to their advantage in times of strife. In the 1920s, when the *Basmachis* (members of the Turkistan National Liberation Movement) had to escape from Russian troops, they fled into the desert.

Demography. Almost 4.7 million people live in Türkmenistan: 77 percent of them are Türkmen, 7 percent Russian, 9 percent Uzbek, with small numbers of Kazakhs, Armenians, Azerbaijani Turks, and other ethnic groups. Türkmen are a fast-growing group, averaging five children per family. Total population growth is at 2.5 percent.

Linguistic Affiliation. Türkmen is a member of the Oguz branch of Turkic. It is closest to the language spoken in Turkey and Azerbaijan, but mutual intelligibility with all Turkic dialects is high. There are many borrowed words from Arabic, Persian, and Russian, especially for technical and scientific terms.

Türkmen writers shared a common Turkic literary language (Chagatai) with other Turks until the eighteenth century when a discernible Türkmen literary language began to emerge. The modern standardized language was developed in the 1920s from the Teke and Yomut dialects as a result of Soviet interest in creating a national literary language. The tribal dialects, which were always mutually comprehensible, now share a standardized written language and grammar. The Türkmen and other Turks, who had used an Arabic-based script for centuries, replaced it with an "international" Latin-based script in 1929. In 1940, when Soviet policy shifted again, the Türkmen were assigned a Cyrillic alphabet. The Türkmen chose to adopt a Latin-based script similar to the one they had used earlier.

Symbolism. In addition to traditional costumes, carpets, and oral traditions, one of the most important Türkmen cultural symbols is the horse, especially the Akhal-Teke breed. Camels were important to a nomadic desert lifestyle, but the Türkmen derived a sense of personal and cultural pride from

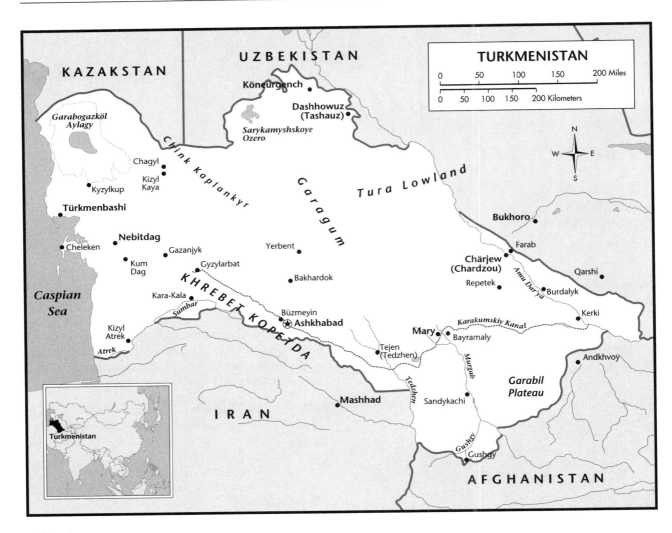

Türkmenistan

horses. A Soviet law outlawing private ownership of livestock in the 1920s, and attempts to erase the Akhal-Teke through breeding with Russian horses, put it at great risk. In 1935 a group of Türkmen rode three hundred miles to Moscow to demonstrate their desire to protect the breed. By 1973, as a result of the slaughter of horses for meat and attempts at crossbreeding, only eighteen pure bred Akhal-Teke were left in the Soviet Union. In 1988 the trek to Moscow was reenacted to demonstrate that Türkmen still considered the horse a defining symbol of their culture.

Examples of the animal's importance are found in the efforts to build an independent Türkmen national culture since 1991. Independence from the Soviet Union restored the right of Türkmen to own horses and encouraged promotion of the Akhal-Teke breed. President Niÿazov gives horses as gifts to heads of state and he institutionalized the animal's symbolic value by having a picture of an

Ahal-Teke printed on the new money (the *manat*). In 1995 he established 27 April as the Holiday of the Türkmen Horse, celebrated with horse races at the hippodrome in Aşgabat.

The state seal, which was created in 1992, also bears the image of the Akhal-Teke. A white horse stands against a background of sky blue (an important color in Turkic culture), encircled by five tribal carpet patterns (*göl*). An outer ring displays cotton and wheat. At the top center of the outer ring is a crescent moon alongside five stars, representing the five tribes and the nation's Islamic heritage. This seal is stamped on official documents, and no paperwork is official without it.

The Türkmen flag also features the five tribal *göls* and the Islamic crescent moon. As an emblematic color of Islam, the green background emphasizes the nation's Muslim heritage.

HISTORY AND ETHNIC RELATIONS

Emergence of the Nation. Türkmen identity and culture have been tied closely to the political history and shifts in power in Central Asia. Although Türkmen had their own religious, cultural, and political traditions, the emergence of powerful neighboring states affected their governing systems, economy, and ecology and sometimes altered their way of life.

The Russian invasion subjugated the Türkmen, ended practices such as slavery, and brought the Transcaspian Railroad as well as Russian colonists. The conquest of the Türkmen occurred at the battle of Gök Tepe in 1881, but the Russian army continued fighting until it had secured Merv (Mary) in 1884. Thousands of women and children were slaughtered at Gök Tepe. That memory is marked by the 12 January day of commemoration and by the extravagant mosque that was erected near the site of the massacre. These experiences have fostered a sense of Türkmenness that in some respects is stronger than the sense of Turkicness.

National Identity. The establishment of the Soviet Union after 1917, and the creation of the Türkmen SSR ushered in a new era of Türkmen culture and identity. Forced collectivization stripped Türkmen of their lands, nomadism ceased, and cotton became the main agricultural product. Intellectual, military, and religious leaders were purged, and political and religious structures were attacked. The government tried to supplant tribal identity with a Soviet one. The Türkmen rebelled in guerilla-like resistance groups (*Basmachi*) into the early 1930s. While the Türkmen were united for the first time and a stronger sense of Türkmenness was fostered, tribal affiliation was not eradicated.

Türkmenistan attained its independence on 27 October 1991 with the break-up of the Soviet Union. Saparmurat Niÿazov, who had been chairman of the Supreme Soviet since 1985, became president in 1990 and then "President for life" in December 1999. His popular name, Türkmenbaşy, means "head of the Türkmen." Today the Türkmen are evolving once again as they learn to run a modern, sovereign country for the first time and take back their identity by redefining their national culture. The country is working to forge a place for itself in the global community, establishing relations with neighbors like Iran and potential investors in the West, and joining the United Nations Organization in 1992.

Ethnic Relations. Türkmen are culturally and linguistically related to other Turkic peoples, such as Uighurs, Kazakhs, Uzbeks, Kirghiz, Tatars, Başkurts, Azerbaijanis, and those in Turkey. They are descended from larger Turkic groups living on the Chinese border that began to migrate westward in the ninth century. While their migrations often were due primarily to a lack of pasturage, military and political conquests shaped the way of life in the new lands.

For many centuries the Türkmen were a fragmented group of tribes that associated and warred according to their immediate needs. They formed the ethnic base of great empires, however, such as the Seljuks and Ottomans, and of modern states such as Azerbaijan and Turkey. Their reputation as magnificent horsemen and warriors earned them a place as frontier fighters when those empires attempted to expand their borders. They also raided settled neighbors, especially Persia, for slaves and wealth.

Modernization, Sovietization, and the introduction of western culture have altered some traditional ways, and others have lost prominence because of the proliferation of urban centers.

URBANISM, ARCHITECTURE, AND THE USE OF SPACE

Furniture was borrowed from the West, and its use varies. Some homes have furniture, and some do not. The traditional bedding consists of padded mats that are laid on the floor at bedtime. In the morning they are folded and placed in a designated corner with the blankets and pillows. This allows sleeping space to be used for other purposes during the day.

Some families, primarily in the cities, have a work table in the kitchen area, but most Türkmen eat sitting on the floor. They spread a large cloth on the floor, with food and dishes placed on top of it. Guests occupy the place of honor, which is made soft with pillows or quilts.

Türkmen traditionally have a toilet outside of the main living space. Although some rural families use outhouses, a separate building containing a toilet and sink is typical. In the cities, where most people live in apartments or small houses, there is no space for this arrangement, but many households separate the toilet by locating it in one room and placing the sink and shower in a nearby room.

Cooking is done in a separate space; some homes have a small building for preparing food, dying yarn, and storing utensils. This is the domain of women, and it is not unusual for neighbors or relatives to arrive uninvited to lend a hand or to bring their own chores so that they can work and

Ashkhabad, Türkmenistan, features many one-story homes. Most homes have a walled courtyard.

socialize at the same time. Cooking done outside (roasting meat and popping corn) is handled by men and often becomes a social activity, with neighbors and friends forming a small crowd.

The separation of space with regard to gender is an aspect of life that varies greatly. Men and women may sit and eat together, or may remain in separate rooms during a social event. Some women continue the tradition of wearing a *yaşmak* (head scarf) in the first year of marriage. The bride holds the corner of her scarf between her teeth to serve as a symbolic barrier between her and any male visitors who are not family or to show deference to her parents-in-law; the scarf also prevents her from speaking. A woman may stop wearing a *yaşmak* after one year of marriage, after the birth of a child, or as a result of an agreement within the family.

Türkmen are conscientious about keeping living spaces clean. They never wear shoes in the house but wear and provide guests with slippers. Acts of personal hygiene such as cutting the hair or cutting or filing the nails are done in the bath area, never in the main living space.

Almost every available space in a home, except the washroom and kitchen, is covered with carpets. Floors are covered with multiple carpets, chairs are draped with a medium-sized rug or a square seat covering, and the walls display large and often valuable carpets.

The architecture of homes does not vary greatly throughout the nation. People live in one-story homes or stark Stalin-era apartment high-rises. Most common are modest houses with walled courtyards that allow families to spend time outdoors, where it is cooler, and private. There are variations in the amenities and the amount of space, both of which are more limited in urban areas.

The traditional structure is a felt tent called a "black house" (*gara oÿ*). A thick felt covering is draped over a wooden frame, leaving an entrance and a round opening at the top to allow smoke to escape. The frame is collapsible so that the tent can be dismantled quickly for travel. Today most Türkmen live in modern housing, and *gara oÿs* are used only for summer recreation and holidays.

FOOD AND ECONOMY

Food in Daily Life. The diet shows a Russian influence and imported items are available at a high price, but Türkmen food generally remains traditional.

Hot green tea (*gök çaÿ*) accompanies most meals. Türkmen drink hot tea year round from shallow bowl-like cups called *käses*. A good hostess

A woman sells jewelry at the Ashkhabad Sunday bazaar market. Silver jewelry is common.

will not fill the guest's cup to the brim to demonstrate that she is being attentive, and will pour many times if she wishes the guest to stay.

Türkmen eat a lot of meat, primarily from sheep and cows but also from camels, goats, chicken, and despite the Muslim tradition, pigs. They also use milk from these animals. Meat is boiled or fried inside a casing of dough. *Manty* is a popular version, eaten with yogurt on top. Soup usually is served with meat and/or noodles and may be eaten for breakfast.

Bread is eaten at every meal. Russian-style loaves can be bought cheaply, and traditional flatbread (çörek) is often made at home in a *tamdyr*. A *tamdyr* is a traditional Central Asian dome-shaped clay oven placed outside the home; in the cities, several apartment buildings may share a single *tamdyr*.

Türkmen also drink black tea, seltzer water, and imported sodas. Despite the ban on alcohol among some Muslim peoples, Türkmen drink wine, beer, and liquor; Türkmen wine has won international competitions.

Food is rarely bought prepared or processed, and there are few restaurants. Fresh and dried fruits, vegetables, nuts, and grains are bought at the bazaar, while butter, bottled water, milk, and sausages are usually purchased from state stores.

Basic Economy. There were drastic economic fluctuations when price controls were lifted by the Soviet government in the late 1980s and when the new government attempted to stabilize the economy and introduce a new currency.

Salaries are very low, with workers in the state sector averaging approximately $40 per month; many people supplement their income by using private cars as taxis or selling goods at bazaars. Many households are multigenerational so several salaries, stipends, and pensions are combined to support the family, although some young professionals who work for Western companies live on their own.

The government provides electricity, gas, water, and bread at a nominal charge. This helps poor families, but has produced a population that is accustomed to wasting basic resources. In some neighborhoods, access to water is highly restricted and the electricity supply is unstable.

Land Tenure and Property. Historically, land and water were held in common by villages and nomadic groups. Under the Soviet system all land and property was under government control. The new government has been moving slowly toward privatization and redistribution of collective farmland. In 1995 the government restructured farms into peasant associations so that individuals, but preferably groups, could lease land. The administration also revived the traditional position of *mirap* (the post responsible for overseeing water distribution and teaching irrigation management). Legalities for foreign ownership of land and buildings are in the process of being settled.

Commercial Activities. Agriculture is the basis of the economy, especially cotton farming. Many Soviet-era state and collective farms still operate, producing grains, melons, grapes, and silk as well as cotton. Livestock raising is a time-honored occupation, and the milk, skins, and wool from cattle, sheep, camels, and goats generate other enterprises.

While many manufactured goods are imported or bought on trips abroad to places like the United Arab Emirates or Turkey, textiles are still produced for daily use. Türkmen carpets are known worldwide for their beauty and quality. Many individuals make carpets at home, but the Türkmenistan Carpet Productional Association oversees carpet factories, operates the only carpet store, and controls exports by requiring its seal of approval on carpets leaving the country. It is illegal to export national treasures such as antique carpets.

Major Industries. The oil and gas industries occupy an important space in Türkmenistan's current economic development as well as in its vision for the future. Attracting foreign investors and constructing pipelines have been at the top of the government's agenda since 1992 when they began holding international conferences to gather oil companies and promote international competition for investment. To encourage such capital investments, efforts have been made to improve the banking industry and tax codes. Türkmenistan's commitment to these industries also impacts its foreign policy as it nurtures relationships with many potential investors and customers as well as neighbors like Iran which may be in a position to host a gas or oil pipeline.

The Petro-chemical industry has been developing slowly but consistently. Two refineries, one in Türkmenbaşy and one in Çärjew (Türkmenabad), have an annual capacity to process 7.7 million tons of oil. A facility to produce poly-ethane was opened in 1997. Chemical facilities have been established to produce artificial fertilizers, sulphuric acid, and ammonia detergents. A super-phosphate factory, a sulphur factory, and iodine and bromine factories have been erected in different regions including Çärjew, Gurdak, and Çeleken.

Trade. Imports include processed food and nonfood products for the consumer market, industrial chemicals such as fertilizers, farm machinery, and metalwork for the agricultural industry. Exports include cotton, natural gas, and oil products. Türkmenistan has vast reserves of oil and natural gas, and arrangements to export gas and oil through pipelines are primary concerns of the government and foreign investors.

Division of Labor. The minimum age for employment is sixteen, but during the cotton harvest many schools close and children spend their day in the field.

SOCIAL STRATIFICATION

Symbols of Social Stratification. Traditionally, distinction among the Türkmen did not fall along class lines. Perhaps the greatest differentiation lay in the lifestyles of nomadic pastoralists (çarwa) and settled agriculturalists (çomur). While Türkmen generally preferred the freedom of roaming with their herds, neither category was necessarily per-

manent. Tribal affiliation was always the supreme marker among Türkmen.

During the Soviet period an elite developed among the party hierarchy and some intelligentsia (writers, artists, scholars), but one could fall from grace easily. As politics shifted over the decades an author's writings from one era could later be used against him or her and lead to persecution. For example, intellectuals who had fostered the Soviet policy of korenizatsiia (a program to promote national languages and fill official positions with natives) in the 1920s were labeled enemies of the state when policies changed in the 1930s. Those who stayed in favor of the Party were allowed privileges like summer homes (dachas) in rural areas like Firuze.

There are emerging economic classes in Türkmenistan today, as new jobs are created and Türkmenistan's new global position redefines job skills. Dramatic changes in agriculture, the oil industry and the business world have created spaces for the post-Soviet Türkmen, especially younger people who know foreign languages, primarily English. Still tribal loyalties and personal contacts remain important for obtaining positions and favors.

Styles of dress do not signify social stratification. Women wear traditional clothing such as long, flowing solid-colored dresses in bright tones decorated with elaborate embroidery (keşde) around the collar. They sometimes cover their heads with colorful scarves for protection against the elements or sand, but there are no social rules that require head coverings. Most women prefer the traditional styles of long upswept hair for adults and long braids for girls. Jewelry, especially made from silver, and pierced ears are very common. Men wear Western-style pants and jackets, but some wear traditional clothing. The high lamb's wool hat (telpek) is worn even during the hot summer months. For ceremonies and special occasions white telpeks are worn with dark, baggy pants tucked into high black boots. Older men wear sheepskin coats with the fur on the inside or red and yellow striped robes that fall to the knees.

POLITICAL LIFE

Government. The legislative branch of government, established in the 1992 constitution, consists of two parliamentary bodies. The People's Council (Halk Maslahaty) includes more than 100 seats, some of which are elected by popular vote and some of which are appointed, and the Assembly (Majlis) has 50 seats whose holders are elected by popular

Women in a Türkmenistan have historically been viewed as equal partners.

vote to five-year terms. Executive power is exercised by a President who is also chairman of the cabinet of ministers. Ministers oversee sectors of the government and economy such as domestic affairs, foreign affairs, the oil industry, and agriculture.

Leadership and Political Officials. Despite the unopposed establishment of Saparmurat Niÿazov as president for life, small unofficial opposition movements exist underground and in foreign countries. The president's portrait appears on most public buildings and is printed on the currency.

Social Problems and Control. The government does not restrict freedom of travel, but the southern border zones and some areas of high security require a permit for visitation and are off limits to foreigners. Citizens carry internal passports primarily as a form of identification.

Military Activity. There is national conscription to staff a small military force that is plagued by corruption and disorganization. Neutrality is the policy of the post–Soviet nation.

SOCIAL WELFARE AND CHANGE PROGRAMS

There is an unofficial group in Aşgabat that supports battered women, and efforts are made to care for orphans and the mentally and physically disabled.

People pay 1 percent of their wages to receive a pension after retirement. Small pensions are also paid to invalids and war veterans.

NONGOVERNMENTAL ORGANIZATIONS AND OTHER ASSOCIATIONS

Several organizations have been founded by foreigners to help establish democracy. Several are concerned with human rights, and others are concerned with the environment.

GENDER ROLES AND STATUSES

Division of Labor by Gender. The traditional nomadic lifestyle demanded a strict division of labor. Men hunted, tended the herds, and kept the horses, while women cooked, tended the home, and made the textiles. Today, women usually tend the house and men have more free time, but employment is not restricted by gender. Women work as teachers, academics, librarians, authors, administrators, scientists, linguists, and salespeople, and there are nine female members of the *Majlis*. Textiles are made primarily by women, while heavy industry is male-

Ancient Islamic buildings in Türkmenistan. Few mosques were open during the Soviet period.

oriented, as are the livestock industries and transportation.

The Relative Status of Women and Men.
Historically women were considered equitable partners. The last independent Türkmen leader was a woman, Güljamal Hatun, who succeeded her husband Nurberdi Han.

Under the Soviet system women began to work outside the home and it became more common for women to attain higher education. Women have retained the right to education and work. In fact, many of the students who have taken part in programs in Turkey and the West have been female.

There are unacknowledged inequalities which are difficult to document. The traditional role of homemaker and caregiver prevents some women from seeking roles outside of the home. There are anecdotal reports of domestic violence, but it is not spoken of publicly.

MARRIAGE, FAMILY, AND KINSHIP

Marriage. Türkmen usually marry in their early twenties, although some delay marriage to begin a career. The traditional expectation is to have a baby within the first year of marriage, and the groom's parents can demand a divorce if they suspect that the bride is infertile.

A Türkmen wedding is a festive occasion characterized by historic Turkic rituals. There is an exchange of value called *galyñ* (bride price), which despite its name, does not mean that a bride is purchased; it is a historic, complex approach to redistribution of wealth in the traditional communities and is an honored tradition even today. The Soviet government established a civil system and discouraged Islamic rites, but they persisted.

There is a new and surprising trend among Türkmen women in urban centers who feel compelled to have children but do not have a husband; they cannot find a man that they think would make a good husband and prefer to be without one.

Polygamy was never common among the Türkmen.

Inheritance. The Soviet government, and the Türkmen government after that, established civil laws of inheritance; however, Türkmen prefer to follow *Adat* (custom) when possible, even over *Sarigat* (Islamic law). Traditionally the youngest son would remain with his parents inheriting the home upon their deaths; daughters would marry and move into their husband's home.

Kin Groups. In more than ten major tribes, there is complex kinship systems with distinct terms to refer to gender, seniority, and to indicate whether a person is related on the mother's or father's side. Families are close, and a holiday or a birthday celebration often fills a large home.

The Türkmen were organized by their kinship system into families, clans, and tribes. These relations governed loyalties, economics, marriages and even migration. Historically these groups interacted and sometimes merged into confederations to suit political needs. The Soviet system and the present government have downplayed tribalism to promote nationalism. Most people continue to marry within the tribe. Although it is officially discouraged, there is some hiring along tribal lines.

SOCIALIZATION

Infant Care. Mothers and other female family members play an important role in a child's life. Male babies are circumcised in a special ceremony led by a *molla*, usually attended only by close family members.

Certain superstitions surround infants: a newborn should not be seen by non-family members for the first forty days, and a Koran should be placed near the cradle to help protect the baby and so that it will never be ''alone.''

Child Rearing and Education. Child rearing is primarily the responsibility of women, but elders and older siblings have authority over children. Fathers tend to take more responsibility for raising boys and teaching them about labor, ethics, and etiquette. Mothers oversee girls' education in homemaking. A young girl spends a great deal of time preparing the items necessary for marriage and practices cooking, sewing, embroidery, and textile making.

The Soviet system of free education remains basically intact. There are kindergartens and elementary schools, and an eighth grade education is mandatory. Seventy-seven percent of schools teach in Türkmen, and 16 percent in Russian. Türkmen is gaining educational prominence, and the role of English has expanded. Adults study Türkmen in free workplace classes, and many take private lessons to learn English.

Higher Education. The Soviet system of state education remains fairly intact and has been free and open to all qualified individuals. However, a July 2000 declaration of reform reports that the numbers at universities will be reduced so that instructors have only five students in a class and admittance will be based on an individual's genealogy. There are several higher institutes in Aşgabat, and there is one teacher training college in Türkmenabad (formerly Çärjew). Most courses of study are five years, although graduate and doctoral work can take many more years.

There are kindergartens and elementary schools (*mekdep*) and graduation of eighth grade is mandatory. Under the Soviet system, elementary schools were organized by language of instruction, either Türkmen or Russian. Russian schools were perceived as better overall, but especially because they taught the language of professionals. However, attachment to the mother tongue was always strong, today 77 percent of schools teach in Türkmen and 16 percent in Russian; there are also some Turkish language schools and a university which charge high tuition. With the country's reorientation, a shift in language prominence has become a national priority. Türkmen is gaining prominence and the role of English has expanded. Even adults try to study in private lessons or with Peace Corps volunteers.

All institutions suffer from lack of financial security, dilapidated buildings, lack of textbooks and undertrained teachers. Some foreign experts are lending aid and advice, although progress, especially in the rural areas, is slow. Turkey is printing new nationally-oriented textbooks in the new alphabet for free (although some schools still use the thirty-year-old Soviet textbooks venerating Lenin).

Since independence, Türkmen students have had the opportunity to study abroad. Some go to England or the United States, but Turkey has provided the greatest opportunity, training dentists, doctors and other professionals.

Teachers have been hit especially hard by the dramatic economic shift since independence. Many are forced to supplement their incomes with private tutorials and still make very low salaries. Despite political and social change, and poor pay, teachers (*mugallyma*) are still held in very high esteem.

ETIQUETTE

Historic customs are still revered by the Türkmen. *Adat* is Türkmen customary law. *Edep* is the guideline of etiquette and behavior, and *Şarigat* is Islamic law. Sometimes in combination or with precedence in separate arenas, these advise Türkmen on how to interact socially and live with a sense of Türkmenness (*Türkmençilik*). Instructions include how to

The rug section of a Sunday market in Ashkhabad. Many carpets are made in private homes.

handle responsibilities related to inheritance, property ownership, marriage, family life, deference to elders, hospitality toward guests, and tribal and clan identity. Children are surrounded by multigenerations and learn at an early age to respect elders, even among siblings the eldest is given status.

RELIGION

Religious Beliefs. The Türkmen state is secular. While independence inaugurated a mild surge of interest in religion, it seems mostly related to the fact that Türkmen feel their Islamic heritage to be a fundamental aspect of their identity, rather than to a widespread affinity for piety.

Other religious groups are represented in Türkmenistan, but Türkmen are Sunni Muslims of the Hanafi school. When Arab and Persian invasions brought Islam to Central Asia (seventh–eighth centuries) the Turkic groups did not all convert at the same time, nor to the same degree. Conversion to Islam depended on time and place, for example, urban centers were more likely to participate in formal rituals whereas nomadic Turks (like Türkmen) mixed aspects of Islam with elements from other practices (like the celebration of Nowruz which came from Zoroastranism) and still retained much of their pre-Islamic heritage (retaining the name of

the sky god *Gök* for the words blue and green). Türkmen began to convert around the tenth century. While their practices still reflect this early syncretism, even non-practicing Türkmen call themselves Muslim and see this as integral to their identity.

Religious Practitioners. Religious leaders are called *mollas*, or *işan* in the mystical Sufi orders, and *käzys* interpret Islamic law but do not act as clergy. The oldest man leads the group in prayer.

In 1992 the government sanctioned the establishment of the *Kazyÿat* as the highest religious authority. In divorcing itself from the Central Asian *Müftiÿat*, the Türkmen leadership declared its interest in promoting Islam as an aspect of national culture. The Committee (Geñes) for Religious Affairs' attachment to the Office of President affords the state oversight of religious affairs in the new state.

Rituals and Holy Places. Islamic holidays are celebrated according to the lunar calendar and fall on a different day each year of the Gregorian calendar. Ramadan is the month of fasting; Oraz Bayramy celebrates the conclusion of fasting; and Gurban Bayramy falls 40 days after Oraz Bayramy with the slaughter of a sheep.

Few mosques were open during the Soviet period, and most Türkmen prayed at home. Several mosques have been opened since independence, but visits to shrines are more popular. At the tomb of a saint, Türkmen pray for the birth of a child, cure from illness, or good fortune.

Death and the Afterlife.
Türkmen perform burial ceremonies according to Islamic law and did so even under communism. Women do not attend funerals, but do participate in the commemoratory feasts held at seven days, forty days, and one year after a death. Türkmen prefer to use the term "to pass on" (aradan çykmak), rather than "to die" (ölmek).

MEDICINE AND HEALTH CARE

The Soviet socialized health care system remains intact and is free to citizens but is insufficient to serve the country's needs. Doctors are undertrained; facilities are in poor condition and are often unsanitary; and medicine and equipment are scarce. Foreign aid has included Turkish ambulances and advice from Western medical personnel. Traditional healers provide treatment using herbs, prayer, and the manipulation of energies.

SECULAR CELEBRATIONS

Among the major holidays are Flag Day (19 February), Women's Day (8 March), the first day of spring (21 March), Victory Day (9 May), Constitution Day (18 May), Remembrance Day (6 October), Independence Day (27 October), and the Day of Neutrality (12 December). The battle at Gök Tepe is commemorated on 12 January; 6 April is celebrated as a Drop of Water Is a Grain Gold Day; and the Day of the First Election of the President is marked on 21 June. Other celebrations are held on 27 April (Day of the Türkmen Horse), 25 May (Carpet Day), 17 November (Student Youth Holiday), and 7 December (Good Neighborliness Day).

THE ARTS AND HUMANITIES

Support for the Arts.
Some artists sell their work independently; one can purchase paintings and jewelry from galleries in the urban centers and at bazaars. However, the arts are supported and supervised by the state. Most efforts are aimed at promoting the newly independent Türkmen national identity imbued with a combination of Islamic heritage and traditional Türkmen culture. There has been some foreign support for building museums and some architecture.

Literature.
Türkmen literary tradition is a rich mosaic of pre-Islamic Turkic elements fused with Islamic influences. Examples of folk traditions still highly valued today include the dastans Gorgut Ata and Göroglu which illustrate early Turkic culture overlaid with Islamic values. A dastan is a combination epic tale and lyric poem which formed the basis of oral tradition. The dastan was sung by a bagşy who memorized thousands of lines and sang them while playing various instruments. In addition to being a pastime which all members of the society could enjoy, the dastan was an oral record of Türkmen history, values, culture, and language. Dastans have played such an important role in Türkmen identity (as for all Turks) that enormous efforts are currently being made to revitalize them (after decades of Soviet suppression) in order to bolster the sense of Türkmen identity and unity.

Highly regarded literary figures include the poets Mammetveli Kemine (1770–1840) and Mollanepes (1810–1862), but it is eighteenth century poet Magtymguly who is considered the Türkmen national poet. His poems urged the politically fragmented Türkmen tribes to unite. Both the Soviets and the current government have promoted his wisdom in efforts to foster nationalism over tribalism.

Performance Arts.
The Soviet system introduced theaters, television, radio, and cinemas to Türkmenistan, which imparted Soviet values. Today satellite dishes are becoming popular in the cities and broadcasts of Indian music videos. Mexican and American soap operas are popular, as well as American pop music.

Traditional dancing is strongly promoted by the state and the troupes of female dancers grace the covers of magazines and travel to many neighboring states where they act as cultural ambassadors. In urban centers, Türkmen singers give concerts which combine a fusion of pop and traditional Türkmen music called estrada.

THE STATE OF THE PHYSICAL AND SOCIAL SCIENCES

The Soviet system of scholarship neglected traditional Türkmen history and culture. Dastans, literature, dance, architecture, language, and the development of the alphabet reflect the nation's intent to authenticate an independent Türkmen identity.

BIBLIOGRAPHY

Akbarzadeh, Shahram. "National Identity and Political Legitimacy in Türkmenistan," *Nationalities Papers*, 27 (2): 271–290, 1996.

Bartold, W. "A History of the Türkmen People," *Four Studies of the History of Central Asia*, vol. 3, 1962.

———. *Turkestan Down to the Mongol Invasion*, 1977.

Baskakov, N. A. *Turkic Languages of Central Asia*, translated by Stephen Wurm, 1960.

———. *Voprosy sovershenstvovaniia alfavitov tiurskikh iazykov SSR*, 1972.

Becker, Seymour. *Russia's Protectorates in Central Asia: Bukhara and Khiva, 1865–1924*, 1968.

Bennigsen, Alexandre, and S. Enders Wimbush. *Muslim National Communism in the Soviet Union: A Revolutionary Struggle for the Colonial World*, 1979.

Caroe, Olaf. *Soviet Empire*, 1967.

Clark, Larry, Mike Thurman, and David Tyson. "Türkmenistan," in Glenn E. Curtis, ed., *Kazakhstan, Kyrgyzstan, Tajikstan, Türkmenistan and Uzbekistan: Country Studies*, 1997.

Clement, Victoria. "The Politics of Script Reform in Soviet Türkmenistan: Alphabet and National Identity Formation." MA thesis, Ohio State University, 1999.

Dankoff, Robert. *Diwan Lugat-it Turk (Compendium of Turkish Dialects)*, translated by Robert Kelly, 1982–1985.

———. *The Wisdom of Royal Glory*, 1983.

D'Encausse, Helene Carrere. *Islam and the Russian Empire: Reform and Revolution in Central Asia*, translated by Quintin Hoare, 1988.

———. *Decline of an Empire: The Soviet Socialist Republics in Revolt*, 1979.

DeWeese, Devin. *Islamization and Native Religion in the Golden Horde: Baba, Tukles and Conversion to Islam in Historical and Epic Tradition*, 1994.

Edgar, Adrienne. "Nationality Policy and National Identity: The Türkmen Soviet Socialist Republic, 1924–1929." *Journal of Central Asian Studies*, 1 (2): 2–20, 1997.

———. "The Creation of Soviet Türkmenistan, 1924–1938." Ph.D. dissertation, University of California, Berkeley, 1999.

Ercilasun, Ahmet B. *Örneklerle Bügünkü Türk Alfebeleri*, 1996.

Evans, John. *Mission of N. P. Ignat'ev to Khiva and Bukhara, 1858*, 1984.

Glantz, Michael H., ed. *Creeping Environmental Problems and Sustainable Development in the Aral Sea Basin*, 1999.

Gleason, Abbott, Peter Kenez, and Richard Stites. *Bolshevik Power*, 1985.

Golden, Peter. *An Introduction to the History of the Turkic Peoples*, 1992.

———. "The Migrations of the Oguz." *Archivum Ottomanicum*, 4: 45–84, 1972.

Henze, Paul. "Alphabet Changes in Soviet Central Asia and Communist China." *Royal Central Asian Journal* XLIV: 124–136, 1957.

Hostler, Charles Warren. *Turkism and the Soviets: The Turks of the World and Their Political Objectives*, 1957.

Hunsicker, David R., Jr. "The Historical Significance of the Akhal-Teke in Türkmen Identity." Presented at the 11th Annual Nicholas Poppe Symposium, University of Washington, 1999.

Irons, Williams. *The Yomut Türkmen: A Study of Social Organization among a Central Asian Turkic Speaking Population*, 1975.

Karryew, A. *Istoriia Sovetskogo Türkmenistana, 1917–1937*, 1970.

Khalk Malslakhaty: Materialy istoricheskogo zasedaniia Khalk maslakhaty Türkmenistana ot 14 dekabria 1992 goda, 1993.

Kirkwood, Michael. ed. *Language Planning in the Soviet Union*, 1989.

Leiser, Gary, ed. and trans. *A History of the Seljuks: Imbrahim Kafesoglu's Interpretation and the Resulting Controversy*, 1988.

Lewis, Geoffrey, trans. *The Book of Dede Korkut*, 1974.

Materialy po istorii Türkmen i Türkmenii, 1939.

Öräev, Arazbaÿ. *Türkmenistanyñ dövlet nysanlary*, 1993.

Park, Alexander. *Bolshevism in Turkestan, 1917–1927*, 1957.

Paksoy, H. B. *ALPAMYSH: Central Asian Identity Under Russian Rule*, 1989.

———. "Basmachi (*Basmatchestvo*) Movement and Z. V. Togan: The Turkistan National Liberation Movement." *Cahiers d'Etudes sur la Méditerranée orientale et le monde turco-iranien*, 27: 301–312, 1999.

———. "The Basmachi Movement from Within: An Account of Zeki Velidi Togan." *Nationalities Papers* 23 (2): 373–399, 1995.

———. "Introduction to *DEDE KORKUT*," *Soviet Anthropology and Archeology* 29 (1): 14–18, 1990.

———. "Central Asia's New Dastans." *Central Asian Survey* 6 (1): 75–92, 1987.

Pipes, Richard. *Formation of the Soviet Union: Communism and Nationalism, 1917–1923*, 1964.

———. "Muslims of Central Asia." *Middle East Journal* IX: (2, 3), 1955.

Poppe, Nicholas. *Introduction to Altaic Linguistics*, 1965.

Saray, Mehmet. *The Türkmens in the Age of Imperialism: A Study of the Türkmen People and Their Incorporation into the Russian Empire*, 1989.

Simon, Gerhard. *Nationalism and Policy toward the Nationalities in the Soviet Union*, translated by Karen Forster and Oswald Forster, 1991.

Simsir, Bilal. *Türk Yazi Devrimi*, 1992.

Sümer, F. *Oguzlar (Türkmenler)*, 3rd ed., 1980.

Tekin, Talat. *A Grammar of Orkhon Turkic*, 1968.

Togan, Z. V. *Türkili Türkistan*, 1981.

Tyson, David. "Shrine Pilgrimage in Türkmenistan as a Means to Understand Islam among the Türkmen." *Central Asian Monitor* 1: 15–32, 1997.

Vambery, Arminius. *Travels in Central Asia*, 1970.

Vanishing Jewels: Central Asian Tribal Weavings, 1990.

Wheeler, Geoffrey. *The Modern History of Soviet Central Asia*, 1964.

Wixman, Ronald. "Applied Soviet Nationality Policy: A Suggested Rationale." *Turco-Tatar Past, Soviet Present: Studies Presented to Alexandre Bennigsen*, 1986.

—Victoria Clement

TUVALU

CULTURE NAME
Tuvaluan

ALTERNATIVE NAMES

For most of the nineteenth century, Western navigators referred to this archipelago as the "Lagoon Islands," a name gradually supplanted by the "Ellice Islands." This latter term became official in 1892 when Great Britain created the Gilbert and Ellice Islands Protectorate (later Colony). The name and its Tuvaluan rendition (Elise) remained in use until the group separated from the Gilberts in 1975.

ORIENTATION

Identification. The name "Tuvalu" is deemed traditional and roughly translates as "eight traditions." There is no historical evidence of its use, however, until the rise of self-determination in the 1970s. Inhabitants assert their identity as members of distinct societies, referred to by the name of each of the eight traditionally inhabited islands.

Location and Geography. Contemporary Tuvalu is a group of nine small islands and atolls, including the historically uninhabited Niulakita. They lie in a northwest-southeast chain stretching over 250 square miles (645 square kilometers) of ocean in the western Pacific, north of Fiji, east of the Solomon Islands, and south and southeast of Kiribati. Closest to the equator is Nanumea, followed southwards by Niutao, Nanumaga, Nui, Vaitupu, Nukufetau, Funafuti, Nukulaelae, and Niulakita, the smallest. The first four constitute a compact northern subgroup, while the latter five form a more scattered southern group. The climate throughout is tropical maritime. Seasonal variations are slight, though wet and stormy conditions with strong westerlies occur from December to February. During the rest of the year, easterly trade winds predominate. Rainfall is heavier in the south than in the north, although it is generally adequate throughout. Limited storage capacity, however, means that water may become scarce even after a relatively short dry spell.

Demography. The 1991 national census enumerated 9,043 persons, but the total population of Tuvaluans was estimated at about 11,000, including those living in other parts of the Pacific, as well as those working on ships around the world. The separate island populations vary considerably, from over 4,000 on Funafuti, the capital, to fewer than 100 on Niulakita. The vast majority is of Tuvaluan ethnic origin, with a small minority of immigrants from other Pacific nations. A sizable group of advisers, officials, development workers, and volunteers from Western countries resides in Tuvalu at any one time, especially on Funafuti. Overseas, significant clusters of Tuvaluans are found on Kioa Island in Fiji (about 400), in Kiribati (about 400), and in New Zealand (estimated at several hundred). In June 2000, the Tuvaluan prime minister asked New Zealand to take another 3,000 migrants as a response to rising sea levels, but an agreement has not yet been reached. A few remain on Nauru (located northwest of Tuvalu), where they once worked in large numbers in the phosphate and supporting industries. In each case, Tuvaluans living outside their home nation adapt to the dominant culture, while retaining symbols of a distinct identity.

The best estimates suggest a precontact population of around 3,000. After European contact, most of Tuvalu escaped the depredations wrought by diseases and other factors elsewhere in the Pacific, but Nukulaelae and Funafuti suffered significant population losses in 1863 when Peruvian "blackbirders" (labor traders using a mixture of force and inducement) kidnaped several hundred natives. The population of these two islands has since more than recovered through natural increase and migration.

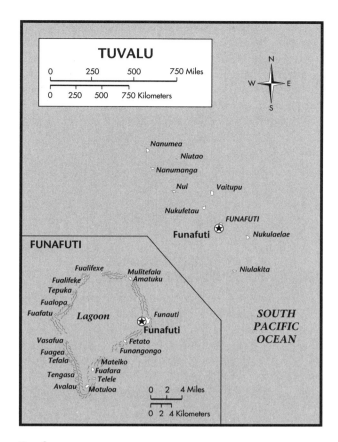

Tuvalu

Linguistic Affiliation. The majority of people speak Tuvaluan, a Polynesian language, except for the inhabitants of Nui who speak a mainly Gilbertese (Micronesian) dialect. Although all varieties of Tuvaluan are mutually intelligible, each island community has a distinct dialect. Nanumea, Nanumaga, and Niutao form a loose subgroup, while the inhabitants of the four Southern islands speak closely related dialects. Tuvaluan is historically related to Polynesian Outlier languages in Melanesia, and is a more distant relative of Samoan and Tokelauan. Many Tuvaluans are competent in Samoan, which functioned as the language of church and (to a lesser extent) government until recently, as well as Gilbertese, the dominant language of the colony for seven decades. Samoan in particular has exerted considerable influence on the structure of Tuvaluan. Since the mid-1970s, Samoan and Gilbertese have declined in importance and English has become the prestige language and the medium of communication with the outside world.

Symbolism. While the symbols that relate persons to their home island are numerous, long-standing, and diffuse, those connecting persons to the nation-state are fewer, more recent, less well established, and comparatively self-conscious. National identity is symbolized by a flag, a national anthem, a seal, and an Independence Day celebrated every year. The flag, devised for independence, represents each of the nine islands with a gold star. It also sports the Union Jack in the upper-left-hand corner, symbolic of membership in the Commonwealth, and a reminder of the British colonial presence. This design has been contested, however: it was modified in 1995, entirely replaced in 1996, but restored in 1997. These changes followed partisan politics, heavily influenced in turn by kinship and island affiliations.

The only medium of popular communication for promoting national integration is the radio station, which broadcasts (highly sanitized) information and entertainment for several hours a day. Print media are confined to an intermittent government news sheet and an even more intermittent church newsletter. Both are difficult to obtain and consequently not widely read. There is no broadcast television technology in the country though videos are popular and have replaced film screenings as a mode of entertainment. The educational system exerts conflicting pressures on national identity. There are only two secondary schools for the entire group, but entry is competitive. Any nation-building that results is, as elsewhere in the Pacific, concentrated in the emergent elite.

HISTORY AND ETHNIC RELATIONS

Emergence of the Nation. Tuvalu was probably settled as part of the backwash by which the Polynesian Outliers in Melanesia and Micronesia were populated after the main eastward historical wave of Polynesian migration. Lack of archaeological investigation makes original settlement dates difficult to establish. Ethno-historical evidence suggests that the islands maintained sporadic contacts with one another, as well as with invaders and other visitors, principally from Samoa, Tonga, and Kiribati. First contact with the world outside of the Pacific probably occurred in 1568, when Spanish explorer Álvaro de Mendaña de Neira sighted Nui. Sustained contact did not take place until the early nineteenth century. From 1865 to the mid-1870s, Samoan missionaries from the London Missionary Society (LMS) established Christian churches on each island, and from 1892 to 1975 Britain administered the group jointly with the Gilbert Islands, first as a protectorate and after 1916 as a colony.

While the Congregationalist ethos and limited resources of the LMS left each island largely to its own devices, British administration fostered a sense of commonality among the inhabitants of the group, encouraged by and in contrast to the often absent colonial officers, but also in contrast to the Gilbertese. The founding of a boys' secondary school on Vaitupu in 1922 brought together children from around the group. The use of three atolls as bases for U.S. forces during World War II also brought islanders into contact both with one another and with Americans (enabling them to place British authority into perspective).

As Great Britain moved to divest itself of its Pacific possessions, Ellice Islanders decided against remaining tied to the more populous Gilbertese, who were judged to be culturally different and inferior. Britain reluctantly allowed the Ellice Islanders to secede in 1975. The newly renamed Tuvalu became independent in 1978 and its neighbor, renamed Kiribati, in 1979.

Ethnic Relations. Small numbers of migrants from other Pacific islands (particularly Kiribati) reside in Tuvalu, often through marriage, and their integration is mostly unproblematic. The only significant pattern of group identification revolves around a person's island of origin, which is reckoned according to one's kinship affiliations. When numbers permit, Tuvaluans use island of origin as an organizational principle for such purposes as exchange and celebrations, but it is not an ethnic marker as such.

URBANISM, ARCHITECTURE, AND THE USE OF SPACE

Before Christianity, island communities probably consisted of dispersed hamlets. Under missionary influence, each island population became concentrated in one or two villages, spatially and socially divided into two or four "sides" (*feituu*). Membership in these is largely symbolic but serves as a way of organizing gift exchanges, games, fund-raising, and some fishing and communal projects. In the neutral village center are located the church building, the *maneapa* or meetinghouse, and the village green (*malae*). Government buildings (e.g., island office, school, first-aid station, rest house) are generally built on the outskirts. Until the 1970s, houses throughout the group were open rectangular structures supported by pandanus posts and roofed with pandanus thatch. Meeting houses were similar in design but larger, while churches and government buildings were and are built with im-

ported materials. After a devastating hurricane on Funafuti in 1972, dwellings were rebuilt with imported materials (timber, wood-chip board, cement, and corrugated iron). Other islands gradually followed suit, and by the mid-1980s the only structures made of local material were small peripheral buildings such as cooking huts.

The only significant variation from the general pattern is on Funafuti, where space is more fragmented and diversely organized owing to the presence of the national government, the large number of residents from other islands, the greater population, and the airstrip of World War II vintage, which occupies much of the main islet.

FOOD AND ECONOMY

Food in Daily Life. The most important cultivated plant is *pulaka* (swamp taro), grown in large pits dug into the top layer of a freshwater lens, and valued for its resistance to drought and high salinity. Also of importance to the daily diet are coconut palms (used for the collection of *kaleve* "toddy" as well as for the nuts), pandanus, bananas, and breadfruit. Fish was traditionally the main source of dietary protein. Today, particularly on Funafuti, imported rice and flour figure prominently in the daily diet, as well as canned and frozen meat. Weakly brewed tea has long been part of daily fare, often in preference to the nutrient-rich coconut toddy. Meals are consumed two or three times a day at home. The few restaurants are all on Funafuti.

Food Customs at Ceremonial Occasions. Feasts consist of the daily staples, but in larger quantities, and with the addition of pork and fowl meat (the product of local animal husbandry), and occasional treats such as wild birds and turtle.

Basic Economy. The daily activities of the inhabitants of the Outer Islands (all islands other than Funafuti) remain primarily subsistence-oriented. Fishing, agriculture, and animal husbandry occupy most individuals' days, supplemented by craft production for local consumption (e.g., mat weaving, house building and repairing, boat and motor maintenance, tackle making, fishing, and net mending). On Funafuti, these activities have lost their prominence, as many inhabitants, particularly non-Funafuti Islanders, do not have access to land, and fishing grounds are not readily reachable. Many residents are dependent on the salaries of relatives employed by the government and the few other bureaucratic or commercial bodies. Even on the Outer Islands, remittances from relatives employed elsewhere have long served to supplement subsistence through the purchase of store-bought food, fuel, and clothing. Little is produced for sale on the Outer Islands; rather, surplus production is used to sustain networks of exchange between families and individuals.

Land Tenure and Property. The original form of tenure may have been communal, as this arrangement still exists and is accorded symbolic priority. From a system in which chiefs probably allocated land rights for use rather than ownership, more complex forms of title have evolved. Land may now be held privately, either by individuals or by groups, although this distinction is blurred by the fact that individuals are always members of groups that wax and wane as the individuals that constitute them are born, reproduce, and die.

Commercial Activities. Small cottage-industry ventures emerge from time to time. They target food needs (e.g., baked items, pigs and fowl, salt fish prepared on the Outer Islands for sale on Funafuti) or cater to the tiny tourist and export industry, through the sale of woven fans, shell necklaces, and model canoes. These efforts are marked by high rates of failure and turnover.

Major Industries. Large-scale ventures, such as the commercial harvesting of the bountiful marine resources, require capital investments (e.g., for harvesting equipment and storage facilities) and adequate transportation between the islands and to the outside world, both of which are currently unavailable. The group's Exclusive Economic Zone does generate revenue, however, through licenses for Distant Water Fishing Nations.

Trade. Trade before Western contact was confined to occasional interisland voyages, which may have been accompanied by exchanges, marriages, and political tribute. Foreign traders became interested in coconut oil and then in copra (dried coconut flesh for the food and cosmetics industries). Copra is still exported but has greatly declined in importance, owing to inefficiencies of scale and fluctuating prices on the world market. Tuvalu's current principal export is its manual labor: since the 1980s, international shipping corporations have employed Tuvaluan seamen, whose remittances make an important contribution to the economy.

Division of Labor. Traditionally, there was little full-time specialization, though certain people were acknowledged experts at fishing, navigation, defense, canoe making, house building, and garden-

A Polynesian man wears a traditional costume at a ceremony on Tuvalu Island.

ing, as well as curing and divination. This division was often formalized into bodies of knowledge jealously guarded by particular descent groups. Traditional chiefs were not necessarily exempt from working at the common range of pursuits, although today high-status individuals (e.g., the pastor, the island president) are expected not to engage in strenuous activities. Younger people, especially men, are expected to take on more physically demanding tasks, while older individuals attend to more sedentary work. Specialization has taken hold mainly in the church and in government.

SOCIAL STRATIFICATION

Classes and Castes. On most islands, traditional chiefs (*aliki*) headed the major descent groups and sometimes deferred to one or two paramount chiefs. In no case did chieftainship give rise to a caste system. The chiefs seem to have been as much religious leaders as political ones, but they shared religious authority with spirit mediums and diviners. While the latter were suppressed by missionaries, the chiefly system survived. Its power was greatly reduced under missionary and colonial hegemony but has never disappeared and is occasionally revived.

Embryonic class formation has appeared on Funafuti, caused by occupational specialization, the increasing importance of cash in the economy, and the fledgling development of business. Obligations to kin, however, continue to have a neutralizing effect on class-generated upward mobility.

Symbols of Social Stratification. Traditional chiefly status is said to have been symbolized by certain objects and prerogatives: pearl-shell fishing-lure necklaces, reserved seating against the head post of the meetinghouse, and the right to the head of all turtles caught. Many of these privileges are now bestowed on the village pastor. No clear markers of incipient class differentiation have emerged, other than the mostly subtle material and symbolic correlates of social achievement (e.g., material comforts, self-confidence, fluency in English).

POLITICAL LIFE

Government. The written constitution established a Westminster-style system. The British monarch is nominally head of state and represented locally by a governor-general, whose role is largely honorific. Each island elects one or two members of a twelve-member parliament (apart from Niulakita residents, who vote for a Niutao delegate). The leader of a parliamentary majority becomes prime minister and selects a cabinet from elected members.

Leadership and Political Officials. Achievement of national leadership positions follows quasi-traditional principles. It requires personal charisma, evidence of divine protection (e.g., educational achievement and fluency in English), enough wealth or income to allow generosity, and favorable kinship connections (including large numbers of voting relatives). As in Western parliamentary practice, compromises and informal deals occupy a central role in Tuvaluan politics. Political parties with agendas and policies do not exist at either local or national levels. Political alignment is best understood as loosely structured and potentially unstable factionalism, configured by local-level kinship ties. Politicians receive the same deference as other high-status persons (positive politeness, some avoidance, etc.), although these patterns are highly informal in comparison to larger Polynesian polities, as befits the relatively egalitarian ethos of Tuvaluan society, traditional and modern.

Social Problems and Control. A small police force maintains order on each island, where magistrate courts regularly sit to deal with drunken and disorderly conduct, breaking and entering, unpaid debts, and failure to keep pigs confined. More serious crimes, such as rape and embezzlement, are sent to the high court on Funafuti. Informal mechanisms such as gossip, shaming, and public admonition are effective. Tuvaluans place high value on the maintenance of harmonious interpersonal relations, and have long taken pride in presenting themselves as a peaceful and law-abiding society. This image began to come into question in the late twentieth century with rising crime rates, particularly in the capital, said to stem from increasing contact with the outside world, the greater availability of liquor, the decreasing power of traditional forms of social control, and the presence of returned seamen.

SOCIAL WELFARE AND CHANGE PROGRAMS

Kinship groups and island communities continue to take primary responsibility for welfare and social services. Tuvalu has a strong tradition of volunteerism, whereby persons and families present food, services, and money to the community on occasions such as a child's educational achievement or a wedding. Feeding the entire island is also a common way of asking for communal forgiveness for a transgression (e.g., causing a serious fight). Competitive fund-raising and other forms of resource pooling occur frequently. The product of these efforts may be destined for a third party, such as a neighboring island in need or the island's pastor, or may be redistributed among the members of the group. Individuals, groups, and communities can gain considerable prestige from generous contributions to such efforts. Conversely, the system can place less fortunate individuals under substantial strain.

NONGOVERNMENTAL ORGANIZATIONS AND OTHER ASSOCIATIONS

Many types of organizations form and reform around specific identities and purposes: women's groups, dancing groups, religious groups, "development" groups. Their purpose is often to raise funds or pool resources. Some, such as village sides and choir groups, are more enduring than others. Individuals may belong to many different groups simultaneously or consecutively, and may thus negotiate their allegiances strategically.

While most groups are confined to particular island communities, some are part of national organizations with links to international bodies (e.g., the Tuvalu Christian Church and the Tuvalu Red Cross Society). A few international organizations, such as the Save the Children Federation and overseas volunteer agencies, have played a notable role in development.

GENDER ROLES AND STATUSES

Division of Labor by Gender. There was and is a general gender-based division of labor, more marked in ideology than in practice. Men engage in open sea and lagoon fishing from canoes as well as the gathering of coconuts and palm toddy and the more strenuous forms of cultivation. Women share the activity of reef fishing and collecting and take responsibility for weaving and infant care, as well as for harvesting some crops and preparing food. This division is less ideologically clear-cut in modern occupational fields, although in practice women are overrepresented in menial positions while men overwhelmingly control key positions in the labor market.

The Relative Status of Women and Men. In daily life, there is relative gender equality. The coercion of women by men is strongly condemned, although forms of it (e.g., domestic violence) do occur. Women's lack of power becomes evident in formal contexts. They are seriously underrepresented in local structures of authority and power (despite the occasional appointment of a female chief), as well as in the higher ranks of government, civil service, and the church.

MARRIAGE, FAMILY, AND KINSHIP

Marriage. The choice of a marriage partner is today dictated by a mixture of kinship alliance and personal choice. Island communities differ in terms of their preference for endogamy (marriage within one's group) and exogamy (marriage outside one's group) but marriage between "avoidance" relatives (up to third cousins) is always strictly prohibited. Marriage is one of the most important rites of passage in Tuvaluan society, since it legitimizes children and establishes new kinship links in relation to land rights and the flow of resources. Very few people fail to marry. Polygyny (having more than one wife) was suppressed by missionization, and present-day attitudes concerning marriage, sexuality, and family obligation are strongly influenced by Christianity. Divorce and remarriage, rare until recently, are on the increase.

Domestic Unit. Marriage establishes a nuclear family that usually lives with the husband's parents (though sometimes with the bride's parents until after the first child is born). Households of one or more such families are generally headed by the most senior man or (sometimes) woman. Household composition can vary greatly over time and space, and may include distant relatives on long-term visits. Children are often redistributed among related families by different levels of adoption, allowing grandparents or childless siblings to maintain multigenerational domestic units.

Inheritance. Descent has an agnatic (male) bias, as shown in property inheritance. Thus, while the apex of a descent group is typically a founding set of siblings, and the estates that accrued to them could be inherited by males and females alike, eldest sons inherited most.

Kin Groups. Kinship is cognatic, with important links being traced through both parents in the construction of ego-centered kindreds. Extended families do not necessarily live contiguously. They continue to function as significant units as long as they share ownership of particular plots of land, from which they "eat together" (*kai tasi*), a condition that encourages the sharing of other resources (e.g., fish, money). When such arrangements are weakened because of genealogical distance or a breakdown in interpersonal relations, the various branches agree on a division of the property held in common and gradually cease to share other resources.

SOCIALIZATION

Infant Care. Mothers are infants' primary caregivers, but a wide range of kin may be mobilized if necessary. Infants are generally showered with attention and affection; but they are also socialized to be attentive to surroundings, as in being held facing the center of interactional groups, and adaptive, as in being expected to go to sleep in the middle of well-lit, crowded, and noisy households.

Child Rearing and Education. Children, especially girls, are involved in the rearing of younger siblings, who are expected to stop depending on the attention of mothers early. Physical punishment is used but it is rarely severe, with amicable relations restored almost immediately. Shaming and peer pressure generally prove more potent sanctions, and the peer group tends to play an important role in socialization. Education is highly valued, although most nonelite households do not provide children the space and time to study. Competence in English, a requirement for advancement in the educational system, is a major stumbling block for

Queen Elizabeth and Prince Philip tour Tuvalu, which is still a British Proctectorate.

many children who have few opportunities to practice the language, particularly on the Outer Islands.

Higher Education. Students who graduate from secondary school may attend tertiary institutions overseas (in Fiji, New Zealand, or Australia), usually with the financial assistance of donor countries. Few Tuvaluans have obtained tertiary qualifications, and those that have are guaranteed employment in the national bureaucracy.

ETIQUETTE

Across all contexts, everyday interactions between most people emphasize convivial informality, positive politeness, and indirection. Importance is given to being attentive to the presence and needs of others, and on maintaining a jovial demeanor. Children are expected not to impinge on the social space of adult strangers, particularly those of high status. Lower status persons should not cross directly in front of higher status persons, stand above them, or touch their head.

Within the family, the most constrained type of interaction is between cross-sex first, second, and sometimes third cousins, who were traditionally expected to avoid each other's presence completely. Today, such pairs must avoid talking to one an-

other beyond the absolutely necessary and should strive to orient themselves away from one another. Joking and speaking about bodies and bodily functions in the presence of such cousins is considered a serious faux pas. More relaxed patterns of avoidance characterize interactions between in-laws. At the same time, avoidance can contextually become the subject of jokes. Interactions between fathers and sons tend to be distant and undemonstrative, while interactions between grandparent and grandchild, between adoptive parent and adoptive child, and between mother's brother and sister's child, are generally warm and affectionate.

RELIGION

Religious Beliefs. Tuvalu is solidly Protestant with a Congregationalist flavor. Other sects and religions have few adherents. While some syncretic pre-Christian beliefs in magic and sorcery remain, the Christian deity is universally acknowledged, with the Tuvalu Christian Church giving equal prominence to Jesus.

Religious Practitioners. For several decades after missionization, the (mainly Samoan) pastors of the London Missionary Society wielded great power. The role of pastor became a prestigious career choice for Tuvaluan males as well, a number of whom were appointed to other parts of the Pacific. Locally, deacons (men and women) and lay preachers (men only) play important parts in religious affairs.

Rituals and Holy Places. Church buildings are important holy places on each island, and are among the most impressive structures in terms of size, cost, and design. Tuvaluans celebrate the regular Christian holidays and days of worship. Religious celebrations are often protracted; Christmas festivities, for example, can last several weeks and mobilize abundant resources.

Death and Afterlife. Christian ideology proclaims the existence of Heaven and Hell as the destinations of souls. Alternative views, if they exist, are not officially condoned, though the spirits of the dead are believed to have the power of action under certain circumstances (lack of filial piety, bad relations between kin, etc.).

MEDICINE AND HEALTH CARE

Western medicine is practiced by trained doctors and nurses, but is not equally reliable or available on every island. Local curing practices are a syncretic combination of traditional, Christian, and scientific ideas: massage, herbal and other medicines, special foods or food prohibitions, faith healing, divination and magic, and prayer.

SECULAR CELEBRATIONS

Each island community celebrates events such as the return of land from traders or the repayment of a communal debt. The only salient government-related national celebration is Independence Day (1 October), celebrated on Funafuti with a state ceremony, the raising of the flag, and a parade of policemen and schoolchildren; and on the Outer Islands with scaled-down versions of these. Independence Day and all other celebrations are marked by several days of feasting, dancing, and games in the meetinghouse. Other nationally celebrated events not associated with nationhood include International Women's Day, Children's Day, and United Nations Day.

THE ARTS AND HUMANITIES

Literature. Despite the very high rate of literacy, there is no tradition of written literature.

Graphic Arts. The only production of graphic artistry is the decoration of mats, dancing skirts, and fans with dyed fibers.

Performance Arts. The major artistic traditions are performance-oriented. Action songs known as *faatele* reign supreme. Seated vocalists sing the repeated verses of a song faster and faster until they reach a climax and stop abruptly, while standing dancers act out the lyrics. *Faatele* may involve competition between different sides, be an adjunct to other festivities, or be an end in themselves, and may be composed and choreographed by anyone with the inspiration to do so. Tuvaluans also enjoy other kinds of musical activity, including hymn singing, Western-style dancing, and pop music. The verbal arts are confined to oratorical performances, which are the exclusive domain of older men.

THE STATE OF THE PHYSICAL AND SOCIAL SCIENCES

No significant local endeavors in this area have taken place.

BIBLIOGRAPHY

Besnier, Niko. "The Demise of the Man Who Would Be King: Sorcery and Ambition on Nukulaelae Atoll." *Journal of Anthropological Research* 49: 185–215, 1993.

———. "Christianity, Authority, and Personhood: Sermonic Discourse on Nukulaelae Atoll." *Journal of the Polynesian Society* 103: 339–378, 1994.

———. *Literacy, Emotion, and Authority: Reading and Writing on a Polynesian Atoll,* 1995.

———. "Authority and Egalitarianism: Discourses of Leadership on Nukulaelae Atoll." In Richard Feinberg and Karen A. Watson-Gegeo, eds., *Leadership and Change in the Western Pacific: Essays Presented to Sir Raymond Firth on the Occasion of His 90th Birthday,* 1996.

———. *Tuvaluan: A Polynesian Language of the Central Pacific,* 2000.

Brady, Ivan A. "Land Tenure in the Ellice Islands: A Changing Profile." In Henry P. Lundsgaarde, ed., *Land Tenure in Oceania,* 1974.

———. "Christians, Pagans, and Government Men: Culture Change in the Ellice Islands." In Ivan Brady and Barry Isaac, eds., *A Reader in Culture Change,* vol. 2, 1975.

———. "Socio-Economic Mobility: Adoption and Land Tenure in the Ellice Islands." In Ivan A. Brady, ed., *Transactions in Kinship: Adoption and Fosterage in Oceania,* 1976.

Chambers, Anne. *Nanumea,* 1984.

————, and Keith Chambers. ''Illness and Healing in Nanumea, Tuvalu.'' In Claire D. F. Parsons, ed., *Healing Practices in the South Pacific*, 1985.

Goldsmith, Michael. ''Transformations of the Meeting-House in Tuvalu.'' In Antony Hooper and Judith Huntsman, eds., *Transformations of Polynesian Culture*, 1985.

————, and Doug Munro. ''Conversion and Church Formation in Tuvalu.'' *Journal of Pacific History* 27: 44–54, 1992.

Kennedy, D. G. *Field Notes on the Culture of Vaitupu*, 1931.

Laracy, Hugh, ed. *Tuvalu: A History*, 1983.

Munro, Doug. ''Migration and the Shift to Dependence in Tuvalu: A Historical Perspective.'' In John Connell, ed., *Migration and Development in the South Pacific*, 1990.

————, and Teloma Munro. ''The Rise and Fall of the Vaitupu Company: An Episode in the Commercial History of Tuvalu.'' *Journal of Pacific History* 20: 174–190, 1985.

Noricks, Jay Smith. ''Unrestricted Cognatic Descent and Corporateness on Niutao, a Polynesian Island of Tuvalu.'' *American Ethnologist* 10: 571–584, 1983.

—MICHAEL GOLDSMITH
AND NIKO BESNIER

UGANDA

CULTURE NAME

Ugandan

ORIENTATION

Identification. Lake Kyoga serves as a rough boundary between Bantu speakers in the south and Nilotic and Central Sudanic language speakers in the north. Despite the division between north and south in political affairs, this linguistic boundary actually runs roughly from northwest to southeast, near the course of the Nile. However, many Ugandans live among people who speak different languages, especially in rural areas. Some sources describe regional variation in terms of physical characteristics, clothing, bodily adornment, and mannerisms, but others claim that those differences are disappearing.

Location and Geography. Bantu speakers probably entered southern Uganda by the end of the first millennium. They had developed centralized kingdoms by the fifteenth or sixteenth century, and after independence from British rule in 1962, Bantu speakers constituted roughly two-thirds of the population. They are classified as either Eastern Lacustrine or Western Lacustrine Bantu. The Eastern Lacustrine Bantu speakers include the Baganda people whose language is Luganda, the Basoga, and many smaller societies in Uganda, Tanzania, and Kenya. The Western Lacustrine Bantu speakers include the Banyoro, the Bastoro, the Banyankole, and several smaller populations in Uganda.

Nilotic language speakers probably entered the area from the north beginning about C.E. 1000. Thought to be the first cattle-herding people in the area, they also relied on crop cultivation. The largest Nilotic populations in Uganda are the Iteso and Karamojong ethnic groups, who speak Eastern Nilotic languages, and the Acholi, Langi, and Alur, who speak Western Nilotic languages. Central Sudanic languages, which arrived in Uganda from the north over a period of centuries, are spoken by the Lugbara, the Madi, and a few small groups in the northwestern part of the country.

Demography. The population was about twenty-three million in mid-1999. The Eastern Lacustrine Bantu include the Baganda, the Basoga, and the Bagisu. The Baganda, the largest ethnic group, account for about 17 percent of the population, or approximately 3.9 million people. The second largest ethnic group, the Basoga, make up about 8 percent of the population, or 1.8 million people, while the Bagisu constitute roughly 5 percent of the population, or just over a million people. The Western Lacustrine Bantu—the Banyoro, Batoro, and Banyankole people—probably constitute around 3 percent of the population, or 700,000 people each.

The Eastern Nilotic language groups include the Karamojong cluster, the Iteso and the Kakwa. The Karamojong account for around 12 percent of the population (2.8 million), the Iteso amount to about 8 percent (1.8 million), and the Kakwa constitute 1 percent (about 230,000). The Western Nilotic language groups include the Langi and Acholi as well as the Alur. Together they account for roughly 15 percent of the population, or about 3.4 million people, with the Langi contributing 6 percent (1.4 million), the Acholi 4 percent (900,000), and the Alur probably about 2 percent (460,000).

Central Sudanic languages are spoken by about 6 percent of the population, mostly in the northwest. The Lugbara (roughly 3.8 percent of the total, or 870,000) and the Madi (roughly 1.2 per cent, or 275,000) are the largest of these groups, representing the southeastern corner of a belt of Central Sudanic language speakers stretching from Chad to Sudan.

About 10,000 Ugandans of Sudanese descent are classified as Nubians. They are descendants of Sudanese military recruits who came in the late nineteenth century as part of the colonial army. Rwandans, who constituted almost 6 percent of the

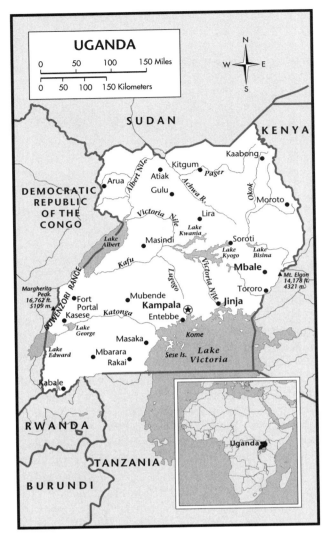

Uganda

1990s, there were about ten thousand Asians in the country.

Linguistic Affiliation. Introduced by the British in the late nineteenth century, English was the language of colonial administration. After independence, it became the official language, used in government, commerce, and education. Official publications and most major newspapers appear in English, which often is spoken on radio and television. Most residents speak at least one African language. Swahili and Arabic also are widely spoken.

HISTORY AND ETHNIC RELATIONS

Emergence of the Nation. After independence in 1962, ending a period of colonization that began in 1885, there was little indication that the country was headed for social and political upheaval. Instead, Uganda appeared to be a model of stability and progress. It had no white settler class attempting to monopolize the cash crop economy, and there was no legacy of conflict. It was the African producers who grew the cotton and coffee that brought a higher standard of living, financed education, and led to high expectations for the future.

Independence arrived without a national struggle against the British, who devised a timetable for withdrawal before local groups had organized a nationalist movement. This near absence of nationalism among the country's ethnic groups led to a series of political compromises.

National Identity. Ethnic and religious divisions as well as historical emnities and rivalries contributed to the country's disintegration in the 1970s. There was a wide gulf between Nilotic speakers in the north and Bantu speakers in the south and an economic division between pastoralists in the drier rangelands of the west and north, and agriculturists, in the better-watered highland and lakeside regions. There was also a historical division between the centralized and sometimes despotic rule of the ancient African kingdoms and the kinship-based politics elsewhere. The kingdoms were often at odds in regard to the control of land. During the colonial period, the south had railways, cash crops, a system of Christian mission education, and the seat of government, seemingly at the expense of other regions. There also were religious groups that had lost ground to rivals in the past, for example, the domination of Muslims at the end of the nineteenth century by Christians allied to British colonialism. All these divisions precluded the formation of a national culture.

population (more than one million) in the late 1950s, included Hutu and Tutsi groups. The government attempted to limit Rwandan influence by restricting those who lacked Ugandan citizenship to refugee camps and expelling some to Tanzania. In the late 1980s, more than 120,000 Rwandans were recognized as refugees. Asians, who in the 1969 census amounted to some seventy thousand people, mainly of Indian and Pakistani descent, were officially considered foreigners despite the fact that more than half were born in Uganda. After independence and especially when the Obote government threatened to nationalize many industries in 1969, Asians exported much of their wealth and were accused of graft and tax evasion. President Idi Amin deported about seventy thousand Asians in 1972, and only a few returned in the 1980s to claim their expropriated land, buildings, factories, and estates. In the

Ethnic Relations. After independence, there were conflicting local nationalisms. The Buganda's large population, extensive territory in the favored south, and self-proclaimed superiority created a backlash among other Ugandan peoples. Nubians shared little sense of identification with other groups. The closely related peoples of nearby Zaire and the Sudan soon became embroiled in civil wars in the 1960s and 1970s, drawing in ethnically related Ugandans. Today relations are relatively harmonious. However, suspicion remains with the president believing to favor certain groups from the west of the country over others.

FOOD AND ECONOMY

Food in Daily Life. Most people, except a few who live in urban centers, produce their own food. Most people eat two meals a day: lunch and supper. Breakfast is often a cup of tea or porridge. Meals are prepared by women and girls; men and boys age twelve and above do not sit in the kitchen, which is separate from the main house. Cooking usually is done on an open wood fire. Popular dishes include *matoke* (a staple made from bananas), millet bread, cassava (tapioca or manioc), sweet potatoes, chicken and beef stews, and freshwater fish. Other foods include white potatoes, yams, corn, cabbage, pumpkin, tomatoes, millet, peas, sorghum, beans, groundnuts (peanuts), goat meat, and milk. Oranges, papayas, lemons, and pineapples also are grown and consumed. The national drink is *waragi*, a banana gin. Restaurants in large population centers, such as Kampala (the capital), serve local foods.

Basic Economy. Most food is produced domestically. Uganda exports various foodstuffs, including fish and fish products, corn, coffee, and tea. The environment provides good grazing land for cattle, sheep, and goats. Agriculture is the most important sector of the economy, employing over 80 percent of the workforce. Much production is organized by farmers' cooperatives. Smallholder farmers predominated in the 1960s and 1970s but declined as a result of civil conflict. In the 1980s, the government provided aid to farmers, and by the middle of the decade nearly a hundred ranches had been restocked with cattle.

Lakes, rivers and swamps cover about 20 percent of the land surface, and fishing is an important rural industry. The basic currency is the shilling.

Land Tenure and Property. At independence, the country was a patchwork of district administrations subdivided into counties and consolidated into

Grand Mosque of Kampala. Roughly 15 percent of Ugandans are Muslims

provinces. As a result of a treaty with the British in 1900, Uganda retained its monarchy together with a modified version of its government and a distinctive form of quasi-freehold land tenure. Land was divided between the protectorate government and the kabaka (king), chiefs, and other tribal notables. This *mailo* land quickly became an important element in the colonial farming economy.

Uganda has a long history of diverse laws and social systems governing land tenure. Since the promulgation of the Land Reform decree of 1975, only two systems of land tenure exist (leasehold and customary tenure), but in practice a complex mixture of systems (including customary, leasehold, and freehold) continue to exist. The government attempted to simplify and unify the land tenure system. A major development in that process has been the inclusion of land tenure in the constitution of 1995. However, issues such as women's right to own land require further consideration.

Commercial Activities. The major goods and services produced for sale are foodstuffs and cash crops for exportation, with coffee as the major export crop. Uganda escaped widespread famine in the late 1970s and 1980s because many people, including urban residents, resorted to subsistence cultivation. Both commercial and subsistence farming operated in the monetary and nonmonetary sectors, presenting the government with problems of organization and taxation. By the late 1980s, government reports estimated that about 44 percent of gross domestic product (GDP) originated outside the monetary economy. Most nonmonetary activity was agricultural.

Major Industries. When the present government seized power in 1986, industrial production was negligible, consisting mostly of the processing of crops and the production of textiles, wood and paper products, cement, and chemicals. Industry was a small part of GDP in the late 1980s, operating at approximately one-third of the level of the early 1970s. Under Museveni, there has been some industrial rejuvenation, although this has amounted to not much more than the repair of damage done during the civil war to the industrial infrastructure. The sugar industry was rehabilitated through joint ventures involving the private sector and the government. By the 1990s there was a refining capacity of at least 140,000 tons of sugar annually. Other rehabilitated industries include beer brewing, tobacco, cotton, and cement. About 4 percent of adults worked in industry by the 1990s. During the 1990s, industrial growth was 13.2 percent.

Trade. In 1998, the country exported products worth $575 million. The main export commodities were coffee (54 percent of the total value), gold, fish and fish products, cotton, tea, and corn. The countries receiving most of these products were Spain, Germany, the Netherlands, France, and Italy. The main imports include chemicals, basic manufactured goods, machinery, and transport equipment.

Division of Labor. In the mid-1990s the labor force was estimated to be about 8.5 million, with more than 85 percent working in agriculture, 4 percent in industry, and 10 percent in the services sector. Jobs are allocated according to ability and preference.

SOCIAL STRATIFICATION

Classes and Castes. Although there are no castes, there is a relatively high degree of social inequality. In the mid-1990s, 55 percent of the population lived below the poverty line. The top 10 percent owned about one-third of the available wealth, while the bottom 10 percent owned 3 percent. Wealth distribution is governed by class position. The richest people live mostly in the capital, Kampala.

Symbols of Social Stratification. Social stratification is governed primarily by level of education and status derived primarily from employment. Among the elites, English is the language of communication, and these people dress in a modern Western fashion. Others tend to wear traditional dress.

POLITICAL LIFE

Government. Under the constitution of 1995, legislative power is in the hands of a unicameral parliament (the National Resistance Council) with 276 members (214 elected directly and 62 appointed). Executive powers are held by the president, who is directly elected for a five-year term. On coming to power in 1986, the government introduced ''no-party'' democracy known as the ''movement system'' with a national network extending from the capital to the rural areas. Only one political organization, formerly the National Resistance Movement (or NRM) and now known as the ''Movement,'' is recognized; it is the party of President Museveni. Among the parties that exist but are not allowed to sponsor candidates, the most important are the Ugandan People's Congress (UPC), the Democratic Party (DP), and the Conservative Party (CP).

Leadership and Political Officials. It is alleged that one of the main criteria for advancement in the current government is whether an individual fought in President Museveni's guerrilla army, which was instrumental in bringing the regime to power in 1986. Those people are said to have achieved their positions through a combination of hard work, influence peddling, and corruption.

Social Problems and Control. After the victory of the National Resistance Army (NRA) in 1986, the NRA assumed responsibility for internal security. The police force was reorganized and, together with other internal security organs, began to enforce law and order in all districts except those experiencing rebel activity. There are two continuing civil wars against the ''Lord's Resistance Army'' and against guerrillas based in the Sudan. In 1995, the government established a legal system based on English common law and customary law. There is a court of appeal and a high court, both with judges appointed by the president. The most common crimes are theft and, in some parts of the country, banditry.

Military Activity. Uganda has an army, a navy, and an air force. The NRA has about seventy thousand troops. Recruitment is voluntary; there is no fixed term of service, and both men and women serve. In 1999, Ugandan military forces supported the rebel forces in the civil war in the Democratic Republic of Congo.

Women preparing food in Kampala. All meals are prepared by women in Uganda; boys over age twelve are banned from the kitchen.

SOCIAL WELFARE AND CHANGE PROGRAMS

In 1987, the government launched a four-year Rehabilitation and Development Plan to restore the nation's productive capacity, especially in industry and agriculture, and rehabilitate the social and economic infrastructure. The plan targeted industrial and agricultural production, transportation, and electricity and water services, envisioning an annual 5 percent growth rate. Transportation would receive the major share of funding, followed by agriculture, industry and tourism, social infrastructure, and mining and energy. Although the international financial community provided debt rescheduling and new loans, the level of economic recovery was modest. Improved security and private sector development contributed to economic growth and the rehabilitation of the social infrastructure in the 1990s, but external shocks, an overvalued currency, and high government spending limited economic progress.

NONGOVERNMENTAL ORGANIZATIONS AND OTHER ASSOCIATIONS

Political conflict and the near disintegration of the state under Milton Obote and Idi Amin in the 1970s and early 1980s, led to the incorporation of autonomous self-help organizations and nongovernmental organizations (NGOs). Foreign and indigenous NGOs concerned with developmental, social, and political goals have flooded Uganda since the mid-1980s. In general, NGOs have been effective in addressing the needs of service provision and alleviating poverty. For groups of traditionally disadvantaged people such as physically disabled persons and women, NGOs have provided guaranteed political representation at every level of the society.

GENDER ROLES AND STATUSES

Division of Labor by Gender. Traditionally, women's roles were subordinate to those of men despite the substantial economic and social responsibilities of women in traditional Ugandan societies. Women were taught to accede to the wishes of their fathers, brothers, husbands, and other men and to demonstrate their subordination to men in public life. Into the 1990s, women in rural areas of Buganda were expected to kneel when speaking to a man. However, women had the primary responsibility for child care and subsistence agriculture while contributing to cash crop agriculture. Many Ugandans recognized women as important religious leaders who sometimes had led revolts that

The people of Kalunga village celebrate the victory of Kintu Musoke in the 1994 nonpartisan general election in Uganda.

overthrew the political order dominated by men. In some areas, women could own land, influence crucial political decisions made by men, and cultivate cash crops.

The Relative Status of Women and Men. In the 1970s and 1980s, political violence had a heavy toll on women. Economic hardship was felt in the home, where women and children lacked the economic opportunities available to most men. Women's work became more time-consuming, and the erosion of public services and infrastructure reduced access to schools, hospitals, and markets. However, some Ugandan women believed that the war years strengthened their position in society, and the Museveni government has pledged to eliminate discrimination against women. During the civil war, women were active in the NRA. The government decreed that one women would represent each district on the National Resistance Council, and the government owned Uganda Commercial Bank established a rural credit plan to make farm loans available to women.

MARRIAGE, FAMILY, AND KINSHIP

Marriage. Family prosperity in rural areas involves the acquisition of wives, which is accomplished through the exchange of bridewealth. Since the 1950s a ceiling on bridewealth has been set at five cows and a similar number of goats. The payment of bridewealth is connected to the fact that men "rule" women. Polygynous marriages have reinforced some aspects of male dominance but also have given women an arena for cooperating to oppose male dominance. A man may grant his senior wife "male" status, allowing her to behave as an equal toward men and as a superior toward his other wives. However, polygynous marriages have left some wives without legal rights to inheritance after divorce or widowhood.

Domestic Unit. The extended family is augmented by a kin group. Men have authority in the family; household tasks are divided among women and older girls. Women are economically dependent on the male next of kin (husband, father, or brother). Dependence on men deprives women of influence in family and community matters, and ties them to male relationships for sustenance and the survival of their children.

Inheritance. Land reform is a continuing aspect of constitutional debate. Suggestions for a new land policy were part of the draft constitution submitted to the president of the Constitutional Commission in late 1992, though little consideration had been given to the issue of women's right to own and

A woman winnowing grain in the Virunga National Park. More than 80 percent of the workforce is employed in agriculture.

inherit land. Although women make a significant contribution in agriculture, their tenure rights are fragile. The determination and protection of property rights have become important issues as a result of civil war and the impact of AIDS. However, the state's legal stand on inheritance recognizes the devolution of property through statutory as well as customary law.

According to the law, a wife equally with a husband is entitled to 15 percent of the spouse's estate after death. The practice, though, is that in the majority of cases a man inherits all of his wife's property, while culture dictates that a woman does not inherit from her husband at all. In other words, regarding inheritance, where there is conflict between cultural unwritten law and the written modern law, the cultural laws tend to take precedence.

Kin Groups. For many people, clan, lineage, and marriage provide the framework of daily life and access to the most significant resources. Farming is largely a family enterprise, and land and labor are available primarily through kin.

SOCIALIZATION

Infant Care. Virtually all infant care is undertaken by women and older girls at home.

Child Rearing and Education. Mothers bore an average of over seven children in the late 1990s, and the use of family planning is low. The death of children is commonplace, with an estimated ninety deaths per one thousand live births. Boys are more likely to be educated to the primary and secondary levels than are girls. Among the 62 percent of the population that is literate, nearly three-quarters are men.

Higher Education. Established in 1922, Makerere University in Kampala was the first college in East Africa. Its primary aim was to train people for government employment. In the 1980s, it expanded to include colleges of liberal arts and medicine serving more than five thousand students. In the early 1990s, there were about nine thousand students. The Islamic University at Mbale, financed by the Organization of the Islamic Conference, opened in 1988. This college provides Islamic educational services primarily to English-speaking students from African countries. In 1989, a second national university campus opened in Mbarara, with a curriculum designed to serve rural development needs. Development plans for higher education rely largely on international and private donors. Most residents value higher education, perceiving it as an essential aspect of national development.

ETIQUETTE

Shaking hands is the normal form of greeting. Casual dress is considered appropriate in the daytime and evening. It is customary to give waiters and taxi drivers a 10 percent tip. Etiquette is important at family meals. When a meal is ready, all the members of the household wash their hands and sit on floor mats. Visitors and neighbors who drop in are expected to join the family at a meal. Normally a short prayer is said before the family starts eating. During the meal, children talk only when asked a question. It is considered impolite to leave the room while others are eating. Leaning on the left hand or stretching one's legs at a meal is a sign of disrespect. When the meal is finished, everyone in turn gives a compliment to the mother.

RELIGION

Religious Beliefs. One-third of the population is Roman Catholic, one-third is Protestant, and 16 percent is Muslim; 18 percent believe in local religions, including various millenarian religions. World religions and local religions have coexisted for more than a century, and many people have established a set of beliefs about the nature of the universe by combining elements of both types. There is a proliferation of religious discourses centering on spirits, spirit possession, and witchcraft.

Religious Practitioners. Religious identity has economic and political implications: church membership has influenced opportunities for education, employment, and social advancement. Religious practitioners thus are expected to provide a range of benefits for their followers. Leaders of indigenous religions reinforce group solidarity by providing elements necessary for societal survival: remembrance of ancestors, means of settling disputes, and recognition of individual achievement. Another social function of religious practitioners is helping people cope with pain, suffering, and defeat by providing an explanation of their causes. Religious beliefs and practices serve political aims by bolstering the authority of temporal rulers and allowing new leaders to mobilize political power and implement political change.

Rituals and Holy Places. In Bantu-speaking societies, many local religions include a belief in a creator God. Most local religions involve beliefs in ancestral and other spirits, and people offer prayers and sacrifices to symbolize respect for the dead and maintain proper relationships among the living. Mbandwa mediators act on behalf of other believers, using trance or hypnosis and offering sacrifice and prayer to beseech the spirit world on behalf of the living.

Uganda has followers of Christianity, Islam, and African traditional religions. Ugandan Muslims make pilgrimages to Mecca when they can. Followers of African religions tend to establish shrines to various local gods and spirits in a variety of locations.

Death and the Afterlife. Death is sometimes interpreted in the idiom of witchcraft. A disease or other cause of death may not be considered the true cause. At a burial, if the relatives suspect someone of having caused the deceased person's death, a spirit medium may call up the spirit of the deceased and ask who really killed him or her.

MEDICINE AND HEALTH CARE

Health services deteriorated in the 1970s and 1980s, as a result of government neglect, violence, and civil war. In the 1990s, measles, respiratory tract infections, and gastro enteritis caused one-half of all deaths attributed to illness, and malaria, AIDS, anemia, tetanus, whooping cough, and respiratory tract infections also claimed many lives. Infant mortality was often caused by low birth weight, premature birth, or neonatal tetanus. The entire health care system was served by less than a thousand doctors in the 1990s. Care facilities included community health centers, maternity clinics, dispensaries, leprosy centers, and aid posts. Today there is at least one hospital in each district except the southern district of Rakai. In the sparsely populated northern districts, people sometimes travel long distances to receive medical care, and facilities are inferior to those in the south. Those who live far from or cannot afford modern health care depend on traditional care. Women are prominent among traditional healers.

SECULAR CELEBRATIONS

The major holidays are New Year's Day, 1 January; Liberation Day, 26 January; International Women's Day, 8 March; Labor Day, 1 May; National Heroes Day, 9 June; and Independence Day, 9 October.

THE ARTS AND HUMANITIES

Support for the Arts. Most artists are self-supporting as there is virtually no state support. Small-scale, local initiatives take place, but it has been

A farm with terraced fields near Kibale. Coffee, cotton, tea, and corn are among the most common agriculture exports.

difficult to establish viable sectors because of the disruptions caused by long-term political conflict and economic decline.

Literature. The development of literature is at an early stage. It has been held back by the years of civil war.

Graphic and Performance Arts. Performing arts often are associated with different ethnic groups throughout the country.

THE STATE OF THE PHYSICAL AND SOCIAL SCIENCES

The physical and social sciences are generally under-developed as a result of civil instability and conflict and the development of other priorities centered on national reconstruction. Makerere University is still in operation but virtually all expatriate staff, once the backbone of the teaching staff, have been long gone. Little research is currently undertaken because of a lack of up-to-date books, journals, or computers.

BIBLIOGRAPHY

Abid, Syed, ed. *Uganda Women in Development*, 1990.

Allen, Tim. "Understanding Alice: Uganda's Holy Spirit Movement in Context." *Africa* 61 (3): 37–39, 1991.

Antrobus, P. "The Empowerment of Women." *Women and International Development* 1 (2): 189–207, 1989.

Bernt Hansen, Holger, and Michael Twaddle eds. *Uganda Now: Between Decay and Development*, 1988.

——. *Developing Uganda*, 1998.

Bwegye, F. A. W. *The Agony of Uganda*, 1985.

Dicklich, Susan. "Indigenous NGOs and Political Participation." In Holger Bernt Hansen and Michael Twaddle, eds. *Developing Uganda* 145–158, 1998.

Furley, Oliver. "Uganda's Retreat from Turmoil?," *Conflict Studies* 196, 1986.

Gertzel, Cherry. "Uganda's Continuing Search for Peace." *Current History* 89 (547): 205–228, 231–232, 1990.

Harlow, Vincent, and E. M. Chilver, eds. *History of East Africa*, 1965.

Ingham, Kenneth. *The Making of Modern Uganda*, 1983.

Jorgensen, Jan Jelmert. *Uganda: A Modern History*, 1981.

Kabwegyere, T. B. *The Politics of State Formation and Destruction in Uganda*, 3rd ed. 1995.

Kasfir, Nelson. *The Shrinking Political Arena: Participation and Ethnicity in African Politics*, 1976.

——. "Land and Peasants in Western Uganda: Bushenyi and Mbarara Districts." In Holger Bernt

Hansen and Michael Twaddle, eds. *Uganda Now: Between Decay and Development*, 1988.

Khadiagala, G. M. "State Collapse and Reconstruction in Uganda." In William I. Zartman, ed. *Collapsed States*, 1995.

Livingstone, Ian. "Developing Industry in Uganda in the 1990s." In Holger Bernt Hansen and Michael Twaddle, eds. *Developing Uganda*, 1998.

Marquardt, Mark A., and Abby Sabina-Zziwa. "Land Reform in the Making." In Holger Bernt Hansen and Michael Twaddle, eds. *Developing Uganda*, 1998.

Mbowa, Rose. "Theatre for Development: Empowering Ugandans to Transform Their Condition." In Holger Bernt Hansen and Michael Twaddle, eds. *Developing Uganda*, 1998.

Nsibambi, Apolo R. "The Restoration of Traditional Rulers." In Holger Bernt Hansen and Michael Twaddle, eds. *From Chaos to Order: The Politics of Constitution-Making in Uganda*, 1996.

Omara-Otunu, Amii. *Politics and the Military in Uganda*, 1987.

———. "The Dynamics of Conflict in Uganda." In Oliver Furley, ed. *Conflict in Africa*, 1995.

Roberts, A. "The Sub-Imperialism of the Baganda." *Journal of African History* 8 (3): 435–450, 1962.

Sathymurthy, T. V. *The Political Development of Uganda, 1900–1986*, 1986.

Southall, Aidan W. "Social Disorganization in Uganda: Before, During, and After Amin." *Journal of Modern Africa Studies* 18 (4): 627–656, 1980.

Tindigarukayo, Jimmy, K. "Uganda, 1979–85: Leadership in Transition." *Journal of Modern African Studies* 26 (4): 607–22, 1988.

Twaddle, Michael, ed. *Expulsion of a Minority*, 1975.

Van Zwanenburg, R. M. A, and Anne King. *An Economic History of Kenya and Uganda, 1800–1970*, 1975.

Watson, Catherine. "Uganda's Women: A Ray of Hope." *Africa Report* 33 (6): 32–35, 1988.

Welbourn, F. B. *Religion and Politics in Uganda, 1952–1962*, 1965.

Werbner, Richard. *Ritual Passage, Sacred Journey*, 1989.

World Bank. *Uganda: Towards Stabilization and Economic Recovery*, 1988.

———. *Uganda: The Economic Impact of AIDS*, 1991.

———. *Uganda: Agriculture Sector Memorandum*, 1991.

—JEFF HAYNES

UKRAINE

CULTURE NAME

Ukrainian

ORIENTATION

Identification. Ukrainian nationhood begins with the Kyivan Rus. This Eastern Slavic state flourished from the ninth to the thirteenth centuries on the territory of contemporary Ukraine, with Kyiv as its capital. The name Ukraine first appeared in twelfth century chronicles in reference to the Kyivan Rus. In medieval Europe cultural boundary codes were based on a native ground demarcation. Ukraine, with its lexical roots *kraj* (country) and *krayaty* (to cut, and hence to demarcate), meant ''[our] circumscribed land.'' The ethnonym *Rus* was the main self-identification in Ukraine until the seventeenth century when the term Ukraine reappeared in documents. This ethnonym of Rus people, *Rusych* (plural, *Rusychi*), evolved into *Rusyn*, a western Ukrainian self-identification interchangeable with Ukrainian into the twentieth century. *Ruthenian*, a Latinization of *Rusyn*, was used by the Vatican and the Austrian Empire designating Ukrainians.

Location and Geography. Ukraine, Europe's second largest country during the twentieth century, occupies 232,200 square miles (603,700 square kilometers). Its main geographical features are the Polissya and Volyn northern forests, the central forest steppes, the Donetsk eastern uplands (up to 1,600 feet [500 meters] above sea level), and the coastal lowlands and steppes along the Black and Azov Seas. The Carpathian mountains in the west reach 6,760 feet (2,061 meters) at Mount Hoverla. Roman-Kosh in the Crimean peninsula reaches 5,061 feet (1,543 meters.) Alpine meadows—called *polonyna* in the Carpathians and *iajla* in the Crimea—are another interesting geographical feature.

Ukraine's climate is moderate. The yearly average temperatures range from 40 to 49 degrees Fahrenheit (6 to 9 degrees Celsius)—except for the southern steppes and in Crimea, where yearly average temperatures range from 50 to 56 degrees Fahrenheit (10 to13 degrees Celsius).

Ukraine has twenty-four administrative units—oblasts—almost all named for their capitals. From east to west, they are Donetsk, Luhansk, Kharkiv, Poltava, Zaporizhzhya, Dnipropetrovsk, Kirovohrad, Kherson, Mykolaiv, Odessa, Cherkasy, Kyiv, Sumy, Chernihiv, Zhytomyr, Vinnytsya, Rivne, Luts'k (Volyns'ka oblast'), Khmel'nyts'kyj, Ternopil', Lviv, Ivano-Frankivs'k, Uzhhorod (Zakarpats'ka oblast'), and Chernivtsi. The Crimean oblast became an autonomous republic in 1991.

Ukraine's regional ethnographic cultures, not always congruent with oblast boundaries are: Donbas, Slobozhanshchyna, Zaporizhzhya, Steppes Ukraine, Poltava, Cherkasy, Polissya, Podillya, Volyn, Halychyna, Bukovyna, Transcarpathia, and Crimea. Crimean Tatar culture predominates in Crimea, and the Hutsul highlanders live in Halychyna, Bukovyna, and Transcarpathia.

Demography. Ukraine's 1989 census showed a population of 51,452,000. A negative population growth was probably caused by economic and environmental crises, including the Chernobyl disaster. The 1989 census shows the following percentages of the population's ethnic composition: Ukrainians, 72.7 percent; Russians, 22.1 percent; Jews, 0.9 percent; Belorussians, 0.8 percent; Moldovans, 0.6; Poles, 0.5 percent; Bulgarians, 0.4 percent; Hungarians, 0.3 percent; Crimean Tatars, 0.2 percent; Romanians, 0.2 percent; Greeks, 0.2 percent; Armenians, 0.1 percent; Roma (Gypsies), 0.1 percent; Germans, 0.1 percent; Azerbaijanis, 0.1 percent; Gagauz, 0.1 percent; and others, 0.5 percent.

Linguistic Affiliation. Ukrainian is an Indo-European language of the Eastern Slavic group. Its Cyrillic alphabet is phonetic; its grammar is synthetic, conveying information through word modification rather than order. Contemporary literary Ukrai-

Ukraine

nian developed in the eighteenth century from the Poltava and Kyiv dialects. Distinctive dialects are the Polissya, Volyn, and Podillya dialects of northern and central Ukraine and the western Boyko, Hutsul, and Lemko dialects. Their characteristics derive from normatively discarded old elements that reappear in dialectic usage. The *surzhyk*, an unstable and variable mixture of Ukrainian and Russian languages, is a by-product of Soviet Russification. A similar phenomenon based on Ukrainian and Polish languages existed in western Ukraine but disappeared almost completely after World War II.

In 1989 statistics showed Ukrainian spoken as a native language by 87 percent of the population, with 12 percent of Ukrainians claiming Russian as their native language. The use of native languages among ethnic groups showed Russians, Hungarians, and Crimean Tatars at 94 to 98 percent and Germans, Greeks, and Poles at 25 percent, 19 percent and 13 percent, respectively. Assimilation

through Ukrainian language is 67 percent for Poles, 45 percent for Czechs, and 33 percent for Slovaks. As a second language Ukrainian is used by 85 percent of Czechs, 54 percent of Poles, 47 percent of Jews, 43 percent of Slovaks, and 33 percent of Russians.

Formerly repressed, Ukrainian and other ethnic languages in Ukraine flourished at the end of the twentieth century. Ukrainian language use grew between 1991 and 1994, as evidenced by the increase of Ukrainian schools in multiethnic oblasts. However, local pro-communist officials still resist Ukrainian and other ethnic languages except Russian in public life.

Symbolism. The traditional Ukrainian symbols—trident and blue-and-yellow flag—were officially adopted during Ukrainian independence in 1917–1920 and again after the declaration of independence in 1991. The trident dates back to the Kyivan Rus as a pre-heraldic symbol of Volodymyr the

Great. The national flag colors are commonly believed to represent blue skies above yellow wheat fields. Heraldically, they derive from the Azure, the lion rampant or coat of arms of the Galician Volynian Prince Lev I. The 1863 patriotic song "Ukraine Has Not Perished," composed by Myxaylo Verbyts'kyi from a poem of Pavlo Chubyns'kyi, became the Ukrainian national anthem in 1917 and was reaffirmed in 1991. These symbols were prohibited as subversive under the Soviets, but secretly were cherished by all Ukrainian patriots.

The popular symbol of Mother Ukraine appeared first in Ukrainian baroque poetry of the seventeenth century as a typical allegory representing homelands as women. When Ukraine was divided between the Russian and Austrian empires, the image of Mother Ukraine was transformed into the image of an abused woman abandoned by her children. Mother Ukraine became a byword, not unlike Uncle Sam, but much more emotionally charged. After 1991 a new generation of Ukrainian writers began to free this image from its victimization aspects.

HISTORY AND ETHNIC RELATIONS

Emergence of the Nation. Ukrainian nationhood begins with the Kyivan Rus realm, which arose from a unification of Antian tribes between the sixth and ninth centuries. Rus is mentioned for the first time by European chroniclers in 839 C.E. The Kyivan state experienced a cultural and commercial flourishing from the ninth to the eleventh centuries under the rulers Volodymyr I (Saint Volodymyr), his son Yaroslav I the Wise, and Volodymyr Monomakh. The first of these rulers Christianized Rus in 988 C.E. The other two gave it a legal code. Christianity gave Rus its first alphabet, developed by the Macedonian saints Cyril and Methodius. Dynastic fragmentation and Mongol and Tatar invasions in the thirteenth century caused Kyiv's decline. The dynastically related western principality of Halych (Galicia) and Volyn resisted the Mongols and Tatars and became a Rus bastion through the fourteenth century. One of its most distinguished rulers was Danylo Romanovich, the only king in Ukrainian history, crowned by the Pope Innocent IV in 1264.

After the fourteenth century, Rus fell under the rule of foreign powers: the Golden Horde Mongols, the Grand Duchy of Lithuania, and the kingdom of Poland. Lithuania controlled most of the Ukrainian lands except for the Halych and Volyn principalities, subjugated after much struggle by Poland. The southern steppes and the Black Sea coast remained under the Golden Horde, an outpost of Genghis Khan's empire. The Crimean khanate, a vassal state of the Ottomans, succeeded the Golden Horde after 1475. Eventually northwestern and central Ukraine were absorbed into the Grand Duchy of Lithuania which then controlled almost all of Ukraine—giving Ukrainians and Belorussians ample autonomy. The Grand Duchy of Lithuania adopted the administrative practices and the legal system of Rus and a state language that was Old Slavonic, heavily imbued with vernacular Ukrainian and Belorussian. However, Lithuania—united with Poland by a dynastic linkage in 1386—gradually adopted Roman Catholicism and Polish language and customs. In 1569 the Lublin Union created the Polish-Lithuanian Commonwealth, and Ukraine was annexed to Poland. The 1596 Brest-Litovsk Union divided Ukrainians into Orthodox and Uniate Catholics. Northern borderlands initially colonized by Rus princes increasingly diverged from the Kyivan culture with the rise of the Duchy of Muscovy.

In the fifteenth century Ukraine clashed with the Crimean Khanate. The 1490 chronicles mention Ukrainian warriors called *kozaks* defending Ukrainian lands from Crimean Tatar slave raids. Kozaks were based on the Zaporozhian Sich, an island fortress below the Dnipro River rapids. Nominally subject to the Polish crown, the Zaporozhian kozaks became symbols of Ukrainian national identity. Strife between the Ukrainians and their Polish overlords began in the 1590s, spearheaded by the kozaks. In 1648, led by the kozak hetman (military leader) Bohdan Khmelnytsky, Ukrainians rose against Poland, forming an independent state. Khmelnytsky sought help against the Poles in a treaty with Moscow in 1654, which was used as a pretext for occupation by the Muscovites. Poland recognized Moscow's suzerainty over Kiev and the lands east of the Dnipro, and the Ukrainian hetmanate was gradually subjugated by Moscow. Despite this, the hetmanate reached its pinnacle under Ivan Mazepa (1687–1709). Literature, art, architecture in the distinctive Kozak baroque style, and learning flourished under his patronage. Mazepa wanted a united Ukrainian state, initially under the tsar's sovereignty. When Tsar Peter threatened Ukrainian autonomy, Mazepa rose against him in alliance with Charles XII of Sweden. The allies were defeated in the Battle of Poltava in 1709. Fleeing from Peter's vengeance Mazepa and his followers became the first organized political immigration in Ukrainian history.

During the eighteenth-century partitions of Poland, the Russian Empire absorbed all Ukraine except for Galicia, which went to Austria. The empress Catherine II extended serfdom to the traditionally free kozak lands and destroyed the Zaporozhian Sich in 1775. During the nineteenth century all vestiges of nationhood were repressed in Russian-held Ukraine. The Ukrainian language was banned from all but domestic use by the Valuev Decree of 1863 and the Ems Ukase of 1876. Ukrainians opposed this policy by developing strong ties with Ukrainian cultural activists in the much freer Austrian Empire. An inclusive national movement arose during World War I, and in 1917 an independent Ukrainian state was proclaimed in Kyiv. In 1918 western Ukraine declared independence striving to unite with the East, but its occupation by Poland was upheld by the Allies in 1922.

After two years of war Ukraine became part of the Soviet Union in 1922. Its Communist party was subordinated to the Russian Communists. Only 7 percent of its 5,000 members were Ukrainian. Favoring city proletarians—mostly alien in nationality and ideology—the Bolsheviks had very little support in a population 80 percent Ukrainian, and 90 percent peasant. However, Ukrainian communists implemented a policy of Ukrainization through educational and cultural activities. This rebirth of Ukrainian culture ended abruptly at the time of the Stalin's genocidal famine of 1933. This famine killed up to seven million Ukrainians, mostly peasants who had preserved the agricultural traditions of Ukraine along with an ethnic and national identity. The destruction of Ukrainian nationalism and intelligentsia lasted through the Stalinist purges of the late 1930s and continued more selectively until the fall of the Soviet Union.

When Germany and the Soviets attacked Poland in 1939, Galicia was united to the rest of Ukraine. The German-Soviet war in 1941 brought hopes of freedom and even a declaration of independence in western Ukraine. However, the brutal Nazi occupation provoked a resistance movement, first against the Germans and then against the Soviets. The Ukrainian Insurgent Army fought overwhelming Soviet forces that subjected western Ukraine to mass terror and ethnic cleansing to destroy the resistance. At the end of World War II almost three million Ukrainians were in Germany and Austria, most of them forced laborers and prisoners of war. The vast majority of them were forcibly repatriated to the Soviet Union, and ended up in Gulag prison camps. Two-hundred thousand refugees from Ukraine managed to remain in Western Europe and immigrated to the United States and to other Western countries.

In 1986, the Chernobyl accident, a partial meltdown at a Soviet-built nuclear power plant, shocked the entire nation. After Mikhail Gorbachev's new openness policy in the 1980s, the democratized Ukrainian parliament declared the republic's sovereignty in 1990. Following a failed coup against Gorbachev in the Soviet Union, the Ukrainian parliament declared independence on 24 August 1991, overwhelmingly approved by referendum and internationally recognized.

National Identity. National identity arises from personal self-determination shared with others on the basis of a common language, cultural and family traditions, religion, and historical and mythical heritages. There is a lively reassessment of these elements in contemporary Ukraine in a new stage of identity development. Language issues focus on the return of phonetics, purged from Soviet Ukrainian orthography by Russification, and on the macaronic Russo/Ukrainian *surzhyk*. A revival of cultural traditions includes Christian holidays, days of remembrance, and church weddings, baptisms, and funerals. The Ukrainian Catholic Church emerged from the underground and the exiled Ukrainian Orthodox Autocephalous Church united formally with the Kyivan patriarchy. Ukrainian Protestants of various denominations practice their religion unhampered.

The 988 baptism of the Rus melded Christian beliefs with existing customs, leading to a Rus identity connected to both homeland and religion. In the seventeenth century Ukrainian identity held its own against Polish identity and the Roman Catholic Church. In the Russian empire Ukrainians preserved their identity through culture and language because religion by itself integrated them with Russians.

Historical facts and myths as bases of national identity were first reflected in the literature of the Ukrainian baroque. In later times, the proto-Slavic origins of the Ukrainian people were ascribed to the settled branch of Scythians (500 B.C.E.–100 B.C.E.) mentioned by ancient Greek and Roman historians. Recent theories connecting origins of Ukrainian culture with the first Indo-European tribes of the Northern Black Sea region and with the Trypillya culture (4,000 B.C.E.) are supported by plausible research.

Ethnic Relations. Ukraine, surrounded by diverse nations and cultures, is home to Belorussians in northern Polissia; Poles, Slovaks, Hungarians, and Romanians in western Ukraine; Moldovians and

Boats and barges line the Dnieper River in Kiev.

Gagauz in southern Ukraine; and Russians in eastern and northern Ukraine. The Russian Empire settled Germans, Swedes, Bulgarians, Greeks, Christian Albanians, and Serbs in southern steppes. Russian landlords brought ethnic Russian serfs to the steppes, and Russian Old Believers also settled there fleeing persecution. In 1830 and 1863 the Russian government exiled Polish insurgents to southern Ukraine. Serbs and Poles assimilated with Ukrainians, but the other groups retained their identities. Tatars, Karaims, and Greeks were native to Crimea. Since the Middle Ages Jews and Armenians settled in major and minor urban centers. Roma (Gypsies) were nomadic until Soviets forced them into collective farms. The last major immigration to Ukraine took place under the Soviets. Ethnic Russians were sent to repopulate the villages emptied by the 1933 genocide and again after 1945 to provide a occupying administration in western Ukraine.

Historically, ethnic conflicts emerged in Ukraine on social and religious grounds. The seventeenth century Ukrainian-Polish wars were caused by oppressive serfdom, exorbitant taxes, and discrimination or even elimination of the Ukrainian Orthodox Church by Polish magnates. Their appointment of Jewish settlers as tax collectors in Ukrainian villages also led to strife between these ethnic groups. The settled Ukrainians and the nomadic steppe tribes conflicted since medieval times. From the fifteenth century on, Crimean Tatars raided Ukraine for slaves, and Zaporozhian kozaks were the only defense against them. Even so, Zaporozhians made trade and military agreements with the Crimean khanate: Tatar cavalry often assisted Ukrainian hetmans in diverse wars. Likewise, Ukrainian cultural and educational connections with Poles existed despite their conflicts: Bohdan Khmelnytsky and many other kozak leaders were educated in Polish Jesuit colleges, and initially Khmelnytsky considered the Polish king as his liege. Ukrainian Jewish relations of the seventeenth and eighteenth centuries also cannot be wholly described in terms of ethnic strife. Jewish merchants regularly traded with kozaks and several high officers of the hetmanate—such as members of the renowned Markevych/Markovych aristocratic families—were of Jewish origin.

In contemporary Ukraine ethnic communities enjoy governmental support for their cultural development. Ethnic language instruction increased considerably in multicultural regions. The first center for preservation and development of Roma culture opened in Izmail near Odessa. Two prominent issues in ethnic relations concern the return to Crimea of the Crimean Tatars exiled in Soviet times and the problem of the Russian-speaking population. The Crimean Tatar *Medjlis* (parliament) demands citizenship for Tatars returning from Stalinist exile while the Russian-dominated parliament of the Crimean autonomous republic opposes that demand.

Pro-Russian elements identify Russophones with Russian ethnicity. However, statistics show a large number of Russophones who do not consider themselves Russian. In 1989, 90.7 percent of Jews, 79.1 percent of Greeks, and 48.9 percent of Armenians and other ethnic groups in Ukraine recognized Russian as a language of primary communication but not an indicator of ethnicity or nationality. Forcing a Russian ethnic identity onto non-Russian Russophones infringes on their human rights. Russians in Ukraine are either economic migrants from Soviet times, mostly blue-collar workers, or the former Russian *nomenklatura* (bureaucratic, military, and secret police elite). The latter were the upper class of Soviet society. Since losing this status after the Soviet Union collapsed, they have rallied around a neo-Communist, pro-Russian political ideology, xenophobic in the case of the Crimean Tatars.

URBANISM, ARCHITECTURE, AND THE USE OF SPACE

A prototypical architectural tradition was found by archeologists studying ancient civilizations in Ukraine. Excavations of the Tripillya culture (4,000–3,000 B.C.E.) show one- and two-room houses with outbuildings within concentric walled and moated settlements. The sophisticated architecture of Greek and Roman colonies in the Black Sea region in 500 B.C.E.–100 C.E. influenced Scythian house building. The architecture of later Slavic tribes was mostly wooden: log houses in forested highlands and frame houses in the forest-steppe. The Kyivan Rus urban centers resembled those of medieval Europe: a prince's fortified palace surrounded by the houses of the townsfolk. Tradesmen and merchants lived in suburbs called *posad*. Stone as a building material became widespread in public buildings from the tenth century, and traditions of Byzantine church architecture—cross plan and domes—combined with local features. Prime examples of this period are the Saint Sophia Cathedral in Kyiv (about 1030s) and the Holy Trinity Church over the Gate of the Pechersk Monastery (1106–1108). Elements of Romanesque style, half-columns and arches, appear in Kyivan Rus church architecture from the twelfth century, principally in the Saint. Cyril Church in Kyiv (middle-twelfth century), the Cathedral of the Dormition in Kaniv, and the Saint Elias Church in Chernihiv.

Ukrainian architecture readily adopted the Renaissance style exemplified by the Khotyn and Kamyanets'-Podil'skyi castles, built in the fourteenth century, Oles'ko and Ostroh castles of the fifteenth century, and most buildings in Lviv's Market Square. Many Ukrainian cities were ruled by the Magdeburg Law of municipal self-rule. This is reflected in their layout: Lviv and Kamyanets' Podil'skyi center on a city hall/market square ensemble.

Ukrainian baroque architecture was representative of the lifestyle of the kozak aristocracy. At that time most medieval churches were redesigned to include a richer exterior and interior ornamentation and multilevel domes. The most impressive exponents of this period are the bell tower of the Pechersk Monastery and the Mariinsky Palace in Kyiv, Saint George's Cathedral in Lviv, and the Pochaiv Monastery. A unique example of baroque wooden architecture is the eighteenth century Trinity Cathedral in former Samara, built for Zaporozhian kozaks. The neoclassical park and palace ensemble became popular with the landed gentry in the late eighteenth century. Representative samples are the Sofiivka Palace in Kamianka, the Kachanivka Palace near Chernihiv, and the palace in Korsun'-Shevchenkivskyi.

Ukrainian folk architecture of the seventeenth and eighteenth centuries shows a considerable influence of baroque ornamentation and neoclassic orders while preserving traditional materials like wood and wattled clay. Village planning remained traditional, centered around a church, community buildings, and marketplace. The streets followed property lines and land contours. Village neighborhoods were named for extended families, clans, or diverse trades and crafts. This toponymy, dating from medieval times, reappeared spontaneously in southern and eastern Ukrainian towns and cities, such as Kherson, Mykolaiv, and Simferopol that were built in the eighteenth century.

Throughout the nineteenth century and into the beginning of the twentieth century, the empire architectural style came to Ukraine from the West. Modern urban planning—a grid with squares and promenades—was applied to new cities. At the beginning of twentieth century, there was a revival of national styles in architecture. A national modernism combined elements of folk architecture with new European styles. A prime exponent of this style is Vasyl' Krychevs'kyi's design of the 1909 Poltava Zemstvo Building.

Soviet architecture initially favored constructivism as shown in the administrative center of Kharkiv and then adopted a heavy neoclassicism pejoratively called totalitarian style for major urban centers. Post-World War II architecture focused on monobloc projects reflecting a collectivist ideology. However, contemporary Ukrainians prefer single houses to apartment blocs. The traditional Ukrainian house has a private space between the street and the house, usually with a garden. Striving for more private space people in apartment buildings partition original long hallways into smaller spaces. *Dachas* (summer cottages) are a vital part of contemporary Ukrainian life. Laid out on a grid, *dacha* cooperatives provide summer rural communities for city dwellers.

FOOD AND ECONOMY

Food in Daily Life. Ukrainians prefer to eat at home, leaving restaurants for special occasions. Meal times are from 7:00 to 10:00 A.M. for breakfast, from 12:00 noon to 3:00 P.M. for dinner or lunch, and from 5:00 to 8:00 P.M. for supper. The main meal of the day is dinner, including soup and meat, fowl, or a fish dish with a salad. Ukrainians

The Opera and Ballet Theatre in Odessa uses the half-columns and arches common to the Romanesque style of architecture.

generally avoid exotic meats and spices. A variety of soups—called *borshch* collectively—is traditional and symbolic, so it is never called "soup."

Menu items in restaurants are usually Eastern European. Expensive restaurants are patronized at supper time by a new breed of business executives who combine dining with professional interaction.

Food Customs at Ceremonial Occasions. Culinary traditions in Ukraine are connected with ancient rituals. The calendar cycle of religious holidays combined with folk traditions requires a vari-

ety of specific foods. Christmas Eve supper consists of 12 meatless dishes, including *borshch*, cabbage rolls, *varenyky* (known in North America as pierogi), fish, mushrooms, various vegetables, and a wheat grain, honey, poppyseed, and raisin dish called *kutya*. The latter dish is served only at Christmas time. On Easter Sunday food that has been blessed previously is eaten after Resurrection services. It includes a sweet bread called *paska*, colored eggs, butter, meat, sausages, bacon, horseradish, and garlic. On the holiday of the Transfiguration (19 August), apples and honey are blessed and eaten along with other fruits of the season. Various alcoholic drinks complement the meals. It is customary to offer a drink to guests, who must not refuse it except for health or religious reasons.

Basic Economy. Traditional Ukrainian food products are domestic. Pressured by the economic crisis, people grow products in their home gardens and dachas. City and village markets are places of bartering consumer goods and food products. In the late 1990s, the development of the food industry was stimulated by economic reforms.

Land Tenure and Property. Private property rights were reinstated in Ukraine after 1991. Collective farms were abolished in 2000, and peasants received land titles. Privatization also has been successful in cities. Inheritance law in Ukraine, as in other countries, applies to transfers of property according to legal testaments.

Commercial Activities. The current government has decontrolled prices, reduced subsidies to factories, and abolished central economic planning. Ukraine imports chemicals, specialized metals, raw rubber, metalworking equipment, cars, trucks, electrical and electronic products, wood products, textiles, medicines, and small appliances. Ukraine exports aircrafts, ships, and agricultural and food products.

Major Industries. Heavy industry in Ukraine includes aircraft plants in Kharkiv; shipbuilding in Kherson, Mykolaiv, and Kerch; and steel and pig iron mills in Donetsk, Luhansk, and Zaporizhya oblasts. The latter depend on large supplies of coal and iron ore from Kryvbas and Donbas. Electronics, machine tools, and buses are produced in Lviv, and one of the world's largest agrochemical plants is located in Kalush. Other important industrial products include ferro-alloys, nonferrous metals, and building materials. Under the Soviet command economy, Ukraine's industry focused on raw materials and on the production of armaments and heavy machinery—25 percent of all Soviet military goods. Lately, successful joint ventures with foreign partners produce consumer goods. Seventy percent of the land is in agricultural use.

Trade. The integration of Ukraine into the world economic system is indispensable for an effective export-oriented economic reform and for foreign investments. Establishing trade relations with the G7 countries (the seven largest industrialized countries: United States, Japan, Great Britain, France,

Germany, Italy, and Canada) is a priority for Ukraine's international economic strategy.

Division of Labor. Contemporary Ukraine has a high level of both official and hidden unemployment, especially in industry and in research institutions formerly oriented to military needs. Equal opportunity employment rules have not been implemented at the end of the twentieth century.

SOCIAL STRATIFICATION

Classes and Castes. Soviet Ukrainian society was officially classless with three equal groups: workers, peasants, and working intelligentsia. In reality the Communist Party elite enjoyed an immensely preferential status, with several internal gradations. In contemporary Ukraine many former Soviet bureaucrats (*nomenklarura*) retained their status and influence as members of the new administration or as newly rich business professionals. Education, health care, and research professionals, all dependent on state budgets, are in the lowest income bracket. Unemployment among blue-collar workers rose when heavy industry shifted its production focus. Farmers are in a transitionary phase in the re-institution of land property rights.

Symbols of Social Stratification. In Soviet times ownership of so-called deficit goods (scarce items available only to party elite in restricted stores) conferred a superior social status. The free market made prestigious goods available to anyone with cash. Social distinctions are popularly based on material status symbols such as cars, houses, luxury items, and fashionable attire. A more modest and traditional social and regional identification shows through apparel: many older suburban and country women wear typical kerchiefs, and Carpathian highlanders of any gender and age often wear characteristic sheepskin vests or sleeveless jackets.

POLITICAL LIFE

Government. Constitutionally, Ukraine is a democratic, social, law-based republic. The people exercise power through elected state and local governments. The right to amend the constitution belongs solely to the people and may be exercised only through popular referenda.

The office of president was instituted in 1917 in the Ukrainian National Republic and reinstated in 1991. The constitution vests executive power on the president and the prime minister and legislative power on the *Verkhovna Rada*, a unicameral body of

Farm workers travel in a village near Orane. Seventy percent of the land in the Ukraine is used for agriculture.

450 directly elected representatives. All suffrage is universal. The president is elected by direct vote for a five years' cadence. The president appoints the prime minister and cabinet members, subject to approval by the *Verkhovna Rada*.

Leadership and Political Officials. Ukraine has more than one hundred registered political parties. Right of center and nationalist parties include the National Front, Rukh, and UNA (Ukrainian National Association). The most prominent of them is Rukh, championing an inclusive national state and free market reforms. The leftist parties are the Communist, Progressive Socialist, Socialist, and United Socialist. Communists oppose land privatization and propose to revive the Soviet Union. Centrists are most numerous and include the Agrarian, Popular Democratic, Hromada, Greens, and Labor-Liberal parties. The Green Party became a political force because of its pro-active concern with ecology.

Political leaders and activists in Ukraine are generally accessible. However, most of them are used to old Soviet models of interaction. By contrast, younger politicians are much more attuned to a democratic style of communication.

Social Problems and Control. The Security Service of Ukraine, the Internal Affairs Ministry, and the Defense Ministry are responsible for national security, reporting to the president through his cabinet. The armed and security forces are controlled by civilian authorities. The Internal Affairs Ministry and its police, called *militsia*, deal with domestic crime and run correctional institutions. The Security Service succeeded the Soviet KGB. It deals with espionage and economic crimes. Public confidence in the authorities is gradually replacing the well-founded fear and mistrust of Soviet times.

Military Activity. The Ukrainian army conscripts males between the ages of eighteen and twenty five for eighteen months of compulsory service, with medical and hardship exemptions and student deferments. In 1992 the Ukrainian armed forces numbered 230,000. The Soviet Black Sea Fleet was incorporated into the Ukrainian naval forces. Ukrainian infantry participated in the United Nations peacekeeping effort in Bosnia and Herzegovina. Ukrainian armed forces conduct frequent joint maneuvers with the North Atlantic Treaty Organization.

SOCIAL WELFARE AND CHANGE PROGRAMS

Ukrainian social welfare programs are in their beginnings. Unemployment assistance is available at governmental centers that offer professional retraining aided by nongovernmental organizations.

International charity organizations provide assistance to the needy. Help to Chernobyl disaster victims is funded by taxes and by international charity. Statistics from 1995 show Chernobyl-accident compensations to 1.5 million persons, 662,000 of them children.

NONGOVERNMENTAL ORGANIZATIONS AND OTHER ASSOCIATIONS

Community associations have a long history in Ukraine. The *Prosvita* (Enlightenment) Society established in 1868 under the Austrian Empire and in 1905 under the Russian Empire promoted literacy in Ukrainian through reading rooms and lending libraries, publishing activities, amateur theatrics, and other cultural activities. It was closed by the Soviets but flourished in western Ukraine until 1939. Prosvita was re-established in independent Ukraine with its original mission. Many contemporary Ukrainian non-governmental organizations derive from the human rights movements of the 1970s. A society, *Memorial*, was organized in the late 1980s to collect evidence and memories of political persecution and to assist former political prisoners.

The Ukrainian Women's Association was established in 1884. Currently, this organization and its diasporan counterpart concentrate on the preservation of national culture, on education, on human issues, and on charity work. Ukrainian women participate in politics through the Ukrainian Women Voter organization. The nongovernmental organization, *La Strada*, supports services for victims of sexual trafficking and helps to run prevention centers in Donets'k, Lviv, and Dnipropetrovs'k.

GENDER ROLES AND STATUS

Division of Labor by Gender. Ukrainian labor laws guarantee gender equality, but their implementation is imperfect. Few women work at higher levels of government and management, and those who do are generally in subordinate positions. As in the Soviet Union, women work in heavy blue-collar jobs, except for coal mining. Nevertheless, there still is a traditional labor division by gender: teachers and nurses are mostly women; school administrators and physicians are mostly men. Women in typically female jobs such as teachers and nurses are paid less and promoted more slowly than men.

The Relative Status of Women and Men. Males in positions of authority generally perceive women as the weaker sex. Women are welcome as secretaries or subordinates but not as colleagues or competitors. Women politicians and business executives are rare. They have to adopt a male style of interaction to function effectively. Sexual harassment in the workplace is widespread.

MARRIAGE, FAMILY, AND KINSHIP

Marriage. Ukrainians favor endogamy. Traditionally, young people chose mates at social events. Historically, parental approval and blessing were sought. Marriages against parents' wishes were rare in the past, and matchmakers mediated between the two families. The parents' role in the marriage has been preserved in contemporary Ukrainian culture through their responsibilities to organize and finance the wedding ceremonies and festivities for their children. The festivities show the family's social status. Most marriage ceremonies today are both civil and religious.

In traditional society public opinion pressured young people to marry early. This still leads to many marriages between the ages of seventeen and twenty five. It also leads to a high number of divorces, very rare in the traditional past. The Ukrainian Catholic Church prohibits divorce and the Ukrainian Orthodox Church discourages it. Civil courts grant divorce, adjudicating property and custodial rights.

Domestic Unit. The traditional Ukrainian domestic unit is a single family. Elderly parents eventually lived with the child who inherited their property. The chronic housing shortage in the Soviet Union and the economic crisis in contemporary Ukraine forced young couples to live with their parents in close quarters. This reduction of personal space frequently caused familial dysfunction.

The Ukrainian agricultural tradition clearly defined men's and women's parallel responsibilities. Men were responsible for tilling the fields and for their sons' socialization. Women were housekeepers, who also took responsibility for home crafts and budgets and for the daughters' socialization.

Inheritance. Ukrainian customs and laws of property inheritance never discriminated by gender. Historically, sons and daughters inherited parents' property equally, and a widow was the principal heir of her deceased husband. At present, inheritance is granted by testament. Without a testament, an estate is divided regardless of gender between children or close relatives in court. Inheritances and

Traders sell food at a Sunday market in Kiev. A marketplace is the centerpiece of almost every town and village.

deeded gifts are not subject to division in divorce cases.

Kin Groups. In Ukraine kinship beyond the immediate family has no legal standing, but it is an important aspect of popular culture. A kin group usually includes cognates of all degrees and godparents. A non-relative who is chosen as a godparent is thereby included into the kin group. Kin group reunions take place on family occasions such as marriages, baptisms, or funerals, and on traditional festive days.

SOCIALIZATION

Infant Care. In 1992, 63 percent of children under age seven in urban areas and 34 percent in rural areas attended day care. These figures have decreased as current legislation provides paid maternity leaves for up to one year and unpaid leaves up to three years, recognizing Ukrainian women's preference for personal care of their children. Grandparents also provide care for grandchildren, especially in lower-income families. A well-cared for child is a traditional source of family pride. The decreasing number of births may be explained by the potential parents' inability to provide appropriate care for their children during economic crisis.

An increasing number of children are abandoned by dysfunctional parents.

Child Rearing and Education. Ancient beliefs regarding child rearing still exist in contemporary Ukraine: a baby's hair is not cut until the first birthday; baptism is seen as a safeguard, and safety pins inside a child's clothing ward off evil spells.

Children attend school from age six. Education is compulsory and universal through nine grades. Students may graduate after the ninth grade at age sixteen and may work with special permission or enter vocational and technical schools. Since the number of specializations in these schools has decreased, most students finish the full eleven grades. A curricular revision is introducing new courses and programs for gifted children.

Higher Education. In post-secondary education undergraduate degrees are granted directly by universities. Candidate and doctor of sciences or arts degrees are granted by the Highest Attestation Commission of the Ministry of Education in a bureaucratically complicated system. Every major field of learning is covered in major universities. Every large and medium-sized urban center has at least one institution of higher learning.

Men talking in a hayfield near Rovno. Workers can now own land again, as collective farms were abolished in 2000.

ETIQUETTE

Social interaction in Ukraine is regulated by etiquette similar to the rest of Europe. Some local idiosyncrasies are a personal space of less than an arm's length in business conversations and the habit of drinking alcohol at business meetings, a relic of Soviet times.

RELIGION

Religious Beliefs. Religious beliefs are central to Ukrainian culture. Ukraine experienced a revival of many religions: Ukrainian Orthodox, Ukrainian Catholic, Protestantism, Judaism—including Hasidism—and Islam. The constitution and the 1991 Law on Freedom of Conscience and Religion provide for separation of church and state and the right to practice the religion of one's choice.

Religious Practitioners. Ukrainian Orthodox clergy are educated in divinity schools such as the Kyiv Theological Academy. The Ukrainian Catholic Church, banned in Soviet times, needs priests and provides a wide array of educational programs at the Lviv Theological Seminary. Protestant denominations, principally Baptists and Seventh-Day Adventists, train their ministers with the assistance of American and Western European mission pro-

grams. The numerically small Roman Catholic clergy is assisted by pastoral visitors from abroad. Since the time of independence, Jewish rabbis have been completing their studies in Israel. Muslim clergy is educated in Central Asia and Turkey.

Rituals and Holy Places. Ukrainian Orthodox and Catholic Churches share historic, ritual, and national heritages. Popular culture incorporated many ancient pagan rituals into a folk version of Christianity. Orthodox priests still perform exorcisms by the canon of Saint Basil the Great. The Holy Virgin icon and the spring of the Pochaiv Orthodox Monastery are believed to have miraculous healing powers. Zarvanytsia in western Ukraine is a place of holy pilgrimage for Ukrainian Catholics. The grave of the founding rabbi of Hassidism, situated near Uman', is a pilgrimage site for Hasidic Jews.

Death and the Afterlife. Ukrainians observe ancient funeral traditions very faithfully. A collective repast follows funeral services and is repeated on the ninth and fortieth days and then again at six and twelve months. An annual remembrance day called Provody on the Sunday after Easter gathers families at ancestral graves to see off once again the souls of the departed. Provody is widely observed in contemporary Ukraine. Under the Soviets it symbolized an ancient tradition. Its Christian symbolism represents Christ's victory over death. Its pre-Christian roots are attuned to the rebirth of nature in the spring and to an ancient ancestors' cult.

MEDICINE AND HEALTH CARE

Ukraine's comprehensive and free health care includes primary and specialized hospitals and research institutions. Yet folk healing is not ignored by professional medicine. The popularity of folk healing is based on a distrust of standard medicine. The folk healers' knowledge of natural resources and lore is an ancient cultural heritage. Rituals, prayers, and charms are used by folk healers only as additional elements of healing. These healers prefer to work individually and let the patient determine the fee.

Another type of healer has become popular since the last days of the Soviet Union. These healers hold collective sessions eliciting mass hysteria from their audiences for an admission fee. Their popularity may be explained as a reaction among the less educated to stressful economic and social situations combined with the spiritual vacuum created by seventy-four years of compulsory atheism.

SECULAR CELEBRATIONS

There are several secular official holidays in Ukraine, some left over from Soviet times. The International Women's Day, 8 March, is celebrated now in the same context as Mother's Day: men present small gifts and flowers to all women family members and work colleagues. Victory Day, 9 May, became a day of remembrance of those who died in World War II. Constitution Day is 28 June. Independence Day, 24 August, is celebrated with military parades and fireworks.

THE ARTS AND HUMANITIES

Support for the Arts. The former Soviet Union provided governmental support for the arts through professional organizations such as unions of writers, artists, or composers. These organizations still exist and try to function despite a general lack of funds. Young and unconventional artists usually organize informal groups funded by individual sponsors and grants from international foundations.

Literature. Ukrainian literature begins with the chronicles of Kyivan Rus and the twelfth century epic *The Tale of Ihor's Campaign*. Principal authors in

A Western Orthodox church in the Carpathian Mountains. Crosses and domes are common on Ukrainian churches.

the baroque period were Lazar Baranovych (1620–1693), Ioannykii Galyatovs'kyi (d. 1688), Ivan Velychkovs'kyi (d. 1707), and Dymitrii Tuptalo (1651–1709), who wrote didactic poetry and drama. Kozak chronicles of the early eighteenth century include *The Chronicle of the Eyewitness*, *The Chronicle of Hryhorii Hrabyanka*, and *The Chronicle of Samijlo Velychko*.

Ivan Kotlyarevskyi (1769–1838) first used the proto-modern Ukrainian literary language in his 1798 poem *Eneida* (Aeneid). He travestied Virgil, remaking the original Trojans into Ukrainian kozaks and the destruction of Troy into the abolition of the hetmanate. Hryhorij Kvitka Osnov'yanenko (1778–1843) developed a new narrative style in prose.

In 1837 three Galician writers known as the Rus'ka Trijtsia (Ruthenian Trinity)—Markiian Shashkevych (1811–1843), Ivan Vahylevych (1811–1866) and Yakiv Holovats'kyi (1814–1888)—published a literary collection under the title *Rusalka Dnistrovaya (The Nymph of Dnister)*. This endeavor focused on folklore and history and began to unify the Ukrainian literary language. The literary genius of Taras Shevchenko (1814–1861) completed the development of romantic literature and its national spirit. His 1840 collection of poems

Kobzar and other poetic works became symbols of Ukrainian national identity for all Ukrainians from gentry to peasants. In his poetry he appears as the son of the downtrodden Mother-Ukraine. Later, his own image was identified with an archetypal Great Father, embodying the nation's spirit. This process completed the creation of a system of symbolic representations in Ukrainian national identity.

In the second half of the nineteenth century, Ukrainian writers under the Russian Empire—Panteleimon Kulish (1819–1897), Marko Vovchok (1834–1907), Ivan Nechuj-Levyts'kyj (1838–1918), Panas Myrnyj (1849–1920), and Borys Hrinchenko (1863–1910)—developed a realistic style in their novels and short stories. Osyp-Yurij Fed'kovych (1834–1888) pioneered Ukrainian literature in the westernmost Bukovyna under Austrian rule. Ivan Franko (1856–1916) is a landmark figure in Ukrainian literature comparable to Shevchenko. His poetry ranged from the most intimate introspection to epic grandeur. His prose was attuned to contemporary European styles, especially naturalism, and his poetry ranged from introspective to philosophical.

Mykhailo Kotsubynskyi (1864–1913); Vasyl Stefanyk (1871–1936), a master of short psychological stories in dialect; and Olha Kobylianska (1865–1942) all wrote in a psychologically true style. Lesya Ukrainka (1871–1913) saw Ukrainian history and society within a universal and emotionally heightened context in her neo-romantic poems like *Davnya Kazka* (*The Ancient Tale*, 1894) or *Vila-Posestra* (*Sister Vila*, 1911) and such dramas as *U Pushchi* (*In the Wilderness*, 1910), *Boiarynia* (*The Noblewoman*, 1910) and *Lisova Pisnya* (*Song of the Forest*, 1910). Popularly, Shevchenko, Franko, and Lesia Ukrainka are known in Ukrainian culture as the Prophet or Bard, the Stonecutter, and the Daughter of Prometheus, images based on their respective works.

After the Soviet takeover of Ukraine, many Ukrainian writers chose exile. This allowed them to write with a freedom that would have been impossible under the Soviets. Most prominent among them were Yurii Lypa (1900–1944), Olena Teliha (1907–1942), Evhen Malaniuk (1897–1968) and Oksana Liaturyns'ka (1902–1970). Their works are distinguished by an elegant command of form and depth of expression along with a commitment to their enslaved nation.

Ukrainian literature showed achievements within a wide stylistic spectrum in the brief period of Ukrainization under the Soviets. Modernism, avant-garde, and neoclassicism, flourished in opposition to the so-called proletarian literature. Futurism was represented by Mykhailo Semenko (1892–1939). Mykola Zerov (1890–1941), Maksym Rylskyj (1895–1964), and Mykhailo Draj-Khmara (1889–1938) were neoclassicists. The group VAPLITE (Vil'na Academia Proletars'koi Literatury [Free Academy of Proletarian Literature], 1925–1928) included the poets Pavlo Tychyna (1891–1967) and Mike Johansen (1895–1937), the novelists Yurij Yanovs'kyi (1902–1954) and Valerian Pidmohyl'nyi (1901–1937?), and the dramatist Mykola Kulish (1892–1937). The VAPLITE leader Mykola Khvyliovyi (1893–1933) advocated a cultural and political orientation towards Europe and away from Moscow. VAPLITE championed national interests within a Communist ideology and therefore came under political attack and harsh persecution by the pro-Russian Communists. Khvyliovyi committed suicide after witnessing the 1933 famine. Most VAPLITE members were arrested and killed in Stalin's prisons.

From the 1930s to the 1960s, the so-called social realistic style was officially mandated in Ukrainian Soviet literature. In 1960 to 1970 a new generation of writers rebelled against social realism and the official policy of Russification. Novels by Oles' Honchar (1918–1995), poetry by Lina Kostenko (1930–) and the dissident poets Vasyl' Stus (1938–1985) and Ihor Kalynets' (1938–) opened new horizons. Unfortunately, some of them paid for this with their freedom and Stus with his life.

Writers of 1980s and the 1990s sought new directions either in a philosophical rethinking of past and present Ukraine like Valerii Shevchuk (1939–) or in burlesque and irony like Yurii Andrukhovych (1960–). Contemporary culture, politics, and social issues are discussed in the periodicals *Krytyka* and *Suchasnist'*.

Graphic Arts. Ancient Greek and Roman paintings and Byzantine art modified by local taste were preserved in colonies in the Northern Black Sea region. The art of the Kyivan Rus began with icons on wooden panels in Byzantine style. Soon after the conversion to Christianity, monumental mosaics embellished churches, exemplified by the Oranta in Kyiv's Saint Sophia Cathedral. Frescoes on the interior walls and staircases complemented the mosaics. Frescoes of the period also were created for the Saint Cyril Church and Saint Michael Monastery in Kyiv.

Medieval manuscript illumination reached a high level of artistry and the first printed books retained these illuminations. Printing presses were established in Lviv and Ostrih in 1573, where the

Kiev University. Every large or medium-sized urban center has at least one university.

Ostrih Bible was published in 1581. In the seventeenth century Kyiv became a center of engraving. The baroque era secularized Ukrainian painting, popularizing portraiture even in religious painting: The icon Mary the Protectress, for example included a likeness of Bohdan Khmelnytsky. Kozak portraits of seventeenth and eighteenth centuries progressed from a post-Byzantine rigidity to a high baroque expressiveness.

In the eighteenth and nineteenth centuries, several Ukrainian artists worked in Saint Petersburg: Antin Losenko (1737–1773), Dmytro Levyts'kyi (1735–1825), Volodymyr Borovykovs'kyi (1757–1825), and Illia Repin (1844–1928). In 1844 Taras Shevchenko, a graduate of the Russian Academy of Arts, issued his lithography album *Picturesque Ukraine*. An ethnographic tradition of the nineteenth and early twentieth centuries is represented by Lev Zhemchuzhnikov (1928–1912) and Opanas Slastion (1855–1933).

Mykola Pymonenko (1862–1912) organized a painting school in Kyiv favoring a post-romantic style. National elements pervaded paintings of Serhii Vasylkyvs'kyi (1854–1917). Impressionism characterized the works of Vasyl (1872–1935) and Fedir Krychevs'ky (1879–1947). The highly individualistic and expressive post-romantics Ivan Trush (1869–1941) and Oleksa Novakivs'kyi

(1872–1935) ushered western Ukrainian art into the twentieth century.

Yurii Narbut's graphics (1886–1920) combined Ukrainian baroque traditions with principles of modernism. Mykhailo Boichuk (1882–1939) and his disciples Ivan Padalka (1897–1938) and Vasyk Sedlyar (1889–1938) combined elements of Byzantine art with modern monumentalism. Anatol' Petryts'kyi (1895–1964), an individualistic expressionist, survived Stalinist persecution to remain a champion of creative freedom to the end of his life.

In Lviv of the 1930s Ukrainian artists worked in different modernist styles: Pavlo Kovzhun (1896–1939) was a symbolist and a constructivist. Several western Ukrainian artists between the two world wars—Sviatoslav Hordynsky, Volodymyr Lasovsky, Mykhailo Moroz, and Olena Kulchytska—studied in Paris, Vienna, Warsaw, and Cracow. Many artists, such as the neo-Byzantinist Petro Kholodnyi, Sr. (1876–1930) and the expressionist Mykola Butovych (1895–1962), left Soviet Ukraine for western Ukraine in the 1920s to avoid persecution. Old icons influenced Vasyl Diadyniuk (1900–1944) and Yaroslava Muzyka (1896–1973). Alexander Archipenko (1887–1966), the most prominent Ukrainian artist to emigrate to the West, attained international stature with paintings and sculptures that combined abstraction with expressionism. Akin to Grandma Moses are the folk painters Maria Pryimachenko (1908–) and Nykyfor Drevniak (1900–1968).

After World War II many Ukrainian artists immigrated into the United States and other Western countries. Jacques Hnizdovsky (1915–1985) achieved wide recognition in engraving and woodcuts. The highly stylized sculpture of Mykhailo Chereshniovsky showed a unique lyrical beauty. Edvard Kozak (1902–1998), a caricaturist in pre-World War II Lviv, became a cultural icon in the diaspora.

After Stalin's genocide of the 1930s, social realism (a didactic kind of cliched naturalism applied to all literary and artistic media) became the only style allowed in the Soviet Union. In the 1960s some young Ukrainian artists and poets, who also defended civil rights, rejected social realism. For some of them this proved tragic: the muralist Alla Hors'ka was assassinated, and the painter Opanas Zalyvakha was imprisoned in the Gulag for long years. During the 1980s, modernism and postmodernism appeared in Ukraine in spontaneous art movements and exhibitions. Post-modern rethinking infused the works of Valerii Skrypka and Bohdan Soroka. An identity search in the Ukrainian diaspora showed in the surrealistic works of Natalka Husar.

Performance Arts. Ukrainian folk music is highly idiosyncratic despite sharing significant formal elements with the music of neighboring cultures. Epic *dumas*—ancient melodies, especially those of seasonal rituals—are tonally related to medieval modes, Greek tetrachords, and Turkic embellishments. The major/minor tonal system appeared in the baroque period. Typical genres in Ukrainian folk music are solo singing; part singing groups; epic *dumas* sung by (frequently blind) bards who accompanied themselves on the bandura (a lute shaped psaltery); and dance music by *troisty muzyky*, an ensemble of fiddle, wind, and percussion including a hammered dulcimer. Traditional dances—*kozachok*, *hopak*, *metelytsia*, *kolomyika*, *hutsulka*, and *arkan*—differ by rhythmic figures, choreography, region, and sometimes by gender, but share a duple meter. Traditional folk instruments include the bandura, a variety of flutes, various fiddles and basses, drums and rattles, the bagpipe, the hurdy-gurdy, the Jew's harp, and the hammered dulcimer.

The medieval beginnings of professional music are both secular and sacred. The former was created by court bards and by *skomorokhy* (jongleurs). The latter was created by Greek and Bulgarian church musicians. Ukrainian medieval and Renaissance sacred a capella music was codified and notated in several Irmologions. The baroque composer and theoretician Mykola Dylets'kyi developed a polyphonic style that composers Maksym Berezovs'kyi (1745–1777), Dmytro Bortnians'kyi (1751–1825), and Artem Vedel (1767–1808) combined with eighteenth-century classicism. The first Ukrainian opera *Zaporozhets za Dunayem* (Zaporozhian beyond the Danube) was composed in 1863 by Semen Hulak-Artemovs'kyi (1813–1873). The Peremyshl School of western Ukraine was represented by Mykhailo Verbyts'kyi (1815–1870), Ivan Lavrivs'kyi (1822–1873), and Victor Matiuk (1852–1912). All three composed sacred music, choral and solo vocal works, and music for the theater.

A scion of ancient kozak aristocracy, Mykola Lysenko (1842–1912) is known as the Father of Ukrainian Music. A graduate of the Leipzig Conservatory, a pianist, and a musical ethnographer, Lysenko created a national school of composition that seamlessly integrated elements of Ukrainian folk music into a mainstream Western style. His works include a cyclic setting of Shevchenko's poetry; operas, including *Taras Bulba*; art songs and choral works; cantatas; piano pieces; and chamber music. His immediate disciples were Kyrylo Stetsenko (1883–1922) and Mykola Leontovych (1877–1919). Twentieth-century Ukrainian music is represented by the post-Romantics Borys Liatoshyns'kyi (1895–1968), Lev Revuts'kyi (1899–1977), Vasyl Barvins'kyi (1888–1963), Stanyslav Liudkevych (1879–1980), and Mykola Kolessa (1904–). Contemporary composers include Myroslav Skoryk, Lesia Dychko, and Volodymyr Huba.

Many Ukrainian performers have attained international stature: the soprano Solomia Krushelnyts'ka (1973–1952), the tenor Anatoliy Solovianenko (1931–1999), and the Ukrainian-American bass Paul Plishka (1941–).

The theater in Ukraine began with the folk show *vertep* and baroque intermedia performed at academies. The baroque style with its florid language and stock allegories lasted longer in Ukraine than in Western Europe. The eighteenth-century classicism featured sentimentalist plays presented by public, private, and serf theaters. Kotliarevs'ky's ballad opera *Natalka-Poltavka* (*Natalka from Poltava*) and the comedy *Moskal'-Charivnyk* (*The Sorcerer Soldier*) premiered in 1819 and began an ethnographically oriented Ukrainian theater. In

1864 the *Rus'ka Besida* (Ruthenian Club) in Lviv under Austria established a permanent Ukrainian theater, while in the Russian Empire Ukrainian plays were staged by amateurs until banned by the *Ems Ukase*. Despite this prohibition, Marko Kropyvnyts'kyi (1840–1910) staged Ukrainian plays in 1881 along with Mykhailo Staryts'kyi (1840–1904) and the Tobilevych brothers. The latter became known under their pen and stage names as the playwright Ivan Karpenko-Karyi (1845–1907) and the actors and directors Panas Saksahans'kyi (1859–1940) and Mykola Sadovs'kyi (1856–1933). They created an entire repertoire of historical and social plays. Sadovs'kyi's productions marked the beginning of Ukrainian cinema: Sakhnenko's studio in Katerynoslav filmed his theater productions in 1910.

From 1917 to 1922 numerous new theaters appeared in both Eastern and western Ukraine. The most prominent new figure in theater was Les' Kurbas, director of The Young Theatre in Kyiv and later of Berezil theater in Kharkiv. His innovative approach combined expressionism with traditions of ancient Greek and Ukrainian folk theaters and included an acting method based on theatrical synthesis, a psychologically reinterpreted gesture, and a rhythmically unified performance. The expressionist style was adopted in the cinema by the internationally recognized director Oleksandr Dovzhenko (1894–1956).

Berezil's leading dramatist Mykola Kulish (1892–1937) reflected in his plays the social and national conflicts in Soviet Ukraine and the appearance of a class that used revolution for personal purposes. In 1933–1934 Kurbas, Kulish, and many of their actors were arrested and later killed in Stalin's prisons. As in every other art, social realism became the only drama style, exemplified by the plays of the party hack Oleksander Korniichuk. In 1956 former members of The Young Theatre and Berezil formed The Ivan Franko Theatre in Kyiv, but without the innovative character of the former ensembles.

Some Berezil members who escaped from the Soviet Union during World War II brought Kurbas's style to western Ukraine. After World War II these and other Ukrainian actors found themselves in refugee camps in Western Europe and made theater an influential force for preservation of national culture and reconstitution of the refugees' identity after cultural shocks of war and displacement. Theaters led by Volodymyr Blavats'kyi (1900–1953) and former Berezil actor Josyp Hirniak continued their performances as professional companies in New York in the 1950s and 1960s.

New ideas appeared in Ukrainian cinema of the 1960s. Director Kira Muratova's work showed existentialist concepts. The impressionistic and ethnographically authentic *Shadows of Forgotten Ancestors* (1964) by Sergij Paradzhanov and Jurii Ilienko was a prize-winner at Cannes. Ilienko is now a leading Ukrainian film director and cinematographer of post-modern style.

THE STATE OF THE PHYSICAL AND SOCIAL SCIENCES

The present National Academy of Sciences of Ukraine succeeds its Soviet eponym. It is an umbrella for research institutes, specializing in all fields of sciences and humanities. Most institutes are funded by the state, and unfortunately their budgets were cut by 38 percent in the year 2000. The scientific institutes usually sign independent contracts to provide research for industry. At present they have developed their own small enterprises in order to finance otherwise unfunded projects. Institutes in humanities and social sciences survive through publication grants from independent foundations. The National Academy of Medical Sciences and the National Academy of Pedagogy are similar to the Academy of Sciences and are financed by the state. Other research institutes are sponsored by diverse industries combining general research with product-oriented work. University-based research groups obtain funds from the Ministry of Education on the basis of open competition. The Ministry of Science has a yearly competition for project awards for research institutes. The competition concept is indicative of the transition from a centralized budget to funding through merit grants.

BIBLIOGRAPHY

Armstrong, John A. *Ukrainian Nationalism, 1939–1945*, 1955.

Asyeyev, Yu S. *Dzherela. Mystetstvo Kyivs'koi Rusi*, 1980.

Before the Storm: Soviet Ukrainian Fiction of the 1920s, 1986.

Bilets'kyi, P. O. *Ukrainske mystetstvo druhoi polovyny XYII–XVIII stolit'*, 1981.

Chirovsky, Nicholas L. *Nineteenth- and Twentieth-Century Ukraine*, 1986.

Constitution of Ukraine, 1996.

Contemporary Ukraine: Dynamics of Post–Soviet Transformation, 1998.

Conquest, Robert. *The Harvest of Sorrow: Soviet Collectivization and the Terror-Famine,* 1986.

von Hagen, Mark. ''The Russian Imperial Army and the Ukrainian National Movement in 1917.'' *The Ukrainian Quarterly,* 54, (3–4): 220–256, 1998.

Hnizdovsky. Woodcuts, 1944–1975, 1976

Hordynsky, Sviatoslav. *The Ukrainian Icon of the Twelfth to Eighteenth Centuries,* 1973.

Hrushevs kyi, Mykhailo. *History of Ukraine-Rus',* 1997.

Iavornyts'kyi, D. I. *Istoria zaporiz'kykh kozakiv,* 1992.

————, M. C. Samokysh, and S. I. Vasyl'kivs'kyi. *Z Ukrains'koi starovyny,*

Ilnytzkyj, Oleh S. *Ukrainian Futurism, 1914–1930: A Historical and Critical Study,* 1997.

Isajiw, Wsevolod W., Yury Boshyk, and Roman Senkus, eds. *The Refugee Experience: Ukrainian Displaced Persons after World War II,* 1992.

Knysh, George D. *Rus and Ukraine in Medieval Times,* 1991.

Kolessa, F. M. *Muzykoznavchi pratsi,* 1970.

Krypiakevych, Ivan, ed., *Istoria ukrains'koi kul'tury,* 1994.

Kulish, Mykola. *Zona/ Blight* 1996.

Kultura i pobut naseleniia Ukrainy, 1991.

Kuzio, Taras. *Ukraine under Kuchma: Political Reform, Economic Transformation, and Security in Independent Ukraine,* 1997.

Lavrynenko, Yurii. *Rozstriliane vidrodzhennia,* 1959.

Luckyj, George S. N. *Ukrainian Literature in the Twentieth Century: A Reader's Guide,* 1992.

Lobanovs'kyj, B. B., and P. I. Hovdia. *Ukrains'ke mystetstvo druhoi polovyny XIX–pochatku XX st.,* 1989.

Lohvyn, Hryhorii ed. *Sophia Kyivs'ka. Derzhavnyj arkhitekturno istorychnyj zapovidnyk,* 1971.

Magosci, Paul Robert. *A History of Ukraine,* 1996.

Maria Prymachenko, 1989.

Michaelsen, Katherine Janszky, and Nehama Guralnik, eds. *Alexander Archipenko: A Centennial Tribute,* 1986.

Motyl, Alexander J. *Dilemmas of Independence: Ukraine after totalitarism,* 1993.

Mudrak, Myroslava. *The New Generation and Artistic Modernism in the Ukraine,* 1986.

Natalka Husar's True Confessions, 1991.

Onyshkevych, Larissa M. L. Z. ed. *Antolohia Modernoi ukrains'koi dramy,* 1998.

Ovsijchuk, V. A. *Ukrains'ke mystetstvo XIV-pershoi polovyny XVII stolittia,* 1985.

Panibud'laska, V. F. ed. *Natsional'ni protsesy v Ukraini. Istoria I suchasnist',* 1997.

Reeder, Ellen, ed. *Scythian Gold: Treasures from Ancient Ukraine,* 1999.

Serech, Yury. *Druha cherha. Literatura. Teatr. Ideolohii,* 1978.

Sevcenko, Ihor. *Ukraine Between East and West: Essays on Cultural History to the Early Eighteenth Century,* 1996.

Shcherbak, Yurii. *Chernobyl: A Documentary Story,* 1989.

Shkandrij, Myroslav. *Modernists, Marxists, and the Nation: Ukrainian Literary Discussion of the 1920s,* 1992.

Sochor, Zenovia A. ''No Middle Ground? On the Difficulties of Crafting a Political Consensus in Ukraine.'' *Peoples, Nations, Identities: The Russian-Ukrainian Encounter. The Harriman Review* 9 (1–2): 57–61.

Spirit of Ukraine: Five Hundred Years of Painting; Selections from the State Museum of Ukrainian Art, Kiev, 1991.

Subtelny, Orest. *Ukraine: A History,* 1988.

Szporluk, Roman. ''Russians in Ukraine and Problems of Ukrainian Identity in the USSR.'' *Ukraine in the Seventies,* 1974.

Towards an Intellectual History of Ukraine: An Anthology of Ukrainian Thought from 1710 to 1995, 1996.

Ukrainian Painting, 1976.

Ukrains'kyi narodnyi odiah XVII-pochatku XIX st. v akvareliakh Yu.Hlohovs'koho, 1988.

Ukrains'kyi seredniovichnyj zhyvopys (Ukrainian Medieval Painting), 1976.

Voropaj, Oleksa. *Zvychai nashoho narodu,* 1958.

Vozniak, Mykhailo. *Istoriia ukraïns koï literatury,* 1992.

Wanner, Catherine. *Burden of Dreams: History and Identity in Post-Soviet Ukraine,* 1998.

Wolowyna, Oleh. ''Ukrains'ka mova v Ukraini: Matirnia mova za natsional'nistiu I movoiu navchannia.'' *Essays on Ukrainian Orthography and Language,* 1997.

—HANNA CHUMACHENKO

UNITED ARAB EMIRATES

CULTURE NAME

Emirati (in Arabic, *Al-Thaqafa Al-Emaratiya*)

ORIENTATION

Identification. The United Arab Emirates (UAE) consists of the seven small emirates of Abu Dhabi, Dubai, Sharjah, Ras Al-Khaimah, Ajman, Umm Al-Qaiwain, and Fujairah, which were united as a federal state on 2 December 1971. Before the establishment of the oil economy in the early 1960s, two main orientations shaped traditional Emeriati culture: the nomadic desert-oriented Bedouins with small oasis farming within the broader context of the desert economy and culture, and the sea-oriented culture that revolved around pearling and sea trading. These subcultures were economically, politically, and socially interdependent, creating a common culture and social identity. The UAE shares significant aspects of its culture with neighboring Arab countries and the larger Arab culture.

Location and Geography. The UAE covers 32,278 square miles (83,600 square kilometers) and is located on the Arabian (Persian) Gulf. It shares land borders with Oman, Qatar, and Saudi Arabia. The seven emirates vary greatly in size. Abu Dhabi represents 85 percent of the land, and the smallest emirate is Ajman. Each emirate is named after its capital city, and Abu Dhabi City is the permanent capital of the nation. The inland area is mostly desert with a few oases, and the barren Hajar Mountains run through the country. The UAE has a dry climate with very high temperatures and humidity in the summer.

Demography. Relative to its size and oil wealth, the UAE has a small population, estimated at 2,624,000 in 1997. Before 1970, the local population was tiny (estimated at eighty-six thousand in 1961) and lacked most of the technical skills needed for a modern society. The commercial production of oil triggered rapid population growth as a result of an increase in the national population from improvements in diet, health care, and living standards and the importation on a large scale of mostly male foreign laborers. The latter factor has generated a dependence on expatriate labor; the UAE has become a multiethnic society, and Emirati nationals account for only about 20 percent of the population. This has created an imbalanced population composition in favor of males; in 1997, there were 1,755,000 males and 869,000 females.

About two-thirds of the immigrants are Asians, mainly from India, Pakistan, Iran, Sri Lanka, Bangladesh, and the Philippines. The remainder are Arabs, Europeans, and Americans.

Linguistic Affiliation. The official language is Arabic. Among the immigrant population, English, Hindi, Urdu, Farsi, and Filipino are spoken. English is the language of commerce.

Symbolism. National Day symbolizes one of the most successful experiments in unity in the modern Arab world. The main metaphor is that of the family, with the president referred to as a father. The colors of the national flag—green, red, white, and black—are shared with other Arab countries. Other cultural symbols are the falcon, camel, Arabian horse, pearling boat, coffeepot, and date palm. They are used to invoke a historical community that survived harsh conditions and now enjoys the benefits of unity and prosperity. These emblems appear on banknotes, coins, and stamps.

HISTORY AND ETHNIC RELATIONS

Emergence of the Nation. Before 1971 the seven emirates were collectively known as the Trucial States, a name that originated from maritime agreements between the British and the leading sheikhs of the tribes inhabiting the southern coast between Qatar and Oman in the first half of the nineteenth century. The economic life of the UAE depended heavily on pearl diving and sea trade in the Gulf and

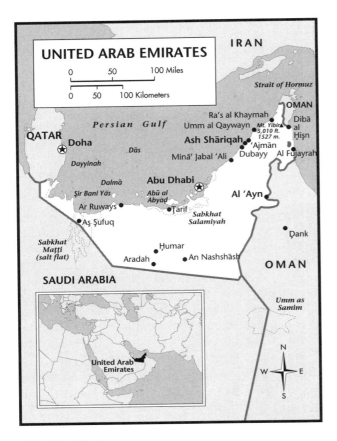

United Arab Emirates

the Indian Ocean. This led to the settlement of different ethnic groups from countries along the trade routes, such as Iran and India. Trade activities with east Africa led to the importation of Africans as laborers in the pearling industry in the late nineteenth century. The African and Iranian ethnic populations have been fully integrated as citizens.

URBANISM, ARCHITECTURE, AND THE USE OF SPACE

Before 1960, the only settlements were small towns and villages. Oil resources have enabled massive modernization. Towns have been transformed from mud-walled communities into commercial capitals integrated in the global economy. Because of the small population and harsh desert interior, 80 percent of the population lives in the coastal capital cities, leading social scientists to describe them as city-states.

Urbanization has been characterized by unparalleled growth. Abu Dhabi is one of the most modern cities in the world. UAE cities have been heavily influenced by the global city type. Dominant urban features include skyscrapers in the commercial city

centers, multistory residential buildings, large shopping malls, wide boulevards, an extensive network of highways, and sprawling new suburbs.

The cities have a multiethnic composition, with segregated housing areas for nationals and the immigrants. Housing is subdivided further according to class, social power, ethnicity, and nationality.

To create a balance between their global and local aspects, in municipalities have adopted policies projecting Arab-Islamic architectural design, particularly arched windows, gates, and decorative stucco. Recently, more urban settings have exhibited decorative designs with local themes related to the national heritage. Preservation of the urban heritage also is seen in the renovation of old forts, palaces, souks (marketplaces), and mosques. Date palm trees, symbols of the local culture, have been planted extensively along city roadsides.

FOOD AND ECONOMY

Food in Daily Life. Before the 1960s, food consisted mainly of fish, rice, bread, dates, yogurt, homegrown vegetables, and meat from sheep, goats, and camels. The diet has improved in quality and variety, with modern supermarkets offering imported foods.

Lunch is the main family meal and is eaten at home at around two o'clock. It usually consists of fish, rice, meat, and a vegetable dish. Many Emiratis prefer the traditional style of eating with the right hand. There are strict Muslim taboos against pork and alcohol, and meat must be slaughtered according to the Islamic *halal* method.

Emiratis are known for their hospitality; they feel honored when receiving guests and socializing with friends and relatives. Guests are welcomed with coffee and fresh dates. Incense is passed around so that guests can catch the fragrance in their headwear. With the immigrant population have come restaurants offering a wide variety of ethnic foods, and fast-food restaurants have also become popular.

Basic Economy. Income is among the highest in the world, but there are large differences between the emirates, with Abu Dhabi, Dubai, and Sharjah producing the most oil. The other emirates have benefitted from oil wealth through the federal welfare system and employment in state institutions.

With declining oil prices, the government has attempted to diversify the national economy. This has led to the growth of industry, construction, commerce, free trade zones, transportation, tourism, farming, fisheries, and communications. The rapid development of these sectors has reduced the nation's dependence on oil. In 1998, the gross domestic product was estimated at $45,590 million, 70 percent from the nonoil sector.

The national currency name is called the Emirian Dirham.

Major Industries and Trade. The UAE is the third largest exporter of crude oil and gas in the Gulf. It is a member of the Organization of Petroleum Exporting Countries (OPEC).

Division of Labor. Citizens account for 10 percent of the total labor force. Almost all nationals (99 percent) work in the state sector because of the attractive benefits and are employed mainly in nontechnical jobs in education, the army, the police, and the civil service. They also own all Emirati businesses. Immigrants are employed in both the public and private sectors in manual, technical, and professional occupations.

SOCIAL STRATIFICATION

Classes and Castes. Emirati society is divided into two social categories: the nationals (*Al-Muwateneen*) and the foreign immigrants, referred to as the incomers (*Al-Wafedeen*). Citizens are subdivided into four main social classes: (1) the ruling sheikhly families, whose members hold the highest political positions and power and have immense wealth and prestige, (2) the merchant class, known as *al-tujjar*, traditionally pearling merchants who now sell international consumer goods, (3) the new middle class, represented by increasing numbers of professionals who have benefitted from free state education, and (4) the low-income groups, represented by newly settled Bedouin nomads and former pearl divers and oasis farmers.

Among the immigrants there are hierarchical groups that receive different economic and social rewards: (1) top professionals and technocrats with international contracts, who earn high salaries and other benefits, (2) middle-range professionals such as school teachers, skilled technicians, and company salesmen, and (3) low-paid semi-skilled and unskilled workers, primarily Asian. In general, nationals are a privileged minority, and benefit from state laws and business regulations.

Symbols of Social Stratification. The symbol of a male national as a distinct social category is seen most visibly in the traditional dress of a white robe (*kandoura*) and white head cloth (*ghutrah*) with a black rope (*aqal*). Men grow short beards and mus-

An old fortress surrounded by modern buildings in Abu Dhabi. After 1960, mud-walled communities transformed into commercial centers.

taches. Women wear long dresses with a head cover (*hijab*) and black cloak (*abayah*).

POLITICAL LIFE

Government. The UAE has a federal government that is made up of several organs: the president and his deputy, the Supreme Council, the cabinet, the Federal National Council, and an independent judiciary with a federal supreme court. The Supreme Council has both legislative and executive powers and includes the rulers of the seven emirates. The cabinet consists of ministers drawn mainly from the ruling families of the emirates.

Leadership and Political Officials. The fact that the traditional tribal system of government each emirate was based on similar political principles facilitated the establishment of the UAE. Hereditary dynastic family rule still operates in each emirate as a local government system under the umbrella of the federal system. Members of the ruling families occupy the most important positions in their political administrations. While the political system continues to retain some of its traditional values at formal and informal levels, it has been able to keep pace with economic and social change. The sheikhs are highly regarded for performing the dual roles of modernizers and guardians of the cultural heritage. They still have traditional *majlis* where citizens have access to their leaders.

SOCIAL WELFARE AND CHANGE PROGRAMS

The development of the infrastructure has been impressive. The welfare system offers womb-to-tomb free state services for all nationals, including high-quality health care, education up to the tertiary level, social security, family allowances, subsided electricity and water, and housing for low-income groups. This is a major way of distributing oil wealth among the national population. The immigrant population also benefits to some extent, particularly in regard to medical care.

NONGOVERNMENTAL ORGANIZATIONS AND OTHER ASSOCIATIONS

There were 103 Associations of Public Benefit in 1999, serving interests of many groups and identified with heritage preservation, immigrant communities, professional groups, culture, women, religion, sports, and general humanitarian services. Their role is seen as complementary to that of governmental institutions.

GENDER ROLES AND STATUSES

Division of Labor by Gender. Modern economic roles and social status reflect both change and continuity for women. Schools and universities are segregated, and levels of enrollment of girls and their performance are impressive. In higher education, female students outnumber males two to one. However, women's participation in the labor force remains one of the lowest in the world at 6 percent in 1990. In spite of new employment opportunities, most women opt for marriage and raising children. UAE society places a high value on those roles. Conservative cultural attitudes lead women to seek jobs that do not involve mixing with men or commuting far from home. Subsequently, most women are employed in education, health, and civil service.

The Relative Status of Women and Men. Official statements affirm that men and women have equal rights and opportunities to advance themselves and the nation, yet patriarchy as a generalized ideology is still visible in social life. Men continue to receive employment preferences in high state administration and private businesses. Women do not play a significant role in politics and religious life, as these areas are considered male domains.

MARRIAGE, FAMILY, AND KINSHIP

Marriage. Arranged endogamous marriage within the kinship (tribal) units was the preferred pattern in the preoil period, but this pattern has changed somewhat. Individuals now have greater choice, yet many nationals still prefer arranged marriages. Emiratis are strongly discouraged from marrying nonnationals, and a young man receives $19,000 from the Marriage Fund if he marries a national. As prescribed by Islam, a man is allowed up to four wives, but most men have only one wife.

Domestic Unit. The traditional household unit of the extended family has been undermined, as over 80 percent of national households live as nuclear families in their own houses. Large families are encouraged by the state as a national policy, and family size is six to eight children. The husband's authority is declining, while the wife is gaining importance as a mother and the manager of the domestic unit. On average, each household employs two live-in domestic servants, usually Asian.

Kin Groups. UAE society is family- and kin-oriented. Tribal kinship units play a significant role in social identification and one's standing in the community. Most families prefer to live in the same neighborhood as their kin.

SOCIALIZATION

Child Rearing and Education. Children are showered with care, affection, and physical contact. They are raised to be respectful toward their parents and elders and grow up to be skilled in interaction with a large number of relatives. Up to age 5, a child is referred to as *jahel* ("the one who does not know"), and there is a tolerant attitude toward children's behavior. Most families employ maids to share child caretaking, and this has introduced a foreign cultural element to child socialization, although a maid's influence is viewed as negative. The school system has undertaken a greater role in children's socialization, significantly reducing the family's role in this process.

Higher Education. The government views higher education as a major instrument for development. The UAE has one of the highest ratios of students entering higher education in the world. There are seven universities and eleven higher colleges of technology.

An old mosque in Fujairah. Islam is the dominant religion in the UAR, so mosques can be found everywhere.

ETIQUETTE

Social customs are shared throughout the Gulf Arab countries. An Islamic greeting (*al-salam alaykom*) is the most appropriate, and men follow this with a quick nose-to-nose touch while shaking hands. Women greet each other by kissing several times on both cheeks. Men normally do not shake hands with women in public. It is customary to ask about the health of a person and his or her family several times before beginning light conversation. Refreshments usually are served before serious matters are discussed.

It is customary not to use first names but to say "father or mother of (oldest son)." Respect and courtesy are shown to elders, and in their presence young men are expected to listen more and speak less. Sex segregation is still evident in social life. Men are entertained in *majlis* (large living rooms, often with a separate entrance), while women entertain friends in the home. It is customary to take off one's shoes before entering a private house.

Emiratis stand close to each other when interacting. It is acceptable for men or women to hold hands. The presence of many ethnic groups has led Emiratis to be tolerant of other social customs, yet they remain conscious of their own customs as markers of cultural identity.

RELIGION

Religious Beliefs. Islam dominates all aspects of life. Most Emiratis are members of the Sunni sect. Matters relating to marriage, divorce, inheritance, economics, politics, and personal conduct are affected by *Sharia* (Islamic) law.

Emaritis are tolerant toward other religions, and immigrants of other faiths are allowed to have their own places of worship. Large numbers of Asian and Arab immigrants also follow Islam.

Rituals and Holy Places. The main Muslim religious ritual is prayer five times a day. This requires *wodou* (ablution) for purification. Usually people go to the nearest mosque or pray at home. The rituals involved in the pilgrimage (*Haj*) to Mecca are the most elaborate. One must remove the shoes before entering a mosque. In large mosques, there are separate areas for women.

MEDICINE AND HEALTH CARE

Before 1960, there were few hospitals, and the population relied on traditional folk medicine. Cautery, bloodletting, and the use of herbs were common, and a religious teacher (*muttawe*) dealt with cases of mental illness. Life expectancy was around forty-five years. Today Emiratis have a free modern

An ancient watchtower on the coast of the United Arab Emirates.

health care system with numerous hospitals, primary health care centers, and private clinics staffed primarily by immigrants. With improved diet and health care, life expectancy is now seventy-two years, and there has been a reduction in infant mortality. The extended family provides its sick members with support in the form of frequent hospital visits, and traditional medical practices are still used to deal with mental illnesses.

SECULAR CELEBRATIONS

The UAE national day, 2 December, is the most important secular celebration. Cities are decorated with colored lights, and folklore troops perform in heritage villages. 1 January is a holiday but is not celebrated by nationals. Expatriate communities celebrate their own religious and secular holidays.

THE ARTS AND HUMANITIES

Support for the Arts. The state generously supports writers, painters, actors, and folk dancers. Sharjah is particularly active in promoting culture and was chosen by UNESCO as the Arab Cultural Capital in 1998.

Literature. The oral tradition remains strong, particularly storytelling and poetry, and most state events are accompanied by poetry readings. Written literature is increasing in popularity.

Performance Arts. Conservative elements of the society still impede women's participation in performance arts. In 1999, the first college for theater arts opened in Sharjah. Emiratis rely on theater and television programs produced in other Arab countries.

BIBLIOGRAPHY

Abdul Rahman, Abdullah. *The Emirates in the Memory of Her Sons* (in Arabic), 1990.

Abdulla, Abdul Khaliq, et al. *Civil Society in the United Arab Emirates* (in Arabic), 1995.

Al-Alkim, Hassan. *The Foreign Policy of the United Arab Emirates*, 1989.

Al-Faris, Abdul Razzaq. *Higher Education and the Labor Market in the UAE* (in Arabic), 1996.

Al-Gurg, Easa. *The Wells of Memory*, 1998.

Al-Hassan, Yusuf. *The Welfare State in the United Arab Emirates* (in Arabic), 1997.

Al-Mur, Mohammad. *National Aspirations: Essays about the Emirates* (in Arabic), 1997.

Al-Otaiba, Mana. *Petroleum and the Economy of the United Arab Emirates*, 1977.

Codrai, Ronald. *The Seven Sheikhdoms: Life in the Trucial States before the Federation of the United Arab Emirates*, 1999.

Corderman, Anthony. *Bahrain, Oman, Qatar and the UAE*, 1997.

Crystal, Jill. *Oil and Politics in the Gulf: Rulers and Merchants in Kuwait and Qatar*, 1990.

Drake, Diana. *Discovery Guide to the United Arab Emirates*, 1998.

Dubai: A Pictorial Tour, 1999.

Dyck, Gertrude. *The Oasis: Al-Ain, Memoirs of Doctora Khalifa*, 1995.

Encyclopedia of the Emirates, vol. 1: *Dubai*, 1993–1994.

Facey, William, and Gillian Grant. *The Emirates by the First Photographers*, 1996.

Ghobash, Moaza. *Immigration and Development in the United Arab Emirates: A Sociological View* (in Arabic), 1986.

Heard-Bey, Frauke. *From Trucial States to United Arab Emirates*, 1996.

Kay, Shirley. *Emirates Archaeological Heritage*, 1986.

———. *Land of the Emirates*, 6th ed., 1992.

Khalaf, Sulayman. "Gulf Societies and the Image of Unlimited Good." *Dialectical Anthropology* 17: 53–84, 1992.

Matthew, Jane. *UAE: A MEED Practical and Business Guide,* 5th ed., 1999.

Mohammed Al-Fahim. *From Rags to Riches,* 1995.

National Atlas of the United Arab Emirates, 1993.

Nowell, John. *Now and Then: The Emirates,* 1998.

Owen, Roger. "Migrant Workers in the Gulf." *Minority Rights Report* 68: 1985.

Progress of UAE Women. Association of Popular Heritage Revival.

Robinson, Gordon. *Arab Gulf States,* 1996.

Spectrum Guide to the United Arab Emirates, 1998.

Studies in Emirates Society (in Arabic), 1997.

Thesiger, Wilfred. *Arabian Sands,* 1959.

UAE in Focus: A Photographic History of the United Arab Emirates, 1998.

Zahlan, Rosemarie. *The Making of Modern Gulf States,* 1989.

—SULAYMAN NAJM KHALAF

UNITED KINGDOM

CULTURE NAME

British

ALTERNATIVE NAME

Formally known as the United Kingdom of Great Britain and Northern Ireland

ORIENTATION

Identification. The United Kingdom of Great Britain and Northern Ireland is the formal name of the sovereign state governed by Parliament in London. The term ''United Kingdom'' normally is understood to include Northern Ireland; the term ''Great Britain'' refers to the island of Britain and its constituent nations of England, Wales, and Scotland but does not include Northern Ireland. Any citizen of Great Britain may be referred to as a Briton.

Location and Geography. The land area of Great Britain is 89,000 square miles (230,500 square kilometers), with an additional 5,400 square miles (13,986 square kilometers) in Northern Ireland, giving it one of the highest population densities in the Western world. Although the country lies mostly at the latitude of Labrador in the western Atlantic, the climate is tempered by the Gulf Stream and does not have extremes of summer heat or winter cold. Except for some areas of barren upland and bog, most of the land is suitable for agriculture and has been grazed or cultivated since the Bronze Age. The natural vegetation is mixed oak woodland, but most of the terrain has been cleared for agriculture or for shipbuilding and charcoal for smelting. The earliest evidence of human settlement is at Boxgrove, Sussex, and the island may have been continuously occupied for 500,000 years.

Demography. The population is approximately 55 million: 46 million in England, 5 million in Scotland, 2.5 million in Wales, and 1.5 million in Northern Ireland.

The nation's cultural diversity has been increased by migration within the British Isles and by immigration from Europe and overseas. Until 1920, Ireland was incorporated within the United Kingdom. Movement across the Irish Sea had existed since the eighteenth century, even among Ireland's poorest people. In the nineteenth century, there was a regular pattern of seasonal migration of farm workers from Ireland to Britain. Irishmen volunteered for the Royal Navy and British Army regiments in the eighteenth and nineteenth centuries and saw service in all parts of the empire. A wide variety of other Irish people spent periods in Britain, which had a more highly developed economy than Ireland. From 1841 onward, the censuses of Scotland, England, and Wales have enumerated Irish-born people in every part of the country. Similarly, Scottish and Welsh people have settled in England. Most British people have ancestries that are mixtures of the four nationalities of the British Isles.

Before and after World War II, political and religious refugees and displaced persons from the Baltic countries, Poland, Czechoslovakia, and Hungary were offered shelter in Britain and remained, along with some prisoners of war. Other immigrants of European ancestry who were born in Canada, New Zealand, Australia, and South and East Africa, along with Greek and Turkish Cypriots, also settled in Britain. After the late 1940s, many of non-European overseas immigrants arrived, predominantly from the colonies, including people of Indian and African ancestry from the West Indies and Guyana; people from India, Pakistan and Bangladesh; and Chinese from Hong Kong and Singapore. The 1991 census, the first to include ethnic background, enumerated three million Britons of non-European birth or ancestry.

Linguistic Affiliation. Regional and cultural relationships are expressed in marked linguistic differences. Although the language has been modified by a gradual convergence toward ''estuary English'' a

United Kingdom

less formal variety of southeastern speech, and educational and socioeconomic factors, it is possible to determine people's geographical origins by the way they speak. In some areas, there are significant differences in speech patterns from one city or county to its neighbor. These differences are associated with loyalties to one's place of birth or residence and for many people are important aspects of self-identity; non-English native languages are little spoken but in recent years have gained significance as cultural and political symbols. These languages include Scots Gaelic, Welsh, Cornish, and Irish (commonly referred to as the Celtic languages); there is also the Old Norse language of the Northern Isles (Orkney and especially Shetland) and the Norman French patois of the Channel Islands. In Wales, 80 percent of the people speak English as their first or only language and those who speak Welsh as their first language are bilingual. In Scotland, Gaelic is not a national symbol because it was never spoken in some parts of that country. People in the Northern Isles are bilingual in English and an unwritten creolized form of Old Norse; in the Channel Islands, the Norman French patois is nearly extinct; and in Cornwall, there are no natural speakers of Cornish, although the language has been reconstructed. In Northern Ireland, the Irish language has been reintroduced as a means of revitalizing Celtic pride among Belfast Catholics.

Symbolism. Symbolic attachment may reinforce localism or take the form of personal commitments that extend across socioeconomic strata. Support for soccer and rugby teams became significant during the twentieth century, and teams now command fierce local loyalties as sport has come to symbolize male pride and self-image in a society where mining and manufacturing have declined. Forms of personal commitment that transcend locality include vegetarianism and environmentalism: the first is predominantly middle class and female, and the second is identified less with gender and socioeconomic status. On the fringes of society, especially among the young, there has been a significant growth in new religious movements, which include radical environmentalist cults, New Age paganism, anarchism, anticapitalist and antinuclear groups, and adopted Far Eastern and South Asian religions and belief systems, including martial arts cults. Cults based on popular music and performers engender personal commitment in culturally patterned ways.

HISTORY AND ETHNIC RELATIONS

Emergence of the Nation. The United Kingdom was formed by Acts of Union between England and Wales (1536) and England, Wales, and Scotland (1707), uniting the three nations under a single monarchy and legislative council (Parliament in London). After 1169, the island of Ireland came under British influence, and it became a colonial dependency in 1690. The British and Irish parliaments were united in 1801. A separatist movement led to the dissolution of the Union of Great Britain and Ireland in 1920; twenty-six of Ireland's thirty-two counties became the independent Irish Free State (later the Republic of Ireland), with six of the nine counties of Ulster remaining within the United Kingdom. The present-day nation also includes the Channel Islands off the coast of France and the Isle of Man between Britain and Ireland, which are substantially self-governing. Northern Ireland and

Scotland have separate legal and educational systems and issue their own currency; Wales is fully incorporated within the English legal, educational, and banking systems. Recent referendums in Scotland and Wales have resulted in the establishment of a Scottish Parliament which is still under the general jurisdiction of London but has limited local tax-raising powers, and the Welsh Assembly, which does not have tax-raising powers.

The native tribes in the central and eastern parts of England were conquered by the Romans in 55 B.C.E., and permanent Roman settlements were established in 43 B.C.E. and continued for four hundred years. The numbers of Romans were never great, but the indigenous upper classes became Romanized and spoke Latin. The principal Roman towns had baths, temples, amphitheaters, and forums and some of the roads designed to connect Roman towns are still in use. With the departure of the Romans, the British Isles were invaded by a succession of warlike peoples from the European mainland, including the Angles, Saxons, and Jutes; there were also persistent Danish raids. All migrations influenced the native Britons, as can be seen in the English language, which is an amalgam of the languages spoken by the waves of colonists. This turbulence ended with the Norman Conquest in 1066. A new line of kings attempted to extend control into the farthest reaches of Wales, Scotland, and Ireland, and struggles for supremacy between rival chieftains and princes culminated in the Magna Carta of 1215, which eventually led to the establishment of Parliament and representative democracy. A period of consensus and stability followed the accession to the throne of the Tudor king Henry VII in 1495. His successor, Henry VIII, broke with the Catholic church in Rome and declared himself the head of the Church of England. The dissolution of the monasteries and the confiscation of the property of the Roman Catholic church occurred during the Reformation, leading to challenges to the monarchy by rivals who supported Catholicism. Instability, civil unrest, and competition with other European powers over claims to overseas territory continued for much of the seventeenth century.

Commerce and manufacturing (principally the domestic woolen and Newfoundland and Boston salt-fish trades) developed rapidly, and the authority of Parliament over the monarchy was consolidated by the beginning of the eighteenth century. Capitalism existed before the Industrial Revolution, but its development was hampered by technologies limited to water power and a lack of surplus labor. During the period of the Enclosures (1740–1789),

A castle overlooks the water in Scotland. Castles dot the countryside in all parts of the United Kingdom.

landlords cleared the peasantry from the rural landscape to create fields enclosed by hedgerows and fences and began to derive profit from new, scientific methods of intensive agricultural production rather than relying the meager tithes and rents paid by peasant smallholders. This displaced large numbers of rural people, who were forced to emigrate to the overseas colonies or migrate to the new sites of industrial production.

The impetus for the Industrial Revolution came from trade with the expanding colonies by a growing middle class of entrepreneurs and investors whose wealth was not derived from land but from commerce; those entrepreneurs reinvested their wealth in new forms of manufacturing and trade rather than in ways that imitated the consumption patterns of the landed gentry. The Industrial Revolution began at the end of the seventeenth century, specifically in the machine-driven manufacturing processes made possible by the steam engine, which was first used in 1698 to draw water from an underground tin mine, and then was adapted to drive power looms in textile mills. Overseas colonization and wars with other European powers stimulated the further development of mining and metallurgy, precision machine tools, navigational instruments, cartography, and managerial and logistical organization, which were exploited for commercial gain by private entrepreneurs. By 1815, Britain had the world's largest and most powerful navy, and within twenty years steam railways and steam-powered ships designed by British engineers were carrying passengers and cargo for profit, allowing British shipping companies to dominate world trade. By midcentury, the country was the world's leading power in business and finance, engineering, science, and medicine.

The Industrial Revolution created a new social order as entrepreneurship and factory production resulted in new forms of wealth and work that were added to the agrarian social order dominated by aristocratic landowners. The 1832 Reform Act ended the political privileges of landed wealth by extending the vote to middle-class male heads of household. The country would be governed by the beliefs, values, and aspirations of the middle class rather than by those of the landed aristocracy. One dimension of this new social order was urbanization: as dispersed cottage industries such as weaving were replaced by mills in central locations, nearby housing was needed for the workers; that housing frequently was built by the mill owner and rented to the workers. The populations of Glasgow, Manchester, Liverpool, and Birmingham doubled or tripled between 1801 and 1841, and many major towns and cities grew up around mines, mills, smelting works, ports and railway junctions.

Work in the "dark, satanic mills" brought new levels of exploitation and hardship. Rapid industrialization caused overcrowding and disease; cholera epidemics between the 1830s and 1860s provoked public unrest and forced the government to improve public health. Another consequence of Victorian working conditions was the rise of trade unionism. A socially stratified and politically divided society, that was preoccupied with distinctions of social class and the rival ideologies of laissez-faire capitalism and state socialism soon crystallized.

Until the middle of the twentieth century, the United Kingdom was one of the world's wealthiest and most influential nations. Machine tools, locomotives, and steamships built in Scotland and the industrial Midlands were exported worldwide; textile products from Lancashire, Staffordshire china and pottery, Welsh anthracite coal, and finished steel products from Sheffield, dominated world markets for a century. British mining, manufacturing, transportation technology; legal, banking and parliamentary systems; and scientific discoveries and advances were exported worldwide. The nation's wealth was further underwritten by its position as the chief European colonial power, with captive markets and extensive sources of cheap labor and raw materials in Australasia, Asia, Africa, and the Americas. The country's position as a world power was reduced in the second half of the twentieth century by two world wars and the gradual decline of its advantages in manufacturing and business, the loss of the empire, and expensive experiments with state socialism. By the late 1970s, the nation was in debt to the International Monetary Fund. The discovery of oil in the North Sea in the 1970s saved the country from bankruptcy and stimulated economic recovery. Tax revenues from the oil industry provided the means to restructure the economy away from an obsolescent manufacturing base and toward a base dominated by service and knowledge-based industries.

National Identity. The United Kingdom is made up of four interdependent nations with many common institutions. While differences in everyday modes of sociality and consumer behavior are not great from one part of the nation to another, some aspects of culture are symbolic of national or local difference on the level of everyday practice or on special occasions. Support for the monarchy, political parties, and soccer teams are the most obvious expressions of contemporary localism; religious adherence and ethnic differentiation are also signifi-

cant. Support for the monarchy and the Conservative Party is highest in England, especially in the south, while in Scotland and Wales it is substantially lower. In Scotland and Wales, there are minority nationalist parties. The Scottish National Party's political program is dominated by economic issues, particularly tax revenues from North Sea oil. The political agenda of Plaid Cymru, the Welsh nationalist party, is mainly concerned with linguistic and cultural matters. In both Scotland and Wales, the Labour Party is dominant, drawing strength from its critique of the class privilege traditionally associated with London and southeastern England. The dominance of the Labour Party in much of Wales and Scotland provides conditions for patronage-style politics.

Ethnic Relations. A high degree of spatial integration is generally held to be indicative of social integration, assimilation, and acculturation, while spatial segregation is indicative of social pluralism. Non-European immigration in Britain has not moved toward a pattern of sharply-defined urban ethnic ghettoes. Nevertheless, many non-European immigrants continue to be subject to discriminatory practices in employment and in other spheres, even if systematic marginalization cannot be inferred from their spatial distribution within the towns and cities of the nation.

URBANISM, ARCHITECTURE, AND THE USE OF SPACE

Rights to land development were in effect nationalized in 1947 by an act of Parliament that removed the right of the owner of a piece of property to change its use and transferred that power to the state. By the end of the twentieth century, 80 percent of the land area was reserved for agricultural use but was responsible for less than 5 percent of the gross national product and less than 2 percent of employment, yet the land-use planning system has continued to grow in size and power. Speculating in land is big business, and the amount of land available for housing is so restricted that any house within commuting range of a job will command a high price.

The countryside is increasingly seen as an aesthetic and recreational resource for people who live in the towns and cities. However, this image of the countryside is very expensive to maintain. The population is crowded together in towns on tiny plots of land, while much of the open land is underpopulated and underused. Many people in small

Cottages in Walthamstow Village, London, England. Housing in or near the cities is in very high demand.

urban houses have high mortgages because of the cost of land.

FOOD AND ECONOMY

Basic Economy. The United Kingdom has one of the largest economies in the world, with a Gross National Product estimate in 1999 at $1.29 trillion (U.S.). Finance, manufacturing, and trade form the base of the economy. The pound sterling is the currency, and it is still being debated whether the nation will join with the its European Union partners and adopt the Euro.

Commercial Activities. Banking and finance, including insurance, are mainstays of the economy.

Major Industries. The United Kingdom is one of the most industrialized nations on earth and has a strong manufacturing base. Major products include machine tools, aircraft and ships, motor vehicles, electronics, chemicals, coal, petroleum, textiles, and food processing.

Trade. One of the leading trading powers in the world, the United Kingdom exported $271 billion (U.S.) and imported $306 billion (U.S.) worth of goods in 1998. Chief exports include manufactured goods, food, chemicals, and fuels. Manufactured goods, machinery, fuel, and food products are imported. Primary trading partners are the European Union and the United States.

Division of Labor. Although the nation produces almost two-thirds of its food needs, in 1998, agriculture accounted for less than 2 percent of the workforce sector. Services account for 73 percent, and industry another 25.3 percent.

SOCIAL STRATIFICATION

Classes and Castes. The idea of social class is much more powerful than that of ethnicity. People frequently characterize themselves as working class or middle class. Although few admit to being upper class, in principle there are three classes, with the highest one reserved for the aristocratic inheritors of old, landed wealth. The term ''social class'' has complex meanings with social, economic, and political dimensions. People who describe themselves as working class perceive themselves to have respectable but unprivileged origins, and typically are born into a family supported by wages from industrial or agricultural labor paid in cash at the end of the week. In these families neither parent has a college degree and the housing that the family occupies is rented. There is a strong association between the idea of being working class and supportive of the

Wide open grounds surround Belfast's Northern Ireland Parliament Building for security reasons.

trade union movement and the Labour Party; the identification thus is with a set of corporate or collective economic, social, and political interests and aspirations. A self-described middle-class person has a social background and political attitudes that suggest parents with white-collar jobs whose salaries are paid monthly by check and who are likely to have professional or advanced education, to live in an owner-occupied suburban house, and to have made strategic choices about their children's education. They are likely to use their education and social skills for upward economic mobility and to support the Conservative Party, which stresses self-sufficiency and individualism. These differences have never been as clear-cut as the rhetoric of the main political parties and professional critics of the social order have asserted. The concept of class has recently fallen out of favor with politicians and sociologists as the nation's social and economic structure has changed dramatically with deindustrialization and the growth of social mobility and the knowledge economy.

POLITICAL LIFE

Government. The United Kingdom is a constitutional monarchy. The monarch is chief of state and the prime minister is head of government. The Cabinet of Ministers is appointed by the prime minister and are responsible to Parliament. Parliament is composed of the House of Lords (hereditary), the House of Commons (elected), and the sovereign.

Leadership and Political Officials. The monarch reigns, but does not rule the nation per se, acting only with the approval of Parliament. The prime minister holds the executive power and is traditionally the leader of the majority party in Parliament. The primary parties are the Labour Party, the Conservative Party, and the Liberal Democrats.

Social Problems and Control. Each of the countries within the United Kingdom has its own judicial system and courts.

Military Activity. The United Kingdom has a strong military, with an army, the Royal Navy, and the Royal Air Force. The nation is an active participant in the North Atlantic Treaty Organization (NATO).

SOCIAL WELFARE AND CHANGE PROGRAMS

The National Insurance, in operation since 1948, provides medical, unemployment, maternity, and retirement benefits, among others. Employers and employees contribute to this fund. The National

City Hall in Cardiff, Wales.

Assistance Board provides financial assistance to the poor.

GENDER ROLES AND STATUSES

The Relative Status of Women and Men. In the 1970s, there were national debates on the changing role of women in society and their women's employment prospects. By the 1980s, the debate had shifted to the implications of the increasing participation of women as the economy was restructured and the balance changed from manufacturing to service occupations. In the 1990s, national debates concentrated on the relationship between work, family life, consumption levels, and the socialization and education of the next generation. Approximately half of British women work; of these, half are part-time workers. Nevertheless, a significant gender divide persists in regard to suitable occupations for men and women, access to occupations by women and men, pay levels for similar kinds of work, and the allocation of domestic tasks. Although the ideal of gender equality is widely shared, social behavior lags behind the ideal. For example, 75 percent of couples say that the preparation of the evening meal should be shared equally, but only one-third of these couples live up to that ideal.

MARRIAGE, FAMILY, AND KINSHIP

Marriage. Premarital sex and unmarried cohabitation are widely accepted even if they are not liked by defenders of traditional family values. Single motherhood caused by unstable cohabiting relationships or marital breakdown is perceived as a major problem because of its impact on the welfare budget rather than as a moral question. Nonetheless, family relationships remain close. Roughly 70 percent of adults live within an hour's journey of their parents or grown-up children, and nearly half see their mothers, fathers, adult children, and best friends at least once a week. While newspaper and television reports claim that the nuclear family is in decline because of increased rates of unmarried cohabitation and divorce, personal commitment to kinship ties has not changed much. Seventy percent of adults think that people should keep in touch with close family members; 55 percent think that they should keep in touch with relatives such as uncles, aunts, and cousins; 60 percent say that they would rather spend time with relatives than with friends; and nearly 80 percent think relatives are more important than friends. These attitudes vary with age and gender—people over age forty-five tend to be more family-centered than are younger people.

Kin Groups. Family life is changing, and there are tensions between kinship ties and some contemporary social values. However, the great majority of people perceive themselves to be part of multigenerational families and regard these relationships as very important.

ETIQUETTE

The United Kingdom is a crowded country. People cope with this situation by being reserved and diffident in public, politely ignoring strangers, quietly minding their own business, and marking out and defending their private spaces, homes, and gardens. They expect others to do the same.

RELIGION

Religious Beliefs. Since the 1950s, church adherence has fallen dramatically, and the British are generally uninterested in formal religious practice. Sixty percent of adults do not believe in God, and one-third have no religious affiliation. Thirty-six percent of the population identifies with the official, state-sanctioned Church of England; 10 percent with the Roman Catholic Church; 4 percent with Presbyterianism; 4 percent with Baptism and Methodism; 3 percent with other Protestant denominations, and 3 percent with other religions. Four percent describe themselves as Christians, and 35 percent say that they have no religion. Geographically, the Church of England is represented as the Church of England, the Church of Scotland, the Church of Ireland, and the Church in Wales, but Anglicanism is the predominant church mainly in England. In Wales, there was a strong nonconformist presence of Methodist and Baptist chapels whose importance in local life has declined considerably since 1950; in Scotland and Northern Ireland, Presbyterianism is strongly represented; and Roman Catholicism is significant in Northern Ireland, the Western Isles of Scotland, parts of Lancashire and Sussex, and cities where large numbers of nineteenth century Irish Catholic immigrants settled. Only in Northern Ireland is religion strongly identified with political aspirations.

MEDICINE AND HEALTH CARE

The National Health Service, which was set up by an act of Parliament in 1947, gave every resident access to free medical care. A system was created that operated local public hospitals throughout the country and directly employed doctors, nurses, and other health workers. Family doctors, specialists, and dentists also received payment from the government for treating patients, although any doctor or patient can practice privately or pay for private medical care. There have been continuing debates on the level of care the service should provide and how it should be funded. The system was intended to provide unlimited medical care to any patient, and the government undertook to pay the full cost. In some ways, the service has been a victim of its own success. Free medical care and successful efforts to promote better health, diet, and working conditions have meant that people live much longer. The care of the frail elderly has consumed an increasing amount of resources; as have advances in treating diseases. Governments' attempts to control the costs of health care inevitably result in the covert rationing of resources, which conflicts with the principle of the citizen's right to high-quality free care when it is needed.

SECULAR CELEBRATIONS

The Celebration of the Birthday of the Queen is held on the second Saturday in June. Other legal holidays include New Year's Day, Good Friday, Late Summer Holiday (the last Monday in August or the first in September), Christmas Day, and Boxing Day (26 December). Scotland and Northern Ireland, celebrate several of their own holidays.

BIBLIOGRAPHY

Baumann, Gerd. *Contesting Culture: Discourses of Identity in Multi-Ethnic London*, 1996.

Bell, Colin. *Middle-Class Families*, 1969.

Boyce, D. George. *The Irish Question and British Politics, 1868–1996*, 2nd ed., 1996.

British Social Attitudes, annual editions.

Bruce, Steve. *The Edge of the Union: The Ulster Loyalist Political Vision*, 1994.

Byron, Reginald. *Irish America*, 1999.

Chapman, Malcolm. *The Gaelic Vision in Scottish Culture* 1978.

———. *The Celts: The Construction of a Myth*, 1992.

Charsley, Simon. *Rites of Marrying: A Scottish Study*, 1991.

Clancy, Patrick, Sheelagh Drudy, Kathleen Lynch, and Liam O'Dowd, eds. *Ireland: A Sociological Profile* 1986.

Cohen, Anthony, ed. *Belonging: Identity and Social Organisation in British Rural Cultures*, 1982.

Colls, Robert, and Philip Dodd, eds. *Englishness: Politics and Culture, 1880–1920*, 1986.

Davies, Charlotte. *Welsh Nationalism in the Twentieth Century*, 1989.

Davis, Graham. *The Irish in Britain, 1815–1914*, 1991.

Dennis, Norman, Fernando Henriques, and Clifford Slaughter. *Coal is Our Life: An Analysis of a Yorkshire Mining Community*, 2nd ed., 1969.

Fenton, Alexander. *The Northern Isles: Orkney and Shetland*, 1978.

———. *Country Life in Scotland: Our Rural Past*, 1987.

Finnegan, Ruth. *The Hidden Musicians: Music-Making in an English Town*, 1989.

Firth, Raymond, Jane Hubert, and Anthony Forge. *Families and their Relatives*, 1969.

Frankenberg, Ronald. *Village on the Border: A Study of Religion, Politics and Football in a North Wales Community*, 1990.

Goldthorpe, John. *Social Mobility and Class Structure in Modern Britain*, 2nd ed., 1987.

———. *Family Life in Western Societies: A Historical Sociology of the Family in Britain and North America*, 1987.

Gmelch, George. *Double Passage: The Lives of Caribbean Migrants at Home and Abroad*, 1992.

Harris, C. C. *Redundancy and Recession in South Wales*, 1987.

———. *Family, Economy and Community*, 1990.

Jenkins, Richard, ed. *Northern Ireland: Studies in Social and Economic Life*, 1989.

Macdonald, Sharon. *Reimagining Culture: Histories, Identities, and the Gaelic Renaissance*, 1997.

Macfarlane, Alan. *The Origins of English Individualism*, 1978.

———. *The Culture of Capitalism*, 1987.

Newby, Howard. *Green and Pleasant Land? Social Change in Rural England*, 1979.

Pahl, R. E., ed. *Patterns of Urban Life*, 1970.

Parman, Susan. *Scottish Crofters: A Historical Ethnography of a Scottish Village*, 1990.

Radcliffe, Peter. *Ethnicity in the 1991 Census*, vol. 3, 1996.

Rees, Alwyn. *Celtic Heritage: Ancient Tradition in Ireland and Wales*, 1961.

———. *Life in a Welsh Countryside*, 1996.

Review of Scottish Culture, annual editions.

Sampson, Anthony. *The Changing Anatomy of Britain*, 1982.

Short, Brian. *The English Rural Community: Images and Analysis*, 1992.

Social Trends, annual editions.

Stanworth, Philip, and Anthony Giddens. *Elites and Power in British Society*, 1974.

Strathern, Marilyn. *Kinship at the Core*, 1981.

Thompson, E. P. *The Making of the English Working Class*, 2nd ed., 1980.

———. *Customs in Common*, 1991.

Tunstall, Jeremy. *The Fishermen: The Sociology of an Extreme Occupation*, 1962.

Wallman, Sandra. *Eight London Households*, 1984.

—REGINALD F. BYRON

SEE ALSO: ENGLAND, NORTHERN IRELAND, SCOTLAND, AND WALES

UNITED STATES OF AMERICA

CULTURE NAME

American

ORIENTATION

Identification. The name "America" is often used to refer to the United States, but until the political formation of the United States after the Revolutionary War, this designation referred to South America only. Contemporary use of the term to refer to the United States underlines that country's political and economic dominance in the western hemisphere. Such use of this designation is impolitic from the perspective of Canadians and Latin Americans.

The United States has an Anglo majority that is politically and economically dominant. One of the defining characteristics of the country as a nation is its legacy of slavery and the persistence of economic and social inequalities based on race.

U.S. culture has significant regional inflections. Most Americans are aware of these differences despite the fact that these regions have experienced economic transformations and that Americans are a mobile people who often leave their regions of origin.

The Northeast is densely populated. Its extensive corridors of urbanization have been called the national "megalopolis." Once a leader in technology and industry, the Northeast has been overtaken in those areas by California's Silicon Valley.

The Midwest is both rural and industrial. It is the home of the family farm and is the "corn belt" and "breadbasket" of the nation. In the Great Lakes area of the upper Midwest, the automobile and steel industries were central to community and economy. As those industries declined, the upper Midwest became known as the rust belt.

The South was shaped by its secession from the Union before the Civil War and is associated with slavery and with subsequent battles over civil rights for African-Americans. In contemporary terms, these are the sunshine states, retirement havens, and new economic frontiers.

The West, the last national frontier, is associated with national dreams and myths of unlimited opportunity and individualism. It has the nation's most open landscapes.

California, along with the southwestern states were ceded to the United States by Mexico in 1848 after the Mexican-American War. The Southwest is distinctive because of its historical ties to colonial Spain, its Native American populations, and its regional cuisine, which has been influenced by Native American and Spanish cultures.

Location and Geography. The United States is the world's fourth largest country, with an area of 3,679,192 square miles (9,529,107 square kilometers). It includes fifty states and one federal district, where the capital, Washington, D.C., is located. Its forty-eight contiguous states are situated in the middle of North America. The mainland United States borders Canada to the north and Mexico, the Gulf of Mexico, and the Straits of Florida to the south. The western border meets the Pacific Ocean, and to the east lies the Atlantic Ocean.

Alaska and Hawaii are not joined to the other forty-eight states. Alaska is at the extreme north of North America, between the Pacific and Arctic oceans, and is bordered by Canada to the east. The island chain of Hawaii is situated in the east-central Pacific Ocean, about two thousand miles southwest of San Francisco.

Although Americans generally do not consider themselves an imperial or colonial power, the country has a number of commonwealths and territories, most of which were acquired through military conquest. These territories include Puerto Rico and the Virgin Islands in the Caribbean basin, and Guam, the Northern Mariana Islands, American Samoa, and Wake island in the Pacific.

United States

The physical environment is extremely diverse and often spectacular. Alaska's glaciers coexist with flowering tundras that bloom in the arctic summer. The forests of the Pacific Northwest and northern California are known for giant ancient trees such as Sitka spruce and sequoia (redwoods). Niagara Falls, Yellowstone National Park, and the Grand Canyon are a few of the better-known landscapes.

The physical regions of the country overlap both national boundaries and cultural regions. For example, the Atlantic coastal plain extends from New England to Mexico's Yucatan Peninsula. It is characterized by flooded river valleys that form major estuaries, such as the Chesapeake Bay.

The Appalachian Mountains span two cultural regions. Located to the west of the Atlantic coastal plain, they extend from the Middle Atlantic state of New York to the southeastern state of Georgia. The Appalachians are an old, eroded mountain range that is now heavily forested. It is possible to traverse the entire range by walking the two-thousand-mile Appalachian Trail.

The interior lowlands area also crosses regions and national borders. It includes the Midwestern corn belt and the Great Plains wheat-growing region. The Great Plains section of the interior lowlands stretches into Canada.

The Western Cordillera is part of a mountain chain that stretches from Chile in South America to Alaska. The highest peak in the country, Mount McKinley (Denali), is in the Western Cordillera in Alaska. The Western Intermontane Plateau, or Great Basin, crosses from the mountain states into the west.

Major navigable inland waterways include the Mississippi River, which cuts north to south through the east-central part of the country; the Great lakes in the upper Midwest, the largest freshwater lake group in the world; and the Saint Lawrence River.

The physical environment has had significant effects on regional cultures. The rich topsoil of the Midwest made it an important agricultural area; its rivers and lakes made it central to industrial development. However, settlers significantly transformed their environments, recreating the landscapes they had left behind in Europe. The vast prairies of the Great Plains, which were characterized by numerous species of tall grasses, have been transformed by irrigation and modern agricultural methods into continuous fields of soybeans and wheat. In the West, a series of pipelines and dams transformed Los Angeles and its desert surroundings into a giant oasis.

American settlers were not the first to transform these landscapes; native American groups also altered the lands on which they depended. Fire was used in hunting, and this expanded the prairie; irrigation was used in settled communities that practiced agriculture; and maize, a crop that cannot grow without human manipulation, was a staple crop.

The idea that the environment shapes culture or character does have cultural currency. Over a century ago, the historian Frederick Jackson Turner theorized that the American frontier experience had been instrumental in forming the rugged, independent, and democratic national character. Wilderness, independence, and democracy are common aspects of American symbolism.

Demography. The United States has a population of over 280 million (2000 census), but it is relatively sparsely populated. The most populous state, California, with 33,871,648 inhabitants, contrasts with Wyoming, which has only 493,782 residents.

These population figures reflect the fact that the United states is an urban nation. Over 75 percent of the inhabitants live in cities, among whom more than 50 percent are estimated to be suburban. Population growth is at below-replacement levels unless immigration is taken into account.

One of the most significant facts about the population is that its average age is on the rise. The baby boomers born in the period from the end of World War II until the early 1960s are beginning to get old.

Life expectancy is seventy-three years for white men and seventy-nine years for white women. African-American men have a life expectancy of sixty-seven years; in inner-city areas, the average life expectancy of African-American males is much lower. Infant mortality rates are higher among African-Americans than among whites.

U.S. Census categories identify populations according to whether they are of European descent (white). Whites constitute a large majority at about 70 percent of the population. According to current census figures, in the year 2000 the largest minority was blacks, who number about 35 million, or 13 percent of the population.

The Hispanic (Latino) population, which includes primarily people of Mexican, Puerto Rican, and Cuban (who may be any color) descent, is estimated to number 31 million, or 12 percent of the population. Latinos are expected to become the largest minority group early in the twenty-first century.

The Asian population (including Pacific Islanders) is defined as people of Chinese, Filipino, Japanese, Indian, Korean, and Vietnamese origin. It is estimated that there are eleven million Asians, making up about 4 percent of the population.

The Native American population, which includes natives of Alaska such as the Inuit and Aleuts, is estimated to consist of over two million people, slightly over 1 percent of the population. Roughly a third of Native Americans live on reservations, trust lands, territories, and mother lands under Native American jurisdiction.

Linguistic Affiliation. There is no official national language. If English is its unofficial first language, Spanish is its unofficial second language. The

United States ranks fifth in the world in the number of Spanish speakers.

Standard English is the language Americans are expected to speak. Within the social hierarchy of American English dialects, Standard English can be described as the exemplar of acceptable for correct usage based on the model of cultural, economic, and political leaders. There is no clear-cut definition of what Standard English is, and it is often defined by what it is not. For example, it often is contrasted with the type of English spoken by black Americans (African-American Vernacular English).

Standard English grammar and pronunciation are taught by English teachers in public schools. Like "whiteness," this implies a neutral, normative and nonethnic position. However, most Americans do not speak Standard English; instead, they speak a range of class, ethnic, and regional variants.

Spoken English includes many dialects that have been influenced by Native Americans, immigrants, and slaves. These languages include not only Dutch, German, and Scandinavian, Asian, and African languages, but less widely spoken languages such as Basque, Yiddish, and Greek. Thus, spoken English reflects the nation's immigration and history.

As linguistic diversity has increased, and particularly as Spanish has become more widely spoken, language has become an important aspect of the debate over the meaning or nature of American culture. Linguistic and cultural diversity is accepted in states such as New York and Illinois, where Spanish bilingual education is mandated in the public schools. In California, however, where tensions between Anglos and Mexican immigrants run high, bilingual education has been abolished in the public school systems. State laws prohibit even bilingual personnel from using Spanish with Spanish-speaking patients in hospitals or with students in schools.

Bilingual education is not new. In the nineteenth century, Germans outnumbered all other immigrant groups except for all the people from the British Isles combined. With the exception of Spanish speakers in the Southwest, at no other time has foreign language been so widely spoken. German-only newspapers and German and bilingual public schools were found throughout the Midwest and Oregon and Colorado and elsewhere from the mid-nineteenth century until World War I, when anti-German sentiment resulted in the elimination of German instruction in public schools.

Other languages used in the press and in public schools included Yiddish, Swedish, and Norwegian.

Thus, proponents of English only, who claim that bilingual education should not be provided to Spanish-speaking immigrants because earlier immigrants did not have this advantage, overlook the fact that those immigrants often were schooled in their native languages.

Education was important in spreading English as a standard language. Public schools played a major role; by 1870, every state in the country had committed itself to compulsory education. The percentage of foreign-born persons who were unable to speak English peaked 31 percent in 1910, by 1920 had decreased to 15 percent, and by 1930 had fallen less than 9 percent. Among Native Americans, English was enforced by the establishment by the Bureau of Indian Affairs of compulsory boarding schools for school-age children. Contemporary Native American speech patterns can be traced to that experience.

Symbolism. The flag is perhaps the most potent and contested national symbol. Made up of stars symbolizing the original thirteen colonies and fifty stripes representing the fifty states, it is displayed on national holidays such as Veterans Day, Memorial Day, Labor Day, and Independence Day. Public places and businesses raise the flag as a matter of course. Individuals who display the flag in their homes or yards make an explicit statement about their patriotic connection to the nation.

The flag is also employed frequently as a symbol of protest. In the nineteenth century, northern abolitionists hoisted the flag upside down to protest the return of an escaped slave to his southern owner, and upside-down flags continue to be used as a sign of protest. The use of the stars and stripes design of the flag in clothing, whether for fashion, humor, or protest, is controversial and is considered by some people to be akin to treason and by others to be an individual right in a state that upholds individual rights.

Nationalism and community solidarity frequently are expressed through sports. In the Olympic games, patriotic symbols abound, and victors are heralded for their American qualities of determination, individualism, and competitiveness. In the same way, football games connect fans to one another and to their communities through a home team. The game expresses the important value of competition: unlike soccer, American football games can never end in a tie. Football also reflects cultural ideals about sex and gender; the attire of players and cheerleaders exaggerates male and female sex characteristics.

Aerial view along the East River of New York City, one of the largest cities in the world and perhaps the most famous.

HISTORY AND ETHNIC RELATIONS

Emergence of the Nation. The first European settlements date from the early sixteenth century and included Spanish towns in Florida and California, French outposts in Louisiana, and British settlements in New England. The United States of America was declared in 1776 by colonists from England who wanted independence from that country and its elite representatives in the colonies.

The class, racial, ethnic, and gender relationships of the contemporary nation have their roots in the colonial period. Unsuccessful efforts by British settlers to enslave Native Americans were followed by the importation of African slaves to work on cotton plantations in the South and of white indentured servants to work in the emerging industries in the North.

British taxation fell disproportionately on poor white laborers and indentured servants. This sector was instrumental in organizing the protests and boycotts of British goods that culminated in the American Revolution. Women participated in the Revolution by running farms and businesses during the war.

The egalitarian rhetoric of the Revolution did not extend to slaves, and after independence, full citizenship rights did not extend to all whites. Men

and women who did not own property had no voting rights. (Women did not gain the right to vote until the early twentieth century.) The area west of the Appalachians was settled by poor whites seeking land and autonomy from wage labor.

After 1820, when poor white men gained the vote in most states, women began to see their own lack of political rights in a new way. Women's ability to connect their powerlessness to that of men in relationship to plantation owners made them active in the abolitionist movement. However, after the Civil War when freed male slaves, but not freed women or white women, were given the right to vote, the women's suffrage movement broke with the civil rights movement in the South.

State laws enacted in the South after the Civil War enforced racial separation by keeping freed men out of skilled and industrial jobs, limited their political rights through restrictive voting registration practices, and enforced segregation at all levels, including in housing and education.

Women were an essential part of the industrial labor force in the early years of the nation. Their work in textile manufacturing helped provide commodities for an expanding population and freed men to work in the agricultural sector. Women were active in labor union organizing in the nineteenth century.

A man holds trays of cooked lobster and corn on the cob at the annual Yarmouth Clam Festival in Yarmouth, Maine.

The emerging nation also was shaped by its territorial expansion. After the Revolution, the United States included only thirteen former British colonies in the Northeast and the Southeast. Territories to the west and south of the original colonies were acquired through later purchases and concessions. The most important of these acquisitions was the Louisiana Purchase of 1803, by which the country doubled its territory. This purchase signaled the beginning of western expansion beyond the Appalachians. It became the country's "manifest destiny" to expand from the eastern to the western shore.

During this time, the Indian wars that eventually subdued the major Native American groups and drove them west to reservation lands were waged. In 1838, President Andrew Jackson rounded up thousands of Cherokees from North Carolina and marched them to "Indian territory," then a large area that included Oklahoma. One of every four Cherokees died of cold, hunger, or disease, and the Cherokees named this march the Trail of Tears.

Another major expansion occurred after the Mexican-American War. In 1848, Mexico was compelled to sell its northern territories to the United States. The Treaty of Guadalupe-Hidalgo conceded California and what is now the Southwest, consid-erably expanding the continental United States and broadening its ethnic and linguistic profile.

In 1890, at the Battle of Wounded Knee, many of the Sioux were massacred, and the survivors were forced onto Pine Ridge Reservation. This battle marked the disappearance of the traditional Native American way of life. In the same year, the Census Bureau observed that the continental United States had been settled by whites in virtually every corner. The American frontier was considered closed.

National Identity. Often referred to as a melting pot, the United States is popularly regarded as a nation that assimilates or absorbs immigrant populations to produce a standard American. This is a powerful cultural idea. The word "American" conjures up an image of a person of white, middle-class status. All other residents, including the area's indigenous inhabitants, are "hyphenated" or characterized by an identifying adjective: African-American, Native American, Asian-American, Mexican-American. The national Census does not hyphenate Americans of European descent.

Huge waves of non-European immigration since the 1960s have made the United States the nation with the highest immigrant population in the world. This fact, combined with the many identity and civil rights movements that emerged in the 1960s and 1970s, has created a new kind of cultural politics that challenges the country's Anglo identity and power base.

Ethnic Relations. From colonial times, indentured servants and other poor whites constituted a buffer between landowners and slaves, who made up the bottom rung of the social ladder. Poor whites self-identified as white to associate themselves with the powerful landowning class rather than see their common interests with slaves. This process accentuated the dominance of white racial identity over class identity.

The "whiteness" of buffer groups has been ambiguous, changing along with their position in the labor market. Although now considered white, the Irish immigrants who arrived in great numbers in the early nineteenth century occupied the lowest rungs of the labor force next to slaves and often were referred to as "white niggers."

Between 1848, when lands from Mexico were annexed, and the 1930s, Americans of Mexican descent were classified as white. As Mexicans became important as laborers in the expanding agribusiness sector, those people were reclassified as Mexican-American. The large waves of immigrants who poured into the country from Southern and Eastern Europe between 1880 and World War I made up a new buffer group. This group included large numbers of Jews who did not come to be considered white for several generations.

Relationships among racial and ethnic groups have been mediated by this association between status, whiteness, and position in the labor market. Between 1916 and 1929, African-American laborers migrated to the North to work in industrial jobs. Paid less than whites for comparable jobs, they were regarded by white workers as union busters and scabs. African-Americans also received less than their share of the social benefits extended to whites after World War II. Federal programs for returning veterans included housing and educational subsidies. Most of these white groups considered their own ascension into the middle class as being the result of sweat and determination.

URBANISM, ARCHITECTURE, AND THE USE OF SPACE

The United States is an urban and suburban nation whose numerous cities each tell a story about its historical and economic development. New York, founded by the Dutch as a trading colony, was once the hunting and fishing grounds of Native Americans. It became an important industrial center in the nineteenth century, but by the mid-twentieth century its industries had declined and much of its middle class population had relocated to the suburbs. As the twenty-first century begins, New York is a ''global'' city resurrected from decline by its role as a center of finance in the world economy. Like New York, Chicago and Los Angeles have emerged as important cities in connected world.

Many cities are notable for their particular regional roles. Saint Louis, situated on the Missouri and Mississippi rivers, was an important transportation hub in the nineteenth century before railroads replaced riverboats as the most efficient form of travel. Once known as the ''Gateway to the West,'' it was the last outpost of civilization as the country expanded to the west. Today, it is possible to see the Arch, a monument to the expansionist past, from nearby Cahokia, which houses the ruins of one of the largest cities in the world of its time. Between 900 and 1300 C.E., this city built by the indigenous Mississippian culture was larger than most contemporary European cities.

In colonial times, cities were divided along racial and class lines. The row house, a series of attached dwellings, was a common form of housing. It symbolized the defensive posture of early settlers, whose enclaves protected them from the untamed wilderness and its Indian inhabitants. The elites lived in the central city, often with slave quarters behind their homes. The working classes and urban slaves who eventually were allowed to live apart from their masters resided in peripheral areas and the early suburbs. In early American cities, there was no separation between the workplace and the home. Most goods were produced by artisans who lived and worked in the same building. As the country industrialized, home and workplace became distinct.

During the nineteenth century, the suburb was transformed from a space for social outcasts and the lower classes to a space for the elite. A number of factors led to the suburbanization that is central to modern American life. A romantic engagement with the countryside arose as the frontier expanded to the west and the wilderness receded from view in the East. The noise and pollution of the industrialized cities of the nineteenth century, as well as the presence of the working classes, made them less attractive to the elites. These factors combined with a transportation revolution made possible by cable cars and railroads.

Cities were stopovers for new immigrants, who soon began to move to the suburbs, and the permanent domains of the working poor and, until recently, black Americans of all classes, who were kept out of suburbs through discriminatory real estate and zoning practices. Suburbs were organized along class and ethnic lines, and cities became the repositories of the most disadvantaged.

The early suburbs of the elite classes were characterized by large and architecturally unique homes. Beginning in the early twentieth century, federal subsidies such as deductible mortgage interest and loan programs made suburban living a possibility for working-class and middle-class immigrants. Standard designs and quick building methods resulted in uninspired architecture but relatively inexpensive housing.

The use of the automobile and the growth of highways made possible a nationwide suburban sprawl of which shopping malls and motels are ubiquitous reminders. Americans have a complex relationship to the suburb. On the one hand, it represents success, family life, and safety from the chaos and danger of the city, fulfilling the peculiarly American promise that every family should be able to own its own home. On the other hand, the monotony of this landscape is a metaphor for cultural conformity, social isolation, and racism.

Fishing boats are anchored in the Lafourche Bayou in Cajun Country, Louisiana. Fishing is an important part of the Lousiana economy.

For women, suburban life is particularly ambiguous. The suburb promises a large home and yard and a safe and healthy place in which to raise children, but the single-family home isolates women from the extended family networks and friends that make child rearing less onerous.

Suburbs are often referred to as bedroom communities, suggesting that suburbanites depend on a nearby city for employment, services, and cultural activities. However, the growth of suburban industries and services that allow suburbanites to work in their own communities points to the declining dependency of suburbs on city centers.

By the 1970s, white flight from the cities created an urban-suburban landscape aptly described as Chocolate City/Vanilla Suburb, referring to the racial separation of blacks and whites. Cities were mythologized in the popular imagination as wild and dangerous places riddled with crime, gang violence, and drugs. Young black males and welfare mothers were the symbols of social problems.

Beginning in the 1980s, young urban professionals began to "reclaim" the cities, rehabilitating the aging and often decrepit housing stock. This process of gentrification turns cities into the new American frontier, where professionals drawn to major financial centers such as New York and Los Angeles are the "pioneers" and black and Hispanic residents are the "Indians."

FOOD AND ECONOMY

Food in Daily Life. Americans eat large amounts of processed, convenience, and fast foods. The average diet is high in salt, fat, and refined carbohydrates. It is estimated that 60 percent of Americans are obese. The preference for packaged and processed foods is culturally rooted. Americans as a whole enjoy the taste of hamburgers, hot dogs, and junk foods. Processed foods generally are perceived to be cleaner or more safe than unprocessed foods.

Industrial food producers use advertising to associate processed foods with the desirable modern and industrial qualities of speed, cleanliness, and efficiency. Speed of preparation was essential in a nation of nuclear family households where wives and mothers did not have relatives to help them and usually were solely responsible for food preparation.

However, gourmet, regional, and alternative styles of eating are highly influential. Gourmet foods, including high quality fresh and local produce, imported cheeses, fine coffees, and European kinds of bread, are available in every city and in many towns.

Regional cuisines, from cheese steaks in Philadelphia to the green chili stews of New Mexico and the grits of the South, are culinary reminders that the country encapsulates many different traditions.

An alternative tradition is the health food movement, which includes a preference for unprocessed foods and fruits and vegetables that have not been chemically treated or genetically altered. Some health food proponents are concerned primarily with avoiding the heavily processed foods that make up the bulk of the traditional diet. Others also see the consumption of organic products, which generally are produced by small, labor-intensive farms, as a way to fight the ecological damage caused by agricultural chemicals and challenge the corporate nature of food production.

Food Customs at Ceremonial Occasions. Americans have few occasions that they term ceremonial. In the case of weddings, funerals, and other rites, few fixed food rules apply. Most weddings, whether religious or secular, include a large tiered cake. After the wedding, the newlyweds feed each other a piece of the cake. At Jewish funerals, fish, usually smoked or pickled, and eggs may be served as symbols of life's continuation. Some Americans, particularly in the South, eat hopping john, a dish made with black-eyed peas, to bring good luck in the New Year.

Americans have many fixed food rituals to accompany events and occasions not generally considered ceremonial. Waking up is accompanied by coffee. Social occasions usually include alcohol. Hot dogs and beer are ubiquitous at sporting events, and popcorn and candy are consumed at movie theaters.

Basic Economy. The United States has an advanced industrial economy that is highly mechanized. The gross national product is the largest in the world. The country more than meets its own economic needs and is the world's leading exporter of food. Moreover, it is a dominant force in world finance.

The major challenges facing the economy are to maintain profits by keeping production costs low and to increase consumer markets. Besides mechanizing production to reduce labor costs, firms subcontract production to less developed countries where those costs are much lower. At the same time, advertising firms that help market these goods to consumers at home and in other countries now constitute one of the biggest industries in the country.

The basic unit of currency is the dollar, with one hundred cents making one dollar.

Land Tenure and Property. Land tenure is based largely on private ownership, but the government owns an enormous amount of land. Private property is culturally valued, and this is best expressed in the high rate of home ownership. Historically, the United States was an agricultural nation, and it culturally has a romantic image of the small, independent farm family battling the elements on the prairie.

The ways in which federal lands were apportioned to settlers and developers constitutes a mixed legacy. Land grants made to pioneer families and the public universities in every state point to a democratic apportionment of land. However, many private companies gained access to large tracts of public lands. For example, federal land grants made to railroads in the nineteenth century resulted in the consolidation of wealth by railroad company directors who sold parcels of that land and by timber companies that bought large tracts of forested land from the railroads at low prices. Contemporary patterns of landholding in the Pacific Northwest reflect this legacy of land accumulation by a few large timber firms.

Commercial Activities. The vast majority of businesses are clustered within the service industry, including finance, advertising, tourism, and various professions.

Major Industries. Important manufacturing industries include petroleum, steel, motor vehicles, aerospace, telecommunications, chemicals, electronics, food processing, lumber, and mining.

The family farm is clearly on the decline. Most people who claim farming as their occupation work for an agricultural firm and do not own their own land. Since 1940, the United States has been the world's largest producer of wheat, corn, and soybeans, it produces over 40 percent of the world's corn and 45 percent of its soybeans. However, between 1940 and 1990, the number of farms fell from over six million to just over two million. Although occasional attention is paid to the ''plight of the family farm,'' the growth of agribusiness has not resulted in major overt conflicts because most Americans see corporate growth as the fair outcome of free enterprise and competition.

Tension arises in cases where property is publicly owned. During the nineteenth century, the federal government reserved large tracts of western land for federal and common uses. Logging or grazing on these lands is regulated and requires permits. During the sagebrush rebellion of the 1980s, private developers and ranchers who wanted free access to

Overview of a summertime baseball game between the Chicago Cubs and the Colorado Rockies at Chicago's Wrigley Field. Baseball is often referred to as the "national pasttime."

these lands claimed that federal restrictions on private property ownership were anti-American. The language of this rebellion resonated with westerners in poor rural areas who believed that the federal government was usurping valuable land at their expense.

Many environmental conflicts become battles between private developers and companies and the federal government. For example, endangered species are protected under federal rules. In the Pacific Northwest, this legislation mandated the protection of the spotted owl habitat, prohibiting logging in areas with owl nests. Loggers regarded owl protection as an assault on their livelihood and their constitutional right to private property.

Division of Labor. The labor force has always been divided on the basis of race, ethnicity, and gender. Skilled jobs in manufacturing and management jobs typically have been more accessible to white men than to black men or women of any race. Within the service industries, there is a technological divide. Blacks and other minorities fill low-skill jobs such as food service and are found less often in managerial positions or the growing hi-tech industries.

SOCIAL STRATIFICATION

Classes and Castes. Most Americans do not believe that theirs is a "class" society. There is a strong cultural belief in the reality of equal opportunity and economic mobility. Rags to riches stories abound, and gambling and lotteries are popular. However, there is evidence that mobility in most cases is limited: working-class people tend to stay in the working classes. Moreover, the top 1 percent of the population has made significant gains in wealth in the last few years. Similar gains have not been made by the poorest sectors. In general, it appears that the gap between rich and poor is growing.

Symbols of Social Stratification. Stratification is visible in many facets of daily life. The social segregation of blacks and whites in cities mirrors their separation in the labor force. The crumbling housing stock of blacks in the inner cities contrasts with giant homes in gated suburbs all across the country. Speech, manners, and dress also signal class position. With some exceptions, strong regional or Spanish accents are associated with working-class status.

POLITICAL LIFE

Government. The United States is a federal republic composed of a national government and fifty state governments. The political system is dominated by two parties: the Republicans and the Democrats. One of the features of American democracy is low voter turnout. On the average, less than half the eligible voters participate in federal elections.

Also referred to as conservatives and liberals, respectively, Republicans and Democrats differ on certain key social issues. Republicans are generally conservative on social spending and moral issues. They support cuts in federally-sponsored social programs such as welfare. They believe in strengthening institutions such as marriage and the traditional family and usually are opposed to abortion and gay rights. Democrats tend to support federal funding for social programs that favor minorities, the environment, and women's rights. However, critics argue that these two parties set a very narrow range for political debate. Third parties that have emerged on both the left and the right include the Green, Socialist, Farm-Labor, Reform, and Libertarian parties.

The powers and responsibilities of the Federal government are set out in the Constitution, which was adopted in 1789. The national government consists of three branches that are intended to provide "checks and balances" against abuses of power. These branches are the executive, the legislative, and the judicial. The executive branch includes the President and federal agencies that regulate everything from agriculture to the military. The legislative branch includes members elected to the upper and lower houses of Congress: the Senate and the House of Representatives. The judicial branch consists of the Supreme Court and the U.S. Court of Appeals. At the state level, government is designed along the same lines, with elected governors, senators, and assemblymen and state courts. The smallest unit of government is the county, which has an elected board, but not all states have a system of county governments.

With the exception of the President, officials are elected directly, on the basis of popular vote. The President is elected by the electoral college. Each state has as many electors as it has senators and representatives, the latter of which are awarded according to population. Electors vote as a bloc within each state. This means that all electoral votes in a state go to the candidate with the plurality of the popular vote within that state. A candidate must win 270 electoral votes to win the election. This system is controversial because it is possible for a President to win a national election without winning a national majority of the popular vote, as happened in the presidential election of 2000.

Leadership and Public Officials. With the exception of local-level offices, politics is highly professionalized: most people who run for political offices are lifelong politicians. Running for a high-level political office is extremely expensive; many politicians in the House and the Senate are wealthy. The expense of winning campaigns requires not only personal wealth, but corporate sponsorship in the form of donations.

Social Problems and Control. Although crime rates have decreased, the United States remains the most violent industrialized nation in the world. The capital city, Washington, D.C., has the highest per capita crime rate in the country. In the nation as a whole, African-Americans, the poor, and teenagers are the most common victims of violent and nonviolent crime.

The country has more people in prison and more people per capita in prison than any other industrialized nation. The prison population is well over one million. These numbers have increased since 1980 as a result of mandatory sentences for drug-related crimes. Although African-Americans make up only about 12 percent of the population, they outnumber white inmates in prison. Both African-American and Hispanic men are far more likely to be imprisoned than are white men. Although rates of imprisonment are on the rise for women, women are far less likely to be imprisoned than men of any race or ethnicity. The United States is also the only Western industrialized nation that allows capital punishment, and rates of execution for African-American men are higher than those of any other group.

Cities are perceived to be very dangerous, but crime rate is not consistently higher in urban areas than in rural areas. The elderly tend to be the most fearful of crime but are not its most common victims. Tough penalties for violent crime are often perceived to be a solution, and it is on this basis that the death penalty is defended. Interestingly, Florida and Arizona, which have the death penalty, have the highest rates of violent crime in the country.

The vast majority of crimes in all categories are committed by white males, but in popular culture and the popular imagination, violent criminal tendencies are often associated with African-American and Hispanic males. This perception legitimates a controversial practice called racial profiling, in

Exterior façade of the United States Capitol in Washington, D.C.

which African-American and Hispanic men are randomly stopped, questioned, or searched by police.

Historically, immigrant groups that constituted the urban "rabble" of their day were the subject of intense policing efforts and were believed to have propensities for vice and crime.

Military Activity. The country has officially been at peace since World War II but has unofficially been in almost continuous military conflict. These conflicts have included frequent interventions in Central and South America, the Middle East, and Africa. During the period between the end of World War II and the breakup of the Soviet Union (1989), military interventions frequently involved Cold War motivations. Since that time, the country has used its military forces against Iraq and has supported efforts by other governments to fight the drug war in Central America.

SOCIAL WELFARE AND CHANGE PROGRAMS

The Great Depression, which lasted from 1929 until World War II, posed a real threat to the legitimacy of the American economic model in the eyes of citizens. During that period, President Franklin Delano Roosevelt established a series of social programs collectively known as the New Deal. Many of those programs, including government-backed pension programs, banking insurance, and unemployment benefits, are still in place. These programs, which were intended to provide a buffer against the inevitable downturns of economic cycles, were also a response to serious social unrest, including strikes and socialist organizing.

Americans generally are not opposed to social benefits such as social security pensions and the insurance of bank deposits. However, general relief programs for the poor, known popularly as welfare, have been very controversial. In a country that believes that all its citizens have an equal chance, where opportunity is unlimited, and where only the lazy are poor, programs for mothers and children and the indigent have been vulnerable to cutbacks. Recently, the federal government made sweeping reforms to the welfare laws that require mothers on welfare to work in order to receive benefits.

NONGOVERNMENTAL ORGANIZATIONS AND OTHER ASSOCIATIONS

Nongovernmental organizations (NGOS) are not as influential as they are in less wealthy nations. Among the NGOs that operate within the country, the most notable is Amnesty International, which has made both political prisoners and torture within American prisons major issues in recent years.

More influential than NGOs are the many nonprofit institutions. These groups are not associated with government agencies or corporate interests. They include a wide spectrum of advocacy and public interest groups that deal with consumer, environmental, and social justice issues. Nonprofits are a main locus for alternative views and left-wing politics. Examples include the American Civil Liberties Union, the various Public Interest Research Groups, Fairness and Accuracy in the Media, Planned Parenthood, and the National Organization of Women.

GENDER ROLES AND STATUSES

Division of Labor by Gender. Although most women work outside the home, household and child-rearing responsibilities are still overwhelmingly the responsibility of women. The "double day" of women consists of working and then returning home to do domestic chores. This situation persists in spite of the cultural belief that men and women are equal. Studies carried out in middle-class homes, in which couples claim to share household duties, show that women still do the vast majority of domestic work. Although young women as a whole spend much less time on domestic chores than their mothers did, this is attributable not to the fact that men do a significant share of domestic work, but to the fact that women spend less time cooking, cleaning, and caring for children than they did in the past.

Women are paid seventy cents to every male dollar for comparable jobs. Occupations continue to be defined along gender lines. Secretarial or low-level administrative jobs are so overwhelmingly female that they have been termed pink-collar jobs. In the white-collar world, women often occupy middle-management positions. With a few exceptions, the "glass ceiling" keeps women out of high management positions. This situation is justified on the grounds that women take time from their working lives to raise children and therefore do not spend the same amount of time developing their working careers that men do. Occupations requiring nurturing skills, such as teaching and nursing, are still predominantly female.

Within the blue-collar sector, women are underrepresented in jobs considered to require physical strength, such as the construction industries and firefighting. Women often fill low-paid positions in industry, such as assembly-line work, sewing, and electronics assembly. This is justified on the basis that women are by nature more dextrous and that their small hands suit them to assembly-line work. It is more likely that the low wages offered by these factories explains the recruitment of female laborers, whose other options may include even less desirable seasonal and temporary work.

The Relative Status of Women and Men. In legal terms, women have the same formal rights as men. They can vote, own property, choose to marry or divorce, and demand equal wages for equal work. They also have access to birth control and abortion. The status of women in relation to men is very high compared to the situation in many other countries.

However, women as a whole do not receive the same social and economic benefits as men. Women are greatly underrepresented in elected political offices and are more likely to live in poverty. Female occupations both in the home and in the workplace are valued less than men's. Women are more likely than men to suffer from a sense of disempowerment and to have a distorted or low self-image.

MARRIAGE, FAMILY, AND KINSHIP

Marriage. Marriage is formally a civil institution but is commonly performed in a church. Statistically, marriage appears to be on the decline. Half of all adults are unmarried, including those who have never married and those who are divorced. Rates of marriage are higher among whites than among blacks.

With the exception of Vermont, civil unions are legal only between heterosexual adults. However, gay marriages are increasingly common whether or not they are formally recognized by the state. Some religious denominations and churches recognize and perform gay marriages. The high rate of divorce and remarriage has also increased the importance of stepfamilies.

Domestic Unit. The typical model of the family is the nuclear family consisting of two parents and their children. Upon marriage, adult couples are expected to form their own household separate from either of their biological families. The nuclear family is the cultural ideal but is not always the reality. Immigrant groups have been reported to rely on extended family networks for support. Similarly, among African-American families, where adult males are often absent, extended kin ties are crucial for women raising children.

Inheritance. Americans trace their ancestry and inherit through both the maternal and paternal lines. Surnames are most commonly adopted through the paternal line, with children taking the father's name. Women usually adopt the husband's surname upon marriage, but it is increasingly common for women to keep their own surnames and for the children to use both the father's and the mother's last names.

Kin Groups. Family can refer to a nuclear family group or an extended kin group. The "ideal" family consists of a mother, a father, and two or three children. Americans often distinguish between blood relatives and relatives through marriage; blood relatives are considered more important. Ties among nuclear families generally are closer than ties among extended family members. Adoption is common, but reproductive technologies that allow infertile couples and gay couples to reproduce are highly valued. This reflects the importance of the concept of biological kinship in the culture.

Alternative models of family life are important in American life. A great deal of scholarship has addressed the historical and economic conditions

A snow-capped mountain rises above an old barn in the Mission Range Valley, Montana. The landscape of the U.S. is extremely diverse and often spectacular.

that have led to a high proportion of female-headed households and the incorporation of nonrelated members into family units among African-Americans. However, these trends are on the rise in the population as a whole. A significant number of Americans of all ethnic backgrounds live in nontra-ditional families. These families may consist of un-married couples or single parents, gay couples and their children, or gay families without children.

SOCIALIZATION

Infant Care. Infant care varies by class. In New York City, it is common to see women of Domini-can and West Indian descent caring for white chil-dren. Wealthy people often employ nannies to care for infants. Nannies, who often have children of their own, may have to rely on family members or their older children to watch over their infants. Wealthy or poor, the majority of mothers work outside the home. This, coupled with the fact that many people cannot rely on their extended families to help care for their newborns, makes infant care a challenge. Some employers offer short maternity leaves for mothers and increasingly, paternity leaves for fathers who are primary caregivers.

Child Rearing and Education. Child rearing practices are diverse, but some common challenges apply to all families. It is common to put children in day care programs at an early age. For wealthy families, this entails finding the most elite day care centers; for less wealthy families, it may involve finding scarce places in federally-funded programs. For all working families, day care can be a cause of anxiety and guilt. Negative media stories about child abuse at these centers spoke more to these anxieties than to the actual quality of care. The country makes few provisions for the care of young children considering the fact that most mothers work outside the home.

From age five to age eighteen, public schooling is provided by the state and is universally available. School is mandatory for children until the age of sixteen. Public school education in suburban areas and small cities and towns is usually adequate or excellent.

Inner-city schools are underfunded and have a high proportion of minority students. This reflects a history of white flight to the suburbs and a system in which schools are funded through local property taxes. Thus, in cities abandoned by wealthier whites, both tax bases and school funding have declined. The reputation of inner-city schools is so poor that families that live in cities send their children to private schools if they can afford it. Private schools are mostly white enclaves.

Access to equal education has long been an issue for African-Americans. Until the Supreme Court struck down the doctrine of "separate but equal" in 1954, all educational institutions in the South were segregated on the basis of race. However, the legally permitted segregation of the past has been replaced by the de facto segregation of the present.

Higher Education. The level of educational achievement is high. Most Americans complete high school, and almost half receive at least some college education. Almost one-quarter of the population has completed four or more years of college. Rates of graduation from high school and college attendance are significantly lower for African-Americans and Hispanics than for whites.

The quality and availability of colleges and universities are excellent, but a university education is not funded by the state as it is in many Western industrialized nations. The cost of higher education has soared and ranges from a few thousand dollars annually at public institutions to more than ten thousand dollars a year at private institutions. In elite private colleges, the cost of tuition exceeds $20,000 a year.

Among the middle classes, paying for college is a source of anxiety for parents from the moment their children are born. Students from middle-income and low-income families often pay for college with student loans, and the size of these debts is on the increase.

ETIQUETTE

Personal comportment often appears crass, loud, and effusive to people from other cultures, but Americans value emotional and bodily restraint. The permanent smile and unrelenting enthusiasm of the stereotypical American may mask strong emotions whose expression is not acceptable. Bodily restraint is expressed through the relatively large physical distance people maintain with each other, especially men. Breast-feeding, yawning, and passing gas in public are considered rude. Americans consider it impolite to talk about money and age.

RELIGION

Religious Beliefs. The overwhelming majority of the people are Christian. Catholicism is the largest single denomination, but Protestants of all denominations (Baptist, Methodist, Lutheran, Presbyterian, and others) outnumber Catholics. Judaism is the largest non-Christian faith, followed by Islam, which has a significant African-American following. Baptism, the largest Protestant sect, originated in Europe but grew exponentially in the United States, especially in the South, among both whites and blacks. Aside from the many Christian movements from England and Europe that reestablished themselves early in the nation's history, a few religious sects arose independently in the United States, including Mormons and Shakers.

Although religion and the state are formally separated, religious expression is an important aspect of public and political life. Nearly every President has professed some variety of Christian faith. One of the most significant religious trends in recent years has been the rise of evangelical and fundamentalist sects of Christianity. As an organized po-

Ranchers herding cattle in the Salt Lake Valley, Utah.

litical–religious force, fundamentalist Christians significantly influence political agendas.

Another trend is the growth in New Age religions, which blend elements of Eastern religions and practices, such as Buddhism, with meditation, yoga, astrology, and Native American spirituality.

Religious Practitioners. In addition to the practitioners of world religions such as priests, ministers, and rabbis, the United States has a tradition of nonordained and nontraditional religious practitioners. These people include evangelical lay preachers, religious leaders associated with New Age religions, and leaders of religious movements designated as cults. Women are increasingly entering traditionally male religious positions. There are now women ministers in many Protestant denominations and women rabbis.

Rituals and Holy Places. The country does not have religious rituals or designated holy places that have meaning to the population as a whole. However, Salt Lake City is a holy city for Mormons, and the Black Hills of South Dakota and other places are sacred native American sites.

There are many shared secular rituals and places that have an almost religious importance. Secular rituals include baseball and football games. Championship games in these sports, the World Se-

ries and the Super Bowl, respectively, constitute major annual events and celebrations. Important places include Disneyland, Hollywood, and Graceland (Elvis Presley's estate).

Death and the Afterlife. Americans have an uncomfortable relationship with their own mortality. Although most residents are Christian, the value placed on youth, vigor, and worldly goods is so great that death is one of the most difficult subjects to talk about.

Death is considered a sad and solemn occasion. At funerals, it is customary to wear black and to speak in hushed tones. Graveyards are solemn and quiet places. Some people believe in an afterlife or in reincarnation or other form of continuity of energy or spirit.

MEDICINE AND HEALTH CARE

The dominant approach to medicine is biomedical, or Western. Although many people are interested in alternative approaches such as acupuncture, homeopathic medicine, and other therapies, the United States continues to be less medically diverse than most other countries. Biomedicine is characterized by the frequent use of invasive surgeries such as cesarean sections and high doses of psychotropic drugs. With the exception of limited government care for the elderly and the disabled, health care is private and profit-based. This makes the United States distinct from other wealthy, industrial nations, nearly all of which provide universal health-care coverage.

SECULAR CELEBRATIONS

A number of secular national holidays are celebrated but are regarded less as celebrations of patriotism than as family holidays. The fireworks displays of the Fourth of July mark the Declaration of Independence from Britain in 1776, but this is also a time for summer outings such as picnics and camping trips with friends and family members.

Thanksgiving is part of the national history that is understood by every schoolchild. This annual feast celebrates the hardships of the early colonists, who were starving in their new environment. According to the legend, American Indians came to their aid, sharing indigenous foods such as maize and turkey. Thanksgiving is important not primarily because of its symbolism but because it is the most significant family holiday of the year, one of the few large and elaborate meals that families prepare.

THE ARTS AND HUMANITIES

Support for the Arts. The level of public support for the arts is much lower than it is in other wealthy nations. Patronage for unknown individual artists, writers, and performers is scarce. The National Endowment for the Arts (NEA) has a very small operating budget with which it funds everything from public broadcasting to individual artists. In recent years, the NEA has been under attack from Congress, whose conservative members question the value and often the morality of the art produced with NEA grants.

Support also comes from private donations. These donations are tax-deductible and are a popular hedge among the wealthy against income and estate taxes. Generous gifts to prestigious museums, galleries, symphonies, and operas that often name halls and galleries after their donors are essential means of subsidizing the arts.

Literature. Much of American literature revolves around questions of the nature or defining characteristics of the nation and attempts to discern or describe the national identity. American literature found its own voice in the nineteenth century. In the early decades of that century, the essayists Henry David Thoreau and Ralph Waldo Emerson set out the enduring themes of personal simplicity, the continuity between man and nature, individualism, and self-reliance. Walt Whitman celebrated democracy in his free verse poems.

Other nineteenth-century writers, such as Herman Melville, Emily Dickinson, Nathaniel Hawthorne, and Mark Twain, articulated moral and ethical questions about the new country and were particularly influential for their critique of American puritanism.

Turn-of-the-century writers such as Edith Wharton, Henry James, and Theodore Dreiser picked up on those themes but were particularly concerned with social class and class mobility. They explored the nature of American culture and the tensions between ideals of freedom and the realities of social conditions.

In the early decades of the twentieth century, writers such as F. Scott Fitzgerald and Ernest Hemingway began to question the values earlier writers had represented. Fitzgerald questioned the reality of the American dream by highlighting the corrupting influence of wealth and casting doubt on the value of mobility and success. Hemingway, like other modernists, addressed the issue of how one ought to live once one has lost faith in religious values and other social guidelines. Other early twentieth-century writers, such as Zora Neil Hurston, Nella Larsen, and William Faulkner, introduced race and racism as central themes in American literature.

In the 1930s, the Great Depression inspired authors such as John Steinbeck and Willa Cather to write about rural America. Their novels romanticized the hard work of poor rural whites. Implicit in these novels is a critique of the wealth and excess of the urban metropolis and the industrial system that supported it. Although these novels are permeated with multiethnic characters and themes, Anglos are generally the focal point.

Issues of identity and race were explored by earlier American black writers. A generation of black authors after World War II made these permanent themes in American literature, illustrating the poverty, inequality and racism experienced by American blacks. Many black writers explored the meaning of living inside a black skin in a white nation with a legacy of slavery. These writers included James Baldwin, Ralph Ellison, and Richard Wright. Perhaps the most influential contemporary writer who deals with these themes is Toni Morrison.

An important literary school known as Southern Gothic discussed the nature of rural southern

A tractor harvesting crops in the western United States. The U.S. is the world's leading food exporter.

life from the perspective of poor and middle-class whites. Writers such as Truman Capote, Tennessee Williams, Carson McCullers, and Shirley Jackson explored the contradictions between privileged whiteness and a culturally deficient southernness. These novels feature lonely, grotesque, and underprivileged white characters who are the superiors of their black playmates, servants, and neighbors but cultural inferiors in America as a whole.

Beginning in the late 1950s and 1960s, a generation known as the Beats challenged the dominant norms of white American masculinity. They rejected conventions of family and sexuality, corporate success, and money. Among the Beats were William Burroughs, Lawrence Ferlingetti, Allan Ginsberg, and Jack Kerouac.

Starting in the 1960s, women writers began to challenge the notion that women's place was in the home. Early feminist writers who critiqued the paternalism of marriage include the nonfiction writer Betty Friedan, the novelist Marge Piercy, and the poets Anne Sexton and Sylvia Plath.

Feminist themes, along with issues of ethnicity and otherness, continue to be important in American literature. Gloria Anzuldúa and Ana Castillo show how female and Latina identities intersect. Novels by Louise Erdrich and Leslie Marmon Silko illustrate how Native American families attempt to

survive and reclaim their traditions amid poverty and discrimination.

Other contemporary novels try to deconstruct the experience of the "norm" in American culture. Ann Tyler's characters are often empty and unhappy but cannot locate the sources of those feelings. Don Delillo writes about the amoral corporate world, the American obsession with consumer goods, and the chaos and anxiety that underlie the quietness of suburban life. Joyce Carol Oates is attracted to the sinister aspects of social conformity.

These novels are not the most widely read looks in the United States. Much more popular are genres such as crime and adventure, romance, horror, and science fiction. These genres tend to repeat valued cultural narratives. For example, the novels of Tom Clancy feature the United States as the moral victor in cold war and post–Cold War terrorist scenarios. Harlequin romances idealize traditional male and female gender roles and always have a happy ending. In horror novels, violence allows for catharsis among readers. Much science fiction revolves around technical-scientific solutions to human problems.

Graphic Arts. The most influential visual artists are from the modern period. Much early art was imitative of European styles. Important artists include Jackson Pollack and Andy Warhol. Warhol's art documented icons of American life such as Cambell's soup cans and Marilyn Monroe. His work was deliberately amusing and commercial. Most graphic art is produced for the advertising industry.

Performance Arts. Performance arts include many original genres of modern dancing that have influenced by classical forms as well as American traditions, such as jazz. Important innovators in dance include Isadora Duncan, Martha Graham, and Alvin Ailey. Theaters in every town that once hosted plays, vaudeville, and musicals now show movies or have closed. In general, performance arts are available only in metropolitan areas.

The United States has produced several popular music genres that are known for blending regional, European, and African influences. The best known of these genres are the African-American inventions blues and jazz. Among the most important jazz composers and musicians are Louis Armstrong, Duke Ellington, Miles Davis, John Coltrane, and Thelonius Monk. Although now considered classics, blues and jazz standards were the popular music of their day.

Music fits into "black" and "white" categories. Popular swing jazz tunes were standardized by band leaders such as Glenn Miller, whose white band made swing music hugely popular with young white people.

Rock 'n' roll, now a major cultural export, has its roots in these earlier popular forms. Major influences in rock and roll include Elvis Presley, Jimi Hendrix, Janis Joplin, and Bruce Springstein. Although rock 'n' roll is primarily white, soul and Motown, with singers such as Aretha Franklin, the Supremes, and the Temptations, produced a popular black music.

Country music, another popular genre, has its roots in the early American folk music of the Southeast now termed country or bluegrass. This genre reworked traditional gospel songs and hymns to produce songs about the everyday life of poor whites in the rural Southeast.

Popular music in the United States has always embodied a division between its commercial and entertainment value and its intellectual or political values. Country and folk, blues, rock 'n' roll, rap, and hip-hop have all carried powerful social and political messages. As old forms become standard and commercialized, their political edge tends to give way to more generic content, such as love songs.

THE STATE OF THE PHYSICAL AND SOCIAL SCIENCES

The United States is a leading producer and exporter of scientific knowledge and technology. Major areas of scientific research include medicine, energy, chemicals, weapons, aerospace technology, and communications. Funding for research comes from government agencies and universities as well as the private corporate sector.

The role of private corporations in research is controversial. Pharmaceutical companies often fund research that leads to cures and treatments for diseases. One consequence is a dearth of research on diseases particular to poor countries. Another consequence is that medicines are marketed at costs that are prohibitive to the poor both inside and outside of the country.

In the face of technology and science as being culturally valued, an increasing cause of social concern is the fact that American schoolchildren do not do well on standardized tests in the sciences.

BIBLIOGRAPHY

Alvarez, Robert R. "The Foundations and Genesis of a Mexican-American Community: A Sociohistorical Perspective." In Leigh Mullings, ed., *Cities of the United States*, 1987.

Asbury, Herbert. *The Gangs of New York*, 1928.

Baer, Hans A., Singer Merrill, and Ida Susser. *Medical Anthropology and the World System: A Critical Perspective*, 1997.

Baker, Lee D. "The Color-Blind Bind." In Ida Susser and Thomas C. Patterson, eds., *Cultural Diversity in the United States*, 2000.

Bolles, A. Lynn. "Perspectives on U.S. Kinship: The Phoenix Rises from the Ashes." In Ida Susser and Thomas C. Patterson, eds., *Cultural Diversity in the United States*, 2000.

Brodkin, Karen. "Diversity in Anthropological Theory." In Ida Susser and Thomas C. Patterson, eds., *Cultural Diversity in the United States*, 2000.

———. "How Did Jews Become White Folks?" In Steven Gregory and Roger Sanjek, eds., *Race*, 1996.

Brown, Dee. *Bury My Heart at Wounded Knee: An Indian History of the American West*, 1981.

Cawley, R. McGreggor. *Federal Land, Western Anger: The Sagebrush Rebellion and Environmental Politics*, 1993.

Chan, Sucheng, et al., *Peoples of Color in the American West*, 1994.

Conklin, Nancy Faires, and Margaret A. Lourie. *A Host of Tongues: Language Communities in the United States*, 1983.

Cronon, William, ed. *Uncommon Ground: Rethinking the Human Place in Nature*, 1996.

Crystal, David. *The Cambridge Encyclopedia of Language*, 1987, revised edition 1997.

Davis, Mike. *City of Quartz: Excavating the Future in Los Angeles*, 1990.

Diamond, Sara. *Roads to Dominion: Right–Wing Movements and Political Power in the U.S.*, 1995.

Fishman, Robert. *Bourgeois Utopias: The Rise and Fall of Suburbia*, 1987.

Garreau, Joel. *The Nine Nations of North America*, 1981.

———. *Edge City: Life on the New Urban Frontier*, 1991.

Ginsberg, Faye, and Anna Lowenhaupt Tsing, eds. *Uncertain terms: Negotiating Gender in American Culture*, 1990.

Gregory, Steven, and Roger Sanjek, eds. *Race*, 1994.

Hazen-Hammond, Susan. *Timelines of Native American History*, 1997.

Hibbard, Michael, and James Elias. "The Failure of Sustained–Yield Forestry and the Decline of the Flannel-Shirt Frontier." In Thomas A. Lyson and William W. Falk, eds., *Forgotten Places: Uneven Development in Rural America*, 1993.

Jackson, Kenneth T. *Crabgrass Frontier: The Suburbanization of the United States*, 1985.

Lauter, Paul, et al. *The Heath Anthology of American Literature*, 1998.

Mitchell, Robert D., and Paul A. Groves, eds. *North America: The Historical Geography of a Changing Continent*, 1987.

Morgen, Sandra, ed. *Gender and Anthropology: Critical Reviews for Research and Teaching*, 1989.

Nash, June. *From Tank Town to High Tech: The Clash of Community and Industrial Cycles*, 1989.

Patterson, Thomas C. "Class and Historical Process in the United States." In Ida Susser and Thomas C. Patterson, eds., *Cultural Diversity in the United States*, 2000.

Piven, Francis Fox. *Why Americans Don't Vote*, 1988.

Ripetto, Robert, and Malcolm Gillis, eds. *Public Policies and the Misuse of Forest Resources*, 1988.

Robbins, Richard H. *Cultural Anthropology: A Problem-Based Approach*, 1997.

Rodriguez, Gregory. "Do the Multiracial Count?"

Rodriguez, Sylvia. "Land, Water and Ethnic Identity in Taos." In Charles Briggs and John Van Ness, eds., *Land, Water and Culture: New Perspectives on Hispanic Land Grants*, 1987.

Rosman, Abraham, and Paula G. Rubel. *The Tapestry of Culture: An Introduction to Cultural Anthropology*, 2001.

Sassen, Saskia. *The Global City*, 1991.

Smith, Neil. *The New Urban Frontier: Gentrification and the Revanchist City*, 1996.

Susser, Ida. "Gender in the Anthropology of the United States." In Morgen, Sandra ed., *Gender and Anthropology: Critical Reviews for Research and Teaching*, 1989.

———, and Thomas C. Patterson, eds. *Cultural Diversity in the United States*, 2000.

Turner, Frederick Jackson. *Frontier and Section: Selected Essays of Frederick Jackson Turner*, 1961.

Urciuoli, Bonnie. "The Complex Diversity of Language in the United States." In Ida Susser and Thomas C. Patterson, eds., *Cultural Diversity in the United States*, 2000.

White, Richard. "The Altered Landscape: Social Change and the Land in the Pacific Northwest." In William G. Robbins, Robert J. Frank, and Richard E. Ross, eds., *Regionalism and the Pacific Northwest*, 1983.

Winn, Peter. *The Americas: The Changing Face of Latin America and the Caribbean*, 1992.

Wright, John W., ed. *The New York Times 1999 Almanac*, 1998.

Zinn, Howard. *A People's History of the United States*, 1980.

Web Sites

Salon.com, http://www.salon.com/news/feature/2000/02/15/census

U.S. Department of the Census. http://www.census.gov

—Molly Doane

UNITED STATES VIRGIN ISLANDS

CULTURE NAME
Virgin Islander

ALTERNATIVE NAMES
Cruzan or Crucian (Saint Croix); Thomian (Saint Thomas)

ORIENTATION

Identification. In 1493, Christopher Columbus landed on an island he named Santa Cruz. Driven away by the Carib Indians, he sailed northward to a nearby group of islands he called *Las Once Mil Virgenes*, in honor of Saint Ursula. The French took Santa Cruz from Spain in 1650, renaming it Saint Croix. The towns of Christiansted and Frederiksted on Saint Croix and Charlotte Amalie, the capital, on Saint Thomas were founded by the Danes and named after Danish royalty.

Location and Geography. The country lies seventy miles east of Puerto Rico, in the Lesser Antilles of the Caribbean, and is composed of three large and fifty small islands totaling 136 square miles (352 square kilometers). Saint Croix, the southernmost and largest island, has land suitable for agriculture. Saint Thomas, forty miles to the north, has the highest point on the islands, with little tillable land. With a good port at Charlotte Amalie, it became a commercial center with reliance on the slave trade. The smallest of the main islands, Saint John, was donated by Laurence Rockefeller in 1956 as a national park. In 1996, Water Island, off the southern coast of Saint Thomas, was officially added to the country.

Demography. In 1999, the population was estimated at 120,000. The main population groups are West Indian (74 percent born in the Virgin Island,s and 29 percent born elsewhere), United States mainland (13 percent), Puerto Rican (5 percent) and others (8 percent). Blacks constitute 80 percent of the population, whites 15 percent, and others 5 percent.

Linguistic Affiliation. English is the official language. A Dutch Creole, Negerhollands, arose in the seventeenth century on Saint Thomas from interactions between Dutch planters and African slaves and spread to Saint John and Saint Croix. In the next century, German missionaries translated the Bible into that language. With emancipation and the influx of English Creole speakers from other islands, the use of Dutch Creole declined. An English Creole arose on Saint Croix and is still spoken, although its use is generally limited to older islanders. The United States takeover in 1917 resulted in American English becoming the standard administrative, educational, and economic language. "Virgin Islands English," which retains some Creole features, is widely used in personal and informal situations. Spanish has become increasingly important because of immigration from nearby islands; Spanish speakers make up 35 percent of the population of Saint Croix.

Symbolism. The territorial bird is the indigenous yellow breast, and the territorial flower is the yellow elder, commonly called "Ginger Thomas." The flag, adopted in 1921, is white with a yellow American eagle grasping three arrows in its left talon and with an olive branch in its right, between the blue initials "V" and "I." On its breast is a shield of the United States.

HISTORY AND ETHNIC RELATIONS

Emergence of the Nation. By 1600, the native population had been wiped out by the Spanish. The Dutch and English settled on Saint Croix, with the Dutch being driven out around 1645. The French and the Knights of Malta took possession from Spain; Denmark, which had established slave plantations on Saint Thomas and Saint John, purchased Saint Croix from France in 1733. Although Den-

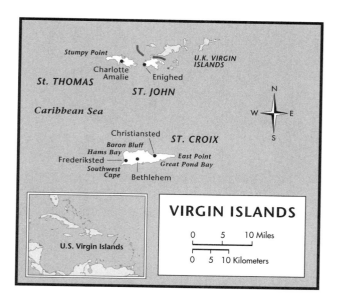

U.S. Virgin Islands

mark suppressed the slave trade in 1803, the practice did not end until the British occupied the islands in 1807. The islands were returned to Denmark in 1815 and remained the Danish West Indies until their purchase by the United States in 1917. Originally under the control of the navy, they passed to the Department of the Interior in 1954.

National Identity. Many documents from the colonial period are in Denmark, not accessible to residents seeking to study the country's history. Since 1917, there has been a lot of migration to and from the islands to other parts of the Caribbean and to the mainland; until recently, less than half of the population was native-born. People emphasize the variety of cultures in the islands, and the advantage of being both ''U.S.'' and ''Caribbean.''

Ethnic Relations. The first elected black governor in the United States, Melvin Evans, took office in 1970. Relations between ethnic groups are generally good, although there has been some racial violence.

URBANISM, ARCHITECTURE, AND THE USE OF SPACE

Several cultures have influenced local architecture. Wattle and daub construction, the use of cisterns to collect water, the ''Big Yard'' or common area, and verandas and porches can be traced to Africa. Danish culture is reflected in the design of towns, especially the ''step streets''; street names; ovens and cookhouses; and red roofs. Yellow ballast brick, carried in ships from Europe, was used in construction

along with locally quarried stone and coral. Open market areas, formerly the sites of slave markets, are found in the main towns. Many urban buildings date back to the colonial period.

FOOD AND ECONOMY

Food in Daily Life. Cassava, pumpkins, and sweet potatoes are native to the islands, and a variety of seafood is found in the surrounding waters. Many recipes are based on African sources. Okra is an ingredient in killaloo, a stew with local greens and fish, and in fungi, a cornmeal-based side dish; conch appears in fritters, chowders, and mixed with rice. Guava, soursop, and mango are eaten, along with mamey and mesple.

Food Customs at Ceremonial Occasions. Sugar cakes made with coconut and boiled sugar, are a traditional midafternoon snack. Maubi, a local drink, is made from the bark of a tree, herbs, and yeast. Souse is a stew of pig's head, tail, and feet, flavored with lime juice that is served on festive occasions.

Basic Economy. Per capita income is high, but the cost of living is expensive and there is constant pressure for new jobs. A major economic problem at the beginning of 1997 was the high level of governmental debt; since that time, expenditures have been cut, revenues have been increased, and fiscal stability has been restored. An increase in the tax on rum is expected to increase revenues. The islands' lack of natural resources makes them dependent on imports for local consumption and later reexportation. The basic unit of currency is the U.S. dollar.

Commercial Activities. The retail sector, including hotels, bars, restaurants, and jewelry stores, accounts for nearly half of the islands' revenues. The service sector is the largest employer; a small but growing area is financial services. Construction increased after the hurricanes of 1995. Tourism is the primary economic activity, accounting for more than 70 percent of the gross-domestic product and 70 percent of employment. Around two million tourists visit the islands annually; two-thirds are cruiseship passengers, but air visitors account for the majority of tourism revenue. Agriculture has declined in importance.

Major Industries. Manufacturing consists of textile, electronics, pharmaceutical, and watch assembly plants. Saint Croix has one of the world's largest oil refineries and an aluminum smelter. The need to rebuild after hurricanes has caused an upsurge in the construction industry.

Trade. Imports include crude oil, food, consumer goods, and building materials. The major source of export revenue is refined petroleum, with manufactured goods contributing a significant amount. The major trading partners are the United States and Puerto Rico.

SOCIAL STRATIFICATION

Classes and Castes. Historically, the society was divided along caste and color lines. Even after emancipation in 1848, ex-slaves' participation in the political process was restricted and their freedom of movement and emigration were limited by legislation. A result of Danish determination to maintain the status quo was the Fireburn of 1878, a labor revolt on Saint Croix that destroyed many plantations.

Symbols of Social Stratification. The use of Standard English characterizes the upper classes. Children often use native forms at home and speak Standard English at school. A higher percentage of males speak dialect than do females. The use of dialect is considered an important part of the culture but an impediment to educational and economic mobility.

POLITICAL LIFE

Government. Congress established the government through the Revised Organic Act of 1954. The Office of Insular Affairs of the U.S. Department of the Interior administers the islands. The governor and lieutenant governor are elected by popular vote for four-year terms. There is a fifteen-seat Senate whose members are elected for two-year terms. The islands elect one representative to the U.S. House of Representatives who may vote in committees and subcommittees. Virgin Islands citizens do not vote in United States' presidential elections. The judicial branch is composed of the U.S. District Court, with judges appointed by the President, and the Territorial Court, with judges appointed by the governor.

Leadership and Political Officials. The current governor and the current representative to the U.S. House are both Democrats. In the Senate, the Democratic Party holds six seats and the Republican Party and the Independent Citizens Movement have two seats each; the remaining five seats are held by independents.

Social Problems and Control. The high cost of living and the low pay scale for service sector jobs have created widespread discontent. Saint Croix has seen drive-by shootings, but most crime is property-related. To protect tourism, the government has increased the law enforcement budget. Local officials work with the Drug Enforcement Agency, Customs, and the Coast Guard to combat the illegal drug trade.

SOCIAL WELFARE AND CHANGE PROGRAMS

The Department of Human Services attempts to provide for the needs of low-income persons, the elderly, children and families, and the disabled.

NONGOVERNMENTAL ORGANIZATIONS AND OTHER ASSOCIATIONS

The Saint Croix Foundation is active in community development and has established anticrime initiatives. Environmental associations on the three main islands promote ecological awareness, sponsor guided outings, and encourage responsible legislation.

GENDER ROLES AND STATUSES

Division of Labor by Gender. Women are increasing their participation in the economic and political areas. The U.S. Small Business Administration established the Virgin Islands Women's Business Center in 1999 to encourage and train women business owners. The heroine of the 1878 labor rebellion in Saint Croix was "Queen Mary," a canefield worker. The current Senate president and the presiding judge of the Territorial Court are women.

MARRIAGE, FAMILY, AND KINSHIP

Marriage. One in three families is headed by a single female parent. The rate of unmarried teenage pregnancy is increasing and is a major social concern. Wedding customs range from the traditional African "jump the broom" to European-influenced church ceremonies.

Domestic Unit. According to 1995 census data, married couples comprise 57 percent of households and unmarried females with children, 34 percent. The average household has two children.

Inheritance. The concept of jointly owned "family land" accommodates the pattern of alternately settling down and moving that has characterized the lives of many families since colonial times.

Boats in the Charlotte Amalie Harbor, Saint Thomas. Two million tourists visit the islands annually; two-thirds of them are cruiseship passengers.

SOCIALIZATION

Infant Care. Women are responsible for infant care. Breast-feeding is supplemented by formula given in bottles; the use of formula results in early weaning. In more traditional households, folk beliefs about infant care, including the use of "bush tea" to induce sleep, are common.

Child Rearing and Education. A "bogeyman" is used as a threat to correct children's bad behavior. Education is compulsory and free. Multicultural education is seen as a necessity, but there is growing concern about the public schools, and those who can afford private schools generally choose that alternative. A higher percentage of females than males finish high school.

Higher Education. The University of the Virgin Islands, founded in 1962, has campuses on Saint Thomas and Saint Croix. It offers bachelor's degrees in a number of areas and master's degrees in business administration and public administration.

ETIQUETTE

Politeness is considered important. Children are told to address adults as "sir" or "ma'am." Visitors are encouraged to smile, use greetings, and maintain a courteous attitude.

RELIGION

Religious Beliefs. The predominant religious affiliations are Baptist (42 percent), Catholic (34 percent), and Episcopalian (17 percent). Remnants of African culture are found in the belief in spirits.

Religious Practitioners. Under Danish rule, the Lutheran church was the state church; to practice any other religion, an official permit had to be granted. Permits were granted fairly easily, and sermons were not censored. With the coming of the Americans in 1917, the Catholic Redemptorists became the predominant religious order, and Catholicism was a major force through the 1940s, in terms of the influence which priests wielded over parishioners.

Rituals and Holy Places. Saint Thomas has the second oldest synagogue in the New World. Lord God of Sabaoth Lutheran Church and the Friedensthal Moravian Church on Saint Croix are the oldest congregations of their kind in the United States. To commemorate their freedom in 1848,

The colonial style architecture of Charlotte Amalie, Saint Thomas. European and African cultures have influenced local architecture.

former slaves built the All Saints Cathedral. The Arawak Indian carvings on Saint John may have religious significance.

MEDICINE AND HEALTH CARE

There are hospitals on Saint Croix and Saint Thomas and a clinic on Saint John. Alternative healing methods are widely used, such as faith healing, chiropractic, and traditional "bush" remedies based on indigenous plants.

SECULAR CELEBRATIONS

Legal holidays include 1 January, New Year's Day; 6 January, Three Kings Day; 15 January, Martin Luther King Day; President's Day on the third Monday in February; Memorial Day on the last Monday in May; Independence Day, 4 July; Veterans Day, 11 November; and Thanksgiving.

Legal holidays commemorating local events include Transfer Day (from Denmark to the United States in 1917); 31 March, Organic Act Day; Virgin Islands/Danish West Indies Emancipation Day, 3 July; and D. Hamilton Jackson Day on 1 November. Carnival was officially reinstated in 1952 and is

celebrated at different times. Carnival celebrations include parades, floats, stilt walking "Mocko Jumbies," steel pan competitions, beauty contests, and food fairs.

THE ARTS AND HUMANITIES

Support for the Arts. A nine-member Arts Council and a thirteen-member Historic Preservation Commission are appointed by the governor. Community arts groups exist on all three islands, with private support from a number of sources.

Literature. *The Caribbean Writer,* sponsored by the University of the Virgin Islands, showcases local writers. Lezmore Emanuel, a folk composer and poet; the literary historians Adelbert Anduze and Marvin Williams; and the poets Gerwyn Todman, Cyril Creque, J. P. Gimenez, and J. Antonio Jarvis have all made significant contributions.

Graphic Arts. The most famous locally born painter, Camille Pissaro, was born on Saint Thomas but moved to Paris. A number of contemporary artists work outside the country. Tourist preference has influenced the development of visual arts; Caribbean themes predominate in local galleries, such as the Caribbean Museum Center on Saint Croix.

Performance Arts. Mocko Jumbie stilt dancers perform at festivals and celebrations. Mocko Jumbies are masked and wear straw hats with cutouts for the eyes and mouth. This clothing was traditionally a woman's dress, but long trousers have become an acceptable part of the costume. The figure symbolizes the spirit world, and so the entire body must be disguised. Small decorative mirrors are worn to indicate invisibility. The stilts give the dancer additional height to frighten away evil spirits and also allow the Mocko Jumbie to chase misbehaving children and to keep crowds back from parade routes.

The Reichhold Center for the Arts, the Island Center Theater, and the Caribbean Community Theater give dance, music, and theater performances. Groups such as the Saint Croix Heritage Dancers and the Caribbean Dance Company preserve and teach traditional folk dances, many with African roots. The traditional folk dance, the quadrille, dates back to eighteenth century European settlers.

THE STATE OF THE PHYSICAL AND SOCIAL SCIENCES

The University of the Virgin Islands maintains an Agricultural Experiment Station, a Cooperative Extension Service, and the William P. MacLean Marine Science Center. Its Eastern Caribbean Center conducts social, survey, and environmental research. The Virgin Islands Ecological Research Station on Saint John provides support services for visiting scientists and students.

BIBLIOGRAPHY

Corbett, Karen Suzanne. "An Ethnographic Field Study of Infant Feeding Practices in St. Croix, United States Virgin Islands." Ph.D. dissertation, University of Texas, Austin, 1989.

Domingo, Jannette O. "Employment, Income and Economic Identity in the U.S. Virgin Islands." *Review of Black Political Economy* 18 (1):37–57, 1989.

Fallon, Joseph E. "The Ambiguous Status of the U.S. Insular Territories." *The Journal of Social, Political and Economic Studies* 23 (2):189–208, 1998.

Jno-Finn, John. "The Current State of Multicultural Education in the Virgin Islands." Ph.D. dissertation, Vanderbilt University, 1997.

Martel, Arlene R. *USVI: America's Virgin Islands*, 1998.

Nicholls, Robert W. "The Mocko Jumbie of the U.S. Virgin Islands: History and Antecedents." *African Arts* 32 (3): 48–71, 1999.

Olwig, Karen Fog. "Caribbean Place Identity: From Family Land to Region and Beyond." *Identities* 5 (4): 435–67, 1999.

Richards, Heraldo Victor. "An Investigation of the Relationship between Virgin Islands English Creole Usage and Reading Achievement among Third, Fifth, and Seventh Graders in the United States Virgin Islands." Ph.D. dissertation, Northwestern University, 1993.

Simmonds, Ruby. "The Words Beneath the Sand: An Examination of the Works of Three Virgin Islands Poets." Doctor of Arts in Humanities dissertation, Clark Atlanta University, 1995.

Willocks, Harold. *The Umbilical Cord: The History of the United States Virgin Islands*, 1995.

———. *Massacre in Paradise*, 1997.

Web Sites

Caribbean Writer, http://www.uvi.edu/CaribbeanWriter

Government of the U.S. Virgin Islands. *Virgin Islands Blue Book*, http://www.gov.vi

Highfield, Arnold R. "Myths and Realities in Virgin Islands History," "The Origins of the Christmas Festival Celebration on St. Croix," and "Toward a Language History of the U.S. Virgin Islands," http://www.sover.net/~ahighfi/indexwrarh.html

"United States Virgin Islands: America's Caribbean Paradise," http://www.usvi.net

—SUSAN W. PETERS

URUGUAY

CULTURE NAME

Uruguayan

ORIENTATION

Identification. The name Oriental Republic of Uruguay *República Oriental del Uruguay*, derives from the fact that the country lies east of the Uruguay River, a major tributary of the Rio de la Plata estuary. Before independence, it was known as *Banda Oriental del Uruguay*. The name "Uruguay" is a Guaraní word meaning "river of shellfish," or "river the uru birds come from."

Uruguayans have a strong sense of national identity and patriotism. There are no alternative traditions or nationalities within the country.

Location and Geography. Uruguay is on the southeastern Atlantic coast of the Southern Cone of South America, bordering Argentina to the west and south and Brazil to the north. The Atlantic Ocean is on the east and the estuary of the Río de la Plata is on the south. The land area is about 68,020 square miles (176,220 kilometers).

Most of the country consists of gently rolling plains interrupted by two ridges of low hills. The remainder consists of fertile coastal and riverine lowlands, including a narrow sandy and marshy coastal plain. The many beaches are an important tourist attraction.

The climate is generally mild, and freezing temperatures are almost unknown. Because of the absence of mountains, all the regions are vulnerable to rapid changes in weather.

Grasslands and agricultural lands cover the majority of the country. There are also some limited extensions of gallery forests and palm tree savannas. The main cultural differences are related to rural (9 percent) versus urban populations (91 percent), and whether people live in the capital or the interior towns. The country is divided into nineteen administrative *departamentos*, each with a capital town. About half of the population lives in the capital, Montevideo, and its metropolitan area.

Demography. The total population is approximately 3.3 million. About half of the population lives in the capital, Montevideo, and its metropolitan area. The second largest city, Salto, has ninety thousand inhabitants. Much of the hinterland is very sparsely populated. As a result of emigration, there could be as many people of Uruguayan descent living outside as inside the country.

Most of the indigenous population was exterminated by the nineteenth century, and those who survived were assimilated. The ethnic composition of the population is 90 percent European (predominantly Spanish and Italian), and 6 percent of the people are partly of Native American descent. Africans, 4 percent of the population, mainly in Montevideo, were imported as slaves to work in the ports, in the processing of meat and hides, and as servants.

Linguistic Affiliation. The prevalent language is a variety of Spanish known as *Rioplatense* or *Platellano*. In rural areas, *gauchesco/criollo*, the creole dialect spoken by the eighteenth- and nineteenth-century gauchos, is still influential. *Gauchesco* has been preserved in literature, music, and jokes, and is part of the national identity. Along the Brazilian border, a local dialect called *portuñol* or *brasilero* is spoken. It is a mixture of Spanish and Portuguese. English has influenced the language of technology and the slang used by young people.

Symbolism. The color sky-blue (*celeste*) is a powerful symbol that represents freedom and independence. It is present in the four horizontal stripes of the flag that alternate with five white ones (a sun with a face in the upper corner also symbolizes independence). It is also the color worn by the national soccer team.

Soccer is the national sport and occupies a central place in the life of the nation. The entire popula-

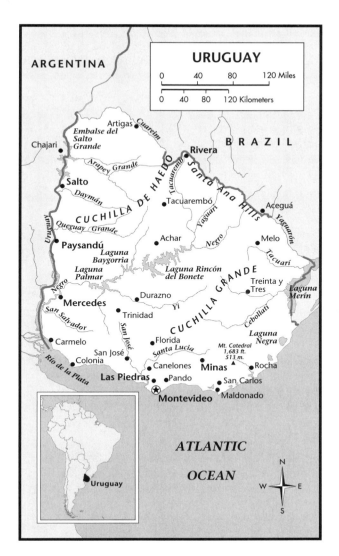

Uruguay

they were equestrian hunters of cattle for hides, beef or salting, and horses for riding. Later they traded in contraband, worked on the cattle and sheep ranches, and served as militia during the struggle for independence and as mercenaries for post-independence *caudillos.* The gaucho image has become the embodiment of the national character. The idealized gaucho is strong, brave, loyal, proud but humble, honorable, generous, straightforward, clever, patient, wise but melancholic from hardship, and free and independent. The Charrúa, a dominant fierce and independent regional First Nation, although annihilated by the Europeans, is imagined to still live in the spirit of the gaucho mestizo and the Uruguayans (who sometimes called themselves ''charruas'').

The national flower is the *ceibo* and the most symbolically significant tree is the *ombu.* The *tero-tero* bird is a common literary symbol for the audacious, bold, attentive, and vivacious nature of the gaucho.

Another important symbol is the historical figure of José Gervasio Artigas, who is considered the father of independence and political nationalism. All political parties refer to Artigas in their platforms. Artigas' flag is still used as a patriotic symbol and was adopted by the Tupamaros. The number 33 has nationalistic connotations, being related to the 33 Patriots (*Los 33 Orientales*), a group that fought for independence.

HISTORY AND ETHNIC RELATIONS

Emergence of the Nation. The colonial period from 1516 to 1810 was characterized by a struggle for control of the area by Spain and Portugal, with minor incursions by the British and French. It was during this time that Montevideo was founded (1726). Between 1811 and 1827, during the wars of independence, the formation of the national identity materialized around the epics of Artigas and the 33 Orientales. In 1828, Uruguay gained independence as a buffer state between Argentina and Brazil. Until the early twentieth century, the country engaged in an internal contest for political power through civil wars, dictatorships, and *caudillismo.* Polarization of the contending factions resulted in the formation of two opposing parties: the Blancos and Colorados.

In the early 1900s, under the leadership of President José Batlle y Ordóñez, the nation achieved political stability and implemented social reforms. A period of prosperity that lasted until about 1950 transformed the country into ''the Switzerland of South America.'' Change in the international markets and an oversized government created economic

tion is united behind the national combined team, but fans' allegiance is divided among the rival local teams (Peñarol and nacional are the most popular ones). Many figures of speech and cultural metaphors revolve around soccer.

Another central symbolic element is the figure of the gaucho. The original gauchos were an equestrian ethnic group similar to North American cowboys and Ukrainian Cossacks. Cattle and horses introduced by the Spanish in the sixteenth and seventeenth centuries multiplied in the grasslands and roamed freely over the land. Some Spaniards became seminomadic exploiters of this resource, and local native residents also learned to ride horses and live off wild cattle.

Gauchos originated as mestizos in these prairies (*pampas*) of southern South America. Originally,

hardship in the 1960s. Political instability ensued and, compounded by civil unrest and the appearance of the Tupamaro guerrilla movement, culminated in a coup and a military dictatorship in 1973. The new democratic period started with the 1984 presidential election. Since that time, the Blancos and Colorados have alternated in controlling the presidency.

National Identity. The national identity is a historical blend resulting from the struggle to maintain freedom from Spain and later from Argentina and Brazil, the gaucho culture, African slave roots, political *caudillismo;* and a European cultural and intellectual model.

Ethnic Relations. Uruguayans maintain harmonious ethnic relations internally and externally. They are well received in neighboring Argentina and Brazil as tourists and immigrants, and there are no ethnic tensions within the country.

URBANISM, ARCHITECTURE AND THE USE OF SPACE

Montevideo is a modern city with a European flavor. The character of the old part of the city, which was originally within a defensive stone wall, has been preserved to some extent. There are many parks, some very large. Public spaces follow the Spanish model and are open to everyone. Brick and mortar and concrete and stone are the dominant construction materials.

The urban centers in the interior are much less imposing and lively. Of note are the historic quarters of Colonia del Sacramento (founded in 1680 by the Portuguese), which UNESCO has declared a World Heritage City. The beach resort towns and cities are modern and active in the summer; Punta del Este has become a center for international meetings, golf tournaments, and film festivals. In remote rural areas, some gauchos still live in the traditional *rancho,* a simple adobe construction with a thatched roof.

FOOD AND ECONOMY

Food in Daily Life. Meat, particularly beef, is the mainstay of the diet. The national dish is the *asado* (barbecued meat). The *parrillada* (beef and entrails) is the most typical dish. It contains a varied assortment of parts, the most common being beef ribs, kidneys, salivary glands or sweetbreads (*mollejas*), small intestine (*chinchulines*) or large intestine (*tripa gorda*), and sweet blood pudding sausage (*morcilla dulce*). Pork sausage usually is served as an appetizer. Barbecued lamb is consumed in large quantities, particularly in rural areas. At rural banquets, entire cows are barbecued slowly with their hides.

As a result of Italian immigration in the late 1800s and early 1900s, pasta is a national food. Sunday is the preferred day for eating pasta. Most home cooking has a Spanish influence, and meals almost invariably include soup.

A standard fast food is *chivito,* a substantial steak sandwich. Another unique snack is wedges of *fainá* a chickpea flour pancake.

People eat a lot of bread and ship biscuits (*galleta marina*), mostly made of white flour, and many consume dairy products, including the national dessert, *dulce de leche.* Other popular desserts are pastries, milk and egg pudding, and rice pudding.

Mate which is a strong tea-like beverage made by infusing coarsely ground leaves of *Yerba Mate* with hot water in a gourd and sipped through a metal straw with a terminal filter (*bombilla*), is drunk at home, at work, at the beach, at soccer games and in public places. Coffee is drunk as espresso or with milk. Tea usually is drunk with milk.

Breakfast is a light meal. Traditionally, lunch and dinner are the main meals. Wine and beer commonly accompany the main meals.

Food Customs at Ceremonial Occasions. More elaborate meals are eaten at anniversaries, birthdays, promotions, and other special occasions. People take advantage of any event or occasion to eat their favorite dishes or have an outdoor barbecue. The most important special meal of the year is the Christmas Eve dinner.

Basic Economy. Services and export-oriented herding and agricultural production and industry, a relatively even distribution of income, and high levels of social spending characterize the economy. The main natural resources are pastures (more than 75 percent of the land), agriculture (10 percent of the land), hydro power, and fisheries. Mineral resources are scanty, and the country does not produce petroleum.

From the earliest period of settlement, the economy offered few employment opportunities, for it was dominated by the exploitation of grazing livestock. Large ranches (*estancias*), were overseen by a small number of herdsmen under the supervision of a steward. In many cases the landlord was absent most of the time, living in an urban center. Raw

Spanish-style plazas are a common meeting place for Uruguayans.

Commercial Activities. The major agricultural products are wheat, rice, barley, corn, sorghum, sugarcane, potatoes, and fruits. The bulk of livestock are cattle, sheep, and horses. Pigs, chickens, turkeys, and rabbits are also significant. Fishery is a major economic activity, and there is some mussel aquaculture and seal harvesting. The major exports are meat, leather products, wool, rice, dairy products, and hydroelectric power. The main imports are vehicles, electrical machinery, metals, heavy industrial machinery, and crude petroleum.

There is a good highway system and some railroads and waterways. There are ports and harbors at Montevideo, Colonia, Punta del Este, Fray Bentos, Nueva Palmira, Paysandu, and Piriapolis.

Major Industries. Industry became a significant factor in the economy in the second half of the twentieth century. This sector manufactures primarily food products, petroleum products, alcoholic (mainly beer and wine) and nonalcoholic beverages, chemicals and chemical products, textiles, clothing, hydraulic cement, gypsum, tobacco products, electrical appliances, and transportation equipment.

Trade. Uruguay is part of the Mercado Común del Sur (Mercosur) free-trade area. Almost half the country's exports go to Argentina and Brazil. Other significant export recipients are the European Union countries (20 percent) and the United States (7 percent). Imports come mainly from the Mercosur partners (43 percent), the European Union (20 percent) and the United States (11 percent).

Division of Labor. Among people 14 to 55 years old, 61 percent are economically active. Among those working, 12 percent are in the primary sector, 25 percent in the secondary sector, and 63 percent in the tertiary sector. Schooling is obligatory, and children are not in the workforce.

Jobs in rural areas often are obtained though historical connections among families or through the system of *compadrazgo*, in which the children of rural workers are given a godfather or godmother from the local elite when they are baptized. The father and the godfather become *compadres*, and the mother and godmother become *comadres*. This symbolic kinship system is intended to assure help later if the child becomes an orphan and for preferential treatment in employment. The obligations of the godchild include loyalty in disputes with neighbors and voting.

Industrial jobs are supposedly granted on the basis of qualifications, but since major industries

wool and beef still represent about a third of exports by value, but sheep and cattle products account for more than 90 percent of exports.

Three-fifths of the economic output is produced by a well-educated workforce in the service sector, mainly in public services and tourism. As a result of welfare state social policies and political favors in the past, there is a disproportionate number of public servants and retired citizens, and only around 32 percent of the population is economically active.

The government owns and operates the railroads, the national airline, a shipping fleet, the telephone and telegraph system, petroleum and alcohol refining and processing, and the cement industry. However, privatization has become more prevalent. The currency is the peso. The exchange rate fluctuates, sometimes markedly.

Land Tenure and Property. Most land is privately owned, and more than half the territory is divided into large landed ranches that belong to a few families. These properties began to be fenced after the introduction of wool-producing sheep. Historically, land was obtained through titles given by Spanish and Portuguese representatives, distributed by caudillos, or informally occupied. Legal land titles now are registered.

are government-owned, many openings are filled through partisan connections with the political party in power. This practice is particularly important in appointments for public positions. This has resulted in an oversized government workforce.

SOCIAL STRATIFICATION

Classes and Castes. Uruguay has long had a high standard of living, and its social, religious, political, and labor conditions are among the freest in South America. The state has provided universal free education since the late 1870s. However, there is social polarization; 13 percent of people in Montevideo and 16 percent in the interior live below the poverty line, and the unemployment rate is high. The relatively small upper class includes the ranching, business, professional, and political elites.

The two major minorities—the mestizos and the African-Uruguayans—are overwhelmingly in the low and lower-middle classes. During the wars for independence and later struggles for power, those ethnic groups were recruited into the militias, and they still often join the armed forces. Many African-Uruguayans are employed in domestic service or work as musicians and entertainers. There is no overt bigotry against minorities.

Symbols of Social Stratification. Montevideans stress their closeness to Europeans in appearance and life styles. Upper-class and middle-class people are very conscious of grooming and dress. In rural areas, many people still wear gaucho-influenced clothing. There is an inverse correlation between social class and the use of slang and *gauchesco* words. Car ownership is still seen as a social class symbol, and being a fan of certain soccer clubs also is said to be related to social class. Belonging to exclusive clubs is a symbol of social status. Where people spend their summer vacations and the beaches they go to are also related to social status.

POLITICAL LIFE

Government. Uruguay is a republic characterized by the presence of representative democracy at all levels of government; elections are held every five years. People are generally well informed about politics, and voting is compulsory after the age of eighteen. The election for president is unique in that the primaries and the voting occur simultaneously. People vote for candidates on open lists from each party; those who receive the most votes are the official candidates, and the presidency goes to the party with an absolute majority of votes.

The executive branch consists of a president and twelve appointed ministers. The legislative branch consists of a bicameral general assembly with ninety-nine representatives and thirty senators and the vice president. The Supreme Court is the highest body in a judicial branch based on Spanish civil law.

Leadership and Political Officials. The major political forces are the mostly centrist Colorado Party (currently in power), the center to right Blanco or Nacional Party (strong in rural areas), and a coalition of leftist parties, the "Broad Front," which dominates the municipal government of the capital.

Social Problems and Control. Before the 1970s, Uruguay was known as the freest and safest South American country, with an exemplary judiciary system. During the military dictatorship (1973–1985), personal and human rights were suspended, and formal social control was directed at suppressing "subversive" activities. As a result, many thousands of people left the country as political refugees, and many who stayed were imprisoned, tortured, or killed by the police and the military. After democracy was reestablished, the country returned to the previous system of social control.

Military Activity. Military expenditures were high during the dictatorship of the 1970s and 1980s. At the present time, those expenditures are much lower (less than 1 percent of the GDP). The Navy and Air Force are very small and military service is not compulsory.

SOCIAL WELFARE AND CHANGE PROGRAMS

Because of its achievements in social security, public education, and health care in the first half of the twentieth century, Uruguay is known as Latin America's "first welfare nation." After the economy entered a period of decline, the growth of the government and public bureaucracy continued. The retirement of these public servants has created a disproportionate number of pensioners, and the country has gained the nickname *El País de los Jubilados* ("The Country of Pensioners").

GENDER ROLES AND STATUSES

Division of Labor by Gender. There is a very high proportion of women in the labor force. Legally, men and women have equal rights to power, authority, and privileges. However, an overwhelming majority of the higher economic, professional, po-

A house on Paseo de San Gabriel. Novo Colonia do Sacramento is a UNESCO World Heritage City.

litical, social, and religious positions are held by men.

MARRIAGE, FAMILY, AND KINSHIP

Marriage. Official marriages have been civil since 1837; marriages are not arranged and are monogamous. About 48 percent of persons older than 15 years old are married, 10 percent live together, 28 percent are single, 4 percent are divorced, 2 percent are separated, and 8 percent are widows and widowers. Serial polygamy is accepted but is not common.

Domestic Unit. Although the typical domestic unit is a nuclear family with one of two children plus the grandparents, extended family networks usually are preserved. Large family reunions are held at least once a year. Authority in the household is divided between the husband and the wife. Many couples live with the parents of the husband or wife, and it is not uncommon for a widowed grandmother to assume the role of a matriarch. Children stay at home until late in life, but older widows and widowers increasingly live alone, to the point where the government has identified old age isolation as a major social and health problem.

Inheritance. Inheritance follows the European ambilinear tradition.

Kin Groups. There are no other kin groups besides the nuclear and informal extended family, except for the symbolic kin system of *compadrazgo*.

SOCIALIZATION

Infant Care. Customary practices of infant care and child rearing are essentially identical to those of Europe. It is common for the mother to leave the work force in order to do dedicate more time to child rearing, frequently with the help of grandmothers. Day care centers (*guarderias*) are not as widespread as in the United States.

Child Rearing and Education. Since the 1870s, primary education and secondary education have been based on the French model. Religion was banned from public schools in 1909. All public primary school children wear a white coat and a blue ribbon as a tie. Private school children wear uniforms, that are similar to those in British schools.

Public education is free at all levels, including the university level. This has resulted in an extremely high literacy rate; under 4 percent of males and 3 percent of females older than age ten are illiterate. The average number of years of study per adult is nine to ten.

Higher Education. A university education is highly valued. There are three universities. The Universidad de La República is public and free and specializes in the natural, physical, and medical sciences. The Universidad Católica, which is run privately by the Catholic Church, specializes in the social sciences. The Universidad ORT, associated with the Jewish ORT constructivist educational movement, specializes in technical studies. There are active links with Argentinean and Brazilian universities.

ETIQUETTE

Uruguayans are quite traditional and do not welcome criticism from foreigners. They also do not appreciate being confused with Paraguayans or Argentineans. Otherwise, people are friendly and easygoing. Although tactful, people are frank and direct and maintain a close distance when speaking. Close acquaintances of the opposite sex greet each other with one kiss on the cheek.

A national behavioral particularity is the conspicuous "following gaze" that males direct to females to indicate that they are attractive. In many cases this is accompanied by verbal expressions called *piropos*, which are sometimes abusive and usually are ignored.

RELIGION

Religious Beliefs. The church and state have been officially separated since 1917. The constitution protects religious freedom, but people are not devout and daily life is highly secular. More than one-third of the people profess no religion. Approximately 60 percent of the population is nominally Catholic, but only a minority attend church regularly (mostly those in the upper classes). Recently, the Padre Pio revitalization movement has been a source of converts for the Catholic Church.

The Jewish community, which once constituted about 2 percent of the population, is dwindling because of emigration to Israel. There is also a small proportion of people who practice African-derived religions. Protestants represent less than 4 percent of the population.

MEDICINE AND HEALTH CARE

Cardiovascular diseases are the leading cause of death, and hypertension is among the primary causes for medical visits. Dietary factors are implicated in this pattern: fat consumption is very high, and fiber intake is low. A high prevalence of obesity is associated with a high incidence of diabetes. Cancer accounts for 23 percent of all deaths. The high rate of lung cancer is related to the prevalence of smoking, particularly among men. Alcoholism is a problem among men age twenty to forty-nine years, which is associated with a high prevalence of cirrhosis of the liver.

Approximately 60 percent of the population is covered by private nonprofit collective health care associations known as *mutualistas*. Free coverage through the Ministry of Public Health covers approximately 20 percent of the population, and military and/or police or private company insurance covers approximately 10 percent. The rest of the population has no formal coverage.

Complementary and alternative medicine has not been practiced traditionally. However, in recent years this pattern has been changing (e.g., acupuncture, homeopathy, and herbal medicine).

SECULAR CELEBRATIONS

Traditional Catholic holidays have been secularized and renamed. For example, Christmas is called Family Day and Holy Week is called Tourism Week.

Holidays also celebrated in other Latin American countries include New Year's Day, Carnaval, Worker's Day (1 May), the Day of the Americas (12 October), and the Day of the Deceased (2 November). Holidays related to the nation's history are the 33 Patriots Day (19 April), Battle of Las Piedras (18 May), José Artigas's Birthday (19 June), Constitution Day (18 July), and Independence Day (25 August).

THE ARTS AND HUMANITIES

Support for the Arts. Artists are self-supporting, but receive some funding from the government and private institutions. The *Ateneo de Montevideo* is a meeting place for those involved in artistic and humanistic activities.

Literature. Among the most important writers are José Enrique Rodó, a philosophical essayist; Juan Zorrilla de San Martín, the author of *Tabaré*, an epic poem about a heroic Charrúa mestizo; Horacio Quiroga, a modernist short story writer; and José Alonso y Trelles, who wrote about the gauchos. Female poets include Delmira Agustini and Juana de Ibarbourou. More recent writers include Mario Ben-

The gaucho is symbolic of the Uruguayan nationality. Rural gauchos still wear the traditional garb as seen above.

edetti, Eduardo Galeano, and Juan Carlos Onetti and Tessa Bridal (who wrote the novel *The Tree of Red Stars*, a depiction of the national culture in the 1960 and 1970s).

Graphic Arts. There are many museums and galleries. Some of the best known painters are Juan Manuel Blanes, a realist known for historical paintings and gaucho motifs; Pedro Figari, a postimpressionist who specialized in bucolic colonial and early twentieth-century scenes (including aspects of black Uruguayans' life); and Joaquín Torres Garcia, a constructivist. Renowned sculptors include José Belloni, José Luis Zorrilla de San Martín, and Edmundo Prati.

Performance Arts. The Teatro Solis and the El Galpón theater are important sites for theatrical and musical presentations. Among classical composers, Eduardo Fabini is the best known internationally. Many musical and dance traditions derive from Europe, with local variations. Others are native to Uruguay and Argentina, particularly the tango. Uruguay was the birthplace of Carlos Gardel, the most famous interpreter of the tango.

There are many folkloric musical styles and dances, such as *Pericón* (the national dance). Another important musical style is *candombe*. This is a typical Afro-Uruguayan musical style played with three kinds of drums. These drums are crafted individually, and each is said to have a unique sound. Candombe can be heard throughout Montevideo during the February Carnaval, when ensembles of marching drummers cruise the streets. *Llamadas* are parades of competing groups of dancers who move to the rhythm of the candombe (the public is also welcome to join the dancers). These events are typical of the neighborhoods where most Afro-Montevideans live. Carnaval includes other cultural expressions, such as *murgas* which are musical groups that make fun of the social and political events of the year.

THE STATE OF THE PHYSICAL AND SOCIAL SCIENCES

Most research in the sciences and humanities is done in the universities, museums, and government institutions. Research budgets are clearly insufficient.

BIBLIOGRAPHY

Davis, William C. *Warnings from the Far South, Democracy versus Dictatorship in Uruguay, Argentina, and Chile*, 1995.

Ferguson, J. Halcro. *The River Plate Republics, Argentina, Paraguay, Uruguay*, 1965.

Fitzgibbon, Russell H. *Uruguay, Portrait of a Democracy,* 1966.

Gilio, Maria E. *The Tupamaro Guerrillas,* 1972.

Hudson, Rex A., and Sandra W. Meditz, eds. *Uruguay: A Country Study,* 2nd ed., 1992.

Pan American Health Organization. *Health in the Americas,* 1998.

Pendle, George. *Uruguay,* 1965.

Sans, Mónica, et al. "Historical Genetics in Uruguay: Estimates of Biological Origins and Their Problems." *Human Biology* 69 (2): 161–170, 1997.

Weinstein, Martin. *Uruguay, the Politics of Failure,* 1975.

Zum Felde, Alberto. *Evolución Histórica del Uruguay y Esquema de su Sociología,* 1941.

———. *Proceso Intelectual del Uruguay, Crítica de su Literatura,* 1967.

Web Site

Kelly, Robert C., et al., eds. *Country Review, Uruguay 2000,* http://www.CountryWatch.com

—MIGUEL BOMBIN

UZBEKISTAN

CULTURE NAME
Uzbek

ALTERNATIVE NAMES
Uzbeq, Ozbek

ORIENTATION

Identification. Uzbeks likely take their name from a khan. A leader of the Golden Horde in the fourteenth century was named Uzbek, though he did not rule over the people who would share his name.

Modern Uzbeks hail not only from the Turkic-Mongol nomads who first claimed the name, but also from other Turkic and Persian peoples living inside the country's borders. The Soviets, in an effort to divide the Turkic people into more easily governable subdivisions, labeled Turks, Tajiks, Sarts, Qipchaqs, Khojas, and others as Uzbek, doubling the size of the ethnicity to four million in 1924.

Today the government is strengthening the Uzbek group identity, to prevent the splintering seen in other multiethnic states. Some people have assimilated with seemingly little concern. Many Tajiks consider themselves Uzbek, though they retain the Tajik language; this may be because they have long shared an urban lifestyle, which was more of a bond than ethnic labels. Others have been more resistant to Uzbekization. Many Qipchaqs eschew intermarriage, live a nomadic lifestyle, and identify more closely with the Kyrgyz who live across the border from them. The Khojas also avoid intermarriage, and despite speaking several languages, have retained a sense of unity.

The Karakalpaks, who live in the desert south of the Aral Sea, have a separate language and tradition more akin to Kazakh than Uzbek. Under the Soviet Union, theirs was a separate republic, and it remains autonomous.

Location and Geography. Uzbekistan's 174,330 square miles (451,515 square kilometers), an area slightly larger than California, begin in the Karakum (Black Sand) and Kyzlkum (Red Sand) deserts of Karakalpakistan. The arid land of this autonomous republic supports a nomadic lifestyle. Recently, the drying up of the Aral Sea has devastated the environment, causing more than 30 percent of the area's population to leave, from villages in the early 1980s and then from cities. This will continue; the area was hit by a devastating drought in the summer of 2000.

Population increases to the east, centered around fertile oases and the valleys of the Amu-Darya River, once known as the Oxus, and the Zeravshan River, which supports the ancient city-states of Bokhara and Samarkand. The Ferghana Valley in the east is the heart of Islam in Uzbekistan. Here, where the country is squeezed between Tajikistan and Kyrgyzstan, the mountainous terrain supports a continuing nomadic lifestyle, and in recent years has provided a venue for fundamentalist guerrillas. Kazakhstan, Turkmenistan, and Afghanistan also border the country. In 1867 the Russian colonial government moved the capital from Bokhara to Tashkent. With 2.1 million people, it is the largest city in Central Asia.

Demography. The current population of Uzbekistan is 24.8 million. Seventy-five to 80 percent are Uzbek, though many of these were originally from other ethnic groups. Russians and Tajiks are each 5 percent, Karakalpaks 2 percent, and other nationalities the remainder. From 1989 to 1996, five hundred thousand more people emigrated than immigrated; most of the emigrants were educated. Of the more than one million people who have left, essentially all were non-Uzbek. Cities like Andijan and Ferghana, whose populations had been only half Uzbek, are now virtually entirely Uzbek. In 1990, 600,000 Germans lived in Uzbekistan; 95

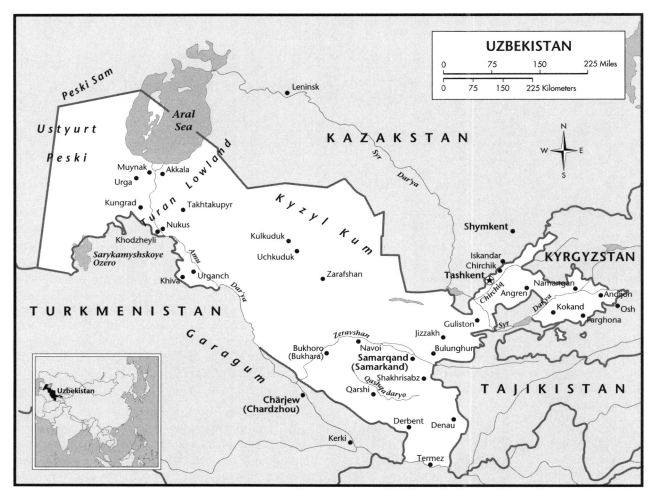

Uzbekistan

percent have left. In 1990, 260,000 Jews lived in Uzbekistan; 80 percent have left.

Linguistic Affiliation. Uzbek is the language of about twenty million Uzbeks living in Uzbekistan, Tajikistan, Kyrgyzstan, and Kazakhstan. The language is Turkic and abounds with dialects, including Qarlug (which served as the literary language for much of Uzbek history), Kipchak, Lokhay, Oghuz, Qurama, and Sart, some of which come from other languages. Uzbek emerged as a distinct language in the fifteenth century. It is so close to modern Uyghur that speakers of each language can converse easily. Prior to Russian colonization it would often have been hard to say where one Turkic language started and another ended. But through prescribed borders, shifts in dialect coalesced into distinct languages. The Soviets replaced its Arabic script briefly with a Roman script and then with Cyrillic. Since independence there has

been a shift back to Roman script, as well as a push to eliminate words borrowed from Russian.

About 14 percent of the population—mostly non-Uzbek—speak Russian as their first language; 5 percent speak Tajik. Most Russians do not speak Uzbek. Under the Soviet Union, Russian was taught as the Soviet lingua franca, but Uzbek was supported as the indigenous language of the republic, ironically resulting in the deterioration of other native languages and dialects. Today many people still speak Russian, but the government is heavily promoting Uzbek.

Symbolism. Symbols of Uzbekistan's independence and past glories are most common. The flag and national colors—green for nature, white for peace, red for life, and blue for water—adorn murals and walls. The twelve stars on the flag symbolize the twelve regions of the country. The crescent moon, a symbol of Islam, is common, though its appearance on the national flag is meant not as a religious symbol but as a metaphor for rebirth. The mythical bird Semurg on the state seal also symbolizes a national renaissance. Cotton, the country's main source of wealth, is displayed on items from the state seal to murals to teacups. The architectures of Samara and Bukhara also symbolize past achievements.

Amir Timur, who conquered a vast area of Asia from his seat in Samarkand in the fourteenth century, has become a major symbol of Uzbek pride and potential and of the firm but just and wise ruler—a useful image for the present government, which made 1996 the Year of Amir Timur. Timur lived more than a century before the Uzbeks reached Uzbekistan.

Independence Day, 1 September, is heavily promoted by the government, as is Navruz, 21 March, which highlights the country's folk culture.

HISTORY AND ETHNIC RELATIONS

Emergence of the Nation. The Uzbeks coalesced by the fourteenth century in southern Siberia, starting as a loose coalition of Turkic-Mongol nomad tribes who converted to Islam. In the first half of the fifteenth century Abu al-Khayr Khan, a descendant of Genghis Khan, led them south, first to the steppe and semidesert north of the Syr-Daria River. At this time a large segment of Uzbeks split off and headed east to become the Kazakhs. In 1468 Abu'l Khayr was killed by a competing faction, but by 1500 the Uzbeks had regrouped under Muhammad Shaybani Khan, and invaded the fertile land of modern Uzbekistan. They expelled Amir Timur's heirs from Samarkand and Herat and took over the city-states of Khiva, Khojand, and Bokhara, which would become the Uzbek capital. Settling down, the Uzbeks traded their nomadism for urban living and agriculture.

The first century of Uzbek rule saw a flourishing of learning and the arts, but the dynasty then slid into decline, helped by the end of the Silk Route trade. In 1749 invaders from Iran defeated Bokhara and Khiva, breaking up the Uzbek Empire and replacing any group identity with the division between Sarts, or city dwellers, and nomads. What followed was the Uzbek emirate of Bokhara and Samarkand, and the khanates of Khiva and Kokand, who ruled until the Russian takeover.

Russia became interested in Central Asia in the eighteenth century, concerned that the British might break through from colonial India to press its southern flank. Following more than a century of indecisive action, Russia in 1868 invaded Bokhara,

then brutally subjugated Khiva in 1873. Both were made Russian protectorates. In 1876, Khokand was annexed. All were subsumed into the Russian province of Turkistan, which soon saw the arrival of Russian settlers.

The 1910s produced the Jadid reform movement, which, though short-lived, sought to establish a community beholden neither to Islamic dogma nor to Russian colonists, marking the first glimmer of national identity in many years. With the Russian Revolution in 1917 grew hopes of independence, but by 1921 the Bolsheviks had reasserted control. In 1924 Soviet planners drew the borders for the soviet socialist republics of Uzbekistan and Karakalpakistan, based around the dominant ethnic groups. In 1929 Tajikstan was split off from the south of Uzbekistan, causing lasting tension between the two; many Uzbeks regard Tajiks as Persianized Uzbeks, while Tajikstan resented Uzbekistan's retention of the Tajik cities of Bokhara and Samarkand. Karakalpakistan was transferred to the Uzbekistan SSR in 1936, as an autonomous region. Over the ensuing decades, Soviet leaders solidified loose alliances and other nationalities into what would become Uzbek culture.

In August 1991 Uzbek Communists supported the reactionary coup against Soviet leader Mikhail Gorbachev. After the coup failed, Uzbekistan declared its independence on 1 September. Though shifting away from communism, President Islom Kharimov, who had been the Communist Party's first secretary in Uzbekistan, has maintained absolute control over the independent state. He has continued to define a single Uzbek culture, while obscuring its Soviet creation.

National Identity. The Soviet government, and to a lesser extent the Russian colonial government that preceded it, folded several less prominent nationalities into the Uzbeks. The government then institutionalized a national Uzbek culture based on trappings such as language, art, dress, and food, while imbuing them with meanings more closely aligned with Communist ideology. Islam was removed from its central place, veiling of women was banned, and major and minor regional and ethnic differences were smoothed over in favor of an ideologically acceptable uniformity.

Since 1991 the government has kept the Soviet definition of their nationhood, simply because prior to this there was no sense or definition of a single Uzbek nation. But it is literally excising the Soviet formation of the culture from its history books; one university history test had just 1 question of 850 dealing with the years 1924 to 1991.

Ethnic Relations. The Soviet-defined borders left Uzbeks, Kyrgyz, Tajiks, and others on both sides of Uzbekistan. Since independence, tightening border controls and competition for jobs and resources have caused difficulties for some of these communities, despite warm relations among the states of the region.

In June 1989, rioting in the Ferghana Valley killed thousands of Meskhetian Turks, who had been deported there in 1944. Across the border in Osh, Kyrgyzstan, the Uzbek majority rioted in 1990 over denial of land.

There is official support of minority groups such as Russians, Koreans, and Tatars. These groups have cultural centers, and in 1998 a law that was to have made Uzbek the only language of official communication was relaxed. Nevertheless, non-Uzbek-speakers have complained that they face difficulties finding jobs and entering a university. As a result of this and of poor economic conditions, many Russians and others have left Uzbekistan.

URBANISM, ARCHITECTURE, AND THE USE OF SPACE

In ancient times the cities of Samarkand and Bokhara were regarded as jewels of Islamic architecture, thriving under Amir Timur and his descendants the Timurids. They remain major tourist attractions.

During the Soviet period, cities became filled with concrete-slab apartment blocks of four to nine stories, similar to those found across the USSR. In villages and suburbs, residents were able to live in more traditional one-story houses built around a courtyard. These houses, regardless of whether they belong to rich or poor, present a drab exterior, with the family's wealth and taste displayed only for guests. Khivan houses have a second-story room for entertaining guests. Since independence, separate houses have become much more popular, supporting something of a building boom in suburbs of major cities. One estimate puts two-thirds of the population now living in detached houses.

The main room of the house is centered around the *dusterhon*, or tablecloth, whether it is spread on the floor or on a table. Although there are not separate areas for women and children, women tend to gather in the kitchen when male guests are present.

Each town has a large square, where festivals and public events are held.

Parks are used for promenading; if a boy and a girl are dating, they are referred to as walking together. Benches are in clusters, to allow neighbors to chat.

FOOD AND ECONOMY

Food in Daily Life. Bread holds a special place in Uzbek culture. At mealtime, bread will be spread to cover the entire dusterhon. Traditional Uzbek bread, *tandir non*, is flat and round. It is always torn by hand, never placed upside down, and never thrown out.

Meals begin with small dishes of nuts and raisins, progressing through soups, salads, and meat dishes and ending with *palov*, a rice-and-meat dish synonymous with Uzbek cuisine throughout the former Soviet Union; it is the only dish often cooked by men. Other common dishes, though not strictly Uzbek, include *monti*, steamed dumplings of lamb meat and fat, onions, and pumpkin, and kabob, grilled ground meat. Uzbeks favor mutton; even the nonreligious eschew pig meat.

Because of their climate, Uzbeks enjoy many types of fruits, eaten fresh in summer and dried in winter, and vegetables. Dairy products such as *katyk*, a liquid yogurt, and *suzma*, similar to cottage cheese, are eaten plain or used as ingredients.

Tea, usually green, is drunk throughout the day, accompanied by snacks, and is always offered to guests.

Meals are usually served either on the floor, or on a low table, though high tables also are used. The table is always covered by a dusterhon. Guests sit on carpets, padded quilts, chairs, or beds, but never on pillows. Men usually sit cross-legged, women with their legs to one side. The most respected guests sit away from the entrance. Objects such as shopping bags, which are considered unclean, never should be placed on the dusterhon, nor should anyone ever step on or pass dirty items over it.

The *choyhona*, or teahouse, is the focal point of the neighborhood's men. It is always shaded, and if possible located near a stream.

The Soviets introduced restaurants where meals center around alcohol and can last through the night.

The Karakalpaks' national dish is *besbarmak*, boiled mutton, beef, or horse served over a plate of broad noodles and accompanied by the reduced broth. Russians have brought many of their foods, such as *pelmeni*, boiled meat dumplings, borscht,

A vendor sells round loaves of bread called tandirnon to a customer at the Bibi Bazaar in Samarkand. Bread is especially important in Uzbek culture.

cabbage and meat soup, and a variety of fried or baked savory pastries.

Food Customs at Ceremonial Occasions. Uzbeks celebrate whenever possible, and parties usually consist of a large meal ending with palov. The food is accompanied by copious amounts of vodka, cognac, wine, and beer. Elaborate toasts, given by guests in order of their status, precede each round of shots. After, glasses are diligently refilled by a man assigned the task. A special soup of milk and seven grains is eaten on Navruz. During the month of Ramadan, observant Muslims fast from sunrise until sunset.

Basic Economy. The majority of goods other than food come from China, Turkey, Pakistan, and Russia. It is very common for families in detached homes to have gardens in which they grow food or raise a few animals for themselves, and if possible, for sale. Even families living in apartments will try to grow food on nearby plots of land, or at dachas.

Land Tenure and Property. Beginning in 1992, Uzbekistanis have been able to buy their apartments or houses, which had been state property, for the equivalent of three months' salary. Thus most homes have become private property.

Agricultural land had been mainly owned by state or collective farms during the Soviet period. In many cases the same families or communities that farmed the land have assumed ownership, though they are still subject to government quotas and government guidelines, usually aimed at cotton-growing.

About two-thirds of small businesses and services are in private hands. Many that had been state-owned were auctioned off. While the former *nomenklatura* (government and Communist Party officials) often won the bidding, many businesses also have been bought by entrepreneurs. Large factories, however, largely remain state-owned.

Major Industries. Uzbekistan's industry is closely tied to its natural resources. Cotton, the white gold of Central Asia, forms the backbone of the economy, with 85 percent exported in exchange for convertible currency. Agricultural machinery, especially for cotton, is produced in the Tashkent region. Oil refineries produce about 173,000 barrels a day.

The Korean car maker Daewoo invested $650 million in a joint venture, UzDaewoo, at a plant in Andijan, which has a capacity of 200,000 cars. However, in 1999 the plant produced just 58,000 cars, and it produced far less in 2000, chiefly for the domestic market. With Daewoo's bankruptcy in November 2000, the future of the plant is uncertain at best.

Trade. Uzbekistan's main trading partners are Russia, South Korea, Germany, the United States, Turkey, and Kazakhstan. Before independence, imports were mainly equipment, consumer goods, and foods. Since independence, Uzbekistan has managed to stop imports of oil from Kazakhstan and has also lowered food imports by reseeding some cotton fields with grain.

Uzbekistan is the world's third-largest cotton exporter.

Uzbekistan exported about $3 billion (U.S.), primarily in cotton, gold, textiles, metals, oil, and natural gas, in 1999. Its main markets are Russia, Switzerland, Britain, Belgium, Kazakhstan, and Tajikistan.

Division of Labor. According to government statistics, 44 percent of workers are in agriculture and forestry; 20 percent in industry; 36 percent in the service sector. Five percent unemployed, and 10 percent are underemployed. Many rural jobless, however, may be considered agricultural workers.

A particular feature of the Uzbekistan labor system is the requirement of school and university students, soldiers, and workers to help in the cotton harvest. They go en masse to the fields for several days to hand-pick cotton.

Many Uzbeks, particularly men, work in other parts of the former Soviet Union. Bazaars from Kazakhstan to Russia are full of Uzbek vendors, who command higher prices for their produce the farther north they travel. Others work in construction or other seasonal labor to send hard currency home.

About 2 percent of the workforce is of pension age and 1 percent is under sixteen.

SOCIAL STRATIFICATION

Classes and Castes. During the Soviet Union, Uzbekistani society was stratified not by wealth but by access to products, housing, and services. The *nomenklatura* could find high-quality consumer goods, cars, and homes that simply were unattainable by others. Since independence, many of these people have kept jobs that put them in positions to earn many times the $1,020 (U.S.) average annual salary reported by the United Nations. It is impossible to quantify the number of wealthy, however, as the vast majority of their income is unreported, particularly if they are government officials.

Children walking home after school. As children grow older, school discipline increases.

Many members of the former Soviet intelligentsia—teachers, artists, doctors, and other skilled service providers—have been forced to move into relatively unskilled jobs, such as bazaar vendors and construction workers, where they could earn more money. Urban residents tend to earn twice the salaries of rural people.

Symbols of Social Stratification. As elsewhere in the former Soviet Union, the new rich tend to buy and show off expensive cars and limousines, apartments, and clothes and to go to nightclubs. Foreign foods and goods also are signs of wealth, as is a disdain for shopping in bazaars.

POLITICAL LIFE

Government. Uzbekistan is in name republican but in practice authoritarian, with Kharimov's Halq Tarakiati Partiiasi, or People's Democratic Party, controlling all aspects of governance. On 9 January 2000 he was reelected for a five-year term, with a 92 percent turnout and a 92 percent yes vote. Earlier, a March 1995 referendum to extend his term to 2000 resulted in a 99 percent turnout and a 99 percent yes vote. The legislature, Oliy Majlis, was inaugurated in 1994. At that time the ruling party captured 193 seats, though many of these candidates ran as independents. The opposition political movement Birlik, or Unity, and the party Erk, or Will, lack the freedom to directly challenge the government.

Makhallas, or neighborhood councils of elders, provide the most direct governance. Some opinion polls have ranked makhallas just after the president in terms of political power. Makhallahs address social needs ranging from taking care of orphans, loaning items, and maintaining orderly public spaces, to sponsoring holiday celebrations. In Soviet times these were institutionalized, with makhalla heads and committees appointed by the local Communist Party. Then and now, however, makhallas have operated less smoothly in neighborhoods of mixed ethnicities.

Leadership and Political Officials. The president appoints the head, or *khokim*, of each of Uzbekistan's 12 regions, called *viloyatlars*, and of Karakalpakistan and Tashkent, who in turn appoint the khokims of the 216 regional and city governments. This top-down approach ensures a unity of government policies and leads to a diminishing sense of empowerment the farther one is removed from Kharimov.

Khokims and other officials were chiefly drawn from the Communist Party following independence—many simply kept their jobs—and many remain. Nevertheless, Kharimov has challenged local leaders to take more initiative, and in 1997 he replaced half of them, usually with public administration and financial experts, many of whom are reform-minded.

Corruption is institutionalized at all levels of government, despite occasional prosecution of officials. Students, for example, can expect to pay bribes to enter a university, receive high grades, or be exempted from the cotton harvest.

Social Problems and Control. The government has vigorously enforced laws related to drug trafficking and terrorism, and reports of police abuse and torture are widespread. The constitution calls for independent judges and open access to proceedings and justice. In practice, defendants are seldom acquitted, and when they are, the government has the right to appeal.

Petty crime such as theft is becoming more common; violent crime is much rarer. Anecdotal evidence points to an increase in heroin use; Uzbekistan is a transshipment point from Afghanistan and Pakistan to Europe, and access is relatively easy despite tough antidrug laws.

People are often reluctant to call the police, as they are not trusted. Instead, it is the responsibility of families to see that their members act appropriately. Local communities also exert pressure to conform.

Military Activity. Uzbekistan's military in 2000 was skirmishing with the Islamic Movement of Uzbekistan, a militant group opposed to the secular regime, and numbering in the hundreds or thousands. Besides clashes in the mountains near the Tajikistani border, the group has been blamed for six car bombings in Tashkent in February 2000.

Uzbekistan spends about $200 million (U.S.) a year on its military and has 150,000 soldiers, making it the strongest in the region.

NONGOVERNMENTAL ORGANIZATIONS AND OTHER ASSOCIATIONS

Most domestic nongovernmental organizations are funded and supported by the government, and all must be registered. Kamolot, registered in 1996, is the major youth organization, and is modeled on the Soviet Komsomol. Ekosan is an environmental group. The Uzbek Muslim Board has been active in building mosques and financing religious education. The Women's Committee of Uzbekistan, a government organization, is tasked with ensuring women's access to education as well as employment and legal rights, and claims three million members.

The government also has set up quasi nongovernmental organizations, at times to deflect attention from controversial organizations. The Human Rights Society of Uzbekistan, for example, was denied registration from 1992 to 1997, before the government set up its own human rights monitor.

The leaders of these groups may receive privileges once granted to the Soviet *nomenklatura*, such as official cars and well-equipped offices.

There are no independent trade unions, though government-sponsored unions are common. The Employment Service and Employment Fund was set up in 1992 to address issues of social welfare, employment insurance, and health benefits for workers.

Ironically, some truly independent organizations from the Soviet period, such as the Committee to Save the Aral Sea, were declared illegal in 1994. Social groups associated with Birlik also have been denied registration.

As a result of the government's lack of reforms, in particular making the national currency convertible, major international donors are becoming reluc-

Weddings are very important in Uzbek culture, as the family is the center of society.

tant to assist Uzbekistan. The International Monetary Fund is pushing hard for convertibility before it gives further assistance. The U.S. Agency for International Development in 2000 said it was hesitant to assist the government in any sectors other than health, as the government was smothering economic reform.

GENDER ROLES AND STATUSES

Division of Labor by Gender. Before the Soviet period, men worked outside the house while women did basic domestic work, or supplemented the family income by spinning, weaving, and embroidering with silk or cotton. From the 1920s on, women entered the workforce, at textile factories and in the cotton fields, but also in professional jobs opened to them by the Soviet education system. They came to make up the great majority of teachers, nurses, and doctors. Family pressure, however, sometimes kept women from attaining higher education, or working outside the home. With independence, some women have held on to positions of power, though they still may be expected to comport themselves with modesty. Men in modern Uzbekistan, though, hold the vast majority of managerial positions, as well as the most labor-intensive

jobs. It is common now for men to travel north to other former Soviet republics to work in temporary jobs. Both sexes work in bazaars.

The Relative Status of Women and Men. Uzbekistan is a male-dominated society, particularly in the Ferghana Valley. Nevertheless, women make up nearly half the workforce. They hold just under 10 percent of parliamentary seats, and 18 percent of administrative and management positions, according to U.N. figures.

Women run the households and traditionally control the family budgets. When guests are present they are expected to cloister themselves from view.

In public women are expected to cover their bodies completely. Full veiling is uncommon, though it is occasionally practiced in the Ferghana Valley. Women often view this as an expression of their faith and culture rather than as an oppressive measure.

MARRIAGE, FAMILY, AND KINSHIP

Marriage. Uzbek women usually marry by twenty-one; men not much later. Marriage is an imperative for all, as families are the basic structure in society. A family's honor depends on their daughters' virginity; this often leads families to encourage early marriage.

In traditional Uzbek families, marriages are often still arranged between families; in more cosmopolitan ones it is the bride and groom's choice. Either way, the match is subject to parental approval, with the mother in practice having the final word. Preference is given to members of the kin group. There is particular family say in the youngest son's choice, as he and his bride will take care of his parents. People tend to marry in their late teens or early twenties. Weddings often last for days, with the expense borne by the bride's family. The husband's family may pay a bride price. Polygamy is illegal and rare, but it is not unknown.

Following independence, divorce has become more common, though it is still rare outside of major cities. It is easier for a man to initiate divorce.

Domestic Unit. Uzbek families are patriarchal, though the mother runs the household. The average family size is five or six members, but families of ten or more are not uncommon.

Inheritance. Children are the primary claimants to the deceased's property. The youngest son receives the family house, along with the obligation to care

A woman places flat bread dough in an oven, while another woman folds dough in a large bowl, Old Town, Khiva. Families are patriarchal, but mothers run the households.

for his parents. Sons typically receive twice as large a share as daughters, though this can vary.

Kin Groups. Close relations extends to cousins, who have the rights and responsibilities of the nuclear family and often are called on for favors. If the family lives in a detached house and there is space, the sons may build their homes adjacent to or around the courtyard of the parents' house.

SOCIALIZATION

Infant Care. Uzbek babies are hidden from view for their first forty days. They are tightly swaddled when in their cribs and carried by their mothers. Men generally do not take care of or clean babies.

Child Rearing and Education. Children are cherished as the reason for life. The mother is the primary caretaker, and in case of divorce, she will virtually always take the children. The extended family and the community at large, however, also take an interest in the child's upbringing.

When children are young, they have great freedom to play and act out. But as they get older, particularly in school, discipline increases. A good child becomes one who is quiet and attentive, and all must help in the family's labor.

All children go to school for nine years, with some going on to eleventh grade; the government is increasing mandatory education to twelve years.

Higher Education. Enrollment in higher-education institutions is about 20 percent, down from more than 30 percent during the Soviet period. A major reason for the decline is that students do not feel a higher education will help them get a good job; also contributing is the emigration of Russians, and declining standards related to budget cutbacks. Nevertheless, Uzbeks, particularly in cities, still value higher education, and the government gives full scholarships to students who perform well.

ETIQUETTE

Elders are respected in Uzbek culture. At the dusterhon, younger guests will not make themselves more comfortable than their elders. The younger person should always greet the older first.

Men typically greet each other with a handshake, the left hand held over the heart. Women place their right hand on the other's elbow. If they are close friends or relatives, they may kiss each other on the cheeks.

If two acquaintances meet on the street, they will usually ask each other how their affairs are. If the two don't know each other well, the greeting will be shorter, or could involve just a nod.

Women are expected to be modest in dress and demeanor, with clothing covering their entire body. In public they may walk with their head tilted down to avoid unwanted attention. In traditional households, women will not enter the room if male guests are present. Likewise, it is considered forward to ask how a man's wife is doing. Women generally sit with legs together, their hands in their laps. When men aren't present, however, women act much more casually.

People try to carry themselves with dignity and patience, traits associated with royalty, though young men can be boisterous in public.

People tend to dress up when going out of the house. Once home they change, thus extending the life of their street clothes.

RELIGION

Religious Beliefs. Uzbeks are Sunni Muslims. The territory of Uzbekistan has been a center of Islam in the region for a thousand years, but under the Soviet Union the religion was heavily controlled: mosques were closed and Muslim education was banned. Beginning in 1988, Uzbeks have revived Islam, particularly in the Ferghana Valley, where mosques have been renovated. The call to prayer was everywhere heard five times a day before the government ordered the removal of the mosques' loudspeakers in 1998.

The state encourages a moderate form of Islam, but Kharimov fears the creation of an Islamic state. Since the beginning of the Islamic Movement of Uzbekistan's terror campaign in February 1999, he has cracked down even further on what he perceives as extremists, raising claims of human rights abuses. The government is particularly concerned about what it labels Wahhabism, a fundamentalist Sunni sect that took hold in the Ferghana Valley following independence.

Nine percent of the population is Russian Orthodox. Jews, Baptists, Roman Catholics, Lutherans, Seventh-Day Adventists, evangelical and Pentecostal Christians, Buddhists, Baha'is, and Hare Krishnas also are present.

Religious Practitioners. Most Sunni Uzbeks are led by a state-appointed mufti. Independent imams are sometimes repressed, and in May 1998, a law requiring all religious groups to register with the government was enacted. In addition to leading worship, the Muslim clergy has led mosque restoration efforts and is playing an increasing role in religious education.

Death and the Afterlife. Uzbeks bury their deceased within twenty-four hours of death, in above-ground tombs. At the funeral, women wail loudly and at specific times. The mourning period lasts forty days. The first anniversary of the death is marked with a gathering of the person's friends and relatives.

Muslims believe that on Judgment Day, each soul's deeds will be weighed. They will then walk across a hair-thin bridge spanning Hell, which leads to Paradise. The bridge will broaden under the feet of the righteous, but the damned will lose their balance and fall.

MEDICINE AND HEALTH CARE

Current health practices derive from the Soviet system. Health care is considered a basic right of the entire population, with clinics, though ill-equipped, in most villages, and larger facilities in regional centers. Emphasis is on treatment over prevention. Yet the state health care budget—80 million dollars in 1994—falls far short of meeting basic needs; vaccinations, for example, fell off sharply following independence. Exacerbating the situation is a lack of potable water, industrial pollution, and a rise in infectious diseases such as tuberculosis.

Perhaps the most common traditional health practices are shunning cold drinks and cold surfaces, which are believed to cause colds and damage to internal organs, and avoiding drafts, or bad winds. Folk remedies and herbal treatments also are common. An example is to press bread to the ailing part of the body. The sick person then gives a small donation to a homeless person who will agree to take on his or her illness.

SECULAR CELEBRATIONS

The major secular holidays are New Year's Day (1 January); Women's Day (8 March), a still popular holdover from the Soviet Union, when women receive gifts; Navrus (21 March), originally a Zoroastrian holiday, which has lost its religious significance but is still celebrated with *Sumaliak* soup, made from milk and seven grains; Victory Day (9 May), marking the defeat of Nazi Germany; and Independence Day (1 September), celebrating separation from the Soviet Union.

A man cuts bread in a choyhana, or tea house. The tea house is the central gathering place for Uzbek men.

Uzbeks typically visit friends and relatives on holidays to eat large meals and drink large amounts of vodka. Holidays also may be marked by concerts or parades centered on city or town squares or factories. The government marks Independence Day and Navrus with massive outdoor jamborees in Tashkent, which are then broadcast throughout the country, and places of work or neighborhoods often host huge celebrations.

THE ARTS AND HUMANITIES

Support for the Arts. During the Soviet period, the government gave extensive support to the arts, building cultural centers in every city and paying the salaries of professional artists. With independence, state funding has shrunk, though it still makes up the bulk of arts funding. Many dance, theater, and music groups continue to rely on the state, which gives emphasis to large productions and extravaganzas, controls major venues, and often has an agenda for the artists to follow.

Other artists have joined private companies who perform for audiences of wealthy business-people and tourists. Some money comes in from corporate sponsorship and international charitable organizations—for example UNESCO and the Soros Foundation's Open Society Institute. Yet many artists have simply been forced to find other work.

Literature. The territory of Uzbekistan has a long tradition of writers, though not all were Uzbek. The fifteenth-century poet Alisher Navoi, 1441–1501, is most revered; among his works is a treatise comparing the Persian and Turkish languages. Abu Rayhan al-Biruni, 973–1048, born in Karakalpakistan, wrote a massive study of India. Ibn Sina, also known as Avicenna, 980–1037, wrote *The Cannon of Medicine*. Omar Khayyam, 1048–1131, came to Samarkand to pursue mathematics and astronomy. Babur, 1483–1530, born in the Ferghana Valley, was the first Moghul leader of India, and wrote a famous autobiography.

Until the twentieth century, Uzbek literary tradition was largely borne by *bakshi*, elder minstrels who recited myths and history through epic songs, and *otin-oy*, female singers who sang of birth, marriage and death.

The Jadids produced many poets, writers, and playwrights. These writers suffered greatly in the Stalinist purges of the 1930s. Later the Soviet Union asked of its writers that they be internationalists and further socialist goals. Abdullah Qahhar, 1907–1968, for example, satirized Muslim clerics. But with the loosening of state control in the 1980s, a new generation of writers renewed the Uzbek language and Uzbek themes. Many writers also were active in Birlik, which started as a cultural movement but is now suppressed.

Graphic Arts. Uzbekistan has begun a revival of traditional crafts, which suffered from the Soviet view that factory-produced goods were superior to handicrafts. Now master craftsmen are reappearing in cities such as Samarkand and Bukhara, supported largely by foreign tourists. Miniature painting is narrative in character, using a wide palette of symbols to tell their stories. They can be read from right to left as a book, and often accompany works of literature. Wood carving, of architectural features such as doors and pillars and of items such as the *sonduq*, a box given to a bride by her parents, also is regaining a place in Uzbek crafts. *Ikat* is a method of cloth dying, now centered in the Yordgorlik Silk Factory in Margilan. Silk threads are tie-dyed, then woven on a loom to create soft-edged designs for curtains, clothing, and other uses.

Performance Arts. Uzbek music is characterized by reedy, haunting instruments and throaty, nasal singing. It is played on long-necked lutes called *dotars*, flutes, tambourines, and small drums. It developed over the past several hundred years in the khanates on the territory of modern Uzbekistan, where musicians were a central feature of festivals and weddings. The most highly regarded compositions are cycles called *maqoms*. *Sozandas*, sung by women accompanied by percussion instruments, also are popular. In the 1920s, Uzbek composers were encouraged, leading to a classical music tradition that continues today. Modern Uzbek pop often combines elements of folk music with electric instruments to create dance music.

Uzbek dance is marked by fluid arm and upper-body movement. Today women's dance groups perform for festivals and for entertainment, a practice started during the Soviet period. Earlier, women danced only for other women; boys dressed as women performed for male audiences. One dance for Navruz asks for rain; others depict chores, other work, or events. Uzbek dance can be divided into three traditions: Bokhara and Samarkand; Khiva; and Khokand. The Sufi dance, *zikr*, danced in a circle accompanied by chanting and percussion to reach a trance state, also is still practiced.

Uzbekistan's theater in the twentieth century addressed moral and social issues. The Jadidists presented moral situations that would be resolved by a solution consistent with Islamic law. During the Soviet period dramatists were sometimes censored.

The Ilkhom Theater, founded in 1976, was the first independent theater in the Soviet Union.

Admission to cultural events is kept low by government and corporate sponsorship. It also has become common for dancers to perform for groups of wealthy patrons.

THE STATE OF THE PHYSICAL AND SOCIAL SCIENCES

Uzbekistan has several higher-education institutions, with departments aimed at conducting significant research. Funding, however, has lagged since independence. The goal of the Academy of Sciences in Tashkent is practical application of science. It has physical and mathematical, chemical-biological, and social sciences departments, with more than fifty research institutions and organizations under them.

BIBLIOGRAPHY

Adams, Laura L. "What Is Culture? Schemas and Spectacles in Uzbekistan." *Anthropology of East Europe Review* 16 (2): 65–71, 1998.

Ali, Muhammad. "Let Us Learn Our Inheritance: Get to Know Yourself." *AACAR Bulletin* 2 (3): 3–18, 1989.

Allworth, Edward A. *The Modern Uzbeks: From the Fourteenth Century to the Present; A Cultural History*, 1990.

Freedom House 2000. *Freedom in the World, The Annual Survey of Political Rights and Civil Liberties, 1999–2000: Uzbekistan Country Report*, 2000.

Griffin, Keith. *Issues in Development Discussion Paper 13: The Macroeconomic Framework and Development Strategy in Uzbekistan*, 1996.

Human Rights Watch. *Human Rights Watch World Report 2000: Uzbekistan*, 2000.

Jukes, Geoffrey J.; Kirill Nourzhanov, and Mikhail Alexandrov. *Race, Religion, Ethnicity and Economics in Central Asia*, 1998.

Kalter, Johannes, and Margareta Pavaloi. *Uzbekistan: Heirs to the Silk Road*, 1997.

Khan, Azizur Rahman. *Issues in Development Discussion Paper 14: The Transition of Uzbekistan's Agriculture to a Market Economy*, 1996.

Kharimov, Islom A. *Uzbekistan on the Threshold of the Twenty-first Century: Challenges to Stability and Progress*, 1998.

Nazarov, Bakhtiyar A., and Denis Sinor. *Essays on Uzbek History, Culture, and Language*, 1993.

Nettleton, Susanna. "Uzbek Independence and Educational Change," *Central Asia Monitor* 3, 1992.

Paksoy, H. B. "Z. V. Togan: The Origins of the Kazaks and the Ozbeks," *Central Asian Survey* 11 (3), 1992.

Prosser, Sarah. "Reform Within and Without the Law: Further Challenges for Central Asian NGOs," *Harvard Asia Quarterly*, 2000.

Schoeberlein-Engel, John. "The Prospects for Uzbek National Identity," *Central Asia Monitor* 2, 1996.

"Tamerlane v. Marx;" *Bulletin of the Atomic Scientists* 50 (1), 1994.

U.N. Development Project. *Human Development Report: Uzbekistan 1997*, 1997.

UNESCO, *Education Management Profile: Uzbekistan*, 1998.

U.S. Department of State. *Background Notes: Uzbekistan*, 1998.

U.S. Department of State, Central Intelligence Agency. *The CIA World Factbook*, 2000.

U.S. Library of Congress. *Kazakstan, Kyrgyzstan, Tajikistan, Turkmenistan and Uzbekistan: Country Studies*, 1997.

—JEFF ERLICH

VANUATU

CULTURE NAME

Ni-Vanatu

ORIENTATION

Identification. The name "Vanuatu" is an important aspect of national identity. Leaders of the Vanua'aku Party, which led the first independent government, invented the term in 1980 to replace the colonial name New Hebrides. *Vanua* means "land" in many of Vanuatu's one hundred five languages, and translations of the new name include "Our Land" and "Abiding Land." Culturally, Vanuatu is complex. Some of the people follow matrilineal descent rules, while others follow patrilineal rules. Leadership on some islands depends on advancement within men's societies, and in others it depends on possession of chiefly titles or personal ability. Although most people depend on subsistence farming and fishing, the economy of the seaboard differs from that of interior mountain plateaus.

Political leaders have consciously cultivated national culture to foster a national identity, including political slogans such as "Unity in Diversity." Many rural people, however, are attached primarily to their home islands, while educated urbanites, refer to supranational identities such as Melanesian.

Location and Geography. Vanuatu is a Y-shaped tropical archipelago of over eighty islands, sixty-five of which are inhabited. The Solomon Islands lie to the north, New Caledonia to the south, Fiji to the east, and the Coral Sea and Australia to the west. The mostly volcanic archipelago extends 560 miles (900 kilometers) from north to south and has an area of 5,700 square miles (14,760 square kilometers). Espiritu Santo is the largest island. Port Vila, the capital, which was also the colonial headquarters, is on the south-central island of Efate.

Demography. The 1997 population of 185,000 is 94 percent Melanesian, 4 percent European (mostly French), and 4 percent other (Vietnamese, Chinese, and other Pacific Islander).

Linguistic Affiliation. Bislama, the nation's pidgin English which emerged in the nineteenth century, is essential for public discourse. Many aspects of the national culture are phrased in Bislama, which has become an important marker of national identity. Alongside Bislama, English and French are recognized as "official languages." These languages overlie one hundred five indigenous Austronesian languages, three of which are Polynesian in origin. There are strong links between local language, place, and identity, but many people are multilingual. Most children pursue elementary schooling in English or French, although few residents are fluent in either language. Most national discourse takes place in Bislama, which is becoming creolized.

Symbolism. The politicians who forged independence emphasized shared culture (*kastom*) and shared Christianity to create a national identity and iconography. The national motto is *Long God Yumi Stanap* ("In (or with) God We Stand/Develop"). Leaders of the Vanua'aku Party, which governed during the nation's first eleven years, came mostly from the central and northern areas. Objects selected to represent the nation come principally from those regions, including circle pig tusks, palm leaves, and carved slit gongs. The name of the national currency, the *vatu* ("stone") derives from central northern languages, as does the name "Vanuatu." After independence, holidays were established to celebrate the nation and promote national identity and unity.

HISTORY AND ETHNIC RELATIONS

Emergence of the Nation. The New Hebrides was a unique "condominium" colony ruled jointly by Great Britain and France after 1906. Although they instituted a joint court and a few other combined services, each ran separate and parallel administra-

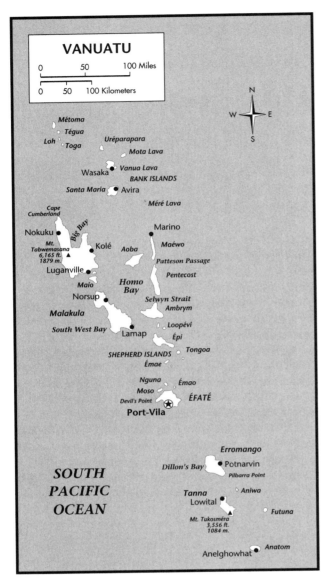

VANUATU

0   50   100 Miles

0   50   100 Kilometers

Métoma
Tégua
Loh Toga   Uréparapara
                  Mota Lava
Wasaka   Vanua Lava
              BANK ISLANDS
Santa Maria   Avira
                  Méré Lava
Cape
Cumberland
Nokuku   Marino
Mt.   Kolé   Aoba   Maéwo
Tabwemasana
6,165 ft.
1879 m.   Patteson Passage
Luganville   Pentecost
Maio   Homo
Norsup   Bay   Selwyn Strait
                  Ambrym
Malakula
South West Bay   Loopévi
          Lamap   Épi
              Tongoa
      SHEPHERD ISLANDS
          Émae
      Nguna   Émao
      Moso
      Devil's Point   *ÉFATÉ*
      Port-Vila

*SOUTH
PACIFIC
OCEAN*

              Erromango
    Dillon's Bay   Potnarvin
              Pilbarra Point

    Tanna   Aniwa
    Lowital
              Futuna
    Mt. Tukosméra
    3,556 ft.
    1084 m.
          Anatom
    Anelghowhat

Vanuatu

tive bureaucracies, medical systems, police forces, and school systems. Competition and conflict between Anglophones and Francophones culminated in the 1970s, when both groups backed different political parties in the run-up to independence. The French had greatly expanded their educational system, leaving a legacy of Francophones who commonly find themselves opposed politically to their Anglophone compatriots.

The main parties in favor of independence in the 1970s were British-supported and Anglophone, drawing on English and Protestant roots more than on French and Roman Catholic. Still, all the citizens distinguish themselves from European colonialists as they assume their national identity. Since inde-

pendence, the French have provided aid in periods when the country has been ruled by Francophone political parties. Australia and New Zealand have largely replaced British assistance and influence.

Ethnic Relations. A relatively small population of Vietnamese (which the French recruited as plantation workers beginning in the 1920s) and overseas Chinese control a significant proportion of the economies of Port Vila and Luganville. These wealthy families are linked by kinship, economic, and other relations with the majority Melanesian population.

URBANISM, ARCHITECTURE, AND THE USE OF SPACE

Vanuatu is still a rural country. Most ni-Vanuatu live on their home islands, although the population of the two towns has increased significantly since independence. Town layout and architecture reflect French and British sensibilities. A huge American military base that grew up around Luganville during the World War II still displays that heritage. Rural architecture remains largely traditional. Local notions of gender and rank influence village layout. Women's mobility is more restricted than that of men, and in many churches, men and women sit on opposite sides of a central aisle. People use "bush" materials in the construction of housing, although they also use cement brick and aluminum sheet roofing. Houses have one or two rooms for sleeping and storage. Cooking is done in fireplaces or lean-to kitchens outdoors.

After independence, the government erected several public buildings, including a national museum, the House of Parliament, and the House of Custom Chiefs. These buildings incorporate slit gongs and other architectural details that display the cultural heritage. The latter two also model the traditional *nakamal* (men's house or meeting ground), a ritual space where public discussion and decision making take place. In many cultures, men and occasionally women retire each evening to the nakamal to prepare and drink kava, an infusion of the pepper plant. Scores of urban kava bars have opened in Port Vila, Luganville, and government centers around the islands. Employed urbanites gather there at the end of the day, just as their rural kin congregate at nakamal on their home islands.

FOOD AND ECONOMY

Food in Daily Life. Ni-Vanuatu combine traditional south Pacific cuisine with introduced elements. Before contact with the West, staple foods included yam, taro, banana, coconut, sugarcane, tropical nuts, greens, pigs, fowl, and seafood. After contact, other tropical crops (manioc, plantain, sweet potato, papaya, mango) and temperate crops (cabbage, beans, corn, peppers, carrots, pumpkin) were added to the diet. Rural people typically produce most of what they eat, supplementing this with luxury foods (rice and tinned fish) purchased in stores. The urban diet relies on rice, bread, and tinned fish supplemented with rural products. Port Vila, and Luganville have restaurants that serve mostly the foreign and tourist communities.

Food Customs at Ceremonial Occasions. Ceremonies typically involve an exchange of food, such as the traditional taro and yam, kava, fowl, pigs, and chicken, along with a feast. Pigs are exchanged and eaten at all important ritual occasions. The national ceremonial dish is *laplap*, pudding made of grated root crops or plantain mixed with coconut milk and sometimes greens and meat, wrapped in leaves, and baked for hours in a traditional earth oven. In rural areas, during the week many people rely on simple boiling to cook roots and greens. On weekends, they prepare earth ovens and bake laplap for the evening meal and a Sunday feast. The exchange, preparation, and consumption of kava are integral parts of ceremonial occasions.

Basic Economy. Most ni-Vanuatu are subsistence farmers who do cash cropping on the side. The mode of production is swidden ("slash-and burn") horticulture, with farmers clearing and then burning new forest plots each season. Vanuatu has significant economic difficulties. Transportation costs are high, the economic infrastructure is undeveloped, and cyclone damage is common. Major export crops include copra, beef, tropical woods, squash, and cacao. Vanuatu is a tax haven that earns income from company registrations and fees and an offshore shipping registry. Tourism has become a major growth area. The government remains the largest employer of wage labor, and few employment activities exist outside the towns and regional government centers.

Land Tenure and Property. After independence, all alienated plantation land reverted to the customary owners. Only citizens may own land, although they can lease it to foreigners and investors. Generally, land belongs jointly to the members of lineages or other kin groups. Men typically have greater management fights to land than do women, although women may control land, particularly in matrilineal areas.

Commercial Activities, Major Industries, and Trade. Rural families produce cash crops (coconut, cacao, coffee, and foodstuffs) for sale in local markets. The opening of urban kava bars has stimulated an internal market for kava. With the growing tourist industry, there is a small market for traditional handicrafts, including woven baskets and mats, wood cavings, and jewelry. Manufacturing and industry contribute only 5 to 9 percent of the gross domestic product, and this mostly consists of fish, beef, and wood processing for export. The major trade partners are Australia, Japan, France, New Zealand, and New Caledonia

SOCIAL STRATIFICATION

Chiefly status exists in many of the indigenous cultures, though differences between chiefly and commoner lineages are slight. Symbolically, a man and his family's possession of a title is often marked in details of dance costume, adornment, and architecture. Leadership in the north rests largely on a man's success in "graded societies" which able individuals work their way up a ladder of status grades by killing and exchanging circle-tusked pigs. In the central and southern regions, the acquisition of titles also depends on individual effort and ability. Everywhere leadership correlates with ability, gender, and age, with able, older men typically being the most influential members of their villages.

Since rural society is still rooted in subsistence agriculture, economic and political inequalities are muted. However, there is increasing economic stratification between the educated and employed, most of whom live in urban areas, and rural subsistence farmers. The middle-class elite is relatively small, and urbanites remain connected by important kin ties to their villages.

POLITICAL LIFE

Government. Vanuatu is a republic with a unicameral parliament with fifty seats. An electoral college elects a nonexecutive president every five years. There are six regions whose elected councils share responsibility for local governance with the national government. An elected national council of chiefs, the Malvatumaori, advises the parliament on land tenure and customs.

Leadership and Political Officials. Since independence, elected officials have mostly been educated younger men who were originally pastors and leaders of Christian churches. The elders remain in the islands, serving as village chiefs, though the

Children from the Jon Frum Cargo Cult Village play in the black sand beach on Tanna Island, which is a short distance from the active volcano Yasur. Vanuatu is a mostly volcanic archipelago of over eighty islands.

country's prime ministers, presidents, and members of parliament have typically acquired honorary chiefly titles from various regions.

Social Problems and Control. The pattern of "circular migration" between rural village and urban center from the colonial era has broken down as more people have become permanent residents of Port Vila and Luganville. Many underemployed people live in periurban settlements, and urban migration has correlated with increasing rates of burglary and other property crimes. Demonstrations associated with political factions occur occasionally. The urban crime rate is very low.

An informal system of "town chiefs" supplements the state police force and judiciary. Leading elders in the towns meet to resolve disputes and punish offenders. Punishment sometimes involves the informal banishment of an accused person back to his or her home island. Unofficial settlement procedures frequently are used to handle disputes in rural areas.

Military Activity. The Vanuatu Mobile Force has been active only occasionally, mostly in international endeavors such as serving as peacekeepers.

SOCIAL WELFARE AND CHANGE PROGRAMS

State and nongovernmental organizations have focused on developing economic infrastructure and public services. Most villages have no electricity, and many people lack access to piped water despite efforts to expand rural water systems. Several organizations work with rural youth and women. The National Council of Women sponsors programs to improve women's access to the cash economy and reduce domestic violence.

A number of international and nongovernmental organizations are active in Vanuatu. Many international donors are encouraging a comprehensive reform program to make government more efficient and honest and lower deficit spending.

NONGOVERNMENTAL ORGANIZATIONS AND OTHER ASSOCIATIONS

The principal nongovernmental organizations are the Christian churches. Religious affiliation is second in importance only to kinship and neighborhood ties. A few labor unions have attempted to organize urban and rural salaried workers (such as schoolteachers) but have not been effective in industrial action and political campaigning.

GENDER ROLES AND STATUSES

Generally, women have less control of land and other property, are less mobile, and have less of a say in marriage. In the northern region, women participate in graded societies that parallel those of men. In matrilineal regions, women have better land and sea rights. Many ni-Vanuatu continue to believe in the deleterious, polluting effects of menstrual blood and other body fluids, and men and women sleep apart during women's menstrual periods, when women often give up cooking. Both men and women farm, although men are responsible for clearing forest and brush for new garden plots. Both men and women fish and reef gather, though only men undertake deep-sea fishing. Although women have excelled in the school system, men continue to monopolize economic and political leadership positions. Few women drive cars, and only a handful have been elected to the parliament and the regional and town councils. Women do much of the work in town and roadside marketplaces.

MARRIAGE, FAMILY, AND KINSHIP

Marriage. The marriage rate approaches 100 percent. Traditionally, leaders of kin groups arrange the marriages of their children. Marriage is an important event in ongoing exchange relations between kin groups and neighborhoods and typically involves the exchange of goods. Some educated urban residents have adopted Western notions of romantic love and arrange their own marriages with or without family approval. Marriage rules identify certain kin groups as the source of appropriate spouses. In the southern region, marriage is patterned as "sister exchange," in which a man who marries a woman from another family owes a woman in return. In some cases, this woman is an actual sister who marries one of her brother's new wife's brothers; in other cases, the woman is a classificatory sister or even a future daughter. In other areas, notable amounts of goods (bride wealth) change hands, including money, pigs, kava, mats, food, and cotton cloth. Traditionally, powerful leading men might marry polygynously, although after missionization, monogamy became the norm. There are three types of marriages: religious, civil, and "customary." Divorce rates are very low.

Domestic Unit. The nuclear family is the principal domestic unit, forming the basic household and being responsible for day-to-day economic production and consumption. Households, however, continue to rely on extended kin groups in significant

A mask from Vanuatu. There is a strong belief in the power of ancestral spirits.

ways. Most people's access to land and sea rights derives from membership in lineages and clans. People call on extended kin as a labor pool when they build new houses, clear garden land, and raise money and collect goods for family exchanges (marriage, child initiation, funerals). Residence typically is patrivirilocal. Women move to live with their new husbands, who themselves live with their fathers' families. Formerly, many men and initiated boys lived in separate men's houses; today families typically live together as one unit. Both spouses may be involved in managing family affairs; men, however, citing custom and Christian scripture, typically assert basic authority their families.

Inheritance. Except in urban areas, where inheritance is modeled on European precedent, people follow local customs. Land rights pass patrilineally or matrilineally to surviving members of kin groups. In some areas, people destroy much of dead person's goods. Surviving spouses and children inherit what is left.

Kin Groups. Families are organized into larger patrilineages or matrilineages, patriclans or matriclans, and moieties. Lineages tend to be localized in one or two villages, as kin live together on or near lineage land. The membership of larger clans is dispersed across a region or island.

SOCIALIZATION

Infant Care. Babies often nurse until they are three years old. Both parents are involved in child care, but siblings, especially older sisters, do much of the carrying, feeding, and amusing of infants. Babies are held by caregivers almost constantly until they can walk. Physical punishment of children is not common. Younger children may strike their older siblings, while older siblings are restrained from hitting back.

Child Rearing and Education. Many communities and ensure the growth of children through ritual initiation ceremonies that involve the exchange of pigs, mats, kava, and other goods between a child's father's and mother's families. Boys age six to twelve typically undergo circumcision as part of a ritual event.

Most children receive several years of primary education in English or French. Many walk to the nearest school or board there during the week. Less than 10 percent of children go on to attend one of the twenty-seven secondary schools.

Higher Education. Tertiary education includes a teachers' training college, an agricultural school, several church seminaries, and a branch of the University of the South Pacific in Port Vila. A few students pursue university education abroad. The adult literacy rate has been estimated at 55 to 70 percent.

ETIQUETTE

Customary relationships are lubricated by the exchange of goods, and visitors often receive food and other gifts that should be reciprocated. Lines in rural stores are often amorphous, but clerks commonly serve overseas visitors first. People passing on the trails or streets commonly greet one another, and the handshake is an important aspect of initial encounters. A woman traveling alone through the countryside may receive unwelcome attention from men.

RELIGION

Religious Beliefs. Most families have been Christian since the late nineteenth century. The largest denominations are Presbyterian, Anglican, Roman Catholic, Seventh-Day Adventist, and Church of Christ. Baha'i and Mormon missionaries have attracted local followings. Some people reject Christianity and retain traditional religious practices. Others belong to syncretic religious organizations that mix Christianity and local belief. Nearly everyone maintains firm beliefs in the power and presence of ancestral spirits.

Religious Practitioners. Christian priests, ministers, pastors, and deacons lead weekly services and conduct marriages and funerals. A number of people are recognized as clairvoyants and diviners, working sometimes within and sometimes outside the Christian churches. These people, who are often women, divine the causes of disease and other misfortunes, locate lost objects, and sometimes undertake antisorcery campaigns to uncover *poesen* (sorcery paraphernalia) hidden in a village. Other people specialize in rain, wind, earthquake, tidal wave, and other sorts of magical practice. Many ni-Vanuatu also suspect the existence of sorcerers.

Rituals and Holy Places. Ni-Vanuatu celebrate the Christian calendar, particularly the Christmas and New Year's season, which they call *Bonane*. At the year's end, urbanites return to their home islands. In villages, people form choruses and visit neighboring hamlets to perform religious and secular songs.

Ni-Vanuatu continue to celebrate traditional holidays. In many places, islanders organize first-fruit celebrations, particularly for the annual yam crop. The most spectacular celebration is the ''land jump'' on southern Pentecost Island. Tourists sometimes attend other traditional rites, such the dancing and feasting that accompany male initiation and grade-taking ceremonies in many of the cultures and the *Toka* (or *Nakwiari*), a large-scale exchange of pigs and kava celebrated with two days of dancing.

Every community recognizes important places associated with ancestral and other spirits. These ''taboo places'' may be mountain peaks, offshore reef formations, or rocky outcroppings. People avoid these locations or treat them with respect.

Death and the Afterlife. Nearly all families turn to Christian funerary ritual to bury their dead. Ancestral ghosts continue to haunt their descendants. Many people experience their spiritual presence and receive their advice in dreams.

MEDICINE AND HEALTH CARE

The national health service emerged from the separate French and British colonial systems. Most sick people turn initially to local diviners and healers

Villagers congregate in the protection of the shade on Ambrym Island. Households rely on extended kin groups.

who determine whether the source of disease is supernatural or natural and concoct medicines. Folk pharmacology includes hundreds of medical recipes, mostly infusions of leaves and other plant material.

SECULAR CELEBRATIONS

In addition to Independence Day (30 July), Constitution Day (5 October), and Unity Day (29 Novem-

ber), the government has established Family Day (26 December) and Custom Chiefs Day (5 March). Organized and impromptu sports matches are popular, as are money-raising carnivals, agricultural fairs, and arts festivals.

THE ARTS AND HUMANITIES

Literature. Although nineteenth-century missionaries created orthographies and dictionaries for some of the languages, indigenous literature is mostly oral. Ni-Vanuatu appreciate oratory and storytelling and have large archives of oral tales, myths, and legends. Since independence, an orthography committee has attempted to standardize Bislama spelling. Publications mostly consist of biblical material and newspapers, newsletters, and pamphlets. Writers working in English or French have published poems and short stories, particularly at the University of the South Pacific.

Graphic Arts. The tourist industry supports an active cottage handicraft and carving industry, including woven baskets and dyed mats, bark skirts, penis wrappers, miniature slit-gongs and other carvings, shell jewelry, bamboo flutes and panpipes. A few art galleries in Port Vila sell the work of local artists.

Performance Arts. The string band is the preeminent musical genre. Hundreds of bands perform at village dances and weddings, and their music has been important in the emergence of a national culture. Young musicians sing of local and national issues in local languages and Bislama. Popularized on cassette tapes or broadcast on the two radio stations, some of those songs have become national standards. Many bands travel to Port Vila in June to compete in an annual competition. Small community theater organizations whose dramas often address national issues perform in Port Vila, and occasionally tour the hinterlands.

THE STATE OF THE PHYSICAL AND SOCIAL SCIENCES

Several international research associations, such as France's ORSTOM, have studied agriculture, volcanism, geology, geography, and marine biology in Vanuatu. A local amateur society, the Vanuatu Natural Science Society, emphasizes ornithology. The University of the South Pacific Centre in Port Vila houses that university's Pacific languages unit and law school. The Vanuatu Cultural Center supports a succesful local fieldwork program in which men and women are trained to study and document anthropological and linguistic information.

BIBLIOGRAPHY

Allen, Michael, ed. *Vanuatu: Politics, Economics and Ritual in Island Melanesia*, 1981.

Bonnemaison, Joël. *The Tree and the Canoe: History and Ethnography of Tanna*, 1994.

————, Kirk Huffman, Christian Kaufmann, and Darrell Tryon, eds. *Arts of Vanuatu*, 1996.

Coiffier, Christine. *Traditional Architecture in Vanuatu*, 1988.

Crowley, Terry. *Beach-La-Mar to Bislama: The Emergence of a National Language in Vanuatu*, 1991.

Foster, Robert J., ed. *Nation Making: Emergent Identities in Postcolonial Melanesia*, 1995.

Haberkorn, Gerald. *Port Vila: Transit Station or Final Stop?*, 1989.

Jolly, Margaret. *Women of the Place: Kastom, Colonialism and Gender in Vanuatu*, 1994.

Lindstrom, Lamont. *Knowledge and Power in a South Pacific Society*, 1990.

Lini, Walter. *Beyond Pandemonium: From the New Hebrides to Vanuatu*, 1980.

McClancy, Jeremy. *To Kill a Bird with Two Stones: A Short History of Vanuatu*, 1980.

Miles, William F. S. *Bridging Mental Boundaries in a Postcolonial Microcosm: Identity and Development in Vanuatu*, 1998.

Rodman, Margaret C. *Masters of Tradition: Consequences of Customary Land Tenure in Longana, Vanuatu*, 1987.

Van Trease, Howard, ed. *Melanesian Politics: Stael Blong Vanuatu*, 1995.

Weightman, Barry. *Agriculture in Vanuatu: A Historical Review*, 1989.

—LAMONT LINDSTROM

VATICAN CITY

CULTURE NAME
Vatican

ALTERNATIVE NAMES
Holy See, the Vatican

ORIENTATION

Identification. The Vatican, or Vatican City, is the center of Roman Catholicism and the residence of the bishop of Rome (the pope). The popes controlled the Papal States in what is now Italy throughout most of the Middle Ages. On 13 May 1871, the new Italian state restricted the pope's temporal authority to the Vatican and Lateran areas of Rome and the rural retreat of Castel Gandolfo. The popes refused to accept the validity of this law until the Concordat of 11 February 1929 gave the Catholic Church special status in Italy and paid an indemnity to the now independent Vatican City.

Location and Geography. The Vatican's 108.7 acres are completely surrounded by Rome.

Demography. There are about 850 Italian and Swiss permanent residents, along with lay workers from Catholic communities around the world.

Linguistic Affiliation. The major languages are Italian and Latin.

Symbolism. The pope represents a link to Saint Peter and Jesus. Vatican ceremonies recall the words and actions of Jesus and his followers. Candles, incense and various rituals carry symbolic meaning. The Vatican is a symbol of Church leadership and its apostolic tradition.

HISTORY AND ETHNIC RELATIONS

Emergence of the Nation. The Vatican is a successor to the Papal States, which made up a large area of central Italy. After the unification of Italy, the new state annexed the Papal States after Germany defeated France, which had protected the pope's interests, in the Franco-Prussian War (1870–1871). The popes refused to leave, declaring themselves ''Prisoners of the Vatican,'' until Benito Mussolini signed agreements in 1929 granting the Church special privileges in Italy and a cash settlement. The Vatican was given independence under papal rule. Since that time, the Vatican has been an independent state that sends and receives ambassadors.

National Identity. The Vatican's identity is religious, not national. It presents itself as transnational and universal.

Ethnic Relations. The Vatican has sought ties with members of all ethnic groups as part of its universal religious identity.

URBANISM, ARCHITECTURE, AND THE USE OF SPACE

The Vatican is entirely urban. It has many artistic and architectural masterpieces, including Saint Peter's Cathedral and the Sistine Chapel. Despite its small area, there is a sense of openness and comfort.

FOOD AND ECONOMY

Food in Daily Life. The major food style is that of Rome. Like other Italians, residents of the Vatican consider their cooking the best in the world. Pope John Paul II caused a furor when he requested Polish cooking from the papal chef.

Food Customs at Ceremonial Occasions. On New Year's Eve, the Italian tradition is to have the meal of the seven fishes, including eels, conch, and squid. Lamb is a traditional Easter dish. For each of these meals, there is always a pasta course.

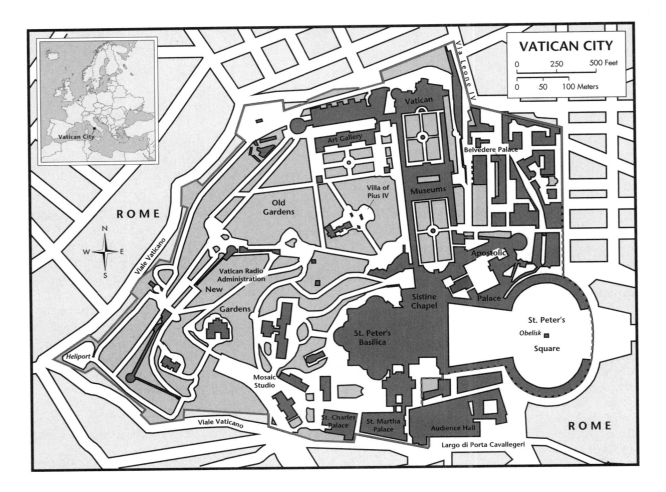

Vatican City

Basic Economy. The economy is based on religious work: the Vatican receives contributions from churches around the world. Tourists come to visit religious shrines and view the art. The major commercial activities are organized around religious concerns, the major industry is governance of the Church, and trade is organized around religious goods.

Land Tenure and Property. The Church owns all property in Vatican City and areas outside the Vatican covered by extraterritorial rights.

Division of Labor. The Curia rules the Church under the pope. Its members come from countries around the world and work in many governmental departments. The pope presides over the bureaucracy, delegating and consulting with his subordinates. The heads of the important bureaus tend to be cardinals.

SOCIAL STRATIFICATION

Classes and Castes. The Vatican is highly stratified. The pope is at the apex of the hierarchy and cardinal-archbishops, bishops, monsignors, priests, and others come below him, followed by the heads of bureaus. Lay workers generally rank below the clergy.

Symbols of Social Stratification. Clerical dress marks a person's rank. The pope's white robes distinguish him clearly. Cardinals wear red, and other ranks are noted by their style of dress and rings. Style of clothing, place in a procession line, and seating are also marks of social position.

POLITICAL LIFE

Government. The basic law is the Code of Canon Law. Church councils meet approximately once per century. Bishops' synods meet periodically and offer advice, but the day-to-day running of the Vati-

The Piazza San Pietro at night. The Piazza is the site of public masses and worldwide papal addresses.

can is in the hands of appointed officials who oversee the Curia.

Leadership and Political Officials. There are no political parties, but the positions held by the clergy and the laity cover a wide spectrum of opinion, although those positions are not always equally represented. There is an elaborate code of etiquette for approaching officials. Generally, go-betweens are used to arrange meetings. Much is done informally. There is a feeling that consensus should be reached before decisions are published. Therefore, things are discussed at length before the pope speaks officially.

Social Problems and Control. There is little crime, and the typical problems are disputes over religious doctrine and governance. Strict statements and actions regarding conformity to doctrine, including censorship and the silencing of dissidents, have alternated with attempts at persuasion and expressions of conciliation.

Military Activity. The Vatican is officially neutral in world affairs but can mediate disputes if invited to do so. Swiss guards in medieval uniforms protect the pope and the city.

SOCIAL WELFARE AND CHANGE PROGRAMS

There are social welfare programs for employees. Catholic charity organizations promote social welfare and change throughout the world.

NONGOVERNMENTAL ORGANIZATIONS AND OTHER ASSOCIATIONS

In the Vatican, there are no distinctions between church and state. The Vatican works with many secular organizations.

GENDER ROLES AND STATUSES

The ethos is male-dominated. There have been efforts toward greater gender equality, especially on the part of nuns. However, as long as the priesthood is reserved for males, it will be difficult to achieve such equality. Men hold the vast majority of key positions.

MARRIAGE, FAMILY, AND KINSHIP

The married people in the Vatican are mainly commuting workers whose family arrangements are the same as those in Italy.

ETIQUETTE

The Vatican insists on modest and appropriate dress in its sacred places. Quiet is enjoined in sacred areas, and deference to the clergy is expected. There is strict adherence to speaking only when addressed and deferring to senior officials.

RELIGION

Religious Beliefs. The Vatican is a Catholic state whose population is virtually 100 percent Roman Catholic. There is a belief in heaven and hell and in just rewards or punishments for one's actions on earth. There is a belief in a supreme triune God, and various saints are honored. The final judgment and resurrection of the dead are tenets of the faith.

Religious Practitioners. The Catholic clergy are the major religious practitioners and can administer the seven sacraments, depending on their rank. Bishops can ordain other priests.

Rituals and Holy Places. The Vatican is a treasure trove of special buildings and shrines. Saint Peter's is the site of Peter's tomb and is built over the original basilica. The Sistine Chapel in the church features the ceiling painted by Michelangelo. The Lateral Palace, once the home of the popes, is another magnificent building. Saint Peter's Square is known around the world, and the pope often addresses the world from the square. It is also the site of many of his public masses. The religious calendar of the Catholic Church is followed, along with the rituals appropriate to that calendar.

Death and the Afterlife. The beliefs of the Catholic Church in a life after death, the existence of Purgatory, and the efficacy of prayers for the dead are followed.

MEDICINE AND HEALTH CARE

The Vatican has an up-to-date health care system that draws on specialists from around the world.

SECULAR CELEBRATIONS

There are no secular holidays. The major religious feasts are Christmas and Easter, and there are other major holy days and feast days of saints.

THE ARTS AND HUMANITIES

The Church has a long history of supporting the arts. The Vatican is among other things a museum. Its library is a major source of knowledge about the Renaissance and European history.

THE STATE OF THE PHYSICAL AND SOCIAL SCIENCES

The Vatican is more interested in social sciences than physical sciences. It is not opposed to the physical sciences and has stated its general support for the physical sciences and their compatibility with religion. Within the Vatican, there has been more immediate application of the social sciences, particularly sociology, psychology, and political science.

BIBLIOGRAPHY

"Future Doubtful for Bishops' Conferences." *America* 179 (4): 3, 1998.

Hersey, George L. *High Renaissance Art in St. Peter's and the Vatican: An Interpretive Guide*, 1993.

Hutchinson, Robert J. *When in Rome: A Journal of Life in the Vatican*, 1998.

McDowell, Bart, James L. Stanfield, Elizabeth L. Newhouse, and Charles M. Kogod, eds. *Inside the Vatican*, 1993.

Reese, Thomas. *Inside the Vatican*, 1996.

Roncalli, Francesco. *Vatican City: Vatican Museums*, 1997.

Steinfels, Margaret O'Brien. "How the Vatican Works: An Interview with Thomas J. Reese." *Commonweal*, 123 (4): 10–13, 1996.

Stickler, Alphonso. *The Vatican Library: Its History and Treasures*, 1989.

—FRANK A. SALAMONE

VENEZUELA

CULTURE NAME
Venezuelan

ORIENTATION

Identification. In 1499, as a member of Christopher Columbus's third voyage to the Americas, Alonso de Ojeda made an initial reconnaissance of what is today Venezuela's northern Caribbean coast. Ojeda named this region Venice because the indigenous houses were located on stilts above the Orinico River's current. This initial name later evolved into that of Venezuela, which was then used to name the colonial territory under Spanish rule as the *Capitanía General de Venezuela.*

Venezuela's national population is very similar to that of most other South American countries, with a mixture of an initial indigenous population, a large Spanish influx, and a significant population of African ancestry. There have also been notable European and Latin American migrations in the last two centuries. Even with these different populations, however, Venezuela has one of the most stable national identities in the continent. This national stability is probably due to two factors: (1) Venezuela has an extremely small contemporary presence of indigenous communities to contest the national stability, and (2) until the 1990s Venezuela boasted an incredibly strong national economy.

Location and Geography. Venezuela is located on the northern (Caribbean) coast of South America. It has an area of 352,144 square miles (912,050 square kilometers) and is bordered by Guyana to the east, Brazil to the south, Colombia to the west, and the Atlantic Ocean and Caribbean Sea to the north. In general, Venezuela is usually divided into four major environmental regions: the coastal zone, the Andean mountain range, the *llanos* (plains), and the Guiana Highlands.

Venezuela's capital, Caracas, and all the other major cities are located along the coast. Historically the coast has been the most populated area in the country and is where most of Venezuela's population lives today. The rest of the country is traditionally referred to as the interior (*el interior*). The northernmost tip of the Andes' continental range runs through the northernmost part of Venezuela. Andean inhabitants are portrayed as conservative and reserved, having more in common culturally with other Andean populations than with the rest of the country.

The llanos is by far the largest region in the country, making up one-third of the territory. The region is mainly great open plains with small foothills toward the north, dividing the region into low and high llanos. The population in the region is typically portrayed as open and rugged plains-people. The population is far from homogenous, however, and even the language spoken in the region still reflects both indigenous and African linguistic influence.

To the east the llanos end at the *Macizo Guayanés* (Guyanese Mount) which is one of the oldest rock formations in the world. The region to the south, the Guiana, is also referred to as *La Gran Sabana* (Great Savanna) since it is composed of savannas and flat mountaintops (referred to as *tepuis* in the indigenous Pemón tongue). It was this environment that Sir Arthur Conan Doyle (1859–1930) immortalized in his epic, *The Lost World.* Further south is the Amazonas with its hot and humid tropical forest. The Amazonas region is sparsely populated even though it includes 70 percent of Venezuela's indigenous population.

Demography. Venezuela is mainly made up of four groups: *mestizos,* or *pardos,* (mixed European and Indian ancestry), comprising 67 percent of the population; white (European descent, mainly Spanish, Italian, and Portuguese), 2l percent; black (African and Caribbean descent), 10 percent; and Indian (Native Americans), 2 percent. These groups tend to be regionally localized: The cities are mainly (but

Venezuela

not exclusively) inhabited by whites and pardos; Indians occupy the remote Guianan and Amazonas interior; and blacks live along the Caribbean coast–line. At least one-fourth of Venezuela's contemporary population consists of immigrants, many of them illegal.

Linguistic Affiliation. Venezuela's official language, Spanish, was introduced into the territory in the sixteenth century. There are still twenty-five surviving indigenous languages belonging to three linguistic families: Caribans, Arawak, and Chibcha. A strong African linguistic presence is also felt along the coastal region. It is English, however, that is slowly becoming the country's second official language. As extremely modern-minded citizens, Venezuelans feel it is necessary to be fluent in English for cultural and commercial purposes. Venezuela's oil boom has also contributed to an increase in English usage, and many private schools use English in a bilingual curriculum.

Symbolism. The most cohesive national symbol is the image of the country's main independence fighter, General Simón Bolívar (1783–1830). Bolívar led the military movement that freed Venezuela and the neighboring countries of Colombia, Ecuador, Peru, and Bolivia of Spanish domination. Statues of him are present in almost every city and town, and the country's currency and the main airport (as well as many other institutions) are named after him.

Venezuelans are also one of the most appearance-minded people in the world. Venezuelans place an extreme national pride on their physical beauty, fashion, and overall outward appearance. They also express pride in the fact that Venezuelan contestants either win or place very well in the yearly Miss World and Miss Universe beauty pageants. Although beauty is predominantly a concern for the female population, males have also increased their awareness of beauty standards, and a yearly male beauty pageant has also been instituted. This beauty concern is also reflected in the growth of the television media in the country. Venezuela was one of the first exporters of *telenovelas* (soap operas) to the South American continent and the world.

Another national symbolic marker is the Caribbean coast along with its grand Lake Maracaibo. Lake Maracaibo itself is approximately 130 miles (209 kilometers) long and 75 miles (120 kilometers) at its widest, and is directly connected by a narrow strait to the Caribbean Sea. The coastline and lake reflect the symbiotic relationship of the country with both South America and the Caribbean. The Caribbean coastline, and its imagery of sand, sun, and pleasurable delights, also supports the second largest industry of the country, tourism.

HISTORY AND ETHNIC RELATIONS

Emergence of the Nation. The current Venezuelan nation as such appeared in 1829. Venezuela had three brief republican configurations before 1829. The first Venezuelan republic was a short-lived rule forged in 1810 by Venezuela's Francisco de Miranda; Miranda surrendered to the Spaniards in 1812 and died in exile in 1816. The second republican junta (1813) was led by Simón Bolívar himself but was as short-lived as the initial republic. Finally, Bolívar was able to oust the Spanish colonial empire in the Battle of Carabobo on 24 June 1821, and proclaimed Venezuela part of the Republic of Gran Colombia (which included the contemporary states of Colombia and Ecuador). Because of internal political conflicts and Bolívar's waning health, however, Venezuela proclaimed itself an independent republic on 5 July 1829.

National Identity. Venezuela has been able to sustain a national identity that owes much to its Spanish colonial heritage. The country has maintained a white (European) national ethos and its top positions have typically been secured for its lighter-skinned citizens. This European-minded identity has been very much part of Venezuela since its initial republican origin. For example, in many of

Bolívar's foundational writings the Indians, pardos, and blacks are referred to in paternalistic fashion and benevolently advised to come into the modern civilized fold. This particular national ethos, however, has not gone unaffected by both the pardo and black communities, which together make up more than two-thirds of Venezuela's population. This demographic reality in itself is reflected in Caribbean and Latin American cultural characteristics even in the face of a white ideology central to the national identity.

Ethnic Relations. The four main cultural groups are very much regionally oriented: whites and pardos are mostly city dwellers; Indians live in the Amazon as region; and blacks along the Caribbean coast. These groups have maintained a surprisingly small amount of modern ethnic friction considering the predominantly white control of the country. This Europanist trend has also significantly impacted Venezuela's large immigrant population.

In the 1840s and again during the early 1900s Venezuela consistently attempted to entice Europeans to migrate to the country. Both of these campaigns proved unsuccessful, with Spanish, Italian and Portuguese immigrants flocking to Venezuela only after World War II. These constant attempts to bring in skilled workers and to "whiten" the national population were further supported by congressional proposals in the late 1800s to prohibit the immigration of Asians and black.

By far the largest immigrant group in the country, however, is Colombians, followed very closely by other South Americans—Ecuadorians and Chileans—and Caribbeans, mainly Dominicans and people from the Lesser Antilles. Since the 1960s, largely due to the oil boom, official immigrant restrictions on nonwhite populations have ended. By then, however, social power was solidly entrenched among the white elite.

URBANISM, ARCHITECTURE, AND THE USE OF SPACE

Venezuela's spatial landscape is clearly demarcated between the urban and the rural. The city of Caracas, with its 4 million inhabitants (almost a fifth of the country's total population) is the emblem of a modern elite and European-style existence. Meanwhile the rural homesteads of the llanos, Andes, and Guiana Highlands represent a farming way of life with a more traditional subsistence strategy. The recent influx of rural migrants (both from Venezuela and abroad) has impacted the urban landscape, especially within the *ranchos* (lower- and middle-

Simple homes with a flaring oil well in the background, Cabimas. Oil is Venezuela's most profitable export product.

income urban housing). Modern ideals and the escalating Americanization of Venezuelan culture have increasingly diminished the presence of traditional rural customs in the city centers.

This blend of modernist aspirations tempered with local traditions, including colonial architectural remnants, has created a unique Venezuelan style. A particular architectural expression of this is the internationally acclaimed construction of the Central University of Caracas, designed by the Venezuelan architect Carlos Raúl Villanueva, with asymmetrical buildings, large standing murals, and sculptures.

FOOD AND ECONOMY

Food in Daily Life. Venezuelans have three main meals: a large breakfast, a large dinner (around noontime), and a very light supper in the evening. Venezuelan hospitality is widespread, so something to drink and eat is expected when visiting someone's home. *Arepas*, the most distinctive Venezuelan food, are thick disks made of precooked cornmeal, either fried or baked. Large arepas, with a variety of fillings (ham and cheese is the most popular one), are eaten as snacks throughout the day; smaller arepas are typically served as side companions at all meals.

Similar to arepas are *empanadas* (deep-fried pasties) and *cachapas* (a pancake/crepe-like dish), which are filled with cheese, ham, and/or bacon. Among the other main Venezuelan dishes are the *pabellón criollo*, which consists of black beans, fried sweet plantains, white rice, and semi-shredded meat (*carne mechada*), all topped with a fried egg. Also popular are *pernil* (roasted pork), *asado* (roasted beef), *bistec a caballo* (steak with fried egg), and pork chops. Fruit juices are also extremely popular and there is also a great variety of salads, although these are traditionally seen as a complementary, not a main, dish.

Tequeños, long small rolls filled with hot cheese or chocolate, take their name from Los Teques, a city just outside Caracas. The typical drink of the llanos, *chicha*, is made out of ground rice, salt, condensed milk, sugar, vanilla, and ice.

Basic Economy. That Venezuela was until 1970 the largest oil exporter in the world positively differentiated its economy from other South American nations. Since the 1940s oil revenues were consistently used to diversify Venezuela's national industry. This national trend has most significantly affected a strong mineral export policy and the development of hydroelectric energy. It was only in the mid-1970s that Venezuela was finally able to break the multinational hold over its oil and gas industry. This transnational privatization trend returned in the 1990s, however, when a drop in oil prices, global recession, inflation, unemployment, government corruption, and a lack of skilled personnel forced the reversal of the initial nationalizing policy. An increasing foreign debt as well as large level of illegal immigration further burdened Venezuela's troubled economy at the turn of the millennium. Venezuela has responded to these circumstances with growing support and continued diversification of its industry, larger agricultural outputs, and greater exploitation of its natural resources.

Land Tenure and Property. Until the 1950s and 1960s when the first agrarian reform projects were implemented, the land distribution was still very similar to that of colonial days, allowing 2 percent of the population to control over 80 percent of the land. Agricultural production is also quite underdeveloped with less than 5 percent of the total territory dedicated to farming. There is still a large group of traditional farmers harvesting small family plots (*conucos*), with their main crops being corn, rice, coffee, and cacao. Large agricultural producers (*fincas comercializadas*) have most significantly benefitted from government and state funding, allowing them to use large amounts of wage labor, fertilizers, and insecticides, and to also mechanize their production. There are also large herding farms (*fincas ganaderas*), some over 6,000 acres (2,430 hectares), located in the vast llanos region.

Major Industries. More than half of Venezuela's labor force is incorporated into the service sector of the economy, while less than 40 percent of the population is dedicated either to agricultural or industrial production. Venezuela has quite a diversified industrial sector, largely due to its reinvestment of oil resources. The first type of industry are the oil refineries and petrochemical plants themselves. These tend to be located around Puerto Cabello (just west of Caracas) and in the state of Zulia (Venezuela's westernmost state). The second largest industry is the production of consumer goods. Import substitution strategies have been established for goods such as textiles, leather, paper, tires, tobacco, light engineering products, and modern appliances. The auto industry has also attempted, albeit less successfully, to establish its own assembly industry. The third type of industry is the production of heavy industrial materials such as iron, steel, and aluminum.

Trade. Venezuela's most lucrative export item is oil. Its main trading partner is the United States,

with which it has been able to maintain favorable trade balances. Venezuela imports machinery, transportation equipment, pharmaceuticals, food products, tobacco, and beverages from the United States in exchange for its oil. Venezuela's other major trading partners are the Netherlands, Japan, Germany, France, Italy, Brazil, and Colombia.

Division of Labor. The main division of labor in the country is between rural and urban populations. By far, rural occupations such as agriculture and cattle herding are considered to be less sophisticated. This same modernist ideal contributes to a division between manual and specialized forms of labor. The immigrant population occupies most of the menial and less remunerative forms of employment which Venezuelans themselves avoid. In the 1990s, however, there was a significant lack of local specialized workers; this was one of the main factors that seriously compromised the country's oil production.

SOCIAL STRATIFICATION

Classes and Castes. Venezuela does not recognize an official caste system although it does participate in a strongly defined class structure that is not without its strong caste implications. The class system places most of the political and economic power in the hands of a very small group (less than 10 percent of the population). The elite is composed of the traditional white population; this also provides white (European) immigrants greater opportunity for participating in Venezuela's economic wealth. Meanwhile this color/racial division is most dramatically felt by Latin American immigrants of African and Indian ancestry, who are forced to form the lowest ranks of Venezuelan society.

Venezuela also developed a large middle class in the twentieth century mainly as a result of the oil revenues. The middle class, and in particular the large lower-middle class, was significantly affected by the social crisis of the 1990s which led to large-scale riots that caused thousand of deaths and the collapse of President Carlos Andrés Perez's government.

Symbols of Social Stratification. Media images of physical beauty and fashion are the most salient symbols of social stratification. How one looks, what one wears, one's profession, and one's wealth are the greatest markers of social status. The country's preoccupation with a modern beauty ideal and personal hygiene is closely related to a colonial complex of idealizing European (white) culture. Since

Thatched huts along the shore of a river. This type of dwelling is home to the indigenous peoples of Venezuela.

World War II, U.S. pop culture has most significantly attracted and been imitated by Venezuelans. The reification and embodiment of North American ideals of beauty, musical genres, and fashion define who maintains the greatest level of social status.

POLITICAL LIFE

Government. Venezuela's government is federalist in nature, composed of executive, legislative, and judicial branches. The executive branch is led by a popularly elected president who holds office for five years. The legislative branch is composed of a Congress that is divided into a Senate and a Chamber of Deputies. The Chamber of Deputies reflects the country's regional representation, while the Senate has two representatives from each state and the capital's federal district. Venezuela's highest judicial institution is that of the Supreme Court, whose members are elected by the representatives of Congress.

Leadership and Political Officials. In 1999 Colonel Hugo Chávez Frías was overwhelmingly voted into office as Venezuela's president. Chávez's election as president was striking because he had recently been imprisoned for leading a failed coup against the government of Carlos Andrés Pérez. But Chávez can best be described as a *caudillo* (popular leader), that is, a leader who expresses an idiosyncratic nature and has wide-level popular support. In fact, until 1935 Venezuela had mainly been lead by strong military caudillos. It was not until 1969 that the first transition between two popularly elected democratic governments occurred.

The two main political parties are the Social Christian (COPEI) and the left-leaning Democratic Action (Acción Democrática), although the left-leaning MAS (Movimiento al Socialismo) and Radical Cause (Causa Radical) also have popular followings. Nevertheless, the fragile political party structure is still evident in the election of strong *caudillo* figures such as Chávez and in his explicit effort to try to dismantle the political party system.

Social Problems and Control. The largest problems in terms of social unrest are those that result from traditional crimes and riots. Crimes come in all shapes and sizes, from petty theft to widespread government corruption. Most street crime is committed at night or in the poorest neighborhoods of the urban centers. These violent crimes, although committed at gun- or knifepoint, tend to be fatal less often than they could be. There is, however, widespread carrying of guns not only by the police but also by private guards and a significant part of the male population. All of this contributes to constant shoot-outs and police chases, which produce a notable increase in wounds and death. At the same time the police and other government officials do not tend to garner much public affection, which only increases the difficulty of maintaining the public order. In the 1990s the economic crises also contributed to traditional forms of public protests and riots. This unfortunately had its climax during Pérez's government when confrontations between the people and the army and police led to over a thousand deaths.

Military Activity. The Venezuelan military includes an estimated eighty thousand members divided into the navy, army, and air force. The country has traditionally maintained low levels of defense expenditures, averaging only 1.5 percent of its gross domestic product. Venezuela has had ongoing historic conflicts with neighboring Colombia and Guyana, which flared up in the 1980s. Since then, however, the military has been less concerned with international conflicts than with maintaining internal political order. The military has also been brought in to investigate cases of ransom kidnaping, which have significantly increased since the 1980s.

Skyscrapers and a fountain in Plaza Venezuela, Caracas, exemplify the ideals of modernization and Americanization.

NONGOVERNMENTAL ORGANIZATIONS AND OTHER ASSOCIATIONS

In striking comparison to most other South American countries, Venezuela has a negligible presence of nongovernmental organizations. The two areas that most vividly benefit from international and local support are the environment and human rights advocacy. The area around Lake Maracaibo and the Amazon regions are the ones most generally presented as in need of local legislative protection. Meanwhile, it is also Amazon indigenous groups such as the Yanomamo who receive the greatest amount of international funds to defend themselves against government and private mining incursions in their territory. Unfortunately the Yanomamo have been the target of genocidal massacres as well as the constant threat of the destruction of their traditional ways of life.

GENDER ROLE AND STATUS

Division of Labor by Gender. Men overwhelmingly occupy the most important political, economic, social, and religious positions in Venezuela. The traditional sexist Western gender division of labor is present in Venezuela, with men occupying the most physical demanding jobs while women are traditionally relegated to household or domestic service jobs. In the rural areas, however, women and men both partake in demanding physical labor, and Western roles are somewhat blurred. Cattle herding, however, is still a predominantly male occupation. Meanwhile, the beauty pageant industry and the preparation of females for international competitions seems to both sustain and subvert traditional Western notions of female and male occupations. In this manner females are still highly regarded as beauty objects but more and more men are also raised to similar standards of sexual objectification.

The Relative Status of Women and Men. Venezuela is a very patriarchal society expressing its own distinct national brand of machismo. Although men and women are legally equal, there are still great differences in terms of actual wage earnings, sexual freedom, and social expectations. In daily life, men are still expected to work outside the home, support the household, and prove their virility with many heterosexual liaisons. The modernist trend of following North American culture, however, is creating conflicts with these traditional gender expectations. Women are more and more a part of the general workforce, increasing their economic standing and discarding the exclusive domestic burden of the household and child rearing.

MARRIAGE, FAMILY AND KINSHIP

Marriage. Venezuelans practice open-ended marriages, meaning there are few legal restrictions as long as the person marries someone of the opposite sex and of legal age. In actuality, however, there are several concerns regarding whom one should get involved with, particularly in terms of class and racial distinctions. It is expected and predominant that people marry others of their same or higher social class standing—including racial status as well. The ideal is generally to marry somebody "whiter" or at least of the same racial status; the opposite, although not completely rare, is seen as going against the norm.

Domestic Unit. In Venezuelan society the family and the role played by the mother are essential in the maintenance of the social fabric. Most people tend to live in nuclear families (parents and siblings), although extended kin (grandparents, aunts, uncles, and cousins) traditionally live close by. When migration has produced a break in the family, the ties are closely maintained through letters, phone calls, and e-mail. In this manner it is not surprising that children (both male and female) live with their parents until their mid-twenties or until they marry and can move out on their own. It is expected that family members do everything in their power to help and support all family members—help that can range from getting each other jobs to making space for them in their own homes.

Inheritance. Inheritance rules are legally prescribed and there is no major distinction in terms of gender, class, or race. The higher status one holds, however, the more successful one is in maneuvering Venezuela's complex legal and social system.

SOCIALIZATION

Child Rearing and Education. Children are traditionally cared for by their parents, although the extended kin may also play a major role in the upbringing. In terms of child rearing the national culture espouses Western ideals of good behavior, education, and competitiveness. On top of this an enormous amount of friendliness, generosity, and overall good nature is expected of children as they grow up.

Venezuela provides free and compulsory education through grade twelve for all its population. In 1995 literacy was estimated at over 90 percent. Private and Catholic schools provide a large array of grade and high schools (*liceos*) mainly in the major urban centers. These private institutions have far better reputations and are where most of the middle and upper classes send their children.

Higher Education. In general only 20-30 percent of Venezuela's population goes on to obtain a university degree. Since the 1950s there has been an increasing proliferation of private universities although by far the ones with the best reputations are public ones such as the Universidad Central de Caracas (the Central University in Caracas). A university degree or title (normally referred to as *carrera*) traditionally takes between four and five years after which one obtains the degree of *licenciado* (equivalent to or higher than the bachelor of arts degree in the United States). There are a series of master's level graduate programs but doctorates at the Ph.D. level are quite rare.

ETIQUETTE

Venezuelans are characterized by their outgoing and gregarious nature. This extroverted behavior is visible in the traditional forms of greeting and in people's body language. When meeting somebody, even if it is for the first time, it is common to give two kisses, one on each cheek; women greet men and women this way, while men only kiss women. Between men a strong-gripped handshake is the custom and many times this is accompanied by the placing of the other hand on the side for greater emphasis. A hug is also used between men, especially if the men have not seen each other for a while. These forms of male greeting, however, are used for people of equal status and indicate familiarity and therefore are not be used with somebody of higher status.

Body language between Venezuelans is also much more fluid and pervasive. People stand very close to each other while talking and will gesticulate with their hands and bodies to make a point. It is also common for people to touch each other to even further emphasize what it is that they are saying. Friendly conversations can also appear to be arguments because of their loud and freewheeling nature. Meanwhile there is also lots of unique sign language. For example, pointing with one's finger is considered rude and vulgar; it is much more acceptable and widely understood if one just points with one's mouth. At the same time a smaller version of the "okay" symbol is usually meant as an insult rather than as a symbol of agreement.

A peddler selling Venezuelan flags. Statues of freedom-fighter Simón Bolívar are pervasive throughout the country.

There is also an enormous amount of public expression of machismo. Women are customarily showered with remarks and gazes from men who want to display admiration and awe at their sexual beauty. This behavior, however, very rarely goes further than a *piropo* (small adulatory phrase) and any touching or pinching is not condoned. Women tend to ignore most of these remarks and from early on learn not to publicly acknowledge them (either favorably or not).

RELIGION

Religious Beliefs. Most Venezuelans—at least 90 percent of the population—are Catholic. Since the 1980s, Protestant religions have been attracting more followers, especially Evangelists and Adventists, and to a lesser degree, Mormons. There are also significant Jewish communities in Caracas and Maracaibo; these communities are traditionally grouped under the banners of the Asociación Israelita Venezolana (Israeli Venezuelan Association) and the Unión Israelita de Venezuela (United Israelis of Venezuela). Venezuela also has a smaller number of Islamic practitioners.

Most indigenous religious practices were lost with the decimation of the Native American population and the few surviving indigenous populations practice their religious traditions in complete isolation from the national culture. Even though indigenous religion did not survive intact, many Venezuelans participate in a symbiotic religious practice known as the *culto* of María Lonza (*culto* meaning more religious practice than cult). This culto has its home base in the hill of Sorte, near the small town of Chivacoa, just east of the larger western city of Barquisimeto. María Lonza is portrayed as a Venezuelan witch/healer who was born from an Indian father and a Creole Spanish mother. She is traditionally represented with two other figures, that of a black henchman, el Negro Felipe, and of an Indian *cacique* (chief), Guaicapuro. The three of them together are traditionally referred to as the Three Powers (*Tres Poderes*).

Another interesting religious belief shared by Venezuelans is the veneration for the figure of Dr. José Gregorio Hernández. This Venezuelan doctor, who lived during the late 1800s, was recently given venerable status by the Vatican but is still not officially recognized as a saint by the church. Nevertheless, this has not deterred a widespread following in Venezuela (and other Latin American countries) that proclaims Brother Gregorio (as he is referred to) a miraculous healer who actually operates and heals people while they sleep.

Rituals, and Holy Places. The Catholicism practiced in Venezuela very much follows the guidelines of the Roman hierarchy. Masses are held everyday but attendance is obligatory only on Sunday. Since the Second Vatican Council masses are no longer said in Latin but in Spanish, and the priest (males only) now faces the public as opposed to celebrating the ritual with his back to them. The mass is believed to recreate Jesus' last supper with his apostles before his crucifixion, and the ritual itself is believed to transform bread and wine into the body and blood of Christ to be partaken of by everybody free of mortal sin. There are Catholic churches throughout Venezuela with the most impressive cathedrals located in Caracas and other major cities. In smaller towns, however, there are also churches with a grand colonial architectural style: these churches had greater importance during Venezuela's colonial period than they do now.

The principal rituals associated with the culto of María Lonza involve the main practitioners falling into trances through hypnotic music, dancing, rum drinking, and painting themselves with different color dyes. During these trances they ''see'' what is in the supplicant's psyche and what the future has in store for them. Even though this culto has a strong rural and Afro-indigenous origin it is not uncommon to see practitioners from all social backgrounds and classes involved. There is also a statue of a naked María Lonza riding on a tapir in the center of Caracas.

Death and the Afterlife. Venezuelans' belief in the afterlife follows the Roman Catholic belief in hell (for those who were evil in life), purgatory (for those who still need to do penance for their sins), and heaven (for those without any fault). Even the syncretic practices of María Lonza and San Gregorio are intertwined with this Catholic understanding of death and the afterworld. In the practices of Maria Lonza and San Gregorio, however, both also express the possibility of communicating with dead spirits and deities. These beliefs in establishing an actual connection with the world beyond death are closer to the beliefs of African-based religions such as voodoo than to those of Christianity.

MEDICINE AND HEALTH CARE

Venezuela's health-care system has a large array of public and private hospitals and clinics. Even though the country's health coverage is better than that of most other South American countries, its public system is still far from exemplary. The public hospitals normally have long lines and waiting periods, and they tend to be understaffed (there is a particular shortage of nurses) with the staff they do have being overworked. Private clinics, however, are quite well operated, and the people who can afford to can get some of the best medical care in the world. Similar to other ''developed'' Western nations, most deaths in Venezuela are due to heart attacks, cancer, and fatal accidents. AIDS is also present but is still not a major epidemic as in the United States or certain African countries.

Parishioners push a portable shrine past a church during a festival. Most Venezuelans practice Catholicism.

In general the death rate is four for every thousand, while the birth rate is twenty-nine for every thousand. Most traditional tropical and third world diseases have been eradicated in Venezuela, although infant mortality is still much higher than in most European countries. Although Western medicine is the most popular mode of health care, other non-Western traditions are surprisingly still present. Surviving in many rural belief systems, herbal remedies (including rubbing the body with plants while saying certain prayers) are still widely believed to cure nontraditional ailments such as the evil eye and various emotional afflictions.

SECULAR CELEBRATIONS

There are several important and officially recognized holidays in Venezuela other than New Year's and Christmas. Carnival is by far one of the liveliest Venezuelan traditions. This holiday falls on the three days prior to Ash Wednesday (in the Catholic calendar). It normally means a holiday exodus from Caracas and other cities to Venezuela's Caribbean coast and even to Trinidad (an island off the northeast coast of Venezuela), which is famous for its Carnival celebrations. In the coastal towns Carnival means general partying with lots of drinking and dancing, parades with drummers and people in costumes, and a generally greater level of sexual undertones.

Other important holidays are Bolívar's birthday (24 July) and Venezuela's Independence Day, which is celebrated on the day of the victorious Battle of Carabobo (24 June). The Day of the Race (Día de la Raza) is celebrated on 12 October with parades. This day also holds great religious significance for María Lonza followers. Venezuela also celebrates a series of religious town festivals that commemorate either the appearance of the Virgin Mary (or of a saint) to an Indian/rural peasant or the miraculous protection of the town from an epidemic or natural disasters. The most famous of these festivals include: the Feast of Corpus Christi in San Francisco de Yare, the Feast of the Divina Pastora (the Divine Sheperdess) in Santa Rosa, and the Feast of San Juan Bautista (Saint John the Baptist), which is celebrated by extensive rhythmic drumming and dancing in Caracas and other parts of the country.

THE ARTS AND HUMANITIES

Support for the Arts. Since the 1920s the Venezuelan state has invested in developing and maintaining a national culture through the arts. The two areas that have most benefited from this support have been literature and music. Caracas features a publicly financed symphony orchestra that plays not only classical genres but also the more nationalistic genre of *joropos*. The state also supports several museums that house some of the national artistic production. The three prime ones are: the Museum of Fine Arts, which was founded in 1938; the Museum of Colonial Art, which is located in an eighteenth century house; and the Museum of Natural Sciences, which was founded in 1940 and houses over fifteen thousand exhibits. All three are located in Caracas.

Literature. Very few Venezuelan artists are known outside of the national borders. Exceptions to this in literature include the writers Rómulo Gallegos and Arturo Uslar Pietri. Gallegos in first part of the twentieth century and Pietri in the second half worked within a continental tradition of nostalgic and national writing about the nature of Venezuelan/American identity.

Graphic Arts. Architects such as Carlos Raúl Villanueva have gained international acclaim, while other architects such as Enrique Hernández, Enrique Zubizarreta, and José Castillo are also widely recognized for their designs.

Performance Arts. In music, Venezuela has produced one of the world's leading salsa bands in the person of Oscar D'Leon whose music has become emblematic of this genre's tradition even in Puerto Rico and New York City (the original sources of salsa music). World pop diva Mariah Carey is the daughter of an Afro-Venezuelan man.

THE STATE OF THE PHYSICAL AND SOCIAL SCIENCES

The actual scientific research carried out in Venezuela has not been significantly registered outside of its national borders. The country includes high quality universities and research institutions such as the National Academy of History, the Royal Academy of Language, and the Central University in Caracas. Interestingly enough, initial research pursuits date back to the 1800s with Dr. José Gregorio Hernández's medical work, which contributed greatly to the present configuration of the Ministry of Health. An intense research spirit is still alive, if not continentally disseminated. A small example of these are the historical works of such scholars as Iraida Vargas and Mario Sanoja.

BIBLIOGRAPHY

Alfonso, Alejandro. "El caso venezolano." *Chasqui* 3, 1983.

Allen, Loring. *Venezuelan Economic Development: A Political-Economic Analysis*, 1977.

Baguley, Kitt. *Culture Shock: Venezuela*, 1999.

Baloyra, Enrique A., and John D. Martz. *Political Attitudes in Venezuela: Societal Cleavages and Political Opinion*, 1979.

Bermúdez, Manuel. *La ficción narrativa en radio y televisión*, 1984.

Betancourt, Rómulo. *Venezuela: Oil and Politics*, 1979.

Blanck, David Eugene. *Venezuela: Politics in a Petroleum Country*, 1984.

Boulton, Alfredo, et al. *Arte de Venezuela*, 1977.

Braveboy-Wagner, Jacqueline Anne. *The Venezuela-Guyana Border Dispute: Britain's Colonial Legacy in Latin America*, 1984.

Bustamante, Edgar, ed. *Maravillosa Venezuela*, 1987.

Cabrera Sifontes, Horacio. *El profeta Enoch: Su travesía por Guayana en el año de la humadera*, 1982.

Coronel, Gustavo. *The Nationalization of the Venezuelan Oil Industry from Technocratic Success to Political Failure*, 1983.

Coronil, Fernando. *The Magical State: Nature, Money, and Modernity in Venezuela*, 1997.

De Grummond, Jane Lucas. *Renato Beluche, Smuggler, Prviateer, and Patriot, 1780–1860*, 1983.

De Janvry, Alain, et al. *The Political Feasibility of Adjustment in Ecuador and Venezuela*, 1994.

Doyle, Sir Arthur Conan. *The Lost World*, 1912.

Ellner, Steve. *Venezuela's Movimiento al Socialismo (MAS): From Guerilla Defeat to Innovative Politics*, 1988.

Ewell, Judith. *Venezuela: A Century of Change*, 1984.

Gallegos, Rómulo. *Canaima*, 1997.

———. *Doña Barbara*, 1997.

García Márquez, Gabriel. *The General in His Labyrinth*, 1990.

Goodman, Louis W. *Lessons of the Venezuelan Experience*, 1995.

Herman, Donald L. *Christian Democracy in Venezuela*, 1980.

Levine, Daniel. *Religion and Politics in Latin America: The Catholic Church in Colombia and Venezuela*, 1981.

Lieuwen, Edwin. *Venezuela*, 1985.

Lombardi, John. *Venezuela: The Search for Order, the Dream of Progress*, 1982.

Lombardi, John, German Carrera Damas, and Roberta E. Adams. *Venezuelan History: A Comprehensive Working Bibliography*, 1977.

Martz, John D., and David J. Myers, eds. *Venezuela: The Democratic Experience*, 1986.

Muñoz, Carlos C. *Televisión, violencia, y agresión*, 1974.

Naim, Moisés. *Paper Tigers and Minotaurs: The Politics of Venezuela's Economic Reforms*, 1993.

Oviedo y Baños, José de. *The Conquest and Settlement of Venezuela*, 1723.

Peeler, John A. *Latin American Democracies: Colombia, Costa Rica, and Venezuela*, 1985.

Pollak-Eltz, Angelina. "The Family in Venezuela." In Man SinghDas and Clinton J. Jesser, eds. *The Family in Latin America*, 1980.

Quintero, Rodolfo. *Antropología del petróleo*, 1972.

Ramón y Rivera, Luis Felipe. *La música popular de Venezuela*, 1976.

Randall, Laura. *The Political Economy of Venezuelan Oil*, 1987.

Rodwin, Lloyd. *Planning Urban Growth and Regional Development: The Experience of the Guayana Program in Venezuela*, 1969.

Salcedo Bastardo, J. L. *Historia fundamental de Venezuela*, 1982.

Sanoja, Mario, and Iraida Vargas. *Antiguas formaciones y modos de producción Venezolanos*, 1974.

Siso, Carlos. *La formación del pueblo Venezolano: Estudios sociológicos*, 1941.

Tugwell, Franklin. *The Politics of Oil in Venezuela*, 1975.

Tulchin, Joseph S., and Gary Bland. *Venezuela in the Wake of Radical Reform*, 1993.

Uslar Pietri, Arturo. *De una a otra Venezuela*, 1985.

———. *Las lanzas coloradas*, 1995.

———. *Venezuela en seis ensayos*, 1995.

Vargas Arena, Iraida. *Arqueología, ciencia, y sociedad*, 1990.

Vázquez Carrizosa, Alfredo. *Colombia y Venezuela: Una historia atormentada*, 1987.

Vegas, Federico. *Venezuelan Vernacular*, 1985.

Wright, Winthrop R. *Café con leche: Race, Class, and National Image in Venezuela*, 1990.

Zahm, John Augustine. *Up the Orinoco and down the Magdalena*, 1910.

—O. Hugo Benavides

VIETNAM

CULTURE NAME
Vietnamese

ORIENTATION

Identification. The name Vietnam originated in 1803 when envoys from the newly founded Nguyen dynasty traveled to Beijing to establish diplomatic relations with the Chinese court. The new emperor had chosen the name *Nam Viet* for his kingdom. The word *Viet* he derived from the traditional name for the Vietnamese imperial domain and its people in what is now northern and central Vietnam. *Nam* (south) had been added to acknowledge the expansion of the dynasty's domain into lands to the south. The Chinese objected to this new name because it was the same as an ancient state that had rebelled against Chinese rule. They therefore changed it to Viet Nam. Vietnamese officials resented the change and it did not attain public acceptance until the late 1800s.

The story of the origin of Vietnam's name captures several prominent themes that have run throughout the nation's history. As the usage of Viet indicates, the Vietnamese have for centuries had a sense of the distinctiveness of their society and culture. However, as the inclusion of Nam shows, the land they inhabit has expanded over time, and also has its own internal divisions into northern, central, and southern regions. Additionally, as evidenced by the name change, their history has been profoundly influenced by their contact with other, often more powerful, groups.

Vietnam today stands at a crossroads. It has been at peace for over a decade, but since the 1986 introduction of the "Renovation" or *Doi Moi* policy that began dismantling the country's socialist economy in favor of a market economy, the country has experienced tremendous social changes. Some have been positive, such as a general rise in the standard of living, but others have not, such as increased corruption, social inequality, regional tensions, and

an HIV-AIDS epidemic. The Communist Party still exercises exclusive control over political life, but the question of whether Vietnam will continue its socio-economic development in a climate of peace and stability remains uncertain at the beginning of the twenty-first century.

Location and Geography. Vietnam occupies approximately 127,243 square miles (329,560 square kilometers), an area roughly equivalent to New Mexico, and is situated between 8 and 24 degrees latitude and 102 and 110 degrees longitude. It borders China in the north, Laos in the northeast and center, and Cambodia in the southwest. Its 2,135 miles (3,444 kilometers) of coastline run from its border with Cambodia on the Gulf of Thailand along the South China Sea to its border with China. The delineation of Vietnam's borders has been a focus of dispute in the post–1975 period, notably the ownership disputes with China, Malaysia, the Philippines, Taiwan, and Malaysia over the Spratly Islands; and with China and Taiwan over the Paracel Islands. Recent progress has been made settling land border disputes with China and Cambodia. The Vietnamese culturally divide their country into three main regions, the north (*Bac Bo*), center (*Trung Bo*), and south (*Nam Bo*), with Hanoi, Hue, and Ho Chi Minh City (formerly Saigon) serving as the main cities of each region. Hanoi, the site of the former capital of one of the country's earliest dynasties, has been the capital of the unified Vietnam since 1976.

Vietnam contains a wide-variety of agroeconomic zones. The river deltas of Vietnam's two great rivers, the Red River in the north and the Mekong in the south, dominate those two regions. Both deltas feature irrigated rice agriculture that depends on the annual monsoons and river water that is distributed through immense and complicated irrigation systems. Irrigated rice agriculture is also practiced in numerous smaller river deltas and plains along the country's coast. Vietnam's western

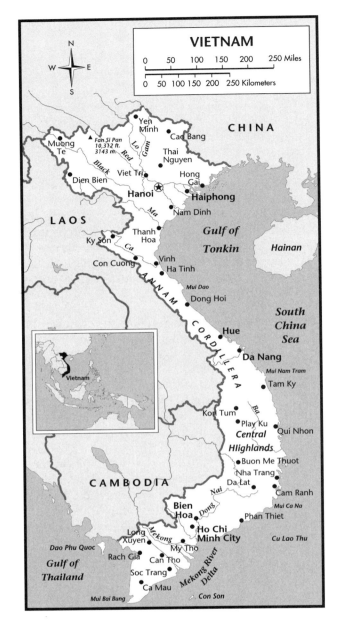

Vietnam

areas. The country is largely lush and tropical, though the temperature in the northern mountains can cool to near freezing in the winter and the central regions often experience droughts.

Demography. The current population is approximately seventy-seven million composed almost exclusively of indigenous peoples. The largest group is the ethnic Vietnamese (*Kinh*), who comprise over 85 percent of the population. Other significant ethnic groups include the Cham, Chinese, Hmong, Khmer, Muong, and Tai, though none of these groups has a population over one million. Expatriates of many nationalities reside in urban areas. The country's two largest population centers are Hanoi and Ho Chi Minh City, but over 75 percent of the population lives in rural areas. The country's birth rate, estimated to increase at 1.37 percent per year, has led to rapid population growth since the 1980s with approximately 34 percent of the population under 14 years of age.

Linguistic Affiliation. Vietnamese is the dominant language, spoken by an estimated 86.7 percent of the population. It is a tonal Mon-Khmer language with strong Chinese lexical influences. The six-toned dialect of the central Red River delta region, particularly around Hanoi, is regarded as the language's standard form, but significant dialectical variations exist between regions in terms of the number of tones, accents, and vocabulary. Dialectical differences often serve as important symbols of regional identity in social life. As the official language, Vietnamese is taught in schools throughout the country. Since the 1940s, Vietnamese governments have made great progress in raising literacy rates and approximately 90 percent of the adult population is literate. During the twentieth century the country's elite have mastered a variety of second languages, such as French, Russian, and English, with the latter being the most commonly learned second language today. Linguists estimate that approximately eighty-five other languages from the Austro-Asiatic, Austronesian, Daic, Miao-Yiao, and Sino-Tibetan language families are indigenous to the country. These range from languages spoken by large numbers of people, such as Muong (767,000), Khmer (700,000), Nung (700,000), Tai Dam (over 500,000), and Chinese (500,000), to those spoken by only a few hundred people, such as O'Du, spoken by an estimated two hundred people. Many minority group members are bilingual, though not necessarily with Vietnamese as their second language.

salient is defined by the mountainous Annamite Cordillera that is home to most of the country's fifty-four ethnic groups. Many of these groups have their own individual adaptations to their environments. Their practices include hunting and gathering, slash and burn agriculture, and some irrigated rice agriculture. The combination of warfare, land shortages, population surpluses, illegal logging, and the migration of lowlanders to highland areas has resulted in deforestation and environmental degradation in many mountainous

Symbolism. The Vietnamese government extensively employs a number of symbols to represent the nation. These include the flag, with its red background and centered, five-pointed gold star; a variety of red and gold stars; the image of Ho Chi Minh; and representations of workers and soldiers. Images and statues of the latter, wearing green pith helmets and carrying weapons, are common in public places. Images of Ho are ubiquitous, adorning everything from currency to posters on buildings to the portraits of him commonly found hanging in northern Vietnamese homes. Ho was a strong advocate of national unity and referred to all Vietnamese as "children of one house." Other commonly visible symbols are the patterns of seabirds and other figures featured on Dong Son drums. These drums, manufactured by early residents of northern Vietnam in the first and second millennia B.C., represent the nation's antiquity. Since Vietnam began developing its tourist industry in the late 1980s, a number of other images have become commonplace, such as farmers in conical hats, young boys playing flutes while riding on the back of buffalo, and women in *ao dai*, the long-flowing tunic that is regarded as the national dress.

HISTORY AND ETHNIC RELATIONS

Emergence of the Nation. Many Vietnamese archeologists and historians assert that the origins of the Vietnamese people can be reliably traced back to at least the fifth or sixth millennium B.C. when tribal groups inhabited the western regions of the Red River delta. A seminal event in the solidification of Vietnamese identity occurred in 42 B.C.E. when China designated the territory as its southern-most province and began direct rule over it. China would rule the region for almost one thousand years, thereby laying the foundation for the caution and ambivalence that Vietnamese have felt for centuries toward their giant northern neighbor. The Vietnamese reestablished their independence in 938. The next thousand years saw a succession of Vietnamese dynasties rule the country, such as the Ly, Tran, Le, and Vietnam's last dynasty, the Nguyen (1802–1945). These dynasties, though heavily influenced by China in terms of political philosophy and organizational structure, participated in the articulation of the uniqueness of Vietnamese society, culture, and history. This period also saw the commencement of the "Movement South" (*Nam Tien*) in which the Vietnamese moved south from their Red River delta homeland and gradually conquered southern and central Vietnam. In the process, they displaced two previously dominant groups, the Cham and Khmer.

The modern Vietnamese nation was created from French colonialism. France used the pretext of the harassment of missionaries to begin assuming control over Vietnam in the 1850s. By 1862 it had set up the colony of Cochinchina in southern Vietnam. In 1882 it invaded northern Vietnam and forced the Vietnamese Emperor to accept the establishment of a French protectorate over central and northern Vietnam in 1883. This effectively brought all of Vietnam under French control. The French colonial regime was distinguished by its brutality and relentless exploitation of the Vietnamese people. Resistance to colonial rule was intense in the early years, but weakened after the late 1890s. The situation began to change dramatically in the late 1920s as a number of nationalist movements, such as the Indochinese Communist Party (formed in 1930) and the Vietnam Nationalist Party (formed in 1927), became more sophisticated in terms of organization and ability. Such groups grew in strength during the turmoil of World War II. On 19 August 1945 an uprising occurred in which Vietnamese nationalists overthrew the Japanese administration then controlling Vietnam. On 2 September 1945 Ho Chi Minh officially established the Democratic Republic of Vietnam. The French attempted to reassert control over Vietnam by invading the country in December 1946. This launched an eight-year war in which the Vietnamese nationalist forces, led primarily by the Vietnamese Communists, ultimately forced the French from the country in late 1954. Vietnam was divided into North and South Vietnam for the next twenty-one years. During this period the North experienced a socialist revolution. In 1959 North Vietnam began implementing its policy to forcibly reunify the country, which led to outbreak of the American War in Vietnam in the early 1960s. This concluded on 30 April 1975 when North Vietnamese soldiers captured the city of Saigon and forced the surrender of the South Vietnamese government. On 1 January 1976 the Vietnamese National Assembly declared the establishment of the Socialist Republic of Vietnam, thereby completing the reunification of the Vietnamese nation.

National Identity. National identity is a complex and contentious issue. One of the most basic components is the Vietnamese language. Many Vietnamese are tremendously proud of their language and its complexities. People particularly enjoy the rich opportunities for plays on words that come from its tonal nature and value the ability to appropriately use the countless number of adages and proverbs enshrined in the language. Vietnamese also have an attachment to their natural world. The expression "Vietnamese land" (dat Viet), with its defining metaphors of mountains and rivers, encapsulates the notion that Vietnamese society and culture have an organic relationship to their environment. Another important component of national identity is the set of distinctive customs such as weddings, funerals, and ancestor worship that Vietnamese perform. These are subject to a great deal of regional and historical variation, but there is a perceived core that many regard as uniquely Vietnamese, especially the worship of patrilineal ancestors by families. Vietnamese food, with its ingredients and styles of preparation distinct from both China and other Southeast Asian nations, also defines the country and its people.

Contemporary national identity's contentiousness derives from the forced unification of the country in 1975. Prior to this, the northern sense of national identity was defined through its commitment to socialism and the creation of a new, revolutionary society. This identity had its own official history that celebrated such heroes as Ho Chi Minh and others who fought against colonialism, but rejected many historical figures associated with the colonial regime, the Nguyen dynasty, and what it regarded as the prerevolutionary feudal order. South Vietnamese national identity rejected Communism and celebrated a different set of historical figures, particularly those that had played a role in the Nguyen dynasty's founding and preservation. After unification, the government suppressed this history and its heroes. The northern definition of national identity dominates, but there remains alternate understandings among many residents in the southern and central regions.

Ethnic Relations. Vietnam is home to fifty-four official ethnic groups, the majority of which live in highland areas, although some large groups such the Cham or Chinese live in lowland or urban areas. Since the mid-1980s, relations between ethnic groups have generally been good, but conflict has been present. The most frequent problem is competition for resources, either between different highland groups or between highland groups and lowland groups that have settled in the midlands and highlands. Some minority group members also feel discriminated against and resent governmental intrusion in their lives. The government, which at one level supports and celebrates ethnic diversity, has had complicated relations with groups it fears might become involved in anti-government activi-

ties. This has been the case with several highland groups in northern and central Vietnam, the ethnic Chinese, many of whom fled Vietnam at the time of the Vietnam War and China's brief border war in 1979, and expatriate Vietnamese who have returned to Vietnam.

URBANISM, ARCHITECTURE, AND THE USE OF SPACE

Vietnam's cities carry the architectural traces of the many phases of its history. The city of Hue, capital of the Nguyen dynasty, features the Citadel and other imperial structures, such as the mausolea of former emperors. In 1993 UNESCO designated the Citadel and other imperial sites as a part of their World Heritage List and have subsequently begun renovations to repair the extensive damage they received in the 1968 Tet Offensive. The French left behind an impressive legacy of colonial architecture, particularly in Hanoi, Hue, and Saigon. Colonial authorities meticulously planned these cities, creating wide, tree-covered avenues that were lined with impressive public buildings and private homes. Many of these structures still serve as government offices and private residences. Following the division of the country in 1954, South Vietnam saw an increase in functional American-style buildings, while North Vietnam's Eastern Bloc allies contributed to the construction of massive concrete dormitory housing. The 1990s brought an array of new architectural styles in the cities as people tore down houses that had for years been neglected and constructed new ones, normally of brick and mortar. New construction has removed some of the colonial flavor of the major cities.

City residents often congregate to sit and relax at all hours of the day in parks, cafes, or on the street side. The busiest locations during the day are the markets where people buy fresh meat, produce, and other essentials. Religious structures such as Christian churches, Buddhist temples, and spirit shrines are often crowded to capacity on worship days. Almost all lowland communities have structures dedicated to the war and revolution. These range in size from a large monument for war dead in Hanoi to the numerous cemeteries and cenotaphs for the war dead in towns and villages across the nation. These sites only commemorate those who fought for the victorious north, leaving those who served the south officially uncommemorated.

Vietnamese rural villages feature a variety of architectural styles. Village residents in lowland river deltas usually live in family compounds that

Traditional thatched-roof homes on piles in a village outside Sapa. These homes are more common among poorer, rural families.

feature one or more rectangular-shaped houses made of brick and mortar. Compounds often have large open areas on the ground for drying rice. Village homes are normally built extremely close to each other, creating nuclear or semi-nuclear settlements surrounded by agricultural fields. Historically, villages planted dense stands of bamboo around their communities to define their boundaries and protect them from trespassers, though these are disappearing. In poor areas, such as in the central provinces of Nghe An and Quang Binh, many families still live in thatched houses. Regardless of their type, the main entrance to most homes is in the center of the long side, directly before the family ancestral altar. Kitchens, regarded as women's spaces, are on the side. Lowland villages have a variety of sacred spaces, such as Buddhist temples, spirit shrines, lineage halls, and the communal house (a sacred structure that houses the village guardian spirit's altar). These spaces normally have behavioral restrictions such as prohibitions against entry while in a polluted state to protect their sacredness. Highland minority groups often live in either thatched houses or in houses raised on stilts. Many of these houses maintain discrete spaces defined by age or gender.

FOOD AND ECONOMY

Food in Daily Life. Rice is the dietary staple which most people eat three meals a day. Rice is usually consumed jointly by family members. The common practice is to prepare several dishes that are placed on a tray or table that people sit around. Individuals have small bowls filled with rice, and then take food from the trays as well as rice from their bowls with chopsticks. Vietnamese often accompany these main dishes with leafy vegetables and small bowls of salty sauces in which they dip their food. Popular dishes include sauteed vegetables, tofu, a seafood-based broth with vegetables called *canh*, and a variety of pork, fish, or meat dishes. A common ingredient for cooked dishes and the dipping sauces is salty fish sauce (*nuoc mam*). Another important family practice is the serving of tea from a small tea pot with small cups to guests. Northern cuisine is known for its subtle flavors, central cuisine for its spiciness, and southern cuisine for its use of sugar and bean sprouts. Diet varies with wealth; the poor often have limited amounts of protein in their diets and some only have the means to eat rice with a few leafy vegetables at every meal.

The major cities feature restaurants offering Vietnamese and international cuisines, but for most Vietnamese, food consumed outside of the home is taken at street-side stalls or small shops that specialize in one dish. The most popular item is a noodle soup with a clear meat-based broth called *pho*. Many Vietnamese regard this as a national dish. Other foods commonly consumed at these sites include other types of rice or wheat noodle soups, steamed glutinous rice, rice porridge, sweet desserts, and "common people's food" (*com binh dan*), a selection of normal household dishes. There are no universal food taboos among Vietnamese, although some women avoid certain foods considered "hot," such as duck, during pregnancy and in the first few months after giving birth. The consumption of certain foods has a gendered dimension. Dishes such as dog or snake are regarded as male foods and many women avoid them. Some minority groups have taboos on the consumption of certain food items considered either sacred or impure.

Food Customs at Ceremonial Occasions.

Food consumption is a vital part of ritual celebrations. Historically, villagers held feasts after the conduct of rites dedicated to village guardian spirits, but revolutionary restrictions on resource consumption in these contexts has largely eliminated such feasts. Feasts held after weddings and funerals remain large and have increased in size in recent years. The most popular feast items are pork, chicken, and vegetable dishes served with rice. Liberal amounts of alcohol are also served. In the countryside this usually takes the form of locally-produced contraband rice spirits, while feasts in the cities often feature beer or imported spirits. Feasts are socially important because they provide a context through which people maintain good social relations, either through the reciprocation of previous feast invitations or the joint consumption of food. Other important occasions for feasting are the death anniversaries of family ancestors and the turning of the Lunar New Year or *Tet*. Many of the foods served on these occasions are similar, although the latter has some special dishes, such as a square of glutinous rice, pork and mung bean cake called *banh trung*. These feasts are comparatively smaller and, unlike the weddings and funerals, generally are confined to family members or close friends.

Basic Economy.

Despite efforts at industrialization after 1954, agriculture remains the foundation of the economy. The 1998 Vietnam Living Standards Survey showed that over 70 percent of the total population engaged in farming or farm-related work. Vietnam imports few basic agricultural commodities, and the majority of the items people consume are grown or produced in Vietnam.

Land Tenure and Property.

The Vietnamese government, in line with socialist ideology, does not legally recognize private land ownership. Since the early 1990s, the government has made moves to recognize de facto land ownership by granting individuals long-term leaseholds. This trend received more formal recognition with the passage of the 1998 Land Law. Control over land is extremely contentious. With the recent growth of a market economy, land has become an extremely valuable commodity, and many cases of corrupt officials illegally selling land-use rights or seizing it for personal uses have been reported. Ambiguities in the law and the lack of transparent legal processes exacerbate tensions and make land disputes difficult to resolve.

Commercial Activities.

Agricultural and manufactured products are sold both retail and wholesale. Cities, towns, and villages all feature markets, most of which are dominated by petty traders, normally women. The most commonly sold commodities are foodstuffs and household items such as salt, sugar, fish sauce, soaps, clothing, fabric, tableware, and cooking implements. Major purchases such as household appliances, bicycles, or furniture are often made in specialty stalls in larger markets or in stores in towns and cities. Currency is used for most transactions, but the purchase of real estate or capital goods requires gold. The number of open market wage-laborers has increased in recent years.

Major Industries.

Industrial output is evenly split between the state-owned, private, and foreign sectors. Since the late 1980s, Vietnam has actively promoted foreign investment, resulting in a very rapid growth in output by that sector. International corporations have been most active in mining, electronics assembly, and the production of textiles, garments, and footwear, usually for export. Corruption and an unclear legal system have severely limited Vietnam ability to attract additional foreign investment since the 1997 Asian financial crisis. Vietnamese state-owned factories produce a number of commodities for local consumption, such as cigarettes, textiles, alcohol, fertilizer, cement, food, paper, glass, rubber, and some consumer appliances. Private firms are still relatively small in size and number, and are usually concentrated in agricultural processing and light industry. Many complain that state interference, an undeveloped commercial infrastructure, and a confusing and ineffective legal system inhibit their growth and success.

Overview of Hanoi's Old Quarter. The French colonial influence is apparent in the architecture of many of the buildings that line the street.

Trade. Vietnam's international trade relations have grown considerably since the early 1990's. Major exports include oil, marine products, rubber, tea, garments, and footwear. The country is one of the world's largest exporters of coffee and rice. It sells most of its rice to African nations. Its largest trading partners for other commodities include Japan, China, Singapore, Australia, and Taiwan.

Division of Labor. Vietnamese of all ages work. As soon as they are able, young children begin helping out around the house or in the fields. Men tend to perform heavier tasks, such as plowing, construction, or heavy industrial work while women work in the garment and footwear sectors. Individuals with post-secondary school educations hold professional positions in medicine, science, and engineering. The lack of a post-secondary education is generally not a barrier to occupying high-ranking business or political positions, though this had begun to change by the late 1990s. National occupational surveys show that only slightly more than 16 percent of the population is engaged in professional or commercial occupations, while just under 84 percent of the population is engaged in either skilled or unskilled manual labor.

SOCIAL STRATIFICATION

Classes and Castes. The vast majority of the contemporary Vietnamese population is poor. The average annual earnings in the 1990s for a family is estimated at $370. There has been an increase in social stratification based upon wealth, particularly in urban areas where some individuals, often with links to business or the government, have become very wealthy. Another important axis of stratification is the distinction between mental and manual labor. Given the recent origin of this wealth-based stratification and the widespread poverty, these groups have yet to congeal into clearly-defined classes.

Symbols of Social Stratification. The most prominent contemporary symbols of social stratification are consumer goods. Two of the most common symbols are the possession of a motorcycle, particularly one of Japanese manufacture, and a mobile phone. Other items include refrigerators, televisions, video players, gold jewelry, and imported luxury goods, such as clothing or liquor. Some individuals also assert their status through large wedding feasts. For the very wealthy, automobiles, foreign travel, and expensive homes are important status symbols. Many of the poor ride bicycles, wear old and sometimes tattered clothing, and live in thatched homes.

POLITICAL LIFE

Government. Vietnam is a socialist republic with a government that includes an elected legislature, the national assembly, a president as head of state, and a prime minister as head of government. However, real political power lies with the Vietnamese Communist Party. Party members hold virtually all executive and administrative positions in the government. The party's Fatherland Front determines which candidates can run in elections and its politburo sets the guidelines for all major governmental policy initiatives. The most powerful position in the country is the Communist Party general secretary. Other important positions are the prime minister, the president, the minister of public security, and the chief of the armed forces. Women and members of Vietnam's ethnic groups are nominally represented in the government. One of the most sensitive issues the government faces is balancing regional interests.

Leadership and Political Officials. The Communist Party pressures its members to serve as examples of political virtue. The image they employ as their ideal leader is Ho Chi Minh. Ho was a devoted revolutionary who lived a life of simplicity, avoided corruption, behaved in a fair and egalitarian manner, and put the nation and revolution above his own personal interests. Party members and others often invoke the numerous moral adages coined by Ho during his life as a benchmark for social and political morality. Ho's popularity is greatest in the north. Residents of other regions sometimes have more ambivalent feelings about him.

Local political officials often are caught between two conflicting sets of expectations regarding their behavior. As party members, they are exhorted to follow the official line and disregard their own interests, but relatives and members of their communities often expect them to use their positions to their advantage; thus nepotism and localism are, at one level, culturally sanctioned. Officials must balance these two sets of demands, as moving too far in one direction can lead to criticism from the other.

The Vietnamese revolution eliminated the extremely inegalitarian forms of interaction such as kowtowing or hierarchical terms of address that had existed between commoners and officials. Most Vietnamese address officials with respectful kinship terms, such as ''older brother'' (*anh*) or ''grandfather'' (*ong*), or in rare cases as ''comrade'' (*dong chi*). Events in the late 1990s, notably several uprisings in rural areas in 1997, have demonstrated that the people's respect for the party and its officials has declined, largely as a result of the high-handedness and corruption of many officials. However, significant alternative political movements have not emerged.

Social Problems and Control. Vietnam has enjoyed a large measure of stability since the late 1970s, but its government today faces a number of significant social problems. Its greatest concern has been unrest in rural areas brought on by official malfeasance and land disputes. The government is also concerned about relations with religious groups in the south, particularly Catholics, Cao Dai, and Hoa Hao, who have demonstrated against the government since the 1990s. Another source of concern is smuggling and the production of counterfeit commodities. Three problems that have increased dramatically in urban areas during the 1990s have been theft, prostitution, and drug abuse. Many who engage in the latter two activities are often from the poorest segments of the population. Official corruption associated with the drug trade and sex industry are another significant problem.

Vietnam has a legal system supported by a police force, a judicial and a security system. Yet, many Vietnamese feel that the system does not work, particularly with regard to its failure either to punish high-ranking offenders or to prevent the wealthy from bribing their way out of being punished for illegal activities. The former is often made possible by the extremely low salaries received by public officials. People also feel that the state deals more severely with political dissidents than many civil and criminal offenders. While there is a limited police and security presence in rural communities, the tightly-packed living spaces and ubiquitous kinship relations hinder the conduct of many crimes. If possible, local officials often prefer to settle disputes internally, rather than involve higher authorities. Public skepticism regarding the police and judicial system is a source of concern for the government.

Military Activity. The People's Army of Vietnam has roughly 484,000 active members with three to four million in the reserves. Over the past decade the military has cut its forces considerably, though recent estimates are that military expenditures constitute an amount equivalent to approximately 9 percent of the GDP ($650 million). Since its withdrawal from Cambodia in 1989, the military has not been

Houses clustered along the shore of Halong Bay. It is common for houses in Vietnam to be built close to one another within a village.

engaged in any large-scale conflicts, but its forces have been involved in numerous small skirmishes with the Chinese and Cambodians over border disputes.

SOCIAL WELFARE AND CHANGE PROGRAMS

The Vietnamese government has a strong commitment to social welfare and social change, particularly health improvements, poverty alleviation, and economic development. It is also concerned with providing assistance to war invalids and the families of war dead. Numerous offices at all levels of government are dedicated to these goals, but their efforts are severely constrained by a lack of funding. As a result, the implementation of many such policies is carried out with the assistance of international donors and organizations. Several governments including those of Sweden, Finland, Norway, and Japan, have provided significant assistance.

NONGOVERNMENTAL ORGANIZATIONS AND OTHER ASSOCIATIONS

The international nongovernmental organization presence is significant, ranging from various organizations of the United Nations that conduct a wide variety of projects across the country, to small groups that work in only one community. The programs they finance and implement include poverty alleviation, infectious disease control, contraception, educational assistance, and water purification, among others.

The development of civil society in Vietnam is still in its nascent stages, thus there are as of yet few indigenous nongovernmental associations that play a significant role in social life. Two types that appear to be gaining importance are patrilineages and religious or ritual organizations, such as local Buddhist Associations or Spirit Medium Associations. Some official organizations such as the Communist Party's Elderly Association that has a presence in villages throughout the country play an important role in organizing funerals and assisting the elderly.

GENDER ROLES AND STATUSES

Division of Labor by Gender. In prerevolutionary Vietnam the "public" (*ngoai*) domain was the male domain while the "domestic" (*noi*) domain was for women. This pattern still largely remains with women performing most of the essential tasks for running the household such as cooking, cleaning, going to market, and caring for children. Outside

Two women sit down to breakfast in Vietnam. While women have a strong role within families, their status in business and government is less significant than men's.

the home, women dominate the business of petty trading which is a common sideline to earn money in many families. In urban areas women are often secretaries or waitresses, occupying lower level service positions. In general, men perform the majority of public activities, particularly business, political office or administration, and occupations that require extended periods away from home, such as long-distance truck driving. Men also control the most prestigious religious roles such as being a Buddhist monk or Catholic priest. While both men and women engage in all phases of agricultural production, the physically demanding activities of plowing and raking are mostly performed by men.

The Relative Status of Women and Men. Vietnamese revolutionary policies endorse the principle of gender equality, but its realization in social life has been incomplete. Men dominate official positions, the Communist Party, business, and all other prestigious realms of social life. Women play a strong role within their families, a point made in the reference to the wife as the "general of the interior" (*noi tuong*). The position and status of women has improved significantly since 1950, but lower literacy rates, less education, and a smaller presence in public life indicate that their inferior status remains.

MARRIAGE, FAMILY, AND KINSHIP

Marriage. Marriage is an expected rite of passage for the attainment of adulthood. Almost all people marry, usually in their late teens or early twenties. According to Vietnamese law, arranged marriage and polygamy are illegal. Young people can court freely, but many women are careful not to court too openly for fear of developing a negative reputation. Many Vietnamese regard the development of romantic love as an important component in deciding to marry, but many will also balance family considerations when making their decision. Vietnamese prefer to marry someone of equal status, though it is better for the husband to be of slightly higher status. Such considerations have become more significant in recent years as wealth differentials have grown. Vietnamese law allows both men and women to ask for a divorce. Divorce rates have increased, particularly in urban areas, but many women are reluctant to divorce because remarriage is difficult for them.

Domestic Unit. The common pattern for the domestic unit is to have two or three generations living together in one home. In some urban settings, particularly if the family resides in government allocated housing, the household might only include two generations, while some homes in the countryside have up to five generations. Residence in most homes is organized around the male line. Authority within the household is exercised by the eldest male, although his wife will often have an important say in family matters. Sons stay in the parent's home, and after marriage their brides move in with them. The eldest son will usually remain in the home, while younger sons might leave to set up their own household a few years after marriage. Women of all generations tend to such matters as cooking, cleaning, and caring for children, though these responsibilities tend to fall on the younger wives.

Inheritance. The general custom is for the eldest son to inherit the parental home and the largest portion of the family property, particularly land. Younger sons will often inherit some land or other items, such as gold. In rare cases daughters receive small items. Many parents like all of their children to receive something in order to prevent discord. If a person dies without a pre-stipulated arrangement, Vietnamese law requires an equal distribution of property among the next of kin.

Kin Groups. Patrilineages are the most important kin groups. At birth, children become members of their father's patrilineage and are forbidden from marrying anyone of that patrilineage within five degrees of relation. Most rural villages have several patrilineages whose members live amongst each other. Patrilineages generally do not exercise a dominant role in social life, although lineage members often meet to conduct commemorative rites for their ancestors. Many highland groups have matrilineages and different rules regarding marriage.

SOCIALIZATION

Infant Care. Vietnamese infants are in constant contact with others. People hold children and pass them around throughout the day. During the night infants sleep with their parents in the parents' bed. Infant care is largely the responsibility of female family members. Mothers play the primary role, although in cases when they must be away, older relatives help care for the children. Older siblings often help out too. People talk and play with infants, calm them when they cry, and always try to make them smile and laugh.

Child Rearing and Education. Adults take a generally indulgent attitude toward children until they reach the age of five or six. At that point, they become more strict and begin more serious moral instruction. The general moral message is for chil-

dren to learn to ''respect order'' (*ton ti trat tu*), a reference to knowing their inferior position in society and showing deference to their superiors. Parents also emphasize the importance of filial piety and obedience to the parents. A good child will always know its inferior place and yield to its seniors. As they get older, the moral socialization of girls is more intense than that of boys. Girls are expected to display a number of feminine virtues, particularly modesty and chastity. Schools continue the instruction of these moral themes, but given that the majority of Vietnamese do not study beyond primary school, they are not a significant site for moral socialization.

Higher Education. Higher education is very prestigious, a tradition that dates back to the competitive examination system to become an official in the precolonial period. Many families want their children to attend university, but such an option is beyond reach for the majority of the population, particularly those in rural or highland areas.

ETIQUETTE

Polite behavior is highly valued. One of the most important dimensions of politeness is for the young to show respect to their elders. In everyday life, younger people show this respect by using hierarchical terms of address when interacting with their seniors and parents regularly instruct their children on their proper usage. Younger people should also be the first to issue the common salutation *chao* when meeting someone older, should always invite their seniors to begin eating before they do, ask for permission to leave the house, announce their arrival when they return, and not dominate conversations or speak in a confrontational manner with their seniors. Prerevolutionary practices demanded that juniors bow or kowtow to their seniors, but the revolution has largely eliminated such practices. Many elders today feel that the revolution produced a general decline in politeness.

People of the same gender often maintain close proximity in social contexts. Both males and females will hold hands or sit very close together. People of different genders, however, especially if they are not married or related, should not have physical contact. In general woman are expected to maintain greater decorum than men by avoiding alcohol and tobacco, speaking quietly, and dressing modestly. In many public spaces, however, people often avoid standing in queues, resulting in a chaotic environment where people touch or press up against one another as they go about their business.

Rice is a staple of Vietnamese cuisine, eaten three meals a day, but rice is also exported as well—mostly to African countries.

RELIGION

Religious Beliefs. The Vietnamese government recognizes six official religions: Buddhism, Catholicism, Protestantism, Islam, and two indigenous religious traditions that emerged during the colonial period, Cao Dai and Hoa Hao. The Mahayana tradition of Buddhism is dominant in Vietnam, and over 70 percent of Vietnamese consider themselves at least nominally Buddhist. The constitution technically allows for the freedom of religion, but this right is often constrained, particularly with regard to any religious activities that could become a forum for dissent. All religious organizations are technically overseen by the Communist Party's Fatherland Front, but opposition, notably from the Cao Dai, Hoa Hao, and some Buddhist sects, has been present.

Denominational variations aside, the core of religious practice for almost all Vietnamese is the worship of spirits. The most important spirits are the souls of the ancestors. Almost all families have altars in their homes where they perform rites for family ancestors, especially on the deceased's death anniversaries and the Lunar New Year. Many Vietnamese also perform or participate in rites for their village guardian spirits, spirits associated with specific locations, spirits of deceased heroes, or the Buddha or different Boddhisatvas, particularly Av-

alokitesvara. Some Vietnamese believe that spirits have the ability to bring good fortune and misfortune to human life. Revolutionaries strenuously objected to such thinking because they felt that it prevented the Vietnamese from becoming masters of their own destinies. Today, acceptance of ideas of supernatural causality is more common among women, while some men, particularly those with party or military backgrounds, reject such ideas.

Religious Practitioners. Each of the main religious traditions has its own set of practitioners such as Christian priests, nuns, and ministers, Buddhist monks and nuns, Islamic clerics, and Cao Dai and Hao Hao priests. Vietnamese society also features spirit priests, Taoist masters, spirit mediums, diviners, and astrologers. The three former specialists have the ability to interact with the spirit world in order to learn the spirits' desires and persuade or coerce them to behave in particular manners. They are usually consulted to help the living cure illness or end a pattern of misfortune. Spirit priests and Taoist masters are usually men who study religious texts to learn their specialty. Most mediums are women, many of whom become mediums after a crisis or revelatory experience. Diviners and astrologers have the ability to predict the future. Diviners make their predictions through a range of divinatory rites or by reading faces or palms. Astrologers make their cal-

Agriculture is one of the few areas in which men and women share tasks in Vietnamese culture.

culations based on the relationship between the date and time of a person's birth and a wider set of celestial phenomena. Many people consult one of the latter two specialists when planning a new venture, such as taking a trip or starting a business.

Rituals and Holy Places. The most important ritual event in Vietnamese society is the celebration of the Lunar New Year (*Tet Nguyen Dan*) when families gather to welcome the coming of the new year and pay their respects to family ancestors. The first and fifteenth of every month in the twelve month lunar year are also important occasions for rites to ancestors, spirits, and Buddhist deities. Other common days for rites are the death anniversaries of family ancestors, historical figures, or Buddhist deities; the fifteenth of the third lunar month when family members clean ancestral graves; and the fifteenth of the seventh lunar month, which is Vietnamese All Soul's Day. Vietnamese conduct rites in a variety of sacred spaces. These include family ancestral altars, lineage halls, a variety of shrines dedicated to spirits, communal houses that hold the altars of village guardian spirits, temples of Buddhist or other affiliations, Christian churches, and mosques. The country also has many shrines and temples that hold annual festivals that pilgrims and interested visitors attend, often from great distances. Among the more fa-

mous are the Perfume Pagoda in the north, the Catholic shrine at La Vang in the center, and the Cao Dai Temple in the south.

Death and the Afterlife. The vast majority of Vietnamese hold that a person's soul lives on after death. One of the most important moral obligations for the living, especially the deceased's children, is to conduct a proper funeral that will facilitate the soul's movement from the world of the living to what Vietnamese refer to as "the other world" (*gioi khac*). This transfer is vital because a soul that does not move to the other world is condemned to becoming a malevolent wandering ghost, while the soul that does move can become a benevolent family ancestor. There is a great deal of variation regarding the conduct of funeral rites, but they share this common goal.

The other world is regarded as identical to that of the living. To live happily there, the dead depend on the living to provide them with essential items. At a minimum this includes food, though some also send money, clothing, and other items. Family members deliver these items through mortuary rituals, especially those performed annually on the deceased's death anniversary. All rituals associated with death have a tremendous moral significance in Vietnamese society.

MEDICINE AND HEALTH CARE

The Vietnamese, like residents of other poor, tropical countries, suffer from a wide range of maladies, including parasitic, intestinal, nutritional, sexually transmitted, and respiratory diseases. In 1999, the average life expectancy at birth was 65.71 years for men and 70.64 years for women. The major endemic diseases include malaria, hepatitis A, and hepatitis B. Other diseases present are HIV-AIDS, syphilis, gonorrhea, measles, typhoid, dengue fever, Japanese encephalitis, cholera, leprosy, and tuberculosis. Since the early 1990s, the Vietnamese government, with assistance from international organizations, has achieved tremendous successes in reducing malaria fatalities and also in eliminating polio. However, some infectious diseases have begun reemerging in recent years, particularly tuberculosis, and the number of HIV-AIDS cases has also grown significantly. Many infectious diseases are associated with poverty and the poor often suffer the most severe consequences.

The Vietnamese revolution created improvements in the quality and availability of health care. The government constructed hospitals in urban areas and health clinics in rural communities where patients were required to pay only minimal fees. Many of the larger facilities were constructed with international assistance. These programs helped reduce infant mortality and the frequency of many infectious diseases, but many of these advances were unevenly spread throughout the country as many poor highland areas continued to receive inadequate care. Budgetary restrictions held back overall health improvements. Many facilities today do not have adequate resources to function and have begun charging patients higher fees. Many specialists have also left rural areas for better opportunities in cities. These changes have put adequate health care out of reach of many Vietnamese.

One of the greatest strains on the contemporary medical system is HIV-AIDS, the first Vietnamese case of which was reported in 1990. Experts estimate that the disease has affected over 165,000 Vietnamese. The government has launched effective education and awareness programs to combat the spread of the disease so Vietnam has not experienced an epidemic as severe as other Asian countries. The two groups most heavily affected by the disease have been prostitutes and intravenous drug users. HIV-AIDS is a largely stigmatized disease due to its association with perceived immoral behavior. Many sufferers seek to conceal their infection, producing a significant difference between the 20,000 officially reported cases and the expert estimates of over 165,000 cases. There are several hospitals devoted to the care of HIV-AIDS patients, but a lack of adequate funding prevents the majority of patients from receiving the most advanced and effective treatments.

The treatment of illnesses illustrates the diverse medical systems that coexist in Vietnam. The most commonly consulted, particularly in urban areas, is western biomedicine with its reliance on surgery and pharmaceuticals. For most Vietnamese, biomedicine is the first resort in cases of acute illness or bacterial or viral infections. With chronic illness, many will first try biomedical treatments, but if these fail, they will turn to herbal treatments. Vietnam has two main herbal traditions: Chinese herbal medicine (*thouc bac* or "northern drugs") and Vietnamese herbal medicine (*thuoc nam* or "southern drugs"). Both traditions have substantial similarities, particularly in their theories that illness results from humoral imbalances in the body, yet the treatments prescribed in the latter rely more on herbal remedies available in Vietnam. In some cases people use biomedical and alternative treatments in a complementary manner. Many Vietnamese comment that herbal medicines are more effective in the long run because they deal with the true cause of illness whereas biomedicine only treats the symptoms. Members of different highland communities also employ biomedical and herbal remedies to treat illness, but the poverty of many communities makes access to the former difficult.

The Vietnamese have a range of indigenous healers, such as spirit mediums or other spirit specialists, who are consulted in cases of prolonged physical or mental illness. These healers believe that disease and misfortune are caused by spirits or other malevolent entities. The techniques they employ involve contacting the spirit world, finding and identifying the offending spirit, and determining what is needed to end the spirit's torments. The government strongly opposes and criticizes these specialists, but they remain active throughout the country.

SECULAR CELEBRATIONS

Vietnam's socialist government has created a range of secular celebrations to glorify official history and values. Official holidays include: Labor Day (1 May), National Day (2 September), and Teacher's Day (19 November). Other important dates are War Invalids' and Martyrs' Day (27 July), and the anniversaries of the founding of the Communist Party (3 February), Ho Chi Minh's birth (19 May), and the August Revolution (19 August). Perhaps the most

Celebrants crowd Hanoi streets during the Tet lunar new year celebration in Vietnam.

sensitive official holiday for Vietnam's people is Liberation Day (30 April) that commemorates the South Vietnamese government's surrender. The government heavily promotes the significance of these dates, but financial limitations often make their celebration rather low-key.

THE ARTS AND HUMANITIES

Support for the Arts. Vietnam's socialist government places a strong emphasis on the arts, particularly because it regards them as a prime vehicle for the propagation of socialist values. All of the main artistic forms such as theater, literature, cinema, and painting have state-controlled organizations that artists are encouraged if not forced to join. The government at times severely constrains the direction of artistic development through censorship, control over printing, and the presence of party members in artistic organizations. This has not prevented a minor artistic renaissance, particularly in literature, since the late 1980s. Some artists find ways to insert critical messages into their work. Many artists struggle financially because of the recent dramatic reductions in government subsidies for the arts, the absence of adequate protection for copyrights, and the fickle tastes of a public that sometimes prefers imported films, music, and literature. Artists, especially painters, who can produce for expatriates or the tourist market, have the greatest freedom to pursue their craft.

Literature. Vietnam has a vibrant literary tradition dating back many centuries. Elite mandarins and scholars in the premodern period composed sophisticated poetry. Many poems from earlier eras such as Nguyen Du's *The Tale of Kieu* or Nguyen Dinh Chieu *Luc Van Tien* are regarded as literary masterpieces. Along with these traditions, the Vietnamese also maintained a rich oral legacy of songs, poems, and morality tales people still recite today. Prose fiction became popular under colonial rule in the first half of the twentieth century. Writers of this period such as those of the "Self-Reliance Literature Group" (*Tu Luc Van Doan*) developed the role of author as social critic. The socialist authorities kept literature under tight control for several decades to ensure that it was in accord with the officially prescribed "socialist realist" canon that described the virtues of the working class and the revolution. Since the late 1980s, Vietnam has experienced a literary revitalization with the publication of numerous works that present war, and revolution, and their consequences in a critical light. The work of several such authors, including Bao Ninh, Duong Thu Huong, and Nguyen Huy Thiep has attracted an international audience.

Graphic Arts. A number of indigenous graphic art traditions remain popular. These include lacquerware, ink block prints, and ceramics, all of which employ distinctive themes developed by Vietnamese artists. Historically, specialist families or villages have produced these items for local sale, though some objects such as ceramics were sold throughout the country and abroad. Painting has become more popular in urban areas since the colonial period. All of these forms are displayed in museums and, with the exception of paintings, are sold in local markets as well as galleries or shops in major cities.

Performance Arts. The most popular performance arts in Vietnam have historically been a variety of musical theater traditions, all of which continue to be performed by government-organized troupes. The main forms included the courtly tradition of classical opera (*hat tuong*); reform theater (*hat cai luong*); an innovative tradition that emerged in the Mekong Delta in the early twentieth century; and *hat cheo*, a rural folk tradition. The former tradition has been in decline for several decades. Reform theater is popular in the south, and hat cheo in the north. Most performances take place in theaters usually in urban areas. Troupes struggle financially and perform less frequently than before the revolution. The French introduced Western drama to Vietnam, but its popularity has never matched musical theater. Musical performances, either of traditional musical forms or contemporary popular music, are also popular. Radio and television have become a common way to listen to or watch the whole range of performance arts.

THE STATE OF THE PHYSICAL AND SOCIAL SCIENCES

The Vietnamese government has a strong commitment to the development of the physical and social sciences. Officially sponsored universities and research institutes have specialists in most major disciplines such as biology, chemistry, physics, mathematics, anthropology, sociology, psychology, and economics. Many specialists have received training abroad, either in the former Eastern Bloc nations or in advanced capitalist nations. Despite this commitment, the overall state of the physical and social sciences is poor due to a lack of funding that hinders the construction of adequate research facilities such as laboratories or libraries, constrains the training of adequate numbers of specialists, and keeps scientists' pay extremely low.

BIBLIOGRAPHY

Beresford, Melanie. *Vietnam: Politics, Economics, and Society*, 1988.

Biddington, Ralph and Judith Biddington. ''Education for All: Literacy in Vietnam, 1975–1995.'' *Compare* 27 (1): 43–61, 1997.

Bryant, John. ''Communism, Poverty, and Demographic Change in North Vietnam.'' *Population and Development Review* 24 (2): 235–269, 1998.

Cadiere, L. M. *Croyances et pratiques religieuses des Vietnamiens*, 1992.

Condominas, Georges. *We Have Eaten the Forest: The Story of a Montagnard Village in the Central Highlands of Vietnam*, 1977.

Dollar, David, Paul Glewwe, and Jennie Litvack, eds. *Household Welfare and Vietnam Transition*, 1998.

Fforde, Adam. *The Agrarian Question in Vietnam, 1974–1979*, 1989.

Forbes, Dean. ''Urbanization, Migration, and Vietnam Spatial Structure. *Sojourn* 11 (1): 24–51, 1996.

Gammeltoft, Tine. *Women's Bodies, Women's Worries: Health and Family Planning in a Vietnamese Rural Community*, 1999.

Goodkind, Daniel. ''Rising Gender Inequality in Vietnam Since Reunification.'' *Pacific Affairs* 68 (3): 342–359, 1995.

Haughton, Dominique Marie-Annick, ed. *Health and Wealth in Vietnam: An Analysis of Living Standards*, 1999.

Hickey, Gerald Cannon. *Village in Vietnam*, 1964.

———. *Free in the Forest: Ethnohistory of the Vietnamese Central Highlands, 1954–1976*, 1982.

Hirschman, Charles and Vu Manh Loi. ''Family and Household Structure in Vietnam: Some Glimpses from a Recent Survey.'' *Pacific Affairs* 69 (2): 229–250, 1996.

Ho-Tai, Hue Tam, ed. *The Country of Memory: Remaking the Past in Late Socialist Vietnam*, Forthcoming.

Jamieson, Neil L. *Understanding Vietnam*, 1993.

Kerkvliet, Benedict J. Tria. ''Village–State Relations in Vietnam: The Effects of Everyday Politics on Decollectivization. *The Journal of Asian Studies* 54 (2): 396–418, 1995.

Kerkvliet, Benedict J. Tria and Doug J. Porter. *Vietnam Rural Transformation*, 1995.

Kleinen, John. *Facing the Future, Reviving the Past: A Study of Social Change in a Northern Vietnamese Village*, 1999.

Knodel, J., J. Friedman, T. S. Anh, and B. T. Cuong. ''Intergenerational Exchanges in Vietnam: Family Size, Sex Composition, and the Location of Children.'' *Population Studies* 54 (1): 89-104, 1998.

Ladinsky, Judith, Nancy D. Volk, and Margaret Robinson. ''The Influence of Traditional Medicine in Shaping Medical Care Practices in Vietnam Today. *Social Science and Medicine* 25 (10): 1105–1110, 1987.

Liljestrom, Rita. *Profit and Poverty in Rural Vietnam: Winners and Losers of a Dismantled Revolution*, 1998.

Luong, Hy Van. *Revolution in the Village: Tradition and Transformation in North Vietnam, 1925–1988*, 1992.

——— ''Economic Reform and the Intensification of Rituals in Two Northern Vietnamese Villages, 1980–90.'' In Borje Ljunggren, ed. *The Challenge of Reform in Indochina*, 259–292, 1993.

Mai Thi Thu, and Le Thi Nham Tuyet. *Women in Viet Nam*, 1978.

Malarney, Shaun Kingsley. ''Culture, Virtue, and Political Transformation in Contemporary Northern Viet Nam.'' *The Journal of Asian Studies* 56 (4): 899–920, 1997.

———. ''State Stigma, Family Prestige, and the Development of Entrepreneurship in the Red River Delta.'' In Robert W. Hefner, ed., *Market Cultures: Society and Morality in the New Asian Capitalisms*, 268–289, 1998.

Marr, David. *Vietnamese Tradition on Trial, 1920–1945*, 1981.

Marr, David and Christine White, eds. *Postwar Vietnam: Dilemmas in Socialist Development*, 1988.

Moise, Edwin. *Land Reform in China and North Vietnam: Consolidating the Revolution at the Village Level*, 1983.

Nguyen Khac Vien. *Tradition and Revolution in Viet Nam*, 1974.

Nguyen Tron Dieu. *Geography of Vietnam: Natural, Human, Economic*, 1992.

Nguyen Xuan Thu. ''Higher Education in Vietnam: Key Areas Need Assistance. Higher Education Policy 10 (2): 137–143, 1997.

Norton, Barley. ''Music and Possession in Vietnam.'' Ph.D. dissertation. University of London, 1999.

Phan Chanh Cong. ''The Vietnamese Concept of the Human Souls and the Rituals of Birth and Death.'' *Southeast Asian Journal of Social Science.* 21 (2): 159–198, 1993.

Phan Van Bich. *The Vietnamese Family in Change: The Case of the Red River Delta*, 1999.

Pike, Douglas. *PAVN: People's Army of Vietnam*, 1986.

Porter, Gareth. *Vietnam: The Politics of Bureaucratic Socialism*, 1993.

Taylor, Keith Weller. *The Birth of Vietnam*, 1983.

Tran Khanh. *The Ethnic Chinese and Economic Development in Vietnam*, 1993.

Turley, William S. and Mark Selden, eds. *Reinventing Vietnamese Socialism: Doi Moi in Comparative Perspective*, 1993.

Vietnam Living Standards Survey, Government of Vietnam. 1998.

Woodside, Alexander Barton. *Vietnam and the Chinese Model*, 1971.

—SHAWN KINGSLEY MALARNEY

WALES

CULTURE NAME

Welsh

ALTERNATIVE NAME

Cymru, the nation; Cymry, the people; Cymraeg, the language

ORIENTATION

Identification. The Britons, a Celtic tribe, who first settled in the area that is now Wales, had already begun to identify themselves as a distinct culture by the sixth century C.E. The word "Cymry," referring to the country, first appeared in a poem dating from 633. By 700 C.E., the Britons referred to themselves as Cymry, the country as Cymru, and the language as Cymraeg. The words "Wales" and "Welsh" are Saxon in origin and were used by the invading Germanic tribe to denote people who spoke a different language. The Welsh sense of identity has endured despite invasions, absorption into Great Britain, mass immigration, and, more recently, the arrival of non-Welsh residents.

Language has played a significant role in contributing to the sense of unity felt by the Welsh; more than the other Celtic languages, Welsh has maintained a significant number of speakers. During the eighteenth century a literary and cultural rebirth of the language occurred which further helped to solidify national identity and create ethnic pride among the Welsh. Central to Welsh culture is the centuries-old folk tradition of poetry and music which has helped keep the Welsh language alive. Welsh intellectuals in the eighteenth and nineteenth centuries wrote extensively on the subject of Welsh culture, promoting the language as the key to preserving national identity. Welsh literature, poetry, and music flourished in the nineteenth century as literacy rates and the availability of printed material increased. Tales that had traditionally been handed down orally were recorded, both in Welsh and English, and a new generation of Welsh writers emerged.

Location and Geography. Wales is a part of the United Kingdom and is located in a wide peninsula in the western portion of the island of Great Britain. The island of Anglesey is also considered a part of Wales and is separated from the mainland by the Menai Strait. Wales is surrounded by water on three sides: to the north, the Irish Sea; to the south, the Bristol Channel; and to the west, Saint George's Channel and Cardigan Bay. The English counties of Cheshire, Shropshire, Hereford, Worcester, and Gloucestershire border Wales on the east. Wales covers an area of 8,020 square miles (20,760 square kilometers) and extends 137 miles (220 kilometers) from its most distant points and varies between 36 and 96 miles (58 and 154 kilometers) in width. The capital, Cardiff, is located in the southeast on the Severn Estuary and is also the most important seaport and shipbuilding center. Wales is very mountainous and has a rocky, irregular coastline with numerous bays, the largest of which is Cardigan Bay to the west. The Cambrian Mountains, the most significant range, run north-south through central Wales. Other mountain ranges include the Brecon Beacons to the southeast and Snowdon in the northwest, which reaches an elevation of 3,560 feet (1,085 meters) and is the highest mountain in Wales and England. The Dee River, with its headwaters in Bala Lake, the largest natural lake in Wales, flows through northern Wales into England. Numerous smaller rivers cover the south, including the Usk, Wye, Teifi, and Towy.

The temperate climate, mild and moist, has ensured the development of an abundance of plant and animal life. Ferns, mosses, and grasslands as well as numerous wooded areas cover Wales. Oak, mountain ash, and coniferous trees are found in mountainous regions under 1,000 feet (300 meters). The pine marten, a small animal similar to a mink, and the polecat, a member of the weasel family, are

Wales

found only in Wales and nowhere else in Great Britain.

Demography. The latest surveys place the population of Wales at 2,921,000 with a density of approximately 364 people per square mile (141 per square kilometers). Almost three-quarters of the Welsh population reside in the mining centers of the south. The popularity of Wales as a vacation destination and weekend retreat, especially near the border with England, has created a new, nonpermanent population.

Linguistic Affiliation. There are approximately 500,000 Welsh speakers today and, due to a renewed interest in the language and culture, this number may increase. Most people in Wales, however, are English-speaking, with Welsh as a second language; in the north and west, many people are Welsh and English bilinguals. English is still the main language of everyday use with both Welsh and English appearing on signs. In some areas, Welsh is used exclusively and the number of Welsh publications is increasing.

Welsh, or Cymraeg, is a Celtic language belonging to the Brythonic group consisting of Breton, Welsh, and the extinct Cornish. Western Celtic tribes first settled in the area during the Iron Age, bringing with them their language which survived both Roman and Anglo-Saxon occupation and influence, although some features of Latin were introduced into the language and have survived in modern Welsh. Welsh epic poetry can be traced back to the sixth century C.E. and represents one of the oldest literary traditions in Europe. The poems of Taliesin and Aneirin dating from the late seventh century C.E. reflect a literary and cultural awareness from an early point in Welsh history. Although there were many factors affecting the Welsh language, especially contact with other language groups, the Industrial Revolution of the eighteenth and nineteenth centuries marked a dramatic decline in the number of Welsh speakers, as many non-Welsh people, attracted by the industry that had developed around coal mining in the south and east, moved into the area. At the same time, many Welsh people from rural areas left to find work in London or abroad. This large-scale migration of non-Welsh-speaking workers greatly accelerated the disappearance of Welsh-speaking communities. Even though there were still around forty Welsh-language publications in the mid-nineteenth century, the regular use of Welsh by the majority of the population began to drop. Over time two linguistic groups emerged in Wales; the Welsh-speaking region known as the Y Fro Cymraeg to the north and west, where more than 80 percent of the population speaks Welsh, and the Anglo-Welsh area to the south and east where the number of Welsh speakers is below 10 percent and English is the majority language. Up until 1900, however, almost half the population still spoke Welsh.

In 1967 the Welsh Language Act was passed, recognizing the status of Welsh as an official language. In 1988 the Welsh Language Board was established, helping to ensure the rebirth of Welsh. Throughout Wales there was a serious effort in the second half of the twentieth century to maintain and promote the language. Other efforts to support the language included Welsh-language television programs, bilingual Welsh-English schools, as well

A procession heading to the National Eisteddfod Festival in Llandudno, Wales.

as exclusively Welsh-language nursery schools, and Welsh language courses for adults.

Symbolism. The symbol of Wales, which also appears on the flag, is a red dragon. Supposedly brought to the colony of Britain by the Romans, the dragon was a popular symbol in the ancient world and was used by the Romans, the Saxons, and the Parthians. It became the national symbol of Wales when Henry VII, who became king in 1485 and had used it as his battle flag during the battle of Bosworth Field, decreed that the red dragon should become the official flag of Wales. The leek and the daffodil are also important Welsh symbols. One legend connects the leek to Saint David, the patron saint of Wales, who defeated the pagan Saxons in a victorious battle that supposedly occurred in a field of leeks. It is more likely that leeks were adopted as a national symbol because of their importance to the Welsh diet, particularly during Lent when meat was not allowed. Another, less famous Welsh symbol consists of three ostrich plumes and the motto ''Ich Dien'' (translation: ''I serve'') from the Battle of Crecy, France, in 1346. It was probably borrowed from the motto of the King of Bohemia, who led the cavalry charge against the English.

HISTORY AND ETHNIC RELATIONS

Emergence of the Nation. The earliest evidence of a human presence in Wales dates from the Paleolithic, or Old Stone Age, period almost 200,000 years ago. It was not until the Neolithic and Bronze Age period around 3,000 B.C.E., however, that a sedentary civilization began to develop. The first tribes to settle in Wales, who probably came from the western coastal areas of the Mediterranean, were people generally referred to as the Iberians. Later migrations from northern and eastern Europe brought the Brythonic Celts and Nordic tribes to the area. At the time of the Roman invasion in 55 B.C.E., the area was made up of the Iberian and Celtic tribes who referred to themselves as Cymry. The Cymry tribes were eventually subjugated by the Romans in the first century C.E. Anglo-Saxon tribes also settled in Britain during this period, pushing other Celtic tribes into the Welsh mountains where they eventually united with the Cymry already living there. In the first centuries C.E., Wales was divided into tribal kingdoms, the most important of which were Gwynedd, Gwent, Dyved, and Powys. All of the Welsh kingdoms later united against the Anglo-Saxon invaders, marking the beginning of an official division between England and Wales. This boundary became official with the construction of Offa's Dyke around the middle of the eighth century C.E. Offa's Dyke was at first a ditch constructed by Offa, the king of Mercia, in an attempt to give his territories a well-defined border to the west. The Dyke was later enlarged and fortified, becoming one of the largest human-made boundaries in Europe and covering 150 miles from the northeast coast to the southeast coast of Wales. It remains to this day the line that divides English and Welsh cultures.

When William the Conqueror (William I) and his Norman army conquered England in 1066, the three English earldoms of Chester, Shrewsbury, and Hereford were established on the border with Wales. These areas were used as strong points in attacks against the Welsh and as strategic political centers. Nevertheless, the only Welsh kingdom to fall under Norman control during the reign of William I (1066–1087) was Gwent, in the southeast. By 1100 the Norman lords had expanded their control to include the Welsh areas of Cardigan, Pembroke, Brecon, and Glamorgan. This expansion into Welsh territory led to the establishment of the March of Wales, an area previously ruled by the Welsh kings.

The Welsh continued to fight Norman and Anglo-Saxon control in the first part of the twelfth century. By the last half of the twelfth century the three Welsh kingdoms of Gwynedd, Powys, and Deheubarth were firmly established, providing a permanent base for Welsh statehood. The principal settlements of Aberffraw in Gwynedd, Mathrafal in Powys, and Dinefwr in Deheubarth formed the core of Welsh political and cultural life. Although the Welsh kings were allies, each ruled separate territories swearing loyalty to the king of England. The establishment of the kingdoms marked the beginning of a period of stability and growth. Agriculture flourished, as did scholarship and the Welsh literary tradition. A period of unrest and contested succession followed the deaths of the three Welsh kings as different factions fought for control. The stability provided by the first kings was never restored in Powys and Deheubarth. The kingdom of Gwynedd was successfully united once again under the reign of Llywelyn ap Iorwerth (d. 1240) following a brief power struggle. Viewing Llywelyn as a threat, King John (1167–1216) led a campaign against him which led to Llywelyn's humiliating defeat in 1211. Llywelyn, however, turned this to his advantage and secured the allegiance of other Welsh leaders who feared total subjugation under King John. Llywelyn became the leader of the Welsh forces and, although conflict with King John continued, he successfully united the Welsh politically and eventually minimized the king of England's involvement in Welsh affairs. Dafydd ap Llywelyn, Llywelyn ap Iorwerth's son and heir, attempted to broaden Welsh power before his premature death in 1246. With Dafydd leaving no heirs, succession to the Welsh throne was contested by Dafydd's nephews and in a series of battles between 1255 and 1258 Llwelyn ap Gruffydd (d. 1282), one of the nephews, assumed control of the Welsh throne, crowning himself Prince of Wales. Henry III officially recognized his authority over Wales in 1267 with the Treaty of Montgomery and in turn Llwelyn swore allegiance to the English crown.

Llwelyn succeeded in firmly establishing the Principality of Wales, which consisted of the twelfth century kingdoms of Gwynedd, Powys, and Deheubarth as well as some parts of the March. This period of peace, however, did not last long. Conflict arose between Edward I, who succeeded Henry III, and Llwelyn, culminating in an English invasion of Wales in 1276, followed by war. Llwelyn was forced into a humiliating surrender that included relinquishing control over the eastern part of his territory and an acknowledgment of fealty paid to Edward I annually. In 1282 Llwelyn, aided this time by the Welsh nobility of other regions, rebelled against Edward I only to be killed in combat. The Welsh forces continued to fight but finally capitulated to Edward I in the summer of 1283, marking the beginning of a period of occupation by the English.

Although the Welsh were forced to surrender, the struggle for unity and independence over the previous one hundred years had been crucial in shaping Welsh politics and identity. During the fourteenth century economic and social difficulties prevailed in Wales. Edward I embarked on a program of castle building, both for defensive purposes and to shelter English colonists, which was continued by his heir Edward II. The result of his efforts can still be seen in Wales today, which has more castles per square mile than any other area of Europe.

At the end of the 1300s Henry IV seized the throne from Richard II, provoking a revolt in Wales where support for Richard II was strong. Under the leadership of Owain Glyndwr, Wales united to rebel against the English king. From 1400 to 1407 Wales once again asserted its independence from England. England did not regain control of Wales again until 1416 and the death of Glyndwr, marking the last Welsh uprising. The Welsh submitted to Henry VII (1457–1509), the first king of the house of Tudor, whom they regarded as a countryman. In 1536 Henry VIII declared the Act of Union, incorporating Wales into the English realm. For the first time in its history Wales obtained uniformity in the administration of law and justice, the same political rights as the English, and English common law in the courts. Wales also secured parliamentary representation. Welsh landowners exercised their authority locally, in the name of the king, who granted them their land and property. Wales, although no longer an independent nation, had finally obtained unity, stability, and, most importantly, statehood and recognition as a distinct culture.

National Identity. The different ethnic groups and tribes that settled in ancient Wales gradually merged, politically and culturally, to defend their territory from first, the Romans, and later the Anglo-Saxon and Norman invaders. The sense of national identity was formed over centuries as the people of Wales struggled against being absorbed into neighboring cultures. The heritage of a common Celtic origin was a key factor in shaping Welsh identity and uniting the warring kingdoms. Cut off from other Celtic cultures to the north in Britain and in Ireland, the Welsh tribes united against their non-Celtic enemies. The development and continued use of the Welsh language also played important roles in maintaining and strengthening the national identity. The tradition of handing down poetry and stories orally and the importance of music in daily

A pile of slate rests above a Welsh town. Mining is an important industry in Wales.

life were essential to the culture's survival. With the arrival of book publishing and an increase in literacy, the Welsh language and culture were able to continue to flourish, through the nineteenth century and into the twentieth century, despite dramatic industrial and social changes in Great Britain. A revival of Welsh nationalism in the second half of the twentieth century once again brought to the forefront the concept of a unique Welsh identity.

Ethnic Relations. With the Act of Union, Wales gained peaceful relations with the English while maintaining their ethnic identity. Until the late eighteenth century Wales was predominantly rural with most of the population living in or near small farming villages; contact with other ethnic groups was minimal. The Welsh gentry, on the other hand, mixed socially and politically with the English and Scottish gentry, producing a very Anglicized upper class. The industry that grew up around coal mining and steel manufacturing attracted immigrants, principally from Ireland and England, to Wales starting in the late eighteenth century. Poor living and working conditions, combined with the arrival of large numbers of immigrants, caused social unrest and frequently led to conflicts—often violent in nature—among different ethnic groups. The decline of heavy industry in the late nineteenth century, however, caused an outward migration of Welsh and the country ceased to attract immigrants. The end of the twentieth century brought renewed industrialization and with it, once again, immigrants from all over the world, although without notable conflicts. The increased standard of living throughout Great Britain has also made Wales a popular vacation and weekend retreat, principally for people from large urban areas in England. This trend is causing significant tension, especially in Welsh-speaking and rural areas, among residents who feel that their way of life is being threatened.

URBANISM, ARCHITECTURE, AND THE USE OF SPACE

The development of Welsh cities and towns did not begin until industrialization in the late 1700s. Rural areas are characterized by a scattering of isolated farms, typically consisting of the older, traditional whitewashed or stone buildings, usually with slate roofs. Villages evolved from the early settlements of the Celtic tribes who chose particular locations for their agricultural or defensive value. More successful settlements grew and became the political and economic centers, first of the kingdoms, then later the individual regions, in Wales. The Anglo–Norman manorial tradition of buildings clustered on a landowner's property, similar to rural villages in England, was introduced to Wales after the conquest of 1282. The village as a center of rural society, however, became significant only in southern and eastern Wales; other rural areas maintained scattered and more isolated building patterns. Timber-framed houses, originally constructed around a great hall, emerged in the Middle Ages in the north and east, and later throughout Wales. In the late sixteenth century, houses began to vary more in size and refinement, reflecting the growth of a middle class and increasing disparities in wealth. In Glamorgan and Monmouthshire, landowners built brick houses that reflected the vernacular style popular in England at the time as well as their social status. This imitation of English architecture set landowners apart from the rest of Welsh society. After the Norman conquest, urban development began to grow around castles and military camps. The *bastide*, or castle town, although not large, is still significant to political and administrative life. Industrialization in the eighteenth and nineteenth centuries caused an explosion of urban growth in the southeast and in Cardiff. Housing shortages were common and several families, often unrelated, shared dwellings. Economic affluence and a popula-

tion increase created a demand for new construction in the late twentieth century. Slightly over 70 percent of homes in Wales are owner-occupied.

FOOD AND ECONOMY

Food in Daily Life. The importance of agriculture to the Welsh economy as well as the availability of local products has created high food standards and a national diet that is based on fresh, natural food. In coastal areas fishing and seafood are important to both the economy and the local cuisine. The type of food available in Wales is similar to that found in the rest of the United Kingdom and includes a variety of food from other cultures and nations.

Food Customs at Ceremonial Occasions. Special traditional Welsh dishes include *laverbread*, a seaweed dish; *cawl*, a rich broth; *bara brith*, a traditional cake; and *pice ar y maen*, Welsh cakes. Traditional dishes are served at special occasions and holidays. Local markets and fairs usually offer regional products and baked goods. Wales is particularly known for its cheeses and meats. Welsh rabbit, also called Welsh rarebit, a dish of melted cheese mixed with ale, beer, milk, and spices served over toast, has been popular since the early eighteenth century.

Basic Economy. Mining, especially of coal, has been the chief economic activity of Wales since the seventeenth century and is still very important to the economy and one of the leading sources of employment. The largest coalfields are in the southeast and today produce about 10 percent of Great Britain's total coal production. Iron, steel, limestone, and slate production are also important industries. Although heavy industry has played a significant role in the Welsh economy and greatly affected Welsh society in the nineteenth century, the country remains largely agricultural with almost 80 percent of the land used for agricultural activities. The raising of livestock, particularly cattle and sheep, is more important than crop farming. The principal crops are barley, oats, potatoes, and hay. Fishing, centered on the Bristol Channel, is another important commercial activity. The economy is integrated with the rest of Great Britain and as such Wales is no longer exclusively dependent on its own production. Although agriculture accounts for much of the economy, only a small segment of the total population actually works in this area and agricultural output is largely destined for sale. Many foreign companies that produce consumer goods, particularly Japanese firms, have opened factories and offices in Wales in recent years, providing employment and encouraging economic growth.

Land Tenure and Property. In ancient Wales land was informally controlled by tribes who fiercely protected their territory. With the rise of the Welsh kingdoms, land ownership was controlled by the kings who granted their subjects tenure. Because of the scattered and relatively small population of Wales, however, most people lived on isolated farms or in small villages. After the Act of Union with England, the king granted land to the nobility and later, with the rise of a middle class, the Welsh gentry had the economic power to purchase small tracts of land. Most Welsh people were peasant farmers who either worked the land for landowners or were tenant farmers, renting small patches of land. The advent of the industrial revolution caused a radical change in the economy and farmworkers left the countryside in large numbers to seek work in urban areas and coal mines. Industrial workers rented living quarters or, sometimes, were provided with factory housing.

Today, land ownership is more evenly distributed throughout the population although there are still large privately owned tracts of land. A new awareness of environmental issues has led to the creation of national parks and protected wildlife zones. The Welsh Forestry Commission has acquired land formerly used for pasture and farming and initiated a program of reforestation.

Major Industries. Heavy industry, such as mining and other activities associated with the port of Cardiff, once the busiest industrial port in the world, declined in the last part of the twentieth century. The Welsh Office and Welsh Development Agency have worked to attract multinational companies to Wales in an effort to restructure the nation's economy. Unemployment, higher on average in the rest of the United Kingdom, is still a concern. Industrial growth in the late twentieth century was concentrated mostly in the area of science and technology. The Royal Mint was relocated to Llantrisant, Wales in 1968, helping create a banking and financial services industry. Manufacturing is still the largest Welsh industry, with financial services in second place, followed by education, health and social services, and wholesale and retail trade. Mining accounts for only 1 percent of the gross domestic product.

Trade. Integrated with the economy of the United Kingdom, Wales has important trade relations with other regions in Britain and with Europe. Agricultural products, electronic equipment, synthetic fibers, pharmaceuticals, and automotive parts are the principal exports. The most important heavy industry is the refining of imported metal ore to produce tin and aluminum sheets.

POLITICAL LIFE

Government. The Principality of Wales is governed from Whitehall in London, the name of the administrative and political seat of the British government. Increasing pressure from Welsh leaders for more autonomy brought devolution of administration in May 1999, meaning that more political power has been given to the Welsh Office in Cardiff. The position of secretary of state for Wales, a part of the British prime minister's cabinet, was created in 1964. In a 1979 referendum a proposal for the creation of a nonlegislating Welsh Assembly was rejected but in 1997 another referendum passed by a slim margin, leading to the 1998 creation of the National Assembly for Wales. The assembly has sixty members and is responsible for setting policy and creating legislation in areas regarding education, health, agriculture, transportation, and social services. A general reorganization of government throughout the United Kingdom in 1974 included a simplification of Welsh administration with smaller districts regrouped to form larger constituencies for economic and political reasons. Wales was reorganized into eight new counties, from thirteen originally, and within the counties thirty-seven new districts were created.

Leadership and Political Officials. Wales has always had strong left wing and radical political parties and leaders. There is also a strong political awareness throughout Wales and voter turnout at elections is higher on average than in the United Kingdom as a whole. In most of the nineteenth and early twentieth centuries the Liberal Party dominated Welsh politics with the industrial regions supporting the Socialists. In 1925 the Welsh Nationalist Party, known as Plaid Cymru, was founded with the intention of gaining independence for Wales as a region within the European Economic Community. Between World Wars I and II severe economic depression caused almost 430,000 Welsh to immigrate and a new political activism was born with an emphasis on social and economic reform. After World War II the Labor Party gained a majority of support. During the late 1960s Plaid Cymru and the Conservative Party won seats in parliamentary elections, weakening the Labor Party's tradi-

The Pembrokeshire landscape in Cribyn Walk, Solva, Dyfed. Wales is surrounded by water on three sides.

tional dominance of Welsh politics. In the 1970s and 1980s Conservatives gained even more control, a trend that was reversed in the 1990s with the return of Labor dominance and the increased support for Plaid Cymru and Welsh nationalism. The Welsh separatist, nationalist movement also includes more extremist groups who seek the creation of a politically independent nation on the basis of cultural and linguistic differences. The Welsh Language Society is one of the more visible of these groups and has stated its willingness to use civil disobedience to further its goals.

Military Activity. Wales does not have an independent military and its defense falls under the authority of the military of the United Kingdom as a whole. There are, however, three army regiments, the Welsh Guards, the Royal Regiment of Wales, and the Royal Welch Fusiliers, that have historical associations with the country.

SOCIAL WELFARE AND CHANGE PROGRAMS

Health and social services fall under the administration and responsibility of the secretary of state for Wales. The Welsh Office, which works with the county and district authorities, plans and executes matters relating to housing, health, education, and welfare. Terrible working and living conditions in

the nineteenth century brought significant changes and new policies regarding social welfare that continued to be improved upon throughout the twentieth century. Issues regarding health care, housing, education, and working conditions, combined with a high level of political activism, have created an awareness of and demand for social change programs in Wales.

GENDER ROLES AND STATUSES

The Relative Status of Women and Men. Historically, women had few rights, although many worked outside the home, and were expected to fulfill the role of wife, mother, and, in the case of unmarried women, caregiver to an extended family. In agricultural areas women worked alongside male family members. When the Welsh economy began to become more industrialized, many women found work in factories that hired an exclusively female workforce for jobs not requiring physical strength. Women and children worked in mines, putting in fourteen-hour days under extremely harsh conditions. Legislation was passed in the mid-nineteenth century limiting the working hours for women and children but it was not until the beginning of the twentieth century that Welsh women began to demand more civil rights. The Women's Institute, which now has chapters throughout the United Kingdom, was founded in Wales, although all of its activities are conducted in English. In the 1960s another organization, similar to the Women's Institute but exclusively Welsh in its goals, was founded. Known as the *Merched y Wawr*, or Women of the Dawn, it is dedicated to promoting the rights of Welshwomen, the Welsh language and culture, and organizing charitable projects.

SOCIALIZATION

Child Rearing and Education. During the eighteenth and nineteenth centuries children were exploited for labor, sent into mines to work in shafts that were too small for adults. Child and infant mortality rates were high; almost half of all children did not live past the age of five, and only half of those who lived past the age of ten could hope to live to their early twenties. Social reformers and religious organizations, particularly the Methodist Church, advocated for improved public education standards in the mid-nineteenth century. Conditions began to gradually improve for children when working hours were restricted and compulsory education enacted. The Education Act of 1870 passed to enforce basic standards, but also sought to banish Welsh completely from the education system.

Today, primary and nursery schools in areas with a Welsh-speaking majority provide instruction completely in Welsh and schools in areas where English is the first language offer bilingual instruction. The Welsh Language Nursery Schools Movement, *Mudiad Ysgolion Meithrin Cymraeg*, founded in 1971, has been very successful in creating a network of nursery schools, or *Ysgolion Meithrin*, particularly in regions where English is used more frequently. Nursery, primary, and secondary schools are under the administration of the education authority of the Welsh Office. Low-cost, quality public education is available throughout Wales for students of all ages.

Higher Education. Most institutions of higher learning are publicly supported, but admission is competitive. The Welsh literary tradition, a high literacy rate, and political and religious factors have all contributed to shaping a culture where higher education is considered important. The principal institute of higher learning is the University of Wales, a public university financed by the Universities Funding Council in London, with six locations in Wales: Aberystwyth, Bangor, Cardiff, Lampeter, Swansea, and the Welsh National School of Medicine in Cardiff. The Welsh Office is responsible for

Town hall of Laugharne, Dyfed, Wales.

the other universities and colleges, including the Polytechnic of Wales, near Pontypridd, and the University College of Wales at Aberystwyth. The Welsh Office, working with the Local Education Authorities and the Welsh Joint Education Committee, oversees all aspects of public education. Adult continuing education courses, particularly those in Welsh language and culture, are strongly promoted through regional programs.

RELIGION

Religious Beliefs. Religion has played a significant role in the shaping Welsh culture. Protestantism, namely Anglicanism, began to gather more support after Henry VIII broke with the Roman Catholic Church. On the eve of the English Civil War in 1642, Puritanism, practiced by Oliver Cromwell and his supporters, was widespread in the border counties of Wales and in Pembrokeshire. Welsh royalists, who supported the king and Anglicanism, were stripped of their property, incurring much resentment among non-Puritan Welsh. In 1650 the Act for the Propagation of the Gospel in Wales was passed, taking over both political and religious life. During the period known as the Interregnum when Cromwell was in power, several non-Anglican, or Dissenting, Protestant congregations were formed which were to have significant influences on modern Welsh life. The most religiously and socially radical of these were the Quakers, who had a strong following in Montgomeryshire and Merioneth, and eventually spread their influence to areas including the Anglican border counties and the Welsh-speaking areas in the north and west. The Quakers, intensely disliked by both other Dissenting churches and the Anglican Church, were severely repressed with the result that large numbers were forced to emigrate to the American colonies. Other churches, such as the Baptist and Congregationalist, which were Calvinist in theology, grew and found many followers in rural communities and small towns. In the latter part of the eighteenth century many Welsh converted to Methodism after a revival movement in 1735. Methodism was supported within the established Anglican Church and was originally organized through local societies governed by a central association. The influence of the original Dissenting churches, combined with the spiritual revival of Methodism, gradually led Welsh society away from Anglicanism. Conflicts in leadership and chronic poverty made church growth difficult, but the popularity of Methodism eventually helped establish it permanently as the most widespread denomination. The Methodist and other Dissenting churches were also responsible for an increase in literacy through church-sponsored schools that promoted education as a way of spreading religious doctrine.

Today, followers of Methodism still constitute the largest religious group. The Anglican Church, or the Church of England, is the second largest sect, followed by the Roman Catholic Church. There are also much smaller numbers of Jews and Muslims. The Dissenting Protestant sects, and religion in general, played very important roles in modern Welsh society but the number of people who regularly participated in religious activities dropped significantly after World War II.

Rituals and Holy Places. The Cathedral of Saint David, in Pembrokeshire, is the most significant national holy place. David, the patron saint of Wales, was a religious crusader who arrived in Wales in the sixth century to spread Christianity and convert the Welsh tribes. He died in 589 on 1 March, now celebrated as Saint David's Day, a national holiday. His remains are buried in the cathedral.

MEDICINE AND HEALTH CARE

Health care and medicine are government-funded and supported by the National Health Service of the United Kingdom. There is a very high standard of health care in Wales with approximately six medical practitioners per ten thousand people. The Welsh National School of Medicine in Cardiff offers quality medical training and education.

SECULAR CELEBRATIONS

During the nineteenth century, Welsh intellectuals began to promote the national culture and traditions, initiating a revival of Welsh folk culture. Over the last century these celebrations have evolved into major events and Wales now has several internationally important music and literary festivals. The Hay Festival of Literature, from 24 May to 4 June, in the town of Hay-on-Wye, annually attracts thousands, as does the Brecon Jazz Festival from 11 to 13 August. The most important Welsh secular celebration, however, is the Eisteddfod cultural gathering celebrating music, poetry, and storytelling.

The Eisteddfod has its origins in the twelfth century when it was essentially a meeting held by the Welsh bards for the exchange of information. Taking place irregularly and in different locations, the Eisteddfod was attended by poets, musicians and troubadours, all of whom had important roles in medieval Welsh culture. By the eighteenth century the tradition had become less cultural and more social, often degenerating into drunken tavern meetings, but in 1789 the Gwyneddigion Society revived the Eisteddfod as a competitive festival. It was Edward Williams, also known as Iolo Morgannwg, however, who reawakened Welsh interest in the Eisteddfod in the nineteenth century. Williams actively promoted the Eisteddfod among the Welsh community living in London, often giving dramatic speeches about the significance of Welsh culture and the importance of continuing ancient Celtic traditions. The nineteenth century revival of the Eisteddfod and the rise of Welsh nationalism, combined with a romantic image of ancient Welsh history, led to the creation of Welsh ceremonies and rituals that may not have any historical basis.

The Llangollen International Musical Eisteddfod, held from 4 to 9 July, and the Royal National Eisteddfod at Llanelli, which features poetry and Welsh folk arts, held from 5 to 12 August, are the two most important secular celebrations. Other smaller, folk and cultural festivals are held throughout the year.

A half-timbered building in Beaumaris, Anglesey, Wales.

THE ARTS AND HUMANITIES

Support for the Arts. The traditional importance of music and poetry has encouraged a general appreciation of and support for all of the arts. There is strong public support throughout Wales for the arts, which are considered important to the national culture. Financial support is derived from both the private and public sectors. The Welsh Arts Council provides government assistance for literature, art, music, and theater. The council also organizes tours of foreign performance groups in Wales and provides grants to writers for both English- and Welsh-language publications.

Literature. Literature and poetry occupy an important position in Wales for historical and linguistic reasons. Welsh culture was based on an oral tradition of legends, myths, and folktales passed down from generation to generation. The most famous early bardic poets, Taliesin and Aneirin, wrote epic poems about Welsh events and legends around the seventh century. Increasing literacy in the eighteenth century and the concern of Welsh intellectuals for the preservation of the language and culture gave birth to modern written Welsh literature. As industrialization and Anglicization began to threaten traditional Welsh culture, efforts were made to promote the language, preserve Welsh poetry, and encourage Welsh writers. Dylan Thomas, however, the best known twentieth century Welsh poet, wrote in English. Literary festivals and competitions help keep this tradition alive, as does the continued promotion of Welsh, the Celtic language with the largest number of speakers today. Nevertheless, the influence of other cultures combined with the ease of communication through mass media, from both inside the United Kingdom and from other parts of the world, continually undermine efforts to preserve a purely Welsh form of literature.

Performance Arts. Singing is the most important of the performance arts in Wales and has its roots in ancient traditions. Music was both entertainment and a means for telling stories. The Welsh National Opera, supported by the Welsh Arts Council, is one of the leading opera companies in Britain. Wales is famous for its all-male choirs, which have evolved from the religious choral tradition. Traditional instruments, such as the harp, are still widely played and since 1906 the Welsh Folk Song Society has preserved, collected, and published traditional songs. The Welsh Theater Company is critically acclaimed and Wales has produced many internationally famous actors.

THE STATE OF PHYSICAL AND SOCIAL SCIENCES

Until the last part of the twentieth century, limited professional and economic opportunities caused many Welsh scientists, scholars, and researchers to leave Wales. A changing economy and the investment of multinationals specializing in high technology are encouraging more people to remain in Wales and find work in the private sector. Research in the social and physical sciences is also supported by Welsh universities and colleges.

BIBLIOGRAPHY

Curtis, Tony. *Wales: The Imagined Nation, Essays in Cultural and National Identity*, 1986.

Davies, William Watkin. *Wales*, 1925.

Durkaez, Victor E. *The Decline of the Celtic Languages: A Study of Linguistic and Cultural Conflict in Scotland, Wales and Ireland from the Reformation to the Twentieth Century*, 1983.

English, John. *Slum Clearance: The Social and Administrative Context in England and Wales*, 1976.

Fevre, Ralph, and Andrew Thompson. *Nation, Identity and Social Theory: Perspectives from Wales*, 1999.

Hopkin, Deian R., and Gregory S. Kealey. *Class, Community, and the Labour Movement: Wales and Canada*, 1989.

Jackson, William Eric. *The Structure of Local Government in England and Wales*, 1966.

Jones, Gareth Elwyn. *Modern Wales: A Concise History, 1485–1979*, 1984.

Owen, Trefor M. *The Customs and Traditions of Wales*, 1991.

Rees, David Ben. *Wales: The Cultural Heritage*, 1981.

Williams, David. *A History of Modern Wales*, 1950.

Williams, Glanmor. *Religion, Language, and Nationality in Wales: Historical Essays by Glanmor Williams*, 1979.

Williams, Glyn. *Social and Cultural Change in Contemporary Wales*, 1978.

———. *The Land Remembers: A View of Wales*, 1977.

Web Sites

U.K. Government. "Culture: Wales." Electronic document. Available from http://uk-pages.net/culture

—M. CAMERON ARNOLD

SEE ALSO: UNITED KINGDOM

WALLIS AND FUTUNA

CULTURE NAME
Wallisian and Futunan

ORIENTATION

Identification. Wallis is named after the eighteenth century English explorer Samuel Wallis. Some people call the island East 'Uvea to distinguish it from an island off the east coast of New Caledonia, known as West 'Uvea, which was settled two hundred years ago by people from East 'Uvea. The population is of Tongan ancestry. Futuna was called the Hoorn Islands by Dutch explorers. Futuna includes the nearby uninhabited island of Alofi.

Location and Geography. The island of Wallis lies in the central Pacific. It is a raised reef, mainly limestone, with an area of ninety-six square miles (250 square kilometers). It is surrounded by a wide lagoon with many small islets. There are no rivers but several lakes in the interior plateau. Better soil is found on the coastal rim, where large trees and crops are cultivated. The villages are in this coastal region, predominantly on the eastern side. The western side is uninhabited; several of the larger islets are inhabited. The lagoon is shallow, and barely navigable. The island is divided into three districts. Mu'a, the most populous; Hahake; and Hihifo. The main town where government offices and the hospital are located is Mata'utu in Hahake in the central district.

Futuna lies one hundred miles southwest of Wallis. Futuna and Alofi are volcanic islands. Futuna is twenty-five square miles (64 square kilometers), and Alofi is eleven square miles (28 square kilometers) in area. A narrow reef encircles both islands, but there is no lagoon. People cultivate the hillsides and use the banks of streams to grow taro. The island is divided by several major rivers, and the population lives in the southern coastal zone. The island is divided into two kingdoms: Sigave in the west and Alo in the east. Leava in Sigave is the main town and port.

Demography. The population of Wallis was 8973 in 1990, and in 1995 was estimated at 9,500. The population of Futuna was estimated at 5,000 in 1995. Similar numbers of Wallisians and Futunans live in New Caledonia. On Wallis, the population lives on the eastern side of the island in communities near a Catholic church. Europeans, mainly French administrators and teachers, account for about 3 percent of the total population.

Linguistic Affiliation. The 'Uvean language is a Western Polynesian language closely related to Tongan. Wallisians use 'Uvean as their everyday language. All school-age and older persons also speak French, the language of the administration. A few people also speak English. The Futunan language is of Samoic origin. It is the language of everyday life, though French is used on official occasions and is taught in schools.

Symbolism. The kava bowl and tapa cloth are important symbols of both cultures. Kava is drunk both ritually and secularly in Futuna. The kava bowl is used to honor chiefs and the existing hierarchy. Tapa cloth is made by women for exchange at rituals that draw extended families together. It is symbolic of women's wealth, along with specially scented oil. Tapa is also sold to tourists. Food gifts are symbols of welcome and good will. The *malae*, or meeting ground, is a place where people gather to honor their chiefs (kings in Futuna). The Lomipeau canoe represents the ties between Wallis/'Uvea and the early maritime empire of Tonga of four hundred years ago. It also symbolizes the strong seagoing tradition of these people, particularly their journeys to Tonga, Samoa, and other islands.

HISTORY AND ETHNIC RELATIONS

Emergence of the Nation. Wallis and Futuna are treated as a single overseas territory of France. Wallis emerged from the Early Tongan Maritime Empire in the 1500s. Before that time it was part of

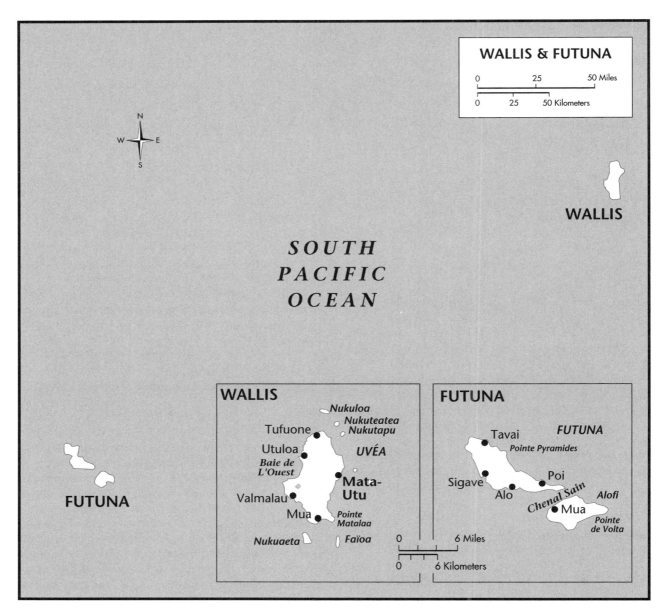

Wallis and Futuna

Tonga and shared its language and customs. Those ties were weakened in the mid-nineteenth century when the French banned overseas voyaging. Futuna has close cultural ties with Samoa and Rotuma. With the arrival of the Catholic mission in the 1830s, a long history of warfare ended.

In 1844, France was invited to protect the people of Wallis and Futuna under the rule of the Catholic Church. France took over political management in 1888 at the insistence of Lavelua (Queen) Amelia, who wanted a French doctor to become the administrator. The French navy provided a series of ad-

ministrators. The result was a tripartite administration of Wallis and Futuna. The Lavelua along with the Tui Sigave and Tuiagaifo of Alo for Futuna, all chiefly families, represented the traditional leadership; the French naval doctors, were the colonial administrators; and the bishop of the Catholic Church also exercised administrative powers.

National Identity. Wallis is the dominant partner because of its larger population and the French colonial administration in Mata'utu. Despite intermarriages, Wallisians and Futunans refer to themselves as separate cultural entities.

Ethnic Relations. There is a small French community in Wallis that consists mainly of administrators and secondary teachers. There are few English speakers and no Chinese community.

URBANISM, ARCHITECTURE, AND THE USE OF SPACE

Wallis is predominantly a rural community. All the villages are linked by road to Mata'utu. The villages surround a Catholic church where people gather at large family occasions. A program to teach building skills has led to the construction of numerous churches built with expensive imported materials.

Houses are substantial, built mainly of concrete with corrugated iron roofs. A few houses of local materials, with pandanus thatch sides and thatched roofs, still exist. Houses are furnished to varying degrees, and people prefer to sit on the floor. Some cooking is done outdoors. Toilet facilities are attached to the home in newer houses. Houses are scattered have one or two acres of land that is used to grow subsistence crops. A house site may consist of four or five houses for the extended family.

Futunan houses follow the Samoan *fale* style. The sleeping house is open-sided with a thatched roof and thatched blinds that can be let down in bad weather. There may be a concrete floor and a low wall to keep the pigs out. Cooking is done in a cook house behind the sleeping house or in an earth oven in the bush. Water and electricity were installed in 1990, though few families can afford electricity.

Wallis has an urban space that contains government buildings and a shopping area. Futuna consists of a string of villages along the southern coast, of which Leava is the main center. Each village has a small shop.

FOOD AND ECONOMY

Food in Daily Life. Family households rely on taro, yams, and sweet potatoes. Villages on Wallis near the lagoon eat fish. If no man in the family is available, women comb the lagoon for crustaceans. Pigs and chickens are raised mainly for celebratory occasions.

Families eat twice a day. Bread and coffee are the mainstays of breakfast. The evening meal consists of taro or yam and fish (on Wallis) and sometimes frozen chicken or corned beef. Tea is the most common beverage.

Food Customs at Ceremonial Occasions. Every family contributes food on public occasions. Pork and turtle are feast foods, with chicken also being reserved for special occasions. Alcohol is an expected part of public feasting on Wallis, and kava is drunk by Futunan men.

Basic Economy. Both Wallis and Futuna have a subsistence-based economy. The land produces taro, yams, sweet potatoes, cassava, and breadfruit. There are no sales of local foods, except to foreigners. The nuns teach cooking and how to use new foods.

On Wallis working for the government and teaching are the main sources of employment. Overseas remittances from family members in New Caledonia contribute to the basic economy. Young men serving in the French military also send or bring goods home. Futunan families farm the hillsides inland and also maintain a small garden in which they grow the kava plant and bananas for daily use.

Land Tenure and Property. Two types of land are distinguished; bush land and house land. Families "possess" some lands that link them to a *pule* and ultimately to the traditional chief. There is also land for use by members of the village. Family land rights are passed to both sons and daughters, but males bear the major responsibility for keeping the land productive. All family members are expected to work on the family land.

Commercial Activities. There are minimal commercial activities. One or two importers, French by nationality, serve the purchasing requirements of the community, namely running one super market, and selling to the small stores in each village. There are no exports, other than an occasional shipment of handicrafts to New Caledonia. Electricity is provided by hydro-generation on Futuna, run by a French-based company.

Major Industries. Tourism is considered essential to the economy but is dependent on irregular air links. There are two small hotels and three or four restaurants on Wallis. There are no hotels on Futuna.

Trade. There are no significant exports except foods to family members in New Caledonia. Imports include hardware, building materials, vehicles, electrical wiring, and appliances. These exports come from France via New Caledonia, Australia or New Zealand. There is one supermarket, and each village has a small store run by a local family. Women make tapa for sale in New Caledonia.

A boy and his dog run past thatch roof huts on Futuna Island, Wallis and Futuna. These huts follow the general style of Futuna homes.

Division of Labor. Men and women on Wallis work together on family land. Men cultivate steep lands on Futuna, while the women remain in the village, making tapa and other handicrafts, and caring for children. Most government jobs are held by men, but women predominate in the education sector. Women produce most of the handicrafts sold in New Caledonia. Men are more prominent than women in political affairs.

SOCIAL STRATIFICATION

Classes and Castes. Traditional hierarchies exist alongside stratification by income. Classes are perhaps more pronounced on Futuna. In Wallis, the traditional hierarchy persists, with the Lavelua at the apex and the general populace referred to as commoners. A distinction exists between families with and without cash income. Remittances from family members overseas also distinguish families. The Catholic Church is the largest landowner. Families that have produced a priest or nun have a high status.

Symbols of Social Stratification. Education levels are not important markers. New Caledonia has been the sole source of tertiary education until a two year post-secondary program opened up in 1990.

Symbols of difference include a car or truck, a large house, furniture, access to electricity, and knowledge of life in New Caledonia. Gifts to the church are important indicators of status.

POLITICAL LIFE

Government. Wallis is run jointly with Futuna as a territory of the French government. The administrator represents the French republic and heads the cabinet, which consists of the three kings and three appointed members. An operational staff of government advisors operate on a budget supplied almost entirely by France. Wallis and Futuna together elect one representative to the French Senate.

The second form of local government is an elected body, the Territorial National Assembly which consists of an elected leader, and a body of elected assemblymen. This body debates finances and the issue of independence.

Leadership and Political Officials. The Lavelua, Tui Sigave, and Tuiagaifo rule their geographic areas. Each is assisted by district councillors. Their area of governance includes traditional access to labor as needed and welcoming visiting dignitaries.

Each village has a primary school.

They are the controlling authority in people's everyday lives and issue passports.

Social Problems and Control. Justice is administered by the prefect under French laws. The Lavelua and the two Futunan Tui, together with the Territorial Assembly, deal with local concerns. There is a small local police force.

Military Activity. All young men serve two years in the French military when they reach eighteen years of age.

Social Welfare and Change Programs

Welfare is the concern of families and falls under the traditional system of local government. France funds the hospital and the medical staff as well as many secondary schools and public works. A minimal welfare system is supported by the French. A small pension is available to those over age sixty, but there are few other means of support.

Nongovernmental Organizations and Other Associations

Trade unions have been active as workers, particularly teachers, seek better conditions. Catholic organizations include parents' groups associated with

schools and a women's organization. There are links to other Catholic communities in the Pacific. A small group of health educators is supported by hospital administrators.

Gender Roles and Statuses

Division of Labor by Gender. Men and women work together in the fields. Work in the home is shared among the sisters and wives of brothers, so that mothering is a joint activity. Often Grandmothers are the care takers during the day if the women of the household are employed or are drawn away from the village by church activities. Men cook outdoors, while women cook indoors.

The Relative Status of Women and Men. Few women run for public office, but many women hold senior posts in government and in the community.

Women's status as sisters gives them higher rank than their brothers within the family. Oldest sisters in particular are honored, but as wives, however, they are expected to be subservient to their husbands.

Marriage, Family and Kinship

Marriage. Marriages are controlled by the family and formalized by the church. Missionaries once raised young boys and girls apart from their families and then arranged their marriages. Today young people meet in high school, and families approve or disapprove of the friendship. Cohabitation occurs but is not approved of by the family or the church. Illegitimate children are likely to be raised by aunts and grandmothers.

Domestic Unit. An extended family household is likely to consist of several houses linked by brothers and sisters and their spouses. Households change in size as young people and their children go to New Caledonia, leaving one or two children to look after the parents. When a young couple marry, they join the household of one of their families. It is rare for a new house to be built. The household usually is headed by the father or the oldest son, though occasionally the oldest sister takes this role. The extended family is the basic unit of interaction. Food and other gifts are exchanged, and children move freely between members of the extended family. A funeral draws the extended family together.

Kin Groups. Kin groups are synonymous with the extended family. Close ties are maintained despite

A festival on Futuna Island. The population of Futuna is approximately 5,000 people.

separation over distance, such as Noumea, France, or Futuna. Kinship is traced bilaterally, with both sons and daughters inheriting rights to the land, and membership of the kinship group. One son and one daughter are expected to look after the parents, including siblings of their parents. Strong kin ties between brothers and sisters hold the extended family together. Kin terms for brother and sister also apply to cousins. Funerals are major occasions when kin make every effort to travel from Noumea or France to honor a departed relative. Similarly, kin on Wallis and Futuna will endeavor to travel to Noumea for funerals of close kin.

SOCIALIZATION

Infant Care. Infants are welcomed as an addition to the extended family. They are cared for by a number of relatives, both old and young. Sisters and aunties look after the infant's every need, so it is rare to hear a child crying. They attend church along with the family. An infant is weaned at about one year of age by an "auntie."

Child Rearing and Education. Children are raised and nurtured in an extended network of kin and are wanted and loved. They sleep alongside adults and accompany adults to the fields and to social events. Children who cry are quickly attended to.

Each village has a primary school run by the state. Primary education is much desired by parents, but classes are large and attendance is irregular because children, usually girls, are expected to meet home commitments as well as get an education.

Higher Education. Higher education is available in New Caledonia, France, and Australia, but graduates have difficulty finding jobs and adjusting to life back home. A two-year post secondary program was established in the islands in 1990.

ETIQUETTE

Respect for elders and generosity are the core principles. Oldest sisters are honored and respected. Elders hold authority in the family, and brothers are expected to look after their sisters and guard their virginity. Men and women socialize in separate groups. Children are expected to sit quietly through church or a meeting; if they become restless, they are taken outside by a young sibling.

RELIGION

Religious Beliefs. The Catholic Church has been dominant on both islands for over 160 years. Villages are built around churches, which are maintained by the community.

Religious Practitioners. Catholic priests are the church leaders, with one serving several villages in a contiguous area. Nuns are also very active serving the Catholic community, particularly as teachers, but also in a wider caring role. The Bishop of Wallis and Futuna is a leading authority figure and still plays an important role in island politics.

Rituals and Holy Places. The original Catholic settlement at Lano in Hahake is still the center of Catholic society on both islands. Until about 1910, a secondary school trained future priests and nuns. Catholic feast days and holy days and first communions are part of the annual cycle of rituals. The beatification of Father Chanel in 1889 has made the basilica at Poi a special symbol of the Catholic religion. The installation of a new Lavelua or a new Tui Sigave or Tui Asoa is likely to involve a kava ceremony.

Death and the Afterlife. Funerals are major extended family events that draw together mourners from Wallis and those who can afford to return from New Caledonia.

MEDICINE AND HEALTH CARE

Traditional medicine is practiced mainly by women, who use massage with local oils, potions made from local vegetable materials, and insertions of local plant materials into the appropriate orifices. Pregnancies are still treated largely by local health practitioners.

Major villages each have a small clinic with a visiting nurse several times a week. Serious cases are referred to the central hospital on Wallis. Less serious cases on Futuna are treated in a small hospital. Victims of road accidents must be airlifted to New Caledonia or Australia.

THE ARTS AND HUMANITIES

Support for the Arts. The church is an outlet for sales on Wallis and in Noumea. Men who carve sell their work in New Caledonia.

Literature. Literature has been poorly developed with few attempts to record myths and legends, or history locally. This is changing as tertiary education becomes available to Wallisians and Futunans.

Graphic Arts. Designs on siapo and tapa are a major art form for Wallisian and Futunan women, who use a template carved out and then applied to the beaten barkcloth. Both local and purchased dyes are used along with the traditional brown and black. Woven mats, often fringed with brightly colored wool, are used as gifts at the funerals of relatives.

Performance Arts. Participation in the Pacific Arts Festivals is a high point of community involvement. Dances are revived and composed to represent the unique features of the Wallisian and Futunan cultures. The South Pacific Games are another arena in which residents compete.

THE STATE OF THE PHYSICAL AND SOCIAL SCIENCES

The sciences are poorly developed. Government officials from France bring ideas but the absence of any tertiary training center has necessitated Wallisians and Futunans to travel overseas to gain western type knowledge of the sciences. A two year college that opened in 1991 will begin to change this.

BIBLIOGRAPHY

Bibliographie, Phonographie, Filmographie et Museographie des iles Wallis et Futuna, 1976.

Burrows, Edwin. *Ethnology of Futuna*, 1936.

Connell, John. *Migrations, Emploi et Developpement dans le Pacifique Sud*, 1985.

Godard, P. *Wallis et Futuna*, 1976.

Kirch, Patrick. "Cultural Adaptation and Ecology in West Polynesia: An Ethnoarcheological Study." Ph.D. dissertation, Yale University, 1975.

Manuaud, S. *Futuna, Ethnologie et Actualite*, 1983.

Mayer, Raymond. *Deux Cent Legendes de Wallis et Futuna*, 1971.

Pollock, Nancy J. "Doctor Administrators on Wallis and Futuna." *Journal of Pacific History* 25 (1): 47–67, 1990.

Poncet, Monsignor. *Histoire de l'Ile Wallis, le Protectorat Francais*, 1972.

Rensch, Karl, ed. *Tikisionalio Fakafutuna-Fakafalani*, 1986.

Roux, J-C. "Migration and Change in Wallisian Society" In R. T. Shand, ed., *The Island States of the Pacific and Indian Oceans*.

Tikisionalio Fakauvea-Fakafalani, 1984.

Viala, M. "Les Iles Wallis et Horn." *Bulletin de la Societe Neufchateloise de Geographie*, vol. xxviii 1919.

—NANCY J. POLLOCK

WEST BANK SEE PALESTINE, WEST BANK, GAZA STRIP

YEMEN

CULTURE NAME

Yemeni

ALTERNATIVE NAMES

South Arabian, al-Yamani

ORIENTATION

Identification. The name of the country is derived from the legendary ancestor Yaman, the son of Qahtan, or from the Arabic root *ymn* (''the right'') since Yemen is located to the right of the Meccan sanctuary of Kaaba. Some scholars compare the Arabic word *yumna* (''happy'') with the Roman name for the southwest Arabia, *Arabia Felix* (''Happy Arabia''). Inhabitants feel that they have a common culture, although local and class identities are still important.

Location and Geography. Medieval Arab geographers thought of Yemen as covering the entire southern strip of the Arabian peninsula, from the mountainous southwest, including Najran and Asir, to Hadhramaut and Oman on the east. Today that area includes the regions that make up the Republic of Yemen (RY), which was formed in 1990 when the Yemen Arab Republic (YAR, or North Yemen) with its capital in Sana'a, and the People's Democratic Republic of Yemen (PDRY, or South Yemen), with its capital in Aden, were unified. The capital is Sana'a, and Aden is referred to as the country's economic capital. The approximate size of the nation, since some of its borders are not demarcated, is 187,000 square miles (North: 75,000 square miles; South: 112,000 square miles), or 482,100 square kilometers.

There are six cultural and economic zones. The Tihama, a coastal plain and hilly area along the Red Sea, is fifteen to twenty-five miles (twenty-five to forty kilometers) wide. It is an area of fishing, commerce, and trade in the ports of al-Mukha (Mocha) and al-Hudayda as well as agriculture in oases (the main crops are millet, maize, sugarcane, watermelons, tobacco, and cotton) as well as livestock breeding. Handicrafts are made in Zabid, Bayt al-Faqih, and other centers. The highlands in the west have regular seasonal rains. Terraced agriculture (millet, wheat, barley, grapes, coffee, tobacco, vegetables, fruits, qat) is practiced, and goats, sheep, cows, and donkeys are raised. The central mountains consist of wide plateaus and basins. Fields are watered from wells and rainfall is sufficient for most crops. This region includes urban centers such as Sana'a and Sa'da. The high plateau in the east gradually merges with the desert *Rub al-Khal*. Date palms are cultivated in small oases, and the population is semi nomadic. There are salt deposits near Shabwa, Safir, and Harib. The limestone tableland of Hadhramaut and Wadi Masila has valleys *(wadis)* carved deep into the plateau. Cultivated patches are irrigated with rain and flood waters and from wells. Hinterlands towns include Shibam, Sayun, and Tarim in the Inner Wadi, and there are seaports at al-Mukalla and al-Shihr. The adjacent Mahra province and Socotra island are culturally related to this zone. The Gulf of Aden coastal plain, which is five to ten miles (eight to sixteen kilometers) wide, is discontinuous. Its ports, from Aden in the west to Sayhut and al-Ghayda in the east, are connected with the inland regions rather than with one another.

Demography. The population is ethnically Arab, divided between Sunni Muslims of the Shafi'i school and Shi'a Muslims of the Zaydi school. There are small groups of Jews, Hindus, and Christians. In 1949 and 1950, about fifty thousand Yemeni Jews left for Israel. In 1998, the population was 17,071,000. The annual growth rate is limited by migration and a high infant mortality rate. The birthrate is high, and almost half the population is under fifteen years of age.

Linguistic Affiliation. Yemenis speak Arabic, which belongs to the Semitic language family. Clas-

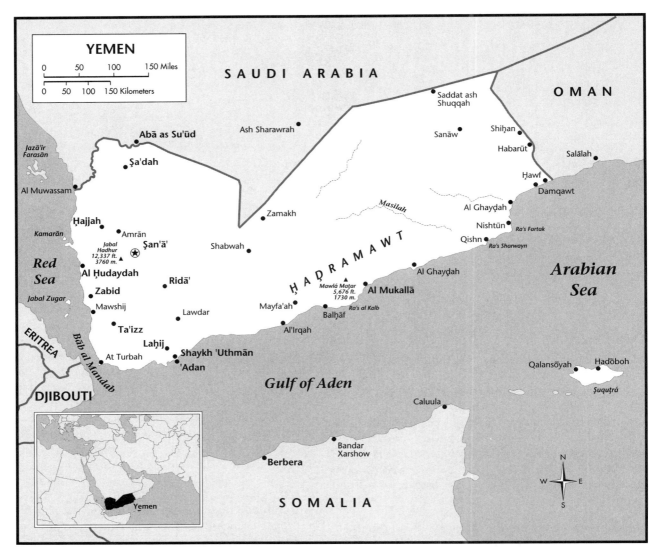

Yemen

sical Arabic, the language of Islam and the Koran, is used on formal occasions. The spoken dialects, whose areas roughly correspond to the six cultural zones, are used in everyday life. Some groups have maintained their ancient oral tongues of the south Arabic branch. The most commonly used foreign language is English, and Russian is still understood in Sana'a and Aden.

Symbolism. The notion of allegiance is shaped by kinship, the native land, language, faith, and a shared culture. The symbol of male honor is a curved dagger, the *jambiyyah*; lineage is symbolized by a clan's tower at the top of a hill; and generosity and hospitality are expressed in making and serving coffee. The coffee tree, the state eagle, the national colors, and the Marib Dam are shown in the new national emblem. The colors of the national flag (horizontal bands of red, white, and black) reflect pan-Arab symbolism, being similar to the flags of Syria, Iraq, and Egypt. The national anthem and national days of celebration emphasize the unification of the country.

HISTORY AND ETHNIC RELATIONS

Emergence of the Nation. The ancient walled city Sana'a is said to be the oldest city in the world, founded by Noah's eldest son, Shem, the forefather of Qahtan. Bilqis, the Queen of Sheba (Saba), is mentioned in the Bible and the Koran. The kingdom of Saba, with its capital, Marib, had existed since the first millennium B.C.E. The Marib Dam provided irrigation for about twenty-five thousand acres of

Most Yemenis are urban dwellers or sedentary agriculturalists.

arable land; its collapse in the first centuries C.E. is depicted in the Koran as a punishment from God. The prosperity of the principal rival kingdoms, Saba, Hadhramaut, Awsan, Qataban, and Ma'in, was based on the cultivation and overland exportation of frankincense, myrrh, and spices to the Mediterranean. Ancient South Arabian culture developed an intricate architecture and created masterpieces of figurative and decorative arts. It maintained contacts with Egypt, Greece, Palmyra, Chaldea, and Abyssinia, which was founded by Sabaeans, as well as India. In 25–24 B.C.E., the Roman emperor attempted to conquer the Sabaean kingdom, which was the southernmost outlet of the trade route to India. At that time, caravan traffic became less important than the shipping route between Egypt and India. The whole of southwestern Arabia was united by the kingdom of Himyar (circa 100 B.C.E.– 525 C.E., which controlled the Red Sea and the coasts of the Gulf of Aden. After the fall of Jerusalem in 70 C.E., many Jews settled in the region, and the Christian (Nestorian) faith was propagated. In the early sixth century, the kings of Himyar converted to Judaism and persecuted local Christians, leading the Abyssinians to take control of South Arabia in 525. The Persian Sassanians followed in 575.

The advent of Islam to South Arabia in the seventh century ousted local pantheons and monotheistic cults. Yemeni tribes took an active part in the Arab conquests and the construction of an Islamic state, and the tribal principal became a distinct form of communal organization in the area. In 898, al-Hadi Yahya proclaimed himself the first Zaydi imam, establishing a Shi'a dynasty that ruled in several regions of northern Yemen until 1962. The Egyptian Ayyubids invaded in 1173 and controlled all of Yemen until 1228. Their local vassals, the Rasulids, ruled until 1454, the golden age of art, science, and prosperity. The Tahirid tribesmen succeeded the Rasulids but were overthrown by the Egyptian Mamluks (1515–1517), who opened Yemen to invasion by the Ottoman Turks.

The Portuguese, the French, and the British as well as the Ottoman Empire tried to seize the main routes to the Indian Ocean. The local coffee *mocha* (named after the town al-Mukha), became an important item in world trade. The split of Yemen into the south and the north was caused by British and Ottoman politics. In 1839, the British occupied Aden. The Ottomans took control over main regions of the north in 1848–1872 in spite of armed resistance by the Zaydi imams, who had defeated the Turks in 1568, 1613, and 1635. Frequent uprisings forced the Ottomans to grant autonomy to the Zaydi regions in 1911. After the collapse of the Ottoman Empire in 1918, the Turks withdrew from the north; its independence under the Zaydi imams was internationally recognized in 1923. The imams claimed the right to all of historical Yemen but ceded the province of Najran to Saudi Arabia in 1934. In 1962, the rule of imams was overthrown, and YAR was paroclaimed.

The South was administered by British Bombay presidency until 1937, when it was designated the Crown Colony of Aden and Protectorate. In 1963, the Aden Colony became part of the British-sponsored Federation of South Arabia, which was scheduled to become independent in 1968. The British had to withdraw in 1967, and power was seized by the Marxist-oriented National Liberation Front. The south was proclaimed the People's Republic of South Yemen in 1967 and the PDRY in 1970. The tribal, religious, and pro-Western YAR and the Marxist, secular, and pro-communist PDRY engaged in border warfare in 1979 and 1987. In 1989, the YAR and the PDRY signed a draft document for unification. On 22 May 1990 the new Yemeni nation was born. Six months after unification, the Gulf War started. Yemeni labor migrants from the Arab oil states were forced to return home, causing a population increase, a slowdown in the migrants' remittances, and a reduction in foreign aid.

URBANISM, ARCHITECTURE, AND THE USE OF SPACE

Apart from a relatively few pastoral nomads who live in tents or caves, most residents are urban dwellers (one-fourth) and sedentary agriculturalists. Since ancient times builders have used local materials to build cities and villages on mountain slopes, dry islets at the bed of a valley, stony plateaus, and sandy seashores. Most localities, from walled cities to tiny hamlets, are still divided into traditional quarters or neighborhoods. Public spaces, especially markets, foster communication among men.

Cultural zones vary in the use of building materials. In villages in northern Tihama timber and straw are used, while in towns shell lime is more common; in southern Tihama timber and brick are used. In the central mountainous region, hewn stone is used; in the highlands, houses are made of stone, burned brick, and stamped clay. In the desert, houses are built from stamped clay and sun-dried mud bricks. These materials also are used in Hadhramaut, whose multistory ''skyscrapers'' in Shibam are reputed to be the highest mud constructions in the world. Natural stone is used mainly in Mahra and on Socotra.

The majority of buildings originate from pre-Islamic fortified towers that combine in a single structure under a whitewashed flat roof the functions of dwelling, storage, and fortress.

The traditional division of Arab dwellings into men's and women's halves led to the use of separate staircases and room entrances hidden behind partitions. There is a minimum of furniture: cushions and mattresses are placed along the walls for sitting, and special mattresses, which are taken away in the daytime, are used for sleeping. The floor is covered with palm leaf matting, goat-hair rugs, or imported rugs. Cubbyholes are made in thick walls for books, utensils, and clothes.

UNESCO has sponsored international campaigns to protect the architectural heritage, encouraging the use of local materials and building methods. These principles were maintained in the building of the Ministry of Justice in Sana'a and Provincial Health Center and Hospital in Dhamar. The 1990s witnessed a construction boom in the urban centers.

FOOD AND ECONOMY

Food in Daily Life. Yemenis usually eat three times a day at home. The traditional diet varies locally and socially and is open to innovations. Generally, there is an early breakfast of sweet strong tea with bread made of sorghum, wheat, or barley; dinner includes a porridge prepared from fenugreek with meat, eggs, vegetables, herbs, and spices, which is served hot in a stone or clay bowl; a light supper consists of vegetables and/or dates. One can drink a glass of tea or a brew of coffee husks outdoors in the daytime. Lentils and peas are traditional staples in addition to sorghum. Many inexpensive restaurants have opened, some of them Lebanese. Local food taboos are those common to the Islamic world: alcohol and pork are officially prohibited.

Food Customs at Ceremonial Occasions. At feasts and celebrations, the festive meal of the nomads, roasted or boiled meat from goat or sheep served on heaps of rice, is eaten. In town and villages it is served with side dishes of roasted or fried eggplant and mixed green salads, with fruit or custard with raisins or grapes for dessert. People now consume more fish, poultry, and dairy products. Among the variety of sweets is *bint as-sahn*, a puff pastry covered with honey. Yemenis prepare special dishes and sweets for nightly breaks during the Ramadan fast. At wedding celebrations and religious feasts, coffee is drunk. In decorated drawing-rooms, people smoke water pipes and chew qat.

Basic Economy. About one-fourth of the gross domestic product is derived from agriculture. However, the nation imports more than sixty percent of its food needs. About twenty percent of the population suffers from malnutrition. Agriculture employs more than half the labor force. The principal crops are sorghum, potatoes, dates, wheat, grapes, barley, maize, cotton, millet, and garden vegetables, but only part of the harvest is produced for sale. This is also the case for sheep, goats, and camels. Coffee, biscuits, grapes, sesame seeds, sugar, honey, and dried and salted fish are exported.

Land Tenure and Property. Land can be state, private, or communal. Traditionally, state lands were used for cultivation and public purposes and were controlled by the state authorities; private property consisted of agricultural, building, and other plots; there were Islamic endowments and tribal land was used for grazing livestock and served as areas of tribal responsibility for travelers and protected groups. In the north, customs, laws, and practices concerning land and water allocation are

Groups of chatting men in Sana'a. Public spaces, especially markets, foster communication among men.

based on Islamic, customary, and, after 1962, civil regulations. In the south, the first two practices were supplemented by British law and, after 1967, socialist legislation. After unification, agricultural land was denationalized and returned in the south to those who owned it under the British. About 6 percent of the national territory is arable, 30 percent is occupied by pastures, and 7 percent is forest and woodland.

Commercial Activities. Shops and permanent and weekly markets offer local and imported foodstuffs, qat and frankincense, livestock, manufactured goods, fabrics, and clothing. Goods traditionally associated with the culture, such as side arms, textiles, leather, and agates, also are available for purchase.

Major Industries. The petroleum refinery in Little Aden produces a major share of the industrial output. Other products are foodstuffs, including soft drink bottling and dairy plants; cement and cinder blocks, tiles, and burned bricks; textiles; aluminum utensils, rubber and plastic; and salt. Yemenis still practice traditional handicrafts such as silver and copperwork, dagger manufacturing, carpentry, boat building, pottery, weaving and dyeing, wickerwork, and leather tanning. Electricity is generated from thermal power plants. The major sea ports are Aden, al-Hudayda, al-Mucha, al-Mukalla; international airports are situated in Sana'a, Aden, al-Hudayda, Ta'izz, and al-Mukalla. Economic prospects depend on the development of oil resources.

Trade. The principal exports are livestock and food, cigarettes, leather, and petroleum products, which are shipped mainly to Saudi Arabia, Japan, and Italy. Yemen traditionally exports labor to the Arab world, East Africa, the Indian Ocean area, and the United States. All manner of staples from food to consumer goods are imported.

Division of Labor. Most of the population is employed in agriculture and herding or works as expatriate laborers. Industry (about 5 percent of total labor power), services, construction, and commerce employ for less than half the workforce. There is a labor hierarchy that conforms to the traditional social strata.

SOCIAL STRATIFICATION

Classes and Castes. Under law all citizens are equal. The traditional social structure, however, has at the top the *Sayyids* stratum, descendants of the Prophet Muhammad. The Sayyids competed for the office of Zaydi imam and control sacred enclaves, solved tribal conflicts by mediation, engaged in theology and law, and owned and leased land. Slightly lower on the social scale are the *Qadis* or *Fuqaha* (in the south, the *Mashayikh*) who perform the same social functions. *Qabilis* (tribesmen) control their territory and caravan routes, own arable land that most of them cultivate, and carry weapons. The lower strata are underprivileged and have an obscure genealogy. Being under tribal protection, they traditionally were deprived of land ownership and were not allowed to bear arms. The members of this group are called the *Bani Khums* in the north and the *Masakeen* and *Du'afa* (the poor and the weak) in the south. They engage in low-status occupations that in most cases are hereditary, working as smiths, carpenters, potters, brokers, barbers (who also perform circumsion), bloodletters, musicians, heralds, butchers weavers and dyers, and tanners. The *Akhdams* (servants) wash and bury the dead and clean latrines. The majority of Akhdams and ex-slaves (*Abeeds*) are of African or Ethiopian descent. All these strata tend to be endogamous or, in the south, observe the marital rule of hypergamy, in which men marry within their strata or lower and women marry their equals or higher-status men. The mass return of expatriates in 1990 has raised the social problem of *muwalladin*, or Yemenis of mixed origins.

Symbols of Social Stratification. Male Sayyids and Qadis traditionally wore long robes and covered their heads with white or green turbans; their authority also was symbolized by a staff, a ring, and a flag. Tribal symbols include weapons (firearms), dances, greetings, call songs, and tribal poetry. Women's dress reflects not so much class differences but social and regional ones except for the fact that women in nomadic tribes and the most underprivileged strata leave their faces unveiled. In the south, the *jambiya* is worn only by tribesmen. In the north, men in most social strata carry daggers. Today all Yemeni men prefer to wear jambiyas that are placed vertically at the center of the belt.

POLITICAL LIFE

Government. United Yemen proclaimed itself a presidential republic and a multiparty parliamentary democracy. The parliament consists of the House of Deputies and an appointed Upper Chamber, or Senate. The constitution was approved by referendum in 1991 and was amended in 1994. The president is elected for a five-year term; the last campaign for the presidency was won in 1999 by the general Ali Abdullah Saleh. Executive authority is vested in the prime minister and the cabinet. The

Women have rights guaranteed by law, but gender disparity is widespread.

Supreme Court heads the judicial branch. The press is among the freest in the Arab world.

Leadership and Political Officials. Politics is practiced mostly outside the new democratic institutions. Real power is exercised through a network of personal relations and patronage and clientele ties that involve family, class, and local affinities. Since a multiparty system was not allowed before unification, the strength of party leadership matters today more than does ideology. Among about forty political parties and organizations, the most significant are: the General People's Congress (GPC) of the president, the Yemeni Congregation for Reform (the *Islah*) with active Islamic and tribal trends, and the Yemeni Socialist Party (YSP), which, after abortive secession of the south in 1994, has regrouped as a loyal opposition.

Social Problems and Control. In 1991, the court system was set up with the Supreme Court of the Republic at the top in Sana'a, provincial courts of appeal in every governorate, and uniform district courts in the main local centers. In 1994, laws regarding crimes, punishments, and criminal procedures were promulgated; the police and security forces were organized. Those measures were aimed at eradicating corruption, bribery, and favoritism. Other common crimes are larceny in large cities, smuggling along the border, and the taking of hostages in tribal areas; robbery and murder are not widespread. Crime statistics are not representative, since disputes traditionally are solved through mediation, customary tribal arbitration, and mutual accord. Yemenis regard customary justice as less expensive than state courts. Legal practice includes contradictory aspects of secular, religious, and customary regulations.

Military Activity. Military campaigns took place in 1979, 1986, 1987, and 1994. The Defense Forces include an army, a navy, an air force, and paramilitary forces that include the police. Most tribes have their own militias.

SOCIAL WELFARE AND CHANGE PROGRAMS

The current development strategies are documented in a five-year plan that calls for a market economy led by the private sector. External assistance, which was withdrawn in the early 1990s, returned after 1994, when the government launched an ambitious economic, financial, and administrative reform program under the auspices of the International Monetary Fund and the World Bank. In 1996, those sources were joined by the Arab Fund for Social and Economic Development, the Arab Monetary Fund, and the European Union. About an eighth of external aid goes for health and human resources development.

NONGOVERNMENTAL ORGANIZATIONS AND OTHER ASSOCIATIONS

There are trade unions, professional syndicates, human rights groups, and sport, religious (including charitable), and other informal organizations and associations, most of which have a top-down structure.

GENDER ROLES AND STATUSES

Division of Labor by Gender. In the cultural stereotype, women are viewed as subordinate and indulgent mothers, sisters, and wives who perform household duties; men are seen as financial providers in the outside world, responsible for the well-being and prestige of the family. Long-term male labor migration has resulted in a modification of the traditional division of labor, since women and older children have had to take over some male tasks, particularly in agriculture. Some women in urban centers have jobs in education and health care. Women Islamic activists are very active in the Islah Charitable Society, which helps the poor.

The Relative Status of Women and Men. The 1994 constitution states that women are men's sisters and have rights and duties guaranteed by Islamic Shari'a and secular law. However, gender disparity in all aspects of life outside the family is striking, since religious authorities strongly recommend gender segregation. For example the testimony of two women in court equals that of one man.

MARRIAGE, FAMILY, AND KINSHIP

Marriage. Most marriages are arranged by the families: a bridegroom's female relatives suggest potential brides to him and his father, who come to a decision according to the rules of martial conformity. In most cases, the woman's father asks her about her wishes before the marriage contract is prepared. Groom and bride are attached to their respective descent groups through the male line: The father of the groom has to pay a brideprice *mahr*, and the family of the bride is expected to help her in times of hardship. Arab custom regards as ideal a parallel cousin marriage in which the father's brother's daughter is the bride as well as other endogamous marriages. Shari'a law allows a man to marry up to four wives if he treats them all as equals; the rate of polygamy is low. Half of the adult population is married, four percent is widowed, and one percent is divorced. Both men and women can request a divorce. If it was initiated by the husband, the ex-wife keeps her brideprice and can remarry after four months and ten days, during which time the ex-husband has to support her. Children up to seven years of age remain with

A traditional Yemeni hut in the village of Tihamah uses timber and straw.

the mother if she does not remarry. Divorce and remarriage are not stigmatized.

Domestic Unit. The most common type family, especially outside urban centers, is patrilocal and extended. There are also nuclear families, as well as fraternal joint families (households consisting of the nuclear families of two or more brothers). The average household has 6.7 persons. Most of the household economy is controlled by men. In villages, men are responsible for qat and cultivation of the crops, whereas women grow vegetables and take care of domestic animals.

Inheritance. Inheritance customs stress the right of primogeniture, which gives preference to the oldest brother. In accordance with Shari'a law, after a husband's death, his mother inherits one-sixth of his estate and one-eighth goes to his widow; a woman inherits half of her brother's share. If she has no brothers or sisters, she gets half the property. Formally inherited property, including land, is at a woman's disposal, but often it is managed by her male relatives.

Kin Groups. This stratified society is based on the tribal idiom of common descent, which serves as the source of mutual rights and obligations within each group. This flexible structure has several levels above the nuclear family: a unit of patrilineal kin (*bayt*), whose members share a house or closely interact in other ways; the larger descent group, the clan or subtribe (*fakhdh*); a tribe (*qabila*); and a tribal confederation (*silf*). Individuals usually identify themselves with the lowest or highest levels of kinship, since alliances are not determined solely by kin principles.

SOCIALIZATION

Infant Care. Children are culturally, socially, and religiously valued, although infant mortality is high. Mothers are responsible for the care of young children, and older daughters take an active part in raising their siblings. Only male children give their mother high status. Small children usually are carried by their caretakers. Girls and small children sleep in the women's half of the house, while adolescent boys sleep apart. Children rarely are punished. If they fight, they are separated by adults.

Child Rearing and Education. Most women give birth at home. A son's birth involves a circumcision festivity during which the mother gets presents. Circumcision (clitoridectomy) of newly born female children usually is done without a special ceremony. Babies are swaddled, and children are regarded as incapable of self-control until age four. Male children are believed to be particularly vulnerable to the evil eye. More emphasis is placed on the education of sons than on that of daughters in free public, or private as well as religious schools, all of which are sexually segregated.

Higher Education. Gender segregation is practiced in higher education, which has been developing rapidly since unification. In addition to national universities in Sana'a and Aden, state and private universities are being organized in al-Mukalla, Taiz, Ibb, Dhammar, and al-Hudayda.

ETIQUETTE

Social and individual interactions are determined by customary law and religious regulations, which include structured series of verbal exchanges and salutations in greeting or saying good-bye and the avoidance of women who are not close relatives. The strata disparity reflected in behavioral norms has been lessening but still exists in regard to marital and other rules. Cultural values include hospitality, respect for elders, decency, and good manners while eating from a communal dish. Guests do not accept more than three cups of coffee or tea and

Two Jewish jewelers at work in north Sana'a. Goods produced by small vendors are an important part of market-based commercial activity.

wobble the cup from side to side to show that nothing more is required, and shoes are left outdoors before one enters a dwelling. Physical distance between social interactors is close. The spatial disposition of social interactors is circular at tribal meetings and linear during ritual ceremonies in mosques and outdoors; indoors, it is at the perimeter, with the best position at the far corner of the wall in which the door is situated. In a market one is expected to enjoy the process of bargaining. During social events, poets, singers, and dancers may transgress the precepts of acceptable behavior.

RELIGION

Religious Beliefs. Sunni Islam of the Shafi'i school dominates in the south and many regions of the north; the Zaydi Shi'a school with its center in Sa'da is practiced mainly among the tribes of central mountains and the adjacent highlands. A much smaller Islamic group near Manakha is the Isma'ilis, who are divided into the Sulaymani (*Makarima*) branch, which is connected with Najaran, and the Dawudi (*Boharas*) which is linked with India.

Religious Practitioners. Islamic scholars, judges, managers of charitable property, elders in sacred enclaves, and leaders of communal prayer used to be recruited primarily from the two upper strata but now may belong to other classes as well.

Rituals and Holy Places. Yemenis observe the Five Pillars of Islam, including five prayers a day and a daytime fast during the month of Ramadan. The weekly day of rest is Friday. Religious celebrations include 27 Ramadan, the Night of Power; 1 Shawwal, the Lesser Feast; 10 Dhu al-Hijja, the Greater Feast, or the Feast of Sacrifice, commemorating the end of the pilgrimage to Mecca; 12 Rabi' al-Awwal, the birthday of the Prophet; 10 Muharram, the day of the martyrdom of Imam Husayn; and 27 Rajab, the day of the Prophet's miraculous journey. In mid-Rajab, pilgrimages are usually made to the tombs of local saints.

Death and the Afterlife. The body of the deceased is washed, perfumed, and wrapped in a white, unseamed shroud. The deceased has to be buried before sunset on the day of death. Women do not accompany the body to the grave, staying outside the cemetery. During the first three days of mourning, the Koran is read and relatives and friends visit the family of the dead person. Remembrance sessions usually are held on the seventh and fortieth days after death.

MEDICINE AND HEALTH CARE

The Sayyids and Qadis/Mashayikh are reputed to be effective in giving verbal therapy; some are said to heal illnesses by placing their hands over or breathing on a patient. Tribesmen are known as healers of wounds and snake bites, barbers specialize in blood letting, and both use cauterization, preventive diets and herbal treatments. Traditionally, disease is seen as the effect of bad winds and an imbalance of the four humors of the body. Modern health programs have been established.

SECULAR CELEBRATIONS

National Day on 22 May commemorates the country's unification. The Revolution of 26 September 1962 in the north and the beginning of revolt in the south on 14 October 1963 also are celebrated.

THE ARTS AND HUMANITIES

Literature. Medieval culture was rich in historical, geographic, and religious works; agricultural almanacs; astronomical treatises; and rhymed prose. Poetry in classical and colloquial styles is the most popular art form. Since the Middle Ages, poetry has been spoken, sung, and improvised during social events, at performances, and in competitions.

Graphic Arts. Rich traditions of decorative art, such as silver jewelry, embroidered garments, handwoven textiles, and architectural decor, are still practiced. There are art galleries in large cities with modern drawings, paintings, and sculptures.

Performance Arts. Traditional performaces include musical-poetical improvisations called *dan* in the Hadhramaut, at which singers chant a tune without words and poets offer them a freshly created text line by line. There are choral ritual processions, tribal call songs, special types of regional songs, and local and strata dances.

THE STATE OF THE PHYSICAL AND SOCIAL SCIENCES

The General Organization for Antiquities, Museums, and Manuscripts (GOAMM), with the help of the main universities, does archaeological, historical, and ethnographic studies. GOAMM also coordinates research run by the American Institute for Yemeni Studies, the German Archaeological Institute, the French Center for Yemeni Studies, the British-Yemeni Society, and Russian scientific expeditions. These institutions study social activities, methods of administration, urbanization, land tenure practices, and other aspects of the social and political sciences. Physical sciences and applications, as well as vocational and technical education, require further development.

BIBLIOGRAPHY

Adib, Naziha, Ferdous al-Mukhtar, et al. *Arabic Cuisine from the Gulf to the Mediterranean,* 1993.

Adra, Najwa. "Qabyala: The Tribal Concept in the Central Highlands of the Yemen Republic." Ph.D dissertation, Philadelphia: Temple University, 1982.

Al-Amri, Husayn. *Yemen in the 18th and 19th Centuries,* 1985.

Almadhagi, Ahmed Noman. *Yemen and the United States: A Study of a Small Power and a Super State Relationship, 1962–1994,* 1996.

Al-Sabban, Abd al-Q Muhammad. *Visits and Customs: The Visit to the Tomb of the Prophet Hud,* translated by Linda Boxberger and Awad Abu Hulayqa, 1998.

Auchterlonie, Paul. *Yemen,* rev. ed., 1998.

Bidwell, Robin. *Travellers in Arabia,* 1994.

Buchman, Davie. "The Underground Friends of God and Their Adversaries: A Case Study and Survey of Sufism in Contemporary Yemen." *Yemen Update (Bulletin of the American Institute for Yemeni Studies)* 39:21–24.

Buringa, Joke (ed. By Marta Colburn). *Bibliography on Women in Yemen,* 1992.

Burrowes, Robert D. *Historical Dictionary of Yemen,* 1995.

Carapico, Sheila. *Civil Society in Yemen. The Political Economy of Activism in Modern Arabia,* 1998.

Caton, Steven C. *"Peaks of Yemen I Summon": Poetry as Cultural Practice in a North Yemeni Tribe,* 1990.

Costa, Paolo M. *Studies in Arabian Architecture,* 1995.

Crociani, Paola. *Portrets of Yemen,* 1996.

Damluji, Salma Samar. *The Valley of Mud Brick Architecture,* 1992.

Daum, Werner, ed. *Yemen: 3000 Years of Art and Civilisation in Arabia Felix,* 1987.

Doe, Brian. *Socotra, Island of Tranquility,* 1992.

Dostal, Walter. *Ethnographica Jemenica,* 1992.

Dresh, Paul K. *Tribes, Government, and History in Yemen,* 1989.

Eickelman, Dale F. *The Middle East: An Anthropological Approach,* 1981.

Elgood, Robert. *The Arms and Armour of Arabia in the 18th–19th, and 20th Centuries,* 1994.

Freitag, Ulrike, and William G. Clarence-Smith, eds. *Hadhrami Traders, Scholars and Statesmen in the Indian Ocean, 1750s–1960s*, 1997.

Gerholm, Tomas. *Market, Mosque, and Mafraj: Social Inequality in a Yemeni Town*, 1977.

Gingrich, Andre, et al., eds. *Studies in Oriental Culture and History: Festschrift for Walter Dostal*, 1993.

———— and Johann Heiss. *Beitrage zur Ethnographie der Provinz Sa'da (Nordjemen)*, 1986.

Glaser, Eduard. *My Journey through Arhab and Hashid*, translated by David Warburton, 1993.

Halliday, Fred. *Arabs in Exile: Yemen Migrants in Urban Britain*, 1992.

Hubaishi, Husain. *Legal System and Basic Law in Yemen*, 1988.

Ingrams, Doreen. *A Time in Arabia*, 1970.

Ingrams, Harold. *Arabia and the Isles*, 1966.

Knysh, Alexandr. "The Cult of Saints in Hadramawt: An Overview." *New Arabian Studies*, 1:37–152, 1993.

————. "The Cult of Saints and Islamic Reformism in Early Twentieth Century Hadramawt." *New Arabian Studies* 4: 139–167, 1997.

Korotayev, Andrey. *Pre-Islamic Yemen: Socio-Political Organisation of the Sabaean Cultural Area in the 2nd and 3rd Centuries AD*, 1996.

Kostiner, Joseph. *Yemen. The Torturous Quest for Unity 1990–1994*, 1996.

Lewis, Herbert. *After the Eagles Landed: The Yemenites of Israel*, 1994.

Makhlouf, Carla. *Changing Veils: Women and Modernisation in North Yemen*, 1979.

Messick, Brinkley M. *The Calligraphic State: Textual Domination and History in a Muslim Society*, 1993.

Muchawsky-Schnapper, Ester. *The Jews of Yemen: Highlights of the Israel Museum Collections*, 1994.

Myntti, Cynthia. *Women in Rural Yemen*, 1978.

————. "Notes on Mystical Healers in the Higariyya." *Arabian Studies* 8: 171–176, 1990.

Naumkin, Vitaly. *Island of the Phoenix: An Ethnographic Study of the People of Socotra*, 1993.

Phillips, Carl. "Archaeological Research in Yemen." *The British-Yemeni Society Journal* 4: 22–28, 1996.

Pieragostini, Karl. *Britain, Aden and South Arabia: Abandoning Empire*, 1991.

Posey, Sarah. *Yemeni Pottery: The Littlewood Collection*, 1994.

Pridham, Brian, ed. *Contemporary Yemen: Politics and Historical Background*, 1984.

Qafisheh, Hamdi A. *Yemeni Arabic Reference Grammar*, 1992.

Rodionov, Mikhair. "Field Data on Folk Medicine from the Hadramawt." *Proceedings of the Seminar for Arabian Studies* 26: 125–133, 1996.

————. "Poetry and Power in Hadramawt. *New Arabian Studies* 3: 118–133, 1996.

———— and Mikhail Suvorov, eds. *Cultural Anthropology of Southern Arabia: Hadramawt Revisited*, 1999.

Sedov, Alexandr, and Ahmad BaTayi. "Temples of Ancient Hadramawt." *Proceedings of the Seminar for Arabian Studies* 24: 183–196, 1994.

Serjeant, Robert B. *Prose and Poetry from Hadramawt: South Arabian Poetry, I*, 1951.

————. *Society and Trade in South Arabia*, 1996.

———— and Ronal Lewcock, eds. *San'a'*, 1983.

Stevenson, Thomas B. *Social Change in a Yemeni Highlands Town*, 1985.

————. *Studies on Yemen, 1975–1900: A Bibliography of European-Language Sources for Social Scientists*, 1994.

————. "Yemen Filmography." *Yemen Update (Bulletin of the American Institute for Yemeni Studies)* 40: 29–31, 1998.

al-Suwaydi, Jamal, ed. *The Yemeni War of 1994. Causes and Consequences*, 1995.

Tobi, Jacob. *West of Aden: A Survey of the Aden Jewish Community*, 1994.

UNICEF. *Thee Situation of Women and Children in the Republic of Yemen 1992*, 1993.

Varisco, Daniel M. "The Adaptive Dynamics of Water Allocation in al-Ahjur, Yemen Arab Republic." Ph.D. dissertation, University of Pennsylvania, 1982.

————. *Medieval Agriculture and Islamic Science: The Almanac of a Yemeni Sultan*, 1994.

Watson, Jannet C. E. *A Syntax of San'ani Arabic*, 1993.

Weir, Shelagh. *Oat in Yemen: Consumption and Social Change*, 1985.

Wenner, Manfred W. *Modern Yemen, 1918–1966*, 1967.

—MIKHAIL RODIONOV

ZAMBIA

CULTURE NAME
Zambian

ALTERNATIVE NAMES
Republic of Zambia

ORIENTATION

Identification. Zambia derives its name from the Zambezi River. The river runs across the western and southern border and then forms Victoria Falls and flows into Lake Kariba and on to the Indian Ocean.

Location and Geography. In size, the country is roughly equivalent to the state of Texas, about 290,585 square miles (752,615 square kilometers). The unique butterfly-shaped boundaries are the result of the European scramble for Africa's natural resources in the early 1900s. The capital is Lusaka. Bordering neighbors are the Democratic Republic of the Congo, Tanzania, Malawi, Mozambique, Zimbabwe, Botswana, Namibia, and Angola.

It is a landlocked country with several large freshwater lakes, including Lake Tanganyika, Lake Mweru, Lake Bangweulu, and the largest manmade lake in Africa, Lake Kariba. The terrain consists of high plateaus, large savannas, and hilly areas; the highest altitude is in the Muchinga Mountains, at 6,000 feet (1,828 meters). The Great Rift Valley cuts through the southwest and Victoria Falls, the most visited site in Zambia, is in the South.

There are several game parks in the country; some consider Southern Luangwa to be the best game park on the continent.

Demography. The population in 2000 was estimated at 9.87 million. There exists a strong migration to urban areas where families go looking for employment. With 43 percent of the population living in cities, Zambia has the highest ratio of urban population in Africa. Those living in the rural areas face a life of mainly low-yielding subsistence farming, which contributes to the high migration.

The population is comprised primarily (97 percent) of seven main tribes and a collection of seventy-five minor tribes. There is also a small percentage of citizens from other African nations. The remaining population is of Asian, Indian, and European descent. Because of conflicts in the border countries of the Democratic Republic of the Congo and Angola, there has been a large influx of refugees in recent years.

Linguistic Affiliation. English is the official language as the country was once an English colony (1924–1964). While many people speak English, in rural areas tribal languages are spoken, in addition to a few other vernacular languages. Each of the seventy-five tribes living in the country has its own dialects and language. The main vernacular languages are Bemba, Lozi, Luanda, Luvale, Nyanja, Tonga, and Tumbuka.

Symbolism. The background of the national flag is green, symbolic of the country's natural beauty, with three vertical stripes in the lower right corner. The three stripes are: red, symbolic of the country's struggle for freedom; black, representing the racial makeup of the majority population; and orange, symbolic of the country's copper riches and other mineral wealth. A copper-colored eagle in the upper right corner symbolizes the country's ability to rise above its problems.

Zambia is noted for its rich wildlife and landscapes, using those resources to promote tourism with the slogan, "the Real Africa." The most notable landmark is Victoria Falls, known locally as Mosi-oa-Tunya, which means "the smoke that thunders." It is one of the seven natural wonders of the world and even though it is shared with Zimbabwe, it is a source of great pride for Zambians.

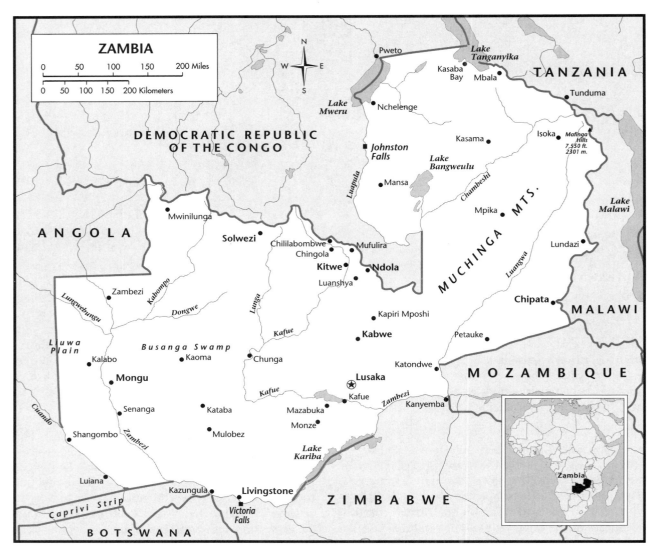

Zambia

For many years, the saying "Copper is king" was symbolic of the country because copper was the main contributor to the economy.

HISTORY AND ETHNIC RELATIONS

Emergence of the Nation. One of the cradles of the human race is in the northern African Rift Valley, which includes modern-day Zambia. This area traces human settlement back almost three million years. In Zambia, sites in the north and south record back to sixty thousand years ago.

Tribal migrations in only the past three hundred years have determined the makeup of present-day Zambia. Between 1500 and 1800 the Lunda and Luba people traveled from the Congo and became a powerful group. The Ngoni, originally from South Africa, escaped from the Boers and Zulus and settled in Eastern Zambia around 1850–1870. Another powerful tribe, the Lozi, dominated western Zambia and also originated from the Congo in the late seventeenth century. By the beginning of the twentieth century, these tribal migrations had transformed the area into a complex society tied together by conflicts and trade.

In the late 1800s, Portuguese and Muslim traders moved further inland and established trade with tribes. The main items were gold, ivory, and slaves. It was also at this time that missionaries established themselves, the most famous probably being David Livingstone. He worked hard to stop the slave trade and opened the door for the British who wanted to prevent the Portuguese from occupying the land and connecting Angola to Mozambique. Livingstone died in the Bangweulu Swamps in 1873 after exploring much of the area that is now Zambia.

Livingstone's exploring was tied directly into British colonial history and "the scramble for Africa." Cecil Rhodes founded the British South Africa Company (BSAC), which wanted to connect the "Cape to Cairo." Rhodes quickly became one of the wealthiest men in southern Africa. In 1898 he was granted a charter by Queen Victoria to govern the territory then under British control. Under the belief that there were gold and minerals along the Zambezi River, he financed British expansion into these areas. The BSAC established its headquarters in the town of Livingstone.

In 1929 the British government took back control and made the area a protectorate named Northern Rhodesia. The capital was moved to Lusaka in 1935. At this time large copper and other mineral deposits (including gold) were found in the Copperbelt, a province in the north central region. The mines became the driving force for the settlement and expansion of the country as a whole. To fill jobs in the mines, Zambians came from all over the country and settled in urban areas.

In 1953 the British Colonial Office decided to unite Nyasaland (Malawi), Southern Rhodesia (Zimbabwe), and Northern Rhodesia into the Central African Federation. There was strong opposition to the federation because a substantial amount of money was funneled out of Northern Rhodesia to support Southern Rhodesia. The struggle against the federation soon turned into one for freedom as the independence fever swept across Africa. Strikes by mine workers turned into a power base that formed the United National Independence Party (UNIP), led by Kenneth Kaunda. Civil disobedience organized by the UNIP led the British government to allow elections. The republic of Zambia gained its independence on 24 October 1964 with Kaunda as the first president.

National Identity. The people retain strong ties to their tribe or clan, but there is also a strong national identity. Zambia became a settling ground for many migrating tribes around 1500 to 1700, and those immigrants helped create a crossroads of culture in the country. These tribes have lived in harmony with each other for decades. When the first president, Kenneth Kaunda, introduced the slogan "One Zambia, One Nation," it was considered a strong symbol of the country's unified national identity.

Ethnic Relations. The seventy-five tribes that make up Zambia coexist relatively well in comparison to tribes in neighboring countries who were purposefully pitted against each other as part of the colonial governing policies. In these calculated cases, the minority tribe would usually develop primary power; this would only fuel tribal hatred. In some countries, that animosity still exists and creates major social problems.

The main tribes in Zambia are Bemba, Nagoni, Lozi, Chewa, Chokwe, Lunda, Luvale, Tonga, and Tumbuka. Most Zambians have joking relations with other tribes; the relationships go back many years. For example, a Bemba may throw verbal abuses to a Nyanja, but this is done in jest for the most part. This is an important distinction from other countries, where greater animosity exists. Zambians may consider their tribe superior to another, but there is an overall sense of unity across all groups.

Another factor in these good relations is the large urban population. The vast bush regions provide for a great deal of open land and tribes generally do not infringe on one another. In the cities, there is a strong interaction between the tribes. Some members choose to marry out of their own tribes, which strengthens the ties between the different groups. The flip side is that Zambian society has become more homogenized.

URBANISM, ARCHITECTURE, AND THE USE OF SPACE

There is a trend to move away from vernacular building styles and techniques to more modern or Western ways of construction. Traditionally, the type of building depended on the availability of materials. For example, basket-weaving construction can be found in homes of the eastern province, while construction using mud-covered small branches can be found in the rest of the country. Construction also depends on the tribe's customs. The Lozi in the southwest build rectangular houses, while the Chewa favor circular structures. Most of the roofs are made of poles and thatch.

A great change occurred with the influence of missionaries and European colonists. The settlers built using Western standards. The missionaries introduced the burnt brick, used to build into square structures, while the colonists built wood-frame structures with metal roofs. These proved to be quite hot, and adaptations were made, incorporating large roofs to allow for ventilation, and spacious verandas to capitalize on the breezes. Examples of colonial architecture can still be seen in Livingstone as well as some examples of Cape Dutch influence from South Africa.

When the British reigned over the countryside, they established British Overseas Management Areas (BOMAs), or small towns that were seats of government and business. Towns were laid out using a grid system. Villages were different, varying from tribe to tribe. The Chewa would form a village in a crescent-moon shape with the chief's lodging in the center. The Lozi developed large homesteads enclosed in a fence. This was for protection from warring tribes, as well as safety for the tribe's cattle.

A homestead usually consists of a main house, other houses, a social insaka, a cooking insaka, and other functional structures such as latrines or granaries. An insaka is a small roofed structure that is similar to a gazebo.

FOOD AND ECONOMY

Food in Daily Life. The availability of food supplies depends on season and location. The main staple is *nshima*, which is made of maize (corn). "Mealie meal" is dried and pounded corn to which boiling water is added. It is cooked to a consistency of thickened mashed potatoes and is served in large bowls. The diner scoops out a handful, rolls it into a ball and dips it into a relish. The preferred relish is usually a meat—goat, fish, or chicken—and a vegetable, usually rape (collard greens) and tomatoes, onions, or cabbage. In rural areas, where meat is not an option on a regular basis, nshima is served with beans, vegetables, or dried fish. Mealie meal is eaten three times a day, at breakfast as a porridge and as *nshima* for lunch and dinner. Buns are also popular at breakfast, taken with tea.

Other foods, such as groundnuts (peanuts), sweet potatoes, and cassava, are more seasonal. Fruits are plentiful, including bananas, mangoes, paw paws, and pineapples, which come from the hilly regions.

In the cities, there are plenty of fast-food establishments or "take-aways" that serve quick Western food such as sausages, samoosas (savory-filled pastries), burgers, and chips with a Coca-Cola. There are also an increasing number of formal Western-style restaurants that are largely accessible only to the wealthy.

Food Customs at Ceremonial Occasions. Food customs vary among tribes. For example, in the Bemba culture it is taboo for a bride to eat eggs because it may affect her fertility. Another Bemba

tradition is to serve the newlyweds a pot of chicken whose bones are then replaced in the pot and given to the bride's mother. A Lozi tradition is to eat porridge off of a stone to bless the couple. Most ceremonies, including weddings, funerals, and initiation ceremonies, involve lots of food and traditionally brewed beer.

Basic Economy. Starting with the rural community, life is supported primarily by subsistence farming. Most villagers have a small plot of land on which they farm maize, groundnuts, cassava, millet, sweet potatoes, and other products. Some villagers organize larger fields to support the community and groups of women may grow their own crops for sale.

The eastern part of the country has a climate suitable for the growing of cotton; coffee is grown in the north. Communities near lakes focus on fishing as a major industry, selling their catch all over the country. Zambia is host to a variety of freshwater fish species, including kapenta and bream. In areas where water is scarce, cattle and other domestic animals are raised.

While industrial manufacturing is limited, many everyday products are produced in the country, such as candles, cooking oil, and matches. People in the smaller urban areas may have small shops or a stand in the local marketplace, selling produce or providing a service such as watch repair. The market is a place not only of trade but of socialization. But while some may be able to support themselves and their families on the farm or in the village, job opportunities in the larger urban areas continue to contribute to the urban migration taking place in the country.

Land Tenure and Property. There are many plots of land, both in cities and rural areas, that are owned by individuals after purchase from the government. In the villages, the chiefs own the land and give out parcels to their supporters. In this distribution, tribal customs and practices are honored. The government supports this form of distribution because the acreage to be distributed is vast and unpopulated. The government still owns most of the valuable land, specifically the mines and other mineral-rich areas.

In the large urban areas, there is a huge housing crisis. Shantytowns have been erected with no sewage and the majority lack electricity. The occupants of these areas are squatters who do not own the land but who have established their homes there and indeed, whole communities.

A tailor's stall market in Lusaka, Zambia. The stall is not only the tailor's business, but it is also a place to socialize.

There are no laws preventing ownership of land by women. Very few women own land in practice primarily because of cultural and historical precedent.

Ten percent of all the land is demarcated by the government for private ownership and most of that is located in the cities. The corridors of development that do exist appear along railways and highways, which are also demarcated, usually by large farmers who want to be tied into the transportation system.

Commercial Activities. Some of the locally produced agricultural products are sold domestically, along with some household goods, cloth, and other food items. In the years of Kaunda, there was an attempt to locally make the goods needed by the country. Zambia also had an agreement with the government of the People's Republic of China, who built the Tarzara railway, connecting Zambia to Dar es Salaam, Tanzania, and the rest of the world. Because Zambia is landlocked, this link helped out with the limited trade that did occur. When democracy was ushered in, President Frederick Chiluba opened the Zambian doors to trade. Since that time, there has been a heavy influx of goods from England, Japan, the United States, and, primarily,

South Africa, whose products have flooded the market and are very popular with Zambians.

Major Industries. The copper mines have traditionally provided for a major part of the economy. In 1996, copper accounted for 80 percent of all exports. A major portion of the mines were opened to privatization, but the government was still working to sell them off. Mines were sold because of years of mismanagement and financial corruption.

Zambia has great agricultural potential and many large-scale farms have been established. The infrastructure for the distribution of goods, though, is very poor and poses a major obstacle for economic advancement in this area.

The country does support some unique industries, such as a flourishing cement trade that exports primarily to Zambia's neighbors. Farms outside of Lusaka also export roses, and are a leading supplier to the European market.

In 1995, 70 percent of the labor force was in agriculture, 18 percent in services, and 12 percent in industry.

Trade. The main exports are copper, cobalt, zinc, tobacco, maize, and emeralds. The primary recipients are South Africa, Japan, and Saudi Arabia. The

A woman wears a mask made of bark fibers, in preparation for an initation ceremony, Zambia.

main imports are automobiles, farming equipment, chemicals and fuels, and food items, from South Africa, Japan, Europe, and the United States.

Division of Labor. Labor is primarily divided between rural and urban workforces. In urban areas, jobs obtained are related to an individual's educational levels. There is high unemployment in the cities, with better-paying jobs found in government work, large businesses, and with nongovernmental organizations (NGOs). These jobs are held by people with higher education, especially those who had schooling overseas. The poor, lesser-trained individuals who come to the cities may manage to earn a living by doing odd jobs or owning a small shop.

SOCIAL STRATIFICATION

Classes and Castes. Since independence came to Zambia, there has been an obvious gap between the rich and the poor. The elite have adopted a Western standard of living and in essence have created their own class. In both rural and urban societies, there are definite lines of wealth and poverty. In the village a man is considered wealthy by having a large,

healthy family, as well as his material goods. In the cities, there is greater emphasis on material wealth.

The white and Asian populations have traditionally owned businesses and have done well over the years.

With the loosening of trade restraints, the gap between rich and poor has only widened. At the same time, the government is working to increase foreign investment in the country, while national priorities such as education and health care declined in importance.

Symbols of Social Stratification. Concrete blocks and tin roofs—once provided by the government for palace construction within the villages—became a symbol of wealth and prestige. If a family did well financially, they would attempt to copy this construction fashion.

In small cities where electricity is available, appliances such as refrigerators, stoves and especially televisions and video cassette recorders are an indication of wealth. In all communities, a vehicle is an obvious indicator of wealth and success. In the cities, foreign imports are frequent sights on the streets.

An individual's house is also a symbol of wealth and success. In the cities, large houses with pools and manicured gardens enclosed in a large fence can be found. In the villages, a family's homestead reflects wealth through the number of structures, particularly if those structures include granaries, which hold a family's maize harvest.

POLITICAL LIFE

Government. The first president, Kaunda, came to power in 1964. He soon banned all other political parties and established what he called "Zambian Humanism," which was loosely based on socialist ideas. The country faired well because of the price of copper. Because of economic hardships and pressure from foreign countries, Kaunda eventually allowed for multiparty elections. Chiluba was the second president, winning the elections under the Movement for Multiparty Democracy (MMD). He encouraged open trade relations which led to increased economic activity. With the new elections, a declaration of independence was created that included a bill of rights for every citizen.

A president is elected for five years and cannot serve more than two terms. In 1996 the country was criticized for holding unfair elections.

The legal system is modeled after English common law and customary law. The judicial branch includes a supreme court with justices appointed by the president. The vice president is also appointed by the president.

Leadership and Political Officials. Government jobs are highly coveted because of the pay and other associated benefits that might include cars, houses, and even travel. Political power, as in other governments, is related to loyalty to the presidential administration and shifts in that power do occur.

In rural areas, political control is directed by the village chiefs or chieftainesses. Some of these rural rulers have immense power, wealth, and influence while others do not. Traditionally, the chiefs and chieftainesses ruled vast amounts of land and people. They held great power, and the British, while in control of the country, allowed for local rule in remote areas. This political structure is still in place today.

Social Problems and Control. AIDS is a major concern not only for sub-Saharan Africa but especially in Zambia, where the caseload is particularly high. The disease has led to a huge orphan crisis, creating an overburden on an already stressed medical system. Efforts to combat this disease are being made, but resources are scarce.

Refugees from warring neighboring countries also have had an impact on the government's ability to deliver human services. In 2000, government-sponsored camps held 200,000 refugees (United Nations High Commissioner for Refugees figure) from the wars in the Democratic Republic of the Congo and in Angola.

Crime is a growing problem for the country, with violent robberies and car-jacking incidents not uncommon. In villages and sometimes urban areas, a thief may find himself the victim of an angry crowd if he is unlucky enough to be caught before the official police show up. Government corruption is another problem that is crippling the country at all levels. From bribes to payoffs at a local roadblock, corruption exists. The misdirection of government funds affects everyday life when the money intended for social problems does not reach its intended use.

Military Activity. The military consists of an army and an air force but both branches suffer from inadequate funding and equipment shortages. In recent history, the troops have been used primarily for United Nations missions to the Democratic Republic of the Congo and to Angola.

There have been no major wars fought on Zambian soil. Kaunda supported Zimbabwe's fight for independence and Southern Rhodesia attacked camps in Zambia in 1978 and 1979.

In 1997, a minority faction of the military attempted a coup, but the result of that effort was a state of emergency which lasted six months.

President Chiluba traditionally has taken an active role in arranging peace talks for local conflicts as well as more international negotiations such as the Angolan conflict resolution. Zambian officials have also tried to help resolve the continuing political conflicts in the Congo.

SOCIAL WELFARE AND CHANGE PROGRAMS

Once independence was achieved, copper prices made Zambia one of the wealthiest countries in Africa, which helped fund many of the subsidized government programs and products. But when copper prices dropped dramatically in the early 1970s, that income source of the government decreased and the subsidies were no longer available. With the government unable to assist, foreign aid was encouraged and some areas became dependent on that foreign support. Zambia became heavily indebted to the World Bank and the International Monetary Fund. It was pressure from these organizations that forced Kaunda to allow democratic elections.

NONGOVERNMENTAL ORGANIZATIONS AND OTHER ASSOCIATIONS

Numerous nongovernmental organizations (NGOs), from various foreign countries and religious groups operate programs in Zambia. The stated goal of these organizations is to provide aid both on a large scale and at the grassroots level. One of the largest recent projects in Zambia has been a road improvement program, since transportation problems in the country are a major issue. Examples of NGOs operating in Zambia include: World Vision, Habitat for Humanity, and the International Red Cross.

GENDER ROLES AND STATUSES

Division of Labor by Gender. Both men and women work hard for basic survival. Traditionally, women have had the role of caring for the household, but in recent times, especially in cities, women work in offices, sell vegetables, and hold numerous other positions, including positions in the military. In the village, a woman's day starts out with sweeping and cleaning, followed by the collection of

A man working at a food processing plant at Kabwe. Industrial jobs are scarce, as few products are produced in Zambia. Only 12 percent of the working population is employed in industry.

water, often from long distances. The washing of clothes and the preparation of meals are also done by women. The primary responsibility for children too, falls to women, although older siblings are expected to help out with these chores.

Both women and men work long hours in the fields, although the task is largely considered men's work. The men traditionally do the fishing, hunting, and raising of livestock, but also are known to socialize more with neighbors, family, and friends.

Women tend to socialize when they are doing chores.

The Relative Status of Women and Men. Men have most of the power. There has been an effort to gain greater influence for women's rights, but it is difficult to incorporate programs that change traditional beliefs. Women's groups work together in sewing or farming a small vegetable plot. This gives the women some financial gain and a voice in the family's money matters. It is also a source of pride and belonging.

MARRIAGE, FAMILY, AND KINSHIP

Marriage. Traditionally, people would marry within their tribe, rarely going outside that circle to find a mate, but marriage within a clan group is considered taboo. Tribal customs vary but there usually is a mediator who serves as a go-between for a man and his desired bride. The man and his negotiator will meet with a prospective bride's family and in addition to getting to know each other, start negotiations for a *lobola* (dowry). This lobola traditionally involves cattle or other livestock, but in modern times money settlements have been accepted. The lobola is considered a compensation to the family for the lost services of the woman.

Christian weddings are very common even in villages, although traditional religious customs are still practiced in both cities and rural areas, with variations from tribe to tribe. A Bemba custom calls for the man to live with his bride's parents for a period, to prove his ability to take care of his wife.

Domestic Unit. The main domestic structure is the extended family, common throughout Africa. The system grew out of a need to help family members in times of trouble. For example, if a family had a year of bad crops, their relatives would be expected to provide assistance. If a mother and father died, their children would be cared for by relatives.

Inheritance. The issue of inheritance is handled differently throughout the country, reflecting the different customs of the numerous tribes. Traditional methods call for disputes to be settled within the clan or at the next level, which is the chief. In disputes involving men and women, the clans traditionally favor the male's position. In urban areas, the courts resolve these disputes. The Goba tribe has what is called *dihwe*, a council to settle problems of succession and inheritance if a prominent member of the household dies. Many Zambians, especially in cities, now create a will and last testament.

Kin Groups. As in most areas of Africa, clans are an important factor in Zambia society. Clans provide another way to identify one's self, in addition to tribal connections. Similar to an extended family, one is expected to assist another clan member whenever needed; it is considered part of one's social duty and identity. These kin groups are traditionally named after animals or natural features, such as crocodiles, elephants, or rain.

A Zambian judge overseeing a judicial tribunal in the attire of the British colonial legal tradition, Zambia.

SOCIALIZATION

Infant Care. Because many families have a large number of children and since many parents work, both in rural and urban communities, a number of children are raised by their siblings. It is not uncommon in the village to see a baby being carried around by children as young as five years old.

Shitangas, which are large pieces of cloth, wrapped around the baby and the mother, allow the mother to carry the baby on her back with the baby's head peering just over her shoulder. Mothers often conduct hard labor, such as carrying water or working in the fields, while carrying an infant.

Child Rearing and Education. It is difficult for families, both rural and urban, to afford fees charged for attending school. In villages, schools are often hampered by out-of-date textbooks and buildings in terrible disrepair. There is usually an inadequate number of teachers, which forces a class schedule of only a half-day. When not in school, children are expected to be at home, helping with chores or working the fields.

Most tribes have an initiation ceremony for both boys and girls to mark an individual's entry into adulthood and official acceptance into the village. These are large events, lasting for days and celebrated with dance, food, and singing. Both male and female ceremonies involve many rituals that teach them about customs, sex, and the responsibilities of being an adult. It is usually right after these ceremonies that marriage takes place.

Higher Education. After primary school (grades one to seven), some Zambians proceed to secondary school, or grades eight to twelve. Since secondary school fees are even higher than primary school fees, some children are unable to attend. In addition to the secondary schools, the country has several boarding schools with even higher fees, but the results are a better-funded educational system. Educational resources are hard to come by and many rural schools simply must do with what they have.

After secondary school, students have limited options for furthering their formal education. There are numerous trade colleges specializing in technical programs, such as machinery, plumbing, construction, and sewing. More recently, computer programs are being offered, but these, as with other programs, specialize in basic skills for the trade fields. There also are teaching colleges that supply professionals for the Zambian school system. There are two universities: the University of Zambia in Lusaka, which specializes in liberal arts degrees, including law and business, and the Copperbelt University, in Kitwe, which offers degrees in technical subjects, such as mining, engineering, and architecture.

There have been several demonstrations by students, protesting the government's cutbacks on subsidies for school and living expenses.

In years past, these universities were well funded by the government, but deterioration has increased sharply. There is limited funding for basic things such as modern textbooks, computers, and basic building maintenance. Many Zambians choose to pursue an education out of the country and while some can afford the cost, others hope for scholarships from foreign countries, especially the United Kingdom, which has been very generous in the past. There is a concern that as many of the country's smarter students seek an education outside of the country, they will not return, opting instead to work overseas for more pay and a better standard of life.

ETIQUETTE

Greetings are very important. One greets another by saying "hello" and "how are you?" Then come inquiries into one's family, the crops or the weather. It is rude to come directly to the point; conversations may go on for several minutes before the point of the conversation is broached.

There is hand etiquette as well. The right hand is for eating—which is traditionally done without utensils—greetings, and exchanges of money. It is impolite to use your left hand when interacting with another person. Washing of one's hands before eating is very common, with a bowl of water passed around as one sits at the table. The guests are given the honor of going first.

Proverbs are an important part of Zambian society. They are part of the oral tradition and have become catchphrases in which a lesson is taught. For example a Kaunde proverb is "Bubela bubwel," which translates to "lies return." This is a proverb used to warn against gossip and telling lies because it can make you look foolish later.

Another important aspect of Zambian culture is respect for elders. When greeting an elder, one shows respect by dropping to one knee, bowing the head, clapping three times, and saying one of the many terms that signify respect.

RELIGION

Religious Beliefs. The influence of Christian missionaries is evident. An estimated 53 percent of the population considers themselves Catholic. The country's official religion has been Catholicism since 1993 when President Chiluba officially declared it so. There are other religions, including a large Muslim population primarily in Eastern Province. This is a result of the immigration of Arabs from Dar es Salaam, Tanzania, largely due to the slave trade. There are Hindus, Jews, and Pentecostals, who, combined, comprise only 1 percent of the population. Animism is practiced by a large amount of the population, even if they are Catholic, Seventh Day Adventists, or practitioners of another religion. Animism beliefs vary from tribe to tribe, but most are based on beliefs in the power of ancestors and in nature. Some people call this witchcraft and indeed such terms as "wizards" and "witches" are used. Many areas believe that crocodiles have strong powers.

Religious Practitioners. Missionaries have a long history in the country although for many years there have been Zambian priests, especially in cities. A mission will periodically send a priest into the bush country for services and other religious duties.

There is a recognition of witch doctors, who use traditional medicines made from roots or plants,

A witchdoctor from the Tonga, Zambia, sits in his grass hut. Various gourds, boxes, and other items are spread before him.

and every rural area has access to a traditional healer.

Rituals and Holy Places. The major holy places are the many waterfalls, where people believe certain spirits live. Traditional healers will often go into the woods or bush to contact spirits.

The various tribes have many rituals. For example, the Litunga tribe performs a ceremony that is called Kuomboka. This signifies the tribe's movement in the rainy season from the floodplains to higher ground. Hundreds of canoes travel down the river with the chief leading the way. Umutomboko is performed once a year by the Kazembe Bemba and is a ceremonial reenactment of a migration that took place in the early 1800s. Much dancing culminates with the chief's dance.

Death and the Afterlife. Funerals are a major event, with family members coming from great distances to attend. A funeral may last for many days, with the men outside drinking and talking, and women inside, wailing. The delay gives people traveling from long distances time to arrive. After a period, the group will proceed to a graveyard where services, usually Christian, will be held. Unfortunately, funerals have become an everyday occurrence due to the high death rate associated with AIDS and other illnesses.

There are separate ceremonies for the burial of village chiefs, along with their ancestors. A Bemba tradition is that if a paramount chief dies, his body will not be buried for a week but is protected because a clipping of his hair or a fingernail could be a very powerful item in traditional religions.

Traditional religions also have their specific beliefs on death and afterlife.

MEDICINE AND HEALTH CARE

Under President Kaunda, the government provided basic health coverage for everyone, including those in rural areas. That, however, was when Zambia was a wealthy country and could afford to do so. Government hospitals have deteriorated significantly in the past few years with major problems of understaffing and increasing numbers of sick patients. Because of limited funding, even hospital maintenance has suffered. Medicines, particularly those for AIDS patients, are in high demand, and funding is inadequate; the situation is worse in the rural areas. The major health problems are AIDS, TB, malaria, and malnutrition.

Much of the support from NGOs and foreign governments comes in the form of medical assistance such as medicines, equipment, and personnel. There is a strong government immunization program for children in very rural areas, with traveling clinics for those five years or younger, where routine immunization shots and basic health care are distributed.

SECULAR CELEBRATIONS

Holidays officially celebrated by the government include: New Year's Day (1 January), Labor Day (1 May), African Freedom Day (21 May), Unity Day (in July), Heroes Day (in July), Youth Day (9 August), and Independence Day (21 October). Government offices and banks are closed on these days and there often are planned celebrations in the larger cities, including parades or festivals. Residents of the cities traditionally return to their clans for these times of celebrations.

THE ARTS AND HUMANITIES

Support for the Arts. Most of the support for the country's art programs comes from tourists or NGOs. Zambians produce beautifully carved pieces for the tourist trade with a sale expected to bring in quite a bit of money for a household. Basket weaving in Zambia is generally considered the best in Africa, with many different materials and styles used. The baskets are typically made out of grass reeds and are used for containers.

Literature. There are few published Zambian authors, largely because of the high illiteracy rate. Another factor is the high cost of books. The books that are written are usually stories of independence or on topics related to life in the city or the village.

Graphic Arts. At one time, a large textile industry existed in the country, owned and operated by the government. The main product was brilliantly colored dyed fabrics in many patterns. This fabric was used for clothing, particularly *chitenges*, which are strips of cloth. These are worn as skirts, wrapped about the bodies of women and especially popular in villages. In the 1990s, the importance of *saulas*, or secondhand clothing, increased, with donations from Western countries and church organizations—thus decreasing the need for new textiles.

Performance Arts. Drum and dance troupes are popular. Many of these are for the benefit of tourists and perform in major cities, since the smaller cities do not have the facilities or money to support the arts. These dances are very lively and use the traditional instruments of drums, an instrument similar to a xylophone, and a thumb piano.

Bands are also popular in urban settings. The most popular sound is rumba music from the Congo, but there is an appreciation of the traditional tribal songs and sounds. In village settings, the basics prevail. In most cases, not even an instrument is used; instead, traditional songs are sung and clapped while sitting around a community fire. The passing on of beliefs and customs in oral performances are still practiced. This is a very important part of tribal culture and preserves a tribe's identity and beliefs.

BIBLIOGRAPHY

Baldwin, Robert E. *Economic Development and Export Growth: A Study of Northern Rhodesia, 1920–1960,* 1966.

Beveridge, Andrew A., and Anthony R. Oberschall. *African Businessmen and Development in Zambia*, 1979.

Bonnick, Gladstone G. *Zambia Country Assistance Review: Turning an Economy Around*, 1997.

Burdette, Marcia M. *Zambia: Between two Worlds*, 1988.

Cancel, Robert. *Allegorical Speculation in an Oral Society*, 1988.

Chiluba, Frederick J. T., *Democracy: The Challenge of Change*, 1995.

Crehan, Kate A. F. *The Fractured Community*, 1997.

De Gaay Fortman, Bastiaan, ed. *After Mulungushi: The Economics of Zambian Humanism*, 1969.

Epstein A. L. *Urbanization and Kinship*, 1981.

Fisher, W. Singleton, and Julyan Hoyte. *Ndotolu*, 1987.

Holmes, Timothy. *Zambia*, 1998.

Ihonvbere, Julius O. *Economic Crisis, Civil Society and Democratization: The Case of Zambia*, 1996.

Knauder, Stefanie. *Shacks and Mansions*, 1982.

Lancaster, Chet S. *The Goba of the Zambezi*, 1981.

Obidegwu, Chukwuma F., and Mudziviri Nziramasanga. *Copper and Zambia: An Econometric Analysis*, 1981.

Roberts, Andrew D. *A History of the Bemba*, 1973.

Schmetzer, Harmut. *Traditional Architecture in Zambia*, 1987.

Smith, Edwin W. *The Ila Peoples of Northern Rhodesia*, 1968.

Turner, Edith. *The Spirit and the Drum*, 1987.

———. *Experiencing Ritual*, 1992.

Turok, Ben, ed. *Development in Zambia: A Reader*, 1979.

Van Binsbergen, Wim M. J. *Religious Change in Zambia*, 1981.

—JON SOJKOWSKI

ZIMBABWE

CULTURE NAME

Zimbabwean

ALTERNATIVE NAMES

Shona, Ndebele

ORIENTATION

Identification. Zimbabwe is named after Great Zimbabwe, the twelfth- to fifteenth-century stone-built capital of the Rozwi Shona dynasty. The name is thought to derive from *dzimba dza mabwe* ("great stone houses") or *dzimba waye* ("esteemed houses"). Cultural and religious traditions among the Shona, Ndebele and smaller groups of Tonga, Shangaan and Venda have similarities in regard to marriage practices and the belief in supernatural ancestors. All those groups called on the support of the spirit world in the struggle for independence, which was achieved in 1980. European culture and values indelibly shaped the urban and rural landscapes, particularly in terms of the use of space, and the structure and practice of government. Black Zimbabweans have assimilated more white Zimbabwean culture than vice versa. In these distinct cultures, which generally are referred to as African and European, the most obvious differences are economic. While the white minority lost political power after Independence, it has retained a disproportionate share of economic resources.

Location and Geography. Zimbabwe is in central southern Africa. Because of the impact of its colonial history on the nation's political, economic, and sociocultural life, it generally is identified more with southern Africa than with central Africa. A landlocked country of 242,700 square miles 390,580 square kilometers between the Zambezi River to the north and the Limpopo River to the south, it is bordered by Mozambique, South Africa, Botswana, Namibia, and Zambia. Most of the country is a high to middle veld plateau with extensive areas of wooded savanna and a temperate climate; the low veld of the Limpopo and the Zambezi Valley is hotter and has less rain. On the Mozambique border, the only mountainous area, the Eastern Highlands, runs from Nyanga in the north to Chimanimani in the south. Rainfall is higher in the north of the Eastern Highlands and lower in the Zambezi Valley and the low veld.

The capital, Harare, is located in Mashonaland, which covers the eastern two-thirds of the country and is the area where most Shona-speaking people live. The second city, Bulawayo, is in Matabeleland in the west, where most Ndebele-speaking people live.

Demography. At the beginning of the twentieth century, the population is estimated to have been about six hundred thousand. The 1992 national census estimated it at over ten million, and with a growth rate of 3 percent, it is expected to be over twelve million in 2000. About 70 percent of the population lives in rural areas, and Harare and Bulawayo account for most of the approximately 30 percent in urban areas. The largest ethnic group is collectively known as the Shona and consists of the Manyika, Zezuru, Karanga, Korekore, Rozwi, and Ndau groups, which make up about seventy-six percent of the population. The second largest ethnic group is the Ndebele, consisting of the Ndebele and Kalanga groups, which constitute about 18 percent. Mashonaland, where most of the Shona live, is a collective term for the eastern two-thirds of the country, and most Ndebele live in the western third of Matabeleland. Other ethnic groups, each constituting 1 percent of the population, are the Batonga in the Zambezi Valley, the Shangaan or Hlengwe in the low veld, and the Venda on the border with South Africa. About 2 percent of the population is of non-African ethnic origin, mainly European and Asian.

In the twentieth century, there were three major changes in the demographic and settlement

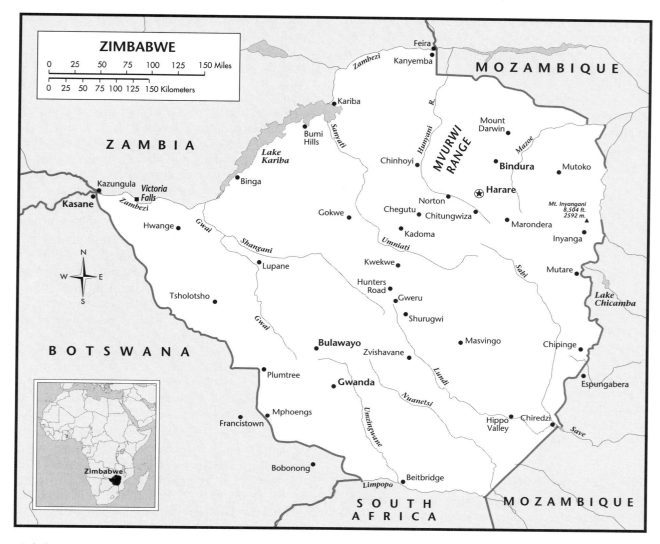

Zimbabwe

pattern. First, the acquisition of large tracts of land by white settlers for commercial agriculture, until shortly after World War II resulted in a situation in which half the land was owned by well under 1 percent of the population, with limited access to land for the vast majority of the rural population. Second, in the colonial period, the development of industry in towns and cities, particularly Harare and Bulawayo, required men seeking work to live in urban areas, leaving women and children in the rural areas. Although this gender imbalance in urban areas no longer exists, and there is more movement between urban and rural areas, de facto women heads of household are still common in rural areas. Most jobs continue to be found in urban areas and employment income rather than income from farming is the most important factor in the standard of living among smallholder families. The

third major change has involved the age profile of the population. A sharp drop in mortality rates and longer life expectancy between 1960 and 1992 meant that almost sixty-three percent of the population sixteen to thirty-four years of age. The statistical impact of the AIDS epidemic on the population will not be clear until the next national census in 2002, but that disease is considered a major factor in higher maternal and infant mortality rates.

Linguistic Affiliation. All the national languages, with the exception of the official language, English, are Bantu, a branch of the Niger-Congo language family. Shona and Sindebele are the most widely spoken, and students are required to take at least one of those languages. The four main dialects of Shona—Zezuru, Kalanga, Manyika, and Ndau—have a common vocabulary and similar tonal and grammatical features. The Ndebele in the nineteenth century were the first to use the name "Shona" to refer to the peoples they conquered; although the exact meaning of the term is unclear, it was probably derogatory. Later, white colonists extended the term to refer to all groups that spoke dialects officially recognized as Shona. One view of the dialects is that they resulted from differing missionary education policies in the nineteenth century. Sindebele is a click language of the Nguni group of Bantu languages; other members of this language group are Zulu and Xhosa, which are spoken mainly in South Africa; siSwati (Swaziland); and siTswana (Botswana). Other languages spoken in Zimbabwe are Tonga, Shangaan, and Venda, which are shared with large groups of Tonga in Zambia and Shangaan and Venda in South Africa.

Symbolism. The national flag and the Zimbabwe bird (the African fish eagle) are the most important symbolic representations of the nation. The Zimbabwe bird is superimposed on the flag, and while the flag symbolizes independence, the Zimbabwe bird represents continuity with the precolonial past. Internationally, particularly in the tourist sector, photographs of Victoria Falls, Great Zimbabwe, and wildlife are symbols of the national history and natural heritage.

HISTORY AND ETHNIC RELATIONS

Emergence of the Nation. San (Bushmen) hunters are believed to have been the earliest inhabitants of the area that is now Zimbabwe. When Bantu-speaking peoples migrated from the north at the end of the second century, the San moved on or were absorbed rapidly into the farming and cattle-herding culture of the Bantu groups. Little is known about those early Bantu groups, but the present-day Shona can be traced to a group that moved into the area around 1200 C.E.

From the eleventh century, after commercial relations were established with Swahili traders on the Mozambique coast, until the fifteenth century, the Shona kingdom was one of southern Africa's wealthiest and most powerful societies. Its political and religious center was probably Great Zimbabwe, a city of ten thousand to twenty thousand people built between the twelfth and fourteenth centuries by the Rozvi dynasty. The city was constructed from granite, using highly developed stone-cutting and construction techniques. Historians are unsure about the reasons for its decline in the fifteenth century, but the human and livestock population might have outstripped available resources. Until

1905, when archaeological research proved that Great Zimbabwe was of Bantu origin, and then until independence in 1980, colonial explanations of the city's origins failed to consider that it could be of Bantu origin. The importance of Great Zimbabwe to the colonists, who referred to it as the Zimbabwe Ruins, was also the basis of its importance in the nationalist struggle for majority rule. Whereas the colonists denied its significance, the nationalist movement promoted it as sacred. According to Shona religion, the ancestors who built Great Zimbabwe still live there, and it therefore is a sacred site. Today Great Zimbabwe is one of the most potent symbols of the nations, and the Zimbabwe bird on the flag depicts one of the excavated soapstone sculptures of the fish eagle found at the site.

New dynasties followed the Rozvi of Great Zimbabwe, but the kingdom declined in importance. Although Swahili and later Portuguese traders tried to exploit internal differences in the kingdom, they never succeeded. The second significant encounter in the making of Zimbabwe was the Ndebele invasion of the early 1880s under the command of Mzlikazi, who established his capital at Inyati to the north of Bulawayo. He was succeeded by Lobengula, who shifted the capital to Bulawayo.

In 1888 Cecil John Rhodes tricked Lobengula into signing an agreement that opened the country to mining prospectors and other speculators. Rhodes then formed the British South Africa Company and organized the "Pioneer Column" and subsequently the first group of white settlers, who moved up from South Africa in search of gold and arable land. After defeating the Ndebele in battle and appropriating land in Mashonaland, the colonists founded Rhodesia in 1895. The first *Chimurenga* (war of liberation) occurred in 1896, when the Ndebele were joined by the Shona. The war was led by two spirit mediums, Nehanda and Kagubi, who were caught and executed and subsequently became powerful symbols in the second Chimurenga, which started in the mid–1960s.

After the establishment of a white legislative council 1899, white immigration increased, and in 1922 the white minority decided that the country would be self-governing (run by the British South Africa Company as a commercial enterprise) and independent of the government in South Africa. In 1923, the British South Africa Company handed the country over to the British Crown, and in 1930, the white minority passed the Land Apportionment Act, which barred blacks from legal access to the best land, simultaneously assuring a source of cheap labor. Between 1946 and 1960, the white population increased from 82,000 to 223,000, and this period witnessed economic expansion, including the construction of the Kariba Dam.

Organized resistance to white supremacy began in the 1920s, and in the absence of meaningful reform, radical active resistance started in the 1940s. By the early 1960s the two groups that were to lead the country to independence, the Zimbabwe African People's Union and the Zimbabwe African National Union, had been established. When Great Britain demanded that Rhodesia guarantee racial equality and put in place a plan for majority rule or face economic sanctions, the government declared a Unilateral Declaration of Independence in 1965. A guerrilla war followed that was characterized by political differences between resistance groups and among the white minority. It also was characterized by a close relationship between the guerrillas and spirit mediums. Embodying the ancestors, the spirit mediums represented a common past, untainted by colonialism, that could be drawn on to shape and legitimize a new national identity.

After the negotiation of a settlement at the Lancaster House Conference in 1979, the first multiparty general elections were held with complete adult suffrage in 1980. The Zimbabwe African National Unity party led by Robert Mugabe won the majority of seats and took over the government in April 1980. Seven years later, that party and the Zimbabwe Africa People's Union merged. While there are minor political parties, Zimbabwe has effectively been a one-party state.

National Identity. The adoption of the name "Zimbabwe" and citizens' identity as Zimbabweans, functioned as a symbol of continuity with the past. The common struggle of all groups was instrumental in forming a sense of national identity. Political tensions between the Ndebele and the Shona, which culminated when the army suppressed dissidence in 1983 and 1984 in the Matabeleland Massacres, have been contained by the state.

URBANISM, ARCHITECTURE, AND THE USE OF SPACE

Urban centers are divided into areas of low and high housing density (formerly referred to as townships) for low-income families. The use of space therefore is closely correlated with socioeconomic status. High-density areas have been planned with water and power supplies. Little artistic emphasis has been placed on architecture, and with the exception of some well-maintained colonial buildings, especially in Harare and Bulawayo, buildings tend to be functional.

Mud and wattle or sun-dried bricks are used in house building in rural areas; well-off families may use concrete blocks. Traditionally, houses were round with thatch roofing, but an increasing number are square or rectangular with zinc sheet roofing, although kitchens are still built as roundavels (round thatched mud huts). The most marked use of space is in the kitchen, where a bench runs around the right side for men to sit on, while women sit on the floor on the left.

Areas of higher rainfall and therefore higher agricultural potential attracted a large number of white settlers at the end of the nineteenth century. That group appropriated land and established a self-governing colonial state and two systems of land use; one for smallholding subsistence farming and one for large-scale commercial production and speculation. Those systems have had different effects on the physical environment, giving rise to controversy about the causes and effects of overgrazing and erosion and raising issues of equity with respect to access to land. Population density is low in the commercial farming areas and relatively high in the smallholder areas and communal areas. Smallholdings are scattered because people prefer to have some bush between themselves and their neighbors. The term "village" is used to refer to an administrative area and does not imply the presence of a number of houses in a small area.

Another important influence on land use and the physical environment was the designation of protected areas as national parks or safari areas, covering about 13 percent of the land area. These areas are important to tourism and the national economy.

FOOD AND ECONOMY

Food in Daily Life. The major grain for consumption is maize, although in parts of the Zambezi Valley millet and sorghum are the principle grains. After grinding, the flour is cooked into a thick porridge that is eaten with green vegetables or meat. A wide range of green vegetables are grown in kitchen gardens and collected wild. They generally are prepared with onion and tomato and sometimes with groundnut (peanut) sauce. Bread is a staple in the urban diet but not as important in rural areas. Foods that are eaten seasonally include milk, boiled or roasted groundnuts, boiled or roasted maize, fruits, termites, and caterpillars. Dry land rice is grown in

Farm workers winnow soya beans. Agriculture and forestry accounts for 14 percent of the GDP.

some parts of the country, but generally rice is not an everyday food.

A few food taboos with serious health consequences are still widely practiced. Traditionally eggs, were believed to cause infertility in women and therefore were avoided, but they are now widely consumed. The meat of one's clan totem was traditionally avoided; even today animals representing totems are rarely eaten.

Eating out is not common, even among men in the urban areas. Travelers purchase soft drinks and prepared food, such as fried cakes, potato chips, roasted maize, and sugarcane from vendors. A higher proportion of the white population regularly buys prepared meals and eats in restaurants.

Food Customs at Ceremonial Occasions. Roasted and stewed meat is the food of celebrations; an ox, cow, or goat may be slaughtered in the rural areas, depending on the significance of the event, and may be accompanied by rice. Beer made from millet usually is prepared by women, and roasted groundnuts are served on special occasions.

Basic Economy. Agriculture is the mainstay of the economy for over 70 percent of the population, although manufacturing accounts for about 25 percent of the gross national product (GDP) and is the most important macroeconomic sector. Economic decline began in the mid-1980s, when foreign demand for minerals dropped, and this situation was worsened by the impact of several droughts and structural adjustment polices that have had a disproportionate impact on the poor. Since the opening up of the South African economy in 1994, increased competition in export markets and the increased availability of South African goods in Zimbabwe have heightened macroeconomic concerns.

Until 1992, the country was self-sufficient in grain, and a massive increase in maize production by smallholders was a postindependence success story. However, since that time, annual grain production has not always met demand because of a decline in producer prices and an increase in the population.

The major crops grown by smallholders on the high and middle veld plateau are maize, sunflower, groundnuts, and cotton. In the Zambezi Valley more millet and sorghum are grown than maize, but only for subsistence, and cotton is the only major cash crop. The west and the low veld are predominantly cattle-raising areas. Self-sufficiency varies at the household level and depends on a variety of factors, including rainfall and the type of grain grown (maize or more drought-resistant millet and sorghum) and the availability of draft animals. To increase grain production for household consumption, the government and nongovernment organizations are encouraging farmers to grow more millet and sorghum. This is meeting with only limited success; most people prefer the taste of maize, and it is less labor-intensive to harvest and prepare for consumption.

Meeting grain deficits is dependent on cash income from the sale of cash crops (for example, groundnuts and cotton) or cash remittances from workers in the towns. There has been a steady movement of maize and goats from rural to urban areas.

The basic unit of currency is the Zimbabwe dollar.

Land Tenure and Property. Land distribution is highly skewed: freehold large-scale commercial farms that cover about 40 percent of the national territory are owned by a tiny fraction of the population, predominantly white. About half the population lives on holdings that are typically between five and fifty acres (two hectares and twenty hectares) in the communal and resettlement sectors,

A family attends to their fields. Young children, like the boy pictured above, learn adult tasks early on—as early as seven or eight years old.

which cover about 40 percent of the country. Freehold small-scale commercial farms that were established as "native purchase areas" by the 1930 Land Apportionment Act cover approximately 4 percent of the country. Other major categories of land use are state-owned areas protected for their wildlife, flora and fauna (about 13 percent of the country), and forests, particularly in the Eastern Highlands.

Freehold land is privately owned, but communal land is vested in the president and allocated through rural district councils that grant consent for use according to customary law. In practice, chiefs have the right to allocate usufruct (rights to use the land) to married adult men; women have access to land only through their husbands. Resettlement areas were established after independence to increase black access to land, and land there is allocated by permit. Although women can obtain permits, most women in the resettlement areas secure access to land through their husbands. Freehold landowners are predominantly men; although women have rights to succession, inheritance by widows and daughters is rare. As with land, property is predominantly male-owned.

Commercial Activities. During the period of the Unilateral Declaration of Independence, the country developed a strong manufacturing base, and it continues to manufacture products ranging from household items to steel and engineering products for the construction industry and commercial agricultural products such as textiles and foodstuffs. The diversified economy provides a solid basis for sustained economic growth, but in recent years it has been underperforming.

Major Industries. Manufacturing is the largest single sector of the economy (23 percent of GDP), followed by agriculture and forestry (14 percent), distribution, hotels and restaurants (11 percent), and public administration (10 percent).

Trade. Major exports include tobacco, gold, ferroalloys, nickel, and asbestos. The main export destinations are Great Britain, South Africa, and Germany. South Africa is by the far the largest source of imports and machinery and transport equipment, manufactured goods, chemicals, petroleum products, and electricity are the largest imports.

Division of Labor. In the formal economy, jobs are assigned on the basis of education, skills, and experience; advertising and interviewing precede hiring. In the informal economy, most people work for themselves and pay workers on a cash basis.

POLITICAL LIFE

Government. Zimbabwe is a parliamentary democracy headed by a president. Although the president is elected by direct vote in advance of party elections and holds office for six years, the term during which a party can control the government is five years. Representative structures consist of a House of Assembly and a cabinet appointed by the president; at rural district level, there are elected councils. Each district is made of a number of wards, and wards are subdivided into villages. Each ward and village has a development committee that is responsible for promoting and supporting local development initiatives. Ten chiefs, traditional representatives elected by their peers, sit in the House of Assembly. Alongside the representative structure is the civil service (the administrative structure), the police, the military, permanent secretaries and other ministry staff, and provincial and district administration staff.

Military Activity. Military branches of the government are the Zimbabwe National Army, the Air Force of Zimbabwe, the Zimbabwe Republic Police (including the Police Support Unit and the Paramilitary Police). About 1.8 million men aged between 15 and 49 are estimated fit for military service, and over 45,000 were serving in the army at the beginning of the twenty-first century.

Expenditure on military activities rose as a result of the country's involvement in the war in the Democratic Republic of the Congo, beginning in 1998. This was the army's first foreign military intervention since 1980.

SOCIAL WELFARE AND CHANGE PROGRAMS

Social welfare programs provide assistance to the destitute and drought relief in the communal areas when there are poor harvests. Zimbabwe provided more relief in the drought of 1991 and 1992 than did international donors. Nongovernmental organizations and churches provide many services that the government cannot, such as rehabilitation of disabled persons and care in the community for the sick.

NONGOVERNMENTAL ORGANIZATIONS AND OTHER ASSOCIATIONS

There are eight hundred to nine hundred organizations and associations that engage in activities ranging from advocacy work, to service delivery, to welfare. Membership organizations include farmer's unions, trade unions, and organizations of the disabled, and nonmembership organizations vary from development organizations to charities that provide welfare services. Many of these groups are closely linked with other southern African and international organizations. Church groups, burial societies, and savings and credit groups are the most common informal organizations in the community, and most people, particularly women, are members of at least one.

GENDER ROLES AND STATUSES

Division of Labor by Gender. The roles of men and women in farming are determined by a land tenure system in which men are allocated land in the communal areas and own most of the land in the commercial areas. Both men and women work the smallholdings in the communal areas, and women are responsible for domestic work. About 70 percent of women are smallholder farmers, compared with 35 percent of men. Commercial farmers rely on hired labor, both male and female. Only in the agricultural sector of the formal economy do women outnumber men; this includes commercial farms and agroprocessing activities.

Many enterprises in the informal sector are based on women's traditional economic activities, such as gardening, raising poultry, and baking, to supplement household income. The informal sector has grown considerably because of retrenchment in the formal sector and a decline in household income and is a crucial source of income for many households.

Men predominate as government representatives and civil servants, from the cabinet to the village and from ministries to district councils. About 15 percent of members of the House of Assembly are women. Political leadership is male-dominated, although there is a growing challenge to this system from organizations seeking to raise more women to influential decision-making positions.

The Relative Status of Women and Men. According to the constitution, men and women are equal. However, in terms of the law there are many areas where women are discriminated against, such as laws governing the conditions of part-time work, inheritance law, and the fact that brideprices (*lobola*) are still allowed. In a recent setback for women's rights, in April 1999 the Supreme Court, in an inheritance dispute, ruled that women cannot be considered equal to men before the law because of African cultural norms. Precedence was given to customary

A view of downtown Harare. Most Zimbabwean architecture is strictly functional, like these commercial and office buildings.

law over the constitution on the basis of a clause in the constitution that allows for certain exceptions.

MARRIAGE, FAMILY, AND KINSHIP

Marriage. Through marriage a family ensures its survival and continuation into the next generation. Shona, Ndebele, Shangaan, and Venda are patrilineal societies in which descent is through the male line and after marriage a women moves into her husband's home. The Tonga people are matrilineal, and the husband moves to the home area of his wife. Patrilocal or virilocal residence rarely applies in urban areas, but most urban families have a smallholding that is the rural home of the husband and wife.

Two types of marriage are recognized under the law. Customary marriages are potentially polygynous and legal for black Zimbabweans only and usually are dissolved only by death (divorce is rare). Civil marriages are monogamous and can be dissolved by death or divorce. Customary marriages are the more common form. Arranged marriages are rare, although families on both sides are heavily involved in marriage negotiations, which include deciding on the brideprice to be paid by the husband to the woman's family; thus, a wife and her children belong to the husband and are affiliated with his kin. Marriage gives women status and access to land, and unmarried men and women are rare. Polygyny is still widespread, although it is declining as land constraints and lower incomes are encouraging smaller households. Divorce is not common and carries a stigma, especially for women.

Domestic Unit. In rural areas the family unit is composed of the husband, the wife or wives, children, and members of the extended family. In urban areas, households are smaller, with a tendency toward a nuclear family of the husband, the wife, and children. In polygynous families, each wife has her own house and a share of a field. Households usually are defined in terms of a domestic unit of the wife, the children, and other dependents; therefore, a polygynous family and a wider extended family living together may consist of two or more households. The average household has 4.76 persons.

Authority is vested in men, and wisdom is vested in age. After marrying, a man assumes domestic authority as the household head, but in wider family affairs the elders are more influential. A woman also gains authority and respect with age, and newly married daughters-in-law take over much of the housework and help in the fields. Assistance continues after a daughter-in-law has established her own house nearby.

Inheritance. In customary marriages, all property rights during marriage or after divorce or death be-

The village in Guruve, which consists of traditional thatch-roofed housing (roundavels).

long to the man. Disposition of the estate and guardianship of children are determined by male relatives of the husband. Women may retain property that is traditionally associated with their domestic role, such as kitchen utensils, and one of the implications of patrilocal residence that has carried into contemporary urban life is that immovable property is regarded as the man's property. Although changes in the law recognize a woman's contribution, it is difficult for a woman to claim rights to property in the face of family opposition. Wills are rare, although they override customary law. In civil marriages ended by divorce or death, wives and widows have the right to a share of the husband's estate, although the same difficulties apply.

Kin Groups. Relationships with maternal kin (or, in the case of the Tonga, paternal kin) are important; although contact may be infrequent, the relationship is normally a close one. Therefore, the wider kin group of an extended family can be very extensive.

SOCIALIZATION

Infant Care. The nurturing and socialization of infants are the responsibility of mothers and, in their temporary absence (for example, when they are working), a female relative. In customary prac-tice orphans are the responsibility of the husband's relatives. A great deal of an infant's time is spent in the company of the mother, being carried on her back in the kitchen and sleeping with her at night. Socialization takes place mostly in the household through the mother and the extended family, and other children nearly always are around to play with an infant. Therefore, in addition to the strong caring bond between mother and child, other adults and older children develop bonds and assume responsibility in the absence of the mother.

Child Rearing and Education. An infant or child is seldom lonely, and being constantly surrounded by relatives lays the foundation for behavior in an adult life that is dependent on cooperation within the family. Children learn respect for their elders, which is considered a very important quality. From the age of about seven or eight, girls start to help in the house, and in rural areas boys of that age begin to learn to herd livestock. Children are encouraged to take on adult tasks from an early age.

Primary school starts when a child is seven, and after seven years there, a child who has passed the examinations may continue in secondary school for two, four or six years. Children walk to school, and a primary school may be a one-hour walk and a secondary school a longer walk. Walking to school and playing generally are not supervised closely by adults and are important ways in which children learn self-reliance. However, a child is usually dependent on the family economically and socially, and later as an adult the demands of urban life, particularly the reliance on cash to support a lifestyle, can lead to conflict with a rural family's need for cash and traditional values.

Higher Education. Higher education is valued as qualification for white-collar and professional occupations and is becoming increasingly important as an entry point to technically skilled employment. Families are proud of children who go on to receive further education, especially in the rural areas. There is no social stigma for the family of a child who was expected to enter college or university but failed to do so.

RELIGION

Religious Beliefs. In traditional religion, the spirit of a deceased person returns to the community and the deceased heads of extended families (the ancestors), have a powerful influence on family life. The spirit ancestors are usually only two or three generations back from the living generation and are the people who passed on the custom of honoring their ancestors and the traditions of the community. They are honored in ceremonies to celebrate a good harvest and in appeals to deal with misfortune. When a spirit becomes angry, it communicates through a medium, or a diviner diagnoses the anger and cause, and appeasement follows. Families seeking to avenge a death or enforce debt payment may consult diviner-healers (*n'anga*). Witches are thought to have the power to raise angry spirits, and the anger of a spirit may or may not be justified in the view of the affected family.

Many Christians continue to believe in spirits and the power of witchcraft and seek spiritual guidance from both belief systems. The largest churches are the Roman Catholic and the Anglican, and the Apostolic Church is the largest independent church. Independent churches tend to interpret the Bible more in accordance with traditional values, and faith healing and savings organizations (for example, burial societies) feature strongly in their activities.

Death and the Afterlife. Customarily, the dead are buried close to home, and people in urban areas may bring the deceased back to rural areas for burial. Graves are prepared close to the family homestead and are both sacred and feared for their association with death and spirits. A diviner may be consulted to determine the cause of death and prescribe a ritual action; this is followed by ceremonies to settle the spirit and mark the end of mourning. After one year a final ceremony is held at which the spirit becomes a spirit guardian of the family. These ceremonies generally combine traditional and Christian practices.

MEDICINE AND HEALTH CARE

Traditional and modern medicines are used, and a distinction is made between minor ailments and serious illnesses. This is done partly because of the belief that illness may have been inflicted by angry spirits (justifiably or through witchcraft). Therefore, treatment for a serious illness may include a consultation with a n'anga. Herbal remedies continue to be used widely for minor ailments, and n'anga are respected for their counseling skills, especially in treating psychological and psychiatric problems.

There is a health care system of clinics, district hospitals, and teaching hospitals in Harare and Bulawayo, although in recent years the service has been affected by financial constraints. There is also an association of registered traditional healers, the Zimbabwe National Traditional Healer's Association of N'anga, that includes spirit mediums in its membership.

SECULAR CELEBRATIONS

Independence Day is celebrated on 18 April, and Heroes Day on 11 August.

THE ARTS AND HUMANITIES

Support for the Arts. Artists are held in high regard. In Harare and Bulawayo and to a lesser extent in rural areas, there are many training centers. Some of those centers are self-run, started with the assistance of a patron; some are run by nongovernmental organizations; and some are cooperatives. The most famous is Tengenenge in Guruve District, which has produced many of the most famous Shona sculptors. The National Gallery in Harare, founded in 1954, has been instrumental in the promotion of art, especially sculpture. Competition is high, especially in the sculpture and women's traditional craft markets (baskets, mats, and pottery).

Literature. The first Shona novel was published in 1956, and the first Ndebele one in 1957. Since that time, especially after independence, there has been a burgeoning of Shona and Ndebele literature. Major themes are folklore, myths and legends (traditional

A woman selling crocheted tablecloths in Harare. Many enterprises in the informal sector are based on women's traditional activities.

oral literature), the preindependence experience and struggle, and living in a postindependent country. Internationally acclaimed novelists include Shimmer Chinyodya *(Harvest of Thorns)* Chenjerai Hove *(Bones, Shadows)*, and Doris Lessing (the Martha Quest trilogy and her autobiographies), who is the most famous white writer. An international book fair is held in Harare every August.

Graphic Arts. Shona sculpture is internationally acclaimed and exhibited. Those works fetch thousands of dollars on the international market, particularly in Europe and the United States. Although this art form is referred to as Shona sculpture, it is not specific to the Shona. The themes are derived largely from African folklore and transformed into figurative, semiabstract, and minimalist works that use a variety of stone, including black serpentine.

Performance Arts. Traditionally inspired music is predominant in the arts and represents cultural continuity with the past. Based on the rhythms and melodies of the *mbira* (finger piano), the instrument associated with the ancestors, traditional music promoted a feeling of solidarity in the struggle for independence. Music groups were formed in urban areas, lyrics contained political messages, and the music scene promoted African rather than Euro-

pean figures. Since 1980, the number of cultural groups has increased and public performances have become common. The ready availability of radios has not replaced playing music (usually the mbira or drums) in the home. Thomas Mapfuma and the Blacks Unlimited group are the most well-known proponents of popular music heavily influenced by traditional music. Other influences on popular music include church music, gospel, Zairean rhumba, and South African mbaqanga and mbube. Black Umfolosi exemplifies the mbubu tradition of Nguni vocals and harmony sung a capella.

Older people have a greater affinity with traditional music, but all Zimbabwean music is influenced by the rhythms and melodies of the *mbira*. Western music is popular, and artists are influenced by it to varying degrees.

Several Zimbabwean films have been commercially successful, including *Flame, Jit, Everyone's Child*, and *Neria*. *Flame* has a political focus, and the other three have social themes.

THE STATE OF THE PHYSICAL AND SOCIAL SCIENCES

Before independence, black Zimbabwean college enrollment was low, particularly in technical colleges:

the tendency was to find course places in universities and technical colleges outside the country, and in academic courses rather than in technical or vocational courses. The expansion of primary, secondary, and tertiary education with independence meant an expansion of the social sciences, in particular education. This was not matched by the same expansion in the scientific and technical fields of the physical sciences, engineering, and medicine. Therefore technical expertise and highly skilled labor has continued to be a constraint, and one which has at least in part been responsible for the white minority retaining a disproportionate share of economic resources.

There are two state-funded universities, the University of Zimbabwe in Harare and the National University of Science and Technology in Bulawayo. The University of Zimbabwe is the older university and it has an international track record in the physical and social sciences, particularly in the natural sciences and in the application of social science to agricultural and rural development, and ecology, and conservation projects. The National University of Science and Technology opened in 1991 and offers courses in applied science, commerce, and industrial technology. Two private universities have also recently been established: Africa University, funded by the United Methodist church in Mutare, and Catholic University in Harare. The Harare Polytechnic and technical colleges in major towns offer vocational and technical training courses.

Support from international donors has been provided to the applied social sciences, media and communication studies, the applied natural sciences, and biotechnology at the University of Zimbabwe.

BIBLIOGRAPHY

Beach, David. "Cognitive Archaeology and Imaginary History at Great Zimbabwe." *Current Anthropology* 39 (1): 47–72, 1998.

———. *The Shona and the Neighbours*, 1994.

Berliner, P. F. *The Soul of the Mbira: Music and Traditions of the Shona People of Zimbabwe*, 1978.

Bourdillon, M. F. C. "Religious Symbols and Political Change." *Zambezia* 12, 1984–1985.

———. *Where Are the Ancestors: Changing Culture in Zimbabwe*, 1997.

———. *Religion and Society: A Text for Africa*, 1990.

Bourdillon, Michael. *The Shona People*, 1976.

Burgess, S. F. *Smallholders and Political Voice in Zimbabwe*, 1997.

Burke, T. *Lifebuoy Men, Lux Women: Commodification, Consumption, and Cleanliness in Modern Zimbabwe*, 1996.

Chavunduka, G. L. *Traditional Medicine in Modern Zimbabwe*, 1994.

Cheater, A. P. "The Ideology of 'Communal' Land Tenure in Zimbabwe: Mythogenesis Enacted?" *Africa* 60 (2): 188–206, 1990.

———. *Idioms of Accumulation: Rural Development and Class Formation among Freeholders in Zimbabwe*, 1984.

———. "Formal and Informal Rights to Land in Zimbabwe's Black Freehold Areas: A Case Study from Msengezi." *Africa* 52 (3): 77–91, 1982.

Chinodya, Shimmer. *Can We Talk and Other Stories*, 1998.

———. *Harvest of Thorns*, 1989.

Cox, J. "Ancestors, the Sacred and God: Reflections on the meaning of the Sacred in Zimbabwean Death Rituals." *Religion* 25 (4): 339–55, 1995.

———. "Significant Change and Religious Certainties." *The Zimbabwean Review* 2 (1): 8–9, 1996.

Dingirai, V. and M. F. C. Bourdillon. "Religious Ritual and Political Control in Binga District, Zimbabwe." *African Anthropology* 4 (2): 4–26, 1997.

Fontein, Joost. "Great Zimbabwe: A Sacred Site or a National Shrine?" M.A. dissertation, University of Edinburgh, Edinburgh, 1997.

Gaidzanwa, R. "Women's Land Rights in Zimbabwe." *Issue*, XXII (2): 12–16, 1994.

Garbett, G. K. "Disparate Regional Cults and a Unitary Field in Zimbabwe." In R. B. Werbner, ed., *Regional Cults*, 1977.

Gelfand, Michael. *Diet and Tradition in an African Culture*, 1971.

Gordon, R. "Girls Cannot Think as Boys Do: Socialising Children through the Zimbabwean School System." *Gender and Development* 6 (2): 53–58, 1998.

Hancock, Ian. *White Liberals and Radical in Rhodesia 1953–1980*, 1984.

Hapanyengwi, Chemhuru O, and Ed Shizha. "Through Zimbabwean Eyes." *Journal of African Religion and Philosophy* 4 (2): 45–47, 1998.

Harbitz N J. "Mediums in Zimbabwe's Media." In *Media Culture and Society* 18 (4): 669–676, 1996.

Hasler, R. *Agriculture, Foraging, and Wildlife Resource Use in Africa: Cultural and Political Dynamics in the Zambezi Valley*, 1995.

Hobsbawm, E., and T. Ranger, eds. *The Invention of Tradition*, 1983.

Horn, N. E. *Cultivating Customers: Market Women in Harare, Zimbabwe*, 1994.

Hove, Chenjerai. *Ancestors*, 1996.

Jones, Claire. *Making Music: Musical Instruments in Zimbabwe Past and Present*, 1992.

Kaarsholm, P. ''Inventions, Imaginings, Codifications: Authorising Versions of Ndebele Cultural Tradition.'' *Journal of Southern African Studies* 23 (2): 243–258, 1997.

Kriger, Norma. *Zimbabwe's Guerilla War: Peasant Voices*, 1992.

Lan, David M. *Guns and Rain: Guerillas and Spirit Mediums in Zimbabwe*, 1985.

Lessing, Doris. *African Laughter*, 1992.

———. *Under my Skin: Volume One of My Autobiography, to 1949*, 1994.

Lonely Planet. *Zimbabwe, Botswana and Namibia*, 3rd ed., 1999.

Martin, David, and Phyllis Johnson. *The Struggle of Zimbabwe: The Chimurenga War*, 1981.

Matshalaga, N., ed. *The Political Economy of Poverty in Zimbabwe*, 1996.

Meekers, D. ''The Noble Custom of Roora: The Marriage Practices of the Shona of Zimbabwe.'' *Ethnology* 32. 35–54, 1993.

Moyo, S., P. Robinson, Y. Katere., S, Stevenson, and D.Gumbo. *Zimbabwe's Environmental Dilemma: Balancing Resource Inequities*, 1993.

Mungoshi, Charles. *Walking Still*, 1997.

Murphree, M. W. ''Strategic Considerations for Enhancing Scholarship at the University of Zimbabwe.'' *Zambezia*, 24 (1): 1–12, 1997.

Mutswairo, Solomon, Emmanual Chiwome, Nhira Edgar Mberi, Albert Masasire, and Munashe Furusa. *Introduction to Shona Culture*, 1996.

Ndoro, W. ''Great Zimbabwe.'' *Scientific American* 277 (5): 62–67, 1997.

O'Keefe, P., and S. Moyo. ''Land Tenure in Zimbabwe.'' *Review of African Political Economy* 70 (23): 579–580, 1996.

Phimister, J. *Wangi Kolia: Coal, Capital and Labour in Colonial Zimbabwe, 1884–1954*, 1994.

Ranger, T. ''Making Zimbabwean Landscapes: Painters, Projectors and Priests.'' *Paideuma* 43: 59–74, 1997.

———. ''Missionaries, Migrants and the Manyika: The Invention of Ethnicity in Zimbabwe.'' In Leroy Vail ed. *The Creation of Tribalism in Southern Africa*, 1989.

———. *Peasant Consciousness and Guerilla War in Zimbabwe*, 1985.

———. *The African Voice in Southern Rhodesia, 1898–1930*, 1970.

Republic of Zimbabwe. *Census 1992: Zimbabwe National Report*, 1994.

Reynolds, P. *Dance Civet Cat: Child Labour in the Zambezi Valley*, 1991.

———. *Traditional Healers and Childhood in Zimbabwe*, 1996.

Riphenburg, C. J. ''Changing Gender Relations and Structural Adjustment in Zimbabwe.'' *Africa* 52 (2): 237–260, 1997.

Roe, E. M. ''More Than the Politics of Decentralization: Local Government Reform, District Development and Public Administration in Zimbabwe.'' *World Development* 23 (5): 833–844, 1995.

Scarnecchia, T. ''Poor Women and Nationalist Politics: Alliances and Fissures in the Formation of a Nationalist Political Movement in Salisbury, Rhodesia, 1950–56.'' *Journal of African History* 37 (2): 283–310, 1996.

Schmidt, Elizabeth. *Peasants, Traders and Wives: Shona Women in the History of Zimbabwe 1870–1939*, 1992.

Scoones, I., et al. *Hazards and Opportunities: Farming Livelihoods in Dryland Africa: Lessons from Zimbabwe*, 1995.

Stoneman, C. ed. *Zimbabwe's Prospects*, 1988.

Stoneman, Colin, and Lionel Cliffe. *Zimbabwe: Politics, Economics and Society*, 1989.

Style, Colin, and O-Ian. *Mambo Book of Zimbabwean Verse in English*, 1986.

UNESCO. *General History of Africa*, 1993.

Walker, P. J. ''The Architectural Development of Great Zimbabwe.'' *Azania* 28 87–102, 1993.

Weinrich, A. K. H. *Tears of the Dead: The Social Biography of an African Family*, 1991.

———. *Chiefs and Councils in Rhodesia: Transition from Patriarchal to Bureaucratic Power*, 1971.

Werbner, R. *Ritual Passage, Sacred Journey: The Process and Organization of Religious Movement*, 1989.

———. *African Farmers in Rhodesia: Old and New Peasant Communities in Karangaland*, 1975.

Werbner, R. P. ''Atonement Ritual and Guardian-Spirit Possession among the Kalanga.'' *Africa* 34 (2): 113–136, 1964.

Zimbabwe Women's Resource Centre and Network and SADCC–WIDSAA. *Beyond Inequalities: Women in Zimbabwe*, 1998.

—ANN MUIR

PHOTO CREDITS

Photographs and illustrations appearing in Countries and Their Cultures were received from the following sources and are used by permission:

Afghanistan: map, c. 1998. © Maryland Cartographics, 2; Baci/Corbis, 3; Caroline Penn/Corbis, 5, 6; Ric Ergenbright/Corbis, 8; Julia Waterlow, Eye Ubiquitous/Corbis, 10.

Albania: map, c. 1998. © Maryland Cartographics, 13; Catherine Karnow/Corbis, 14; Richard Bickel/Corbis, 16; Peter Turnley/Corbis, 17, 18; Richard Bickel/Corbis, 20.

Algeria: map, c. 1998. © Maryland Cartographics, 24; Adam Woolfitt/Corbis, 26; Marc Garanger/Corbis, 28; Margaret Courtney-Clarke/Corbis, 29; Tiziana and Gianni Baldizzone/Corbis, 30; Robert Holmes/Corbis, 33.

American Samoa: map, © Maryland Cartographics, 36; Jack Fields/Corbis, 37, 38, 39, 40; Lowell Holmes, 41, 42, 43.

Andorra: map, c. 1998. © Maryland Cartographics, 46; Fancesc Muntada/Corbis, 47; Morton Beebe, S.F./Corbis, 49; Ric Ergenbright/Corbis, 50.

Angola: map, c. 1998. © Maryland Cartographics, 53; Francoise de Mulder/Corbis, 55, 56, 57, 61; Paul Velasco; Gallo Images/Corbis, 60.

Anguila: map, © Maryland Cartographics, 64; Dave G. Houser/Corbis, 65; Layne Kennedy/Corbis, 67, 68.

Antigua and Barbuda: map, c. 1998. © Maryland Cartographics, 71; © Reinhard Eisele/Corbis, 73; © Michael Boys/Corbis, 74; © Neil Rabinowitz/Corbis, 75.

Argentina: map, c. 1998. © Maryland Cartographics, 78; Macduff Everton/Corbis, 80; Pablo Corral Vega/Corbis, 82, 86, 87; Ric Ergenbright/Corbis, 88; Vittoriano Rastelli/Corbis, 88.

Armenia: map, c. 1998. © Maryland Cartographics, 94; Dave Bartruff/Corbis, 95; Dean Conger/Corbis, 96, 98; 99, 100.

Aruba: map, © Maryland Cartographics, 104; © Cees Van Leeuwen, Cordaiy Photo Library Ltd./Corbis, 106; © Dave G. Houser/Corbis, 108; © Buddy Mays/Corbis, 109.

Australia: map, c. 1998. © Maryland Cartographics, 113; Catherine Karnow/Corbis, 115; Michael S. Yamashita/Corbis, 117; Paul A. Souders/Corbis, 119, 120; Roger Garwood and Trish Ainslie/Corbis, 122.

Austria: map, c. 1998. © Maryland Cartographics, 128; Bob Krist/Corbis, 129; K.M. Westermann/Corbis, 131; Marc Garanger/Corbis, 132; Michael S. Yamashita/Corbis, 133; Paul Almasy/Corbis, 136.

Azerbaijan: map, c. 1998. © Maryland Cartographics, 141; © Caroline Penn/Corbis, 143, 144; Marc Garanger/Corbis, 145; Dean Conger/Corbis, 146, 150; reproduced by permission, 148.

Bahama Islands: map, c. 1998. © Maryland Cartographics, 154; Kit Kittle/Corbis, 156; Philip Gould/Corbis, 157; Ted Spiegel/Corbis, 158.

Bahrain: map, c. 1998. © Maryland Cartographics, 161; Adam Woolfitt/Corbis, 163, 164; Roger Wood/Corbis, 165.

Bangladesh: map, c. 1998. © Maryland Cartographics, 168; © Tiziana and Gianni Baldizzone/Corbis, 170, 172; reproduced by permission, 173; © Howard Davies/Corbis, 175; © Arvind Garg/Corbis, 176; © Liba Taylor/Corbis, 177; Roger Wood/Corbis, 179.

Barbados: map, c. 1998. © Maryland Cartographics, 183; Bob Krist/Corbis, 185; Tony Arruza/Corbis, 186; Wolfgang Kaehler/Corbis, 188.

Belarus: map, c. 1998. © Maryland Cartographics, 191; Nik Wheeler/Corbis, 193, 194, 196, 198, 200.

Belgium: map, c. 1998. © Maryland Cartographics, 203; Charles & Josette Lenars/Corbis, 205; Gillian Darley; Edifice/Corbis, 207; Dave Bartruff/Corbis, 208; Michael Busselle/Corbis, 210; Paul Almasy/Corbis, 211.

Belize: map, c. 1998. © Maryland Cartographics, 214; Kevin Schafer/Corbis, 215, 216; © Macduff Everton/Corbis, 218.

Benin: map, c. 1998. © Maryland Cartographics, 221; Caroline Penn/Corbis, 223, 224, 225, 226; Mark Newham, Eye Ubiquitous/Corbis, 227.

Bermuda: map, © Maryland Cartographics, 230; The Purcell Team/Corbis, 233; Catherine Karnow/Corbis, 234; Dave G. Houser/Corbis, 236.

Bhutan: map, c. 1998. © Maryland Cartographics, 239; Tom Owen Edmunds/Corbis, 241, 242, 243.

Bolivia: map, c. 1998. © Maryland Cartographics, 246; © Tiziana and Gianni Baldizzone/Corbis, 248; © Caroline Penn/Corbis, 250; © Vanni Archive/Corbis, 252; © Enzo & Paolo Ragazzini/Corbis, 253, 255.

Bosnia and Herzegovina: map, c. 1998. © Maryland Cartographics, 260; Chris Rainier/Corbis, 263; David Reed/Corbis, 264; Emmanuel Ortiz/Corbis, 265; Michael S. Yamashita/Corbis, 266; Richard Bickel/Corbis, 267; Hans Georg Roth/Corbis, 268.

Botswana: map, c. 1998. © Maryland Cartographics, 272; Craig Lovell/Corbis, 276; David Reed/Corbis, 278; Peter Johnson/Corbis, 280.

Brazil: map, c. 1998. © Maryland Cartographics, 284; Daniel Laini/Corbis, 287, 290; Stephanie Colasanti/Corbis, 291; Stephanie Maze/Corbis, 293, 296; Wolfgang Kaehler/Corbis, 298; Yann Arthus-Bertrand/Corbis, 299.

British Virgin Islands: © Maryland Cartographics, 303; Neil Rabinowitz/Corbis, 305; Dave G. Houser/Corbis, 306; Bob Krist/Corbis, 308; Jan Butchofsky-Houser/Corbis, 309.

Brunei Darussalam: map, c. 1998. © Maryland Cartographics, 312; © Michael S. Yamashita/Corbis, 314; © Michael S. Yamashita/Corbis, 316, 317.

Bulgaria: map, c. 1998. © Maryland Cartographics, 320; © Morton Beebe, S.F./Corbis, 323; © Michael Freeman/Corbis, 325; © Adam Woolfitt/Corbis, 326; © Reuters Newmedia Inc./Corbis, 328; © Charles & Josette Lenars/Corbis, 329.

Burkina Faso: map, c. 1998. © Maryland Cartographics, 333; Charles & Josette Lenars/Corbis, 336, 338, 340; Margaret Courtney-Clarke/Corbis, 342, 343.

Burma: map, c. 1998. © Maryland Cartographics, 347; Christophe Loviny/Corbis, 348, 350; George W. Wright/Corbis, 351, 353, 355; Jack Fields/Corbis, 356; Robert van der Hilst/Corbis, 358.

Burundi: map, c. 1998. © Maryland Cartographics, 362; Howard Davies/Corbis, 365, 366, 368; Kennan Ward/Corbis, 369; Paul Almasy/Corbis, 370.

Cambodia: map, c. 1998. © Maryland Cartographics, 374; AFP/Corbis, 376, 377, 379; Catherine Karnow/Corbis, 381; Michael S. Yamashita/Corbis, 382.

Cameroon: map, c. 1998. © Maryland Cartographics, 385; Daniel Laini/Corbis, 388, 390; Michael & Patricia Fogden/Corbis, 391; Paul Almasy/Corbis, 393; Paul Almasy/Corbis, 394.

Canada: map, c. 1998. © Maryland Cartographics, 398; The Purcell Team/Corbis, 403, 411; Lowell Georgia/Corbis, 404; Nik Wheeler/Corbis, 407, 409; Wolfgang Kaehler/Corbis, 413, 415.

Cape Verde: map, c. 1998. © Maryland Cartographics, 418; Arthur Thivenart/Corbis, 420; Dave G. Houser/Corbis, 421; Dave G. Houser/Corbis, 422.

Cayman Islands: map, © Maryland Cartographics, 425; Bob Krist/Corbis, 427; Kit Kittle/Corbis, 429; W. Wayne Lockwood/Corbis, 430.

Central African Republic: map, c. 1998. © Maryland Cartographics, 433; Earl & Nazima Kowall/Corbis, 435, 436; Yann Arthus-Bertrand/Corbis, 437.

Chad: map, c. 1998. © Maryland Cartographics, 440; Daniel Laini/Corbis, 443; Paul Almasy/Corbis, 445, 447, 448, 450.

Chile: map, c. 1998. © Maryland Cartographics, 453; Bettmann/Corbis, 456; Gary Braasch/Corbis, 458; Hubert Stadler/Corbis, 460; Macduff Everton/Corbis, 462, 464.

China: map, c. 1998. © Maryland Cartographics, 467; Bettmann/Corbis, 470; Hanan Isachar/Corbis, 472; Galen Rowell/Corbis, 474; Jack Fields/Corbis, 476; Jerry Cooke/Corbis, 478; Kelly-Mooney Photography/Corbis, 480; Peter Turnley/Corbis, 482.

Colombia: map, c. 1998. © Maryland Cartographics, 485; The Purcell Team/Corbis, 487, 496; Enzo & Paolo Ragazzini/Corbis, 489, 492; Jeremy Horner/Corbis, 491; Ted Spiegel/Corbis, 494, 495.

Comoros: map, c. 1998. © Maryland Cartographics, 500; Robert van der Hilst/Corbis, 502, 503, 504.

Democratic Republic of the Congo: map, c. 1998. © Maryland Cartographics, 507; Craig Lovell/Corbis, 509; Dave Bartruff/Corbis, 511; Paul Almasy/Corbis, 512, 514, 516, 520, 521; Howard Davies/Corbis, 517; Liba Taylor/Corbis, 518.

Republic of Congo: map, c. 1998. © Maryland Cartographics, 525; Vittoriano Rastelli/Corbis, 527, 528, 529.

Cook Islands: map, © Maryland Cartographics, 532; Nik Wheeler/Corbis, 534, 536; Robert Holmes/Corbis, 535.

Costa Rica: map, c. 1998. © Maryland Cartographics, 539; Dave G. Houser/Corbis, 541; Martin Rogers/Corbis, 543; Jan Butchofsky-Houser/Corbis, 544.

Côte d'Ivoire: map, c. 1998. © Maryland Cartographics, 548; Albreacht G. Schaefer/Corbis, 551; Fulvio Roiter/Corbis, 552; Lisa Trocchi; Gallo Images/Corbis, 554; Marc Garanger/Corbis, 556, 558.

Croatia: map, c. 1998. © Maryland Cartographics, 561; Francoise de Mulder/Corbis, 563, 569, 570; Hans Georg Roth/Corbis, 565; Emmanuel Ortiz/Corbis, 566; Jonathan Blair/Corbis, 568.

Cuba: map, c. 1998. © Maryland Cartographics, 574; Bettmann/Corbis, 578; Jon Spaull/Corbis, 580; Robert van der Hilst/Corbis, 583; Tim Page/Corbis, 584, 586.

Cyprus: map, c. 1998. © Maryland Cartographics, 590; Chris Hellier/Corbis, 592; Jonathan Blair/Corbis, 593, 595; Richard List/Corbis, 596.

Czech Republic: map, c. 1998. © Maryland Cartographics, 599; Peter Wilson/Corbis, 602; Paul Almasy/Corbis, 604; David Cumming, Eye Ubiquitous/Corbis, 606; David Bartruff/Corbis, 608; Liba Taylor/Corbis, 610.

Denmark: map, c. 1998. © Maryland Cartographics, 616; Bob Krist/Corbis, 618, 620; Dave Bartruff/Corbis, 622; Peter Johnson/Corbis, 624; Steve Raymer/Corbis, 625.

Djibouti: map, c. 1998. © Maryland Cartographics, 630; Wolfgang Kaehler/Corbis, 632, 633; Scheufler Collection/Corbis, 635.

Dominica: map, c. 1998. © Maryland Cartographics, 638; Wolfgang Kaehler/Corbis, 640, 642; Michael S. Yamashita/Corbis, 643.

Dominican Republic: map, c. 1998. © Maryland Cartographics, 647; Abbie Enock; Travel Ink/Corbis, 648; Massimo Listri/Corbis, 651; Tony Arruza/Corbis, 653; Richard Bickel/Corbis, 654, 656.

Ecuador: map, c. 1998. © Maryland Cartographics, 660; Dave G. Houser/Corbis, 661; Marc Garanger/Corbis, 663; Owen Franken/Corbis, 664, 666; Stepanie Colasanti/Corbis, 668; Manuel Zambrana/Corbis, 669.

Egypt: map, c. 1998. © Maryland Cartographics, 674; Charles & Josette Lenars/Corbis, 675;

Jonathan Blair/Corbis, 677; Julia Waterlow, Eye Ubiquitous/Corbis, 679, 683; Hans Georg Roth/Corbis, 681; Richard T. Nowitz/Corbis, 686; Owen Franken/Corbis, 688.

El Salvador: map, c. 1998. © Maryland Cartographics, 692; The Purcell Team/Corbis, 693, 695; Lynda Richardson/Corbis, 696, 699; Tim Wright/Corbis, 698.

England: map, © Maryland Cartographics, 702; Bob Krist/Corbis, 704; Michael Busselle/Corbis, 706; Vince Streano/Corbis, 708; Warren Morgan/Corbis, 710; Wolfgang Kaehler/Corbis, 712; Susan D. Rock, 714.

Equatorial Guinea: map, c. 1998. © Maryland Cartographics, 718; Vittoriano Rastelli/Corbis, 721.

Eritrea: map, c. 1998. © Maryland Cartographics, 725; Caroline Penn/Corbis, 727, 729; Wolfgang Kaehler/Corbis, 730.

Estonia: map, c. 1998. © Maryland Cartographics, 734; Jack Fields/Corbis, 736; Ludovic Maisant/Corbis, 737; Dean Conger/Corbis, 738.

Ethiopia: map, c. 1998. © Maryland Cartographics, 741; Carmen Redondo/Corbis, 743, 745; Caroline Penn/Corbis, 747, 748; Jonathan Blair/Corbis, 750; Dave Bartruff/Corbis, 751; Francoise de Mulder/Corbis, 753.

Falkland Islands: map, © Maryland Cartographics, 758; © Michael S. Yamashita/Corbis, 758; reproduced by permission, 759.

Faroe Islands: map, © Maryland Cartographics, 761; Adam Woolfitt/Corbis, 763, 765, 766.

Fiji: map, c. 1998. © Maryland Cartographics, 769; Jack Fields/Corbis, 770; Jon Sparks/Corbis, 772; Morton Beebe, S.F./Corbis, 775; Robert Holmes/Corbis, 777.

Finland: map, c. 1998. © Maryland Cartographics, 780; Sandro Vannini/Corbis, 782; Steve Raymer/Corbis, 784; Nik Wheeler/Corbis, 786, 787; Caroline Penn/Corbis, 789.

France: map, c. 1998. © Maryland Cartographics, 792; Adam Woolfitt/Corbis, 794; Catherine Karnow/Corbis, 795; David Gallant/Corbis, 797; Gail Mooney/Corbis, 799; Massimo Listri/Corbis, 800; Michael Busselle/Corbis, 803; Nik Wheeler/Corbis, 804.

French Guiana: map, © Maryland Cartographics, 808; © Laurence Fordyce, Eye Ubiquitous/Corbis, 809, 811; © Roger Ressmeyer/Corbis, 810.

French Polynesia: map, © Maryland Cartographics, 814; © Wolfgang Kaehler/Corbis, 815, 817; © Nik Wheeler/Corbis, 818.

Gabon: map, c. 1998. © Maryland Cartographics, 822; © The Purcell Team/Corbis, 823, 825, 826.

Gambia: map, © Maryland Cartographics, 829; Caroline Penn/Corbis, 831; Liba Taylor/Corbis, 833; Nik Wheeler/Corbis, 834.

Georgia: map, c. 1998. © Maryland Cartographics, 837; Dean Conger/Corbis, 838, 840; Jon Spaull/Corbis, 842; Peter Turnley/Corbis, 844; Michael S. Yamashita/Corbis, 845.

Germany: map, c. 1998. © Maryland Cartographics, 848; Dave G. Houser/Corbis, 850; Gregor Schmid/Corbis, 854; Marc Garanger/Corbis, 857; Wolfgang Kaehler/Corbis, 859; Ric Ergenbright/Corbis, 861; Wolfgang Kaehler, 863.

Ghana: map, c. 1998. © Maryland Cartographics, 867; Liba Taylor/Corbis, 870, 872; Margaret Courtney-Clarke/Corbis, 874, 878; Daniel Laini/Corbis, 876.

Gibraltar: map, Maryland Cartographics, 882; Adam Woolfitt/Corbis, 883; Jan Butchofsky-Houser/Corbis, 884; Patrick Ward/Corbis, 885.

Greece: map, c. 1998. © Maryland Cartographics, 888; Dave Bartruff/Corbis, 890; Dave G. Houser/Corbis, 892; Kevin Schafer/Corbis, 894; Daniel Laini/Corbis, 896; Ted Spiegel/Corbis, 897.

Greenland: map, © Maryland Cartographics, 901; Michael Lewis/Corbis, 903; Wolfgang Kaehler/Corbis, 905; Hubert Stadler/Corbis, 906.

Grenada: map, c. 1998. © Maryland Cartographics, 909; Catherine Karnow/Corbis, 911; Buddy Mays/Corbis, 912; Dave G. Houser/Corbis, 913.

Guadeloupe: map, © Maryland Cartographics, 916; Dave G. Houser/Corbis, 918; Philip Gould/Corbis, 919, 920.

Guam: map, Maryland Cartographics, 923.

Guatemala: map, c. 1998. © Maryland Cartographics, 929; Bob Winsett/Corbis, 932; Dave G. Houser/Corbis, 933, 936; Galen Rowell/Corbis, 937; Owen Franken/Corbis, 939.

Guinea: map, c. 1998. © Maryland Cartographics, 942; Bettman/Corbis, 945; David Reed/Corbis, 948.

Guinea-Bissau: map, c. 1998. © Maryland Cartographics, 953; Dave G. Houser/Corbis, 954, 955, 956, 957, 958.

Guyana: map, c. 1998. © Maryland Cartographics, 961; Charles & Josette Lenars/Corbis, 963; John Tinning, Frank Lane Photo Agency/Corbis, 964.

Haiti: map, c. 1998. © Maryland Cartographics, 968; Daniel Laini/Corbis, 970, 975; Morton Beebe, S.F./Corbis, 972; Kelly-Mooney Photography/Corbis, 973; Phillip Gould/Corbis, 977.

Honduras: map, c. 1998. © Maryland Cartographics, 980; Macduff Everton/Corbis, 982; Owen Franken/Corbis, 984, 989; Tony Arruza/Corbis, 985; Laurence Fordyce, Eye Ubiquitous/Corbis, 987.

Hong Kong: map, © Maryland Cartographics, 992; Alissa Crandall/Corbis, 993; James Davis, Eye Ubiquitous/Corbis, 995; Morton Beebe, S.F./Corbis, 996; James Marshall/Corbis, 998; Julia Waterlow, Eye Ubiquitous/Corbis, 999.

Hungary: map, c. 1998. © Maryland Cartographics, 1002; Paul Almasy/Corbis, 1003, 1006; Barry Lewis/Corbis, 1005; Catherine Karnow/Corbis, 1008; Adam Woolfitt/Corbis, 1009.

Iceland: map, c. 1998. © Maryland Cartographics, 1012; Ian Yates, Eye Ubiquitous/Corbis, 1013; Paul Almasy/Corbis, 1015, 1017.

India: map, c. 1998. © Maryland Cartographics, 1020; Jeremy Horner/Corbis, 1021; 1022; Wolfgang Kaehler/Corbis, 1023; Winifried Wisniewski; Frank Lane Picture Agency/Corbis, 1025; Bob Krist/Corbis, 1027; Lindsay Hebberd/Corbis, 1028; Ric Ergenbright/Corbis, 1030; Catherine Karnow/Corbis, 1031.

Indonesia: map, c. 1998. © Maryland Cartographics, 1035; Albrecht G. Schaefer/Corbis, 1037; Buddy Mays/Corbis, 1040; Tiziana and Gianni Baldizzone/Corbis, 1042, 1044; Jack Fields/Corbis, 1047, 1051; Morton Beebe, S.F./Corbis, 1052.

Iran: map, c. 1998. © Maryland Cartographics, 1058; Brian Vikander/Corbis, 1060, 1063, 1064, 1067; Earl & Nazima Kowall/Corbis, 1070, 1071; Roger Wood/Corbis, 1074.

Iraq: map, c. 1998. © Maryland Cartographics, 1079; Caroline Penn/Corbis, 1080, 1085; Francoise de Mulder/Corbis, 1082; Nik Wheeler/Corbis, 1084; Daniel Laini/Corbis, 1087; Charles & Josette Lenars/Corbis, 1088.

Ireland: c. 1998. © Maryland Cartographics, 1092; Jacqui Hurst/Corbis, 1094; Richard T. Nowitz/Corbis, 1096; Jan Butchofsky-Houser/Corbis, 1098; Michael St. Maur Sheil/Corbis, 1100; Michael S. Yamashita/Corbis, 1102.

Israel: map, c. 1998. © Maryland Cartographics, 1105; Annie Griffiths Belt/Corbis, 1107; David Rubinger/Corbis, 1109, 1111, 1113; Richard T. Nowitz/Corbis, 1114.

Italy: map, c. 1998. © Maryland Cartographics, 1118; Patrick Ward/Corbis, 1120; Bryan Pickering, Eye Ubiquitous/Corbis, 1122; James Davis, Eye Ubiquitous/Corbis, 1124; Vince Streano/Corbis, 1126, 1127; Sandro Vannini/Corbis, 1129; Peter Wilson/Corbis, 1130.

Jamaica: map, c. 1998. © Maryland Cartographics, 1134; Bojan Brecelj/Corbis, 1136; Howard Davies/Corbis, 1137; Daniel Laini/Corbis, 1138.

Japan: map, c. 1998. © Maryland Cartographics, 1141; Corbis, 1144; Jerry Cooke/Corbis, 1146; Michael S. Yamashita/Corbis, 1148; Morton Beebe, S.F./Corbis, 1150; Vince Streano/Corbis, 1152, 1153; Paul A. Souders/Corbis, 1155.

Jordan: map, c. 1998. © Maryland Cartographics, 1160; Charles & Josette Lenars/Corbis, 1162; David Rubinger/Corbis, 1163; Miki Kratsman/Corbis, 1164.

Kazakhstan: map, c. 1998. © Maryland Cartographics, 1168; David Samuel Robbins/Corbis, 1171; Earl & Nazima Kowall/Corbis, 1173; Jon Spaull/Corbis, 1175; Wolfgang Kaehler/Corbis, 1178, 1180.

Kenya: map, c. 1998. © Maryland Cartographics, 1184; Adrian Arbib/Corbis, 1185; The Purcell Team/Corbis, 1188, 1189; Dave G. Houser/Corbis, 1191; Paul Almasy/Corbis, 1193.

Kiribati: map, c. 1998. © Maryland Cartographics, 1196; Charles & Josetta Lenars/Corbis, 1197; Caroline Penn/Corbis, 1199, 1200.

North Korea: map, c. 1998. © Maryland Cartographics, 1203; Jeremy Horner/Corbis, 1204, 1210; Michael S. Yamashita/Corbis, 1206; Nathan Benn/Corbis, 1208; Jim Sugar Photography/Corbis, 1212.

South Korea: map, c. 1998. © Maryland Cartographics, 1215; Kevin R. Morris/Corbis, 1217, 1218; Nathan Benn/Corbis, 1220, 1222; Wolfgang Kaehler/Corbis, 1224, 1226.

Kuwait: map, c. 1998. © Maryland Cartographics, 1230; Heini Schneebeli, Edifice/Corbis, 1231; Penny Tweedie/Corbis, 1232, 1233.

Kyrgyzstan: map, c. 1998. © Maryland Cartographics, 1236; Caroline Penn/Corbis, 1237, 1240; Janet Wishnetsky/Corbis, 1241, 1242; Nevada Wier/Corbis, 1244.

Laos: map, c. 1998. © Maryland Cartographics, 1248; The Purcell Team/Corbis, 1250; Caroline Penn/Corbis, 1252; Michael S. Yamashita/Corbis, 1253, 1257; Nevada Wier/Corbis, 1255.

Latvia: map, c. 1998. © Maryland Cartographics, 1260; Dean Conger/Corbis, 1261; Staffan Widstrand/Corbis, 1263; Steve Raymer/Corbis, 1264.

Lebanon: map, c. 1998. © Maryland Cartographics, 1267; Carmen Redondo/Corbis, 1268; Michael Nicholson/Corbis, 1270; Morton Beebe, S.F./Corbis, 1271.

Lesotho: map, c. 1998. © Maryland Cartographics, 1275; Liba Taylor/Corbis, 1277; Nik Wheeler/Corbis, 1278; Kim Sayer/Corbis, 1279.

Liberia: map, c. 1998. © Maryland Cartographics, 1282; Albrecht G. Schaefer/Corbis, 1284; Paul Almasy/Corbis, 1286; Eldad Rafaeli/Corbis, 1288.

Libya: map, c. 1998. © Maryland Cartographics, 1291; Roger Wood/Corbis, 1293, 1294, 1297; Peter Turnley/Corbis, 1298, 1301.

Lithuania: map, c. 1998. © Maryland Cartographics, 1305; Dean Conger/Corbis, 1307, 1308, 1314; Peter Turnley/Corbis, 1310, 1313.

Luxembourg: map, c. 1998. © Maryland Cartographics, 1317; Dave G. Houser/Corbis, 1319; Farrell Grehan/Corbis, 1321, 1322.

Macau: map, © Maryland Cartographics, 1326; Hans Georg Roth/Corbis, 1327; Macduff Everton/Corbis, 1330; Michael S. Yamashita/Corbis, 1332.

Macedonia: map, c. 1998. © Maryland Cartographics, 1335; Francoise de Mulder/Corbis, 1337, 1339; Paul Almasy/Corbis, 1338.

Madagascar: map, c. 1998. © Maryland Cartographics, 1343; Chris Hellier/Corbis, 1345, 1347; John R. Jones; Papilio/Corbis, 1348; Wolfgang Kaehler/Corbis, 1350, 1352.

Malawi: map, c. 1998. © Maryland Cartographics, 1356; Gina Glover/Corbis, 1357; Liba Taylor/Corbis, 1359, 1362; Martin B. Withers; Frank Lane Picture Agency/Corbis, 1360; Earl & Nazima Kowall/Corbis, 1361.

Malaysia: map, c. 1998. © Maryland Cartographics, 1365; Dave G. Houser/Corbis, 1367; Nik Wheeler/Corbis, 1369; Sergio Dorantes/Corbis, 1370; John Hulme, Eye Ubiquitous/Corbis, 1372; Neil Rabinowitz/Corbis, 1374.

Maldives: map, c. 1998. © Maryland Cartographics, 1377; Adam Woolfitt/Corbis, 1378, 1381; Earl & Nazima Kowalls/Corbis, 1380; Nik Wheeler/Corbis, 1382.

Mali: map, c. 1998. © Maryland Cartographics, 1385; Charles & Josette Lenars/Corbis, 1387, 1389; © Wolfgang Kaehler/Corbis, 1390, 1394, 1396; Nik Wheeler/Corbis, 1392.

Malta: map, c. 1998. © Maryland Cartographics, 1401; Paul Almasy/Corbis, 1402; Roger Wood/Corbis, 1404; Bob Krist/Corbis, 1405.

Marshall Islands: map, c. 1998. © Maryland Cartographics, 1409; Jack Fields/Corbis, 1410, 1412, 1414.

Martinique: © Maryland Cartographics, 1417; Dave G. Houser/Corbis, 1418, 1420; Philip Gould/Corbis, 1422.

Mauritania: map, c. 1998. © Maryland Cartographics, 1425; Margaret Courtney-Clarke/Corbis, 1427; Bernard and Catherine Desjeux/Corbis, 1430; Juan Echeverria/Corbis, 1432.

Mauritius: map, c. 1998. © Maryland Cartographics, 1435; Daniel Laini/Corbis, 1436; Chris Hellier/Corbis, 1438; Wolfgang Kaehler/Corbis, 1439.

Mayotte: map, © Maryland Cartographics, 1442; Mike Southern, Eye Ubiquitous/Corbis, 1443, 1445.

Mexico: map, c. 1998. © Maryland Cartographics, 1448; Charles & Josette Lenars/Corbis, 1450, 1451; Dave G. Houser/Corbis, 1453; Nik Wheeler/Corbis, 1454, 1456; Robert Holmes/Corbis, 1459, 1460.

Micronesia: map, c. 1998. © Maryland Cartographics, 1466; Jack Fields/Corbis, 1468, 1470, 1472; Nik Wheeler/Corbis, 1474.

Moldova: map, c. 1998. © Maryland Cartographics, 1478; Nik Wheeler/Corbis, 1481, 1482, 1484, 1486; Barry Lewis/Corbis, 1485; used by permission, 1487.

Monaco: map, c. 1998. © Maryland Cartographics, 1490; Charles & Josette Lenars/Corbis, 1492; Chris Hellier/Corbis, 1494; Jerome Prevost; TempSport/Corbis, 1496.

Mongolia: map, c. 1998. © Maryland Cartographics, 1499; Dean Conger/Corbis, 1501; Nik Wheeler/Corbis, 1502, 1503.

Montserrat: map, © Maryland Cartographics, 1507; Kelly-Mooney Photography/Corbis, 1508, 1509, 1510.

Morocco: map, c. 1998. © Maryland Cartographics, 1513; Michelle Garrett/Corbis, 1515; © K. M. Westermann/Corbis, 1517; Robert Holmes/Corbis, 1519; Penny Tweedie/Corbis, 1521; Nevada Wier/Corbis, 1522.

Mozambique: map, c. 1998. © Maryland Cartographics, 1525; Adrian Arbib/Corbis, 1527; Paul Velasco/Corbis, 1528, 1530; Liba Taylor/Corbis, 1531, 1533.

Namibia: map, c. 1998. © Maryland Cartographics, 1538; © Wolfgang Kaehler/Corbis, 1540; © Yann Arthus-Bertrand/Corbis, 1542, 1543.

Nauru: map, c. 1998. © Maryland Cartographics, 1546; Quadrillion/Corbis, 1548; Bettmann/Corbis, 1549, 1550.

Nepal: map, c. 1998. © Maryland Cartographics, 1553; Craig Lovell/Corbis, 1554; Nik Wheeler/Corbis, 1555; The Purcell Team/Corbis, 1556; David Samuel Robbins/Corbis, 1558, 1559; Roman Soumar/Corbis, 1561.

Netherlands: map, © Maryland Cartographics, 1565; Wolfgang Kaehler/Corbis, 1567; Michael S. Yamashita/Corbis, 1569, 1573; Morton Beebe, S.F./Corbis, 1570; Michael John Kielty/Corbis, 1572.

Netherlands Antilles: map, © Maryland Cartographics, 1577; James L. Amos/Corbis, 1578; Neil Rabinowitz/Corbis, 1580; Bob Krist/Corbis, 1581.

New Caledonia: map, © Maryland Cartographics, 1584; Jack Fields/Corbis, 1585, 1587, 1588.

New Zealand: map, c. 1998. © Maryland Cartographics, 1591; Hans Georg Roth/Corbis, 1593; James L. Amos/Corbis, 1594; Charles O'Rear/Corbis, 1597; Michael S. Yamashita/Corbis, 1598, 1599.

Nicaragua: map, c. 1998. © Maryland Cartographics, 1602; Daniel Laini/Corbis, 1604; Jeremy Horner/Corbis, 1606; Owen Franken/Corbis, 1608; Bill Gentile/Corbis, 1610.

Niger: map, c. 1998. © Maryland Cartographics, 1613; Bernard and Catherine Desjeux/Corbis, 1614, 1620; Nik Wheeler/Corbis, 1615, 1617; Yann Arthus-Bertrand/Corbis, 1619; Paul Almasy/Corbis, 1621.

Nigeria: map, c. 1998. © Maryland Cartographics, 1625; Paul Almasy/Corbis, 1627, 1630, 1632, 1634, 1637, 1639; Margaret Courtney-Clarke/Corbis, 1641.

Niue: maps, © Maryland Cartographics, 1644; Wolfgang Kaehler/Corbis, 1647.

Northern Ireland: map, © Maryland Cartographics, 1651; Tim Page/Corbis, 1654; Michael St. Maur Sheil/Corbis, 1655, 1657.

Northern Mariana Islands: map, © Maryland Cartographics, 1661; Michael S. Yamashita/Corbis, 1663, 1665; Charles & Josette Lenars/Corbis, 1664.

Norway: map, c. 1998. © Maryland Cartographics, 1668; Peter Guttman/Corbis, 1670; Adam Woolfitt/Corbis, 1672; Farrell Grehan/Corbis, 1674; Richard T. Nowitz/Corbis, 1675; Paul A. Souders/Corbis, 1677; Wolfgang Kaehler/Corbis, 1678.

Oman: map, c. 1998. © Maryland Cartographics, 1682; Arthur Thevenart/Corbis, 1684; © K.M. Westermann/Corbis, 1686; Nik Wheeler/Corbis, 1687.

Pakistan: map, c. 1998. © Maryland Cartographics, 1692; Caroline Penn/Corbis, 1695; David Samuel Robbins/Corbis, 1696; Keren Su/Corbis, 1697; Robert Holmes/Corbis, 1699; Staffan Widstrand/Corbis, 1700.

Palau: map, c. 1998. © Maryland Cartographics, 1704; Jack Fields/Corbis, 1706; Dave G. Houser/Corbis, 1709; Wolfgang Kaehler/Corbis, 1710.

Palestine: map, © Maryland Cartographics, 1712; Caroline Penn/Corbis, 1714; Morton Beebe, S.F./Corbis, 1715; David Rubniger/Corbis, 1717.

Panama: map, c. 1998. © Maryland Cartographics, 1720; Adam Woolfitt/Corbis, 1722; Bettmann/Corbis, 1724; Danny Lehman/Corbis, 1725.

Papua New Guinea: map, c. 1998. © Maryland Cartographics, 1728; Caroline Penn/Corbis, 1730; Otto Lang/Corbis, 1731; Wolfgang Kaehler/Corbis, 1733, 1734; Michael S. Yamashita/Corbis, 1735; Charles & Josette Lenars/Corbis, 1736, 1737.

Paraguay: map, c. 1998. © Maryland Cartographics, 1742; Johnathan Smith, Cordaiy Photo Library Ltd./Corbis, 1745; Laurence Fordyce, Eye Ubiquitous/Corbis, 1747; Richard Bailey/Corbis, 1749; Terry Whittaker; Frank Lane Picture Agency/Corbis, 1751, 1753.

Peru: map, c. 1998. © Maryland Cartographics, 1756; Bettmann/Corbis, 1759; Galen Rowell/Corbis, 1761; Jeremy Horner/Corbis, 1763; Wolfgang Kaehler/Corbis, 1764; Ted Speigel/Corbis, 1765.

Philippines: map, c. 1998. © Maryland Cartographics, 1769; Bennett Dean, Eye Ubiquitous/Corbis, 1771; Catherine Karnow/Corbis, 1773; Charles & Josette Lenars/Corbis, 1775; Morton Beebe, S.F./Corbis, 1776; Paul A. Souders/Corbis, 1778; Paul Almasy/Corbis, 1780; Vince Streano/Corbis, 1781.

Poland: map, c. 1998. © Maryland Cartographics, 1785; Bernard and Catherine Desjeux/Corbis, 1788, 1790, 1791; Frank Lane Picture Agency/Corbis, 1793; Raymond Gehman/Corbis, 1795; Roger Tidman/Corbis, 1796; Yiorgos Nikiteas, Eye Ubiquitous/Corbis, 1798.

Portugal: map, c. 1998. © Maryland Cartographics, 1802; Dave G. Houser/Corbis, 1805; Tony Arruza/Corbis, 1807, 1811; © John Heseltine/Corbis, 1808; Hans Georg Roth/Corbis, 1810.

Puerto Rico: map, © Maryland Cartographics, 1815; James Marshall/Corbis, 1817; Macduff Everton/Corbis, 1818; Neil Rabinowitz/Corbis, 1819; Corbis, 1821; AFP/Corbis, 1822.

Qatar: map, c. 1998. © Maryland Cartographics, 1826; Christine Osborne/Corbis, 1828, 1829.

Reunion Island: map, © Maryland Cartographics, 1834; Chris Hellier/Corbis, 1835; Daniel Laini/Corbis, 1836; Hubert Stadler/Corbis, 1836; Yann Arthus-Bertrand/Corbis, 1837.

Romania: map, c. 1998. © Maryland Cartographics, 1839; Barry Lewis/Corbis, 1842; Caroline Penn/Corbis, 1844; Dean Conger/Corbis, 1845; Peter Turnley/Corbis, 1847; Peter Wilson/Corbis, 1848.

Russia: map, c. 1998. © Maryland Cartographics, 1851; Buddy Mays/Corbis, 1855; Steve Raymer/Corbis, 1857, 1859, 1862; Vince Streano/Corbis, 1864; Wolfgang Kaehler/Corbis, 1866, 1868.

Rwanda: map, c. 1998. © Maryland Cartographics, 1873; Adrian Arbib/Corbis, 1876; Bacm/Corbis, 1878; Dave Bartruff/Corbis, 1879; Howard Davies/Corbis, 1880, 1882.

Saint Kitts and Nevis: map, © Maryland Cartographics, 1886; Catherine Karnow/Corbis, 1888, 1889; Tony Arruza/Corbis, 1890.

Saint Lucia: map, © Maryland Cartographics, 1892; Corbis, 1895; Tony Arruza/Corbis, 1896, 1897.

Saint Vincent and the Grenadines: map, © Maryland Cartographics, 1901; Dean Conger/Corbis, 1904.

Samoa: map, © Maryland Cartographics, 1908; Catherine Karnow/Corbis, 1909, 1910; Nik Wheeler/Corbis, 1911.

San Marino: map, c. 1998. © Maryland Cartographics, 1914; Paul Almasy/Corbis, 1916; Vittormano Rastelli/Corbis, 1918.

Sao Tome and Principe: map, c. 1998. © Maryland Cartographics, 1921.

Saudi Arabia: map, c. 1998. © Maryland Cartographics, 1928; K. M. Westermann/Corbis, 1930; AFP/Corbis, 1933; Wolfgang Kaehler/Corbis, 1934, 1936, 1938.

Scotland: map, © Maryland Cartographics, 1941; Dave Bartruff/Corbis, 1943; © Catherine Karnow/Corbis, 1944; Macduff Everton/Corbis, 1946; Buddy Mays/Corbis, 1948; Bjorn Backe; Papilio/Corbis, 1949.

Senegal: map, c. 1998. © Maryland Cartographics, 1953; Bernard and Catherine Desjeux/Corbis, 1955, 1957; Corbis, 1959; Owen Franken/Corbis, 1960, 1961.

Serbia and Montenegro: map, © Maryland Cartographics, 1964; Bojan Brecelj/Corbis, 1967, 1968; O. Alamany & E. Vicens/Corbis, 1970; Paul Almasy/Corbis, 1972, 1974.

Seychelles: map, c. 1998. © Maryland Cartographics, 1977; Nik Wheeler/Corbis, 1978, 1979; Buddy Mays/Corbis, 1980.

Sierra Leone: map, © Maryland Cartographics, 1983; Caroline Penn/Corbis, 1985; Charles & Josette Lenars/Corbis, 1987; Christine Osborne/Corbis, 1988, 1990; Ted Speigel/Corbis, 1991.

Singapore: map, © Maryland Cartographics, 1995; Adam Woolfitt/Corbis, 1996; Dave Bartruff/Corbis, 1997; Michael S. Yamashita/Corbis, 1998.

Slovakia: map, © Maryland Cartographics, 2001; Scheufler Collection/Corbis, 2004; Adam Woolfitt/Corbis, 2006; Farrell Grehan/Corbis, 2007; Liba Taylor/Corbis, 2009; Owen Franken/Corbis, 2010.

Slovenia: map, © Maryland Cartographics, 2014; Bojan Brecelj/Corbis, 2017, 2018; Janez Skok/Corbis, 2019.

Solomon Islands: map, © Maryland Cartographics, 2022; Wolfgang Kaehler/Corbis, 2025, 2028, 2030.

Somalia: map, © Maryland Cartographics, 2033; David Turnley/Corbis, 2036; Studio Patellani/Corbis, 2039; Kevin Fleming/Corbis, 2041; Michael S. Yamashita/Corbis, 2043, 2044.

South Africa: map, © Maryland Cartographics, 2048; Charles O'Rear/Corbis, 2051, 2052; David Turnley/Corbis, 2054; Hans Georg Roth/Corbis, 2056; Jonathan Blair/Corbis, 2057; Paul Velasco; Gallo Images/Corbis, 2059; Tony Arruza/Corbis, 2060.

Spain: map, c. 1998. © Maryland Cartographics, 2065; David Gallant/Corbis, 2069; Elke Stoltzenberg/Corbis, 2071; Hans Georg Roth/Corbis, 2074; Michelle Chaplow/Corbis, 2076; Owen Franken/Corbis, 2078; Paul Almasy/Corbis, 2081; Stephanie Maze/Corbis, 2083.

Sri Lanka: map, © Maryland Cartographics, 2087; Howard Davies/Corbis, 2090; Jeremy Horner/Corbis, 2092; Richard Powers/Corbis, 2094, 2095; Sheldan Collins/Corbis, 2097.

Sudan: map, © Maryland Cartographics, 2101; Caroline Penn/Corbis, 2104; Christine Osborne/Corbis, 2105; Paul Almasy/Corbis, 2107, 2108; Penny Tweedie/Corbis, 2110.

Suriname: map, © Maryland Cartographics, 2113; Adam Woolfitt/Corbis, 2115, 2116, 2117.

Swaziland: map, © Maryland Cartographics, 2120; Paul Almasy/Corbis, 2121; Philip Perry; Frank Lane Picture Agency/Corbis, 2123; Nik Wheeler/Corbis, 2124.

Sweden: map, © Maryland Cartographics, 2127; Hubert Stadler/Corbis, 2130; Macduff Everton/Corbis, 2132, 2134, 2136.

Switzerland: map, © Maryland Cartographics, 2139; Charles & Josette Lenars/Corbis, 2141; Keren Su/Corbis, 2142; Morton Beebe, S.F./Corbis, 2143; Sandro Vannini/Corbis, 2144; Tim Thompson/Corbis, 2145.

Syria: map, © Maryland Cartographics, 2150; Christine Osborne/Corbis, 2153; George W. Wright/Corbis, 2154; K.M. Westermann/Corbis, 2156, 2157, 2158.

Taiwan: map, © Maryland Cartographics, 2162; Jack Fields/Corbis, 2164, 2165; The Purcell Team/Corbis, 2167; Kevin R. Morris/Corbis, 2170, 2171; Dave Bartruff/Corbis, 2168; Paul Almasy/Corbis, 2174.

Tajikistan: map, © Maryland Cartographics, 2178; Jim Richardson/Corbis, 2180, 2181; Jon Spaull/Corbis, 2183; Nevada Wier/Corbis, 2185, 2186.

Tanzania: map, © Maryland Cartographics, 2189; Jack Fields/Corbis, 2191; Caroline Penn/Corbis, 2193; Kennan Wood/Corbis, 2195; Paul Almasy/Corbis, 2197, 2199.

Thailand: map, © Maryland Cartographics, 2203; Catherine Karnow/Corbis, 2204; Hanan Isachar/Corbis, 2207; John Hulme, Eye Ubiquitous/Corbis, 2209; Michael S. Yamashita/Corbis, 2211; Nevada Wier/Corbis, 2212; Tim Page/Corbis, 2214; Wolfgang Kaehler/Corbis, 2215.

Togo: map, © Maryland Cartographics, 2219; Caroline Penn/Corbis, 2221; Daniel Laini/Corbis, 2223, 2225.

Tokelau: map, illustration. © The Gale Group, 2228; Catherine Karnow/Corbis, 2229.

Tonga: map, © Maryland Cartographics, 2232; Ted Streshinsky/Corbis, 2233; Jack Fields/Corbis, 2235; Giovanni Bennardo, 2236.

Trinidad and Tobago: map, © Maryland Cartographics, 2239; Reinhard Eisele/Corbis, 2241; Pablo Corral V/Corbis, 2243, 2244, 2245.

Tunisia: map, © Maryland Cartographics, 2249; Christine Osborne/Corbis, 2251; Inge Yspeert/Corbis, 2253, 2254, 2255; Jonathan Blair/Corbis, 2257.

Turkey: map, © Maryland Cartographics, 2260; Caroline Penn/Corbis, 2262; Dave Bartruff/Corbis, 2264; Farrell Grehan/Corbis, 2265; Richard T. Nowitz/Corbis, 2266; Nik Wheeler/Corbis, 2267, 2269; Corbis, 2272.

Turkmenistan: map, © Maryland Cartographics, 2276; David Samuel Robbins/Corbis, 2278, 2279; Girard Degeorge/Corbis, 2281, 2282; Nevada Wier/Corbis, 2284.

Tuvalu: map, © Maryland Cartographics, 2289; Charles & Josette Lenars/Corbis, 2291; Quadrillion/Corbis, 2294.

Uganda: map, © Maryland Cartographics, 2298; Jack Fields/Corbis, 2299; Liba Taylor/Corbis, 2301; Peter Gallo; Gallo Images/Corbis, 2302;

INDEX

F

M

N

Najd (Saudi Arabia), IV:1927
Namibia, **III:1537–1544**
Nampula (Mozambique), III:1528
Napali language, III:1552
Napoleonic Code of 1803, II:800
Nassau family, III:1318
National anthems. *See* National symbols
National Cathedral (Mexico), III:*1450*
National Day (Switzerland), IV:2140
National defense. *See* Military
National dishes. *See* Food and drink
National heroes and heroines. *See* History and ethnic relations; National symbols
National identity. *See* History and ethnic relations; National symbols
National symbols
  Afghanistan, I:2
  Albania, I:14–15
  Algeria, I:23
  American Samoa, I:35
  Andorra, I:45
  Angola, I:52–53
  Anguilla, I:63
  Antigua and Barbuda, I:70–71
  Argentina, I:79–82
  Aruba, I:103
  Austria, I:128
  Azerbaijan, I:141–142
  Bahama Islands, I:153
  Bangladesh, I:168
  Belarus, I:191
  Belgium, I:203–204
  Belize, I:213
  Benin, I:220
  Bermuda, I:229
  Bhutan, I:239
  Bolivia, I:246–247
  Bosnia and Herzegovina, I:259–260
  Botswana, I:273
  Brazil, I:286
  British Virgin Islands, I:302
  Brunei, I:311–312
  Bulgaria, I:320–321
  Burkina Faso, I:333–334
  Burma, I:347
  Burundi, I:361
  Cambodia, I:374–375
  Cameroon, I:386
  Canada, I:399–400
  Cayman Islands, I:424
  Central African Republic, I:432–433
  Chad, I:440–441
  Chile, I:454
  China, I:467–468
  Colombia, I:486

  Comoros, I:499
  Cook Islands, I:531
  Côte d'Ivoire, I:548
  Croatia, I:562
  Cuba, I:573–574
  Cyprus, I:590
  Czech Republic, I:599–600
  Democratic Republic of the Congo, I:508
  Denmark, II:615–616
  Ecuador, II:661–662
  Egypt, II:676
  El Salvador, II:691
  England, II:703
  Equatorial Guinea, II:717
  Eritrea, II:724–725
  Estonia, II:733–734
  Ethiopia, II:742
  Falkland Islands, II:757
  Faroe Islands, II:760
  Fiji, II:768–769
  Finland, II:780
  France, II:793
  French Guiana, II:807
  French Polynesia, II:813
  Gabon, II:821
  Georgia, II:837–838
  Germany, II:849–850
  Ghana, II:868
  Gibraltar, II:881
  Greece, II:889
  Greenland, II:901–902
  Grenada, II:908
  Guadeloupe, II:915
  Guam, II:922
  Guatemala, II:930
  Guinea, II:943
  Guinea-Bissau, II:952–953
  Guyana, II:960
  Haiti, II:967–968
  Honduras, II:981
  Hong Kong, II:991
  Hungary, II:1001–1002
  Iceland, II:1011–1012
  India, II:1019
  Indonesia, II:1037–1038
  Iran, II:1059
  Iraq, II:1078–1079
  Ireland, II:1093
  Israel, II:1104
  Italy, II:1117–1118
  Jamaica, II:1133
  Japan, II:1142
  Jordan, II:1159
  Kazakhstan, II:1169
  Kenya, II:1183–1184
  Kiribati, II:1196
  Kyrgyzstan, II:1235–1236
  Laos, III:1248
  Latvia, III:1259–1260

  Lebanon, III:1266
  Lesotho, III:1274–1275
  Liberia, III:1282
  Lithuania, III:1304–1305
  Luxembourg, III:1317
  Macau, III:1326
  Macedonia, III:1334
  Madagascar, III:1344
  Malaysia, III:1365
  Maldives, III:1376
  Mali, III:1386
  Malta, III:1400
  Marshall Islands, III:1408–1409
  Martinique, III:1416–1417
  Mauritania, III:1426
  Mayotte, III:1441
  Mexico, III:1449
  Micronesia, III:1465–1466
  Moldova, III:1479
  Monaco, III:1489
  Mongolia, III:1498
  Monserrat, III:1506
  Morocco, III:1514
  Mozambique, III:1524, 1526
  Namibia, III:1537
  Nauru, III:1545
  Nepal, III:1552
  Netherlands, III:1566
  Netherlands Antilles, III:1576
  New Caledonia, III:1584
  New Zealand, III:1592
  Nicaragua, III:1602–1603
  Niger, III:1612
  Nigeria, III:1626
  North Korea, II:1203–1204
  Northern Ireland, III:1652
  Northern Mariana Islands, III:1661
  Norway, III:1669
  Oman, III:1681
  Pakistan, III:1693
  Palau, III:1704
  Panama, III:1719
  Papua New Guinea, III:1816
  Paraguay, III:1743
  Peru, III:1757
  Poland, III:1785–1786
  Portugal, III:1802–1803
  Puerto Rico, III:1815–1816
  Qatar, III:1825
  Republic of Congo, I:524
  Reunion Island, III:1833
  Romania, III:1838
  Russia, III:1852–1853
  Rwanda, III:1873
  Saint Kitts and Nevis, IV:1885
  Saint Lucia, IV:1892
  Samoa, IV:1907
  San Marino, IV:1913
  Sao Tomé e Príncipe, IV:1920–1921
  Saudi Arabia, IV:1929